Lecture Notes in Computer Science 3776

Commenced Publication in 1973
Founding and Former Series Editors:
Gerhard Goos, Juris Hartmanis, and Jan van Leeuwen

Editorial Board

David Hutchison
  Lancaster University, UK
Takeo Kanade
  Carnegie Mellon University, Pittsburgh, PA, USA
Josef Kittler
  University of Surrey, Guildford, UK
Jon M. Kleinberg
  Cornell University, Ithaca, NY, USA
Friedemann Mattern
  ETH Zurich, Switzerland
John C. Mitchell
  Stanford University, CA, USA
Moni Naor
  Weizmann Institute of Science, Rehovot, Israel
Oscar Nierstrasz
  University of Bern, Switzerland
C. Pandu Rangan
  Indian Institute of Technology, Madras, India
Bernhard Steffen
  University of Dortmund, Germany
Madhu Sudan
  Massachusetts Institute of Technology, MA, USA
Demetri Terzopoulos
  New York University, NY, USA
Doug Tygar
  University of California, Berkeley, CA, USA
Moshe Y. Vardi
  Rice University, Houston, TX, USA
Gerhard Weikum
  Max-Planck Institute of Computer Science, Saarbruecken, Germany

Sankar K. Pal   Sanghamitra Bandyopadhyay
Sambhunath Biswas (Eds.)

Pattern Recognition and Machine Intelligence

First International Conference, PReMI 2005
Kolkata, India, December 20-22, 2005
Proceedings

 Springer

Volume Editors

Sankar K. Pal
Indian Statistical Institute
Kolkata 700 108, India
E-mail: sankar@isical.ac.in

Sanghamitra Bandyopadhyay
Sambhunath Biswas
Indian Statistical Institute, Machine Intelligence Unit
Kolkata 700 108, India
E-mail: {sanghami,sambhu}@isical.ac.in

Library of Congress Control Number: 2005937700

CR Subject Classification (1998): I.4, F.1, I.2, I.5, J.3, C.2.1, C.1.3

ISSN   0302-9743
ISBN-10   3-540-30506-8 Springer Berlin Heidelberg New York
ISBN-13   978-3-540-30506-4 Springer Berlin Heidelberg New York

This work is subject to copyright. All rights are reserved, whether the whole or part of the material is concerned, specifically the rights of translation, reprinting, re-use of illustrations, recitation, broadcasting, reproduction on microfilms or in any other way, and storage in data banks. Duplication of this publication or parts thereof is permitted only under the provisions of the German Copyright Law of September 9, 1965, in its current version, and permission for use must always be obtained from Springer. Violations are liable to prosecution under the German Copyright Law.

Springer is a part of Springer Science+Business Media

springer.com

© Springer-Verlag Berlin Heidelberg 2005
Printed in Germany

Typesetting: Camera-ready by author, data conversion by Scientific Publishing Services, Chennai, India
Printed on acid-free paper   SPIN: 11590316   06/3142   5 4 3 2 1 0

Message from the General Chair

Pattern recognition and machine intelligence form a major area of research and developmental activity that encompasses the processing of multimedia information obtained from the interaction between science, technology and society. An important motivation for the spurt of activity in this field is the desire to design and make intelligent machines capable of performing certain tasks that we human beings do. Potential applications exist in forefront research areas like computational biology, data mining, Web mining, global positioning systems, medical imaging, forensic sciences, besides classical problems of optical character recognition, biometry, target recognition, face recognition, remotely sensed data analysis, and man–machine communication. There have been several conferences around the world in the past few decades individually in these two areas of pattern recognition and artificial intelligence, but hardly any combining the two, although both communities share similar objectives. Therefore holding this international conference covering these domains is very appropriate and timely, considering the recent needs of information technology, which is a key vehicle for the economic development of any country. The first integrated meeting of 2005, under this theme, was PReMI 2005.

The objective of this international meeting is to present state-of-the-art scientific results, encourage academic and industrial interaction, and to promote collaborative research and developmental activities, in pattern recognition, machine intelligence and related fields, involving scientists, engineers, professionals, researchers and students from India and abroad. The conference will be held every two years to make it an ideal platform for people to share their views and experiences in these areas. Particular emphasis in PReMI 2005 was placed on computational biology, data mining and knowledge discovery, soft computing, case-based reasoning, biometry, as well as various upcoming pattern recognition/image processing problems. There were tutorials, keynote talks and invited talks, delivered by speakers of international repute from both academia and industry. These were accompanied by interesting special sessions apart from the regular technical sessions.

It may be mentioned here that in India the activity on pattern recognition started in the 1960s, mainly in ISI, Calcutta, TIFR, Bombay and IISc, Bangalore. ISI, having a long tradition of conducting basic research in statistics/mathematics and related areas, has been able to develop profoundly activities in pattern recognition and machine learning in its different facets and dimensions with real-life applications. These activities have subsequently been consolidated under a few separate units in one division. As a mark of the significant achievements, special mention may be made of the DOE-sponsored KBCS Nodal Center of ISI founded in the 1980s and the Center for Soft Computing Research (CSCR) of ISI established in 2004 by the DST, Government of India.

CSCR, which is the first national center in the country in this domain, has many important objectives including distance learning, establishing linkage to premier institutes/industries, organizing specialized courses, as well as conducting fundamental research.

The conference proceedings of PReMI-05, containing rigorously reviewed papers, is published by Springer in its prestigious *Lecture Notes in Computer Science* (LNCS) series. Different professional sponsors and funding agencies (both national and international) came forward to support this event for its success. These include, International Association of Pattern Recognition (IAPR); Web Intelligence Consortium (WIC); Institute of Electrical and Electronics Engineering (IEEE): International Center for Pure and Applied Mathematics (CIMPA), France; Webel, Government of West Bengal IT Company; Department of Science & Technology (DST), India; Council of Scientific & Industrial Research (CSIR), India. To encourage participation of bright students and young researchers, some fellowships were provided.

I believe the participants found PReMI-05 an academically memorable and intellectually stimulating event. It enabled young researchers to interact and establish contacts with well-known experts in the field

I hope that you have all enjoyed staying in Calcutta (now Kolkata), the city of Joy.

September 2005   Sankar K. Pal, Kolkata
General Chair, PReMI-05
Director, Indian Statistical Institute

Preface

This volume contains the papers selected for the 1st International Conference on Pattern Recognition and Machine Intelligence (PReMI 2005), held in the Indian Statistical Institute Kolkata, India during December 18–22, 2005. The primary goal of the conference was to present the state-of-the-art scientific results, encourage academic and industrial interaction, and promote collaborative research and developmental activities in pattern recognition, machine intelligence and related fields, involving scientists, engineers, professionals, researchers and students from India and abroad. The conference will be held every two years to make it an ideal platform for people to share their views and experiences in these areas.

The conference had five keynote lectures, 16 invited talks and an evening talk, all by very eminent and distinguished researchers from around the world. The conference received around 250 submissions from 24 countries spanning six continents. Each paper was critically reviewed by two experts in the field, after which about 90 papers were accepted for oral and poster presentations. In addition, there were four special sessions organized by eminent researchers. Accepted papers were divided into 11 groups, although there could be some overlap.

We take this opportunity to express our gratitude to Professors A. K. Jain, R. Chellappa, D. W. Aha, A. Skowron and M. Zhang for accepting our invitation to be the keynote speakers in this conference. We thank Professors B. Bhattacharya, L. Bruzzone, A. Buller, S. K. Das, U. B. Desai, V. D. Gesu, M. Gokmen, J. Hendler, J. Liu, B. Lovell, J. K. Udupa, M. Zaki, D. Zhang and N. Zhong for accepting our invitation to present invited papers in this conference. Our special thanks are due to Professor J. K. Aggarwal for the acceptance of our invitation to deliver a special evening lecture. We also express our deep appreciation to Professors Dominik Ślęzak, Carlos Augusto Paiva da Silva Martins, P. Nagabhushan and Kalyanmoy Gupta for organizing interesting special sessions during the conference. We gratefully acknowledge Mr. Alfred Hofmann, Executive Editor, Computer Science Editorial, Springer, Heidelberg, Germany, for extending his co-operation for publication of the PReMI-05 proceedings. Finally, we would like to thank all the contributors for their enthusiastic response.

We hope that the conference was an enjoyable and academically fruitful meeting for all the participants.

September 2005

Sankar K. Pal
Sanghamitra Bandypodhyay
Sambhunath Biswas
Editors

Organization

PReMI 2005 was organized by the Machine Intelligence Unit, Indian Statistical Institute (ISI) in Kolkata during December 18–22, 2005.

PReMI 2005 Conference Committee

General Chair:	Sankar K. Pal (ISI, Kolkata, India)
Program Chairs:	S. Mitra (ISI, Kolkata, India)
	S. Bandyopadhyay (ISI, Kolkata, India)
	W. Pedrycz (University of Alberta, Edmonton, Canada)
Organizing Chairs:	C. A. Murthy (ISI, Kolkata, India)
	R. K. De (ISI, Kolkata, India)
Tutorial Chair:	A. Ghosh (ISI, Kolkata, India)
Publication Chair:	S. Biswas (ISI, Kolkata, India)
Industrial Liaison:	M. K. Kundu (ISI, Kolkata, India)
	R. Roy (PWC, India)
International Liaison:	G. Chakraborty (Iwate Prefectural University, Takizawamura, Japan)
	J. Ghosh (University of Texas at Austin, USA)

Advisory Committee

A. K. Jain, USA
A. Kandel, USA
A. P. Mitra, India
A. Skowron, Poland
B. L. Deekshatulu, India
C. Y. Suen, Canada
D. Dutta Majumder, India
H. Bunke, Switzerland
H.-J. Zimmermann, Germany
J. Keller, USA
J. K. Ghosh, India
J. M. Zurada, USA
K. Kasturirangan, India
L. Kanal, USA
L. A. Zadeh, USA
M. G. K. Menon, India
M. Jambu, France
M. Vidyasagar, India

N. Balakrishnan, India
R. Chellappa, USA
R. A. Mashelkar, India
S. Prasad, India
S. I. Amari, Japan
T. S. Dillon, Australia
T. Yamakawa, Japan
V. S. Ramamurthy, India
Z. Pawlak, Poland

Program Committee

A. Pal, India
A. K. Majumdar, India
A. M. Alimi, Tunisia
B. B. Bhattacharyya, India
B. Chanda, India
B. Lovell, Australia
B. Yegnanarayana, India
D. Mukhopadhyay, India
D. Ślęzak, Canada
D. Zhang, Hong Kong, China
D. P. Mukherjee, India
D. W. Aha, USA
E. Diday, France
G. S. di Baja, Italy
H. Frigui, USA
H. Kargupta, USA
H. L. Larsen, Denmark
J. Basak, India
J. K. Udupa, USA
L. Bruzzone, Italy
L. Hall, USA
L. I. Kuncheva, UK
M. Banerjee, India
M. Nikravesh, USA
M. N. Murty, India
N. Nasrabadi, USA
N. Zhong, Japan
O. Nasraoui, USA
O. Vikas, India
P. Chaudhuri, India
P. Mitra, India
R. Kothari, India
R. Setiono, Singapore

R. Krishnapuram, India
R. Weber, Chile
S. Bose, India
S. B. Cho, Korea
Santanu Chaudhuri, India
Subhasis Chaudhuri, India
S. Mukhopadhyay, India
S. Sarawagi, India
S. Ray, Australia
S. Sinha, India
S. K. Parui, India
T. Heskes, Netherlands
T. K. Ho, USA
U. B. Desai, India
V. D. Gesù, Italy
Y. Hayashi, Japan
Y. V. Venkatesh, Singapore
Y. Y. Tang, Hong Kong, China

Reviewers

A. M. Alimi
A. Bagchi
A. Bhaduri
A. Bishnu
A. Biswas
A. Ghosh
A. Konar
A. Laha
A. Lahiri
A. Liu
A. K. Majumdar
A. Mukhopadhyay
A. Negi
A. Pal
B. B. Bhattacharyya
B. Chanda
B. Lovell
B. Raju
C. A. Murthy
C. V. Jawahar
D. W. Aha
D. Chakraborty
D. M. Akbar Hussain

D. Mukhopadhyay
D. P. Mukherjee
D. Ślęzak
D. Zhang
E. Diday
F. R. B. Cruz
F. A. C. Gomide
G. S. di Baja
G. Chakraborty
G. Gupta
G. Pedersen
G. Siegmon
H. Frigui
H. Kargupta
H. L. Larsen
J. Basak
J. Ghosh
J. Mukhopadhyay
J. K. Sing
J. Sil
J. K. Udupa
Jayadeva
K. Kummamuru

K. Mali
K. Polthier
K. S. Venkatesh
L. Bruzzone
L. Dey
L. Hall
L. I. Kuncheva
L. V. Subramaniam
L. E. Zarate
M. Acharyya
Mahua Banerjee
Minakshi Banerjee
M. Deodhar
M. Gehrke
M. K. Kundu
M. Mandal
M. Mitra
M. N. Murty
M. Nasipuri
M. K. Pakhira
M. P. Sriram
N. Das
N. Zhong

O. Nasraoui
P. Bhowmick
P. Biswas
P. Chaudhuri
P. Dasgupta
P. Dutta
P. Guha
P. Mitra
P. P. Mohanta
P. Nagabhushan
P. A. Vijaya
Rajasekhar
R. Krishnapunam
R. Setiono
R. Kothari
R. Weber
R. K. De
R. U. Udupa
R. M. Lotlikar
R. H. C. Takashi
Sameena
S. Asharaf

S. Bandyopadhyay
S. Biswas
S. Bose
Santanu Chaudhuri
Subhasis Chaudhuri
S. Datta
S. Ghosh
S. Maitra
S. Mitra
S. Mukhopadhyay
S. Mukherjee
S. Palit
S. Ray
S. Roychowdhury
S. Sarawagi
S. Sandhya
S. Sen
S. Sinha
S. Sur-Kolay
S. B. Cho
S. K. Das
S. K. Mitra

S. K. Pal
S. K. Parui
T. Acharya
T. A. Faruquie
T. Heskes
T. K. Ho
T. Pal
U. Bhattacharyya
U. B. Desai
U. Garain
U. Pal
V. S. Devi
V. D. Gesù
V. A. Popov
V. V. Saradhi
W. Pedrycz
Y. Y. Tang
Y. Hayashi
Y. V. Venkatesh
Y. Zhang

Sponsoring Organizations

- Indian Statistical Institute (ISI), Kolkata
- Center for Soft Computing Research-A National Facility, ISI, Kolkata
- Department of Science and Technology, Government of India
- International Center for Pure and Applied Mathematics (CIMPA), France
- International Association for Pattern Recognition (IAPR)
- Web Intelligence Consortium (WIC), Japan
- Webel, Government of West Bengal IT Company, India
- Council of Scientific & Industrial Research (CSIR), Government of India
- Institute of Electrical and Electronics Engineers (IEEE), USA
- And others

Table of Contents

Keynote Papers

Data Clustering: A User's Dilemma
Anil K. Jain, Martin H.C. Law 1

Pattern Recognition in Video
Rama Chellappa, Ashok Veeraraghavan, Gaurav Aggarwal 11

Rough Sets in Perception-Based Computing
Andrzej Skowron 21

Conversational Case-Based Reasoning
David W. Aha 30

Computational Molecular Biology of Genome Expression and Regulation
Michael Q. Zhang 31

Human Activity Recognition
J.K. Aggarwal 39

Invited Papers

A Novel T^2-SVM for Partially Supervised Classification
Lorenzo Bruzzone, Mattia Marconcini 40

S_Kernel: A New Symmetry Measure
Vito Di Gesù, Bertrand Zavidovique 50

Geometric Decision Rules for Instance-Based Learning Problems
*Binay Bhattacharya, Kaustav Mukherjee,
Godfried Toussaint* 60

Building Brains for Robots: A Psychodynamic Approach
Andrzej Buller 70

Designing Smart Environments: A Paradigm Based on Learning and Prediction
Sajal K. Das, Diane J. Cook 80

Towards Generic Pattern Mining
Mohammed J. Zaki, Nilanjana De, Feng Gao, Nagender Parimi, Benjarath Phoophakdee, Joe Urban Vineet Chaoji, Mohammad Al Hasan, Saeed Salem 91

Multi-aspect Data Analysis in Brain Informatics
Ning Zhong 98

Small Object Detection and Tracking: Algorithm, Analysis and Application
U.B. Desai, S.N. Merchant, Mukesh Zaveri, G. Ajishna, Manoj Purohit, H.S. Phanish 108

Illumination Invariant Face Alignment Using Multi-band Active Appearance Model
Fatih Kahraman, Muhittin Gökmen 118

Globally Optimal 3D Image Reconstruction and Segmentation Via Energy Minimisation Techniques
Brian C. Lovell 128

Go Digital, Go Fuzzy
Jayaram K. Udupa, George J. Grevera 137

A Novel Personal Authentication System Using Palmprint Technology
David Zhang, Guangming Lu, Adams Wai-Kin Kong, Michael Wong 147

World Wide Wisdom Web (W4) and Autonomy Oriented Computing (AOC): *What, When, and How?*
Jiming Liu 157

Semantic Web Research Trends and Directions
Jennifer Golbeck, Bernardo Cuenca Grau, Christian Halaschek-Wiener, Aditya Kalyanpur, Bijan Parsia, Andrew Schain, Evren Sirin, James Hendler 160

Contributory Papers

Clustering, Feature Selection and Learning

Feature Extraction for Nonlinear Classification
Anil Kumar Ghosh, Smarajit Bose 170

Anomaly Detection in a Multi-engine Aircraft
  Dinkar Mylaraswamy 176

Clustering Within Quantum Mechanical Framework
  Güleser K. Demir 182

Linear Penalization Support Vector Machines for Feature Selection
  Jaime Miranda, Ricardo Montoya, Richard Weber 188

Linear Regression for Dimensionality Reduction and Classification of
Multi Dimensional Data
  Lalitha Rangarajan, P. Nagabhushan 193

A New Approach for High-Dimensional Unsupervised Learning:
Applications to Image Restoration
  Nizar Bouguila, Djemel Ziou 200

Unsupervised Classification of Remote Sensing Data Using Graph
Cut-Based Initialization
  *Mayank Tyagi, Ankit K Mehra, Subhasis Chaudhuri,
  Lorenzo Bruzzone* 206

Hybrid Hierarchical Learning from Dynamic Scenes
  *Prithwijit Guha, Pradeep Vaghela, Pabitra Mitra, K.S. Venkatesh,
  Amitabha Mukerjee* 212

Reference Extraction and Resolution for Legal Texts
  *Mercedes Martínez-González, Pablo de la Fuente,
  Dámaso-Javier Vicente* 218

Classification

Effective Intrusion Type Identification with Edit Distance for
HMM-Based Anomaly Detection System
  Ja-Min Koo, Sung-Bae Cho 222

A Combined fBm and PPCA Based Signal Model for On-Line
Recognition of PD Signal
  Pradeep Kumar Shetty 229

Handwritten *Bangla* Digit Recognition Using Classifier Combination
Through DS Technique
  *Subhadip Basu, Ram Sarkar, Nibaran Das, Mahantapas Kundu,
  Mita Nasipuri, Dipak Kumar Basu* 236

Arrhythmia Classification Using Local Hölder Exponents and Support
Vector Machine
  *Aniruddha Joshi, Rajshekhar, Sharat Chandran, Sanjay Phadke,
  V.K. Jayaraman, B.D. Kulkarni* 242

A Voltage Sag Pattern Classification Technique
  *Délio E.B. Fernandes, Mário Fabiano Alvaes,
  Pyramo Pires da Costa Jr.* 248

Face Recognition Using Topological Manifolds Learning
  Cao Wenming, Lu Fei 254

A Context-Sensitive Technique Based on Support Vector Machines for
Image Classification
  Francesca Bovolo, Lorenzo Bruzzone 260

Face Recognition Technique Using Symbolic PCA Method
  P.S. Hiremath, C.J. Prabhakar 266

A Hybrid Approach to Speaker Recognition in Multi-speaker
Environment
  Jigish Trivedi, Anutosh Maitra, Suman K. Mitra 272

Design of Hierarchical Classifier with Hybrid Architectures
  M.N.S.S.K. Pavan Kumar, C.V. Jawahar 276

Neural Networks and Applications

Human-Computer Interaction System with Artificial Neural Network
Using Motion Tracker and Data Glove
  Cemil Oz, Ming C. Leu 280

Recurrent Neural Approaches for Power Transformers Thermal Modeling
  *Michel Hell, Luiz Secco, Pyramo Costa Jr.,
  Fernando Gomide* 287

Artificial Neural Network Engine: Parallel and Parameterized
Architecture Implemented in FPGA
  *Milene Barbosa Carvalho, Alexandre Marques Amaral,
  Luiz Eduardo da Silva Ramos,
  Carlos Augusto Paiva da Silva Martins, Petr Ekel* 294

Neuronal Clustering of Brain fMRI Images
  *Nicolas Lachiche, Jean Hommet, Jerzy Korczak,
  Agnès Braud* 300

An Optimum RBF Network for Signal Detection in Non-Gaussian
Noise
   D.G. Khairnar, S.N. Merchant, U.B. Desai 306

A Holistic Classification System for Check Amounts Based on Neural
Networks with Rejection
   M.J. Castro, W. Díaz, F.J. Ferri, J. Ruiz-Pinales, R. Jaime-Rivas,
   F. Blat, S. España, P. Aibar, S. Grau, D. Griol 310

A Novel 3D Face Recognition Algorithm Using Template Based
Registration Strategy and Artificial Neural Networks
   Ben Niu, Simon Chi Keung Shiu, Sankar Kumar Pal 315

Fuzzy Logic and Applications

Recognition of Fault Signature Patterns Using Fuzzy Logic for
Prevention of Breakdowns in Steel Continuous Casting Process
   Arya K. Bhattacharya, P.S. Srinivas, K. Chithra, S.V. Jatla,
   Jadav Das 318

Development of an Adaptive Fuzzy Logic Based Control Law for a
Mobile Robot with an Uncalibrated Camera System
   T. Das, I.N. Kar 325

Fuzzy Logic Based Control of Voltage and Reactive Power in
Subtransmission System
   Ana Paula M. Braga, Ricardo Carnevalli,
   Petr Ekel, Marcelo Gontijo, Marcio Junges,
   Bernadete Maria de Mendonça Neta, Reinaldo M. Palhares 332

Fuzzy-Symbolic Analysis for Classification of Symbolic Data
   M.S. Dinesh, K.C. Gowda, P. Nagabhushan 338

Handwritten Character Recognition Systems Using Image-Fusion and
Fuzzy Logic
   Rupsa Chakraborty, Jaya Sil 344

Classification of Remotely Sensed Images Using Neural-Network
Ensemble and Fuzzy Integration
   G. Mallikarjun Reddy, B. Krishna Mohan 350

Intelligent Learning Rules for Fuzzy Control of a Vibrating Screen
   Claudio Ponce, Ernesto Ponce 356

Fuzzy Proximal Support Vector Classification Via Generalized
Eigenvalues
  Jayadeva, Reshma Khemchandani, Suresh Chandra 360

Segmentation of MR Images of the Human Brain Using Fuzzy Adaptive
Radial Basis Function Neural Network
  J.K. Sing, D.K. Basu, M. Nasipuri, M. Kundu 364

Optimization and Representation

Design of Two-Dimensional IIR Filters Using an Improved DE
Algorithm
  Swagatam Das, Debangshu Dey 369

Systematically Evolving Configuration Parameters for Computational
Intelligence Methods
  Jason M. Proctor, Rosina Weber 376

A Split-Based Method for Polygonal Approximation of Shape Curves
  R. Dinesh, Santhosh S. Damle, D.S. Guru 382

Symbolic Data Structure for Postal Address Representation and
Address Validation Through Symbolic Knowledge Base
  P. Nagabhushan, S.A. Angadi, B.S. Anami 388

The Linear Factorial Smoothing for the Analysis of Incomplete Data
  Basavanneppa Tallur 395

An Improved Shape Descriptor Using Bezier Curves
  *Ferdous Ahmed Sohel, Gour C. Karmakar,
  Laurence S. Dooley* 401

Isothetic Polygonal Approximations of a 2D Object on Generalized
Grid
  Partha Bhowmick, Arindam Biswas, Bhargab B. Bhattacharya 407

An Evolutionary SPDE Breeding-Based Hybrid Particle Swarm
Optimizer: Application in Coordination of Robot Ants for Camera
Coverage Area Optimization
  Debraj De, Sonai Ray, Amit Konar, Amita Chatterjee 413

An Improved Differential Evolution Scheme for Noisy Optimization
Problems
  Swagatam Das, Amit Konar 417

Image Processing and Analysis

Facial Asymmetry in Frequency Domain: The "Phase" Connection
  Sinjini Mitra, Marios Savvides, B.V.K. Vijaya Kumar 422

An Efficient Image Distortion Correction Method for an X-ray Digital Tomosynthesis System
  J.Y. Kim 428

Eigen Transformation Based Edge Detector for Gray Images
  P. Nagabhushan, D.S. Guru, B.H. Shekar 434

Signal Processing for Digital Image Enhancement Considering APL in PDP
  Soo-Wook Jang, Se-Jin Pyo, Eun-Su Kim, Sung-Hak Lee, Kyu-Ik Sohng 441

A Hybrid Approach to Digital Image Watermarking Using Singular Value Decomposition and Spread Spectrum
  Kunal Bhandari, Suman K. Mitra, Ashish Jadhav 447

Image Enhancement by High-Order Gaussian Derivative Filters Simulating Non-classical Receptive Fields in the Human Visual System
  Kuntal Ghosh, Sandip Sarkar, Kamales Bhaumik 453

A Chosen Plaintext Steganalysis of Hide4PGP V 2.0
  Debasis Mazumdar, Soma Mitra, Sonali Dhali, Sankar K. Pal 459

Isolation of Lung Cancer from Inflammation
  Md. Jahangir Alam, Sid Ray, Hiromitsu Hama 465

Learning to Segment Document Images
  K.S. Sesh Kumar, Anoop Namboodiri, C.V. Jawahar 471

A Comparative Study of Different Texture Segmentation Techniques
  Madasu Hanmandlu, Shilpa Agarwal, Anirban Das 477

Run Length Based Steganography for Binary Images
  Sos.S. Agaian, Ravindranath C. Cherukuri 481

Video Processing and Computer Vision

An Edge-Based Moving Object Detection for Video Surveillance
  M. Julius Hossain, Oksam Chae 485

An Information Hiding Framework for Lightweight Mobile Devices with
Digital Camera
   Subhamoy Maitra, Tanmoy Kanti Das, Jianying Zhou 491

Applications of the Discrete Hodge Helmholtz Decomposition to Image
and Video Processing
   Biswaroop Palit, Anup Basu, Mrinal K. Mandal 497

A Novel CAM for the Luminance Levels in the Same Chromaticity
Viewing Conditions
   Soo-Wook Jang, Eun-Su Kim, Sung-Hak Lee, Kyu-Ik Sohng 503

Estimation of 2D Motion Trajectories from Video Object Planes and
Its Application in Hand Gesture Recognition
   M.K. Bhuyan, D. Ghosh, P.K. Bora 509

3D Facial Pose Tracking in Uncalibrated Videos
   Gaurav Aggarwal, Ashok Veeraraghavan, Rama Chellappa 515

Fusing Depth and Video Using Rao-Blackwellized Particle Filter
   Amit Agrawal, Rama Chellappa 521

Specifying Spatio Temporal Relations for Multimedia Ontologies
   Karthik Thatipamula, Santanu Chaudhury, Hiranmay Ghosh 527

Motion Estimation of Elastic Articulated Objects from Image Points
and Contours
   Hailang Pan, Yuncai Liu, Lei Shi 533

Parsing News Video Using Integrated Audio-Video Features
   S. Kalyan Krishna, Raghav Subbarao, Santanu Chaudhury,
   Arun Kumar 538

Image Retrieval and Data Mining

A Hybrid Data and Space Partitioning Technique for Similarity Queries
on Bounded Clusters
   Piyush K. Bhunre, C.A. Murthy, Arijit Bishnu,
   Bhargab B. Bhattacharya, Malay K. Kundu 544

Image Retrieval by Content Using Segmentation Approach
   Bhogeswar Borah, Dhruba K. Bhattacharyya 551

A Wavelet Based Image Retrieval
   Kalyani Mali, Rana Datta Gupta 557

Use of Contourlets for Image Retrieval
  Rajashekhar, Subhasis Chaudhuri 563

Integration of Keyword and Feature Based Search for Image Retrieval
Applications
  A. Vadivel, Shamik Sural, A.K. Majumdar 570

Finding Locally and Periodically Frequent Sets and Periodic Association
Rules
  A. Kakoti Mahanta, F.A. Mazarbhuiya, H.K. Baruah 576

An Efficient Hybrid Hierarchical Agglomerative Clustering (HHAC)
Technique for Partitioning Large Data Sets
  P.A. Vijaya, M. Narasimha Murty, D.K. Subramanian 583

Density-Based View Materialization
  A. Das, D.K. Bhattacharyya 589

On Simultaneous Selection of Prototypes and Features in Large Data
  T. Ravindra Babu, M. Narasimha Murty, V.K. Agrawal 595

Knowledge Enhancement Through Ontology-Guided Text Mining
  Muhammad Abulaish, Lipika Dey 601

Bioinformatics Application

A Novel Algorithm for Automatic Species Identification Using Principal
Component Analysis
  Shreyas Sen, Seetharam Narasimhan, Amit Konar 605

Analyzing the Effect of Prior Knowledge in Genetic Regulatory
Network Inference
  Gustavo Bastos, Katia S. Guimarães 611

New Genetic Operators for Solving TSP: Application to Microarray
Gene Ordering
  *Shubhra Sankar Ray, Sanghamitra Bandyopadhyay,
  Sankar K. Pal* 617

Genetic Algorithm for Double Digest Problem
  S. Sur-Kolay, S. Banerjee, S. Mukhopadhyaya, C.A. Murthy 623

Intelligent Data Recognition of DNA Sequences Using Statistical Models
  Jitimon Keinduangjun, Punpiti Piamsa-nga, Yong Poovorawan 630

Parallel Sequence Alignment: A Lookahead Approach
  Prasanta K. Jana, Nikesh Kumar 636

Evolutionary Clustering Algorithm with Knowledge-Based Evaluation
for Fuzzy Cluster Analysis of Gene Expression Profiles
  Han-Saem Park, Sung-Bae Cho 640

Biological Text Mining for Extraction of Proteins and Their
Interactions
  Kiho Hong, Junhyung Park, Jihoon Yang, Sungyong Park 645

DNA Gene Expression Classification with Ensemble Classifiers
Optimized by Speciated Genetic Algorithm
  Kyung-Joong Kim, Sung-Bae Cho 649

Web Intelligence and Genetic Algorithms

Multi-objective Optimization for Adaptive Web Site Generation
  Prateek Jain, Pabitra Mitra 654

Speeding Up Web Access Using Weighted Association Rules
  Abhinav Srivastava, Abhijit Bhosale, Shamik Sural 660

An Automatic Approach to Classify Web Documents Using a Domain
Ontology
  *Mu-Hee Song, Soo-Yeon Lim, Seong-Bae Park, Dong-Jin Kang,
  Sang-Jo Lee* 666

Distribution Based Stemmer Refinement
  B.L. Narayan, Sankar K. Pal 672

Text Similarity Measurement Using Concept Representation of
Texts
  Abhinay Pandya, Pushpak Bhattacharyya 678

Incorporating Distance Domination in Multiobjective Evolutionary
Algorithm
  *Praveen K. Tripathi, Sanghamitra Bandyopadhyay,
  Sankar K. Pal* 684

I-EMO: An Interactive Evolutionary Multi-objective Optimization
Tool
  Kalyanmoy Deb, Shamik Chaudhuri 690

Simultaneous Multiobjective Multiple Route Selection Using Genetic Algorithm for Car Navigation
  Basabi Chakraborty 696

Rough Sets, Case-Based Reasoning and Knowledge Discovery

Outliers in Rough k-Means Clustering
  Georg Peters 702

Divisible Rough Sets Based on Self-organizing Maps
  Rocío Martínez-López, Miguel A. Sanz-Bobi 708

Parallel Island Model for Attribute Reduction
  Mohammad M. Rahman, Dominik Ślęzak, Jakub Wróblewski 714

On-Line Elimination of Non-relevant Parts of Complex Objects in Behavioral Pattern Identification
  Jan G. Bazan, Andrzej Skowron 720

Rough Contraction Through Partial Meets
  Mohua Banerjee, Pankaj Singh 726

Finding Interesting Rules Exploiting Rough Memberships
  Lipika Dey, Amir Ahmad, Sachin Kumar 732

Probability Measures for Prediction in Multi-table Infomation Systems
  R.S. Milton, V. Uma Maheswari, Arul Siromoney 738

Object Extraction in Gray-Scale Images by Optimizing Roughness Measure of a Fuzzy Set
  D.V. Janardhan Rao, Mohua Banerjee, Pabitra Mitra 744

Approximation Spaces in Machine Learning and Pattern Recognition
  Andrzej Skowron, Jarosław Stepaniuk, Roman Swiniarski 750

A Rough Set-Based Magnetic Resonance Imaging Partial Volume Detection System
  Sebastian Widz, Kenneth Revett, Dominik Ślęzak 756

Eliciting Domain Knowledge in Handwritten Digit Recognition
  Tuan Trung Nguyen 762

Collaborative Rough Clustering
  Sushmita Mitra, Haider Banka, Witold Pedrycz 768

Learning of General Cases
  Silke Jänichen, Petra Perner 774

Learning Similarity Measure of Nominal Features in CBR Classifiers
  *Yan Li, Simon Chi-Keung Shiu, Sankar Kumar Pal,
  James Nga-Kwok Liu*.. 780

Decision Tree Induction with CBR
  B. Radhika Selvamani, Deepak Khemani 786

Rough Set Feature Selection Methods for Case-Based Categorization of
Text Documents
  *Kalyan Moy Gupta, Philip G. Moore, David W. Aha,
  Sankar K. Pal*... 792

An Efficient Parzen-Window Based Network Intrusion Detector Using
a Pattern Synthesis Technique
  P. Viswanath, M. Narasimha Murty, Satish Kambala.............. 799

Author Index... 805

Data Clustering: A User's Dilemma*

Anil K. Jain and Martin H.C. Law

Department of Computer Science and Engineering, Michigan State University,
East Lansing, MI 48823, USA
{jain, lawhiu}@cse.msu.edu

Abstract. Cluster analysis deals with the automatic discovery of the grouping of a set of patterns. Despite more than 40 years of research, there are still many challenges in data clustering from both theoretical and practical viewpoints. In this paper, we describe several recent advances in data clustering: clustering ensemble, feature selection, and clustering with constraints.

1 Introduction

The goal of data clustering [1], also known as cluster analysis, is to discover the "natural" grouping(s) of a set of patterns, points, or objects. Cluster analysis is prevalent in any discipline that involves analysis or processing of multivariate data. Image segmentation, an important problem in computer vision, is often formulated as a clustering problem [2,3]. Clustering has also been used to discover subclasses in a supervised setting to reduce intra-class variability. Different writing styles were automatically discovered by clustering in [4] to facilitate online handwriting recognition. Contours of MR brain images are clustered into different subclasses in [5]. Documents can be clustered to generate topical hierarchies for information access [6] or retrieval. The study of genome data [7] in biology often involves clustering – either on the subjects, the genes, or both.

Many clustering algorithms have been proposed in different application scenarios (see [8] for a survey). Important partitional clustering algorithms in the pattern recognition community include the k-means algorithm [9], the EM algorithm [10], different types of linkage methods (see [11]), the mean-shift algorithm [12], algorithms that minimize some graph-cut criteria (such as [13]), path-based clustering [14] and different flavors of spectral clustering [3,15]. However, a universal clustering algorithm remains an elusive goal. The fundamental reason for this is the intrinsic ambiguity of the notion of natural grouping. Another difficulty is the diversity of clusters: clusters can be of different shapes, different densities, different sizes, and are often overlapping (Figure 1). The problem is even more challenging when the data is high-dimensional, because the presence of irrelevant features can obscure the cluster structure. Above all, even for data without any cluster structure, most clustering algorithms still generate spurious clusters (see [16,17] for a discussion)! All these issues make clustering a dilemma [18] for the user.

---

* Research supported by the U.S. ONR grant no. N000140410183.

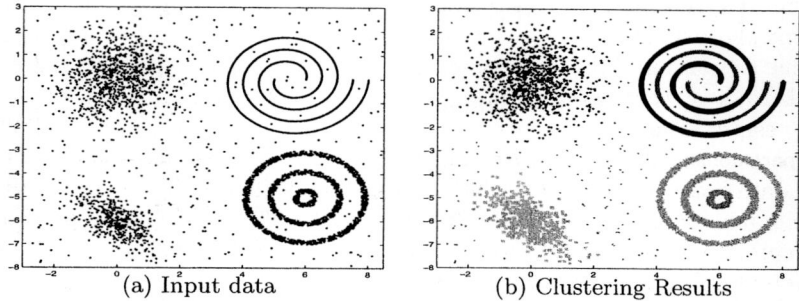

Fig. 1. Diversity of clusters. The clusters in this data set, though easily identified by a human, are difficult to be detected automatically. The clusters are of different shapes, sizes and densities. Background noise makes the clustering task even more difficult.

In the rest of this paper, we shall describe some recent advances in clustering that alleviate these limitations for partitional clustering. In Section 2, we examine how different data partitions in a clustering ensemble can be combined to discover clusters with high diversity. Feature selection can be performed when high dimensional data is to be clustered (Section 3). The arbitrariness of clustering can be reduced by introducing side-information – notably constraints on the cluster labels (Section 4). Finally, we conclude in Section 5.

2   Clustering Ensemble

In supervised learning, it is often beneficial to combine the outputs of multiple classifiers in order to improve the classification accuracy. The goal of *clustering ensemble* is similar: we seek a combination of multiple partitions that provides improved overall clustering of the data set. Clustering ensembles are beneficial in several aspects. It can lead to better average performance across different domains and data sets. Combining multiple partitions can lead to a solution unattainable by any single clustering algorithm. We can also perform parallel clustering of the data and combine the results subsequently, thereby improving scalability. Solutions from multiple distributed sources of data or attributes (features) can also be integrated.

We shall examine several issues related to clustering ensemble in this section. Consider a set of n objects $\mathcal{X} = \{x_1, \ldots, x_n\}$. The clustering ensemble consists of N different partitions of the data set $\mathcal{X}$. The k-th partition is represented by the function π_k, where $\pi_k(x_i)$ denotes the cluster label of the object x_i in the k-th partition, which consists of m_k clusters.

2.1   Diversity

How can we generate each of the partitions in the ensemble? While the optimal strategy is probably dependent on the problem domain and the goal for performing clustering, there are also some general procedures. One can apply different algorithms (like k-means, complete-link, spectral clustering) to create different partitions of the data. Some clustering algorithms like k-means require initialization of parameters. Different initializations can lead to different clustering results. The parameters of a clustering algorithm, such as the number of clusters, can be altered to create different data partitions. Different "versions" of the data can also be used as the input to the clustering algorithm, leading to different partitions. For example, the data set can be perturbed by re-sampling with replacement or without replacement. Different feature subsets or projection to different subspaces can also be used.

Note that these strategies can be combined. For example, the k-means algorithm with different number of clusters and different initializations is used to create the clustering ensemble in [19].

2.2 Consensus Function

A consensus function is a mapping from the set of N partitions $\{\pi_1, \ldots, \pi_N\}$ in the clustering ensemble to a consensus partition π^*. Different consensus functions have been proposed in the literature (Table 1). In this paper, we shall present two examples of consensus functions: consensus by co-association matrix [19], and consensus by quadratic mutual information [20].

In consensus by co-association, we compute the $n \times n$ co-association matrix $\mathbf{C}$, whose (i, j)-th entry is given by

$$c_{ij} = \frac{1}{N} \sum_{k=1}^{N} I\big(\pi_k(x_i) = \pi_k(x_j)\big); \quad i, j = 1, \ldots, n. \quad (1)$$

Here, $I(.)$ is the indicator function, which is 1 if the argument is true and 0 otherwise. Intuitively, c_{ij} measures how many times x_i and x_j are put in the same cluster in the clustering ensemble. The co-association matrix can be viewed as a new similarity matrix, which is superior than the original distance matrix based on Euclidean distance. The consensus partition is found by clustering with $\mathbf{C}$

Table 1. Different consensus functions in the literature

Method	Key ideas
Co-association matrix [19]	Similarity between patterns is estimated by co-association; single-link with max life-time is used for finding the consensus partition
Mutual Information [20]	Maximize the quadratic mutual information between the individual partitions and the consensus partition
Hyper-graph methods [21]	Clusters in different partitions are represented by hyper-edges; consensus partition is found by a k-way min-cut of the hyper-graph
Finite mixture model [20]	Maximum likelihood solution to latent class analysis problem in the space of cluster labels via EM
Re-labeling and voting [22]	Assuming the label correspondence problem is solved, a voting procedure is used to combine the partitions

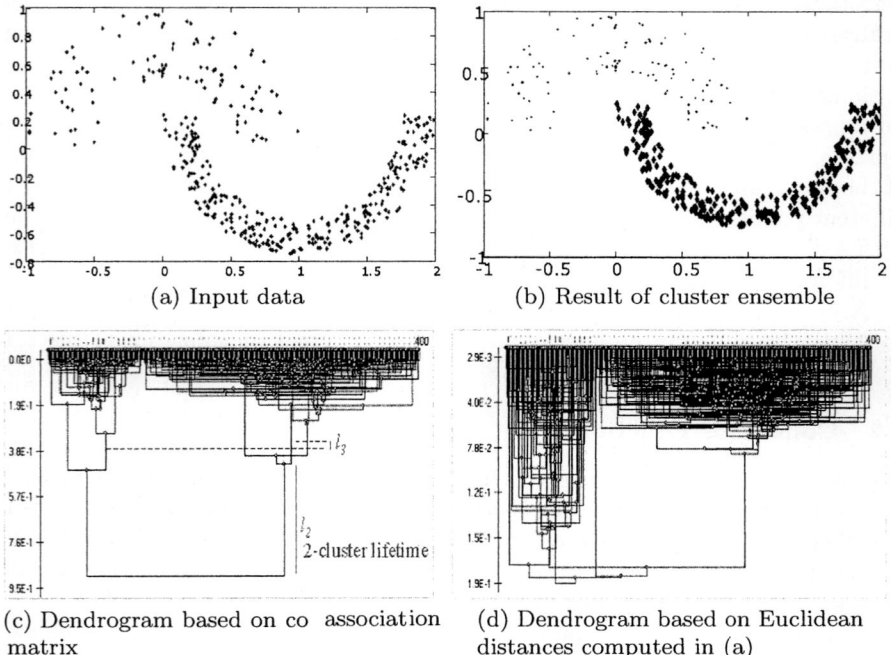

Fig. 2. Example of consensus partition by co-association matrix in [19]. The number of clusters (2 in this case) is determined by the lifetime criteria. Note that the co-association values lead to a much more clear-cut dendrogram than Euclidean distances.

as the similarity matrix. The single-link algorithm is used, because the "chaining" behavior in $\mathbf{C}$ is often desirable. The number of clusters is determined by maximizing the *lifetime*. The lifetime of a partition with K clusters is defined as the range of threshold values on the dendrogram that leads to the identification of the partition. The longer the lifetime, the more stable the partition upon data perturbation. A simple illustration of this consensus function can be seen in Figure 2. Additional experimental results can be found in [19].

One drawback of the co-association consensus function is its $O(n^2)$ memory requirement. A consensus function that uses only $O(n)$ memory was proposed in [20]. It is based on the notion of *median partition*, which maximizes the average utility of the partitions in the ensemble with respect to the consensus partition. Formally, we seek π^* that maximizes $J(\pi^*) = \sum_{k=1}^{N} U(\pi^*, \pi_k)/N$, where $U(\pi^*, \pi_k)$ denotes a utility function. The utility function based on mutual information is advocated in [20]. Define a random variable X_t that corresponds to the cluster labels of the objects in π_t. The joint probability $p(X_t = i, X_s = j)$ is proportional to the number of objects that are in the i-th cluster for the partition π_t and in the j-th cluster for π_s. The similarity/utility between π_t and π_s can be quantified by Shannon mutual information $I(X_t, X_s)$: it takes the largest value when π_t and π_s are identical, and the smallest value when π_t is "independent" of π_s. However, maximizing $I(X_t, X_s)$ is difficult. Instead, the qualitatively similar generalized mutual information is used:

$$I^\alpha(X_t, X_s) = H^\alpha(X_t) - H^\alpha(X_t|X_s)$$
$$H^\alpha(X_t) = (2^{1-\alpha} - 1)^{-1} \left(\sum_{i=1}^{m_t} P(X_t = i)^\alpha - 1 \right) \quad \alpha > 0, \alpha \neq 1 \qquad (2)$$

Note that $H^\alpha(X_t)$ is the Renyi entropy with order α. When $\alpha = 2$, the above quantity is known as the "quadratic mutual information", and it is proportional to the category utility function proposed in [23]. Because of this equivalence, the consensus partition that maximizes the sum of the quadratic mutual information can be found by the k-means algorithm in a new feature space. Specifically, let $\mathbf{y}_{ik}$ be a vector of length m_k, where the j-th component of $\mathbf{y}_{ik}$ is 1 if $\pi_k(x_i) = j$, and 0 otherwise. A new feature vector for the object x_i is obtained by concatenating $\mathbf{y}_{ik}$ for different k. The new pattern matrix is then standardized to have zero column and row means. Running k-means on this new pattern matrix gives us the consensus partition that maximizes the quadratic mutual information. Note that the number of clusters in the consensus partition π^* is assumed to be known for this consensus function. Empirical study in [20] showed that this consensus function outperformed other consensus functions over a variety of data sets.

2.3 Strength of Components

Combining multiple partitions can lead to an improved partition. Is the improvement possible only when the individual partitions are "good" and close to the target partition? Another way to phrase this question is: will the clustering ensemble still work if the clustering algorithms used to generate the partitions in the ensemble are "weak", meaning that they give only a slightly better than random partition? In [20], two different types of "weak" algorithms were considered. The first is to project the data randomly on a 1D space and run k-means on the resulting 1D data set. The second is to split the data in the space of given features into two clusters by a random hyperplane. Note that computing a partition by these weak algorithms is very fast, and this allows one to create a large clustering ensemble. It turns out that, despite the poor quality of each of the partitions in the ensemble, the consensus partition is meaningful and can even outperform the results of combining strong partitions [20]. A similar idea of combining the clustering results by projecting to random subspaces was explored in [24].

2.4 Convergence

Is the success of clustering ensemble purely empirical? In [25], a theoretical analysis of the utility of clustering ensemble was performed. The analysis is based on the premise that each partition in the ensemble is a "corrupted" version of the true, but unknown, partition $\tilde{\pi}$. Two different partition generation models were considered. In both cases, the consensus partition π^* is more likely to be equal to $\tilde{\pi}$ than individual partitions in the ensemble, and π^* converges to $\tilde{\pi}$ as the number of partitions in the ensemble increases.

In the first model, a noise process $F(.)$ first corrupts the labels of $\tilde{\pi}$ in an identical and independent manner, followed by a process $T(.)$ that permutes the labels, in order to generate π_k. The consensus function is plurality voting [22], where the Hungarian algorithm is first applied to inverse $T(.)$. The label of each object in the consensus partition π^* is found by voting on the cluster labels in the ensemble. It can be shown that, as N goes to infinity, the probability that π^* is the same as $\tilde{\pi}$ goes to one, despite the fact that (i) plurality voting is used instead of majority voting, and (ii) the Hungarian algorithm may undo the effect of $T(.)$ erroneously.

In the second model, a distance function $d(\pi_t, \pi_s)$ on two partitions in the space of possible partitions $\mathbb{P}$ is assumed. Note that $d(\pi_t, \pi_s)$ needs not satisfy the triangle inequality. Some example distance functions for two partitions can be found in [26]. The observed partition π_k is a corrupted version of $\tilde{\pi}$, which is generated according to a probability distribution $p(\pi_k|\tilde{\pi})$. Under some mild assumptions on $p(\pi_k|\tilde{\pi})$, the consensus by median partition, $\pi^* = \arg\min_\pi \sum_{k=1}^{N} d(\pi, \pi_k)$, converges to $\tilde{\pi}$ at an exponential rate when N goes to infinity.

3 Feature Selection in Clustering

Clustering, similar to supervised classification and regression, can be improved by using a good subset of the available features. However, the issue of feature selection in unsupervised learning is rarely addressed. This is in sharp contrast with supervised learning, where many feature selection techniques have been proposed (see [27,28,29] and references therein). One important reason is that it is not at all clear how to assess the relevance of a subset of features without resorting to class labels. The problem is made even more challenging when the number of clusters is unknown, since the optimal number of clusters and the optimal feature subset are inter-related. Recently, several feature selection/weighting algorithms [30,31,32,33] for clustering have been proposed. We shall describe the algorithm in [33], which estimates both the importance of different features and the number of clusters automatically.

Consider model-based clustering using a Gaussian mixture. The algorithm in [33] begins by assuming that the features are conditionally independent given the (hidden) cluster label. This assumption is made regularly for models involving high-dimensional data, such as naive Bayes classifiers and the emission densities of continuous hidden Markov models. Formally, the density of the data $\mathbf{y}$ is assumed to take the form $p(\mathbf{y}) = \sum_{j=1}^{k} \alpha_j \prod_{l=1}^{d} p(y_l|\theta_{jl})$, where α_j is the weight of the j-th component/cluster and θ_{jl} is the parameter of the j-th component for the l-th feature. The j-th cluster is modeled by the distributions $p(y_l|\theta_{jl})$ with different l, and they are typically assumed to be Gaussians.

The l-th feature is irrelevant if its distribution is independent of the class labels. In other words, it follows a common density $q(y_l|\lambda_l)$ which is parameterized by λ_l, and is the same irrespective of the value of j. The form of $q(y_l|\lambda_l)$ reflects our prior knowledge about the distribution of the non-salient features, and it can be assumed to be a Gaussian. Denote the saliency of the l-th feature by ρ_l. The higher the saliency, the more important a feature is. With the introduction of ρ_l and $q(y_l|\lambda_l)$, the density of **y** can be written as

$$p(\mathbf{y}) = \sum_{j=1}^{k} \alpha_j \prod_{l=1}^{d} \left(\rho_l p(y_l|\theta_{jl}) + (1 - \rho_l) q(y_l|\lambda_l) \right), \tag{3}$$

where there are k clusters for the d-dimensional vector **y**. The saliencies of different features, together with the cluster parameters, can be estimated by maximizing the log-likelihood. Because of the need to estimate k automatically, the minimum message length (MML) criterion [34] is adopted. The optimal parameters $\{\alpha_j, \rho_l, \theta_{jl}, \lambda_l\}$ can be found by an EM algorithm [33].

One key property of that EM algorithm is its pruning behavior, which can force some of the α_j to go to zero and some of the ρ_l to go to zero or one during parameter estimation. Therefore, the algorithm is initialized to have a large number (greater than the true number) of clusters. The redundant clusters will be pruned by the algorithm automatically. This initialization strategy (first proposed in [35]) can also alleviate the problem of poor local minimum. Experimental results and further details on the algorithm can be found in [33].

4 Clustering with Constraints

In many applications of clustering, there is a preference for certain clustering solutions. This preference or extrinsic information is often referred to as *side-information*. Examples include alternative metrics between objects, orthogonality to a known partition, additional labels or attributes, relevance of different features and ranks of the objects. The most natural type of side-information in clustering is a set of *constraints*, which specifies the relationship between cluster labels of different objects. A pairwise must-link (must-not-link) constraint corresponds to the requirement that two objects should be placed in the same (different) cluster. Constraints are naturally available in many clustering applications. For instance, in image segmentation one can have partial grouping cues for some regions of the image to assist in the overall clustering [36]. Clustering of customers in market-basket database can have multiple records pertaining to the same person. In video retrieval tasks, different users may provide alternative annotations of images in small subsets of a large database; such groupings may be used for semi-supervised clustering of the entire database.

There is a growing literature on clustering with constraints (see [37] and the references therein). We shall describe the algorithm in [37], which tackles the problem of model-based clustering with constraints. Let $\mathcal{Y}^c$ and $\mathcal{Y}^u$ be the set of data points with and without constraints, respectively. Clustering with constraints is performed by seeking the cluster parameter Θ that explains both the constrained and unconstrained data well. This is done by maximizing

$$J(\Theta) = (1 - \gamma)\mathcal{L}(\mathcal{Y}^c; \Theta) + \gamma \mathcal{L}(\mathcal{Y}^u; \Theta), \tag{4}$$

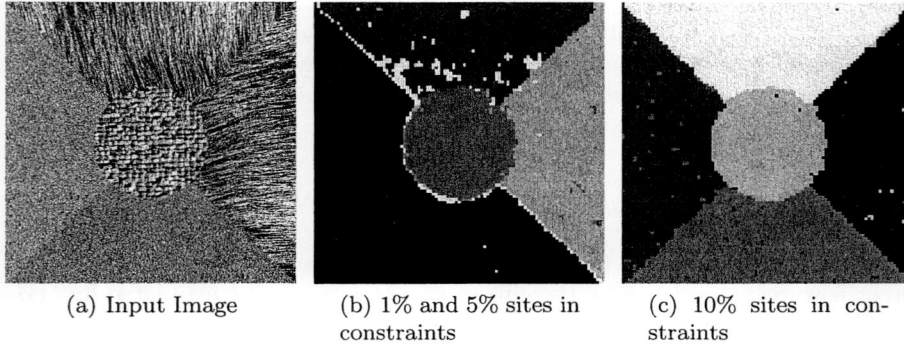

(a) Input Image (b) 1% and 5% sites in constraints (c) 10% sites in constraints

Fig. 3. Results of image segmentation. (a): input image. (b): segmentation result with 1% and 5% of sites in constraints. (c): segmentation result with 10% sites in constraints.

where $\mathcal{L}(\mathcal{Y}^c; \Theta)$ and $\mathcal{L}(\mathcal{Y}^u; \Theta)$ are the log-likelihood of the data points with and without constraints, respectively, and γ is the tradeoff parameter. The term $\mathcal{L}(\mathcal{Y}^u; \Theta)$ is defined as in the standard mixture distribution. To define $\mathcal{L}(\mathcal{Y}^c; \Theta)$, a more elaborate distribution that considers the constraints is needed.

Let z_i be the cluster label of the data $\mathbf{y}_i$. Let $\mathcal{S}$ and $\mathcal{D}$ be the set of must-link and must-not-link constraints, respectively. The number of violations of must-link and must-not-link constraints can be written as $\sum_{(i,j)\in\mathcal{S}} I(z_i \neq z_j)$ and $\sum_{(i,j)\in\mathcal{D}} I(z_i = z_j)$, respectively. By using the maximum entropy principle with λ^+ and λ^- as the Lagrange parameters, one can arrive at a prior distribution for the cluster labels $z_1, \ldots, z_m$ that participate in the constraints:

$$p(z_1, \ldots, z_m) \propto \exp\bigl(-\lambda^+ \sum_{(i,j)\in\mathcal{S}} I(z_i \neq z_j) - \lambda^- \sum_{(i,j)\in\mathcal{D}} I(z_i = z_j)\bigr). \quad (5)$$

This prior distribution on z_i, together with the component density $p(\mathbf{y}_i|z_i)$, yields the log-likelihood $\mathcal{L}(\mathcal{Y}^c; \Theta)$. A mean-field approximation is applied to the posterior distribution of the cluster labels to keep the computation tractable. An EM algorithm can be derived to find the parameter Θ that maximizes $J(\Theta)$. The algorithm is fairly efficient, and is of similar computational complexity to the standard EM algorithm for estimating a mixture distribution. Figure 3 shows the results of applying this algorithm to an image segmentation task.

5 Conclusion

Data clustering is an important unsupervised learning problem with applications in different domains. In this paper, we have reviewed some of the recent advances in cluster analysis. Combination of data partitions in a clustering ensemble can produce a superior partition when compared with any of the individual partitions. Clustering of high-dimensional data sets can be improved by estimating the saliencies of different features. Side-information, in particular constraints on cluster labels, can lead to a more desirable data partition. The research topics presented here give a glimpse of the state-of-the-art in cluster analysis, and we hope that this will stimulate the readers to investigate other problems in the area of data clustering.

References

1. Jain, A., Dubes, R.: Algorithms for Clustering Data. Prentice Hall (1988)
2. Jain, A., Flynn, P.: Image segmentation using clustering. In: Advances in Image Understanding, IEEE Computer Society Press (1996) 65–83
3. Shi, J., Malik, J.: Normalized cuts and image segmentation. IEEE Transactions on Pattern Analysis and Machine Intelligence **22** (2000) 888–905
4. Connell, S., Jain, A.: Writer adaptation for online handwriting recognition. IEEE Transactions on Pattern Analysis and Machine Intelligence **24** (2002) 329–346
5. Duta, N., Jain, A., Dubuisson-Jolly, M.P.: Automatic construction of 2D shape models. IEEE Transactions on Pattern Analysis and Machine Intelligence **23** (2001) 433–446
6. Sahami, M.: Using Machine Learning to Improve Information Access. PhD thesis, Computer Science Department, Stanford University (1998)
7. Baldi, P., Hatfield, G.: DNA Microarrays and Gene Expression. Cambridge University Press (2002)
8. Jain, A., Murty, M., Flynn, P.: Data clustering: A review. ACM Computing Surveys **31** (1999) 264–323
9. MacQueen, J.: Some methods for classification and analysis of multivariate observations. In: Proc. Fifth Berkeley Symposium on Math. Stat. and Prob., University of California Press (1967) 281–297
10. McLachlan, G., Peel, D.: Finite Mixture Models. John Wiley & Sons, New York (2000)
11. Duda, R., Hart, P., Stork, D.: Pattern Classification. 2nd edn. John Wiley & Sons, New York (2001)
12. Comaniciu, D., Meer, P.: Mean shift: A robust approach toward feature space analysis. IEEE Transactions on Pattern Analysis and Machine Intelligence **24** (2002) 603–619
13. Wu, Z., Leahy, R.: An optimal graph theoretic approach to data clustering: Theory and its application to image segmentation. IEEE Transactions on Pattern Analysis and Machine Intelligence **15** (1993) 1101–1113
14. Fischer, B., Buhmann, J.: Path-based clustering for grouping smooth curves and texture segmentation. IEEE Transactions on Pattern Analysis and Machine Intelligence **25** (2003) 513–518
15. Verma, D., Meila, M.: A comparison of spectral clustering algorithms. Technical Report 03-05-01, CSE Department, University of Washington (2003)
16. Smith, S., Jain, A.: Testing for uniformity in multidimensional data. IEEE Transactions on Pattern Analysis and Machine Intelligence **6** (1984) 73–81
17. Jain, A., Xu, X., Ho, T., Xiao, F.: Uniformity testing using minimum spanning tree. In: Proc. the 16th International Conference on Pattern Recognition. (2002) IV:281–284
18. Dubes, R., Jain, A.: Clustering techniques: The user's dilemma. Pattern Recognition **8** (1976) 247–260

19. Fred, A., Jain, A.: Evidence accumulation clustering. To appear in IEEE Transactions on Pattern Analysis and Machine Intelligence (2005)
20. Topchy, A., Jain, A., Punch, W.: Clustering ensembles: Models of consensus and weak partitions. To appear in IEEE Transactions on Pattern Analysis and Machine Intelligence (2005)
21. Strehl, A., Ghosh, J.: Cluster ensembles – a knowledge reuse framework for combining multiple partitions. Journal of Machine Learning Research **3** (2002) 583–617
22. Fridlyand, J., Dudoit, S.: Applications of resampling methods to estimate the number of clusters and to improve the accuracy of clustering method. Technical report, University of California, Berkeley (2001)
23. Mirkin, B.: Reinterpreting the category utility function. Machine Learning **45** (2001) 219–228
24. Fern, X., Brodley, C.: Random projection for high dimensional data clustering: A cluster ensemble approach. In: Proc. the 20th International Conference on Machine Learning, AAAI press (2003) 186–193
25. Topchy, A., Law, M.H., Jain, A.K., Fred, A.: Analysis of consensus partition in cluster ensemble. In: Proc. the 5th IEEE International Conference on Data Mining. (2004) 225–232
26. Meila, M.: Comparing clusterings by the variation of information. In: Proc. The 16th Annual Conference on Learning Theory, Springer (2003) 173–187
27. Guyon, I., Elisseeff, A.: An introduction to variable and feature selection. Journal of Machine Learning Research **3** (2003) 1157–1182
28. Blum, A., Langley, P.: Selection of relevant features and examples in machine learning. Artificial Intelligence **97** (1997) 245–271
29. Jain, A., Zongker, D.: Feature selection: Evaluation, application, and small sample performance. IEEE Transactions on Pattern Analysis and Machine Intelligence **19** (1997) 153–157
30. Dy, J., Brodley, C.: Feature selection for unsupervised learning. Journal of Machine Learning Research **5** (2004) 845–889
31. Roth, V., Lange, T.: Feature selection in clustering problems. In: Advances in Neural Information Processing Systems 16. MIT Press, Cambridge, MA (2004)
32. Modha, D., Scott-Spangler, W.: Feature weighting in k-means clustering. Machine Learning **52** (2003) 217–237
33. Law, M., Figueiredo, M., Jain, A.: Simultaneous feature selection and clustering using mixture models. IEEE Transactions on Pattern Analysis and Machine Intelligence **26** (2004) 1154–1166
34. Wallace, C., Freeman, P.: Estimation and inference via compact coding. Journal of the Royal Statistical Society. Series B (Methodological) **49** (1987) 241–252
35. Figueiredo, M., Jain, A.: Unsupervised learning of finite mixture models. IEEE Transactions on Pattern Analysis and Machine Intelligence **24** (2002) 381–396
36. Yu, S., Shi, J.: Segmentation given partial grouping constraints. IEEE Transactions on Pattern Analysis and Machine Intelligence **26** (2004) 173–183
37. Lange, T., Law, M., Jain, A., Buhmann, J.: Learning with constrained and unlabelled data. In: Proc. the IEEE Computer Society Conference on Computer Vision and Pattern Recognition. (2005)

Pattern Recognition in Video*

Rama Chellappa, Ashok Veeraraghavan, and Gaurav Aggarwal

University of Maryland,
College Park MD 20742, USA
{rama, vashok, gaurav}@umiacs.umd.edu
http://www.cfar.umd.edu/~rama

Abstract. Images constitute data that live in a very high dimensional space, typically of the order of hundred thousand dimensions. Drawing inferences from correlated data of such high dimensions often becomes intractable. Therefore traditionally several of these problems like face recognition, object recognition, scene understanding etc. have been approached using techniques in pattern recognition. Such methods in conjunction with methods for dimensionality reduction have been highly popular and successful in tackling several image processing tasks. Of late, the advent of cheap, high quality video cameras has generated new interests in extending still image-based recognition methodologies to video sequences. The added temporal dimension in these videos makes problems like face and gait-based human recognition, event detection, activity recognition addressable. Our research has focussed on solving several of these problems through a pattern recognition approach. Of course, in video streams patterns refer to both patterns in the spatial structure of image intensities around interest points and temporal patterns that arise either due to camera motion or object motion. In this paper, we discuss the applications of pattern recognition in video to problems like face and gait-based human recognition, behavior classification, activity recognition and activity based person identification.

1 Introduction

Pattern recognition deals with categorizing data into one of available classes. In order to perform this, we need to first decide on a feature space to represent the data in a manner which makes the classification task simpler. Once we decide the features, we then describe each class or category using class conditional densities. Given unlabeled data, the task is now to label this data (to one of available classes) using Bayesian decision rules that were learnt from the class conditional densities. This task of detecting, describing and recognizing visual patterns has lead to advances in automating several tasks like optical character recognition, scene analysis, fingerprint identification, face recognition etc.

In the last few years, the advent of cheap, reliable, high quality video cameras has spurred interest in extending these pattern recognition methodologies to

---

* This work was partially supported by the NSF-ITR Grant 0325119.

video sequences. In video sequences, there are two distinct varieties of patterns. Spatial patterns correspond to problems that were addressed in image based pattern recognition methods like fingerprint and face recognition. These challenges exist in video based pattern recognition also. Apart from these spatial patterns, video also provides us access to rich temporal patterns. In several tasks like activity recognition, event detection/classification, anomaly detection, activity based person identification etc, there exists a temporal sequence in which various spatial patterns present themselves. It is very important to capture these temporal patterns in such tasks. In this paper, we describe some of the pattern recognition based approaches we have employed for tasks including activity recognition, face tracking and recognition, anomaly detection and behavior analysis.

2 Feature Representation

In most pattern recognition (PR) problems, feature extraction is one of the most important tasks. It is very closely tied to pattern representation. It is difficult to achieve pattern generalization without using a reasonably correct representation. The choice of representation not only influences the PR approach to a great extent, but also limits the performance of the system, depending upon the appropriateness of the choice. For example, one cannot reliably retrieve the yaw and pitch angles of a face assuming a planar model.

Depending on the problem at hand, the representation itself can manifest in many different ways. Though in the case of still images, only spatial modeling is required, one needs ways to represent temporal information also when dealing with videos. At times, the representation is very explicit like in the form of a geometric model. On the other hand, in a few feature based PR approaches, the modeling part is not so explicit. To further highlight the importance of representation, we now discuss the modeling issues related to a few problems in video-based recognition.

2.1 Affine Appearance Model for Video-Based Recognition

Recognition of objects in videos requires modeling object motion and appearance changes. This makes object tracking a crucial preceding step for recognition. In conventional algorithms, the appearance model is either fixed or rapidly changing, while the motion model is a random walk model with constant variance. A fixed appearance template is not equipped to handle appearance changes in the video, while a rapidly changing model is susceptible to drift. All these factors can potentially make the visual tracker unstable leading to poor recognition results. In [1], we use adaptive appearance and velocity models to stabilize the tracker and closely follow the variations in appearance due to object motion. The appearance is modeled as a mixture of three different models, viz., (1) object appearance in a canonical frame (first frame), (2) slow-varying stable appearance within all the past observation, and (3) the rapidly changing component characterizing the two-frame variations. The mixture probabilities are updated at each frame based on the observation. In addition, we use an adaptive-velocity

Fig. 1. Affine appearance model for tracking

model, where the adaptive velocity is predicted using a first-order linear approximation based on appearance changes between the incoming observation and the previous configuration.

The goal here is to identify a region of interest in each frame of the video and not the 3D location of the object. Moreover, we believe that the adaptive appearance model can easily absorb the appearance changes due to out-of-plane pose and illumination changes. Therefore, we use a planar template and allow affine transformations only. Fig. 1 shows an example where tracker using the described representation is used for tracking and recognizing a face in a video.

2.2 3D Feature Graphs

Affine model suffices for locating the position of the object on the image, but it does not have the capability to annotate the 3D configuration of the object at each time instant. For example, if the goal is to utilize 3D information for face recognition in video, the described affine representation will not be adequate. Accordingly, [2] uses a cylindrical model with elliptic cross-section to perform 3D face tracking and recognition. The curved surface of the cylinder is divided into rectangular grids and the vector containing the average intensity values for each of the grids is used as the feature. As before, appearance model is a mixture of the fixed component (generated from the first frame) and dynamic component (appearance in the previous frame). Fig. 2 shows a few frames of a video with the cylinder superimposed on the image displaying the estimated pose.

Fig. 2. Estimated 3D pose of a face using a cylindrical model for face recognition in videos

Another possibility is to consider using a more realistic face model (e.g., 3D model of an average face) instead of a cylinder. Such detailed 3D representations make the initialization and registration process difficult. In fact, [3] shows experiments where perturbations in the model parameters adversely affect the tracking performance using a complex 3D model, whereas the simple cylindrical model is robust to such perturbations. This highlights the importance of the generalization property of the representation.

2.3 Representations for Gait-Based Recognition

Gait is a very structured activity with certain states like heel strike, toe off repeating themselves in a repetitive pattern. Recent research suggests that the gait of an individual might be distinct and therefore can be used as a biometric for person identification. Typical representations for gait-based person identification include use of the entire binary silhouette [4][5], sparser representations like the width vector [5] or shape of the outer contour [6]. 3D part based descriptions of human body [7] is also a viable representation for gait analysis.

2.4 Behavior Models for Tracking and Recognition

Statistical modeling of the motion of the objects enables us to capture the temporal patterns in video. Modeling such behaviors explicitly is helpful in accurate and robust tracking. Typically each object could display multiple behaviors. We use Markovian models (on low level motion states) to represent each behavior of the object. This creates a mixture modeling framework for the motion of the object. For illustration, we will discuss the manner in which we modeled the behavior of insects for the problem of tracking and behavior analysis of insects. A typical Markov model for a special kind of dance of a foraging bee called the waggle dance is shown in Fig. 3.

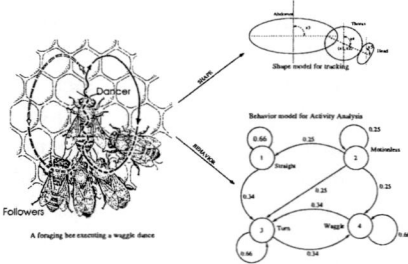

Fig. 3. A Bee performing waggle dance: The Shape model for tracking and the Behavior model to aid in Activity analysis are also shown

3 Particle Filtering for Object Recognition in Video

We have so far dealt with issues concerned with the representation of patterns in video and dealt with how to represent both spatial and temporal patterns in a manner that simplifies identification of these patterns. But, once we choose a certain set of representations for spatial and motion patterns, we need inference algorithms for estimating these parameters. One method to perform this inference is to cast the problem of estimating the parameters as a energy minimization problem and use popular methods based on variational calculus for performing this energy minimization. Examples of such methods include gradient descent, simulated annealing, deterministic annealing and Expectation-Maximization. Most such methods are local and hence are not guaranteed to converge to the global optimum. Simulated annealing is guaranteed to converge to the global optimum if proper annealing schedule is followed but this makes the algorithm extremely slow and computationally intensive. When the state-observation description of the system is linear and Gaussian, estimating the parameters can be performed using the Kalman filter. But the design of Kalman filter becomes complicated for intrinsically non-linear problems and is not suited for estimating posterior densities that are non-Gaussian. Particle filter [8][9] is a method for estimating arbitrary posterior densities by representing them with a set of weighted particles. We will precisely state the estimation problem first and then show how particle filtering can be used to solve such problems.

3.1 Problem Statement

Consider a system with parameters θ. The system parameters follow a certain temporal dynamics given by $F_t(\theta, D, N)$. (Note that the system dynamics could change with time.)

$$SystemDynamics: \qquad \theta_t = F_t(\theta_{t-1}, D_t, N_t) \qquad (1)$$

where, N is the noise in the system dynamics. The auxiliary variable D indexes the set of motion models or behaviors exhibited by the object and is usually omitted in typical tracking applications. This auxiliary variable assumes importance in problems like activity recognition or behavioral analysis (Section 4.3).

Each frame of the video contains pixel intensities which act as partial observations Z of the system state θ.

$$ObservationEquation: \qquad Z_t = G(\theta_t, I, W_t) \qquad (2)$$

where, W represents the observation noise. The auxiliary variable I indexes the various object classes being modeled, i.e., it represents the identity of the object. We will see an example of the use of this in Section4.

The problem of interest is to track the system parameters over time as and when the observations are available. Quantitatively, we are interested in estimating the posterior density of the state parameters given the observations i.e., $P(\theta_t/Z_{1:t})$.

3.2 Particle Filter

Particle filtering [8][9] is an inference technique for estimating the unknown dynamic state θ of a system from a collection of noisy observations $Z_{1:t}$. The particle filter approximates the desired posterior pdf $p(\theta_t|Z_{1:t})$ by a set of weighted particles $\{\theta_t^{(j)}, w_t^{(j)}\}_{j=1}^{M}$, where M denotes the number of particles. The interested reader is encouraged to read [8][9] for a complete treatment of particle filtering. The state estimate $\hat{\theta}_t$ can be recovered from the pdf as the maximum likelihood (ML) estimate or the minimum mean squared error (MMSE) estimate or any other suitable estimate based on the pdf.

3.3 Tracking and Person Identification

Consider a gallery of P objects. Supposing the video contains one of these P objects. We are interested in tracking the location parameters θ of the object and also simultaneously recognize the identity of the object. For each object i, the observation equation is given by $Z_t = G(\theta_t, i, W_t)$. Suppose we knew that we are tracking the pth object, then, as usual, we could do this with a particle filter by approximating the posterior density $P(\theta_t/Z_{1:t}, p)$ as a set of M weighted particles $\{\theta_t^{(j)}, w_t^{(j)}\}_{j=1}^{M}$. But, if we did not know the identity of the object we are tracking, then, we need to estimate the identity of the object also. Let us assume that the identity of the object remains the same throughout the video, i.e., $I_t = p$, where $p = \{1, 2, ...P\}$. Since the identity remains a constant over time, we have

$$P(X_t, I_t = i/X_{t-1}, I_{t-1} = j) = P(X_t/X_{t-1})P(I_t = i/I_{t-1} = j) \qquad (3)$$

$$= \begin{cases} 0 & \text{if } i \neq j; \\ P(X_t/X_{t-1}) & \text{if } i = j; j = \{1, 2, ...P\} \end{cases}$$

As was discussed in the previous section, we can approximate the posterior density $P(X_t, I = p/Z_{1:t})$ using a M_p weighted particles as $\{\theta_{t,p}^{(j)}, w_{t,p}^{(j)}\}^{j=1:M_p}$. We maintain such a set of M_p particles for each object $p = 1, 2, ..P$. Now the set of weighted particles $\{\theta_{t,p}^{(j)}, w_{t,p}^{(j)}\}_{j=1:M_p}^{p=1:P}$ with weights such that $\sum_{p=1:P}\sum_{j=1:M_i} w_{t,p}^{(j)} = 1$, represents the joint distribution $P(\theta_t, I/Z_{1:t})$. MAP and MMSE estimates for the tracking parameters $\hat{\theta}_t$ can be obtained by marginalizing the distribution $P(\theta_t, I/Z_{1:t})$ over the identity variable. Similarly, the MAP estimate for the identity variable can be obtained by marginalizing the posterior distribution over the tracking parameters. Refer to [10] for the details of the algorithm and the necessary and sufficient conditions for which such a model is valid.

3.4 Tracking and Behavior Identification

Simultaneous tracking and behavior/activity analysis can also be performed in a similar manner by using the auxiliary variable D in a manner very similar to performing simultaneous tracking and verification. Refer to [11] for details about the algorithm. Essentially, a set of weighted particles $\{\theta_t^{(j)}, w_t^{(j)}, D_t^{(j)}\}$ is used to represent the posterior probability distribution $P(\theta_t, D_t/Z_{1:t})$. Inferences about the tracking parameters θ_t and the behavior exhibited by the object D_t can be made by computing the relevant marginal distribution from the joint posterior distribution. Some of the tracking and behavior analysis results for the problem of analyzing the behaviors of bees in a hive are given in a later section.

4 Pattern Recognition in Video: Working Examples

In this section, we describe a few algorithms to tackle video-based pattern recognition problems. Most of these algorithms make use of the material described so far in this paper, in some form or the other.

4.1 Visual Recognition Using Appearance-Adaptive Models

This work [10] proposes a time series state space model to fuse temporal information in a video, which simultaneously characterizes the motion and identity. As described in the previous section, the joint posterior distribution of the motion vector and the identity variable is estimated at each time instant and then propagated to the next time instant. Marginalization over the motion state variables yields a robust estimate of the posterior distribution of the identity variable. The method can be used for both still-to-video and video-to-video face recognition. In the experiments, we considered only affine transformations due to the absence of significant out-of-plane rotations. A time-invariant first-order Markov Gaussian model with constant velocity is used for modeling motion transition. Fig. 4 shows the tracking output in a outdoor video. [1] incorporates appearance-adaptive models in a particle filter to perform robust visual tracking and recognition. Appearance changes and changing motion is handled adaptively in the manner as described in Section 2.1. The simultaneous recognition is performed by including the identity variable in the state vector as described in Section 3.3.

Fig. 4. Example tracking results using the approach in [10]

4.2 Gait-Based Person Identification

In [12], we explored the use of the width vector of the outer contour of the binarized silhouette as a feature for gait representation. Matching two sequences of width vectors was performed using the Dynamic Time Warping (DTW). The DTW algorithm is based on dynamic programming and aligns two sequences by computing the best warping path between the template and the test sequence. In [5], the entire binary image of the silhouette is used as a feature. The sequence of binary silhouette images were modeled using a Hidden Markov Model (HMM). States of the HMM were found to represent meaningful physical stances like heel strike, toe off etc. The observation probability of a test sequence was used as a metric for recognition experiments. Results using both the HMM and DTW were found to be comparable to the state of the art gait-based recognition algorithms. Refer to [12] and [5] for details of the algorithms.

4.3 Simultaneous Tracking and Behavior Analysis of Insects

In [11], we present an approach that will assist researchers in behavioral research study and analyze the motion and behavior of insects. The system must also be able to detect and model abnormal behaviors. Such an automated system significantly speeds up the analysis of video data obtained from experiments and also prevents manual errors in the labeling of data. Moreover, parameters like the orientation of the various body parts of the insects(which is of great interest to the behavioral researcher) can be automatically extracted in such a framework. Each behavior of the insect was modeled as a Markov process on low-level motion states. The transition between behaviors was modeled as another Markov process. Simultaneous tracking and behavior analysis/identification was performed using the techniques described in Section 3.4. Bees were modeled using an elliptical model as shown in Fig. 3. Three behaviors of bees Waggle Dance, Round Dance and Hovering bee were modeled. Deviations from these behaviors were also identified and the model parameters for the abnormal behaviors were also learnt online. Refer [11] for the details of the approach.

4.4 Activity Recognition by Modeling Shape Sequences

Human gait and activity analysis from video is presently attracting a lot of attention in the computer vision community. [6] analyzed the role of two of the most important cues in human motion- shape and kinematics using a pattern recognition approach. We modeled the silhouette of a walking person as a sequence of deforming shapes and proposed metrics for comparing two sequences of shapes using a modification of the Dynamic Time Warping algorithm. The shape sequences were also modeled using both autoregressive and autoregressive and moving average models. The theory of subspace angles between linear dynamical systems was used to compare two sets of models. Fig. 5 depicts a graphical visualization of performing gait recognition by comparing shape sequences. Refer to [6] for the details of the algorithm and extended results.

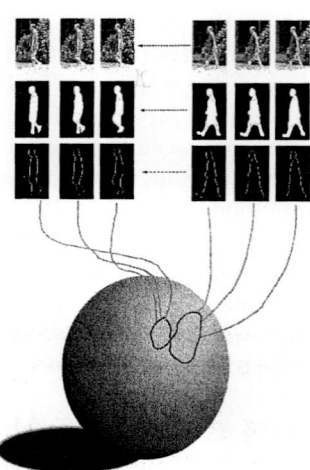

Fig. 5. Graphical illustration of the sequence of shapes obtained during gait

4.5 Activity Modeling and Anomaly Detection

In the previous subsection, we described an approach for representing an activity as a sequence of shapes. But, when new activities are seen, then we need to develop approaches to detect these anomalous activities. The activity model under consideration is a continuous state HMM. An abnormal activity is defined as a change in the activity model, which could be slow or drastic and whose parameters are unknown. Drastic changes can be easily detected using the increase in tracking error or the negative log of the likelihood of current observation given past (OL). But slow changes usually get missed. [13] proposes a statistic for slow change detection called ELL (which is the Expectation of negative Log Likelihood of state given past observations) and shows analytically and experimentally the complementary behavior of ELL and OL for slow and drastic changes. We have also established the stability (monotonic decrease) of the errors in approximating the ELL for changed observations using a particle filter that is optimal for the unchanged system. Asymptotic stability is shown under stronger assumptions. Finally, it is shown that the upper bound on ELL error is an increasing function of the rate of change with increasing derivatives of all orders, and its implications are discussed. Fig. 6 shows the tracking error, Observation likelihood and the ELL statistic for simulated observation noise.

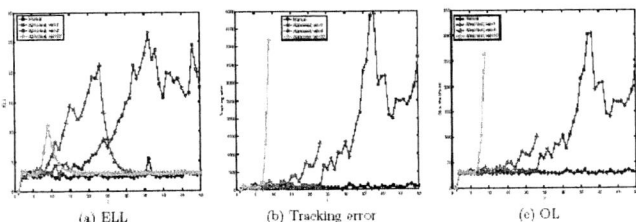

Fig. 6. ELL, Tracking error (TE) and Observation Likelihood (OL) plots: Simulated Observation noise. Notice that the TE and OL plots look alike.

5 Conclusions

We have presented very brief descriptions of some of the approaches based on pattern recognition to various problems like tracking, activity modeling, behavior analysis and abnormality detection. The treatment in this paper is not comprehensive and the interested readers are encouraged to refer the respective references and references therein for details on each of these approaches.

Acknowledgments. The authors thank Shaohua Zhou, Namrata Vaswani, Amit Kale and Aravind Sundaresan for their contributions to the material presented in this manuscript.

References

1. Zhou, S., Chellappa, R., Moghaddam, B.: Visual tracking and recognition using appearance-adaptive models in particle filters. IEEE Trans. on IP (2004)
2. Aggarwal, G., Veeraraghavan, A., Chellappa, R.: 3d facial pose tracking in uncalibrated videos. Submitted to Pattern Recognition and Machine Intelligence (2005)
3. Cascia, M.L., Sclaroff, S., Athitsos, V.: Fast, reliable head tracking under varying illumination: An approach based on registration of texture-mapped 3D models. IEEE Trans. on Pattern Analysis and Machine Intelligence **22** (2000) 322–336
4. Lee, L., Dalley, G., Tieu, K.: Learning pedestrian models for silhouette refinement. IEEE International Conference on Computer Vision 2003 (2003)
5. Kale, A., Rajagopalan, A., Sundaresan.A., Cuntoor, N., Roy Cowdhury, A., Krueger, V., Chellappa, R.: Identification of humans using gait. IEEE Trans. on Image Processing (2004)
6. Veeraraghavan, A., Roy-Chowdhury, A., Chellappa, R.: Role of shape and kinematics in human movement analysis. CVPR **1** (2004) 730–737
7. Yamamoto, T., Chellappa, R.: Shape and motion driven particle filtering for human body tracking. Intl. Conf. on Multimedia and Expo (2003)
8. Doucet, A., Freitas, N.D., Gordon, N.: Sequential Monte Carlo methods in practice. Springer-Verlag, New York (2001)
9. Gordon, N.J., Salmond, D.J., Smith, A.F.M.: Novel approach to nonlinear/nongaussian bayesian state estimation. In: IEE Proceedings on Radar and Signal Processing. Volume 140. (1993) 107–113
10. Zhou, S., Krueger, V., Chellappa, R.: Probabilistic recognition of human faces from video. Computer Vision and Image Understanding **91** (2003) 214–245
11. Veeraraghavan, A., Chellappa, R.: Tracking bees in a hive. Snowbird Learning Workshop (2005)
12. Kale, A., Cuntoor, N., Yegnanarayana, B., Rajagopalan, A., Chellappa, R.: Gait analysis for human identification. 3rd Intl. conf. on AVBPA (2003)
13. Vaswani, N., Roy-Chowdhury, A., Chellappa, R.: Shape activity: A continuous state hmm for moving/deforming shapes with application to abnormal activity detection. IEEE Trans. on Image Processing (Accepted for Publication)

Rough Sets in Perception-Based Computing
Extended Abstract

Andrzej Skowron

Institute of Mathematics, Warsaw University,
Banacha 2, 02-097 Warsaw, Poland
skowron@mimuw.edu.pl

Intelligent systems for many real life problems can be modeled by systems of complex objects and their parts changing and interacting over time. The objects are usually linked by certain dependencies, can cooperate between themselves and are able to perform complex and flexible actions (operations) in an autonomous manner. Such systems are identified as complex dynamical systems [2,40], autonomous multiagent systems [20,40], or swarm intelligent systems (see, e.g., [28,7]).

One of the main challenges to be solved in intelligent systems research is the development of methods for approximate reasoning from measurements to perception, i.e., from concepts that can be directly approximated using sensor measurements to concepts, expressed by human beings in natural language, that are the perception results [42].

The existing methodologies and technologies are not adequate to solve many problems associated with this challenge. Among such problems are, e.g., classification and understanding of medical images [30], control of autonomous systems such as unmanned aerial vehicles or robots (see, e.g., [47,44]) or problems pertaining to monitoring or rescue tasks in multiagent systems [11].

Nowadays, new emerging computing paradigms are investigated in an attempt to develop methods for solving such problems. The further progress depends on a successful cooperation of specialists from different scientific disciplines such as mathematics, logic, philosophy, computer science, artificial intelligence, biology, physics, chemistry, bioinformatics, medicine, neuroscience, linguistics, psychology, and sociology. In particular, different aspects of reasoning from measurements to perception are investigated in psychology [1,3,16], neuroscience [30,24], theories of cognition [21], layered learning [39], mathematics of learning [30], machine learning, pattern recognition [14], data mining [17] and also by researchers working on recently emerged computing paradigms, like computing with words and perception [43], granular computing [25], rough sets, rough mereology, and rough-neural computing [25].

In this lecture we overview some of these new computing paradigms and some of the interactions between the various disciplines that have been mentioned.

The concept approximation problem is the basic problem investigated in machine learning, pattern recognition [14] and data mining [17]. It is necessary to induce approximations of concepts (models of concepts) from available experimental data. The data models developed so far in such areas as statistical learning, machine learning, pattern recognition are not satisfactory for approximation of complex concepts that occur in the perception process. Researchers from the different areas have recognized the necessity to work on new methods for concept approximation (see, e.g., [8,41]). The main reason for this is that these complex concepts are, in a sense, too far from measurements which makes the searching for relevant features infeasible in a very huge space. There are several research directions aiming at overcoming this difficulty. One of them is based on the interdisciplinary research where the knowledge pertaining to perception in psychology or neuroscience is used to help to deal with complex concepts (see, e.g., [30]). There is a great effort in neuroscience towards understanding the hierarchical structures of neural networks in living organisms [12,30]. Also mathematicians are recognizing problems of learning as the main problem of the current century [30]. These problems are closely related to complex system modeling as well. In such systems again the problem of concept approximation and its role in reasoning about perceptions is one of the challenges nowadays. One should take into account that modeling complex phenomena entails the use of local models (captured by local agents, if one would like to use the multi-agent terminology [20]) that should be fused afterwards. This process involves negotiations between agents [20] to resolve contradictions and conflicts in local modeling. This kind of modeling is becoming more and more important in dealing with complex real-life phenomena which we are unable to model using traditional analytical approaches. The latter approaches lead to exact models. However, the necessary assumptions used to develop them result in solutions that are too far from reality to be accepted. New methods or even a new science therefore should be developed for such modeling [15].

One of the possible approaches in developing methods for complex concept approximations can be based on the layered learning [39]. Inducing concept approximation should be developed hierarchically starting from concepts that can be directly approximated using sensor measurements toward complex target concepts related to perception. This general idea can be realized using additional domain knowledge represented in natural language. For example, one can use some rules of behavior on the roads, expressed in natural language, to assess from recordings (made, e.g., by camera and other sensors) of actual traffic situations, if a particular situation is safe or not [22]. To deal with such problems one should develop methods for concept approximations together with methods aiming at approximation of reasoning schemes (over such concepts) expressed in natural language. The foundations of such an approach, creating a core of perception logic, are based on rough set theory [27] and its extension rough mereology [31,25], both invented in Poland, in combination with other soft computing tools, in particular with fuzzy sets.

Rough set theory due to Zdzisaw Pawlak [27], is a mathematical approach to imperfect knowledge. The problem of imperfect knowledge has been tackled for a long time by philosophers, logicians and mathematicians. Recently it became also a crucial issue for computer scientists, particularly in the area of artificial intelligence. There are many approaches to the problem of how to understand

and manipulate imperfect knowledge. The most successful one is, no doubt, the fuzzy set theory proposed by Lotfi A. Zadeh [42]. Rough set theory presents still another attempt to solve this problem. It is based on an assumption that objects are perceived by partial information about them. Due to this some objects can be indiscernible. From this fact it follows that some sets can not be exactly described by available information about objects; they are rough not crisp. Any rough set is characterized by its (lower and upper) approximations. The difference between the upper and lower approximation of a given set is called its boundary. Rough set theory expresses vagueness by employing a boundary region of a set. If the boundary region of a set is empty it means that the set is crisp, otherwise the set is rough (inexact). A nonempty boundary region of a set indicates that our knowledge about the set is not sufficient to define the set precisely. One can recognize that rough set theory is, in a sense, a formalization of the idea presented by Gotlob Frege [13].

One of the consequences of perceiving objects using only available information about them is that for some objects one cannot decide if they belong to a given set or not. However, one can estimate the degree to which objects belong to sets. This is another crucial observation in building foundations for approximate reasoning. In dealing with imperfect knowledge one can only characterize satisfiability of relations between objects to a degree, not precisely. Among relations on objects the rough inclusion relation, which describes to what degree objects are parts of other objects, plays a special role. A rough mereological approach (see, e.g., [31,35,25]) is an extension of the Leśniewski mereology [19] and is based on the relation *to be a part to a degree*. It will be interesting to note here that Jan Łukasiewicz was the first who started to investigate the inclusion to a degree of concepts in his discussion on relationships between probability and logical calculi [18].

The very successful technique for rough set methods was Boolean reasoning [9]. The idea of Boolean reasoning is based on construction for a given problem P a corresponding Boolean function f_P with the following property: the solutions for the problem P can be decoded from prime implicants of the Boolean function f_P. It is worth to mention that to solve real-life problems it is necessary to deal with Boolean functions having a large number of variables.

A successful methodology based on the discernibility of objects and Boolean reasoning has been developed in rough set theory for computing of many key constructs like reducts and their approximations, decision rules, association rules, discretization of real value attributes, symbolic value grouping, searching for new features defined by oblique hyperplanes or higher order surfaces, pattern extraction from data as well as conflict resolution or negotiation [32]. Most of the problems involving the computation of these entities are NP-complete or NP-hard. However, we have been successful in developing efficient heuristics yielding sub-optimal solutions for these problems. The results of experiments on many data sets are very promising. They show very good quality of solutions generated by the heuristics in comparison with other methods reported in literature (e.g., with respect to the classification quality of unseen objects). Moreover, they are very time-efficient. It is important to note that the methodology makes it possible to construct heuristics having a very important approximation property. Namely, expressions generated by heuristics (i.e., implicants) close to prime implicants define approximate solutions for the problem (see, e.g., [46]).

A question arises if the methods developed so far based on Boolean and approximate Boolean reasoning can be scaled to the case of complex problems considered here.

Rough set theory has attracted attention of many researchers and practitioners all over the world, who have contributed essentially to its development and applications. The rough set approach seems to be of fundamental importance to AI and cognitive sciences, especially in the areas of machine learning, knowledge acquisition, decision analysis, knowledge discovery from databases, expert systems, inductive reasoning and pattern recognition.

The rough set approach can be used in searching for complex patterns relevant for approximation of vague concepts. Different stages of this searching process are strongly related to perception.

Let us consider two simple illustrative examples supporting this claim.

In searching for relevant features often a function f, transforming objects from a given set U into simpler objects from another set U_0, is defined. In image or signal analyzis, objects from U are represented by relational structures while objects from U_0 are parts of objects from U or some other relational structures. The selection of relevant transformations f can be interpreted as the relevant structural perception of objects or their parts. Next, a set A of features (attributes) is defined on U_0. Any feature (attribute) a is a function from U_0 into V_a, where V_a is the value set of a. The indiscernibility relation $IND(B) \subseteq U_0 \times U_0$ for $B \subseteq A$ [27] can be extended to the indiscernibility relation $IND^*(B, f) \subseteq U \times U$ by $uIND^*(B, f)u'$ if and only if $f(u)IND(B)f(u')$. Hence, the indiscernibility classes of $IND^*(B, f)$ can be adjusted using parameters f and B. However, the search space for f and B is very large. Therefore, some hints from research on perception that would make this search more efficient will be of great importance [6].

Perception of relevant context for a given object is an important task in pattern recognition of complex objects. To see how such a context can be defined in the rough set approach, let us consider slightly modified information systems [27]. We assume that for any attribute a not only the value set V_a is given but also a relational structure $\mathcal{R}_a$ over V_a. One can define neighborhoods over such relational structures. Such neighborhoods can be sets defined by formulas interpreted in $\mathcal{R}_a$ or some substructures of $\mathcal{R}_a$. For example, one can define in this way time windows or some neighborhoods over time windows representing relational structures over time windows. Next, such neighborhoods can be fused and used to induce neighborhoods of objects [36]. The searching process for relevant object neighborhoods and their properties is computationally expensive. Hence, again some hints from research on perception can help to make this process more efficient.

There are many more examples linking the research on rough sets with the research on perception. For example, reasoning about changes [37], or relevant granulation of complex objects (information granules) [29].

Further cooperation between researchers working in different areas on perception can lead to advancement in constructing more efficient algorithms involved in searching for complex patterns and corresponding to different stages of the perception processes.

In a more general setting, objects we are dealing with are information granules. Such granules are obtained as the result of information granulation (see, e.g., [43,33,35,25]). Information granulation can be viewed as a human way of achieving data compression and it plays a key role in implementing the divide-and-conquer strategy in human problem-solving [43].

Computing with Words and Perceptions "derives from the fact that it opens the door to computation and reasoning with information which is perception - rather than measurement-based. Perceptions play a key role in human cognition, and underlie the remarkable human capability to perform a wide variety of physical and mental tasks without any measurements and any computations. Everyday examples of such tasks are driving a car in city traffic, playing tennis and summarizing a story" [43].

The rough mereological approach (see, e.g., [31,25]) is based on calculi of information granules for constructing complex concept approximations. Constructions of information granules should be robust with respect to their input information granule deviations. Hence, the information granule construction process itself can also be granulated. As the result the so called AR schemes (AR networks) [31,32,33,35] are obtained. AR schemes can be interpreted as complex patterns [17]. Searching methods for such patterns relevant to a given target concept have been developed [35]. Methods for deriving relevant AR schemes are computationally expensive. This complexity can be substantially reduced by using domain knowledge. In such a case AR schemes are derived in conformity with reasoning schemes in natural language that are ellicited from domain knowledge. Developing methods for deriving such AR schemes is one of the main goals of our current projects.

The ontology approximation problem is one of the fundamental problems related to approximate reasoning in distributed environments [38,34]. One should construct (in a given language that is different from the ontology specification language) not only approximations of concepts from ontology but also vague dependencies specified in the ontology. It is worthwhile to mention that ontology approximation should be induced on the basis of incomplete information about concepts and dependencies specified in the ontology. Information granule calculi based on rough sets have been proposed as tools making it possible to solve this problem.

We discuss ontology approximation in the granular computing framework. In particular, approximation of any vague dependency is a method which allows any object to compute the arguments "for" and "against" its membership to the dependency conclusion on the basis of the analogous arguments relative to the dependency premisses. Any argument is a compound information granule (compound pattern). Arguments are fused by local schemes (production rules) discovered from data. Further fusions are possible through composition of local schemes, called approximate reasoning schemes (AR schemes) (see, e.g., [31,4,33,35]). To estimate the degree to which (at least) an object belongs to concepts from an ontology the arguments "for" and "against" those concepts are collected and next a conflict resolution strategy is applied to them for predicting the degree. Several information granule calculi are involved in solving the problem of ontology approximation. Information granules are represented by compound patterns. By granulation of the discovered patterns to layers of vague concepts one can obtain more relevant approximations of dependencies by using the rough–fuzzy approach based on granulation.

Let us mention some illustrative examples related to our current projects in which ontology approximation is involved.

The prediction of behavioral patterns of a complex object evaluated over time is usually based on some historical knowledge representation used to store information about changes in relevant features or parameters. This information is usually represented as a data set and has to be collected during long-term observation of a complex dynamic system. For example, in case of road traffic, we associate the object-vehicle parameters with the readouts of different measuring devices or technical equipment placed inside the vehicle or in the outside environment (e.g., alongside the road, in a helicopter observing the situation on the road, in a traffic patrol vehicle). Many monitoring devices serve as informative sensors such as GPS, laser scanners, thermometers, range finders, digital cameras, radar, image and sound converters (see, e.g. [40]). Hence, many vehicle features serve as models of physical sensors. Here are some exemplary sensors: location, speed, current acceleration or deceleration, visibility, humidity (slipperiness) of the road. By analogy to this example, many features of complex objects are often dubbed sensors. In the lecture we discuss (see also [5]) some rough set tools for perception modelling that make it possible to recognize behavioral patterns of objects and their parts changing over time. More complex behaviour of complex objects or groups of complex objects can be presented in the form of *behavioral graphs*. Any behavioral graph can be interpreted as a *behavioral pattern* and can be used as a complex classifier for recognition of complex behaviours. We outline [5] the complete approach to the perception of behavioral patterns, that is based on behavioral graphs and the dynamic elimination of behavioral patterns. The tools for dynamic elimination of behavioral patterns are used for switching-off in the *system attention* procedures searching for identification of some behavioral patterns. The developed rough set tools for perception modeling are used to model networks of classifiers. Such networks make it possible to recognize behavioral patterns of objects changing over time. They are constructed using an ontology of concepts provided by experts that engage in approximate reasoning on concepts embedded in such an ontology. Experiments on data from a vehicular traffic simulator [45] are showing that the developed methods are useful in the identification of behavioral patterns.

Our second example concerns human computer-interfaces that allow for a dialog with experts to transfer to the system their knowledge about structurally complex objects. For pattern recognition systems [10], e.g., for Optical Character Recognition (OCR) systems it will be helpful to transfer to the system a certain knowledge about the expert view on border line cases. The central issue in such pattern recognition systems is the construction of classifiers within vast and poorly understood search spaces, which is a very difficult task. Nonetheless, this process can be greatly enhanced with knowledge about the investigated objects provided by an human expert. We outline a framework for the transfer of such knowledge from the expert and it is shown how to incorporate it into the learning process of a recognition system using methods based on rough mereology [23]. Is is also demonstrated how this knowledge acquisition can be conducted in an interactive manner, with a large dataset of handwritten digits as an example.

The outlined research directions create, in our projects, foundations toward understanding the nature of reasoning from measurements to perception. Understanding such reasoning processes is fundamental for developing intelligent systems based on perception logic. A further understanding of perception logic in interdisciplinary projects will make it possible to use discoveries from the different scientific disciplines mentioned in this article for improving the performance of intelligent systems.

Acknowledgment

The research has been supported by the grant 3 T11C 002 26 from Ministry of Scientific Research and Information Technology of the Republic of Poland.

References

1. J.R. Anderson, C. Lebiere, *The Atomic Components of Thought*, Mahwah, NJ: Lawrence Erlbaum, 1998.
2. Y. Bar-Yam, *Dynamics of Complex Systems*, Addison Wesley, 1997.
3. L.W. Barsalou, "Perceptual symbol systems," *Behavioral and Brain Sciences* 22: 577-660 1999.
4. J. Bazan, A. Skowron, "Classifiers based on approximate reasoning schemes," In: B. Dunin-Keplicz, A. Jankowsk, A. Skowron, and M. Szczuka (eds.), *Monitoring, Security, and Rescue Tasks in Multiagent Systems MSRAS*, Advances in Soft Computing, Springer, Heidelberg, pp. 191-202, 2005.
5. J. Bazan, J. Peters, A. Skowron, "Behavioral pattern identification through rough set modelling," *Proceedings of RSFDGrC 2005*, Regina, Canada, September 1-3, 2005 (to appear).
6. S. Behnke, *Hierarchical Neural Networks for Image Interpretation*, LNCS 2766, Springer, Heidelberg, 3003.
7. E. Bonabeau, M. Dorigo, and G. Theraulaz, *Swarm Intelligence. From Natural to Artificial Systems*, Oxford University Press, UK, 1999.
8. L. Breiman, "Statistical Modeling: The Two Cultures," *Statistical Science* 16(3): 199-231, 2001.

9. F.M. Brown, *Boolean Reasoning*, Kluwer Academic Publishers, Dordrecht, 1990.
10. R.O. Duda, P.E. Hart, and D.G. Stork, *Pattern Classification*, Wiley, New York, 2001.
11. B. Dunin-Keplicz, A. Jankowski, A. Skowron, and M. Szczuka (eds.), *Monitoring, Security, and Rescue Tasks in Multiagent Systems MSRAS*, Advances in Soft Computing, Springer, Heidelberg, 2005.
12. M. Fahle, T. Poggio (eds.), *Perceptual Learning*, MIT Press, Cambridge, 2002.
13. G. Frege, *Grundlagen der Arithmetik 2*, Verlag von Herman Pohle, Jena, 1893.
14. J.H. Friedman, T. Hastie, and R. Tibshirani, *The Elements of Statistical Learning: Data Mining, Inference, and Prediction*, Springer-Verlag, Heidelberg, 2001.
15. M. Gell-Mann, *The Quark and the Jaguar - Adventures in the Simple and the Complex*, Little, Brown and Co., London, 1994.
16. S. Harnad (ed.), *Categorical Perception: The Groundwork of Cognition*, Cambridge University Press, New York, 1987.
17. W. Kloesgen, J. Żytkow (eds.), *Handbook of Knowledge Discovery and Data Mining*, Oxford University Press, 2002.
18. J. Łukasiewicz, "Die Logischen grundlagen der Wahrscheinlichkeitsrechnung," Kraków, 1913, in: L. Borkowski (ed.), *Jan Lukasiewicz - Selected Works*, North Holland Publishing Company, Amsterdam, London, Polish Scientific Publishers, Warsaw, 1970.
19. S. Leśniewski: "Grungzüge eines neuen Systems der Grundlagen der Mathematik", *Fundamenta Matemaicae* XIV: 1-81, 1929.
20. M. Luck, P. McBurney, and Ch. Preist, *Agent Technology: Enabling Next Generation Computing: A Roadmap for Agent Based Computing*, AgentLink 2003.
21. A. Newell, *Unified Theories of Cognition,* Harvard University Press, Cambridge, MA, 1990.
22. S. Hoa Nguyen, J. Bazan, A. Skowron, and H. Son Nguyen, "Layered learning for concept synthesis," Transactions on Rough Sets I, LNCS3100, Springer, Heidelberg, 2004,187–208.
23. T. T. Nguyen, A. Skowron, "Rough set approach to domain knowledge approximation," In: G. Wang, Q. Liu, Y. Yao, and A. Skowron (eds.), *Proceedings of the 9th International Conference: Rough Sets, Fuzzy Sets, Data Mining, and Granular Computing, RSFDGRC'03*, Chongqing, China, Oct 19-22, 2003, LNCS 2639, pp. 221-228, Springer Verlag, Heidelberg, 2003.
24. R.W. Paine, S. Grossberg, , and A.W.A. Van Gemmert: "A quantitative evaluation of the AVITEWRITE model of handwriting learning," *Human Movement Science* (in press), 2004.
25. S.K. Pal, L. Polkowski, and A. Skowron (eds.) *Rough-Neural Computing: Techniques for Computing with Words*, Cognitive Technologies series, Springer-Verlag, Heidelberg, Germany, 2004.
26. S.K. Pal, A. Skowron (eds.), *Rough Fuzzy Hybridization: A New Trend in Decision-Making*, Springer-Verlag, Singapore, 1999.
27. Z. Pawlak, *Rough Sets: Theoretical Aspects of Reasoning about Data*, Kluwer Academic Publishers, Dordrecht, The Netherlands, 1991.
28. J.F. Peters, "Rough ethology: Towards a biologically-inspired study of collective behavior in intelligent systems with approximation spaces," *Transactions on Rough Sets* III: 153-174, LNCS 3400, springer, Heidelberg, 2005.
29. J.F. Peters, A. Skowron, P. Synak, and S. Ramanna, "Rough sets and information granulation," In: T.B. Bilgic, D. Baets, and O. Kaynak (eds.), *Tenth International Fuzzy Systems Association World Congress IFSA*, Istanbul, Turkey, June 30 - July 2, 2003, LNAI 2715, Springer-Verlag, Heidelberg, pp.370-377, 2003.

30. T. Poggio, S. Smale, "The mathematics of learning: Dealing with data," *Notices of the AMS* 50(5): 537-544, 2003.
31. L. Polkowski, A. Skowron, "Rough mereology: A new paradigm for approximate reasoning," *International Journal of Approximate Reasoning* 15(4): 333-365, 1996.
32. A. Skowron, "Rough sets in KDD" (plenary lecture), In: Z. Shi, B. Faltings, and M. Musen (eds.), *16-th World Computer Congress (IFIP'2000): Proceedings of Conference on Intelligent Information Processing (IIP'2000)*, Publishing House of Electronic Industry, Beijing, pp. 1-17, 2000.
33. A. Skowron, "Toward intelligent systems: Calculi of information granules," *Bulletin of the International Rough Set Society* 5(1-2): 9-30, 2001.
34. Skowron, A., "Approximate reasoning in distributed environments," In: Zhong, N., Liu, J. (Eds.), *Intelligent Technologies for Information Analysis*, Springer, Heidelberg, pp. 433-474, 2004.
35. A. Skowron, J. Stepaniuk, "Information granules and rough-neural computing," In: S.K. Pal, L. Polkowski, and A. Skowron (eds.), *Rough-Neural Computing: Techniques for Computing with Words*, Cognitive Technologies series, Springer-Verlag, Heidelberg, Germany, pp. 43-84, 2004.
36. A. Skowron, P. Synak, "Complex patterns," *Fundamenta Informaticae* 60(1-4): 351-366, 2004.
37. A. Skowron, P.Synak, "Reasoning in information maps," *Fundamenta Informaticae* 59(2-3): 241-259, 2004.
38. Staab, S., Studer, R., (Eds.): *Handbook on Ontologies*. International Handbooks on Information Systems, Springer, Heidelberg, 2004.
39. P. Stone, *Layered Learning in Multi-Agent Systems: A Winning Approach to Robotic Soccer*, MIT Press, Cambridge, 2000.
40. C. Urmson, et al., "High speed navigation of unrehearsed terrain: Red team technology for Grand Challenge 2004", *Report CMU-RI-TR-04-37*, The Robotics Institute, Carnegie Mellon University, 2004.
41. V. Vapnik, *Statistical Learning Theory*, Wiley, New York, 1998.
42. L.A. Zadeh, "Fuzzy sets," *Information and Control* 8: 338-353, 1965.
43. L.A. Zadeh, "A new direction in AI: Toward a Computational Theory of Perceptions," *AI Magazine* 22(1):73-84, 2001.
44. RoboCup: www.robocup.org
45. Road simulator: logic.mimuw.edu.pl/~bazan/simulator
46. RSES: logic.mimuw.edu.pl/ rses/
47. WITAS: www.ida.liu.se/ext/witas/

Conversational Case-Based Reasoning

David W. Aha

Head, Intelligent Decision Aids Group,
Navy Center for Applied Research in Artificial Intelligence,
Naval Research Laboratory (Code 5515),
Washington, DC 20375
david.aha@nrl.navy.mil

Overview

Case-based reasoning (CBR) is a problem solving methodology that focuses on reusing lessons obtained from previous (possibly generalized) experiences towards solving new problems (Kolodner, 1993; Aamodt & Plaza, 1994; Watson, 1999; Bergmann, 2002). Originally conceived by cognitive scientists, since 1993 the CBR community has focused primarily on issues of interest to artificial intelligence researchers and practitioners. Some research topics of particular interest include case representation and indexing, solution retrieval and adaptation, learning (e.g., case acquisition), and integrating case-based approaches with others. Some motivating applications have included those related to customer support, recommender systems, knowledge management, diagnosis, the health sciences, and legal reasoning.

Among these areas, most deployed CBR applications have been for the customer support niche of help-desk systems. These applications have the characteristic that problem descriptions are *incrementally* elicited from a user rather than available in complete form a priori. This category of CBR approaches is referred to as *conversational* (Aha *et al.*, 2001) because they use a dialogue with the end user to identify the problem to be solved. Many case-based diagnosis and recommendation systems have used a conversational CBR (CCBR) methodology, and met with considerable success.

In this presentation, I will introduce the CCBR methodology, describe its evolution, examine its various manifestations and their motivations, highlight recent work, and describe unsolved issues that could be the focus of enlightened dissertations.

References

Aamodt, A., & Plaza, E. (1994). Case-based reasoning: Foundational issues, methodological variations, and system approaches. *AI Communications,* **7**, 39-59.
Aha, D.W., Breslow, L.A., & Munoz-Avila, H. (2001). Conversational case-based reasoning. *Applied Intelligence,* **14**(1), 9-32.
Bergmann, R. (2002). *Experience management: Foundations, development methodology, and Internet-based applications.* Berlin: Springer.
Kolodner, J. (1993). *Case-based reasoning.* San Mateo, CA: Morgan Kaufmann.
Watson, I., (1999). CBR is a methodology not a technology. *Knowledge Based Systems Journal,* **12**(5-6), 303-308.

Computational Molecular Biology of Genome Expression and Regulation

Michael Q. Zhang

Cold Spring Harbor Laboratory,
1 Bungtown Road, Cold Spring Harbor, NY 11724 USA
mzhang@cshl.edu

Abstract. Technological advances in experimental and computational molecular biology have revolutionized the whole fields of biology and medicine. Large-scale sequencing, expression and localization data have provided us with a great opportunity to study biology at the system level. I will introduce some outstanding problems in genome expression and regulation network in which better modern statistical and machine learning technologies are desperately needed.

Recent revolution in genomics has transformed life science. For the first time in history, mankind has been able to sequence the entire human own genome. Bioinformatics, especially computational molecular biology, has played a vital role in extracting knowledge from vast amount of information generated by the high throughput genomics technologies. Today, I am very happy to deliver this key lecture at the First International Conference on Pattern Recognition and Machine Intelligence at the world renowned Indian Statistical Institute (ISI) where such luminaries as Mahalanobis, Bose, Rao and others had worked before. And it is very timely that genomics has attracted new generation of talented young statisticians, reminding us the fact that statistics was essentially conceived from and continuously nurtured by biological problems. Pattern/rule recognition is at the heart of all learning process and hence of all disciplines of sciences, and comparison is the fundamental method: it is the similarities that allow inferring common rules; and it is the differences that allow deriving new rules.

Gene expression, normally referring to the cellular processes that lead to protein production, is controlled and regulated at multiple levels. Cells use this elaborate system of "circuits" and "switches" to decide when, where and by how much each gene should be turned on (activated, expressed) or off (repressed, silenced) in response to environmental clues. Genome expression and regulation refer to coordinated expression and regulation of many genes at large-scales for which advanced computational methods become indispensable. Due to space limitations, I can only highlight some of the pattern recognition problems in transcriptional regulation, which is the most important and best studied.

Currently, there are two general outstanding problems in transcriptional regulation studies: (1) How to find the regulatory regions, in particular, the promoters regions in the genome (throughout most of this lecture, we use promoter to refer to proximal promoters, *e.g.* ~ 1kb DNA at the beginning of each gene); (2) How to identify functional *cis*-regulatory DNA elements within each such region.

1 Introduction

Recent revolution in genomics has transformed life science. For the first time in history, mankind has been able to sequence the entire human genome. Bioinformatics, especially computational molecular biology, has played a vital role in extracting knowledge from vast amounts of information generated by high throughput genomics technologies. Today, I am very happy to deliver this key lecture at the First International Conference on Pattern Recognition and Machine Intelligence at the world renowned Indian Statistical Institute (ISI) where such luminaries as Mahalanobis, Bose, Rao and others have worked before. And it is very timely that genomics has attracted a new generation of talented young statisticians, reminding us of the fact that statistics was essentially conceived from and is continuously nurtured by biological problems. Pattern/rule recognition is at the heart of all learning processes and hence, of all disciplines of sciences, and comparison is the fundamental method: It is the similarities that allow inferring common rules and it is the differences that allow deriving new rules.

Gene expression (normally referring to the cellular processes that lead to protein production) is controlled and regulated at multiple levels. Cells use this elaborate system of "circuits" and "switches" to decide when, where and by how much each gene should be turned on (activated, expressed) or off (repressed, silenced) in response to environmental clues. Genome expression and regulation refer to coordinated expression and regulation of many genes of large-scales for which advanced computational methods become indispensable. Due to space limitations, I can only highlight some pattern recognition problems in transcriptional regulation, which is the most important and best studied. Currently, there are two general outstanding problems in transcriptional regulation studies: (1) how to find the regulatory regions, in particular, the promoters (throughout most of this lecture, we use promoter to refer to proximal promoter, *e.g.* ~ 1kb DNA at the beginning of each gene) regions in the genome; (2) how to identify functional *cis*-regulatory DNA elements within each such region.

2 Finding Promoter and First Exon (FE) of a Multi-exon Gene in Vertebrate Genome

Transcription is the process of pre-mRNA (a gene transcript) synthesis. A typical vertebrate pre-mRNA contains about 9 exons, the intervening sequences (introns) between exons are spliced out during RNA processing to produce a matured RNA (mRNA). Most of the regulatory elements are found in the flanking regions of the FE of the target gene. Finding the FE is therefore the key for locating the transcriptional regulatory regions. Promoter upstream of (and overlapping with) FE functionally directs RNA polymerase II (PolII) to the correct transcriptional start site (TSS, the first base of FE) and the core promoter extending ~35bp on either side of TSS plays a central role in regulating initiation of transcription of pre-mRNA transcripts [35]. As the most important regulatory region, promoter is enriched by many transcription factor binding sites (TFBSs). They form so-called modules, each of which is acting relatively autonomously and responding to a specific set of TFs. Core promoter may be regarded as a general module and is the docking region for the Pre-Initiation Complex (PIC) of largely basal TFs and PolII itself. Core promoter contains one or more of the following *cis*-elements: TFIIB Recognition Element (BRE: ~-37SSRCGCC) and TATA-box (TBP-site: ~-31TATAWAAR) at about -35 upstream of the TSS, Initiator (Inr: -2YYANWYY) at the TSS and Downstream Core Promoter Element (DPE: +28RGWYV). Although these four elements are relatively position specific (with respect to TSS) and they have been used for TSS prediction [46], they are not enough for accurate TSS prediction at the genome-scale because many core promoters may only have one or two such elements and many such putative sites may occur frequently by chance in a large genome. One could use a large-scale promoter finder, such as CpG_Promoter [20, 47] or PromoterInspector [32].

Three general promoter/TSS recognition approaches, briefly described below, may represent the current state-of-the-art; they all are based on some specific statistical pattern learning/prediction procedures. The first is called Dragon Promoter Finder (DPF) [2, 3]. Its algorithm uses sensors for three functional regions (promoters, exons and introns) and an Aritficial Neural Network (AAN) for integrating signals. The second is called Eponine [14]. Its algorithm uses a hybrid of Relevance Vector Machine (RVM) [41] and Monte Carlo sampling from extremely large model space of possible motif weight matrices and Gaussian position distributions. The third is called First Exon Finder (FirstEF) [13]. Its algorithm uses two-level discriminant analysis: At the first level filtering, it computes a Quadratic Discriminant Analysis (QDA) score for the splice donor site from several 3'-sensors and another QDA score for the promoter from several 5'-sensors; at the second level, it integrates these flanking region sensors with additional exon-sensors using yet another QDA to arrive at the *a posteriori* probability p(FirstExon|data). It has been demonstrated recently that addition of ortholog comparison with other evolutionarily related species can further improve the prediction accuracy [44]. FirstEF not only can provide promoter/TSS predictions, but also predict the 5' splice site (donor site) of the first intron, which also often contains many regulatory *cis*-elements.

Currently, promoter prediction has been hampered by very limited training data and poor understanding of molecular details of regulation mechanisms. The performance of even the best prediction programs are still far from satisfactory [4], leaving ample room for further improvements. Because of high false-positives when predicting promoters in the whole genome, it should always locate the beginning (ATG) of protein coding regions first [48]. Multiple comparisons of evolutionarily related genomic DNA sequences can be very useful for finding conserved promoters. Some open problems are: (1) identification of alternative promoters [21]; (2) identification of non-CpG island related promoters [13]; (3) tissue/developmental specific classification and lineage relationship [38]; (4) epigenetic controls [16]; (5) coupling to RNA processing [27]; (6) good cross-species promoter alignment algorithms [31, 40]; (7) promoter evolution [43]; (8) gene regulation networks [23] and dynamics [26].

3 Identifying TFBSs in Vertebrate Promoters

Once approximate regulatory regions, such as promoters, are located, the next task is to identify *cis*-regulatory elements (largely TFBSs) within such regions. A single TFBS pattern (also called motif) can be characterized by either IUPAC consensus (as given above for the core promoter motifs) or position weight matrix (PWM), although more complicated models, such as WAM [45], HMM [24], ANN [30], VOBN [6], etc., are also possible, but less popular. Here I will focus on PWM model as it is the most useful and is directly related to protein-DNA binding affinity measurements [7]. There are many different PWM definitions, all of which are derived from frequency weight matrixes (FWM).

The three classical methods for promoter motif discovery are all based on multiple sequence alignment [49]: (1) CONSENSUS based on a greedy algorithm [37]; (2) MEME based on Expectation-maximization (EM) of likelihood for a mixture model [1]; (3) Gibbs sampling based on a simple Monte Carlo Markov Chain model [22]. In the mixture model, it is assumed that in the motif region, the base-pairs are generated with probabilities specified by $P(x, B_x)$ (x is the position within the motif and B_x is the base-pair at x) for which the matrix elements of FWM are the maximum likelihood estimator; outside the motif region, the base-pairs are generated according to a uniform random background model $P_0(B)$ which can be estimated by the composition of B (If B were a word of length k, the background model would be a Markov model of order $k-1$.). The mixing coefficient and motif starting positions will be the model parameters to be optimized by maximizing the Log-likelihood function. All of these three methods have since been further improved with more functionalities and user-friendliness. Better initial seeding may be done by word-based motif-finding methods [5].

The above motif-finding methods are used when the motif is known to be enriched in a given set of sequences. To increase specificity and sensitivity, it is better to construct two input sequence sets: One is the positive (foreground) and the other is the negative (background). Then the interesting problem is to find motif(s) that can maximally discriminate/classify the positive set from the negative set. For example, the positive set may be the genes that are co-regulated or bound by a TF and the negative set contains the genes that are not regulated or bound by the TF. If the consensus pattern (word or spaced words) are good enough for motif description, a very fast Discriminate Word Enumerator (DWE) algorithm [38] can be used in which all possible words are efficiently enumerated and ranked by the p-values derived from hyper-geometric function (Fisher exact test). The first discriminant matrix method ANN-Spec [42] is based on a perceptron (a single layer ANN) and uses a Gibbs sampling to optimize parameters (matrix elements) for maximum specificity (differential binding of the positive set vs. the negative set) through local multiple sequence alignment. Since the positives and the negatives are usually not linearly separable, the simple perceptron maybe generalized by nonlinear models using SVM [29] or Boosting approaches [19]. More recently, a novel matrix-centric approach – Discriminate Matrix Enumerator (DME) [36] has also been developed, which allows to exhaustively and efficiently enumerate and rank all possible motifs (satisfying user specified minimum information-content requirement) in the entire (discretized) matrix space (hence guaranteeing global optimality). This binary classification problem may be generalized to multi-classification problems [33].

If one has a continuous quality score for each gene (such as fold-change in expression microarray data or binding probability in ChIP-chip data), one can further generalize the classification/discrimination problem to a regression one. The first successful application of linear regression for motif finding algorithm in yeast is REDUCE [10], using MobyDick [9] to build the initial word motifs. A similar method Motif_Regressor [11], but using MDscan [25] as a feature extraction tool, can improve the sensitivity and specificity due to matrix-based motifs. Recently, nonlinear regression methods, such as, MARS_Motif [12] based on Multiple Adaptive Regression Splines [17], have also been developed, that can model synergistic motifs with a *cis*-regulatory module (CRM). Regression methods are very powerful. They can either be used for selecting functional motifs or for predicting mRNA expression levels.

Some open problems are: (1) identification of distal enhancers/silencers [28, 8]; (2) identification of tissue/developmental specific CRMs [23]; (3) higher order structural constraints [34]; (5) TFBS evolution [18].

4 Future Directions

I have only touched upon one special (albeit an important) area of genome expression and regulation. Even for protein-coding gene transcription, there are also many other regulatory steps (such as: promoter escape, pausing, elongation and termination in addition to chromatin remodeling and initiation), let alone those for many other RNA genes [15]. There are yet many steps of post-transcription control and regulation, such as, Capping, RNA splicing, polyadenylation, RNA transport, in the nucleus; and various translational regulation and post-translational modifications [27, 50]. The future challenge will include integration of data coming from various levels, especially how DNA, RNA (including miRNAs, or ncRNA in general) and protein are interrelated in the gene regulation networks.

Acknowledgements

My Lab is supported by grants from NIH and NSF. I would like to thank present and past members who have contributed to various methods discussed in this text.

References

1. Bailey TL, Elkan C. Fitting a mixture model by expectation maximization to discover motifs in biopolymers. Proc Int Conf Intell Syst Mol Biol. (1994) 2:28-36.
2. Bajic VB, Seah SH, Chong A, Zhang G, Koh JL, Brusic V. Dragon Promoter Finder: Recognition of vertebrate RNA polymerase II promoters. Bioinformatics. (2002) 18(1):198-199.
3. Bajic VB, Brusic V. Computational detection of vertebrate RNA polymerase II promoters. Methods Enzymol. (2003) 370:237-250.

4. Bajic VB, Tan SL, Suzuki Y, Sagano S. Promoter prediction analysis on the whole human genome. Nat Biotechnol. (2004) 22(11):1467-1473.
5. Barash Y, Bejerano G, Friedman N. A simple hyper-geometric approach for discovering putative transcription factor binding sites. In: Gascuel O, Moret BME (eds): Algorithms in Bioinformatics. Proc First Intl Wksp, #2149 LNCS. (2001) 278-293.
6. Ben-Gal I, Shani A, Gohr A, Grau J, Arviv S, Shmilovici A, Posch S, Grosse I. Identification of transcription factor binding sites with variable-order Bayesian networks. Bioinformatics. (2005) 21(11):2657-2666.
7. Berg OG, von Hippel PH. Selection of DNA binding sites by regulatory proteins. Statistical-mechanical theory and application to operators and promoters. J Mol Biol. (1987) 191(4):723-750.
8. Boffelli D, Nobrega MA, Rubin EM. Comparative genomics at the vertebrate extremes. Nat Rev Genet. (2004) 5(6):456-465.
9. Bussemaker HJ, Li H, Siggia ED. Building a dictionary for genomes: Identification of presumptive regulatory sites by statistical analysis. Proc Natl Acad Sci U S A. (2000) 97(18):10096-10100.
10. Bussemaker HJ, Li H, Siggia ED. Regulatory element detection using correlation with expression. Nat Genet. (2001) 27(2):167-171.
11. Conlon EM, Liu XS, Lieb JD, Liu JS. Integrating regulatory motif discovery and genome-wide expression analysis. Proc Natl Acad Sci U S A. (2003) 100(6):3339-3344.
12. Das D, Banerjee N, Zhang MQ. Interacting models of cooperative gene regulation. Proc Natl Acad Sci U S A. (2004) 101(46):16234-16239.
13. Davuluri RV, Grosse I, Zhang MQ. Computational identification of promoters and first exons in the human genome. Nat Genet. (2001) 29(4):412-417. Erratum: Nat Genet. (2002) 32(3):459.
14. Down TA, Hubbard TJ. Computational detection and location of transcription start sites in mammalian genomic DNA. Genome Res. (2002) 12(3):458-461.
15. Eddy SR. Computational genomics of noncoding RNA genes. Cell. (2002) 109(2):137-140.
16. Fazzari MJ, Greally JM. Epigenomics: Beyond CpG islands. Nat Rev Genet. (2004) 5(6):446-455.
17. Friedman MJ. Multivariate adaptive regression splines. Ann Stat. (1991) 19:1-67.
18. Gasch AP, Moses AM, Chiang DY, Fraser HB, Berardini M, Eisen MB. Conservation and evolution of cis-regulatory systems in ascomycete fungi. PloS Biol. (2004) 2(12):e398.
19. Hong P, Liu XS, Zhou Q, Lu X, Liu JS, Wong WH. A boosting approach for motif modeling using ChIP-chip data. Bioinformatics. (2005) 21(11):2636-2643.
20. Ioshikhes IP, Zhang MQ. Large-scale human promoter mapping using CpG islands. Nat Genet. (2000) 26(1):61-63.
21. Kim TH, Barrera LO, Zheng M, Qu C, Singer MA, Richmond TA, Wu Y, Green RD, Ren B. A high-resolution map of active promoters in the human genome. Nature. (2005) [e-pub ahead of print].
22. Lawrence CE, Altschul SF, Boguski MS, Liu JS, Neuwald AF, Wootton JC. Detecting subtle sequence signals: A Gibbs sampling strategy for multiple alignment. Science. (1993) 262(5131):208-214.
23. Levine M, Davidson EH. Gene regulatory networks for development. Proc Natl Acad Sci U S A. (2005) 102(14):4936-4942.
24. Li W, Meyer CA, Liu XS. A hidden Marcov model for analyzing ChIP-chip experiments on genome tiling arrays and its application to p53 binding sequences. Bioinformatics. (2005) 21 Suppl 1:i274-i282.

25. Liu XS, Brutlag DL, Liu JS. An algorithm for finding protein-DNA binding sites with applications to chromatin-immunoprecipitation microarray experiments. Nat Biotechnol. (2002) 20(8):835-839.
26. Lucchetta EM, Lee JH, Fu LA, Patel NH, Ismagilov RF. Dynamics of Drosophila embryonic patterning network perturbed in space and time using microfluidics. Nature. (2005) 434(7037):1134-1138.
27. Maniatis T, Reed R. An extensive network of coupling among gene expression machines. Nature. (2002) 416(6880):499-506.
28. Nobrega MA, Ovcharenko I, Afzal V, Rubin EM. Scanning human gene deserts for long-range enhancers. Science. (2003) 302(5644):413.
29. Pavlidis P, Furey TS, Liberto M, Haussler D, Grundy WN. Promoter region-based classification of genes. Pac Symp Biocomput. (2001) 151-163.
30. Pedersen AG, Engelbrecht J. Investigations of Escherichia coli promoter sequences with artificial neural networks: New signals discovered upstream of the transcriptional startpoint. Proc Int Conf Intell Syst Mol Biol. (1995) 3:292-299.
31. Prakash A, Tompa M. Statistics of local multiple alignments. Bioinformatics (2005) 21 Suppl 1:i344-i350.
32. Scherf M, Klingenhoff A, Werner T. Highly specific localization of promoter regions in large genomic sequences by PromoterInspector: A novel contact analysis approach. J Mol Biol. (2000) 297(3):599-606.
33. Segal E, Barash Y, Simon I, Friedman N, Koller D. From promoter sequence to expression: A probabilistic framework. Proc 6th Intl Conf Res Comp Mol Biol. (2002) 263-272.
34. Siggers TW, Silkov A, Honig B. Structural alignment of protein-DNA interfaces: Insights into the determinants of binding specificity. J Mol Biol. (2005) 345(5):1027-1045.
35. Smale ST, Kadonaga JT. The RNA Polymerase II core promoter. Annu Rev Biochem. (2003) 72:449-479.
36. Smith AD, Sumazin P, Zhang MQ. Identifying tissue-selective transcription factor binding sites in vertebrate promoters. Proc Natl Acad Sci U S A. (2005) 102(5):1560-1565.
37. Stormo GD, Hartzell GW 3rd. Identifying protein-building sites from unaligned DNA fragments. Proc Natl Acad Sci U S A. (1989) 86(4):1183-1187.
38. Sumazin P, Chen G, Hata N, Smith AD, Zhang T, Zhang MQ. DWE: Discriminating word enumerator. Bioinformatics. (2005) 21(1):31-38.
39. Taatjes DJ, Marr MT, Tjian R. Regulatory diversity among metazoan co-activator complexes. Nat Rev Mol Cell Biol. (2004) 5(5):403-410.
40. Tharakaraman K, Marino-Ramirez L, Sheetlin S, Landsman D, Spouge JL. Alignments anchored on genomic landmarks can aid in the identification of regulatory elements. Bioinformatics. (2005) 21 Suppl 1:i440-i448.
41. Tipping ME. Space Bayesian learning and the relevance vector machine. J Machine Learning Res. (2001) 1:211-244.
42. Workman CT, Stormo GD. ANN-Spec: A method for discovering transcription factor binding sites with improved specificity. Pac Symp Biocomput. (2000) 467-478.
43. Wray GA. Transcriptional regulation and the evolution of development. Int J Dev Biol. (2003) 47(7-8):675-684.
44. Xuan Z, Zhao F, Wang JH, Chen GX, Zhang MQ. Genome-wide promoter extraction and analysis in human, mouse and rat. Genome Biol. (2005) In Press.
45. Zhang MQ, Marr TG. A weight array method for splicing signal analysis. Comput Appl Biosci. (1993) 9(5):499-509.
46. Zhang MQ. Identification of human gene core promoters *in silico*. Genome Res. (1998) 8(3):319-326.

47. Zhang MQ. Discriminant analysis and its application in DNA sequence motif recognition. Brief Bioinform. (2000) 1(4):331-342.
48. Zhang MQ. Computational prediction of eukaryotic protein-coding genes. Nat Rev Genet. (2002) 3(9):698-709.
49. Zhang MQ. Computational methods for promoter recognition. In: Jiang T, Xu Y, Zhang MQ, (eds.): Current Topics in Computational Molecular Biology, MIT Press Cambridge, Massaschusetts (2002) 249-268.
50. Zhang MQ. Inferring gene regulatory networks. In: Lengquer, T. (ed.) Bioinformatics – from Genome to Therapies. Wiley-VCH. (2005) Submitted.

Human Activity Recognition

J.K. Aggarwal

Department of Electrical and Computer Engineering,
The University of Texas at Austin,
Austin, Texas, 78712
aggarwaljk@mail.utexas.edu

Motion is an important cue for the human visual system Mobiles have fascinated children, Zeno (circa 500 B.C.) studied moving arrows to pose a paradox and Zeke is investigating the human brain devoted to the understanding of motion. In computer vision research, motion has played an important role for the past thirty years. An important application of motion research has emerged in the past decade. This area is devoted to the study of people – facial expression recognition, gesture recognition, whole-body tracking and human activity recognition. The broad area is at times called "looking at people." In addition, study of human motion is of interest to number of disciplines including psychology, kinesiology, choreography, computer graphics and human-computer interaction.

Recent interest in certain applications like surveillance, sports-video analysis, monitoring a car driver has heightened our interest in human activity recognition. A major goal of current computer vision research is to recognize and understand human motion, activities and continuous activity. Initially, we focused on tracking a single person; today we focus on tracking, recognizing and understanding interactions among several people, for example at an airport or at a subway station. Interpreting such a scene is complex, because similar configurations may have different contexts and meanings. In addition, occlusion and correspondence of body parts in an interaction present serious difficulties to understanding the activity.

Prof. Aggarwal's interest in motion started with the study of motion of rigid planar objects and it gradually progressed to the study of human motion. The current work includes the study of interactions at the gross (blob) level and at the detailed (head, torso, arms and legs) level. The two levels present different problems in terms of observation and analysis. For blob level analysis, we use a modified Hough transform called the Temporal Spatio-Velocity transform to isolate pixels with similar velocity profiles. For the detailed-level analysis, we employ a multi-target, multi-assignment strategy to track blobs in consecutive frames. An event hierarchy consisting of pose, gesture, action and interaction is used to describe human-human interaction. A methodology is developed to describe the interaction at the semantic level.

Professor Aggarwal will present analysis and results, and discuss the applications of the research.

A Novel T^2-SVM for Partially Supervised Classification

Lorenzo Bruzzone and Mattia Marconcini

Dept. of Information and Communication Technology, University of Trento,
Via Sommarive, 14, I-38050, Povo, Trento, Italy
Phone: +39-0461-882056, Fax: +39-0461-882093
lorenzo.bruzzone@ing.unitn.it

Abstract. This paper addresses partially supervised classification problems, i.e. problems in which different data sets referring to the same scenario (phenomenon) should be classified but a training information is available only for some of them. In particular, we propose a novel approach to the partially supervised classification which is based on a Bi-transductive Support Vector Machines (T^2-SVM). Inspired by recently proposed Transductive SVM (TSVM) and Progressive Transductive SVM (PTSVM) algorithms, the T^2-SVM algorithm extracts information from unlabeled samples exploiting the transductive inference, thus obtaining high classification accuracies. After defining the formulation of the proposed T^2-SVM technique, we also present a novel accuracy assessment strategy for the validation of the classification performances. The experimental results carried out on a real remote sensing partially supervised problem confirmed the reliability and the effectiveness of both the T^2-SVM and the corresponding validation procedure.

1 Introduction

In the pattern recognition literature, classification problems are usually addressed according to supervised or unsupervised approaches, depending on both the availability of prior information and the specific investigated application. If a reliable training set is available, supervised methods are preferred, otherwise it is mandatory to adopt unsupervised clustering techniques. However, there are also hybrid problems which lie between these two opposite families. In this context, a novel issue concerns partially supervised classification problems [1], [2]. The term partially supervised is used to indicate situations in which many data sets referring to the same scenario (phenomenon) are available, but a reliable training set is not available for all of them. This is a common situation in several real applications (e.g., video surveillance, remote sensing, speech recognition), where gathering reliable prior information is often too expensive both in terms of economic costs and time. The aim of partially supervised techniques is to obtain an acceptable classification accuracy for all the considered data sets, included those for which a specific training set is not available. Therefore, the investigated problem becomes strongly ill-posed and ill-conditioned, because no labeled samples are available for some data sets.

In this paper, we addressed the aforementioned problem in the framework of Support Vector Machines (SVMs). SVMs proved to be very effective in addressing standard supervised classification problems. Recently, the Transductive SVM (TSVM) [3] and Progressive Transductive SVM (PTSVM) [4] algorithms, which exploit the transductive inference (i.e., extracting information from the spectral distribution of unlabeled samples), proved capable to improve the classification accuracies with respect to standard inductive SVM when only few training samples are available. In order to take advantage of the transductive inference in addressing the partially supervised problem, inspired by both TSVMs and PTSVMs, we propose a bi-transductive SVM (called T^2-SVM) that, starting from an inductive learning inference, is able to update the decision function according to a double transductive inference based on unlabeled samples. In particular, a three-step procedure is defined by considering the different types of data that are taken into account (only training samples, only transductive samples or both of them).

Given the complexity of the investigated problem, the accuracy assessment of the classification algorithm plays a very important role, considering that: i) the problem is strongly ill-posed; ii) standard statistical methods for validation cannot be employed because no labeled samples are available for defining a test set. For this reason, in this work we also present a novel empirical validation strategy, which assumes that there exist an intrinsic structure underlying a classification process that rules the partially supervised problem.

The paper is organized into six sections. Section 2 describes the simplifying assumptions and the notation adopted, whereas Section 3 addresses the proposed T^2-SVM technique. Section 4 introduces the derived validation approach. Section 5 reports the experimental results, and, finally, Section 6 draws the conclusions.

2 Problem Formulation

In the following, without loss of generality, we consider as an example of partially supervised problem the classification of two different data sets, $\mathbf{R}_1$ and $\mathbf{R}_2$ (e.g. two remote sensing images, two audio signals), referring to the same scene observed at different times (t_1 and t_2, respectively). We assume that prior information is available only for $\mathbf{R}_1$. It is worth nothing that the extension to the case of more data sets is straightforward.

Let $\mathbf{X}_1 = \{\mathbf{x}_1^1, \mathbf{x}_2^1, \ldots, \mathbf{x}_M^1\}$ and $\mathbf{X}_2 = \{\mathbf{x}_1^2, \mathbf{x}_2^2, \ldots, \mathbf{x}_N^2\}$ denote two proper subsets of $\mathbf{R}_1$ and $\mathbf{R}_2$ composed of M labeled and N unlabeled patterns, respectively. We refer to $\mathbf{X}_1$ as "training set" and to $\mathbf{X}_2$ as "transductive set", whereas we call $\mathbf{x}_1^2, \ldots, \mathbf{x}_N^2$ "transductive patterns". Let $\mathbf{x}_i^1$ and $\mathbf{x}_i^2$ be the $1 \times d$ feature vectors associated with the i-th sample of $\mathbf{X}_1$ and $\mathbf{X}_2$ (where d represents the dimensionality of the input space) and let $A = |\mathbf{X}_1|$ be the cardinality of $\mathbf{X}_1$. We assume that in our system the set of classes that characterize the considered data sets is fixed; therefore only the spatial and spectral distributions of such classes are supposed to vary over time. This assumption is reasonable in several real applications [1], [2]. We name $\Omega = \{\omega_1, \omega_2, \ldots, \omega_L\}$ the set of L classes that characterize the two data sets at both t_1 and t_2; $y_i^1, y_i^2 \in \Omega$ are the classification labels of the i-th pattern of $\mathbf{X}_1$ and $\mathbf{X}_2$, respectively. In the formulation of the proposed technique, we make the following assumptions:

- a set of training labels $Y_1 = \{y_1^1, y_2^1, \ldots, y_M^1\}$ for X_1 is available;
- a set of training labels $Y_2 = \{y_1^2, y_2^2, \ldots, y_N^2\}$ for X_2 is not available;
- the statistical distribution of the classes in R_1 and R_2 is consistent.

Under the aforementioned hypothesis, our goal is to perform an accurate and robust classification of R_2 by exploiting X_1, Y_1 and X_2.

3 The Proposed T²-SVM Technique

The proposed technique is divided into three main phases, which refer to the different types of samples exploited in the learning process: i) only training patterns (*inductive inference*); ii) training and transductive patterns (*bi-transductive inference*); iii) only transductive patterns (*algorithm convergence*). For the sake of simplicity, we formulate the T²-SVM technique addressing a two-class problem.

3.1 Phase 1: Inductive Inference

The initial step of the entire process ($t = 0$) corresponds to the first phase of the T²-SVM technique. In order to determine the starting position of the separating hyperplane, at the beginning a standard inductive SVM is applied only to training samples of the first data set (acquired at time t_1). As we assume to deal with linearly non-separable data, the inductive SVM solves the following minimization problem [5]:

$$\begin{cases} \min_{(w^{(0)}, b^{(0)}, \xi^{(0)})} \left\{ \frac{1}{2} \|w^{(0)}\|^2 + C^{(0)} \sum_{i=1}^{A^{(0)}} \xi_i^{(0)} \right\} \\ y_i^1 \cdot \left(w^{(0)} \cdot x_i^1 + b^{(0)} \right) \geq 1 - \xi_i^{(0)}, \quad \forall i = 1, \ldots, A^{(0)}, \ x_i^1 \in X_1^{(0)} \end{cases} \quad (1)$$

where $\xi_i^{(0)}$ are positive slack variables, $C^{(0)}$ is the regularization parameter, $w^{(0)}$ represents the vector normal to the separating hyperplane and $b^{(0)}$ is the bias of the separating hyperplane [5].

The value of $C^{(0)}$ can be chosen a priori depending on the standard methods commonly used in literature [5]. All the transductive patterns $x_1^2, \ldots, x_N^2$ are classified according to the resulting decision function $f^{(0)}(x) = w^{(0)} \cdot x + b^{(0)}$.

3.2 Phase 2: Bi-transductive Inference

The second iterative phase represents the core of the proposed algorithm. At the generic iteration t, for all the transductive patterns the corresponding value of the decision function determined at the iteration $t-1$ is computed. The P unlabeled transductive samples lying into the margin band which are closest both to the lower or the upper margin bound are given the label "-1" and "$+1$", respectively (P is a free parameter defined a priori by the user). It may happen that the number of unlabeled patterns in one side of the margin is lower than P. In such situations the labeling is done anyway. As a consequence, let $D \leq P$ and $U \leq P$ denote the number of transductive patterns labeled at the current iteration which belong to the lower and the upper side of the margin, respectively.

The main purpose of the T^2-SVM technique is to define and solve a bound minimization problem involving only the patterns that describe the classification problem at t_2. Consequently, at each iteration a subset of the training samples of the first data set is deleted. In particular, from the original training set $\mathbf{X}_1^{(0)}$, the D samples with label "-1" and the U samples with label "$+1$" furthest from the separating hyperplane are erased (they are the training patterns that less affect the position of the separating hyperplane). Figure 1 and Figure 2 show an example on a simulated data set. If the training set is not completely erased yet and the margin band is empty, the number of patterns to delete becomes E. This parameter is defined a priori by the user and is not critical. It is worth nothing that in this way the position of the separating hyperplane changes at each iteration, therefore a dynamical adjusting is mandatory. It may happen, in fact, that the classification results at the current iteration do not match the labels assigned earlier: if the new label is different from the previous one, the transductive pattern is reset as unlabeled. As it will be underlined in the following, our aim is to gradually increase the regularization parameter for the transductive patterns that algorithm for a simulated data set. Training patterns $x_i^1 \in \mathbf{X}_1$ are shown as white and black circles; transductive patterns $x_i^2 \in \mathbf{X}_2$ are shown as grey squares. The separating hyperplane is shown as a solid line, while the dashed lines define the margin. The dashed circles highlight the P ($P=3$) transductive patterns selected from both the upper and the lower side of the margin labeled at the first iteration. The dashed squares surround the training patterns to erase. have been given a label, according to a time-dependent criterion. We say that all the samples of $\mathbf{X}_2^{(0)}$ which have been assigned until iteration $t-1$ always to the same label, belong to set $\mathbf{J}^{(t)}$. This set is partitioned into a finite number of subsets G, where G is a free parameter called *Growth Rate* and represents the maximum number of iterations for which the user

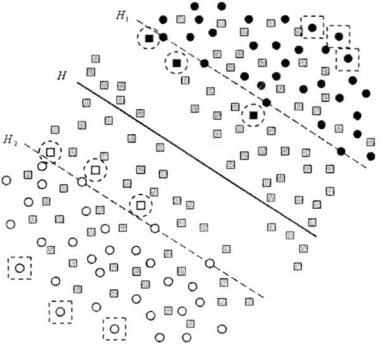

Fig. 1. Margin and separating hyperplane resulted after the first phase ($t=0$) of the T^2-SVM algorithm for a simulated data set. Training patterns $x_i^1 \in \mathbf{X}_1$ are shown as white and black circles; transductive patterns $x_i^2 \in \mathbf{X}_2$ are shown as grey squares. The separating hyperplane is shown as a solid line, while the dashed lines define the margin. The dashed circles highlight the P ($P=3$) transductive patterns selected from both the upper and the lower side of the margin labeled at the first iteration. The dashed squares surround the training patterns to erase.

allows the regularization parameter to increase. Each subset $\mathbf{J}_l^{(t)}$ contains all the samples that belong to the subset with index $l-1$ at iteration $t-1$ and are consistent with the results of the current separating hyperplane. The cost function to minimize and the corresponding bounds become the following:

$$\begin{cases} \min_{\left(\mathbf{w}^{(t)}, b^{(t)}, \bar{\xi}^{(t)}, \bar{\xi}^{*(t)}\right)} \left\{ \frac{1}{2}\left\|\mathbf{w}^{(t)}\right\|^2 + C^{(t)} \sum_{i=1}^{A^{(t)}} \xi_i^{(t)} + \sum_{l=1}^{G} C_l^* \sum_{j=1}^{B_l^{(t)}} \xi_{lj}^{*(t)} \right\} \\ y_i^1 \cdot \left(\mathbf{w}^{(t)} \cdot \mathbf{x}_i^1 + b^{(t)}\right) \geq 1 - \xi_i^{(t)}, \quad \forall i = 1, \ldots, A^{(t)} \\ \left(y_{lj}^2\right)^{(t)} \cdot \left(\mathbf{w}^{(t)} \cdot \mathbf{x}_{lj}^2 + b^{(t)}\right) \geq 1 - \xi_{lj}^{*(t)}, \forall l = 1, \ldots, G, \forall j = 1, \ldots, B_l^{(t)} \end{cases} \quad (2)$$

where $\mathbf{x}_i^1 \in \mathbf{X}_1^{(t)}$, $\mathbf{x}_{lj}^2 \in \mathbf{J}_l^{(t)} \subseteq \mathbf{X}_2^{(0)}$ and

$$\begin{cases} \bar{\xi}^{*(t)} = \left\{ \xi_{11}^{*(t)}, \ldots, \xi_{1,B_1}^{*(t)}, \ldots, \xi_{G,1}^{*(t)}, \ldots, \xi_{G,B_G}^{*(t)} \right\} \\ B_l^{(t)} = \left|\mathbf{J}_l^{(t)}\right|, \quad \forall l = 1, \ldots, G \\ \left(y_{lj}^2\right)^{(t)} = f^{(t-1)}\left(\mathbf{x}_{lj}^2\right), \quad \forall l = 1, \ldots, G, \forall j = 1, \ldots, B_l^{(t)} \end{cases} \quad (3)$$

At the generic iteration t, the algorithm associates the patterns of $\mathbf{J}_l^{(t)}$ with a regularization parameter C_l^* depending on the l-th subset $\mathbf{J}_l^{(t)}$. The regularization parameter $C^{(t)}$ corresponding to the original training samples that describe the classification problem at t_1, changes at each iteration. A proper choice for $C^{(t)}$ and C_l^* has an important role for an effective behavior of the algorithm. In order to decrease the influence of the patterns of $\mathbf{X}_1^{(0)}$ in determining the position of the separating hyperplane, at each iteration, on the one end, we let their cost-factor $C^{(t)}$ drop gradually down. On the other hand, in order to better control possible mislabelings, we let the regularization parameter associated with the transductive patterns gradually increase. Training

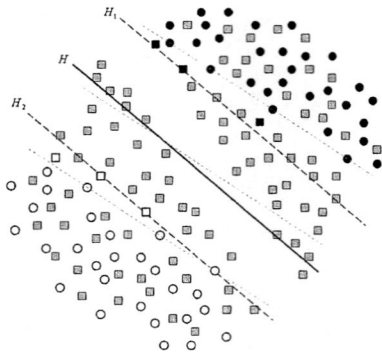

Fig. 2. Margin and separating hyperplane resulting at the end of the first iteration $(t=1)$ of the T^2-SVM algorithm. The dashed grey lines represent both the separating hyperplane and the margin at the beginning of the learning process.

and transductive data might exhibit very different distribution functions. As a consequence, we reasonably expect that a transductive pattern starts assuming a significant weight during the learning process only after it has the same label for some iterations. Accordingly, we decided to increase the cost-factor for the transductive patterns in a quadratic way, depending on the number of cycles they last inside $\mathbf{J}$. Likewise, we let the cost factor for the training samples, $C^{(t)}$, decrease in a quadratic way too. The described procedure requires that three parameters have to be chosen a priori: $C \equiv C^{(0)}$, $C^* \equiv C_1^*$ and G (with the constraint $C > C^*$). At step G, we make $C^{(t)}$ and C_l^* assume the values C^* and C_G^*, respectively. In order to better control the classification error, we set $C_G^* = C/2$. The second phase ends at iteration K, when $\mathbf{X}_1^{(0)}$ is empty.

3.3 Phase 3: Algorithm Convergence

The second phase ends when all the original training patterns associated to $\mathbf{R}_1$ have been erased. Consequently, in the last phase, only the transductive samples are considered. We can rewrite the initial minimization problem as follows:

$$\begin{cases} \min_{\left(\mathbf{w}^{(l)}, b^{(l)}, \xi^{*(l)}\right)} \left\{ \frac{1}{2} \left\| \mathbf{w}^{(l)} \right\|^2 + \sum_{l=1}^{G} C_l^* \sum_{j=1}^{B_l^{(t)}} \xi_{lj}^{*(l)} \right\} \\ \left(y_{lj}^2 \right)^{(t)} \cdot \left(\mathbf{w}^{(l)} \cdot \mathbf{x}_{lj}^2 + b^{(l)} \right) \geq 1 - \xi_{lj}^{*(l)}, \forall l = 1, \ldots, G, \forall j = 1, \ldots, B_l^{(t)} \end{cases} \quad (4)$$

When both the remaining unlabeled samples of $\mathbf{X}_2^{(0)}$ lying into the margin band at the current iteration and the number of mislabeled patterns with respect to the previous iteration are lower than or equal to $\lceil a \cdot N \rceil$, we assume that convergence is reached and denote the corresponding iteration $t = conv$. The coefficient a is fixed a priori and tunes the sensitivity of the learning process (a reasonable empirical choice has proven to be $a = 0.02$). At the iteration $t = conv + 1$ the final minimization problem becomes the following:

$$\begin{cases} \min_{(\mathbf{w}, b, \xi^*)} \left\{ \frac{1}{2} \|\mathbf{w}\|^2 + \frac{C}{2} \sum_{j=1}^{|\mathbf{J}^{(conv)}|} \xi_j^* \right\} \\ \left(y_j^2 \right)^{(conv)} \cdot \left(\mathbf{w} \cdot \mathbf{x}_j^2 + b \right) \geq 1 - \xi_j^*, \forall j = 1, \ldots, \left| \mathbf{J}^{(conv)} \right|, \mathbf{x}_j^2 \in \mathbf{J}^{(conv)} \end{cases} \quad (5)$$

The aforementioned problem is solved by employing a standard inductive SVM because the algorithm associates to all the patterns the same cost-factor $C/2$. Now, all the patterns of $\mathbf{R}_2$ can be labeled according to the current separating hyperplane (see Figure 3). Note that $\mathbf{X}_2$ and $\mathbf{R}_2$ might coincide. The bigger is $\mathbf{X}_2$, the higher is the number of transductive patterns taken into account in positioning the separating hyperplane and the more accurate becomes the classification of $\mathbf{R}_2$. However, an effective trade-off is necessary, because the computational load increases together with the size of $\mathbf{X}_2$.

The above-described algorithm is defined only for two-class problems. When a multiclass problem has to be investigated, the choice of adopting a One-Against-All strategy [5] is mandatory. At each iteration, in fact, all the transductive patterns should be labeled. Hence, we cannot employ a One-Against-One strategy: it is not possible to consider only samples that are supposed to belong to two specific information classes without labeling all the others.

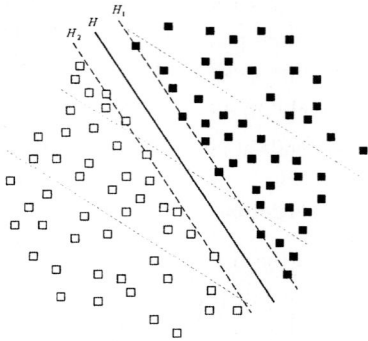

Fig. 3. Final margin and separating hyperplane resulting after the third phase of the T^2-SVM algorithm. The dashed grey lines represent both the separating hyperplane and the margin at the beginning of the learning process.

4 The Proposed Accuracy Assessment Strategy

As we pointed out before, since no prior information for the second data set R_2 is available, a technique for validating the classification results of the T^2-SVM technique is necessary. We investigated such challenging issue assuming that there exist an intrinsic structure which underlies the classification process and relates the solutions to the partially supervised problem that are consistent for R_1 and R_2. Let us suppose to obtain an acceptable solution for R_2 by exploiting a T^2-SVM. Our idea is that by applying again the T^2-SVM algorithm in the reverse sense (using the classification labels in place of the missing prior knowledge for R_2 and keeping the same transductive parameters), in the most cases it is possible to obtain a reasonable classification accuracy over R_1. At the beginning, we train an inductive SVM using the labeled patterns $x_i^1 \in X_1^{(l)}$; the resulting solution is supposed to be acceptable for R_1: we say that the system is in the state $\overline{A}$. Afterwards, we apply the bi-transductive algorithm as described in Section III. For both the kernel-function parameters and the regularization parameter C we keep the same values used in the learning phase of the inductive SVM. If the four parameters C^*, G, P and E are set properly, the solution is expected to be consistent for R_2 and the system moves to the state $\overline{B}$; otherwise, if the solution is not-consistent, the system moves to the state $\overline{D}$. Let $y_1^2,...,y_M^2$ denote the classification labels corresponding to the transductive samples $x_i^2 \in X_2^{(l)}$. Successively, we apply the T^2-SVM algorithm again using X_2 with the labels $y_1^2,...,y_M^2$ as training set and $\mathbf{X}_1$ as transductive set (it is worth nothing that the labels $y_1^1,\ldots,y_N^1$ are not taken into account for the learning purpose). All the transductive parameters remain the same. Let $CA \in [0 \div 1]$ denote the classification accuracy parameter selected by the user (e.g., the Kappa coefficient, the Overall Accuracy), whereas let CA_{th} represent a prefixed threshold for it. We can compute the value for CA associated to the results obtained by the T^2-SVM addressing the reverse bi-transductive process because the labels $y_1^1,\ldots,y_N^1$ are known. When $CA < CA_{th}$, the classification accuracy for $\mathbf{R}_1$ is considered non-acceptable and the system moves to the state $\overline{C}$, otherwise the solution is consistent and the system moves back to the state $\overline{A}$. When the system, starting from the state $\overline{A}$, is able to return into the state $\overline{A}$, we can empirically assume that the classification accuracy over $\mathbf{R}_2$ is satisfactory and, as a consequence, the solution is acceptable. This aspect is very crucial because in such situations we are able to assess that $\mathbf{R}_2$ is classified with a proper accuracy for our classification task even if no a priori information is available. Let us denote $P(\overline{Y} | \overline{X})$ be the probability that the system joins the generic state $\overline{Y}$ starting from the generic state $\overline{X}$ by applying the T^2-SVM algorithm. The proposed validation technique is effective under the two following conditions:

- $P(\overline{A} | \overline{D}) = 0$ and $P(\overline{C} | \overline{D}) = 1$: if the solution obtained by the first T^2-SVM is not acceptable, it must be never possible to obtain an acceptable solution for $\mathbf{R}_1$ by applying the bi-transductive algorithm in the reverse sense;
- $P(\overline{A} | \overline{B}) > 0$: starting from an acceptable solution for $\mathbf{R}_2$ it must be possible, by applying the T^2-SVM algorithm in the reverse sense, to obtain an acceptable solution for $\mathbf{R}_1$. The transductive parameters are not optimized for the reverse bi-transductive process, therefore we always assume that $P(\overline{C} | \overline{B}) > 0$. Moreover, it is desirable that $P(\overline{A} | \overline{B}) > P(\overline{C} | \overline{B})$.

It is worth nothing that in the aforementioned assumptions the system reasonably discards solutions that are actually consistent, but never accepts and validates solutions that are non-consistent, which is definitely a more critical aspect of validation in partially supervised problems. The best value for CA obtained by the inductive SVM for $\mathbf{R}_1$ is denoted as CA_{best}. We reasonably expect that the final value of CA should be lower than CA_{best} in the most cases, therefore, we suggest to fix the threshold $CA_{th} = CA_{best} - \varepsilon$, $\varepsilon \in [0.1 \div 0.2]$. The higher the threshold is, the more reliable the final results are but, at the same time, the number of the correct consistent solutions for the partially supervised problem discarded increases.

5 Experimental Results

In order to assess the effectiveness of the proposed approach, without loss of generality, we focused our attention on the analysis of remote-sensing images acquired over the same geographical area at different times. We carried out several experiments on a data set made up of two multispectral images acquired by the Thematic Mapper (TM) sensor of the Landsat 5 Satellite. The investigated area refers to Lake Mulargia (Italy). The two images were acquired in September 1995 (R_1) and in July 1996 (R_2), respectively. The available prior knowledge was used to derive a training and a test set for both the images, but in all the experiments, we assumed that only the information for the first date was available. We identified five land-cover classes that characterize the considered classification problem (see Table 1). We used the training set of R_1 as X_1 ($N = 2249$) and the test set of R_2 as X_2 ($M = 1949$). Five texture features in addition to the six TM channels (the thermal IR band was discarded) were taken into account, in order to exploit the non-parametric properties of the SVMs. The well-known SMO algorithm [5] was employed in the learning phase of both the inductive SVMs and the proposed T^2-SVMs (with proper modifications). For all the experiments we used Gaussian kernel functions.

An inductive SVM called SVM-1 was firstly trained over R_1: on the related test samples we obtained an Overall Accuracy and a Kappa coefficient equal to 95.33% and 0.938, respectively. Table 2 reports the results obtained at t_2 over X_2 by: i) SVM-1; ii) an inductive SVM trained using the available prior knowledge at t_2 (SVM-2) keeping the same parameters determined for SVM-1; iii) the T^2-SVM (whose parameter values were $G = 250$, $C^* = 0.25$, $E = N \cdot 0.005$ and $P = N \cdot 0.035$), which exhibited the highest classification accuracy. The T^2-SVM proved the effectiveness of the proposed technique exhibiting both an Overall Accuracy and a Kappa coefficient higher than those obtained by the inductive SVMs trained over X_1. Furthermore, the accuracies are even slightly higher than those obtained with the inductive SVM trained over X_2. This result is very important because it proves that T^2-SVMs can model the addressed problem better than an inductive SVM trained on

Table 1. Number of Patterns in the Training and Test Sets for Both the September 1995 and July 1996 Images

Class	Number of patterns	
	Training	Test
Pasture	554	589
Forest	304	274
Urban Area	408	418
Water Body	804	551
Vineyard	179	117

Table 2. Overall Accuracy and Kappa Coefficient over the Test Set of the July 1996 Image

Classifier	Overall Accuracy	Kappa Coefficient
SVM-1	87.84%	0.843
SVM-2	94.56%	0.928
T^2-SVM	94.77%	0.932

the proper labeled patterns. It is worth nothing that the experiment with SVM-2 has been carried out only to assess the effectiveness and the reliability of the proposed technique: in partially supervised problems, in fact, a training set at t_2 is not available for definition. The classification accuracies of the T^2-SVM approach resulted high and stable even into a large neighborhood of the optimal values for the transductive parameters (i.e., G, C^*, P and E), thus proving the robustness of the proposed algorithm.

We also carried out several experiments for validating the proposed accuracy assessment procedure and the results obtained over 300 trials proved that it is particularly promising. The Kappa coefficient was chosen as the reference classification accuracy parameter CA, fixing $CA_{th} = 0.79$ (i.e. $\varepsilon = 0.15$). The system moved from state $\overline{A}$ to state $\overline{B}$ in 260 cases. In the remaining 40 cases it moved to state $\overline{D}$. It is worth nothing that for simulating malfunctions of the T^2-SVM learning process, we selected values for the transductive parameters very far from the optimal ones. The system did never obtain consistent solutions for $\mathbf{R}_1$ when it started from non-acceptable solutions for $\mathbf{R}_2$, thus satisfying the first requirement addressed in Section 4. We point out that starting from state $\overline{B}$ the system went back to state $\overline{A}$ in the 54% of the cases. It is a very important result considering that 140 correct solutions for $\mathbf{R}_2$ were correctly identified without any prior training information, thus confirming the validity of the proposed accuracy assessment technique.

6 Conclusion

In this paper, a T^2-SVM approach to partially supervised classification and the corresponding validation strategy have been presented. The results obtained on the investigated data set confirmed the effectiveness of both: i) the bi-transductive approach to partially supervised classification problems; ii) the accuracy assessment strategy for identifying correct solutions without having any training information.

References

1. L. Bruzzone and D. Fernàndez Prieto, "Unsupervised retraining of a maximum-likelihood classifier for the analysis of multitemporal remote-sensing images," *IEEE Trans. Geosci. Remote Sensing*, vol. 39, 2001.
2. L. Bruzzone and R. Cossu, "A multiple-cascade-classifier system for a robust and partially unsupervised updating of land-cover maps," *IEEE Trans. Geosci. Rem. Sens*, vol. 40, 2002.
3. T. Joachims, "Transductive inference for text classification using support vector machines," *Proceedings of the 16th International Conference on Machine Learning*, Bled, 1999.
4. Y. Chen, G. Wang and S. Dong, "Learning with progressive Transductive support vector machine," *Pattern Recognition Letters*, vol. 24, 2003.
5. N. Cristianini and J. Shawe-Taylor, *An Introduction to Support Vector Machines*, Cambridge University Press, 2000.

S_Kernel: A New Symmetry Measure

Vito Di Gesù[1,2] and Bertrand Zavidovique[2]

[1] DMA, Università di Palermo, Italy
[2] IEF, University of Paris XI, ORSAY, France
digesu@math.unipa.it, zavido@ief.u-psud.fr

Abstract. Symmetry is an important feature in vision. Several detectors or transforms have been proposed. In this paper we concentrate on a measure of symmetry. Given a transform S, the kernel SK of a pattern is defined as the maximal included symmetric sub-set of this pattern. It is easily proven that, in any direction, the optimal axis corresponds to the maximal correlation of a pattern with its flipped version. For the measure we compute a modified difference between respective surfaces of a pattern and its kernel. That founds an efficient algorithm to attention focusing on symmetric patterns.

Keywords: Symmetry transforms, symmetry measure, correlation, feature extraction.

1 Introduction

Symmetry is a prevalent perceptive feature for humans. For instance the human face or body is approximately symmetric that is exploited to assist in face recognition and facial feature detection. Asymmetry is instinctively interpreted for a sign of disease. Psychologists of the Gestalt school have assigned a relevant role to symmetry in attentive mechanism both in visual and auditory systems [1]. For example, psycho-physical experiments show that infants (1-2 years old) tend to fixate symmetrically around an arbitrary single distinctive stimulus (ex. corners of a triangle). From the survey by Zabrodsky [2], we stress upon some saliency of the vertical symmetry associated with a mental rotation of linear complexity with the angle. Symmetry detection skills are ranked in the order vertical, horizontal, bent and then rotational. Moreover, symmetry of parts near the axis contribute more than symmetry of further parts near edges, themselves more critical than regions in between, and half a pattern is really scanned as soon as some symmetry was conjectured. That corroborates our own findings in the machine domain.

Like most visual features as edges, regions from color or texture, or motion, symmetry appears more an impression and a clue on some phenomenon than really a quantified variable. In psychophysics, the concern for symmetry measures emerges as early as in the late fifties [3] . They should help predicting response to (plane) figures. Thus the question of binary vs. continuous concept is raised: is a pattern symmetric or asymmetric, or could it be symmetric to a certain degree?

Zusne [4] exemplifies a research school that tends to evaluate symmetry based on moments — the third in his case — of area or perimeter of the pattern itself or of its projections. Moments can be determinate or statistical. Partly by-product of the Gelstalt theory, the informational concept of redundancy bridges both types. Single form symmetry involves redundancy, but also the shape is likely considered an item in a sample which the "best" figure is extracted from (e.g. maximum self overlapped). When symmetry is assumed single form parameter, the shape is broken into quadrants thanks to tentative axes and for instance a variance of portions in different quadrants is computed. Still in the informational vein of psychophysics studies, Yodogawa [5] departs from simple measures of the type "number of axes", "size of equivalent sub-set" etc. that usually involve frequencies (e.g. Fourier or Gabor). Redundancy is again taken for the measurable property, and the 2-D Walsh-Hadamar transform is preferred from noticing that its basic functions fall equally into 4 subsets along with the type of symmetry — vertical, horizontal, πrotational and double — . Hence the transform decomposes any single pattern into four symmetry components which an entropy function of the power spectrum is applied to, resulting in the so-called *symmetropy*. However, test patterns are small blocks of dots or squares, making it easy to compare with human responses but telling little about the method to process real images.

The concept of symmetry is important in machine vision too. Several surveys have been proposed, a recent quite interesting one being [6]. Same as other image features, to be extracted by computers, symmetry obeys geometric or analytic mathematical models: some distance from the actual image to the model is minimized. In the present paper we rather introduce a new symmetry measure based on the concept of kernel (SK) of a pattern, defined as the maximal included symmetric sub-set of this pattern [32].

Section 2 provides a review on symmetry works. In section 3, we introduce the notion of a "kernel" that stems logically from IOT ([32]) through a classical gauge in functional analysis, and a preliminary study of the main parameter - the optimal axis to spot - leads to an ultimate detection algorithm based on correlation and to a general enough symmetry measure. A series of experiments in section 4, on both binary and grey scaled pictures, show the relevance of primary results. Concluding remarks are given in Section 5.

2 State of the Art

The *Symmetry Axial Transform (SAT)* [7] can be considered one of the first approaches for the detection of symmetry starting from the borders of a digital object. SAT is a subset of the medial axis, derived from the selection of the center of maximal circles for inclusion. SAT is able to retrieve only maximal axes of symmetry, i.e. those symmetries that are already included in the medial axis. Some limitations of the SAT algorithm have been solved by the introduction of the *Smoothed Local Symmetry* [8]. The main idea is retrieving a global symmetry (if it exists) from the local curvature of contours, through the locus of mid-edge-point pairs. An innovating approach by Sewisy [9] makes a late avatar of that algorithmic line.

Authors couple the Hough transform with geometric symmetry to exhibit candidate ellipse centers. All remaining feature points are grouped into sub-regions where ellipse-like patterns are actually detected. In [10] polygonal approximations of pattern contours are broken into elements (e.g. with Delaunay/Voronoi type of method) of which axial features are pieced together. In [11,12,13] the mathematical background to extract object skewed symmetries under scaled Euclidean, affine and projective images transformation is proposed. An algorithm for back-projection is given and the case of non-coplanarity is studied. The authors introduce also the concept of invariant signature for matching problems.

The use of gray level information was firstly investigated in [14], where the symmetry descriptor of a given object is based on a cross correlation operator evaluated on the gray levels. In [15], the search for symmetries is based on the evaluation of the *axial moment* of a body around its center of gravity. In the case of images, gray levels are considered the point masses. This descriptor has been applied at a local level to define the *Discrete Symmetry Transform* (*DST*). Object symmetries can hence be studied with axial moments of regions previously selected. In [16], local symmetry is computed in convolving with the first and second derivative of Gaussians to detect reflectional symmetry. Both a "measure" of symmetry and an axis orientation are provided at each point. Shen [17] or DuBuff [18] use complex moments associated with Fourier or Gabor transforms of images for an approximation. Although it implies axes to pass through the center of mass, and although they are not invariant to affine transforms, the phase of such (generalized) complex moments proves efficient in detecting most axes of isolated, centered and well contrasted figures.

In [19], authors introduce several descriptors from Marola's one, further extended to finite supports and varying scales for the analysis of object symmetries that are based on the Radon and the Fourier transforms. Scale dependency is claimed to detect global symmetries in an image without using any segmentation procedure. The proposed algorithm is based on a *global optimization* approach that is implemented by a probabilistic genetic algorithm to speedup the computation. Along the same line, Shen and al. [20] detect symmetry in seeking out the lack of it. A measure is defined that is comprised of two terms - symmetric and asymmetric energy. The latter is null for a set of pixels invariant through horizontal reflection. Hence, the method consists of minimizing the asymmetric term of the energy over an image. In [21], a multi-scale similar idea (see also [22]) is considered: a vector potential is constructed from the gradient field extracted from filtered images. Edge and symmetry lines are extracted through a topographical analysis of the vector field (i.e. curl of the vector potential). This is performed at various heights above the image plane. Symmetry axes are lines where the curl of the vector vanishes and edges are where the divergence of the potential vanishes.Yeshurun and al. [23] build on the Blum-Asada vein, but in quantifying a potential for every pixel to be center —or part of an axis— of symmetry, based on pairs of edge points tentatively symmetric from their respective gradient vectors. A degree of symmetry is assigned to every pair within a given pixel neighborhood and a weighted combination of these makes the pixel potential, whose local maxima provide a measure depending on both intensity and shape. The technique further extends to textures [24].

Some described methods provide more symmetry descriptors that measures can be computed from, others aim at straight symmetry measures. The difference is obvious when comparing for instance Cross's and Yeshurun's. One major reason is the objective mathematical difference between a metric and a measure, the first is some integral version of the second. Another reason is whether it is required for measures in pattern recognition to mimic perceptual evaluations. An analysis of the wider concept of similarity is proposed in [25]. Authors challenge distance axioms as for comparing patterns or pattern and ideal model. Tversky's psychological indexes are used to substitute distances with ordinal structures based on three properties - dominance, consistency and transitivity - that rely extensively on the "max". Hence, through set theory a connection is made with fuzzy sets to implement comparisons between segments from shapes or textures. The comparison departs mainly from others in that not only absolute segment properties as length or coarseness found it but also inter relations between neighbor segments. That was targeted and makes it interesting for any other image feature as symmetry. Tuzikof [26] designs an illustration of such concepts applied to symmetry sensed by machines. They propose to consider the co-volume of a shape P and its transformed version τP, to quantify the invariance through that transform τ. The co-volume is the symmetric term in the expression of the volume of the Minkowski's sum (morphological expansion) of P and τP, and the measure is the co-volume normalized by the product of volumes. That makes it a symbolic correlation of P and τP. So, the link is made with inertia and further with the canonical form to support proofs of invariance. The developed theory applies only to compact convex sets but it provides a perfect example of a true symmetry measure that takes advantage of not obeying the triangle inequality.

Zabrodsky [27] tackles explicitly symmetry detection as a continuous feature. She selects equidistant points along contours or equiangular edge points around the pattern center-of- mass (centroid). From these n points the nearest $C_n - symmetric$ pattern is built in rotating the average of the counter rotation version of the points by $2i\pi/n, [0 \leq i \leq n-1]$. The method extends easily in 2.5-D by facets, and to grey level objects in treating inner level lines separately the same way. The measure considered is the point to point L_2-distance from the pattern to its nearest symmetric version. An iterative procedure of the gradient descent type can improve the center of symmetry by maximizing the measure, in case of a predicted pattern truncation. In the many applications they completed in Chemistry, corners seem to be favored as most as possible for the point basis. Yet the method remains line based if not strictly edges. It depends heavily on the centroid and on the choice of points, hence of the order, for which optimality appears hard to provide. About the order, an interesting comment by Kanatani [28] reminds that symmetries make an hierarchy. Then for a given set of n points, information criteria exist to ground a maximization of the robustness to perturbations. An optimal order of symmetry can thus be derived. That is also an answer to those who claim that moments are the only order free technique. Yet an other answer to the same is that the hierarchy justifies to privilege vertical then horizontal symmetry as nature does. Apart from the relativity of symmetry direction, the review of preceding works points out that: 1) searching for invariance in comparing a pattern with its transformed version, prevents from imposing the centroid for the a priori focus of interest; 2) introducing true measures helps building more abstract versions of distances, more suitable for approximate comparison of objects; 3) sets which measures apply on may be "sets of pixels or vectors" making the shapes under consideration or "sets of patterns comparable through some class of transforms": in either case "set operations" , as Minkowski's ones, are worth considered. They do not limit to contours and bridge logic with geometry.

Before to show in the next sections why and how we put these ingredients together, we conclude this bibliography by recalling three more works that fit very well the algorithmic line above and are the closest to ours. It makes clear the main contributions of this paper respective to previous work. In [29] the authors had this intuitive idea of correlating the image with its transformed version to by-pass the centroid. But they do that on the inner product of (gaussian) gradients, hence on edges. R. Owens [30] searches explicitly for a measure of symmetry to indicate approximate bilateral symmetry of an extracted object. But she defines tentative symmetries from the principal axes of inertia, whence the centroid again, before to compute the sum of absolute differences of grey levels in symmetric pairs over the object, normalized by their maximum. When the symmetric point falls out of the object the difference is set to this latter maximum value. Note that, although it is not mentioned, such a measure amounts to a slightly modified L_1-difference between the object and a maximal-for-inclusion symmetric version of it in the given direction. Kazhdan et al. [31] target a true visualization of symmetry over every point of the pattern. They use explicitly the same idea of a difference (L_2 in their case) between the image and its closest symmetric version, proven to be the average of the picture and its transform. But they need a measure that integrates all reflective invariance about a bundle of straight lines (or planes in 3-D). It is robust to noise and suitable for object matching, yet a center is necessary to this symmetry representation. The representation plots for each and every direction the measure of symmetry about the plane normal to that direction passing through the center of mass. Note that its local maxima point out the potential pattern symmetries.

3   The New Symmetry Measure

In previous papers [32] we defined the *IOT* that is a map product of iterated morphological erosion and symmetry detection.

Definition 1. The *Symmetry Transform*, S, on a continuous object $X \subset R^2$ is given by:

$$S_\alpha(\mathbf{X}) = \int_X m(x) \times \rho^2(x, r(\alpha)) dx \quad for \quad \alpha \in [0, \pi[\tag{1}$$

where, $r(\alpha)$ is the straight line with slope α passing through the center of gravity of the object X, $m(x)$ is the mass of the object in $x \in X$, and ρ is a distance function of x from the straight line. ◇

Definition 2. The *Iterated Object Transform*, IOT, is given by:

$$IOT_{\alpha,1}(X) = S_\alpha(X), \quad IOT_{\alpha,n}(X) = S_\alpha\left[(E)^{n-1}(X)\right] \quad for \ n > 1 \quad (2)$$

$(E)^n$ stands for the morphological erosion by the unit sphere (or any other suitable structuring element would any suitable a priori information be available), iterated n times. The number of iterations depends on the size of the input image and on the distribution of the gray levels. The S transform is thus computed on progressively shrunk versions of the binary input image or on steadily intensity reduced versions of the gray level input image, until some predefined decrease or a minimum of intensity is reached.

3.1 Definition of the Kernel

Following commonly used gauges in functional analysis, a possible object to support a symmetry measure could be *maximal included symmetric pattern* resp. *minimal including symmetric pattern* : *extremal* then subjects to the measure.

Definition 1. The S-kernel of the pattern P - $SK(P)$ - is the maximal for inclusion symmetric (pattern) subset of P (see Fig. 1).

Remark 1: the center of mass likely varies from the kernel to the pattern.

For instance, let be $\mu = argMaxSymmetry(ptrn)$. How does $K_\mu(ptrn)$ compare with $K(ptrn)$? How do their respective Symmetry relate? In most cases $K_\mu(ptrn)$ should be a good enough gauge of $K(ptrn)$, or the difference between them will be most indicative.

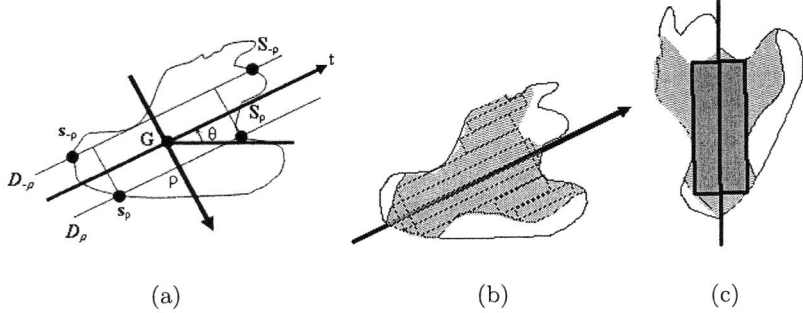

(a) (b) (c)

Fig. 1. (a) Sketch of the kernel detection algorithm; (b) the kernel of the pattern in (a); (c) expanding the $IOTK$ of the pattern in (a) into the kernel

3.2 Formal Setting and an Algorithm

Considering operators to be used in the end, correlation, our conjecture here is of an attention focusing process based on symmetry. Introducing the latter notion of interest implies that all non interesting regions around be faded to zero, and that the pattern scan be started for instance at the very left of it. Hence, the pattern $f(x)$ gets a bounded support and the origin of the x-axis can be where the interest starts.

Let be (Fig 2): $S_f^x(t) = \frac{f(x+t)+f(x-t)}{2}$ the symmetric version of f with respect to x. For the L_2-norm, the best axis x^* corresponds to:

$$S_{x*}(f) = \min_x \int_a^b [f(x+t) - f(x-t)]^2 \, dt$$

It is easily proven that $S_{x*}(f)$ corresponds to

$(f \otimes f) maximal$ or equivalently to $\int_{sup(0,2x-b)}^{inf(2x,b)} f(2x-u) \times f'(u) du = 0$

One gets yet another algorithm: find the maximum correlation of the picture in a given direction (i.e. over all translations in this direction) with its mirror symmetric in that direction (i.e. scanned right to left). Considering existing efficient algorithms for image geometric transforms (eg. *cordic*), rotations to span directions can then be performed on the image before scans and correlation: approximations need to be checked for the error introduced remain acceptable (comparable to the one from sampled angles and discrete straight lines).

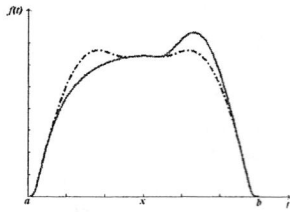

Fig. 2. Searching for the symmetry axis of a function $y = f(t)$ (plain line): its symmetric version around $x, S_f^x(t)$ (dotted line)

Remark 2: Note that if the image is tiled adapted to the predicted size of potential symmetric objects, one can derive an efficient focusing process.

3.3 Symmetry Measure

Following the preliminary simplifying assumption above, while the kernel is exhibited the picture is considered to be binarized or at least the pattern was cropped if it was not before. So, in order to test the proposed algorithm we compute a measure of symmetry classically defined as: $\lambda_1 = 1 - \frac{Area(D)}{Area(A)}$, with A, the pattern or a binding sub-picture, B, its kernel, and $Area(D) = Area(A - B)$. Provided suitable binarization or windowing, it remains a robust first approximation where $\lambda_1 = 1$ if $Area(B) = Area(A)$.

4 Experimental Results and Further Comments

In this section we show some results of the application of the S-kernel algorithm (SKA) to attention focusing.

We tested the possibility of using kernel based operators to detect points of interest in complex images. Examples of such images are shown in Fig.s 3a,b; they represent a famous painting by Tintoretto and a group photo under natural illuminating conditions. In both images the goal was to detect the directions of the most symmetric objects of a given size. For example in the group photo the direction of people faces (see Fig. 3c,d).

(a) (b)

Fig. 3. Point of attention derived by the kernel transformation based on the correlation for images: (a) Group of women (Tintoretto 1545-1588); (b) group photo

The implemented algorithm is not general: the size of the target is first estimated. This is not a big constraint in many applications, among which is face detection. The procedure consists in raster scanning the input image with a window, size of which is set on the basis of the human face dimensions scaled to the input frame. Inside each window kernel-based operators are computed. The algorithm returns all windows for which the value of λ (ρ) is greater than a given threshold $\phi \in [0, 1]$. Here, the threshold was set to the mean value of λ (ρ) in all experiments. A great value of λ (ρ) in a given direction indicates a bilateral symmetry typical of face like objects. Fig.s 3c,d show the results from SKA. Not all objects with high bilateral symmetry are faces. Nevertheless the method was able to extract all face positions, introducing an error of 17% in the evaluation of the face direction. And over all experiments the percentage of not faces was 21%.

5 Concluding Remarks

This paper describes a new measure of axial symmetry derived from a new object feature named the "symmetry-kernel". The symmetry kernel of an object is its maximal subpart symmetric respective to a given direction. A new algorithm is derived from, based on the computation of the cross-correlation of an object with its flipped version. It is fast and not sensitive to numerical factors because computations are inner products. The algorithmw as tested on both synthetic and real data. Experiments show the ability of the symmetry-kernel to detect the main directionality of an object. It has been also implemented as a local operator to detect the presence of objects in a scene and their direction. The evaluation of the distance between an object and its kernel is a crucial point and needs further investigation.

References

1. W.Khöler and H.Wallach, "Figural after-effects: an investigation of visual processes", *Proc. Amer. phil. Soc.*, Vol.88, pp.269–357, 1944.
2. H. Zabrodsky, "Symmetry - A review", *Technical Report 90-16*, CS Dep. The Hebrew University of Jerusalem, 1990.
3. R.M. Boyton, C.L. Elworth, J. Onley, C.L. Klingberg, "Form discrimination as predicted by overlap and area", *RADC-TR-60-158*, 1960.
4. L.Zusne, "Measures of symmetry", *Perception and Psychophysics*,Vol.9, N.3B, 1971.
5. E. Yodogawa, "Symmetropy, an entropy-like measure of visual symmetry", *Perception and Psychophysics*, Vol. 32, N.3, 1983.
6. David O'Mara, "Automated facial metrology, chapter 4: Symmetry detection and measurement" PhD thesis, Feb. 2002.
7. H.Blum and R.N.Nagel, "Shape description using weighted symmetric axis features", *Pattern recognition*, Vol.10, pp.167–180, 1978.
8. M.Brady, H.Asada, "Smoothed Local Symmetries and their implementation", *The International Journal of Robotics Research*, Vol.3, No.3, pp.36–61, 1984.
9. A. Sewisy, F. Lebert, "Detection of ellipses by finding lines of symmetry inthe images via an Hough transform applied to staright lines", *Image and Vision Computing*, Vol.19, N.12, pp. 857–866, 2001.
10. S. Fukushima, "Division-based analysis of symmetry and its applications", *IEEE PAMI*, Vol.19, N.2, 1997.
11. D.P.Mukhergee, A.Zisserman, M.Brady, "Shape form symmetry: detecting and exploiting symmetry in affine images", *Philosofical Transaction of Royal Society of London Academy*, Vol.351, pp.77–101, 1995.
12. T.J.Chan, R.Cipolla, "Symmetry detection through local skewed symmetries", *Image and Vision Computing*, Vol.13, N.5, pp.439–455, 1995.
13. J.Sato, R.Cipolla, "Affine integral invariants for extracting symmetry axes", *Image and Vision Computing*, Vol.15, N.5, pp.627–635, 1997.
14. G.Marola, "On the detection of the axes of symmetry of symmetric and almost symmetric planar images", *IEEE Trans.of PAMI*, Vol.11, pp.104–108, 1989.
15. V.Di Gesù, C.Valenti, "Symmetry operators in computer vision", in *Vistas in Astronomy*, Pergamon, Vol.40, N.4, pp.461–468, 1996.
16. R. Manmatha, H. Sawhney, "Finding symmetry in Intensity Images", *Technical Report*, 1997.
17. D. Shen, H. Ip, K.T. Cheung, E.K. Teoh, "Symmetry detection by Generalized complex moments: a close-form solution", *IEEE PAMI*, Vol. 21, N.5, 1999.

18. J. Bigun, J.M.H. DuBuf, "N-folded symmetries by complex moments in Gabor space and their application to unsupervized texture segmentation" *IEEE PAMI*, Vol. 16, N.1, 1994.
19. N.Kiryati, Y.Gofman, "Detecting symmetry in grey level images (the global optimization approach)", *preprint*, 1997.
20. D. Shen, H. Ip, E.K. Teoh, "An energy of assymmetry for accurate detection of global reflexion axes, *Image Vision and Computing*, Vol.19, pp.283–297, 2001.
21. A. D. J. Cross and E. R. Hancock, "Scale space vector fields for symmetry detection", *Image and Vision Computing*, Volume 17, N.5-6, pp. 337–345, 1999.
22. V.Di Gesù, C.Valenti, "Detection of regions of interest via the Pyramid Discrete Symmetry Transform", in *Advances in Computer Vision* (Solina, Kropatsch, Klette and Bajcsy editors), Springer-Verlag, 1997.
23. D.Reisfeld, H.Wolfson, Y.Yeshurun, "Detection of interest points using symmetry", *3rd IEEE ICCV* Osaka, 1990.
24. Y. Bonneh, D.Reisfeld, Y.Yeshurun, "Texture discrimination by local generalized symmetry", *4th IEEE ICCV* Berlin, 1993.
25. S. Santini, R. Jain. "Similarity measures", *IEEE PAMI* Vol.21, N.9, 1999.
26. H.J.A.M. Heijmans, A. Tuzikof, "Similarity and Symmetry measuresfro convex shapes using Minkowski addition", *IEEE PAMI*, Vol.20, N.9, pp.980–993, 1998.
27. H. Zabrodsky, S. Peleg, D. Avnir, "Symmetry as a continuous feature", *IEEE PAMI*, Vol.17, N.12, 1995.
28. K. Kanatani, "Comments on Symmetry as a continuous feature", *IEEE PAMI*, Vol.19, N.3, 1997.
29. T. Masuda, K. Yamamoto, H. Yamada, "Detection of partial symmetyr using correlation with rotated-reflected images", *Pattern Recognition*, Vol.26, N.8, 1993.
30. D. O'Maraa, R. Owens, "Measuring bilateral symmetry in digital images". *IEEE TENCON*, Digital signal processing aplications, 1996.
31. M. Kazhdan, B. Chazelle, D. Dobkin, A. Finkelstein, T. Funkhouser, "A reflective symmetry descriptor", 7th *ECCV*, pp. 642–656, 2002.
32. V. DiGesu and B. Zavidovique, "A note on the Iterative Object Symmetry Transform", *Pattern Recognition Letters, Pattern Recognition Letters*, Vol.25, pp.1533–1545, 2004.

Geometric Decision Rules for Instance-Based Learning Problems

Binay Bhattacharya[1,*], Kaustav Mukherjee[1], and Godfried Toussaint[2,**]

[1] School of Computing Science, Simon Fraser University,
Burnaby, B.C., Canada
[2] School of Computer Science, McGill University,
Montréal, Québec, Canada

Abstract. In the typical nonparametric approach to classification in instance-based learning and data mining, random data (the training set of patterns) are collected and used to design a decision rule (classifier). One of the most well known such rules is the k-nearest neighbor decision rule (also known as *lazy learning*) in which an unknown pattern is classified into the majority class among the k-nearest neighbors in the training set. This rule gives low error rates when the training set is large. However, in practice it is desired to store as little of the training data as possible, without sacrificing the performance. It is well known that thinning (condensing) the training set with the Gabriel proximity graph is a viable partial solution to the problem. However, this brings up the problem of efficiently computing the Gabriel graph of large training data sets in high dimensional spaces. In this paper we report on a new approach to the instance-based learning problem. The new approach combines five tools: first, editing the data using Wilson-Gabriel-editing to smooth the decision boundary, second, applying Gabriel-thinning to the edited set, third, filtering this output with the ICF algorithm of Brighton and Mellish, fourth, using the Gabriel-neighbor decision rule to classify new incoming queries, and fifth, using a new data structure that allows the efficient computation of *approximate* Gabriel graphs in high dimensional spaces. Extensive experiments suggest that our approach is the best on the market.

1 Introduction

In the typical non-parametric classification problem (see Devroye, Gyorfy and Lugosi [4]) we have available a set of d measurements or observations (also called a feature vector) taken from each member of a data set of n objects (patterns) denoted by $\{X, Y\} = \{(X_1, Y_1), ..., (X_n, Y_n)\}$, where X_i and Y_i denote, respectively, the feature vector on the ith object and the class label of that object. One of the most attractive decision procedures, conceived by Fix and Hodges in 1951, is the nearest-neighbor rule (1-*NN*-rule). Let Z be a new pattern (feature vector) to be

---
[*] Research supported by NSERC and MITACS.
[**] Research supported by NSERC and FCAR.

classified and let X_j be the feature vector in $\{X,Y\} = \{(X_1,Y_1), ..., (X_n,Y_n)\}$ closest to Z. The nearest neighbor decision rule classifies the unknown pattern Z into class Y_j. The resulting feature space is partitioned into convex polyhedra. This partitioning is called the *Voronoi* diagram. Each pattern (X_i, Y_i) in (X, Y) is surrounded by its Voronoi polyhedron consisting of those points in the feature space closer to (X_i, Y_i) than to (X_j, Y_j) for all $j \neq i$. The *1-NN*-rule classifies a new pattern Z that falls into the Voronoi polyhedron of pattern X_j into class Y_j. Therefore, the decision boundary of the *1-NN*-rule is determined by those portions of the Voronoi diagram that separate patterns belonging to different classes.

A key feature of this decision rule (also called *lazy learning, instance-based learning, and memory-based learning*) is that it performs remarkably well considering that no explicit knowledge of the underlying distributions of the data is used. Furthermore, a simple generalization of this rule called the *k-NN*-rule, in which a new pattern Z is classified into the class with the most members present among the k nearest neighbors of Z in $\{X,Y\}$, can be used to obtain good estimates of the Bayes error and its probability of error asymptotically approaches the Bayes error (Devroye et al. [4]).

In practice the size of the training set $\{X,Y\}$ is not infinite. This raises two fundamental questions of both practical and theoretical interest. How fast does the k-nearest neighbor error rate approach the Bayes error rate as n approaches infinity, and what is the finite-sample performance of the *k-NN*-rule ([9,6]) These questions have in turn generated a variety of additional problems concerning several aspects of *k-NN*-rules in practice. How can the storage of the training set be reduced without degrading the performance of the decision rule? How large should k be? How can the rule be made robust to overlapping classes or noise present in the training data? How can new decisions be made in a practical and computationally efficient manner? Geometric proximity graphs such as Voronoi diagrams and their many relatives provide elegant approaches to these problems.

2 Editing the Training Data to Improve Performance

Methods that have as their goal the improvement of recognition accuracy and generalization, rather than the reduction of the size of the stored training set, are called *editing* rules in the pattern recognition literature. In 1972 Wilson [12] first conceived the idea of editing with this goal in mind, and proposed an elegant and simple algorithm. Delete all points (in parallel) misclassified by the *k-NN*-rule. Classify a new unknown pattern Z using the *1-NN* rule with the *edited* subset of $\{X,Y\}$.

This simple editing scheme is so powerful that the error rate of the *1-NN* rule that uses the edited subset converges to the Bayes error as n approaches infinity. One problem with with Wilson-editing is that, although the final decision is made using the *1-NN*-rule, the editing is done with the *k-NN*-rule, and thus one is faced again with the problem of how to choose the value of k in practice. In our approach we will modify Wilson-editing as described in the following.

3 Thinning the Training Data to Reduce Storage

3.1 Decision-Boundary-Consistent Subsets Via Proximity Graphs

In 1979 Toussaint and Poulsen [11] used d-dimensional Voronoi diagrams to delete "redundant" members of $\{X, Y\}$ in order to obtain a subset of $\{X, Y\}$ that implements *exactly* the same decision boundary as would be obtained using all of $\{X, Y\}$. For this reason they called their method *Voronoi condensing*. The algorithm in [11] is very simple. Two points in $\{X, Y\}$ are called *Voronoi neighbors* if their corresponding Voronoi polyhedra share a face. First mark each point X_i if all its Voronoi neighbors belong to the same class as X_i. Then discard all marked points. The remaining points form the Voronoi condensed subset. Voronoi condensing does not change the error rate of the resulting decision rule because the nearest neighbor decision boundary with the reduced set is identical to that obtained by using the entire set. For this reason the Voronoi condensed subset is called *decision-boundary consistent*. While this approach to editing sometimes does not discard a large fraction of the training data, that information in itself is extremely important to the pattern classifier designer because the fraction of the data discarded is a measure of the resulting reliability of the decision rule. If few points are discarded it means that the feature space is relatively empty because few points are completely "surrounded" by points of the same class. This means that either there are too many features (the dimensionality of the space is too high) or more training data are urgently needed to be able to obtain reliable and robust estimates of the future performance of the rule. The main problem with Voronoi-condensing is that the complexity of computing all the Voronoi neighbors of a point is prohibitive in high dimensions.

3.2 Condensing Prototypes Via Proximity Graphs

Bhattacharya [2] and Toussaint, Bhattacharya and Poulsen [10] generalized Voronoi condensing so that it would discard more points in a judicious and organized manner so as not to degrade performance unnecessarily. To better understand the rationale behind their proximity-graph-based methods it is useful to cast the Voronoi condensing algorithm in its dual form. The dual of the Voronoi diagram is the Delaunay triangulation. Therefore an equivalent description of Voronoi-condensing is to discard all points (in parallel) if all their Delaunay neighbors belong to the same class. The idea is then to use subgraphs of the Delaunay triangulation in exactly the same manner. Experimental results obtained in [2] and [10] suggest that the Gabriel graph is the best in this respect. This procedure will be referred to as Gabriel-thinning in the following. Two points p and q are Gabriel neighbors if the "region of influence" of p and q is empty, i.e. there does not exist any point r of the set such that $d^2(p,q) > d^2(p,r) + d^2(r,q)$ where $d(p,q)$ denotes the distance measure between p and q. In the Euclidean space the region of influence of p and q is the smallest hypersphere that contains them. The Gabriel graph is obtained by connecting two points with an edge if they are Gabriel neighbors.

In 1998 Bhattacharya and Kaller [1] proposed a proximity graph they call the *k-Gabriel* graph and show how inexact thinning can be performed with this graph. The *k-Gabriel* graph is much easier to use than the *k-Delaunay* graph and yields good results.

4 Filtering the Training Data for Fine Tuning

Brighton and Mellish [3] proposed a new hybrid method and compared it to several other hybrid methods on 30 different classification data sets. Their elegant and simple algorithm, which appears to be the previous best in practice, is called *iterative case filtering* (ICF), and may be described as follows. The first part of the algorithm consists of preprocessing with the original Wilson editing scheme. The second part of their algorithm, their main contribution, is an adaptive condensing procedure. The rule for discarding an element (X_k, Y_k) of $\{X, Y\}$ depends on the relative magnitude of two functions of (X_k, Y_k) called the *reachable* set of (X_k, Y_k) and the *coverage* set of (X_k, Y_k). The *reachable* set of (X_k, Y_k) consists of all the data points contained in a hypersphere centered at X_k with radius equal to the distance from X_k to the nearest data point belonging to a class different from that of X_k. More precisely, let $S(X_k, Y_k)$ denote the hypersphere with center X_k and radius $r_k = min\{d(X_k, X_j)|Y_j \neq Y_k\}$ minimized over all j. Then all the data points of $\{X, Y\}$ that are contained in $S(X_k, Y_k)$ constitute the reachable set of (X_k, Y_k) denoted by $R(X_k, Y_k)$. The *coverage* set of (X_k, Y_k), denoted by $C(X_k, Y_k)$, consists of all the data points in $\{X, Y\}$ that have (X_k, Y_k) in their own reachable set. More precisely, $C(X_k, Y_k)$ consists of all data points $(X_i, Y_i), i = 1, 2, ..., n$ such that (X_k, Y_k) is a member of $R(X_i, Y_i)$. The condensing (thinning) step of the ICF algorithm of Brighton and Mellish [3] can now be made precise. First, for all i mark (X_i, Y_i) if $|R(X_i, Y_i)| > |C(X_i, Y_i)|$. Then discard all marked points. This condensing step is repeated until no marked points are discarded. We will refer to this second iterative step of their overall procedure as the *filtering* step of ICF.

5 The New Hybrid Gabriel Graph Algorithm

Our new approach to the problem of instance-based learning depends heavily on the use of the Gabriel graph. First we describe the approach using the exact Gabriel graph, and after that we turn to the practical version for high dimensional problems.

Step 1: The original training set $\{X, Y\}$ is subjected to editing with a modification of Wilson editing. Instead of editing with the k nearest neighbors of a point, we use the Gabriel neighbors, thus dispensing with the problem of choosing a value of k. Let $\{X, Y\}'$ denote the edited training set.

Step 2: The set $\{X, Y\}'$ is subjected to thinning (condensing) using the Gabriel graph rule: points are discarded (in parallel) if all their Gabriel neighbors belong to the same class. Let $\{X, Y\}''$ denote the resulting edited-thinned training set.

Step 3: Subject the set $\{X, Y\}''$ to the *filtering* step of the ICF algorithm of Brighton and Mellish [3]. Let $\{X, Y\}'''$ denote the final training set obtained.

Decision rule: A new query point Z is classified according to the majority vote among the Gabriel neighbors of Z in $\{X, Y\}'''$.

The above algorithm is called Hybrid Gabriel-Graph Algorithm. If $\{X, Y\}''$ is used instead of $\{X, Y\}'''$ in the decision rule, the algorithm is called Gabriel-Graph Algorithm. As discussed earlier, the set $\{X, Y\}''$ maintains the decision boundary of the the set $\{X, Y\}$ extremely well [2,10,11].

In high dimensional spaces computing the exact Gabriel graph may be costly for large training sets. The brute force approach to compute the Gabriel graph of n points in d dimension is $O(dn^3)$. There is no known faster algorithm for the exact computation of the Gabriel graph in arbitrary dimensions. In this paper a data structure called *GSASH* is introduced that allows efficient computation of approximate Gabriel neighbors. The practical version of our algorithm uses the *approximate* Gabriel graph instead of the exact Gabriel graph at every step. The resulting algorithms are called Approximate Hybrid Gabriel-Graph Algorithm and Approximate Gabriel-Graph Algorithm.

5.1 GSASH Structure

The data structure GSASH [8] is a modification of SASH [5] to handle Gabriel neighbors rather than the originally intended k nearest neighbors. GSASH is basically a multi-level directed acyclic graph with the following characteristics:

(a) Each node in the graph corresponds to a data item.
(b) The graph consists of $O(\log n)$ levels for a dataset X of size n. Actually at most $2n$ nodes in GSASH are maintained, with n items at the bottom most level, say h, and one item at level 1. With the possible exception of the first level, each level i has half of the nodes as in level $i + 1$. The overall structure is as follows: All the n data items are stored at level h. We then "copy" half of these i.e. $\frac{n}{2}$ items uniformly at random to level $h - 1$. We repeat this process of "copying" all the way up to the root. If a level has at most c nodes (the constant c is chosen in advance of the construction), we pick one of these c nodes to be the root. The root is at level 1. The levels of GSASH are therefore numbered from 1 (the top level) to h (the bottom level). Let S_i denote the data items stored at level i.
(c) The nodes of S_i at level i have edges directed to the nodes of S_{i+1} at level $i + 1$. Each node (object p) links to at most c nodes at level below. These nodes represent the c closest approximate Gabriel neighbors of p among the points of the set S_{i+1}.

The issue of determining the value of c is an important one. One of the considerations behind the GSASH design is that connections to a given node v from a sufficient number of its approximate Gabriel neighbors could help guide a query search to v. In SASH a fixed choice of $c = 16$ led to good performance. In GSASH the same value for the parameter c has been used.

5.2 GSASH Querying

Given a query object q, the search for a set of closest k approximate Gabriel neighbors can be performed on GSASH. The query process starts at the root. Let $P_i(q)$ denote the set of k_i closest approximate Gabriel neighbors of q selected from among the elements of S_i. Let $C_i(q)$ denote the distinct child nodes of $P_i(q)$. $P_{i+1}(q)$ is then constructed by first determining the approximate Gabriel neighbors of q among the points of the set $C_i(q)$ with respect to the set S_{i+1} and then selecting the closest k_{i+1} of them to q.

We can easily use $k_i = k$ for all i. Like SASH [5] the GSASH experimentation uses a geometric search pattern that allows a larger proportion of the search to be devoted on the largest samples of the elements, namely those located closer to the bottom of the GSASH.

Theorem 1. *The GSASH data structure of n objects can be constructed in $O(dn \log n)$ time requiring $O(dn)$ extra storage space. An arbitrary k approximate Gabriel neighbors query can be answered in $O(dk \log n)$ time.*

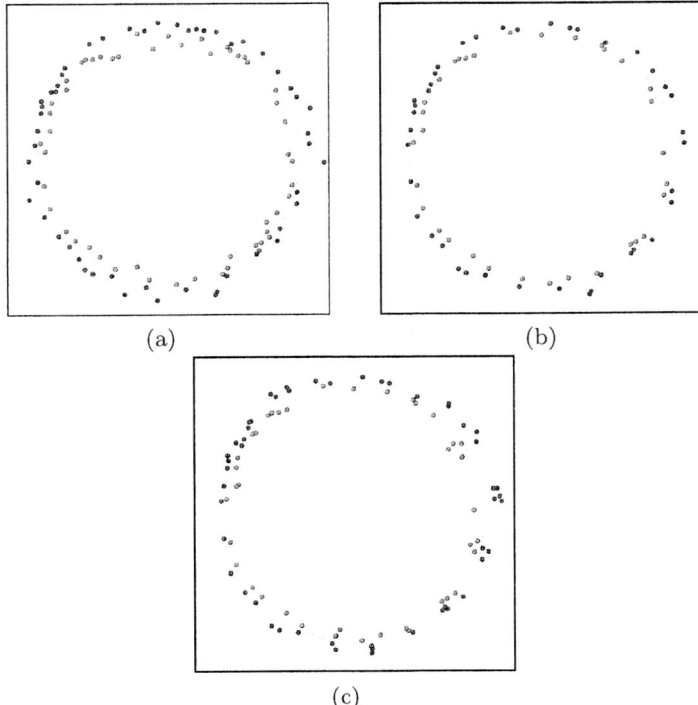

Fig. 1. (a) Gabriel thinned data set. 104 out of 1000 points remained. Error rate 2.75% on 200 randomly generated points (b)Hybrid thinned data set. 73 out of 1000 points remained. Error rate 3.25% on 200 randomly generated points (c)ICF thinned data set. 98 out of 1000 points remained. Error rate 4.75% on 200 randomly generated points.

6 Experimental Results

In this section we compare three algorithms: Approximate Gabriel-Graph Algorithm (called Gabriel), ICF-Algorithm (called ICF) and Approximate Hybrid Gabriel-Graph Algorithm (called Hybrid). In order to investigate the inner workings of these algorithms we generated some synthetic data sets in the plane. All data are generated inside a unit square. The decision boundary considered is circular. Points generated uniformly on either side of the boundary are given opposite class labels. Each generated set has 1000 points. The results obtained are 10-fold cross validated. Figs. 1(a), (b) and (c) show the points that are kept by the algorithms Gabriel, Hybrid and ICF respectively. The figures also show the error rates and storage reductions for the three algorithms. As expected, Gabriel produces the condensed subset of points that tightly maintains the decision boundary at the cost of slightly extra storage. The ICF distorts the boundary significantly. There are significant number of "non-border" points that are maintained which are not close enough to the boundary so as to classify the border points correctly. This is a significant weakness of the ICF algorithm. This

Table 1. Particulars of the data sets used

Data Set	Size	Number of Classes	Dimension
abalone	4177	29	8
anneal	898	6	38
audiology	226	24	69
auto-mpg	398	9	7
balance-scale	625	3	4
breast-cancer-w	699	2	9
bupa	345	2	6
car	1728	4	6
cell	2999	2	6
cmc	1473	3	10
crx	690	2	15
dermatology	366	6	33
ecoli	336	8	7
glass	214	7	10
haberman	306	2	3
heart-cleveland	303	5	13
hepatitis	155	2	19
house-votes-84	435	2	16
ionosphere	351	2	34
iris	150	3	3
pima-diabetes	768	2	8
thyroid	215	3	6
waveform	5000	3	21
wine	178	3	13
wisconson-bc-di	569	2	30

Table 2. Results on real-world data

Data Set	Gabriel			Hybrid			ICF-1			ICF-2		
	Accu	Sdev	Stor	Accu	Sdev	Stor	Accu	Sdev	Stor	Accu	Sdev	Stor
abalone	25.8%	1.1	28.7%	23.7%	1.7	14.8%	21.2%	1.8	24.3%	21.5%	2.3	17.8%
anneal	83.1%	3.2	23.2%	94.3%	2.2	10.3%	94.1%	3.3	20.7%	91.8%	2.0	13.7%
audiology	51.6%	4.3	23.2%	55.1%	8.4	15.0%	73.8%	6.2	31.3%	53.8%	5.3	14.8%
auto-mpg	47.3%	6.4	25.5%	53.2%	4.0	30.0%	50.9%	3.7	36.9%	48.9%	10.0	34.7%
balance-scale	85.1%	1.8	61.3%	80.0%	2.0	19.0%	78.1%	2.1	16.0%	79.7%	1.7	18.6%
breast-cancer-w	95.8%	2.9	10.4%	96.0%	2.1	1.8%	94.5%	1.9	3.0%	94.5%	3.4	2.5%
bupa	64.6%	5.5	46.6%	63.8%	6.4	22.9%	56.8%	4.4	22.4%	64.6%	5.5	26.2%
car	94.4%	1.4	81.5%	94.3%	1.2	13.7%	95.5%	1.3	17.4%	94.6%	1.2	13.7%
cell	94.1%	1.2	8.2%	94.6%	0.6	3.3%	94.2%	0.5	4.6%	93.8%	0.5	2.2%
cmc	51.2%	3.0	45.3%	52.4%	2.5	17.8%	47.8%	5.0	28.5%	51.8%	3.0	22.0%
crx	69.9%	2.7	27.5%	85.9%	3.5	8.2%	82.6%	2.5	8.5%	74.5%	4.6	16.8%
dermatology	97.3%	2.6	86.6%	94.5%	3.5	13.2%	94.0%	3.9	10.2%	95.6%	3.7	14.1%
ecoli	83.6%	4.7	34.0%	82.7%	4.8	11.8%	83.3%	6.9	14.2%	84.2%	4.3	13.8%
glass	64.3%	8.9	48.1%	66.2%	5.9	26.3%	63.8%	9.0	27.4%	68.6%	8.8	26.5%
haberman	74.8%	5.9	18.7%	70.5%	3.3	10.6%	68.9%	4.8	13.9%	69.2%	4.2	12.9%
heart-cleveland	54.0%	5.8	14.3%	50.0%	3.9	9.4%	54.7%	5.2	18.2%	54.7%	7.6	7.3%
hepatitis	76.1%	7.4	11.3%	74.8%	12.8	6.0%	80.0%	9.0	9.0%	80.0%	8.3	5.3%
house-votes-84	94.3%	3.5	48.1%	87.6%	4.8	8.0%	87.1%	6.9	10.9%	84.4%	7.6	7.8%
ionosphere	85.7%	4.3	54.7%	81.1%	10.1	8.5%	82.0%	6.2	5.3%	84.6%	2.6	8.8%
iris	95.3%	4.5	20.8%	92.0%	5.6	14.7%	92.0%	6.1	18.5%	90.0%	2.4	16.7%
pima-diabetes	73.2%	2.7	31.3%	72.3%	2.3	14.3%	70.5%	3.0	13.9%	71.9%	3.6	17.2%
thyroid	93.5%	5.0	19.2%	93.5%	3.0	9.9%	92.1%	2.8	9.1%	93.5%	3.4	11.5%
waveform	79.7%	1.0	84.9%	76.1%	1.9	14.6%	75.5%	0.8	13.2%	75.6%	1.0	14.8%
wine	73.1%	5.9	22.5%	94.9%	3.1	13.8%	89.1%	7.9	12.4%	92.0%	4.2	12.7%
wisconson-bc-di	92.9%	1.7	6.4%	93.3%	2.8	4.6%	93.5%	1.7	5.5%	92.6%	1.6	6.8%

is where Hybrid algorithm wins out. Not only does it reduce storage appreciably but also it faithfully maintains the decision boundary.

We have also compared the three algorithms using the data sets available in UCI machine learning depository [7]. The cell data was obtained from the Biomedical Image Processing laboratory at McGill University. The chosen data sets appeared to be the universal choice for performing experimental analysis of IBL algorithms (Wilson and Martinez [13] and Brighton and Mellish [3]). Table 1 shows the particulars of the data sets.

Table 2 gives us a measure of the accuracy of the algorithms. The results are obtained by the so-called cross validation technique. 20% of the data (for the testing purpose) is selected randomly from the data set. The remaining data points (called training set) are used to design the classifier. The experiment was repeated 10 times. The editing step of the algorithms Gabriel and Hybrid uses the approximate Gabriel neighbors. There are two versions of ICF reported in Table 2. The first version ICF-1 implements Wilson editing using *3-NN*-rule. This is similar to the one used in [3]. The second version of ICF-2 implements Wilson editing using *Gabriel-NN*-rule. Thus the edited sets used in Gabriel,

Hybrid and ICF are the same. In all cases the classification is done using the nearest neighbor rule. The distance between feature vectors (numerical, nominal or mixed) are computed using the VDM approach proposed by Wilson and Martinez [13]. The results indicate that ICF algorithm is able to aggressively throw away instances but has higher classification error. The Hybrid algorithm strikes the best balance between classification accuracy and storage reduction.

The results indicate that ICF algorithm is able to aggressively throw away instances but has higher classification error. The Hybrid algorithm strikes the best balance between classification accuracy and storage reduction.

7 Conclusion

The main objective of our study is to show that proximity graphs captures the appropriate proximity information in a data set. However, it is costly to exactly compute the proximity information. A data structure GSASH is proposed which allows one to compute the approximate Gabriel proximity information in an efficient manner. The Gabriel condensed set, using the approximate Gabriel graph, preserves the classification decision boundary remarkably well. We have shown here that ICF algorithm [3] aggressively removes instances from the training set thereby compromising on the quality of the classification correctness. The proposed Hybrid algorithm, based on the approximate Gabriel graph information, is shown to exhibit the best features of both of its constituents. It preserves the decision boundary remarkably well and is also able to aggressively reduce the storage space.

Acknowledgement

The authors acknowledge the help provided by Benjamin Lewis and Yuzhuang Hu.

References

1. Binay Bhattacharya and Damon Kaller. Reference set thinning for the k-nearest neighbor decision rule. In *Proceedings of the 14th International Conference on Pattern Recognition*, volume 1, 1998.
2. Binay K. Bhattacharya. Application of computational geometry to pattern recognition problems. Ph.d. thesis, School of Computer Science, McGill University, 1982.
3. Henry Brighton and Chris Mellish. Advances in instance selection for instance-based learning algorithms. *Data Mining and Knowledge Discovery*, 6:153–172, 2002.
4. Luc Devroye, László Györfi, and Gábor Lugosi. *A Probabilistic Theory of Pattern Recognition*. Springer-Verlag New York, Inc., 1996.
5. Michael Houle. SASH: A spatial approximation sample hierarchy for similarity search. Tech. Report RT-0517, IBM Tokyo Research Laboratory, 2003.

6. Sanjeev R. Kulkarni, Gábor Lugosi, and Santosh S. Venkatesh. Learning pattern classification - a survey. *IEEE Transactions on Information Theory*, 44:2178–2206, 1998.
7. C. J. Merz and P. M. Murphy. UCI repository of machine learning database. Internet http://www.ics.uci.edu/mlearn/MLRepository.html, Department of Information and Computer Science, University of California.
8. Kaustav Mukherjee. Application of the gabriel graph to instance-based learning. M.sc. project, School of Computing Science, Simon Fraser University, 2004.
9. Demetri Psaltis, Robert R. Snapp, and Santosh S. Venkatesh. On the finite sample performance of the nearest neighbor classifier. *IEEE Transactions on Information Theory*, 40:820–837, 1994.
10. G. T. Toussaint, B. K. Bhattacharya, and R. S. Poulsen. The application of Voronoi diagrams to nonparametric decision rules. In *Computer Science and Statistics: The Interface*, pages 97–108, Atlanta, 1985.
11. G. T. Toussaint and R. S. Poulsen. Some new algorithms and software implementation methods for pattern recognition research. In *Proc. IEEE Int. Computer Software Applications Conf.*, pages 55–63, Chicago, 1979.
12. D. L. Wilson. Asymptotic properties of nearest neighbor rules using edited data. *IEEE Transactions on Systems, Man and Cybernetics*, 2:408–420, 1972.
13. D. Randall Wilson and Tony R. Martinez. Reduction techniques for instance-based learning algorithms. *Machine Learning*, 38:257–286, 2000.

Building Brains for Robots: A Psychodynamic Approach

Andrzej Buller

Advanced Telecommunications Research Institute International
Network Informatics Laboratories,
2-2-2 Hikaridai, Keihanna Science City, 619-0288 Kyoto, Japan
buller@atr.jp

Abstract. I argue that the disregard of the psychodynamic perspective by the Artificial Intelligence (AI) community is a kind of prejudice, and that AI/Robotics could benefit by dealing with some Freudian concepts. This point is supported by the results of some experiments with robots. An approach to AI/Robotics research called *Machine Psychodynamics* emerges from the discussion. The approach is compared with some other approaches in reference to mission, motivation, economy of behavior, world model, imitation, conflict resolution, role of perception, and human-robot communication.

1 Introduction

By an irony of fate the seemingly most insightful view of human mind, i.e., that proposed by Sigmund Freud and known as *psychodynamic perspective*, has never seen a serious debate in the Artificial Intelligence (AI) community. Indeed, the label "unscientific" could frighten away even the most open-minded seeker of *strong AI*. I argue that the disregard of the psychodynamic view is a kind of unfortunate prejudice, and, moreover, AI could benefit a lot by dealing with some Freudian concepts. This point is supported by some experimental results I briefly present. An approach to AI/Robotics research I call *Machine Psychodynamics* emerges from the discussion.

The psychodynamic perspective on the human mind (quite well represented in syllabi offered to students of social sciences) proposes that *people's actions reflect the way thoughts, feelings, and wishes are associated in their minds; that many of these processes are unconscious; and that mental processes can conflict with one another, leading to compromises among competing motives* [26, p. 15]. The key concepts in psychodynamics are *tensions* and *defense mechanisms*. Freud wrote: "The raising of these tensions is in general felt as *unpleasure* and their lowering as *pleasure*. It is probable, however, that what is felt as pleasure or unpleasure is not the *absolute* height of this tension but something in the rhythm of the changes of them." [16, p. 15]. Defense mechanisms are to keep an individual mentally balanced when a given tension cannot be reduced using the available repertoire of behaviors [5, pp. 184-5].

Psychodynamics is not to be confused with psychoanalysis. The latter is a theory and therapeutic method based on four assumptions: (i) the fundamental role of unconscious processes, (ii) the existence of conflicting mental forces and defense mechanisms, (iii) the existence of the Oedipus complex, and (iv) the key role of sexual drive and aggressive drive in the development of personality. It has been proposed that psychodynamics solely accepts the first two of the assumptions, whereas it does not consider the last two. It must also be said that in psychology there is still no universally accepted definition of the psychodynamic approach. For example, besides the obvious assumption about the influence of unconscious processes, Matt Jarvis [17, pp. 2-3] also proposes that the psychodynamic approach should assume the primacy of affect, the continuity between childhood and adult experience, the significance of early relationships, and the significance of subjective experience.

Perhaps psychodynamic concepts could not to date significantly influence the evolution of AI because of conclusions broadcasted by passionate critics of Freud and his work. Yet psychodynamic propositions "do not rise and fall with textual analysis of Freud's arguments. They rise and fall from evidence" [25]. Though Hans Eysenck and Glenn Wilson [15] provided devastating arguments against early attempts to verify Freudian theory empirically [19], several new results, obtained through proper scientific procedure, support basic Freudian concepts. Among several examples, Joel Weinberger and Drew Westen [25] quote literature from the last decade of the 20th century dealing with object relations, in which investigators have coded hours of psychotherapeutic sessions and several projective responses, generally with reliabilities well above $r=.80$, and which have shown predictive validity with respect to a whole host of measures ranging from diagnosis to interpersonal behavior. They also quote longitudinal data showing that adult motivation positively correlates, as Freud hypothesized, with childhood training and parental permissiveness.

The myth about the "unscientific" character of the psychodynamics approach now faces a fast track to oblivion. After reviewing the recent findings in neurobiology vs. Freud's ideas, Eric Kandel, 2000 Nobel laureate, has concluded that psychoanalysis is "still the most coherent and intellectually satisfying view of the mind" [24]. Stuart Kaufmann [18] predicts that one day "psychoanalysis will be regarded as a forefront arena of science." There is no longer a reason to shy away from implementing selected psychodynamic concepts in artifacts, especially in view of the fact that the psychodynamic perspective is a severely expurgated version of Freudian work, i.e., free of the most controversial statements about sexuality and aggression.

2 Psychodynamic Agent

Psychodynamic concepts in related literature are provided in a narrative way. In order to make them useful for building artificial agents, they should be interpreted in more technical terms. It is virtually impossible to formulate definitions that are at once satisfactory or ultimate. So, let the following descriptions be treated as initial ideas facilitating the analysis of psychodynamic machines.

Tension is a physical quantity associated with a physical or simulated *tension-accumulating device*. In such a device tension accumulates or discharges as a reaction to certain input signals. A collection of appropriately interconnected tension-accumulating devices may constitute a *memory*.

Thoughts are meaningful patterns formed by states of tension-accumulating devices constituting *working memory*, i.e., the part of memory that the agent can more or less ably manipulate.

Feelings are subjective experiences an agent can have when it is conscious and when certain elements of its working memory get important bodily signals and/or certain kinds of thoughts appear. In the case of unconscious artificial agents a given feeling may be substituted by a sum of signals produced by specialized devices connected to related tension-accumulating devices.

Pleasure is one of the feelings. It appears during a discharge of certain tensions. Even an unconscious agent can use a signal substituting pleasure as a reinforcing reward in training selected mechanisms.

Wishes are meaningful thought-like patterns in working memory representing imaginary objects or situations which are or were believed by the agent to possibly cause pleasure.

Conflicts are situations such that two or more contradictory wishes appear in working memory, while the agent can undertake an action in favor to only one of them.

The notion of working memory was introduced by Alan Baddeley and Graham Hitch [2] as a replacement for the dated notion of short-term memory, so it does not belong to the Freud legacy. Nevertheless, working memory well supplements the psychodynamic view as a platform for both conscious and unconscious processes, including a fight between conflicting thoughts and wishes.

Let *psychodynamic agent* mean an entity that meets or that can potentially meet the following assumptions:

i. The agent's only "mission" is to strive for its own pleasure.
ii. Pleasure comes from the discharge of tensions and its record is used as an award reinforcing the agent's learning.
iii. The agent's brain and body contain several tension-accumulating devices of various transfer functions working in such a way that given input signals produces a unique effect on the dynamics of changes of the level of the related tension; he signals are various spatiotemporal patterns coming from the environment or from the agent's brain or body; some of the signals represent states of other tension-accumulating devices.
iv. There are tensions that can have an effect on the agent's actuators, transfer functions of tension-accumulating devices, or on the growth of the neurons that form new devices.
v. The agent's sensors, actuators and tension-accumulating devices are configured in such a way that some tensions are always increasing and, in order to have pleasure, the agent more or less efficiently performs an action aimed at acquiring or producing signals capable of discharging the tensions.
vi. When two or more tensions become high at the same time, each of them tries to suppress all others and cause an action that can discharge it first.
vii. Some tension-accumulating devices form a memory that stores acquired knowledge and enables processing of the knowledge toward a tension-discharge-oriented action.
viii. When no action intended to discharge a given tension succeeds, then certain defense mechanisms may change the layout of the tension levels (thus giving the agent the opportunity to have a substitute pleasure from the discharge of another kind of tension) or modify the inconvenient memories.
ix. During the agent's development its memory system becomes sufficiently complicated to plan multi-step actions.

x. Through interactions with its caregiver, the agent acquires the ability to judge other agents and social situations according to the criteria accepted in a particular society and becomes capable of feeling pleasure when it is positively judged by others.

Let us imagine a robot successfully built according to the above assumptions. First, it can be noted that it makes no sense to ask what its application is. A psychodynamic robot is a creature living its own life. This doesn't mean that it must be selfish and useless. In its simple version it may be a pet demonstrating a host of life-like behaviors. A developed psychodynamic robot, if properly raised, may feel satisfaction from successfully accomplishing tasks given by its human master.

The behavior of the psychodynamic robot is not necessarily caused by perception. For example, a lack of meaningful percepts may result in an increase of the tension labeled "boredom". In order to discharge this tension the robot explores its surroundings, which may result in encountering an object of interest and then acquiring signals discharging this tension. An more advanced psychodynamic robot may deliberately expose itself to inconveniences and dangers simply to accumulate related tensions and receive the pleasure that comes from discharging them.

When the robot learns a given behavior, or when its brain circuitry grows, pleasure-related signals serve as reinforcing awards. Hence, an appearance of specialized memories is expected in the growing brain. A long-term memory stores patterns representing acquired knowledge, thoughts and wishes, whereas a working memory enables interactions among the patterns. Via the interactions the robot generates plans of multi-step actions and tests them in its imagination before executing them. The robot can gain pleasure from a purely mental action, that is, when it manages to produce thoughts capable of serving as tension-discharging patterns.

The working memory may also serve as a theater in which conflicting beliefs or behavioral patterns may fight for access to long-term memory or actuators, respectively. The fight may end with a compromise or with a victory for the most promising idea; however, the victorious idea may after some time lose to a rival idea and then after more time win again, and so on [12].

Based on perceived and deduced facts, some sections of the memory system may form an inaccurate yet still useful model of surrounding world including the robot itself. The model may serve as a canvas for the evolution of models of desired reality and ideal reality. The differences between these two models may also cause tensions to be discharged and conflicts to be resolved. If the desired reality is based on the perceived behavior of observed humans or other robots, pleasure may come from the successful imitation of such behaviors.

3 Some Experimental Results

To test basic psychodynamic solutions one does not need a walking humanoid robot. A simple two-motor mobile vehicle with camera and speaker can demonstrate how tensions and pleasures work. Robots of such kind, *Neko*, *Miao*, and *Miao-V*, were used for the first experiments with tension-driven behaviors.

Neko was physically constructed. It had two wheels propelled by two dedicated motors, a speaker, color camera, and two touch sensors. *Neko*'s brain consisted of functional blocks simulated on a cluster of three PCs and an on-board module for collision avoidance connected to the touch sensors. The implemented tensions represented boredom, excitation, fear, and a three-dimensional anxiety. Boredom increased when *Neko* did not perceive any object of interest and discharged when it saw one. When the camera detected a green object, the level of excitation increased and remained high as long as the object remained in the visual field. The level of fear became high immediately as a reaction to the appearance of a red object, remained high as long as the object remained in the visual field, and solely dropped after the object's disappearance. Anxiety was represented by the states of three tension-accumulating devices: Anx_L, Anx_R, and Anx_B. Each of the three parts of anxiety increased spontaneously and independently from the other. A discharge of Anx_L, Anx_R, or Anx_B took place any time *Neko* turned left, right or back, respectively.

An arbitrary hardwiring determined the hierarchy of *Neko*'s tensions. The priority list was: fear, excitation, anxiety, and boredom. The tension that achieved maximum volume suppressed the outputs of all tension-accumulating devices related to tensions located at lower positions at the list. As for the elements of the vector of anxiety, the one that first achieved maximum volume suppressed the outputs of the tension-accumulating devices related to the other two.

An unsuppressed signal from a tension-accumulating device related to a tension of its maximum volume activated a dedicated functional module. The module activated by fear caused the robot to turn back and escape until fear fell below a defined level. The module activated by excitation forced the robot to chase the exciting object. In the case of activation of the module connected to $Anxiety_L$, $Anxiety_R$, or $Anxiety_B$, *Neko* looked left, right, or back, respectively. When the signal produced by the tension-accumulating device representing boredom was high and unsuppressed, it went through a controlled associator connected to three functional modules: a scream generator, a driver for looking around, a driver for going forward. The associator initially activated the scream generator connected to the speaker. When for a defined time the associator did not receive a tension discharge signal, it activated the driver for looking around. If a tension discharge signal still did not come, the associator activated the driver for going forward. If even then a tension discharge signal did not come, it again activated the scream generator, and so on.

Equipped as described above *Neko* learned by itself how to cope with boredom that grew when no object of interest was perceived. It could choose between producing a sound, looking around, and going forward. Indeed, going forward increased the chance of seeing an object of interest. The learning was reinforced by a tension discharge signal. Since tensions representing "irrational" anxiety were also accumulated, in the event of a lack of an object of interest, *Neko* behaved as an animal in a cage, i.e. it wandered back and forth and "nervously" looked around [11].

Miao is a simulated creature living in a simulated world. Its tension-accumulation devices and functional modules cover fear-, excitation-, anxiety-, and boredom-related behaviors similar to those demonstrated by *Neko*, as well as hunger-related behavior and a fight between hunger and excitation. The hunger volume is a function of the state of the simulated battery. If tensions representing fear and excitation are negligible, hungry Miao activates a module that drives it toward the battery charger. However, the activation signal must pass through a conflict-resolution device called *MemeStorm*. Also the signal representing excitation must pass through *MemeStorm* and only then can it activate the module that makes it chase the object of excitation. Inside *MemeStorm*, hunger and excitation try to suppress each other. The device has such an intrinsic dynamics that in the case of a substantial difference between competing tensions, the stronger one quickly wins, i.e., suppresses its rival and becomes high. However, when the competing tensions are close to a balance, one of the tensions wins, but after a couple of seconds loses to the other tension, with a possibility of winning again in a short time [20].

A related report states: *Miao punches the ball / it stopped punching and looks toward the battery charger / Miao turns back to the ball and punches it (though not too vigorously) / suddenly it resigns, turns, and slowly approaches the charger / It gets very close to the charger / Miao sadly looks back at the ball, then turns and starts recharging...* Isn't it life-like? Of course, the word "sadly", if treated literally, would be by all means farfetched. But what the experiment intended to show was not a "true" sadness. The point is that the robot's gaze *looked* sad and looked so not because somebody intentionally programmed a masquerade sadness, but because the robot's brain allowed for a psychodynamic process resulting in such expression.

Miao-V, like *Miao*, is a simulated creature living in a simulated world, with the same set of sensors, actuators, and tension-accumulating devices. However, the tensions that in the case of Miao represented fear, hunger, and excitation, in *Miao-V* represent desire for a red object, yellow object, and green object, respectively and increase randomly. Furthermore, unlike its predecessor, *Miao-V* has a brain that develops in a literal sense. Each new pleasure-related sensorimotor experience adds new cells and connections to its neural network. The network provides control signals to the speaker and to each of the two motors. What is essential is that there is no ready-made circuitry for approaching an object of interest. A "newborn" *Miao-V*, like a newborn human baby, has no idea of how to purposefully use its actuators, so in the face of increasing tensions it can only produce random sounds and moves.

In the development of the brain of *Miao-V* the role of its caregiver is fundamental. Hearing sequences of sounds produced by the robot, the caregiver gives it items she supposes it wants to get at the moment. If by accident the given item causes a discharge of the dominant tension, the subsequently generated pleasure signal reinforces changes in the neural network, thus increasing the strength of association between the tension and the most recently produced vocal expression. In this way, *Miao-V* gradually learns to differentiate vocal expressions as distinguishable sequences of sounds, each dedicated to a different object of desire. At the same, time the caregiver gradually learns to properly guess the robot's needs based on the sequences of sounds she hears. In other words, within the pair—*Miao-V* and its caregiver—a common, mutually understandable proto-language emerges.

When, in this stage of the robot's brain development, the caregiver fails to give it a desired item, *Miao-V* has no choice but to try and get the item itself. The growing network provides the motors with senseless signals, but, when by accident (or owing to a discrete caregiver's help) the item is touched, the related pleasure signal reinforces the changes in the network that caused the recent sequence of motor-driving signals and the locational changes of the image of the item in the robot's visual field. This way *Miao-V* learns how to use its motors and camera to approach objects of desire with increasing efficiency. Having learned to approach immobile items, the robot then learned to chase mobile objects. When, having learned the art of approaching and chasing, *Miao-V* still faces difficulties in catching the object of desire, it "recalls" the possibility of asking its caregiver to bring the object to it, so it again produces the appropriate sound sequences [21].

Although the brains of *Neko* and *Miao* can be expanded to cover more psychodynamic functionalities, because of the necessity of manually attaching the new tension-accumulating devices and behavior-generating blocks the constructions cannot be called psychodynamic agents. The above conclusion does not apply to *Miao-V* whose brain develops driven by pleasures.

4 A New Discipline?

This final section compares the psychodynamic approach to building brains for robots, labeled here *Machine Psychodynamics*, with some other approaches that I suppose might represent "mainstream AI/Robotics" in reference to such issues as: mission, motivation, economy of behavior, world model, imitation, conflict resolution, role of perception, and human-robot communication.

Mission. It seems natural that the purpose of research in the field of AI/Robotics is to build better and better devices that would better and better serve humans. Hence, anyone who presents a new construction or idea is asked: What is the application of the thing you propose? For what kind of missions has your robot been designed? It is seen as obvious that a robot must without reluctance accomplish missions instructed by its owner within an assumed area of application. Even the purchaser of an artificial pet seemingly assumes its full obedience. Machine Psycho-dynamics challenges this view of the human-robot relationship. Psychodynamic robots are assumed to live their own life and strive for pleasure for themselves. As long as robots are dependent on the resources we possess, it will be easy to use the resources as pleasurable awards and make psychodynamic robots do what we want.

Motivations. It seems to be commonly accepted that there is a hierarchy of goals and there are scales of values that guide the agent's decision-making process toward a particular goal (cf. [22, p. 192]). Another assumption, followed for example in the construction of Kismet [3, pp. 108-9], is that there are defined drives (social, stimulation, and fatigue) and the system should always try to maintain them in a bounded range called a homeostatic regime. Machine Psychodynamics does not deny the usefulness of goals and homeostatic regimes, however, it proposes that the most essential motivator is a measurable pleasure signal that is generated when a given tension is being discharged.

Economy of behavior. It seems natural that a robot to be deployed on the surface of a distant planet is designed to accomplish a defined mission in a possibly safe and economical way. The same applies to entertaining robots or even contemporary sociable robots. Nobody wants to witness a fall by his beloved robot (especially when it cost a fortune) from the table. Even a constructor of an advanced sociable robot would not appreciate a situation where the robot irrationally refuses to cooperate with children invited to her lab. Machine Psychodynamics challenges this economy-oriented way of thinking and admits the possibility that a robot may deliberately expose itself to inconveniences and dangers—just to accumulate a lot of tensions and have a great pleasure from discharging them. Stanislaw Lem once wrote a story whose characters debated on the possible reasons why one of their robots stupidly started climbing a rock, which resulted in a fatal fall. Did it do it for pleasure? Did it do it for curiosity? In psychodynamic terms the answer is obvious.

World model. There is still no dominating attitude about the idea of a world model in mainstream AI/Robotics. For example Alexander Meystel and James Albus [22, p. 11] still see a world model as an indispensable block in the general scheme of intelligent systems. This view has been challenged by subsumption architecture [6] that is believed to enable the development of any robot behavior without building a world model. Based on empirical evidence it is argued that the human view of the surrounding world is never accurate and never complete [8]. Rodney Brooks convincingly argues that a robot may use the world as its own model [7, p. 42]. But for a roboticist who still has not given up the dream about machine consciousness the hypothesis of Richard Dawkins [13, p. 59] may be quite tempting: "Perhaps consciousness arises when the brain's simulation of the world becomes so complete that it must include a model of itself". In view of the debate and the need to cover such phenomena as generating intentions and analyzing them versus socially acceptable rules, as well as generating plans and testing them in imagination, Machine Psychodynamics recommends that mechanisms for facilitating the emergence of a world model in a growing memory system be sought. The model can never become accurate and complete, but it may become more and more useful.

Imitation. Maybe the most attractive and efficient method of teaching people certain motor skills is demonstration. The same may apply to teaching robots, provided they have developed mechanisms for imitation. Hence, machine imitation is a hot topic in AI/Robotics. Humanoid robots are seen as the most suitable platforms for developing imitation mechanisms [4]. Kerstin Dautenhahn and Chrystopher Nehaniv [14, pp. 22-3] provide the "Big Five" central issues for designing experiments on imitation with autonomous agents: whom to imitate, when to imitate, what to imitate, how to map observed and imitated behavior, and how to evaluate the success. From the psychodynamic point of view, the authors omitted the most important issue: for what purpose to imitate? In Machine Psychodynamics imitation is seen as one of the ways of discharging tensions and, as a result, having pleasure. It was proposed [9] that an agent could be equipped with an innate mechanism that would create an imaginary desired scene in which it itself possesses the same item as a currently perceived individual or is doing the same things as the individual. The difference between the perceived and desired reality may cause a tension that can be discharged when the perceived reality becomes similar to the desired reality, which would be a drive to imitate. In further development, the agent could achieve the ability to cease imitating if it violated socially accepted rules or endangered its more essential interests.

Conflict resolution. A conflict appears when two or more behavior-generating modules attempt to drive a robot's actuators. Ronald Arkin [1, pp. 111-9] presents two approaches to behavior coordination: (a) using competitive methods that decide about output by arbitration or action-selection and (b) using cooperative methods that find a superposition of forces or gradients based on the notion of field. In both cases, the point is to work out in a reasonable time an explicit decision of what the robot is to do. This works well in the case of robots with a defined area of application. Nevertheless, it can be noted that such "self-confident" decisiveness is not life-like.

One of the conflict-related psychological phenomena is the so-called *mouse effect*. Human subjects were asked to read a story about a controversial person and then to express their feelings using a computer mouse. Positive feelings were to be expressed by locating the cursor at the center of the screen, whereas the cursor located at the border of the screen would mean highly negative feelings. The records of cursor locations revealed a counterintuitive truth about social judgment. Even if no new data about the person of interest were heard, it occurred that after a period of keeping the cursor near the screen center a subject suddenly moved it to the screen's border [23, pp. 97-98]. Therefore, Machine Psychodynamics recommends developing mechanisms that enable conflicting ideas to fight, with the possibility that the victorious idea may after some time lose to another idea and after some time win again [10][20]. This is the way to a life-like machine ambivalence and hesitation that, as Andrzej Nowak and Robin Vallacher [23, pp. 101-2] suppose, play a non-negligible role in cognitive development.

Communication. One can often see demonstrations of so-called "communicating robots" that "speak" pre-recorded sentences. This obvious masquerade is one of the by-products of mainstream AI/Robotics. More ambitious constructions use speech generators to articulate sentences generated by programs manipulating strings of symbols toward the more or less efficient parsing of perceived questions and a knowledge-based synthesis of sensible answers. A different sort of research is aimed at developing mechanisms for a growth of the ability of meaningful communication through social interactions reinforced by simulated motivations. Machine Psychodynamics goes in a similar direction, however, it assumes that communication behaviors (including natural language) are to emerge from pleasure-oriented interactions between a robot and its caregiver.

Acknowledgement

This research was supported by the National Institute of Information and Communications Technology of Japan (NICT), Grant 13-05. The described experiments used the tools and models engineered by Juan Liu, Michal Joachimczak, Daniel Jelinski, Beata Grzyb, Adam Stefanski, and Tarun Tuli.

References

1. Arkin, R.: Behavior-Based Robotics. The MIT Press, Cambridge, Mass. London (1998).
2. Baddeley, A.D., Hitch, G.J.: Working Memory. In Bower G.A. (ed.): The Psychology of Learning and Motivation. Academic Press, New York (1974) 47-89
3. Breazeal, C. L.:. Designing Sociable Robots. A Bradford Book/The MIT Press, Cambridge, Mass. London: (2002)
4. Breazeal C.L. & Scassellati B.: Robots that imitate humans. Trends in Cognitive Sciences, 6 (11) (2002) 481- 487
5. Brody, N. & Ehrlichman, H.: Personality Psychology: The Science of Individuality. Prentice Hall, Upper Saddle River, NJ (1988)
6. Brooks, R: A Robust Layered Control System For a Mobile Robot. In Brooks R.: Cambrian Intelligence: The Early History of the New AI. A Bradford Books/The MIT Press, Cambridge, Mass. London (1999) 3-26
7. Brooks, R.: Flesh and Machines: How Robots Will Change Us. Pantheon Books, New York (2002)
8. Brooks R.A., Breazeal (Ferrel) C., Irie R., Kemp C.C., Marianović M., Scassellati B., Williamson, M.M: Alternative Essences of Intelligence. AAAI-98 (1998) 961-968
9. Buller, A.: Psychodynamic robot. Proc. FIRA Robot World Congress, Seoul (2002) 26-30

10. Buller, A.: Dynamic Fuzziness. In Ishizuka M., Satter A.: PRICAI 2002: Trends in Artificial Intelligence, Proc. of the 7th Pacific Rim Int. Conf. on Artificial Intelligence, Tokyo, Lecture Notes in Artificial Intelligence, Vol. 2417. Springer-Verlag, Berlin (2002) 90-96
11. Buller, A.: From q-cell to artificial brain. Artificial Life and Robotics, Vol. 8 (1) (2004) 89-94
12. Buller A., Shimohara K.: On the dynamics of judgment: does the butterfly effect take place in human working memory? Artificial Life and Robotics, Vol. 5 (2) (2001) 88-92
13. Dawkins, R.: The Selfish Gene. Oxford University Press, Oxford (1976/1989)
14. Dautenhahn, K., Nehaniv Ch.: Imitation in Animals and Artifacts. A Bradford Books/The MIT Press. Cambridge, Mass., London (2002)
15. Eysenck, H., Wilson, G.: The Experimental Studies of Freudian Theories. Barnes & Noble, New York (1974)
16. Freud, S.: An Outline of Psycho-Analysis. W.W. Norton, New York (1940/1989)
17. Jarvis, M.: Psychodynamic Psychology. Classical theory and contemporary research. London, Thomson (2004)
18. Kauffman, S.: The emergent ego. In Palombo S.R.: The Emergent Ego: Complexity and Coevolution in the Psychoanalytic Process. Int. Univ. Press, Madison (1999) xii
19. Kline, P.: Fact and Fancy in Psychoanalytic Theory. Methuen, London (1972)
20. Liu, J., Buller, A.: Tensions and conflicts: Toward a pleasure-seeking artifact. 5th IFAC Symposium on Intelligent Autonomous Vehicles (IAV'2004). Lisboa, Portugal (2004)
21. Liu, J. & Buller, A.: Emergent communication and motor behavior of a simulated robot. Unpublished research note (2004)
22. Meystel, A.M., Albus, J.S.: Intelligent Systems. Architecture, Design, and Control. John Wiley & Sons, New York (2002)
23. Nowak, A., Vallacher, R.A. Dynamical Social Psychology. Guilford Press, New York (1998)
24. Solms, M.: Freud returns. Scientific American Vol. 290 (5) May, (2004) 82-8
25. Weinberger, J., Westen, D.: Science and Psychodynamics: From Arguments About Freud to Data. Psychological Inquiry 12 (3) (2001) 129-132
26. Westen, D.: Psychology. Mind, Brain, & Culture. Second Edition. John Wiley & Sons. New York (1999)

Designing Smart Environments: A Paradigm Based on Learning and Prediction

Sajal K. Das and Diane J. Cook

Department of Computer Science and Engineering,
The University of Texas at Arlington
{das, cook}@cse.uta.edu

Abstract. We propose a learning and prediction based paradigm for designing smart home environments. The foundation of this paradigm lies in information theory as it manages uncertainties of the inhabitants' contexts (e.g., locations or activities) in daily lives. The idea is to build compressed dictionaries of context-aware data collected from sensors and devices monitoring and/or controlling the smart environment, efficiently learn from these profiles, and finally predict inhabitant's future contexts. Successful prediction helps automate device control operations and tasks within the environment as well as to identify anomalies. Thus, the learning and prediction based paradigm optimizes such goal functions of smart environments as minimizing maintenance cost, manual interactions and energy utilization. After identifying important features of smart environments, we present an overview of our MavHome architecture and apply the proposed paradigm to the inhabitant's location and activity tracking and prediction, and automated decision-making capability.

1 Introduction

We live in an increasingly connected and automated society. Smart environments embody this trend by linking computers and other devices to everyday settings and commonplace tasks. Although the desire to create smart environments has existed for decades, research on this multidisciplinary topic has become increasingly intense in the recent years. Indeed, tremendous advances in smart devices, wireless mobile communications, sensor networks, pervasive computing, machine learning, robotics, middleware and agent technologies, and human computer interfaces have made the dream of smart environments a reality. To our understanding, a smart environment is a small world where sensor-enabled and networked devices work continuously and collaboratively to make lives of inhabitants more comfortable. "Smart" or "intelligent" means "the ability to autonomously acquire and apply knowledge", while an "environment" refers to our surroundings. Thus, a "smart environment" is able to acquire and apply knowledge about an environment and adapt to its inhabitants, thereby improving their experience [7].

The type of experience that individuals wish from an environment varies with the individual and the type of environment considered. This may include the safety of inhabitants, reduction of cost of maintaining the environment, optimization of resources (e.g., utility/energy bills or communication bandwidth), or task automation.

Reflecting the increased interest in smart environments, research labs in academia and industry are picking up the theme and creating environments with their own individual spin and market appeal. For example, the Aware Home [1, 21], Adaptive House [26], and MavHome [9, 32] use sensors to learn models of the inhabitants and automate activities accordingly. Other designs include smart offices, classrooms, kindergartens, tables, and cars [1, 3, 13, 22, 30]. Connected homes with device communications capability have become the focus of companies such as Philips, Cisco [5], Verizon, Sun, Ericsson, and Microsoft [4]. Projects on smart environments to assist individuals with health challenges are discussed in [10, 12, 14, 17, 20]. Refer to [7], for a comprehensive treatment of necessary technologies, architectures, algorithms, and protocols to build smart environments for a variety of applications.

This paper presents our research experience in developing MavHome [9, 32], a smart home project funded by the US National Science Foundation. In particular, we propose "learning and prediction" as a paradigm for designing efficient algorithms and smart protocols in smart environments. This paradigm lies in information theory as it manages inhabitants' uncertainties in mobility and activities in daily lives. The underlying idea is to build intelligent (compressed) dictionaries of inhabitants' mobility and activity profiles collected from sensor data, learn from this information, and predict future mobility and actions. Such prediction helps device automation and efficient resource management, thus optimizing the goals of the smart environment.

2 Features of Smart Environments

Important features of smart environments are that they possess a degree of autonomy, adapt themselves to changing environments, and communicate with humans in a natural way [7]. Intelligent automation can reduce the amount of interactions required by the inhabitants, as well as reduce resource consumption and other potential wastages. These capabilities can provide additional features such as detection of unusual or anomalous behavior for health monitoring and home security, for example.

Remote Control of Devices: The most basic feature is the ability to control devices remotely or automatically. By plugging devices into simple power-line controllers like X10, inhabitants can turn lights, coffee makers, and other appliances on or off in much the same way as couch potatoes switch television stations with a remote control. Computer software can additionally be employed to program sequences of device activities and capture device events. This capability allows inhabitants to be free from the requirement of physical access to devices. Individuals with disabilities can control devices from a distance. Automated lighting sequences can give the impression that an environment is occupied while inhabitants are gone, thus handling routine procedures without human intervention.

Device Communications: With the maturity of wireless communications and middleware technology, smart environment designers and inhabitants have been able to raise their standards and expectations. In particular, devices use these technologies to communicate with each other, share data to build a more informed model of the state of the environment and/or inhabitants, and retrieve information from outside sources over the Internet or wireless network infrastructure. With these capabilities, for example, the environment can access the weather page to determine the forecast and query the moisture sensor in the lawn to determine how long the sprinklers should run. Devices can access information from the Internet such as menus, operational manuals, or software upgrades, and can post information such as a grocery store list generated from monitoring inventory with an intelligent refrigerator or trash bin.

Activation of one device can also trigger other sequences, such as turning on the bedroom radio, kitchen coffee maker, and bathroom towel warmer when the alarm goes off. Inhabitants can benefit from the interaction between devices by muting the television sound when the telephone or doorbell rings; temperature as well as motion sensors can interact with other devices to ensure that the temperature is kept at a desired level wherever the inhabitants are located within the environment.

Sensory Information Acquisition: Recent advancements in sensor technology have made it possible to make low-level decisions from monitored data. As a result, environments can provide dynamic adjustments based on sensor readings and can better customize behaviors to the nuances of the inhabitants' surroundings. Motion detectors or force sensors can detect the presence of individuals in the environment and accordingly adjust lights, music, or climate control. Water and gas sensors can monitor potential leaks and force the valves, thus closing them when a danger arises. Low-level control of devices offers fine-tuning in response to changing conditions, such as adjusting window blinds as the amount of daylight coming into a room changes. Networks composed of these sensors can share data and offer information to the environment at speeds and complexity not experienced before. For example, a Smart Sofa [29] can identify individuals based on the weight and thus customize device settings around the house.

Enhanced Services by Intelligent Devices: Smart environments are usually equipped with numerous networked and sensor-enabled devices/appliances that provide varied and impressive capabilities. For example, Frigidaire and Whirlpool offer intelligent refrigerators with features that include web cameras to monitor inventory, bar code scanners, and Internet-ready interactive screens. Through interactive cameras, inhabitants away from home can view the location of security or fire alerts; similarly remote caregivers can check on the status of their patients or family. Merloni's washing machine uses sensor information to determine appropriate cycle times. In addition, specialized equipments have been designed in response to the growing interest in assistive environments. Researchers at MIT's Media Lab are investigating new specialized devices, such as an oven mitt that can tell if food has been warmed all the way through. A breakthrough development from companies such as Philips is an interactive tablecloth that provides cable-free power to all chargeable objects placed on the table's surface. An environment that can combine the features of these devices with information gathering and remote control capability will realize many of the intended goals of smart environment designers.

Predictive Decision Making Capabilities: Full automation and adaptation of smart environments rely on the software itself to learn, or acquire information that allows the software to improve its performance with experience. Specific features of recent smart environments that meet these criteria incorporate predictive and automatic decision-making capabilities into the control paradigm. Contexts (mobility or activity) of inhabitants as well as of the environment can be predicted with good accuracy based on observed activities and known features. Models can also be built of inhabitant patterns that can be used to customize the environment for future interactions. For example, an intelligent car can collect information about the driver including typical times and routes to go to work, theatre, restaurant, and store preferences, and commonly used gas stations. Combining this information with data collected by the inhabitant's home and office as well as Internet-gathered specifics on movie times, restaurant menus and locations, and sales at various stores, the car can make recommendations based on the learned model of activity patterns and preferences. Similarly, building device performance model can allow the environment to optimize its behaviors and performance. For example, smart light bulbs may warn expiry time, letting the factory deliver replacements before the need is critical.

As a complement to predictive capabilities, a smart environment will be able to decide on how to automate its own behaviors to meet the specified goals. The environment should control device settings and timings; it should also elect between alternate methods of achieving a goal, such as turning on lights in each room entered by an inhabitant or anticipating where the inhabitant is heading and illuminating just enough of the environment to direct the individual to their goal.

3 The MavHome Smart Home

The MavHome [9, 32] at the University of Texas at Arlington represents an environment that acts as an intelligent agent, perceiving the state of the home through sensors and acting upon the environment through device controllers with a goal to maximize inhabitants' comfort and minimize home's operating cost. To achieve this goal, the house must reason about, learn, predict, and adapt to its inhabitants.

In MavHome, the desired smart home capabilities are organized into an agent based software architecture that seamlessly connects the components. Figure 1 describes the architecture of a MavHome agent that separates the technologies and functions into four cooperating layers: (i) the *Decision* layer selects actions for the

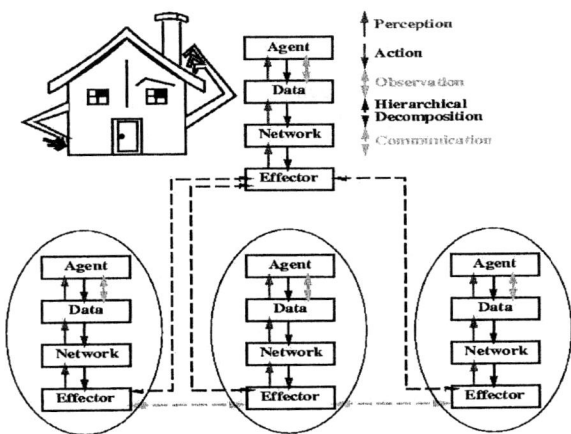

Fig. 1. MavHome agent architecture

agent to execute; (ii) the *Information* layer collects information and generates inferences useful for making decisions; (iii) the *Communication* layer is responsible for routing and sharing information between agents; and (iv) the *Physical* layer consists of devices, transducers, and network equipments. The MavHome software components are connected using a distributed inter-process communication interface. Because controlling an entire house is a large-scale complex learning and reasoning problem, it is decomposed into reconfigurable tasks. Thus, the Physical layer for one agent may represent another agent somewhere in the hierarchy, which is capable of executing the task selected by the requesting agent.

Perception is a bottom-up process. Sensors monitor the environment (e.g., lawn moisture level) and transmit information to another agent through the Communication layer. The database records the information in the Information layer, updates its learned concepts and predictions, and alerts the Decision layer of the presence of new data. During action execution, information flows top down. The Decision layer selects an action (e.g., run the sprinklers) and relates the decision to the Information layer. After updating the database, the Communication layer routes the action to the appropriate effector to execute. Specialized interface agents allow interaction with users and external resources such as the Internet. Agents communicate with each other using the hierarchical flow as shown in Fig. 1. In the following, a smart home will generically represent a smart environment.

4 Automation Through Learning and Prediction

In order to maximize comfort, minimize cost, and adapt to the inhabitants, a smart home must rely upon sophisticated tools for intelligence building such as learning, prediction, and making automated decisions. We will demonstrate that learning and prediction indeed play an important role in determining the inhabitant's next action and anticipating mobility patterns within the home. The home will need to make this prediction based solely on the history of mobility patterns and previously seen inhabitant interactions with various devices (e.g., motion detectors, sensors, device controllers, video monitors), as well as the current state of the inhabitant and/or the house. The captured information can be used to build powerful models that aid in efficient prediction algorithms. The number of prediction errors must be minimal, and the algorithms must be able to deliver predictions with minimal processing delays. Prediction is then handed over to a decision-making algorithm that selects actions for the house to meet its desired goals. The underlying concepts of MavHome prediction schemes lie in the text compression, on-line parsing and information theory. Well-investigated text compression methods [8, 31] have established that good compression algorithms are also good learners and hence good predictors. According to information theory [8], a predictor with an order (size of history used) that grows at a rate approximating the entropy rate of the source is an optimal predictor. We summarize below a novel paradigm for inhabitant's mobility and activity predictions.

4.1 Inhabitant Location Prediction

Location is perhaps the most common example of context. Hence, it is crucial for a smart environment to track inhabitant's mobility accurately by determining and predicting his location. The prediction also helps in optimal allocation of resources and activation of effectors in location-aware applications [11, 24]. In [2], we proposed a model-independent algorithm for location prediction in wireless cellular networks, which we later adopted for indoor location tracking and predicting inhabitant's future locations [15, 28]. Our approach uses symbolic representation of location information that is relative to the access infrastructure topology (e.g., sensor ids or zones through which the inhabitant passes), making the approach universal or model-independent. At a conceptual level, prediction involves some form of statistical inference, where some sample of the inhabitant's movement history (profile) is used to provide intelligent estimates of future location, thereby reducing the location uncertainty associated with the prediction [11, 27].

Hypothesizing that the inhabitant's mobility has repetitive patterns that can be learned, and assuming the inhabitant's mobility process as stochastically random, we proved that [2]: *It is impossible to optimally track mobility with less information exchange between the system (i.e., smart environment) and the device (detecting inhabitant's mobility) than the entropy rate of the stochastic mobility process.* Specifically, given the past observations of inhabitant's position and the best possible predictors of future position, some uncertainty in the position will always exist unless the device and the system exchange location information. The actual method by which this exchange takes place is irrelevant to this bound. All that matters is that the exchange exceeds the entropy rate of the mobility process. Therefore, a key issue in establishing bounds is to characterize the mobility process (and hence entropy rate) in an adaptive manner. To this end, based on information-theoretic framework, we proposed an optimal on-line adaptive location management algorithm, called LeZi-update [2]. Rather than assuming a finite mobility model, LeZi-update learns his movement history stored in a Lempel-Ziv type of compressed dictionary [31], builds a universal model by minimizing entropy, and predicts future locations with high accuracy. In other words, LeZi-update offers a model-independent solution to manage mobility related uncertainty. This framework is also applicable to other contexts such as activity prediction [16], resource provisioning [11, 27], and anomaly detection.

The LeZi-update framework uses a symbolic space to represent sensing zone of the smart environment as an alphabetic symbol and thus captures inhabitant's movement history as a string of symbols. That is, while the geographic location data are often useful in obtaining precise location coordinates, the symbolic information removes the burden of frequent coordinate translation and is capable of achieving universality across different networks [24, 27]. The blessing of symbolic representation also helps us hierarchically abstract the indoor connectivity infrastructure into different levels of granularity. We assume that the inhabitants' itineraries are inherently compressible and allow application of universal data compression algorithms [31], which make very basic and broad assumptions, and yet minimize the source entropy for stationary Ergodic stochastic processes [26].

In LeZi-update, the symbols (sensor-ids) are processed in chunks and the entire sequence of symbols withheld until the last update is reported in a compressed (encoded) form. For example, referring to the abstract representation of mobility in Figure 2(a), let the inhabitant's movement history at any instant be given as ajlloojhhaajlloojaajlloojaajll.... . This string of symbols can be parsed as distinct substrings (or phrases) "a, j, l, lo, o, jh, h, aa, jl, loo, ja, aj, ll, oo, jaa, jll, ...". As shown in

Figure 2(b), such a symbol-wise context model, based on variable-to-fixed length coding, can be efficiently stored in a dictionary implemented by a trie. Essentially, the mobile node acts as an encoder while the system acts as a decoder and the frequency of every symbol is incremented for every prefix of every suffix of each phrase. By accumulating larger and larger contexts, one can affect a paradigm shift from traditional position update to route update. For stationary Ergodic sources with n symbols, this framework achieves asymptotic optimality, with improved location update cost bounded by $o(lg\ n - lg\ lg\ n)$ where $lg\ n$ denotes logarithm base 2.

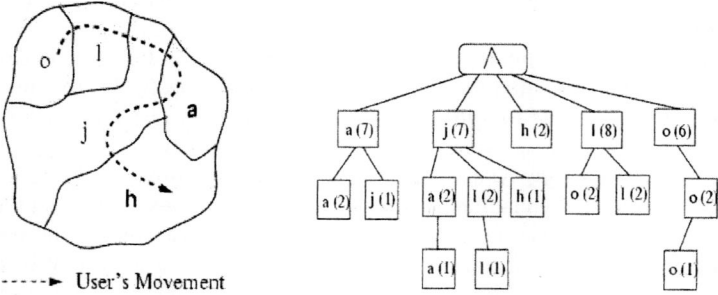

Fig. 2. (a) Symbolic representation of mobility, (b) Trie holding zones and their frequencies

Table 1. Phrases and their frequencies at context "jl", "j" and Λ

jl	j	Λ		
ljl(1)	alj(1)	a(4)	aa(2)	aj(1)
Λljl(1)	aalj(1)	j(2)	ja(1)	jaa(1)
	Llj(1)	jl(1)	jh(1)	l(4)
	lllj(1)	lo(1)	loo(1)	ll(2)
	hlj(1)	o(4)	oo(2)	h(2)
	Λlj(2)	Λ(1)		

One major objective of the LeZi-update scheme is to endow the prediction process, by which the system finds nodes whose position is uncertain, with sufficient information regarding the node mobility profile. Each node in the trie preserves the relevant frequencies provided by the update mechanism in the current context. Thus, considering "jll" as the latest update phrase (route), the usable contexts are its prefixes: "jl", "j" and Λ (null symbol). A list of all predictable contexts with frequencies is shown in Table 1. Following the blending technique of prediction by partial match (PPM) [6], the probability computation starts from the leaf nodes (highest level) of the trie and escapes to the lower levels until the root is reached. Based on the principle of insufficient reasoning [26], every phrase probability is distributed among individual symbols (zones) according to their relative occurrence in a particular phrase. The total residence probability of every zone (symbol) is computed by adding the accumulated probabilities from all possible phrases at this context. The optimal prediction order is now determined by polling the zones in decreasing order of residence probabilities.

So overall, the application of information-theoretic methods to location prediction allowed quantification of minimum information exchanges to maintain accurate location information, provided an on-line method by which to characterize mobility, and in addition, endowed an optimal prediction sequence [11]. Through learning this approach allows us to build a higher order mobility model rather than assuming a finite model, and thus minimizes entropy and leads to optimal performance.

While the basic LeZi-Update algorithm was used to predict only the current location from past movement patterns, this approach has also been extended in [28] to predict the likely future routes (or trajectories) of inhabitants in smart homes and also for heterogeneous environments [23]. The route prediction exploits the asymptotic equi-partition property in information theory [8], which implies the algorithm predicts a relatively small set (called *typical* set) of routes that the user is likely to take. A smart home environment can then act on this information by activating resources in an efficient manner (for example, by turning on the lights lying only on these routes). Our experiments [28] demonstrate that the predictive framework can save up to 70% electrical energy in a typical smart home environment. The prediction accuracy is up to 86% while only 11% of routes constitute the typical set.

4.2 Inhabitant Action Prediction

A smart home inhabitant typically interacts with various devices as part of routine activities. These interactions may be considered as a sequence of events, with some inherent repeatability pattern, that can be modeled as a stationary stochastic process. Inhabitant action prediction consists of first mining the data to identify sequences of actions that are regular and repeatable enough to generate predictions, and using a sequence matching approach to predict the next action.

To mine the data, a window can be moved in a single pass through the history of inhabitant actions, looking for sequences within the window that merit attention. Each sequence is evaluated using the Minimum Description Length principle [26], which favors sequences that minimize the description length of the sequence once it is compressed by replacing each instance of the discovered pattern with a pointer to the pattern definition. A regularity factor (daily, weekly, monthly) helps compress the data and thus increases the value of a pattern. Action sequences are first filtered by the mined sequences. If a sequence is considered significant by the mining algorithm, then predictions can be made for events within the sequence window. Using this algorithm as a filter for two alternative prediction algorithms, the resulting accuracy increases on an average by 50%. This filter ensures that MavHome will not erroneously seek to automate anomalous and highly variable activities [18,19].

As above, the action prediction algorithm parses the input string (history of interactions) into substrings representing phrases. Because of the prefix property used by the algorithm, parsed substrings can be efficiently maintained in a trie along with the frequency information. To perform prediction, the algorithm calculates the probability of each symbol (action) occurring in the parsed sequence, and predicts the action with the highest probability. To achieve optimal predictability, the predictor must use a mixture of all possible order models (phrase sizes) when determining the probability estimate. To accomplish this, techniques from the PPM family of predictors are incorporated, that generate weighted Markov models of different orders. This blending strategy assigns greater weight to higher-order models, in keeping with the advisability of making the most informed decision.

In our experiments run on sample smart home data, predictive accuracy of this approach converged on 100% for perfectly-repeatable data with no variation, and converged on 86% accuracy for data containing variations and anomalies [16].

4.3 Automated Decision Making

The goal of MavHome is to enable automation of basic functions so as to maximize the inhabitants' comfort and minimize the operating cost of the home. We assume comfort is a function of the number of manual interactions with the home, and the operating cost of energy usage. Because the goal is a combination of these two factors, blind automation of all inhabitant actions is frequently not the desired solution. For example, an inhabitant might turn on the hallway light in the morning before opening the blinds in the living room. MavHome could, on the other hand, open the blinds in the living room before the inhabitant leaves the bedroom, thus alleviating the need for the hallway lights. Similarly, turning down the air conditioning after leaving the house and turning it back up before returning would be more energy efficient than turning the air conditioning to maximum after arriving home in order to cool it as quickly as possible [28].

To achieve its goal, MavHome uses reinforcement learning to acquire an optimal decision policy. In this framework, the agent learns autonomously from potentially delayed rewards rather than from a teacher, reducing the requirement for the home's inhabitant to supervise or program the system. To learn a strategy, the agent explores the effects of its actions over time and uses this experience to form control policies that optimize the expected future reward.

5 Conclusion

This paper summarizes our experience on the effectiveness of learning and prediction based paradigm in designing a smart home environment. Efficient prediction algorithms provide information useful for future locations and activities, automating activities, optimizing design and control methods for devices and tasks within the environment, and identifying anomalies. These technologies reduce the work to maintain a home, lessen energy utilization, and provide special benefits for elderly and people with disabilities. In the future, these abilities will be generalized to conglomeration of environments, including smart offices, smart roads, smart hospitals, smart automobiles, and smart airports, through which a user may pass through in daily life. Another research challenge is how to characterize mobility and activity profiles of multiple inhabitants (e.g., living in the same home) in the same dictionary and predict or trigger actions to meet the common goals of the house under conflicting requirements of individual inhabitants.

Acknowledgements. This research was supported by the US National Science Foundation grants under award numbers IIS-0121297 and IIS-0326505.

References

[1] G. D. Abowd, "Classroom 2000: An Experiment with the Instrumentation of a Living educational Environment," *IBM Systems Journal*, 38(4), pp. 508-530, 1999.

[2] A. Bhattacharya and S. K. Das, "LeZi-Update: An Information-Theoretic Approach for Personal Mobility Tracking in PCS Networks," *Wireless Networks*, 8, pp. 121-135, 2002.

[3] A. Bobick, et al., "The KidsRoom: A Perceptually-Based Interactive and Immersive Story Environment," *Presence*, 8 (4), pp. 369-393, Aug 1999.

[4] B. Brumitt, et al., "Ubiquitous Computing and the Role of Geometry," *IEEE Personal Communications*, 7 (5), pp. 41-43, Aug 2000.

[5] Cisco, http://www.cisco.com/warp/public//3/uk/ihome

[6] J. G. Cleary and I. H. Witten, "Data Compression Using Adaptive Coding and Partial String Matching," *IEEE Transactions on Communications*, 32 (4), pp. 396-402, Apr 1984.

[7] D. J. Cook and S. K. Das, *Smart Environments: Technology, Protocols, and Applications*, Wiley, 2005.

[8] T. M. Cover and J. A. Thomas, *Elements of Information Theory*, Wiley, 1991.

[9] S. K. Das, D. J. Cook, et al., "The Role of Prediction Algorithms in the MavHome Smart Home Architecture," *IEEE Wireless Communications*, 9 (6), pp. 77-84, Dec 2002.

[10] S. K. Das and D. J. Cook, "Agent Based Health Monitoring in Smart Homes," *Proc Int. Conf. on Smart Homes and Health Telematics* (ICOST), Singapore, Sept 2004 (Keynote Talk).

[11] S. K. Das and C. Rose, "Coping with Uncertainty in Wireless Mobile Networks," *Proc. of IEEE Personal, Indoor and Mobile Radio Communications*, Barcelona, Spain, Sept 2004 (Invited Talk).

[12] Edinvar, http://www.stakes.fi/tidecong/732bonne.html

[13] A. Fox, B. Johanson, P. Hanrahan, T. Winograd, "Integrating Information Appliances into an Interactive Space," *IEEE Computer Graphics and Applications*, 20 (3), pp. 54-65, 2000.

[14] http://www.dementua-voice.org.uk/Projects_GloucesterProject.html

[15] K. Gopalratnam and D. J. Cook, "Online Sequential Prediction via Incremental Parsing: The Active LeZi Algorithm", *IEEE Intelligent Systems*, 2005.

[16] K. Gopalratnam and D. J. Cook, "Active LeZi: An Incremental Parsing Algorithm for Sequential Prediction", *International Journal of Artificial Intelligence Tools*, 14 (1-2), 2004.

[17] S. Helal, et al., "Enabling Location-Aware Pervasive Computing Applications for the Elderly," *Proc. of IEEE Int. Conf. on Pervasive Computing and Communications* (Per-Com'03), pp. 531-538, Mar 2003.

[18] E. Heierman, M. Youngblood, and D. J. Cook, "Mining Temporal Sequences to Discover Interesting Patterns", *KDD Workshop on Mining Temporal and Sequential Data*, 2004.

[19] E. Heierman and D. J. Cook, "Improving Home Automation by Discovering Regularly Occurring Device Usage Patterns", *Proc. of International Conf. on Data Mining*, 2003.

[20] Intel, http://www.intel.com/research/prohealth

[21] C. Kidd, et al., "The Aware Home: A Living Laboratory for Ubiquitous Computing," *Proceedings of the Second International Workshop on Cooperative Buildings*, 1999.

[22] C. Le Gal, J. Martin, A. Lux and J. L. Crowley, "Smart Office: Design of an Intelligent Environment," *IEEE Intelligent Systems*, 16 (4), July-Aug 2001.

[23] A. Misra, A. Roy and S. K. Das, "An Information Theoretic Framework for Optimal Location Tracking in Multi-System 4G Wireless Networks," *Proc. IEEE INFOCOM*, 2004.

[24] A. Misra and S. K. Das, "Location Estimation (Determination and Prediction) Techniques in Smart Environments," *Smart Environments* (Eds. D. J. Cook and S. K. Das), Ch. 8, pp. 193-228, Wiley, 2005.
[25] M. Mozer, "The Neural Network House: An Environment that Adapts to its Inhabitants," *Proc. of the AAAI Spring Symposium on Intelligent Environments*, 1998.
[26] J. Rissanen, Stochastic Complexity in Statistical Inquiry, World Scientific, 1989.
[27] A. Roy, S. K. Das and A. Misra, "Exploiting Information Theory for Adaptive Mobility and Resource Management in Future Wireless Cellular Networks," *IEEE Wireless Commun.*, 11 (8), pp. 59-64, 2004.
[28] A. Roy, S. K. Das, et al., "Location Aware Resource Management in Smart Homes," *Proc. IEEE Int. Conf. on Pervasive Computing and Communications*, pp. 481-488, 2003.
[29] Smart sofa, http://www.dsg.cs.tcd.ie/?category_id=350
[30] M. B. Srivastava, et al., "Smart Kindergarten: Sensor-Based Wireless Networks for Smart Problem-Solving Environments," *Proc. ACM Int. Conf. on Mobile Computing and Networking*, Rome, July 2001.
[31] J. Ziv and A. Lempel, "Compression of Individual Sequences via Variable Rate Coding," *IEEE Transcations on Information Theory*, 24(5), pp. 530-536, Sept 1978.
[32] M. Youngblood, D. J. Cook, and L. B. Holder, "Managing Adaptive Versatile Environments", *Proc. IEEE Int. Conf. on Pervasive Computing and Communications*, 2005.

Towards Generic Pattern Mining*
(Extended Abstract)

Mohammed J. Zaki, Nilanjana De, Feng Gao, Nagender Parimi,
Benjarath Phoophakdee, Joe Urban Vineet Chaoji,
Mohammad Al Hasan, and Saeed Salem**

Computer Science Department, Rensselaer Polytechnic Institute,
Troy NY 12180

1 Introduction

Frequent Pattern Mining (FPM) is a very powerful paradigm which encompasses an entire class of data mining tasks. The specific tasks encompassed by FPM include the mining of increasingly complex and informative patterns, in complex structured and unstructured relational datasets, such as: Itemsets or co-occurrences [1] (transactional, unordered data), Sequences [2,8] (temporal or positional data, as in text mining, bioinformatics), Tree patterns [9] (XML/semistructured data), and Graph patterns [4,5,6] (complex relational data, bioinformatics). Figure 1 shows examples of these different types of patterns; in a generic sense a pattern denotes links/relationships between several objects of interest. The objects are denoted as nodes, and the links as edges. Patterns can have multiple labels, denoting various attributes, on both the nodes and edges.

We have developed the Data Mining Template Library (DMTL) [10], a generic collection of algorithms and persistent data structures for FPM, which follows a generic programming paradigm[3]. DMTL provides a systematic solution for the whole class of pattern mining tasks in massive, relational datasets. DMTL allows for the isolation of generic containers which hold various pattern types from the actual mining algorithms which operate upon them. We define generic data structures to handle various pattern types like itemsets, sequences, trees and graphs, and outline the design and implementation of generic data mining algorithms for FPM, such as depth-first and breadth-first search. It provides persistent data structures for supporting efficient pattern frequency computations using a tightly coupled database (DBMS) approach. One of the main attractions of a generic paradigm is that the generic algorithms for mining are guaranteed to work for **any** pattern type. Each pattern is characterized by inherent properties that it satisfies, and the generic algorithm exploits these properties to perform the mining task efficiently. Full details of the DMTL approach appear in [10]. Here we selectively highlight its main features.

---
* This work was supported in part by NSF CAREER Award IIS-0092978, DOE Career Award DE-FG02-02ER25538, and NSF grants EIA-0103708 and EMT-0432098.
** We thank Paolo Palmerini and Jeevan Pathuri for their previous work on DMTL.

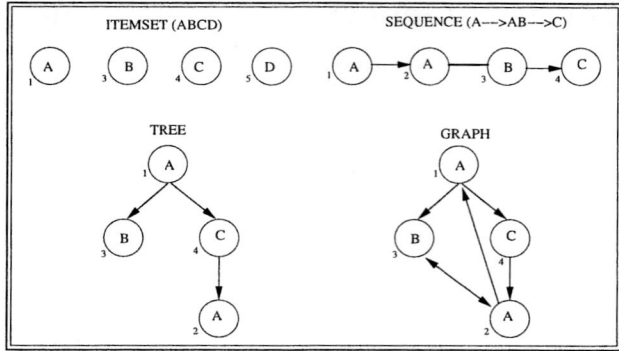

Fig. 1. FPM Instances

2 DMTL: Data Structures and Algorithms

DMTL is a collection of generic data mining algorithms and data structures. In addition, DMTL provides persistent data and index structures for efficiently mining any type of pattern or model of interest. The user can mine custom pattern types, by simply defining the new pattern types, but the user need not implement a new algorithm - the generic DMTL algorithms can be used to mine them. Since the mined models and patterns are persistent and indexed, this means the mining can be done efficiently over massive databases, and mined results can be retrieved later from the persistent store.

Containers: Figure 2 shows the different DMTL container classes and the relationship among them. At the lowest level are the different kinds of pattern-types one might be interested in mining. A pattern is a generic container instanti-

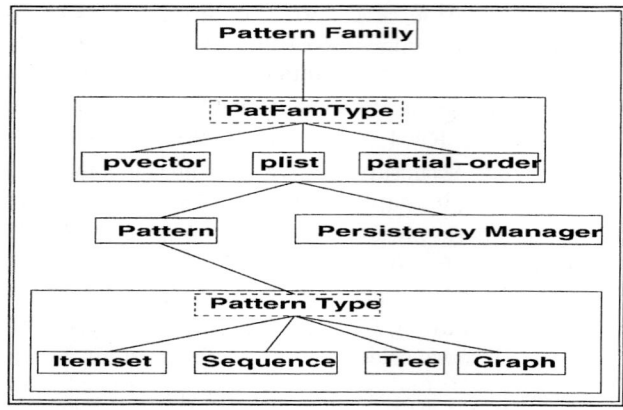

Fig. 2. DMTL Container Hierarchy

ated for one of the pattern-types. There are several pattern family types (such as pvector, plist, etc.) which together with a persistency manager class make up different pattern family classes. In DMTL a pattern is a generic container, which can be instantiated as an itemset, sequence, tree or a graph, specified as Pattern<class P> by means of a template argument called Pattern-Type (P). A generic pattern is simply a Pattern-Type whose frequency we need to determine in a larger collection or database of patterns of the same type. A pattern type is the specific pattern to be mined, e.g. itemset, and in that sense is not a generic container. DMTL has the itemset, sequence, tree and graph pattern-types defined internally; however the users are free to define their own pattern types, so long as the user defined class provides implementations for the methods required by the generic containers and algorithms. In addition to the basic pattern classes, most pattern mining algorithms operate on a collection of patterns. The pattern family is a generic container PatternFamily <class PatFamType> to store groups of patterns, specified by the template parameter PatFamType. PatFamType represents a persistent class provided by DMTL, that provides seamless access to the members, whether they be in memory or on disk. This class provides the required persistency in storage and retrieval of patterns. DMTL provides several pattern family types to store groups of patterns. Each such class is templatized on the pattern-type (P) and a persistency manager class PM. An example is pvector <class P, class PM>, a persistent vector class. It has the same semantics as a STL vector with added memory management and persistency. Another class is plist<P,PM>. Instead of organizing the patterns in a linear structure like a vector or list, another persistent family type DMTL class, partial-order <P,PM>, organizes the patterns according to the sub-pattern/super-pattern relationship.

Algorithms: The pattern mining task can be viewed as a search over the pattern space looking for those patterns that match the minimum support constraint. For instance in itemset mining, the search space is the set of all possible subsets of items. Within DMTL we attempt to provide a unifying framework for the wide range of mining algorithms that exist today. DMTL provides generic algorithms which by their definition can work on any type of pattern: Itemset, Sequence, Tree or Graph. Several variants of pattern search strategies exist in the literature, depth-first search (DFS) and breadth-first search (BFS) being the primary ones. BFS has the advantage of providing better pruning of candidates but suffers from the cost of storing all of a given level's frequent patterns in memory. Recent algorithms for mining complex patterns like trees and graphs have focused on the DFS approach, hence it is the preferred choice for our toolkit as well. Nevertheless, support for BFS mining of itemsets and sequences is provided.

3 DMTL: Persistency and Database Support

DMTL employs a back-end storage manager that provides the persistency and indexing support for both the patterns and the database. It supports DMTL by seamlessly providing support for memory management, data layout, high-performance I/O, as well as tight integration with database management systems (DBMS). It supports multiple back-end storage schemes including flat files, embedded databases, and relational or object-relational DBMS. DMTL also provides persistent pattern management facilities, i.e., mined patterns can themselves be stored in a pattern database for retrieval and interactive exploration.

Vertical Attribute Tables. To provide native database support for objects in the vertical format, DMTL adopts a fine grained data model, where records are stored as *Vertical Attribute Tables* (VATs). Given a database of objects, where each object is characterized by a set of properties or attributes, a VAT is essentially the collection of objects that share the same values for the attributes. For example, for a relational table, cars, with the two attributes, color and brand, a VAT for the property color=red stores all the transaction identifiers of cars whose color is red. The main advantage of VATs is that they allow for optimizations of query intensive applications like data mining where only a subset of the attributes need to be processed during each query. These kinds of vertical representations have proved to be useful in many data mining tasks [7,8,9]. In DMTL there is one VAT per pattern-type. Depending on the pattern type being mined the vat-type class may be different. Accordingly, their intersection shall vary as well.

Storage & Persistency Manager. The database support for VATs and for the horizontal family of patterns is provided by DMTL in terms of the following classes, which are illustrated in Figure 3. Vat-type is a class describing the vat-type that composes the body of a VAT, for instance int for itemsets and pair<int,time> for sequences. VAT<class V> is the class that represents VATs. This class is composed of a collection of records of vat-type V. Storage<class PM> is the generic persistency-manager class that implements the physical persistency for VATs and

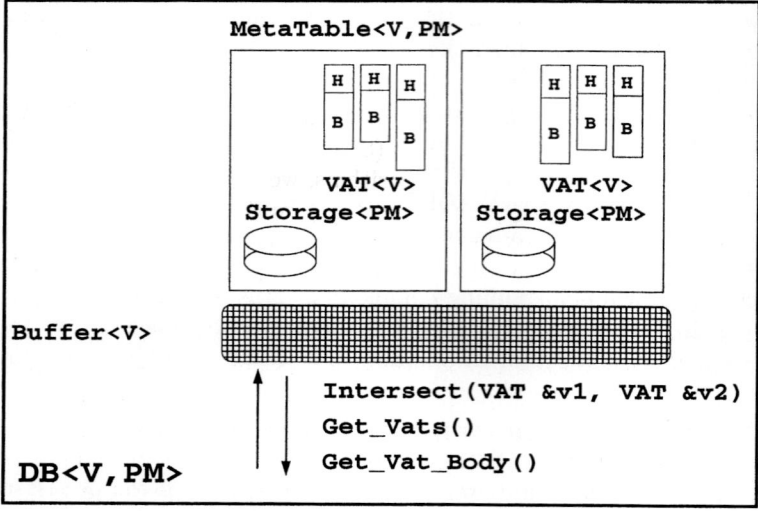

Fig. 3. DMTL: High level overview of the different classes used for Persistency

other classes. The class PM provides the actual implementations of the generic operations required by Storage. For example, PM_metakit and PM_gigabase are two actual implementations of the Storage class in terms of different DBMS like Metakit (http://www.equi4.com/metakit/), a persistent C++ library that natively supports the vertical format, and Gigabase (http://sourceforge.net/projects/gigabase), an object-relational database. Other implementations can easily be added as long as they provide the required functionality.

Buffer<class V> provides a fixed-size main-memory buffer to which VATs are written and from which VATs are accessed, used for buffer management to provide seamless support for main-memory and out-of-core VATs (of type V). MetaTable<class V, class PM> represents a collection of VATs. It stores a list of VAT pointers and the adequate data structures to handle efficient search for a specific VAT in the collection. It also provides physical storage for VATs. It is templatized on the vat-type V and on the Storage implementation PM. In the figure the H refers to a pattern and B its corresponding VAT. The Storage class provides for efficient lookup of a particular VAT object given the header. DB<class V, class PM> is the database class which holds a collection of Metatables. This is the main user interface to VATs and constitutes the database class DB referred to in previous sections.

4 Experiments

Templates provide a clean means of implementing our concepts of genericity of containers and algorithms; hence DMTL is implemented using the C++ Standard Template Library [3]. We present some experimental results on different types of pattern mining. We used the IBM synthetic database generator [1] for itemset and sequence mining, the tree generator from [9] for tree mining and the graph generator by [5], with sizes ranging from $10K$ to $500K$ (or 0.5 million) objects. The experiment were run on a Pentium4 2.8Ghz Processor with 6GB of memory, running Linux.

Figure 4 shows the DMTL mining time versus the specialized algorithms for itemset mining (ECLAT [7]), sequences (SPADE [8]), trees (TreeMiner [9]) and graphs (gSpan [6]). For the DMTL algorithms, we show the time with different persistency managers/databases: flat-file (Flat), metakit backend (Metakit) and the gigabase backend (Gigabase). The left hand column shows the effect of minimum support on the mining time for the various patterns, the column on the right hand size shows the effect of increasing database sizes on these algorithms. Figures 4(a) and 4(b) contrast performance of DMTL with ECLAT over varying supports and database sizes, respectively. As can be seen in, Figure 4(b), DMTL(Metakit) is as fast as the specialized algorithm for larger database sizes. Tree mining in DMTL (figures 4(e) and 4(f)) substantially outperforms TreeMiner; we attribute this to the initial overhead that TreeMiner incurs by reading the database in horizontal format, and then converting it into the vertical one. For graph and sequence patterns, we find that DMTL is at most, within a factor of 10 as compared to specialized algorithms and often much closer (Figure 4(d)).

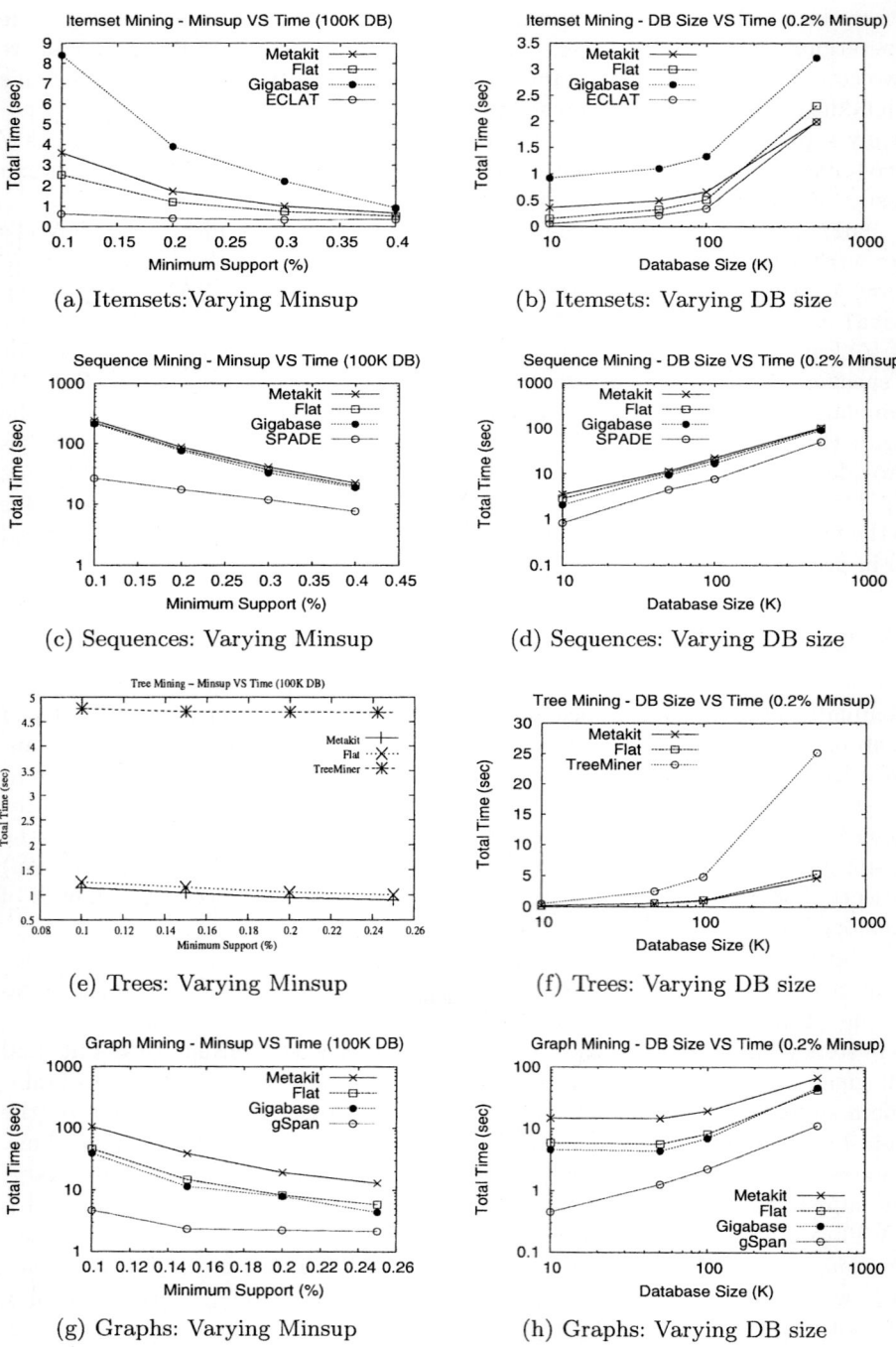

Fig. 4. Performance: Itemset, Sequence, Tree and Graph Mining

Overall, the timings demonstrate that the performance and scalability benefits of DMTL are clearly evident with large databases. For itemsets, our experiments reported that ECLAT breaks for a database with 5 million records, while DMTL terminated in 23.5s with complete results.

5 Conclusions

The generic paradigm of DMTL is a first-of-its-kind in data mining, and we plan to use insights gained to extend DMTL to other common mining tasks like classification, clustering, deviation detection, and so on. Eventually, DMTL will house the tightly-integrated and optimized primitive, generic operations, which serve as the building blocks of more complex mining algorithms. The primitive operations will serve all steps of the mining process, i.e., pre-processing of data, mining algorithms, and post-processing of patterns/models. Finally, we plan to release DMTL as part of open-source, and the feedback we receive will help drive more useful enhancements. We also hope that DMTL will provide a common platform for developing new algorithms, and that it will foster comparison among the multitude of existing algorithms. For more details on DMTL see [10].

References

1. R. Agrawal, H. Mannila, R. Srikant, H. Toivonen, and A. Inkeri Verkamo. Fast discovery of association rules. In U. Fayyad and et al, editors, *Advances in Knowledge Discovery and Data Mining*, pages pp. 307–328. AAAI Press, Menlo Park, CA, 1996.
2. R. Agrawal and R. Srikant. Mining sequential patterns. In *11th Intl. Conf. on Data Engg.*, 1995.
3. M. H. Austern. *Generic Programming and the STL*. Addison Wesley Longman, Inc., 1999.
4. A. Inokuchi, T. Washio, and H. Motoda. An apriori-based algorithm for mining frequent substructures from graph data. In *4th European Conference on Principles of Knowledge Discovery and Data Mining*, September 2000.
5. M. Kuramochi and G. Karypis. Frequent subgraph discovery. In *1st IEEE Int'l Conf. on Data Mining*, November 2001.
6. X. Yan and J. Han. gspan: Graph-based substructure pattern mining. In *IEEE Int'l Conf. on Data Mining*, 2002.
7. M. J. Zaki. Scalable algorithms for association mining. *IEEE Transactions on Knowledge and Data Engineering*, 12(3):372-390, May-June 2000.
8. M. J. Zaki. SPADE: An efficient algorithm for mining frequent sequences. *Machine Learning Journal*, 42(1/2):31–60, Jan/Feb 2001.
9. M. J. Zaki. Efficiently mining frequent trees in a forest. In *8th ACM SIGKDD Int'l Conf. Knowledge Discovery and Data Mining*, July 2002.
10. Mohammed J. Zaki, Nagender Parimi, Nilanjana De, Feng Gao, Benjarath Phoophakdee, Joe Urban, Vineet Chaoji, Mohammad Al Hasan, and Saeed Salem. Towards generic pattern mining. In *Int'l Conf. on Formal Concept Anaysis*, February 2005.

Multi-aspect Data Analysis in Brain Informatics

Ning Zhong

The International WIC Institute & Department of Information Engineering,
Maebashi Institute of Technology,
460-1 Kamisadori-Cho, Maebashi-City 371-0816, Japan
zhong@maebashi-it.ac.jp

Abstract. In order to investigate human information processing mechanism systematically, various methods of brain data measurement and analysis are required. It has been observed that multiple brain data such as fMRI brain images and EEG brain waves extracted from human multi-perception mechanism involved in a particular task are *peculiar* ones with respect to a specific state or the related part of a stimulus. Based on this point of view, we propose a way of *peculiarity oriented mining* for multi-aspect analysis in multiple human brain data, without using conventional image processing to fMRI brain images and frequency analysis to brain waves. The proposed approach provides a new way in Brain Informatics for automatic analysis and understanding of human brain data to replace human-expert centric visualization. We attempt to change the perspective of cognitive scientists from a single type of experimental data analysis towards a holistic view.

1 Introduction

Brain Informatics (BI) is a new interdisciplinary field to study human information processing mechanism systematically from both macro and micro points of view by cooperatively using experimental brain/cognitive technology and Web Intelligence (WI) and Data Mining centric advanced information technology. In particular, it attempts to understand human intelligence in depth, towards a holistic view at a long-term, global field of vision to understand the principle, models and mechanisms of human multi-perception, language, memory, reasoning and inference, problem solving, learning, discovery and creativity [17].

Although brain sciences have been studied from different disciplines such as cognitive science and neuroscience, Brain Informatics (BI) represents a potentially revolutionary shift in the way that research is undertaken. As a crucial step in understanding human intelligence in depth, we must first fully master the mechanisms in which human brain operates. These results reported, over the last decade, about studying human information processing mechanism, are greatly related to progress of measurement and analysis technologies. Various noninvasive brain functional measurements are possible recently, such as fMRI and EEG. If these measurement data are analyzed systematically, the relationship between a state and an activity part will become clear. Furthermore, it is useful to discover more advanced human cognitive models based on such measurement and analysis. Hence, new instrumentation and new data analysis methods are causing a revolution in both AI and Brain Sciences. The synergy between AI and Brain Sciences will yield profound advances in our understanding of intelligence over the coming decade [9,11].

In recent papers [8,14,15,16], we have reported an approach for modeling, transforming, and mining multiple human brain data obtained from visual and auditory psychological experiments by using fMRI and EEG. We observed that each method (fMRI and EEG) has its own strength and weakness from the aspects of time and space resolution. fMRI provides images of functional brain activity to observe dynamic activity patterns within different parts of the brain for a given task. It is excellent in the space resolution, but inferior time resolution. On the other hand, EEG provides information about the electrical fluctuations between neurons that also characterize brain activity, and measurements of brain activity at resolutions approaching real time. Hence, in order to discover new knowledge and models of human multi-perception activities, not only individual data source obtained from only single measuring method, but multiple data sources from various practical measuring methods are required.

It is also clear that the future of Brain Informatics will be affected by the ability to do large-scale mining of fMRI and EEG brain activations. The key issues are how to design the psychological and physiological experiments for obtaining various data from human information processing mechanism, as well as how to analyze such data from multiple aspects for discovering new models of human information processing. Although several human-expert centric tools such as SPM (MEDx) have been developed for cleaning, normalizing and visualizing the fMRI images, researchers have also been studying how the fMRI images can be automatically analyzed and understood by using data mining and statistical learning techniques [7,9,12]. Furthermore, spectral analysis [1] and wavelet analysis [5] are the main stream as the frequency analysis methods of EEG brain waves.

We are concerned to extract significant features from multiple brain data measured by using fMRI and EEG in preparation for multi-aspect data mining that uses various data mining techniques for analyzing multiple data sources. Our purpose is to understand activities of human information processing by

- investigating the features of fMRI brain images and EEG brain waves for every state or part;
- studying the neural structures of the activated areas to understand how a peculiar part of the brain operates and how it is linked functionally to individual differences in performance.

As a step in this direction, we observe that fMRI brain imaging data and EEG brain wave data extracted from human information processing mechanism are *peculiar* ones with respect to a specific state or the related part of a stimulus. Based on this point of view, we propose a way of *peculiarity oriented mining* for knowledge discovery in multiple human brain data, without using conventional imaging processing to fMRI brain images and frequency analysis to EEG brain waves [8,14,16]. The proposed approach provides a new way for automatic analysis and understanding of fMRI brain images and EEG brain waves to replace human-expert centric visualization. The mining process is a multi-step one, in which various psychological experiments, physiological measurements, data cleaning, modeling, transforming, and mining techniques are cooperatively employed to investigate human information processing mechanism.

The rest of the paper is organized as follows. Section 2 describes the design of visual and auditory calculation experiments as a case study. Section 3 introduces our peculiarity oriented mining approach and its application in multiple brain data analysis is discussed in Section 4. Finally, Section 5 gives concluding remarks.

2 Visual and Auditory Calculation Experiments

In order to study the relevance between auditory and visual information processing in a more advanced information processing activity, we deal with fMRI brain images and EEG brain waves measured by the visual and auditory stimuli about human's calculation activities (2-figures addition). Each experiment took about 7 or 8 minutes, and we execute each of visual and auditory experiments 3 times, respectively. Thus, in the experiments, five states (tasks), namely, *auditory on-task*, *auditory off-task*, *visual on-task*, *visual off-task*, and *no-task*, exist by the difference in the stimulus given to a subject.

We try to compare and analyze how brain waves change along with the different tasks stated above. And in the experiments, we defined the position of electrode as shown in Fig. 1, which is an extension of the international 10-20 system. Moreover, the sampling frequency is determined as 500Hz in consideration of the ingredient of brain waves. On the other hand, in the fMRI experiments, the presenting speed of the visual and auditory stimuli are decided to identify the rate of correct answers for each subject by using the results of the rate of correct answers measured by traditional psychological experiments. For our experiments, the rate of correct answers both of the auditory and visual stimuli sets is 85-90%. Numbers of stimuli and control periods are decided by the presenting speed of the auditory and visual stimuli. Thus, we got 30 fMRI images in one experiment from one subject.

3 Peculiarity Oriented Mining (POM)

The main task of peculiarity oriented mining is the identification of peculiar data. An attribute-oriented method, which analyzes data from a new view and is different from traditional statistical methods, is recently proposed by Zhong *et al.* and applied in various real-world problems [10,13,14].

Peculiar data are a subset of objects in the database and are characterized by two features: (1) very different from other objects in a dataset, and (2) consisting of a relatively low number of objects. The first property is related to the notion of distance or dissimilarity of objects. Intuitively speaking, an object is different

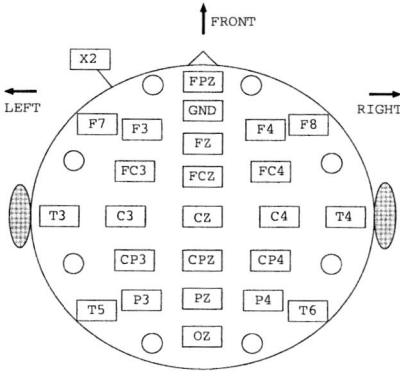

Fig. 1. Position of electrode

from other objects if it is far away from other objects based on certain distance functions. Its attribute values must be different from the values of other objects. One can define distance between objects based on the distance between their values. The second property is related to the notion of support. Peculiar data must have a low support.

At attribute level, the identification of peculiar data can be done by finding attribute values having properties (1) and (2). Let x_{ij} be the value of attribute A_j of the i-th tuple in a relation, and n the number of tuples. Zhong et al [13] suggested that the peculiarity of x_{ij} can be evaluated by a *Peculiarity Factor*, $PF(x_{ij})$,

$$PF(x_{ij}) = \sum_{k=1}^{n} N(x_{ij}, x_{kj})^\alpha \qquad (1)$$

where N denotes the conceptual distance, α is a parameter to denote the importance of the distance between x_{ij} and x_{kj}, which can be adjusted by a user, and $\alpha = 0.5$ as default.

Based on peculiarity factor, the selection of peculiar data is simply carried out by using a threshold value. More specifically, an attribute value is peculiar if its peculiarity factor is above minimum peculiarity p, namely, $PF(x_{ij}) \geq p$. The threshold value p may be computed by the distribution of PF as follows:

$$threshold = mean\ of\ PF(x_{ij}) + \qquad (2)$$
$$\beta \times standard\ deviation\ of\ PF(x_{ij})$$

where β can be adjusted by a user, and $\beta = 1$ is used as default. The threshold indicates that a data is a peculiar one if its PF value is much larger than the mean of the PF set. In other words, if $PF(x_{ij})$ is over the threshold value, x_{ij} is a peculiar data. By adjusting parameter β, a user can control and adjust threshold value.

4 Application in Multiple Human Brain Data Analysis

4.1 Data Modeling and Transformation

The existing multimedia data such as fMRI brain images and EEG brain waves might not be suitable for data mining. Hence, a key issue is how to transform such data into a unique representation format (i.e. table). For such transformation, we develop a system and cooperatively utilize a software tool called MEDx (SPM) to formalize, clean and conceptualize fMRI brain images, so that such images can be represented in a relational data model and stored in a relational database. Figure 2 shows examples of brain images transformed by using the MEDx. Furthermore, the ER (Entity-Relationship) model conceptualized fMRI brain images [14].

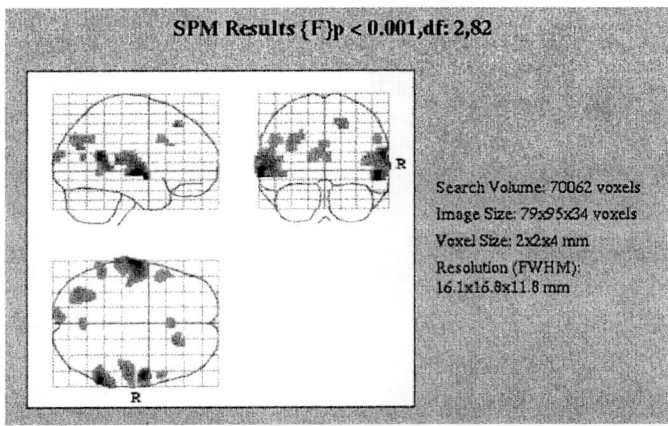

Fig. 2. Examples of brain images transformed by MEDx

Although the brain images transformed by using the MEDx can be represented in a relational data format, a problem is that the number of such data is too big. For instance, the number of the data for each subject is 122880 (i.e. 64 (pixels) × 64 (pixels) × 30 (images)). A way to reduce the number of data is to use a software tool called Talairach Daemon that is based on the Brodmann map as prior knowledge.

Brodmann assigned numbers to various brain regions by analyzing each area's cellular structure starting from the central sulcus (the boundary between the frontal and parietal lobes). Table 1 provides a general view of brain functions that refers to the Brodmann map as shown in Fig. 3. In our experiments, the Brodmann map is used as prior knowledge to obtain the Brodmann area values from the Talairach Daemon, before using our peculiarity oriented mining system to analyze the visual and auditory calculation related databases.

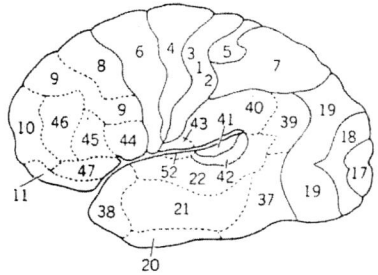

Fig. 3. Brodmann human brain map

Table 1. Functional areas with respect to the Brodmann human brain map

Function	Brodmann Area
Vision	17, 18, 19
Audition	22, 41, 42
Body Sensation	1, 2, 3, 5, 7
Sensation, tertiary	7, 22, 37, 39, 40
Motor	4, 6, 8, 44
Motor, tertiary	9, 10, 11, 45, 46, 47

4.2 The Mining Process of fMRI Imaging Data

Two peculiarity oriented mining processes, namely mining (1) and mining (2), are carried out on the fMRI data, respectively. In the process of mining (1), the prior knowledge of Brodmann areas is used before peculiarity oriented analysis. This process can be divided into the following steps [14]:

Step 1. Formalize/transform fMRI data by using the MEDx system.
Step 2. Obtain the Talairach Daemon coordinate and active values from the MEDx data.
Step 3. Get Brodmann area values from the Talairach Daemon.
Step 4. Create the visual and auditory calculation related databases, respectively, by using the Brodman area values. If there are multiple values in a Brodman area, use the sum of the values.
Step 5. Carry out peculiarity-oriented mining in the visual and auditory calculation related databases, respectively.
Step 6. Compare/evaluate the results.

On the other hand, in the process of mining (2), our peculiarity oriented mining is carried out on the fMRI data transformed in MEDx, directly (i.e. without prior knowledge of Brodmann areas is used before data mining), so that we will be able to analyze and compare the results of using the Brodmann area or not.

4.3 The Mining Process of Brain Waves Data

The mining process of brain-wave data as shown in Fig. 4 is a multi-step one with data modeling and transformation. Brain wave data are typically a kind of time series data with noises. Hence, the removal of noises and data modeling are required. Usually, the low pass filter (LPF) and the band pass filter (BPF) are employed to remove noises by frequency analysis. However, we applied the FIR band pass filter that does not need to take into account the gap of a phase, because we paid our attention to the form of brain waves.

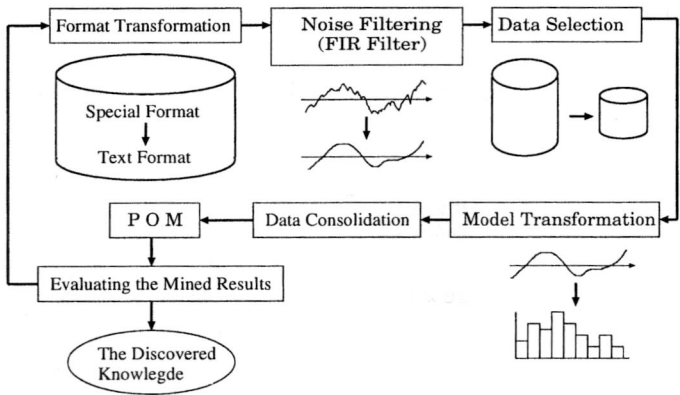

Fig. 4. The mining process of brain wave data

Brain wave data are clustered for every task after noise removal. Furthermore, it is necessary to differentiate valid brain waves from invalid ones, because the eye movement like a blink has a remarkable influence on brain waves. The 512 data per sample were extracted from the effective data. Thus we were able to obtain about 120 samples for each task.

The next important work is the model transformation of brain wave data. A problem of using peculiarity oriented mining in time series data is that it is influenced by a phase. That is, it is necessary to shift the cut area of each data so that the correlation may become strong. Hence, we change the wave data into 2-variate histogram that makes slope of a line and a potential in order to leverage the feature of raw data. Such 2-variate histogram data with respect to a channel can be collected in a two-dimension table as shown in Fig. 5, where v_i denotes the class value of a potential, and d_j denotes the class value of a slope. Furthermore, the frequency of appearance is denoted in a rate a_{ij}, so that they can be compared equally since the number of each task is different.

In order to investigate how subject A's brain waves are different from subject B's brain waves, it is necessary to calculate the difference between histograms. For example, let p be the number of subject A's sample, q be the number of subject B's sample, and x_{ij} be the difference of 2 histograms (histograms A

	a_{l1}	a_{l2}	a_{l3}	$\cdots$	a_{lm}
	$\vdots$	$\vdots$	$\vdots$	$\ddots$	$\vdots$
	a_{31}	a_{32}	a_{33}	$\cdots$	a_{3m}
	a_{21}	a_{22}	a_{23}	$\cdots$	a_{2m}
	a_{11}	a_{12}	a_{13}	$\cdots$	a_{1m}
	d_1	d_2	d_3	$\cdots$	d_m

slope [μV/2msec]

Fig. 5. The sample of 2-variate histogram

and B). It is not possible to compare each of them by the frequency equally, because the number of samples of two tasks is different. Hence, frequency a_{ij} and frequency b_{ij} are converted into percentage $\overline{a_{ij}}$ and percentage $\overline{b_{ij}}$, respectively, such as $\overline{a_{ij}} = (100 \times a_{ij})/(512 \times p)$ and $\overline{b_{ij}} = (100 \times b_{ij})/(512 \times q)$. Thus, the difference can be computed as $x_{ij} = \overline{a_{ij}} - \overline{b_{ij}}$. As a result, the new histograms are able to be utilized as the data chunks for peculiarity oriented mining. Such histogram data with respect to a channel can be collected in a two-dimension table as shown in Fig. 6, where z is the maximum number of channels and is set to 24 for our experiments.

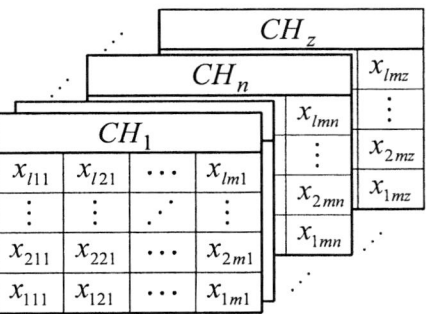

Fig. 6. Structure of mining data

Since our purpose is to find the *peculiar channel* by finding the difference of the states in the transformed datasets, the formula of calculating peculiarity factor needs to be extended from Eq. (1) into Eq. (3).

$$PF(CH_n) = \sum_{k=1}^{z} \sum_{j=1}^{m} \sum_{i=1}^{l} N(x_{ijn}, x_{ijk})^{\alpha} \qquad (3)$$

which means calculating the distances among channels after the calculation of distances for histogram data in each channel. After the calculation of peculiarity factors of all 24-channels, the threshold value is computed for judging whether some channel is peculiar one or not by Eq. (2) in which the β is set to 0.1 for our experiments.

5 Concluding Remarks

We presented a new methodology for investigating human multi-perception mechanism by combining cognitive technology and peculiarity oriented mining. We showed that multi-aspect analysis in multiple data sources is an important data mining methodology in Brain Informatics. The proposed methodology attempts to change the perspective of cognitive scientists from a single type of experimental data analysis towards a holistic view.

Since this project is very new, we just had preliminary results [8,14,15,16]. Our future work includes studying the neural structures of the activated areas and trying to understand how a peculiar part of the brain operates and how it is linked functionally to individual differences in performance by combining various mining methods with reasoning. Some of lessons in cognitive science and neuroscience are applicable to novel technological developments in Brain Informatics, yet others may need to be enhanced or transformed in order to manage and account for the complex and possibly more innovative practices of sharing, analyzing and creating data/knowledge that are made technically possible by the Wisdom Web and Knowledge Grids [6,15].

Acknowledgments

I am grateful to all my research collaborators, assistants, and students who have, over the years, together contributed to the development of Web Intelligence (WI) and Brain Informatics (BI). I would like to express my gratitude to Jiming Liu, Yiyu Yao, and Jinglong Wu for our joint projects and discussions. Finally, I would like to acknowledge the support of the following research grants: (1) the grant-in-aid for scientific research on priority area "Active Mining" from the Japanese Ministry of Education, Culture, Sports, Science and Technology, (2) Open Foundation of Beijing Municipal Key Laboratory for Multimedia and Intelligent Software Technology (KP0705200379), (3) Maebashi Institute of Technology Faculty Research Grants.

References

1. J.P. Banquet, "Spectral Analysis of the EEG in Meditation", *Electroencephalography and Clinical Neurophysiology*, 35, (1973) 143-151.
2. J. Banfield and A. Raftery, "Model-based Gaussian and Non-Gaussian Clustering", Biometrics, 49 (1993) 803-821.
3. L.A. Consularo, R.A. Lotufo, and L.F. Costa, "Data Mining Based Modeling of Human Visual Perception", K.J. Cios (ed) *Medical Data Mining and Knowledge Discovery*, Physica-Verlag (2001) 403-431.

4. S. Cerutti, G. Chiarenza, D. Liberati, P. Mascellani, and G. Pavesi, "A Parametric Method of Identification of Single Trial Event-related Potentials in the Brain", *IEEE Trans. Biomed. Eng.*, 35(9) (1988) 701-711.
5. R. Hornero, M. Martin-Fernandez, A. Alonso, A. Izquierdo, and M. Lopez, "A DSP Implementation of Wavelet Transform to Detect Epileptiform Activity in the EEG", *Proc. 8th Annual International Conference on Signal Processing Applications and Technology*, ICAPAT'97 (1997) 692-696.
6. J. Liu, "Web Intelligence (WI): What Makes Wisdom Web?", *Proc. 18th International Joint Conference on Artificial Intelligence (IJCAI'03)* (2003) 1596-1601.
7. V. Megalooikonomou and E.H. Herskovits, "Mining Structure-Function Associations in a Brain Image Database", K.J. Cios (ed.) *Medical Data Mining and Knowledge Discovery*, Physica-Verlag (2001) 153-179.
8. S. Motomura, N. Zhong, and J.L. Wu, "Brain Waves Data Mining for Human Multi-perception Activity Analysis", *Proc. Inter. Workshop on Advanced Technologies for e-Learning and e-Science (ATELS'04)* (2004) 65-72.
9. T.M. Mitchell, R. Hutchinson, M. Just, and R.S. Niculescu, F. Pereira, and X. Wang, "Classifying Instantaneous Cognitive States from fMRI Data", *Proc. American Medical Informatics Association Annual Symposium* (2003) 465-469.
10. M. Ohshima, N. Zhong, Y.Y. Yao, and S. Murata, "Peculiarity Oriented Analysis in Multi-people Tracking Images", H. Dai et al (eds) *Advances in Knowledge Discovery and Data Mining (PAKDD'04)*, LNAI 3056, Springer (2004) 508-518.
11. R.J. Sternberg, J. Lautrey, and T.I. Lubart, *Models of Intelligence*, American Psychological Association (2003).
12. H. Tsukimoto and C. Morita, "The Discovery of Rules from Brain Images", *Proc. First Inter. Conf. on Discovery Science*, LNAI 1532, Springer (1998) 198-209.
13. N. Zhong, Y.Y. Yao, and M. Ohshima, "Peculiarity Oriented Multi-Database Mining", *IEEE Transaction on Knowlegde and Data Engineering*, 15(4) (2003) 952-960.
14. N. Zhong, J.L. Wu, A. Nakamaru, M. Ohshima, and H. Mizuhara, "Peculiarity Oriented fMRI Brain Data Analysis for Studying Human Multi-Perception Mechanism", *Cognitive Systems Research*, 5(3), Elsevier (2004) 241-256.
15. N. Zhong, J. Hu, S. Motomura, J.L. Wu, and C. Liu, "Building a Data Mining Grid for Multiple Human Brain Data Analysis", *Computational Intelligence*, 21(2), Blackwell Publishing (2005) 177-196.
16. N. Zhong, S. Motomura, and J.L. Wu, "Peculiarity Oriented Multi-Aspect Brain Data Analysis for Studying Human Multi-Perception Mechanism", *Proc. SAINT 2005 Workshops (Workshop 8: Computer Intelligence for Exabyte Scale Data Explosion)*, IEEE Computer Society Press, (2005) 306-309.
17. N. Zhong, J. Liu, Y.Y. Yao, and J. Wu, "Web Intelligence (WI) Meets Brain Informatics (BI)", *Proc. CME'05* (in press).

Small Object Detection and Tracking: Algorithm, Analysis and Application

U.B. Desai, S.N. Merchant, Mukesh Zaveri, G. Ajishna,
Manoj Purohit, and H.S. Phanish

SPANN Lab, Electrical Engineering Dept., IIT Bombay - 400076
ubdesai@ee.iitb.ac.in

Abstract. In this paper, we present an algorithm for detection and tracking of small objects, like a ping pong ball or a cricket ball in sports video sequences. It can also detect and track airborne targets in an infrared image sequence. The proposed method uses motion as the primary cue for detection. The detected object is tracked using the multiple filter bank approach. Our method is capable of detecting objects of low contrast and negligible texture content. Moreover, the algorithm also detects point targets. The algorithm has been evaluated using large number of different video clips and the performance is analysed.

1 Introduction

Detection and tracking of small and fast moving objects is increasingly becoming important for the sports industry. Critical decisions are now based on the exploitation of such algorithms. Decision based on very slow motion replays in football and cricket is already highly pervasive. The objective of this paper is to develop algorithms which can further assist in making such decisions as well as in analyzing sports video sequences. The paper focuses on a small segment of this large task, namely, detection and tracking of small objects in sports video sequences.

Another important application of detection and tracking is in IR (infrared) images where,the target of interest could be either a point target or an approaching one (varying target size). This problem is challenging as the intensity of the target and that of the cluttered background varies with time. Even the shape and size of the clouds and target may vary from one time instant to another. Because of these reasons, the methods based on spatial processing, [1] and optical flow [2] do not help.

In literature, various approaches have been proposed for object detection and tracking. Techniques such as background registration [3] or background extraction [4] may not be feasible in sports video sequence due to the non-stationary nature of the background. Detection of a small moving object based on segmentation of each frame [5] will not be viable, in our case, due to low contrast image and lack of any texture information. In this paper we propose a method to detect small and fast moving object in sports video sequences using motion as the primary cue. This work is based on our earlier work on point target detection [6].

Along with detection, tracking algorithm also plays an important role. A variety of methods for tracking multiple targets based on multiple hypothesis tracking (MHT) and joint probability data association filter (JPDA) have been proposed in literature [7,8]. A dynamic programming approach (DPA) has been proposed in [9], and the truncated sequential probability ratio test (SPRT) is presented in [10] to detect and track targets with straight line trajectories. All these methods are computationally expensive and have little scope for real time application. Moreover, these methods are able to track only linear trajectory.

We track the targets using two different methods; (i) modified pipeline algorithm [11] and (ii) filter bank approach [12,13]. The key feature of the filter bank approach is its ability to track maneuvering as well as non-maneuvering trajectories in the absence of any apriori information about the target dynamics.

2 Object Detection

2.1 Wavelet Based Detection

We use wavelet transform for temporal filtering [6] as it enables one to detect and characterize the dynamical behavior of elements present in the scene. We have used the Haar wavelet because with increase in the number of wavelet filter coefficients, larger number of image frames are needed by the transform to do a proper job of detection. The temporal multiscale decomposition facilitates the construction of the intensity change maps which indicate whether there is temporal change or not. A two-hypotheses likelihood ratio test is then applied to validate the temporal changes at each scale. By exploiting this likelihood ratio test, the issue of motion detection is solved in statistical frame work.

In order to make the detection scheme robust to clutter and noise, post processing is incorporated. As stated above temporal multiscale decomposition and hypothesis testing provide the (binary) change detection map. In this map, nearby small regions are merged using binary morphological operation, namely, closing (dilation followed by erosion). Next, the change detection map is segmented and all segments having a size larger than a pre-defined threshold are removed. Small size clutter which appear like small targets are eliminated by comparing local contrast with a predefined threshold. If it crosses the threshold it will be a moving target.

2.2 Gradient Based Detection of Small Targets

It is often difficult to detect small objects of low contrast in a highly evolving background. This algorithm[14], based on spatial gradient thresholding and region merging, is proposed to overcome the problem and effectively detect small objects of low contrast in evolving clouds.

The algorithm uses image-differencing technique to register motion. The regions corresponding to variation between frames, wherein there is a target motion or any displacement would be captured in the difference image. Also, this eliminates any stationary clutter, assuming the imaging facility is stationary.

The spatial gradient of the difference image is then obtained by applying the Sobel operator which identifies the edges in the difference image. The edges of a target are usually well defined and stronger than those of clouds. Hence, the target motion registered in the difference image can be separated from the temporal differences registered by moving (or evolving) clouds, using this as a cue. A gradient magnitude thresholding is done to highlight target regions i.e., the regions of interest (ROI) among the low magnitude variations contributed by clouds.

The processed images however contain stray pixels corresponding to isolated noise pixels as well as cloud edge variations. These pixels can be eliminated and the regions of interest can be located by using a region merging technique like binary morphological closing. Once the ROI are located in the original frame, local contrast of these regions within specific windows are inspected. The pixel is then declared as a target pixel if the local contrast exceeds a predefined threshold.

3 Object Tracking

For object tracking we proposed two algorithms, first one deals with linear and slow maneuvering target. And the second algorithm is able to track arbitrary trajectories of the objects.

3.1 Modified Pipeline Based Tracking

The pipeline algorithm is able to detect and track targets having 1-2 pixel movement per frame. To track a target with large movement (±20 pixels per frame), the window size needs to be increased and hence it leads to false alarm due to increased search neighborhood in continuity filtering algorithm (CFA). Consequently, taking centroid position of Temporal Window Column (TWC) as a detected target position is not correct, as number of additions per pixel increase by $O(N^2)$ with increase in maximum detectable target movement, where N is the number of pixels in a frame. To overcome these limitations, modified pipeline algorithm is developed, a variable slope pipe shown in Figure 1 is used. Pipeline

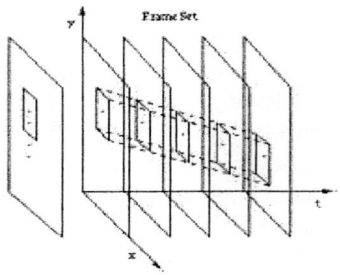

Fig. 1. Modified Test Pipe

algorithm consists of two major components: (i) fixed length TEST PIPE of temporally adjacent image frames. At each iteration a frame from the bottom of the test pipe is discarded and new frame is added to the top of the pipe and other frames are shifted in the pipe by one position. (ii) AND PIPE (AP), consists of two image frames and a single blank frame called Target Frame (TF). The CFA uses the AND PIPE to test continuity of the target pixel. The algorithm is as follows: (1) Initialize the AND PIPE (AP) by adding a frame to the top at each cycle. (2) Initialize the TEST PIPE (TP) with $n-1$ frame cycles, where n is the number of frames in TP. (3) At each time step, (a) A constant acceleration based Kalman filter is used in a predictor mode, which predicts the target position in the next frame.(i) Update the AP (ii) Apply the CFA in AP. (b) (i) Update the TP by adding the output frame of the AP in each cycle to the top of the TP. (ii) Form a search window around the predicted position given by the Kalman filter. Apply the TWC at each pixel (X_i, Y_i) in the search window and sum the intensities. This greatly reduces the computational load. This sum is given by:

$$S(X_i, Y_i) = \sum_{k=1}^{n} \sum_{x=-w/2}^{w/2} \sum_{y=-l/2}^{l/2} I(X_i + x, Y_i + y, k)$$

where n, w and l are the dimension of the TWC in the TP. (iii) If sum is greater than threshold (determined by possible target intensities) then go to Step 3(d), else consider it as occlusion and go back to Step 3(a) for the next time step. (d) Compute the intensity centroid. Find the Euclidean distance between the current position and the previous position and compare it against a threshold. If it is below the threshold then, accept as trajectory pixel and record in the TF else reject.

The modified pipeline algorithm requires coarse estimate of initial velocity, to overcome this, the output of target detection phase is used in following manner: First, the candidate target list is formed using the first two frames, and secondly using nearest neighbour technique with maximum velocity constraint, candidate is associated from one list to another list, which provides estimation of velocity and a new target track is initiated if association is not possible for any candidate target in the list.

3.2 Multiple Filter Bank Approach

Using a single tuned filter, it is difficult to track complex maneuvering trajectories. We propose a method to track multiple point target movement using multiple filter bank [12]. The filter bank consists of different types of filters. For example, in a bank of two filters, one could be a constant velocity filter and the other could be based on a maneuver model.

In the filter bank, all the filters run in parallel. Nevertheless, at any given time, only one filter is designated as an active filter - this is the filter whose output is selected as the predicted position of the target. The validation gate is formed around this predicted position and only validated observations (i.e. observation falling inside this validation gate) are used for data association. In

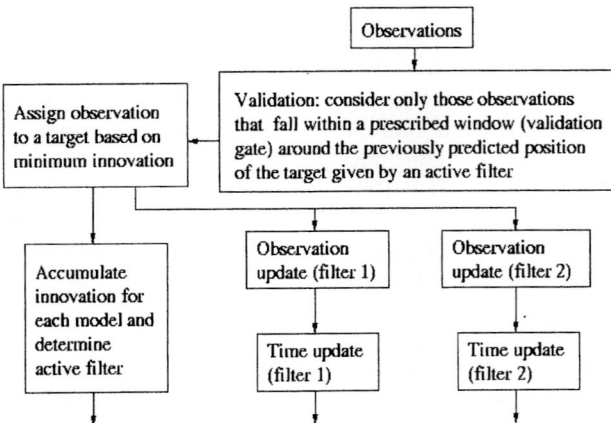

Fig. 2. Multiple Filter Bank algorithm with two filters

our case, Munkres' optimal data association algorithm is used for data association based on nearest neighbor method. The state vector of other models in a filter bank is also updated using the same observation. The decision on which filter becomes the active filter is based on minimum average innovation. The logical steps for multiple filter bank algorithm are described in Figure 2. An approach based on the use of multiple filters has been explored earlier [15]. But in the proposed method switch-over between the filters in the bank is based on single-step decision logic, and consequently, is computationally more efficient and performance-wise more robust. For filter switch-over, the innovation error is accumulated over the past iterations for each filter in the filter bank. It is averaged and compared with that of other filters. Based on minimum averaged innovation error for the filter, the switch-over takes place. From our simulations, we observe that a filter bank with two filters, one based on constant acceleration model and the other based on acceleration being modeled as colored noise, is able to track both non-maneuvering and maneuvering targets.

3.3 FPGA Based Tracking Hardware Implementation

Xilinx Virtex-II Pro FPGAs provide one or more embedded PowerPC processor cores along with FPGA fabric. Combining a PowerPC processor core with the Virtex-II FPGA fabric brings a huge amount of flexibility, the processor and FPGA are used together in a way that makes the best use of the power of each element. The PowerPC provides many different interfaces that are designed for use in different ways, which are used to enhance the overall performance of the system and to achieve right balance between the workload of the PowerPC and FPGA. FPGA logic can be connected to PowerPC interfaces, with software for the CPU interacting with HDL written for the FPGA.

The Hardware acceleration block takes the Image pixels processes them and writes them back and thus achieving result better than processor in terms of

Small Object Detection and Tracking: Algorithm, Analysis and Application 113

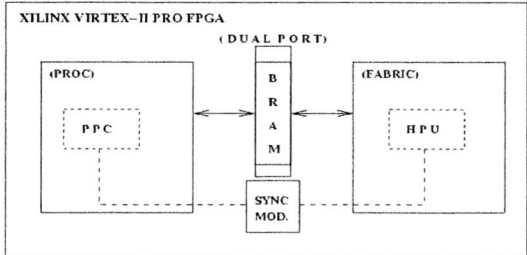

Fig. 3. Virtex-II pro Based Embedded system

speed. Function of the synchonisation module is to control data access to the Block RAM and is used for data synchronisation between PowerPC and FPGA based hardware processing unit. Architecture based decoupling (Figure 3) is possible as Block RAMs are dual ported, with one side connected to the processor and other to logic.

PowerPC feeds the hardware acceleration block with data and also controls and monitors the operation of that logic. This provides a hardware framework that can be used to implement many other different types of FPGA function block (wavelet detection, etc.).

Thus the main features of Virtex-II pro (platform FPGA) based implementation is that both PowerPC and logic used for design, use of RTOS (e.g. Xilkernel) for embedded processor, use of customized logic (hardware acceleration unit) for time critical part alongwith synchonisation unit for data synchronisation between processor and hardware acceleration unit.

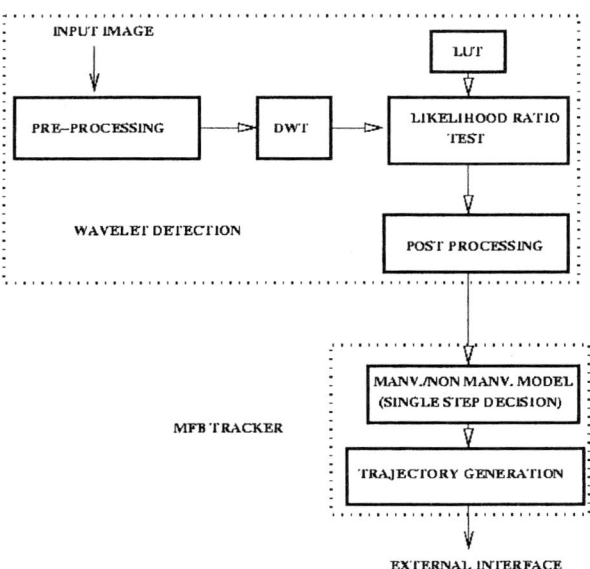

Fig. 4. Algorithm block diagram

4 Simulation Results and Performance Analysis

In our simulations, we have used two filters: constant acceleration (CA) and Singers' maneuver model (SMM) for the multiple filter bank. For the simulations, the tracker is setup after object continuity is found in three consecutive frames in the sequence. We have evaluated the performance of the proposed algorithm using a number of sequences. Simulation results are presented for two sport sequences; cricket and ping pong.

The ping pong sequence has 100 frames and was captured with a stationary camera. In the sequence, the ball does not appear as a full circle due to low contrast and shadow effects. Our proposed detection algorithm is able to detect and track the ping pong ball with such low contrast. Figures 5-(a) and 5-(b) represent the output of wavelet based detection algorithm at frame 46 and tracking of the ping pong throughout the sequence. The ping ball enters and leaves the sequence number of times. To discriminate entering and leaving time instant, each trace of the tracked ball is represented using different colors. In Figures 5-(b) and 6-(b) the real trajectory is shown with a solid line, whereas the predicted trajectory is shown using a dotted line with the same color. In the cricket video sequence we have 32 frames for detection and tracking. In the cricket sequence, unlike the ping pong ball sequence, the background has significant motion. Another challenging aspect is the varying size of the ball due to zoom in and zoom out of the camera. Our algorithm is able detect and track the cricket ball effectively in spite of these challenges. The detection output for the cricket sequence is shown in Figure 6-(a). Figure 6-(b) depicts the tracked trajectory of the cricket ball upto frame 15.

We used our algorithms to detect and track approaching targets in IR sequence also. Simulation results for two clips are depicted here. (Note, due to space limitations, we have depicted the details of trajectories in clip 1 only.) For clip 1, for all trajectories, initial target signature is of 3×3, gradually increasing to a maximum size of 15×11. The enlarged view of the target signature is shown in Figure 7(c). First trajectory is generated using constant velocity, coordinated turn and constant acceleration model. The initial position and initial velocity are set to $(9km, 7km)$ and $(280.0m/s, 280.0m/s)$. Trajectory takes total of four

 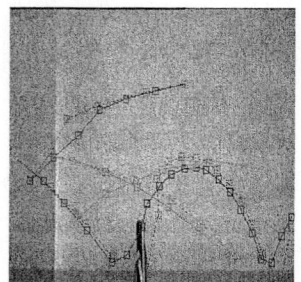

(a) Detection at frame 46   (b) Trajectory plot upto frame 98

Fig. 5. Ping Pong Ball Detection and Tracking

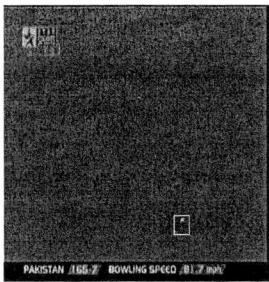 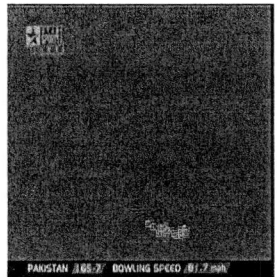

(a) Detection at frame 26 (b) Trajectory plot upto frame 15

Fig. 6. Cricket Ball Detection and Tracking

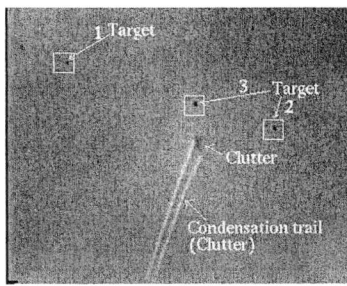 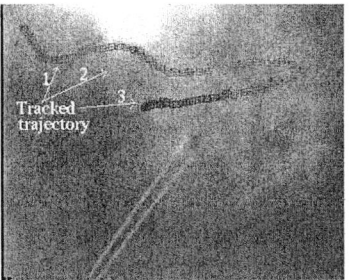 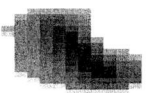

(a) Detection at frame 20 (b) Trajectory Plot upto frame 69 (c) IR target signature (Enlarged view)

Fig. 7. Approaching Target Detection and Tracking (clip 1)

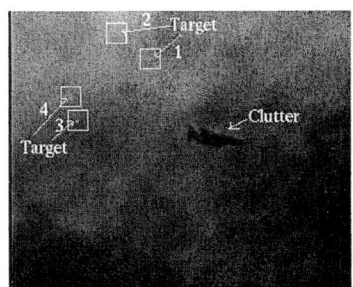 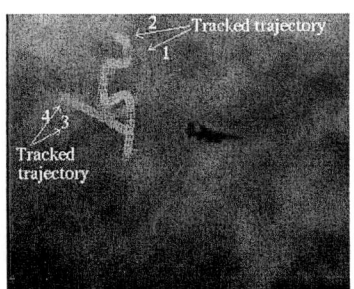 

(a) Detection at frame 4 (b) Trajectory Plot upto frame 69 (c) IR target signature (Enlarged view)

Fig. 8. Approaching Target Detection and Tracking (clip 2)

turns: (a) from frame 15 to 22 with turn angle 15°, it results in $\approx 10.5g$ acceleration, (b) from frame 30 to 36 with turn angle $-15°$ ($\approx 10.27g$ acceleration), (c) from frame 43 to 52 with 12° ($\approx 8.8g$ acceleration) and (d) from frame 58 to 67 with $-12°$ ($\approx 6.1g$ acceleration). For projecting the trajectory on to the image plane, the trajectory plane is assumed at 8km depth and rotated about (X,Y,Z) axis by (15°, 25°, 12°) respectively. Second trajectory is generated with initial

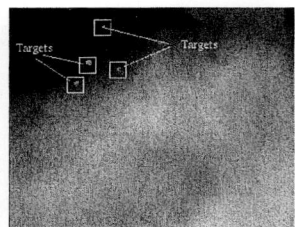

Fig. 9. Detected and marked targets

position $(7km, 7km)$, initial velocity $(300m/s, 270m/s)$ and initial acceleration $(100.0m/s^2, 80.0m/s^2)$. The trajectory plane is assumed to be at 7km and it is rotated by 10° about X-axis and by 40° about Y-axis for projection on to the image plane. Finally, the third trajectory is generated with initial position $(10km, 7km)$ and initial velocity $(320m/s, -260m/s)$. For projecting the trajectory on to the image plane, the trajectory plane is rotated by 20° about X-axis and by 30° about Y-axis. Figures 7(a) and 7(b) represent the detection output at frame 20 and the tracked trajectory upto frame 69. The condensation trail formed at the wing tips appears as clutter in the sequence. Clip 2 is similar to clip 1 except for: (a) it has 4 targets, (b) maximum target size is 16 × 7. Figures 8(a) and 8(b) depict the detected target at frame 4, and the tracked trajectories. The enlarged view of the target signature is shown in Figure 8(c). The gradient based detection algorithm was used to detect targets in an IR clip. The sequence consisting of four targets embedded in evolving cloud clutter, were detected are shown in Figure 9.

References

1. Braga-Neto, U., Choudhary, M., Goutsias, J.: Automatic target detection and tracking in forward-looking infrared sequences using morphological connected operators. Journal of Electronic Imaging ((In press) 2004)
2. Vaswani, N., Agrawal, A.K., Zheng, Q., Chellappa, R.: Moving object detection and compression in IR sequences. In Bhanu, B., Pavlidis, I., eds.: Computer Vision beyond the Visible Spectrum. Springer (2003) 153–177
3. Chien, S.Y., et al.: Efficient moving object segmentation algorithm using background registration technique. IEEE Transactions on Circuits and Systems for Video Technology **12** (2002) 577–586
4. Durucan, E., Ebrahimi, T.: Change detection and background extraction by linear algebra. Proceedings of IEEE **89** (2001) 1368–1381
5. Tsaig, Y., Averbuch, A.: Automatic segmentation of moving objects in video sequences: A region labeling approach. IEEE Transactions on Circuits and Systems for Video Technology **12** (2002) 597–612
6. Mukesh A. Zaveri , S.N. Merchant and Uday B. Desai: Multiple single pixel dim target detection in infrared image sequence. In: Proc. IEEE International Symposium on Circuits and Systems, Bangkok (2003) 380–383
7. S. Blackman, R. Dempster and T. Broida: Multiple Hypothesis Track Confirmation for Infrared Surveillance Systems. IEEE Transactions on Aerospace and Electronic Systems **29** (1993) 810–824

8. Y. Bar-shalom and T. E. Fortmann: Tracking and Data Association. Academic Press (1989)
9. Yari Barniv: Dynamic Programming Solution for Detecting Dim Moving Targets. IEEE Transactions on Aerospace and Electronic Systems **21** (1985) 144–156
10. S. Blostein and T. Huang: Detecting small, moving objects in image sequences using sequential hypothesis testing. IEEE Transactions on Signal Processing **39** (1991) 1611–1629
11. Mukesh A. Zaveri, Anant Malewar, S.N. Merchant and Uday B. Desai: Wavelet Based Detection and Modified Pipeline Algorithm for Multiple Point Targets Tracking in InfraRed image sequences. In: Proceedings of 3rd Conference ICVGIP 2002, Ahmedabad, India (2002) 67–72
12. Mukesh A. Zaveri, Uday B. Desai and S.N. Merchant: Tracking multiple maneuvering point targets using multiple filter bank in infrared image sequence. In: Proc. IEEE International Conference on Acoustics, Speech, & Signal Processing, Hongkong (2003) 409–412
13. Uday B. Desai, S. N. Merchant, Mukesh A. Zaveri: Detection and Tracking of Point Targets. In: Proceedings of the 5th International Conference on Advances in Pattern Recognition (ICAPR - 2003) Invited Paper (to appear), Calcutta, India (2003)
14. Ajishna G.: Target detection in ir sequences. Master's thesis, Indian Institute of Technology Bombay (June 2005)
15. James R. Cloutier, Ching-Fang Lin and Chun Yang: Enhanced Variable Dimension Filter for Maneuvering Target Tracking. IEEE Transactions on Aerospace and Electronic Systems **29** (1993) 786–797

Illumination Invariant Face Alignment Using Multi-band Active Appearance Model

Fatih Kahraman[1] and Muhittin Gökmen[2]

[1] Istanbul Technical University, Institute of Informatics, Computer Science,
80626 Istanbul, Turkey
kahraman@be.itu.edu.tr
[2] Istanbul Technical University, Computer Engineering Department,
80626 Istanbul, Turkey
gokmen@ce.itu.edu.tr

Abstract. In this study, we present a new multi-band image representation for improving AAM segmentation accuracy for illumination invariant face alignment. AAM is known to be very sensitive to the illumination variations. We have shown that edges, originating from object boundaries are far less susceptible to illumination changes. Here, we propose a contour selector which mostly collects contours originating from boundaries of the face components (eyes, nose, chin, etc.) and eliminates the others arising from texture. Rather than representing the image using grey values, we use Hill, Hue and Grey value (HHG) for image representation. We demonstrate that HHG representation gives more accurate and reliable results as compared to image intensity alone under various lighting conditions.

1 Introduction

Face recognition is an active research topic in image processing and computer vision. Recent years have seen large efforts in searching for a face recognition system which is capable of working with images captured under various lighting conditions including different poses for apparent security reasons. Proposed algorithms could be summarized as sketch-based, feature-based and appearance-based. Most of the proposed algorithms either assume that there is a constant background or face image is already segmented from the background. Also, they require that the frontal view of the face is used under homogeneous illumination condition. Since the transformations (e.g., Fourier, Wavelet, and Karhunen-Loeve) used in these algorithms are linear, all nonlinear degradations on the input face image cause recognition performance to drop drastically [1].

There are several leading studies in transform-based approaches. Probably most well known is eigenface [2]. It has been known that eigenface is very sensitive to shape, pose, mimic and illumination changes. Ezzat and Poggio [3] developed a similar method which is capable of synthesizing face images from training face database. Unfortunately generalization performance of their approach is poor. In the work of Nastar et al. [5] shape and appearance model based on a 3D

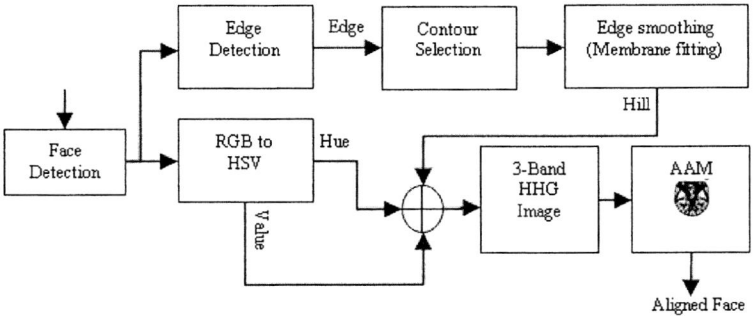

Fig. 1. Overview of the proposed method

appearance of grey level surface was used to synthesize human face. They tried to exactly synthesize face shape and texture by using three dimensional grey level surface model. Since the matching algorithm they offered gets easily trapped at local minimum, the use of method is very limited. Lanitis et al. [6] presented a similar method which models shape and normalized texture separately. Edwards improved this model further by exploiting the relationship between shape and texture. Edwards et al. [7] then offered a fast method to grap face by fitting the Active Shape Model (ASM) through least square minimization. The face is then normalized with respect to the fitted shape model in order to extract grey level texture. Although this approach yields satisfactory results, one cannot always obtain stable model parameters in the presence of variations [4]. This is due to the fact that the model does not completely utilize the face texture inside the face region.

In this study, Haar cascade classifier is used to detect face region from the input image using Haar wavelet features. Once the face region is detected, face components are extracted by applying AAM [15] [20] [4] [16]. Since AAM contains shape information, the pose and direction of the face can be directly estimated from the shape and then the face could be easily aligned to the mean shape. Our work is based on the use of Hill images obtained from selected edge segments together with modified Hue values as in [17], instead of grey values. The overview of the proposed method is depicted in Fig.1 The remainder of this paper is organized as follows: Section 2 describes how AAM is initialized by using Haar Cascade Classifier. Section 3 describes how salient face components are extracted. Details of the multi-band (HHG) representation are discussed in Section 4. Experimental results are presented in Section 5. Conclusions and future works are given in Section 6.

2 Face Detection and Model Initialization

The first step in our face alignment system is to detect face region from the still image. This is achieved by using Haar Cascade Classifier (HCC) which is scale invariant and can cope with pose variations to some degree. HCC has been successfully used in many object recognition applications. The classifier was first proposed by Viola and Jones [10] [11] and then enhanced by Lienhart [12].

The classifier is trained by the images taken from face (positives) and non-face (negatives) regions of the size 20 by 20. After successful training, the classifier produces 1 where there exists a face and 0 otherwise [12]. HCC can only give a rough estimate of the face region.

We have used Active Appearance Model (AAM) to extract face landmark points. Initialization of AAM is very important for the convergence. Any improper initialization results in erroneous model convergence and consequently yields wrong landmarks. To avoid dependence on initialization, HCC result is used in order to initialize the AAM automatically (Fig.2). It helps both better initialization and fast convergence of the model.

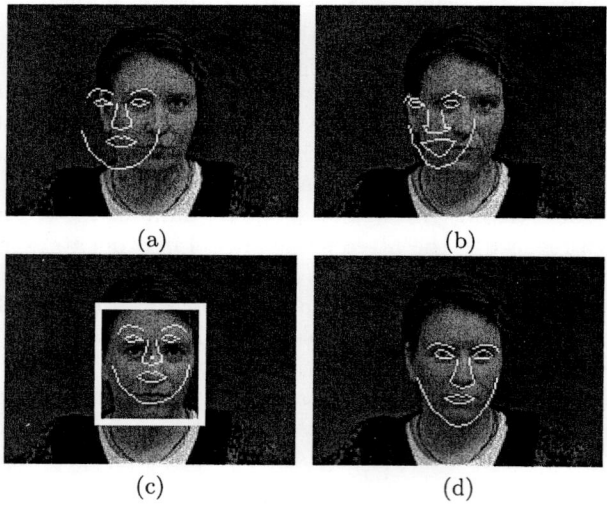

Fig. 2. AAM initialization: (a) Initialization of AAM by using mean shape without HCC, (b) AAM result for (a), (c) Initialization of AAM by using HCC, (d) AAM result of (c)

3 Face Modeling

In this section, we concentrate on face alignment problem. Face alignment is required to obtain high recognition rates in any face recognition system. Recent studies are centered on around this problem. Proposed solutions are generally model-based algorithms. Active Appearance Model (AAM) is the most promising algorithm among the model-based solutions. AAM can compute fast, deformable and robust matching between the model and the original image by utilizing the relationship between the shape and the texture. In this study, we use AAM to extract salient points on human face.

3.1 Active Appearance Model

Any human face can be synthesized from the model which is trained by the training database. The database is prepared by a human observer selecting the landmark points. Once the model is constructed, any given face can be mapped to the model space by minimizing the residual error between the original face image and the synthesized face image. The landmark points on the face images are selected by the human observer. Assume that the points belonging to the ith face image are denoted as $\{(S_i, T_i)\}$. Where S_i is a set of points containing shape information such that $S_i = \{(x_1, y_1), (x_2, y_2), \ldots, (x_K, y_K)\}$ and T_i contains texture information at S_i. AAM is obtained by applying principal component analysis on $\{(S_i, T_i)\}$

$$S = \bar{S} + P_s s \qquad (1)$$
$$T = \bar{S} + P_t t \qquad (2)$$

where $\bar{S}$ is called mean shape and $\bar{T}$ is called mean texture. s and t are the eigenvectors corresponding to the m largest eigenvalues. Any face image can be easily mapped to the model by multiplying the difference between the original image and the mean signal with the covariance

$$S = P_s^T (S - \bar{S}) \qquad (3)$$
$$T = P_t^T (T - \bar{T}). \qquad (4)$$

Any change on the shape leads to a change on texture since AAM model space is composed of the texture and shape subspaces [9]. Hence the appearance model (A) for any given image can be obtained by the formula

$$A = \begin{pmatrix} \Lambda s \\ t \end{pmatrix} \qquad (5)$$

where Λ denotes diagonal shape weight matrix. Principal component analysis can be applied to A in order to reveal the relationship between shape and texture subspaces

$$A = P_a a \qquad (6)$$

where a are the eigenvectors corresponding to the m largest eigenvalues.

4 Multi-band HHG Image Representation

In this section, we explain the basic components of our Hill, Hue and Grey value (HHG) based multi-band image representation.

4.1 Face Contour Detection

Classical AAM trained with raw RGB values fails at modeling the faces captured under different illuminations even if the face exists in the training database. This is due to the fact that AAM makes use of texture resemblance in minimization. This makes AAM very sensitive to illumination variations. It suggests that a feature less sensitive to illumination changes is required rather than using texture alone. We have showed that contours originating from object boundaries are far less susceptible to illumination variations [19] [20]. Fortunately face components such as eyes, eyebrows, nose and lips correspond to object boundaries. Another observation is that contours arising from texture disappears at large scales. This shown in Fig.3(c). We utilized the Generalized Edge Detector (GED) [13] [14], which combines the most of the existing high performance edge detectors under a unified framework. Most important part of the contour extraction algorithm is to select the perceptually important contours among these contours obtained by tracing these edges. This is achieved by assigning a priority to each contour by simply calculating the weighted sum of the normalized contour length, the average contrast along normal direction and the average curvature. The priority assigned to the contour C_i is given by (7).

$$Priority(C_i) = w_{length} \cdot Length(C_i) + w_{contrast} \cdot Contrast(C_i) + w_{curvature} \cdot Curvature(C_i) \qquad (7)$$

By means of our contour ordering we can obtain perceptually important contours mostly resulting from object boundaries by selecting only the leading contours in this order and omitting the others, as shown in Fig.3.

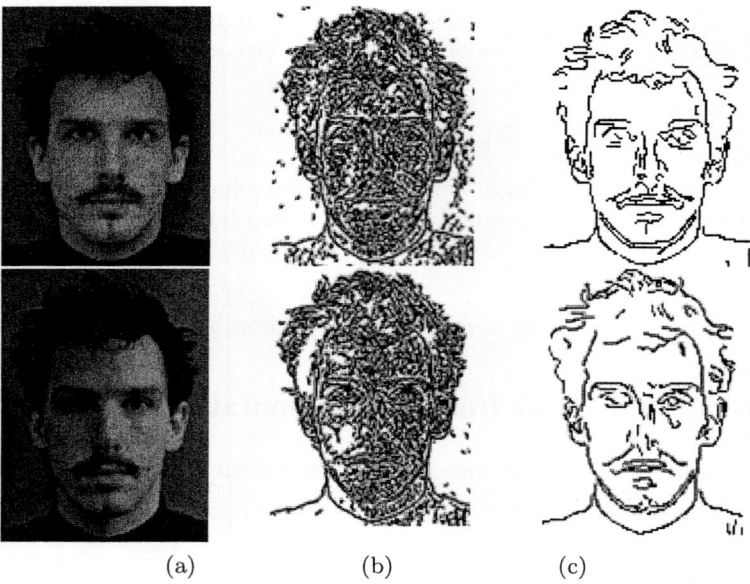

(a)   (b)   (c)

Fig. 3. Contour detection under different illumination: (a) Original image, (b) Detected edges at a small scale, (c) Selected contours

4.2 Membrane Fitting over Edges

By using an appropriate surface reconstruction algorithm, a dense image can be obtained from sparse edge map. To overcome the locality problem of edges, a membrane functional (9), can be applied to edge maps by minimizing.

$$E_m(x,y) = \int\int_\Omega (f-d)^2 dxdy + \lambda \int\int_\Omega (f_x^2 + f_y^2) dxdy \qquad (8)$$

$$R_1(x,y;\lambda) = 1/2\lambda e^{-[(|x|+|y|)/\lambda]} \qquad (9)$$

The spread edge profiles obtained by this membrane fitting gives rise to a dense image called "Hill" [19]. Hills have high values on boundary locations and decrease as we move apart from edges. It is known that, minimizing the membrane functional is equivalent to convolving the data with a first order regularization filter [14], which is shown in Fig.4(b). The details of the Hill representation are given in [19]. In our approach, first the goal oriented edge detection is applied by sorting edges and selecting meaningful contours describing a face. The detected contours are filtered with R-filter which has a very good localization performance while smoothing the edges. Resulting hill image is shown in Fig.4(c). Filtering the selected edges instead of using the contours alone improves the convergence of AAM under varying illumination conditions [21].

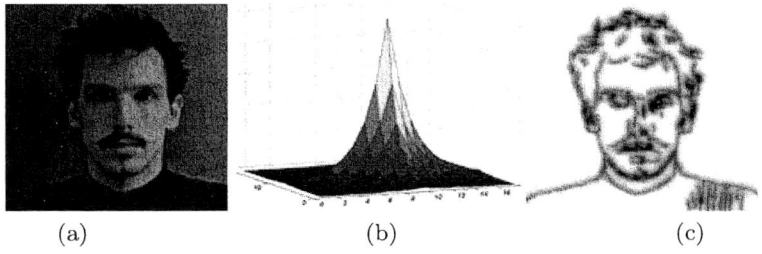

Fig. 4. Membrane fitting: (a) Original face image, (b) Regularization filter kernel, (c) Hill image

4.3 HSV Color Conversion

A disadvantage of the use of raw RGB values in AAM is its sensitivity to illumination changes. On the other hand, the HSV color space has some advantageous to expose the significant features for face recognition. It is well known that Hue band is less sensitive to illumination changes than raw intensity values. One way to increase tolerance toward intensity changes in image is to transform the RGB into a color space where intensity and chromaticity are separated and then use chromaticity part. Changes in illumination can have harsh inferences on the skin color distribution. These changes can be reduced in HSV color space. Thus we used Hue component for our multi-band image representation to get further

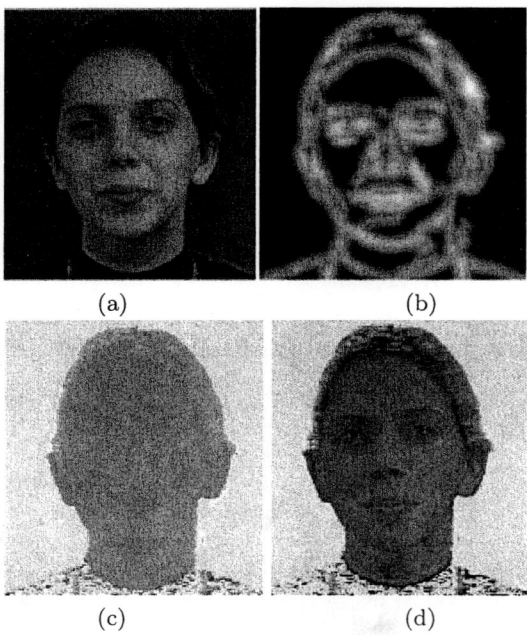

Fig. 5. Multi-band image representation: (a) Value band, (b) Hill band, (c) Hue band. (d) HHV image representation.

robustness to the illumination variation. The image, represented in RGB is converted to HSV. Hue is represented as an angle (0-360 degrees) and saturation as a real number between 0 and 1. We used modified version of Hue band for multi-band image representation as in [17]. Thus our multi-band model consists of the hill band, modified hue band and grey value band.

5 Experimental Results

In our experiments we have used IMM face database [18]. The image resolution is 320x240. 74 color images which have full frontal face, neutral expression are selected and used in our experiments. 37 images with no spotlight are used for training and the remaining 37 images which have spot light added at the person's left side are used for testing. Face detection module gives a rough estimate of the face region. AAM performs the search in the region HCC suggests. Since the search starts at a point closer to the optimal solution, fast convergence is obtained and we escape from poor local minimum. Classical AAM yields satisfactory results provided that test images whose illumination is similar to the training images.

Since AAM is principal component analysis based approach, illumination changes cause AAM to match the model to wrong face components. Models based on raw intensity tend to be sensitive to changes in lighting conditions.

Thus models built based on one data set may not give good results on different face data set which is taken under different lighting condition.

Edge based representation tends to be less sensitive to lighting changes than raw intensity [20]. We experimentally prove that object boundaries are less sensitive to light conditions when compared to intensity. We obtain high accuracy segmentation results with AAM when multi-band HHG images are used. When classical AAM is used, it can be easily verified from the Fig.6(a) that segmented face components move towards the spot light direction. Fig.6(b) shows the segmentation result obtained with proposed algorithm where hills from selected contours are used. Since contours arising from object boundaries are less sensitive to illumination variations, the proposed AAM can still capture the face model accurately.

The accuracy of the segmentation is computed as the point-to-point (pt.-pt.) and point to curve (pt.-crv) distance measures. Pt.-pt measures Euclidean distance between corresponding landmarks of the model and the ground truth,

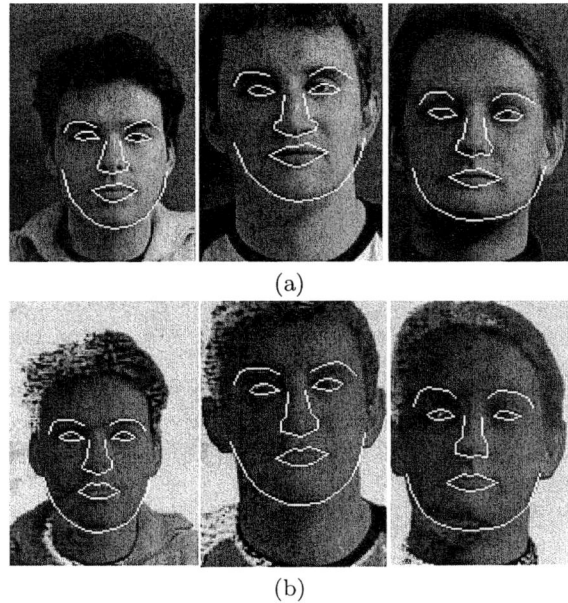

Fig. 6. Face segmentation results: Top:(a) Original AAM results, Bottom:(b) HHG based AAM results

Table 1. Face segmentation results for test images (320x240)

Method	Mean pt.-pt. Error	Mean pt.-crv. Error
Original AAM (RGB)	2.84 ± 0.78	1.35 ± 0.49
Stegmann's Method (VHE)	2.63 ± 0.64	1.27 ± 0.40
Proposed Method (HHG)	2.28 ± 0.10	1.00 ± 0.03

whereas pt.-crv. measures the shortest distance to the curve in a neighborhood of the corresponding ground truth landmark [17]. The comparative results are given in Table.1. It's seen that HHG outperforms both original AAM and the VHE multi-band based AAM with grey values, hue and edge strength.

6 Conclusion and Future Work

We proposed a novel multi-band image representation (HHG) for AAM. The HHG utilizes the hill images obtained by fitting a membrane to the selected contours detected by the Generalized Edge Detector (GED). We compared the performance of original AAM, VHE [17] based AAM and HHG based AAM. We have shown that HHG representation based AAM gives the best performance as compared to the original intensity and VHE based models. Our method can be thought as a extension of the Stegmann's paper [17]. HHG based AAM locates the points more accurately than the others for test images which taken under different illumination condition, because Hill images are obtained by smoothing the most prominent edge contours in the face image gathered by means of an efficient and effective edge ordering scheme. When compared to the original AAM and VHE, the proposed method is more accurate in segmentation, more robust to initialization and less sensitive to illumination condition. The performance of the proposed scheme on larger face databases is currently under investigation.

Acknowledgements. This work is partly supported by the State Planning Agency (DPT) of Turkey. We would like to thank Binnur KURT for his contributions and suggestions.

References

1. Xiaoguang L., Hsu R., Jain A. K. "Face Recognition with 3D Model-Based Synthesis," International Conference on Bioinformatics and its Applications, pp. 315–333, Florida, USA, 2004
2. Turk M.A. and Pentland A. P., "Face recognition using eigenfaces. In IEEE Computer Society Conference Computer Vision and Pattern Recognition, pp. 586–591, 1991.
3. Ezzat T. and Poggio T., "Facial Analysis and Synthesis Using Image-Based Models," In International Workshop on AutomaticFace and Gesture Recognition 1996, pp. 116–121, Killington, Vermont, 1996.
4. Ezzat Cootes T. F., Kittipanyangam P., "ComparingVariations on the Active Appearance Model Algorithm", Proc.BMVC2002, **Vol.2**, pp. 837–846.
5. Nastar C., Moghaddam B., and Pentland A., "Generalized Image Matching: Statistical Learning of Physically-Based Deformations," In European Conference on Computer Vision, **Vol.1**, pp. 589–598, Cambridge, UK, 1996.
6. Lanitis A., Taylor C., and Taylor T., "Automatic Interpretation and Coding of Face Images Using Flexible Models," IEEE Transactions on Pattern Analysis and Machine Intelligence, **19(7)**, pp. 743–756, 1997.

7. Edwards G. J., Taylor C. J., and Cootes T., "Learning to Identify and Track Faces in Image Sequences," British Machine Vision Conference 1997, Colchester, UK, 1997.
8. Ming Z., Stan Z. L., Chun C., "Subspace analysis and optimization for active appearance model based face alignment," The 6th International Conference on Automatic Face and Gesture Recognition. Seoul, Korea, May, 2004.
9. Ahlberg J., "A System for Face Localization and Facial Feature Extraction," Report No. LiTH-ISY-R-2172, July 1999.
10. Viola P., and Jones M. J., "Rapid Object Detection using a Boosted Cascade of Simple Features," in Conference on Computer Vision and Pattern Recognition, 2001.
11. Viola P. and Jones M.J., "Robust real-time object detection", ICCV Workshop on Statistical and Computation Theories of Vision, 2001.
12. Lienhart R. and Maydt J. "An Extended Set of Haar-like Features for Rapid Object Detection," Proceedings of the ICIP'02, 2002.
13. Kurt B., Gökmen M., and Jain A.K. "Image Compression Based On Centipede Model," Proceedings of International Conference on Image Analysis and Processing, ICIAP'99, Vol.I, pp.303–310, 1997.
14. Gökmen M., Jain A.K., "$\lambda\tau$-Space Representation of Images and Generalized Edge Detection," IEEE Trans.on Pattern Analysis and Machine Intelligence, vol.19, No. 6, June 1997, pp.545-563.
15. Cootes T., Cooper D., Taylor C., and Graham J., "Active shape models - their training and application," Computer Vision and Image Understanding, 61(1), pp. 38–59, 1995.
16. Stegman M. B., "Analysis and segmentation of face images using point annotations and linear subspace techniques," Technical Report, DTU, 2002.
17. Stegmann M. B., Larsen R., Multi-band Modelling of Appearance, Image and Vision Computing, vol. 21(1), pp. 61-67, Elsevier Science, 2003.
18. Stegmann M. B., Ersboll B. K., and Larsen R.. FAME "A flexible appearance modeling environment," IEEE Trans. on Medical Imaging, 22(10):1319-1331, 2003.
19. Yilmaz A. and Gökmen M, "Eigenhills vs Eigenface and Eigenedge," Pattern Recognition, Vol.34, pp.181–184, 2001.
20. Cootes T. F. and Taylor C. J., "On representing edge structure for model matching," in Proc. IEEE Computer Vision and Pattern Recognition - CVPR, 2001, vol. 1, pp. 1114-1119.
21. Kahraman F., Kurt B. and Gökmen M., "Active Appearance Model Based Face Recognition," in Proc. IEEE 13th Signal Processing And Communications Applications Conference, 2005, vol. 1, pp. 209-212, Kayseri, Turkey.

Globally Optimal 3D Image Reconstruction and Segmentation Via Energy Minimisation Techniques

Brian C. Lovell

Intelligent Real-Time Imaging and Sensing Group, EMI,
The School of Information Technology and Electrical Engineering,
The University of Queensland
lovell@itee.uq.edu.au
http://www.itee.uq.edu.au/~lovell

Abstract. This paper provides an overview of a number of techniques developed within our group to perform 3D reconstruction and image segmentation based of the application of energy minimisation concepts. We begin with classical snake techniques and show how similar energy minimisation concepts can be extended to derive globally optimal segmentation methods. Then we discuss more recent work based on geodesic active contours that can lead to globally optimal segmentations and reconstructions in 2D. Finally we extend the work to 3D by introducing continuous flow globally minimal surfaces. Several applications are discussed to show the wide applicability and suitability of these techniques to several difficult image analysis problems.

1 Introduction and Time-Line

In 1992 we began a research project to automatically segment cell images from Pap Smear slides for the detection of cancer of the cervix. We investigated simple techniques based on edge detection, grayscale thresholding, and grayscale morphology (*e.g.*, watersheds), but could only achieve accurate segmentation on about 60% of cell images. In 1997 we started looking at dual snake energy minimisation techniques as proposed by Gunn [1], but this method suffered from poor robustness. However, Gunn did suggest a fast globally optimal method based on converting the circular contour finding problem into a linear trellis and then applying the Viterbi shortest path finding algorithm. This approach worked extremely well as reported by Bamford and Lovell [2] and yielded 99.5% correct segmentation on a cell database of nearly 20,000 cell images.

As this method was so remarkably effective on cell images there was little incentive to improve the method for the Pap Smear problem itself, but we still held a desire to develop energy minimisation techniques which were more general. In 2002, Appleton and Sun [3] put the problem of representing closed contours on a linear trellis on to a firm mathematical basis. Then, in 2003, Appleton and Talbot [4,5] extended and generalized the energy minimisation approach to handle the optimal segmentation of planar concave objects as well as convex images such as cells. This extension avoided dependance on a coarse discretization grid so that grid-bias could be removed. The extension to 3D was achieved in late 2003 by Appleton and Talbot [6] by converting the shortest path techniques into an equivalent continuous maximum flow/minimal surface problem.

In this paper we outline the various energy minimisation segmentation techniques and show how they can be applied to solve quite difficult segmentation and reconstruction problems from diverse domains such as volumetric medical imaging to multiview reconstruction.

2 Cell Image Segmentation Using the Viterbi Shortest Path Method

Although the use of active contours [7] is well established, it is well known that these methods tend to suffer from local minima, initialisation, and stopping criteria problems. Fortunately global minimum energy, or equivalently shortest-path, searching methods have been found which are particularly effective in avoiding such local minima problems due to the presence of the many artefacts often associated with medical images [8,9,10].

An energy minimization method employed was based on a suggestion in [1]. A circular search space is first defined within the image, bounded by two concentric circles centralised upon the approximate centre of the nucleus found by an initial rough segmentation technique (*e.g.,* converging squares algorithm). This search space is sampled to form a circular trellis by discretising both the circles and a grid of evenly-spaced radial lines joining them (figure 1). This circular trellis is then unwrapped in a polar to rectangular transformation yielding a conventional linear trellis.

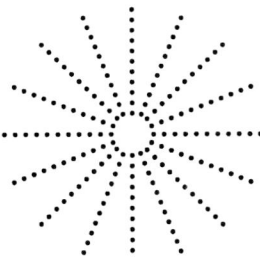

Fig. 1. Discrete search space

Every possible contour that lies upon the nodes of the search space is then evaluated and an associated energy or cost function is calculated. This cost is a function of both the contour's smoothness and how closely it follows image edges. The relative weighting of the cost components is controlled by a single regularization parameter, $\lambda \in [0,1]$. By choosing a high value of λ, the smoothness term dominates, which may lead to contours that tend to ignore important image edges. On the other hand, low values of λ allow contours to develop sharp corners as they attempt to follow all high gradient edges, even those which may not necessarily be on the desired object's edge. Once every contour has been evaluated, the single contour with least cost is chosen as the global solution. The well-known Viterbi algorithm provides an efficient method to find this global solution as described in [2].

A data set of 19946 Pap stained cervical cell images was available for testing. The single parameter λ was empirically chosen to be 0.7 after trial runs on a small sub-set of the images. The effect of the choice of λ on segmentation accuracy on this trial set is shown by the graph of figure 2. Figure 3 shows a value of $\lambda = 0.7$ as being the most suitable for these particular images. Every image in the data set was then segmented at $\lambda = 0.7$ and the results verified by eye. Of the 19946 images, 99.47% were found to be correctly segmented.

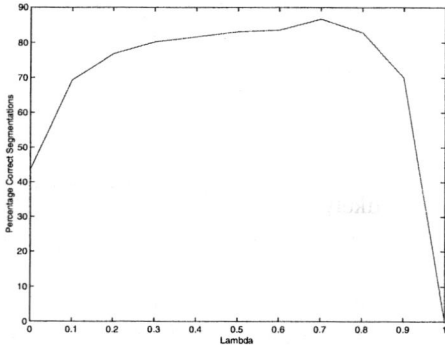

Fig. 2. Plot of percentage of correct segmentations against λ for a set of images consisting of known 'difficult' images and randomly selected images

With λ set at 0.0, the smoothness constraint is completely ignored and the point of greatest gradient is chosen along each search space radius. Previous studies [11] have shown that for approximately 65% of images, all points of greatest gradient actually lie upon the nucleus cytoplasm border, so these "easy" cell images will be correctly segmented. For the remaining 35% of images, a large gradient due to an artefact or darkly stained chromatin will draw the contour away from the desired border. As λ increases, the large curvatures present in these configurations become less probable (figure 3).

Comments: We show in [12] that the above segmentation method can be viewed as the application of hidden Markov model techniques where the transition matrix is determined by the curvature constraints and the observation matrix is determined by the gradient image. Conceptually the Viterbi algorithm progresses like a planar wavefront through the linear trellis in a manner not unlike an electromagnetic wave passing through a waveguide. Later when we look at the fast marching [13,14] and Dijkstra's[15] shortest path algorithm, we see that these two algorithms are more akin to spherical electromagnetic wavefronts propagating in free space.

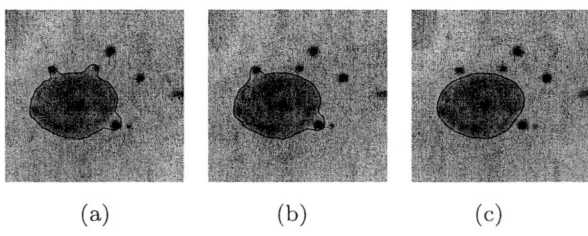

Fig. 3. The effect of increasing λ. a) $\lambda = 0.1$, b) $\lambda = 0.2$, c) $\lambda = 0.5$.

A rather unsatisfactory step in the above development is the formation of the linear trellis from the circular domain and the actual determination of the shortest path. A simple way to find shortest paths on the linear trellis that correspond to closed contours in the image domain is to replicate the M nodes where we unwrap the circular domain such that the last column of nodes in the trellis ia a copy of the first column. Then if there are M such nodes in a column, we would need to evaluate each of the M paths starting and finishing on the same node $i \in [0 \dots M - 1]$. This would require M evaluations of the Viterbi algorithm.

Gunn [1] suggests a heuristic whereby we choose node i where the image gradient is maximal (*i.e.*, likely to be on the cell boundary), then we find the shortest path beginning and ending at i. Even if the first node i is not actually on the cell boundary, halfway around the cell image the nodes on the shortest path are very likely to be on the boundary. So we rotate the wrapping point 180° and rerun the Viterbi algorithm starting from this node. In our case we selected $M=30$, so we can replace 30 Viterbi evaluations with just 2. Although this heuristic works very well in practice, in theory there are clearly situations where it could fail.

Appleton and Sun [3] investigated this general problem of circular shortest paths. Their method is guaranteed to find the shortest circular path and uses a branch and bound technique to quickly locate it. The root of the branch and bound search tree consists of the entire first column of nodes. The shortest path to the other end of the trellis is found and this forms a lower bound on the circular shortest path. The root node is then split in two and the shortest path algorithm run again keeping only paths that are circular. By applying this process recursively the node on the circular shortest path is quickly identified.

However despite this improvement a major shortcoming of all methods based on a polar to rectangular mapping is the inability to handle concave contours, thus severely limiting their application domain.

3 Globally Optimal Geodesic Active Contours

The classic active contour or snake model proposed by Kass [7] modelled a segmentation boundary by a series of point masses connected by springs. This explicit view of curves as a polygon was replaced by an implicit view of curves as the level set of some 3D surface by Osher and Sethian [16]. Level sets offer significant advantages over traditional snakes including improved stability and much better handling of topology (*e.g.,* segmentation of multiple objects with just one contour). Another advance came in the form of geodesic active contours as proposed by Caselles *et al* [17]. They demonstrated the equivalence of their energy function to the length of a geodesic (*i.e.,* path of least cost, path of least time) in an isotropic space. A problem with traditional geodesic active contours is that they are a gradient descent method and thus have all the usual problems of initialisation, termination, and local maxima associated with such methods. They just do not have the stability and simplicity of application of globally optimal segmentation methods.

The globally optimal method we outline here finds closed contours in the image domain itself rather than unwrapping the image through polar to rectangular transformation. Working in the image domain means that we cannot find simple shortest paths as that would cause a bias towards small contours. Instead we use a contour energy of the form [18]

$$E[C] = \oint_C \frac{g}{r}\,ds \qquad (1)$$

where g is a measure of probability of being on the boundary (*e.g.,* gradient) and r is the radius of the contour C. Thus all circles centred on the origin would have the same contour energy. Another innovation is to find the minimal contour as an open path in an augmented helicoidal representation that allows us to represent concave contours as illustrated in figure 4.

We use the Fast Marching Algorithm [13] to find the surface of minimal action, also known as the distance function, whose gradient curves form minimal geodesics. This algorithm finds the surface of minimal action by considering it as the first time-of-arrival of a wavefront emanating from the starting point and travelling with speed $\frac{1}{g}$, where g is usually the image gradient as before. The algorithm is identical to Dijkstra's shortest distance algorithm [15] apart from

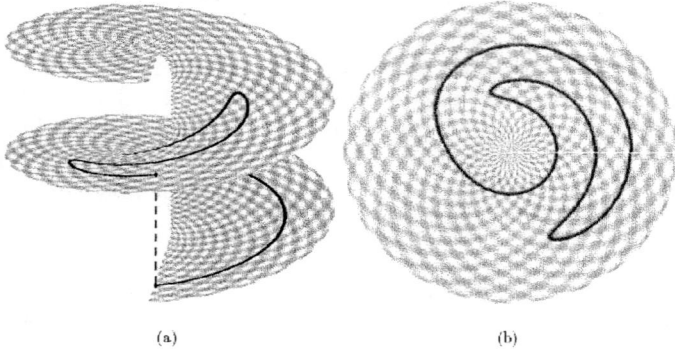

Fig. 4. The helicoidal representation of the cut-concave shape from [18]. (a) open curve (b) closed curve.

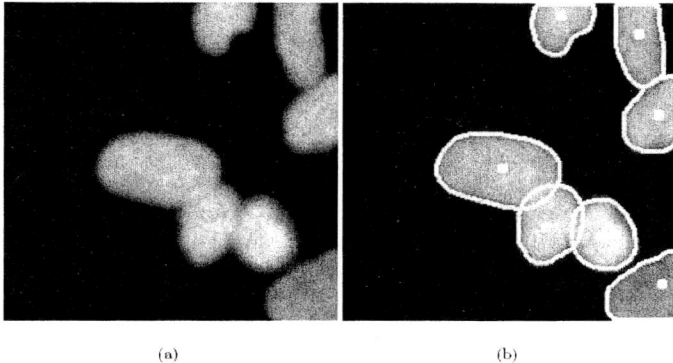

(a) (b)

Fig. 5. Globally optimal geodesic active contours applied to overlapping objects from [18]. The cells (a) are separated despite the weak intesity gradient between them (b).

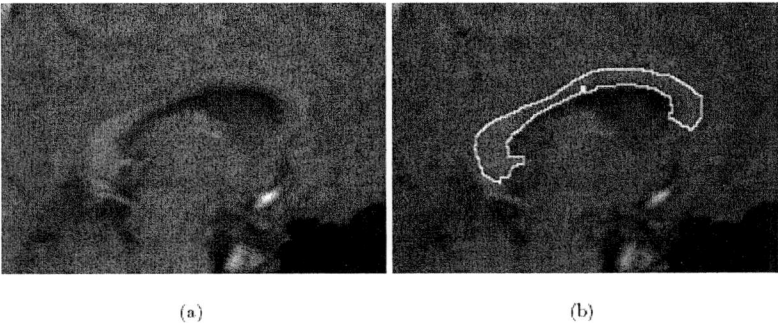

(a) (b)

Fig. 6. Segmentation of MRI image of a concave contour, the corpus callosum in a human brain, from [18]. (a) is the original Image and (b) is the segmentation via globally optimal geodesic active contours.

the need to update g. Figures 5 and 6 show some segmentation results from the globally optimal geodesic active contours method.

4 Globally Minimal Surfaces

The planar segmentation technique outlined in the last section cannot be extended to higher dimensions, so we need an entirely new approach. Minimum cuts and maximum flow techniques are naturally suited to globally optimal segmentation in higher dimensions. Although this has been tried in the past with discrete approximations, Appleton and Talbot [6] have developed a method based on continuous maximal flows by solving a system of partial differential equations. It is shown [18] that this method gives identical results to the pre-

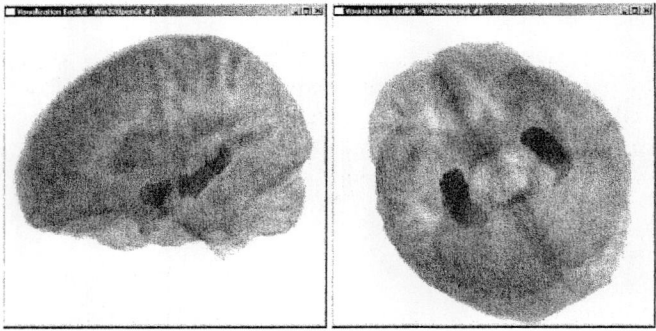

Fig. 7. Segmentation of the hippocampi from an MRI dataset from [18]

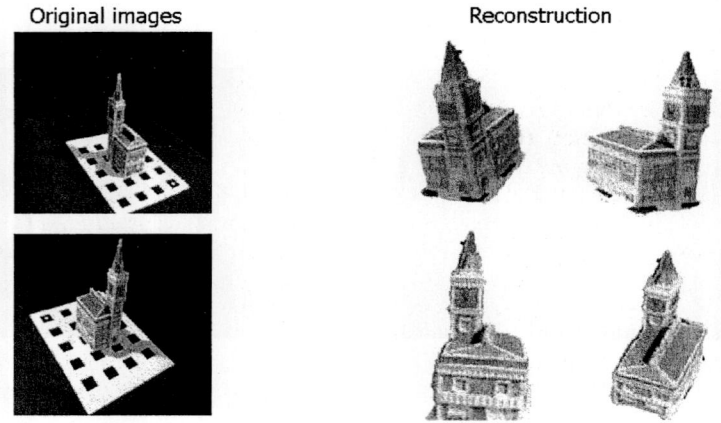

Fig. 8. Multiview reconstruction using globally minimal surfaces for post-processing based on [19]

vious globally optimal geodesic active contour method in the case of planar images. Figure 7 shows the segmentation of volumetric MRI data and figure 8 shows the 3D reconstruction from multiview images using minimal surfaces as a postprocessor.

5   Conclusions

These globally optimal energy minimisation methods are fast, very easy to apply, and tend to yield robust solutions. Future work is focussed on integrating these techniques with statistical shape models to develop an 3D EM-like algorithm incorporating prior knowledge for detection and segmentation of known shapes.

Acknowledgements

This paper outlines a number of research themes currently being pursued within the Intelligent Real-Time Imaging and Sensing Group. I would like to acknowledge the contributions of Terry Caelli, Hugues Talbot, Peter Kootsookos and my current and former PhD students Ben Appleton, Carlos Leung, David McKinnon, Pascal Bamford, and Christian Walder.

References

1. Gunn, S.R.: Dual Active Contour Models for Image Feature Extraction. University of Southampton (1996) PhD Thesis.
2. Bamford, P., Lovell, B.: Unsupervised cell nucleus segmentation with active contours. Signal Processing Special Issue: Deformable Models and Techniques for Image and Signal Processing **71** (1998) 203–213
3. Appleton, B., Sun, C.: Circular shortest paths by branch and bound. Pattern Recognition **36** (2003) 2513–2520
4. Appleton, B.: Optimal geodesic active contours: application to heart segmentation. In Lovell, B.C., Maeder, A.J., eds.: APRS Workshop on Digital Image Computing. Volume 1., Brisbane, APRS (2003) 27–32
5. Appleton, B., Talbot, H.: Globally optimal geodesic active contours. Journal of Mathematical Imaging and Vision (2005)
6. Appleton, B., Talbot, H.: Globally optimal surfaces by continuous maximal flows. In Sun, C., Talbot, H., Ourselin, S., Adriaansen, T., eds.: Digital Image Computing: Techniques and Applications. Volume 2., Sydney, CSIRO Publishing (2003) 987–996
7. Kass, M., Witten, A., Terzopoulos, D.: Snakes: Active contour models. International Journal of Computer Vision **1** (1987) 321–331
8. Cohen, L.D., Cohen, I.: Finite-element methods for active contour models and balloons for 2-D and 3-D images. IEEE Transactions on Pattern Analysis and Machine Intelligence **15** (1993) 1131–1147
9. Davatzikos, C.A., Prince, J.L.: An active contour model for mapping the cortex. IEEE Transactions on Medical Imaging **14** (1995) 65–80
10. Geiger, D., Gupta, A., Costa, L., Vlontzos, J.: Dynamic programming for detecting, tracking, and matching deformable contours. IEEE Transactions on Pattern Analysis and Machine Intelligence **17** (1995) 294–302
11. Bamford, P., Lovell, B.: Improving the robustness of cell nucleus segmentation. In Lewis, P.H., Nixon, M.S., eds.: Proceedings of the Ninth British Machine Vision Conference, BMVC '98, University of Southampton (1998) 518–524
12. Lovell, B.C.: Hidden markov models for spatio-temporal pattern recognition and image segmentation. In Mukherjee, D.P., Pal, S., eds.: International Conference on Advances in Pattern Recognition. Volume 1., Calcutta (2003) 60–65
13. Sethian, J.A.: A fast marching level set method for monotonically advancing fronts. Proceedings of the National Academy of Sciences **93** (1996) 1591–1595
14. Sethian, J.A.: Level Set Methods and Fast Marching Methods — Evolving Interfaces in Computational Geometry, Fluid Mechanics, Computer Vision, and Materials Science. Cambridge University Press (1999)
15. Dijkstra, E.: A note on two problems in connexion with graphs. Numerische Mathematik **1** (1959) 269–271

16. Osher, S., Sethian, J.A.: Fronts propagating with curvature dependent speeed: Algorithms based on hamilton-jacobi formulations. Journal of Computational Physics **79** (1988) 12–49
17. Caselles, V., Kimmel, R., Sapiro, G.: Geodesic active contours. International Journal of Computer Vision **22** (1997) 61–79
18. Appleton, B.C.: Globally Minimal Contours and Surfaces for Image Segmentation. The University of Queensland (2004)
19. Leung, C., Appleton, B., Lovell, B.C., Sun, C.: An energy minimisation approach to stereo-temporal dense reconstruction. In: International Conference on Pattern Recognition. Volume 1., Cambridge (2004) 72–75

Go Digital, Go Fuzzy

Jayaram K. Udupa[1] and George J. Grevera[2]

[1] Medical Image Processing Group,
Department of Radiology, University of Pennsylvania,
423 Guardian Drive 4th Floor Blockley Hall,
Philadelphia, PA 19104-6021
jay@mipg.upenn.edu
[2] Mathematics and Computer Science Department, BL 215,
St. Joseph's University,
5600 City Avenue,
Philadelphia, PA 19131
ggrevera@sju.edu

Abstract. In many application areas of imaging sciences, object information captured in multi-dimensional images needs to be extracted, visualized, manipulated, and analyzed. These four groups of operations have been (and are being) intensively investigated, developed, and applied in a variety of applications. In this paper, we put forth two main arguments: (1) Computers are digital, and most image acquisition and communication efforts at present are toward digital approaches. In the same vein, there are considerable advantages to taking an inherently digital approach to the above four groups of operations rather than using concepts based on continuous approximations. (2) Considering the fact that images are inherently fuzzy, to handle uncertainties and heterogeneity of object properties realistically, approaches based on fuzzy sets should be taken to the above four groups of operations. We give two examples in support of these arguments.

1 Introduction

In imaging sciences, particularly medical, there are many sources of multidimensional images [1]. For ease of further reference, we will refer to a multidimensional image simply as a *scene* and represent it by a pair $C = (C, f)$, where C, the *scene domain*, is a multidimensional rectangular array of spatial elements (*spels* for short), and f, the *scene intensity,* is a function that assigns to every spel a vector whose component elements are from a set of integers. There is usually an *object* of study for which the scene is generated. This may be a physical object such as an organ/tissue component, a tumor/fracture/lesion/an abnormality, a prosthetic device, or a phantom. It may also be a conceptual object such as an isodose surface in a radiation treatment plan, an activity region highlighted by PET or functional MRI, or a mathematical phantom. The objects may be rigid, deformable, static, or dynamic. For example, the bones at a moving joint represent a dynamic, rigid object assembly. The heart muscle and the blood pool in the various chambers constitute a dynamic, deformable object assembly. We note that, most frequently, we are given one scene with scalar-valued intensities relating to an object of study. Often multiple scenes (each with scalar- or vector-valued intensities) from multiple modalities such as CT, MRI, PET, CTA, MRA, and fMRI are also given. We will refer to any operation, which, for a given set of multimodality scenes of an object of study, produces information about the object of study, as *3D imaging*. The information may be qualitative - for example, a 3D rendition of a static object, an animation sequence of a dynamic object or an animation sequence of a static object corresponding to different viewpoints. It may be quantitative - for example, the volume of a static object, and the rate of change of volume of a dynamic, deformable object, the extent of motion of a rigid dynamic object. The purpose of 3D imaging is, therefore, given multiple scenes as input, to output qualitative/quantitative information about the object of study.

In this exposition, we will argue with strong evidence that, since the scenes are inherently digital, we should take entirely digital approaches to realize all 3D imaging operations. We also suggest that, since object information in scenes is always fuzzy, we should take approaches that are based on fuzzy set concepts. The need to fulfill these strategies opens numerous problems that are inherently digital in both hard and fuzzy settings. The reader is referred to [2] for a detailed account of 3D imaging operations and their medical applications.

3D imaging operations may be classified into four groups: *preprocessing, visualization, manipulation*, and *analysis*. All preprocessing operations aim at improving or extracting object information from the given scenes. The purpose of visualization operations is to assist humans in perceiving and comprehending the object structure/characteristics/function in two, three and higher dimensions. The manipulation operations allow humans to interactively alter the object structures (mimic surgery, for example). The analysis operations enable us to quantify object structural/morphological/functional information.

2 Go Digital, Go Fuzzy

Any scene of any body region exhibits the two following important characteristics of the objects contained in the body region.

Graded Composition: The spels in the same object region exhibit heterogeneity of scene intensity due to the heterogeneity of the object material, and noise, blurring, and background variation introduced by the imaging device. Even if a perfectly homogeneous object were to be imaged, its scene will exhibit graded composition.

Hanging-togetherness (Gestalt): In spite of the graded composition, knowledgeable humans do not have any difficulty in perceiving object regions as a whole (Gestalt). This is a fuzzy phenomenon and should be captured through a proper theoretical and computational framework.

There are no binary objects or acquired binary scenes. Measured data always have uncertainties. Additionally, scenes are inherently digital. As seen from the previous section, no matter what 3D imaging operation we consider, we cannot ignore these two fundamental facts – fuzziness in data and their digital nature.

We have to deal with essentially two types of data - scenes and structures. We argue that, instead of imposing some sort of a continuous model on the scene or the structure in a hard fashion, taking an inherently digital approach, preferably in a fuzzy setting, for all 3D imaging operations can lead to effective, efficient and practically viable methods. Taking such an approach would require, in almost all cases, the development of the necessary mathematical theories and algorithms from scratch. We need appropriate theories and algorithms for topology, geometry and morphology, all in a fuzzy, digital setting, for dealing with the concept of a "structure" in scenes. Note that almost all the challenges we raised in the previous section relate to some form of object definition in scenes. Therefore, they all need the above mathematical and algorithmic developments. Additionally, since we deal with deformable objects (all soft-tissue organs, and often even bone, as in distraction osteogenesis – the process of enlarging or compressing bones through load applied over a long period of time), we also need fuzzy digital mechanics theories and algorithms to handle structure data realistically for the operations relating to registration, segmentation, manipulation and analysis. Because of the digital setting, almost all challenges raised previously lead to discrete problems. Since we are dealing with n-dimensional scenes, the mathematics and algorithms need to be developed for hard and fuzzy sets of spels defined in n-dimensions.

In the rest of this section, we shall give two examples of digital/fuzzy approaches that motivated us to the above argument. The first relates to modeling an object as a 3D surface and visualizing it. The second relates to the fuzzy topological concept of connectedness and its use in segmentation.

2.1 Polygonal Versus Digital Surfaces

In hard, boundary-based 3D scene segmentation (e.g., thresholding approaches), the output structure is often a 3D surface. The surface is represented usually either as a set of polygons (most commonly triangles [3]), or in a digital form [4] as a set of cubes or as a set of oriented faces of cubes. We shall describe in some detail how both the representation and rendering of such surfaces is vastly simpler and more efficient using digital approaches than using polygonal or other continuous approximations for them.

Let us consider the representation issues first. We shall subsequently consider the rendering issues. It is very reasonable to expect these surfaces to satisfy the following three properties since surfaces of real objects possess these properties. (1) The surface is connected. (2) The surface is oriented. This means that it has a well defined inside and outside. (3) The surface is closed; that is, it constitutes a Jordan boundary. The latter implies that the surface partitions the 3D space into an "interior" set and an "exterior" set such that any path leading from a point in the interior to a point in the exterior meets the surface.

The definitions of connectedness, orientedness, and Jordan property are much simpler, more natural and elegant in the digital setting using faces of cubes (or cubes) than using any continuous approximations such as representations via triangles. These global concepts can be arrived at using simple local concepts for digital surfaces. For example, orientedness can be defined by thinking of the faces to be oriented. That is, a face with a normal vector pointing from inside of the surface to its outside in the $-x$ direction is distinguished from a face at the same location with a face normal in exactly the opposite direction. Usually the surface normals at various points p on these surfaces (in both the polygonal and the digital case) are estimated independent of the geometry of the surface elements, for example, by the gradient at p of the intensity function f of the original scene from which the surface was segmented. The gradient may also be estimated from other derived scenes such as a Gaussian smoothed version of the segmented binary scene. Since the surface normals dictate the shading in the rendering process, the surface elements are used here only as a geometric guide rather than as detailed shape descriptors of the surface. Therefore the digital nature of the geometry introducing "staircase" effects in renditions can be more or less completely eliminated. Since the surface elements in the digital case are simple *and* all of identical size and shape, they can be stored using clever data structures that are typically an order of magnitude more compact (Figure 1) than their polygonal counterparts [5]. Finally, there is a well-developed body of literature describing the theory of digital surfaces that naturally generalizes to n-dimensions for any n. Such a generalization is very difficult for polygonal representations.

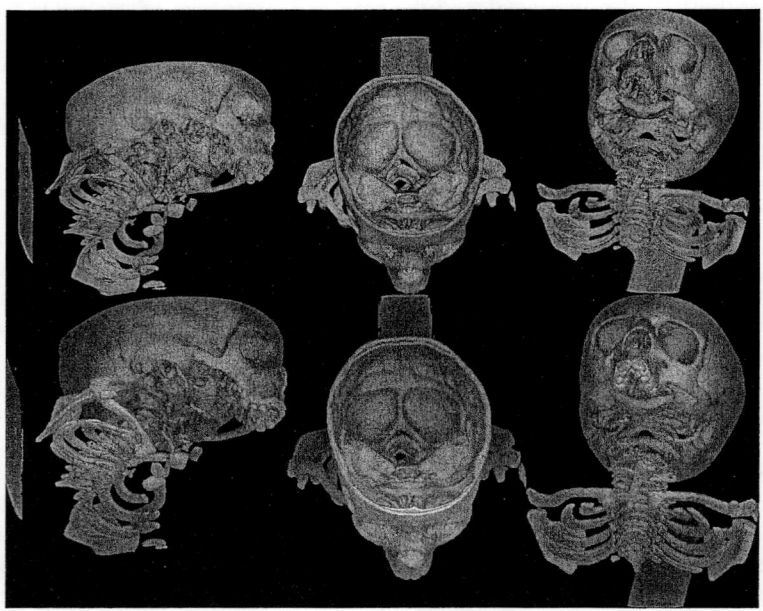

Fig. 1. Comparison of shell rendering and vs. triangulated surfaces. Top row: Triangulated surface via Marching Cubes/OpenGL requiring **3.4 sec on an SGI Reality Engine II**. Bottom row: Shell Rendering requiring **0.85 sec on a 300MHz Pentium**.

Let us now come to the rendering issues. Rendering of digital surfaces is considerably simpler and more efficient than that of polygonal surfaces, the main reason being the simplicity of the surface elements and of their spatial arrangement in the former case. There are mainly two computational steps in any rendering algorithm: hidden surface removal and shading. Both these steps can be considerably simplified exploiting the special geometry of the surface elements, reducing most expansive computations to table lookup operations. For example, the faces in a digital surface can be classified into six groups based on their face normals (corresponding to the directions (+*x*, +*y*, +*z*, -*x*, -*y*, -*z*)). For any viewpoint, all faces from at least three of these groups are not visible and hence can be discarded without doing any computation per face. There are other properties that allow the rapid projection of discrete surfaces in a back-to-front or front-to-back order by simply accessing the surface elements in some combination of column, row, and slice order from a rectangular array. Triangular and other continuous approximations to surfaces simply do not possess such computationally attractive properties. It was shown in [5] based on 10 objects of various sizes and shapes that, digital surface rendering entirely in software on a 300 MHz Pentium PC can be done about 4-17 times faster than the rendering of the same objects, whose surfaces are represented by triangles, on a Silicon Graphics Reality Engine II hardware rendering engine for about the same quality of renditions. Note that the Reality Engine II workstation is vastly more expensive than the Pentium PC. Figure 1 contains an example of digital and polygonal surface rendering.

The design of rendering engines such as Reality Engine II was motivated by the need to visualize, manipulate, and analyze structure systems representing human-made objects such as automobiles and aircrafts. Early efforts in modeling in computer graphics took, for whatever reason, a continuous approach. Digital approaches to modeling have originated mostly in medical imaging [6] and have recently been applied also to the modeling of human-made objects [7] with equal effectiveness. Digital approaches are more appropriate for modeling natural objects (such as internal human organs) than continuous approaches. Natural objects tend to be more complex in shape and morphology than human-made objects. The applications of digital approaches to human-made objects [22] have demonstrated that the latter are equally appropriate even for human-made objects.

2.2 Traditional Volume Rendering Versus Digital Volume Rendering

Surface rendering as described in the previous section is distinguished from volume rendering in that geometric surface primitives such as triangles, rectangular faces of voxels, or geometric representations of the voxels themselves are employed as an intermediate representation in surface rendering [8]. Surface rendering typically employs a binary representation of a surface that is produced via some segmentation scheme. On the other hand, volume-rendering methods do not employ geometric primitives [9] and therefore do not need a binary or explicit hard representation of objects within the three-dimensional space. Although an explicit binary representation of the surface of objects is not required in volume rendering, classification techniques are employed [9] to assign object membership values to points in the three-dimensional space. This process is naturally viewed as the process of determining a "transfer function" that assigns to each point an opacity value based on the scene intensity at that point in the given three-dimensional scene. Given the fact that volume rendering employs classification techniques, one might argue that this is analogous to a segmentation scheme employed in surface rendering although done in a fuzzy manner (see [2], Chapter 1 for a detailed discussion of such matters). The main difference between surface and volume rendering lies in the number and types of elements that are projected onto the screen. Surface rendering methods project only those elements that comprise the surface. Volume rendering techniques, on the other hand, project typically all of the voxels that are elements of the three-dimensional volume onto the screen. The transfer function is "consulted" as each voxel is projected to determine its contribution or influence on what appears on the screen. The transfer function (or lookup table) may indicate little or no contribution, a large contribution, or any amount in between. For a detailed comparison of a particular surface rendering method and a particular volume rendering method, one may refer to Udupa [10].

The general method of volume rendering was first proposed in Levoy [8], and Drebin [11]. The classification process associates a quadruple $\langle R(x), G(x), B(x), \alpha(x) \rangle$ with each scene intensity x occurring in C. R, G, B are the red, green, and blue components, respectively, and $\alpha \in [0,1]$ is referred to as opacity with $\alpha = 1$ corresponding to 100% opacity (opaque) and $\alpha = 0$ representing complete transparency. Rays are then cast through the classified volume orthogonal to the projection plane from every pixel in the projection plane. Values for discrete sample points along each ray are computed typically by trilinear interpolation, as the ray does not usually pass through voxel centers or grid points exactly. Compositing along each ray typically occurs in back-to-front order with respect to the screen or viewing direction. A variety of operators such as *over*, *attenuate*, *MIP* or *sum* (similar to radiographic projection) have been proposed. A specific hardware implementation of the above algorithm called "texture-mapped volume rendering" was first outlined in Cabral [12] using the SGI Reality Engine architecture. Briefly, the input scene, C, is loaded into texture memory (an area of dedicated, special purpose memory in the graphics hardware). Textures may be either one-, two-, or three-dimensional with two and especially three being germane to volume rendering.

We contrast traditional volume rendering with the same object-based technique, namely Shell Rendering [13, 14] that was compared with polygonal surface rendering in the previous section. Shell rendering is a flexible method that encompasses both surface rendering and volume rendering. A *shell* is a special data structure that contains voxels near the border of the object together with other items of information associated with each such voxel. At one extreme, the shell may be quite crisp (hard) in that it contains just the voxels on the object's surface. A crisp shell forms the basis for digital surface rendering. At the other extreme, the shell may be so thick as to contain all voxels in the foreground region of the entire scene. At this extreme, Shell Rendering becomes, in effect, a method of volume rendering. In between these two extremes, the shell becomes a fuzzy boundary between the object and the background.

In Shell Rendering, the information that is associated with each voxel includes the scene intensity gradient vector at the voxel, a code representing the scene intensity configuration of the voxels in the neighborhood, and the voxel coordinates. Shell rendering is done via voxel projection either in front-to-back or back-to-front order rather than by ray casting. Since all shell elements are identical in shape (a cuboid), many computations can be implemented as table lookup operations. These two factors contribute significantly to the speed of shell rendering over ray casting approaches.

Shell rendering is efficient because of the following factors (see Udupa [14] for details):

(1) The shell domain is typically a small subset of the entire scene domain.
(2) For every viewpoint, there exists an order of indexing of the columns, rows, and slices (one of 8 possible combinations) that projects the voxels in either front-to-back or back-to-front order.
(3) During front-to-back projection, an opacity-based stopping criterion implements early projection termination.
(4) Given a particular viewing direction, some elements of the shell domain may be discarded because they are completely occluded by opaque neighbors, as determined by the neighborhood configuration.
(5) Conversely, once a voxel with opaque neighbors behind it (with respect to the current viewing direction) is projected, projection along this ray can be terminated.

Shell rendering has been implemented in the freely available *3DVIEWNIX* software [15]. A tutorial regarding the specific steps in using the *3DVIEWNIX* software to perform shell rendering is also available [16].

Digital volume rendering via shell rendering in software was compared to traditional hardware assisted volume rendering. Input data consisted of four data sets: an MR head, a CT head, a CT knee, and MR angiography data. Shell rendering was executed on a 450 MHz Pentium PC. Hardware assisted volume rendering was executed on a 195 MHz SGI Octane, a dual 300 MHz processor SGI Octane, and a quad 194 MHz processor SGI Onyx 10000. Shell rendering was shown to perform at about the same speed as the 195 MHz Octane but slower than the other two SGI systems but did so by executing entirely in software on a much less expensive

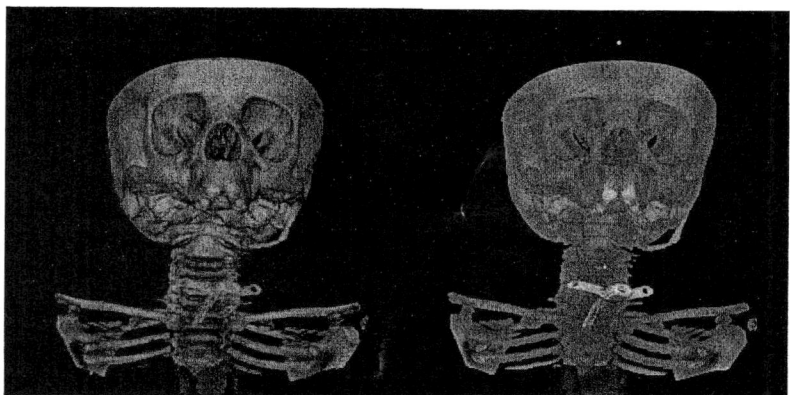

Fig. 2. Renditions of *192411* CT head data (left: shell rendering **requiring 0.9 to 2.9 sec, depending upon settings, on a 450MHz Pentium**; right: volume rendering requiring **0.8 to 1.7 sec on a dual processor 300MHz SGI Octane or a single processor 195MHz SGI Octane**, respectively

computing platform. Figure 2 contains sample shell and volume renderings. Note that traditional volume rendering in these experiments did not include a shading model. This contributed to its speed but did so at reduced image quality.

2.3 Fuzzy Connected Object Definition

Although much work has been done in digital geometry and topology based on hard sets, analogous work based on fuzzy sets is rare [17]. As pointed out earlier, the uncertainties about objects inherent in scenes must be retained as realistically as possible in all operations instead of making arbitrary hard decisions. Although many fuzzy strategies have been proposed particularly for image segmentation, none of them has considered the spatio-topological relationship among spels in a fuzzy setting to formulate the concept of hanging-togetherness. (We note that the notion of hard connectedness has been used extensively in the literature. But hard connectedness already assumes segmentation and removes the flexibility of utilizing the strength of connectedness in segmentation itself.) This is a vital piece of information that can greatly improve the immunity of object definition (segmentation) methods to noise, blurring and background variation.

Given the fuzzy nature of object information in scenes, the frameworks to handle fuzziness in scenes should address questions of the following form: How are objects to be mathematically defined in a fuzzy, digital setting taking into account the graded composition and hanging-togetherness of spels? How are fuzzy boundaries to be defined satisfying a Jordan boundary property? What are the appropriate algorithms to extract these entities from scenes in such a way as to satisfy the definitions? These questions are largely open. We will give one example below of the type of approaches that can be taken. This relates to fuzzy connected object definition [17]. This framework and the algorithms have now been applied extensively on 1000's of scenes in several routine clinical applications attesting to their strength, practical viability, and effectiveness.

We define a fuzzy *adjacency* relation α on spels independent of the scene intensities. The strength of this relation is in [0, 1] and is greater when the spels are spatially closer. The purpose of α is to capture the blurring property of the imaging device. We define another fuzzy relation κ, called *affinity*, on spels. The strength of this relation between any two spels c and d lies in [0, 1] and depends on α as well as on how similar are the scene intensities and other properties derived from scene intensities in the vicinity of c and d. Affinity is a local fuzzy relation. If c and d are far apart, their affinity is 0. Fuzzy *connectedness* is yet another fuzzy relation on spels, defined as follows. For any two spels c and d in the scene, consider all possible connecting paths between them. (A path is simply a sequence of spels such that the successive spels in the sequence are "nearby".) Every such path has a strength, which is the smallest affinity of successive pairwise spels along the path. The strength of fuzzy connectedness between c and d is the largest of the strength of all paths between c and d.

A *fuzzy connected object* of a certain strength θ is a pool O of spels together with an objectness value assigned to each spel in O. O is such that for any spels c and d in O, their strength of connectedness is at least θ, and for any spels e in O and g not in O, their strength is less than θ.

Although the computation of a fuzzy connected object in a given scene for a given κ and θ appears to be combinatorially explosive, the theory leads to solutions for this problem based on dynamic programming. In fact, fuzzy connected objects in 3D scenes (256×256×60) can be extracted at interactive speeds (a few seconds) on PCs such as a 400 MHz Pentium PC.

3 Concluding Remarks

In this article, we have first given an overview of the operations available for 3D imaging - a discipline wherein, given a set of multidimensional scenes, the aim is to extract, visualize, manipulate, and analyze object information captured in the scenes. We have also raised numerous challenges that are encountered in real applications. Computers are digital. Current attempts in image acquisition, storage, and communication are completely digital or are proceeding in that direction. We have presented an argument with evidences that there are considerable advantages in taking an inherently digital approach to realizing all 3D imaging operations. We have also argued that, since object information in scenes is fuzzy, the digital approaches should be developed in a fuzzy framework to handle the uncertainties realistically. This calls for the development of topology, geometry, morphology and mechanics, all in a fuzzy and digital setting, all of which are likely to have a significant impact on imaging sciences such as medical imaging and their applications.

Acknowledgments

The authors' research is supported by NIH grants NS37172 and EB004395. We are grateful to Mary A. Blue for typing the manuscript.

References

[1] Cho, Z.H., Jones J.P. and Singh, M.: *Foundations of Medical Imaging*, New York, New York: John Wiley & Sons, Inc. (1993).
[2] Udupa, J. and Herman, G. (eds.): *3D Imaging in Medicine*, 2nd Edition, Boca Raton, Florida: CRC Press (1999).
[3] Lorensen, W. and Cline, H.: "Marching Cubes: A High Resolution 3D Surface Construction Algorithm," *Computer Graphics* 21(1987), 163-169.
[4] Udupa, J.K., Srihari, S.N. and Herman G.T.: "Boundary Detection in Multidimensions," *IEEE Transactions on Pattern Analysis and Machine Intelligence* PAMI-4 (1982), 41-50.
[5] Grevera, G.J. and Udupa, J.K.: "Order of Magnitude Faster Surface Rendering Via Software in a PC Than Using Dedicated Hardware," *SPIE Proceedings* 3658 (1999), 202-211.
[6] Herman, G. and Liu, H.: "Three-Dimensional Display of Human Organs from Computed Tomograms," *Computer Graphics and Image Processing* 9 (1979), 679-698.
[7] Kaufman, A.: "Efficient Algorithms for 3-D Scan Conversion of Parametric Curves, Surfaces, and Volumes," *Computer Graphics* 21 (1987), 171-179.

[8] Levoy, M.: "Display of surfaces from volume data," *IEEE Computer Graphics and Applications* 8 (1988), no. 3, 29-37.
[9] Elvins, T.T.: "A Survey of Algorithms for Volume Visualization," *Computer Graphics* 26 (1992), no. 3, 194-201.
[10] Udupa, J.K., and Hung, H.-M.: "Surface Versus Volume Rendering: A Comparative Assessment," *IEEE Computer Soc. Proc. First Conference on Visualization in Biomedical Computing* (1990), 83-91.
[11] Drebin, R., Carpenter, L., and Hanrahan, P: "Volume rendering," *Computer Graphics* 22 (1988), 65-74.
[12] Cabral, B., Cam, N., and Foran, J.: "Accelerated Volume Rendering and Tomographic Reconstruction Using Texture Mapping Hardware," *Symposium on Volume Visualization* (1994), 91-98.
[13] Udupa, J.K. and Odhner, D.: "Fast Visualization, Manipulation, and Analysis of Binary Volumetric Objects," *IEEE Computer Graphics and Applications* 11 (1991), no. 6, 53-62.
[14] Udupa, J.K. and Odhner, D.: "Shell Rendering," *IEEE Computer Graphics and Applications* 13 (1993), no. 6, 58-67.
[15] Udupa, J.K., Goncalves, R.J., Iyer, K., Narendula, S., Odhner, D., Samarasekera, S., and Sharma, S.: "3DVIEWNIX: An open, transportable software system for the visualization and analysis of multidimensional, multimodality, multiparametric images," *SPIE Proc. 1897, Medical Imaging 1993:Image Capture, Formatting, and Display* (1993), 47-58.
[16] "Part B: Generate a Fuzzy Surface for Volume Rendering, Tutorial 2: How to create 3D objects," *http://www.mipg.upenn.edu/~Vnews/tutorial/tutorial2.html*, Medical Image Processing Group, Dept. of Radiology, University of Pennsylvania, Philadelphia, PA.
[17] Udupa, J.K. and Samarasekera, S.: "Fuzzy Connectedness and Object Definition: Theory, Algorithms, and Applications in Image Segmentation," *Graphical Models and Image Processing* 58 (1996), no. 3, 246-261.

A Novel Personal Authentication System Using Palmprint Technology

David Zhang[1], Guangming Lu[2], Adams Wai-Kin Kong[1,3], and Michael Wong[1]

[1] Biometric Research Centre, Department of Computing,
The Hong Kong Polytechnic University, Kowloon, Hong Kong
{csdzhang, csmkwong}@comp.polyu.edu.hk
http://www.comp.polyu.edu.hk/~biometrics
[2] Biocomputing Research Lab,
School of Computer Science and Engineering,
Harbin Institute of Technology, Harbin, China
Luguangm@hit.edu.cn
[3] Electrical and Computer Engineering,
University of Waterloo, Ontario, Canada N2L 3G1
adamskong@ieee.org

Abstract. In recent times, an increasing, worldwide effort has been devoted to the development of automatic personal identification systems that can be effective in a wide variety of security contexts. Palmprints have a number of unique advantages: they are rich in features such as principal lines, wrinkles, and textures and these provide stable and distinctive information sufficient for separating an individual from a large population. In this paper, we present a novel biometric authentication system to identify a person's identity by his/her palmprint. Being a robust and reliable system, it was tested by more than 8,000 palmprint images with very low false acceptance rate (0.02%), and a relative high genuine acceptance rate (98.83%). The whole authentication process is less than 1 second. Finally, some possible applications are discussed which could be benefited by using palmprint technology.

1 Introduction

Personal authentication plays a critical role in our society. e-Commerce applications such as e-Banking or security applications such as building entrance demand fast, real time, and accurate personal identification. Knowledge-based approaches use "something that you know" (such as passwords and personal identification numbers [1]) for personal identification; token-based approaches, on the other hand, use "something that you have" (such as passports or credit cards) for the same purpose. Tokens (e.g. credit cards) are time consuming and expensive to replace. These approaches are not based on any inherent attribute of an individual in the identification process made them unable to differentiate between an authorized person and an impostor who fraudulently acquires the "token" or "knowledge" of the authorized person. This is why biometrics identification or verification system started to be more focused in the recent years. Various biometric systems including, fingerprint, iris, hand geometry, voice and face recognition systems have been deployed for various applications [1].

Palmprint is concerned with the inner surface of a hand and looks at line patterns and surface shape. A palm is covered with the same kind of skin as the fingertips and it is larger than a fingertip in size. Therefore, it is quite natural to think of using palmprint to recognize a person, which receives a high user acceptance rate, similar to that of the fingerprint, hand geometry and hand vein [2-5]. Because of the rich features including texture, principal lines and wrinkles on palmprints, they contain enough stable and distinctive information for separating an individual from a large population.

There have been some companies, including NEC and PRINTRAK, which have developed several palmprint systems for criminal applications [6-7]. On the basis of fingerprint technology, their systems exploit high resolution palmprint images to extract the detailed features like minutiae for matching the latent prints. Such approach is not suitable for developing a palmprint authentication system for civil applications, which requires a fast, accurate and reliable method for the personal identification. Based on our previous research work [8-9], we develop a novel palmprint authentication system to fulfill such requirements.

The rest of the paper is organized as follows. The system design and analysis is shown in Section 2. The recognition module is described in Section 3. Experimental results of verification, identification, and robustness are provided in Section 4. Some possible applications of personal authentication using palmprints are revealed in Section 5, and finally conclusions are given in Section 6.

2 System Design and Analysis

2.1 System Design

The schematic diagram of the proposed system is shown in Fig. 1. There is a user interface for the input of the palm. Inside our system, there are various components including a flat platen surface, lighting unit, CCD camera, A/D converter, processing

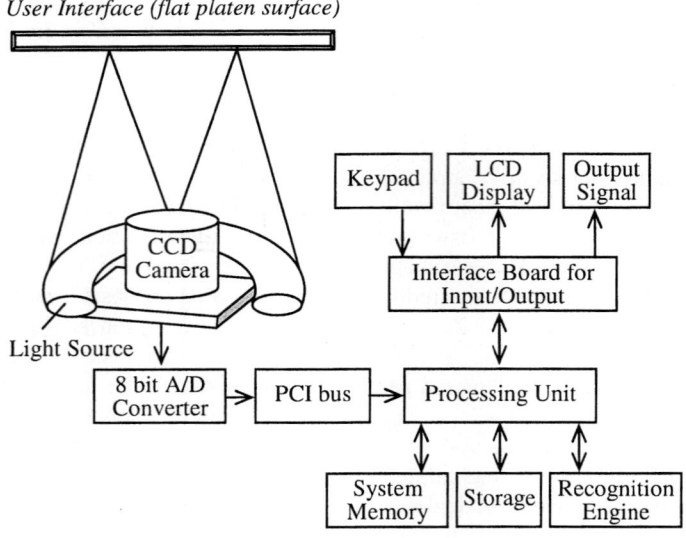

Fig. 1. The schematic diagram of the palmprint authentication system

unit, memory, storage, keypad, LCD display, output signal and recognition engine. The ring light source is designed to provide white light source of high intensity, and it can increase the contrast of the palmprint features from the uneven palm skin surfaces. The optical components (CCD camera and light source) are fabricated in a controlled environment in order to minimize the effects of ambient light. When the signal is generated by the CCD, it is digitized by an 8-bit A/D converter and then the digitized data is transferred to the processor through the PCI bus. The palmprint image is stored in the storage of the system. An interface board is designed to communicate the user with the system through a keypad and a LCD display unit. Recognition engine is the core part of our system which performs personal identification. The output signal is sent when a correct match is obtained.

2.2 System Framework

The proposed palmprint authentication system has four major components: *User Interface Module*, *Acquisition Module*, *Recognition Module* and *External Module*:

(a) *User Interface Module* provides an interface between the system and users for the smooth authentication operation. It is crucial to develop a good user interface so that users are pleasure to use the device. A flat platen surface is designed for palm acquisition accordingly [10].

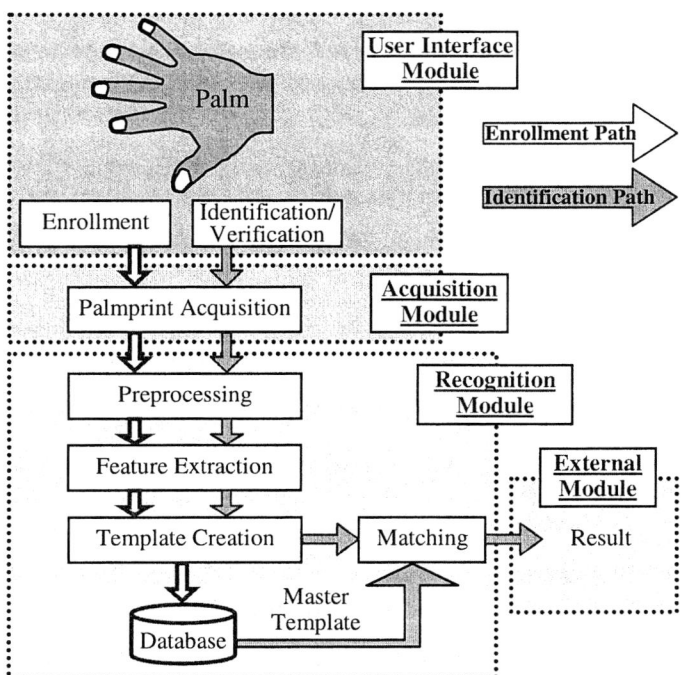

Fig. 2. The breakdown of each module of the palmprint authentication system

(b) *Acquisition Module* is the channel for the palm to be acquired for the further processing. It calls the frame grabber to transfer one frame of image to the processor, and then examines whether a hand has put on the device.
(c) *Recognition Module* is the key part of our system. It consists of image preprocessing algorithm, feature extraction algorithm, template creation, database updating, and matching of features.
(d) *External Module* receives the signal from the recognition module. This module actually is an interfacing component, which may be connected to another hardware or software components. Currently, our system uses a relay to control an electronic door lock for the physical access control.

Fig. 2 shows the details of each module of the palmprint authentication system. The design methodology and implementation of the user interface module and the acquisition module have been described in detail in [10]. The external module is an interfacing component which is application dependent. In this paper, we only concentrate on the recognition module and the performance issues of the proposed system.

3 Recognition Module

After the palmprint images are captured by the *Acquisition Module*, they are fed into the recognition module for palmprint authentication. The recognition module consists of the stages of: palmprints preprocessing, feature extraction, and matching. In the preprocessing stage, different palmprints are aligned for feature extraction. In this paper, we use the preprocessing technique described in [9].

3.1 Feature Extraction

The feature extraction technique implemented on the proposed palmprint system is modified from [9], where a single circular zero DC Gabor filter is applied to the preprocessed palmprint images and the phase information is coded as feature vector called PalmCode. The modified technique exploited four circular zero DC Gabor filters with the following general formula:

$$G_D = \frac{1}{2\pi\sigma^2}\exp\left\{-\frac{1}{2}\left[\frac{(x'-x_o)^2}{\sigma^2}+\frac{(y'-y_o)^2}{\sigma^2}\right]\right\}\left\{\exp(i2\pi\omega x')-\exp(-2\pi^2\omega^2\sigma^2)\right\} \quad (1)$$

where, $x' = x\cos\theta + y\sin\theta$ and $y' = -x\sin\theta + y\cos\theta$; (x_o, y_o) is the center of the function in the spatial domain of the function; ω is the frequency of the sinusoidal plane wave along the orientation, θ ; σ is the standard deviations of the circular Gaussian function; θ is the direction of the filter. The four Gabor filters share the same parameters, σ and ω, only different in θ. The corresponding values of θ are 0, π/4, π/2 and 3π/4.

In the previous approach, only the phase information is exploited but the magnitude information is totally neglected. The proposed method is to use the magnitude to be a fusion condition to combine different PalmCodes generated by the four Gabor filters. Mathematically, the implementation has the following steps.

1. The four Gabor filters are applied to the preprocessed palmprint image, I described as G_j*I, where G_j (j=1, 2, 3, 4) is the circular zero DC Gabor filter and "*" represents an operator of convolution.
2. The square of the magnitudes of the sample point is obtained by $M_j(x,y) = G_j(x,y)*I \times \overline{G_j(x,y)*I}$, where "—" represents complex conjugate.
3. According to the fusion rule, $k = \arg\max_j(M_j(x,y))$, the phase information at point (x, y) is coded as the followings:

$$h_r = 1 \quad if \quad Re[G_k*I] \geq 0 \quad (2)$$
$$h_r = 0 \quad if \quad Re[G_k*I] < 0$$
$$h_i = 1 \quad if \quad Im[G_k*I] \geq 0$$
$$h_i = 0 \quad if \quad Im[G_k*I] < 0$$

More discussion and comparisons between this method and PalmCode are given in [11].

3.2 Matching

The feature matching determines the degree of similarity between two templates – the authentication template and the master template. Since the format of Fusion Code and PalmCode are exactly the same, a normalized hamming distance implemented in PalmCode is still useful for comparing two Fusion Codes. Fusion Code is represented by a set of bits. Mathematically, the normalized hamming distance is represented by:

$$D_o = \frac{\sum_{i=1}^{N}\sum_{j=1}^{N} P_M(i,j) \cap Q_M(i,j) \cap \left((P_R(i,j) \otimes Q_R(i,j) + P_I(i,j) \otimes Q_I(i,j))\right)}{2\sum_{i=1}^{N}\sum_{j=1}^{N} P_M(i,j) \cap Q_M(i,j)} \quad (3)$$

where P_R (Q_R), P_I (Q_I) and P_M(Q_M) are the real part, imaginary part and mask of the Fusion Code $P(Q)$, respectively; $\otimes$ and $\cap$ are Boolean operators, XOR and AND, respectively. The ranges of normalized hamming distances are between zero and one, where zero represents perfect matches. Because of the imperfect preprocessing, one of the Fusion Code is vertically and horizontal translated to match the other again. The ranges of the vertical and the horizontal translations are defined from –2 to 2. The minimum D_0 value obtained from the translated matching is considered to be the final matching score.

4 Performance Evaluation

We collected palmprint images from 200 individuals using our palmprint capture device described in [9]. The subjects are mainly students and staff volunteers from

The Hong Kong Polytechnic University. In this dataset, 134 people are male, and the age distribution of the subjects is: about 86% are younger than 30, about 3% are older than 50, and about 11% are aged between 30 and 50. In addition, we collected the palmprint images on two separate occasions. On each occasion, the subject was asked to provide about 10 images each of the left palm and the right palm. Therefore, each person provided around 40 images, resulting in a total number of 8,025 images from 400 different palms in our database. All the testing images used in the following experiments were 384 × 284 with 75 dpi.

4.1 Experimental Results of Verification

Verification refers to the problem of confirming or denying a claim of individuals and considered as one-to-one matching. Two groups of experiment are carried out separately. In the first experiment, each palmprint image is matched with all other palmprint images in the database. A correct matching occurs if two palmprint images are from the same palm; incorrect matching otherwise. Fig. 3 (a) shows the probability of genuine and imposter distributions estimated by the correct and incorrect matchings. Some thresholds and corresponding false acceptance rates (FARs) and false rejection rates (FRRs) are listed in Table 1 (a). According to Table 1 (a), using one palmprint image for registration, the proposed system can be operated at a low false acceptance rate 0.096% and a reasonably low false rejection rate 1.05%.

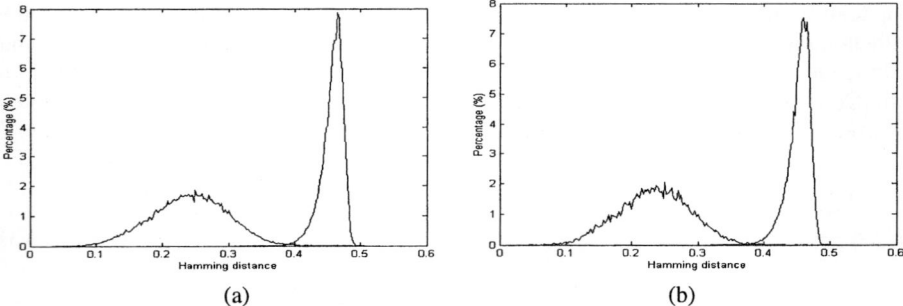

Fig. 3. Verification test results. (a) and (b) show the genuine and imposter distributions for verification tests with one and three registered images per palm, respectively.

In the second experiment, the testing database is divided into two databases, 1) registration database and 2) testing database. Three palmprint images of each palm collected in the first occasion are selected for the registration database. Fig. 3 (b) shows the probability of genuine and imposter distributions estimated by the correct and incorrect matchings, respectively. Some threshold values along with its corresponding false acceptance and false rejection rates are also listed in Table 1 (a). According to Table 1 (a) and Fig. 3, we can conclude that using three templates can provide better verification accuracy. It is also the reason for those commercial biometric verification systems requiring more than one sample for registration.

Table 1. False acceptance rates (FARs) and false rejection rates (FRRs) with different threshold values, (a) verification results and (b) 1-to-400 identification results

(a)

Threshold	Registered image=1		Registered images=3	
	FAR (%)	FRR (%)	FAR (%)	FRR (%)
0.32	0.000027	8.15	0.000012	5.12
0.34	0.00094	4.02	0.0016	2.18
0.36	0.011	1.94	0.017	0.86
0.38	0.096	1.05	0.15	0.43
0.40	0.68	0.59	1.03	0.19

(b)

Threshold	Trial=1		Trial=2		Trial=3	
	FAR (%)	FRR (%)	FAR (%)	FRR (%)	FAR (%)	FRR (%)
0.320	0.0049	3.69	0.0098	1.80	0.020	1.17
0.325	0.0439	2.93	0.088	1.34	0.131	1.06
0.330	0.15	2.29	0.28	1.02	0.42	0.68
0.335	0.37	1.90	0.68	0.72	0.96	0.48
0.340	0.84	1.51	1.43	0.57	1.93	0.37
0.345	1.45	1.16	2.32	0.42	3.02	0.26

4.2 Experimental Results of Identification

Identification test is a one-against-many, N comparison process. In this experiment, N is set to 400, which is the total number of different palms in our database. The registration database contains 1,200 palmprint images, three images per palm. The testing database has 6,825 palmprint images. Each palmprint image in the testing database is matched to all of the palmprint images in the registration database. The minimum hamming distances of correct matchings and incorrect matchings are

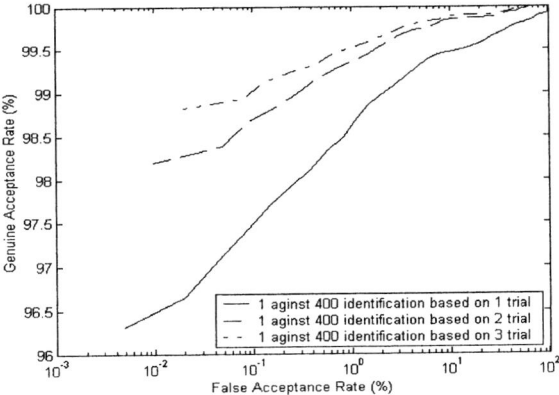

Fig. 4. The ROC curves on a 1-against-400 identification testing with different numbers of trials

regarded as the identification hamming distances of genuine and impostor, respectively. In this experiment, we implement one-, two- and three-trial tests. Fig. 4 shows ROC curves of the three tests and Table 1 (b) lists the threshold values along with its corresponding FARs and FRRs of the tests. According to Fig. 4 and Table 1 (b), more input palmprints can provide more accurate results.

4.3 Robustness

As a practical biometric system, other than accuracy and speed, robustness of the system is another important issue. To verify the robustness of our proposed algorithm against noisy palmprints, we wrote some texts on a palmprint of a hand. Fig. 5 (a) shows a clear palmprint image while Figs. 5 (b)-(f) show five palmprint images, with different texts. Their hamming distances are given in Table 2; all of them are smaller than 0.29. Comparing the hamming distances of imposter in Tables 1 (a) and (b), it is ensured that all the hamming distances in Table 2 are relatively small. Figs. 5 and Table 2 illustrate that the proposed palmprint authentication system is very robust to the noise on the palmprint.

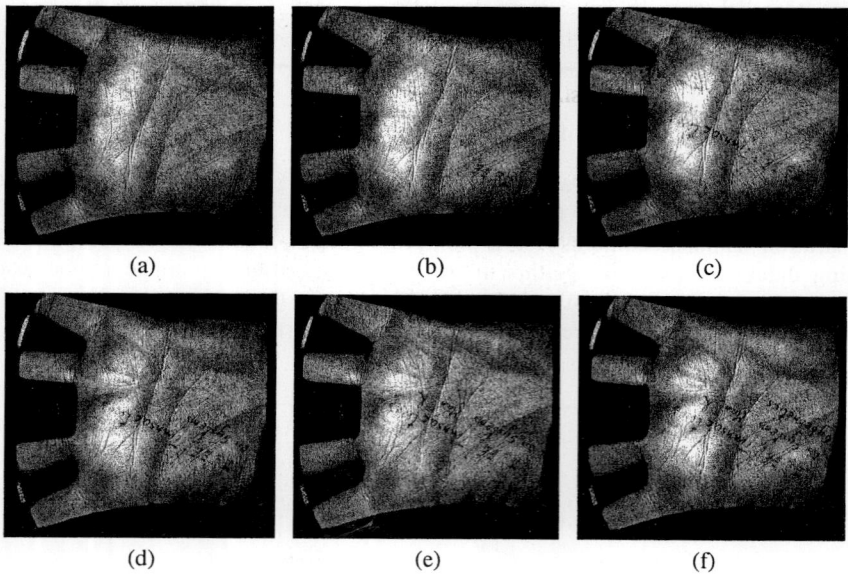

Fig. 5. Palmprint images with different texts for testing the robustness of the system

Table 2. The hamming distances of Figs. 5

Figs	5 (b)	5 (c)	5 (d)	5 (e)	5 (f)
5 (a)	0.19	0.21	0.27	0.29	0.28
5 (b)		0.18	0.27	0.26	0.27
5 (c)			0.27	0.28	0.28
5 (d)				0.23	0.19
5 (e)					0.19

5 Applications

Biometrics can be used in systems ranging from customer oriented to employee oriented applications to improve the work flow and eliminate frauds. Our system can be treated as a supplement of existing service or even a replacement of current method such as smart card or password based authentication systems.

One of the most popular biometric applications is the time and attendance system implemented to prevent frauds from buddy punching. In fact, our palmprint authentication system is most suitable to be used in this type of application because it can be operated in real time for identification/verification, has high accuracy rate and high user acceptance rate. In addition, our system has two modes of operations: identification and verification so that employees do not need to bring any card but their hand to identify their identity. Log files are stored on the file system and can be linked with external software for the automatic salary calculation.

Our system can be extended from a standalone system to a networked version. In addition, we provide different means of input methods such as barcode reader, smart card, and keyboard to allow the most flexible deployment arrangements for the need of different business organizations. In summary, our system can be used in the following applications: ATMs, credit card purchases, airports, building access control, time and attendance management, citizen ID program, biometric passport, voting and voter registration, etc. Fig. 6 shows a standalone version of our prototype system.

Fig. 6. A standalone version of our prototype system

6 Conclusions

In this paper, we have presented a novel personal authentication system using palmprint technology. The proposed system can accurately identify a person in real time, which is suitable for various civil applications such as access control and employee management systems. Experimental results show that the proposed system can identify 400 palms with very low false acceptance rate (0.02%), and a relative high genuine acceptance rate (98.83%). For verification, the system can operate at a false acceptance rate, 0.017% and a false rejection rate, 0.86%. The experimental results including accuracy, speed and robustness demonstrate that the palmprint authentication system is superior to other hand-based biometrics systems, such as hand geometry and fingerprint verification system [2, 12] and is practical for real-world applications. The system has been installed at the Biometric Research Center, Department of Computing, The Hong Kong Polytechnic University since March 2003 for access control [10].

References

1. Jain, R. Bolle and S. Pankanti (eds.), *Biometrics: Personal Identification in Networked Society*, Boston, Mass: Kluwer Academic Publishers, 1999.
2. R. Sanchez-Reillo, C. Sanchez-Avilla and A. Gonzalez-Marcos, "Biometric identification through hand geometry measurements", *IEEE Transactions on Pattern Analysis and Machine Intelligence*, vol. 22, no. 10, pp. 1168-1171, 2000.
3. S.K. Im, H.M. Park, Y.W. Kim, S.C. Han, S.W. Kim and C.H. Kang, "An biometric identification system by extracting hand vein patterns", *Journal of the Korean Physical Society*, vol. 38, no. 3, pp. 268-272, 2001.
4. A. Jain, L. Hong and R. Bolle, "On-line fingerprint verification", *IEEE Transactions on Pattern Analysis and Machine Intelligence*, vol. 19, no. 4, pp. 302-314, 1997.
5. A.K. Jain, A. Ross and S. Prabhakar, "An introduction to biometric recognition", *IEEE Transactions on Circuits and Systems for Video Technology,* vol. 14, no. 1, January 2004.
6. NEC Solutions (America), Inc., 2002. *Automated Palmprint Identification System*, http://www.necsam.com/idsolutions/ download/palmprint/palmprint.html
7. Omnitrak AFIS/Palmprint Identification Technology, http://www.motorola.com/LMPS/RNSG/pubsafety/40-70-10.shtml
8. G. Lu, D. Zhang, K.Q. Wang, "Palmprint recognition using eigenpalms features", *Pattern Recognition Letters*, vol. 24, no. 9-10, pp. 1473-1477, 2003.
9. D. Zhang, W.K. Kong, J. You and M. Wong, "Online palmprint identification", *IEEE Transactions on Pattern Analysis and Machine Intelligence*, vol. 25, no. 9, pp. 1041-1050, 2003.
10. D. Zhang, *Palmprint Authentication*, Kluwer Academic Publishers, USA, 2004.
11. W.K. Kong and D. Zhang, "Feature-level fusion for effective palmprint identification", *Proceedings International Conference on Biometric Authentication*, 15-17, July, 2004, pp. 761-767, Hong Kong.
12. A.K. Jain, S. Prabhakar, L. Hong and S. Pankanti, "Filterbank-based fingerprint matching", *IEEE Transactions on Image Processing*, vol. 9, no. 5, pp. 846-859, 2000.

World Wide Wisdom Web (W4) and Autonomy Oriented Computing (AOC): *What, When, and How?*

(Invited Talk)

Jiming Liu

Department of Computer Science,
Hong Kong Baptist University,
Kowloon Tong, Hong Kong
jiming@comp.hkbu.edu.hk

The World Wide Wisdom Web (W4) (or *Wisdom Web*) and Autonomy Oriented Computing (AOC) were proposed and advocated by Liu et al. and have been recognized, in the fields of WWW, AI, and AAMAS, as promising directions of research in problems that are heavily dominated by large scale, distribution, connectivity, interactivity, and redundancy [1,7,8,2,4].

Generally speaking, W4 encompasses the systems, environments, and activities (1) that are empowered through the global or regional connectivity of computing resources as well as distribution of data, knowledge, and contextual presence, and (2) that are specifically dedicated to enable human beings to gain practical wisdoms of working, living, and playing throughout their professional and personal activities, such as running a business and living with a certain lifestyle. W4 will become the next generation Web Intelligence (WI), providing not only a medium for seamless knowledge and experience sharing but also a supply of self-organized resources for driving sustainable knowledge creation and scientific or social development/evolution.

The present challenges of W4 lie primarily in:

1. how to autonomously derive just-in-time, optimal or sub-optimal solutions to an application-dependent problem, and delegate/carry out related tasks in a distributed way;
2. how to dynamically discover and mobilize distributed, constantly changing (hence sometimes unreliable), redundant or incomplete, heterogeneous resources that can exist in the forms of computational utilities, data repositories, and knowledge sources;
3. how to support the emergence of new social interactions and norms, and cultivate collective and social intelligence on the basis of (1) and (2) above.

The above problems have been known as the three benchmarks or dimensions for operationally defining and evaluating W4[1].

In W4, the tasks of computing are seamlessly carried out through a variety of agent embodiments. There is no single multi-purpose or dedicated machine that can manage to accomplish a job of this nature. The key to success in such an application lies in a large-scale deployment of Wisdom agents capable of autonomously performing localized interactions and making rational decisions in order to achieve their collective goals [5]. In other words, W4 readily exploits and explores the new paradigm of *Autonomy Oriented Computing (AOC)* [2,4].

In essence, the AOC paradigm is intended to effectively and efficiently achieve emergent computational autonomy that is useful in tackling hard computational problems, such as those that are:

1. of high-complexity – problems that involve a large number of autonomous entities, large-scale, high-dimension, highly nonlinear interactions or relationships, and highly interrelated/constrained variables;
2. highly-distributed and locally-interacting – problems that are not solvable in a centralized manner nor ready/efficient for batch processing.

AOC is a self-organizing computing paradigm, which has been found appealing in the areas of large-scale computation, distributed constraint satisfaction, decentralized optimization, and complex phenomena or emergent behavior characterization [3,5,6,4].

This talk presents the theoretical and experimental work on W4, as carried out in the AAMAS/AOC lab of HKBU, and highlights the methodologies of AOC in terms of formulation, macroscopic modeling, discrete-event simulations, and empirical studies of dynamics.

Acknowledgements

I am grateful to my research collaborators, research assistants, and students who have, over the years, worked together with me on the development of Web Intelligence (WI), World Wide Wisdom Web (W4), and Autonomy Oriented Computing (AOC). I would like to acknowledge the support of Hong Kong Research Grant Council (RGC) Central Allocation Grant ("Web Intelligence for E-Transformation - A Research Centre" - HKBU 2/03C).

References

1. Liu, J. (2003). Web Intelligence (WI): What makes Wisdom Web? *Proceedings of the Eighteenth International Joint Conference on Artificial Intelligence (IJCAI-03)*, Acapulco, Mexico, Aug. 9-15, 2003, Morgan Kaufmann Publishers, pp. 1596-1601 (invited talk).
2. Liu, J. (2001). *Autonomous Agents and Multi-Agent Systems: Explorations in Learning, Self-Organization and Adaptive Computation*, World Scientific.
3. Liu, J., Han, J., and Tang, Y. Y. (2002). Multi-agent oriented constraint satisfaction, *Artificial Intelligence*, **136**, 1, pp. 101-144.
4. Liu, J., Jin, X., and Tsui, K.C. (2005a). *Autonomy Oriented Computing (AOC): From Problem Solving to Complex Systems Modeling*, Springer.

5. Liu, J., Jin, X., and Wang, S. (2005b). Agent-based load balancing on homogeneous minigrids: Macroscopic modeling and characterization, *IEEE Transactions on Parallel and Distributed Systems*, **16**, 6.
6. Liu, J., Zhang, S., and Yang, J. (2004). Characterizing Web usage regularities with information foraging agents, *IEEE Transactions on Knowledge and Data Engineering*, **16**, 5, pp. 566-584.
7. Liu, J., Zhong, N., Yao, Y. Y., and Ras, Z. W. (2003). The Wisdom Web: New challenges for Web Intelligence (WI), *Journal of Intelligent Information Systems*, Kluwer Academic Publishers, **20**, 1.
8. Zhong, N., Liu, J., and Yao, Y. Y. (2003). (Eds.), *Web Intelligence*, Springer.

Semantic Web Research Trends and Directions

Jennifer Golbeck[1], Bernardo Cuenca Grau, Christian Halaschek-Wiener,
Aditya Kalyanpur, Bijan Parsia, Andrew Schain,
Evren Sirin, and James Hendler

MINDSWAP, University of Maryland, College Park, MD 20742, USA
`bernardo.cuenca@uv.es, bparsia@isr.umd.edu, andrew@schain.org,`
`{golbeck, halasche, aditya, evren, hendler}@cs.umd.edu`
`http://www.mindswap.org`

Abstract. The Semantic Web is not a single technology, but rather a collection of technologies designed to work together. As a result, research on the Semantic Web intends both to advance individual technologies as well as to integrate them and take advantage of the result. In this paper we present new work on many layers of the Semantic Web, including content generation, web services, e-connections, and trust.

1 Introduction

Defining the Semantic Web is a difficult task. It is the next generation of the web. It is a set of languages and standards. It has a strong logic and reasoning component. Web services, web portals, markup tools, and applications are all components. As a result, there are many interesting, intertwined research areas.

In this paper, we address several emerging trends of research in the Semantic Web space. We begin by presenting two tools for creating content on the Semantic Web: SWOOP, an ontology browser and editor, and PhotoStuff, an image annotation tool that integrates with a web portal. We follow with descriptions of E-Connections, a logical formalism for combining ontologies, and of work in web services. Finally, we describe a project using social trust on the semantic web that builds upon the previous work to create end user applications that benefit from the semantic foundation.

2 Swoop – Web Ontology Editor

Swoop is a hypermedia-inspired Ontology Browser and Editor based on OWL, the first standardized Web-oriented ontology language. Swoop takes the standard Web browser as the UI paradigm, believing that URIs are central to the understanding and construction of OWL Ontologies.

All design decisions are in keeping with the OWL nature and specifications. Thus, multiple ontologies are supported easily, various OWL presentation syntax are used to render ontologies, open-world semantics are assumed while editing and OWL reasoners can be integrated for consistency checking. A key point in our work is that the hypermedia basis of the UI is exposed in virtually every aspect of ontology engineering — easy navigation of OWL entities, comparing and editing related entities, search and cross referencing, multimedia support for annotation, etc. — thus allowing ontology developers to think of OWL as just another Web format, and thereby take advantage of its Web-based features.

2.1 Summary of Features

Swoop functionality is characterized by the following basic features (for an elaborate discussion of the features see [4]).

- Multiple Ontology Browsing and Editing
- Renderer Plugins for OWL Presentation Syntaxes
- Reasoner plugins in Swoop
- Semantic Search
- Ontology Versioning

Additionally, Swoop has the following advanced features, which represent work in progress:

- Resource Holder (Comparator/Mapping utility)
- Automatic Partitioning of OWL Ontologies (using E-Connections): Swoop has a provision for automatically partitioning OWL Ontologies by transforming them into an E-connection. For more details on the theory and significance of E-connections, their use in the context of OWL Ontologies see section 4.
- Ontology Debugging and Repair
- Annotea Client in Swoop: Collaborative Annotations and Change Sets.

3 PhotoStuff Semantic Image Annotation Tool

PhotoStuff is a platform-independent image annotation tool that allows users to annotate regions of an image with respect to concepts in any ontology specified in RDFS or OWL. It provides the functionality to import images (and their embedded metadata), ontologies, instance-bases, perform markup, and export the resulting annotations to disk or a Semantic Web portal.

3.1 Overview

PhotoStuff is designed to load multiple ontologies at once, enabling a user to markup images with concepts distributed across any of the loaded ontologies.

The ontologies are visualized in both a class tree and list (depicted below in Figure 1 in the far left pane of the tool). User can load images (from the Web and/or local disk) in PhotoStuff. The terms listed in both the tree and list can be dragged into any region, or into the image itself, creating a new instance of the selected class. An instance creation form is dynamically generated from the properties of the selected class (range restrictions are imposed). Especially valuable, existing instances can be loaded from any URI on the Web. Using these preloaded instances, depictions can reference existing instances.

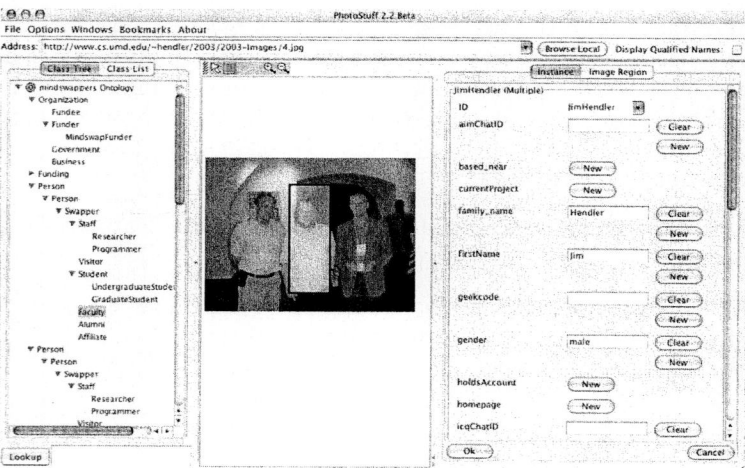

Fig. 1. PhotoStuff Screenshot

PhotoStuff maintains a loose coupling with a Semantic Web portal There are three ways in which PhotoStuff interacts with the portal, namely retrieving all instances that have been submitted to the portal, submitting generated RDF/XML, and uploading local images so they can be referenced by a URI (thus allowing them to be referenced using RDF/XML).

3.2 Image Metadata Browsing and Searching

After metadata of annotated images is submitted to the Semantic Web portal, semantics based image browsing and searching is provided. The portal uses information from the various ontologies image content is annotated against to guide the display of and interaction with metadata All instances that are depicted within an image are presented. As noted earlier, the underlying class of each instance drives the actual order of the depictions, thus providing a high level view of all the metadata of images that have been annotated using PhotoStuff.

When an instance is selected, the user is presented with all images in which the instance is depicted (illustrated in Figure 2). All of the metadata regarding that instance is presented to the user as well (currently in tabular form). We note here that this links the images with pre-existing metadata maintained in the portal.

In Figure 2, it can be seen that specific regions are highlighted. This is accomplished using an SVG outline of the region drawn on the various images (this data is embedded in RDF/XML as well). By selecting an image region, the various co-regions of the selected image region are displayed (shown in Figure 2). This allows browsing of the metadata associated with the various regions depicted in the image. Lastly, the portal provides support for searching image metadata. Images are searchable at the instance and class level.

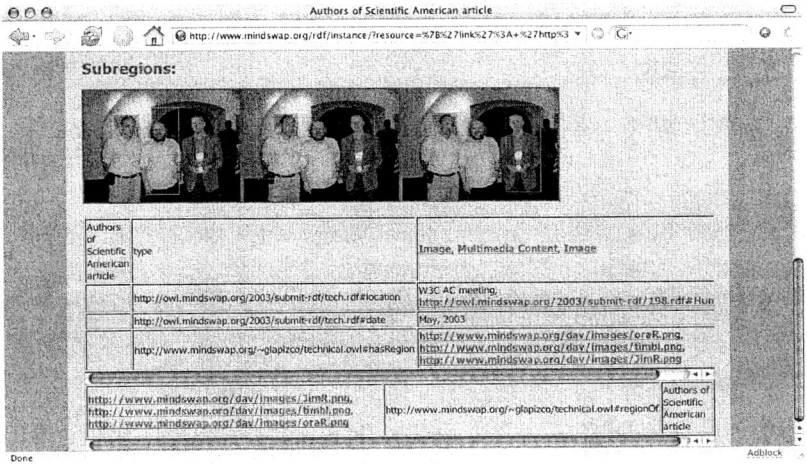

Fig. 2. Instance Descriptions and Image Co-Region Browsing

4 E-Connections of Web Ontologies

An E-Connection is a knowledge representation (KR) formalism defined as a combination of other logical formalisms. The component logics that can be used in an E-Connection include Description Logics (and hence OWL-DL), some temporal and spatial logics, Modal and Epistemic logics. E-Connections were originally introduced as a way to go beyond the expressivity of each of the component logics, while preserving the decidability of the reasoning services. Obviously, different component logics will give rise to different combined languages, with different expressivity and computational properties.

In a Semantic Web context, E-Connections allow the user to combine OWL-DL ontologies. A combination of OWL-DL ontologies is called a combined knowledge base. A combined knowledge base is a set of "connected ontologies. These connected ontologies are basically OWL-DL ontologies extended with the ability to define and use link properties.

In OWL-DL, object properties are used to relate individuals within a given ontology, while datatype properties relate individuals to data values. In a combined knowledge base, link properties are used to relate individuals belonging to different ontologies in the combination.

A link property can be used to define classes in a certain ontology in terms of other classes corresponding to different ontologies in the combination. For example, a "Graduate Student" in an ontology about "people" could be defined as a student who is enrolled in at least one graduate course, by using the class "Student" in the people ontology and a someValuesFrom restriction on the link property "enrolledIn" with value "GraduateCourse": a class in a different ontology dealing with the domain of "academic courses".

Link properties are logically interpreted as binary relations, where the first element belongs to the "source" ontology and the second to the "target ontology" of the link property. Conceptually, a link property will be defined and used in its "source" ontology. For example, the link property "enrolledIn" would be defined as a link property in the "people" ontology with target ontology "academic courses".

From the modeling perspective, each of the component ontologies in an E-Connection is modeling a different application domain, while the E-Connection itself is modelling the union of all these domains. For example, an E-Connection could be used to model all the relevant information referred to a certain university, and each of its component ontologies could model, respectively, the domain of people involved in the university, the domain of schools and departments, the domain of courses, etc.

4.1 Applications

Integration of OWL Ontologies. E-Connections can be used as a suitable representation for combining and integrating OWL-DL ontologies on the Semantic Web. For example, suppose a set of ontologies that have been independently developed and are now required to interoperate within an application. In order to provide support for integrating Web ontologies, OWL defines the owl:imports construct, which allows to include by reference in a knowledge base the axioms contained in another ontology, published somewhere on the Web and identified by a global name (a URI). However, the only way that the owl:imports construct provides for using concepts from a different ontology is to bring into the original ontology all the axioms of the imported one. This keeps the ontologies in separate files, providing some syntactic modularity, but not a logical modularity, as in the case of E-Connections.

Analysis and Decomposition of OWL Ontologies. E-Connections have also proved useful for analyzing the structure of knowledge bases and, in particular, to discover relevant sub-parts of ontologies, commonly called modules. For example, suppose one wants to annotate a word in a document using a class from an ontology, published elsewhere on the Web. It would be natural for a Semantic Web application to retrieve only the minimal set of axioms that "capture" the meaning of that specific class in the remote ontology.

In general, the ability to identify relevant sub-parts of ontologies is important for virtually every Semantic Web application. For example, in ontology engineering, achieving some sort of "modularity" is a key requirement to facilitate collaborative, large scale, long term development. Modularity worthy of the name should provide benefits in the following aspects: processability of the ontology by applications, evolvability and maintenance, knowledge reuse and understandability for humans.

E-Connections provide a sensible way for identifying modules within an ontology. The main idea of the method is to transform the original ontology into an E-Connection with the largest possible number of connected knowledge bases such that it preserves the semantics of the original ontology in a very specific way. The obtained connected ontologies are used to generate, for each entity, a subset of the original ontology that encapsulates the entity, i.e., that preserves a certain set of crucial entailments related to the entity. The key advantage of relying on E-Connections for such a task is that modules are obtained in a completely automatic way, without relying on any heuristics or user intervention.

Tool Support. We have provided support for E-Connection in both an OWL ontology editor, SWOOP, and an OWL reasoner, Pellet. Our aim has been to build an E-Connection aware infrastructure that people with a large commitment to OWL will find understandable and useful. We have been mostly concerned with reusing as much of our current tool support for OWL as possible. Our experience in implementing OWL tools has taught us that implementing a SemanticWeb Knowledge Representation formalism is different from implementing the very same formalism outside the Semantic Web framework. In particular, any new formalism for the Semantic Web needs to be compatible with the existing standards, such as RDF and OWL. For such a purpose, we have extended the syntax and semantics of the OWL-DL recommendation. Thus, we have explored both the issues related to the implementation of a new KR formalism, E-Connections, and those concerning its integration in a Semantic Web context.

5 Web Services

In this section, we describe various different projects and applications we developed for Web Services. Our work on Web Services concentrates on three core tasks: matchmaking, composition, and execution; always focusing on the end-to-end experience. To enable the automation of such tasks, we needed expressive descriptions of Web Services. For this reason, we have been involved with the development of the OWL-S language. The OWL-S is a collection of ontologies written in OWL to describe Web Services. Currently it is the most mature and probably the most widely deployed comprehensive Semantic Web Service technology.

The OWL-S descriptions are invaluable for many web service tasks. However, the intended semantics of OWL-S service descriptions is not expressed (or expressable, often) in OWL. Furthermore, working with OWL-S descriptions at the RDF or even the OWL level is quite difficult and tedious as they tend to be at the wrong level of abstraction. For this reason, we have developed the Mindswap OWL-S API [6], a Java API developed for parsing, validating, manipulating, executing, matching, and in general reasoning over OWL-S descriptions. OWL-S API provides a programmatic interface that has been designed closely to match the definitions in the OWL-S ontology. This interface helps developers build applications using OWL-S without having to deal with all the details of the syntax. The API provides an execution engine to invoke atomic services as well as composite processes that are built using the OWL-S control constructs.

Our work on Semantic Web Services focuses on the automated composition of services using Hierarchical Task Network (HTN) planning formalism [2]. Instead of looking at each service in isolation, we focus on the descriptions of workflow templates. Workflow templates are used for various different tasks such as encoding business rules in a B2B application, specifying domain knowledge in a scientific Grid application, and defining preferences for users that interact with Web Services. A template describes the general outline of how to achieve a certain task and the planners job is to find which of these possible execution paths will be successful in the current state of the world with the current requirements and preferences.

We have developed a mapping [7] from OWL-S to the HTN formalism as implemented in the SHOP2 planner [5]. Using this translation, we implemented a system that plans over sets of OWL-S descriptions using SHOP2 and executes the resulting plans over the Web. The planning system is also capable of executing information-providing Web Services during the planning process to decide which world-altering services to use in the plan. It is possible to completely automate the information gathering process by inspecting the preconditions of a service and finding the relevant information-providing services during planning [8].

The problem of using a planner for composing OWL-S services is the limited reasoning capabilities provided by the planner. The typical logic for expressing preconditions and effects in a planning system has a radically different expressiveness then RDF and OWL do. In order to evaluate such formulas, the planners must understand the semantics of OWL. We have integrated the SHOP2 planner with our OWL-DL reasoner Pellet to overcome this problem [9]. In this integrated system, the precondition evaluation is done by the OWL reasoner against the local and remote OWL ontologies. Such integration poses some efficiency challenges because the planner constantly simulates the effects of services resulting in modifications to its internal OWL KB and continues to query the KB as it continues the planning process. We have developed several query optimization methods to increase the performance of the system.

Most recently, we are looking at how to handle more expressive workflow templates where HTN task selection is extended to incorporate OWL-S based matchmaking [10]. We aim to extend the OWL-S language to describe the abstract processes using profile hierarchies and complex OWL concept descriptions. This extension will allow a clearer way to define soft and hard preferences in a template along with a prioritization of these preferences. Consequently, we can have more elaborate ranking mechanisms for choosing out of the possible options during planning. We are currently working on the implementation of this extended HTN formalism (HTN-DL) [10].

6 Trust: Computations and Applications

One of the ultimate goals of the Semantic Web is to produce a so-called "Web of Trust". Much work in this space has been made in the spheres of security, authentication, and privacy. However, the social component of trust is one that is both important and ideally suited for the Semantic Web. When the Semantic Web-based social networks are augmented with trust information, it is possible to make computations over the values, and integrate the results into applications.

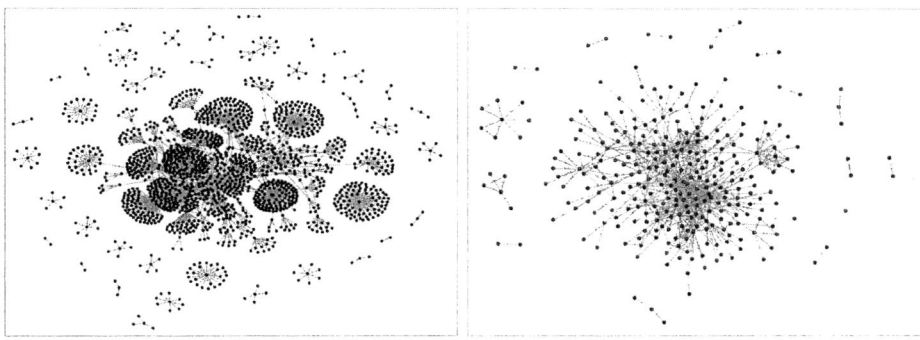

Fig. 3. Visualizations of the Trust Project's network (left) and the FilmTrust network (right)

6.1 Adding Trust to FOAF

In the FOAF vocabulary, the only mechanism for describing social connections between people is the foaf:knows property which indicates one person knows another. The FOAF Trust Module extends the FOAF vocabulary by providing a mechanism for describing the trust relationships. It allows people to rate the trustworthiness of another person on a scale from 1 to 10 where 1 is low trust and 10 is a high trust. This scale is intuitive for human users, but our algorithms can be applied to any scale of values.

The Trust Project[1] regularly spiders the Semantic Web for trust files, and maintains a network with over 2,000 people. The ontology is also used by the FilmTrust social network [3] with over 400 members. These networks can be seen in Figure 3, and are used as testbeds for our algorithms for computing trust.

6.2 Computing with Trust

If one person, the *source*, wants to know how much to trust another person, the *sink*, how can that information be obtained? Clearly, if the source knows the sink, the solution is simple. However, if the two do not know one another, the trust values within the social network can be used to compute a recommendation to the source regarding the trustworthiness of the sink.

Because social trust is an inherently personal concept, a computed trust value must also be personal. Thus, we do not compute a global measure of how trustworthy the sink is; rather, we use the source's perspective on the network to find paths of trust that are in turn used for making the trust computation.

TidalTrust is an algorithm for computing trust over a range of values, such as those provided by the FOAF Trust Module. It is a simple recursive algorithm: the source asks each of its neighbors for their trust rating of the sink. The source then computes a weighted average of these values, giving more weight to neighbors with higher trust ratings, and less weight to neighbors with lower

---

[1] see http://trust.mindswap.org

trust ratings. If a neighbor has a direct trust rating of the sink, it returns that value; otherwise, the sink repeats the algorithm for *its* neighbors, and returns the weighted average that it computes. Because this algorithm is essentially a modified Breadth First Search, it runs in linear time with respect to the site of the network. More detail on the algorithm can be found at [3].

Previous work[3] has shown that the results returned by TidalTrust when it is run on both the Trust Project network and the FilmTrust network can be expected to be relatively accurate. The error varies from network to network, but is usually within 10%.

6.3 Applying Trust

These trust computations are made generally, with networks on the Semantic Web. As such, they can be integrated into a variety of applications.

There are two major projects we have undertaken to illustrate the benefit of trust ratings to the user. The first is FilmTrust, a website built on a semantic social network with movie ratings and reviews from users. On the websit, the user's movie ratings are combined with trust values to generate predictive movie ratings. We have shown that, in FilmTrust, the trust-based predictive ratings outperform other methods of generating these predictions in certain situations[3]. The second application is TrustMail, and email client that uses the trust rating of a message's sender as a score for the email. The trust ratings work as the complement to a spam filter by allowing users to identify potentially important messages by the trustworthiness of their sender.

Because trust and social networks are general and available publicly on the Semantic Web, there is great potential for any application to integrate this data, make computations with it, and use the results to improve the user experience.

7 Conclusions

In this paper, we have presented tools and research projects for creating Semantic Web content with SWOOP and PhotoStuff, combining ontologies with E-Connections, working with web services, and computing with trust in Semantic Web-based social networks. These topics illustrate both the breadth and depth of research topics on the Semantic Web, and serve as clear examples of trends in Semantic Web research.

Acknowledgements

This work, conducted at the Maryland Information and Network Dynamics Laboratory Semantic Web Agents Project, was funded by Fujitsu Laboratories of America – College Park, Lockheed Martin Advanced Technology Laboratory, NTT Corp., Kevric Corp., SAIC, the National Science Foundation, the National Geospatial-Intelligence Agency, DARPA, US Army Research Laboratory, NIST, and other DoD sources.

References

1. Cuenca Grau, Bernardo and Bijan Parsia. From shoq(d) toward e-connections. In Proceedings of the 2004 International Workshop on Description Logics, (DL2004), (Poster)., 2004.
2. Erol, Kutluhan, James Hendler, and Dana Nau. HTN planning: Complexity and Expressivity In Proceedings of the 12th National Conference on Artificial Intelligence (AAAI94), Seattle, 1994.
3. Golbeck, Jennifer. Computing and Applying Trust in Web-Based Social Networks, Ph.D. Dissertation, University of Maryland, College Park, 2005.
4. Kalyanpur, Aditya, Bijan Parsia, and James Hendler. A tool for working with web ontologies. In In Proceedings of the International Journal on Semantic Web and Information Systems, Vol. 1, No. 1, Jan - March, 2005.
5. Nau, Dana, Tsz-Chiu Au, Okhtay Ilghami, Ugur Kuter, J. William Murdock, Dan Wu, Fusun Yaman. SHOP2: An HTN planning system. Journal of AI Research, 20:379404, 2003.
6. Sirin, Evren and Bijan Parsia. The OWL-S Java API. (Poster) In Proceedings of the Third International Semantic Web Conference (ISWC2004), Hiroshima, Japan, 2004.
7. Sirin, Evren , Bijan Parsia, Dan Wu, James Hendler, and Dana Nau. HTN Planning for Web Service Composition using SHOP2. Journal of Web Semantics, 1(4):377-396, 2004.
8. Kuter, Ugur, Evren Sirin, Dana Nau, Bijan Parsia, and James Hendler. Information Gathering During Planning for Web Service Composition. In Proceedings of the Third International Semantic Web Conference (ISWC2004), Hiroshima, Japan, 2004.
9. Sirin, Evren, and Bijan Parsia. Planning for Semantic Web Services. In Semantic Web Services Workshop at the Third International Semantic Web Conference (ISWC2004),
10. Sirin, Evren, Bijan Parsia, and James Hendler. Template-based Composition of Semantic Web Services. Submitted to AAAI Fall Symposium on Agents and the Semantic Web, 2005.

Feature Extraction for Nonlinear Classification

Anil Kumar Ghosh and Smarajit Bose

Theoretical Statistics and Mathematics Unit,
Indian Statistical Institute,
203, B. T. Road, Calcutta 700108, India
anilkghosh@rediffmail.com, smarajit@isical.ac.in

Abstract. Following the idea of neural networks, multi-layer statistical classifier [3] was designed to capture interactions between measurement variables using nonlinear transformation of additive models. However, unlike neural nets, this statistical method can not readjust the initial features, and as a result it often leads to poor classification when those features are not adequate. This article presents an iterative algorithm based on backfitting which can modify these features dynamically. The resulting method can be viewed as an approach for estimating posterior class probabilities by projection pursuit regression, and the associated model can be interpreted as a generalized version of the neural network and other statistical models.

1 Introduction

In high-dimensional classification problems, often a smaller number of features (linear combination of measurement variables) contain most of the information about class separability. Proper identification of these features helps to reduce the dimensionality of the problem which in turn reduces the computational complexity and storage requirement. If we restrict ourselves to linear classification, results for feature extraction are available in the literature [6], [12], [9]. However in practice, linear classifiers are often found to be inadequate and one needs to extract relevant features for nonlinear classification. In regression, projection pursuit model [7] was developed to compensate for this inadequacy, and artificial neural network models [14] provide much more flexibility for classification. Both of them have their own strengths and limitations. In this article, we try to combine these two approaches in order to develop an iterative feature selection (IFS) method, which is more flexible and statistically meaningful.

2 Nonlinear Classification and IFS

In classification problems, one aims to achieve maximum accuracy in assigning p-dimensional observations $\mathbf{x}$ into one of J competing classes. The optimal Bayes rule [1] assigns an observation to the class with the largest posterior probability. In practice, one estimates these unknown probabilities using the available training data. Many nonparametric classification methods like neural nets [14] and classification using splines (CUS) [2] put the classification problem in a regression framework and regress the indicator variables $Y_1, \ldots, Y_J$ (defined for J classes) on the measurement space to estimate $E(Y_j \mid \mathbf{x}) = p(j \mid \mathbf{x})$, the posterior probabilities. CUS uses additive models to estimate these posteriors and associated class boundaries. But in practice, these boundaries may be more complex, and one needs to find suitable classification algorithms in such cases. Bose [3] proposed the multi-layer statistical classifier (MSC), which uses the estimated posterior probabilities obtained by CUS as new features and repeats the CUS procedure with them to get the final posterior probability estimates. In the process, some interactions are indirectly introduced in the model which helps to improve the performance of CUS. However, unlike neural nets, MSC can not re-adjust the features selected by CUS. As a result, the improvement over CUS is often not that significant. On the other hand, neural network training algorithms try to re-adjust these features iteratively, but this popular method lacks meaningful statistical interpretations.

This article presents an iterative feature selection (IFS) algorithm, which tries to estimate the best possible features from the data and then performs CUS with the extracted features to estimate the posterior probabilities. Backfitting is used for dynamic feature adjustment, which makes the method more flexible. IFS can be viewed as an approach to estimate the posterior probabilities $p(j \mid \mathbf{x})$ by projection pursuit regression model $\psi_j(\mathbf{x}) = \phi_{j0} + \sum_{i=1}^{p} \phi_{ji}(\boldsymbol{\alpha}_i' \mathbf{x})$, where ϕ_{j0} is a constant, $\boldsymbol{\alpha}_i$'s are feature directions and ϕ_{ji}'s are smooth univariate functions. IFS uses cubic splines as univariate functions ϕ_{ji} and estimates $\boldsymbol{\alpha}_i$, ϕ_{j0} and ϕ_{ji} iteratively. Note that the additive model used in CUS is a special case of IFS when $\boldsymbol{\alpha}_i$'s are unit vectors along the co-ordinate axes. If sigmoidal transformations are used as the smooth univariate functions, this model turns out to be the popular perceptron model with one hidden layer. Since, our aim is to extract low dimensional features for visualizing class separability, instead of starting with too many features, here we restrict this number to the dimension of the original measurement space.

3 Description of IFS Algorithm

Like neural nets, IFS regresses the indicators $Y_1, Y_2, \ldots, Y_J$ on the measurement variables. We take the eigen vectors of $W^{-1}(W+B)$ (where B and W are between class and within class sum of square matrices respectively) as the initial feature directions $\boldsymbol{\alpha}_i$ ($i = 1, 2, \ldots, p$) and place K knots (based on order statistics) on the range of each feature $Z_i = \boldsymbol{\alpha}_i' \mathbf{x}$ to construct the basis functions. Following the idea of Breiman [4], we use the set of power basis functions $\{1, Z_i, (Z_i - t_k)_+^3, \ k = 1, 2, \ldots, K; \ i = 1, 2, \ldots, p\}$ for fitting cubic splines. We regress Y_j ($j = 1, 2, \ldots, J$) on these basis functions to get the initial estimates for $\phi_{j0}, \phi_{j1}, \ldots, \phi_{jp}$. Posterior probability estimates $\widehat{Y}_{jn} = \psi_j(\mathbf{x}_n)$ and residuals $r_{jn} = Y_{jn} - \widehat{Y}_{jn}$, $n = 1, 2, \ldots, N$ (N being the training sample size) are computed to find the residual sum of squares $(RSS) = \sum_{j=1}^{J} \sum_{n=1}^{N} r_{jn}^2$.

Backfitting is used to re-adjust the features $Z_1, Z_2, \ldots, Z_p$ iteratively. At any stage α_i is adjusted by a factor δ_i, where δ_i is obtained by minimizing $RSS \simeq \sum_{j=1}^{J} \sum_{n=1}^{N} [r_{j_n} - \delta_i' \eta_{j_n}^{(i)}]^2$, where $\eta_{j_n}^{(i)} = \frac{\partial \phi_{ji}}{\partial \alpha_i}|_{\mathbf{x}=\mathbf{x}_n}$ is computed using the current estimates of α_i and ϕ_{ji}. This new estimate of α_i is normalized and Z_i is recomputed. Knots are placed on its range to find the new basis functions. $Y_j - \sum_{k \neq i} \phi_{jk}(Z_k)$ is then regressed on these basis functions to get new estimates of ϕ_{j0} and ϕ_{ji} ($j = 1, 2, \ldots, J$). In this manner, all the p features ($Z_1, Z_2, \ldots, Z_p$) are updated one by one. This step is repeated until no significant improvement in RSS is observed over some consecutive iterations. At the end, Y_j is regressed on the resulting basis functions to get the final estimates for $\phi_{j0}, \phi_{j1}, \ldots, \phi_{jp}$ ($j = 1, 2, \ldots, J$). Like CUS, IFS puts no restriction on ψ_j ($j = 1, 2, \ldots, J$) to ensure that they are in $[0, 1]$. Imposing positivity restrictions by any manner results in much more complicated but not necessarily better classification [13]. However, inclusion of intercept terms ϕ_{j0} ($j = 1, 2, \ldots, J$) in the set of basis functions guarantees the additivity constraint ($\sum_{j=1}^{J} \psi_j(\mathbf{x}_n) = 1$, $\forall n = 1, 2, \ldots, N$).

After fitting the initial model using large number of knots, backward deletion is used to delete the knots and hence the basis functions one by one. At any stage, we delete the basis function whose deletion leads to least increase in RSS. However, the linear basis function Z_i ($i = 1, 2, \ldots, p$) is not considered as a candidate for deletion until all knots on that variable get deleted. This backward deletion process is done by using a modified Gaussian sweep algorithm [4]. It generates a sequence of nested models indexed by their dimensionalities. To arrive at the final and parsimonious model, we adopt the cost complexity criterion proposed in [5], where the ideal cost parameter is selected by 10-fold cross-validation technique [14]. To explain local patterns of the measurement space, the number of initial knots should be reasonably large. However, use of too many knots may make the algorithm numerically unstable. Our empirical experience suggests that $10 - 12$ knots per variable is enough for a moderately large sample size and the final result is not too sensitive on this choice.

4 Experimental Results

For illustration, we present the result of a two-class problem in five dimension, where the first two measurement variables in the two classes are distributed as
$\mathbf{\Pi}_1 : (X_1, X_2) \sim N_2(0, 0, 1, 1, 1/2)$ and $\mathbf{\Pi}_2 : (X_1, X_2) \sim U[-5, 5] \times U[-5, 5]$. Other three variables are i.i.d. $N(0, 1)$ in both classes, and these variables are used to add to the noise. Clearly, the optimal class boundary is of the form $X_1^2 + X_2^2 - X_1 X_2 = C_0$ for some constant C_0. This can be re-written (not uniquely) as $A\{(X_1 - 0.5X_2)\}^2 + BX_2^2 = C$, where A, B and C are appropriate constants. Thus, we see that only two linear features contain the information about class separability. When we ran IFS algorithm on different sets of 500 observations generated from these two-classes, the final model contained exactly two features in most of the cases. Figure 1 shows the estimated features and class boundary for one such data set. Clearly, IFS could obtain appropriate estimates of features and that of the optimal class boundary in this case.

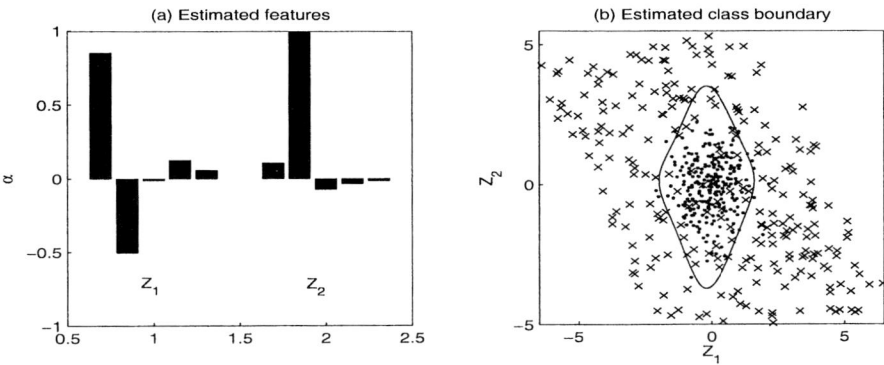

Fig. 1. Estimated features and class boundary

To compare the performance of IFS with other classification techniques like linear discriminant analysis (LDA), quadratic discriminant analysis (QDA), kernel discriminant analysis (KDA) [11], CUS, MSC and neural nets (as implemented in [8]), we report the misclassification rates of these methods for this and two other data sets. For kernel discriminant analysis, we standardize the observations in a class using the usual moment based estimate of the class dispersion matrix to make the data cloud more spherical and then use same bandwidth in all directions to find out the density estimate for the standardized data vector. Density estimate at the original data point can be obtained from that using a simple transformation formula when the measurement variables undergo a linear transformation. Least square cross validation [15] is used to find the bandwidths that minimize the mean integrated square errors of kernel density estimates of different classes and those bandwidths are used for density estimation and classification.

In our second simulated example, each class is an equal mixture of two bivariate normal populations. The location parameters for components of class-1 are $(1,1)$ and $(3,3)$, whereas those for class-2 are $(2,2)$ and $(4,4)$. All components have the same scatter matrix $0.25\mathbf{I}$. For both of these examples, we used training sets of size 500 and test sets of size 3000 taking equal number of observations from each class. In each case, we repeated the experiment 10 times, and the average test set error rates over these 10 trails are reported in Table-1 along with their corresponding standard errors. Since these are simulated examples, one can also plug-in the true densities of the two populations in the Bayes rule to classify the observations. In Table-1, we also present the average misclassification rates of this optimal Bayes classifier for these two examples with their corresponding standard errors. For the third example, we consider a benchmark data set related to a vowel recognition problem (available at http://www.ics.uci.edu), where we have 10 dimensional observations from 11 different classes. This data set has specific training and test sets, and we report the test set error rates of different methods in Table-1. In Example-2 and Example-3, IFS led to the best performance among the classifiers considered here. Misclassification rates for different

Table 1. Misclassification (in %) rates for different classification methods

	Example-1	Example-2	Example-3
Optimal	10.74 (0.14)	12.08 (0.19)	—
LDA	49.98 (0.33)	45.23 (0.57)	55.63
QDA	11.61 (0.17)	45.44 (0.54)	52.81
KDA	12.43 (0.16)	12.68 (0.23)	62.12
CUS	14.30 (0.27)	18.35 (0.41)	51.30
MSC	14.02 (0.28)	18.54 (0.40)	45.67
Neural Net	12.48 (0.19)	12.58 (0.21)	48.92
IFS	11.88 (0.22)	12.38 (0.18)	43.29

types of kernel methods and other nonparametric classifiers on vowel recognition data are available in [12] and [10]. Results of our proposed method is better than those reported error rates. Since the optimal class boundary in Example-1 is quadratic, QDA is expected to perform well, but IFS could nearly match the performance of QDA.

It is difficult to find out the expression for computation complexity of IFS algorithm. Since IFS is an iterative algorithm, in addition to depending on the sample size, number of classes and number of basis functions, the computing time depends on the closeness of the initial and final solution and the convergence criterion as well. However, as a nonparametric classifier IFS works reasonably fast. When 10 knots are used on each of the 10 variables in vowel recognition data, it took nearly 30 minutes on a pentium 4 machine for model selection and classification. Note that we had to run IFS algorithm 11 times including 10 times for cross-validation. We terminated the iteration in IFS if the relative change in RSS is less than 0.1% over 10 consecutive iterations. Of course, one can relax this convergence criterion to cut down the computing time. The overall performance of IFS turned out to be excellent which should be explored and tested further.

References

1. Anderson, T. W. (1984) *An Introduction to Multivariate Statistical Analysis*. Wiley, New York.
2. Bose, S. (1996) Classification using splines. *Comp. Statist. Data Anal.*, **22**, 505-525.
3. Bose, S. (2003) Multilayer Statistical Classifiers. *Comp. Statist. Data Anal.*, **42**, 685-701.
4. Breiman, L. (1993) Fitting additive models to regression data: diagnostics and alternating views. *Comp. Statist. Data Anal.*, **15**, 13-46.
5. Breiman, L., Friedman, J. H., Olshen, R. A. and Stone, C. J. (1984) *Classification and Regression Trees*. Wadsworth and Brooks Press, Monterrey, California. .
6. Duda, R., Hart, P. and Stork, D. G. (2000) *Pattern classification*. Wiley, New York.
7. Friedman, J. and Stuetzle, W. (1981) Projection Pursuit Regression. *J. Amer. Statist. Assoc.*, **76**, 817-823.
8. Ghosh, A. K. and Bose, S. (2004) Backfitting neural networks. *Computational Statistics*, **19**, 193-210.

9. Ghosh, A. K. and Chaudhuri, P. (2005) Data depth and distribution free discriminant analysis using separating surfaces. *Bernoulli*, **11**, 1-27.
10. Ghosh, A. K., Chaudhuri, P. and Sengupta, D. (2005) Multi-scale kernel discriminant analysis. *Proceedings of Fifth International Conference on Advances in Pattern Recognition (ICAPR-03)* (Ed. D. P. Mukherjee and S. Pal), Allied Publishers, Kolkata, pp. 89-93.
11. Hand, D. J. (1982) *Kernel Discriminant Analysis*. Wiley, Chichester.
12. Hastie, T., Tibshirani, R. and Friedman, J. H. (2001) *The elements of statistical learning : data mining, inference and prediction*. Springer Verlag, New York.
13. Kooperberg, C., Bose, S. and Stone, C. J. (1997) Polychotomus regression. *J. Amer. Statist. Assoc.*, **92**, 117-127.
14. Ripley, B. D. (1996) *Pattern recognition and neural networks*. CUP, Cambridge.
15. Silverman, B. W. (1986) *Density Estimation for Statistics and Data Analysis*. Chapman and Hall, London.

Anomaly Detection in a Multi-engine Aircraft

Dinkar Mylaraswamy

Honeywell Laboratories, 3660 Technology Drive, Minneapolis, MN 55418
dinkar.a.mylaraswamy@honeywell.com

Abstract. This paper describes an anomaly detection algorithm by monitoring the spin-down of jet engines. The speed profile from multiple engines in an aircraft is cast as a singular value monitoring problem. This relatively simple algorithm is an excellent example of onboard, lightweight feature extractor, the results of which can feed more elaborate trouble shooting procedures. The effectiveness of the algorithm is demonstrated using aircraft data from one of Honeywell's airline customers.

1 Introduction

Monitoring jet engines is a topic of growing interest among engine makers, aircraft manufacturers and airline operators [1]. Architecture that addresses the fault diagnostic problem using a combination of onboard pre-processors and off-board reasoners is gaining considerable attention [2]. Within this architecture, onboard algorithms process large amount of frequently available data to retain key features. These relatively small features or anomalies are then analyzed by ground-based reasoning systems. In this paper, we describe one such anomaly detection for analyzing the spin-down speed profile of a jet engine.

At the end of the flight, the pilot issues a shutoff command. In response the engine controller starts to reduce fuel to individual engines. At some point during this shutdown, fuel is completely cut out and the engine spins down on its own inertia. This is called the spin-down phase. By monitoring aberration of the speed profile during spin-down, one can detect anomalies for incipient engine faults that cause abnormal drag. Basic principle, algorithm design, and results on one of Honeywell's airline customer are discussed in this paper.

2 Basic Principle

The rate at which engine speed decreases during the spin-down phase is governed by the frictional losses at the bearing and the parasitic drags imposed by the gear-box. Let N_i denote the core speed of the ith engine. A simple torque balance gives:

$$J_i \frac{d\,(2\pi N_i/60)}{dt} = -k_i^{par}(2\pi N_i/60) \qquad (1)$$

where J_i is the moment of inertia of the core shaft, k_i^{par} is the frictional loss coefficient. Integrating equation (1) will generate the spin-down profile. Define a time origin t_i^0 for the ith engine such that $N_i(t) = \mathcal{N}$, where $\mathcal{N}$ is a pre-defined constant. Now we start observing the engine spin-down for T time interval starting from t_i^0. Re-arranging and integrating (1) we get:

$$N_i(t) = \mathcal{N}\,e^{-(k_i^{par}/J_i)t}, \quad t_i^0 \le t \le T + t_i^0 \tag{2}$$

Define τ_i as the closed set $[t_i^0, T + t_i^0]$. We shall use the short hand notation $N_i(t), t \in \tau_i$ to describe equation (2).

On the regional jets (RJ) operated by a Honeywell's customer we have 4 interchangeable engines. From the interchangeability property of the engines, it follows that moment of inertia J_i will be *almost* identical to each other. Similarly frictional losses characterized by k_i^{par} will also be close to each other. In other words, the interchangeability property implies:

$$k_i^{par} \approx k_j^{par} \text{ and } J_i \approx J_k, \quad i,j = 1,2,3,4 \tag{3}$$
$$\text{and hence } \{N_i(t), t \in \tau_i\} \approx \{N_j(t), t \in \tau_j\} \quad i,j = 1,2,3,4 \tag{4}$$

That is, the spin-down profile of all four engines should evolve *almost* identically over a pre-defined time. Note that the length of this time interval is identical, but $t_i^0 \ne t_j^0; i,j = 1,2,3,4$. In the next section, we will design an anomaly detection algorithm based on this principle.

3 Algorithm Design

One of the widely used algorithms for fault diagnosis, given a nominal model is parameter estimation. Stated simply, such model-based fault diagnosis algorithms estimate the model parameters using actual observations. Deviations from design values are indicative of incipient faults[3,4]. In this paper, we investigated a much simpler approach, based on singular values. For the ith engine, starting from t_i^0 we sample the engine speeds N_i at a uniform rate. Let T time interval contain m samples. Define an $m \times 4$ observation matrix X as follows:

$$X = [\boldsymbol{x}_1\ \boldsymbol{x}_2\ \boldsymbol{x}_3\ \boldsymbol{x}_4]; \text{ where } \boldsymbol{x}_i = [N_i(1)\ N_i(2)\ \ldots\ N_i(m)]^T \tag{5}$$

It follows from (4) that the matrix X has only one independent row. Hence the rank of this matrix will be very close to 1. That is, rank$(X) \approx 1$. A computational tractable way of calculating the rank of a matrix is using singular value decomposition (SVD) of the covariance matrix, cov(X). Since rank$(X) \approx 1$ the singular values of the covariance matrix satisfy the following property:

$$\sigma_1 > 0, (\sigma_2, \sigma_3, \sigma_4) \approx 0, \quad \text{where } \sigma_1, \sigma_2, \sigma_3, \sigma_4 = \text{SVD}(X^T X/(m-1))$$

From the property of SVD, we have $\sigma_1 \ge \sigma_2 \ge \sigma_3 \ge \sigma_4 \ge 0$. Hence, closeness of σ_2 to zero is sufficient to monitor the rank of the covariance matrix. By monitoring σ_2, the algorithm compares the spin-down profile of engine i with engine $j, \forall i, \forall j, j \ne i$. The spin-down equation ((2)) does not enter the algorithm

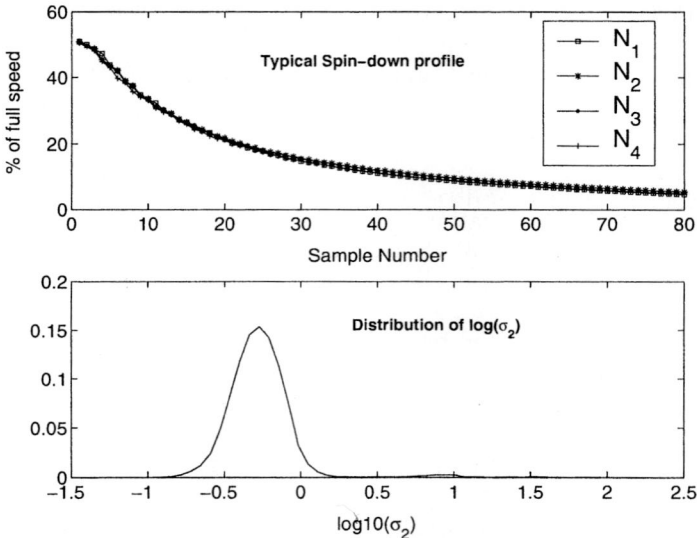

Fig. 1. Data used for algorithm design

explicitly. However, the insight provided by the model is used in designing the detection algorithm. Large deviations in the spin-down profile of engine i indicated by larger value of σ_2 is an indication of possible incipient fault. In real life small perturbations will be introduced as a result of sensor noise and typical engine-to-engine variation. Although internal conditions within the engine core remain constant, external factors like wind speed and engine position cause perturbations in the spin-down profile. Thus one needs to threshold σ_2 to suppress such effects.

Historical data from airline A spanning 10672 flights from 31 aircrafts was used to design the detection threshold. Within this data set, there were no reports of major engine failures. Based on conversations with engine experts, $\mathcal{N}$ was set at 50% of full speed. m was fixed at 80 samples, primarily constrained by onboard memory availability. Frequency of data collection was fixed by existing data collection system. A typical spin-down profile is shown in the top subplot in Fig. 1. The speed decay profiles from the four engines are *similar*, but not identical. Bottom subplot in Fig. 1 shows distribution of $\log(\sigma_2)$ from all 31 aircrafts[1]. Based on this distribution, we identified threshold θ such that the probability $P(\log(\sigma_2) > \theta) < 0.001$. We imposed an additional condition to eliminate outliers and look for sustained excursions in σ_2. If 5 successive values of $\log(\sigma_2)$ exceed 0.6, we declare an anomaly and Transmit $N_i(t)$ to the ground station for further analysis. Results of applying this algorithm on test aircrafts is discussed in the next section.

---

[1] Since the covariance matrix is symmetric, all the singular values are positive.

4 Results and Conclusions

The algorithm described in the previous section was tested on data collected from airline A. Figure 2 shows the trace of $\log(\sigma_2)$ from two engines over this test period. Aircraft 501 has some outliers, whereas aircraft 505 has sustained excursions. Small variations between two engines spin-down cause these outliers. At this point, it is believed that there may be a small influence of wind direction. Although, an interesting hypothesis, we were more interested in sustained variations caused by inherent malfunction within an engine. Possible engine anomaly in aircraft 505 is clearly identified by a jump in the σ_2.

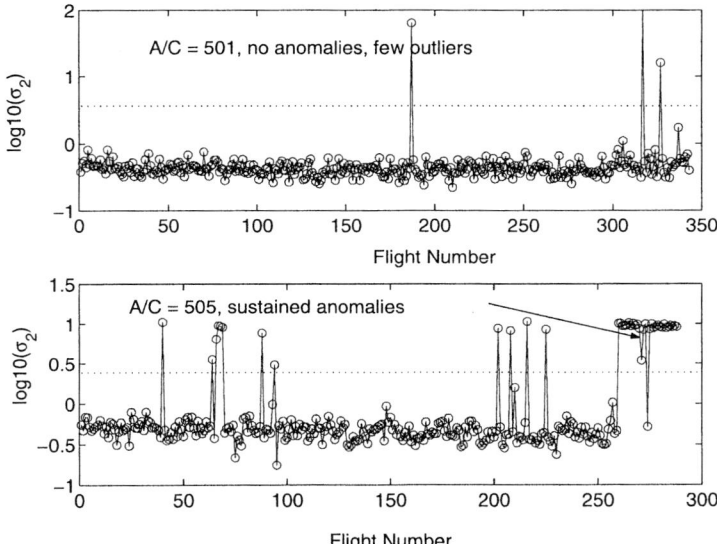

Fig. 2. σ_2 trace on test aircraft data

The trace of $N_i(t)$ for these sustained excursions is shown in Figure 3. Subplots left to right in Figure 3 indicate 8 consecutive flights. It is clear from the N_i trace that N_3 or engine #3 is spinning down rapidly and towards the end it comes to a grinding halt. This anomaly persisted for 16 consecutive flights after which this engine was removed for further trouble shooting. The anomaly clearly localized the problem to the bearing and the gearbox section of the engine. Further analysis at the repair shop revealed a malfunctioning oil pump. Malfunctioning oil pump imposes abnormal parasitic drag on the engine shaft and this gets pronounced as the engine spins down. At 100% speed, this parasitic drag gets masked by the turbine and the compressor. Historically, such incipient faults have gone un-noticed until secondary effects like high oil temperatures cause preventive shutdown. In this respect, the algorithm was successful in achieving what we had designed it for—anomaly detection for engine health monitoring.

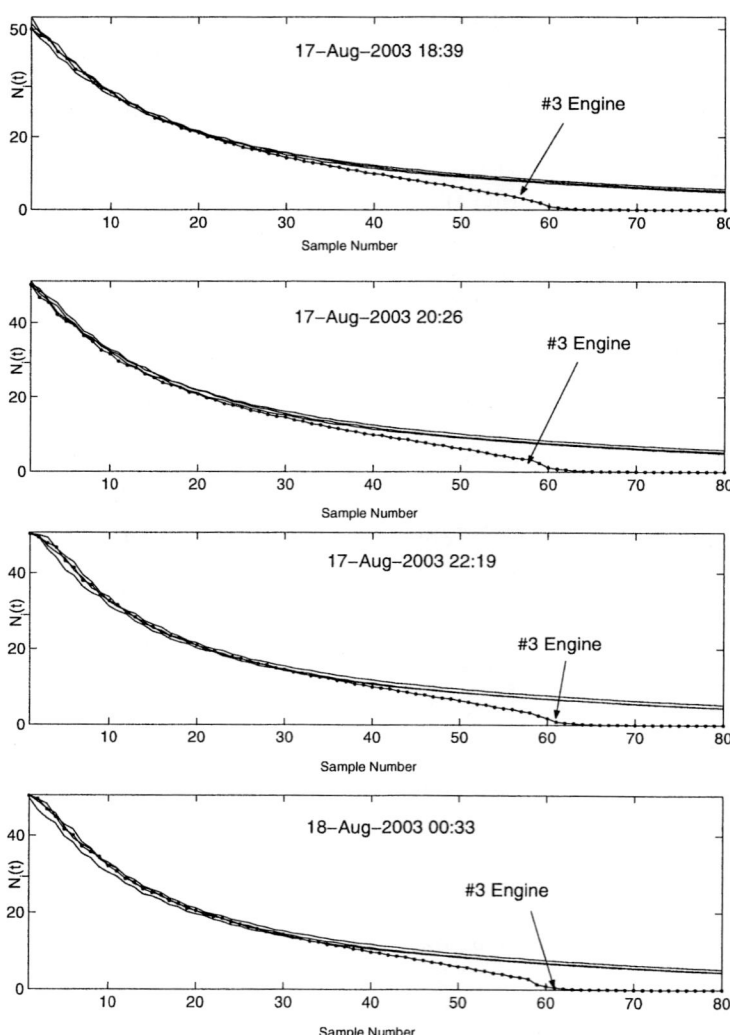

Fig. 3. N_1-square, N_2-star, N_3-circle, N_4-plus. Engine at position 3 (indicated by an arrow) in aircraft 505 is markedly different. There is a strong indication of abnormal drag on the shaft.

The algorithm described in this paper is a good example of how principles of linear algebra, statistics together with engineering knowledge can be used to design simple on-board anomaly detectors. To date, the algorithm has triggered anomalies in two aircrafts (A/C 505, 509), both with confirmed oil module malfunctions.

Future enhancements to this algorithm include analyzing the sample number at which an engine comes to a screeching halt. This abrupt trend is shown by the trace of $N_3(t)$ in Figure 3, which hits a zero value at about 60th sample. It is generally believed among repair engineers that this information can be used to isolate forward and rear bearing. We plan to embark on such investigations in the future.

References

1. Chase, D.: Predictive trend monitoring for commercial engines. In: European Operators Conference, Heidelberg, Germany (2004)
2. A.J.Hess, Calvello, G., Dabney, T., Frith, P.: PHM the key enabler for the joint strike force (JSF) autonomic logistics support concept. MFPT Technologies to Meet Corporate Goals **58** (2004)
3. Gorinevsky, D., Dittmar, K., Mylaraswamy, D., Nwadiogbu, E.: Model-based diagnostics for an aircraft auxiliary power unit. IEEE Conference on Control Applications (2002)
4. Mathioudakis, K., Kamboukos, P., Stamatis, A.: A turbofan performance deterioration tracking using nonlinear models and optimization. In: ASME Turbo Expo, Amsterdam, The Netherlands (2002)

Clustering Within Quantum Mechanical Framework

Güleser K. Demir

Dokuz Eylül University,
Department of Electrical and Electronics Engineering,
TR35460, Izmir, Turkey,
`demir@eee.deu.edu.tr`

Abstract. We study clustering problem within quantum mechanical framework by utilizing the Schroedinger equation written for the lowest energy state. We extend the analysis of Horn and Gottlieb [1] by providing an explicit discussion of probability distribution within full quantum mechanical context and examine the clustering performances for various probability distribution functions with numerical experiments.

1 Introduction

Recently, a clustering method that extents the scale-space clustering by using quantum mechanical analogies has been proposed by Horn and Gottlieb [1]. This approach is interesting in that they have viewed probability distribution function as the stationary-state eigenfunction of Schroedinger equation with potential energy $V(x)$, and thereby, they have shown that minima of the potential energy identify the clusters. In the scale-space or density-based clustering the clusters are defined as dense regions, and each dense region is separated from one another by low density regions [2], [3]. In the quantum mechanical framework, the dense regions are identified as the valley regions of the quantum potential as follows from the Schroedinger equation. As a result, we envisage the minima of the quantum potential as the center points of the clusters, and equipotential levels of the potential as cluster boundaries.

In this work we will extend the analysis of Horn and Gottlieb [1] by providing an explicit discussion of probability distribution within full quantum mechanical context. Furthermore, we compute the potential energy for each data point x_i, and determine the clustering performance by identifying probability distribution with various nonlinear mapping functions used in pattern recognition. As a by-product of the application of full quantum formalism, we also show how the probability distribution changes with time, though we do not provide a full numerical study of this point at this stage yet.

In the next section we provide the quantum mechanical formalism. In Section 3 we provide numerical study of proposed clustering method for various probability distributions. In Section 4 we conclude the work.

2 The Quantum Potential

The dynamics of a quantum system is described by the Schroedinger equation

$$i\frac{\partial}{\partial t}\psi(\boldsymbol{x},t) = \left[-\frac{\gamma^2}{2}\nabla^2 + V(\boldsymbol{x},t)\right]\psi(\boldsymbol{x},t) \qquad (1)$$

where $\psi(\boldsymbol{x},t)$ is the wavefunction and $V(\boldsymbol{x},t)$ is the potential energy of the system [4], [5]. It is convenient to parameterize the wavefunction as $\psi(\boldsymbol{x},t) = \sqrt{\rho(\boldsymbol{x},t)}\,e^{iS(\boldsymbol{x},t)}$ where $\rho(\boldsymbol{x},t)$ and $S(\boldsymbol{x},t)$ are real functions of $\boldsymbol{x}$ and time t. Replacement of this form of the wavefunction in the Schroedinger equation results in two coupled equations

$$-\frac{\partial}{\partial t}S = V + \frac{\gamma^2}{2}(\nabla S)^2 - Q, \qquad -\frac{\partial}{\partial t}\rho = \gamma^2 \nabla(\rho \nabla S) \qquad (2)$$

where Q is the "quantum potential"

$$Q(\boldsymbol{x},t) = \frac{\gamma^2}{2}\frac{\nabla^2 \sqrt{\rho(\boldsymbol{x},t)}}{\sqrt{\rho(\boldsymbol{x},t)}}. \qquad (3)$$

In quantum mechanics the modulus-squared of the wavefunction is the probability density of the system, that is, $\rho(\boldsymbol{x},t)$ gives the probability to find the system within the differential volume $d^D\boldsymbol{x}$. The real function $S(\boldsymbol{x},t)$ is the phase of the wavefunction. It does not contribute to the probability density rather it determines the current density of probability flow. Depending on the temporal properties of the system, one can consider the following special cases:

1. *Stationary-state quantum system with homogeneous phase:* In this case system evolves in time with a definite energy. In particular, $V(\boldsymbol{x},t)$ and thus $\rho(\boldsymbol{x},t)$ is independent of time; moreover, the phase function depends solely on time $S(\boldsymbol{x},t) = -Et$ where E is the total energy of the system (kinetic plus potential energy). Under these conditions (2) gives rise to a static potential

$$V(\boldsymbol{x}) = Q(\boldsymbol{x}) - Q(\boldsymbol{x})_{min} \qquad (4)$$

if $V(\boldsymbol{x})$ is chosen to vanish at its minimum, implying $Q(\boldsymbol{x})_{min} = -E$.

2. *Stationary-state quantum system with inhomogeneous phase:* In this case the phase field is given by $S(\boldsymbol{x},t) = -Et + W(\boldsymbol{x})$ where W is independent of time. Then (2) give rise to

$$V(\boldsymbol{x},t) = Q(\boldsymbol{x},t) - \frac{\gamma^2}{2}(\nabla W)^2 - \left(Q(\boldsymbol{x},t) - \frac{\gamma^2}{2}(\nabla W)^2\right)_{min} \qquad (5)$$

$$\frac{\partial}{\partial t}\rho(\boldsymbol{x},t) = -\gamma^2 \nabla(\rho(\boldsymbol{x},t)\nabla W(\boldsymbol{x})). \qquad (6)$$

It is clear that now $V(\boldsymbol{x},t)$ is determined by both the quantum potential and the phase field. Moreover, the probability density evolves in time with a rate determined by the inhomogeneity of the phase field.

3 Data Clustering Using Quantum Potential

We analyze the implications of the following probability distribution functions

$$\rho_1(x) = \sum_{i=1}^{N} e^{-\frac{(x-x_i)^2}{2\gamma^2}}, \qquad \rho_2(x) = \left|\sum_{i=1}^{N} e^{-\frac{(x-x_i)^2}{2\gamma^2}}\right|^2,$$
$$\rho_3(x) = \left|\sum_{i=1}^{N} e^{-\frac{(x-x_i)^2}{2\gamma^2}}\right|^4, \qquad \rho_4(x) = \left|\sum_{i=1}^{N} \frac{1}{((x-x_i)^2+\gamma^2)^2}\right|^2, \quad (7)$$

by using each of them in (4) where N is the total number of points. Here, we emphasize that all of these ρ functions have local property. Namely, larger the ρ larger the number of points in the neighborhood (whose size is determined by γ) of x. Therefore, they are capable of representing structural relationships of the data points. The main tool for probing the cluster centers is the minima of the potential energy. The quantum potentials corresponding to the probability distribution functions ρ_1, ρ_2, ρ_3 and ρ_4 are given respectively by

$$Q_1(x) = -\frac{D}{4} + \frac{1}{4\gamma^2(\rho_1(x))^2} \sum_{i=1}^{N} (x-x_i)^2 e^{-\frac{(x-x_i)^2}{2\gamma^2}}$$
$$- \frac{1}{8\gamma^2(\rho_1(x))^4} \sum_{i=1}^{N}\sum_{j=1}^{N} (x-x_i)\cdot(x-x_j)\, e^{-\frac{1}{2\gamma^2}[(x-x_i)^2+(x-x_j)^2]}, \quad (8)$$

$$Q_2(x) = -\frac{D}{2} + \frac{1}{2\gamma^2 \rho_2(x)} \sum_{i=1}^{N} (x-x_i)^2 e^{-\frac{(x-x_i)^2}{2\gamma^2}}, \quad (9)$$

$$Q_3(x) = -D + \frac{1}{\gamma^2(\rho_3(x))^{1/2}} \sum_{i=1}^{N} (x-x_i)^2 e^{-\frac{(x-x_i)^2}{2\gamma^2}}$$
$$- \frac{1}{\gamma^2 \rho_3(x)} \sum_{i=1}^{N}\sum_{j=1}^{N} (x-x_i)\cdot(x-x_j)\, e^{-\frac{1}{2\gamma^2}[(x-x_i)^2+(x-x_j)^2]}, \quad (10)$$

$$Q_4(x) = \sum_{i=1}^{N} \frac{-4\gamma^2\left(\gamma^2 - 2(x-x_i)^2\right)}{\left(\gamma^2 + (x-x_i)^2\right)^4}. \quad (11)$$

In what follows we will perform a numerical study of these potentials for the Leptograpsus crab data set which has also been used by Horn and Gottlieb [1]. For the ease of comparison, we follow the same preprocessings applied in that study. This data set consists of four classes each containing 50 instances in a five-dimensional data space. Its dimension is reduced to two by using Principal Component Analysis (PCA) [7]. While applying PCA, the data are projected onto the second and third eigenvectors of the correlation matrix of the data set and then the projections are normalized by dividing them by the square roots of the corresponding eigenvalues. In Figure 1 we depict the data and the tomographic map of the quantum potential divided by its maximum value for

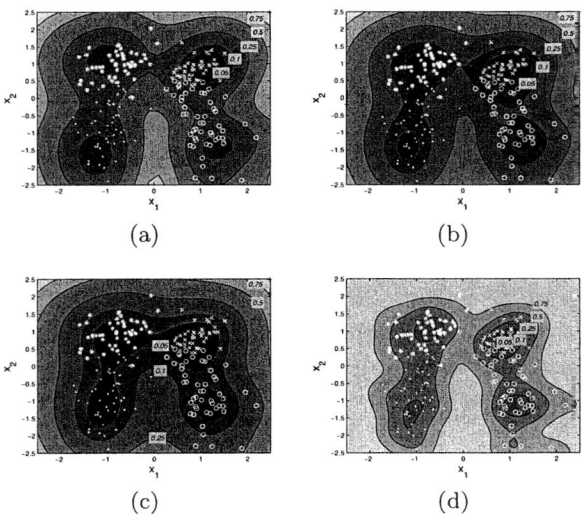

Fig. 1. Tomographic maps of the quantum potential for the probability distribution functions of (a) $\rho_1(x)$, (b) $\rho_2(x)$, (c) $\rho_3(x)$ and (d) $\rho_4(x)$

each of the probability distributions in (7). Figures 1-(a), (b) and (c) show the resulting maps for Q_1, Q_2, and Q_3 with $\gamma = 1/\sqrt{2}$, respectively. Figure 1-(d) shows the tomographic map for Q_4 with $\gamma = 1$. Here, we illustrate the actual class of each data point with four different markers for enabling the visualization of clustering performance. The required four minima are seen clearly in the quantum potential energy distributions. Indeed, these minima correspond to four different cluster centers where equipotential lines are related to the cluster boundaries. One notes from the first three panels of Figure 1 that Q_1 exhibits a much sharper distribution than Q_2 and Q_3. This shows that for clustering purposes direct identification of quantum mechanical probability distribution $\rho(x)$ with the Parzen-window estimator works better than other alternatives. En passant, we note that the analysis of Horn and Gottlieb [1] corresponds to using ρ_2 for clustering, as one can see by rewriting quantum potential in (3) in their form. Figure 1-(d) is obtained for the inverse-quadratic probability distribution function, ρ_4. This potential shows a relatively different behavior than the Gaussian ones though it still clearly identifies the four cluster centers.

In this work, for each point in the data set we find an associated steepest-ascent trajectory which originates at the datum and ends in one of the local maxima. And then, a cluster is formed for all those points whose steepest-ascent trajectories converge to the same local minimum. Interesting enough, the same convergence behavior of trajectories can also be realized by the guiding trajectory driven by quantum potential in Bohmian quantum mechanics [8]. Figures 2-(a) and (b) show the resulting clustering assignments for the Gaussian probability function, ρ_2, and inverse quadratic probability function, ρ_4, respectively.

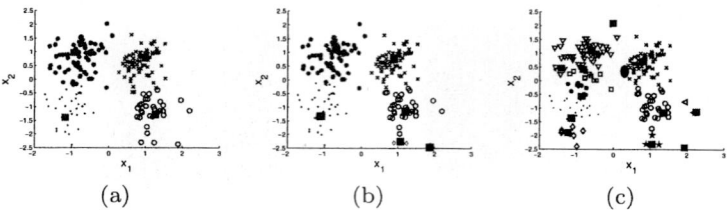

Fig. 2. Cluster assignments via gradient descent algorithm. Different markers show different clusters and filled square markers indicate cluster centers for (a) $\rho_1(x)$ with $\gamma = 1$, (b) $\rho_4(x)$ with $\gamma = 1$, (c) $\rho_4(x)$ with $\gamma = 1/\sqrt{2}$. Big filled ellipse in (c) shows the single cluster center for $\rho_4(x)$ with $\gamma = 4$.

Additional two cluster centers are seen $x_1 \cong 1$ and $x_1 \cong 2$ in Figure 2-(b) due to the rather shallow local minima in these regions. We further examine the dependence of the clustering performance on the width parameter γ. For this we compare inverse-quadratic distribution function for $\gamma = 1/\sqrt{2}$ and $\gamma = 4$. In Figure 2-(c) different markers show different clusters and filled squares show the cluster centers for $\gamma = 1/\sqrt{2}$. In the same sub-figure big filled ellipse shows the single cluster center for $\gamma = 4$. Since the number of minima increases with decreasing γ one needs to choose γ judiciously for good clustering (which might cost a number of experiments). As a second experiment, we tested the proposed method on image compression application. The performances of the clustering by quantum potential and by the well-known k-means algorithm are compared for real images. 4-dimensional data points are obtained by choosing the block size as 2x2 in 64x64 images. The data vectors are normalized so that their means and variances are zero and one, respectively. For performing quantitative analyzes of the methods we use peak signal-to-noise ratio (PSNR). Table 1 shows the number of clusters for different values of γ and corresponding PSNR values by using quantum potential and by using well-known k-means algorithm for the Lena image. Since γ determines the size of neighboring region the number of clusters increases with the decrease of the γ.

The use of quantum mechanical framework for clustering purposes is a rather new approach. Though, as shown here, its performance is not as good as that of the k-means algorithm it opens up the possibility of quantum mechanical computations in neural systems and implementation of clustering at quantum level with significant profits on computational time and size.

Table 1. The number of clusters for different values of γ and corresponding PSNR values by using quantum potential and by using k-means algorithm

γ	Number of Clusters	$PSNR_Q$	$PSNR_{k-means}$
0.5	24	58.82	60.37
1	18	56.13	59.32
2	7	54.01	57.21

4 Conclusion

In this work we discussed the clustering problem within quantum mechanical context and gave experimental results. In the experiments, we have computed the potential energy for each data point x_i, and depicted the clustering performances by using various probability distribution functions. We have assigned data points to the clusters by using gradient descent procedure.

Recently several researchers have studied on the idea of quantum mechanical computations in biological neural networks and proposed some associative neural/quantum network structures with possible implementations at quantum level [9], [10]. Clustering in the quantum mechanical framework is an extension of these studies and it might become a basis for advanced research opportunities. For example, while representing the flow of probability distribution with the use of continuity equation one may trace and segment objects in motion analysis. Additionally, one may include the training data set into the calculations, again considering the minima of quantum potential as the regions which we want to minimize (such as training error).

References

1. D. Horn and A. Gottlieb, Algorithm for Data Clustering in Pattern Recognition Problems Based on Quantum Mechanics, Phys.Rev. Lett., 88, 2002.
2. S.J. Roberts, Non-parametric unsupervised cluster analysis, Pattern Recognition, 30,2, 261-272, 1997.
3. A. Hinneburg , D.A. Keim, An Efficient Approach to Clustering in Multimedia Databases with Noise, Proc. 4rd Int. Conf. on Knowledge Discovery and Data Mining, New York, AAAI Press, 1998.
4. S. Gasiorowicz, *Quantum Physics, 3rd ed*, (John Wiley and Sons, 2003).
5. E. Merzbacher, *Quantum Mechanics, 3rd ed*, (John Wiley and Sons, 1998).
6. B.D. Ripley, Ftp Archive, Department of Statistics, Univ. of Oxford, http://www.stats.ox.ac.uk/pub/PRNN/.
7. Morrison, D.F., *Multivariate Statistical Methods , 2nd ed.*, (McGraw-Hill, New York, 1976).
8. Holland, Peter R. *The Quantum Theory of Motion : An Account of the de Broglie-Bohm Causal Interpretation of Quantum Mechanics*, (Cambridge: Cambridge U. Press, 1993).
9. R. Penrose, *Shadows of the Mind*, (Oxford University Press, 1994).
10. M. Perus, S.K. Dey, Quantum systems can realize content-addressable associative memory; Applied Math. Letters, 13, 8, 31-36, 2000.

Linear Penalization Support Vector Machines for Feature Selection

Jaime Miranda, Ricardo Montoya, and Richard Weber

Department of Industrial Engineering,
Faculty of Physical and Mathematical Sciences,
University of Chile
{jmiranda, rmontoya, rweber}@dii.uchile.cl

Abstract. Support Vector Machines have proved to be powerful tools for classification tasks combining the minimization of classification errors and maximizing their generalization capabilities. Feature selection, however, is not considered explicitly in the basic model formulation. We propose a linearly penalized Support Vector Machines (LP-SVM) model where feature selection is performed *simultaneously* with model construction. Its application to a problem of customer retention and a comparison with other feature selection techniques demonstrates its effectiveness.

1 Introduction

One of the tasks of Statistics and Data Mining consists of extracting patterns contained in large data bases. In the case of classification, discriminating rules are constructed based on the information contained in the feature values of each object. By applying the discriminating rule to new objects, it is possible to conduct a classification that predicts the class to which these new objects belong.

Building a classifier, it is desirable to use the smallest number of features possible in order to obtain a result considered acceptable by the user. This problem is known as feature selection [5] and is combinatorial in the number of original features [8].

Recently, Support Vector Machines (SVM) have received growing attention in the area of classification due to certain significant characteristics such as an adequate generalization to new objects, the absence of local minima and representation that depends on few parameters [3, 11, 12]. Nevertheless, among SVM systems there are few approaches established in order to identify the most important features to construct the discriminating rule.

In the present paper we develop a methodology for feature selection based on SVM. The focus chosen is the penalization for each feature used, which is carried out *simultaneously* with the construction of the classification model.

The paper is structured as follows: Section 2 presents the proposed methodology. Section 3 describes its application for customer retention in a Chilean bank. Section 4 shows the areas of future development and summarizes the main conclusions.

2 Penalized Support Vector Machines (LP-SVM) for Feature Selection

To determine the most relevant features, and to take advantage of SVM capabilities to solve classification problems, we propose a modification of the mathematical model. A penalization for each feature used is incorporated into the objective function. This way, the following three objectives are proposed at the moment of constructing the mathematical formulation of the problem to solve:

1. The capacity for generalization: Minimizing the norm of the normal to the separating hyper plane.
2. Classification errors: Minimizing the sum of the slack variables added to the problem, penalizing each slack variable used.
3. Feature selection: Minimizing the number of features when building the discrimination model, penalizing each feature used.

The current mathematical formulation of the Support Vector Machines only includes the first two of the three objectives. On the other hand, our approach differs from that proposed by Bradley and Mangasarian where only the objectives 2. and 3. are used [1]. The formulation presented in [2] uses second order cone programming for feature selection where a bound assures low misclassification errors and selecting the most appropriate features is performed by minimizing the respective L_1 norm. However, only by explicitly optimizing all three objectives, we can assure that the advantages provided by SVM are combined with the attempt to select the most relevant features.

We need the following notation in order to develop our model.

Let $\vec{x} \in \Re^m$:
$$\left|\vec{x}\right|_j = \begin{cases} x_j & \text{if } x_j > 0 \\ 0 & \text{if } x_j = 0, \quad j=1,...,m \\ -x_j & \text{if } x_j < 0 \end{cases}$$

Step Function:

$$\left(\vec{x}_*\right)_j = \begin{cases} 1 & \text{if } x_j > 0 \\ 0 & \text{if } x_j = 0, \quad j=1,...,m \\ -1 & \text{if } x_j < 0 \end{cases}$$

We note that if $\vec{x} \in \Re_+^m$ $\left(\vec{x}_*\right)_j \in \{0,1\}$ $j=1,...,m$

Number of Components:

$$x_j \in \{0,1\} \ \forall_j \Rightarrow \vec{e}^T \cdot \vec{x} = \sum_{j=1}^{m} x_j = \text{number of strictly positive components of } \vec{x}$$

Objective function of the proposed model:

$$\frac{1}{2}\|\vec{w}\|^2 + C_1 \sum_{i=1}^{n} \xi_i + C_2 \vec{e}^T \cdot |\vec{w}|_* \tag{1}$$

where $\frac{1}{2}\|\vec{w}\|^2 + C_1 \sum_{i=1}^{n} \xi_i$ corresponds to the traditional formulation of SVM objective function and $\vec{e}^T \cdot |\vec{w}|_*$ is the sum of non-negative components of w and refers to the number of selected features.

However, the formulation (1) has the inconvenience of not being a continuous function, because it

- incorporates the modulus $(|\vec{w}|)$ and
- a discontinuous step function $(|\vec{w}|_*)$.

Replacing the modulus by auxiliary variables and the step function by a concave exponential approximation we obtain the following model:

$$\underset{\vec{w},\vec{v},\varepsilon_i,b}{\text{Minimize}} \quad \frac{1}{2}\|\vec{w}\|^2 + C_1 \sum_{i=1}^{n} \xi_i + C_2 \vec{e}^t \cdot \left(\vec{e} - \varepsilon^{-T\vec{v}}\right)$$

Subject to:
$$y_i(\vec{x}_i \cdot \vec{w} + b) - 1 + \xi_i \geq 0 \qquad i = 1,...,n$$
$$\xi_i \geq 0 \qquad i = 1,...,n \tag{2}$$
$$-\vec{v} \leq \vec{w} \leq \vec{v}$$

Where $\vec{w}, \vec{v} \in \Re^m$ and $\xi_i, b \in \Re$. This model will be called LP-SVM. We shall use Cross Validation in order to obtain the best model parameters in a particular application [7].

3 Applying LP-SVM for Customer Retention

In the case of customer retention, companies spend much of their budget trying to understand customers. It is known that the cost of acquiring a new customer is between 5 and 7 times higher than retaining an old one [10] and that, moreover, to increase customer retention by 5% means increasing financial results by 25% [6]. Data coming from customers is very diverse, so it has to be processed previously, selecting the most important features that represent the customer in order to respond to the market requirements more accurately and efficiently.

For financial institutions such as banks, it is important to understand the typical behavior of customers that are about to leave the institution and want to close their current account. In this case the bank would take actions in order to retain these customers. Although we know how the behavior of each one of our customers evolves, it is not possible to manually follow up on each of them because of the portfolio size and, furthermore, we do not know for certain what behavior is associated with a customer who is about to close his/her account so as to be able to pinpoint him/her exactly.

We apply the proposed methodology LP-SVM to a database of a Chilean bank concerned about retention of its customers. We built a classification model using Support Vector Machines, adding the approach suggested in this publication for feature selection and compared it with two other techniques for feature selection.

We analyzed a data set from the respective database that contains information on the customers who voluntarily closed their current accounts over a 3 months period prior to September 2001 and those who were still active at that day. The information contained in this database includes, among others, the following features for each customer: age, sex, antiquity, marital status, level of education, average salary over the last 3 months, number of products acquired and transaction data.

Each customer in the database belongs to a class depending on whether he/she closed his/her current account or remains active. The variable that indicates the class to which the customer belongs is equal to 1 if the customer closed his/her account and -1 if the customer is still active.

The database we shall study in this application is that for September 2001. It contains 1,937 customers, 995 (51.37%) of which closed their current accounts within the 3 months period prior to September 2001 and the remaining 942 (48.63%) are considered to be active customers. For each customer we have 36 feature values.

The following table presents the results applying three methods to a validation set (holdout sample): LP-SVM, Clamping [9] as a wrapper technique combined with a MLP-type neural network as classifier (C-NN), and a decision tree (DT). The underlined value indicates the best model regarding the respective number of selected features.

As can be seen, LP-SVM performs best among the three methods in 7 of 9 cases.

Table 1. Percentage of correct classification in validation set

Number of selected features:	10	12	13	14	15	20	25	30	36
LP-SVM	50.0	84.0	83.7	82.4	82.0	81.1	82.4	82.9	72.8
C-NN	65.0	67.3	67.1	60.5	63.4	67.0	68.3	68.6	68.7
DT	70.3	72.0	72.8	72.8	73.8	73.8	72.8	73.8	73.8

4 Conclusions and Future Work

We presented LP-SVM, a new approach for feature selection using SVM where the feature selection step is performed *simultaneously* with model construction. A comparison with other techniques for feature selection and classification shows the advantages of LP-SVM.

Future work has to be done in various directions. First, it would be interesting to apply the proposed formulation to the non-linear case where Kernel functions are used for feature space transformation.

It would also be interesting to apply feature selection *simultaneously* to model construction for regression problems. A hybrid methodology where feature selection and model building using Support Vector Regression are performed sequentially has been presented in [4].

Acknowledgements

This project has been funded by the Millennium Science Nucleus on Complex Engineering Systems (www.sistemasdeingenieria.cl) and the project Fondecyt 1040926.

References

1. Bradley, P., Mangasarian, O. (1998): Feature selection vía concave minimization and support vector machines. In *Machine Learning proceedings of the fifteenth International Conference* (ICML'98) 82 –90, San Francisco, California, 1998. Morgan Kaufmann.
2. Bhattacharya, Ch. (2004): Second Order Cone Programming Formulations for Feature Selection. Journal of Machine Learning Research , 1417-1433
3. Cristianini, N., Shawe-Taylor, J. (2000): *An Introduction to Support Vector Machines.* Cambridge University Press, Cambridge, UK.
4. Guajardo, J., Miranda, J., Weber, R. (2005): A Hybrid Forecasting Methodology using Feature Selection and Support Vector Regression. Presented at HIS2005 Hybrid Intelligent Systems, Rio de Janeiro, November 2005
5. Hand, D. (1981): *Discrimination and Classification.* Wiley, Chichester
6. Kotler, P. (2000): *Marketing Management: Analysis, Planning, Implementation, and Control.* Prentice Hall International, New Jersey, 10th edition
7. Montoya, R., Weber, R. (2002): Support Vector Machines Penalizado para Selección de Atributos. XI CLAIO, Concepción, Chile, 27-30 de octubre de 2002 (in Spanish)
8. Nemhauser, G., Wolsey, L. (1988): *Integer and Combinatorial Optimization.* John Wiley and Sons, New York.
9. Partridge, D., Cang, S. (2002): Revealing Feature Interactions in Classification Tasks. In: A. Abraham, J. Ruiz-del-Solar, M. Köppen (eds.): Soft Computing Systems - Design, Management and Applications. IOS Press, Amsterdam, Berlin, 394-403
10. Reichheld, F., Sasser, E. (1990): Zero defections: Quality comes to services. Harvard Business Review September-October:105 –111
11. Shawe-Taylor, J., Cristianini, N. (2004): Kernel Methods for Pattern Analysis. Cambridge University Press, Cambridge
12. Vapnik, V. (1998): Statistical Learning Theory John Wiley and Sons, New York.

Linear Regression for Dimensionality Reduction and Classification of Multi Dimensional Data[*]

Lalitha Rangarajan and P. Nagabhushan

Department of Studies in Computer Science,
University of Mysore, Mysore, India
lali85arun@yahoo.co.in, pnagabhushan@hotmail.com

Abstract. A new pattern recognition method for classification of multi dimensional samples is proposed. In pattern recognition problems samples (pixels in remote sensing) are described using a number of features (dimensions/bands in remote sensing). While a number of features of the samples are useful for a better description of the image, they pose a threat in terms of unwieldy mass of data. In this paper we propose a method to achieve dimensionality reduction using regression. The method proposed transforms the feature values into representative patterns, termed as symbolic objects, which are obtained through regression lines. The so defined symbolic object accomplishes dimensionality reduction of the data. A new distance measure is devised to measure the distances between the symbolic objects (fitted regression lines) and clustering is preformed. The efficacy of the method is corroborated experimentally.

Keywords: Pattern Classification, Dimensionality Reduction, Feature Sequence, Regression, Clustering, Data Assimilation, Multi Dimensional Data, Symbolic Data.

1 Introduction

Measurements made in pattern recognition applications are inherently multi dimensional in nature. Larger the numbers of features, more severe are the problems of storage and analysis time requirements. It is a tacit assumption that all these features are useful in obtaining a good classification [2]. In fact, it is more rewarding to use a few significant features or their functions in suitable combinations [1]. Further, reducing the feature set to two or three facilitates visual inspection of the data. Aim of dimensionality reduction is to describe the samples by means of minimum number of features that are necessary for discrimination of objects (patterns) in the image. A variety of methods for dimensionality reduction are proposed in the literature [many described in 2]. Most of these belong to subsetting methods or feature space transformation methods.

In pattern recognition applications, each sample is described using a set of values (features), the size of the set being the dimension of the data set. Each sample can be viewed as quantitative multi valued symbolic variable, as termed in an advanced

---
[*] This research is supported by ISRO project RESPOND 10/4/317, Oct 1999.

exploratory data analysis technique called Symbolic Data Analysis [3]. The gist of symbolic approach in pattern classification is to extend the problems and methods defined on classical data to more complex data called 'symbolic objects', which are well adapted to represent knowledge [3: Michalski, 1981; Diday, 1988, 1989b; Tu Bao Ho et al., 1988]. A symbolic object is a description of the properties of a set of elementary objects. The description of symbolic objects may depend on the relations existing between elementary objects, frequency of occurrence of values [3: Bertrand and Goupil, 2000] and so on. Each variable of a symbolic object may take a set of values [6, 1994; 3: De Carlvaho, 1998] or an interval of values [3: Gowda and Diday, 1991] or even a sub object [6, 1988; 3: Gowda and Diday, 1991]. Symbolic representation of multi dimensional temporal observations can be found in [5, 10].

Each sample in our data set is described by a set of feature values. Ichino, Yaguchi and De Carlvaho have suggested interesting metric on set type symbolic data. These distance measures are inadequate to determine the distance between two samples. We have introduced a new symbolic data type of the set of feature values and a suitable distance measure. We have made an attempt to summarize the feature values of a sample into a new symbolic object namely "regression curves". This results in data assimilation of feature values of a sample. [9] is concerned with the dimensionality reduction of temporal data through regression lines. Here lines of best fit are identified for temporal observations of a specific feature. However in the proposed method we have achieved dimensionality reduction by assimilating the features of a sample into a regression curve. Perhaps feature sequence may affect the nature of best fit.

Section 2 describes the method proposed. In Section 3 we have described computation of distance between two regression lines, which is the foundation for clustering samples, and clustering procedure. Experiments and results are discussed in Section 4. We have concluded the paper with suggestions for further improvements in Section 5.

2 Description of the Method

In an n dimensional image the collection of all n feature values $\{f_1, f_2, ..., f_n\}$ decide the class the sample belongs to. This collection can be regarded as quantitative multi valued symbolic variable (set) [3]. The distance between such symbolic variables (sets) can be measured using (i) the number of total elements in both the sets (Cartesian join $\oplus/\cup$) and (ii) the number of common elements in both the sets (Cartesian meet $\otimes/\cap$) [6]. The distance between features can also be measured using agreement ($\cap$ of both sets) and disagreement ($\cap$ of a set and complement of the other set) as suggested by [3: De Carvalho, 1998] The component distances can be aggregated with generalized Minkowski's metric. Both these distance measures are not suitable for our symbolic object although our data is also multi valued quantitative. Our 'set' is sensitive to arrangement of elements within the set, unlike the 'set' in [3]. That is the following two samples x and y described by the features sets namely, {1.6, 2.4, 4.7, 10.8} and {10.8, 4.7, 2.4, 1.6} are not identical and also unlikely to be from the same class. Our features are not only sets but also vectors. Hence the symbolic representation should take care of not only the set contents but also the arrangement of the set elements.

We have used 'regression curves' for describing each feature of a sample. This symbolic transformation can take care of both the contents of the set and the arrangement of the set elements. For the above example of feature values of samples x and y, our symbolic objects are regression curves fitted for points (1,1.6), (2, 2.4), (3, 4.7), (4, 10.8) and for points (1, 10.8), (2, 4.7), (3, 2.4), (4, 1.6). These regression curves are entirely different. We have used 'least square error' regression curves to symbolize features of a sample. The transformation results in the assimilation of f features into a regression curve.

A good regression curve provides an apt description of the samples. But it is difficult to determine the nature of regression curves. Even if we do, the feature values of different samples could yield different types of regression curves. For instance the best regression curves of two samples may become a quadratic curve and a line. This amounts to keeping track of type of regression curves and also the parameters of regression curves. This results in too much of book keeping, making the problem of classification too tedious. Probably this may even contradict the possibilities of the very theme of the research, that is, dimensionality reduction and data assimilation. Therefore all samples are represented by symbolic data object namely "least square error regression lines" fitted for points $(1, f_1), (2, f_2), ..., (n, f_n)$. Our goal is not a better description of pixels (samples), but a description that is good enough that retains the vital information hidden in the feature values so that the classification is truthful. Our regression lines for points $(1,f_1), (2,f_2), ..., (n, f_n)$ possesses this property. A new distance measure has been proposed to measure the distance between the set of regression lines similar to the one in [9], where dimensionality reduction of multi temporal data using regression is discussed.

Samples belonging to different classes differ significantly in atleast one dimension. The corresponding regression lines reflect this significant difference in feature values. This is illustrated in the figure 1. Samples belonging to same class have the respective feature values close to each other and hence the regression lines are close too. An example of this case is illustrated in the figure 2. Observe that the regression lines of samples belonging to same class are close to each other only in the interval [1,n]. The lines may differ significantly beyond this interval. Yet the samples are similar.

Suppose that the data items are represented by d[i,j] where i is the sample and j is the feature and $1 \leq i \leq s$, $1 \leq j \leq f$. Regression lines are fitted for the points (1, d[i,1]), (2, d[i,2]), ..., (x,d[i,x]), ..., (f, d[i,f]). The above process of fitting regression lines is repeated for all samples. In the end we have s regression lines. The number of features of a sample is reduced from f to 2.

3 Computation of Distance Measure for Clustering and Sequencing the Features

The distance between the samples m,n is defined to be maximum of the lengths LmLn, RmRn (refer figure 3). Here Lm, Ln are the points of intersections of the regression lines of samples m, n with the (left) ordinate at x=1 and Rm, Rn are the points of intersections of the regression lines of samples m, n with the (right) ordinate at x=f. The new reduced set of feature values of the sample m are Lm, Rm. Our distance measure is a supremum distance measuring dissimilarity between samples. It is obvious from figure 4 that the distance measure is a metric.

Sequencing of Features

Suppose that there exists a sequence of features such that they are approximately linear (true for all classes) and is according to the order of variances. Then we have an ideal and most preferred scenario for our transformation into symbolic data, namely regression lines (refer figure 5). But in reality this may not be possible. That is sequencing features according to variances may not preserve linearity for all classes. As we measure distances between samples by looking at ordinates at 1 and f, we require an ordering that would discriminate samples from distinct classes at either the ordinate at 1 or at f. The feature with maximum variance is likely to discriminate many classes. The exhaustive experimentation suggests that the best sequence of features is according to variance. The way the first few PCs are employed for classification, support the argument on sequencing the features based on magnitude of variances. However if classes are well separable any sequence is good enough.

For figures 1 to 6 feature numbers are along X axis and feature values along Y

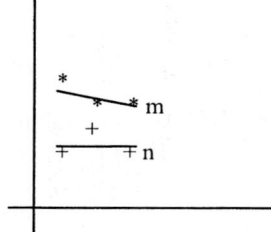
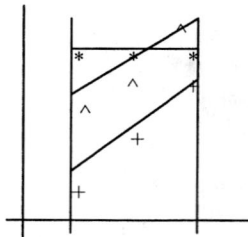
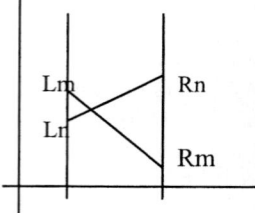

Fig. 1. m,n from different class

Fig. 2. m,n from same class

Fig. 3. Distance between m,n dis(m,n)=max{LmLn, RmRn} =RmRn

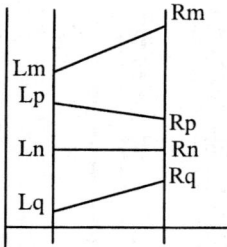
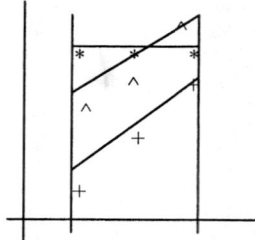
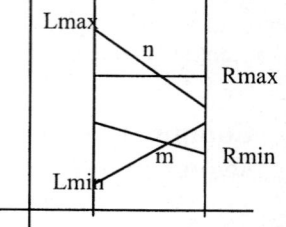

Fig. 4. Dist measure is metric dis(m,n)=dis(m,p)+dis(p,n) dis(m,n)<dis(m,q)+dis(q,n)

Fig. 5. Favorable scenario Features according to order variances and linear. Classes well separable at f=1

Fig. 6. First two centers m,n LminLmax > RminRmax Initial two centers: m,n

4 Experiments

To illustrate the feasibility of the proposed method we conducted experiments on supervised data sets (Iris and synthetic remote sensed image).

The first experiment is on a well separable subset (size 30, 10 from each class) of Iris data with 3 classes. Our method and PCA yield the same result (misclassification is nil). Also classification is found to be independent of feature sequence.

The second experiment is on a synthesized remotely sensed image. The synthesized image (figure 7) is of size 50 x 50 pixels, consisting of 7 classes found in the Coorg forest area in the state of Karnataka, India. The classes are arranged as found in nature and spectral responses generated randomly to be within the predetermined ranges [11]. After transformation and reduction of bands, we performed clustering in two rounds. Initially we made a partition of the data into twice the number of expected clusters. The reason for making too many clusters is that some classes in the data set are hardly separable. The regression lines of such classes tend to average out the small differences that exist in feature values. With more clusters such classes also become distinct (with the new transformed reduced set of features). Initial two centers are selected to be the two most distant regression lines

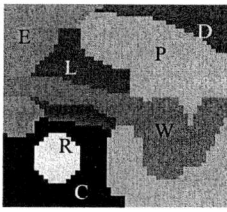

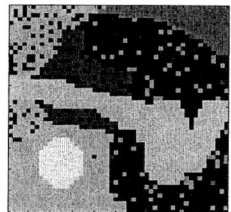

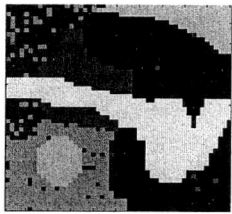

Fig. 7. Synthetic image E-Evergreen forest W-Water R-Rubber P-Paddy C-Coffee L-Cropland D-Deciduous forest

Fig. 8. Classification map of image in fig 7 using first 2 PCs

Fig. 9. Classification map of image in fig 7 using proposed method

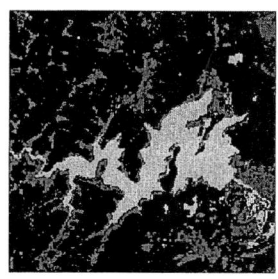

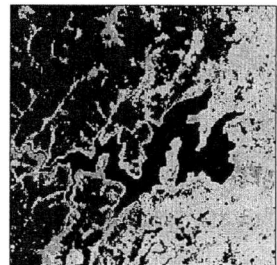

Fig. 10. Registered IRS 1A LISS II B1 – FCC of Coorg forest cover. Size: 260x260 Date: Feb 3rd 1991

Fig. 11. Classification map of image in fig 9 using first two PCs

Fig. 12. Classification map of image in fig 9 using proposed method

(figure 6). Subsequent centers are selected to be the regression lines of the samples that are beyond a threshold distance from all previous centers. The pre specified distance is chosen to give twice as many centers as there are number of classes in the data set. Some amount of misclassification observed only in classes that are overlapping namely Paddy - Cropland and Evergreen - Coffee both with our method and using PCA. These overlapping classes are better separated with our method, than with PCA. The misclassification is 4.4% with our method. Clustering with first two PCs resulted in misclassification of 15.1% (misclassification is more when clustering is done with more or less than 2 PCs). Out of all sequence of features the order of features according to variances is found to outperform any other sequence. Figures 8 and 9 are the classification maps of the synthetic image using first two PCs and the proposed method.

The proposed method is tested on an image from which the synthetic image was derived. Figure 10 is registered IRS 1A image of Coorg forest cover. Classification maps using PCs and the proposed methods are given in figures 11 and 12.

5 Conclusion

The method suggested in this paper performs dimensionality reduction of multi dimensional data. Feature values of a sample are assimilated in the form of a regression line, thus reducing the dimensions from f (the number of features) to 2. A new distance measure is devised to measure distances between the regression lines. Experiments demonstrated the ability of the method to produce fairly good classifications. The method is very versatile and can be used with any multi spectral data. The method is simple and can perform well on classes that are separable. A disadvantage of the method is that the regression lines tend to average out the existing small differences between the classes. Perhaps the method suggested can be used as pre clustering procedure on data sets with large number of classes to isolate well separable few classes and then coarse clusters obtained may be clustered again using original features. Also if the number of features is too many a single regression line for a sample may bring two well-separated classes together. A higher order regression curve may be a better fit. Such as arbitrary curve can be approximated by piecewise linear segments [4,8], the higher order regression curve can be approximated by piece wise regression line segments. Probable solution is to go for slicing number of features and multiple regression lines for each sample as done in [9] for temporal data.

References

1. Dallas E. Johnson, "Applied Multivariate Methods for Data Analysis", Duxbury Press (1998)
2. P.Nagabhushan, "An effient method for classifying Remotely Sensed Data (incorporating Dimensionality Reduction)", Ph.D thesis, University of Mysore, Mysore, India (1988)
3. H.H.Bock, E.Diday (editors), "Analysis of Symbolic Data", Springer Verlag, (2000)
4. Dunham J.G, "Piecewise linear approximation of planar curves", IEEE Trans. PAMI, vol 8 (1986)

5. Getter-Summa, M., MGS in SODAS, Cahiers du CEREMADE no. 9935, Universite' Paris IX Dauphine, France (1994)
6. Ichino, M., Yaguchi, H., Generalized Minkowski metrics for mixed feature type data analysis, IEEE Trans. Systems Man Cybernet, 24(4) (1994)
7. Jolliffee, I.T., Principal Component Analysis, Springer Verlag, NY (1986)
8. Leung, M.K., Yang, Y.H., Dynamic strip algorithm in curve fitting, Computer Vision Graphics and Image Processing, 51 (1990)
9. Lalitha Rangarajan, Nagabhushan, P., Dimensionality reduction of multi dimensional temporal data through regression, J of PRL, Elsevier, vol 25/8 (2004), 899 - 910
10. Srikantaprakash, H.N., Nagabhushan, P., Gowda, K.C., Symbolic data analysis of multi spectral temporal data, IEEE International Geosci and Remote Sensing symposium, Singapore (1997)
11. Lalitha Rangarajan, Nagabhushan, P., Content driven dimensionality reduction at block level in the design of an efficient classifier for multi spectral images, J of PRL, Elsevier, vol 25 (2004), 1833 - 1844

A New Approach for High-Dimensional Unsupervised Learning: Applications to Image Restoration

Nizar Bouguila and Djemel Ziou

Département d'Informatique, Faculté des Sciences,
Université de Sherbrooke,
Sherbrooke, Qc, Canada J1K 2R1
{nizar.bouguila, djemel.ziou}@usherbrooke.ca

Abstract. This paper proposes an unsupervised algorithm for learning a high-dimensional finite generalized Dirichlet mixture model. The generalized Dirichlet distribution offers high flexibility and ease of use. We propose a hybrid stochastic expectation maximization algorithm (HSEM) to estimate the parameters of the generalized Dirichlet mixture. The performance of our method is tested by applying it to the problems of image restoration.

1 Introduction

High-dimensional data appears in many areas such as pattern recognition, computer vision and signal processing. In problems involving the detection of real-world objects, for example, very high-dimensional feature vectors are necessary. In these conditions, use of probabilistic approaches is always delicate. They suffer from a limitation known as the curse of dimensionality. To avoid problems of dimensionality, the most common approaches involve the use of dimensionality reduction, which has been the subject of much research for the past few decades. A good overview of dimensionality reduction techniques is available in [1].

The approach presented in this paper is not aimed at dimensionality reduction. The data is transformed in such a way that density estimation in the transformed space is simpler and more accurate. This transformation is possible thanks to the convenient mathematical proprieties of the generalized Dirichlet density. In previous works, we have shown that the Dirichlet [2] distribution can be good choices to overcome the disadvantages of the Gaussian. Despite its flexibility, the Dirichlet distribution has a very restrictive negative covariance structure. In this paper, we present a generalization of the Dirichlet distribution which has a more general covariance structure than the Dirichlet distribution. We propose a hybrid stochastic expectation maximization (HSEM) algorithm which is a generalization of the EM algorithm. The algorithm is called stochastic because it contains a step in which the data elements are randomly assigned to components in order to avoid convergence to a saddle point. The adjective "hybrid" is justified by the introduction of a Newton-Raphson step. Moreover, the HSEM algorithm allow high-dimensional probabilistic modeling. The number of clusters is determined by the introduction of an agglomerative term.

2 Learning the Finite Generalized Dirichlet Mixture

If the random vector $\boldsymbol{X} = (X_1, \ldots, X_{dim})$ follows a generalized Dirichlet distribution the joint density function is given by [3]:

$$p(X_1, \ldots, X_{dim}) = \prod_{i=1}^{dim} \frac{\Gamma(\alpha_i + \beta_i)}{\Gamma(\alpha_i)\Gamma(\beta_i)} X_i^{\alpha_i - 1} (1 - \sum_{j=1}^{i} X_j)^{\gamma_i} \quad (1)$$

for $\sum_{i=1}^{dim} X_i < 1$ and $0 < X_i < 1$ for $i = 1 \ldots dim$, where $\gamma_i = \beta_i - \alpha_{i+1} - \beta_{i+1}$ for $i = 1 \ldots dim-1$ and $\gamma_{dim} = \beta_{dim} - 1$. A generalized Finite Dirichlet mixture with M components is defined as: $p(\boldsymbol{X}/\Theta) = \sum_{j=1}^{M} p(\boldsymbol{X}/j, \boldsymbol{\Theta}_j) P(j)$, where the $P(j)$ are the mixing probabilities and $p(\boldsymbol{X}/j, \boldsymbol{\Theta}_j)$ is the generalized Dirichlet distribution. Each $\boldsymbol{\Theta}_j = (\alpha_{j1}, \beta_{j1}, \ldots, \alpha_{jdim}, \beta_{jdim})$ defines the j-th component, and $\Theta = (\boldsymbol{\Theta}_1, \ldots, \boldsymbol{\Theta}_M, P(1), \ldots, P(M))$ is the complete set of parameters needed to specify the mixture. Given a set of N independent vectors $\mathcal{X} = (\boldsymbol{X}_1, \ldots, \boldsymbol{X}_N)$, the log-likelihood corresponding to a M-component mixture is:

$$L(\Theta, \mathcal{X}) = \log \prod_{i=1}^{N} p(\boldsymbol{X}_i/\Theta) = \sum_{i=1}^{N} \log \sum_{j=1}^{M} p(\boldsymbol{X}_i/j, \boldsymbol{\Theta}_j) P(j) \quad (2)$$

It's well-known that the ML estimate: $\hat{\Theta}_{ML} = argmax_\Theta \{L(\Theta, \mathcal{X})\}$. The maximization defining the ML estimates are under constraints ($0 < P(j) < 1$ and $\sum_{j=1}^{M} P(j) = 1$). Obtaining ML estimates of the mixture parameters are possible through EM and related techniques [4]. The EM algorithm produces a sequence of estimate $\{\Theta^t, t = 0, 1, 2 \ldots\}$ by alternatingly applying two steps:

1. **E-step:** Compute the a posteriori probabilities $p(j/\boldsymbol{X}_i, \boldsymbol{\Theta}_j)$.
2. **M-step:** Update the parameters estimates according to: $\hat{\Theta} = argmax_\Theta L(\Theta, \mathcal{X})$

In our approach, we determine the appropriate number of components and the parameters of each component simultaneously by using an agglomerative technique [5]. The objective function, using the Lagrange multiplier Λ to incorporate the constraints about the mixing parameters, is then:

$$\Phi(\Theta, \mathcal{X}) = \sum_{i=1}^{N} \log \sum_{j=1}^{M} p(\boldsymbol{X}_i/j, \boldsymbol{\Theta}_j) P(j) + \Lambda(1 - \sum_{j=1}^{M} P(j)) + \mu \sum_{j=1}^{M} P^2(j) \quad (3)$$

The first term in Eq. 3 is the log-likelihood function, and it assumes its global maximum value when each component represents only one of the feature vectors. The last term (the agglomerative term) reaches its maximum when all of the feature vectors are modeled by a single component, i.e., when $P(j_1) = 1$ for some j_1 and $P(j) = 0, \forall j, j \neq j_1$. The algorithm starts with an over-specified number of components in the mixture, and as it proceeds, components compete to model the data. The update for the *a priori* probabilities can be shown to be:

$$P(j)^{(t)} = \frac{\sum_{i=1}^{N} p(j/\boldsymbol{X_i}, \boldsymbol{\Theta}_j)^{(t-1)} + 2\mu p^2(j)^{(t-1)}}{N + 2\mu \sum_{j=1}^{M} p^2(j)^{(t-1)}} \qquad (4)$$

The value of μ should be chosen such that both terms are of the same order of magnitude. Thus, we choose μ to be the ratio of the first term to the last term in Eq. 3 of each iteration t, i.e.,

$$\mu(t) = y(t) \frac{\sum_{i=1}^{N} ln(\sum_{j=1}^{M} p^{(t-1)}(\boldsymbol{X_i}/j, \boldsymbol{\Theta}_j) P^{(t-1)}(j))}{\sum_{j=1}^{M} P^2(j)^{(t-1)}} \qquad (5)$$

The function $y(t)$ is introduced in order to provide a good transition from the non-agglomerative scheme to the agglomerative one. So the value of μ is increased gradually. The plot of the profile of $y(t)$ versus iteration number is shown in Fig. 1.

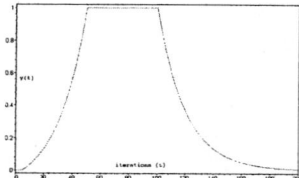

Fig. 1. Plot of the function y(t) versus iterations t

In order to estimate the $\boldsymbol{\Theta}_j$ parameters we will use an interesting property of the generalized Dirichlet distribution. In fact, if a vector $\boldsymbol{X}_i$ has a generalized Dirichlet distribution, then we can construct a vector $\boldsymbol{W}_i = (W_{i1}, \ldots, W_{idim})$ using the following geometric transformation:

$$W_{ij} = T(X_{ij}) = \begin{cases} X_{ij} & \text{if } j = 1 \\ \frac{X_{ij}}{(1-\ldots-X_{ij-1})} & \text{for } j = 2, 3, \ldots, dim \end{cases} \qquad (6)$$

In this vector $\boldsymbol{W}_i$ each W_{id}, $d = 1, \ldots, dim$ has a Beta distribution with parameters α_{id} and β_{id} and the parameters $\{\alpha_{id}, \beta_{id}, d = 1, \ldots, dim\}$ define the generalized Dirichlet distribution which $\boldsymbol{X}_i$ has [3]. Then, the problem of estimating the parameters of a generalized Dirichlet mixture can be reduced to the estimation of the parameters of dim Beta mixtures. For this, we must maximize this equation for every dimension:

$$\Phi_W(\theta_d, \mathcal{W}) = \sum_{i=1}^{N} ln(\sum_{j=1}^{M} p_{beta}(W_{id}/j, \theta_{jd}) P(j)) \qquad (7)$$

where $\mathcal{W} = (W_{1d}, \ldots, W_{Nd})$, $0 < d < dim$, $\theta_d = (\alpha_{1d}, \beta_{1d}, \ldots, \alpha_{Md}, \beta_{Md})$, $\theta_{jd} = (\alpha_{jd}, \beta_{jd})$ and $P(j)$ are the mixing parameters founded by Eq. 4. The

maximization of Eq. 7 is equivalent to: $\frac{\partial}{\partial \theta_{jd}} \Phi_W(\theta_d, \mathcal{W}) = 0 \quad \forall \quad 0 < d < dim$.
In order to estimate the θ_{jd} parameters we have used Fisher's scoring method [6]. The iterative scheme of the Fisher method is given by the following equation:

$$\begin{pmatrix} \hat{\alpha}_{jd} \\ \hat{\beta}_{jd} \end{pmatrix}^{(t)} = \begin{pmatrix} \hat{\alpha}_{jd} \\ \hat{\beta}_{jd} \end{pmatrix}^{(t-1)} + V^{(t-1)} \times \begin{pmatrix} \frac{\partial \Phi_W}{\partial \hat{\alpha}_{jd}} \\ \frac{\partial \Phi_W}{\partial \hat{\beta}_{jd}} \end{pmatrix}^{(t-1)} \tag{8}$$

where j is the class number and d is the current dimension. The matrix V is obtained as the inverse of the Fisher's information matrix. Under sufficiently accurate starting values, the sequence of iterates produced by the Fisher Scoring method enjoys local quadratic convergence to a solution $\hat{\theta}_{jd}$. This rapid convergence can be improved by introducing a Stochastic step in the EM algorithm [7]. In fact, the Stochastic step prevents the sequence of estimates Θ^t from staying near an unstable stationary point of the likelihood function [7]. In order to make our algorithm less sensitive to local maxima, we have used some initialization schemes including the FC-means and the method of moments [2].

INITIALIZATION Algorithm

1. INPUT: X_i, $i = 1, \ldots, N$ and the number of clusters M.
2. Apply the Fuzzy C-means to obtain the elements, covariance matrix and mean of each component.
3. Compute the $W_i = (W_{i1}, \ldots, W_{idim})$ form the X_i.
4. Apply the method of moments for each component j and for each dimension d to obtain the vector of parameters θ_{jd}.
5. Assign the data to clusters, assuming that the current model is correct.
6. If the current model and the new model are sufficiently close to each other, terminate, else go to 4.

With this initialization method in hand, our Hybrid SEM (HSEM) algorithm for estimating of generalized Dirichlet mixture can be summarized as follows:
HSEM Algorithm

1. INPUT: X_i, $i = 1, \ldots, N$ and an over-specified number of clusters M.
2. Apply the INITIALIZATION Algorithm.
3. E-Step: Compute the *a posteriori* probabilities:
$p(j/X_i, \Theta_j) = \frac{p(X_i/j, \Theta_j)P(j)}{\sum_{j=1}^{M} p(X_i/j, \Theta_j)P(j)}$
4. S-Step: For each sample value X_i draw Z_i from the multinomial distribution of order one with M categories having probabilities specified by the $\hat{Z}_{ij}$.
5. M-Step:
    (a) Update the θ_{jd} using Eq. 8, $j = 1, \ldots, M$. and $d = 1, \ldots, dim$.
    (b) Update the $P(j)$ using Eq. 4, $j = 1, \ldots, M$.
6. If $P(j) < \epsilon$ discard component j, go to 3.
7. If the convergence test is passed, terminate, else go to 3.

3 Experimental Results: Image Restoration

Suppose an image has been degraded and we wish to restore it. For this goal, we compare two approaches based on our high-dimensional algorithm and Wiener filtering. We assume that we have a large number of image pairs (original, degraded) for training. In our test, we consider images which are degraded by additive white noise, yet the procedure can be applied for other type of distortion which cannot be expressed simply in mathematical form. For this application, we use an approach proposed in [8]. First, vectors are formed for each original pixel in the training set, as shown in Fig. 2. Next, we apply our algorithm to these vectors. After the mixture's parameters are estimated, they can be used to restore a previously unseen degraded test image in the following way. For each pixel location in a given degraded image, let $X_1, \ldots, X_{dim-1}$ denote the observed values of the neighborhood pixels, and let X_{dim} be the original (unknown) pixel value. The value of X_{dim} is then chosen according to this rule: $X_{dim} = argmax_{X_{dim}} p((X_1, \ldots, X_{dim})/\Theta)$. Figure 3 shows the result of generalized Dirichlet mixture-based restoration in an example where two 256 × 256 images (see Fig 3.a and Fig 3.e) are degraded by additive white Gaussian noise with a variance of 100 (see Fig 3.b and Fig 3.f). The result of Wiener filtering is

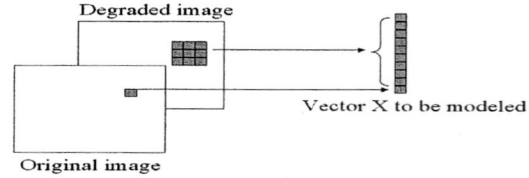

Fig. 2. Formation of data vector X from degraded and original pixels

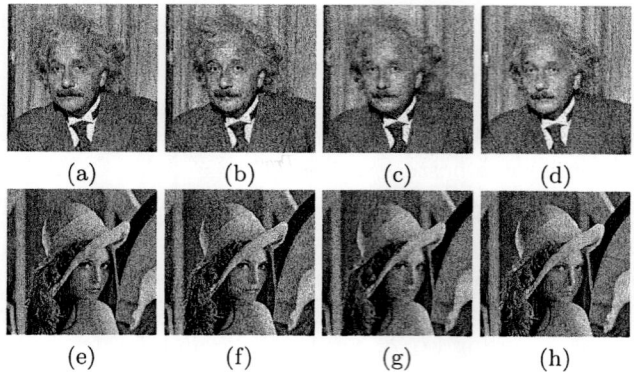

Fig. 3. Image restoration examples. (a) and (e) original images; (b) and (f) degraded; (c) and (g) Wiener filtered; (d) and (h) restored using generalized Dirichlet mixture.

shown in figures 3.c and 3.g. For the generalized Dirichlet mixture model a 3×3 neighborhood was used (dim=9+1=10). We see clearly that the restored images 3.d and 3.h exhibits significant noise reduction and maintain good quality. In order to compare the two approaches (Wiener filtering and our algorithm), we have used the SSIM (Structural SIMilarity) index which is a novel method for measuring the similarity between two images and presented by Wang et al. [9]. Then, we applied this method to compare the original images to the restored ones. The SSIM was 0.72 and 0.8 when we compared the original image in Fig 3.a with the restored images by the Wiener filtering (see Fig. 3.c) and the restored image by our method (see Fig. 3.d), respectively. We have compared the results given by the two methods for the second images (see Fig. 3.e), too. The wiener filtering and our method gave a SSIM index of 0.74 and 0.78, respectively.

4 Conclusion

In this paper, we have focused on high-dimensional data unsupervised learning. The algorithm proposed is motivated by the great number of pattern recognition and image processing applications which involve such types of data. From the experimental results which involve image restoration, we can say that the generalized Dirichlet distribution offers strong modeling capabilities.

References

1. S. Aeberhard, D. Coomans and O. De Vel. Comparative Analysis of Statistical Pattern Recognition Methods in High Dimensional Settings. *Pattern Recognition*, 27(8):1065–1077, 1994.
2. N. Bouguila, D. Ziou and J. Vaillancourt. Unsupervised Learning of a Finite Mixture Model Based on the Dirichlet Distribution and its Application. *IEEE Transactions on Image Processing*, 13(11):1533–1543, November 2004.
3. R. J. Connor and J. E. Mosimann. Concepts of Independence for Proportions With A Generalization of The Dirichlet Distribution. *American Statistical Association Journal*, 64:194–206, 1969.
4. G. J. McLachlan and T. Krishnan. *The EM Algorithm and Extensions.* New York: Wiley-Interscience, 1997.
5. H. Frigui and R. Krishnapuram. A Robust Competitive Clustering Algorithm With Applications in Computer Vision. *IEEE Transactions on PAMI*, 21(5):450–465, 1999.
6. G.J. McLachlan and D. Peel. *Finite Mixture Models.* New York: Wiley, 2000.
7. G. Celeux and J. Diebolt. A Stochastic Approximation Type EM Algorithm for the Mixture Problem. *Stochastics and Stochastics Reports*, 41:119–134, 1992.
8. K. Popat and R. W. Picard. Cluster-Based Probability model and its Application to Image and Texture Processing. *IEEE Transactions on Image Processing*, 6(2):268–284, February 1997.
9. Z. Wang, A. C. Bovik, H. R. Sheikh and E. P. Simoncelli. Image Quality Assessment: From Error Visibility to Structural Similarity. *IEEE Transactions on Image Processing*, 13(4):600–612, April 2004.

Unsupervised Classification of Remote Sensing Data Using Graph Cut-Based Initialization*

Mayank Tyagi[1], Ankit K Mehra[1], Subhasis Chaudhuri[1], and Lorenzo Bruzzone[2]

[1] IIT-Bombay, India
[2] University of Trento, Italy
{mayanktyagi, ankitmehra, sc}@iitb.ac.in,
lorenzo.bruzzone@ing.unitn.it

Abstract. In this paper we propose a multistage unsupervised classifier which uses graph-cut to produce initial segments which are made up of pixels with similar spectral properties, subsequently labelled by a fuzzy c-means clustering algorithm into a known number of classes. These initial segmentation results are used as a seed to the expectation maximization (EM) algorithm. Final classification map is produced by using the maximum likelihood (ML) classifier, performance of which is quite good as compared to other unsupervised classification techniques.

1 Introduction

In literature, two main approaches to the classification problem have been proposed: the supervised approach and the unsupervised approach [1]. The supervised classification methods require the availability of a suitable ground truth (training data) for the classification. On the other hand, the pattern classification using unsupervised techniques can be performed by only considering the information contained in the image itself. Normally, all supervised methods offer a higher accuracy compared to unsupervised classification methods. Unfortunately, in many applications, we do not have ground truth information. In fact, gathering a sufficient number of training samples for each specific image considered, by either photo-interpretation or through the collection of ground truth information, is very expensive in terms of time and economy. Also we have to regularly update this ground truth information since atmospheric conditions and hence digital signatures of different classes change with time. Therefore, in many cases, it is not possible to obtain training data for each image to be classified. So we need good unsupervised methods to perform classification in such cases.

In this paper, we propose a novel multistage unsupervised classifier, based on the maximum likelihood (ML) criterion. This classifier exploits both the region-wise and pixel-wise spectral information included in the image to give reliable classification results. The classical unsupervised classifiers like fuzzy c-means [2] [3], and classifiers using artificial neural network techniques [4] [5] are pixel-based classifiers and do not consider any parametric modeling of the

---

* Funding under Indo-Trento ITPAR project is acknowledged.

population distribution of a class. We present here a hierarchical approach, in which classification is performed on segments generated by graph cut based segmentation, instead of performing on pixel-level. Our approach is based on graph theory based image segmentation and fuzzy classification technique. These initial classification results are used as a seed to an expectation maximization (EM) algorithm. Experimental analysis is carried out on a data set related to the Island of Sardinia (Italy). The results obtained by the proposed unsupervised classifier confirms the effectiveness of the proposed approach.

2 Problem Formulation

Let $\mathbf{X} = \{\mathbf{x}_{1,1}, \mathbf{x}_{1,2}, \ldots, \mathbf{x}_{R,S}\}$ denote a multi spectral image composed of $R \times S$ pixels. Let $\mathbf{x}_{r,s}$ be the $(1 \times j)$ feature vector associated with the pixel at position (r, s) of the image $\mathbf{X}$ (where j is the number of spectral bands present). Let us assume that the set $\Omega = \{\omega_1, \omega_2, \ldots, \omega_M\}$ of M land-cover classes characterizes the considered geographical area in image $\mathbf{X}$. Moreover, it is assumed that the total number of land-cover classes (M) in the set are known *a priori*. Let $l_{r,s}$ be the class label of pixel $\mathbf{x}_{r,s}$.

In the context of the Bayes decision theory [7], the decision rule adopted by the ML classifier for classification is expressed as follows:

$$l_{r,s} \in \omega_m, \text{ if } \omega_m = \arg \max_{\omega_i \in \Omega} \{\hat{P}(\omega_i)\hat{p}(\mathbf{x}_{r,s}|\omega_i)\} \tag{1}$$

where $\hat{P}(\omega_i)$ and $\hat{p}(\mathbf{X}|\omega_i)$ are the estimates of the *a priori* probability and the conditional density function of the class ω_i in the image $\mathbf{X}$, respectively. The training phase of an ML classifier consists in the estimations of the *a priori* probability $P(\omega_i)$ and the conditional density function $p(\mathbf{X}|\omega_i)$ for each class $\omega_i \in \Omega$. In all practical classification approaches, these estimates are obtained by using classical supervised methods that exploit the information included in the appropriate training set for the image. However in our case no training data is available and the probabilities have to be estimated from the data itself.

3 Proposed Unsupervised Classifier

Consider the case in which all classes included in Ω, the land-cover classes set, can be described by Gaussian distributions. The density function associated with each class ω_i can be completely described by the mean vector μ_i, and the covariance matrix Σ_i. Therefore, the parameters to be estimated are:

$$\theta = [\mu_1, \Sigma_1, P(\omega_1), \ldots, \mu_M, \Sigma_M, P(\omega_M)] \tag{2}$$

The estimation of the probabilities becomes a mixture density estimation problem. The expectation maximization (EM) algorithm is one of the most powerful solutions to such type of problems [6]. It can be proved that the required equations for the estimation of means and the covariance matrices for different classes in Ω are the following [7]:

$$P^{k+1}(\omega_i) = \frac{\sum_{\mathbf{x}_{r,s} \in \mathbf{X}} \frac{P^k(\omega_i) p^k(\mathbf{x}_{r,s}|\omega_i)}{p^k(\mathbf{x}_{r,s})}}{R \times S} \qquad (3)$$

$$[\mu_i]^{k+1} = \frac{\sum_{\mathbf{x}_{r,s} \in \mathbf{X}} \frac{P^k(\omega_i) p^k(\mathbf{x}_{r,s}|\omega_i)}{p^k(\mathbf{x}_{r,s})} \mathbf{x}_{r,s}}{\sum_{\mathbf{x}_{r,s} \in \mathbf{X}} \frac{P^k(\omega_i) p^k(\mathbf{x}_{r,s}|\omega_i)}{p^k(\mathbf{x}_{r,s})}} \qquad (4)$$

$$[\Sigma_i]^{k+1} = \frac{\sum_{\mathbf{x}_{r,s} \in \mathbf{X}} \frac{P^k(\omega_i) p^k(\mathbf{x}_{r,s}|\omega_i)}{p^k(\mathbf{x}_{r,s})} \left(\tilde{\mathbf{x}}_{r,s,i} \cdot \tilde{\mathbf{x}}_{r,s,i}^T \right)}{\sum_{\mathbf{x}_{r,s} \in \mathbf{X}} \frac{P^k(\omega_i) p^k(\mathbf{x}_{r,s}|\omega_i)}{p^k(\mathbf{x}_{r,s})}} \qquad (5)$$

where

$$p(\mathbf{x}_{r,s}) = \sum_{i=1}^{M} P(\omega_i) p(\mathbf{x}_{r,s}|\omega_i) \text{ and } \tilde{\mathbf{x}}_{r,s,i} = \mathbf{x}_{r,s} - [\mu_i]^k \qquad (6)$$

k is the iteration index and $R \times S$ is the total number of the pixels in image $\mathbf{X}$.

The EM algorithm is not guaranteed to converge to the global maximum. This is due to the fact that the maximum, whether global or local, to which the algorithm converges depends on the initial seed given for the iterations, i.e. $P^0(\omega_i), \mu^0(\omega_i)$ and $\Sigma^0(\omega_i)$. The proposed classifier obtains the seeds for the iterations through an unsupervised method, from the image $\mathbf{X}$ itself, using the graph cut based image segmentation followed by the fuzzy c-means algorithm.

As the first step, the proposed classifier applies the graph-cut based segmentation technique [8] on the image $\mathbf{X}$ to obtain an over segmentation $\mathbf{G}$ from the image $\mathbf{X}$. This segmentation $\mathbf{G}$ consists of components $\mathbf{C_i}$ such that each $\mathbf{C_i}$ is a connected subgraph of the original graph. It is called an over segmentation because even if two components $\mathbf{C_i}$ and $\mathbf{C_j}$ belong to the same class but are not connected spatially, these components will be considered as two different segments. Therefore, the number of components present will be typically much greater than the number of classes present in the image. This segmentation is done on the basis of spectral properties of the image pixels only. The algorithm by Felzenszwalb and Huttenlocher [8], being fast and accurate, is used for this step. Now, as the number of segments into which the image is divided is greater than the number of classes present, the segments are merged together on the basis of similarity between the means and variances of the two segments being considered. That is, a segment $\mathbf{C}$ belonging to $\mathbf{G}'$, segmentation obtained after merging, is obtained from $\mathbf{G}$ by merging two segments $\mathbf{C}_i \in G$ and $\mathbf{C}_j \in G$, if the differences between the means and variances of two segments is less than some thresholds, which is empirically determined.

At the end of the above step, if the final segmentation $\mathbf{G}' = \{C_1, C_2, \ldots, C_N\}$ has N segments where $N > M$ then the total number of segments N has to be reduced to M segments so that it can be used as seeds for the EM algorithm iterations. For this step fuzzy c-means algorithm is used [2]. That is, say, if $\{\mu_1, \mu_2, \ldots, \mu_N\}$ denotes the mean vector of segments in $\mathbf{G}'$, the fuzzy c-means algorithm is applied on these segments to cluster them and obtain M number of new segments with new means $\{\mu'_1, \mu'_2, \ldots, \mu'_M\}$. To take into account the different sizes of the segments while clustering, each pixel value of a new cluster is multiplied by a weight factor, which is directly proportional to the size of its original cluster, while calculating the new mean for the resulting segment.

After obtaining **M** number of segments and their respective means, the covariance matrices and the membership probabilities for each segment are calculated from the clustered pixels. Now as these segments can be considered as the land cover classes for the area, the corresponding means and covariances can be taken as initial estimates for class conditional density function $p(\mathbf{X}|\omega_\mathbf{i})$ parameters, and the membership probability as the *a priori* class probability $P(\omega_i)$ for all **M** land-cover classes. Thus the initial estimate of θ in equation 2 is obtained. These estimates are then given as seed, $P^0(\omega_i)$ and $p^0(\mathbf{X}|\omega_\mathbf{i})$ to the EM algorithm iterations, which calculates the new parameters for the ML classifier, using the spectral information included in image.

4 Experimental Results

Experiments were carried out on a data set made up of a multi-spectral image acquired by the Thematic Mapper (TM) multi spectral sensor of the Landsat 5 satellite. The selected test site was a section (493×412 *pixels*) of a scene including Lake Mulargias on the Island of Sardinia, Italy acquired in July 1996. Fig. 1(a) shows band 5 of the image. In particular, five land cover classes (i.e. pasture, forest, urban area, water, vineyard) were identified (by domain expert) that characterized the test site at the above date.

The results obtained using proposed classifier, when applied to the image, are shown in Table 1. The table lists the total number of test samples for each class, as well as number of pixels classified accurately by the classifier. As shown in Table 1, the total accuracy obtained by the proposed classifier on the data set is about 80.21%. As a comparison,the fuzzy c-means algorithm on the image gave an accuracy of only 70.12%. Although the proposed classifier outperforms the unsupervised fuzzy c-means classifier by about 10%, the overall accuracy obtained was not too high.

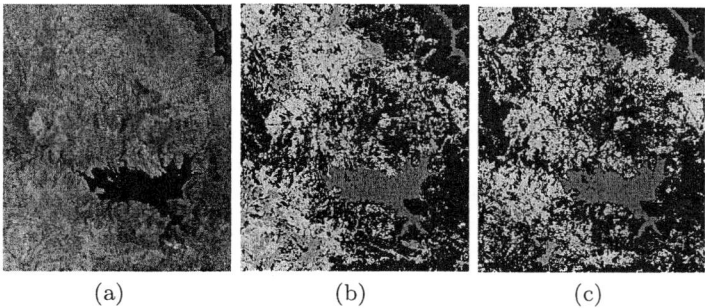

(a) (b) (c)

Fig. 1. (a) Band 5 of a Landsat image. Results of (b) proposed classifier and (c) supervised ML classifier [6].

Table 1. Performance comparison of the proposed method for five classes

Land-Cover Class	Number of test samples	Proposed Unsupervised Classifier(%)	Fuzzy c-means Classifier (%)	Supervised ML Classifier (%)
Pasture	149	46.98	6.71	96.39
Forest	304	63.82	56.56	86.51
Urban Area	408	99.75	75.00	98.78
Water	804	100.00	100.00	100
Vineyard	179	2.23	0.56	82.13
Overall	1844	80.21	70.12	95.64

Table 2. Performance comparison of the proposed method for four classes

Land-Cover Class	Number of test samples	Proposed Unsupervised Classifier(%)	Fuzzy c-means Classifier (%)	Supervised ML Classifier (%)
Pasture+Vineyard	328	59.45	66.46	94.27
Forest	304	65.13	77.63	86.51
Urban Area	408	96.81	47.30	98.28
Water	804	100	100	100
Overall	1844	86.33	78.69	95.99

In order to understand this, when we studied the distributions (in the feature space) of subset of pixels corresponding to all the classes, we observed that two of the land-cover classes (pasture and vineyard) had very similar spectral characteristics and the two corresponding distributions are getting overlapped. Due to this, pixels belonging to one class are getting inaccurately classified to other class, yielding a low classification accuracy. Also, the vineyards are very small regions in the image and some of these regions were not segmented properly by the graph-cut method, further aggravating the cause.

In order to overcome this problem, pixels belonging to these two classes (pasture and vineyard) were taken to be belonging to one class only. Therefore, the problem reduces to classifying four land-cover classes only. The application of the proposed classifier within such a framework gave an accuracy of 86.33% (as shown in Table 2). As a comparison, the corresponding fuzzy c-means classifier gave an overall accuracy of 78.69%, which is notably much lower to that of the proposed classifier. It may be noted that test data set is available only at 1844 pixels, whereas we have classified the entire 493×412 pixels. Since the domain knowledge is not available at all points, the accuracy cannot be computed for the entire land cover. However, a quick look at the classification results shown in Fig. 1(b) suggest that the actual accuracy of the proposed classifier is much higher since it appears to segment a particular class at a given region quite well. In Fig. 1(c), we reproduced the results of supervised classification as developed in [7] using a proper training data, whose accuracy is 95.64%. Compare this to the classification results using the proposed technique given in Fig. 1(b). Given the fact that no training data was provided, the results are still very good. It may be noted that an unsupervised clustering techniques can do segmentation but not the labeling of segments into actual class labels such as waterbody or pasture. The class labels were assigned manually.

5 Conclusions

A novel unsupervised classifier, based on estimating the unknown classifier parameters by using graph cut based segmentation and fuzzy c-means algorithm, has been developed. The EM algorithm is used to learn the class distribution. The proposed method is different from other unsupervised classifiers in the sense that it exploits both the regional as well as pixel wise spectral information contained in the image, giving quite a high accuracy. Our method gave better results than fuzzy c-means and other unsupervised method but the accuracy is still lower than the supervised methods (normally above 90% compared to our 80%). But these initial results can be very helpful to a domain expert who has to assign classes to training samples. If the domain expert has good initial estimates then he/she will have the convenience of assigning classes mostly at a region level rather than at a pixel level.

References

1. R.O. Duda, P.E. Hart, D.G. Stork "Pattern Classification", *John Wiley & Sons, Inc.*, (2001).
2. R. Ehrlich, J.C. Bezedek, W. Full, "FCM: The Fuzzy C-Means Clustering Algorithm", *Comp. Geoscience, vol.10*, (1984) 191-203.
3. I. Gath, A. B. Geva, "Unsupervised Optimal Fuzzy Clustering", *IEEE PAMI, vol. 11*, (1989) 773-780.
4. S. Haykins, "Neural Networks", *Pearson Education*, (1999).
5. D. Kilpatrick, R. Williams, "Unsupervised Classification of Antarctic Satellite Imagery Using Kohonen's Self-Organising Feature Map", *Proceedings, IEEE International Conference on Neural Networks, vol. 1*, (1995) 32-36.
6. T.K. Moon, "The Expectation-Maximization Algorithm", *IEEE Signal Processing Magazine*, (November 1996) 47-60.
7. L. Bruzzone, D.F. Prieto, "Unsupervised Retraining of a Maximum Likelihood Classifier for the Analysis of Multitemporal Remote Sensing Images", *IEEE Transactions On Geoscience And Remote Sensing, Vol. 39, No. 2*, (February 2001) 456-460.
8. P.F. Felzenszwalb and D.P. Huttenlocher, "Efficient Graph-Based Image Segmentation", *International Journal of Computer Vision, Vol. 59, Number 2*, (September 2004)

Hybrid Hierarchical Learning from Dynamic Scenes

Prithwijit Guha[1], Pradeep Vaghela[1], Pabitra Mitra[2],
K.S. Venkatesh[1], and Amitabha Mukerjee[2]

[1] Department of Electrical Engineering,
Indian Institute of Technology, Kanpur,
Kanpur - 208016, UP, India
{pguha, pradeepv, venkats}@iitk.ac.in
[2] Department of Computer Science and Engineering,
Indian Institute of Technology, Kanpur,
Kanpur - 208016, UP, India
{pmitra, amit}@cse.iitk.ac.in

Abstract. The work proposes a hierarchical architecture for learning from dynamic scenes at various levels of knowledge abstraction. The raw visual information is processed at different stages to generate hybrid symbolic/sub-symbolic descriptions of the scene, agents and events. The background is incrementally learned at the lowest layer, which is used further in the mid-level for multi-agent tracking with symbolic reasoning. The agent/event discovery is performed at the next higher layer by processing the agent features, status history and trajectory. Unlike existing vision systems, the proposed algorithm does not assume any prior information and aims at learning the scene/agent/event models from the acquired images. This makes it a versatile vision system capable of performing in a wide variety of environments.

1 Introduction

In recent years, there has been an increasing interest in developing cognitive vision systems capable of interpreting the high level semantics of dynamic scenes. A good overview of cognitive vision system architectures can be found in [1]. Traditional approaches to dynamic scene analysis operate only in restricted environments with predefined and/or learned quantitative object and behavior models. Such models are often fragile and lead to modeling errors; thereby degrading the performance in most practical situations. A hybrid multi-layered vision architecture, consisting of both quantitative and qualitative models which are more robust and immune to modelling errors, essentially processes the visual data at lower levels and extracts worthwhile semantic information for analysis in higher layers.

This work proposes a multi-layered cognitive vision system for agent/event discovery from dynamic scenes, which processes information at various stages of knowledge abstraction, each layer deriving its percept model from the observations obtained from lower level(s). The system initializes with a few preset capabilities involving scene feature (color and shape) extraction, and applies multi-agent tracking with symbolic reasoning, unsupervised agent categorization and event discovery with variable length Markov models. Raw visual data is processed at the lowest level to yield a perception of the background model of the scene. A hybrid analysis involving symbolic reasoning and feature extraction from the image data is performed at the mid-level for multi-agent tracking. The higher layer essentially categorizes the quantitative agent features and qualitative event descriptors in an unsupervised learning framework. The system can be further extended into upper layers depending on the application context, which typically requires user interaction for tagging learned categories and generating linguistic descriptions. Figure 1 shows the functional architecture of the proposed framework.

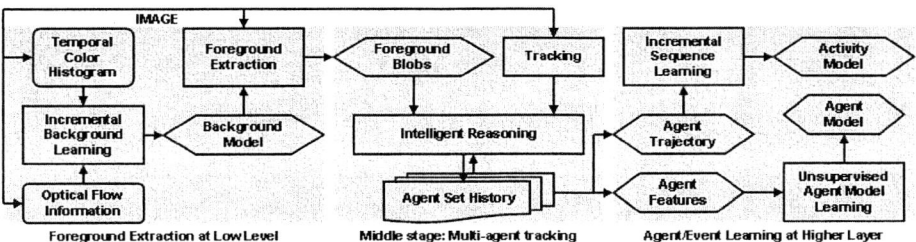

Fig. 1. The Proposed hierarchical scene analysis architecture

The paper is organized in the following manner. Section 2 explains the processing at the lower level of the proposed system. The symbolic reasoning for multi-agent tracking at the mid-level are explored in Section 3. Agent categorization and event discovery are described in Section 4. The results of experimentation are briefly described in Section 5. Finally, we conclude the paper in Section 6.

2 Background Learning for Low Level Vision

Traditional vision systems with an object centered approach learn the background with a specific signal model from a few initially unintruded (pure background) frames. However, in most practical cases, signal models do change and pure background frames can't be availed of for training. Thus, a view centered approach is to be adopted for estimating the background model in an adaptive learning framework. The usual approach to incremental background modeling involves fitting (temporally evolving) Gaussian mixture models [2] on the temporal pixel color histogram. Recently, Gutches et al. [3] have proposed an online background learning algorithm, which combines the temporal histogram features along with optical flow information leading to improved modeling performance. This approach is adopted in our work for modeling the background $\mathbf{B}_t$ learned till the tth instant. This is used to perform the background-foreground segmentation of the image Ω_t followed by a connected component analysis to generate the set $\mathcal{F}_t = \{F_i(t)\}_{i=1}^{n_t}$ of disjoint foreground blobs. The extracted foreground blobs are used for symbolic reasoning to track multiple agents at the mid-level of visual

Fig. 2. Background learning. (a) Sample traffic scene, (b) Background learned after 100 frames, (c) Foreground blobs extracted from (a) using (b).

processing. The results of foreground extraction with incremental background learning (from a traffic video sequence) are illustrated in figure 2.

3 Symbolic Reasoning for Multi-agent Tracking

Agent/event discovery primarily depends on the availability of reliable features and is often challenged by occlusions arising out of crowding and obstructions by background objects. Unlike conventional object oriented approaches [4] to occlusion handling that assume prior shape and motion models and also a ground plane, we propose a reasoning scheme that is not restricted by specific agent/environment models and detects several event primitives. This assists the learning process in selective agent feature updates. [5] provides a detailed discussion of multi-agent tracking which we summarize here.

Intelligent reasoning is performed over an *active* set $\mathcal{S}_A(t) = \{\mathcal{A}_j(t)\}_{j=1}^{m_t}$ containing agents tracked till the tth instant and also a *putative* set $\mathcal{S}_P(t)$ of agents of which the system has lost track. The system initializes itself with empty sets and the agents are added (removed) as they appear (disappear) in (from) the field of view. The jth agent in the active set is characterized by its occupied pixel set $A_j(t)$, weighted color distribution $h_j(t)$ and the order-τ trajectory of the center $C_j(t)$ of the minimum bounding rectangle of $A_j(t)$. Mean-shift iterations [6] initialized with the motion predicted position from the trajectory $\{C_j(t-t')\}_{t'=1}^{\tau}$ are used to localize $A_j(t)$ in the tth frame. To associate the jth agent with the ith foreground blob, we construct the thresholded *localization confidence matrix* $\Theta_{AF}(t)$ and the *attribution confidence matrix* $\Psi_{FA}(t)$. Measures of foreground regions per agent ($\Theta_A[j](t)$ and $\Psi_A[j](t)$) and agents per foreground region ($\Theta_F[i](t)$ and $\Psi_F[i](t)$) can be computed from these matrices.

$$\Theta_{AF}[j,i](t) = \begin{cases} 1; & \frac{|A_j(t) \cap F_i(t)|}{|A_j(t)|} \geq \eta_A \\ 0; & \text{Otherwise} \end{cases} ; \Psi_{FA}[i,j](t) = \begin{cases} 1; & \frac{|A_j(t) \cap F_i(t)|}{|F_i(t)|} \geq \eta_F \\ 0; & \text{Otherwise} \end{cases} \quad (1)$$

$$\Theta_A[j](t) = \sum_{i=1}^{n_t} \Theta_{AF}[j,i](t), \qquad \Theta_F[i](t) = \sum_{j=1}^{m_{t-1}} \Theta_{AF}[j,i](t) \quad (2)$$

$$\Psi_A[j](t) = \sum_{i=1}^{n_t} \Psi_{FA}[i,j](t), \qquad \Psi_F[i](t) = \sum_{j=1}^{m_{t-1}} \Psi_{FA}[i,j](t) \quad (3)$$

We construct four Boolean predicates: IsUnOccTrk$_j(t)$ for agent *isolated, unoccluded and well tracked*; LostTrack$_j(t)$ for agent *lost track of*; IsoPartOcc$_j(t)$ for agent *partially occluded*; Crowd$_j(t)$ for agent *in a crowd*.

$$\text{IsoUnOccTrk}_j(t) = \exists i [\Theta_{AF}[j,i](t) = 1] \wedge [\Theta_F[i](t) = 1] \wedge [\Psi_F[i](t) = 1] \quad (4)$$
$$\text{LostTrack}_j(t) = [\Theta_A[j](t) = 0] \wedge [\Psi_A[j](t) = 0] \quad (5)$$
$$\text{IsoPartOcc}_j(t) = \forall i [\Psi_{FA}[i,j](t) = 1] \wedge [\Psi_F[i](t) = 1] \wedge [\Psi_A[j](t) > 1] \quad (6)$$
$$\text{Crowd}_j(t) = \exists i [\Theta_{AF}[j,i] = 1] \wedge [\Theta_F[i](t) > 1] \quad (7)$$

Fig. 3. Cases of occlusions. (a-b) Partial occlusions: agent detected as multiple foreground blobs; (c-d) Crowding: multiple agents merge to form a single blob.

Color, shape and trajectory of individual agents under IsoUnOccTrk, but only the trajectory of agents under IsoPartOcc and Crowd are continuously updated. Agents under LostTrack are moved from the active set to the putative set.

The **entry/reappearance** of an agent is attributed to the existence of a foreground blob $F_i(t)$ in the scene having no association with any agent from $\mathcal{S}_A(t-1)$. Hence, the corresponding Boolean predicate $\text{NewBlob}_i(t)$ is,

$$\text{NewBlob}_i(t) = [\Theta_F[i](t) = 0] \wedge [\Psi_F[i](t) = 0] \quad (8)$$

The features of the new blob $F_i(t)$ are matched against those in $\mathcal{S}_P(t-1)$ to search for the reappearance of agents. If a match is found, the agent is moved from $\mathcal{S}_P(t-1)$ to $\mathcal{S}_A(t)$. Otherwise, a new agent's entry is declared and is added to $\mathcal{S}_A(t)$. Similarly, an agent is declared to **exit** the scene, if its motion predicted region lies outside the image region and is thus removed from the active set.

The vision system often encounters the phenomenon of **splitting**, when two (or more) agents enter the scene in a group and separate later within the field of view. In such cases, they are initially learned as a single agent and the split is eventually detected as a fragmentation (such as that caused by partial occlusion) for the first few frames (the exact number depends on the relative velocity between separating agents). Afterwards, the tracker converges on one agent and loses track of the other(s), which eventually emerge as a new region(s) and is (are) added as new agent(s).

4 Discovery of Agents and Events

The agents are essentially represented by their color, shape and motion features. The instances of the same class can have significantly different color and motion features, thereby leaving the shape as a more reliable descriptor. In this work, we opt for the second to seventh order Zernike moments [7], which serve as a shape feature. The shape feature vector $X_j(t)$ of the jth agent is only computed when the agent is isolated and well localized and a Gaussian mixture model is incrementally learned over this feature set. Empirically, the selected feature set seems to provide consistent classification which agrees well with that of a human observer. The categorization algorithm has successfully classified the instances of *man*, *man on bike*, *vehicle* and *rickshaw* (figure 4(a)-(d)).

Events are of two different categories, viz. *actions* (characteristic state space trajectories of individual agents) and *interactions* (activities involving multiple agents). Typical examples of actions are the path taken by a vehicle in a traffic scenario or the pose sequence exhibited by a dancer. The events of chasing, overtaking of vehicles refer to interactions in a homogeneous group and the examples for a heterogeneous group include activities like boarding a vehicle, riding a bike etc. Variable length Markov models (VLMMs) have been used previously for the purpose of learning actions [8] and interactions [9]. In this work, we apply the VLMMs for online event discovery by learning the frequent sequences of symbolic descriptors acquired earlier. A detailed discussion on learning with VLMMs can be found in [8].

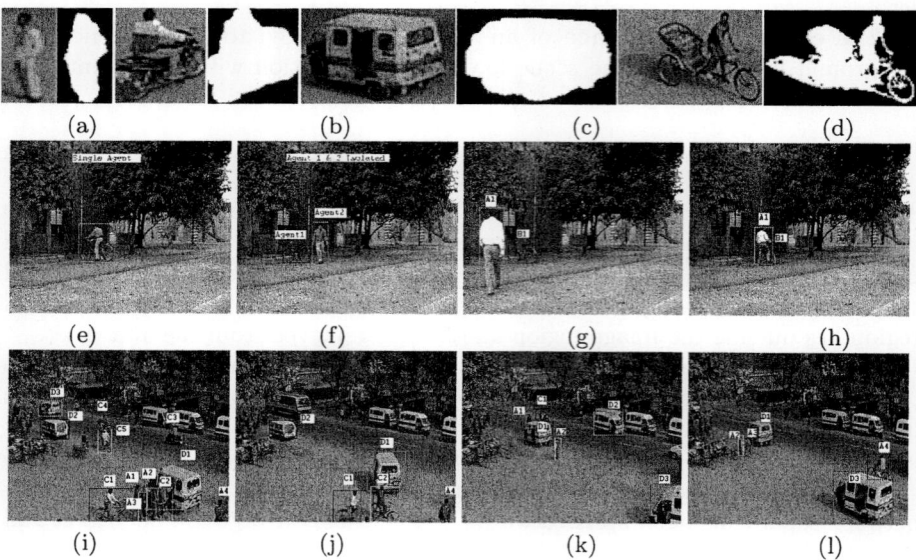

Fig. 4. Instances of learned agents. (a) Man, (b) Man on Bike, (c) Vehicle, (d) Rickshaw. Discovered multi-agent interactions. (e-f) Person on cycle detected followed by person-cycle split: person getting off a cycle, (g-h) Person and cycle isolated followed by person-cycle crowded: The event of person embarking a bicycle, (i-j) A heterogeneous crowd followed by track loss of several agents: people embarking a vehicle, (k-l) Isolated vehicle followed by vehicle-person split: The event of disembarking from a vehicle.

5 Results

The proposed algorithm for event discovery from dynamic scenes is applied to a traffic scenario. The agents and events are discovered online from a video sequence acquired with a static camera. The multi-agent tracking algorithm provides us with symbolic descriptors of object states at each time instant. We assume the interacting agents to be present within a specific attentional window. spatio-temporal interactions are learned as frequently co-occurring sets of agent states. Results show the discovery of events like a *man boarding a bicycle*, *man disembarking the bicycle*, *people boarding vehicle* and *people getting off from vehicle*. The results of discovered sequences are shown in figure 4.

6 Conclusion

We have proposed a hierarchical architecture for discovering events from dynamic scenes. Symbolic and sub-symbolic learning is performed at different processing levels in the hierarchy. The architecture requires minimal prior knowledge of the environment and attempts to learn the semantic informations of dynamic scenes. Qualitative reasoning at a higher level induces tolerance to learning error at lower levels . This makes it suitable for a wide range of applications.

References

1. Granlund, G.: Organization of architectures for cognitive vision systems. In: Proceedings of Workshop on Cognitive Vision, Schloss Dagstuhl, Germany (2003)
2. Stauffer, C., Grimson, W.: Adaptive background mixture models for real-time tracking. In: Proceedings of IEEE Conference on Computer Vision and Pattern Recognition. Volume 2., IEEE Computer Society (1999) 246–252
3. Gutchess, D., Trajkovics, M., Cohen-Solal, E., Lyons, D., Jain, A.K.: A background model initialization algorithm for video surveillance. In: Proceedings of Eighth IEEE International Conference on Computer Vision. Volume 1. (2001) 733–740
4. Haritaoglu, I., Harwood, D., Davis, L.: W4 : Real time surveillance of people and their activities. IEEE Transactions on Pattern Analysis and Machine Intelligence **22** (2000) 809–830
5. Guha, P., Mukerjee, A., Venkatesh, K.: Efficient occlusion handling for multiple agent tracking with surveillance event primitives. In: The Second Joint IEEE International Workshop on Visual Surveillance and Performance Evaluation of Tracking and Surveillance. (2005)
6. Comaniciu, D., Ramesh, V., Meer, P.: Kernel-based object tracking. IEEE Transaction on Pattern Analysis Machine Intelligence **25** (2003) 564–575
7. Teague, M.R.: Image analysis via the general theory of moments. Optical Society of America **70** (1980) 920–930
8. Galata, A., Johnson, N., Hogg, D.: Learning variable-length markov models of behavior. Computer Vision and Image Understanding **81** (2001) 398–413
9. Johnson, N., Galata, A., Hogg, D.: The acquisition and use of interaction behavior models. In: Proceedings of IEEE Conference on Computer Vision and Pattern Recognition, IEEE Computer Society (1998) 866–871

Reference Extraction and Resolution for Legal Texts

Mercedes Martínez-González[1], Pablo de la Fuente[1], and Dámaso-Javier Vicente[2]

[1] Grupo de Investigación en Recuperación de Información y Bibliotecas Digitales (GRINBD), Universidad de Valladolid, Spain
{mercedes, pfuente}@infor.uva.es
[2] Dpto. de Derecho Mercantil, Derecho del Trabajo e Internacional Privado, Universidad de Valladolid, Spain
damaso@der.uva.es

Abstract. An application to the legal domain of information extraction is presented. Its goal is to automate the extraction of references from legal documents, their resolution, and the storage of their information in order to facilitate an automatic treatment of these information items by services offered in digital libraries. References are extracted matching the texts in the collection against sets of patterns, using grammars.

1 Introduction

Legal documents[1] are highly related by references within them. These references are precious information: a rule can not be correctly interpreted without reading some of the referenced items, or they can be used to answer queries as *What documents reference this one?*, *What is the most referenced document in this category?*.

References in legal texts always refer to intellectual entities (laws, decrees, conventions, ...). One of these entities can be addressed in several different manners, all of them correct and without ambiguity. A document can be referenced, e.g., by its year and number or by its title. The *internal structure* of legal texts is used by legal texts authors to precise in references "where" inside a document can be found the rules governing a given subject-matter [5].

We present a information extraction problem. The information extracted are references, which follow regular patterns [9]. References are used to extend services in digital libraries: querying, hypertext services.

2 The Reference Extraction and Resolution Software

The extraction of references and their resolution consists in an analysis of document content. The document is checked from start to end, searching strings

---

[1] The term "document" here designates the intellectual entity users or authors have in mind. It may or not correspond unidirectionally to any of the physical objects stored in a digital system databases.

corresponding to references, either to the analyzed document (internal references) or to other documents (external references). The extraction is a sequence of three subprocesses: the **detection** inside document content of the references (strings), the **resolution** of those references to some item (document, document fragment) between the collection of available documents, and, finally, the **storage** of the information associated to the reference in some database.

These tasks are the responsibility of software tools shown in figure 1. The *document analyzer* gets a document to extract references. It collaborates with a *pattern recognizer*, which extracts patterns from pieces of text it receives from the document analyzer. This component has information about the vocabulary used to name legal items, and knows the grammar associated to each type of reference (references are classified according to a taxonomy). The result of the analysis is a set of data: for each reference, the string found, and some data containing information about it (source document, fragment that contains the reference, target document, referred fragment).

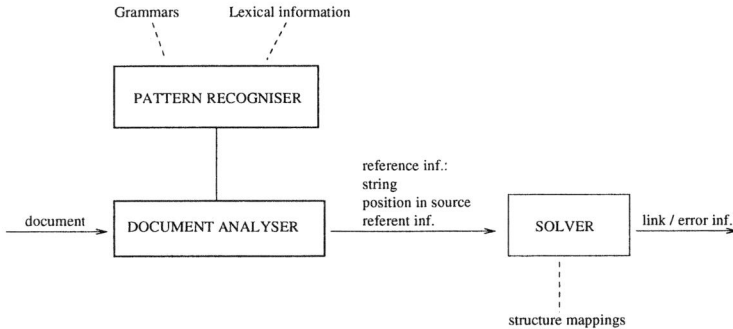

Fig. 1. Software for a reference extraction prototype

These data are processed by the *solver*, which tries to match each reference to some legal item. If it is not able to do it, the solver generates an error message which is associated to the reference, so as the other services in the digital library know that the reference has not been correctly solved. Otherwise, it generates a link that is stored in a link database.

3 Methodology

The extraction of references, their resolution, and the validation of both processes is organized in the following steps:

1. A human examination of 50 documents is made to extract references (strings). In parallel we studied some manuals about legal texts creation [5], that provide some rules about citing legal texts.
2. *Patterns* and vocabularies are characterized and a set of grammar rules is obtained.

Table 1. Results of the experiments

Collection	References detected	Relevant references	Recall
Collection 1	312	423	74%
Collection 2	268	496	54%

3. The extraction is *implemented* (using the grammars obtained in the previous step) and tested on two collections of legal texts. A set of data about references is obtained. The first collection (*'Collection 1'*) is the set of 50 documents used in the previous steps to obtain the patterns. The second collection (*'Collection 2'*) is a set of 14 documents provided by a legal text publisher –*LexNova S.A.*–, in which references are already tagged. This phase includes the three extraction steps described in section 2.

   As the aim was also to evaluate the process, we extracted other data useful for this goal:

   (a) >From the *Collection 1* we select a subset of six documents, on which we carefully revise the set of references extracted manually (this manual work is the reason to limit the number of documents used for the evaluation). That is, we have two types of output data: the reference data set, which is the normal output of the extraction process, and the set of references found manually, generated for validation purposes.

   (b) For the 14 documents provided by the legal publisher we mine the marks that this publisher had included in documents to point to references. This is indeed another extraction, in which we analyze every document to find the marks (and associated references).

4. The last step is the *validation*, which also differs for the two collections:

   (a) For the references extracted from *Collection 1*, the strings set obtained during the extraction is compared to the set of references obtained by human examination.

   (b) With the references of the publisher's collection what we do is to compare the data generated by the application with the data mined from the legal publisher's marks.

Table 1 shows the results for both collections. It shows the number of references detected by the automatic extractor, the number of references present in the collection and the percentage of success (number of relevant references detected over the number of relevant references present in the collection), name *recall*. The results are better with the collection used to obtain the grammars (*Collection 1*), which is logical. Some variations in the patterns of references that appear in the legal text publisher's collection are not present in the first collection. For example, a reference as '*art. 20 y la DA sexta*' (*article 20 and the Sixth Additional Disposition*) contains abbreviations ('*art.*', '*DA*') which are specific to this collection, and in consequence, they are not discovered by the recognizer.

4 Related Work

Some experiences in the area of automatic hypertext creation using information extraction techniques are applied to legal documents [3,1,2]. Pattern recognition is done with grammars in some of them; grammars are appropriate because patterns in legal documents have a high level of regularity. Outside the legal domain, references (mainly scientific references) have also been the target of several efforts [7,6,4,8].

5 Conclusions and Future Work

An application of pattern matching for reference extraction was presented. The work includes the extraction of references, but also their resolution, and validation, whose results are encouraging. There is a wide range of open possibilities for future work. Currently, we are working on extending the tests and evaluation to more types of legal documents, including European Union legal texts.

References

1. Agosti, M., Crestani, F., and Melucci, M. On the use of information retrieval techniques for the automatic construction of hypertext. *Information Processing and Management 33*, 2 (1997), 133–44.
2. Bolioli, A., Dini, L., Mercatali, P., and Romano, F. For the automated mark-up of italian legislative texts in XML. In *Legal Knowledge and Information Systems. JURIX 2002: 15th Annual Conference.* (London, UK, Dec. 2002), T. Bench Capon, D. A., and W. R., Eds., IOS Press, Amsterdam, Netherlands, pp. 21–30.
3. Choquette, M., Poulin, D., and Bratley, P. Compiling legal hypertexts. In *Database and Expert Systems Applications, 6th International Conference, DEXA'95* (Sept. 1995), N. Revell and A. M. Tjoa, Eds., vol. 978 of *Lecture Notes in Computer Science*, Springer, pp. 449–58.
4. Ding, Y., Chowdhury, G., and Foo, S. Template mining for the extraction of citation from digital documents. In *Proceedings of the Second Asian Digital Library Conference* (Nov. 1999), pp. 47–62.
5. Grupo de Estudios de Técnica Legislativa. *Curso de técnica legislativa GRETEL*. Serie de Técnica Legislativa I. Centro de Estudios Constitucionales, Madrid, 1989.
6. Lawrence, S., Giles, C. L., and Bollacker, K. Digital libraries and autonomous citation indexing. *IEEE Computer 32*, 6 (1999), 67–71.
7. Lawson, M., Kemp, N., Lynch, M., and Chowdhury, G. Automatic extraction of citations from the text of english language patents: An example of template mining. *Journal of Information Science 22*, 6 (1996), 423–36.
8. Moens, M.-F., Angheluta, R., and Dumortier, J. Generic technologies fonr single- and multi-document summarization. *Information processing & Management 41* (2005), 569–86.
9. Wilson, E. Links and structures in hypertext databases for law. In *European Conference on Hypertext, ECHT'90* (Paris (France), 1990), A. Rizk, N. A. Streitz, and J. André, Eds., The Cambridge Series on Electronic Publishing, Cambridge University Press, pp. 194–211.

Effective Intrusion Type Identification with Edit Distance for HMM-Based Anomaly Detection System

Ja-Min Koo and Sung-Bae Cho

Dept. of Computer Science, Yonsei University,
Shinchon-dong, Seodaemoon-ku, Seoul 120-749, Korea
{icicle, sbcho}@sclab.yonsei.ac.kr

Abstract. As computer security becomes important, various system security mechanisms have been developed. Especially anomaly detection using hidden Markov model has been actively exploited. However, it can only detect abnormal behaviors under predefined threshold, and it cannot identify the type of intrusions. This paper aims to identify the type of intrusions by analyzing the state sequences using Viterbi algorithm and calculating the distance between the standard state sequence of each intrusion type and the current state sequence. Because the state sequences are not always extracted consistently due to environmental factors, edit distance is utilized to measure the distance effectively. Experimental results with buffer overflow attacks show that it identifies the type of intrusions well with inconsistent state sequences.

1 Introduction

As the computer environment changes rapidly, the security mechanism plays an important role. Intrusion means the behavior which impairs the computer system by anomalous way [1] and it damages to the integrity, secrecy and availability of information [2]. To protect the computer system from the intrusions, a variety of security mechanisms such as firewalls have been developed. Intrusion detection system (IDS) is the representative among them [3]. Intrusion detection techniques are divided into two groups according to the type of data they use: misuse detection and anomaly detection. The former uses the knowledge about attacks and the latter does normal behaviors. However, most of IDSs have some technical inertia such as inability of detecting the cause and the path of intrusion because they have been developed to improve the detection rates. In case of misuse detection, it detects known intrusions very well because it is based on the known intrusion information, but it has vulnerability to transformed or novel intrusions. On the other hand, in case of anomaly detection, it can warn the intrusions but it cannot identify the type of intrusions. Moreover, it is very difficult to detect intrusions because it is possible to penetrate the system in other ways even if intrusions are of identical types. Accordingly, it is hard to take actions for each intrusion type in anomaly detection system.

To solve this problem, we analyzed the state sequences of each intrusion type using Viterbi algorithm in HMM-based intrusion detection system, and identified the type of intrusions by comparing the similarity using Euclidean distance [4]. However, since sequences are not always consistently extracted due to environmental factors, it is difficult to identify the type of intrusions even though identical intrusions are attempted. In this paper, we propose a method to identify the type of intrusions using Viterbi algorithm with edit distance, and verify the usefulness by comparing with the results of other distance measures.

2 Related Works

There are several techniques for IDSs based on anomaly detection such as expert system, statistics, neural network and hidden Markov model (HMM) as shown in Table 1.

Hidden Markov Model (HMM): HMM proposed by C. Warender in New Mexico University is good at modeling and estimating with event sequences which are unknown. It performs better to model the system than any others [5]. However, it takes long time to train and detect intrusions. To overcome such disadvantages, we can extract the events of changing the privilege before and after them, and we are able to model the normal behavior with them. By using this method, we can reduce the time to model and maintain good performance [6].

Table 1. Summary of the representative anomaly detection system (ES: Expert System, NN: Neural Network, ST: Statistics, HMM: hidden Markov model)

Organization	Name	Period	Technique			
			ES	NN	ST	HMM
AT&T	Computer Watch	1987-1990	X			
UC Davis	NSM	1989-1995			X	
	GrIDS	1995-	X			
SRI International	IDES	1983-1992			X	
	NIDES	1992-1995			X	
	EMERALD	1996-			X	
CS Telecom	HyperView	1990-1995		X	X	
New Mexico Univ.	C. Warender, et. al [5]	1999			X	X
Yonsei Univ.	YSCIDS [6]	1999-				X

3 Proposed Method

An IDS based on HMM collects and abridges normal auditing data, and it makes normal behavior models for a specific system, and then it detects intrusions with auditing data to detect the intrusions from it. Finally, to identify the type of intrusions, we analyze the state sequences of the system call events using the Viterbi algorithm [4]. Figure 1 shows the overall structure of the proposed method.

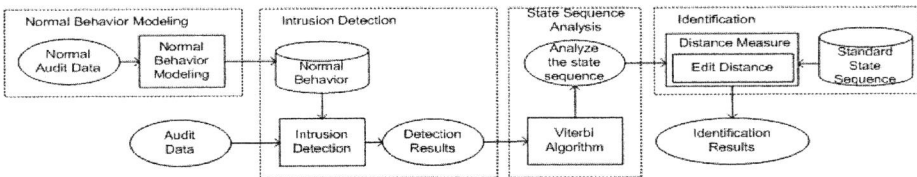

Fig. 1. Overall structure of the proposed method

We measure the similarity between the state sequences extracted and the standard state sequences of each intrusion type using edit distance. Edit distance is based on dynamic programming, and the result of edit distance is the minimal cost of sequence of operations that are used to compare strings x and y.

- $\delta(\varepsilon, a)$: inserting the letter a into string ε
- $\delta(a, \varepsilon)$: deleting the letter a from string ε
- $\delta(a, b)$: replacing a by b, for $a \neq b$

A matrix $C_{0...|x|, 0...|y|}$ is filled, where $C_{i,j}$ represents the minimum number of operations needed to match $x_{1...i}$ to $y_{1...j}$. This is computed as follows for $C_{|x|,|y|} = ed(x,y)$ at the end

$$C_{i,0} = i \quad C_{0,j} = j \quad C_{i,j} = \text{if}(x_i = y_j) \text{ then } C_{i-1,j-1} \text{ else } 1 + \min(C_{i-1,j}, C_{i,j-1}, C_{i-1,j-1})$$

The rationale of the above formula is as follows. First, $C_{0,j}$ represents the edit distance between a string of length i or j and the empty string. Clearly, i and j deletions are needed for the nonempty string. For two non-empty strings of length i and j, we assume inductively that all the edit distances between shorter strings have already been computed, and try to convert $x_{1...x}$ into $y_{1...j}$.

Dynamic programming algorithm must fill the matrix in such a way that the upper, left and upper-left neighbors of a cell are computed prior to computing that cell. This is easily achieved by either a row-wise left-to-right traversal or a column-wise top-to-bottom traversal.

In our problem, we use the edit distance to measure the similarity of intrusion types. When intrusions occur, it calculates the distances between the standard state sequences and the current state sequence. Afterward, input state sequence is identified with the corresponding intrusion type of which the distance is the smallest. However, this algorithm has a weakness in case of input sequences as shown in Table 2.

Table 2. An example of the edit distance's in malfunction

A	1	2	3	4	5
B	1	2	3	2	4
C	1	2	3	5	5
Input	1	3	3	5	

Assuming that the input sequences are given as Table 2, we can recognize that one of input state sequences is deleted and substituted with all classes, A, B and C, and the results of edit distance are all 2. Therefore, we cannot identify the type using normal edit distance. Therefore, we use a modified edit distance with weighting facility to identify the type of intrusions well, and the formula is as follows.

$C_{0,0} = 0$
$C_{i,j} = \text{if } x_i = y_j$
   $\min(C_{i-1,j-1})$
else
   $\min(w_{\delta(a,b)} \times C_{i-1,j-1} \times abs(a,b), w_{\delta(a,\varepsilon)} \times C_{i-1,j} \times abs(a,\varepsilon), w_{\delta(\varepsilon,a)} \times C_{i,j-1} \times abs(\varepsilon,a))$
where $w_{\delta(\varepsilon,a)} = 1; w_{\delta(a,\varepsilon)} = 2; w_{\delta(a,b)} = 3$

4 Experiments

We have collected normal behaviors from six users for 2 weeks using Solaris 7 operating system. They have mainly used text editor, compiler and program of their own writing. In total 13 megabytes (160,448 events are recorded) of BSM audit data are used. Among many intrusions, buffer overflow gets root privileges by abusing systems' vulnerability. We try to penetrate 30 times of each intrusion type. There are 3 kinds of intrusion types called OpenView xlock Heap Overflow, Lpset –r Buffer Overflow Vulnerability and Kcms_sparc Configuration Overflow. The first is used to overflow the buffer by inputting the environmental value which is larger than 1024 bytes. At that time when the buffer is overflow, we can obtain the root privileges by inputting arbitrary commands. The second is the package for setting the printer. Local user can obtain the root privileges with this package operating with long commands with –r flag value. The third overflow is in an sprintf() call that occurs when kcms_sparc configuration is called with -o -S flag value which is larger than 1024 bytes.

In this paper, we use the edit distance for identifying the type of intrusions. To verity the usefulness, we use other 3 kinds of distance measures for comparing the performance: Euclidean distance, Hamming distance and Longest Common Subsequence (LCS).

(1) Euclidean Distance
When intrusions are occurred, the similarity can be compared between the standard state sequence for every intrusion type and the state sequence of current intrusion using Euclidean distance. The formula is as follows.

$$ed = \sqrt{\sum_{i=1}^{N}(x_i - y_i)^2}$$

Assuming the analyzed state sequence of current intrusion to x_i, and the state sequence of every intrusion type to y_j, we calculate the Euclidean distance ed. The smaller the value is, the higher the similarity is. Hence, the intrusion type that we have found has the least value of ed.

(2) Hamming Distance
Hamming distance is used to compare the similarity between two strings whose lengths are the same. The formula is as follows.

$$hd(x, y) = \sum_{i=0}^{n-1} hd(x_i, y_i) \qquad hd(x_i, y_i) = \begin{cases} 0 & x_i = y_i \\ 1 & x_i \neq y_i \end{cases} \quad (\textit{iff}.\ |x|=|y|=k)$$

(3) Longest Common Sequence (LCS)
It is the way to calculate the longest common sequence between two sequences: the more common the sequences are, the higher the similarity is. The formula is as follows.

$$C[i, j] = \begin{cases} 0 & \text{if } i = 0 \text{ or } j = 0 \\ C[i-1, j-1] + 1 & \text{if } i, j > 0 \text{ and } x_i = y_j \\ \max(C[i, j-1], C[i-1, j]) & \text{if } i, j > 0 \text{ and } x_i \neq y_j \end{cases}$$

At first, we conduct the experiments of HMM with varying the number of states from 5 to 30, and observation lengths of 10 and 15. If the number of states is set by small value, the state sequences of all intrusion types are extracted consistently because of the possible state transition paths limitation. Therefore, we have difficulties in identifying the type of intrusions with the number of states less then 20. Figure 2(a) shows the performance of the HMM-based IDS with the number of states 15 and 20, and observation lengths 10 and 15.

We have set the experimental environment with the number of states 20 and the number of observation lengths 10 for identifying the type of intrusions, and compared the performance using various distance measures. Figure 2(b) shows the performance among 4 kinds of distance measures.

We can observe that the performance of using edit distance is better than those of the others as shown in Figure 2(b). Especially, since LCS and Hamming distance only

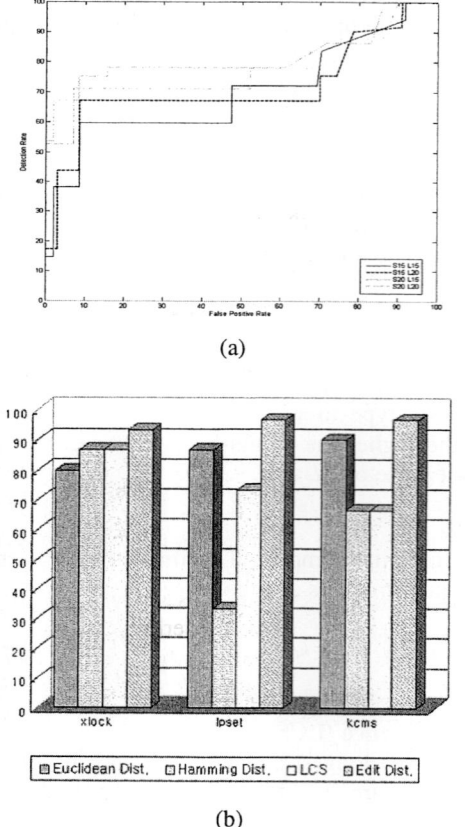

Fig. 2. (a) Performance of HMM-based IDS (X-axis: False Positive Rate Y-axis: Detection Rate) (b) Results of the success rates of each distance measure (X-axis: Intrusion Type Y-axis: Accuracy of Identification)

compare the state sequence one by one and check up whether the sequences are identical or not, the performance is lower than any other when trying to identify the lpset intrusion type.

Table 3. Examples of the input state sequence

	1	2	3	4	5	6	7	8	9	10	Type
Case 1	0	2	4	6	8	8	10	10	12	14	
Case 2	0	2	4	6	8	8	10	12	14	16	KCMS
Case 3	0	2	3	5	7	9	11	13	17	18	

For example, assume that the standard state sequences are given as Table 3 and input state sequence is like case 1 of Table 3. When we try to identify the type of intrusions with Euclidean distance, input state sequence is identified as kcms: D(xlock)=6.7082, D(lpset)=6.6332 and D(kcms)=5.6596, but with Hamming distance the input state sequence is identified as xlock, because of HD(xlock)=6, HD(lpset)=5 and HD(kcms)=5. In general, the performance of Hamming distance is lower than that of Euclidean distance.

In addition, with LCS the type of intrusions is identified as specific class which has the largest common subsequences. If the standard state sequences are like Table 3, and the input state sequence is like case 2 of Table 3, it cannot identify the type of intrusions correctly since the xlock and lpset results with LCS are the same: LCS(xlock)=LCS(lpset)=8.

On the other hand, in the case 3 of Table 3, the input state sequence is identified as xlock with Euclidean distance: 2.8284. However, if we use the edit distance to identify the type of intrusion, we can identify the input state sequence as kcms: $E.D$(xlock)=24 and $E.D$(kcms)=21. We can reduce the error rate using the edit distance which performs proper operations.

5 Concluding Remarks

In this paper, we have proposed a method to identify the type of intrusions in the anomaly detection system based on HMM. The proposed method calculates the edit distance to compare the similarity between the standard state sequences modeled and the current state sequence obtained by using Viterbi algorithm when intrusion occurs. Experiments are performed in the intrusion detection system based on HMM in 100% intrusion detection rates. We change the number of states from 5 to 30 and the length of observation symbols from 10 to 20 in the experiments. As a result, since the possible state transition paths are of small number, the system identifies all the types of intrusions when the number of states is more than 20. We have conducted additional experiments with other 3 distance measures, LCS, Hamming distance and Euclidean distance to verify the usefulness. The experiments indicate that it is very difficult to identify the type of intrusions by using LCS and Hamming distance, while the edit distance produces good performance with proper operations.

References

1. D. Denning, "An intrusion-detection model," *IEEE Trans. on Software Engineering,* vol. 13, no. 2, pp. 212-232, Feb. 1987.
2. B. Balajinath and S. V. Raghavan, "Intrusion detection through learning behavior model," *Computer Communications,* vol. 24, pp. 1202-1212, Jul. 2001.
3. H. S. Vaccaro and G. E. Liepins, "Detection of anomalous computer session activity," In *Proc. of IEEE Symp. on Research Security and Privacy,* pp. 280-289, 1989.
4. J.-M. Koo and S.-B. Cho, "Viterbi algorithm for intrusion type identification in anomaly detection system," *Lecture Notes in Computer Science 2908,* pp. 97-110, Dec. 2003.
5. C. Warrender, S. Forrest and B. Pearlmutter, "Detecting intrusion using calls: Alternative data models," *In Proc. of IEEE Symp. on Security and Privacy,* pp. 133-145, May 1999.
6. S.-B. Cho and H.-J. Park, "Efficient anomaly detection by modeling privilege flows using hidden Markov model," *Computers & Security,* vol. 22, no. 1, pp. 45-55, 2003.

A Combined fBm and PPCA Based Signal Model for On-Line Recognition of PD Signal

Pradeep Kumar Shetty

Honeywell Technology Solutions Lab, Bangalore, India
pradeep.shetty@honeywell.com

Abstract. The problem of on-line recognition and retrieval of relatively weak industrial signal such as Partial Discharges (PD), buried in excessive noise has been addressed in this paper. The major bottleneck being the recognition and suppression of stochastic pulsive interference (PI), due to, overlapping broad band frequency spectrum of PI and PD pulses. Therefore, on-line, on-site, PD measurement is hardly possible in conventional frequency based DSP techniques. We provide new methods to model and recognize the PD signal, on-line. The observed noisy PD signal is modeled as linear combination of systematic and random components employing probabilistic principal component analysis (PPCA). Being a natural signal, PD exhibits long-range dependencies. Therefore, we model the random part of the signal with fractional Brownian motion (fBm) process and pdf of the underlying stochastic process is obtained. The PD/PI pulses are assumed as the mean of the process and non-parametric analysis based on smooth FIR filter is undertaken. The method proposed by the Author found to be effective in recognizing and retrieving the PD pulses, automatically, without any user interference.

1 Introduction

Inspite of advances in the areas of manufacturing, processing optimal design and quality control, the high voltage (HV), high power apparatus have continued to fail in service prematurely. Investigations reveal that, in most cases insulation failure is the primary cause. In this context, power utilities are increasingly resorting to on-line, on-site diagnostic measurements to appraise the condition of insulation system. Amongst others, the PD measurement is emerged as an indispensable, non-destructive, sensitive and most powerful diagnostic tool.

A major constrain encountered with on-line digital PD measurements is the coupling of external interferences, that directly affect the sensitivity and reliability of the acquired PD data. The more important of them being, discrete spectral interferences (DSI), periodic pulse shaped interferences, external random pulsive interferences and random noise generic to measuring system itself. In most of the cases, external interferences yield false indications, there-by reducing the credibility of the PD as a diagnostic tool. Many researchers, have proposed signal processing techniques to suppress the different noise component such as, FFT thresholding, adaptive digital filter, IIR notch filter, wavelet based method with varying degree of success [1]. Due to the inherent difficulties involved in signal modeling and pattern analysis of PD signal, on-line, on-site PD measurement is still elusive which forms the subject matter of this paper.

1.1 Problem Enunciation

Discrete spectral interfrences can be identified and eliminated in frequency domain as they have a distinct narrow-band frequency spectrum concentrated around the dominant frequency, whereas, PD pulses have relatively a broad band spectrum. Periodic pulse shaped interferences can be gated-off in time domain (any PD occurring in that time interval is lost). But, it is very difficult to identify and suppress PI, as they have many characteristics in common (both in time and frequency domain) with PD pulses. Also, PI is a random occurrence like PD, which aggravates the process of separation. Thus, PI continues to pose serious problems for reliable on-line, on-site PD measurement.

In this paper, we analyze the PD time series in statistical perspective to model and classify the PD data. Locating the PD/PI pulses are the first step in further analysis of the signal. In this regard, we enhance the observed noisy signal using wavelet based soft thresholding method and the pulses are detected using simple peak-detector. Windowed signal of appropriate length is then taken around the detected location and further analysis is undertaken on the windowed signal. Considering the signal structure of the observed PD signal, we incorporate a combination of PPCA and fBm process based methodology, which effectively models the systematic component and random component in the observed PD signal. Since the PD signal is combination of different sinusoidal and random noises, this method is quite realistic, also, the long-range dependence of this natural signal is effectively modeled by fBm process. The pure PD/PI pulses are modeled as mean of the process and Non-parametric analysis based on smooth FIR filters is undertaken to extract the features of the pulse. The procedure adopted in this work is completely different from the research work reported in the literature, which is generally based on deserved signal frequency and noise frequency.

1.2 PD/PI Pulse Detection

It has been observed that, PD and PI pulses randomly occur in time. Therefore detection of the pulses is a primary requirement in further analysis of the signal. The signal-to-noise ratio of the PD signal is generally less (around -25dB) and it is difficult to visualize the location and the form of pulses in the observed noisy signal. In this regard, we denoise the noisy observed signal using wavelet based *sureshrink* soft thresholding method and make use of a simple peak detector to detect the location of pulsive activity. A minimum of S scale discrete wavelet transform is taken, where, $S = \lfloor \frac{log(F_s) - log(F_d)}{log(2)} - 1 \rfloor$. Here, F_s is the sampling frequency and F_d is the upper cutoff frequency of the PD detector. A windowed signal of appropriate size is taken around the detected location for further analysis.

2 Probabilistic PCA

Principal Component Analysis (PCA) is a widely used tool for data analysis. Given a set of $d-$dimensional data vector y, the q principal axes U_j, $j = 1, 2, ..., q$, are those onto which the retained variance under projection is maximal. These principal axes are the q eigenvectors corresponding to the q dominant eigenvalues of the sample covariance matrix of the data y. The analysis using PCA does not involve any probability model for the data. Tipping and Bishop [2] showed that by assuming a latent variable model for the data vectors, the data vectors can be represented in terms of its principal components. This approach is very useful because, we not only represent the data in terms of its principal components, but also a probability model for the data can be derived. This model in turn can be used for the tasks like estimation and detection of signals.

2.1 Probability Model for PCA

Any $d-$dimensional data vector y can be related to $q-$dimensional ($q < d$) latent variables z as:

$$y = h + Lz + \gamma \tag{1}$$

where, γ and z are independent random processes. h is the mean of the data vectors. By defining a prior pdf to z, the above equation induces a corresponding pdf to y. If we assume $z \sim N(0, I_q)$ and $\gamma \sim N(0, C_\gamma)$, then, y is also a Gaussian with, $y \sim N(h, LL^T + C_\gamma)$, where, I_q and I are $q \times q$ and $d \times d$ identity matrices. With the above pdf's for z and γ, we can show that the columns of L are the rotated and scaled principal eigenvectors of the covariance matrix of the data vector y. In the above model, the observed vector y is represented as the sum of systematic component (Lz) and random noise component (γ). It is shown in [2] that the ML estimate of L and σ^2 are given by, $L = U_q(\Lambda_q - \sigma^2 I)^{1/2} R$, where, the q column vectors in U_q are the eigenvectors of the covariance matrix of the data with the corresponding eigenvalues in the diagonal matrix Λ_q. R is an arbitrary rotation matrix. The energy in the remaining $(d-q)$ eigen vectors is given by σ^2. The model order (q) is estimated using Akaike information criterion (AIC), which is found to be two.

3 A Combination of PPCA and fBm Time-Series Model

We propose a model for the analysis of PD/PI pulses buried in noise, as:

$$y(t) = \sum_{t=0}^{d} x(t-k)h(k) + w(t), \quad t = 0....d-1 \tag{2}$$

where, y, x and w are observed time series, system impulse response and noise component respectively. We model h by non parametric model based on smooth FIR filter. The eqn. 2 can be written in matrix form as, $y = Xh + w$, where, X is the convolution matrix, which is identity matrix I_d. In this, the noise w can be represented using the latent variable model as explained in section 2. i.e, $w = Lz + \gamma$, where z is a q-dimensional ($q < N$) latent variable and γ is a random noise component. This method is quite realistic in modeling the PD signal, since the observed PD signal is combination of pulses, DSI and other random components. The matrix L is called as systematic noise matrix, which characterizes the systematic noise component by considering q principal components of w, corresponding to the first q dominant eigenvalues. Assuming Gaussian pdf models as described in the section 2, the pdf of noise can be given as, $w \sim N(0, C_y)$, where, $C_y = LL^T + C_\gamma$. Finally, the observed time series can be represented as,

$$y = Xh + Lz + \gamma \tag{3}$$

Therefore, the probability model for the observed PD/PI time-series y for a given h is distributed as,

$$y|h \sim N(Xh, C_y) \qquad (4)$$

The physical phenomena like PD exhibits long-term dependencies and $1/f$ type of behaviour over wide range of frequencies [3]. Also, the natural signals are non-stationary in nature. Therefore, the standard assumption of independence of noise random variables are not valid in modeling the natural signals. We model the noise component (γ) as, $\gamma = \gamma_d + \gamma_i$, where, γ_d describe the long-memory process and γ_i represent the independent random noise. One well-known model of long-memory processes proposed by Mandelbrot and VanNess [4] is fractional Brownian motion. Among others, self-similarity property makes wavelet transform, a preferred tool for analysis of the fBm processes. Thus, By taking DWT of scale m, we have $W\gamma = W\gamma_d + W\gamma_i$. Exploiting the Karhunen-Loeve-like properties of the wavelet decomposition for $1/f$ type of process, we have, $W\gamma_d$ and $W\gamma_i$ uncorrelated and independent of each other. The variance of the wavelet coefficients for each scale is: $var(W\gamma) = \sigma_\gamma^2 = \sigma_d^2 \beta^{-m} + \sigma_i^2$. The parameter β is related to Hurst component (H), which describes the fBm process completely. The Hurst component is given by, $H = (log_2\beta - 1)/2$. The covariance function of the self-similar process with H is: $R_d(t,s) = \frac{\sigma_H^2}{2}(|s|^{2H} + |t|^{2H} - |t-s|^{2H})$, where, $\sigma_H^2 = \Gamma(1-2H)cos(\pi H)/(\pi H)$. The parameter set $\Theta = [H, \sigma_d^2, \sigma_i^2]$ are estimated using ML technique in wavelet domain. The likelihood function L is given by,

$$L(\Theta) = p(W\gamma; \Theta) = \prod_{m,n \in R} \frac{1}{\sqrt{2\pi\sigma_\gamma^2}} exp\left(-\frac{(W\gamma_n^m)^2}{2\sigma_\gamma^2}\right) \qquad (5)$$

where, n represents the number of wavelet coefficients in scale m. The covariance matrix (C_γ) is obtained as, $C_\gamma = C_d + C_i$. The covariance structure (C_d) is estimated using H and C_i is given by, $C_i = \sigma_i^2 I_d$.

A set of training data (y_t) for noise (i.e. non-pulsive region of the data) is required to estimate C_y, which requires the prior knowledge of absence of PD/PI pulse in the observed data. To extract the random noise component from y_t, we project y_t on to DSI space (given by $U_q U_q^T$) and γ is obtained using the additive model as given in Eqn. 3. Finally, the overall covariance matrix C_y is obtained using, $C_y = LL^T + C_\gamma$.

4 Feature Extraction Based on Smooth FIR Filter

In this section we attempt to extract the feature of PD and PI pulses by completely representing them using a smooth FIR filter, irrespective of the shape of the pulse. This method aspire to estimate the function at each time sample making no assumption of the PD/PI shape and robust enough to withstand low SNR, without over constraining the problem. The basic approach to model pulses by a FIR filter is taken from Marrelec [6] in which, the noise space is assumed to be spanned by a third order polynomial functions. In our work, we evaluate the basis vectors for the noise subspace at each windowed section using PPCA and fBm combination model.

In this methodology, the coefficients of the filter emulate the desired pulse. Therefore, estimating the filter coefficients at each windowed signal is the task at hand. The estimation problem is ill poised, since, the number of coefficients to be estimated are large. We assume that, PD/PI pulses are smooth and regularize the problem by introducing smoothing priors. Therefore, we choose to work in a Bayesian framework. The smoothing constraint is imposed by setting up a Gaussian prior for the norm of second derivative of the pulse. The relative weight of this prior to data is controlled by the hyperparameter ϵ.

The pdf of observed data (y) conditioned on h can be written as:

$$p(y|h) = \frac{1}{(2\pi)^{\frac{k}{2}}|C_y|^{\frac{1}{2}}} exp[-\frac{1}{2}(y-Xh)^T C_y^{-1}(y-Xh)] \qquad (6)$$

The smoothing prior for h is given by, $p(h|\epsilon) \propto (\epsilon^2)^{\frac{k-1}{2}} exp(-\frac{\epsilon^2}{2}h^T M_p h)$, where, ϵ is the hyper parameter which is a measure of relative weight of the prior. The higher ϵ, the more the prior constraint taken into account. M_p is called as concentration matrix of the dimension $k-by-k$. A Jeffrey's non-informative prior [7] is used for ϵ, which is given by, $p(\epsilon) = \frac{1}{\epsilon}$. Using Bayes rule, the joint posterior pdf for h and ϵ can be written as, $p(h, \epsilon|y) \propto p(y|h, \epsilon)p(h|\epsilon)p(\epsilon)$. Therefore, the required marginal posterior pdf for h is given by, $p(h|y) = \int p(h, \epsilon|y)d\epsilon$. The closed form solution to this marginal pdf is not possible and therefore numerical optimization is required to find the maximum aposteriori probability (MAP) estimate of h. To over come this problem, we first estimate ϵ by MAP and approximate the aposteriori pdf for h as, $p(h|y) \approx p(h|y, \epsilon = \hat{\epsilon})$, where $\hat{\epsilon}$, the MAP estimate of ϵ which is given by, $\hat{\epsilon} = arg\ max_\epsilon p(\epsilon|y)$, The marginal posterior probability for ϵ is given by:

$$p(\epsilon|y) \propto |M(\epsilon)|^{-1/2}\epsilon^{k-2}exp(\frac{-1}{2}y^t C_y^{-1}y - \hat{\mu_B}^t M(\epsilon)\hat{\mu_B}) \qquad (7)$$

wherein,

$$M(\epsilon) = X^t C_y^{-1} X + \epsilon^2 M_p$$

$$\hat{\mu_B} = M(\epsilon)^{-1}(X^t C_y^{-1}\mathbf{y})$$

Equation 7 is maximized w.r.t ϵ, to get the MAP estimate. Now the task is to estimate the filter coefficients h. We have, $p(h|y, \epsilon = \hat{\epsilon}) \propto p(y|h, \epsilon = \hat{\epsilon})p(h|\epsilon = \hat{\epsilon})$. i.e $p(h|y, \epsilon = \hat{\epsilon}) \propto exp[-\frac{1}{2}(y-Xh)^T C_y^{-1}(y-Xh)] + \hat{\epsilon}^2 h^T M_p h$. The filter coefficient h is obtained by maximizing the posterior probability of h, which is given by,

$$\hat{h} = [X^T C_y^{-1} X + \hat{\epsilon}^2 M_p]^{-1} X^T C_y^{-1} Y \qquad (8)$$

Estimates of a PD and PI pulses considering both real and simulated signal is shown in Fig. [1].

In simulated data (as shown in first part of Fig. [1]), the estimated pulse (h) was found to be very close to the added pulse. This shows the power of the method in modeling the PD data. The estimated PD and PI pulse considering the real data is shown in second part of Fig. [1]. A PCA based binary classifier, one correspond to PD and other one corresponding to PI is employed to extract PD and reject PI. In this methodology,

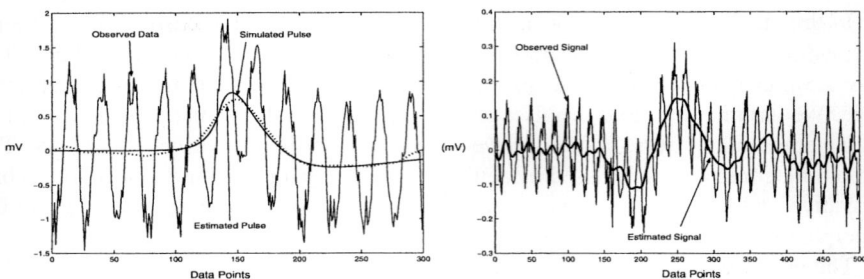

Fig. 1. Demonstration of pulse extraction using simulated and real data

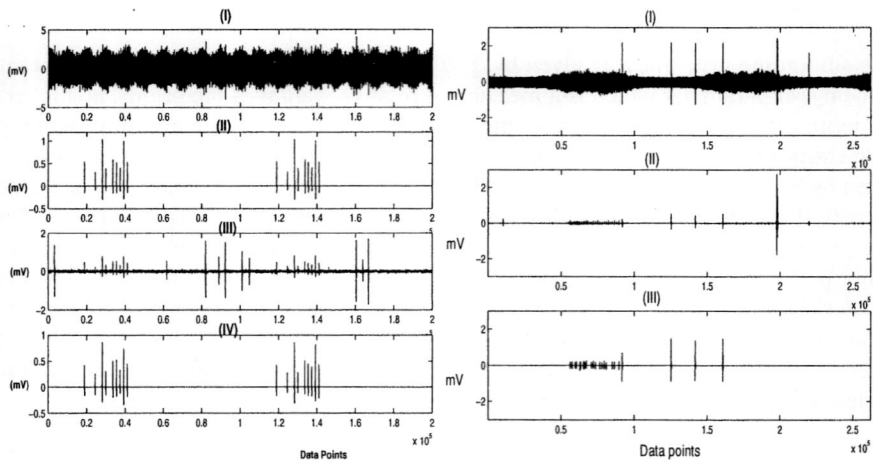

Fig. 2. Output of non-parametric method considering real and simulated data

subspaces are found for the training data of each class which are estimated from the using the non-parametric model as explained earlier. The overall output of the method on simulated data is shown in the first part of fig. [2]. The added PD pulses (we have this as we simulate the data), denoised signal and the retrieved signal are shown in (II), (III) and IV respectively. It can be seen that, all of the PD pulses have been retrieved rejecting all PI pulses. Also, the height of the retrieved pulses are close to that of added pulses, which is very important in making and diagnostic/prognostic decisions. The performance of the method in dealing with the real signal is shown in the second part of Fig. [2]. To the best of Authors knowledge, there is no general technique which can automatically retrieve the PD pulses rejecting PI. Therefore, we have not compared the performance of the method demonstrated in this paper with other techniques reported in the literature.

5 Conclusion

The problem of on-line recognition of PD signal is approached in a different perspective than conventional DSP techniques. A combination of PPCA and fBm process based techniques have been developed and applied to the problem in hand. The methodology is found to be effective in PD signal modeling and recognition. Thus, Author has developed an statistical pattern recognition methodology for on-line, on-site measurements of PD signal.

References

1. Satish, L., Nazneen, B.:Wavelet denoising of PD signals buried in excessive noise and interference. IEEE Transaction on DEI. Vol. 10. No. 2. April 2003. pp 354–367.
2. Tipping, M.E., Bishop, C. M.: A hierarchical latent variable model for data visualization. IEEE trans. PAMI. Vol. 20. no-3. 1998. pp.25-35. 281-293.
3. Flandrin, P.: Wavelet analysis and synthesis of fractional Brownian motion. IEEE transaction on Information Theory. Vol. 38. no-2. 1992. pp.910-917.
4. Wornell, G: Signal Processing with Fractals: A Wavelet Based Approach. Prentice Hall PTR. Newjersy. 1996. Chap. 3. pp. 30-46.
5. Wornell, G. W.: A Karhunen-Loeve-like expansion for 1/f processes via wavelets. IEEE. Trans. Inform. Theory. vol. 36. July 1990. pp. 859-861.
6. Marrelec, G., Benali, H., Ciuciu, P., Poline, J: Bayesian estimation of haemodynamic response function in functional MRI, CP617, Bayesian Inference and Maximum Entropy methods in Science and Engineering: 21st International Workshop, 2002. pp. 229-247.
7. Bretthorst,G. L,: Bayesian interpolation and deconvolution. The U.S Army Missile Command (1992). Tech. Rep. CR-RD-AS-92-4.

Handwritten *Bangla* Digit Recognition Using Classifier Combination Through DS Technique

Subhadip Basu[1], Ram Sarkar[2], Nibaran Das[2], Mahantapas Kundu[2], Mita Nasipuri[2,*], and Dipak Kumar Basu[2]

[1] Computer Sc. & Engg. Dept., MCKV Institute of Engineering,
Liluah, Howrah-711204, India
[2] Computer Sc. & Engg. Dept., Jadavpur University,
Kolkata-700032, India

Abstract. The work presents an application of Dempster-Shafer (DS) technique for combination of classification decisions obtained from two Multi Layer Perceptron (MLP) based *classifiers* for optical character recognition (OCR) of handwritten *Bangla* digits using two different feature sets. *Bangla* is the second most popular script in the Indian subcontinent and the fifth most popular language in the world. The two *feature sets* used for the work are so designed that they can supply complementary information, at least to some extent, about the classes of digit patterns to the MLP classifiers. On experimentation with a database of 6000 samples, the technique is found to improve recognition performances by a minimum of 1.2% and a maximum of 2.32% compared to the average recognition rate of the individual MLP classifiers after 3-fold cross validation of results. The overall recognition rate as observed for the same is 95.1% on average.

1 Introduction

The work presented here deals with an OCR technique of handwritten *Bangla* digits. In doing so, classification decisions from two complementary sources of information are combined using DS technique of belief combination [1]. It is in line with the recent trend for improving classification decisions through the *classifier combination approach*.

Bangla is the second most popular script in the Indian subcontinent. As a script, it is used for *Bangla, Ahamia* and *Manipuri* languages. *Bangla* is also the national language of Bangladesh and is the fifth most popular language in the world. Evidences of research on OCR of handwritten *Bangla* digits are a few in numbers, as found in the literature [2,3].
Techniques developed for OCR of handwritten digits are in general required for many potential *applications* related to reading amounts from bank cheques, extracting numeric data from filled in forms, interpreting handwritten pin codes from mail pieces and so on. Considering the need of a wide cross section of world population using

---

* Corresponding Author. *Email address:* nasipuri@vsnl.com

Bangla either as a language or a script, OCR of handwritten *Bangla* digits has a high value of *commercial importance* in the present time. Fig. 1 shows the typical digit patterns of the decimal digits of *Bangla* script.

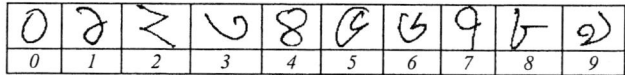

Fig. 1. The decimal digit set of Bengali script

Previously Bhattacharya et al. [2] employed group specific MLP classifiers for recognition of handwritten *Bangla* digits after they are hierarchically classified into some groups of digit classes on the basis of features like loops, junctions etc., extracted from *skeletal shapes* of the digit patterns. The system so developed is trained with a data set of 1880 samples. On being tested with a separate data set of 3440 samples, it shows a recognition performance of 90.56%.

The authors previously developed a *two pass approach* to pattern classification [3] and applied the same for OCR of handwritten *Bangla* digits. In this approach, an unknown digit pattern is first coarsely classified into a group of digit classes on the basis of some preselected *global features* and then classified into some digit class within the group on the basis of some group specific *local features*. Performances of the system developed under the work are tested with a *training set* and a *test set* of 300 and 200 randomly selected sample patterns respectively. It is experimentally observed that application of the two-pass approach improves the classification rate of digit patterns to 93.5% in the second pass from 90.5% observed in the first pass. Due to lack of a common database used for the above two techniques, performances of the same cannot be compared straightway. A major *limitation* of the two-pass approach is that it cannot refine a classification decision on an unknown digit pattern, which is wrongly classified into a group of candidate patterns in the first pass. The *present technique*, aims to overcome this limitation by combining classification decisions of the two MLP classifiers through DS techniques.

The work presented here not only targets the development of suitable *feature sets* for representation of handwritten *Bangla* digits in the feature space but also the development of techniques for dealing with *uncertainty* and *imprecision* in recognizing the same.

2 The Present Work

The two feature sets considered for the present work are so designed that they contain *complementary information* on *Bangla* digit features for improving recognition performances through combination of classification decisions of two MLP classifiers by DS technique. One of the two feature sets selected for the present work consists of 40 features and the other 36 features. Out of these two, the first one consists of octant based 24 *shadow feature* and octant based 16 *centroid features* as described in [3]. The other feature set consists of 36 *longest run features* [4] computed from 9 overlapping windows on the image frame.

To deal with imprecision present in handwritten digit patterns due to variation in writing styles of different individuals, MLPs, a kind of *feed forward* Artificial Neural Networks (ANNs), are used as classifiers for the present work. ANNs are in general famous for their *learning* and *generalization abilities,* necessary for dealing with imprecision in input patterns. The two MLPs employed here to work as two pattern classifiers with the two above mentioned feature sets are of the sizes (40-40-10) and (36-50-10).

Uncertainty of classification decisions occurs because of the fact that unknown handwritten digit patterns may appear close to some other digit pattern(s), which does not belong to its actual class. So, no classification decision taken by any of the two classifiers designed for the present work is considered to be true with the highest degree of probability. One of the major points of *criticism* of probability theory is that it represents *ignorance* by *indifference* or by *uniform probabilities*. Another heavily debated point about the probability theory involves the way it follows in fixing the probability of a hypothesis negation (p (~H)) once the probability of its occurrence (p(H)) is known. In DS theory, it is claimed that, in many situations, evidence that only partially favours a hypothesis should not be construed as also partially supporting its negation.

2.1 DS Technique and Its Application for Combination of Classification Decisions

To deal with the above problems, DS technique involves the following. *Firstly*, it assigns separate *probability masses* to all subsets of a universe of discourse (U) containing all possible hypotheses. For handwritten digit recognition, the value of |U| is 10. The basic probability assignment can be represented as follows:

$$m: 2^U \rightarrow [0,1]$$

The *basic probability assignment* (m) satisfies the relations given as **m(ϕ) = 0** where ϕ denotes a null hypothesis and $\sum_{A \subseteq U} m(A) = 1$.

Secondly, DS technique introduces the concept of *belief* (B) associated with each subset of U as **Bel(A)** = $\sum_{B \subseteq A} m(B)$ and **Bel(ϕ) = 0**

The belief function (B) when applied to a set (A) gives a measure of the *total support* or belief committed to all hypotheses constituting A. It sets a *minimum value* for its *likelihood*. The belief function (B) satisfies the relation given as.**Bel (A) + Bel (~A) <= 1**

In DS technique, only those subsets of U, which have non zero basic probability assignments, are of interest. Each such subset is called a *focal element* of the belief function (Bel) over 2^U.

Thirdly, DS technique introduces a concept of *plausibility* (Pl) of a set of hypotheses (A) giving the maximum amount of belief that can possibly be assigned to A as **Pl(A) = 1 – Bel(~A)**. Introduction of the concept of plausibility makes it possible to define the *confidence* in A as the belief subinterval **[Bel(A),Pl(A)]** of [0,1]. The quantity **(Pl(A) − Bel(A))** is considered as the *uncertainty* in A. This quantity can never be negative. That is, **Pl(A) − Bel(A) >= 0**.

Fourthly, and finally, DS technique also defines rules for combination of belief functions when evidence is available from two or more independent knowledge sources. If m_1 and m_2 be two probability mass assignment functions designed for two such knowledge sources then a function '$m_1 \oplus m_2$' for combining these two can be given as

$$\mathbf{m_1 \oplus m_2} (A) = K. \sum_{X \cap Y = A} m_1(X).m_2(Y), \text{ where } K^{-1} = \sum_{X \cap Y \neq \phi} m_1(X).m_2(Y).$$

For totally contradictory evidences $\mathbf{K^{-1} = 0}$.

An Example. The technique described above can be illustrated with the following examples formed out of the experimentation conducted for the present work.

The universe of discourse for the handwritten digit recognition problem consists of ten hypotheses given as U={'0', '1', '2', '3', '4', '5', '6', '7', '8', '9'}. Each hypothesis in U denotes the assignment of an unknown digit pattern to a specific digit class represented by the class number placed within a pair of quotation marks.

From the responses of two MLPs employed here to recognize independently an unknown digit pattern on the basis of two different feature sets, basic probability assignments, denoted by m_1 and m_2, for the focal elements of Bel_1 and Bel_2 are determined. Instead of considering all elements of the power set 2^U for forming the focal elements of the two belief functions, only the following *three subsets* are considered from the responses of each of the two classifiers.

{ The first highest-ranking class }, { The first highest-ranking class, the second highest-ranking class }, { The first highest ranking class, the second highest-ranking class, the third highest-ranking class }.

The probability assignment for a singleton subset is computed by dividing the *maximum output* of the MLP classifier by the *sum* of its all outputs. For computing the same for the other subsets, a subset is first expressed as the union of singletons, each of which contains an element of the subset. Then the probability assignments for all these singletons are to be computed. And, finally by taking the *minimum* of the probability assignments of the constituent singletons of a subset, the probability assignment of the entire subset is determined.

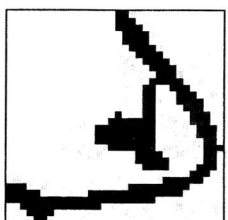

Fig. 2. A sample digit image of '9'

Following the above procedure, the basic probability assignments are made from the responses of the two MLP classifiers to a common *input digit patterns* of '9', shown in Fig. 2. All these basic probability assignment are given below.

$m_1(\{'6'\})=0.578644$, $m_1(\{'6','9'\})=0.356895$, $m_1=(\{'6','9','1'\})=0.051056$, $m_1(U)$ = 0.013405 and $m_2(\{'3'\})=0.375894$, $m_2(\{'3','9'\})=0.271633$,
$m_2=(\{'3','9','1'\})=0.205506$ $m_2(U) =0.146967$.

To combine basic probability assignments for the non null intersections of the focal elements of the two belief functions formed with the responses of the two MLP classifiers, Table 1 is formed. In Table 1, probability mass assignments of the all possible intersections are shown by computing the numerators of previously given formula for computation of 'm1 $\oplus$ m2'. Out of these probability mass assignments, the assignments for singleton cross sections {3}, {6} and {9} are only of interest for the present work. By considering the maximum of the probability mass assignments of singleton intersections, the input pattern is finally classified in to the digit class '9', which is its *true class*. It is worth noting that both the classifiers have misclassified the input pattern by their top choices. But by considering other choices through DS technique, it has been possible to obtain the correct one. Moreover, it is due to power of DS technique of belief combination that it has been possible to reach the correct classification decision by enhancing the beliefs for the second top choices of the two MLP classifiers. With a simpler classifier function based on the policy of reaching a consensus through majority *voting*, it could have not been possible.

Table 1. Combined probability mass assignments ($m_1 \oplus m_2$) of all possible intersections of focal elements

m_1 \ m_2	{'3'} (0.375894)	{'3','9'} (0.271633)	{'3','9','1'} (0.205506)	U (0.146967)
{'6'} (0.578644)	Φ (0.217509)	Φ (0.157179)	Φ (0.118915)	{'6'} (0.085042)
{'6','9'} (0.356895)	Φ (0.134155)	{'9'} (0.096944)	{'9'} (0.073344)	{'6','9'} (0.052452)
{'6','9','1'} (0.051056)	Φ (0.019192)	{'9'} (0.013868)	{'9','1'} (0.010492)	{'6','9','1'} (0.007504)
U (0.013405)	{'3'} (0.005039)	{'3','9'} (0.003641)	{'3','9','1'} (0.002755)	U (0.375894)

3 Results and Discussion

For preparation of the *training* and the *test sets* of samples, a database of 6,000 *Bangla* digit samples is formed by randomly selecting 600 samples for each of 10 digit classes from a larger database of 10,000 samples. The larger database is prepared in CVPR unit , ISI, Kolkata. Samples constituting the database are collected from pin codes used on postal mail pieces. A *training set* of 4000 samples and a *test set* of 2000 samples are finally formed. Three such pairs of the training and the test sets are formed in all with the entire database of 6000 samples for *3-fold cross validation* of results at the time of experimentation. All these samples are first enclosed within a *minimum bounding* box each and then scaled to 32x32 pixel images. These images are finally converted to *binary images* through thresholding.

Table 2. Recognition Performances on Test sets

Classifier	% Recognition Rate		
	Test Set # 1	Test Set # 2	Test Set # 3
MLP # 1	93.1	93.2	94.8
MLP # 2	91.35	92.8	93.7
DS Technique	94.55	95.3	95.45

Recognition performances of the individual MLP classifiers and their combined classification decisions, as recorded experimentally on the three sets of test data are shown in Table 2. The overall recognition rate the technique finally achieves is **95.1%** on average.

Compared to the average recognition performances of the two classifiers, classifier decision combination through DS technique shows a minimum of **1.2%** and a maximum of **2.32%** increase in recognition rates of the classifier ensemble after *3-fold cross validation* of results. Improvement thus achieved is significant especially in the context of high precision applications relating to OCR of handwritten digits.

Acknowledgements

Authors are thankful to the "Center for Microprocessor Application for Training Education and Research", "Project on Storage Retrieval and Understanding of Video for Multimedia" of Computer Science & Engineering Department, Jadavpur University, for providing infrastructure facilities during progress of the work. Authors are also thankful to the CVPR Unit, ISI Kolkata, for providing the necessary dataset of handwritten Bengali Numerals. One of the authors, Mr. S. Basu, is thankful to MCKV Institute of Engineering for kindly permitting him to carry on the research work.

References

1. Kenng-Chi Ng and Bruce Abramson, "Uncertainty management in expert systems", IEEE Expert, p.p. 29-48, April, 1990.
2. U. Bhattacharya et. al. "Recognition of hand printed Bangla numerals using neural network models", AFSS 2002, p.p. 228-235.
3. S. Basu et al., "A two pass approach to pattern classification", Proc 11th ICONIP, Nov-2004.
4. S. Basu et al., "Handwritten 'Bangla' alphabet recognition using an MLP based classifier", Proc. 2nd NCCPB, Dhaka, Feb-2005.

Arrhythmia Classification Using Local Hölder Exponents and Support Vector Machine

Aniruddha Joshi[1], Rajshekhar[2,*], Sharat Chandran[1], Sanjay Phadke[3], V.K. Jayaraman[2], and B.D. Kulkarni[2,**]

[1] Computer Science and Engg. Dept.,
IIT Bombay, Powai, Mumbai, India 400076
[2] Chemical Engineering Division, National Chemical Laboratory,
Pune, India 411008
bdk@ems.ncl.res.in
[3] Consultant, Jahangir Hospital, Pune, India 411001

Abstract. We propose a novel hybrid Hölder-SVM detection algorithm for arrhythmia classification. The Hölder exponents are computed efficiently using the wavelet transform modulus maxima (WTMM) method.

The hybrid system performance is evaluated using the benchmark MIT-BIH arrhythmia database. The implemented model classifies 160 of Normal sinus rhytm, 25 of Ventricular bigeminy, 155 of Atrial fibrillation and 146 of Nodal (A-V junctional) rhythm with 96.94% accuracy. The distinct scaling properties of different types of heart rhythms may be of clinical importance.

1 Introduction

Arrhythmia is a common term for any cardiac rhythm which deviates from normal sinus rhythm. Characterization and classification of such arrhythmia signals is an important step in developing devices for monitoring the health of individuals. Typical and abnormal signals are shown in Fig. 1. Arrhythmias are of different kinds, and exhibit long-term non-stationary patterns. Concepts and techniques including Fourier [1], wavelets [1], chaos parameters [2] have been employed to extract information present in such physiologic time series. All these methods exhibit different degrees of advantages and disadvantages, the main concern being low specificity and accuracy.

Our interest is in the recently developed analytic tools based on nonlinear dynamics theory and fractals. These are attractive because they have the ability to perform a reliable local singularity analysis. For example, gait analysis [3] and localization of outliers [4] have been performed using this approach. This approach offers a new and potentially promising avenue for quantifying features of a range of physiologic signals that differ [5] in health and disease.

Features detected using such approaches exhibit *local* hidden information in time series and thus are suitable for classification. Support vector machine

---

* Under Graduate Summer Trainee from Chemical Engg. Dept., IIT Kharagpur, India.
** Corresponding author.

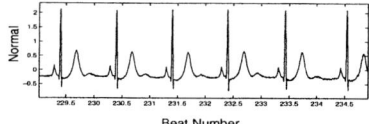 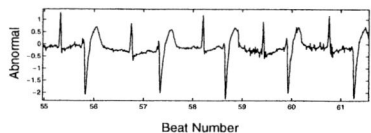

Fig. 1. A normal consistent P-QRS-T rhythm is exhibited on the left. Abnormal rhythm for a patient in every alternate beat appears on the right.

(SVM) rigorously based on statistical learning theory simultaneously minimizes the training and test errors. Apart from that, SVM produces a unique globally optimal solution and hence is extensively used in diverse applications including medical diagnosis.

In this work, *we have developed a novel hybrid Hölder-SVM detection algorithm* for arrhythmia classification. We first pre-process a rhythm data series to remove obvious noise patterns. Next, we compute wavelet coefficients at selected scales and use them to compute local Hölder exponents and subsequently pass selected points of the probability density curve of these exponents as input features to a multi-class support vector machine for classification. Experiments show the validity of our straightforward scheme.

The rest of the paper is organized as follows. In Section 2, we briefly describe the methodology for computation of the local singularities and provide a short introduction to SVM. Section 3 highlights our approach for classification along with results achieved. We conclude with some final remarks in Section 4.

2 Local Hölder Exponents

For a time series f, if there exists a polynomial P_n of degree $n < h$ and constant C, such that:

$$|f(x) - P_n(x - x_0)| \leq C|x - x_0|^h \tag{1}$$

the supremum of all exponents $h(x_0) \in (n, n+1)$ is termed the Hölder exponent, which characterizes the singularity strength. It is evident [3] that the Hölder exponent describes the local regularity of the function (or distribution) f. The higher the value of h, more regular is the local behavior the function f. Thus it characterizes the scaling of the function locally and the distinct scaling behavior of different signals can be exploited to characterize and classify time series.

The wavelet transformation (WT) i.e. $W_{s,x_0}(f)$ provides a way to analyze the local behavior of a signal f, which is a convolution product of the signal with the scaled(s) and translated(x_0) kernel. One of the main aspects of the WT is the ability to reveal the hierarchy of (singular) features, including the scaling behavior. This is formalized by its relation [6] with the Hölder exponent:

$$W_{s,x_0}(f) \propto |s|^{h(x_0)}, \quad s \to 0 \tag{2}$$

Fig. 2 shows an example of the WT and the Hölder exponents. We used the second derivative of the Gaussian function, i.e. Mexican hat, as the analyzing

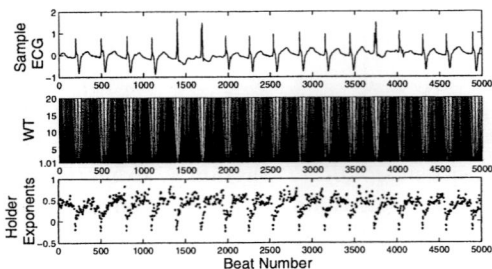

Fig. 2. Sample ECG waveform, its wavelet transform and the corresponding local Hölder exponents at first scale

wavelet. This wavelet is also extensively used by the other authors, since it possesses good localization capabilities in both position and frequency.

Efficiency Considerations. As continuous WT in its original form is an extremely redundant representation, Mallat and Hwang [7] have come up with an alternative approach called wavelet transform modulus maxima (WTMM). Here, the computation of the hierarchical distribution of local behavior, as explained above, can be effectively computed by considering the space-scale partitions. The dependence of the scaling function on the moments q can be captured using WTMM tree as:

$$Z(s,q) = \sum_{\Omega(s)} |W_{s,x_0}(f)|^q \propto s^{\tau(q)} \quad (3)$$

where $Z(s,q)$ is the partition function and $\Omega(s)$ is the set of all maxima at the scale s. The computation of singularity strength and the transformation from $\tau(q)$ to spectrum of singularities $D(h)$ is given by the Legendre transformation[8]:

$$h(q) = d\tau(q)/dq; \qquad D[h(q)] = qh(q) - \tau(q) \quad (4)$$

Stable Computation. The WTMM based formalism developed by Muzy [6] as described above provides global estimates of scaling properties of time series. Recently, it has been found that even though such global estimates of scaling is often a required property, local analysis may provide more useful information.

In the traditional form, the estimation of local singularity strengths and their spectra may not be possible due to the fact that in real life data, the singularities are not isolated but densely packed. This causes the logarithmic rate of increase or decrease of the corresponding wavelet transform maximum line to fluctuate. But very recently, Struzik [9, 10] has provided a stable methodology for estimating the local exponents, in which he has modeled the singularities as if they were created through a multiplicative cascading process. This method has been successfully applied for classification of human gait [3].

The method[10, 3] is as explained below. The mean Hölder exponent $\overline{h}$ is given by $\log[M(s)] = \overline{h}\log(s) + C$, where $M(s) = \sqrt{\frac{Z(s,2)}{Z(s,0)}}$. Employing the multiplicative cascade model, the approximate local Hölder exponent $\hat{h}(x_0, s)$ at the singularity x_0 can now be evaluated as the slope:

$$\hat{h}(x_0, s) = \frac{\log(|W_{s,x_0}(f)|) - (\overline{h}\log(s) + C)}{\log(s) - \log(s_N)} \quad (5)$$

where s_N is the length of the entire wavelet maxima line tree, that is, the maximum available scale that coincides with the sample length $s_N = N$, and x_0 belongs to the set $\Omega(s)$ of all wavelet maxima at the scale s that assume the value $W_{s,x_0}(f)$. (In our calculations we used $s=1$ in the WT.)

2.1 Support Vector Machines

The local Hölder exponents are appropriate as the most informative features for classification using the support vector machines (SVM)[11]. SVM is being extensively used for several classification and regression applications. As the theory is well developed, we provide only the basic ideas [12, 13] involved in binary classification.

1. Transform the input data into a higher dimensional feature space to enable linear classification; specifically define an appropriate kernel in the input space in place of the dot product in the high dimensional feature space.
2. Maximize the margin of the linear hyperplane separating the instances belonging to the two classes by solving the dual formulation of the convex quadratic programming problem to obtain the unique global solution for the classifier.

For multi-class classification, we used popular One-Against-One method [14].

3 Results and Discussion

Data Set. The data set used was extracted from ECG recordings of MIT-BIH Arrhythmia Database according to the beat and rhythm annotations. Each record of these rhythms is at least 10 seconds long. Here, the complete dataset includes 160 of Normal sinus rhythm(NSR), 25 of Ventricular bigeminy (VB), 155 of Atrial fibrillation (AF) and 146 of Nodal (A-V junctional) rhythm (NR) records. Out of the whole dataset, $2/3^{rd}$ of randomly selected data was used as the training set and the remaining $1/3^{rd}$ was used as the testing set.

For each of the extracted rhythms, we computed the features to be used by SVM for classification in the following manner. First, we de-noised the data series using soft threshold wavelet method [15]. Then we computed the wavelet coefficients using WTMM approach, which were subsequently used for the computation of local Hölder exponents as explained in 2. We then computed the probability density of these local Hölder exponents and then fitted this density with Gaussian kernel. For all the rhythms belonging to different classes the local Hölder exponents were in the range [-0.5:1.5]. We divided this range into 12 equal sub-parts and chose 12 points (as shown in Fig. 3(a)) on the fitted probability density curve corresponding to the mid-points of the 12 sub-ranges.

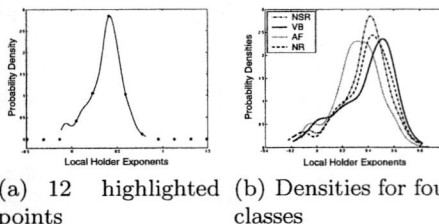

(a) 12 highlighted points (b) Densities for four classes

Fig. 3. probability density of local Hölder exponents

Table 1. confusion matrix (avg.case)

	NSR	VB	AF	NR
NSR	31.93	0.70	0.51	0.11
VB	0.62	3.69	0.18	0
AF	0.84	0	31.75	0
NR	0.48	0	0.15	29.01
Sensitivity Avg	96.04	82.11	97.42	97.9
Sensitivity Best	98.29	100	99.23	99.20
Specificity Avg	97.1	99.27	98.75	99.84
Specificity Best	98.89	100	99.63	99.64

Binary Classification. We considered NSR as the 'normal class' and all other arrhythmias as 'arrhythmia class'. We employed LIBSVM [16] toolbox for the classification purpose and used radial basis function (RBF) as the kernel. Selection of other SVM parameters was done using cross-validation on training data. Using multiple runs of 5-fold cross validation with chosen parameters, the overall accuracy of classifier model combinations ranged between 96% to 98%, and which show average (and best respectively) classification for 96.3% (and 98.48%) of normal class and 98.25%(and 98.89%) of arrhythmia class on the test set.

Multi-class Classification. For classification of four types of rhythms (for which the probability densities vary as shown in Fig. 3(b)), again, the parameters were tuned in the same way as explained in binary classification. The results show overall 96.94% accuracy, and average (and best respectively) classification for 95.98% (and 98.89%) of NSR, 82.05% (and 100%) of VB, 98.51% (and 99.23%) of AF and 98.92% (and 99.20%) of NR rhythms.

The results for multi-class classification can be summarized as the confusion matrix of four classes and sensitivity & specificity of each class as given in Table 1.

We also used the features derived from Fourier analysis, as mentioned in introduction, with SVM classification for comparison with our method. Fourier analysis(by selecting best 300 features) gives average correct classifications respectively 86.48%, 89.33%, 95.7% and 96.74% for the above four classes. Hölder-SVM methodology was found to provide superior performance. An interesting point to note is that in both the binary and multi-class classification, we used data provided by both sensing leads. It was observed that even if we use just a single lead data, classification gives results with comparable accuracy. Arrhythmia being a disorder in the normal rhythm, can thus be captured in any of the two leads.

4 Conclusion

In this study, it is demonstrated that support vector machine in conjunction with wavelet transform modulus maxima based local singularity feature extraction provides an excellent combination in arrhythmia classification. The recognition of the normal and different types of rhythms representing the arrhythmias has been done with a good accuracy. These investigations show that the presented method may find practical application in the recognition of many more types of arrhythmias.

Acknowledgment. We gratefully acknowledge the financial assistance provided by Department of Science and Technology, New Delhi, INDIA.

References

[1] Morchen, F.: Time series feature extraction for data mining using DWT and DFT. Technical Report 33, Dept. of Mathematics and Computer Science, Philipps-University Marburg., Germany (2003)
[2] Owis, M., Abou-Zied, A., Youssef, A.B., Kadah, Y.: Robust feature extraction from ECG signals based on nonlinear dynamical modeling. In: 23rd Annual Int. Conf. IEEE Eng. Med. Biol. Soc. (EMBC'01). Volume 2. (2001) 1585–1588
[3] Scafetta, N., Griffin, L., West, B.J.: Hölder exponent spectra for human gait. Physica A: Statistical Mechanics and its Applications **328** (2003) 561–583
[4] Struzik, Z.R., Siebes, A.P.J.M.: Outlier detection and localisation with wavelet based multifractal formalism. Technical Report INS-R0008, CWI (2000)
[5] Struzik, Z.R.: Revealing local variability properties of human heartbeat intervals with the local effective Hö lder exponent. Fractals **9** (2001) 77–93
[6] Muzy, J., Bacry, E., Arneodo, A.: The multifractal formalism revisited with wavelets. International Journal of Bifurcation and Chaos **4** (1994) 245–302
[7] Hwang, W.L., Mallat, S.: Characterization of self-similar multifractals with wavelet maxima. Applied and Computational Harmonic Analysis **1** (1994) 316–328
[8] Arneodo, A., Bacry, E., Muzy, J.: The thermodynamics of fractals revisited with wavelets. Physica A: Statistical and Theoretical Physics **213** (1995) 232–275
[9] Struzik, Z.R.: Removing divergences in the negative moments of the multi-fractal partition function with the wavelet transform. Technical Report INS-R9803, CWI (1998)
[10] Struzik, Z.R.: Determining local singularity strengths and their spectra with the wavelet transform. Fractals **8** (2000)
[11] Vapnik, V.: The nature of statistical learning theory. Springer-Verlag, New York (1995)
[12] Kulkarni, A., Jayaraman, V.K., Kulkarni, B.D.: Support vector classification with parameter tuning assisted by agent based techniques. Computers and Chemical Engineering **28** (2004) 311–318
[13] Mitra, P., Uma Shankar, B., Sankar, K.P.: Segmentation of multispectral remote sensing images using active support vector machines. Pattern recognition letters **25** (2004) 1067–1074
[14] Hsu, C.W., Lin, C.J.: A comparison of methods for multiclass support vector machines. IEEE Transactions on Neural Networks **13** (2002) 415–425
[15] Novak, D., Cuesta-Frau, D., Eck, V., Perez-Cortes, J., Andreu-Garcia, G.: Denoising electrocardiographic signals using adaptive wavelets. BIOSIGNAL (2000) 18–20
[16] Chang, C.C., Lin, C.J.: LIBSVM: a library for support vector machines. (2001)

A Voltage Sag Pattern Classification Technique

Délio E.B. Fernandes, Mário Fabiano Alves, and Pyramo Pires da Costa Jr.

Pontifical Catholic University of Minas Gerais, PUC-MG,
Av. Dom José Gaspar, 500, Prédio 3, 30535-610, Belo Horizonte, MG, Brazil
{delio, mfabiano, pyramo}@pucminas.br

Abstract. This paper presents an investigation on pattern classification techniques applied to voltage sag monitoring data. Similar pattern groups or sets of classes, resulting from a voltage sag classification, represent disturbance categories that may be used as indexes for a cause/effect disturbance analysis. Various classification algorithms are compared in order to establish a classifier design. Results over clustering performance indexes are presented for hierarchical, fuzzy c-means and k-means unsupervised clustering techniques, and a principal component analysis is used for features (or attributes) choice. The efficiency of the algorithms was analyzed by applying the CDI and DBI indexes.

1 Introduction

As a result of customers' expectations on services level provided by power systems, utilities have begun to develop and apply extensive power quality (PQ) monitoring programs [1]. Voltage sags are reductions in the root mean square value of a voltage, and a great part of the related power quality problems faced by utilities and indus-tries are associated to this PQ disturbance [1]. Modern power quality measurement equipments used to monitor these disturbances can generate a large amount of data. A monitoring system, composed by anything from a few PQ monitors to a hundred or more units, covering several points of an electrical network, generates gigabytes of data. This great amount of data must be systematically and automatically organized in a power quality database, using structures of information developed for characterization of each particular PQ phenomenon, such as voltage sags. A computational system with these characteristics has been developed by the authors [2]. The information introduced in this database comes from a characterization process that defines attributes to the voltage sag event, in an automated pre-processing task, from a signal processing assessment.

Generally, voltage sag cause or effects on a power system plant is analyzed by comparing several event patterns on a bi-dimensional basis. Traditional analysis uses a pair of attributes, magnitude and duration of the voltage sag, to classify it. Several other attributes can be derived from a time analysis of a voltage sag digital recorder, with the possibility of further improving the classification process. Some of these attributes are: the point of the wave where the event begins, the deviation of the phase angle, the average value, hour of the day of event occurrence, energy loss, type of voltage sag (three phase, phase to phase, phase to ground) etc. The use of a larger number of attributes, in a multivariate analysis, increases the discriminatory capacity among the events. Real data sets (data collection) retrieved from the mentioned power quality database, are used as input classification data, and are aggregated by monitoring site, time period, monitor channel or magnitude.

Patterns classification consists on allocation of events to clusters or classes with similar characteristics. A classifier design cycle includes: data collection, features choice, model choice, classifier training and a classifier evaluation [3].

There are extensive investigations on pattern classification using both statistical and artificial intelligence techniques. A complete investigation review linking artificial intelligence and other mathematical tools to PQ is detailed in [4]. Classical statistics classifying and clustering formulations are presented in [3,5,6,7]. Artificial intelligence technique, specifically using neural networks and fuzzy logic on pattern classification are described in [3,5,8].

In order to obtain pattern classes we use different techniques of unsupervised learning data clustering: hierarchical clustering, k-means and fuzzy c-means. In the unsupervised learn classification tecniques, patterns form clusters in a "natural grouping", with results depending on the specific clustering system and data set used. Thus, for a given specific classification problem some systems are more appropriate than others. Classification procedure is followed by its test under different performance indexes [5]. The indexes applied to a number of data clusters that better fits a natural partitioning of the original data set space define which classifier model to be used.

The data set under analysis must be tested to define how useful each feature is to achieve discrimination. With the total variance as a measure, a principal component analysis - PCA applied over the data set, is then used to reduce the dimensionality of the problem [6]. After that, a new clustering session, with a lower dimensionality, defines feature choice assessment.

This work presents the results of the investigations performed on unsupervised classification techniques for data clustering. The data set used originated from digital recording of voltage sags on a specific bus from a regional transmission system (138 kV and higher) and it is composed of eighty patterns. This large power system can be divided into several regional systems, with most of the buses have a similar behavior regarding voltage sags. The authors are presently working with supervised classifiers to complete the design cycle mentioned previously, so as to reproduce the target knowledge, and test the classifier for other regional systems, with different voltage sag characteristics. The results will be presented in a future publication.

2 Classification Techniques

The following terms and notation are used trough this paper. A feature vector $x = (x_1, x_2, ..., x_H)$ is a pattern composed by H attributes (dimensionality). A pattern set is denoted $x = (X_1, X_2, ..., X_N)$, in a $N \times H$ pattern matrix, corresponding to N voltage sag events.

There are several metrics used to quantify the similarity of patterns on a feature space, each one resulting in different cluster extraction characteristics. Euclidian norm is used as a common metric for all the classifiers. Some Euclidean based distances measures that define clustering criterion functions are:

Vector to vector defines a distance between two patterns.

$$d(x,y) = \sqrt{\sum_{h=1}^{H}(x_h - y_h)^2} \qquad (1)$$

Mean vector for cluster D_i, or cluster i centroid, where n_i is the cluster i number of patterns.

$$m_i = \frac{1}{n_i}\sum_{x \in D_i}(x) \qquad (2)$$

Vector to set gives a mean distance between a sample and a cluster.

$$d(x,X) = \sqrt{\frac{1}{n_i}\sum_{y \in X} d^2(x,y)} \qquad (3)$$

Intraset distance gives the mean distance between patterns inside of each cluster

$$\hat{d}(X) = \sqrt{\frac{1}{n_i}\sum_{j=1}^{n_i} d^2(x_j,X)} \qquad (4)$$

In hierarchical clustering, considering a data set with N samples partitioned into C clusters, successively merged clusters based on a similarity measure, will be called agglomerative hierarchical clustering technique. A similarity level matrix provides a mean to group data into clusters, in a procedure with space complexity $O(CN2d)$, where d is the searching number needed to find the min/max distance. The most common hierarchical clustering algorithms are single linkage, complete linkage and average linkage. Single linkage performs the clustering using the minimum distance criterion, complete linkage uses maximum distance criterion. Single link is a more versatile algorithm, however complete link produces more useful hierarchies in many applications [7]. In the average linkage method, the distance between clusters is the average distance between all pairs of patterns, where one member of a pair belongs to each cluster. Depending on the clustering algorithm and metric used, a new result is reached. This iterative process defines a partition extremized by any criterion function.

The k-means clustering is a partitional algorithm that employs the squared error criterion, in relative low time, with space complexity $O(NHCt)$, where t is the number of iterations. Clusters centers are initially randomly chosen, the result de-pending on the choice, and each pattern assigned to its closest cluster center. The clusters centroids are recomputed and a convergence criterion tested to continue or not the process [7].

In the fuzzy c-means clustering, each pattern has a fuzzy membership grade, from a matrix u, where an element u_{ij} represents the probability of a pattern x_j to be classified as belonging to cluster c_i. The fuzzy c-means algorithm seeks a minimum of a global objective function. Patterns are reassigned to clusters in order to reduce this criterion function and recompute u, in an iterative process. The process stops when less significant changes in u is reached.

3 Clustering Validity Assessment

In order to examine the clustering techniques used for voltage sag patterns classification, intensive classifying sessions, with different criterion indexes and a progressive increase in the number of clusters, are used. Cluster dispersion indicator - CDI [5], based on a squared mean of K clusters centers distances set C:

$$CDI = \frac{1}{\hat{d}(C)} \sqrt{\frac{1}{K} \sum_{k=1}^{K} \hat{d}^2(X_k)} \qquad (5)$$

Davies-Bouldin Index - DBI [5], represents the system-wide average similarity measure of each cluster with its most similar cluster.

$$DBI = \frac{1}{K} \sum_{k=1}^{K} \max_{i \neq j} \{ \frac{\hat{d}(X^i) + \hat{d}(X^j)}{d(C^i, C^j)} \} \qquad (6)$$

In these indexes, a smaller value represents a better clustering quality. When applying the indexes to k-means and fuzzy k-means algorithms, care must be taken regarding to the dependency on starting conditions. Random sorted centers can lead to different solutions.

In Figures 1 and 2 the results for both CDI and DBI indexes indicate the superiority of the hierarchical algorithms in grouping voltage sag patterns for the data set under

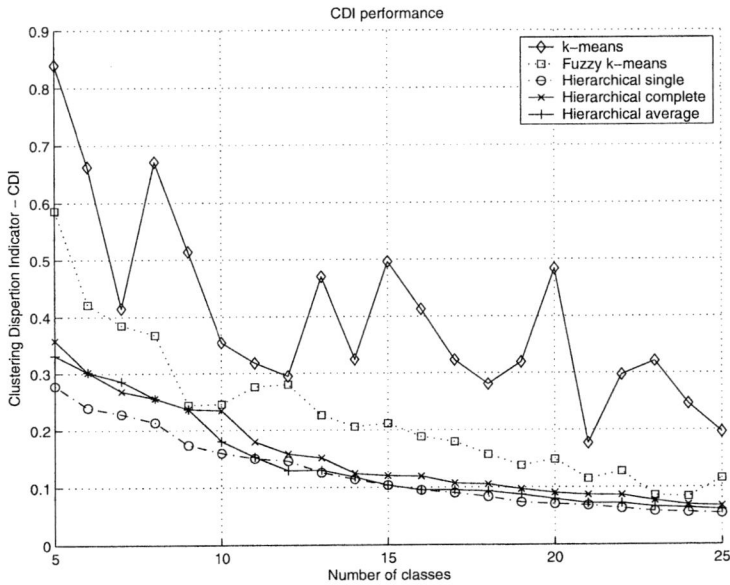

Fig. 1. Clustering dispersion Index - CDI computed from a 5 to 25 clustering using several clustering techniques

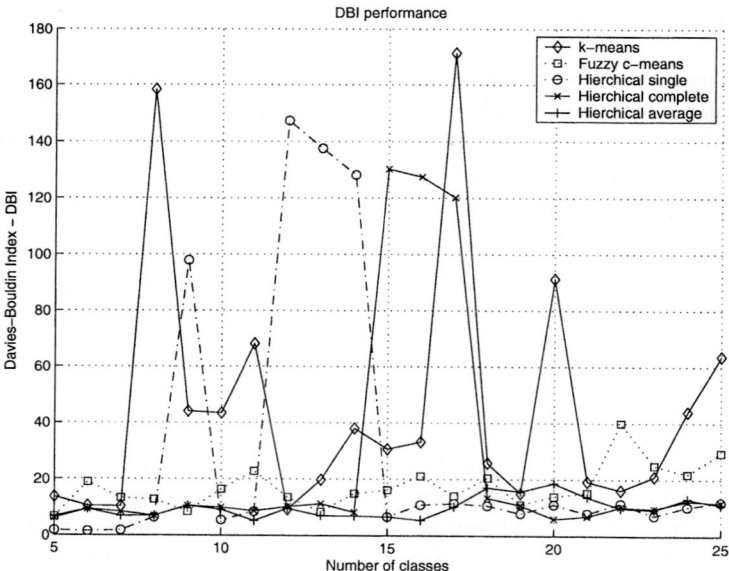

Fig. 2. Davies-Bouldin Index - DBI computed from a 5 to 25 clustering using several clustering techniques

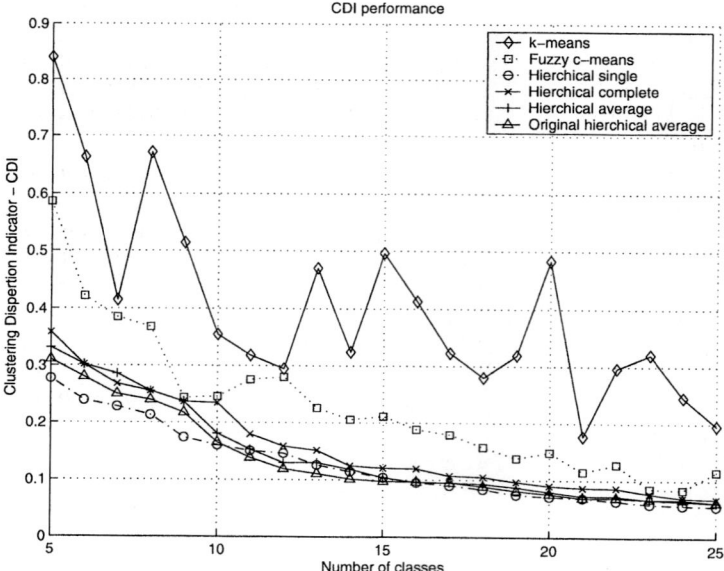

Fig. 3. Clustering dispersion Index - CDI applied over the five first principal component subspace of original data set. Original hierarchical average linkage plotted as a comparative parameter.

analysis. It can also be concluded that use of the CDI index resulted in a better tendency of cluster definition.

The use of principal component analysis, or *Karhunen − Lovetransform*, leads to a feature choice selection by projecting H dimensional data onto a lower R dimensional subspace (the inherent dimensionality). PCA eigenvalues show that the amount of total variance of the used data set is explained by using the first R components. PCA analysis reduced the dimensionality of the problem from eleven variables to five first principal components. Clustering validity over the new R dimensional data set was then performed using CDI and DBI index. Hierarchical single clustering obtained with the original data set, was used for comparison. Figure 3 shows the results of this new clustering process computing the CDI performance index.

4 Conclusions

Voltage sag pattern classification has been investigated using five unsupervised algorithms. The efficiency of the algorithms was analyzed by applying the CDI and DBI indexes. The hierarchical algorithms presented the best performance. This conclusion holds for the two situations considered, that is, for the case of the original data set and for the case with the dimensionality reduced by PCA analysis.

References

1. Dugan, R.C. McGranaghan, M.F. Beaty, H.W.: *Eletrical Power Systems Quality*, McGraw-Hill, (1996).
2. Alves, M.F., Fernandes, D.E.: *Development of an Automated Power Quality Management System*, 1999 IEEE/PES Transmission and Distribution Conference, New Orleans, (1999).
3. Duda, R.O., Hart, P.E., Stork, D.G.: *Pattern Classification*, John Willey & Sons, New York, USA, (2001), 654p.
4. Morcos, M. M., Ibrahim, W. R. A.,: *Artificial Intelligence Advanced Mathematical Tools for Power Quality Applications*, IEEE Transactions on Power Delivery, v17, n2, june, (2002).
5. Chicco,G., Naopli,R., Piglioni,F.: *Comparisons among Clustering Techniques for Electricity Customer Classification*, IEEE Bologna Power Tech, Bologna, Italy, june, (2003).
6. Johnson, R.A., Wichern, D.W.: *Applied Multivariate Statistical Analysis*, Prentice Hall, 3rd edition, New Jersey, USA, (1992), 642p.
7. Jain, A.K. , Murty, M.N., Flynn, P.J.: *Data Clustering: A Review*, ACM Computer Survey, 31, 3, june, (1999), 264-323.
8. Haykin, S.: *Neural Networks - A Comprehensive Foundation*, Macmillan Publishing Company, USA, (1994), 696p.

Face Recognition Using Topological Manifolds Learning

Cao Wenming and Lu Fei

Institute of Intelligent Information System, Information College,
Zhejiang University of Technology,
Hangzhou 310032, China
luf@zjut.edu.cn

Abstract. An algorithm of PCA face recognition based on topological manifolds theory is proposed, which based on the sample sets' topological character in the feature space which is different from "classification". Compare with the traditional PCA+ NN algorithm, experiments prove its efficiency.

1 Introduction

Automatic human face recognition is attractive in personal identification, which widely used in security, bank and commerce department. Compared with other biometric identification techniques such as fingerprint recognition and retina recognition, it is directly, friendly and convenient. So the research of face recognition is become very hot[1]. Face recognition Based on geometrical features is proposed by D.L.Domoho[2], there are other algorithm such as based on deformable template, the character of eyes, neural networks[5][6][7] and the generalized symmetry transform[3], In this paper we introduced an novel face recognition algorithm based on topological manifolds theory[4], experiments prove its efficiency.

2 Principal Component Analysis(PCA)

At common ,a face image is described a high dimensional vector in image space. Facial image can be regarded as a point in the space. Fig 1. shows this idea graphically. Because there are strong symmetry structure of face(eyes, nose, and mouth and so on),so usually the vectors is relative. We can find that images of a people congregate in a certain area in space. So we can project face images into an array of eigenvector, which we obtain from covariance matrix of the trained face images.

Suppose the face image to be size of L by L, this image can be described as a L^2 high dimensional vector or a point in a space of L^2 high dimension. A set of image correspond to a set of point. Because the distribution is not at random, so we can project it to a low dimensional subspace. PCA is a usual dimension reduction method which gives the basis vector for this subspace. Each basis vector is eigenvector of the covariance matrix corresponding to the original face images.

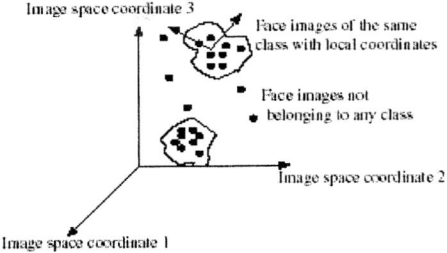

Fig. 1. Image space

Supposed I_1, I_2 ......, Is as a training set, its' average face can be defined by:

$$A = \frac{1}{S}\sum_{i=1}^{S} Ii \qquad (1)$$

The margin of a face image and average face is $Y_i = I_i - A$. Covariance matrix C is defined by:

$$C = \frac{1}{S}\sum_{i=1}^{S} Y_i \cdot Y_i^T \qquad (2)$$

Select the maximum M eigenvector, and then get corresponding value of every image:

$$W_{iK} = E_K^T \cdot (I_i - A) \quad \forall i, K \qquad (3)$$

E_K^T is the maximum M eigenvector, the range of K is from 1 to M.

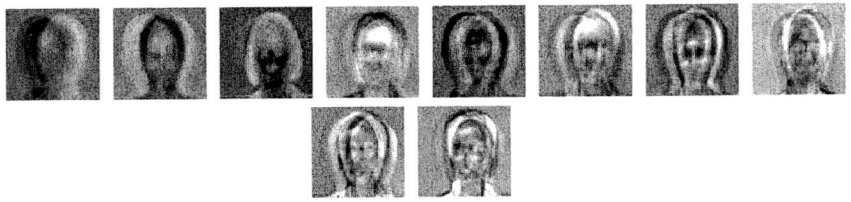

Fig. 2. illuminates face reconstruction corresponding to the maximum 10 eigenvector in experiments

Test image I_{test} project to face space as the algorithm :

$$W_{testK} = E_K^T \cdot (I_{test} - A) \quad \forall K. \qquad (4)$$

3 Algorithm of PCA Face Recognition Based on Topological Manifolds Learning

1) Reduce image space dimension via PCA, project the training image into a low dimensional space, and get the new image vector of low dimension.
2) Form Topological Manifolds in low dimensions space. The method of form Topological Manifolds is:

Consider the training sample set is S, the size of this set is N, let i=1.

Step 1: Select an image a in set S at random,

Step 2: Calculate distance between a and the remain training set $S - \{a\}$. Get sample b which is nearest to a.

Step 3: Form Topological Manifolds A[i] used sample a and b, let i=i+1

Step 4: Abandon image a from set S, then $S = S - \{a\}, N = N - 1$, let $a = b$

step 5: if $N = 1$, the process is complete, otherwise repeat from step1 to step 5.

Fig 3 shows the result of different people's Topological Manifolds

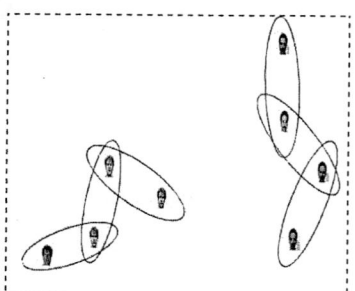 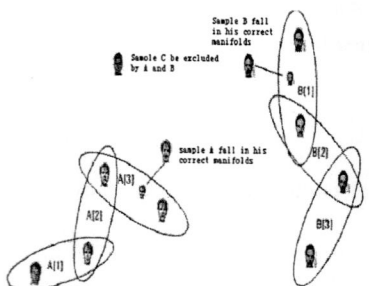

Fig. 3. Different people's on Topological Manifolds

Fig. 4. The recognition process based Topological Manifolds

3) Project every test sample TS_i in test set T_S to image space of the same low dimension, and then calculate the distance between the new image vector and every people Topological Manifolds. If it lies in the a people's Topological Manifolds, we can confirm it belong to this people. If the test image vector does not lie in any people's Topological Manifolds, we can say we do not recognize this sample (Fig 4 demonstrates this process graphically.).

4 Experiment Result

In experiments we used both UMIST and Yale database. The image of Yale database have different illumination and expression, so we use it to analyse the affection of illumination and expression. Meanwhile we use UMIST database to analyse the affection of face position. We compare the traditional PCA+ NN algorithm with PCA+ Topological manifolds theory.

Experiment 1: In Yale database we select 8 people, and select 6 images of every of the 8 people to train the neural network. And we test the remain 5 images and the other 7people's images.

Table 1. Comparison of the efficiency used Yale database

	Correct rate	Rejection rate	Error rate
PCA+ NN	70%	0	30%
PCA+Topological Manifolds	95%	100%	5%

Under the variation of illumination and expression, we can see from above table, the correct rate of PCA+Topological manifolds is higher than that of PCA+ NN. Also it can correctly confirm all of the unacquainted image. So we can say that, under the variation of illumination and expression, PCA+Topological manifolds is superior to PCA+ NN.

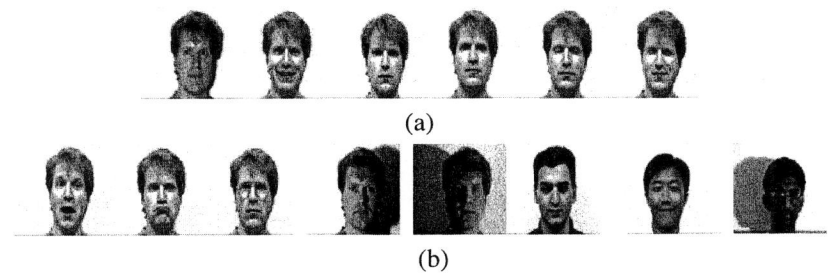

Fig. 5. The training image (a) and testing image(b) in Yale database

Experiment 2: In UMIST database we select 15 people, and select 8 images of every of the 15 people to train the neural network. And we test the remain 2 images and the other 5 people's images.

Table 2. Comparison of the efficiency used UMIST database

	Correct rate	Rejection rate	Error rate
PCA+ NN	72.5%	0	27.5%
PCA+Topological Manifolds	85%	100%	15%

Under the variation of face position , we can see from above table, the correct rate of PCA+Topological manifolds is higher than that of PCA+ NN. Also it can correctly confirm all of the unacquainted image. So we can say that, under the variation of illumination and expression, PCA+Topological manifolds is superior to PCA+ NN.

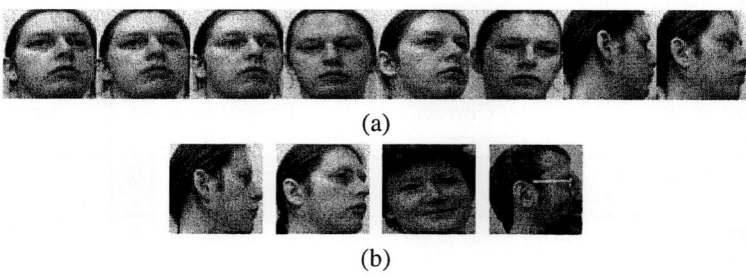

Fig . 6. The training image (a) and testing image(b) in UMIST database

Experiment 3: We test the efficiency between the traditional PCA+ NN algorithm and PCA+ Topological manifolds theory when the dimension of eigenvector changed. If heighten the size of eigenvector ,recognition rate increased, however complexity increased as well. when M>30, the recognition rate do not increase obviously. Because an algorithm of PCA face recognition based on topological manifolds theory is based on the sample sets' topological character in the feature space which is different from "classification", its recognition rate is much better.

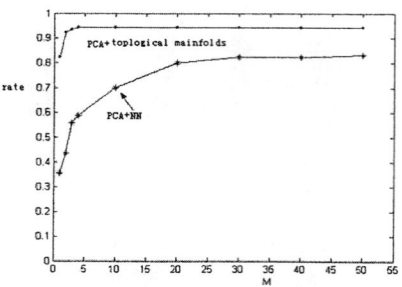

Fig. 7. Comparison of the efficiency when M is changed

5 Conclusion and Problem

In the experiment we can draw conclusion below

1) Face recognition based on topological manifolds do not recognize every people not trained, which is better closer to the function of human being.

2) When add the new trained sample ,topological manifolds structure of original samples do not change.

3) In our experiments, we must make sure of the preprocess is continuous project, otherwise it will affect the efficiency.

Meanwhile there are some problem existed. When forming Topological Manifolds, the size of topological manifolds is important. If the size is bigger ,the chance of a image to fall in the topological manifolds increased, which will bring increase of correct recognition rate, as well as error recognition rate.

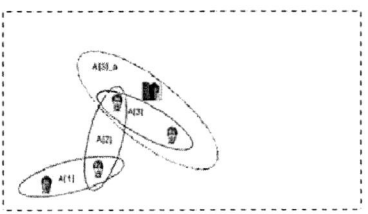

Fig. 8. The structure of different size

The number of a people's sample affect the structure of a people's topological manifolds. When the number of sample is increasing, the chance of the image to fall in it is increasing also., so the correct recognition rate is higher.

References

1. 1.Deslauiers,G.andDubuc,s. Symmetric iterative interpolation processes. Constr. Approx., (1989) 5(1):49-682
2. Monterey,Californla,Wavelet mathe -matics and application CRC Press, Inc,1994
3. Ami Hartegen. Multi-resolution Represe -ntation of data: Ageneral Frame works, SIAM. J. numer. Anal (1996) 33(3) 1205 -1255
4. Wang ShouJue, A new development on ANN in China - Biomimetic pattern recognition and multi weight vector neurons, LECTURE NOTES IN ARTIFICIAL INTELLIGENCE 2639: 35-43, 2003
5. Wang shoujue, Xu jian, Wang xianbao, Qin hong, Multi Camer Human Face Personal Identification System based on the biomimetic pattern recognition , ACTA ELECTRONICA SINICA, Vol.31 No.1,Jan. 2003 1-3
6. Wenming Cao, Feng Hao, Shoujue Wang: The application of DBF neural networks for object recognition. Inf. Sci. (2004) 160(1-4): 153-160
7. Wenming Cao, Jianhui Hu, Gang Xiao, Shoujue Wang. Iris Recognition Algorithm Based on Point Covering of High-Dimensional Space and Neural Network, LECTURE NOTES IN ARTIFICIAL INTELLIGENCE 3587, pp. 305 – 313, 2005.

A Context-Sensitive Technique Based on Support Vector Machines for Image Classification

Francesca Bovolo and Lorenzo Bruzzone

Department of Information and Communication Technologies,
University of Trento,
Via Sommarive 14, 38050 Povo (TN), Italy
lorenzo.bruzzone@ing.unitn.it

Abstract. In this paper, a novel context-sensitive classification technique based on Support Vector Machines (CS-SVM) is proposed. This technique aims at exploiting the promising SVM method for classification of 2-D (or n-D) scenes by considering the spatial-context information of the pixel to be analyzed. The context-based architecture is defined by properly integrating SVMs with a Markov Random Field (MRF) approach. In the design of the resulting system, two main issues have been addressed: i) estimation of the observation term statistic (class-conditional densities) with a proper multiclass SVM architecture; ii) integration of the SVM approach in the framework of MRFs for modeling the prior model of images. Thanks to the effectiveness of the SVM machine learning strategy and to the capability of MRFs to properly model the spatial-contextual information of the scene, the resulting context-sensitive image classification procedure generates regularized classification maps characterized by a high accuracy. Experimental results obtained on Synthetic Aperture Radar (SAR) remote sensing images confirm the effectiveness of the proposed approach.

1 Introduction

Image classification plays a very important role in many application domains, like biomedical and remote sensing image analysis, industrial visual inspection, video surveillance, *etc.* Although often in real applications and commercial software packages image classification problems are addressed according to pixel-based (context-insensitive) classifiers, from a theoretical and practical point of view it is very important to develop classification techniques capable to exploit the spatial-context information present in the images. In this framework, it seems particularly relevant to develop context-sensitive classification methods capable to properly exploit the most promising pixel-based classification methodologies recently proposed in the literature. In this context, a promising machine learning approach to classification is that based on Support Vector Machines (SVMs). SVMs, originated from the statistical learning theory formulated by Vapnik and co-workers [1], are a distribution-free classification approach, which proven very effective in many context-insensitive classification and regression problems. SVM-based classifiers have three main advantages with respect to standard machine learning techniques based on neural networks: i) simple architecture design; ii) moderate computational complexity; iii) excellent generalization cabilty [1]. In particular, advantage iii) is very relevant with respect to image classification problems. In greater detail, designing a classifier characterized by good generalization properties requires assuming: i) a high number of training sample is available; ii) that the training samples are statistical independendent. In image classification problems this last assumption is frequently violated due to high dependency between neighboring pixels; thus the excellent generalization ability of SVMs and their robustness to the Hughes phenomenon [1] seem very suitable to the solution of image classification problems. However, at the present SVMs have been proposed as a context-insensitive classification procedure. Nonetheless, their effectiveness makes it attractive to extend them to address context-sensitive image classification problems.

One of the most promising approaches to context-sensitive classification is to exploit the spatial-context information in the decision rule [2]. In this framework, the correlation among labels can be modeled according to the analysis of either the prior model (regularization term) of the scene and/or the conditional density component (observation term) present in the acquired signal. In this context, in the literature there has been a wide emphasis on using statistical techniques based on Markov Random Fields (MRFs) [2].

In this paper, we propose to properly integrate the SVM technique within a MRFs framework, in order to obtain accurate and reliable classification maps taking into account context-spatial dependence between neighboring pixels. SVMs are used in the MRF for modeling the observation term, which results in a complex problem because the structural risk minimization principle driving SVM is not directly related to a Bayesian estimation of the conditional density functions of classes. This requires additional steps for a proper and effective modeling of the observation component.

Experimental results and comparisons, carried out on Synthetic Aperture Radar (SAR) remote sensing images, confirm the effectiveness of the proposed classification architecture.

2 The Proposed Context-Sensitive Technique Based on SVM

Let us consider a supervised image classification problem. Let X be the image (of size $I \times J$ pixels) to be classified. The training set is composed of L vectors x_i ($i = 1,2,...,L$) from a n-dimensional feature space. Feature space definition is a data dependent task strictly related to user requirements and to the considered image. Here, we assume to have a feature set that properly describes the considered information classes. Each vector in the available training set is associated with a target which identifies the membership of the pattern x_i to one of the K land-cover classes $\omega_j \in \Omega$, $\Omega = \{\omega_1, \omega_2, ..., \omega_K\}$, to be discriminated in the considered classification problem.

The proposed technique integrates the SVM approach in the MRF framework according to the use of a proper classification architecture (see Fig. 1). The proposed architecture is composed of three main blocks: i) a multiclass SVM architecture based on the one-against-all (OAA) strategy; ii) a block devoted to the estimation of the conditional densities of classes; and iii) an MRF context-based classifier. As both the multiclass SVM classifier and the block for the estimation of class conditional density functions require a training phase for parameters estimation, the available training set is divided in two subsets T_1 and T_2, built up of L_1 and L_2 pattern (with $L_1+L_2=L$), respectively.

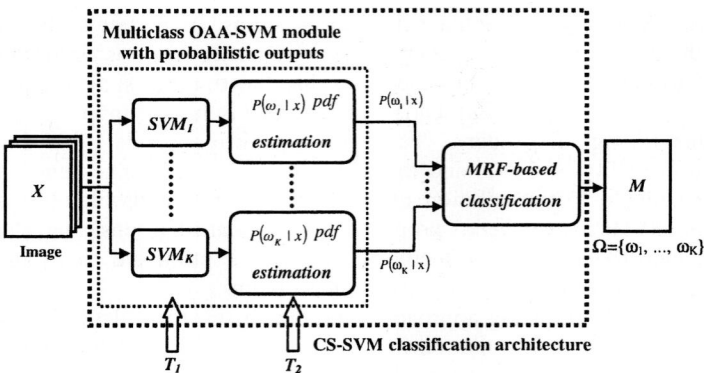

Fig. 1. Block scheme of the proposed CS-SVM based technique for image classification

2.1 Context-Insensitive Multiclass SVM Module

As can be seen in Fig. 1, the first block of the proposed architecture is based on a multiclass SVM classifier that defines a context-insensitive classification model by exploiting the concept of geometrical margin maximization rather than a *bayesian* statistical decision rule. SVMs have been originally designed to solve binary problems. To address multiclass problems, in the literature, among the others, two principal strategies have been proposed: the one-against-all (OAA) and the one-against-one (OAO). Here we focus our attention on the first one as it simplifies both the architecture and the phase of class conditional density estimation. The OAA-SVM architecture involves K binary SVMs, one for each class. Each SVM is trained to discriminate between one information class ω_j, $\omega_j \in \Omega$, and all the others $\Omega - \omega_j$. In the general case of nonlinear separable classes, the discriminant function defined by the *j-th* binary SVM can be expressed as:

$$f_j(x) = w_j \cdot \Phi_j(x_i) + b_j \qquad (1)$$

where $\Phi_j(\cdot)$ is a proper nonlinear kernel (which satisfies the Mercer's theorem) that maps the input feature space into a higher dimensional space where classes can be linearly separated by means of an optimal hyperplane defined by a normal vector w_j and a bias b_j. Once the kernel $\Phi_j(\cdot)$ is defined, training the SVM means estimating the $\Phi_j(\cdot)$ parameters and the values of w_j and b_j so that the following cost function is minimized [1]:

$$\Psi_j(w_j, \xi_j) = \frac{1}{2}\|w_j\|^2 + C_j \sum_{i=1}^{L_1} \xi_{ji} \qquad (2)$$

where ξ_{ji} are the so-called *slack-variable* introduced to account for the non-separability of data, and the constant C_j represents a regularization parameter that allows to control the penalty assigned to errors. For further details on the minimization of (2) and on SVM theory the reader is referred to [1]. The training of the K

considered SVMs (which is carried out on the training set T_l) results in the definition of the set of discrimination functions f_j (with $j = 1, ..., K$). For each pattern the sign of $f_j(x_i)$ indicates whether the given pattern x_i belongs to the class ω_j or not, whereas its absolute value quantifies how far the pattern is from the j-th discriminating function. Since the output of each SVM defines the distance between the pattern and the hyperplane, to derive an estimation of the conditional class probabilities $p(x \mid \omega_j)$, $\omega_j \in \Omega$, to be used in the MRF, it is necessary to exploit a proper estimation procedure. A way to compute the j-th posterior probability from j-th SVM's outputs is to model it as a sigmoid function of the distance from the j-th hyperplane as:

$$P(\omega_j \mid x_i) = \frac{1}{1 + \exp[S_j f_j(x_i) + R_j]} \tag{3}$$

where S_j and R_j are the sigmoid parameters computed on T_2 by minimizing the cross-entropy error function [3]. It is worth noting that, for each class, the observation term (proportional to the conditional class probabilities) is obtained dividing the posterior probabilities by the prior probabilities (computed as relative frequency of the patterns belonging to the considered class in T_l).

2.2 Context-Sensitive MRF-Based Module

This module integrates the SVM based estimates within the MRF framework according to the Bayesian decision theory. The MRF-based classification strategy exploits the assumption that a pixel belonging to a given class $\omega_j \in \Omega$ is likely to be surrounded by pixel belonging to the same class. Therefore exploiting this dependence may yield to more reliable and accurate classification results.

Let $C = \{C_l, 1 \leq l \leq Z\}$ with $Z=K^{IJ}$ be composed of all the sets of labels in the image X, where $C_l = \{C_l(m,n), 1 \leq m \leq I, 1 \leq n \leq J\}$ (with $C_l(m,n) \in \Omega$) is a generic set of label in X. The formulation of the Bayes decision rule for minimum error in terms of Markovian approach to classification is equivalent to minimizing the following energy function [2],[4]:

$$U(X \mid C_l) = \sum_{n=1}^{I} \sum_{m=1}^{J} [U_{ci}(X(n,m) \mid C_l(n,m)) + U_{cs}(C_l(n,m) \mid \{C_l(g,h), (g,h) \in N(n,m)\})] \tag{4}$$

where $U_{ci}(.)$ is the context-insensitive energy term that represents the statistics of the considered image (observation term), and $U_{cs}(.)$ is the context-sensitive energy term computed over the local neighborhood system $N(n,m)$ of the generic pixel in spatial position (n,m). The shape and the size of $N(.)$ depends on the considered image and application [2]. As we are modeling the random variable X as an MRF over the neighborhood system, the context-sensitive term should be a Gibbs energy function and shows an exponential dependency from the prior model for the class labels $P(C_l)$ [2]. In practice $U_{cs}(.)$ is defined as:

$$U_{cs}\left(C_l(n,m) \mid \{C_l(g,h), (g,h) \in N(n,m)\}\right) = \sum_{(g,h) \in N(n,m)} \beta \delta(C_l(n,m) \mid C_l(g,h)) \tag{5}$$

where δ is the Kronecker delta function [2] and β is a constant that controls the influence of the spatial-contextual information in the classification process. Under the assumption of class conditional independence [2], $U_{ci}(.)$ can be expressed as the product of the conditional class probabilities $p(x \mid \omega_j)$. In this paper this term has been estimated by means of the probabilistic OAA-SVM classifier system introduced in the previous paragraph.

Concerning the optimization procedure for minimizing (4), in the proposed approach we analyzed the effectiveness of the three main strategies proposed in the literature: i) iterated conditional modes (ICM) [4]; ii) simulated annealing (SA) [2]; and iii) maximizer of posterior marginals (MPM) [5].

3 Experimental Results

Several experiments on a remote sensing application case were carried out in order to assess the effectiveness of the proposed CS-SVM classifier with respect to the context-insensitive SVM (CI-SVM) classifier. The considered data consists of SAR images acquired by the ERS-1 satellite over the city of Berna (Switzerland). The considered classification problem is characterized by four land-cover classes: forest, urban area, water and fields. The analysis was carried out on a data set made up of 8 temporally filtered images, acquired in the period between June 1995 and May 1996, plus a feature based on the average long-term coherence (the reader is referred to [6] for greater detail on the data set). In all experiments, SVMs with Gaussian radial basis kernel functions were used and context-based classification was carried out using a second order neighborhood system. Several trials were carried out to find the best values of all the binary SVMs classifiers and sigmoidal functions parameters; also the optimal context weight β was derived for each of the three MRF optimization procedures.

Table 1 summarizes the best accuracies obtained with the different techniques on the test set. As expected, the use of the spatial-context information allows to properly model the autocorrelation function between pixels regularizing the classification map and increasing the overall accuracy. In greater detail, the proposed CS-SVM approach (with all the optimization) significantly increased the overall accuracy and the kappa

Table 1. Overall and Kappa accuracies obtained using a standard context-insensitive (CI-SVM) and the proposed context-sensitive technique based on SVM (CS-SVM) with different optimization algorithms

Classification strategy		Kappa coefficient	Overall Accuracy (%)	Forest	Urban area	Water	Fields
Standard CI-SVM		0.88	91.97	96.11	91.20	81.14	90.45
Proposed CS-SVM	ICM	0.91	94.38	98.54	93.48	83.56	92.90
	MPM	0.93	95.52	99.43	94.13	83.49	94.47
	SA	0.94	95.92	99.43	94.60	84.00	95.03

accuracy with respect to the CI-SVM technique. In particular, the highest accuracy was obtained with the simulated annealing optimization procedure, with a significant increase, i.e. 6%, with respect to the classical pixel-based classification strategy. It is worth noting that also class-by-class accuracies increased significantly when introducing the context information in the classification process. Finally, from an analysis of the obtained classification maps, it is possible to observe that the proposed approach properly regularizes the resulting classification maps.

4 Conclusions

In this paper, a novel context-sensitive image classification approach based on SVMs has been proposed. This approach exploits a properly defined multiclass SVM architecture for estimating the distribution of the observation term to be jointly optimized with the prior term in the global energy function used for modeling the classification problem under the MRF framework.

Experimental results carried out on remote sensing SAR images confirmed the effectiveness of the proposed context-sensitive approach, which significantly outperformed the standard CI-SVM classifier. This mainly depends on the capability of the proposed method to both properly take into account the contextual information (included in the model of the *a-priori* term) in the decision process and model the observation term with an effective and reliable machine learning methodology.

As future development of this work we plan to further extend the experimental investigation of the proposed image classification approach to other application domains. In addition, we will investigate the possibility to include the spatial-context information directly in the cost function optimized in the learning phase of SVMs.

References

1. Vapnik, V. N.,: Statistical Learning Theory, Wiley, 1998.
2. Geman, S., Geman, D.: Stochastic Relaxation, Gibbs Distribution, and Bayesian Restoration of Images. *IEEE Trans. Pattern Anal. Machine Intell.* PAMI-6 (1984) 768-778.
3. Platt, J.C.: Probabilistic Outputs for Support Vector Machines and Comparison to Regularized Likelihood Methods. In: Smola, A., Bartlett, P., Scholkopf, B., Schuurmans, D. (eds.): Advances in Large Margin Classifiers. Cambridge, MA, MIT Press (1999).
4. Besag, J.: On the Statistical Analysis of Dirty Pictures. *J. Roy. Statist. Soc. B.* 48 (1986) 259-302.
5. Marroquin,J., Mitter, S., Poggio, T.: Probabilistic Solution of Ill-posed Problems in Computational Vision. *J. Amer. Stat. Assoc..* 82 (1987) 76-89.
6. Bruzzone, L., Marconcini, M., Wegmuller, U., Wiesmann, A.: An advanced system for the automatic classification of multitemporal SAR images. *IEEE Trans. Geosci. Rem. Sens.* 42 (2004) 1321-1334

Face Recognition Technique Using Symbolic PCA Method

P.S. Hiremath[1] and C.J. Prabhakar[2]

[1] Department of Studies in Computer Science, Gulbarga University,
Gulbarga – 585106, Karnataka, India
`hiremathps@yahoo.co.in`
[2] Department of Studies in Computer Science, Kuvempu University,
Shankaraghatta – 577451, Karnataka, India
`psajjan@yahoo.com`

Abstract. A face recognition technique based on symbolic PCA approach is presented in this paper. The proposed method transforms the face images by extracting knowledge from training samples into symbolic objects, termed as symbolic faces. Symbolic PCA is employed to compute a set of subspace basis vectors for symbolic faces and then to project the symbolic faces into the compressed subspace. New test images are then matched with the images in the database by projecting them onto the basis vectors and finding the nearest symbolic face in the subspace. The feasibility of the new symbolic PCA method has been successfully tested for face recognition using ORL database. As compared to eigenface method, the proposed method requires less number of features to achieve the same recognition rate.

1 Introduction

Face recognition involves computer recognition of personal identity based on statistical or geometrical features derived from the face images. Face recognition technology is primarily used in law enforcement applications especially mug shot albums (static matching) and video surveillance (real time matching by video image sequences). Template based face recognition techniques using the Principal Component Analysis was first proposed by Kirby and Sirovich [5] to efficiently represent pictures of human faces. Turk and Pentland [8] presented the well known eigenface method for face recognition in 1991. Since then, PCA has been widely investigated and has become one of the most successful approaches in face recognition.

The classical PCA (eigenface) approach uses data, which is single quantitative value, representing every pixel of a face image as a feature. The proposed method is based on symbolic data, where each feature can be viewed as quantitative multivalued symbolic variable [1]. This is because same face is captured in different orientation, lighting, expression and background which leads to number of poses of same face with same set of features measured in all poses and in the same sequence. This results in coverage of complete information about features of a face represented by a symbolic object. Features characterizing symbolic object may be large in number, which leads to creation of a multi-dimensional feature space. Larger the dimensionality, more severe is the problem of storage and analysis. Hence a lot of importance has been attributed to the process of dimensionality or feature reduction of symbolic objects, which is achieved by subsetting or transformation methods [4] [7]. Gowda and Nagabhushan [6] proposed a dimensionality reduction method on interval data based on Taylor series. Ichino [3] proposed an extension of a PCA based on a generalized Minkowski metrics in order to deal with interval, set valued structure data. Choukria, Diday and Cazes [2] proposed different methods, namely, Vertices Method (V-PCA), Centers Method and Range Transformation Method. Face recognition system using symbolic data analysis involves high number of features; V-PCA requires high computational cost. So to overcome this difficulty we propose to use centers method.

The objective of the present paper is to perform symbolic data analysis of face images stored in a database by representing the face image by symbolic object of interval valued variables. The proposed method first transforms the face images by extracting knowledge from training samples into symbolic faces, each symbolic face summarizing the variation of feature values through the different images of the same subject. Symbolic PCA extracts features from symbolic faces, called as symbolic PCA features, and these are used for recognition purpose. The efficacy of the method is demonstrated by conducting experiments on face images of ORL database.

2 Symbolic Faces

Consider the face images $\Gamma_1, \Gamma_2, \ldots, \Gamma_n$, each of size $N \times M$, from a face image database. Let $\Omega = \{\Gamma_1, \ldots, \Gamma_n\}$ be the collection of n face images of the database, which are first order objects. Each object $\Gamma_l \in \Omega$, $l = 1, \ldots, n$, is described by a feature vector $(\tilde{Y}_1, \ldots, \tilde{Y}_p)$, of length $p = NM$, where each component $\tilde{Y}_j$, $j = 1, \ldots, p$, is a single valued variable representing the intensity values of the face image Γ_l. An image set is a collection of face images of m different subjects; each subject has same number of images but with different orientations, expressions and illuminations. There are m number of second order objects (face classes) denoted by $c_1, \ldots, c_m$, each consisting of different individual images $\Gamma_l \in \Omega$. We denote the set $E = \{c_1, c_2, \ldots, c_m\}$ and $c_i \subseteq \Omega$, $i = 1, \ldots, m$. The feature vector of each face class $c_i \in E$ is described by a vector of p interval variables $Y_1, \ldots, Y_p$, and is of length $p = NM$. The interval variable Y_j of face class c_i is described by $Y_j(c_i) = [\underline{x}_{ij}, \overline{x}_{ij}]$, where $\underline{x}_{ij}$ and $\overline{x}_{ij}$ are minimum and maximum intensity values, respectively, among j^{th} pixels of all the images of face class c_i. This interval incorporates information of the variability of jth feature inside the ith face class. We denote $X(c_i) = (Y_1(c_i), \ldots, Y_p(c_i))$. The vector $X(c_i)$ of symbolic variables is recorded for each $c_i \in E$, and can be described by a symbolic data vector which is called as *symbolic face* : $X(c_i) = (\alpha_{i1}, \ldots, \alpha_{ip})$, where $\alpha_{ij} = Y_j(c_i)$, $j = 1, \ldots, p$. We represent the m *symbolic faces* by a $m \times p$ matrix:

$$\underline{X} = \begin{pmatrix} \alpha_{11} & \cdots & \alpha_{1p} \\ \vdots & \ddots & \vdots \\ \alpha_{m1} & \cdots & \alpha_{mp} \end{pmatrix} = (\alpha_{ij})_{m \times p}. \tag{1}$$

3 Symbolic PCA

The Symbolic PCA takes as input the matrix $\underline{X}$ containing m *symbolic faces* pertaining to the given set Ω of images. We use centers method [2], which essentially applies the classical PCA method to the centers $x_{ij}^c \in \Re$ of the interval $[\underline{x}_{ij}, \overline{x}_{ij}]$, that is,

$$x_{ij}^c = \frac{\overline{x}_{ij} + \underline{x}_{ij}}{2}. \tag{2}$$

where $j = 1, \ldots, p$ and $i = 1, \ldots, m$

The $m \times p$ data matrix $\underline{X}^C$ containing the centers x_{ij}^c of the intervals α_{ij} for m symbolic faces is given by:

$$\underline{X}^c = \begin{pmatrix} x_{11}^c & \cdots & x_{1p}^c \\ \vdots & \ddots & \vdots \\ x_{m1}^c & \cdots & x_{mp}^c \end{pmatrix}. \tag{3}$$

The mean vector Ψ of $\underline{X}^C$ is defined by $\Psi = [\Psi_j]$, where $\Psi_j = \frac{1}{m} \sum_{i=1}^{m} x_{ij}^c$, $j = 1, \ldots, p$. Each row vector of $\underline{X}^C$ differs from the mean vector Ψ by the vector $\Phi_i = (x_{i1}^c, x_{i2}^c, \cdots, x_{ip}^c) - \Psi$. We define the matrix Φ as $\Phi = [\Phi_1', \ldots, \Phi_m']$. The covariance matrix C is obtained as $C = \Phi'\Phi$. Then, we calculate the eigenvalues $\lambda_1 \geq \lambda_2 \geq, \ldots, \lambda_m \geq 0$ and the corresponding orthonormalized eigenvectors $y_1, y_2, \ldots, y_m \in \Re^m$ of the covariance matrix C. The eigenvectors of symbolic PCA can be obtained as $V_m = \Phi Y_m$, where $Y_m = (y_1, \ldots, y_m)$ is the $m \times m$ matrix with columns $y_1, \ldots, y_m$ and V_m is the $p \times m$ matrix with corresponding eigenvectors $v_1, v_2, \ldots, v_m$, as its columns. The subspace is extracted from the $p \times m$ dimensional space by selecting S number of eigenvectors, which contain maximum variance and are denoted by $v_1, v_2, \ldots, v_S$, corresponding to eigenvalues $\lambda_1 \geq \lambda_2 \geq, \ldots, \lambda_S$. The weights W_{ik} for i^{th} symbolic face, $i = 1, \ldots, m$, are computed as

$$W_{ik} = v_k^T (x_{ij}^c - \Psi). \tag{4}$$

where $k = 1, 2, \ldots, S$. The weights of ith symbolic face form the feature vector $(W_{i1}, \ldots, W_{iS})$ of the of ith symbolic face. The weights of test image I_{test} are computed by projecting the test image into face subspace as:

$$W_{testk} = v_k^T (I_{test} - \Psi). \tag{5}$$

4 Experimental Results

The proposed symbolic PCA method is experimented on the face images of the ORL database and compared with eigenface method. In the training phase, firstly construction of symbolic faces (as explained in section 2) for the given training samples is done and then symbolic PCA is applied to obtain the features (as explained in section 3). Further, a nearest neighbor classifier is employed for classification.

The ORL face database (developed at the Olivetti Research Laboratory, Cambridge, U.K.) is composed of 400 images with ten different images for each of the 40 distinct subjects. All the images were taken against a dark homogeneous background with the subjects in an upright, frontal position, with tolerance for some tilting and rotation of up to about 20°. There is some variation in scale of up to about 10%. The spatial and gray level resolutions of the images are 92×112 and 256, respectively. Some typical images of one subject of ORL database are given in Fig 1.

Fig. 1. Five sample images of one subject of the ORL Database

4.1 Comparison of Variance in Eigenvectors of Symbolic PCA and Eigenfaces

Firstly, the experiment is performed using all the 400 image samples (i.e., 40 face classes each with 10 face images) as training sample. Fig. 2 shows the comparison of percentage of variance in eigenvectors of symbolic PCA and eigenfaces. It is ob served that the first eigenvectors of symbolic PCA contain more information (energy) of training samples than the eigenfaces. Thus, fewer eigenvectors of symbolic PCA are required as compared to the large number of eigenfaces necessary to contain the same amount of information, which leads to the dimensionality reduction.

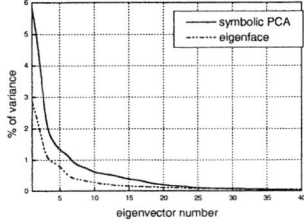

Fig. 2. Comparison of variance in eigenvectors of symbolic PCA and eigenfaces

4.2 Performance of Symbolic PCA Using Four Similarity Measures

In recognition phase, a nearest neighbor classifier based on appropriate similarity measure is used. The experiments are performed using the first five image samples per face class for training and remaining images for testing (i.e., 200 training images and 200 testing images). The experiments are repeated for four different similarity measures, namely, City block (L1), Euclidean (L2), Mahalanobis and cosine similarity measures, and top recognition rates (%) of 55.00, 49.25, 79.45, 92.15, respectively, are achieved. It is observed that the symbolic PCA performed with cosine similarity measure yields better recognition rate as compared to other similarity measures.

4.3 Performance of Symbolic PCA Method for Varying Number of Features

The experiments are performed by adopting leave-one-out strategy. The Fig. 3 shows symbolic PCA method with cosine similarity measure has recognition rate 85.5% using only 13 features, where as eigenface method with Euclidean similarity measure requires 42 features to achieve the same recognition rate. Further, the symbolic PCA with cosine measure achieves a recognition rate of 94.15% using 40 features. This is due to the fact that first few eigenvectors of symbolic PCA account for highest variance of training samples and these few eigenvectors are enough to represent image for recognition purposes. Hence, improved recognition results can be achieved at less computational cost by using symbolic PCA, by virtue of its low dimensionality.

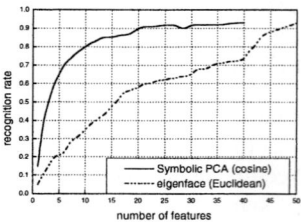

Fig. 3. Comparison of symbolic PCA and eigenface method for varying number of features

5 Conclusion

In this paper, the symbolic PCA approach for face recognition is presented and compared with eigenface method. The experimentation is done using ORL face database. The recognition accuracy obtained by symbolic PCA is better than that obtained by eigenface method for face images with variations in orientations, facial expressions and illuminations. By virtue of dimensionality reduction achieved in symbolic PCA, the improved recognition rates are attained at lower computation cost as compared to eigenface method. Hence, the proposed symbolic PCA is efficient and robust, and can be effectively used in face recognition systems. Further, the usage of symbolic similarity measures in the analysis will be considered in our future studies, in order to exploit the full strength of the symbolic data analysis approach.

Acknowledgement

The authors are grateful to the referees for their valuable comments and suggestions. Also, the authors are indebted to Prof.K.Chidananda Gowda, Vice-chancellor, Kuvempu University, Karnataka, for his helpful discussions and encouragement. Further, the authors are also grateful to Dr.P.Nagabhushan, Professor, and Dr.D.S.Guru, Dept. of Computer Science, University of Mysore, Mysore, for their useful suggestions and encouragement.

References

1. Bock, H.H., Diday, E. (Eds.): Analysis of Symbolic Data. Springer Verlag (2000).
2. Choukria, Diday, Cazes: Extension of the principal component analysis to interval data. NTTS'95: New Techniques and Technologies for statistics, Bonn (1995).
3. Ichino, Yaguchi: Generalized Minkowski metrics for mixed feature type data analysis, vol-(4).IEEE Trans. Systems Man Cybernet. (1994) 698-708.
4. Jain, Dubes: Algorithms for clustering data. Prentice-Hall, Englewood Cliffs, NJ (1998).
5. Kirby, Sirovich: Applications of the Karhunen–Loeve procedure for the characterization of human faces, v-12(1). IEEE Trans. Pattern Anal. Machine Intell. (1990)103-108.
6. Nagabhushan, Gowda, Diday: Dimensionality reduction of symbolic data, vol -16. Pattern Recognition Letters, (1995) 219-223.
7. Sudhanva, Gowda: Dimensionality reduction using geometric projection: a new technique, vol-5(8). Pattern Recognition (1995).
8. Turk, Pentland: Eigenfaces for Recognation, J Cognitive Neuro Science, (1991) 71-86

A Hybrid Approach to Speaker Recognition in Multi-speaker Environment

Jigish Trivedi, Anutosh Maitra, and Suman K. Mitra

Dhirubhai Ambani Institute of Information and Communication Technology,
Gandhinagar, Gujarat, India
{jigish_trivedi, anutosh_maitra, suman_mitra}@da-iict.org

Abstract. Recognition of voice in a multi-speaker environment involves speech separation, speech feature extraction and speech feature matching. Though traditionally vector quantization is one of the algorithms used for speaker recognition; its effectiveness is not well appreciated in case of noisy or multi-speaker environment. This paper describes the usability of the Independent Component Analysis (ICA) technique to enhance the effectiveness of speaker recognition using vector quantization. Results obtained by this approach are compared with that obtained using a more direct approach to establish the usefulness of the proposed method.

Keywords: Speech recognition, ICA, MFCC, Vector Quantization.

1 Introduction

The automatic recognition process of human voice by a machine involves both speech recognition and speaker recognition. Speech recognition is the process by which a computer maps an acoustic speech signal to text. Speaker recognition [1] is the process of recognizing the speaker on the basis of individual information present in the speech waves. In a multi-speaker environment, speech signal may be corrupted by the speech of other speakers, by presence of noise and reverberation, or a combination of both. The quality of the degraded speech will affect the performance of feature extraction for various applications like tracking a moving speaker, speech recognition, speaker recognition, and audio indexing. Thus, it is imperative to enhance the voice from the degraded speech before using it in any application. In this paper, a hybrid approach for speaker recognition is presented where the speech recognition and separation issue has been addressed by a trial application of Independent Component Analysis (ICA); and the speaker recognition technique involves Mel Frequency Cepstrum Coefficient (MFCC) representation of the speech signals and a Vector Quantization (VQ) approach to the feature matching to identify individual speakers. Interestingly, an earlier work in the field of computational auditory scene analysis that focused on the problem of speech segregation concluded that blind source separation techniques could be remarkably powerful if certain requirements on the properties of the source signal are met [2]. This observation was one of the motivating factors in applying the ICA in the speech separation process.

2 Problem Formulation

The speech separation and speaker recognition problems are modeled individually.

Speech Separation: The Independent Component Analysis (ICA) [3,4] has been used for separating the source signals from the information of the mixed signals observed in each input channel. Assuming that we observe n linear mixtures $X=\{x_1, x_2..., x_n\}$ of n independent components $S=\{s_1, s_2..., s_n\}$; the basic problem of source separation could be viewed as modeling the above information in the form of $X=AS$, where A is the mixing matrix. The task here is to obtain an unmixing matrix W such that $W^TX=S$. An improved variant for ICA, known as the FastICA [5] algorithm, is used for the specific task of speech separation in the current work. FastICA uses a learning rule to find the unmixing matrix to separate mixed signals [5]. The source speech signals are assumed to be nongaussian and the nongaussianity is measured by the approximation of negentropy [5].

Speaker Recognition: This comprises of speaker identification and speaker verification. Speaker identification is the process of determining which registered speaker provides a given utterance and it involves speech feature extraction. Speaker verification is the process of accepting or rejecting the identity claim of a speaker with the help of feature matching. The aim of speech feature extraction is to convert the quasi-stationary speech waveform to a parametric representation. A range of techniques exists to suit this purpose; the principal ones being Linear Prediction Coding (LPC) and Mel-Frequency Cepstrum Coefficients (MFCC). MFCCs are based on the filters spaced linearly at low frequencies and logarithmically at high frequencies to capture the phonetically important characteristics of speech. The structure of an MFCC processor consists of 5 well-established different steps, *viz.* Frame blocking, Windowing, FFT, Mel Frequency Wrapping and Cepstrum computation [1]. Feature matching follows the feature extraction process. Amongst the many available feature matching techniques, a vector quantization (VQ) based approach for feature matching with LBG binary split [6] has been preferred here due to its reported high accuracy with relative ease of implementation.

3 Proposed Methodology

For the speech recognition process, only clean speech features are required. In the proposed model, it was conceived that instead of denoising the noisy speech signal in the pre-processing step, it could be computationally more efficient and accurate to directly separate the clean speech features from noisy speech or separate the speech uttered by different speakers.

In a conventional direct approach as depicted in Figure 1, the source signals are randomly mixed to generate an equal number of mixed signals. In real environment, this mixing is achieved using equal number of speakers and microphones. The word 'Direct' signifies that the mixed signals are directly fed to the MFCC-VQ algorithm. In contrast, in the proposed hybrid approach as shown in Figure 2, the mixed signals are processed using the FastICA technique and only the estimated signals are used by the MFCC-VQ algorithm for speaker identification.

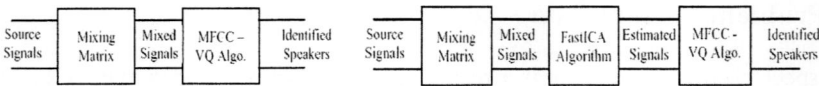

Fig. 1. Direct Approach **Fig. 2.** The Proposed Hybrid Approach

4 Experimental Results

The proposed hybrid approach was tested in a multi-speaker, limited vocabulary recognition scenario. The vocabulary was available from the SR4X sample speech corpus [7] with the speech recorded on four different channels of 5 speakers repeating nine words. The speech was recorded at a sampling frequency of 8KHz and stored at 16 bits per sample. The mixed speech signals are generated from original speech signals by multiplying with random square mixing matrix. These mixed signals are used as testing set for speaker recognition. The FastICA is used for the speech separation task. MFCC-VQ is used for feature extraction and matching.

The implementation of the MFCC algorithm was based on the following setup:

a) The speech signal is blocked into frames of N samples, with adjacent frames being separated by M (M < N) samples and with an overlap of N − M samples. Typical values used for N and M are 256 and 100 respectively, with an 8KHz sampling rate.
b) A hamming window function is used to minimize spectral distortion.
c) A standard FFT routine is used to convert the signals into frequency domain.
d) The approximation used to compute the mel for a given frequency f in Hz is:
$$\text{mel}(f) = 2595 * \log_{10}(1 + f/700)$$
The number of mel spectrum coefficients, K, is chosen as 20.
e) A set of MFCC, called the acoustic vector, is calculated from the log mel spectrum for each speech frame of around 30msec with overlap.

The results of the MFCC-VQ approach for five speakers without using FastICA are shown in Table 1. The training set consists of 31 sound files and the testing set

Table 1. Results of MFCC VQ without using FastICA

Actual Speaker	Training Words	No. of Samples	Testing Words	Identified Speaker
1	71523	4	abracadabra	1
	Computer	4	generation	1
	Nebula	4	processing	1
2	Supernova	4	sungeeta	2
			tektronix	2
3	abracadabra	4	71523	3
			computer	3
4	Sungeeta	3	supernova	4
	Tektronix	4	tektronix	4
5	71523	4	71523	5
			abracadabra	1

Table 2. Comparison of recognition accuracy

No. of Speakers	Recognition Accuracy (%)	
	Direct Approach	Hybrid Approach
2	50	100
3	33 to 66	66 to 100
4	25 to 50	75
5	20 to 40	60

comprises of 11 sound files. During the training and the testing session, the average number of samples per sound file was approximately 22158 and 30714 respectively. After MFCC processing, the dimension for 31 generated set of acoustic vectors for each sound file was 20 × Number of Frames. For each sound file, these acoustic vectors are transformed into the codebook of size 20 × 16 using VQ algorithm.

The performance of the proposed hybrid (FastICA followed by MFCC-VQ) algorithm is compared with that of a direct approach as discussed in Section 3. The comparison result is shown in Table 2. It is observed that the hybrid approach outperformed the direct approach in all cases. Even with a small number of speakers, the accuracy of the direct approach is poor. An overall improvement of 43% in the recognition accuracy is noted in case of the proposed hybrid approach.

5 Conclusion

The study of MFCC – VQ algorithm shows that in a multi-speaker environment, the task of reliable speaker recognition using conventional techniques becomes difficult. However, one can exploit the state of the art of a single speaker environment in a multi-speaker scenario by using the technique of speech separation. The proposed hybrid approach eventually combines the technique of FastICA for speech separation and MFCC-VQ in multi-speaker environment. A fair degree of improvement in recognition accuracy is achieved. The investigation may be further extended to measure the performance of the hybrid approach in noisy environments.

References

1. S. Furui, "An overview of speaker recognition technology", ESCA Workshop on Automatic Speaker Recognition, Identification and Verification, pp. 1-9, 1994.
2. Andre J.W.van der Kouwe, DeLiang Wang, Guy J. Brown, "A comparison of auditory and blind separation techniques for speech segregation", IEEE Transaction of Speech and Audio Processing, Vol.9, No.3, pp. 189-195.
3. J. F. Cardoso, "Eigenstructure of the 4th-order cumulant tensor with application to the blind source separation problem", Proc. ICASSP '89, pp.2109-2112, 1989.
4. A. Bell, T. Sejnowski, "An information maximization approach to blind separation and blind deconvolution", Neural Computation, vol.7, pp.1129-1159, 1995.
5. A. Hyvärinen, E. Oja, "A fast fixed-point algorithm for Independent Component Analysis", Neural Computation, vol. 9, no. 7, pp. 1483-1492, 1997.
6. Y. Linde, A. Buzo, R. Gray, "An algorithm for vector quantizer design", IEEE Transactions on Communications, Vol. 28, pp.84-95, 1980.
7. http://cslu.cse.ogi.edu/corpora/sr4x/

Design of Hierarchical Classifier with Hybrid Architectures

M.N.S.S.K. Pavan Kumar and C.V. Jawahar

Centre for Visual Information Technology,
International Institute of Information Technology,
Hyderabad, INDIA

Abstract. Performance of hierarchical classifiers depends on two aspects — the performance of the individual classifiers, and the design of the architecture. In this paper, we present a scheme for designing hybrid hierarchical classifiers under user specified constraints on time and space.

1 Introduction

Classifiers for multiclass problems, built using combinations of two-class solutions are found to be superior to direct multiclass classifiers in terms of training time and performance [1]. Classifier combination can efficiently be done using hierarchical techniques. Hierarchical classifiers are usually built of simple classifiers. Only a subset of these classifiers evaluate a sample, resulting in low classification time. Hierarchical classifiers are being preferred to the two-stage approaches as demonstrated in BHC-SVM [2]. The topology using which the classifiers are combined is generally referred to as the architecture of the combined classifier. Most of the hierarchical algorithms follow a binary tree architecture. Algorithms for design of hierarchical classifiers focus on evolving the tree by learning the classifiers at each node.

The performance of the hierarchical classifiers depends on the performance of the individual classifiers and the overall combination architecture. In this paper we propose a scheme that incorporates both these factors in designing a hierarchical architecture. Generalization at individual classifiers is obtained with the help of Support Vector Machines(SVM) [1]. The proposed scheme allows selection of a suitable architecture at each node of the tree. A mechanism to specify the suitability of an architecture, as per the requirements like high-accuracy or low-classification time, is provided.

1.1 Background

There are two architectures popular for hierarchical classifiers — Binary Hierarchical Classifier (BHC) [2] and a Decision Directed Acyclic Graph (DDAG) [1]. A BHC is fast but of poorer in accuracy compared to a DDAG. For large class problems, a DDAG requires a prohibitively large number of classifiers.

A BHC recursively partitions the dataset into two at each stage of the hierarchy building, and thereby learns a complete classifier. This results in a classification tree with a binary tree architecture. A sample is presented to the root, and based on the decision at the root node, left or right subtree is selected. This continues till the sample reaches a leaf node, where it gets its label assigned.

A DDAG is an efficient way to combine the pairwise classifiers in the form of a rooted binary directed acyclic graph. Although a DDAG uses $\binom{N}{2}$ classifiers, the number of classifier evaluations is of $O(N)$ for each sample. In [3], an algorithm for improving the performance of a DDAG has been discussed. In a specific case, where misclassification probabilities of all pairwise classifiers are equal, a DDAG design algorithm has been proposed. The algorithm results in an optimal DDAG. The design algorithm attempts to maximize a global objective function J, which is defined as $J = \sum_{i=1}^{N} P_i(1 - Q_i)$ where Q_i is misclassification probability of class ω_i by the DDAG. A greedy algorithm to maximize the global objective function is shown in Table 1.

Table 1. Algorithms for improving the DDAG([3]), and Building the BHC Tree([2])

Algorithm improveDDAG(Ω)	**Algorithm** BuildTree(Ω)
Intialize S = ();	(Ω_l, Ω_r) = partition(Ω);
while Ω not empty **do**	**if** $\|\Omega_l\| > 1$ **then**
select ω_i, ω_j with highest priors	BuildTree(Ω_l);
$S = (\omega_i, S, \omega_j)$	**end if**
$\Omega = \Omega - \omega_i, \omega_j$	**if** $\|\Omega_r\| > 1$ **then**
end while	BuildTree(Ω_r);
output S;	**end if**

In a DDAG the classifier components are fixed and hence the design algorithm involves only arrangement of nodes. In a BHC, the node design decides the architecture of the tree. A BHC partitions the available set of classes into two subsets at each step. This is continued recursively until only a single class remains at each partition. The partitioning step is crucial, and decides the performance of the classifier. The algorithm is described in Table 1.

2 Hybrid Algorithm

In a BHC, at each step of tree building, the classification problems are different, which means a single classifier may not suit all the problems. The proposed hybrid architecture employs different classifiers for building the hybrid tree. We compare a binary partition and a DDAG and at each step, and use the better one among them. The algorithm therefore measures the classifiability of the datasets for these two architectures, and prefers one of them depending on the parameter λ.

Estimating Classifiability. A key step in the algorithm is to compute the advantage obtained by using various architectures at each step of tree building. Let L denote a measure which can estimate the classifiability of a dataset.

Algorithm 1. BHCD($\mathcal{X}, \lambda$)

$f = \phi$
$(\Omega_l^{(i)}, \Omega_r^{(i)}) = \text{Cluster}(\mathcal{X}_i^{(i)}, 2);$ // Make two clusters
$L_{binary} = ComputeClassifiabilityEstimate(\mathcal{X}_i^{(i)}, l, r)$
$L_{ddag} = ComputeClassifiabilityEstimate(\mathcal{X}_i^{(i)}, \Omega_i)$
if ($L_{ddag} < \lambda L_{binary}$) **then**
  $f = f \oplus \theta_i$
  $\theta_i = \text{trainBinary}(\mathcal{X}_l^{(i)}, \mathcal{X}_r^{(i)})$
  if ($n(\Omega^{(i)}) > 2$) **then**
    BHCD($\mathcal{X}_l, \lambda$)
    BHCD($\mathcal{X}_r, \lambda$)
  end if
else
  $\theta_i = \text{trainDDAG}(\mathcal{X}^{(i)})$
  $f = f \oplus \theta_i$
end if

One such measure is proposed in [4]. We extend this measure for applicability to pairwise classifiers, L_{pw}, by taking the average pairwise classifiabilties of individual datasets. This is used in obtaining the estimate for a DDAG. Let L_{lm} denote the classifiability computed for the classes ω_l, ω_m, then $L_{pw} = \frac{2}{N(N-1)} \sum_{l,m \in \Omega^{(i)}, l \neq m} L_{lm}$.

A recursive procedure is used to build the BHCD. At each node i, $\Omega^{(i)}$ denotes the set of labels of the classes that reach that node. The root node of the hierarchy handles all the classes $\Omega^{(0)} = \Omega$. The dataset is split into two subsets using any data clustering algorithm. We use K-Means clustering, with $K = 2$. The classifiability of the data with this split(partition) is L_{split}. The pairwise classifiability, L_{pw} is computed for all the classes at the current node. Using the user specified parameter λ, if $L_{pw} < \lambda L_{split}$, then the DDAG is chosen as architecture for that set of classes. Otherwise, of classes are split into $\Omega_l^{(i)}, \Omega_r^{(i)}$, the left and right subsets of the classes. The algorithm recursively repeats these steps until each node is left with only two classes to train at the leaf level.

When $\lambda = 1$, the algorithm is equivalent to searching for the best design at each node. In this case, the resulting hybrid tree is at least as good as BHC or a DDAG. When $\lambda \neq 1$, then user preferences are taken into account. Considering accuracy, the algorithm is better than a BHC, and could be better than than both BHC and DDAG. More importantly the constraints on size are taken into account in the design.

3 Results

We demonstrate the performance of the BHCD algorithm on the Letter dataset of UCI [5] repository, and an Indian Language Character dataset. The letter dataset contains 26 classes, and 20000 samples in total. In the experiments, 60% of the dataset is used for training and the remaining for testing. At each node of the classifier, a linear SVM is used. When λ is set to a low value, the algorithm results in a DDAG classifier. The DDAG has 325 classifiers, and give a performance of about 75% on the test dataset. For a high value of λ, a pure BHC with 24 nodes is output with an accuracy of 71%. For a medium value of λ, a classifier with 105 nodes is obtained with an accuracy of 73.23%.

We tested the algorithm on Malayalam character recognition dataset with 116 classes and 100 samples per class. 100 samples per class. In this experiment, 60% of the training set is used in training, and the rest for testing. Different classifiers were built on this dataset with varying λ. For a low λ, a pure DDAG is obtained, and has 6555 nodes in total. The length of the evaluation path of the DDAG is 115 nodes. In each case, if each node has parameters which require 3.2KB of storage space, the size of the whole classifier is 21Mb. The accuracy of this classifier is found to be 98.6%. Using a pure BHC tree, an accuracy of 98.2% is obtained. The number of classifiers required were 115, and the storage space is 368KB. Using a medium value for λ, an accuracy of 98.6 is obtained, for a classifier with 990 nodes. This classifier took 3.1MB of storage space. The average length of the evaluation path is 24 nodes, as compared to 8 for a BHC and 115 for a DDAG.

The results show that it is possible to obtain different performances by varying the value of λ. It is upto the user to pick the classifier with the required performance, with respect to size, accuracy and evaluation time. It is shown that a compact classifier without much loss in the performance can be built using this algorithm.

4 Conclusions

We describe a flexible scheme for building hybrid hierarchical classifiers, which can give the best possible classifier meeting the constraints on parameters like classification time and size of the classifier, by capturing and combining different benefits offered by different architectures.

References

1. Platt, J.C., Cristianini, N., Shawe-Taylor, J.: Large margin DAGs for multi-class classification. In: Advances in NIPS-12. (2000) 547–553
2. Kumar, S., Ghosh, J., Crawford, M.: A hierarchical multiclassifier system for hyperspectral data analysis. Lecture Notes in Computer Science **1857** (2000) 270–278
3. M N S S K Pavan Kumar, Jawahar, C.V.: On improving design of multiclass clasifiers. In: Proceedings of the 5th International Conference on Advances in Pattern Recognition. (2003) 109–112
4. Dong, M., Li, Y., Kothari, R.: Theoretical results on a measure of classification complexity. In: Proceedings of 5th International Conference on Advances in Pattern Recognition. (2003) 85–88
5. Hettich, S., Blake, C., Merz, C. In: UCI repository of machine learning databases, http://www.ics.uci.edu/~mlearn/MLRepository.html. (1998)

Human-Computer Interaction System with Artificial Neural Network Using Motion Tracker and Data Glove

Cemil Oz and Ming C. Leu

Department of Mechanical and Aerospace Engineering,
University of Missouri-Rolla, Rolla, Missouri 65409, USA
{ozc, mleu}@umr.edu

Abstract. A Human-Computer Interaction (HCI) system has been developed with an Artificial Neural Network (ANN) using a motion tracker and a data glove. The HCI system is able to recognize American Sign Language letter and number gestures. The finger joint angle data obtained from the strain gauges in the sensory glove define the hand shape while the data from the motion tracker describe the hand position and orientation. The data flow from the sensory glove is controlled by a software trigger using the data from the motion tracker during signing. Then, the glove data is processed by a recognition neural network.

1 Introduction

Using our hands is a primary way of interacting with the outside world. We perform many everyday tasks with our hands; however, we usually use constrained peripheral devices such as a mouse, keyboard or joystick to work with a computer and computer-controlled applications. Sensory glove based input devices could be used overcome this limitation [1]. Commercial devices, such as the VPL data glove and Mattel power glove, have led to an explosion of research and development projects using electronic glove interfaces to computer applications and computer controlled devices. These applications include virtual reality, video games, scientific visualization, puppetry, and gesture-based control.

There has been a significant amount of research work done in the area of gesture recognition in the last decade due to the recent advances in hardware and software for human-computer interaction (HCI). Most of these studies were mainly in the area of sign language recognition [2-6] and game control as well as some other HCI tasks [7].

In this study, an HCI system is designed and implemented with an artificial neural network for recognition of ASL letter and number gestures using Cyberglove and Flock of Birds devices. The neural network for gestures recognition is activated by a software trigger. When the software finds the velocity of the hand below a threshold value, the data from the Cyberglove™ is sent to the gestures recognition network. The data flow from the input devices to the recognition process is then turned off until a high-speed hand movement reactivates it. The software for gesture recognition is based on an ANN method. The system is able to recognize 31 hand gestures. The system is developed for human-computer interaction in a robotic workcell.

2 Overall System

The objective of this project is to control a robotic workcell with commands issued through hand gestures, which are recognized by a hand gesture recognition system. The system consists of the following components: object recognition, target detection, inverse kinematics solution, path planning, and robot control [8]. Figure 1 illustrates the overall system. The dashed-line blocks are not discussed in this paper.

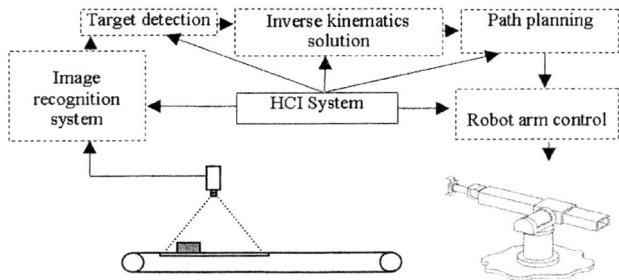

Fig. 1. Overall system block diagram

3 System Hardware

We use a right-hand Cyberglove™ (Figure 2) to retrieve the values of finger joint angles for gesture features. The glove measures the bending angles at various positions and the frequency of data collection can reach 150 Hz. The glove contains fifteen sensors: three for the thumb, two for each of the other four fingers, and four sensors located between the fingers. To track the position and orientation of the hand in 3-D space, we mount the Flock of Birds® motion tracker (Figure 3) on the wrist. The receiver is located in a DC pulsed magnetic field and its effective range is up to 8 feet around the transmitter. The measuring frequency can reach 144 Hz.

Open Inventor SDK (Software Development Kit) is used in the software development for 3-D scene rendering and interactive programming. It is a high-level

Fig. 2. The Cyberglove™ with 18 sensors   **Fig. 3.** The Flock of Birds® 3-D motion tracker

tool kit developed in OpenGL for graphic rendering and user interaction. The software system is implemented using the Object Oriented Programming (OOP) technology; therefore, it is easily extendable.

4 ANN Based Gesture Recognition

We have designed an HCI system for American Sign Language (ASL) letter and number gestures. ASL has twenty-six letters and ten numbers. Although most of the ASL letter and number gestures depend on finger positions only, some of them also depend on hand orientation, and two of them are dynamic. There are great similarities between the signs of g and q, h and u, and k and p. The letters of each of these pairs have the same hand shape, but their hand orientations are different. There are also great similarities between i and j, and x and z. The letters of each of these pairs have the same hand shape, but the signs for j and z are dynamic. Figure 4 shows the hand signs for ASL letters.

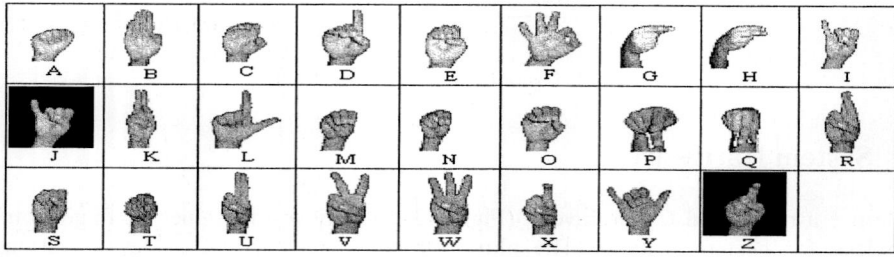

Fig. 4. ASL alphabet gestures

Our HCI system is based on finger positions only; therefore the alphabet characters g, h, p, j and z are not used. In other words, thirty-one gestures in total are used in the HCI system. The HCI system provides the user with the capability of generating many different commands using the 31 letters and numbers. In total, there are 55 commands: 10 commands for the conveyor, 30 commands for the robot arm, 10 commands for the image processing, and 5 commands for the whole system. Each hand shape either corresponds to a unique command such as start, stop, etc. or it is part of a more complex command composed of multiple hand shapes. There are complex commands which may use up to four hand gestures. For example, RT11 command means "take object number 1 and place in bin number 1". Some commands are given in Table 1.

A multi-layer ANN is designed to recognize the ASL letter and number gestures. The ANN model was detailed in previous papers [9, 10]. The input to the network consists of 15 Cyberglove data elements. The proposed ANN, a multi-layer feedforward network, consists of 15 input neurons, 20 hidden neurons, and 31 output neurons. A Levenberg-Marquardt backpropagation algorithm is used for training. The ANN has been trained and tested for two different data sets: single-user data and

Table 1. Representative commands for the HCI system

Whole system	Conveyor	Robot arm	Image processing
S- stop	CS- start conveyor	ROC- cubic path	IS- start image capturing
E- end	CE- stop conveyor	ROS- sinusoidal path	IE- stop image capturing
		RAN- add noise	ICF- extract image features
		RT11- take object 1 to bin 1	IA- add image to database

multi-user data. The output vector consists of 31 elements. The maximum of these elements corresponds to an alphabet or sign. The training set is composed of two files, input and output. The input file contains Cyberglove data which belong to 31 characters, and each character has 15 values which are provided as input to the ANN. The target vector consists of 31 values. All of these values are set to 0 except one value, which is set to 1. The position of the element with 1 defines the hand shape. The overall design of the HCI system is given in Figure 5. It consists of four parts: selection of input data, trained network, output decoding and command generation.

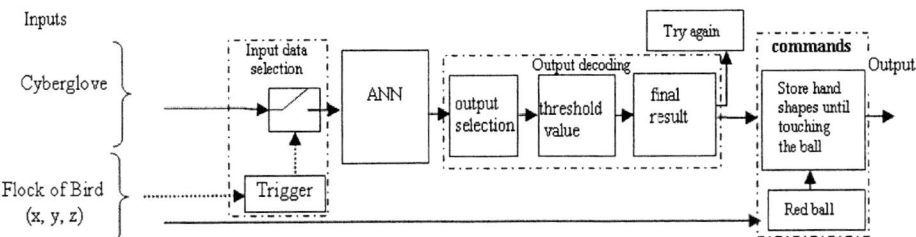

Fig. 5. The HCI system block diagram

A software trigger controls the reading of input data to the recognition network. When the trigger finds the velocity of the hand below a threshold value, in our case 0.05 (unit/second), the data from the Cyberglove and Flock of Birds is sent to the gesture recognition network. The data flow between the input devices and the recognition process is turned off until a hand velocity reactivates it. The reactivation velocity is set at 0.5. The three-layer word recognition network has 15 inputs, 20 hidden neurons and 31 output neurons. The selection block determines the maximum output of the ANN, and then the treshold block checks whether the maximum output value is acceptable or not. In the final part, the system output is stored in a variable to form a command. After issuing the command, the corresponting procedure of the command is procesed by touching a virtual red ball. The recognized letters and commands are displayed on the screen using an Open Inventor interface. Some of the ASL letters recognized by our system are illustrated in Figure 6, and some of cereated commands are showned in Figure 7.

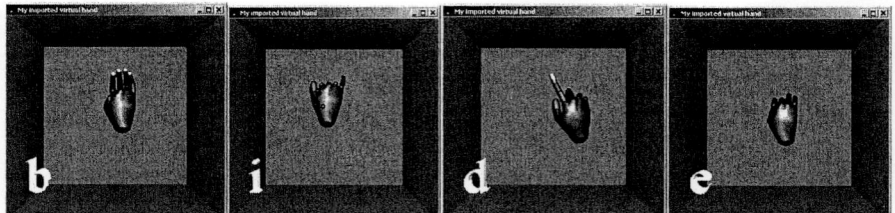

Fig. 6. Sample outputs representing four recognized hand shapes representing ASL letters

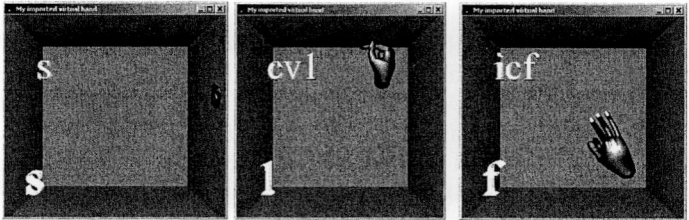

Fig. 7. Three command samples

5 System Test Results

Two ASL letter and number recognition systems have been developed, one with a single-user model and one the other with a multiple-user model. The recognition system with a single user model was first trained with data from three samples. When that was not effective, we trained the ANN with six, nine, then twelve and finally, fifteen samples. Similarly, the recognition system with a multi-user model was first trained with data from three samples, then six, nine, twelve and finally, fifteen samples. At the testing stage, real-time data from alphabet and number gestures are used. Each of these two systems was tested starting with *A* and ending with 9. The testing results are given in Table 2 and Table 3. The recognition accuracy of the single-user system is about 96% when the system is trained with 15 samples and tested in real time.

Table 2. Test result for a single user

Samples	ASL alphabet																														
	A	B	C	D	E	F	I	L	M	N	O	P	Q	R	S	T	U	V	W	X	Y	1	2	3	4	5	6	7	8	9	10
3	/	-	-	/	-	-	-	/	-	/	/	-	/	-	-	/	-	/	/	-	/	-	-	-	/	/	/	/	/	/	/
6	-	-	-	-	-	/	-	-	/	-	-	/	-	-	/	-	-	-	/	/	-	/	/	-	-	/	/	-	-	-	/
9	-	-	-	-	-	/	-	/	-	/	-	-	-	-	-	-	/	-	-	-	-	-	-	-	-	-	-	-	/	-
12	-	-	-	-	-	-	-	-	-	-	-	-	-	-	-	-	-	-	-	-	-	-	-	-	-	-	-	-	-	-	-
15	-	-	-	-	-	-	-	-	-	-	-	-	-	-	-	-	-	-	-	-	-	-	-	-	-	-	-	-	-	-	-

(/) unrecognized, (-) recognized

Table 3. Test result for multiple users

Samples	\multicolumn{31}{c}{ASL alphabet}

Samples	A	B	C	D	E	F	I	L	M	N	O	P	Q	R	S	T	U	V	W	X	Y	1	2	3	4	5	6	7	8	9	10
3	/	/	-	/	-	-	-	/	/	-	/	/	/	-	/	/	-	/	/	-	/	/	-	/	-	-	/	/	/	/	/
6	/	-	-	/	/	-	-	/	-	/	/	-	-	/	-	-	-	/	-	/	/	/	/	/	-	-	/	/	-	-	-
9	-	-	-	-	-	-	/	-	/	-	/	-	-	-	-	-	/	-	/	-	-	-	/	-	/	-	/	-	-	-	/	-
12	-	-	-	-	-	-	-	-	-	-	-	-	-	-	-	-	-	-	-	-	-	-	-	-	-	-	-	-	-	-	/
15	-	-	-	-	-	-	-	-	-	-	-	-	-	-	-	-	-	-	-	-	-	-	-	-	-	-	-	-	-	-	-

(/) unrecognized, (-) recognized

6 Conclusion

A Human-Computer Interaction system has been developed with an artificial neural network using position/orientation sensors and sensory glove data for recognition of 31 ASL alphabet and number gestures. The system uses a Cyberglove, and a Flock of Birds 3-D motion tracker to provide the data input, and it has been trained and tested for single and multiple users for 31 hand gestures. The test results have shown that the proposed technique is capable of performing accurate real-time recognition of hand gestures.

Acknowledgments

This research was partially supported by a Ford Foundation grant, as well as by the Intelligent Systems Center at the University of Missouri–Rolla.

References

[1] D. J. Sturman and D. Zelter, "A Survey of Glove-Based Input," IEEE Computer and Applications, 1994, pp. 30-39.
[2] S. G. Wysoski, M. V. Lamar, S. Kuroyanagi, and A. Iwata, "A Rotation Invariant Approach on Static Gesture Recognition Using Boundary Histograms and Neural networks," Proceeding of the 9th International Conference on Neural Information Processing (ICONIP'02), vol. 4, 2002, pp. 2137-2141.
[3] C. Vogler and D. Metaxas, "ASL Recognition Based on a Coupling Between HMMs and 3D Motion Analysis," Proceedings of the sixth IEEE International Computer Vision Conference, January 1998, pp.363-369.
[4] G. Lalit and M Suei, "Gesture-Based Interaction and Communication: Automated Classification of Hand Gesture Contours," IEEE Transactions on Systems, Man, and Cybernetics, Part c: Application and Reviews, vol. 31, no. 1, February 2001, pp. 114-120.
[5] Y. Cui and J. Weng, "A Learning-Based Prediction and Verification Segmentation Scheme for Hand Sign Image Sequence," IEEE Transactions on Pattern Analysis and Machine Intelligence, vol. 21, no.8, August 1999, pp. 798-804.
[6] C. Vogler and D. Metaxas, "Parallel Hidden Markov Models for American Sign Language Recognition," IEEE Proceeding of International Computer Vision Conference, 1999, pp. 116-122.

[7] L. K. Lee, S. Kim, Y. K. Choi, and M. H. Lee, "Recognition of Hand Gesture to Human-Computer Interaction," IECON 2000, 26th Annual Confjerence of the IEEE 2000, pp. 2177-2122

[8] R. Koker, C. Oz, and A. Ferikoglu," Object Recognition Based on Moment Invariants Using Artificial Neural Networks," Proceedings International Symposium on Intelligent Manufacturing Systems, August 30-31, 2001.

[9] C. Oz, N. N. Sarawate, and M. C. Leu, "American Sign Language Word Recognition with a Sensory Glove Using Artificial Neural Networks," Proceedings of ANNIE Conference, St. Louis, MO, November 7-10, 2004; also Book on Intelligent Engineering Systems through Artificial Neural Networks, Vol. 14, ISBN 0-7918-0228-0, 2004, pp. 633-638.

[10] C. Oz and M. Leu, "Recognition of Finger Spelling of American Sign Language with ANN Using Position/Orientation Sensors and Data Glove," Proceedings of 2nd International Symposium on Neural Networks, Chongqing, CHINA, May 30 - June 1, 2005; also Lecturer Notes in Computer Science 3497, Springer, ISBN 3-540-25913-9, 2005, pp. 157-164.

Recurrent Neural Approaches for Power Transformers Thermal Modeling

Michel Hell[1], Luiz Secco[2], Pyramo Costa Jr.[2], and Fernando Gomide[1]

[1] State University of Campinas - UNICAMP,
Av. Albert Einstein, 400, 13083-852, Campinas, SP - Brazil,
{mbhell, gomide}@dca.fee.unicamp.br
[2] Pontifical Catholic University of Minas Gerais - PUC-MG,
Av. Dom José Gaspar, 500, Prédio 3, 30535-610, Belo Horizonte, MG - Brazil
pyramo@pucminas.br

Abstract. This paper introduces approaches for power transformer thermal modeling based on two conceptually different recurrent neural networks. The first is the Elman recurrent neural network model whereas the second is a recurrent neural fuzzy network constructed with fuzzy neurons based on triangular norms. These two models are used to model the thermal behavior of power transformers using data reported in literature. The paper details the neural modeling approaches and discusses their main capabilities and properties. Comparisons with the classic deterministic model and static neural modeling approaches are also reported. Computational experiments suggest that the recurrent neural fuzzy-based modeling approach outperforms the remaining models from both, computational processing speed and robustness point of view.

1 Introduction

Power transformers are essential to transmit and distribute electric energy. Transformer faults may deeply affect power systems, causing power outages and socio-economic losses. Condition monitoring of power transformers is a key issue to guarantee safe operation, power availability, and service life.

A major factor in power transformer operation concerns its working temperature, that is, its *hot-spot temperature*. The hot-spot temperature has a vital role in insulation aging and service life of power transformers. Monitoring of hot-spot temperature is imperative to develop overload protection systems. High hot-spot temperature also means increasing rate of aging of transformers.

A central element to monitor power transformers condition is dynamic models to describe their thermal behavior. Differences between measured and predicted working temperature provide key information on transformer conditions and may indicate potential abnormalities.

Transient heat equations and specific thermal characteristics constitute an important approach to characterize the thermal capability of power transformers [1]. Conventional modeling techniques are useful to estimate internal temperatures of power transformers, but they still pose substantial challenges. Frequently, security encourages adoption of conservative safety factors. In practice this means underutilized transformers since hot-spot parts of the coils are kept from overheating and failing prematurely. In general the maximum power transfer found are 20-30% lower than the nominal power transformer capacity [2]. To bring power transformers beyond their nominal specifications to increase system operational margin during overload periods requires new loading schemes.

Among the different modeling techniques available today, artificial neural networks and fuzzy systems are examples that have been shown to be relevant and efficient in many application domains. The reason why neural, fuzzy models, and their hybridizations are extensively used in practice concerns their ability to learn complex non-linear relationships and to naturally treat imprecise data, a situation that is much more difficult to handle using conventional approaches [3]. An alternative that has received considerable attention, and shown significant progress in the recent years, is the use of recurrent connections in artificial neural networks and fuzzy models. In recurrent models, feedback connections introduce dynamics and the model become sensitive to the history of input data, an essential ingredient in modeling dynamic systems [3].

This work addresses two different recurrent neural models to model the thermal condition of power transformers. The first is the Elman recurrent neural network (ELM) [6] and the second is a recurrent neural fuzzy network (RNF) suggested by Ballini and Gomide [7]. The paper describes both neural modeling approaches and summarizes their main capabilities and properties. The models have been tested using actual data reported in the literature. Comparisons of these models with the deterministic [1] and static neural networks models are also included.

2 Recurrent Neural Model – ELM

We first review he recurrent neural model introduced by Elman [6]. The ELM is attractive to model dynamic systems because they are capable to learn temporal input/output relationships between patterns.

The structure of Elman neural network is composed by four layers: input layer, hidden layer, context layer, and output layer, as depicted in Figure 1. Learning is performed adjusting the weights connecting the neighboring layers. The self (recurrent) connections of the context nodes turn the network sensitive to the history of input/output data.

If the network inputs are $u(t) \in \mathbb{R}^m$, $y(t) \in \mathbb{R}^n$, $x(k) \in \mathbb{R}^r$, the outputs of each layer are found using:

$$\begin{aligned} x_j(t) &= f\left(\sum_{i=1}^{m} w1_{ij}u_i(t) + \sum_{l=1}^{r} w3_{lj}c_l(t)\right) \\ c_l(t) &= x_j(t-1) \\ y_q(t) &= g\left(\sum_{j=1}^{r} w2_{jq}x_j(t)\right) \end{aligned} \quad (1)$$

where $w1_{ij}$ is the weight connecting node i in the input layer to node j in the hidden layer, $w2_{jq}$ is the weight connecting node j in the hidden layer with node q in the output layer, $w3_{lj}$ is the weight connecting context node l to node j in the hidden layer, and m, n, r are the number of nodes in the input, output, and hidden layers, respectively. $u_i(t), y_j(t)$ are the inputs and outputs, with $i = 1, \cdots, m$ and $j = 1, \cdots, n$, $x_i(t)$ is the

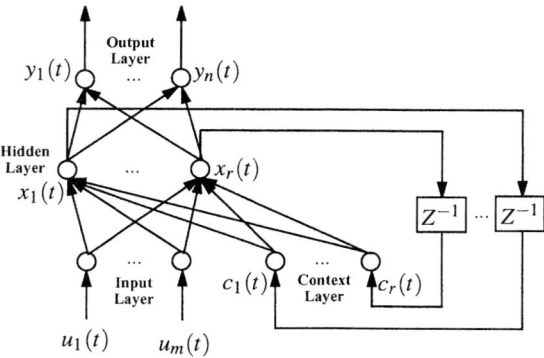

Fig. 1. Structure of the Elman network

output of the hidden node i, $i = 1, \cdots, r$, $c_i(t)$ the output of the context node i, i.e., the output of the hidden node i at t, Z^{-1} the unit delay operator, $f(\bullet)$ and $g(\bullet)$ are activation functions of hidden layer and output layer neurons, respectively.

3 Recurrent Neural Fuzzy Model – RNF

The structure of the recurrent neural fuzzy network consists of two neural systems. The first has an input and two hidden layers and performs fuzzy inference. The second is a classic neural network that acts as operator to aggregate the outputs of the fuzzy inference system (Figura 2). This structure and learning procedure were initially introduced in [7]. Below we detail processing and learning scheme the recurrent neural fuzzy network addressed in this paper.

The first hidden layer consists of neurons whose activation functions are membership functions of fuzzy sets that defines the input space granulation. That is, for each

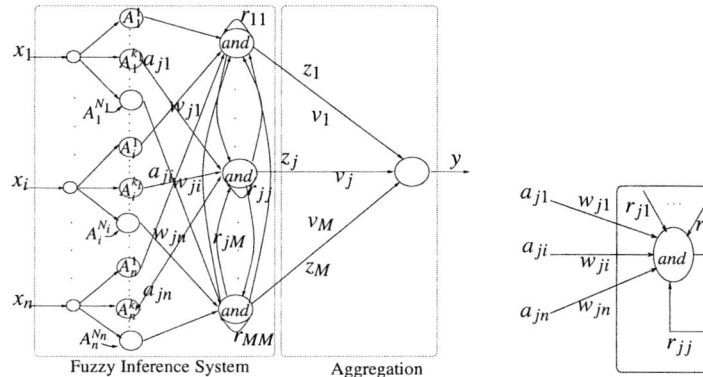

Fig. 2. RNF Model Structure   **Fig. 3.** Recurrent Fuzzy Set-Based Neuron

dimension $x_i(t)$ of a n-dimensional input vector $\mathbf{x}(t)$ there are N_i fuzzy sets $A_i^{k_i}, k_i = 1, \ldots, N_i$ whose membership functions are activation functions of corresponding input layer neurons. The variable t is the discrete-time, that is, $t = 1, 2, \ldots$, but it will be omitted from now on to simplify notation. The outputs of the first hidden layer are the membership degrees of the input values, $a_{ji} = \mu_{A_i^{k_i}}(x_i)$, $i = 1, \ldots, n$ and $j = 1, \ldots, M$; where M is the number of neurons in the hidden layer.

Neurons of the second hidden layer are fuzzy set-based neurons, namely recurrent *and* neurons (Figure 3) with inputs a_{ji} weighted by w_{ji} and feedback connections weighted by $r_{jl}, l = 1, \ldots, M$. Notice that fuzzy set-based neurons use triangular norms (t−norms and s−norms) to process its inputs. Characterization and different instances of t−norms and s−norms are discussed in [5] and references therein. Processing steps of the neural fuzzy network are as follows:

1. N_i is the number of fuzzy sets that composes the partition of i−th input;
2. $a_{ji} = \mu_{A_i^{k_i}}(x_i)$ is the membership degree of x_i in the fuzzy set $A_i^{k_i}$, where a_{ji} is the input of neuron j of the second hidden layer;
3. z_j is the j−th output of the second hidden layer:

$$z_j = \mathop{\mathbf{T}}_{i=1}^{n+M} (w_{ji} \, \mathbf{s} \, a_{ji}) \tag{2}$$

4. y, the output of nonlinear neuron, is given by:

$$y = \psi(u) = \psi\left(\sum_{j=1}^{M} (v_j \cdot z_j)\right) \tag{3}$$

where, $\psi : \Re^M \to [0, 1]$ is a nonlinear, monotonically increasing function. In this paper, we use the logistic function $\psi(u) = 1/(1 + \exp(-u))$;
5. w_{ji} is the weight between the j−th *and*-neuron and the i−th neuron of the first hidden layer;
6. v_j is the weight between the output y of the network and the j−th neuron of the second hidden layer;
7. r_{jl} is the weight of the feedback connection between the j−th *and*-neuron and the l−th neuron of the same, second hidden layer;

Note that the neural fuzzy network is quite flexible once it allows choosing appropriate triangular norms, and allows extraction of linguistic fuzzy rules directly from its topology, the fuzzy inference system part.

4 Simulation Results

This section addresses the performance of the recurrent neural models described in the previous section when they are used to estimate the hot-spot temperature of power transformers. For this purpose, we adopt the same data reported in [2]. Comparisons are made considering the recurrent neural models, the deterministic model suggested in [1], and three static (non-recurrent) neural models: multi layer perceptron network (MLP), radial basis function network (RBF), and neural fuzzy network (SNF) described in [5].

All five models were trained using measurements of the hot-spot temperature during 24 hours and a sampling period of 5 minutes [2]. The inputs of the neural models are the load currents $(K(t))$, $(K(t-1))$, and the top oil temperature $(T_{TO}(t))$. The output is the hot-spot temperature $(T_H(t))$.

After learning, the approximation, generalization and robustness capability of the neural models were verified using two data sets, each set describing different load capability conditions (with and without overload) as those embedded in the learning data of [2]. Test data were collected in the same way as training data.

Table 1 shows the values of performance index obtained after the simulation experiments. In Table 1, $MSE - Dt1$ is the mean square error (MSE) obtained after models are run with test data with no overload condition. $MSE - Dt2$ is the MSE obtained when models process test data with overload. $MSE - Dts$ is the MSE obtained when models simultaneously process both data sets.

Table 1. Simulation Results

Model	Learning Time (seg.)	MSE-Dt1	MSE-Dt2	MSE-Dts
MD	-	17,3489	6,7434	12,0462
MLP	92,76	0,7900	2,4880	1,6390
RBF	82,63	0,2565	0,9914	0,6239
SNF	61,50	0,2689	1,1025	0,6857
ELM	59,39	0,4780	2,1069	1,2925
RNF	31,37	0,0481	0,2635	0,1557

As Table 1 suggests, all neural models satisfactorily estimate hot-spot temperature values. Note, however, that when training data contains spurious data, that is, noisy values not consistent with the actual behavior (non ideal training data), recurrent models become more attractive than static models. Recurrent models are more precise to capture transformer dynamics and gives more robust estimates of the hot spot temperature.

Table 2. Results using non ideal training data

	MD	MLP	RBF	SNF	ELM	RNF
MSE	6,7434	$1,2487 \times 10^2$	$4,6579 \times 10^4$	$0,2804 \times 10^2$	1,8986	0,7912

To further investigate this important issue, we deliberately use a data set that does not fully represent the transformer dynamics to train the neural models. More specifically, we assume data with no overload conditions during training and data with overload to test approximation, robustness and generalization capabilities. Figure 4 depicts the estimates of the hot-spot temperature given by each model. Table 2 shows the mean square approximation errors. Interestingly, static models were unable to keep the same

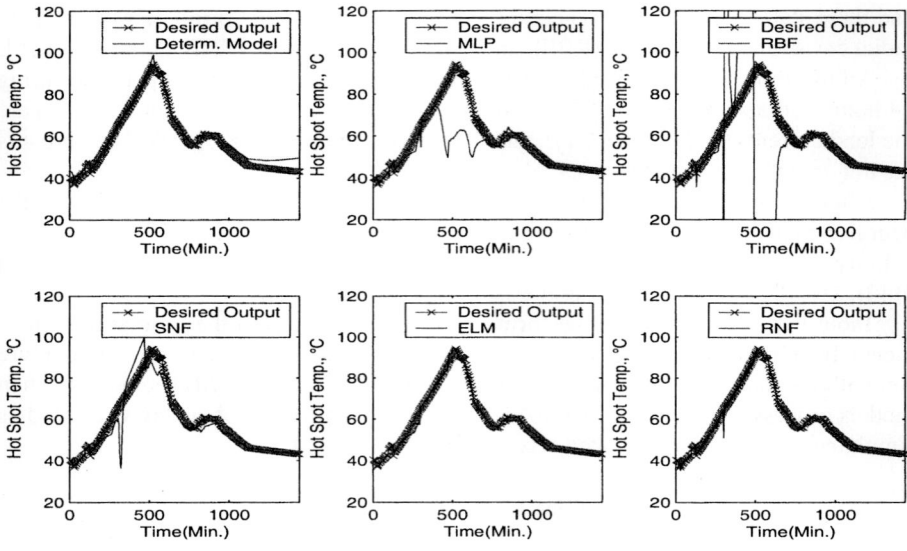

Fig. 4. Robustness Avaliation

performance when dealing with ideal training data while recurrent models did keep the same prediction performance as before. We also note that the recurrent neural fuzzy network - RNF - performs better, learns faster, and is more robust than- ELM.

5 Conclusion

In this work different neural approaches have been investigated as models for the thermal behavior of power transformers. Simulation experiments indicate that recurrent models are more robust than static neural models, especially when non-ideal data set is used during learning. Recurrent models capture the input/output relationship, their temporal relationship, and are more robust to noisy training data. Between the two recurrent models, the recurrent fuzzy neural network outperformed the Elman network. The recurrent fuzzy neural network offers an effective and robust power transformer model, learns quickly, runs fast, and needs modest computational requirements.

Acknowledgment

The first author acknowledges FAPESP, the Research Foundation of the State of São Paulo, for fellowship 03/05042-1, and the last thanks CNPq, the Brazilian National Research Council, for grant 475295/2003-0. The remaining authors also thank the Pontifical Catholic University of Minas Gerais (IPUC, PUC-MG) for its support. The authors are also in debt wit Álvaro Martins and Ronald Moura, from the Energetic Company of Minas Gerais (CEMIG), for their continuous help and motivation during the development of this work.

References

1. G. W. Swift et. al., *Adaptative Transformer Thermal Overload Protection*, IEEE Transactions on Power Delivery, Vol. 16, No. 4, pp. 516-521, 2001.
2. V. Galdi, L. Ippolito, A. Piccolo and A. Vaccaro, *Neural Diagnostic System for Transformer Thermal Overload Protection*, IEE Proceedings of Electric Power Applications, Vol. 147, No. 5, pp. 415-421, 2000.
3. K.S. Narendra, K. Parthasarathy, *Identification and Control of Dynamic Systems using Neural Networks*, IEEE Transactions on Neural Networks, Vol. 1, pp. 4-27, 1990.
4. S. Haykin, *Neural Networks: A Comprehensive Foundation*, Prentice Hall, NJ-USA, ed. 2, 1998.
5. J.-S. R. Jang, *ANFIS: Adaptative-Network-Based Fuzzy Inference System*, IEEE Transactions on System, Man, and Cybernetics, Vol. 23, No. 3, 665-685, 1993.
6. J. Elman, *Finding Structure in Time*, Cognitive Science, Vol. 14, pp. 179-211, 1990.
7. R. Ballini and F. Gomide, *Learning in recurrent, hybrid neurofuzzy networks*, IEEE International Conference on Fuzzy Systems, pp. 785-791, 2002.

Artificial Neural Network Engine: Parallel and Parameterized Architecture Implemented in FPGA

Milene Barbosa Carvalho[1], Alexandre Marques Amaral[1],
Luiz Eduardo da Silva Ramos[1,2], Carlos Augusto Paiva da Silva Martins[1],
and Petr Ekel[1]

[1] Pontifical Catholic University of Minas Gerais (BRAZIL), [2] Rutgers University (USA),
Av. Dom José Gaspar, 500, Prédio 3, 30535-610, Belo Horizonte, MG – Brazil
{milene, alexmarques, luizesramos}@ieee.org,
{capsm, ekel}@pucminas.br

Abstract. In this paper we present and analyze an artificial neural network hardware engine, its architecture and implementation. The engine was designed to solve performance problems of the serial software implementations. It is based on a hierarchical parallel and parameterized architecture. Taking into account verification results, we conclude that this engine improves the computational performance, producing speedups from 52.3 to 204.5 and its architectural parameterization provides more flexibility.

1 Introduction

Artificial neural networks (ANN) implemented in digital computers normally generate a high demand of computational performance. Its serial software implementations executed in programmable hardware, e.g. microprocessor, normally produce relative high response time and unsatisfactory performance [1]. This performance problem is a critical factor for most ANN based applications and it is our motivator problem for the present work. In many situations, first of all, in real-time systems, a high response time can invalidate the responses and solutions. Our main goals in this work are to propose, design and implement an artificial neural network hardware engine in order to improve the computational performance.

2 Proposed Engine

Among different types of artificial neural networks (ANN), we initially propose and design an engine to implement multilayer perceptron (MLP) networks [2,3]. This choice is based on the high utilization of MLP on ANN applications [4].

MLP networks are composed of at least three layers: one input, one or more hidden and one output layers. Input layer does not perform processing, but represents an input data set for neurons of the first hidden layer. Hidden and output layers perform processing of inputs and weights and are composed of perceptron neurons, shown in fig.1a. MLPs are feedforward networks (fig.1b). This means that the inputs of the neurons of any layer (except the input layer) are the output values from neurons of the previous layer [3] [4].

As presented in fig.1a, the output of a perceptron neuron is calculated by the function $f(S)$, where f is the transfer function and S represents the summation of all input-weight products. The transfer function can be any function, but the more popular are threshold and sigmoid functions [4].

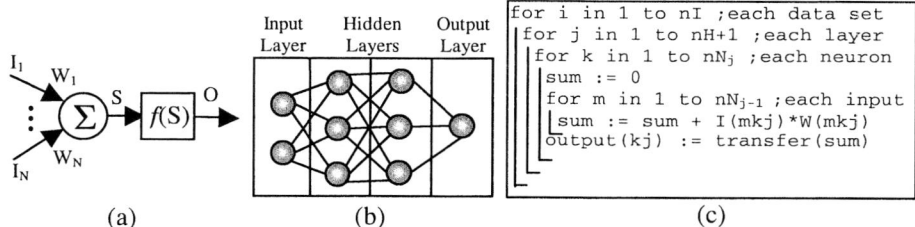

Fig. 1. a) Perceptron neuron. b) MLP topology example. c) MLP execution pseudo-code.

Analyzing fig.1a, we are able to state that there is inherent spatial parallelism in the execution of the neuron's products, called intra-neural parallelism. In fig.1b we notice that a neuron inside a layer is independent from the others within the same layer, (intra-layer parallelism). However, there is dependency among the neurons from a layer and those from the previous layer. It happens because the outputs from a layer are the inputs of the next layer. Nevertheless, the computation of different layers can be done simultaneously, since each neuron has all inputs (temporal parallelism or pipeline). It means that if the layers process different data sets, they can execute simultaneously (inter-layer parallelism).

Fig.1c presents a MLP pseudo-code. The first (outer) loop executes the entire network for all data sets. The second loop executes all hidden and output layers. The third loop executes all neurons of the layer specified in the second loop. The fourth loop executes the products and sums of each neuron, where weights and inputs are determined by previous loops. After that, the transfer function is applied to the total sum of a neuron, generating the neuron's output. Serial code implemented like this and executed in general purpose processors (GPPs) fails to explore the several different levels of inherent parallelisms inside an MLP, as previously indicated. In this implementation, the operations of each neuron are sequentially processed and also the operations within each layer and all over the network. Since this implementation fails to explore parallelism, the overall performance cannot reach the ideal high performance.

Some works implement ANN in parallel computers [1], e.g., clusters and multi-processors [5], which yield great speedup over the sequential monoprocessed one. However, since MLP network present fine-grained parallelism, their implementation in parallel computers not always is efficient, due to speedup, scalability and cost.

Our solution hypothesis is to design and implement MLP networks using hierarchical parallel and parameterized dedicated hardware architectures, to improve the computational performance.

The neuron designed to compose our architecture (fig.2a) has three main modules, named: multiplication, addition and transfer function. In the first module, the inputs are multiplied by their respective weights. In the second, all products are summed.

Then, the summation of the products is processed by the transfer function module, which calculates the neuron's output. Among all possible hierarchical parallelism parameters, there are spatial parallelism in the multiplications and temporal parallelism (pipeline) in each neuron among its three modules.

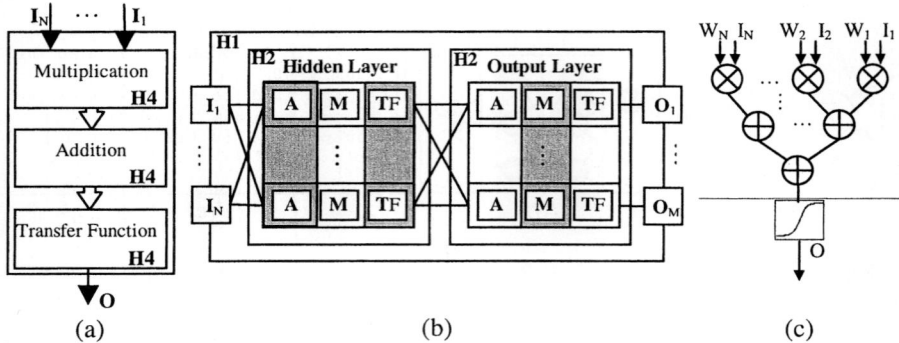

Fig. 2. a) Proposed neuron. b) Proposed MLP architecture. c) Neuron implementation.

The main features of our architecture are its spatial and temporal parallelisms in different hierarchical levels, and their parameterizations. The parameters are divided in two groups, named network and architecture parameters. The first group determines the main features of the network, such as: number of inputs, number of neurons, number of layers, type of transfer function and so on. The second group determines the main features of the architecture, such as: parallelism degree among layers, neurons and modules, implementation of the sub-operations, word length (to represent input, weight and output values), and so on.

The proposed architecture is hierarchically composed of layer, neurons and modules (fig.2b). Observing fig.2, we notice that there are four possible parallelism hierarchical levels in our architecture: (1) H1 is the network, composed of layers (temporal parallelism); (2) H2 is the layer, composed of several neurons (spatial parallelism); (3) H3 is the neuron, with operation modules pipelined execution (temporal parallelism); (4) finally H4 is neuron module with parallel implementation (temporal and spatial parallelism) of each module (fig.2a). Fig2.c is a possible implementation of a neuron with parallelism in H4 in multiplication and addition modules.

Although there are parallelism levels in our architecture, they can be used or not. Thus, the designer must analyze the tradeoffs between performance and cost. Total parallelism implies in high performance, but higher relative cost. For example, it is possible to design an engine without H1 parallelism. In this case, only one layer would be executed at a time, which does not affect other parallelism levels or their execution.

Using the previously described architecture, we have implemented our artificial neural network engine. To design, verify and synthesize our engine, we have codified it in a Hardware Description Language (HDL). The chosen language was VHDL (VHSIC – Very High Speed Integrate Circuit Hardware Description Language) because of its design portability and simplicity to describe a design. Thus, it was possible to define an engine with network and architecture's parameters easily modified. Our implementation has the maximum parallelism that the architecture allows: (1) the layers association composes a pipelined structure; (2) the neurons are disposed in parallel inside each layer, (3) the neuron modules are disposed in a pipelined structure and inside them was applied parallelism. All multiplications are executed in parallel and the summation is executed in a binary tree of synchronous pipelined adders.

Besides the internal parallelism of neuron modules, their design is important for the performance. We designed multipliers and adders considering the tradeoffs between cost and performance. The values of their latencies are two and one clock pulses, respectively. Another limitation of the neurons' implementation is the transfer function (e.g. the sigmoid equation is complex to implement in hardware). There are two frequently used solutions: the implementation of a lookup-table containing the function values for a range, or the implementation of a piecewise function. The former consumes large hardware resources and it implies in high cost and the latter provides less precision. But as errors are inherent of neural networks, some implementations using approximation are acceptable. Thus, we implemented a piecewise function known as PLAN function [6].

The performance of the engine is determined by parallelism degree and clock frequency necessary for neuron's modules execution. In order to determine the pipeline latency of our engine, it is necessary to consider the number of network layers. In Section 3 we discuss the latency and global performance for two engine FPGA implementations.

3 Verification Results

Our verification method consists of the following steps: (1) engine verification using VHDL logic simulations; (2) verification of the FPGA implementation using VHDL, post Place and Route (synthesis), simulations; (3) experimental measurements of software implementations; and (4) performance evaluation and comparative analysis of the hardware and software implementations.

Firstly, we synthesized our engine in a Xilinx XC2V3000 FPGA, and used it to solve a simple problem (XOR operation). We chose this operation in order to verify the implementation's behavior and functionality. We also implemented the same ANN in software and executed on top of a Pentium IV 2.66GHz and an Athlon 2.0GHz. The weights were obtained from the training of the neural network software implemented in C++. In both cases the implemented neural network is a three-layer MLP with a number of inputs (i) varying from 2 to 5 and only one output. The input layer has i neurons, the hidden layer has 2i-1 neurons and the output has one neuron.

We executed the network in hardware and software, and compared the results. Our implementation had a maximum error of 0.02 from the results regarding the software implementation. This architecture's error is insignificant for this problem, considering the required precision and output range from 0 to 1. If a higher precision were required, the word length could be increased.

Fig.3a presents the response time of a single execution of the implemented MLP. In the FPGA implementation, this response time represents the latency of its structure.

Analyzing the results, we notice that the response times of the serial software implementation in both GPP processors increase, as the number of inputs increases, because of its serial processing, as well as the involved overheads (e.g. memory access, operating system etc). Differently, the response time of the FPGA implementation was almost invariable, because of its parallel execution. The FPGA implementation performed better than the software implementations, with a speedup ranging from 7.480 to 19.714.

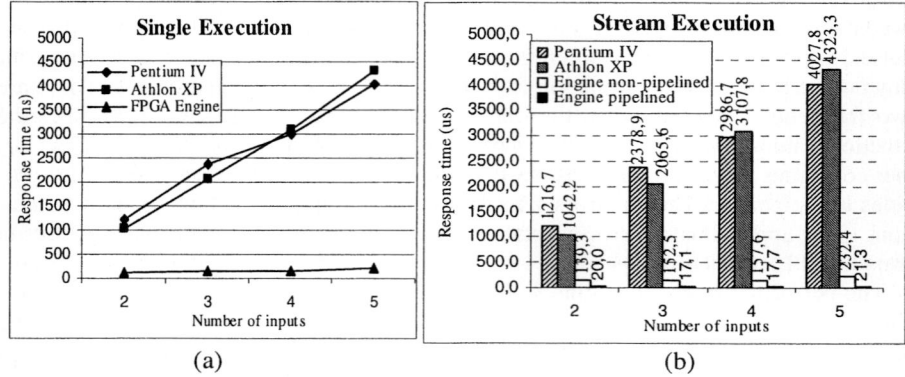

Fig. 3. Response time of the ANN in FPGA and on top of traditional processors

In Fig.3b we present the response time of a thousand consecutive executions of the MLP in software and hardware. The software implementation behaved similarly as before, with proportional increases in the response times. In the same figure, we notice that the speedup of the non-pipelined FPGA implementation also kept the same proportion, ranging from 7.480 to 19.714. Nevertheless, the pipelined FPGA implementation performed even better, yielding a speedup ranging from 7 to 11 regarding the non-pipelined implementation and from 52.354 to 204.576 regarding the serial software implementations.

Table 1. Resource utilization of the FPGA implementation

	2 inputs	3 inputs	4 inputs	5 inputs	Available
Slices	2448	5256	9179	13453	14336
Flip-Flops	935	2150	3425	5748	28672
4-Input LUTs	4326	9279	16061	23437	28672
Bonded IOBs	48	64	80	96	720
Max. Frequency (MHz)	50.236	59.027	57.091	47.323	-
Clock cycles	7	9	9	11	-

In Table1, we notice that the resource utilization within the FPGA is proportional to the overall number of processing neurons and to the number of inputs of each neuron. We also highlight that the engine implemented in FPGA executes with an average frequency of 46.3 times lower than the processors. Thus, our implementation also contributes for lower energy consumption, temperature dissipation and the final cost of the product. Even with a much lower frequency, our engine still has a much better performance, as mentioned before.

4 Conclusions

Considering presented and analyzed results, we conclude that the proposed engine correctly implemented the MLP network and yielded better computational performance than software implementations, with speedups from 52.3 to 204.5. Thus, our main goals were totally reached. Also, our engine yield better performance than some related works [1] [5] [7] based on dedicated parallel architectures and FPGA implementations. The main contributions of this work are the originality of our proposed architecture, considering the parallelism and parameterization architectural features, and its higher computational performance improvements. Also, there are the flexibility and scalability provided by the parameterization. Among future works we highlight: study other parameter combinations and their performance impact, implement our engine using different design styles and implementation technologies and design engines to implement other ANN models.

References

1. Misra, M.: Parallel Environments for Implementing Neural Networks. Neural Computing Surveys, Vol. 1 (1997) 48-60
2. Rosenblatt, F.: The Perceptron: A Probabilistic Model for Information Storage and Organization in the Brain. Psychological Review, Vol. 65, (1958), 386-408
3. Rumelhart, D.E., Hinton, G.E., Williams, R.J.: Learning Internal Representations by Error Propagation. In: Rumelhart, D.E., McCleland, J.L. (eds.): Parallel Distributed Processing: Explorations in the Microstructure of Cognition, Volume 1: Foundations, Cambridge, MA, MIT (1986) 318-364
4. Haykin, S.: Neural Networks: A Comprehensive Foundation. 2nd edn. Prentice Hall (1998)
5. Seiffert, U.: Artificial Neural Networks on Massively Parallel Computer Hardware. Neurocomputing, Vol. 57 (2004) 135-150
6. Tommiska, M.T.: Efficient Digital Implementation of the Sigmoid Function for Programmable Logic, IEE Proceedings Computer and Digital Techniques, Vol. 150, No. 6, (2003), 403-411
7. Linares-Barranco, B., Andreou, A.G., Indiveri, G., Shibata, T. (eds.): Special Issue on Neural on Neural Networks Hardware Implementations, IEEE Transactions on Neural Networks, Vol. 14, No. 5, (2003)

Neuronal Clustering of Brain fMRI Images

Nicolas Lachiche, Jean Hommet, Jerzy Korczak, and Agnès Braud

LSIIT, Pôle API, Bd Brant, F-67400 Illkirch, France
{lachiche, hommet, jjk, braud}@lsiit.u-strasbg.fr

Abstract. Functional Magnetic Resonance Imaging (fMRI) allows the neuroscientists to observe the human brain in vivo. The current approach consists in statistically validating their hypotheses. Data mining techniques provide an opportunity to help them in making up their hypotheses. This paper shows how a neuronal clustering technique can highlight active areas thanks to an appropriate distance between fMRI image sequences. This approach has been integrated into an interactive environment for knowledge discovery in brain fMRI. Its results on a typical dataset validate the approach and open further developments in this direction.

1 Introduction

Functional Magnetic Resonance Imaging (fMRI) provides a unique opportunity to observe the internal behaviour of living organisms. In particular it can be used to observe how the human brain works. This is useful either to gain a better understanding of the human brain in general, or to prepare a surgical operation for a particular patient.

fMRI aims at localizing areas of activity. This is done by considering variations in the blood flow and in the oxygen concentration. Indeed internal activities increase the consumption of oxygen and thus induce the so-called BOLD effect (Blood Oxygenation Level Dependent) which increases the fMRI signal. The studied area is splitted up into cubes with sides usually around 3mm. The intensity of the signal is measured for each of those cubes. A 3D image is formed by associating each cube to a 3D pixel called a voxel. This image shows the intensity of the signal and thus the areas of activity. Compared to other current methods fMRI offers a very good trade-off between spatial and temporal resolutions.

We are interested in brain images. Sequences of fMRI images of the brain are used to check the evolution of the neuronal activity of a patient. The problem is then that the signal on noise ratio is very low, which makes it difficult to identify the areas with a real activity. Moreover, it generates a large amount of data (around 300000 voxels, for which between 100 and 1000 observations are acquired).

Aiming at identifying active areas, the use of mining algorithms seems to be interesting, but they have not reached their full potential yet [9]. Due to the amount of data, most of the studies do not try to explore the data, but use them to test a model with univariate statistics, e.g. Statistical Parametric Mapping

(SPM) [5], AFNI [2], Brain Voyager [7]. Methods to identify the variations which are meaningful can be divided into two families. The most common approach is based on multivariate statistics such as MANCOVA, PCA, PLS, canonical analysis or more recently ICA [1].The second family gathers all the data mining methods, such as clustering, genetic algorithms and neuromimetic networks [9].

Visual Data Mining allows the integration of the user, an expert, in the knowledge discovery process. In this paper, we present a new interactive approach to fMRI images mining, guided by the data. The originality of our approach relies in the fact that we do not only use data mining techniques which have not been used for that purpose yet, but above all those techniques will be extended by injecting a priori knowledge in the mining process and interactivity. The expert will thus be directly involved in the learning process to identify functional areas of the brain and their organization.

In the next section we explain how a neuronal clustering technique can be applied to identify brain areas that have the same activity, and how it has been integrated into an interactive environment for knowledge discovery in brain fMRI. The results of experiments on a typical dataset are reported in section 4 and validate the use of data mining techniques to complement other approaches in this domain.

2 Neuronal Clustering

Clustering algorithms usually depend on a distance. A distance between voxels has to be defined. A 3D distance between voxels is irrelevant to identify voxels having the same activity. Taking the 3D distance into account would make close voxels -close from a 3D perspective- look more similar than far-away voxels having the same activity. The distance between voxels should only be defined according to their activities. Let us also emphasize that a clustering based on the activity of the voxels without any influence of their localisation is clearly different from segmentation techniques also used to "identify areas" in fMRI images that relies on a comparison of neighbouring voxels.

The activity of a voxel is a continuous signal, in practice a sampling of that signal. One approach consists in generating different attributes describing the signal, e.g. its average, minimum and maximum values, and then using those attribute-values in a traditional attribute-value clustering system. In such an approach, the built-in distance of the clustering system is calculated on the intermediate attributes, e.g. the euclidian distance between the respective average, minimum and maximum values of each voxel. Its success depends on how well the built-in distance and the generated attributes fit together. Lots of attributes can be tested. For instance, [3] made use of wavelets to transform the signal, though they made use of hidden markov models rather than a clustering technique.

We considered an alternative approach, where the distance is directly calculated on the signal. Its obvious disadvantage is that it is then impossible to use an existing clustering system right out of the box. This is balanced by having a distance that exactly measures the difference between two signals. First we

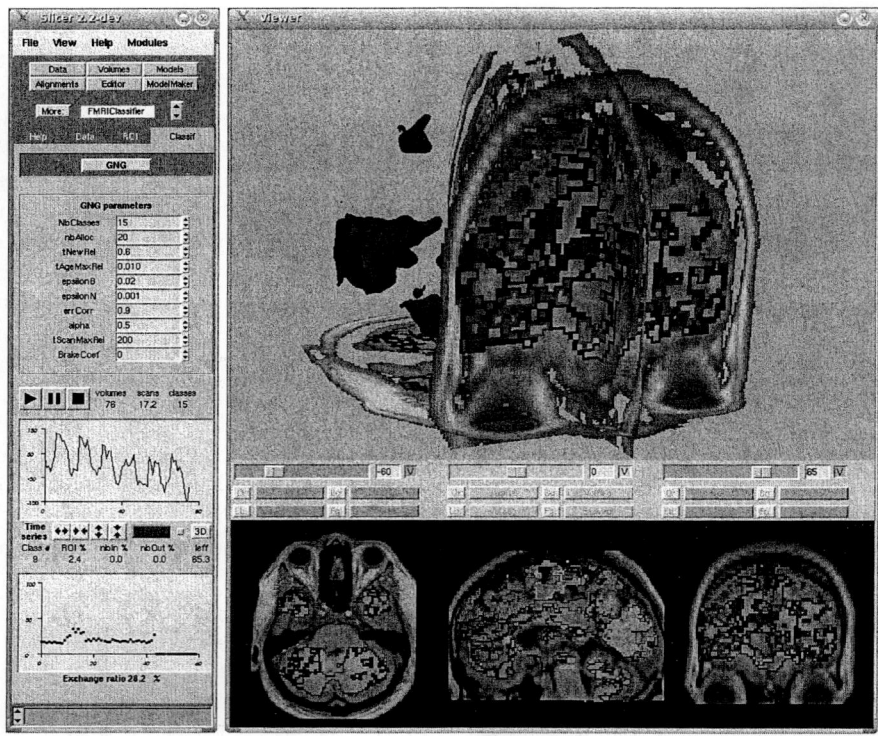

Fig. 1. An environment for interactive knowledge discovery in brain fMRI

remove the average value, then the distance we use is the area between the two variations of the signals around their means.

We have chosen a neuronal clustering algorithm. Kohonen's Self-Organising Maps [8] is the most known neuronal clustering algorithm. However its fixed topological structure would not help in our application, since there is no a priori topological relationship between the classes[1]. Thus we prefered the Growing Neural Gas (GNG) algorithm [6]. Its main advantage is that the number of classes is not fixed in advance as in most clustering algorithms. The class centers can increase as well as decrease during the learning process. Moreover this algorithm easily fits in an interactive knowledge discovery application.

Our aim is indeed to provide a software environment that enables the neuroscientist to improve his understanding of the human brain. While the current approach supposes that the human expert builds up the hypothesis and the software, e.g. SPM [5], is only used to validate that hypothesis, data mining

---

[1] In order to avoid any confusion between the biological neurons of the brain and the artificial neurons of the clustering algorithms, we will denote the former by the voxels -which actually represent/contain thousands of biological neurons- and the latter by the class centers.

techniques can complement that approach by guiding the expert in his generation of new hypotheses, in particular by automatically showing up activated areas, and hightlightening dependencies between those areas.

We have extended the SLICER system for visualisation (http://www.slicer.org/) with clustering and interactive exploration of fMRI images features. In its current version, our software environment allows the user to interact graphically with the clustering process, e.g. by modifying parameters of the GNG algorithms, by focusing on specific parts of the brain, etc. A screenshot of our system is presented on figure 1.

3 Experiments

In this section we demonstrate our approach on a typical dataset: an auditory dataset from the Wellcome Department of Imaging Neuroscience of the University College London (http://www.fil.ion.ucl.ac.uk/spm/). It consists of 96 brain MRI acquisitions with a 7s time interval. Each acquisition consists of 64 contiguous slices (64x64x64 3mm x 3mm x 3mm voxels). The auditory stimulation consists of

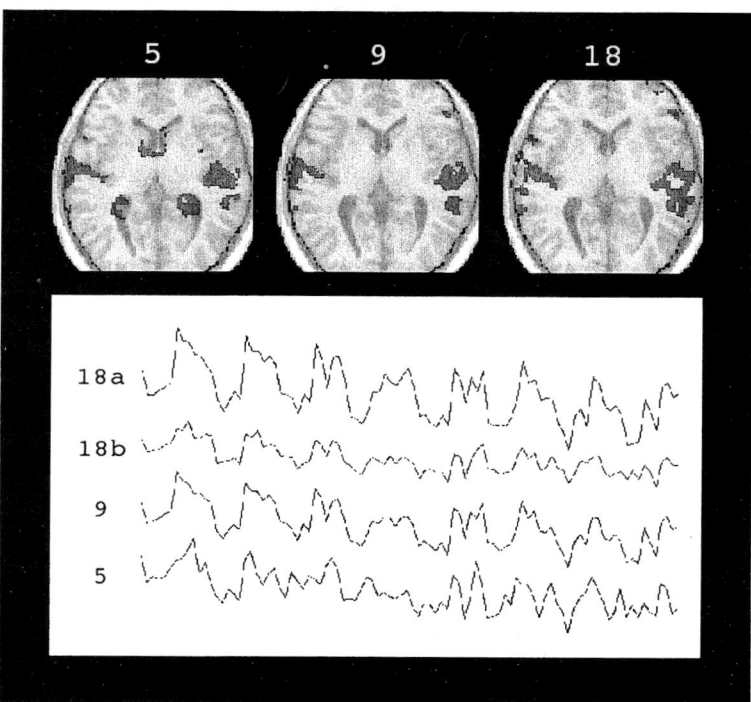

Fig. 2. Active areas and their activities wrt to the number of classes considered in the clustering

bi-syllabic words presented binaurally at a rate of 60 per minute during 42 seconds (6 images), followed by a 42 second silence. It is repeated 8 times.

We illustrate that the clustering algorithm successfully identifies the active areas and their signal. The figure 2 shows the results for three runs with a different number of classes considered in the clustering: 5, 9 and 18. With 5 classes only, the active class overlaps on inactive areas, thus the activity signal do not correspond to the stimulation signal as tightly as with 9 classes. With 18 classes, the active area is decomposed into two parts corresponding to two intensity levels of activation.

4 Conclusion

While the current approach in brain fMRI consists in statistically validating hypotheses made up by the human experts, data mining techniques can help the neuroscientist in the generation of hypotheses. In this paper we showed that a clustering algorithm such as the Growing Neural Gas can successfully highlight active areas in brain fMRI images. It required to express the neuroscientist's interest in terms of a problem that can be solved by a machine learning approach. In particular we had to define a distance between voxels of fMRI images. We argued that such a distance should be based on the signal only, without any influence of the 3D localisation, and that the difference between the variation of the signals is a straightforward alternative to all propositionalisation approaches that could be used to generate attributes then apply usual attribute-value distances. We have integrated our approach on a well-known visualisation plateform in order to get a complete interactive environment for knowledge discovery in brain fMRI.

However the identification of active areas is very difficult. fMRI data are inherently very complex: there is a very low signal to noise ratio, lots of different noises are involved, etc. Considering evenemential signals reduces even further the signal to noise ratio. Taking the stimulation signal into account as in [3] can help by synchronising the signals. However it is no longer possible with spontaneous events [4].

Acknowledgements

The authors kindly thank K. Friston et G. Rees for the auditory dataset, C. Scheiber, J. Foucher and D. Gounod for their help in understanding the fMRI domain, and the following students for their contribution to the software development: H. Hager, P. Hahn, V. Meyer, J. Schaeffer and O. Zitvogel.

References

[1] C. Beckmann and S. M. Smith. Probabilistic independent component analysis for functional magnetic resonance imaging. *IEEE Trans. on Medical Imaging*, 2003.
[2] R. W. Cox. AFNI: Software for analysis and visualization of functional magnetic resonance neuroimages. *Computers and Biomedical Research*, 29:162–173, 1996.

[3] S. Faisan, L. Thoraval, J.-P. Armspach, and F. Heitz. Unsupervised learning and mapping of brain fmri signals based on hidden semi–markov event sequence models. In *Medical Image Computing and Computer Assisted Intervention (MICCAI)*, pages 75–82, 2003.
[4] J. R. Foucher, H. Otzenberger, and D. Gounot. Where arousal meets attention: a simultaneous fmri and eeg recording study. *Neuroimage*, 22(2):688–697, 2004.
[5] K. J. Friston, A. P. Holmes, K. J. Worsley, J. P. Poline, C. D. Frith, and R. S. J. Frackowiak. Statistical parametric maps in functional imaging: A general linear approach. *Human Brain Mapping*, 2:189–210, 1995.
[6] B. Fritzke. A growing neural gas network learns topologies. In G. Tesauro, D. S. Touretzky, and T. K. Leen, editors, *Advances in Neural Information Processing Systems 7*, pages 625–632. MIT Press, Cambridge MA, 1995.
[7] R. Goebel. *BrainVoyager: Ein Programm zur Analyse und Visualisierung von Magnetresonanztomographiedaten.* T. Plesser and P. Wittenburg, Forschung und wissenschaftliches Rechnen, 1997.
[8] T. Kohonen. Self-organized formation of topologically correct feature maps. *Biological Cybernetics*, 43:59–69, 1982.
[9] F. T. Sommer and A. Wichert. *Exploratory Analysis and Data Modeling in Functional Neuroimaging.* The MIT Press, Massachusetts Institute of Technology, Cambridge, Massachusetts, 2003.

An Optimum RBF Network for Signal Detection in Non-Gaussian Noise

D.G. Khairnar, S.N. Merchant, and U.B. Desai

SPANN Laboratory, Dept. of Electrical Engg, I.I.T. Bombay, India
{dgk, merchant, ubdesai}@ee.iitb.ac.in

Abstract. In this paper, we propose a radial basis function (RBF) neural network for detecting a known signal in the presence of non-Gaussian and Gaussian noise. In case of non-Gaussian noise, our study shows that RBF signal detector has significant improvement in performance characteristics; detection capability is better to those obtained with multilayer perceptrons (MLP) and the matched filter (MF) detector.

1 Introduction

Real world signals usually contain departures from the ideal signal due to non-Gaussian noise. Optimum linear detectors, under the assumption of additive Gaussian noise are suggested in [1] and [2]. A class of locally optimum detectors are used in [2]. In [3] Watterson generalizes an optimum MLP neural receiver for signal detection. Lippmann and Beckman [4] employed a neural network as a preprocessor to reduce the influence of impulsive noise components. Michalopoulou et al [5] trained a multilayer neural network to identify one of M orthogonal signals embedded in additive Gaussian noise. Gandhi and Ramamurti [6] has shown that the neural detector trained using BP algorithm gives near optimum performance. In this paper, we propose a neural network detector using RBF network and we employ this neural detector to detect the presence or absence of a known signal corrupted by Gaussian and non-Gaussian noise components. Our study shows that in non-Gaussian noise environments the RBF signal detector show better performance characteristics and good detection capability compared to neural detector using BP.

2 Preliminaries and a RBF for Signal Detection

The two commonly used measures to assess performance of a signal detector are the probability of detection P_d and the probability of false alarm P_{fa} [1]. Consider a data vector $\mathbf{X(t)} = [x_1(t), x_2(t), ..., x_N(t)]^T$ as an input to the detector in Figure 1-(a). Using the additive observational model, we have $\mathbf{X(t)} = \mathbf{S(t)} + \mathbf{C(t)}$ for the hypothesis that the target signal is present and $\mathbf{X(t)} = \mathbf{C(t)}$ for the hypothesis that the signal is absent, where $\mathbf{S(t)} = [s_1(t), s_2(t), ..., s_N(t)]^T$ is the target signal vector and $\mathbf{C(t)} = [c_1(t), c_2(t), ..., c_N(t)]^T$ is the noise vector. With $f_N(x)$ as the marginal probability density function (pdf) of $N_i, i = 1, 2, ..., n$, here we consider the following pdf's:

An Optimum RBF Network for Signal Detection in Non-Gaussian Noise

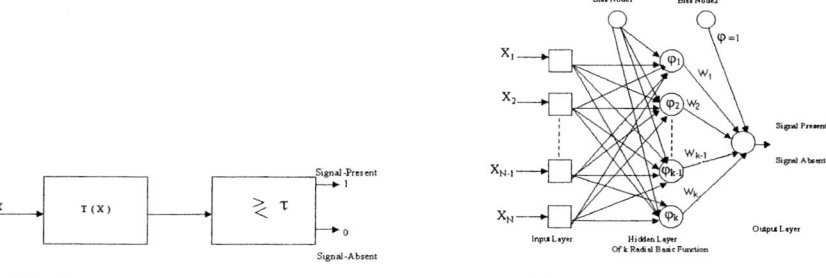

(a) Conventional signal detector   (b) RBF signal detector

Fig. 1. Conventional and RBF signal detector

1. Gaussian pdf with $f_N(x) = e^{-x^2/2\sigma^2}/\sqrt{2\pi\sigma^2}$ and $E[N_i^2] = \sigma^2$.
2. Double exponential pdf with $f_N(x) = e^{-\|x\|/\sigma}/2\sigma$ and $E[N_i^2] = 2\sigma^2$.
3. Contaminated Gaussian pdf with $f_N(x) = (1-\epsilon)e^{-x^2/2\sigma_0^2}/\sqrt{2\pi\sigma_0^2} + \epsilon e^{-x^2/2\sigma_1^2}/\sqrt{2\pi\sigma_1^2}$.

The structure of the signal detector based on an RBF network is shown in Figure 1-(b). The input layer has N neurons with a linear function. One hidden layer of K neurons with Gaussian transfer functions. The output layer has only one neuron whose input-output relationship approximates the two possible states. The two bias nodes are included as part of the network. A real-valued input vector $\mathbf{x}$ to a neuron of the hidden or output layer produces neural output $G(\mathbf{x})$, where $0 < G(\mathbf{x}) < 1$. The Gaussian function we choose is $G(\mathbf{x}, \mathbf{x}_i) = exp(-1/2\sigma_i^2 \|\mathbf{x} - \mathbf{x}_i\|^2)$. The RBF neural network detector test statistic $T_{NN}(\mathbf{x})$ may now be expressed as,

$$T_{NN}(\mathbf{x}) = \sum_{i=1}^{K} w_i \varphi_i(\mathbf{x}) + w^{b_2} \qquad (1)$$

where $\{\varphi_i(\mathbf{x}), i = 1, 2, 3, ..., K\}$ is a set of basis functions. The $\mathbf{w}$ constitutes a set of connection weights for the output layer. When using RBF the basis is

$$\varphi_i(\mathbf{x}) = G(\|\mathbf{x} - \Sigma \mathbf{t_i}\|^2) + w_i^{b_1}, i = 1, 2, 3, ..., K \qquad (2)$$

where $\mathbf{t}_i = [t_{i1}, t_{i2}, ..., t_{iN}]^T$ with $\mathbf{t}_i$ as unknown centers to be determined. Σ is a symmetric positive definite weighting matrix of size $N \mathrm{x} N$, $G(.)$ represents a multivariate Gaussian distribution with mean vector $\mathbf{t}_i$ and covariance matrix Σ. By using above equations we redefine $T_{NN}(\mathbf{x})$ as

$$T_{NN}(\mathbf{x}) = \sum_{i=1}^{K} w_i G(\mathbf{x}, \mathbf{t}_i) = \sum_{i=1}^{K} w_i G(\|\mathbf{x} - \mathbf{t}_i\|). \qquad (3)$$

We determine the set of weights $\mathbf{w} = [w_1, w_2, ..., w_k]^T$ and the set $\mathbf{t}$ of vectors $\mathbf{t}_i$ of centers.

3 Simulation Results and Performance Evaluations

Neural weights are obtained by training the network at 10-dB SNR using $\theta = \sqrt{10}$ and $E[N_i^2] = 1$. During simulation, the threshold τ_{NN} is set to 0.5, and the bias weight w^{b_2} value that gives a P_{fa} value in the range $0.001 - 1$. For each w^{b_2} value that gives a P_{fa} value in the above range, the corresponding P_d value are also simulated. The 10-dB-SNR-trained neural network is tested in the 5-dB and 10-dB SNR environment.

3.1 Performance in Gaussian Noise (Constant and Ramp Signal)

Performance characteristics of neural detectors using RBF, MLP and MF detectors are presented in Figure 2-(a) and 2-(b) for Gaussian noise. The RBF and MLP neural detectors are trained using the constant signal and ramp signal with SNR = 10 dB. And then both neural detectors and match filter detector are tested with 10-dB SNR inputs. In both cases, the RBF and MLP neural detectors performance is very close to that of the MF detector.

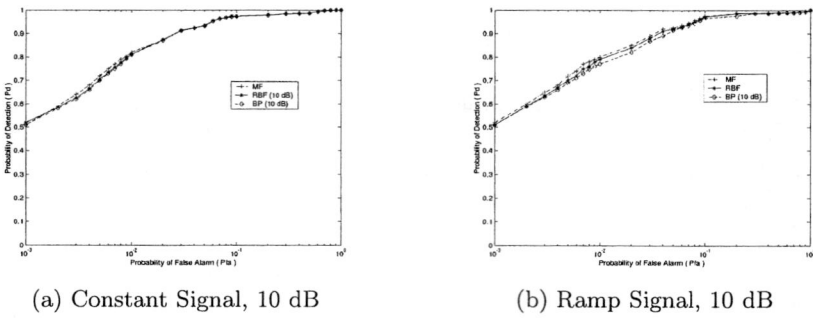

(a) Constant Signal, 10 dB (b) Ramp Signal, 10 dB

Fig. 2. Performance comparison in Gaussian Noise

3.2 Testing of Signal Detector in Non-Gaussian Noise

Here we illustrate the performance comparisons of the likelihood ratio (LR), MF, local optimum (LO), and neural detectors using RBF and MLP for ramp signal embedded in additive double exponential noise. Figure 3-(a) and 3-(b) show the comparison for a 10-dB-SNR-trained neural detectors operating in the 5-dB and 10-dB SNR environment.

The same experiment is repeated for the ramp signal embedded in contaminated Gaussian noise with parameters $\epsilon = 0.2$, $\sigma_0^2 = 0.25$ and $\sigma_1^2 = 4$ and the results are shown in Figure 3-(c) and 3-(d). In all these cases, the RBF based neural detector performance is superior compared to all other detectors (excluding LR detector which is optimal).

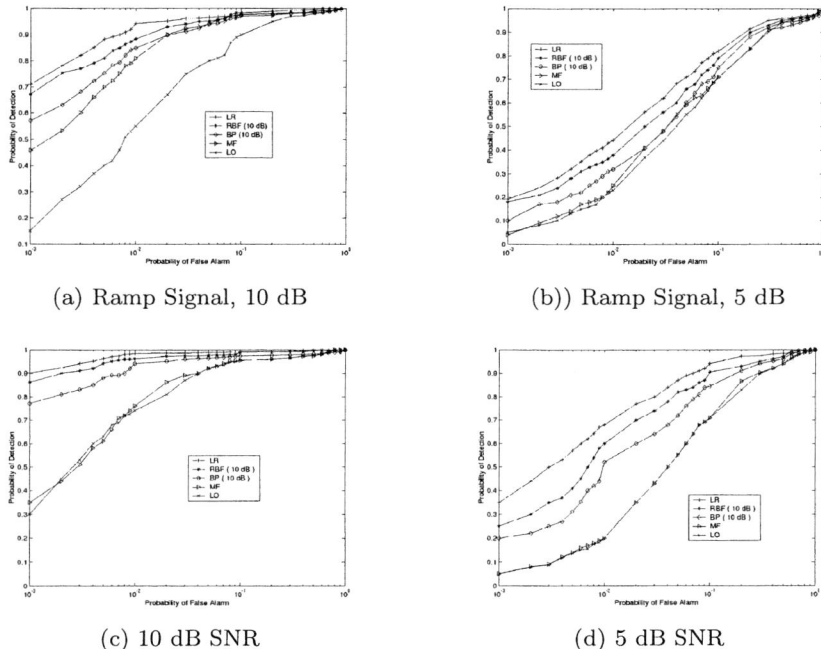

Fig. 3. Performance comparison in double exponential and contaminated Gaussian

4 Conclusion

We have proposed RBF based neural network for detection of known signal in non-Gaussian noise. Our simulation results show that its performance is superior compared to conventional detectors.

References

1. H. V. Poor,: An Introduction to Signal Detection and Estimation, Springer-Verlag (1988).
2. S. A. Kassam,: Signal Detection in Non-Gaussian Noise, Springer-Verlag (1988).
3. J. W. Watterson,: An Optimum Multilayer Perceptron Neural Receiver for Signal Detection, IEEE Transactions on Neural Networks, Vol.1,No.4 (1990) 298-300.
4. R. P. Lippmann and P. Beckman,: Adaptive neural net preprocessing for signal detection in non-Gaussian noise, In Advances in Neural Information Processing Systems, Vol.1, (1989).
5. Z. Michalopoulou, L. Nolta and D. Alexandrou,: Performance evaluation of multilayer perceptrons in signal detection and classification, IEEE Transactions on Neural Networks, Vol.6, No.2 (1995).
6. P. P. Gandhi and V. Ramamurti,: Neural networks for signal detection in non-Gaussian noise, IEEE Transactions on Signal Processing, Vol.45, No.11 (1997).

A Holistic Classification System for Check Amounts Based on Neural Networks with Rejection*

M.J. Castro[1], W. Díaz[2], F.J. Ferri[2], J. Ruiz-Pinales[3], R. Jaime-Rivas[3],
F. Blat[1], S. España[1], P. Aibar[4], S. Grau[1], and D. Griol[1]

[1] Dep. Sistemas Informáticos y Computación, Univ. Politécnica de Valencia, Spain
[2] Dep. Informática, Univ. de València, Burjassot, Valencia, Spain
[3] FIMEE - Univ. de Guanajuato, Salamanca, Guanajuato, Mexico
[4] Dep. Lenguajes y Sistemas Informáticos, Univ. Jaume I, Castellón, Spain
mcastro@dsic.upv.es

Abstract. A holistic classification system for off-line recognition of legal amounts in checks is described in this paper. The binary images obtained from the cursive words are processed following the human visual system, employing a Hough transform method to extract perceptual features. Images are finally coded into a bidimensional feature map representation. Multilayer perpeptrons are used to classify these feature maps into one of the 32 classes belonging to the CENPARMI database. To select a final classification system, ROC graphs are used to fix the best threshold values of the classifiers to obtain the best tradeoff between accuracy and misclassification.

1 Introduction

The processing of legal amounts in checks involves the recognition of handwritten cursive words, which remains a challenging problem due to the great variability in writing styles and devices. In general, there are two main approaches in handwriting word recognition: analytic and holistic [1]. Analytical approaches assume that words are constructed from characters and characters are produced by strokes, so an explicit or implicit segmentation is needed to perform classification. However, correct segmentation requires that individual characters be first identified, which leads to a paradox besides that it is not always possible to recognize every character. Thus, errors made by most analytic systems are mainly due to segmentation errors of the connected characters. On the other hand, holistic approaches, which avoid the segmentation problem and treat the word as a single, have been limited to small size lexicons. However, there still exists a big difference between the performances of human readers and automatic recognition systems even for small-sized vocabulary tasks.

---

* Thanks to the Spanish CICYT under contract TIC2002-04103-C03-03 and the Generalitat Valenciana under contract 20040479 for partial funding.

In the rest of the paper, we will describe the handwritten CENPARMI database and its preprocessing, the methods used to classify, present some experimental results, and discuss the obtained system.

2 The CENPARMI Database

The off-line handwritten English legal word database of CENPARMI [2] has been created from 2 500 handwritten checks written in English. The number of writers is estimated to be close to 800. All checks images were scanned at 300 dpi, transformed into binary images, and segmented into tagged word images. The database is composed of the 32 different legal word classes (from "one" to "twenty", "thirty", "forty" and so on, plus the words "and", "dollars" and "only"). In the recognition experiments, 3 069 images of cursive words were used for training and 341 images for testing.

A check may contain different backgrounds consisting of pictures printed in various colors and intensities. In order to isolate the handwritten information, it is necessary to eliminate or reduce the background. The next step is to locate the handwritten items of information (in this case, the legal amount written in words) to be processed, which can greatly vary in different check forms. The items are found through locating the baselines under the items. This task of baseline detection of cursive words is very important, because the detection of ascenders and descenders and other important features (such as the surface of closed loops above, within and below the central zone) requires a reliable detection of the baseline, something that is very difficult to obtain. In a previous work [3], we proposed that the position of these features can be encoded into several feature maps in order to avoid detecting them explicitly and a new method to extract these features in gray-level images is accomplished.

Global features are extracted from each word using a feature extraction approach to the problem of representing shape (for a survey see [1]). The binary images obtained from the cursive words are processed following the human visual system, employing a Hough transform method to extract perceptual features and they are coded into a bidimensional feature map representation. Images are represented in two different encodings as 7 feature maps of size 12×3 and 24×6. Details of the preprocessing can be found in [3].

3 A Holistic Classification System Based on NNs

The holistic approach to word recognition treats the word as a single entity and attempts to recognize it as whole [1]. This approach avoids the difficult problem of segmenting the word into characters, graphemes or other smaller units. However, since each word is encoded as a different class, it is usually restricted to applications involving small lexicons, as the case for the CENPARMI database is.

Classification using neural networks. Multilayer perceptrons (MLPs) are commonly used in handwritten character or word recognition tasks. For this purpose, the number of output units is defined as the number of classes, $|\mathcal{C}|$, and the input layer must hold the input samples. If a softmax activation function [4] is used, the activation level of an output unit is an approximation of the a posteriori probability that the input sample belongs to the corresponding class [5]. Therefore, given an input sample $\mathbf{x}$, the trained MLP computes $g_k(\mathbf{x},\omega)$ (the k-th output of the MLP with parameters ω given the input sample $\mathbf{x}$) which is an approximation of the a posteriori probability $\Pr(k|\mathbf{x})$. Thus, for MLP classifiers we can use the Bayes decision rule:

$$k^\star(\mathbf{x}) = \operatorname*{argmax}_{k \in \mathcal{C}} \Pr(k|\mathbf{x}) \approx \operatorname*{argmax}_{k \in \mathcal{C}} g_k(\mathbf{x},\omega). \qquad (1)$$

The set of classes $\mathcal{C}$ are the 32 words of the task and classification follows the "winner-takes-all" (WTA) strategy. Nevertheless, in real applications, such as recognition of checks amounts, misclassifications are considered much more costly than rejections, and it is preferred to introduce some rejection criteria [6]. This can be done through the concept of confidence threshold (below which the classifier abstains) and equation (1) is converted to:

$$k^\star(\mathbf{x}) = \begin{cases} \operatorname*{argmax}_{k \in \mathcal{C}} g_k(\mathbf{x},\omega), & \text{if } g_k(\mathbf{x},\omega) \geq \mathcal{T}_k, \\ 0, & \text{in other case.} \end{cases} \qquad (2)$$

With this rule, the classification is always given by the class with greatest a posteriori probability, but the rejection will depend on thresholds which are different for each class. We will refer to classification rules from equations (1) and (2) as "WTA Rule" and "WTA + $\mathcal{T}$ Rule", respectively.

Training the multilayer perceptrons. The corpus was divided into a training set, a validation set and a test set. The trained neural networks differed in the number of hidden layers (one or two hidden layers) and the number of hidden neurons in each layer (from 10 to 200 hidden units). In every case, the online version of the backpropagation learning algorithm with momentum was used [7]. For the same topology, several trainings were performed varying the learning rate, the momentum term and using different initializations of the weights. The stopping criteria was the classification error in the validation set.

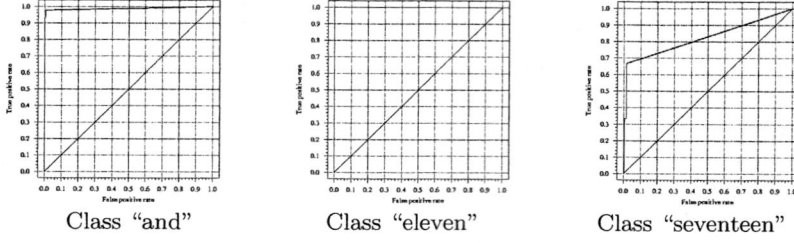

Fig. 1. ROC curves on the threshold values for classification for three classes

Fixing threshold parameters with ROC graphs. Receiver Operating Characteristics (ROC) graphs [8] are a useful technique for visualizing, organizing and selecting classifiers based on their performance. In this work, we use ROC graphs in order to select the threshold values for "WTA + $\mathcal{T}$ Rule" classifiers to obtain the best tradeoff between accuracy and misclassification: we performed classification with the optimal configuration of MLPs on the patterns of the validation set and analyzed the ROC curves. Finally, we measure network performance on the test set for the best configuration of MLP and the best threshold for each class. Figure 1 shows some examples of the ROC curves for classification with feature maps of size 24×6 for three classes.

4 Experiments

In this section, the best result obtained with each approach is given. Performances with MLPs for both tested parametrizations with and without using thresholds for rejection are shown in Table 1. The recognition rate of each legal word class for the best classifier (MLP with two hidden layers of 150 and 100 units for the 24×6-sized feature maps with rejection) is 86.26% (with no rejection) and 69.88% with rejection. It is worth noting that there are very few samples of each word in the test set (for instance, only 3 and 5 instances of the words "seventeen" and "thirteen", respectively).

Table 1. Classification measures (W=Wrong, R=Right, U=Unknown)

Experiment		Classification	Test		
Classifier	Feature maps	rule	%W	%R	%U
MLP 80-60	12×3	WTA	18.77	81.23	0.00
		WTA + $\mathcal{T}$	0.88	51.32	47.80
MLP 150-100	24×6	WTA	13.74	86.26	0.00
		WTA + $\mathcal{T}$	0.00	69.88	30.12

5 Summary and Conclusions

A holistic neural network classification system with rejection has been proposed for handwriting images recognition. Each image is represented as a whole with feature maps of different sizes. As we are interested in cautious classifiers, ROC graphs are employed to obtain the best tradeoff between accuracy and misclassification. The best performance, close to 70% of classification with rejection of 30% and no errors, is achieved with an MLP for a representation of seven feature maps of size 24×6. This result shows the effectiveness of the proposed approach to avoid misclassifications and still achieving a competitive performance.

The task of legal amount recognition from checks is a limited domain application, so a model of language can greatly help in recognition. For future work we are also considering to use multiple classifier systems, that is, combining the expertise of multiple classifier methods (through voting, linear confidence accumulation or weighted schemes).

References

1. Madhvanath, S., Govindaraju, V.: The role of holistic paradigms in handwritten word recognition. IEEE Trans. on PAMI **23** (2001) 149–164
2. Suen, C.Y., et al.: Computer recognition of unconstrained handwritten numerals. Special Issue of Proc IEEE **7** (1992) 1162–1180
3. Ruiz-Pinales, J., Lecolinet, E.: Cursive handwriting recognition using the Hough transform and a neural network. In: ICPR. (2002) 231–234
4. Bridle, J.S.: Training stochastic model recognition algorithms as networks can lead to maximum mutual information estimation of parameters. In: Advances in Neural Information Processing Systems 3, Morgan Kaufmann (1990)
5. Duda, R.O., Hart, P.E., Stork, D.G.: Pattern Classification. Second edn. John Wiley and Sons, New York, NY, USA (2001)
6. Ferri, C., Hernández-Orallo, J.: Cautious classifiers. In: ROCAI. (2004) 27–36
7. Rumelhart, D.E., Hinton, G.E., Williams, R.J.: Learning internal representations by error propagation. MIT Press (1986) 319–362
8. Fawcett, T.: ROC Graphs: Notes and Practical Considerations for Researchers. HP Technical Report HPL-2003-4, HP Labs (2003) Revised March, 2004.

A Novel 3D Face Recognition Algorithm Using Template Based Registration Strategy and Artificial Neural Networks

Ben Niu[1], Simon Chi Keung Shiu[1], and Sankar Kumar Pal[2]

[1] Department of Computing, Hong Kong Polytechnic University, Hong Kong, China
{csniuben, csckshiu}@comp.polyu.edu.hk
[2] Machine Intelligence Unit, Indian Statistical Institute, Kolkata, India
sankar@isical.ac.in

Abstract. In this paper, we present a novel algorithm for 3D face recognition that is robust to the rotations and translations of the face models. Based on the Iterative Closest Point algorithm, a template based registration strategy is proposed for data normalization. Back-Propagation neural networks are then constructed to perform recognition tasks. The proposed algorithm is general purpose and can be applied for common 3D object recognitions. Experimental results illustrate that the algorithm is effective and robust.

1 Introduction

A 3D face model, or a point cloud, is a depth image consisting of a set of 3D points generated from laser scanners or structured lights. The images are usually captured from different viewpoints and distances. Each of them has its own local coordinate system. In order to use the 3D data for building recognition systems it is necessary to transform them into a common coordinate system. This procedure is usually referred to as registration, or normalization. After data normalization, similarity measures are developed for face matching and recognition.

Various approaches have been proposed for 3D point cloud registration and matching. Moreno and Sanchez [1] compute the Gaussian and the mean curvatures of the surface to extract feature points for local coordinate construction and alignments. Euclidean distances among the feature vectors are used for similarity measurement. Zhang *et al* [2] apply Principal Component Analysis to roughly obtain the medial axis of the face model and then use ICP algorithm to refine the registration. The matching process is also based on the Euclidean distance. Lu *et al* [3] use ICP algorithm directly for both face alignment and face matching. The similarity measure is the ICP distance error between the data and the template models.

2 Iterative Closest Point Algorithm

The iterative closest point (ICP) algorithm proposed by Besl and McKay [4] is a widely used method for 3D point cloud registration. The basic ICP algorithm is described as:

Given a template model X and a data model P find the optimal rotation matrix and the translation matrix that minimize the distance error between X and P.

Algorithm. Iterative Closest Point

Step 1. $\forall p \in P$ find its closest point $x \in X$

Step 2. Find transformation Q to minimize the distances between each p and x

Step 3. $P_{k+1} \leftarrow Q(P_k)$

Step 4. Repeat the above steps until the distance error reduce to a minimal level.

3 Registration

We develop a template based strategy to normalize 3D point clouds for neural network training. A face model is selected as the standard coordinate template. All the other face models in the database are aligned to it. The algorithm makes use of the ICP algorithm. Other optional surface alignment algorithms such as the Least-square-based surface matching [6] proposed by Gruen and Akca can also be applied. The complexity of the ICP algorithm employed is $O(N_p N_x)$, where N_p and N_x are the number of points in the data model and template, respectively. In the experiment, to reduce the complexity we also coarsen the 3D point clouds uniformly before aligning them to the standard template. The ultimate transformation matrixes for 3D rotations and translations can be obtained by combining a series of intermediate transformation matrixes generated in the alignment iterations. Let there be n iterations to transform from P_0 to X where X and P_0 are the template and the original data models. Denote R_i and T_i as the rotation and the translation matrixes corresponding to the ith ICP iteration. P_i is the transformed image from P_{i-1} using R_i and T_i. Therefore,

$$P_1 = R_1 \cdot P_0 + T_1, \; P_2 = R_2 \cdot P_1 + T_2, \; ..., \; P_i = R_i \cdot P_{i-1} + T_i, \; ..., \; X = R_n \cdot P_{n-1} + T_n.$$

Combine them together, we get.

$$X = \left(\prod_{i=1}^{n} R_i\right) \cdot P_0 + \left[\sum_{j=2}^{n}\left(\prod_{i=j}^{n} R_i\right) \cdot T_{j-1} + T_n\right]. \quad (1)$$

The ultimate transformation matrixes for rotation and translation are denoted as,

$$R = \prod_{i=1}^{n} R_i. \quad (2)$$

$$T = \sum_{j=2}^{n}\left(\prod_{i=j}^{n} R_i\right) \cdot T_{j-1} + T_n. \quad (3)$$

The transformations R and T are then applied back to the full scale point set for registration.

4 Experiment

The 3D face data set [1] we are working on contains 427 three dimensional facial surface images corresponding to 61 individuals (45 male and 16 female). Using the neural networks for classification the Maximum accuracy rate achieved for distinguishing a subset of faces is 100%.

5 Conclusion

In this paper, we have presented a novel algorithm for 3D face recognition. A template based registration strategy is proposed for data normalization. Back-Propagation neural networks are trained for face matching and retrieval. Experimental results show that the algorithm is invariant to rotations, translations, illuminations. It is also robust to the incomplete and ill-formed 3D point cloud data. The template based registration strategy and the neural network approach for face similarity measurement can be generalized for common 3D object recognitions.

Acknowledgement

This research work is supported by the Hong Kong Polytechnic University research grant A-PD55.

References

1. Moreno, A. B., Sanchez, A.: GavabDB: A 3D Face Database. In: Garcia, C., et al (eds): Proc. 2nd COST Workshop on Biometrics on the Internet: Fundamentals, Advances and Applications, Ed. Univ. Vigo (2004) 77-82
2. Zhang, L., Razdan, A., Farin, G., Bae, M. S., Femiani, J.: 3D Face Authentication and Recognition Based in Bilateral Symmetry Analysis, submitted to IEEE PAMI, (2004)
3. Lu, X., Colbry, D., Jain, A. K.: Three Dimensional Model Based Face Recognition. 17th International Conference on Pattern Recognition, Vol. 1, Cambridge, UK, (2004) 362-366
4. Besl, P., McKay, N.: A Method for Registration of 3-D Shapes. IEEE Trans. PAMI, Vol. 14, no. 2, (1992) 239-256
5. Mitra, N. J., Gelfand, N., Pottmann, H., Guibas, L.: Registration of Point Cloud Data from a Geometric Optimization Perspective. In the proceedings of Symposium on Geometry Processing, Nice, France (2004) 23-32
6. Gruen, A.: Least Squares Matching: A Fundamental Measurement Algorithm. In: K. Atkinson (ed.), Close Range Photogrammetry & Machine Vision, Whittles, Scotland (1996) 217-255

Recognition of Fault Signature Patterns Using Fuzzy Logic for Prevention of Breakdowns in Steel Continuous Casting Process

Arya K. Bhattacharya, P.S. Srinivas, K. Chithra, S.V. Jatla, and Jadav Das

Automation Division, Tata Steel, Jamshedpur 831001, India
{arya, srini, chithra, shiva, jadav}@aut.tatasteel.com

Abstract. In the continuous casting process of steel, a thin solid shell gradually forms around the cooling copper mould inner perimeter as liquid steel flows through it. By the time steel emerges from mould bottom, the perimetric solid shell acquires sufficient thickness and strength to support ferrostatic pressure of liquid steel in its interior. However, the formative shell can tear, stick to mold wall or fail to thicken adequately - in all cases leading to massive leakage of liquid steel out of mold bottom and consequent breakdown of continuous casting. All such phenomena leading to process disruption are preceded by typical patterns in temperature history data recorded at arrays of thermocouples embedded in mould walls. A fuzzy system is developed to accurately recognize these patterns in real time and regulate the speed of casting to prevent breakdowns. The system designed and implemented is fail-safe, has a low false-alarm ratio, and provides online diagnostics of the continuous casting process.

1 Introduction

Continuous casting in the steel industry is the process whereby molten steel is solidified into 'semifinished' slabs for subsequent rolling in finishing mills downstream.

Molten steel is poured into a mold of rectangular cross-section and length of 900 mm. Water flowing in embedded pipes in the mold transfers heat out from the solidifying steel through a copper lining on mold inner wall. Steel that is close to the mold walls gets solidified and forms a shell around the liquid interior, thus forming a downwards-moving semi-solidified steel slab called the *strand*. The main function of the mold is to establish a solid shell sufficient in strength to contain the liquid core when the strand exits from the mold into secondary cooling zones downstream.

When the partially solidified strand comes out of the mold the solid shell has to withstand the ferrostatic pressure of liquid steel within the strand above. If this shell cannot withstand the pressure due to any abnormality in solidification, it may cause a leak leading to a *'breakout'* – a spillage of liquid steel from and around mold bottom. Alternatively, in the early stages of solidification in the mold the formative shell may tear leading to liquid steel leaking onto the mold wall and consequent breakouts. Breakouts of the first type are referred to as crack or thin-shell breakouts, while those of the second type are called sticker breakouts. Either way, a breakout is a catastrophic incident and needs to be avoided. Consequently, all modern continuous casting systems are equipped with on-line breakout detection systems – BDS.

A BDS [1-3] receives the temperature profile of the copper mold walls usually at two or three horizontal levels through a series of thermocouples that encompass the mold perimeter at that level. The temperature readings are obtained at very small time intervals. The BDS analyzes in real time the temperature time-history and concludes whether a breakout is likely or not. If likely, it commands a reduction of the casting speed to near-zero to heal the sticker/shell-weakness and prevent the breakout.

Breakouts are a consequence of a complex combination of metallurgical, chemical and mechanical phenomena and operational characteristics. These vary continuously with time as casting proceeds. The temperature time series matrix, that may be formed by representing in each row a thermocouple's temperature history – reflects in some sense, i.e. is a function of, the internal dynamics of these nonlinear physical phenomena. Almost all existing BD systems map this matrix in real time into a binary output – alarming or no alarming – using some form of pattern recognition.

The Breakout Detection systems existing worldwide vary from one another primarily in the nature of the above mapping. A paradigm of these binary-output mappings is the neglect of continuity, i.e. the fact that the continuous evolution of the physical phenomena – and consequent temperature time matrix – naturally transforms into a continually evolving 'tendency to breakout'. In this development, fuzzy logic is used to transform the features of this matrix into a value of 'breakoutability', an index on 0-100 scale of this continuous 'tendency to breakout'. When this value crosses a threshold, an alarm is raised.

Expert knowledge of the relationship between casting physics and casting health is 'banded' rather than 'precise', i.e. if input variable i is within bounds $[L_i, U_i]$, for all i in the input variable space, then the breakoutability can be said to lie within bounds $[L_o, U_o]$. A binary system imposes undue determinism that can be misplaced leading either to detection failure or excessive false alarming. Fuzzy logic is the correct conceptual formalism for representing this form of knowledge. It captures both the natural continuity of fault evolution and the form of expert knowledge of the process, in effect transforming a fault detection system into a *real time casting health diagnostics system*.

The next section describes the methodology of the developed breakout detection system, named as *Casting Online Diagnostics System* or CODS. The results of testing are described in section three. The last section concludes the discussion.

2 Casting Online Diagnostics System

The conceptual architecture of the developed CODS is shown in Fig. 1. Thermocouples embedded in mold walls at two horizontal layers provide temperature inputs in real time. They serve as common inputs to three fuzzy modules for detection of the three types of breakouts – sticker, crack and thin-shell, and to an intelligent agent that is also based on fuzzy logic. The three modules and the intelligent agent are described below. Apart from temperatures, the three modules also take parameters like casting speed and percentage carbon as inputs. Each of these modules generates a value of instantaneous maximum breakoutability, of type corresponding to the module, as output. The outputs from each module are composed in the breakoutability analyzer,

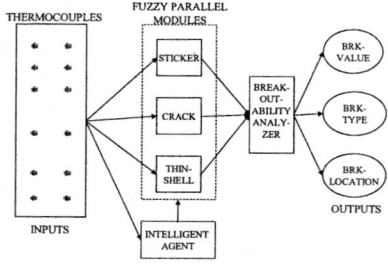 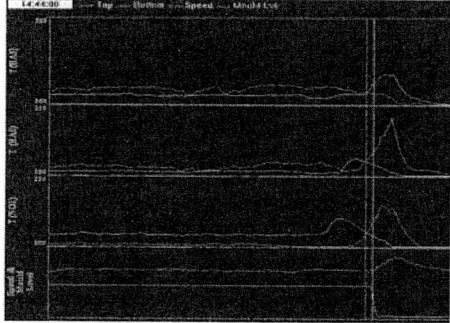

Fig. 1. The CODS Architecture

Fig. 2. Temperature time-history pattern of a Sticker

which generates in real-time a value of overall maximum breakoutability, its type and location of the point of maximum abnormality in the mold. These results are displayed to the operator on a HMI screen.

The description of each of the three modules is provided below.

Sticker Module

A sticker is accompanied by a specific pattern in the temperature time series of the thermocouple it closely passes by. This is illustrated in the snapshot in Fig. 2. The top three of four plots in this figure show temperatures (y-axis) against time (in secs). Since a sticker corresponds to a tear in the formative shell that exposes liquid steel at a higher-than-usual temperature to the mold wall, it shows up as a high-temperature pulse peaking at the instant the sticker is closest to the thermocouple during its downward trajectory. The temperature gradient shoots up appreciably as the sticker approaches, and then falls off. These are shown in the blue lines in the second and third graphs – each representing temperatures from a thermocouple in the second horizontal layer. The yellow lines (darker in black-and-white print) represent temperatures from the first layer of thermocouples.

The sticker fuzzy module compares instantaneous temperature-time patterns against this typical sticker signature. In a computation cycle, this module runs over all thermocouples. In each thermocouple, it takes three inputs, first, the extent of temperature rise, second, the temperature gradient, and third, the percentage of Carbon in the steel. (The properties of steel vary with %C). The breakoutability, i.e. the output, varies directly with all three inputs and is related to them through a fuzzy associative rule matrix. In a sense, the breakoutability represents the 'degree-of-conformity' of an instantaneous temperature-time pattern with the defined sticker signature. A breakoutability value greater than 85 in the second layer generates an alarm.

The variables temperature rise and gradient are both normalized into the [-1:1] space by comparison against their respective bounds of existence. The normalized space for both inputs is discretized using 7 triangular sets as shown in Fig. 3. The variable '%Carbon' is divided into 3 fuzzy sets in a manner consistent with the variation of steel properties with Carbon.

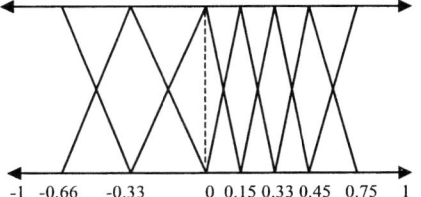
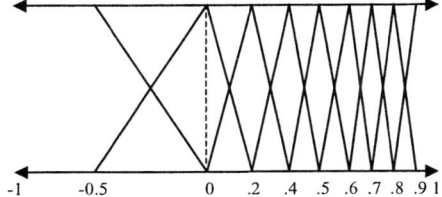
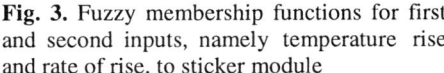

Fig. 3. Fuzzy membership functions for first and second inputs, namely temperature rise and rate of rise, to sticker module

Fig. 4. Fuzzy membership functions for output breakoutability, common to all breakout prediction modules

The output variable 'breakoutability' is scanned by 9 fuzzy membership functions (MF) traversing its domain of existence from 0 to 100. Since 85 to 90 is the alarming threshold (depending on the module), the MF are concentrated in the region above 75, while only 2 MF scan the space below 50. This distribution is shown in Fig. 4.

The fuzzy rule matrix for sticker is shown in Table 1. The columns represent MF of the first input, i.e. temperature rise, while the rows represent rate of rise. The third input, Carbon, is incorporated in each element of the table. It may be seen that each element is composed of three integers. The first denotes the activated MF of the output variable when Carbon lies in the first MF. The second and third integers denote the value added to the first integer to obtain the output MF when Carbon belongs to the second or third MF.

Crack Module

A typical crack signature is illustrated in Fig. 5. A crack (or any depression) is associated with an insulation in heat flux between strand shell and mold, resulting in low heat transfer from that region and consequently a thinner and weaker shell. The recorded temperatures show a dip followed by a rise as the crack passes by the

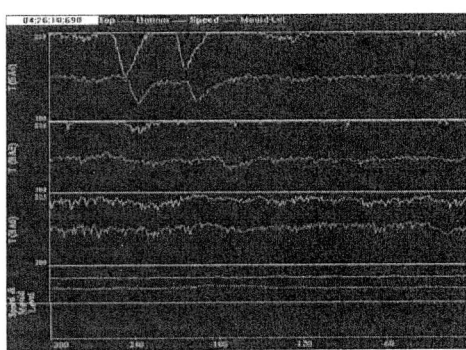

Fig. 5. Temperature time-history pattern for a Crack

Table 1. Fuzzy Associative Matrix for sticker module

$1^{0,1}$	$2^{0,1}$	$3^{1,2}$	$5^{1,3}$	$6^{1,3}$	$8^{0,1}$	9
$1^{0,1}$	$1^{0,1}$	$2^{1,2}$	$3^{1,2}$	$4^{1,3}$	$6^{1,3}$	$8^{0,1}$
$1^{0,1}$	$1^{0,1}$	$1^{0,1}$	$2^{1,2}$	$2^{1,3}$	$4^{1,3}$	$6^{1,3}$
$1^{0,1}$	$1^{0,1}$	$1^{0,1}$	$1^{0,1}$	$2^{1,2}$	$3^{1,2}$	$5^{1,3}$
1	1	1	$1^{0,1}$	$1^{0,1}$	$1^{0,1}$	$3^{0,1}$
1	1	1	1	$1^{0,1}$	$1^{0,1}$	$2^{0,1}$
1	1	1	1	1	1	$1^{0,1}$

Increasing Input One ⟶

thermocouple. This is shown in the first graph in Fig. 5 - which shows two cracks passing in quick succession.

The fuzzy module for cracks is designed to recognize the typical crack signature. It takes four inputs. First, the extent of temperature dip, second, the casting speed, and third, %C. The last input is the layer location relative to total mold length, a fraction varying from 0 to 1; 0 corresponds to mold top. The output varies directly with all four inputs, and a threshold value of 90 is considered for alarming.

Thin Shell Module

A thin shell cannot be easily distinguished as a pattern on a thermocouple. Here the shell across its perimeter, at a given layer, is thinner than normal under same casting condi-tions, and if this thinness falls below a threshold, the layer will be unable to support the ferro-static pressure of the molten core above. A thin shell implies that the molten core is closer to mold wall during casting than is normal, and hence the instantaneous average layer temperature taken over all thermocouples in the layer will be higher than the 'normal average'. In other words, the time-localized average layer temperature varies inversely as average layer physical thickness, and the deviation of this temperature from a 'normal average' is a mapping of the degree of thinness or thickness of the shell. Thus if a method can be found to evaluate this 'normal average' temperature, a measure of shell thinness can be obtained.

The normal average temperature is a strong function of casting parameters after filtering out transients. It varies dynamically as casting parameters change. An *intelligent agent* (see Fig. 1) is used to evaluate it. This agent is essentially a Takagi-Sugeno type fuzzy system and is imbued with the ability to quickly learn the caster features and dynamically adapt to casting conditions while neglecting transients.

In the fuzzy module for thin-shell breakoutability evaluation, the first input is the difference between instantaneous and normal average temperatures. The second, third and fourth inputs are, respectively, the casting speed, %Carbon, and vertical position. The output is breakoutability, varying directly with all inputs.

At every computation cycle, the three fuzzy modules generate in parallel a value of breakoutability corresponding to each type, along with the location of the point (thermocouple) of maximum breakoutability. These are sent to the breakoutability analyzer (Fig. 1), which decides on the global maximum as well as its point of location in the mold. These are displayed to the operator through a HMI.

The global maximum breakoutability, along with its type and location, serve as inputs to a speed control module which commands changes in casting speed, at deceleration rates based on values of these parameters. .

3 Results and Validation

The CODS has been implemented in the slab casters of Tata Steel after passing through a rigorous validation process. An earlier version of a BDS [5] was installed in the premises. This showed good performance in detecting stickers, but did not detect other types of breakouts. Further, the number of false alarms was an area of concern.

The earlier BDS was used as a baseline for validation of the new system. For a period of two months, thermocouple data along with other casting parameters was sent to both detection systems installed on parallel computing platforms, and outputs from both were analyzed. Only outputs from the previous system were sent to speed control units. When either system raised an alarm, the corresponding slab that was cast at the time of alarm was visually surveyed for tell-tale marks of stickers or cracks. This was to confirm whether the alarm was true or false. In some cases both systems raised alarms at near-identical instances, in other cases alarms raised by one system found no mention in the other.

To rationally analyze the consequent data, a few conceptual cases were constructed and every alarm was classified into one or other of these cases [6]. A qualitative value on the validation scale – for the new BDS – was attributed to each of these cases, and at the end of the testing period the results were summarized to decide if the new BDS had passed the acceptance criteria. Table 2 lists out the cases. The second column in this table provides the feature – or definition – of the case. The last column states its implication towards system acceptance. In the table, ES and NS denote Earlier and New Systems, respectively.

Table 2. Validation Strategy: Definition of cases and impact on acceptance

Cases	Definition	Implication on Acceptance
A	ES[1]: False Alarm	None
B	ES: True Alarm	Indirect
C	NS: Missed True Alarm	**Unacceptable**
D	NS: True Alarm	Desirable
E	Breakout: ES Missed, NS Captured	Desirable from validation viewpoint
F1	NS: False Alarm	Less the better
F2	NS: Desirable[2] Alarm	Desirable
G	Breakout: ES Missed, NS also Missed	**Unacceptable**

Table 3. Testing Results Summary: Sixty days continuous casting

Detection System	Slabs inspected after alarm	Stickers		Cracks and Thin Shells	
		True	False	True	False
Earlier BDS	36	7	29	NA	NA
New BDS: CODS	24	7	5	8	4

The defined cases cover the entire space of conditional possibilities. It is seen that Cases C and G are roadblocks to acceptance. When a true alarm is raised in both systems, Cases B and D occur simultaneously. The converse is also expected to occur sometimes, i.e. a false alarm is raised in both systems leading to Cases A and F1 being flagged at the same time.

The results of testing are summarized in Table 3. The second column presents total number of alarms generated by either system. It may be noted that some of these alarms were common to the two systems, as discussed above. The next two columns show sticker alarms from either system, and classify them into true or false based on inspection. The last two columns show crack and thin shell alarms from only the new system, as these are not captured by the earlier one.

In the concerned period of testing there was no occurrence of breakout. The seven true sticker alarms were common to both systems, and hence belong to Cases B and D. There was no occurrence of Case C (Table 2). The number of false sticker alarms has come down. There were eight cases of desirable crack alarms, and four cases of undesirable ones. Most importantly, there were no occurrences of Cases C and G – the unacceptable conditions; and the number of false alarms are seen to have reduced significantly. In other words, the new BDS passed the acceptance criteria for implementation.

4 Conclusions

Application of the concepts and principles of fuzzy logic has facilitated the development and implementation of an advanced breakout detection system for continuous casting of steel. Signatures on temperature time-history data specific to each type of breakout are compared in real time against instantaneous patterns on each thermocouple, to provide a 'degree of conformity'. When the conformity exceeds a threshold, an alarm is generated.

This breakout detection system successfully prevents all types of breakouts, and hence satisfies the fundamental requirement of a reliable breakout detection system. It also raises low number of false alarms in comparison to existing BD systems.

Furthermore, the developed system provides operational personnel with real-time diagnostic information on health of casting and evolution of potential faults. Accordingly, it is named as Casting Online Diagnostics System, or CODS.

Acknowledgment

The authors acknowledge their gratitude to Tata Steel for continuous support and encouragement in this work.

References

1. J.D.Madill, "Application of Mold Thermal Monitoring to Avesta Sheffield SMACC Slab Caster", 1996 Vol. 23, No. 3, *Ironmaking and Steelmaking*, pp. 223-234.
2. M.J.Lu, K.J.Lin., "Sticker Breakout Theory and its Prediction in Slab Continuous Casting", *1993 Steelmaking Conference Proceedings*, pp. 343-352.
3. Richard T. Grass, George W. Skoczylas, "Reduction of Breakouts at Ispat Inland Inc", *2001 Steelmaking Conference Proceedings*, pp. 41-52.
4. P.S. Srinivas, K. Chithra, Shiva Jatla, A.K. Bhattacharya, "Global Design for mould breakout detection system for slab casters", Tata Steel Internal Report No. AUT/PRJ/01019/GDD, July 2004.
5. Mahashabde, V.V., Bhaduri, R., Das, S., Kukreja, B.K., Agarwal, A.K., "Breakout Detection System at Tata Steel's slab caster using Neural Network", *Tata Search*, 1999, pp. 91-94.
6. P.S. Srinivas, K. Chithra, Shiva Jatla, A.K. Bhattacharya, "Field Testing Strategy for Mould Breakout Detection System", Tata Steel Internal Report No. AUT/PRJ/01019/FTS, Sep 2003.

Development of an Adaptive Fuzzy Logic Based Control Law for a Mobile Robot with an Uncalibrated Camera System

T. Das and I.N. Kar

Department of Electrical Engineering, Indian Institute of Technology, Delhi,
New Delhi- 110016, India
ink@ee.iitd.ac.in

Abstract. In this paper, a new adaptive fuzzy controller is proposed for trajectory tracking of wheeled mobile robots by visual servoing. The control algorithm is developed so that it can take care of parametric uncertainty associated with the vision system and the mobile robot dynamics. The system uncertainty associated with nonlinear robot dynamics is estimated by an adaptive fuzzy logic system (FLS) and the uncertain camera parameters are updated online. The controller is designed based on Lyapunov stability theory. Simulation results are presented to illustrate the performance of the proposed controller.

1 Introduction

Wheeled mobile robots (WMRs) have been used extensively in various industrial and service applications which include security, transportation, inspection and planetary exploration etc. Due to the versatility of applications in various structured and unstructured environments, vision system has been proved to be a very useful sensor for controlling the WMRs. A brief review and some references of vision based tracking and control can be found in [3][2]. It is evident that a model based controller gives rise very good control performance when the sensors are accurately calibrated and the exact model of the system is known. In reality, these two assumptions cease to be valid in many cases. In a vision based robot control system, the parametric uncertainty associated with the calibration of the camera incorporates uncertainty in the WMR position/orientation information. Again, the assumption of having exact models of the robot system means that the robot is not able to adapt to any changes and uncertainties in its models and environment. Hence, the uncertainties discussed above can result in degraded control performance. In this direction, Kelly [7] proposed a set point controller for a planar robot manipulator with uncertain camera calibration parameters. Dixon *et.al* [3] proposed a trajectory tracking controller for a wheeled mobile robot with uncertain robot dynamics and camera calibration parameters. Recently, Cheah *et.al* [5]proposed a trajectory tracking controller for a serial link robot manipulator with uncertain robot Jacobian and dynamics. However similar concept has not been applied to the trajectory-tracking problem of a wheeled mobile robot.

In this paper, a new adaptive control algorithm has been proposed for trajectory tracking by a wheeled mobile robot via visual servoing with uncertain robot dynamics and camera calibration parameters. An adaptive fuzzy logic system (FLS) is capable of uniformly approximating any nonlinear function over compact input space as shown in Wang and Mendel [6]. So, an adaptive FLS has been used to approximate the nonlinear robot dynamics including friction. Thus the controller is robust not only to structured uncertainty such as mass variation but also to unstructured one such as friction. To reduce the error between the value of the real uncertain function and its estimator, we design simple and robust adaptive laws based on Lyapunov stability theory. A *velocity transformation matrix*, which consists of functions of uncertain camera parameters, relates the velocity of the robot in the task space to the velocity in the camera space. The main new point in this paper is the adaptation to the uncertainty in this velocity transformation matrix in addition to the dynamics uncertainty. Thus the uncertainties in the camera calibration parameters are taken care of. Novel adaptive laws to deal with the uncertainty in the velocity transformation matrix are proposed. The simulation results show the effectiveness of the proposed controller even with nonlinear friction and uncertainty associated with camera calibration.

2 Basics of Adaptive Fuzzy Logic System

The basic configuration of a fuzzy system consists of four principal elements: *fuzzifier, fuzzy rule base, fuzzy inference engine* and *defuzzifier*. In this paper, multiple-input-single-output (MISO) fuzzy logic systems are considered, because a multiple-output system can always be separated into a collection of single output systems. Following definition is adopted for fuzzy logic system.

Definition 1: The output of a MISO-FLS with singleton fuzzifier, product inference, centroid defuzzifier and Gaussian membership function can be written in the form

$$f(x) = \frac{\sum_{j=1}^{M} \overline{y}^j \left(\prod_{i=1}^{n} \mu_{A_i^j}(x_i) \right)}{\sum_{j=1}^{M} \left(\prod_{i=1}^{n} \mu_{A_i^j}(x_i) \right)} = \sum_{j=1}^{M} \phi_j(x) \overline{y}^j = r^T \boldsymbol{\Phi}(x) \quad (1)$$

where $x = [x_1, \ldots, x_n]^T$ are the input vectors of the fuzzy system, $\overline{y}^j$ is the point in the output space V at which $\mu_{B^j}(y_l)$ achieves its maximum value and $\mu_{A_i^j}(x_i)$ is the Gaussian membership function, defined by mean and variance. In the above $\boldsymbol{\Phi}(x) = \left[\phi_1(x), \phi_2(x), \ldots, \phi_M(x) \right]^T \in \mathfrak{R}^M$ is called the fuzzy basis vector [7] and $r = \left[\overline{y}^1, \overline{y}^2, \ldots, \overline{y}^M \right]^T \in \mathfrak{R}^M$ is called the unknown parameter vector which is to be updated. It has been proved that an adaptive fuzzy logic system is capable of uniformly approximating any real continuous function over a compact input set to arbitrary accuracy [6]. In this paper, we use this adaptive fuzzy logic system as an estimator for approximating the functions involving unknown robot parameters.

3 Kinematics and Dynamics of a Mobile Robot

The mobile robot is a typical example of a nonholonomic mechanical system. It consists of a vehicle with two driving wheels mounted on the same axis, and a front free wheel. A camera (CCD type) providing an image of the entire robot workspace, is mounted fixed in the ceiling above the robot workspace, such that, (i) its image plane is parallel to the plane of motion of the robot, (ii) the camera can capture images throughout the entire robot workspace. The representation of the mobile robot kinematic model [1][3] in the camera-space takes the following form

$$\dot{\bar{q}} = S(\bar{q})\bar{v} \qquad (2)$$

where, $\bar{q}(t) = \begin{bmatrix} \bar{x}_c(t) & \bar{y}_c(t) & \bar{\theta}(t) \end{bmatrix}^T$, $\bar{v}(t) = \begin{bmatrix} \bar{v}_1(t) & \bar{v}_2(t) \end{bmatrix}^T$ denote the variables.

3.1 Task Space to Camera-Space Transformation

We utilize the so-called pin-hole lens model for the robot-camera system to express the robot camera-space position vector in terms of the task-space position vector as shown below [4]

$$\begin{bmatrix} \bar{x}_c(t) \\ \bar{y}_c(t) \end{bmatrix} = LR(\theta_0) \left(\begin{bmatrix} x_c(t) \\ y_c(t) \end{bmatrix} - \begin{bmatrix} O_{o1} \\ O_{o2} \end{bmatrix} \right) + \begin{bmatrix} O_{i1} \\ O_{i2} \end{bmatrix}, \text{ where } L = \begin{bmatrix} \alpha_1 & 0 \\ 0 & \alpha_2 \end{bmatrix} \text{ with the }$$

camera constants α_1, α_2. After few algebraic manipulation, we obtain a formulate for a global invertible transformation between the camera-space robot velocities and the task-space robot velocities as follows:

$$\bar{v} = T_0 v \qquad (3)$$

where,

$$T_0 = diag(T_1, T_2), T_1 = \alpha_1 \cos(\bar{\theta}) \cos(\theta + \theta_0) + \alpha_2 \sin(\bar{\theta}) \sin(\theta + \theta_0),$$

$$T_2 = \frac{\alpha_2}{\alpha_1} \cos^2(\bar{\theta}) \cos^2(\theta + \theta_0) + \frac{\alpha_1}{\alpha_2} \sin^2(\bar{\theta}) \sin^2(\theta + \theta_0) + \frac{1}{2} \sin(2\bar{\theta}) \sin 2(\theta + \theta_0)$$

The matrix T_0 is called the *velocity transformation matrix*. The right hand side of (3) is linear in a set of unknown parameters $\zeta = \begin{bmatrix} \zeta_1, ..., \zeta_q \end{bmatrix}^T$. Hence, equation (3) can be expressed as $\bar{v} = T_0(\bar{q})v = Y_v(\bar{q}, v)\zeta$ where, $Y_v(\bar{q}, v)$ is called the velocity regressor matrix. Taking into account the equation (3), the dynamic model of the mobile robot is transformed to the following equation:

$$\bar{M}(q)\dot{v} + \bar{V}(q,\dot{q})v + \bar{F} = \bar{B}\tau \tag{4}$$

where, $\bar{M} = S^T M S$, $\bar{V} = S^T M \dot{S}$, $\bar{F} = S^T F$ and $\bar{B} = S^T B$.

4 Control Design

The primary objective is to force the mobile robot to track a trajectory generated in the camera-space in the presence of parametric uncertainty. The desired trajectory of the robot is generated by a reference model $\dot{\bar{q}}_r = S(\bar{q}_r)\bar{v}_r$ where, $\bar{q}_r(t)$ and $\bar{v}_r(t)$ denote the reference trajectory and velocity in the camera-space respectively. Now the problem is to find a smooth velocity control input $\bar{v}_c(t) = f_c(\bar{e}_p, \bar{v}_r, K)$ such that $\lim_{t \to \infty}(\bar{q}_r - \bar{q}) = 0$.

Defining an auxiliary error signal by $e_p(t) = [e_1(t) \ e_2(t) \ e_3(t)]^T$, and auxiliary velocity control $\bar{v}_c(t)$ as [1], the auxiliary velocity tracking error in the camera-space is given as $\bar{s} = \bar{v} - \bar{v}_c$. In the presence of camera calibration parameters uncertainty, the matrix T_0 in (4) is uncertain, and under that circumstance, equation (4) can be expressed as

$$\hat{\bar{v}} = \hat{T}_0(\bar{q}, \hat{\zeta})v = Y_V(\bar{q}, v)\hat{\zeta}$$

where $\hat{\bar{v}}$ denotes an estimated velocity vector in camera-space, $\hat{T}_0(\bar{q}, \hat{\zeta})$ is an approximate velocity transformation matrix and $\hat{\zeta} \in \Re^q$ is an estimated kinematic parameters. Defining two variables $e_c = v - v_c$ and $v_c = \hat{T}_0^{-1}\bar{v}_c$, the error equation is derived as $\bar{M}(q)\dot{e}_c + \bar{V}(q,\dot{q})e_c + f(x) = \bar{B}\tau$ where, the nonlinear function is $f(x) = \bar{M}(q)\dot{v}_c + \bar{V}(q,\dot{q})v_c + \bar{F}$ which is approximated by using a FLS as in (1).

4.1 Proposed Control Law

we propose an adaptive controller structure, based on the approximate velocity transformation matrix as,

$$\tau = \bar{B}^{-1}(-\hat{T}_0^T(\bar{q}, \hat{\zeta})K\hat{\bar{s}} - \hat{T}_0^T(\bar{q}, \hat{\zeta})K_p\bar{s} + \hat{R}^T\Phi) \tag{5}$$

where $\hat{\bar{s}} = Y_v(\bar{q}, v)\hat{\zeta} - \bar{v}_c$, $\bar{s} = \bar{v} - \bar{v}_c$ and K, K_p are positive definite matrices. The estimated parameter $\hat{\zeta}$ of the approximate velocity transformation matrix $\hat{T}_0(\bar{q}, \hat{\zeta})$ and the FLS parameter vector are updated by,

$$\dot{\hat{\zeta}} = L_v Y_v^T(\bar{q},v)K_p\bar{s}$$
$$\dot{\hat{R}} = -\Gamma\Phi(q,v_c,\dot{v}_c)e_c^T \quad (6)$$

where $L_v \in \Re^{q \times q}$ and Γ positive definite design matrices. The closed loop stability of the system is stated in the form of a proposition which can be proved by using a suitable Lyapunov function [8].

Proposition 1: For a nonholonomic mobile robot (4), let the adaptive control law (5) and the parameter update laws (6) be used. Then the system is stable in the sense of Lyapunov. Also, the control law results in the convergence of the position errors e_1 and e_3 i.e. $e_1 \to 0$, $e_3 \to 0$ and $\bar{s} \to 0$ as $t \to \infty$.

5 Simulation Results

The proposed control law is verified with computer simulation using MATLAB. For simulation purposes, the value of camera calibration parameters, described in equations - are taken as $\alpha_1 = \alpha_2 = 1.0\,pixels/m$; $\theta_0 = 0.5\,rad$; $[O_{o1}\ O_{o2}] = [0.2\ 0.1]^T$ and $[O_{i1}\ O_{i2}] = \mathbf{0} \in \Re^2$. The parameter values given above are selected for simplicity. The parameters of the mobile robot (5) are taken as $m = 9kg$, $I = 5.0kgm^2$, $r = 0.052m$, $R = 0.153m$. The friction term is taken as $\bar{F} = [0.3\text{sgn}(v_1)\ 0.5\text{sgn}(v_2)]^T$. A circular reference trajectory in the camera-space is taken. The reference trajectory is given by $\bar{x}_{cr}(t) = \cos(t/20)$; $y_{cr}(t) = \sin(t/20)$, $\bar{\theta}_r = \pi/2 + t/20$; so that reference velocities are given by $\bar{v}_{r1} = 0.05\,pixels/\sec$, $\bar{v}_{r2} = 0.05\,rad/\sec$. The reference trajectory y in the camera-space starts from $\bar{q}_r(0) = [1.0\ 0\ \pi/2]^T$. The initial posture of the robot in the camera-space is $\bar{q}(0) = [1.1\ 0\ \pi/2]^T$ and the initial velocities is taken as $v(0) = [0\ 0]^T$. To examine the effects of the uncertainty in camera calibration, the estimated vector $\hat{\zeta}$ is taken as $\hat{\zeta}(0) = [0.5\ 1.0\ 0.5\ 1.0\ 1.0]^T$. The values of the parameters of the controller are chosen as $k_1 = 20$; $K_p = diag\{35,35\}$; $L_v = diag\{10,10,10,10,10\}$; $\Gamma = diag\{20,20,20\}$. The controller is capable of compensating any sudden change of the robot dynamics because its online learning ability. To demonstrate this, the mass of the mobile robot is kept varying. The mass of the mobile robot is taken as $m = 9.0kg$ for $t \le 70\sec$, $m = 14.5kg$ for $70 < t \le 130\sec$ and $m = 9.0kg$ for $t > 130\sec$. The simulation results are

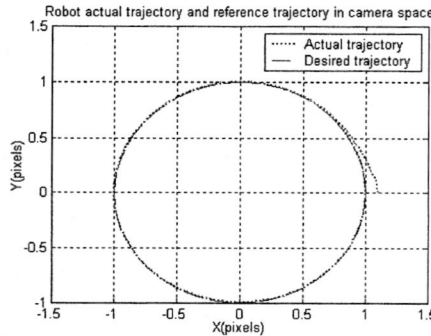 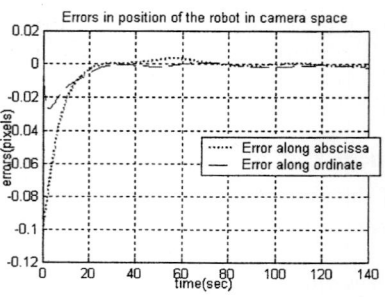

Fig. 1. Performance of the robot in camera-space   **Fig. 2.** Tracking errors

shown in figures 1 and 2. Figure 1 show the mobile robot tracks the virtual reference robot moving on the circular path satisfying the nonholonomic constraints, and the tracking errors sharply drop to very small values as shown in Figure 2.

6   Conclusions

In this paper, a trajectory tracking control algorithm is proposed for wheeled mobile robots via visual servoing in the presence of parametric uncertainty associated with the camera calibration (e.g. scale factor, focal length, orientation angle) and the nonlinear robot dynamics. An adaptive fuzzy logic system approximates the nonlinear robot dynamics. Novel adaptive laws to deal with the uncertainty in the velocity transformation matrix, which involves functions of uncertain camera parameters, are proposed. Simulation results are presented to illustrate the performance of the proposed adaptive controller.

References

[1] Y. Kanayama, Y. Kimura, F. Miyazaki, and T. Noquchi, "A stable tracking control method for an autonomous mobile robot," *Proc. IEEE Int. Conf. Robotics and automation,* vol.1, May 1990, pp. 384-389.

[2] G. Hagar, S. Hutchison, and P. Corke, "A tutorial on visual servo control," *IEEE Trans. Robotics and Automation,* vol. 12, no.5, 1996, pp. 651-670.

[3] W.E. Dixon, D.M. Dawson, E. Zergeroglu, and Aman Behal, "Adaptive tracking control of a wheeled mobile robot via an uncalibrated camera system," *IEEE Trans. Systems, Man, and Cybernetics –Part B: Cybernetics,* vol. 31, no.3, June 2001, pp. 341-352.

[4] R.K. Lenz, and R.Y. Tsai, "Techniques for calibration of the scale factor and image center of high accuracy 3-D machine vision metrology," *IEEE Trans. Pattern Analysis and Machine Intelligence,* vol. 10, no.5, Sep. 1988, pp. 713-720.

[5] C.C. Cheah, C. Liu, and J.J.E. Slotine, "Approximate Jacobian Control for Robot Manipulators," *Proc. IEEE Int. Conf. Robotics and Automation, pp. 3075-3080, April 2004.*

[6] Li-Xin Wang, and Jerry M. Mendel, "Fuzzy Basis Functions, Universal Approximation, and Orthogonal Least-Squares Learning," *IEEE Trans. Neural Networks,* vol. 3, no.5, Sept. 1992, pp. 807-814.
[7] R. Kelly, "Robust asymptotically stable visual servoing of planar robots," *IEEE Trans. Robotics and Automation*, Vo. 12, pp. 756-766. Oct. 1996.
[8] T. Das, "Intelligent tracking control of robotic systems", MS thesis, Indian Institute of Technology, Delhi, 2005.

Fuzzy Logic Based Control of Voltage and Reactive Power in Subtransmission System

Ana Paula M. Braga[1], Ricardo Carnevalli[2], Petr Ekel[1], Marcelo Gontijo[1], Marcio Junges[1], Bernadete Maria de Mendonça Neta[2], and Reinaldo M. Palhares[3]

[1] Graduate Program in Electrical Engineering,
Pontifical Catholic University of Minas Gerais,
Ave. Dom José Gaspar, 500, 30535-610 – Belo Horizonte – MG, Brazil
anapaulamb@terra.com.br, ekel@pucminas.br, montalva@ig.com.br,
marcio.junges@jtech.eng.br

[2] Operation Coordination and Engineering Department,
Minas Gerais State Energy Company,
Ave. Barbacena, 1200, 30190-131 - Belo Horizonte - MG, Brazil
{rcarne, bmmn}@cemig.com.br

[3] Department of Electronics Engineering,
Federal University of Minas Gerais,
Ave. Antônio Carlos, 6627, 31270-010 – Belo Horizonte – MG, Brazil
palhares@cpdee.ufmg.br

Abstract. This paper presents results of research related to the second stage of the project dedicated to developing and employing the xOMNI system (software of the SCADA type). This stage is associated with the elaboration of the Energy Management System (EMS) for the subtransmission system of the Minas Gerais State Energy Company. One of the most important EMS functions is voltage and reactive power control. Its implementation is based on the use of fuzzy logic technology. Taking this into account, the paper covers the consideration of questions of building diverse types of sensitivity indices and forming production rules providing comprehensive and flexible solutions in conditions of regulated and deregulated environments. Some aspects of rational carrying out fuzzy logic procedures are considered as well.

1 Introduction

The Minas Gerais State Energy Company (CEMIG) attends more than 320,000 km of subtransmission and distribution networks and 340 subtransmission substations. These substations are controlled by distribution operation centers (DOCs). The xOMNI system (software of the SCADA type) [1] has been developed to realize this goal. The corresponding project has been divided into two stages. The first stage is associated with the SCADA phase and the second stage is related to the Energy Management System (EMS) phase.

The EMS functions that have already been developed are discussed in [1]. The main goal of this paper is to consider the function of voltage and reactive power control. Since its realization is based on integrating traditional numerical methods with fuzzy logic technology [2], the consideration includes questions of constructing diverse types of sensitivities (which serve for multi-attribute evaluating control actions efficiency), forming rules (that provide comprehensive and flexible solutions) as well as rational implementing fuzzy logic procedures.

2 Fuzzy Logic Based Voltage and Reactive Power Control

Critical investigations on fuzzy logic based voltage and reactive power control have been reported in [3]. They demonstrate that fuzzy logic is one of the most successful of today's technologies for elaborating sophisticated control systems. With its aid, complex requirements are implemented in systems with reasoning capabilities bound by a minimum of production rules that is reached on the basis of the interpolative nature of fuzzy set theory [2]. The approach [3] opened up an important direction in solving the problem of voltage and reactive power control. However, its application is limited by the following considerations:

- the approach is directed to solving the problem within the framework of simplified statement without considering an economical objective (minimization of losses) and restrictions on power-handling capability of system elements;
- the rules included in knowledge base are general, and questions of using rules, which reflect operational philosophy of a concrete system, are not considered;
- an important component of fuzzy modeling is the quality of models and their tuning, making possible improvement in control efficiency, that has not found consideration;
- availability of discrete operating values of regulating and compensating devices does not allow one to utilize the approach without modifications.

Overcoming of these aspects can permit one to use fuzzy logic for solving the problem under comprehensive statement.

3 Construction of Sensitivity Indices

The evaluation of influence of the control action of regulating or compensating device j on the voltage change at bus i is associated with the voltage sensitivity S_{ij}^V. In the system with I controlled buses and J buses with regulating and compensating devices, it is necessary to have a matrix $[S_{ij}^V]$, $i=1,\ldots, I, j=1,\ldots, J$. In [3], its building is based on the use of system Jacobian matrices. However, deficient linearization accuracy in utilizing this approach allows one to apply it when perturbations are small. At the same time, our experience shows that experimental design [4] provides a means for rational building sensitivity models. Its use also permits one to eliminate from consideration actions at buses j , which have no influence on the voltage level at buses i , evaluate the adequacy of models, and, if necessary, change intervals of parameter varying to obtain adequate models. Finally, because the comprehensive solution needs sensitivities

$[S^S_{kj}]$, $k=1,...,K$, $j=1,...,J$ (reflecting the power flow change on line k) and $[S^S_{kj}]$, $k=1,...,K$, $j=1,...,J$ (reflecting the reactive power flow change on line k allowing the estimation of loss increments [5]), their building is possible on the basis of the same computing experiments, which are necessary to obtain voltage sensitivities.

The full experiment is based on carrying out experiments with varying factors on two levels. It demands the performance of 2^J experiments to construct a model

$$y = b_0 + \sum_{j=1}^{J} b_j x_j + \sum_{\substack{j=1 \\ j<q}}^{J} b_{jq} x_j + \sum_{\substack{j=1 \\ j<q<r}}^{J} b_{jqr} x_j x_q x_r + \ldots . \qquad (1)$$

It is assumed that factors can take the minimum x'_j and maximum x''_j values ($x'_j \leq x_j \leq x''_j, j = 1, \ldots, J$) and are presented in the normalized form [4]. Thus, x'_j and x''_j correspond to -1 and +1, respectively.

A matrix for the full experiment with two factors is shown in Table 1.

Table 1. Matrix for the 2^2 design

n	Factors			Factor Product	
	x_0	x_1	x_2	$x_1 x_2$	y
1	+1	-1	-1	+1	y_1
2	+1	+1	-1	-1	y_2
3	+1	-1	+1	-1	y_3
4	+1	+1	+1	+1	y_4

Considering that $2^J > J + 1$, data obtained in the full experiment have information excessiveness. It permits one to build linear models on the basis of fractional experiments. Their matrices are parts of the full experiment matrices and are obtained as a result of reducing a number of experiments in two, four, etc. times by replacing effects of little significance (for example, $\tilde{x}_1 \tilde{x}_2$ in Table 1) by new parameters. The number of replacements g defines the 2^{J-g} design. For example, to estimate coefficients of a model $y = b_0 + b_1 x_1 + b_2 x_2 + b_3 x_3$ we have to perform eight experiments, although it is enough to perform four experiments in accordance with the 2^{3-1} design coinciding with the 2^2 design if $\tilde{x}_1 \tilde{x}_2 = \tilde{x}_3$.

A traditional technique for evaluating experiment results includes several stages [4]. These stages are common if we can perform parallel experiments in corresponding factorial space points. If we speak about computing experiments with a model, this circumstance has a significant impact. One way around this problem is discussed in [5].

The described approach was tested on the CEMIG subtransmission system. Simulation results show its high computing performance: it was necessary less than 6 min. of computer (Pentium IV 1.8 GHz with RAM of 512 MB) time (with executing other tasks) to calculate all types of sensitivities for the CEMIG subtransmission system (72 buses with regulating and compensating devices) on the basis of the 2^{72-65} design. This permits one to use the approach without system decomposition.

4 Rules and Linguistic Variables

Comprehensive statement of the problem of voltage and reactive power control is to cover the following control hierarchy levels: (A) all restrictions are observed, and it is necessary to minimize losses, (B) restrictions on bus voltage levels and/or on power-handling capability of system elements are not observed, but the violations can be eliminated, and (C) restrictions on bus voltage levels and/or on power-handling capability of system elements are not observed, and the violations cannot be eliminated.

The approach [3] provides corrective control and is based on the use of rules of the following type:

(I) IF   bus voltage violates the operational limit
    AND   a controller is available for effective voltage control adjusting its output
    AND   there is adequate margin of output adjustment to eliminate the restriction violation
    THEN increase (decrease) the controller output.

Other works related to using knowledge based methodology also distinguish the phases of corrective control and loss minimization with eliminating the last objective from a knowledge based control loop. However, more comprehensive and flexible solutions may be obtained if knowledge base includes the following type of rules for the hierarchy level (B):

(II) IF   bus voltage violates the operational limit
    AND   a controller is available for effective voltage control adjusting its output
    AND   there is adequate margin of output adjustment to eliminate the restriction violation
    AND   the controller is available for loss reduction (increase)
    THEN increase (decrease) the controller output.

It should be pointed out that the hierarchy level (A) is particular in relation to the level (B). The level (C) is also reduced to the level (B) if priorities are introduced, for example, for buses under infeasibility minimization conditions.

Generally, the use of the rules of the type (II) provides solutions different from the results obtained on the basis of the rules of the type (I). Our experience shows that using the rules of the type (II), it is possible to reduce losses even at the phase of corrective control.

Since the rules (I) and (II) reflect general strategies, each of them is presented by a set of rules defined by fuzzy values [2] of linguistic variables, which are *control efficiency, adequate margin,* and *loss increment* as the input variables and *utilization intensity* as the output variable.

The reactive power planning and operation are important functions of ancillary service markets. The philosophy of [6] justifies the expediency of their structuring within the framework of preparation markets and actuation markets.

In operating actuation markets, a function of observing restrictions on reactive power levels is to be realized. The restrictions may be considered in a traditional way as the restrictions on voltage levels with using $[S_{kj}^Q]$, $p=1,\ldots,P, j=1,\ldots,J$. However, there is another way associated with considering the restrictions on reactive power levels on the basis of minimizing

$$D = (\sum_{p=1}^{P} Q_p^0 |Q_p - Q_p^0|) / \sum_{p=1}^{P} Q_p^0, \qquad (2)$$

which reflects the weighted average magnitude of deviations of reactive power (WAMDRP) from their desirable levels Q_p^0, $p=1,\ldots,P$.

Applying (2), it is possible to realize observing the desirable reactive power levels with using $[S_j^D]$, $j=1,\ldots,J$ and rules of the following type:

(III) IF   bus voltage violates the operational limit
    AND   a controller is available for effective voltage control adjusting its output
    AND   there is adequate margin of output adjustment to eliminate the restriction violation
    AND   the controller is available for reduction (rise) of WAMDRP
    AND   the controller is available for loss reduction (increase)
    THEN   increase (decrease) the controller output.

5 Fuzzy Logic Procedures

The collection of rules may be presented by the following fuzzy algorithm:

IF $x_1 = a_{11}$ ... AND $x_k = a_{1k}$ AND ... AND $x_m = a_{1m}$ THEN $y = b_1$ ELSE
...
IF $x_1 = a_{p1}$ ... AND $x_k = a_{pk}$ AND ... AND $x_m = a_{pm}$ THEN $y = b_p$ ELSE
...
IF $xt_1 = a_{t1}$ ... AND $x_k = a_{tk}$ AND ... AND $x_m = a_{tm}$ THEN $y = b_t$,   (3)

where $a_{pk}, p = 1,\ldots,t, k = 1,\ldots,m$ and $b_p, p = 1,\ldots,t$ have estimates A_{pk} and B_p with the membership functions $\mu_{A_{pk}}(x_{pk})$ and $\mu_{B_p}(y)$, respectively.

The collection (3) is equivalent to the $(m+1)$-dimensional implication relation matrix R [2]. Its use permits one to carry out inference under arbitrary values of $x_1 = a_1'$, $x_2 = a_2'$, ..., $x_m = a_m'$ on the basis of

$$\mu_{B'}(y) = \mu_{A_1}(x_1) \circ \mu_{A_2}(x_2) \circ \ldots \circ \mu_{A_m}(x_m) \circ R, \qquad (4)$$

where the symbol o defines the type of composition.

To avoid manipulations with multidimensional matrices in accordance with (4), it is appropriate to introduce [7] the possibility measure "a_{pk} is a_k'":

$$Poss(a_{pk}|a_k') = \vee_{x_k} \mu_{A_{pk}}(x_k) \wedge \mu_{A_k'}(x_k). \qquad (5)$$

Using (5), it is possible to define

$$Poss(a_{p1},\ldots,a_{pk},\ldots,a_{pm}|a_1',\ldots,a_k',\ldots,a_m') = \wedge_k Poss(a_{pk}|a_k'), \quad (6)$$

which reflects the possibility measure that the constituent concept described by $a_{p1},...,a_{pk},...,a_{pm}$ is constituent concept characterized by $a_1',...,a_k',...,a_m'$.

Considering (5) and (6), it is possible to build

$$\mu_{B'}(y) = \vee_p [\mu_{B_p}(y_p) \wedge \wedge_k Poss(a_{pk}|a_k')], \quad (7)$$

which is equivalent to (4).

The estimates of the computational complexity in carrying out fuzzy inference on the basis of (4) and (7) are given in [8]. They demonstrate the efficiency of realizing fuzzy inference on the basis of (7). This as well as a convenience of implementing (7) explains its application.

6 Conclusion

Questions of using fuzzy logic technology for voltage and reactive power control have been considered. An approach based on experimental design has been applied to build diverse types of sensitivities to evaluate efficiency of control actions and construct rules included in knowledge base. Diverse types of rules applicable to regulated and deregulated environments have been presented. Some aspects of rational carrying out fuzzy logic procedures have been discussed as well.

References

1. Morra, J.L.T., Carnevalli, R.L.J., Mendonça Neta, B.M., Costa, S.T.M., Garcia, A.V., Ekel, P.I.: xOMNI Sistema SCADA/EMS, Revista CIER 41 (2002) 42-48.
2. Tsoukalas, L.H., Uhrig, R.E.: Fuzzy and Neural Approaches in Engineering. Wiley, New York (1997).
3. Yokoyama, R., Nimura, T., Nakanishi, Y.: A Coordinated Control of Voltage and Reactive Power by Heuristic Modeling and Approximate Reasoning. IEEE Trans. Power Systems 8 (1993) 636-645.
4. Box, G.E.P., Hunter, W.G., Hunter, J.S.: Statistics for Experiments. An Introduction to Design, Data Analysis and Model Building. Wiley, New York (1978).
5. Ekel, P.Ya., Junges, M.F.D., Morra, J.L.T., Paletta, F.P.G.: Fuzzy Logic Based Approach to Voltage and Reactive Power Control in Power Systems. Int. J. of Computer Research 11 (2002)159-170.
6. Kaye, R.J., Zammit, M.A.B., Hill, D.J.: Co-ordinated Spot and Ancillary Service Market to Optimise Power Systems Security. Proc. Int. Symp. on Bulk Power Systems Dynamics and Control IV: Restructuring. Santorini (1998) 539-544.
7. Sanchez, E.: Resolution of Eigen Fuzzy Sets Equations. Fuzzy Sets and Systems 1 (1978) 69-74.
8. Ekel, P., Popov, V.: Fuzzy Set Theory and Problems of the Design and Control of Power Systems and Subsystems, Proc. 4th IEEE Conf. on Control Applications (1995) 46-51.

Fuzzy-Symbolic Analysis for Classification of Symbolic Data[*]

M.S. Dinesh[1], K.C. Gowda[2], and P. Nagabhushan[3]

[1] Siemens Information Systems Ltd.,Bangalore-560 100, India
`dineshms@rocketmail.com`
[2] Jnana Sahyadri, Kuvempu University, Shimoga-577451, India
[3] Department of studies in computer science, University of Mysore, India

Abstract. A recent study on symbolic data analysis literature reveals that symbolic distance measures are playing a major role in solving the pattern recognition and analysis problems. After a careful study on the existing symbolic distance measures, we have identified that most of the existing symbolic distance measures either suffer from generalization or do not address object variability. To alleviate these problems we are proposing new generalized Similarity symbolic distance measure. The proposed distance measure is asymmetric, addresses object variability, and obeys partial order. To leverage the advantages of both fuzzy set theory and symbolic data analysis, conventional classification algorithm that works on the principles of fuzzy equivalence relation has been extended to handle Symbolic data. Efficacies of the proposed techniques are validated by conducting several experiments on the well-known assertion type of symbolic data sets with known classification results.

Keywords: Fuzzy-Symbolic data analysis, Fuzzy hierarchical analysis, Symbolic distance measures.

1 Introduction

From the literature it is evident that the two fields in Pattern Recognition (PR) namely, Fuzzy Data Analysis (FDA) and Symbolic Data Analysis (SDA) have been individually supplementary to the growth of PR, while seeming to have remained complementary to each other. Thus the essence of this paper is to leverage the advantages of both Symbolic Data Analysis and the Fuzzy Set Theory.

Distance measure plays a key role in Clustering or Classification of Data and gives an index of proximity, or alikeness, or affinity, or association between pairs of patterns. With the use of a proper distance measure, a proximity matrix can be computed from the pattern matrix where, proximity index is used to represent either dissimilarity or similarity between the patterns/objects/samples [2]. Most of the existing symbolic distance measures are metric in nature and therefore fail to grasp the asymmetric relation between the objects.

---

[*] This work was carried out at SJCE, Mysore, India.

Asymmetric relation between the objects exists due to object variability in size and for many other inherent reasons. Detailed study on the object variability is available in the reference paper [7]. In this paper, we have proposed non-metric similarity distance measure, which successfully overcome the drawbacks of the existing Symbolic Distance Measures. Proposed distance measure has been experimented with the data sets of known classification results and these results are compared with the existing distance measures that are available in literature.

2 Proposed Symbolic Similarity measure

2.1 Feature Space

Let the symbolic object be described with respect to d features $X_1, X_2 \ldots X_d$ and U_k denote the domain of the feature X_k. The domain U_k is assumed to be a bounded closed interval and is of the form $U_k[a_k, b_k]$ where a_k and b_k are minimum and maximum possible values for X_k, when X_k is continuous quantitative, discrete quantitative and ordinal qualitative. On the other hand, U_k is a finite set of all possible values, when X_k is a nominal qualitative. Then the feature space is the Cartesian product of $U_1, U_2 \ldots U_d$ that is,

$$U^{(d)} = U_1 \times U_2 \times \ldots \times U^d. \tag{1}$$

2.2 Similarity Measure

The similarity measure S between two Symbolic objects $A = A_1 \times A_2 \times \ldots \times A_d$ and $B = B_1 \times B_2 \times \ldots \times B_d$ in U_d is written as:

$$S(A, B) = \frac{1}{d} \sum_{k=1}^{d} \frac{W_k}{U_k} S(A_k, B_k) \quad (2) \qquad \sum_{k=1}^{d} W_k = 1 \; , \; W_k > 0, k = 1, \ldots d,$$

thus $0 < S(A, B) < 1$. Weighting constant (W_k) controls the relative importance of the features and U_k helps in the normalization of the output proximity values. For the kth feature, $S(A_k, B_k)$ is defined using two components such as $S_p(A_k, B_k)$ due to position p. and $S_s(A_k, B_k)$ due to span S.

The similarity component due to "position" arises only when the feature is quantitative interval or quantitative absolute/ratio type. It indicates the relative positions of two feature values. The similarity component due to "span" indicates the relative sizes and overlaps of the feature values. Computation of span component is required for both quantitative and qualitative types of features.

Let, a_m = Median value of interval A_k, b_m = Median value of interval B_k, $\emptyset$ = Cartesian join operator,

$\emptyset (x)$ = Cardinal(x), if x is categorical,
$\emptyset (x)$ = Length(x), if x is quantitative.
Where x = A_k or B_k or $A_k \emptyset B_k$

Similarity due to position is defined as:

$$S_p(A_k, B_k) = \frac{1}{1 + |A_m - B_m|} \quad (3) \qquad S_p(A_k, B_k) = S_p(B_k, A_k) \quad (4)$$

For the special cases given in Eqn 4 a_m and b_m the position component will change as follows:

Case 1: When the values of $a_m = b_m$, a_m and b_m in the position component become $a_m = a_L$ and $b_m = b_L$

Similarity due to span is given by:

$$S_s(B_k, A_k) = \frac{\phi(B_k)}{\phi(A_k \oplus B_k)} \quad (5) \qquad S_s(A_k, B_k) = \frac{\phi(A_k)}{\phi(A_k \oplus B_k)} \quad (6)$$

Net Similarity between A_k and B_k is:

$$S(B_k, A_k) = \frac{S_p(B_k, A_k) + S_s(B_k, A_k)}{2.0} \quad (7) \qquad S(A_k, B_k) = \frac{S_p(A_k, B_k) + S_s(A_k, B_k)}{2.0} \quad (8)$$

Concepts of Similarity, Dissimilarity, and Cartesian join operations illustrated through figures are given below:

Let the object be described in terms of d features X_k, k=1, 2, ... d. and E_k is the feature value taken by the feature X_k. Then we represent a pattern by a Cartesian product set $E = E_1 \times E_2 \times \cdots \times E_d$.

Let $A = A_1 \times A_2 \times \ldots \times A_d$ and $B = B_1 \times B_2 \times \ldots \times B_d$ be a pair of events of $U^{(d)}$.

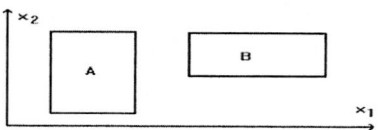

Fig. 1. Events in the Euclidean plane

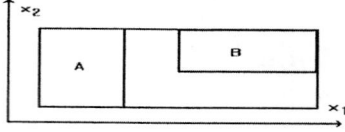

Fig. 2. Cartesian Join operator (A⊕B)

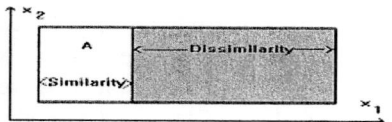

Fig. 3. Similarity/Dissimilarity from A to B

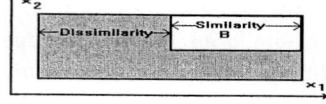

Fig. 4. Similarity/Dissimilarity from B to A

2.3 Specific Features

The proposed distance measures possess the following properties:

- Conveniently takes care of mixed features like, quantitative interval, quantitative absolute/ratio, and qualitative types.
- Satisfy the rules of partial order (reflexive, asymmetric and transitive).

- As a special case the equality $S_{AB} = S_{BA}$ occurs only when the object A has the same description as B, meaning that the two objects A and B having the attributes of same size are exactly identical in all respects.
- Distance measures produce normalized output in the range [0 -1], which helps to employ the fuzzy concepts for further analysis.
- Weightage factors in the distance measure helps in assigning the relative importance to the features.
- Distance measures can be decomposed into symmetric and skew-symmetric parts, this feature will be useful to study the object variability due to unequal spread of feature values.

3 Fuzzy Agglomerative Symbolic Classification

Based on the similarity relation proposed by Lofti Zadeh, Shinuchi Tamura et. al.,[11]; Dunn[6], Abraham Kandel et. al.[1], and Bezdek et. al.[3] we have employed fuzzy hierarchical techniques to analyze symbolic data sets.

Algorithm
1. Let { $y_1, y_2, \ldots, y_n$ } be a set of symbolic objects in 'd' dimensions and the initial number of clusters/classes be 'n'.
2. Compute the symbolic similarities between all pairs of symbolic objects in the data set (similarity measure between objects is computed as described in section 2.2).
3. Asymmetric similarity measure is decomposed into symmetric and skew symmetric parts.
4. Check the Similarity values computed in step 2 for transitiveness. If the similarity relation is not transitive, perform the transitive closure on the similarity values to make the similarity measure as fuzzy equivalence relation(R_T).
5. Since R_T is symmetric, consider either lower or upper triangle elements as distinct α - cut values.
6. Arrange all α - cut values in descending order.
7. Apply each α - cut, one by one on the data set and obtain the partitions.
8. From the partitions construct a dendrogram.
9. Merge all the symbolic objects in a class to form a Composite Symbolic Object (CSO). CSO represents the class description.

4 Experiments and Relation to Other Works

Experiments are conducted on the well-known Symbolic Data Sets whose classification results are known [8, 9, 10]. Assertion type of symbolic data sets of Fat-oil, Microprocessors and Microcomputer are used for the experiments. Fuzzy hierarchical classification scheme described has been extended used to obtain different clusters/classes of the Symbolic Data Sets. The results are compared and contrasted with the existing symbolic clustering techniques.

Experiment No. 1: The data set used for this experiment consists of information about fats and oils[10]. Fat-oil data set consists of four quantitative features of interval type and one nominal qualitative feature. Dendrogram shown in Fig.5. has been obtained after applying the proposed algorithm on Fat-Oil data. By cutting the dendrogram at an appropriate level we can obtain different classes/clusters. The samples grouped for two class and three class are: Two Class: {0,1,2,3,4,5,}, {6,7}, Three class:{0, 1}, {2, 3, 4 ,5}, {6, 7}. The results obtained by Ichino, Ichino & Yaguchi[10] on Fatoil data for two classes are identical with the results obtained by the proposed method. Results obtained by Gowda & Diday[8] on the same data set for three classes are identical with the results obtained by the proposed method.

Experiment No. 2: Experiment on the microprocessor data resulted in the dendrogram as shown in Fig. 6. Samples obtained for two and three classes are: Two class: {0, 1, 2, 3, 4, 5, 6, 7}, {8}, Three Class: {0, 1, 4, 7}, {2, 3, 5, 6}, {8} . The classification results obtained using Ichino's [17] method resulted in three clusters as {0, 1, 4, 5}, {2, 3, 6,}, and {7, 8}. The classification result obtained using the Gowda & Diday dissimilarity measure [8] resulted in two clusters as {0, 1, 2, 3, 4, 5, 6}, {7, 8}. The classification results obtained using the Gowda & Ravi [9] method resulted in three clusters as {0, 1, 4, 5, 7}, {2, 3, 6,}, and {8}. The results of the proposed method vary marginally when compared with the results of Ichino, Gowda and Diday, and Gowda and Ravi.

Experiment No. 3: Application of the proposed algorithm on microcomputer data set produced the dendrogram as shown in Fig. 7. Samples grouped for three classes are {0, 1, 3, 4, 5, 7, 9, 10, 11}, {2, 8}, {6}. The classification results obtained using the Gowda and Ravi [9] divisive algorithm and Ichino's method resulted in two clusters as {0, 1, 2, 4, 5, 7, 8, 9, 10, 11}, and {6} and the classification result obtained using Gowda Diday dissimilarity measure [8] resulted in four clusters as {0, 1, 9, 10}, {6}, {2, 8}, {3, 4, 5, 7, 11}. The results obtained by the proposed method vary marginally when compared with the results of Ichino, Gowda and Diday and Gowda and Ravi.

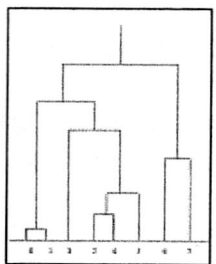
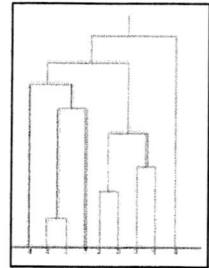
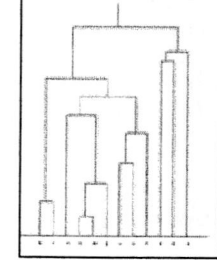

Fig. 5. Fat-Oil Data **Fig. 6.** Microprocessor Data **Fig. 7.** Macrocomputer Data

5 Summary

New similarity measure for Symbolic objects is presented. Conventional algorithm, which works on the principles of Fuzzy equivalence relation, has been extended to handle Symbolic data. To validate the proposed distance measures, they are applied on the well-known assertion type of Symbolic Data Sets with known classification results and these results are compared with the existing techniques. Proposed techniques were also applied and validated on the large data sets like multi spectral satellite images and Magnetic resonance images. Results on large data set are not discussed in this paper due to space constraints. However, authors are planning to discuss these results during the presentation.

References

1. Abraham Kandel and Lawrence Yelowitz,"*Fuzzy Chains,*" IEEE Tran. Sys., Man, Cybern., Vol. SMC-4, No. 5, pp 472-475, Sept. 1974.
2. Anil K. Jain and Richard C. Dubes,"Algorithms for Clustering Data," Prentice Hall, Englewood Cliffs, New Jersey, 1988.
3. J. C. Bezdek, J. Douglus Haris, "*Fuzzy Partitions and Relations: An Axiomatic Basis For Clustering,*" Fuzzy Sets and Systems, Vol. 1, pp. 111-127, 1978.
4. E. Diday, C. Hayashi, M. Jambu and N. Ohsumi, Eds, "Recent Developments in Clustering and Data Analysis, Academic Press, New York, 1987.
5. E. Diday, "*Knowledge representation and symbolic data analysis,*" Proc. 2nd int. workshop on Data, Expert Knowledge, and Decision, Hamburg, Sep. 1989a.
6. J.C. Dunn, "Some Recent Investigations of a New Fuzzy Partitioning Algorithms and its Application to Pattern Classification Problems," Journal of Cybernetics, Vol. 4, pp. 1-15, 1974.
7. Francesco Palumbo and Maria Benedetto, "*A Generalization Measure for Symbolic Objects,*" Proc. of KESDA'98 Conference, Luxembourg, April 1998.
8. K. C. Gowda and E. Diday, "Symbolic Clustering Using a New Similarity Measure," IEEE Trans. Sys. Man Cybern. 22, 368-378, 1992.
9. K. C. Gowda, and T.V.Ravi, "*Agglomerative clustering of symbolic objects using the concepts of both similarity and dissimilarity,*" Pattern Recognition Lett. 16, 647-652, 1995.
10. M. Ichino and H. Yaguchi, Generalized Minkowski Metrics for Mixed Features, Trans. IECE Jpn, J72-A, 398-405(in Japanese), 1989.
11. Shinichi Tamura, Seihaku Kiguchi, and Kokichi Tanaka, "*Pattern Classification Based on Fuzzy Relations,*" IEEE Trans. Sys., Man, Cybern., Vol. SMC-1, No. 1, pp. 61-66, Jan. 1971.
12. L.B. Turksen, "*Interval Valued Fuzzy Sets Based on Normal Forms,*" Fuzzy Sets and Systems, Vol. 20, pp 191-210, 1986.

Handwritten Character Recognition Systems Using Image-Fusion and Fuzzy Logic

Rupsa Chakraborty and Jaya Sil

Department of Computer Science and Technology,
Bengal Engineering and Science University, Shibpur,
Howrah -7111 03, India
rupsa_c@yahoo.com, js@becs.ac.in

Abstract. To date, image segmentation is used as a vital step to developing handwritten character recognition systems. In the paper, image segmentation has been avoided by applying image fusion and fuzzy method to recognize handwritten characters. At first, several digital images corresponding to each handwritten character are fused to generate patterns, which are stored in 10×10 matrices, irrespective of the size of the images. The character to be recognized is matched with each pattern and the best match pattern is considered as the most likely choice. In the second phase of the work subjective judgment using fuzzy logic has been incorporated to improve the recognition rate where Gaussian distribution function, with varied mean and standard deviation are considered as fuzzy membership functions. Several binary images have been tested to demonstrate the effectiveness of the proposed system.

1 Introduction

The problem caters to the automated recognition of handwritten characters (hereafter called characters) that require little or no manual intervention and save considerable amount of time, money and energy. To recognize a particular character, traditional image segmentation methods may be used like region-based methods [5]-[9] (e.g., texture analysis) and edge-based methods [2],[9] (e.g., dynamic programming). Some neural-network-based [6] segmentation techniques and intensity based segmentation procedures using Gabor filters [8] are also reported. Segmentation either implemented by arbitrarily subdividing the image into primitives [4] or by computing connected components. The features like the height, width of each segment and gap between two segments are obtained from the segmentation process. In dynamic programming technique, the matcher takes the input image, a lexicon (a list of strings representing all candidate characters), features of each image and returns a confidence value [0,1] indicating the degree of matching to which the image represents that particular character [4]. Fuzzy integral aggregation is a procedure where a rule base of the characters are constructed and stored. The output of the rule base gives the confidence to the extent an image matches with a known character. A set of features is mapped as antecedents of the fuzzy rules while the consequents of the rules generate a numeric confidence that the sub-image belongs to a particular string.

No matter how efficient the technique is, segmentation consumes a lot of time. The methods which tried to avoid segmentation had to deal with lots of features [1] which add complexity in some way or other. The paper aims at developing a character recognition system with improved performance using image fusion and fuzzy logic. The system can be broadly classified into two phases. In the first phase images of a particular character are fused to generate a pattern and stored in a fixed size probability matrix, irrespective of the size of the image. The image to be recognized is then matched with every pattern generating a recognition score for each of the cases. The character that corresponds to the highest score is then accepted as the recognized character. In the second phase, for improving the recognition rate, subjective judgement has been incorporated using fuzzy method.

The paper is divided into four sections. In section 2 the proposed method is described in detail. Results are documented in section 3 while conclusions are summarized in section 4.

2 Proposed Work

Character set Ch: A set containing images of characters to be recognized.

Pattern matrix ($M_P[10][10]$): A matrix of elements within [0,1] representing the probability of occurrence of a black pixel in the respective cell.

Test image: The image fed to the system for recognition.

Training image: The image representing a known character of *Ch* to be fused for generating M_P.

Pattern-matrix table: A file containing information for each character of *Ch*, such as the character itself, number of images till fused (*num*), and M_P.

Recognition score: Value denoting the extent to which the *test image* represents a member of *Ch*.

2.1 Coarse State of Recognition

Generation of Probability Matrix
In the first phase of recognition, following procedures are executed for the training images to generate M_P of each character.

a. *Pre-processing*: As a preprocessing step noise has been removed from the original image (fig.1(a)) by thresholding operation. Fig.1(b) shows one such image.

b. *Thinning*: The procedure converts the object in the image (which may be a few pixels thick) to a thickness of one pixel to eliminate redundancy.

c. *Image fitting*: The image is fitted within a frame that touches the character at its left, right, top and bottom. The time and space complexity is reduced effectively by eliminating redundant/useless information, see fig.1(c).

d. *Image reduction*: The image is divided into a 10 × 10 grid structure, shown in fig.1(d). A 10×10 matrix M_{tr}, of training images has been formed which

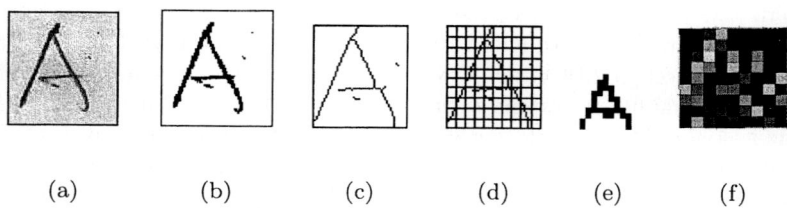

Fig. 1. (a)Original image. (b) Noise-reduced image. (c) After image fitting. (d) A 10×10 grid structure. (e) Reconstructed image (f) A pictorial representation of 'A'.

stores '1' in its (i,j) position provided more than 5 percent of the pixels in the cell(i,j) contains black pixels, else it stores '0'. Effective size of the character is thus reduced significantly and at the same time retaining all the features of the character. Interestingly, it has been observed that the same character is formed from $M_{tr}[10][10]$, only its size is greatly reduced. A reconstructed image obtained from fig.1(e) is shown in fig.1(f).

e. *Image fusion*: A look-up table (*pattern-matrix table*) stores a pattern matrix M_p corresponding to each element of *Ch*. Equation (1) explains the formation procedure of M_p, executed for fusing training images. It is worth mentioning that a training image may be fused with the existing pattern at any point of time.

$$M_p^{new} = \frac{1}{num+1} * (num * M_p^{old} + M_{tr}) \quad (1)$$

Here, M_p^{new} is the pattern matrix obtained after fusing training images contained in M_{tr} and M_p^{old} (already stored in the *pattern-matrix table*). M_p^{new} is copied back to the table along with *num* increased by one. Finally, every cell of M_p represents the probability of occurrence of a black pixel that maps the *test image* to a typical character. Fig.1(f) gives a pictorial representation of M_p for character 'A'. The content ([0-1])of each cell of M_p is represented by colors ranging from blue to red in the order of VIBGYOR. For example, deep blue and deep red represent probability '0' and '1', respectively. Thus, the overall patterns of each character are restored in the pattern file.

f. *Matching*: The *test image* is processed similarly up to the *image-reduction* step to generate M_{tst}. M_{tst} is matched with M_p of each character stored in the *pattern-matrix table* and a recognition score is obtained, as suggested by equation (2).

$$RecognitionScore^k = \frac{\sum_{i=0}^{10}\sum_{j=0}^{10}(M_p^k[i][j] * M_{tst}[i][j])}{\sum_{i=0}^{10}\sum_{j=0}^{10} M_{tst}[i][j]} \quad (2)$$

$RecognitionScore^k$ denotes the extent of matching of the kth pattern matrix with that of M_{tst}. The most likely recognized character is the one corresponding to the element with the highest *recognition score*.

2.2 Fine Tuning Using Fuzzy Logic

To improve the recognition rate, fuzzy approach is invoked. An image containing a standard representation of each element of Ch has been reduced(section 2.1) and stored in matrix namely, $st\_img[10][10]$. The Gaussian distribution function is mapped as fuzzy membership function(g) and assigned to each column of st_img, shown in fig.2(a).

$$g(r) = e^{-\frac{(r-m)^2}{\delta}} \qquad (3)$$

where, r is the row number of a particular column, m and δ denotes the mean and standard deviation, respectively. The function denotes the approximate chance of occurrence of a '1' in that row of the respective column. Membership functions of other columns of the standard image are obtained by changing m and δ only, shown in fig.2(b). A *region* is represented by a set of contiguous rows, for each column, containing '1'(fig 3(a)). A variable, no_reg, denotes the number of such regions in each column having a separate membership function. For each character, a *fuzzy-confidence table* contains no_reg for each column and pair(m,δ) for each region. For recognition, every column of Mtst is scanned from row 0 to 9 which generates a confidence value for every element of the matrix st_img and stored in MF[10][10]. While scanning, the number of regions for the column is computed and stored in a variable $test\_no\_reg$. Here three situations may arise and are tackled in the following manner:

(i) if $test\_no\_reg > no\_reg$, then the fuzzy membership value (fig.3(b)) for every cell in that row is set to zero.
(ii) if $test\_no\_reg = no\_reg$ then for each region the fuzzy membership value (fig.3(b)) is computed from the membership function corresponding to that region.
(iii) if $test\_no\_reg < no\_reg$ then divide the column into number of parts equal to no_reg.

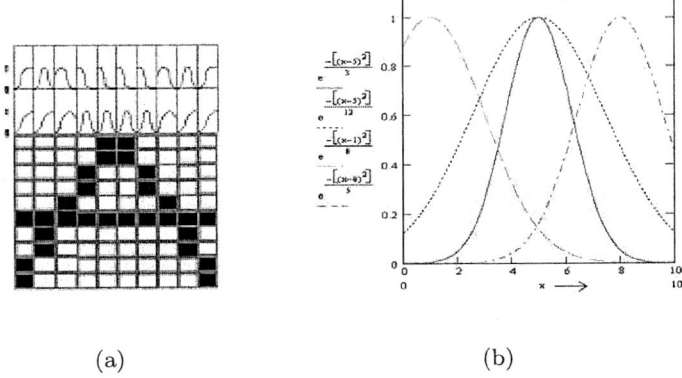

(a)   (b)

Fig. 2. (a) Membership function of each column. (b) Gaussian distribution functions with varied m and δ.

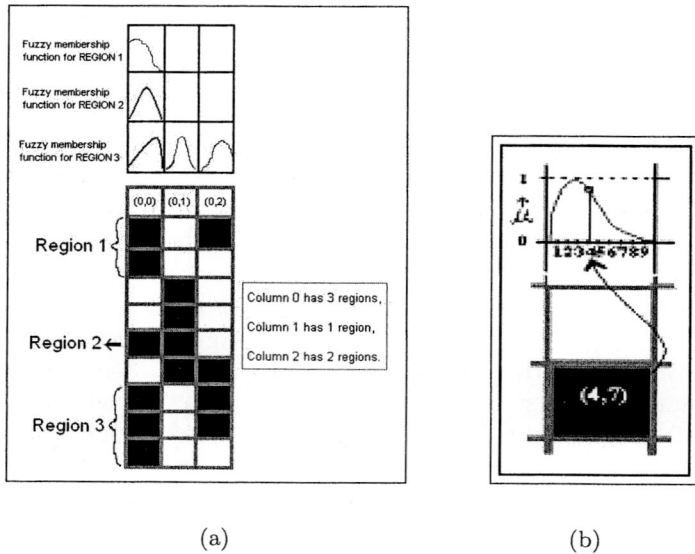

(a)   (b)

Fig. 3. (a) Illustrating computation of *no_reg*. (b) Illustrating the computation of *g*.

After computation of membership value, matching and computation of final recognition score is obtained by equation (4),

$$RecognitionScore^k = \frac{\sum_{i,j=0}^{10} max(M_{tst}[i][j] * M_F[i][j], M_{tst}[i][j] * M_p[i][j])}{\sum_{i=0}^{10} \sum_{j=0}^{10} M_{tst}[i][j]}$$

(4)

The most likely recognized character is the one corresponding to the element with the highest *recognition score*.

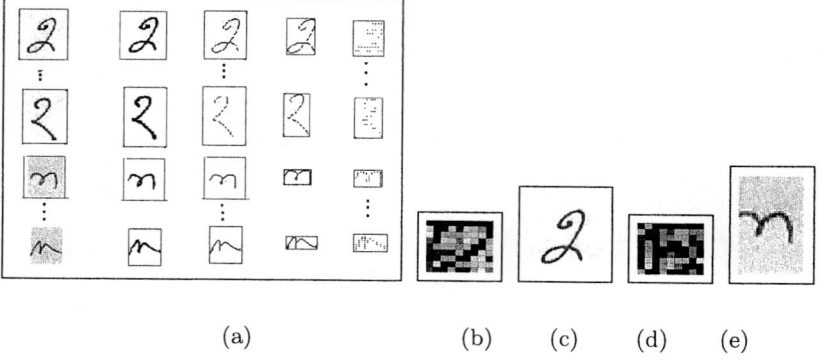

(a)   (b)   (c)   (d)   (e)

Fig. 4. (a) Image reduction of training images for '2' and 'n'. (b)&(d) pictorial representation of M_p for '2' and 'n' respectively. (c)&(e) Test image of '2' and 'n', respectively.

3 Results

The proposed algorithm has been applied on the elements of $Ch = \{0,2,E,T,S,Y, a,d,n\}$ (two instances shown in fig.4). Fuzzy method has been applied on the same instances which generates the recognition scores 0.6979 & 0.5999 for the test image of fig.4(c) and 4(e), respectively. The result reveals that the recognition rate is around 60 percent for the correct answer to be the one with best match and around 75 percent when the correct answer is either the best or the second best match.

4 Conclusion

The paper presents a generic method for recognition of handwritten characters within a finite character set. More insight in the existing systems shows that segmentation needed for such systems, perhaps, is not a very natural way of proceeding toward the ultimate goal. The performance of the system consists of various salient points: i) little time($O(|C|\log_2|C|)$) and memory requirements, ii) works efficiently irrespective of the size of the image, iii) can be extended to characters with varied shape, iv) avoids segmentation, v) multiple thinning is not required.

References

1. Ariki Y, Motegi Y, IEEE Trans. Pattern Anal., Machine Intell, 1995. Segmentation and recognition of handwritten characters using Subspace Method.
2. Bellmann Y (1957), Dynamic Programming, Princeton Univ. Press.
3. Chiang JH, Gader PD (Nov. 1997), Hybrid Fuzzy-Neural Systems in Handwritten Word Recognition, IEEE Trans. Comm.
4. Gader P, Keller JM, Cai J(Feb. 1995), A Fuzzy Logic System for the Detection and Recognition of Handwritten Street Numbers, IEEE Trans. Comm.
5. Halarick RM and Shapiro LG, Image segmentation techniques, Comp. Vision, Graphics, and Image Proc., vol.29, pp.100-132, 1985.
6. Jackel ID,et.al (1991), A neural network approach to handprint character recognition, IEEE Trans. PAMI.
7. Pal SK and Dutta Majumdar DK (1986), FUZZY Mathematical Approach to Pattern Recognition, Wiley Eastern Limited.
8. Richard Buse, Zhi-Qiang Liu and Jim Bezdek (February 2002), Word Recognition using Fuzzy Logic, IEEE Transactions on Fuzzy Systems, Vol 10, No.1.
9. Sonka M, Hlavac V, and R. Boyle (1998), Image Processing, Analysis, and Machine Vision, 2nd ed. Pacific Grove, CA:PWS.
10. Zamperoni P (1986),Analysis of some region growing operators for image segmentation, in Advances in Image Processing and Pattern Recognition, V. Cappelini and R. Marconi, Eds. Amsterdam: North Holland, pp. 204-208.

Classification of Remotely Sensed Images Using Neural-Network Ensemble and Fuzzy Integration

G. Mallikarjun Reddy[1] and B. Krishna Mohan[2]

[1] Kanwal Rekhi School of Information Technology,
Indian Institute of Technology Bombay,
Powai, Mumbai-400076, India
[2] Centre of Studies in Resource Engineering,
Indian Institute of Technology Bombay,
Powai, Mumbai-400076, India

Abstract. An algorithm for fusing multiple remotely sensed image classifiers is addressed herein using fuzzy integral with error proportionate fuzzy measures. This method includes a procedure for calculating the λ-fuzzy measures which are adjusted depending on error correlation among the individual classifiers. Based on these fuzzy measures, the fuzzy integral is then used as non-linear function to search for maximum degree of agreement between multiple conflicting sources of evidence. Results obtained are used for decision making in classification problem. Experimental results on classification of remotely sensed images show that the performance of proposed multi-classifier method performs better than conventional method where fixed fuzzy measures are used.

1 Introduction

Data fusion for optimal information extraction has been gaining attention over the past decade[6]. This study will particularly discuss information fusion in the sense of combining results from multiple classifiers with application to classification of remotely sensed images. Information from multiple classifiers may agree or conflict with each other. Therefore, the task of fusion is to search for maximum degree of agreement between the conflicting supports for each pixel. Let p be an unknown pixel to be classified, $\Omega = \{\omega_i : i = 1, 2, .., m\}$ a set of classes, $C = \{c_i : i = 1, 2, .., n\}$ a set of classifiers. The fusion of multiple classifiers can be expressed as

$$\Phi(\omega_i/p) = F[f(\omega_i/p, c_1), f(\omega_i/p, c_2), ..., f(\omega_i/p, c_n)] \quad (1)$$

Where $\Phi(\omega_i/p)$ is the combined information about p being classified as class ω_i, F is fusion operator, $f(\omega_i/p, c_n)$ is the output of classifier indicating the degree of confidence with which pixel p belongs to class ω_i. The performance of fuzzy integral is greatly affected by changing the values of the fuzzy measures [2] as explained in next section. Some methods for identifying fuzzy measures have been proposed (e.g.: [1],[5]) for classification. One main contribution of this study is to further investigate the role of fuzzy measures in improving the fusion performance of fuzzy integral by introducing corrective measure for calculating these fuzzy measures with application to classification of remotely sensed images. The classifiers being used in this study are neural networks. The generalization abilities can be improved using neural network ensemble instead of a single neural network [3].

2 Fuzzy Measure and Fuzzy Integral

For sake of completeness, some basic definitions and properties of fuzzy integral are discussed below. For full description of the fuzzy integral and related fuzzy measure, the reader is referred to [2].

2.1 Fuzzy Measure

Fuzzy measures are generalizations of classical measures. A measurable space is a pair (X, Ω) consisting of a set X and a σ-algebra of subsets of X. A set function g defined on Ω is a fuzzy measure if it satisfies the following conditions:

1. $g(\phi) = 0, g(X) = 1$
2. $g(A) \leq g(B)$ if $A \subset B$ and $A, B \in \Omega$

A g_λ-fuzzy measure was proposed by Sugeno [4] with additional condition.

$$g(A \cup B) = g(A) + g(B) + \lambda g(A)g(B), \lambda > -1 \quad (2)$$

where $A \cap B = \Phi$ The constant λ can be determined by solving the following equation:

$$\lambda + 1 = \Pi_{i=1}^{n}(1 + \lambda g_i) \quad (3)$$

where g_i ($0 \leq g_i \leq 1$) is fuzzy density and is defined as grade of importance of classifier c_i towards the final evaluation of the system. $g(X)$ is importance of arbitrary set of X classifiers. For given set of g_is, there exists unique root $\lambda > -1$ and $\lambda \neq 0$.

2.2 Fuzzy Integral

Let $C = (c_1, c_2, ...c_n)$ be a finite set of classifiers and $0 \leq f(c_1) \leq f(c_2).. \leq f(c_n) \leq 1$ (if not, the elements of C are rearranged to make this relation hold), where $f(c_i)$ is numerical output of classifier c_i for a particular class, then the Sugeno fuzzy integral can be computed by

$$\int_A f(x) og(.) = max_{i=1}^{n}[min(f(x_i), g(A_i))] \quad (4)$$

where $A_i = \{c_i, c_{i+1}..., c_n\}$.

3 Error Proportionate Fuzzy Measures

In classification of remotely sensed images, it is realized that assigning a fixed value for each fuzzy density is less effective due to the fact that each classifier may not perform equally well in recognizing all the classes. Therefore the weight of importance or the fuzzy density of each classifier will need to be adjusted according to class and also the simultaneous information given by other classifiers.

In the case of multi neural network fusion, let $\Omega = (\omega_1, \omega_2, ...\omega_m)$ be the set of classes of interest and let $C = (c_1, c_2, ...c_n)$ be set of classifiers. Now considering that for each c_i, the degree of importance g_i, must be evaluated. These values can be evaluated easily from the training data. Consider the confusion matrix of classifier c_k denoted as P^k which contains the results of correctly classified and misclassified pixels obtained from the validation set. It is constructed for each classifier and expressed in the form:

$$P^k = [p_{ij}^k] \qquad (5)$$

where, again for short notation i and j stand for ω_i and ω_j respectively (i,j = 1,2,3,....m). For $i = j$, p_{ij}^k is correctly classified pixels in class ω_i by classifier c_k. When $i \neq j$, p_{ij}^k is the number of pixels in class ω_i being misclassified as class Ω_j by c_k. In conventional methods proposed earlier[1], the fuzzy density of each classifier was considered as ratio of correctly classified pixels to the total pixels in the validation data.

Instead of using a single fuzzy density for an individual classifier, we will assign different fuzzy densities for different classes for each classifier. The fuzzy density can be initially defined as:

$$g_i^k = p_{ii}^k / \Sigma_{j=1}^m p_{ij}^k \qquad (6)$$

where g_i^k is the fuzzy density of classifier c_k in the classification of class $\Omega_i, i = 1, 2, ...m$. Furthermore, it is always observed that each classifier is more robust than the others in classifying certain classes, but more error-prone in the classification of some other classes. Therefore it is necessary to take into account this effect to adjust the values of the initially defined fuzzy densities as given in (7). In this study we propose that fuzzy densities be updated by considering the pair wise proportion of the misclassified objects between the considered classifier and other. Thus, the fuzzy densities can now be updated so as to get error-proportionate fuzzy densities as follows:

$$g_i^{k*} = g_i^k * (\Pi_l \alpha^{k/l})^w \qquad (7)$$

where g_i^{k*} is updated fuzzy density of the classifier c_k for class ω_i, and $\{\alpha^{k/l}\}, 0 < \alpha^{k/l} \leq 1$, is set of updating parameters according to the information within considered classifier c_k and other classifier c_l. The weight w is used to make the process more flexible. The set of updating parameters $\alpha^{k/l}$ is derived based on the idea that if both classifiers are assumed to make different mistakes then initial fuzzy density of classifier which used to make more mistakes will be reduced.

And there is no change in the updating process if the considered classifier c_k makes same or less mistake than the other classifier c_l. Thus, it is expressed as

$$\alpha^{k/l} = \begin{cases} 1 & \text{if classifier } c_k \text{ makes same or less mistakes than classifier } c_l; \\ p_{i,j}^l / p_{i,j}^k & \text{if classifier } c_k \text{ makes more mistakes than other classifier } c_l; \\ \delta & \text{if classifier } c_l \text{ makes zero mistakes.} \end{cases} \quad (8)$$

where δ is a small real value which prevents $\alpha^{k/l}$ from becoming zero.

4 Fuzzy Fusion Using Error Proportionate Fuzzy Measures

Let $F_i = \{f(i/k) : k = 1, 2.....n\}$ be set of numerical outputs estimated from all classifiers c_k indicating how likely the input in question should belong to class ω_i, where $0 \leq f(i/k) \leq 1$. For $f(i/k) = 0$, classifier c_k gives no support about the pixel in question belonging to class ω_i, and for $f(i/k) = 1$, classifier c_k gives full support about unknown input belonging to class ω_i. Start with the fuzzy measures, and a sequence $0 \leq f(i/1) \leq f(i/2).... \leq f(i/n) \leq 1$, the fuzzy integral based fusion model combines all of these pieces of evidence from different classifiers into single real value $\Phi(F_i)$, in terms of sugeno integral defined as

$$\Phi(F_i) = max_{k=1}^n [min(f(i/k), g(Z_{i/k}))] \quad (9)$$

where $Z_{i/k} = \{\omega_i/c_1, \omega_i/c_2, ...\omega_i/c_k\}$ i.e., set of first k classifiers after ordering of the numerical outputs, $f(i/k)$.

Using (9), the object can be classified to a class ω_i^* or denoted simply as i^* if its integrated value is maximum, that is

$$i^* = arg_i\{max(\Phi(F_i))\} \quad (10)$$

The detailed algorithm is given below:

1. Construct the confusion matrix for each classifier as described by (5) using the training data.
2. Calculate the initial fuzzy densities as defined by (6).
3. Calculate $\alpha^{k/l}$ as defined by (8) for each classifier k with respect to all other classifiers l.
4. Update the initial fuzzy densities using (7) with given weight w.
5. Repeat steps 2-4 for all classifiers with respect to same class.
6. Compute the g_λ-fuzzy measures using updated fuzzy densities.
7. Repeat steps 2-6 for all classes.
8. For each unknown input pixel compute the fuzzy integral defined by (9) for each class.
9. Using (10), assign the unknown input pixel to a class i^*.

Table 1. Classification performance of individual BPNNs and the fuzzy integration. FI1 is integration using fixed fuzzy measures and FI2 is using error-proportionate fuzzy measures.

Class	BPNN1	BPNN2	BPNN3	FI1	FI2
Early Wheat	50.42	76.06	69.23	67.5	68.37
Late Wheat	75	27.77	62.5	55.56	55.56
Rice	100	100	64.28	100	100
Masoor	58.33	75	78.1	63.88	63.88
Forest	100	100	100	100	100
Water	69.13	60.49	77.7	67.90	74.07
Urban	48.14	59.25	22.2	40.74	40.74
APA	71.57	71.22	67.71	70.79	71.79
OA	75.51	74.2	70.62	76.45	77.58

Table 2. Classification performance of individual BPNNs, RBFs and the fuzzy integration. FI1 is integration using fixed fuzzy measures and FI2 is integration using error-proportionate fuzzy measures.

Class	BPNN1	RBF1	BPNN2	RBF2	FI1	FI2
Early Wheat	42.7	37	43.7	56.2	48.6	47.5
Late Wheat	85.1	75.7	76.5	67.1	84.4	89.06
Rice	89.7	89.7	97.3	89.3	94.1	96.87
Masoor	75	73.4	78.1	68.7	82.8	82.8
Forest	100	99.21	100	100	100	100
Water	59.7	84.7	64.6	87.5	68.75	68.75
Urban	81.2	72.9	81.2	75	79.16	85.41
Background	100	100	100	100	100	100
APA	79.17	79.08	80.18	80.48	82.22	83.79
OA	80	80.4	81.4	83.02	83.12	84.18

Table 3. Classification performance of individual BPNNs, RBFs and the fuzzy integration using multi dated images. FI1 is integration using fixed fuzzy measures and FI2 is integration using error-proportionate fuzzy measures.

Class	BPNN1	RBF1	BPNN2	RBF2	FI1	FI2
Early Wheat	42.7	44.71	43.7	67.30	52.4	66.82
Late Wheat	85.1	45.31	23.43	95.31	55.46	78.12
Rice	89.7	83.48	75.45	57.58	87.05	89.28
Masoor	75	92.18	98.43	53.12	93.75	92.1
Forest	100	100	100	98.43	100	100
Water	59.7	65.27	78.47	57.63	76.39	72.91
Urban	81.2	70.83	93.75	37.5	100	93.75
Background	100	100	100	100	100	100
APA	79.18	75.23	76.64	70.85	83.13	86.62
OA	80	76.14	74.50	76.22	81.72	86.22

5 Experimental Results

The proposed fusion technique is applied to combine the results given by multiple classifiers for classification of remotely sensed images. The data used is taken from Space Applications Centre (ISRO) Ahmedabad. The image used in this study is a 990 x 500 pixel image of Varanasi area, Uttar Pradesh in India. Table 1 gives the results on test data using the back propagation neural networks(BPNN) with 8, 14, 22 hidden units in three layered architecture. Table 2 gives results on test data using two BPNNs with 2 hidden layers with 10 and 30 hidden nodes in each hidden layer and two Radial basis function (RBF) networks with 30 and 25 hidden nodes in hidden layer. Table 3 gives results on test data using same architecture as Table 2, but using the two different dated images. The proposed method can be seen to improve in classification performance as reflected in high overall accuracy (OA) and average percentage accuracy (APA) for most of classes in all the experiments.

6 Conclusions

A fuzzy-integral algorithm for the fusion of information from multiple image classifiers using error proportionate fuzzy measures has been discussed. From the experimental results on the classification of remotely sensed images, it has been shown that proposed method is superior to conventional method of calculation of fuzzy-densities. A procedure for deriving and updating the fuzzy densities which are considered very important in calculation of fuzzy measure and the fuzzy integral is discussed in this paper. One issue worth considering in future investigation is optimal selection of the exponential weight w used for updating fuzzy densities, as at present stage this weight is selected manually through many experiments.

References

1. A. Senthil Kumar, S.K.Basu, and K.L.Majumdar: Robust Classification of Multispectral Data Using Multiple Neural Networks and Fuzzy Integral. IEEE Transactions on Geoscience and Remote Sensing Vol. 35, No.3 (May 1997) 787–790
2. James M.Keller, Hossein Tahani: Information Fusion in Computer Vision Using Fuzzy Integral. IEEE Transactions on Systems, Man, and Cybernetics Vol. 20, No.3 (May 1990) 733–741
3. L.K.Hansen, P.Solomon: Neural Network Ensembles. IEEE Transactions on Pattern Anal. and Machine Intelligence Vol. 12 (1990) 993–1001
4. M.Sugeno: Fuzzy Measures and Fuzzy Integrals: A Survey. Fuzzy Automata and Decision Process, Amsterdam: North Holland (1977) 89–102
5. S.Cho and J.H.Kim: Combining Multiple Neural Networks by Fuzzy Integral for Robust Classification. IEEE Transactions on Systems, Man, and Cybernetics Vol. 25, (1995) 380–384
6. A.Sharkey,Turner.K and Ghosh J: Linear and Order Statistics Combiners for Pattern Classification. Combining Artificial Neural Networks, Springer, London(May 1999) 127–161

Intelligent Learning Rules for Fuzzy Control of a Vibrating Screen

Claudio Ponce and Ernesto Ponce

Electronic Department, Mechanical Department, Tarapaca University,
Postal Code 6-D, Arica, Chile
eponce@uta.cl

Abstract. This work shows a system of intelligent control for a vibrating screen. The design is based in fuzzy logic. The set of rules was obtained by the method of group by means of the neighbor closest. The vibration of the screen (frequency and amplitude), the flow of material and the size of stones are the entrance variables. The variable of exit is the motor speed who controls the excitation force.

1 Introduction

In the Chilean economy the cooper is very important, CODELCO, the principal mining company has many vibratory screens. They presents several problems of efficiency and maintenance. This generates great losses due to the constant failures that take place. In order to give solution to this problem, a scale prototype of vibratory screen of last generation, was designed, [1]. The vibratory screen consists of a machine with two trays with variable slope for the selection of material. It is excited by a motor and two exciting boxes. The movement of the structure is cushioned by a set of springs. The sensors measures the vibration of the structure and the level of material that arrives. An adjustable frequency drive operates on the motor, by means of a strap moves the exciting boxes.

Fig. 1. Prototype on scale of a vibrating screen, used to test the intelligent control system

2 Structure of the Control System

The control is made by a lodged software in a microcomputer BASIC STAMP 2E. Software is operated with fuzzy logic. It requires of few iterations and few resources of memory. This allows a control in real time in a platform of software of low weight lodged in a very simple hardware [7].

The problem is to have a set of rules of the system. It was solved with software of intelligent learning. This one is lodged in the same microcomputer that makes the control fuzzy. Observing the variables of entrance and exit the set of control rules was deduced. The scheme of control consists of three parts:

1. A Software who takes the control of the system (Controller). This one consists of three basic stages: (a) An interface that turns the numerical variables in fuzzy variable. (b) A masterful system of control that handles the variables of entrance and exit. This operation is consulting the set of control rules. (c) An interface that turns the fuzzy variables to numerical variables.
2. A software that learns and models the system of vibratory screen (network of learning). The learning is plotted on a map of knowledge or set of rules. This knowledge is codified in machine language with instructions IF-THEN-ELSE-WHILE. The codified information keeps in RAM (EEPROM) of the microcomputer.
3. A Software of basic control (Trainer). It gives the instructions to the controller while the learning network is training. Once the network finishes learning, the Trainer becomes disconnected. When it happens, the controller consults the new rules learned by the network of Learning.

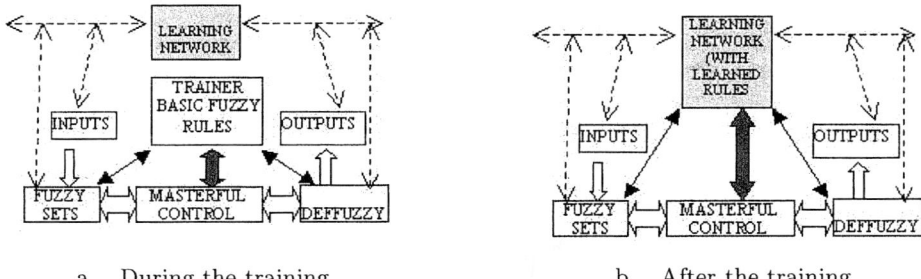

a. During the training   b. After the training

Fig. 2. Scheme of Control training of the intelligent controller

In the first time the controller is into operation, the program TRAINER takes the control of the MASTERFUL CONTROLLER, and the LEARNING NETWORK [4], [6], [8] will only observe the variables of entrance and exit in numerical and fuzzy form (Figure 2.a). When the LEARNING NETWORK concludes its training, the TRAINER will be disconnected and the LEARNING NETWORK will take the control of the MASTERFUL SYSTEM CONTROLLER (Figure 2.b).

The variables of entrance and exit are:

a. Vibration: The screen normally vibrates around 880 rpm with a displacement of 3mm and an acceleration of 1.05G. The Amplitude and frequency are measured by means an accelerometer Memsic 2125. This accelerometer measures in two axes the impact of the vibration (amplitude and g) and rotation. The frequency can be calculated indirectly counting the maximums of the amplitude that happens in a second. This sensor is positioned in the flat x-y of the vibration of the screen.
b. Flow Level: it is measured by means an ultrasonic sonar sensor SFR04. It works emitting a trigger of ultrasonic pulses and detecting the echo. This sensor detects the distance to the material that circulates in the belt.
c. Motor Speed: it is a three phase induction machine, with 2Hp of power. The speed can be controlled, adjusting the source frequency.

The motor is controlled by means an adjustable frequency drive, POWERFLEX40. The microcomputer sends an analogical signal to the drive. This signal varies between 0 volts (0 Hz) and 10 volts (50 Hz).

3 Hardware

The software system is lodged in a microcomputer BASICSTAMP2E, mounted in a stamp card. Its doors of exit are reinforced to give 24 volts and 1 ampere. The BASIC Stamp II is a small computer that executes programs in language PBASIC. It has 16 pins of (entered/exit) I/O that can be connected directly to digital devices or of logical levels, [2], [5].

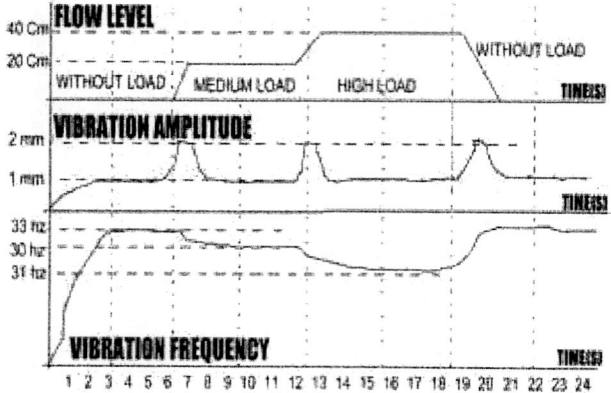

Fig. 3. Screen without load, with medium load and with high load

4 Experimental Results and Conclusions

The intelligent controller was proved with satisfactory results. The Training lasted 18 hours chronological distributed in 4 days, to a programmed percentage error of a 0.5%. The balance point varies between 900 and 1100 rpm depending on the load that is applied to him. In the figure 3, it shows the screen without load, medium load and high load. In each variation of load, the vibration amplitude rises to 2mm and return to 1 mm when the intelligent system is auto regulated.

The intelligent control is very important to optimize the operation and enlarge the life of these machines. Use a control reduces high cost in maintenance by easily avoidable failures. Thousand dollars is the loss per hour for a stopped vibrating screen and the cost of a intelligent control is around nine hundred dollars.

References

1. Ponce, E., Valdes, C., Cortes R., Development of a Vibrating Screen, FACING, Vol. 11, No. 2, pp. 35–40, 2003.
2. Nemsic Instruments, www.parallax.com
3. Narendra, K.S. and Mukhopadhyay, S., Adaptive Control Using Neural Networks and Approximate Models, IEEE Transactions on Neural Networks, Vol. 8, pp. 475–485, 1997.
4. Soloway, D. and Haley, P.J., Neural Generalized Predictive Control, Proceedings of the 1996 IEEE International Symposium on Intelligent Control, pp. 277–281, 1996.
5. Basic Stamp Handbook, Parallax, www.rambal.cl
6. Hilera J. M., Redes Neuronales Artificiales, 2nd. Edition, Ed.Ra-Ma, Madrid, Spain, 2002.
7. D.Dubois and H.Prade, Fuzzy sets and systems, 3rd Edition, Ed.Public Press, USA, 2003.
8. Kosko, B., Neural Networks and Fuzzy Systems, 4th Edition, Ed.Prentice-Hall, 2003.

Fuzzy Proximal Support Vector Classification Via Generalized Eigenvalues

Jayadeva[1], Reshma Khemchandani[2], and Suresh Chandra[2]

[1] Department of Electrical Engineering
[2] Department of Mathematics,
Indian Institute of Technology Delhi,
Hauz Khas, New Delhi 110 016, India
jayadeva@ee.iitd.ernet.in, reshmaiitd@gmail.com,
chandras@maths.iitd.ernet.in

Abstract. In this paper, we propose a fuzzy extension to proximal support vector classification via generalized eigenvalues. Here, a fuzzy membership value is assigned to each pattern, and points are classified by assigning them to the nearest of two non parallel planes that are close to their respective classes. The algorithm is simple as the solution requires solving a generalized eigenvalue problem as compared to SVMs, where the classifier is obtained by solving a quadratic programming problem. The approach can be used to obtain an improved classification when one has an estimate of the fuzziness of samples in either class.

Keywords: Support vector machines, fuzzy data classification, machine learning, generalized eigenvalue problem, proximal classifier.

1 Introduction

Recently, Mangsarian and Wild [1] proposed a non-parallel plane classifier for two category data classification problem. The classifier obtained from the non parallel planes comprises of the eigenvectors corresponding to smallest eigenvalue of two generalized eigenvalue problems which are close to data points of one class and is far from the data points of other class, respectively, whereas in the case of the proximal support vector machine classifier (PSVM) [2], two parallel planes are generated such that each plane is closest to one of the two data sets to be classified, and the planes are as far apart as possible.

Real data sets are usually corrupted with noise and are associated with a fuzziness in the membership of data points to a class. Data samples which are noisy are less informative. A classifier which is able to utilize information regarding this fuzziness can improve its performance and lessen the effect of outliers. Traditional SVM based classifiers lack such a mechanism [3].

In this paper, we propose a fuzzy extension of PSVM via generalized eigenvalues (GEPSVM), by incorporating a membership matrix S that indicates the fuzzy membership of data points (a number between 0 and 1) to the two classes. Experimental results show that the performance of Fuzzy GEPSVM (FGEPSVM) compares favourably with that of GEPSVM, PSVM, and SVM.

The paper is organized as follows: Section 2 briefly dwells on the theory of the multiplane linear kernel classifier for binary data classification. Section 3 introduces Fuzzy Proximal Support Vector Machines via Generalized Eigenvalues (FGEPSVM). Experimental results of the algorithm established in the paper are presented in Section 4. Section 5 contains concluding remarks.

2 The Multi-plane Linear Kernel Classifier

Let the data set consisting of m points in a n-dimensional space be represented by a $m \times n$ pattern matrix A. In this case data points belonging to classes 1 and -1 are represented by $A(+)$ and $A(-)$, respectively. The classifier yields two non parallel planes

$$x^T w_1 - \gamma_1 = 0 \text{ and } x^T w_2 - \gamma_2 = 0, \tag{1}$$

the idea being to minimize the Euclidean distance of the planes from the data points of classes 1 and -1, respectively. This leads to the following optimization problem

$$\min_{(w,\gamma) \neq 0} \left[||A(+)w - e\gamma||^2 / \left\| \begin{bmatrix} w \\ \gamma \end{bmatrix} \right\|^2 \right] / \left[||[A(-)w - e\gamma||^2 / \left\| \begin{bmatrix} w \\ \gamma \end{bmatrix} \right\|^2 \right] \tag{2}$$

where e is a vector of ones. It is implicitly assumed that $(w,\gamma) \neq 0 \Rightarrow A(-)w - e\gamma \neq 0$. The optimization problem (2) can be regularized by introducing a Tikhonov regularization term [4] $\delta(>0)$ to give the following Rayleigh Quotient

$$\min_{z \neq 0} z^T G z \Big/ z^T H z, \tag{3}$$

where G and H are symmetric matrices in $\mathbf{R}^{(n+1) \times (n+1)}$ defined as: $G := [A(+) \ -e]^T * [A(+) \ -e] + \delta * I$; $H := [A(-) \ -e]^T * [A(-) \ -e]$; is positive semi-definite and z is an augmented vector defined as $z := [w \ \gamma]^T$. Using well known properties of the Rayleigh Quotient [5], the solution of (3) is obtained by solving the generalized eigenvalue problem

$$Gz = \mu H z, z \neq 0. \tag{4}$$

where μ is a vector of generalized eigenvalues.

If z_1 denotes the eigenvector corresponding to the smallest eigenvalue (μ_1) (4), then $z_1 = [w_1 \ \gamma_1]^T$ determines the plane $x^T w_1 - \gamma_1 = 0$, which is closest to all data points of class 1. Using an entirely similar argument we define a minimization problem analogous to (2) by interchanging the roles of $A(+)$ and $A(-)$, for determining eigenvector z_2 corresponds to the smallest eigenvalue. The eigenvector z_2 will yield the plane $x^T w_2 - \gamma_2 = 0$, which is closest to all data points of class -1, respectively.

3 Fuzzy Proximal Support Vector Classification Via Generalized Eigenvalues

The FGEPSVMs is obtained by solving the optimization problem

$$\min_{(w,\gamma)\neq 0} \left[||[S_1 * A(+)]w - e\gamma||^2 \Big/ \left\|\begin{bmatrix} w \\ \gamma \end{bmatrix}\right\|^2 \right] \Big/ \left[||[S_2 * A(-)]w - e\gamma||^2 \Big/ \left\|\begin{bmatrix} w \\ \gamma \end{bmatrix}\right\|^2 \right] \tag{5}$$

where $||\cdot||$ denotes the Euclidean distance, and S_1 and S_2 are the matrices of membership values of two classes, respectively.

We observe from (5) that the term in the numerator (denominator) is the weighted euclidean distance in the input space of points in the class 1 (class -1) to the plane $x^T w - \gamma = 0$. On simplification, and working on the lines of [1] we obtain the following generalized eigenvalue problem.

$$Kz = \mu Lz, z \neq 0. \tag{6}$$

where the symmetric matrices K and L in $\mathbf{R}^{(n+1)\times(n+1)}$ are defined as
$K := [S_1 * A(+) \quad - e]^T * [S_1 * A(+) \quad - e] + \delta * I;\quad L := [S_2 * A(-) \quad - e]^T * [S_2 * A(-) \quad - e] \ ; z = [w \ \gamma]^T$. By an entirely similar argument we define a minimization problem analogous to (5) for determining z_2 and hence (w_2, γ_2).

$$\min_{(w,\gamma)\neq 0} \left[||[S_2 * A(-)]w - e\gamma||^2 \Big/ \left\|\begin{bmatrix} w \\ \gamma \end{bmatrix}\right\|^2 \right] \Big/ \left[||[S_1 * A(+)]w - e\gamma||^2 \Big/ \left\|\begin{bmatrix} w \\ \gamma \end{bmatrix}\right\|^2 \right] \tag{7}$$

Solving (7) is equivalent to solving the following generalized eigenvalue problem

$$Pz = \mu Qz, z \neq 0. \tag{8}$$

where the symmetric matrices P and Q in $\mathbf{R}^{(n+1)\times(n+1)}$ are defined as
$P := [S_2 * A(-) \quad - e]^T * [S_2 * A(-) \quad - e] + \delta * I;\quad Q := [S_1 * A(+) \quad - e]^T * [S_1 * A(+) \quad - e] \ ; z = [w \ \gamma]^T$.

Hence the plane (1) gets characterized with the eigenvectors z_1, and z_2, corresponding to minimum eigenvalues of (6) and (8), respectively. A new data sample $x \in \mathbf{R}^n$ is assigned to a class depending on its proximity to the non-parallel planes corresponding to z_1 and z_2 i.e,

$$x^T w_r - \gamma_r = \min_{l=1,2} |x^T w_l - \gamma_l|. \tag{9}$$

4 Experimental Results

To demonstrate the performance of our approach, we report results on publicly available datasets from the UCI Repository [7]. The classification methods were implemented using MATLAB 6.5 [6] running on a PC with an Intel P4 processor (2.4 MHz), and 512 MB RAM. These results are based on ten fold cross-validation approach. In our case, the optimal value of δ is obtained by using a tuning set comprising of 5% of the dataset.

Table 1. Test Set Classification Accuracy(%) using Linear kernel

Dataset	FGEPSVM (s_1, s_2)	GEPSVM	PSVM	SVM
Heart-c	85.13±04.99 (1,0.8)	84.80±05.21	84.48±05.11	82.87±06.64
Heart-statlog	84.44±05.93 (1,0.9)	83.70±06.67	82.59±07.04	81.48±10.64
Heart-h	81.61±10.26 (1,0.8)	78.85±15.83	84.36±05.94	83.39 ± 08.61
Pima-indians	73.04±03.50 (1,0.9)	72.13±03.95	56.56±02.97	71.36±04.83
Sonar	78.93±08.46 (1,0.9)	75.12±11.14	62.93±09.74	75.52±10.15

In particular, FGEPSVMs may prove valuable when one is willing to obtain an improved classification performance for one class even at the expense of the other. In order to understand the importance of the membership function values, we took a simple illustration in which all samples belonging to class 1 are assigned a membership value s_1, while all samples belonging to class -1 are assigned a membership value s_2 [8]. In general, there may be many ways to calculate fuzzy membership matrix S [8]. The experimental results in Table 1 demonstrate that FGEPSVM for data classification provides improved generalization ability in comparison with that of GEPSVM, PSVM and SVM on the UCI datasets.

5 Conclusion

In this paper, we have proposed a fuzzy extension of Proximal Support Vector Machines via Generalized Eigenvalues, which uses knowledge of the uncertainty associated with the membership of a data sample to a given class, to improve generalization.

References

1. Mangasarian, O.L., and Wild, E.W.: Multisurface Proximal Support Vector Classification via Generalized Eigenvalues. Data Mining Institute Technical Report. 04-03 June 2004.
2. Fung, G., and Mangasarian, O.L.: Proximal Support Vector Machines. Proc. KDD-2001 August 26-29, San Francisco (2001) 77-86.
3. Burges, C.: A Tutorial on Support Vector Machines for Pattern Recognition. Data Mining and Knowledge Discovery, **2** (1998).
4. Tikhonov, A.N., and Arsenin, V.Y.: Solution of Ill Posed Problems, John Wiley and Sons, New York, 1977.
5. Parlett, B.N.: The symmetric Eigen value Problem, SIAM, Philadelphia, PA, 1998.
6. http://www.mathworks.com
7. Blake, C.L, and Merz, C.J.: UCI Repository for Machine Learning database, Irvine, CA: University of California, Department of Information and Computer Sciences. On-line at http://www.ics.uci.edu/ mlearn/MLRepository.html
8. Jayadeva, Khemchandani, R. and Chandra. S.: Fast and Robust Learning Through Fuzzy Linear Proximal Support Vector Machines. Journal of Neurocomputing. **61**(2004) 401-411.

Segmentation of MR Images of the Human Brain Using Fuzzy Adaptive Radial Basis Function Neural Network

J.K. Sing[*], D.K. Basu, M. Nasipuri, and M. Kundu

Department of Computer Science & Engineering, Jadavpur University,
Kolkata 700 032, India
jksing@ieee.org

Abstract. A method for segmentation of magnetic resonance (MR) images of the human brain using a fuzzy adaptive radial basis function neural network (FARBF-NN) has been proposed. Since the quality of MR images always gets affected by intensity in-homogeneities (artifacts or noises), generated due to the non-uniformity of magnetic fields during the acquisition process, thereby making segmentation task more difficult. The outputs of the hidden layer neurons of the FARBF-NN have been modified using a fuzzy membership function to eliminate the effect of noises present in the input image. The proposed method has been tested both on simulated and real patient MR brain images for segmentation and found to be better than the k-means clustering algorithm, the fuzzy c-means (FCM) clustering algorithm, and the RBF neural network that uses k-means clustering algorithm to select the centers of the RBFs in the hidden layer, in most of the cases.

1 Introduction

Image segmentation is a technique, which partitions a given image into a set of meaningful non-overlapping sub-regions, which are uniform with respect to certain characteristics, such as distribution of gray level or texture. In most of the cases, noises creep into the sampled images during the acquisition of medical images, thereby, making segmentation a difficult task. A number of methodologies, based on histogram analysis, region growing, edge detection, and pixel classification, have been proposed in the past. A survey of different segmentation techniques for MR images by Clarke *et al.* [1] gives many techniques for image processing.

In this work, to reduce the influence of noises, the output of each hidden layer neuron has been fuzzified (diluted / concentrated) by a fuzzy membership function. This has been done for each input feature vector depending on its position from the center of a radial basis function.

2 Design of the FARBF Neural Network

The architecture of an RBF-NN is shown in Fig.1. The role of an RBF neural network can be viewed as a function, which maps a feature vector x_i from p-dimensional feature space to c-dimensional decision space as z_j.

---

[*] Corresponding author.

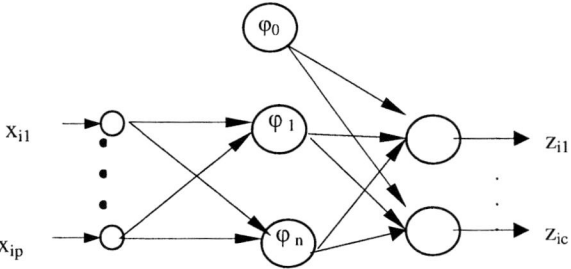

Fig. 1. Standard Radial Basis Function (RBF) Neural Network

The output of the jth hidden layer neuron for i^{th} input pattern x_i is generated by a Gaussian radial-basis function, which is defined as follows:

$$\varphi_j(x_i) = \exp\left(-\frac{\|x_i - t_j\|^2}{2\sigma_j^2}\right), j = 1, 2, \ldots, n; i = 1, 2, \ldots, N \quad (1)$$

where t_j and σ_j are the center and the width of the receptive field, respectively of the jth neuron of the hidden layer, n and N are the total number of hidden layer neurons and total number of input patterns, respectively.

To make the RBF-NN fuzzy adaptive, $\varphi_j(x_i)$ has been diluted (increased) or concentrated (decreased) by a fuzzy membership function, which is defined as follows:

If $(\varphi_j(x_i)) < 0.5$ then

$$y_j(x_i) = (\varphi_j(x_i))^r \quad (2)$$

else

$$y_j(x_i) = (\varphi_j(x_i))^{1/r} \quad (3)$$

where r (r>0) defines the degree of fuzziness imposed on the output of hidden layer neurons and its value has been selected experimentally for which minimum mean square error (MSE) is achieved in the output layer during the training period. Therefore, the output of the kth output layer neuron has been defined as follows:

$$z_{ik} = \sum_{j=1}^{n} \left[y_j(x_i) w_{kj} + b_k w_k\right], k = 1, 2, \ldots, c, i = 1, 2, \ldots, N \quad (4)$$

where w_{kj} is the weight between the jth neuron of the hidden layer and the kth neuron of the output layer, b_k and w_k are unit positive bias and weight to the kth output neuron from the bias neuron, respectively.

The centers of the different RBFs (hidden layer neurons) are selected by using a modified version of the k-means algorithm [2]. The width σ_j (j=1, 2, ..., n) of the receptive field of the hidden layer neuron is defined as follows:

$$\sigma_j = \beta \times \min \|t_j - t_i\|, i, j = 1, 2, \ldots, n \text{ and } i \neq j \quad (5)$$

where β (>1) is a constant and its value has been determined experimentally.

The weights of the links that connect hidden layer with output layer are estimated by using least mean square (LMS) algorithm.

3 Results and Discussion

Performances of the proposed FARBF-NN, the RBF neural network using k-means algorithm, and the two frequently used methods for segmentation i.e., the k-means and the FCM have been compared on simulated and real patient MR images of the human brain. Simulated MR images of human brain are obtained from the McConnel Brain Imaging Centre of the Montreal Neurological Institute, McGill University. The MR images are segmented into four regions, corresponding to background and three tissue classes namely, gray matter (GM), white matter (WM), and cerebrospinal fluid (CSF). The proposed FARBF-NN uses seven hidden layer neurons to segment MR images. The learning rate parameter (η) is taken as 0.002 in all the experiments.

3.1 Quantitative Evaluation of Performance on Simulated Data

Table 1 summarizes the error measures obtained by applying the FCM, k-means, RBF neural network using k-means algorithm, and the proposed FARBF-NN on a simulated T1-weighted image data, which is shown in Fig. 2(a). This error measure is the misclassification rate (MCR), which is defined as the number of pixels misclassified by the algorithm divided by the total number of pixels in the image.

Table 1. Error measure (%) for T1-weighted simulated MR brain image

Method	CSF	WM	GM	Average error
FCM	2.897	6.148	2.404	3.816
k-means	2.891	6.160	2.320	3.790
RBF-NN +k-means	5.024	7.974	1.827	4.942
Proposed FARBF-NN	4.267	3.972	1.827	3.355

Table 2. Error measure (%) for T2-weighted simulated MR brain image

Method	CSF	WM	GM	Average error
FCM	2.362	7.962	2.338	4.221
k-means	2.320	7.890	2.350	4.186
RBF-NN + k-means	3.606	5.114	2.614	3.778
Proposed FARBF-NN	3.047	7.680	1.256	3.994

We have also compared the performances of the above four methods on simulated T2-weighted brain images. The error measures obtained by the four methods are shown in table 2.

3.2 Visual Comparison of Performance

Fig. 2 shows the segmentation results of the FARBF-NN, the RBF neural network using k-means algorithm, the k-means, and the FCM methods on a T1-weighted simulated normal MR brain image. It shows that the performance of the proposed method is better than its counterpart, which uses conventional k-means algorithm. Fig. 3

shows the segmentation results by the above four methods on a T2-weighted real patient MR brain image. The noises have been removed from WM region of Fig. 3(a) by the proposed method, as shown in Fig. 3(b), while other methods fail to remove these noises.

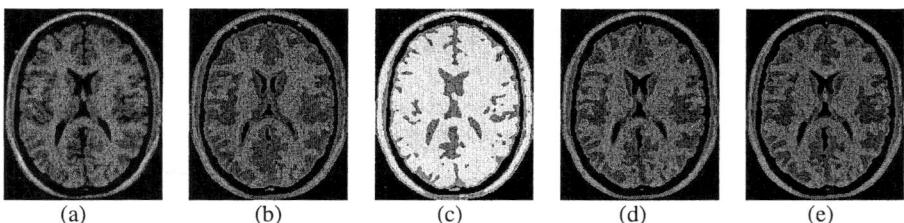

Fig. 2. Comparison of segmentation results. (a) The T1-weighted simulated MR image, and the (b), (c), (d), and (e) are the segmented images obtained by the proposed FARBF-NN, RBF neural network using k-means algorithm, k-means, and FCM, respectively.

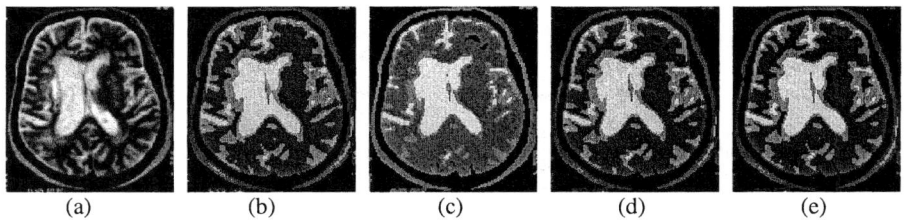

Fig. 3. Segmentation results. (a) The T2-weighted real patient MR brain image, and the (b), (c), (d), and (e) are the segmented images obtained by the proposed FARBF-NN, the RBF neural network using k-means algorithm, the k-means, and the FCM, respectively.

4 Conclusion

In this paper, an approach using a fuzzy adaptive RBF neural network has been proposed for MR brain image segmentation. The output of each hidden layer neuron has been fuzzified (diluted / concentrated) by a fuzzy membership function to reduce the effects of noises present in the MR image. The results of the segmentation have indicated its effectiveness in comparison to the other methods.

Acknowledgement

This work is partially supported by CMATER, SRUVM, and ADTUMI projects of the CSE Dept., Jadavpur University, Kolkata 700032. The authors are also thankful to Dr. P. K. Gharai and Dr. T. Dhibar of the Dept. of Neuroradiology, Bangur Institute of Neurology, Kolkata, India, for their invaluable discussion, suggestions and comments on the results of the segmentation of the MR brain images.

References

1. L. P. Clarke *et. al*: MRI Segmentation: Methods and applications, Magn. Reson. Imag., (1995) 343-368
2. J. K. Sing, D. K. Basu, M. Nasipuri and M. Kundu: Center Selection of RBF Neural Network Based on Modified K-Means Algorithm With Point Symmetry Distance Measure, Foundation of Computing and Decision Sciences, (2004) 247-266

Design of Two-Dimensional IIR Filters Using an Improved DE Algorithm

Swagatam Das[1] and Debangshu Dey[2]

[1] Dept. of Electronics and Telecommunication Engineering
[2] Dept. of Electrical Engineering,
Jadavpur University,
Kolkata-700032, India
swagatamdas19@yahoo.co.in

Abstract. The paper investigates a novel technique of designing 2-dimensional IIR digital filters using a modified version of Differential Evolution (DE) where the scalar factor used for weighing the difference vector is made to vary randomly. This approach makes the classical DE more stochastic and provides it with additional exploration capability over the search space. The task of the design has been reformulated as a constrained minimization problem and is solved by the convergence of the proposed algorithm. Numerical example has been provided in support of the theoretical results. The paper also attempts to demonstrate the superiority of the proposed design method by comparing with a few previous design methods based on GA and neural networks.

1 Introduction

Two-dimensional zero-phase digital filters find an extensive application in the domain of digital image processing, biomedical imaging and digital mammography, X-rays image enhancement, seismic data processing etc [1]-[3]. The most popular design methods for 2-D IIR filters are either based on an appropriate transformation of 1D filter [2], [3]; or based on appropriate optimization techniques. However one of the major problems underlying the design task is to satisfy the stability criterion for the filter transfer function. Although researchers have attempted to tackle the stability problem in a number of ways, most of these efforts resulted into a filter usually having very small stability margin with hardly any practical importance [4]. In this work the design task of 2D recursive filter has been formulated as a constrained optimization problem and an improved DE scheme is applied to solve the same. Numerical results show that [7] the DE-RANDSF (DE with Random Scale Factor) algorithm used here yields a better approximation of the transfer function as compared to works presented in [4] and [5].The proposed technique also satisfies the stability criterion which has been presented as constraints to the minimization problem. Compared to GA based method, the proposed algorithm is easy to implement and takes lesser number of error function evaluations to find an acceptable solution.

2 Problem Formulation

Let the general prototype 2-D transfer function for the digital filter be

$$H(z_1, z_2) = H_0 \frac{\sum_{i=0}^{N} \sum_{j=0}^{N} p_{ij} z_1^i z_2^j}{\prod_{k=1}^{N}(1 + q_k z_1 + r_k z_2 + s_k z_1 \cdot z_2)} \quad (1)$$

with $P_{00} = 1$ always. Also let us assume that the user specified amplitude response of the filter to be designed is M_d which is obviously a function of digital frequencies ω_1 and ω_2, ($\omega_1, \omega_2 \in [0, \pi]$). Now the main design problem is to determine the coefficients in the numerator and denominator of (1) in such a fashion that $H(Z_1 = e^{j\omega_1}, Z_2 = e^{j\omega_2})$ follows the desired response $M_d(\omega_1, \omega_2)$ as closely as possible. Such approximation of the desired response can be achieved by minimizing,

$$J(p_{ij}, q_k, r_k, s_k, H_0) = \sum_{n_1=0}^{N_1} \sum_{n_2=0}^{N_2} [|M(\omega_1, \omega_2)| - M_d(\omega_1, \omega_2)]^b \quad (2)$$

where

$$M(\omega_1, \omega_2) = H(z_1, z_2) \Big|_{\substack{z_1 = e^{j\omega_1} \\ z_2 = e^{j\omega_2}}} \quad (3)$$

where

$$\omega_1 = (\pi/N_1) n_1;$$
$$\omega_2 = (\pi/N_2) n_2;$$

and b is an even positive integer (usually b = 2 or b = 4).

Here the prime objective is to reduce the difference between the desired and actual amplitude response of the filter at $N_1.N_2$ points. Since the denominator contains only first degree factors, we can assert the stability conditions following [1]-[3] as

$$|q_k + r_k| - 1 < s_k < 1 - |q_k - r_k|, \quad k = 1, 2 \ldots N \quad (4)$$

Thus the design of a 2-D recursive filter is equivalent to the following constrained minimization problem:

Minimize J

$$= \sum_{n_1=0}^{N_1} \sum_{n_2=0}^{N_2} [|M(\frac{\pi n_1}{N_1}, \frac{\pi n_2}{N_2})| - M_d(\frac{\pi n_1}{N_1}, \frac{\pi n_2}{N_2})]^b \quad (5)$$

subjected to the constraints imposed by (4).

In [4] the design problem has been tackled with neural networks and [5] attempts to solve it using GA. In the present work a better solution has been presented using a modified version of Differential Evolution (DE) algorithm.

3 A Brief Overview of Modified DE Algorithm

Classical DE [6] searches for a global optimum point in an N-dimensional hyperspace. It begins with a randomly initialized population of N-dimensional real-valued parameter vectors. Each vector forms a candidate solution to the multi-dimensional optimization problem. Unlike the conventional GA, the reproduction scheme in DE is maintained as follows. For each individual vector G_k^D belonging to generation D, randomly sample three other individuals G_i^D, G_j^D and G_m^D from the same generation (for distinct i, j, k and m), calculate the difference of the components (chromosomes) of G_i^D and G_o^d, scale it by a scalar R ($\in [0,1]$) and create a trial vector by adding the result to the chromosomes of G_k^D.

$$G_{k,n}^{D+1} = G_{m,n}^D + R.(G_{i,n}^D - G_{j,n}^D) \quad \text{if } rand_n(0,1) < CR$$
$$= G_{k,n}^D, \quad \text{otherwise.} \tag{6}$$

for the n-th component of each parameter vector.

CR ($\in [0,1]$) is the crossover constant. Parameters R and CR govern the convergence speed and robustness of DE. The trial solution is evaluated and replaces its parent G_k^D deterministically if its fitness is better. This alteration and selection procedure is also known as the 'DE/rand/1/bin' operator. There are also other frequently used DE operators, such as 'DE/rand/1/bin' and 'DE/best/2/exp', which we did not investigate in this study.

In the original DE the difference vector (G_i-G_j) is scaled by a constant factor 'R'. Usually the most popular choice for this control parameter in DE is in the range of (0.4, 1). However we set this scale factor to change in a random manner in the range (0.5, 1) by using the relation

$$R = 0.5*(1 + rand(0,1)) \tag{7}$$

where rand (0,1) is a uniformly distributed random number within the range (0,1). The mean value of the scale factor remains at 0.75. This allows for stochastic variation in the amplification of the difference vector and hence helps retain the population diversity as the search progresses. This new version of DE will be hereafter referred as DE-RANDSF ((DE with Random Scale Factor) algorithm.

4 Application of the Algorithm to the Design Problem

4.1 Converting the Problem to a Soluble Form

Without loss of generality let us assume N = 2 in equation (1). Now if we substitute Z_1 and Z_2 as in (3), then M (ω_1, ω_2) can be expressed in a compact form as,

$$M(\omega_1, \omega_2) = H_0 \frac{N_R - jN_I}{(D_{1R} - jD_{1I}).(D_{2R} - jD_{2I})} \tag{8}$$

where

$$N_R = p_{00} + p_{01}f_{01} + p_{02}f_{02} + p_{10}f_{10} + p_{20}f_{20} + p_{11}f_{11} + p_{12}f_{12} + p_{21}f_{21} + p_{22}f_{22}$$
$$N_I = p_{00} + p_{01}g_{01} + p_{02}g_{02} + p_{10}g_{10} + p_{20}g_{20} + p_{11}g_{11} + p_{12}g_{12} + p_{21}g_{21} + p_{22}g_{22}$$
$$D_{1R} = 1 + q_1 f_{10} + r_1 f_{01} + s_1 f_{11}$$
$$D_{1I} = 1 + q_1 g_{10} + r_1 g_{01} + s_1 g_{11} \quad (9a)$$
$$D_{2R} = 1 + q_2 f_{10} + r_2 f_{01} + s_2 f_{11}$$
$$D_{2I} = 1 + q_2 g_{10} + r_2 g_{01} + s_2 g_{11}$$

with $f_{xy} = \cos(x\omega_1 + y\omega_2)$

$$g_{xy} = \sin(x\omega_1 + y\omega_2) \quad (9b)$$

and $x, y = 0, 1, 2$

Hence the actual magnitude may be written as,

$$|M(\omega_1, \omega_2)| = H_0 \sqrt{\frac{(N_R^2 + N_I^2)}{(D_{1R}^2 + D_{1I}^2)(D_{2R}^2 + D_{2I}^2)}} \quad (10)$$

Now let us consider a specific example of the design problem where the user specification for the desired circular symmetric low pass filter response may be given as,

$$M_d(\omega_1, \omega_2) = 1, \quad \text{if } \sqrt{\omega_1^2 + \omega_2^2} \leq 0.04\pi$$
$$= 0.5, \quad \text{if } 0.04\pi \leq \sqrt{\omega_1^2 + \omega_2^2} \leq 0.08\pi$$
$$= 0, \quad \text{otherwise.} \quad (11)$$

Also from (4) the constraints may be put in a continuously differentiable form as,

$$-(1+s_k) < (q_k + r_k) < (1+s_k)$$
$$-(1-s_k) < (q_k - r_k) < (1-s_k)$$
$$(1+s_k) > 0 \quad (12)$$
$$(1-s_k) > 0$$

Now in this example problem we select $b = 2$, $N_1 = 50$ and $N_2 = 50$. Hence finally the constrained minimization task becomes,

Minimize J

$$= \sum_{n_1=0}^{50} \sum_{n_2=0}^{50} [|M(\frac{\pi n_1}{50}, \frac{\pi n_2}{50})| - M_d(\frac{\pi n_1}{50}, \frac{\pi n_2}{50})]^2 \quad (13)$$

subject to constraints imposed by (15) with $k = 1, 2$.

4.2 Solution Vectors Representation and Initialization for DE

In order to apply the DE-RANDSF algorithm to the problem formulated in (13) we need to represent each trial solution as a point in multi dimensional search space. Since p_{00} is always set to 1 in (1) the dimensionality of the present problem is 14 and each particle has 14 positional coordinates represented by the vector,

$$X = (p_{01}, p_{02}, p_{10}, p_{11}, p_{12}, p_{20}, p_{21}, p_{22}, q_1, q_2, r_1, r_2, s_1, s_2, H_0)^T \quad (14)$$

Each component of a trial solution vector was initialized with a random floating point number whose absolute value was kept below 3.00.

4.3 Handling the Constraints

The constraint-handling method is following the criteria: a) any feasible solution is preferred to any infeasible solution; b) between two feasible solutions, the one having better objective function value is preferred; c) between two infeasible solutions, the one having smaller constraint violation is preferred. To tackle the constraints presented in (12) we start with a population of around 200 trial vectors with randomly initiated positions over the search space. Out of these, 40 vectors were selected, components of which obey the constraints imposed by (12). If more than 40 vectors were initially found to obey the constraints, obviously the selection will take into account the initial fitness value of these particles. During the run of the program, an offspring vector replaces its parent in the next generation only if besides yielding a better fitness value as compared to that of the parent it also satisfies the constraints. If the offspring vector is better than its parent but violates any of the constraints, the parent vector is retained in the next generation.

4.4 GA Parameter Setup

To illustrate the superiority of the proposed technique we also minimize the same fitness function given in (13) using a simple genetic algorithm as proposed in [5]. Chromosomes have the same parameters as shown in (15) and are initialized randomly. Each parameter or gene in a chromosome is converted into a 32 bit binary number. In each iteration, the chromosomes are subjected to usual crossover and mutation [6] operations and from the new population comprising parents and children, the members failing to satisfy the constraints given in (15) are deleted. From the remaining members, candidates for the next generation are selected according to their fitness value.

5 Results of the Simulation and Comparison

Fig. 1(a) below shows the desired amplitude response of the filter to be designed. Now in the present work 50 trials of the DE-RANDSF algorithm was run and the maximum permissible error limit was achieved within 400 iterations on average.

We took the average value of the best particle positions found in these 50 trials. The vector X found in this way is given by,

$X = [0.1596, 1.2154, 0.4302, 0.5630, -0.3282, 0.2889, -2.0931, 1.7801, -0.9366,$
$-0.9833, -0.8653, -0.8115, 0.8551, 0.8214, 0.0005]^T$

The corresponding amplitude response is presented in Fig. 1(b). For the purpose of comparison we also present the amplitude response obtained by using the methods suggested in [4] and [5] in Fig. 1(c) and Fig. 1(d) respectively. A closer look at these figures reveals that the DE-RANDSF algorithm used by us yields a better

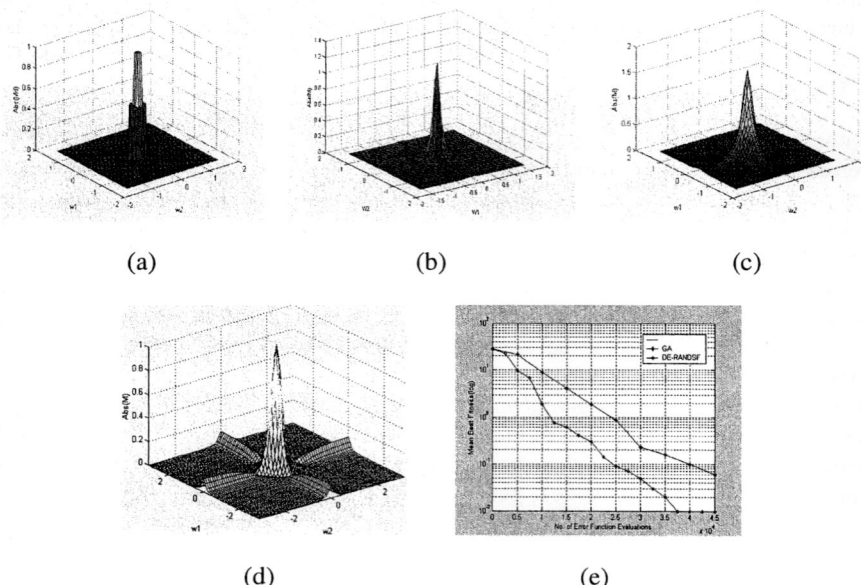

Fig. 1. (a) Desired amplitude response $|M_d (\omega_1, \omega_2)|$ of the 2-D filter (b) Amplitude response $|M (\omega_1, \omega_2)|$ of the 2-D filter using DE-RANDSF (c) Amplitude response $|M (\omega_1, \omega_2)|$ of the 2-D filter using GA (d) Amplitude response $|M (\omega_1, \omega_2)|$ of the 2-D filter using the method in [5] (e) Performance Comparison for GA and DE-RANDSF algorithms

approximation of the desired response as compared to works presented in [4] or [5] and takes considerably smaller time for convergence. The ripple in the stop-band of Fig. 1(b) is much lesser as compared to Fig. 1(c) and Fig. 1(d).

6 Conclusion

In this work one of a newly proposed modified DE algorithm has been successfully applied to a practical optimization problem concerning the design of 2-D zero phase recursive filters. The filter thus obtained has a reasonably good stability margin. Our method also leads to a simpler filter since, in practice, we have to realize a factorable denominator and in particular of first-order filters. Compared to methods suggested in [4] and [5] the algorithm used here yields a much better design in a considerably small convergence time.

References

1. Kaczorek, T.: Two-Dimensional Linear Systems. Berlin, Germany: Springer-Verlag (1985)
2. Tzafestas, S, G.: Ed., Multidimensional Systems, Techniques and Applications. New York: Marcel Dekker (1986)

3. Lu, W, S, Antoniou, A.: Two-Dimensional Digital Filters. NewYork: Marcel Dekker (1992)
4. Mladenov, V, Mastorakis, N.: Design of two-dimensional recursive filters by using neural networks, IEEE Trans. Neural Networks. Vol. 12. 585–590 (2001)
5. Mastorakis, N, Gonos, I, F, Swamy, M, N, S.: Design of two-dimensional recursive filters using genetic algorithms, IEEE Trans. Circuits and Systems. Vol. 50. 634–639 (2003)
6. Storn, R., Price, K.: Differential evolution – A Simple and Efficient Heuristic for Global Optimization over Continuous Spaces, Journal of Global Optimization, 11(4) (1997) 341–359.
7. Das, S., Konar, A., Chakraborty, U.K., Two improved differential evolution schemes for faster global search, to appear in the ACM-SIGEVO Proceedings of GECCO, Washington D.C., June 2005.

Systematically Evolving Configuration Parameters for Computational Intelligence Methods

Jason M. Proctor and Rosina Weber

College of Information Science & Technology, Drexel University
{jp338, rw37}@drexel.edu

Abstract. The configuration of a computational intelligence (CI) method is responsible for its intelligence (e.g. tolerance, flexibility) as well as its accuracy. In this paper, we investigate how to automatically improve the performance of a CI method by finding alternate configuration parameter values that produce more accurate results. We explore this by using a genetic algorithm (GA) to find suitable configurations for the CI methods in an integrated CI system, given several different input data sets. This paper describes the implementation and validation of our approach in the domain of software testing, but ultimately we believe it can be applied in many situations where a CI method must produce accurate results for a wide variety of problems.

1 Introduction

Computational intelligence (CI) methods exploit abilities such as tolerance for imprecision, uncertainty, robustness, and partial truth to achieve tractability [11]. Although there is no consensus on the definition of CI, systems that include evolutionary computing, fuzzy computing, and neurocomputing are commonly identified as CI [5, 7].

In order to support their abilities, CI methods are tailored in each application through their configuration. For example, artificial neural networks (ANN) use configuration parameters such as training accuracy and number of epochs, while genetic algorithms (GA) require the specification of a rate of mutation in each generation. These parameters, which are responsible for the flexibility and tolerance of CI methods, are also responsible for their accuracy. In practice, assigning values for these parameters typically relies on suggestions from the literature, which are then adjusted by trial and error. Sometimes, systems allow users to change these values, but usually without providing individualized recommendations. The result is that CI methods typically assume the same default configuration for all executions.

In order to ensure quality, we believe CI methods should incorporate systematic means to find configurations that can produce high accuracy, and thereby recommend an individualized configuration for each input data set. Our approach to systematically finding configurations for a given input set builds on prior tests of that input set. Given the limited availability of test results for multiple configurations as raw data for our analysis, we use a GA to evolutionarily generate and evaluate parameter configurations.

The contributions of this paper are associated with the following questions. First, can individualized configurations for different inputs improve the overall accuracy of a CI method? Second, is there a way to systematically find individualized configurations for inputs to improve accuracy? In the next section we discuss some background to these questions and describe our approach to finding configuration parameters for CI methods. After that, we evaluate these questions by using our approach, and finalize with conclusions and future work.

2 The Meta-level Genetic Algorithm (MGA)

2.1 Motivation and Background

The potential for a CI method with one fixed parameter configuration to have a lower accuracy than the same method using individualized configurations became a concern in the context of the CI-Tool. The CI-Tool is an integrated suite of CI methods (including ANN, GA, and Info-Fuzzy Networks) for generating test cases for software programs [3, 4, 6, 8]; it must be highly accurate in order to benefit users. The CI-Tool's ANN module is used to analyze the association between inputs and outputs of data-driven programs [8]. The ANN methodology includes construction, training, pruning, and rule-extraction, in order to build a mathematical representation of a target software program (called a testbed) and generate test cases based on that model. These test cases are given as input to the actual testbed program, and the ANN's predicted output for the test cases is compared to the real outcome. The success rate, the ratio of correct test cases to total test cases, represents how well the ANN models the testbed.

The ANN module in the CI-Tool has ten configuration parameters that can be set by the user. An exhaustive evaluation of these would require over fifteen billion processor-years. Clearly, a practical method for finding parameter configurations must be able to converge on a suitable set much faster than that; this is easier if the method can build on past performance. If an automated method for finding suitable configuration values can be developed, then we have the potential to learn more about complex problems and adapt prior solutions to solve them quickly and accurately [9].

In developing and testing the CI-Tool, it was discovered that changing the ANN's configuration parameter values had an apparent effect on accuracy for some testbeds. Detailed exploration of the strength and nature of the effect was hindered by the size of the problem space. Additional evidence of the different impact caused when changing parameter values for different testbeds is given in a study that validated the ANN task with different numbers of training records [2].

Over the last twenty years, many authors have explored many possible interconnections between genetic or evolutionary algorithms and ANNs [1, 10]. Our approach differs from most of these because it only acts indirectly on network weights, architecture, and learning rules, and because it is designed as a reusable component in an integrated CI system, as opposed to a part of the ANN module itself.

2.2 Developing the MGA

A genetic algorithm works by exploring the space of input values and evaluating the results to improve the quality of those results in the context of a target task. Because our GA's target task could be a GA, or any other CI method, we call it a Meta-level GA (MGA). The parameters for the target CI method become the variable space that the MGA explores. The accuracy in which the target CI method performs its original task becomes the reference of fitness for the MGA to evaluate configuration parameters in each improvement step.

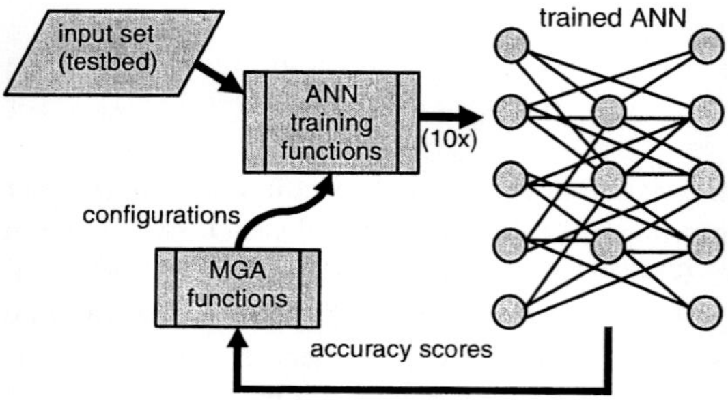

The key functions of the MGA are its fitness function, reproduction function, hybridization function, and mutation function. Most of these could be reused from the CI-Tool's existing GA module [4], but the implementation required a new fitness evaluation function to execute and interpret the results of the ANN. Figure 1 shows the cyclical interaction of MGA and ANN. Because the ANN's initial network weights are seeded randomly, we included a loop to execute each set of configuration parameters ten times for the same training data, and used the average success rate across those iterations as the success rate for that population member. We used the square of the average success rate for breeding selection.

Fig. 1. MGA and ANN

3 Evaluation

3.1 Methodology

In order to answer our research questions, we executed the MGA to systematically find suitable configurations for the ANN for four input sets. The MGA evolved parameter configurations by modifying the ANN's parameters and repeatedly testing it using consistent training data. Attempts to simultaneously vary all ten of the ANN's parameters in the same run caused the MGA not to converge in a reasonable time. Therefore, we studied the data of several test runs and consulted with the module's designers to identify the best candidates for exploration. The designers suggested three parameters: *training accuracy* was suggested to be the most important indicator of success, followed by *pruning accuracy* and *learning rate*.

The MGA was executed for each testbed with ten iterations per candidate ANN configuration, ten candidates per generation, and at least eight generations. Each iteration produced an accuracy score: the percentage of time the ANN's model matched the reality of the testbed. The candidate with the best average score was selected for verification. In two of the four cases, the best fitness score was in a generation other than the last. In each of these cases, this parameter configuration was present in the last generation, but its success rate was slightly lower due to the non-determinism resulting from random seeding of initial network weights in the ANN.

To verify the parameter values, the MGA created twenty more executions of the ANN: ten with the default configuration and ten with the MGA-recommended configuration. To decrease the chance of random error affecting the comparison of results, we used the same training data across all twenty of a testbed's verification runs.

3.2 Results

The results show that the MGA approach can significantly improve the average overall accuracy of the ANN task. Table 1 shows the resulting averages for configurations defined by ANN designers (default) and obtained with the MGA for each input, as well as ANOVA significance values. For testbeds 1 and 2, note that the new accuracy is significantly higher at $p < 0.01$, while for the others, the new accuracy is slightly lower, but the difference is not statistically significant. For the latter two, the MGA-recommended values were similar to the system defaults.

Table 1. Accuracy across four testbeds

	default	MGA	p
Testbed 1	82.2	92.7	0.001
Testbed 2	73.1	90.3	0.004
Testbed 3	90.6	86.8	0.086
Testbed 4	89.2	88.4	0.491
Overall Average	83.8	89.6	0.005

Averaged across all four testbeds, the resulting average accuracy increased from 83.8% to 89.6%; $F(1, 74) = 8.569$, $p = 0.005$. This result demonstrates that CI methods can improve their overall accuracy using individualized configurations for different testbeds. It also demonstrates that our proposed MGA can be used as a systematic means to find individual parameter configurations.

4 Conclusions and Future Work

4.1 Conclusions

Based on the results, we believe the methods typically employed by ANN designers produce results that leave room for improvement. With respect to our first question, we have shown that individualized configuration parameters can improve the overall accuracy of a CI method, making one blanket configuration not ideal for all possible input data sets.

In response to our second question, we conclude that there is a way to systematically find parameters to configure a CI method for a specific input to ensure high accuracy, and that our MGA approach is one way to it. We are not claiming this is the only way or the best way—our approach does not attempt to find optimal parameters, but a configuration that is at least as good as or better than defaults assigned for all inputs. In fact, as these parameters cannot be optimized, empirical evidence is required to suggest their quality. Our assertion is that one fixed configuration tends to lower overall accuracy, and that it is possible to do better.

It is well known that GAs may get stuck in local maxima, being also susceptible to their own configuration parameter values. Acknowledging this fact, we relied on the designer's experience to guide us through the choice of the ANN parameters we would initially vary. Additionally, we have the accuracy obtained with the default parameters, which although not being a baseline, serve as a valid reference for the GA learning.

4.2 Future Work

When using the MGA to find configurations for the CI-Tool's ANN, for practical reasons, we constrained the number of parameters to encourage a workable limit on the time the MGA takes to converge to a suitable configuration. Future work suggests a more flexible stopping strategy, allowing the MGA more time to try to find convergence. The high dimensionality of the problem of configuring the ANN should also be explored more thoroughly.

One possible future step is to determine classes of inputs that are amenable to different configurations so we can recommend these configurations when users submit an input to a CI method. This work suggests deeper methodological ramifications: configurable CI methods should have some kind of self-evaluation (either by MGA or some other method) built in, to improve the quality of systems whenever possible.

ANN is not the only CI method to which the MGA can be applied, although it may be necessary to use some fitness metric other than success rate. Ideally, an MGA could be applied to any CI methods which include their own fitness functions. Because the CI-Tool is an integrated suite of CI method modules, it is an ideal platform for exploring the potential of the MGA on the same set of input problems; this could lead to the ability to recommend one CI method over another.

Acknowledgements

The authors would like to thank Mr. Tom Barr for his guidance in extending the CI-Tool, and Drs. Mark Last and Abraham Kandel for their suggestions on working with the ANN. This work is supported in part by the National Institute for Systems Test and Productivity at USF under the USA Space and Naval Warfare Systems Command grant no. N00039-02-C-3244, for 2130 032 L0, 2002.

References

[1] Abraham, A. and Nath, B., "Hybrid Heuristics for Optimal Design of Neural Nets," in *Developments in Soft Computing: Proceedings of the Third International Conference on Recent Advances in Soft Computing*, R. John and R. Birkenhead, Eds. Berlin: Springer Verlag, 2000, pp. 15–22.

[2] Agarwal, D., "A Comparative Study of Artificial Neural Networks and Info Fuzzy Networks on Their Use in Software Testing," in *Computer Science & Engineering*. Tampa FL: University of South Florida, 2004.

[3] Barr, T., "Architectural Overview of the Computational Intelligence Testing Tool," in *Proceedings of the Eighth IEEE International Symposium on High Assurance Systems Engineering*. Los Alamitos CA: IEEE Computer Society, 2004, pp. 269–270.

[4] Berndt, D., Fisher, J., Johnson, L., Pinglikar, J., and Watkins, A., "Breeding Software Test Cases with Genetic Algorithms," in *Proceedings of the 36th Hawaii International Conference on System Sciences (HICSS '03)*, R. A. Sprague, Jr., Ed. Los Alamitos CA: IEEE Computer Society, 2002.

[5] Bezdek, J. C., "Computational Intelligence Defined - by Everyone!," in *Computational Intelligence: Soft Computing and Fuzzy-Neuro Integration with Applications*, O. Kaynak, L. A. Zadeh, B. Türksen, and I. J. Rudas, Eds. Berlin: Springer Verlag, 1998, pp. 10–37.

[6] Last, M., Friedman, M., and Kandel, A., "The Data Mining Approach to Automated Software Testing," in *Proceedings of the Ninth ACM SIGKDD International Conference on Knowledge Discovery and Data Mining*. New York NY: ACM Press, 2003, pp. 388–396.

[7] Pedrycz, W., "Computational Intelligence As an Emerging Paradigm of Software Engineering," in *Proceedings of the 14th International Conference on Software Engineering and Knowledge Engineering*. New York: ACM Press, 2002, pp. 7–14.

[8] Saraph, P., Last, M., and Kandel, A., "Test Set Generation and Reduction with Artificial Neural Networks," in *Artificial Intelligence Methods in Software Testing*, M. Last, A. Kandel, and H. Bunke, Eds.: World Scientific, 2004.

[9] Weber, R., Proctor, J. M., Waldstein, I., and Kriete, A., "CBR for Modeling Complex Systems," in *Proceedings of the Sixth International Conference on Case-Based Reasoning (ICCBR 2005); LNCS 3620*, H. Muñoz-Avila and F. Ricci, Eds. Berlin: Springer (in press), 2005, pp. 625–639.

[10] Yao, X., "Evolving Artificial Neural Networks," *Proceedings of the IEEE*, vol. 87, pp. 1423–1447, 1999.

[11] Zadeh, L. A., "Roles of Soft Computing and Fuzzy Logic in the Conception, Design and Deployment of Information/Intelligent systems," in *Computational Intelligence: Soft Computing and Fuzzy-Neuro Integration with Applications*, O. Kaynak, L. A. Zadeh, B. Türksen, and I. J. Rudas, Eds. Berlin: Springer Verlag, 1998, pp. 1–9.

A Split-Based Method for Polygonal Approximation of Shape Curves

R. Dinesh, Santhosh S. Damle, and D.S. Guru

Department of Studies in Computer Science, University of Mysore,
Manasagangotri, Mysore – 570 006, India
{dinesh_r21, emailssd}@yahoo.com,
guruds@lycos.com

Abstract. A new split-approach based method for approximating a boundary curve by a polygon is proposed in this paper. The proposed method recursively splits boundary curve into smaller segment with the help of small eigenvalue of covariance matrix of the boundary curve. Set of boundary points at which boundary curve is split into smaller segments are considered as vertices of the approximating polygon. Experimental results show that the proposed method is robust and efficient.

Keywords: Polygonal approximation, Split approach, Eigenvalue, Integral square error, Compression ratio.

1 Introduction

Polygonal approximation is a simple and convenient method for shape curve representation. It offers advantages like simplicity of computation, coding efficiency, good preservation of local properties and reduction in complexity while extracting features. Moreover it offers simpler representation when compared to higher order splines and functional representation.

Several techniques have been proposed for approximating a given boundary curve by a polygon. These schemes can be broadly classified into three classes; (1) Merge-based approaches, (2) Split-based approaches and (3) Split-and-merge based approaches (Pikaz and Dinstein, 1995). Merge approaches are based on linear scanning of digital curve, where, at each point a decision is made whether to merge the point with the current straight line or to draw a new line by treating the previous point as a vertex. Split-approaches are based on recursive partitioning of a curve at points, which are farthest from a given chord connecting two points on the boundary curve. Whereas Split-and-merge based approaches make use of both merge-approach and split-approach for polygonal approximation.

Ray and Ray (1992) proposed a k-cosine based algorithm for polygonal approximation of shape curves. This method makes use of k-cosine for determination of asymmetric region of support and identifies dominant points on the boundary, which are considered as the vertices of approximating polygon. Though the method produces fairly good approximation, it is computationally inefficient as it involves huge trigonometric calculations. Wang et al., (1995) proposed a computationally efficient method, which uses bending value to detect corner points on a curve. However, the method fails to detect sharp corner points, which results in poor approximation. A method proposed by Pikaz and Dinstein (1995) for polygonal approximation builds a heap data structure with the contour points and recursively approximates the curve. Nevertheless the method requires two error criteria to be chosen by the user. Tsai et al., (1999) proposed a method for detection of corner points based on small eigenvalue. The result of this method is very sensitive to the input parameter and in fact it is very difficult to choose a parameter, which effectively works for all kinds of shapes. Methods based on dynamic programming (Perez and Vidal (1994), Marc Salotti (2002) Kolesnikov and Franti(2003)) were also proposed for approximating a boundary curve by a polygon. The main drawback of the methods based on dynamic programming is that, they are computationally very expensive as they include exhaustive searching while identifying the vertices of the approximating polygon and hence they are of little use in real pragmatic applications. Some other interesting workds could be Ray and Ray (1995), Zhang and Guo (2001), Marji and Siy (2003) and Guru and Dinesh (2004).

From the above discussion it is clear that the existing schemes for approximating a shape by a polygon exhibit some shortcomings. The methods that are effective are not computationally efficient and the methods that are computationally efficient suffer from poor approximation. In view of this, in this paper, a successful attempt is made to device a scheme for polygonal approximation. The proposed approach in addition to being computationally efficient, produce acceptable quality results. The proposed method is based on split-approach, it splits the boundary recursively at points which would act as vertices of approximating polygon. Small eigenvalue of covariance matrix of the boundary segment is used as stopping criterion.

2 Proposed Method

The proposed method uses Split-approach to detect vertices of a polygon approximating a boundary curve. Boundary curve is recursively split into smaller segments. During each split, a decision is taken as to go for further splitting or not and the decision is based on the small eigenvalue (λ) of covariance matrix of boundary points. The points at which the boundary curve is split into smaller segments are considered as the vertices of the approximating polygon.

For a set of points $S = \{P_{i=}(x_i, y_i) \mid i=1,2,\ldots,n\}$ small eigenvalue λ is computed as:

$$\lambda = \tfrac{1}{2}\left[C_{11} + C_{22} - \sqrt{(C_{11} - C_{22})^2 + 4C_{12}^2}\right]$$

where, $\begin{bmatrix} C_{11} & C_{12} \\ C_{21} & C_{22} \end{bmatrix}$

is the covariance matrix of S, and the coefficients C_{11}, C_{12}, C_{21} and C_{22} are calculated as below:

$$C_{11} = \frac{1}{n}\sum_{i=1\ldots n} x_i^2 - c_x^2$$

$$C_{12} = C_{21} = \frac{1}{n}\sum_{i=1\ldots n} x_i \cdot y_i - c_x \cdot c_y$$

$$C_{22} = \frac{1}{n}\sum_{i=1\ldots n} x_i^2 - c_x^2$$

Here, $c_x = \frac{1}{n}\sum_{i=1\ldots n} x_i$ and $c_y = \frac{1}{n}\sum_{i=1\ldots n} y_i$ are the respective mean values of the x and y coordinates of the points in S.

Theoretically straight lines have associated small eigenvalue (λ) equal to zero and digital lines have their λ value closer to zero. Proposed method uses this statistical property for determining whether a boundary segment needs further splitting or not. If the boundary segment is approximately a straight line then it does not require further splitting.

Let B be a closed boundary with n points, i.e., B = {P_i = (x_i, y_i), i = 1,2,3...,n}, where points P_i and P_{i+1} (modulo n) as neighbors.

The proposed method, initially identifies two farthest points P_q and P_r on the boundary curve B. This splits the boundary curve into two segments $S_{q,r}$ = {P_k| k = q to r (modulo n)} and $S_{r,q}$ = {P_k| k = r to q (modulo n)}. Both the segments are subjected as input to a recursive procedure one by one to locate the vertices of the approximating polygon. We specifically choose farthest points on the boundary curve for initial splitting to make the procedure invariant to starting point and generally two such farthest points are corner points.

Recursive procedure takes a segment $S_{x,x+y}$ at a time for processing. First it marks both end points P_x and P_{x+y} as vertices of approximating polygon. Small eigenvalue for the segment is calculated; if the computed small eigenvalue exceeds predefined threshold value λ_t, then the segment needs further splitting, as the segment is not a straight line. Otherwise the segment does not require further processing, because the segment is roughly a straight line. To determine the split point P_s between P_x and P_{x+y} the procedure calculates distances from each point on the segment to the chord joining P_x and P_{x+y}. Point P_s on the segment, which has a maximum distance to the chord joining P_x and P_{x+y}, is selected as the splitting point. Now the procedure has ended up with two curve segments $S_{x,s}$ and $S_{s,x+y}$, which would be processed by the same procedure one after the other. When this procedure ends, a set of segments are obtained, none of which have their λ value exceeding the threshold value λ_t. End points of these segments are considered as the vertices of approximating polygon, and polygonal approximation of the shape curve is obtained by joining successive vertices by a straight line. The proposed method ensures good approximation as boundary points between any pair of successive vertices form a straight line.

Optional post processing stage is also proposed in this work to further reduce error to improve the compression ratio. Let us assume that m is the number of vertices obtained by the above split procedure i.e., V_i, i = 1 to m. Square Error between pair of points j and k are denoted as $E_{j,k}$.

Following are the optional post processing rules suggested:

Rule 1: *Rule to reduce overall error*
Some of the candidate vertices obtained by split procedure may not be the exact vertices. In such cases, exact vertex would be in the vicinity of obtained vertex. Overall error would reduce, if exact vertices are identified and vertices obtained by split procedure are replaced by them. Procedure for identification of exact vertices is explained as follows:

Let E_i be sum of square errors between segments (V_i, V_{i+1}) and (V_i, V_{i-1}). Shift the vertex V_i to its neighboring points P_j ($j = -2..+2$) and calculate error E_j in each case. Select the point P_j as actual vertex for which the computed error E_j ($j = -2..+2$) is least. This reduces the error between successive vertices and thus overall error due to approximation is also reduced, and hence approximation is improved.

Rule 2: *Rule to improve compression ratio*
If there are any V_is on straight line or on a curve segment with negligible curvature formed by its neighboring vertices V_{i-1} and V_{i+1} (modulo m) such point can be eliminated. For each set of vertices V_{i-1}, V_i, V_{i+1}, calculate the distance between V_i and the chord joining V_{i-1} and V_{i+1}. If this distance is less than a predefined threshold D_t, then we recommend it to be eliminated. So the number of vertices m is reduced to m-1. This process is an iterative procedure, each iteration works for all the vertices obtained from split procedure or from previous iteration. Iterative procedure is terminated when no vertex is eliminated during an iterative loop. This rule helps us in improving the compression ratio keeping the error unchanged.

Therefore, algorithm for the proposed method of approximating a given shape by a polygon is as trivial as follows.

Algorithm: *Polygon approximation.*
Input: *An object / shape.*
Output: *Corresponding polygonal approximation of the input object/shape.*
Method:
1. *Extract boundary (B) of input image.*
2. *Select two farthest points on the image boundary; let them be P_i and P_j.*
3. *Recursively split segments (P_{i+1}, P_j) and (P_{j+1}, P_i) as explained above.*
4. *Apply optional post-processing rules to further improve the quality of approximation.*

Algorithm ends.

3 Experiments

In order to establish the superiority of the proposed algorithm several experiments were conducted on various standard shapes/boundaries, which also included shapes considered by other researchers. Out of various shapes considered for experimentation, a few shapes and the obtained results are given in Table 1. Through out the experimentation, values of the parameters λ_t and D_t were set to 0.25 and 1.1 respectively.

Table 1. Some of the test shapes on which proposed algorithm was applied and their results

	Original boundary	Original boundary and vertices identified for approximation	Approximated boundary curve
Shape 1			
Shape 2			
Shape 3			
Shape 4			
Shape 5			

Table 2. Compression ratio and error of approximation for the shapes considered in Table 1

	N	V	CR	ISE
Shape1	638	15	42.53	25.24
Shape2	456	24	19	23.71
Shape3	622	37	16.81	12.02
Shape4	444	14	31.71	5.39
Shape5	441	30	14.7	10.30

In order to do a quantitative evaluation of the proposed method, Integral Square Error (ISE) and compression ratio (CR) were used as measures for evaluation (Rosin 1997). Table-2 summarizes the ISE and CR due to application of the proposed methodology on the shapes shown in Table-2, along with the number of boundary points (N) and the number of vertices (V) identified for polygonal approximation. Both optional rules were applied to improve the Integral Square Error and Compression Ratio.

4 Summary and Conclusions

A new method for approximating a boundary curve by a polygon has been proposed in this work. The proposed method is based on split-approach. It detects vertices of approximating polygon by recursively splitting the boundary curve into smaller segments and uses small eigenvalue of covariance matrix of the segment as stopping criterion for splitting. Method has produced good results in terms of approximation error and compression ratio for the images used in experimentation.

References

1. Alexander Kolesnikov and Pasi Franti – 2003, Reduced-search dynamic programming for approximation of polygonal curves, Pattern Recognition Letters 24 (2003) 2243-2254.
2. Guru D.S. and Dinesh R. – 2004, Non-parametric adaptive region of support useful for corner detection: a novel approach, Pattern Recognition 37(2004) 165-168.
3. Juan-Carlos Perez and Enrique vidal – 1994, Optimum polygonal approximation of digitized curves, Pattern Recognition Letters 15(1994) 743-750.
4. Majed Marji and Pepe Siy – 2003, A new algorithm for dominant points detection and polygonization of digital curves, Pattern Recognition 36(2003) 2239-2251.
5. Marc Salotti – 2002, Optimal polygonal approximation of digitized curves using the sum of square deviation criterion, Pattern Recognition 35 (2002) 435-443.
6. Pikaz A. and Dinstein I. – 1995, an algorithm for polygonal approximation based on iterative point elimination, Pattern Recognition Letter 16(1995) 557-564.
7. Ray B.K. and Ray K.S. – 1992, an algorithm for detection of dominant and polygonal approximation of digitized curves, Pattern Recognition Letters 13(1992) 849-856.
8. Ray B.K. and Ray K.S. – 1995, a new split-and-merge technique for polygonal approximation of chain coded curves, Pattern Recognition Letters 16(1995) 161-169.
9. Rosin P.L., Techniques for Assessing Polygonal Approximation of curves, IEEE Transaction on Pattern Analysis and Machine Intelligence, Vol. 19, No. 6, June 1997.
10. Tsai D.M., Hou H.T., Su H.J. – 1999, Boundary-based corner detection using eigenvalue of covariance matrices, Pattern Recognition Letters 20(1999) 31-40.
11. Wang M.J.J., Wu W.Y., Huang L.K. and Wang D.M. – 1995, Corner detection using bending value, Pattern Recognition Letters 16(1995) 575-583.

Symbolic Data Structure for Postal Address Representation and Address Validation Through Symbolic Knowledge Base

P. Nagabhushan[1], S.A. Angadi[2], and B.S. Anami[3]

[1] Department of Studies in Computer Science, University of Mysore, Mysore*
[2] Department of Studies in Computer Science, University of Mysore, Mysore
and Department of Computer Applications BEC, Bagalkot
[3] Department of Computer Science & Engineering, BEC, Bagalkot
{pnagabhushan, anami_basu}@hotmail.com,
vinay_angadi@yahoo.com

Abstract. The postal address data and the domain information for address validation contain qualitative, numeric, interval and other types of data. The efficient processing of such data required for postal automation needs a robust data structure that facilitates their storage and access. A symbolic data structure is proposed to represent the postal address and the information relevant for validating the postal address is stored in a newly devised symbolic knowledge base. The symbolic representation gives a formal structure to the information and hence is more beneficial than other representations such as frames, which do not reflect the structure inherent in the domain knowledge. The process of postal address validation checks the different components of the postal address for consistency before using it for further processing. In the present work a symbolic knowledge base supported address validation system is developed and tested for about 500 addresses. The system efficiency is observed to be 95.6% in validating the addresses automatically.

Keywords: Postal Address validation, Symbolic object, knowledge base, Frames.

1 Introduction

Postal automation aims at rendering the postal service that delivers mail to the doorstep of the addressee, efficient. There is a spurt of activity in postal automation area in recent times [1-4]. The different aspects of postal services that need to be automated are identified in [3]. The most important step in postal automation is interpretation of the destination address. Apart from the pattern recognition and image processing activities for reading the postal address, one of the major tasks is to find a generic data structure to store all types of addresses. The data structure is to be further employed for various sub tasks of postal automation, particularly mail sorting, such as address validation, address component identification, etc [9,11]. Some works in this direction are reported. An algorithmic prototype for automatic validation of postal

---

* Work carried out during sabbatical at Amrita Vishwa Vidyapeetam , Coimbatore.

addresses is presented in [5]. A knowledge based approach to generation of destination postal codes from the addresses is presented in [6]. A truthing, testing and evaluation mechanism for postal addresses is proposed in [7].

Most of the postal automation efforts are seen in the countries that have standard address formats [8], where the correctness and consistency of the address is not in question. The same is not true in India, where the destination addresses are written using any known information about the geographical location of the addressee. Typical unstructured descriptions of the addresses include, Near Playground, Besides City Hospital etc. Also the destination place might be specified by any of the alias names a place has, for example, Madras/ Chennai, Calcutta/ Kolkata etc. Some times even the place name might be mis-spelt like, Bangalore as Banglore, Mysore as Mysooru and the like. Symbolic data objects are very much suitable to model the concepts of the real world [12] such as those described by the postal address.

The components of the postal address (especially in the Indian context) may not be consistent especially with respect to the Postal Index Number (PIN), hence there is a need to validate the address for its correctness before it is used for sorting and distribution. This paper presents a symbolic knowledge base supported methodology for automatically validating the postal address and sorting of postal mail using postal address as a symbolic object.

The paper is organized into 5 sections. The section 2 describes postal address as a symbolic data object. Section 3 presents the knowledge base supported automated solution to postal address validation and sorting. It also describes the symbolic object knowledge base. Section 4 presents the experimental results and their analysis. Section 5 gives the conclusion.

2 The Postal Address as a Symbolic Object

The postal address contains many fields, all of which may not be present in every postal address. Some of these fields are qualitative such as Addressee name, Care of name and other fields may be numeric such as house number, road number and PIN. Although these data are numeric, most often their role in the address could be non-numeric in nature. Symbolic objects offer a formal methodology to represent such type of Information. Symbolic objects are extensions of classical data types. Symbolic objects can be of three different types, Assertion Object, Hoard Object and Synthetic Object. An assertion object is a conjunction of events pertaining to a given object. An event is a pair which links feature variables and feature values. A Hoard object is a collection of one or more assertion objects, whereas a synthetic object is a collection of one or more hoard objects [10,12,13]. The postal address object is described as a hoard object consisting of three assertion type objects as described in (1).

POSTAL ADDRESS OBJECT= {[Addressee],[Location],[Place]} (1)

Each of the assertion objects describes an important component of the destination address. The Addressee specifies the name and personal details of the mail recipient; the Location specifies the geographical position of the mail delivery point and Place specifies the city/ town or village where the mail recipient resides. Each of these assertion objects is defined as a collection of many events. The features (address fields) of the different assertion objects are listed in (2),(3) and (4). Each of the feature describes some aspect of the object and all the features together completely specify the assertions objects namely, Addressee, Location and Place. However, certain features remain missing in a typical postal address because they are not available.

[Addressee=(Addressee Name)(Care of Name)(Qualification)(Profession)
(Salutation)(Designation)] (2)
[Location=(House Number)(House Name)(Road)(Area)(LandMark)
(PBNo)(Firm)] (3)
[Place=(Post)(Taluk)(District)(State)(Place)(PIN)(Via)] (4)

A typical postal address and its symbolic object representation is given in Table 1.

Table 1. A Typical Postal Address Object

Postal Address	Symbolic Representation
Shri M.M.Patil Lakshmi Extension Gokak-591307 Belgaum Karnataka	PostalAddressObject={[Addressee=(Salutation=Shri), (AddresseeName=MMPatil)],[Location=(Area=LaxmiExtension)], [Place=(place=Gokak),(PIN=591307),(District=Belgaum), (State=Karnataka)]}

The symbolic object defined for representing a postal address can be further used to perform various sub tasks of postal automation such as address component identification, address validation etc.

3 The Knowledge Base Supported Symbolic Data Analysis Approach to Postal Address Validation

The proposed system employs symbolic data analysis techniques for address validation and a predefined procedure for mail forwarding in the dispatch sorting office. Every mail specifies the destination location (area) by providing area and place names as well as PIN code. The validation process checks for the correctness of the place names and area names and their mapping to PIN code. The system further corrects the PIN code of the address if there is any inconsistency in the information conveyed by the area/place name and PIN code. If the mail does not contain PIN code, and the other address components are validated, then the PIN is generated to the extent possible depending on the information available at the sorting office. The system works on the premise that the destination place and geographical area are probably more correct than the PIN code. The validated/corrected address is then employed for mail sorting at the dispatch sorting office.

The symbolic knowledge base supported address validation and sorting system processes the input postal address object and validates/ corrects the PIN code for further sorting of postal mail, Figure-1 gives the block diagram of the proposed system. The system comprises of an inference engine consisting of two processes namely address validation and mail sorting. The address validation module checks for consistency among the various address components which are part of the Place and Location objects, whereas the mail sorting module sorts the mail using the rule base employed by the mail sorting office.

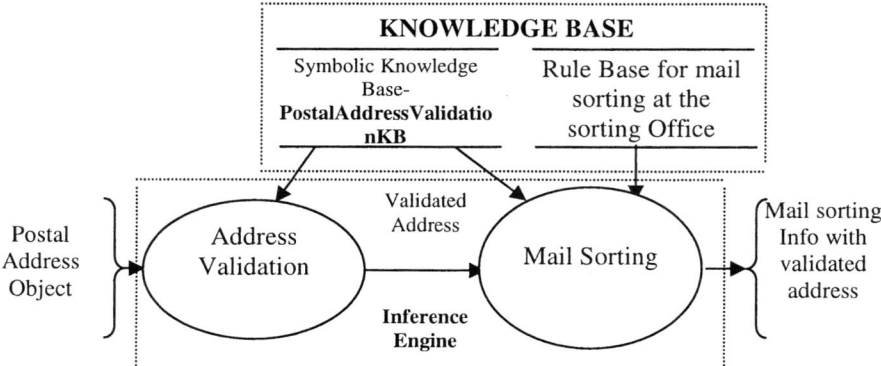

Fig. 1. Symbolic Knowledge base supported Address Validation and Sorting System

Further for validating the mail address the required local knowledge is stored in a knowledge base of symbolic objects. The rule base used for sorting is based on the mail sorting rules of India Posts and has been implemented as a set of external rules separate from the validating knowledge base. The structure of the knowledge base devised is presented in section 3.1.

3.1 The Symbolic Postal Knowledge Base for Dispatch Sorting

The information required for address validation such as various forms of place names, area names, PIN codes etc. and their relationships are to be stored in the knowledge base. A frame structured knowledge base for address validation is proposed in [11]. Though the frame structure helps in storing the variety of information required for postal address validation it does not explicitly bring out the relationships between different pieces of knowledge and hence the inherent structure in the domain information is lost. Also the frame-structured knowledge base has resulted in complex validation procedure because of the complexity in data. The symbolic knowledge base offers a more systematic knowledge representation technique for storing the domain knowledge. The validation procedure is also made easier because of the structure of the knowledge base. A knowledge base of symbolic synthetic object PostalAddressValidationKB has been devised for the purpose. The synthetic object comprises of two hoard objects namely, PLACE_DETAILS and AREA_DETAILS. The knowledge embedded in the two hoard objects is employed for validation depending on the context. The developed knowledge base stores information about various forms of place names, area names, PIN codes, places to which direct bags are closed and the like which are needed for address validation. The symbolic data object that represents the structure of the knowledge base is given in Figure-2. The content of the knowledge base is sorting office dependant, but the proposed structure can be employed by any sorting office.

PostalAddressValidationKB={ {Place_Details=[Icity=((Name)(Length)] [States=((Name)(2digpin))] [Nplaceid=((Placename)(Length))(Npid))] [Nplace=((Npid)(Name)(Pin)(Forwardingplace) (Forwadingplacepin))] [Distid=((Distname)(Length))(Distid))] [Dist=((Distid)(Name)(Pin)(Forwardingplace) (Forwadingplacepin))]	[Dbplaceid=((Placename)(Length))(Placeid))] [Dbplace=((Placeid)(Name)(Pin)(Sdflag) (Bagtype))] [Oplace=((Place_Id)(3digitpin))] [Coveredplace=((Place_Name) (Covering_Place)(Coveringplaceid))]} {Area_Details=[Areainfo=((Areaname) (Dpoid))] [Dpo=((Name)(Dpoid)(Pin) (Placeid))] [Plpin=((Plid)(Plpins))]}]

Fig. 2. Symbolic Data Object Knowledge Base

3.2 Symbolic Data Analysis Technique for Postal Address Validation and Sorting

The process of address validation and sorting employs the symbolic knowledge base and rule base. The process involves systematic comparison of the information about the place in the postal address object with the feature values in place_details object of symbolic knowledge base, generating the PIN to the extent possible. The generated PIN is compared with input PIN if it exists and is corrected if necessary. If the PIN does not exist in the input, the generated PIN is added to the postal address. Further if the mail is destined to a place within the sorting district, then the input information about the location of the addressee is used to validate the PIN upto 6 digits using the information stored in the location_details object of the knowledge base.

4 Experimental Results and Analysis

The knowledge base for Bagalkot (a district place in Karnataka State of India) sorting office is built. The validation and sorting system is implemented in C language and is tested on a P-III machine with 128 MB RAM. The symbolic knowledge base is stored as a separate sorted flat file for every assertion object. The text strings forming the postal address object are input to the system. The system outputs the validated addresses after correction, if necessary. Some of the mails may require manual intervention for validation and sorting.

The system is exhaustively tested for sorting and validation for dispatch at Bagalkot sorting office and the results are summarized in Table-2. The results show that about 95.60% of the mail is either fully or partially validated by the proposed system, which is better than 90.80%[11] of the frame based system. Hence the methodology developed is sufficiently robust and can be used by any sorting office in India with appropriate knowledge base.

The algorithm failed to properly validate the mail destined to a place outside the sorting district, but had a name similar to the name of a place within the sorting district and had incorrect pin code, such a mail required manual intervention.

Table 2. Implementation results

Sl No.	Particulars	Observed Value	% of total test mails
1	The number of mails tested	500	100
2	The number of mails completely validated	390	78.00
3	The number of mails partially validated	88	17.60
4	The number of mails that required human intervention	20	4.00
5	The number of mails that cold not be resolved	2	0.40

5 Conclusions

The symbolic knowledge base supported method for address validation and sorting of mail for dispatch proposed in this paper is robust and takes care of mis-spelt, correctly spelt, abbreviated names and also alias names of places and geographical areas. The system validates or generates, as many PIN digits as are possible using the information extracted from the mail destination address, with the help of symbolic data analysis. The success of the address validation and sorting system is largely dependant on the efficiency of the address reading system. The address validation technique also finds application for bulk mailers in customer relationship management context and even to private courier service providers. The symbolic data analysis approach proposed here can be further used in automation of other sub tasks of mail handling.

Acknowledgement

The work is supported by grant from AICTE, New Delhi under the RPS scheme for the project titled "Development of Techniques for optimal postal mail distribution in the Indian context", vide FNO. 8022/RID/NPROJ/RPS-60/2003-04 dated 22/3/04.

References

1. Kanehiro Kubota and Kazunari Egami, (1999), " Technology trend of postal automation", NEC Research and Development, Vol 40, No. 2, Spl Issue on Postal Technology, pp 127-136
2. Giovani Garibotto, 2002, *"Computer Vision in Postal Automation"* Elsag Bailey-TELEROBOT, 2002.
3. P.Nagabhushan, 1998, " Towards Automation in Indian Postal Services : A Loud Thinking", Technovision , Spl Volume, pp 128-139
4. Rangachar Kasturi, Lawrence O'Gorman and Venu Govindaraju,2002, "Document Image Analysis: A Primer", Sadhana, Vol 27, Part 1, Februrary 2002, pp 3-22.
5. M.R.Premalatha and P. Nagabhushan, 2001, *"An algorithmic prototype for automatic verification and validation of PIN code: A step towards Postal Automation"*, NCDAR-2001, 13th and 14th July 2001, pp 225-233

6. M.R.Nagamani and P.Nagabhushan, 2003, *"Knowledge based approach to Determine the Destination Postal Code Through Address Block Extraction : A case study towards Postal Automation"*, NCDAR-2003 held at PESCE, Mandya, 11th and 12th July 2003, pp 152-163
7. Srirangaraj Setlur, A Lawson, Venu Govindaraju and Sargur N Srihari,, 2001," Truthing, Testing and Evaluation Issues in Complex Systems", Sixth IAPR International Conference on Document Analysis and Recognition, Seattle, WA, pp 1205-1214
8. Universal Postal Union Address Standard, "FGDC Address Standard Version 2".
9. P.Nagabhushan,S.A.Angadi and B.S.Anami, 2005"A Knowledge base supported Inferencing of Address Components in Postal Mail" NVGIP-2005, Shimoga, 2nd and 3rd March 2005
10. Lecture Notes of short term course on symbolic and fuzzy approaches to data analysis, 21-26 April 1997
11. P.Nagabhushan,S.A.Angadi and B.S.Anami, 2004, "A Knowledge based Fast PIN code Validation System for Dispatch Sorting of Postal Mail", International Conference on Cognitive systems New Delhi, 14th and 15th December 2004
12. Edwin Diday,2000, "Knowledge Discovery from the Symbolic Data and the SODAS Software", PKDD 2000 workshop on Symbolic data Analysis, Lyon, 12th September 2000.
13. Bock H.-H. ,Diday E.,2000, "Analysis of symbolic Data", Heidelberg 2000

The Linear Factorial Smoothing for the Analysis of Incomplete Data

Basavanneppa Tallur

IRISA, Université de Rennes 1, Avenue Général Leclerc,
35042 Rennes Cedex, France
tallur@irisa.fr
http://www.irisa.fr/symbiose/people/tallur

Abstract. Huge amounts of data are generated in every field of science and technology and the need for the proper data analysis tools and their adaptation to the ever-increasing data size is more and more crucial. Statistical exploratary data analysis techniques –such as principal component analysis, correspondence analysis, clustering and classification among others– are greatly useful in discovering useful information –or knowledge– hidden in data but they require the data set to be complete. In many situations the data is incomplete for various reasons. Erroneous and uncertain data may also be considered as missing since their use may lead to incorrect results. Many research works have addressed this issue in specific applications. This paper presents a simple and efficient iterative method for estimating the missing values in the data set based on linear *factorial smoothing*. Though this work was prompted by the recurrent problem faced in the field of bioinformatics while analysing the gene expression data, the method proposed for missing value imputation in this paper may be useful in any area.

1 Introduction

Statistical data analysis techniques are gaining more and more importance with the tremendous development in information technology. These techniques are also getting more and more computation-intensive. Most data need to be pre-processed before any analysis is carried out so as to obtain reliable results. One of the recurrent problems in all areas of data analysis applications is that of missing values. The reasons are varied and multiple, such as : non-response to a questionnaire, failure of a measuring apparatus, physical impossibility to observe a value, just to enumerate a few. Erroneous measurements and doubtful observations may also be treated as missing data since such data may lead to incorrect conclusions. We consider the widely used multidimensional data analysis techniques which are very fundamantal in exploring huge data sets in order to discover useful information ; they are part of what is called the *data mining engine*. Many researchers in different areas of application of statistical data analysis techniques have proposed different strategies for dealing with the missing values before performing the analyses. These strategies range from simply deleting the entire observations (i.e. rows in a data table) containing missing values, to estimating the missing values by some elaborate optimization techniques. We consider that the method of missing value imputation should take into consideration the type of analysis that will follow. The idea is that if one needs to perform a supervised classification, then one has to estimate the missing values in such a way that the classifiers resulting from the estimated data be as *close as possible* to the real classifiers i.e. the classifiers obtained from the complete data. Similarly, if one intends to apply principal component analysis (PCA), the estimated data should produce the principal factors as similar as possible to the factors the complete data would have produced. In this paper, we will describe an iterative smoothing method to estimate the missing values for PCA and correspondence analysis (CA) which are the basic techniques used in dimension reduction prior to other analyses such as clustering and classification. In order to assess the quality of the estimation we have used the complete data sets in which some of the randomly chosen values are considered as missing. The results obtained from both known complete data set and the estimated one are compared.

One particular area of research in which the data analysis tools are indispensable is bioinformatics where the data is generated in very large scales, and typically, these data sets contain missing values. In postgenomic research, gene expression microarray experiments can generate data sets with many missing values. Clustering techniques are widely used in gene expression data analysis because, by clustering the genes based on the similarity of their expression profiles the biologists may find functionally related genes and potentially the function of the genes (cf. Eisen et al. [3], Mao et al. [6], Tallur [11]). The recent research in bioinformatics shows that the linear factorial model allows interpretation in terms of biological processes (see e.g. Alter et.al. [1], Girolami and Breitling [2], Lee and Batzoglou [4], Roberts and Everson [7]). To address the problem arising from the high dimensional data, S. Roweis [8] has proposed the EM algorithms. These algorithms naturally accomodate missing data. A more recent survey on missing data estimation methods as applied in bioinformatics is given by Troyanskaya et al. [12]. In the next sections we will briefly describe the principles of PCA and CA before presenting the algorithm of missing value estimation. Finally, we will present the experiments on which the algorithm has been tested.

2 Principal Component Analysis (PCA)

Let us consider a rectangular data matrix X having n rows (each row corresponds to one *observation* or *data point*) and p columns (each column corresponds to a *variable* or an *attribute*). Let $X_1, X_2, \ldots, X_p$ be the variables. Principal component analysis is the fundamental technique for dimension reduction based on the principle of singular value decomposition of the data matrix. This analysis is appropriate when variables are numerical or quantitaive. In order to obtain the statistically interpretable results, the data matrix is standardized with respect to the mean and standard deviation of each variable. Moreover, the euclidean distance between data points is independent of measurement units when the variables are standardized.

2.1 Formulation of PCA

Each data point is represented as a vector in a p-dimensional vector space. The principal factorial axes are defined by the normalized eigenvectors of the $p \times p$ correlation matrix $R = ((r_{jk}))_{j,k=1,\ldots,p}$ where r_{jk} is the correlation coefficient between X_j and X_k.

2.2 Data Reconstruction from Principal Factors

From the normed eigenvectors $u_j, (j = 1, \ldots, k)$, relative to the k largest eigenvalues $\lambda_j, (j = 1, \ldots, k)$ of the matrix R and the first k principal components c_j, for $j = 1, \ldots, k$, (with $k < p$) the data matrix X may be reconstructed approximately as follows :

$$X = \sum_{j=1}^{k} c_j u\prime_j \qquad (1)$$

where $u\prime_j$ is the transpose of the vector u_j. In other words, the estimated value of X_j for i^{th} observation is given by

$$x_{ij} = \sum_{l=1}^{k} c_{li} u_{lj} \text{ for } i = 1, \ldots, n \text{ and } j = 1, \ldots, p \ . \qquad (2)$$

We will call the integer k *the level of approximation*.

3 Correspondence Analysis (CA)

The CA may be considered as an adaptation of PCA applicable to the contingency tables ; the rows and columns of the data table correspond to the values (called *modalities*) of two qualitative variables, say, Q_1 and Q_2 ; and the $(i,j)^{th}$ cell contains the frequency x_{ij} (i.e. the number of simultaneous occurrences) of the ith modailty of Q_1 and the jth modailty of Q_2. Though the CA was developed originally in the framework of the contingency tables, it is widely applied to any data table with all positive values.

3.1 Formulation of CA

Before applying the PCA, the data is transformed so as to represent the rows and columns by their *profile vectors*. The ith row profile is a vector $\left(\frac{x_{i1}}{x_{i.}}, \ldots, \frac{x_{ip}}{x_{i.}}\right)\prime$ in the p-dimensional vector space, where $x_{i.} = \sum_{j=1}^{p} x_{ij}$. The ith row profile is given the weight $p_{i.} = \frac{x_{i.}}{x_{..}}$ where $x_{..} = \sum_{i=1}^{n} \sum_{j=1}^{p} x_{ij}$. Analogously, the jth column profile is a vector $\left(\frac{x_{1j}}{x_{.j}}, \ldots, \frac{x_{nj}}{x_{.j}}\right)\prime$ in the n-dimensional vector space where $x_{.j} = \sum_{i=1}^{n} x_{ij}$. The jth column profile is given the weight $p_{.j} = \frac{x_{.j}}{x_{..}}$. The χ-squared metric is used to measure the distance btween row profiles in this row vector space ; according to this metric, the distance between the row profiles i and $i\prime$ is given by :

$$d^2(i, i\prime) = \sum_{j=1}^{p} \frac{1}{p_{.j}} \left(\frac{x_{ij}}{x_{i.}} - \frac{x_{i\prime j}}{x_{i\prime.}} \right)^2 \qquad (3)$$

Similarly, the distance between the column profiles j and k is :

$$d^2(j, k) = \sum_{i=1}^{n} \frac{1}{p_{i.}} \left(\frac{x_{ij}}{x_{.j}} - \frac{x_{ik}}{x_{.k}} \right)^2 \qquad (4)$$

With this set up which is perfectly symmetrical with respect to rows and columns, the PCA is applied to the row and column spaces. The row factors F_α, ($\alpha = 1, 2, \ldots, p-1$) are defined by the normed eigenvectors of the matrix S whose general term is s_{jk} :

$$S = ((s_{jk}))_{j,k=1,\ldots,p} \text{ where } s_{jk} = \sum_{i=1}^{n} \left(\frac{x_{ij} x_{ik}}{x_{i.} x_{.k}} \right) - p_{.j} \qquad (5)$$

By interchanging the rows and columns, one can obtain the column factors G_α. For further details the readers may be referred to the book by Lebart et.al. [5]

3.2 Data Reconstruction from Factors

The original data matrix may be reconstructed from the row and column factors to the order of approximation (or, appoximation level) k, with $k < p-1$ as follows :

$$x_{ij} = \frac{x_{i.} x_{.j}}{x_{..}} \left[1 + \sum_{\alpha=1}^{k} \lambda_\alpha^{1/2} F_\alpha(i) G_\alpha(j) \right] \text{ for } i = 1, \ldots, n \text{ and } j = 1, \ldots, p. \qquad (6)$$

4 Missing Value Estimation Algorithm

There are two versions of the algorithm namely, ESTIMPCA and ESTIMCA depending on the ultimate analysis performed on the data. The former is appropriate for PCA and the latter for CA.

4.1 ESTIMPCA Algorithm

1. *Initialization*: Assign zeros (or the variable means, or medians) to each of the missing values and assign the value s_{max} to the parameter s, the approximation level. Note that s_{max} should be strictly less than p.
2. repeat the following steps until convergence :
   (a) Compute the matrix R, and its eigenvalues. (Let $\lambda_j, (j = 1, \ldots, s_{max})$ be the s_{max} largest eigenvalues of R) ;
   (b) Compute the corresponding eigenvectors u_j and principal components $c_j, (j = 1, \ldots, s_{max})$.
   (c) estimate each missing value x_{ij} from equation (2) with $k = s_{max}$).

4.2 ESTIMCA Algorithm

1. *Initialization*: Assign zeros to each of the missing values and assign the value s_{max} to the parameter s, the approximation level. Note that s_{max} should be strictly less than $p-1$.
2. repeat the following steps until convergence :
   (a) Compute the matrix S, and its eigenvalues. (Let $\lambda_\alpha, (\alpha = 1, \ldots, s_{max})$ be the s_{max} largest eigenvalues of S) ;
   (b) compute the row factors F_α and column factors G_α, $(\alpha = 1, \ldots, s_{max})$.
   (c) estimate the missing value x_{ij} from equation (6) with $k = s_{max}$.

5 Experimental Validation

In order to validate the alhoritms ESTIMPCA and ESTIMCA, we have used two real world data sets : the first one was obtained by the microarray experimentation conducted at the INSERM laboratory, Rennes (France) and the second one contains the data about the french agriculture. The former data set is particularly suitable for PCA and the latter for CA. Both data sets were complete.

5.1 Gene Expression Data

The first test data set contains gene expression levels of 2175 genes (rows) for each of 12 patients (columns). We generated random sample of upto 5220 numbers without replacement (that corresponds to 20% of the total number of data values) lying between 1 and 26,100. Then the values corresponding to the randomly chosen cells were considered as missing. The algorithm ESTIMACP with $s_{max} = 5$ produced not only the estimation of the missing values but also the estimated principal axes and principal components. Real components and the estimated ones were found to be very close to each other as measured by the high positive linear correlation coefficients, generally higher than 0.95.

5.2 Agricultural Data

This data set contains the number of agricultural farms in each of the 89 french *departmants* (rows) having 8 different sizes (columns) ranging from the smallest (*less than 1 hectare*) to the largest (*more than 100 hectares*). The same method was used to simulate the missing values in the data table and the ESTIMCA algorithm was used for estimation. Again, upto 20% of the total 712 data values were randomly deleted before estimating them. We rather are interested in estimating the factors than the data values themselves. The results were found to be almost comparable to those of the first experiment.

6 Conclusion and Remarks

We have proposed a simple but efficient itertive method for estimating the missing values in view of a specific analysis –PCA and CA– which are generally considered as dimension reduction techniques prior to classification and/or clustering. This work was triggered by the real necessity that arose in gene expression data analysis. Moreover, it has been shown by the recent research works in bioinformatics that the linear factorial methods provide the biologically interpretable models. Each of the algorithms we have proposed necessitates the determination of the parameter s_{max} i.e., the number of factrors used for estimation. Higher the value of s_{max}, faster the algorith will converge. But it should not be too close to p. Neither should it be too small a number. We may use a pilot study to determine this parameter.

References

1. Alter, O., Brown, P., Botstein, D.: Singular value decomposition for genome-wide expression data processing and modelling. PNAS **97** (2000) 10101–10106
2. Girolami, M., Breitling, R.: Biologically valid linear factor models of gene expression. Bioinformatics **20** (2004) 3021–3033
3. Eisen, M., Spellman, P., Brown, P., Botstein, D.: Cluster analysis and display of genome-wide expression patterns. PNAS. **95** (1998) 14863–14868
4. Lee, S.I., Batzoglou, S. Application of independent component analysis to microarrays. Genome Biol. **4** (2003)
5. Lebart, L., Morineau, A., Warwick, KM.: Multivariate descriptive statistical analysis, Correspondence analysis and related techniques for large matrices. Wiley series in probability and mathematical statistics (1984)
6. Mao, R., Zielke, C.L., Zielke, H.R., Pevnser, J. Global upregulation of chromosome 21 gene expression in the developing Down syndrome brain. Genomics **81** (2003) 457–467
7. Roberts, S., Everson, R. (eds) Independent component analysis Principles and practice. Cambridge university press, Cambridge (2001)
8. Roweis, S. EM Algorithms for PCA and SPCA. in Advances in neural informartion processing systems, **10** (1998)
9. Tallur, B. Analyse des correspondances en cas de données manquantes: application en biologie. Thèse doctorat de 3ème cycle, (1973) Université de Paris 6
10. Tallur, B. Contribution à l'analyse exploratoire de tableaux de contingence par la classification. Thèse doctorat ès science, (1988) Université de Rennes 1
11. Tallur, B. Analyse des données de l'expression génomique par la classification: pourquoi et comment? in Méthodes et perspectives en classification (2003) Presse académique de Nauchâtel
12. Troyanskaya, O., Cantor, M., Sherlock, G., Brown, P., Hastie, T., Tibshirani,R., Botstein, D., Altman, R. Missing value estimation methods for DNA microarrays Bioinformatics **17** (2001) 520–525

An Improved Shape Descriptor Using Bezier Curves

Ferdous Ahmed Sohel*, Gour C. Karmakar, and Laurence S. Dooley

Gippsland School of Information Technology, Monash University,
Churchill, Victoria - 3842, Australia
Ferdous.Sohel@infotech.monash.edu.au

Abstract. Existing shape description techniques using Bezier curves do not adequately consider the domain specific shape information such as the cornerity or gradualness of a shape in the control point generation process. This can lead to large distortion in shape representation even when a large descriptor is used. This paper addresses the issue by introducing a novel *improved shape descriptor using Bezier curves (ISDBC)* algorithm which divides a shape into segments depending on the cornerity and generates the control points for the segments based on shape information. It also provides an efficient control point encoding strategy which exploits the inherent periodic nature of the distances between consecutive control points. The performance of the ISDBC algorithm has been rigorously tested upon a number of arbitrary shapes, with both quantitative and qualitative results confirming its superiority over existing algorithms.

1 Introduction

A Bezier curve (BC) is defined by a set of control points (CPs), with the number and orientation of these points governing the shape of the curve. It is costly however, to represent a complex shape using a single BC, since a high degree BC generation is computationally expensive, with the calculation of the CPs alone incurring substantial overheads. To reduce this computational complexity, composite BC [1] has been used to represent more complex shapes, whereby the whole shape is divided into a number of segments, with each individually represented by a BC.

Cinque et al. [2] divided a shape into a priori number of segments containing equal number of shape points and also distributed the CPs evenly over the shape irrespective of the shape complexity. Since the division into segments and the generation of CPs consider only the number of shape points, not the shape complexity, it can produce large distortion even with a large number of segments. To overcome this problem Sohel et al. proposed a generic shape descriptor using Bezier curves (SDBC) [3], which had introduced the concept of significant points and supplementary points considering the domain specific information on the shape. However, since the segments are of equal length in [2]

---

* Corresponding author.

and [3], they cannot address cornerity and repetitions (loops) of the points on the shape due to the fact that segment ends are not necessarily at the corner points. Composite BC has been used in [4] and [5] to describe the outline of Arabic and Chinese characters respectively and in [6] to model the active shape of lips. Though in these algorithms the shape is divided into a number of segments considering the cornerity of the shape at shape points, they do not consider the shape information in each segment to compute the control points. For each segment, respective segment end points are considered the start and end CPs and the middle CPs are calculated in different approaches. In [5] and [6], the locations of the middle CPs are calculated, and hence highly depended, on the tangents at the segment endpoints. While [6] gets the control a point at the intersections of the tangents, [5] calculates these using computationally expensive trial-and-error methods. Though [4] has adopt an approach to minimise the distortion, it may require further divisions of the segments to keep the distortion low. Moreover, one common problem of these algorithms is that they allow CPs to be out side of the shape and consequently, the descriptor length can be increased.

As CPs describe the shape of any object, efficient encoding of CPs will reduce the descriptor length and hence reduce the communication cost and improve efficiency and quality. While [2] adopted a parametric means of encoding the CPs, there is no explicit way to encode them in [4], [5] and [6]. The parametric descriptor of [2] consists of the absolute coordinate values of the first and the fourth CPs, and the angle of direction and magnitude of distance of the second and the third CPs respectively from the first and the fourth CPs. Both distance and angle were encoded as floating point numbers, which means it is unsuitable for very low bit rate video applications, such as video streaming over the Internet, video-on-demand and mobile video transmission for hand-held devices, where there is an innate bandwidth limitation, so alternative methods to reduce the bit rate must be explored. In [3] for equi-length segments, a dynamic fixed length coding (DFLC) has been introduced which reduces the descriptor length utilising the periodic interval between CPs.

This paper presents *an improved shape descriptor using Bezier curves (IS-DBC)* which seeks to reduce distortion by defining a new strategy for CP generation and use an efficient CP coding scheme. This CP generation strategy improves SDBC [3] by dividing the shape into segments depending on the cornerity at the shape points rather than considering equi-length segments, along with considering the domain specific shape information. The CP coding strategy capitalises the periodic nature of the distances between CPs and uses a modified form of the DFLC approach. Performance of the ISDBC algorithm has been extensively tested upon shapes having sharp corners (e.g., *fish*, *Arabic character*) and loops (e.g., *lip*) and both quantitative and qualitative results confirm its improvement compared with the aforementioned shape description methods.

The rest of this paper is organised as follows: Section 2 presents the new ISDBC shape description framework including CP generation and coding strategies. Experimental results are presented in Section 3, confirming the improved performance of the ISDBC model, with some conclusions drawn in Section 4.

2 Improved Shape Description Scheme

The proposed shape description framework comprises two major parts. Firstly, calculation of CPs for each segment and secondly, a modified DFLC coding strategy for CPs based on a combination of Freeman *chain code* and *run-length* coding. These are respectively detailed in the following two subsections.

2.1 Control Point Determination

In the first step of CP generation the shape is divided into segments at the corner points on the shape. Bius-Tiu corner detection [7] method has been used in ISDBC since it produces the closest result to a human viewer. For each segment, CPs are selected from shape points, however, rather than considering all shape points in calculating CPs, concept of *significant* and *supplementary* points of [3] is used, so that regions having more rapidly changing shape features are given more emphasis than flat regions. Actually, significant points are the least number of shape points that can generate the original shape without distortion. This takes account of domain specific shape information during CP generation process and also means that consecutive significant points will not necessarily be separated by 1 pel as with shape points. The larger the distance between consecutive significant points, the greater will be their influence upon the shape. In these situations, shape descriptions based only on significant points can produce higher distortion because influential significant points may be excluded from being CPs. To reduce the likelihood of losing influential significant points as CPs, supplementary points are inserted at equal distances between the significant points. Let the combination of significant and supplementary points be referred to as *potential boundary points* (PBP) and these will be used in calculation of CPs. Note, the greater the number of supplementary points, PBP tends towards the original shape points, while fewer supplementary points may not be able to represent the influential significant points adequately. To balance these two extrema, average distance between consecutive significant points over the entire shape is used as the metric to insert supplementary points. The whole process can mathematically be explained as follows:

The segments can be represented as $S_i = \{s_{i,1}, s_{i,1}, \cdots, s_{i,|S_i|}\}, 1 \leq i \leq N$ where N is the number of segments and $|S_i|$ is the number of shape points in the ith segment and $s_{i,|S_i|} = s_{(i+1)\%N,1}$. Thus, if the significant points of ith segment is denoted as Sig_i, $Sig_i = \{sig_{i,0}, sig_{i,1}, \cdots, sig_{i,|Sig_i|}\} \subseteq S_i, 1 \leq i \leq N$ where $|Sig_i|$ is the cardinality of set Sig_i. If $d(sig_{i,k-1}, sig_{i,k})$ denotes the Euclidean distance between $sig_{i,k-1}$ and $sig_{i,k}$, average distance between significant points over the entire shape is $d_{avg} = \frac{1}{N} \sum_{i=1}^{N} \frac{1}{|Sig_i|} \sum_{k=2}^{|Sig_i|} d(sig_{i,k-1}, sig_{i,k})$. When $d(sig_{i,k-1}, sig_{i,k}) > d_{avg}$, supplementary points are inserted between $sig_{i,k-1}$ and $sig_{i,k}$. The first point (sp_1) is placed at a distance of d_{avg} from $sig_{i,k-1}$ and if $d(sp_1, sig_{i,k}) > d_{avg}$, then a further supplementary point is inserted at distance d_{avg} from (sp_1). This process continues until the distance between two consecutive significant (one of which may be a supplementary point) points is $\leq d_{avg}$. PBP for each segment can be defined as $B_i = \{b_{i,1}, b_{i,1}, \cdots, b_{i,|B_i|}\}, 1 \leq i \leq N$ and is used to calculate CPs. In this paper, cubic BC is used for shape description as lower-order curves are too inflexible to represent the shape, while higher degree curves introduce unwanted oscillations and higher computation overhead. Following from technique [2] CPs of cubic BC for the ith segment can be calculated as: $v_{i,0} = b_{i,1}; v_{i,1} = b_{i,\lceil \frac{|B_i|}{4} \rceil}; v_{i,2} = b_{i,\lceil \frac{3*|B_i|}{4} \rceil}; v_{i,3} = b_{i,|B_i|}$.

2.2 Control Point Encoding

DFLC encodes the control point differentially, where the direction of a CP from its previous (immediate) CP is coded using the chain code, with the distance between them being the run-length of the code. An 8-bit code is used for the directions and for the length it had utilised the periodic nature of intervals between CPs. DFLC considered the segments to be of equal length, however, in ISDBC the segments are of variable length in terms of PBP. So the DFLC is required to be modified. In the following paragraph a suitably modified DFLC has been presented.

Modified dynamic fixed length coding: There are periodic intervals between CPs in terms of PBPs. Consider the ith segment, if l_i is the number of PBP between the first and second CPs, the distance between the second and third CPs is $2 * l_i$ points and the distance between the third and fourth CPs is also l_i points. The same thing is true for any segment. So if the maximum length of all l_is is allotted for every l_i, all CPs can be fitted into a frame consisting of only one l, instead of several l_is. Now z is the largest number of PBP in a segment rather than the equal number of approximated boundary points in SDBC. So $z = max_{1 \leq i \leq N} |B_i|$ and $l = \lceil \frac{z}{4} \rceil$. The maximum length of l, $L = l*d_{avg}$ and $L_1 = \lceil lgL \rceil$ bits require to encode it. Similarly, to encode the length $2*L$ requires $L_1 + 1$ bits. Bezier CPs encoding uses the periodic pattern shown in the next table, where **Dir** is the direction bits of a particular CP. The first segment comprises the absolute location of the first PBP followed by L_1 bits and its direction after which comes $L_1 + 1$ bits with direction and finally L_1 bits with direction. Each subsequent segment will not require a starting point and can be defined in ordered sequence of $L_1, L_1 + 1, L_1$ with directions as shown in the following tabular.

4-bits: length of L_1	Starting point	Dir $+L_1$	Dir $+L_1+1$	Dir $+L_1$	Dir $+L_1$	Dir $+L_1+1$	Dir $+L_1$	...	Dir $+L_1$	Dir $+L_1+1$
		First segment			Next segment			...	Last segment	

It is noteworthy that, the leading 4-bits in the encoded sequence are reserved to represent the length of L_1. Normally 4 bits are sufficient to denote the length of L_1. Using this, a distance of up to 2^{16} pel for L_1 can be encoded, thus the segment length can be up to $4 * 2^{16}$ pel.

Decoding the shape information: Due to the parametric representation of the encoded information and its periodicity, the decoder knows the length and hence the delimiter of each parameter, so it can correctly parse these parameters and reconstruct the shape using them.

3 Results and Analysis

The widely-used shape distortion measurement metrics D_{max} and D_{ms} of [8] were used respectively for the peak and mean-square distortions for numerical analysis. The performance of ISDBC was tested upon the popular object shapes in the literature. Figure 1 shows comparative presentation of the decoded shape by the descriptors with 5 segments on the *lip* object having loops. The numerical results, along with for some other shapes, are presented in Table 1. Table 1 shows that both SDBC and algorithm in [2] produced large D_{max} of 12.1 and 10.2 *pel* respectively and D_{ms} of 7.5 and 5.4 pel^2 respectively for the *lip* shape while ISDBC showed better results of 1.5 *pel* and 0.9 pel^2 distortions; this is due to considering the cornerity and loops on the shape in ISDBC. In fact, ISDBC produced the lowest distortion among all the methods (including those also consider curvature information in dividing a shape into segments) and this is because of considering the domain specific shape information in CP generation. The results on the *fish* shape using the cited [2]-[6] techniques with 7 segments are compared in Figure 2 and Table 1. For instance, ISDBC produced D_{max} and D_{ms} of 3.85 *pel* and 2.76 pel^2 respectively. From the results, it is evident that ISDBC produced the lowest distortions and thus outperformed the aforementioned shape descriptors using BC. A same conclusion is true for the Arabic character which has been used in [4].

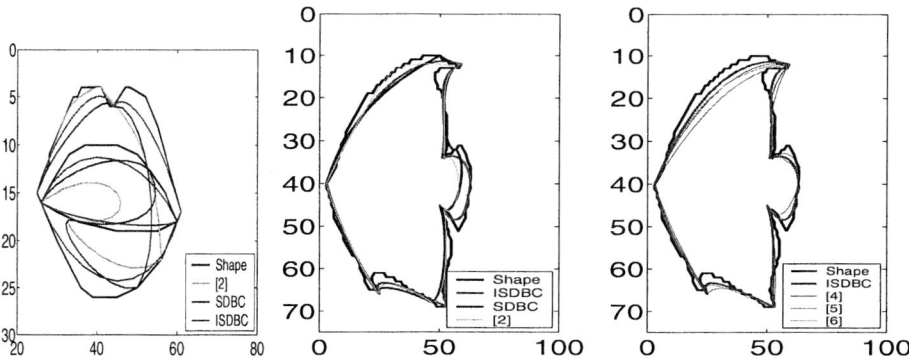

Fig. 1. Results for lip-shape used in [6]

Fig. 2. Comparative results for fish extracted from [2]

For the descriptor length, it was assumed that coordinate values would require one byte each, also despite of the direction and magnitudes in [2] are floating point numbers, only one byte was assumed for each. Thus for *fish* shape with 7 segments, the descriptor length was 340 bits while ISDBC required only 267 bits, with $z = 35$ and $d_{avg} = 1.8$ pel, so $L_1 = 4$ bits. Thus there is a reduction of 20% in the descriptor size. Moreover, for each additional segments, [2] required 48 bits more, while it is 37 bits for ISDBC and hence, about 23% improvement for each additional segment. ISDBC is computationally efficient over

Table 1. Distortion in shape representations (unit: $D_{max} = pel$, $D_{ms} = pel^2$)

Object → Technique ↓	Fish of [2]		Arabic of [4]		Lip of [6]	
	D_{max}	D_{ms}	D_{max}	D_{ms}	D_{max}	D_{ms}
ISDBC	3.85	2.76	1.2	0.83	1.5	0.9
SDBC [3]	5.4	3.6	1.9	1.25	**12.1**	**7.5**
[2]	6.0	4.3	2.1	1.35	**10.2**	**5.4**
[4]	4.22	3.34	1.3	0.95	1.65	1.05
[5]	3.9	3.46	1.35	1.2	1.7	1.2
[6]	6.05	6.55	2.0	1.4	1.8	1.5

[4]-[6], because of the process of CP generation and coding. However, there is a little increase in computational time requirement over [2]-[3] which is secondary when compared with the improvement in the rate-distortion sense.

4 Conclusions

While Bezier curves have been applied in many different applications including describing object shapes, a critical aspect in using them is the proper selection of the segments and control points. This paper has presented *an improved shape descriptor using Bezier curves (ISDBC)* algorithm which provides a novel strategy in defining the control points along with dividing the shape into segments by considering domain specific information concerning the shape and an efficient strategy for encoding the control points. Both qualitative and quantitative results have shown the improved performance of ISDBC compared with existing shape description techniques.

References

1. R. H. Bartels, J.C.B., Barsky, B.A.: An Introduction to Splines for use in Computer Graphics and Geometric Modeling. Morgan Kaufmann Publishers (1987)
2. L. Cinque, S.L., Malizia, A.: Shape description using cubic polynomial bezier curves. Pattern Recognition Letters, Elsevier Science Inc. (1998) 821–828
3. F.A. Sohel, G.K., Dooley, L.: A generic shape descriptor using bezier curves. In: Int. Conf. on Info. Tech.: New Trends in Image Proc., ITCC. Volume II. (2005) 95–100
4. Sarfraz, M., Khan, M.A.: Automatic outline capture of arabic fonts. Information Sciences, Elsevier Science Inc. (2002) 269–281
5. H. M. Yang, J.J.L., Lee, H.J.: A bezier curve-based approach to shape description for chinese calligraphy characters. In: Int. Conf. Doc. Anal. Recog. (2001) 276–280
6. I. Shdaifat, R.G., Langmann, D.: Active shape lip modeling. In: Proc. of International Conference on Image Processing, ICIP-2003. (2003) 875–878
7. Beus, H.L., Tiu, S.S.H.: An improved corner detection algorithm based on chain coded plane curves. Pattern Recognition **20** (1987) 291–296
8. Schuster, G.M., Katsaggelos, A.K.: Rate-Distortion Based Video Compression-Optimal Video Frame Compression and Object Boundary Encoding. Kluwer Academic Publishers (1997)

Isothetic Polygonal Approximations of a 2D Object on Generalized Grid

Partha Bhowmick[1], Arindam Biswas[1], and Bhargab B. Bhattacharya[2]

[1] Computer Science and Technology Department,
Bengal Engineering and Science University, Shibpur, Howrah, India
{partha, abiswas}@becs.ac.in
[2] Advanced Computing and Microelectronics Unit,
Indian Statistical Institute, Kolkata, India
bhargab@isical.ac.in

Abstract. Determination of an isothetic polygonal approximation of the outer or inner contour of an object is a challenging problem with numerous applications to pattern recognition and image processing. In this paper, a novel algorithm is presented for constructing the outer (or inner) tight isothetic polygon(s) containing (or filling) an arbitrarily shaped 2D object on a background grid, using a classical labeling technique. The background grid may consist of uniformly or non-uniformly spaced horizontal and vertical lines. Experimental results for both uniform and non-uniform grids of varying sizes have been reported to demonstrate the applicability and efficiency of the proposed algorithm.

1 Introduction

Given a closed 2D contour (object) $\mathcal{C}$, we consider the problem of constructing the set of isothetic polygons that either fills the object (set of inner polygons, $\{\mathcal{P}_{in}(\mathcal{C})\}$) or contains the object (set of outer polygons, $\{\mathcal{P}_{out}(\mathcal{C})\}$), imposed by a set of horizontal and vertical grid lines, $\mathcal{G}$. The difficulty of successfully finding the isothetic polygon(s) corresponding to an arbitrarily shaped object lies in tracing a valid path defining the polygon boundary, especially in a convoluted region (on the background for outer polygons and on the object for inner polygons) that may propagate in every possible direction at every possible instant. An improper path surpassing a "dead end" may lead to a point whence no further advancement is possible. Further, if any backtracking is adopted, then in the case of complex and convoluted objects, the tracing procedure may become protracted, which would increase computational burden and difficulty in implementation.

It may be noted that the set of isothetic polygons corresponding to a given set of objects is useful to many interesting applications, such as area location [6], grasping objects by a robot [5,8,9,?], newspaper page decomposition and article tracking [7], document image analysis [1], deriving free configuration space (path-planner) for robot navigation, lower and upper approximation in rough sets [14,15] (in non-uniform grid spacing), image mining using rough sets [10],

VLSI layout design [13, 16], and computational geometry [2]. For rough set applications, the grid lines or decision lines imposed on the object are usually non-uniformly spaced. The proposed algorithm, therefore, would be helpful for rough set applications in 2D, as well as in higher dimensions, if properly modified, for its fitness and aptitude in non-uniform grid.

Very recently, another algorithm [3] for finding the outer isothetic polygon has been published. However, the algorithm proposed here is different in several aspects. In [3], the outer isothetic polygon is derived from two matrices, namely "unit edge matrix" and "unit square matrix", defined on the uniformly spaced grid. On the contrary, the algorithm, proposed here, is based on labeling of grid points by 15 unique labels, meant for determining the class and type of a vertex of the polygon. Further, in the proposed algorithm, non-uniform grids, multiple polygons, self-intersections of polygons, polygons for holes, etc., have been addressed and solved, which are not considered earlier [3].

2 Proposed Algorithm

The algorithm consists of three stages. For an outer (inner) polygon, Stage 1 labels a grid point p if and only if the following conditions are satisfied simultaneously:

(**C1**) p lies on the background (object);
(**C2**) object (background) lies in the 4-neighborhood of p.

In Stage 1, each grid point that satisfies (**C1**) and (**C2**) simultaneously is assigned with left/right/bottom/top (L/R/B/T) or a combination of them. Stage 2 extracts the vertices of the polygon on the basis of their labels in Stage 1. Stage 3, called the construction stage, constructs the isothetic outer polygon with the help of the vertex types assigned in the Stage 2. In the subsequent discussions, we adhere to the process of finding the outer isothetic polygon only, since that for the inner one is very much similar, as evident from the object–background duality mentioned above.

2.1 Stage 1: Labeling the Grid Points

Let p_1 be a grid point on the background that lies in the 4-neighborhood of the object. A depth-first search (DFS)-Visit [4] is initiated from p_1, followed by its (ordered) adjacency list, Adj[p_1], containing eight neighboring grid points of p_1 in counter-clockwise order. For each of these eight neighbors, the DFS-Visit is recursively executed, provided (**C1**) and (**C2**) are satisfied simultaneously.

A grid point p is labeled as L/R/B/T or a combination of them depending upon which of the four grid edges incident on p intersect the object, as illustrated in Fig. 1. For example, in Fig. 1(a), only the right edge of p intersects the object, which implies that p lies left of the object, whence p is labeled as L. Similarly, in Fig. 1(b), since p lies left and top of the object simultaneously, it is labeled by LT, and in Fig. 1(c), since p lies bottom and top of the object simultaneously, it is labeled by BT.

It may be noted that a grid point p can be labeled in $2^4 - 1 = 15$ different ways, namely, L, R, B, T, LR, LB, LT, RB, RT, BT, LRB, LRT, LBT, RBT,

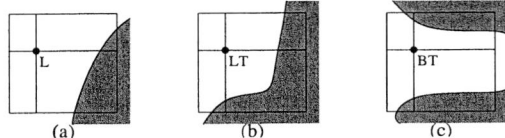

Fig. 1. An illustration of labeling for some cases of p

and LRBT. Out of these 15 cases, 4 cases (LB, LT, RB, RT) are candidate vertices (with internal angle 270^0) of $\mathcal{P}_{out}(\mathcal{C})$, and 4 other cases (L, R, B, T) are ordinary edge points of $\mathcal{P}_{out}(\mathcal{C})$. The remaining 7 cases (the labels containing LR or BT) are considered as **dead ends**. A dead end primarily signifies that it does not qualify for being a vertex or an edge point of $\mathcal{P}_{out}(\mathcal{C})$ as evident in Fig. 1(c), where a dead end, namely BT, has been illustrated. Further, a dead end signals a sharp change in curvature of the contour, which may call for a detailed examination in its neighborhood with a denser grid, if required.

2.2 Stage 2: Extracting the Candidate Vertices of $\mathcal{P}_{out}(\mathcal{C})$

Since $\mathcal{P}_{out}(\mathcal{C})$ is an isothetic polygon, each vertex of $\mathcal{P}_{out}(\mathcal{C})$ can have internal angle either 90^0 or 270^0. Based on this observation, Stage 2 extracts and classifies the vertices using object containments of the four quadrants, namely Q_1, Q_2, Q_3, Q_4 (see Fig. 1), associated with p, which, in turn, are derived from the labels of the grid points awarded in Stage 1. These vertices are of three classes, which are as follows.

(i) 90^0 **vertex:** It can be shown that, if a grid point p is a 90^0 vertex, then part of the object lies in exactly one of the neighboring four quadrants of p (Fig. 2). A 90^0 vertex can be sub-classified into four types, namely NE, NW, SE, SW, when the object lies in Q_1, Q_2, Q_3, Q_4 respectively.
(ii) 270^0 **vertex:** For a 270^0 vertex, p, object lies in exactly three quadrants of p (Fig. 2). This class is also sub-classified to NE, NW, SE, SW, when the object not lies in Q_1, Q_2, Q_3, Q_4 respectively.
(iii) **Cross vertex:** A cross vertex is a point of self-intersection. Since an isothetic polygon may have self-intersection(s), a cross vertex is merely the point of intersection of a horizontal edge and a vertical edge of $\mathcal{P}_{out}(\mathcal{C})$. A cross vertex is sub-classified into two types, namely NWSE (object is in Q_1 and Q_3) and NESW (object is in Q_2 and Q_4, see Fig. 2).

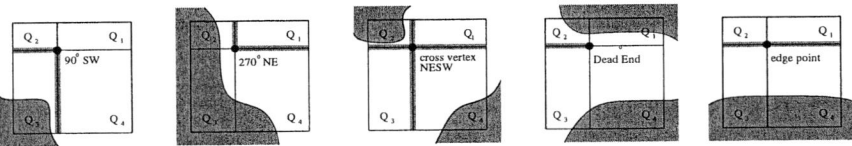

Fig. 2. Different vertex types

The sub-classification of the vertex types into NE, NW, SE, and SW aids the process of construction of the polygon. For example, if p is labeled as NE, then the outgoing edge from p will be its east-bound edge, provided the incoming edge for p is its north-bound edge; similarly, the outgoing edge from p will be its north-bound edge, provided the incoming edge for p is its east-bound edge.

2.3 Stage 3: Construction of $\mathcal{P}(\mathcal{C})$

Stage 3 constructs the outer polygon using the types of the detected vertices in Stage 2. It may be noted that the class of a vertex is not required, and only the type of the vertex is sufficient, for construction of the polygon.

The construction starts from a grid point, which is classified as a 90^0 vertex in stage 2. This vertex is specially marked as the start vertex, v_s, for the construction. It can be shown that a 270^0 vertex may not appear in the set of detected vertices in Stage 2. Hence a 90^0 vertex is always considered as a start vertex (v_s). Now, let v_c be the vertex that is currently under visit during the construction. Depending on the (incoming) edge along which v_c is visited and the type of v_c, the outgoing edge from v_c is determined. The traversal proceeds along the direction of this outgoing edge until the next vertex, v_n, is found. This process is repeated until v_n coincides with v_s.

2.4 Time Complexity

In Stage 1, since p_1 is the grid point lying in the 4-neighborhood of the object from where the DFS-Visit is initiated, the next grid point visited would be one of its eight neighbors in Adj[p_1], which being recursively executed, would finally terminate when p_1 is reached. Since each node p in this recursive DFS-Visit satisfies conditions (**C1**) and (**C2**), the number of nodes visited in the entire process would be linearly bounded by the number of grid points satisfying conditions (**C1**) and (**C2**). In Stage 2, the labels are used for deciding the vertices, which are finally used in Stage 3 to construct the polygon. Hence, for an object with no hole and having one isothetic polygon (inner or outer), the time complexity for finding out its single isothetic polygon is given by $O(|\mathcal{C}|/\alpha^2)$, where $|\mathcal{C}|$ denotes the length of the contour $\mathcal{C}$ and α denotes the spacing (minimum for non-uniform) between the grid lines.

If the object is having holes and/or requires multiple polygons (inner or outer) for its representation, then the time complexity for finding out its complete set of isothetic polygons, containing m polygons, is given by $O(m|\mathcal{C}|/\alpha^2)$, provided the starting grid point p_1 is given for each polygon. If the starting grid point p_1 is unknown for each polygon, then the complexity is $O(MN/\alpha^2)$, where M and N denote the width and height of the 2D plane containing $\mathcal{C}$.

3 Results

The above algorithm has the ability to extract the inner and outer polygons of a digital object of any complex shape, whether defined on uniform or non-uniform background grid. In addition, this algorithm also produces self-intersecting polygons when a cross vertex is treated as a point of self-intersection. We have tested it on a number of complex 2-D objects producing correct results in all cases, one of which being shown in Fig. 3.

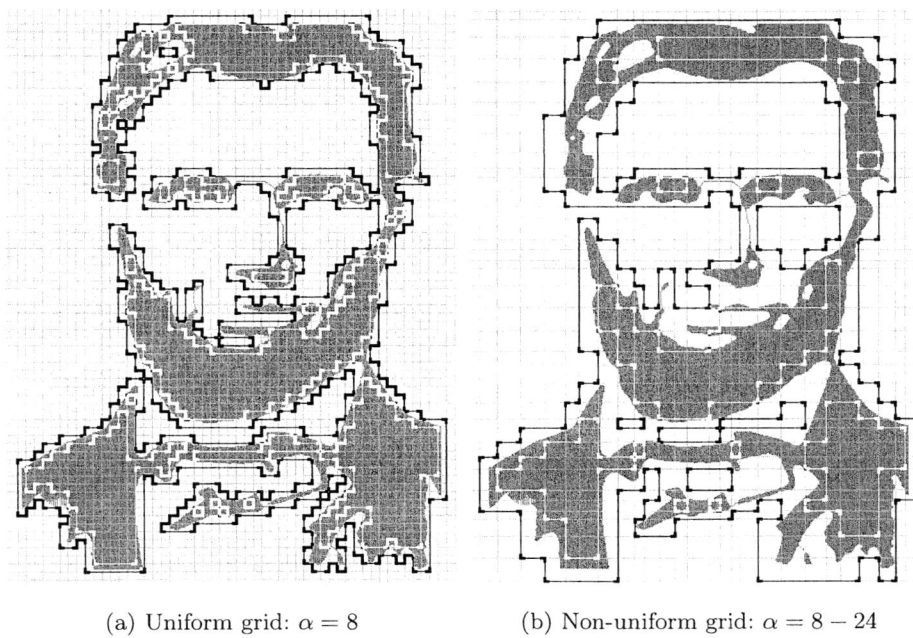

(a) Uniform grid: $\alpha = 8$ (b) Non-uniform grid: $\alpha = 8 - 24$

Fig. 3. Inner and outer polygons of Lincoln image on uniform and non-uniform grids

It may be noted that the number of vertices of both the outer and the inner polygons decrease with increase in grid size, thereby reducing the complexity of the isothetic polygon. For the image (size 430×570) in Fig. 3, CPU times for construction of isothetic polygons for grid size 1 are 956 and 507 milliseconds, which drops drastically to 4 and 6 milliseconds for grid size 16, for inner and outer polygons respectively.

4   Conclusion and Future Work

In this paper, we have presented an elegant algorithm to capture approximate outer and inner isothetic polygons covering a 2D object on both uniformly and non-uniformly spaced grid lines. This algorithm is fast and can be extended to higher dimensions, facilitating the determination of outer and inner approximations in rough sets. A detailed analysis can be done with respect to the point of inflections to make it amenable to different critical applications like VLSI design and verification, and robot grasping.

References

1. O. T. Akindele and A. Belaid, *Page Segmentation by Segment Tracing*, ICDAR 1993, pp. 341–344.
2. A. Bemporad, C. Filippi, and F. D. Torrisi, *Inner and Outer Approximations of Polytopes using Boxes*, Computational Geometry - Theory and Applications, vol. 27, 2004, pp. 151–178.
3. A. Biswas, P. Bhowmick, and B. B. Bhattacharya, *TIPS: On Finding a Tight Isothetic Polygonal Shape Covering a 2D Object*, 14th Scandinavian Conf. on Image Analysis (SCIA 2005), LNCS, vol. 3540, pp. 930–939.
4. T. H. Cormen, C.E. Leiserson, and R.L. Rivest *Introduction to Algorithms*, Prentice Hall India, New Delhi, 2000.
5. L. Gatrell, *Cad-based Grasp Synthesis Utilizing Polygons, Edges and Vertices*, Proc. IEEE Intl. Conf. Robotics and Automation, 1989, pp. 184–189.
6. B. Gatos and S. L. Mantzaris, *A Novel Recursive Algorithm for Area Location using Isothetic Polygons*, ICPR 2000, pp. 492–495.
7. B. Gatos, S. L. Mantzaris, K. V. Chandrinos, A. Tsigris, and S. J. Perantonis, *Integrated Algorithms for Newspaper Page Decomposition and Article Tracking*, ICDAR 1999, pp. 559–562.
8. Y. Kamon, T. Flash, and S. Edelman, *Learning to Grasp using Visual Information*, Proc. IEEE Intl. Conf. Robotics and Automation, 1995, pp. 2470–2476.
9. J. Lengyel, M. Reichert, B. R. Donald, and D. P. Greenberg, *Real-time Robot Motion Planning Using Rasterizing Computer*, Computer Graphics, ACM, vol. 24(4), pp. 327–335.
10. M. Liu, Y. He, H. Hu, and D. Yu, *Dimension Reduction Based on Rough Set in Image Mining*, Intl. Conf. on Computer and Information Technology (CIT'04), 2004, pp. 39–44.
11. A. Morales, P. J. Sanz, and A. P. del Pobil, *Vision-Based Computation of Three-Finger Grasps on Unknown Planar Objects*, IEEE Intl. Conf. on Intelligent Robots and Systems, 2002, pp. 1711–1716.
12. S. C. Nandy and B. B. Bhattacharya, *Safety Zone Problem*, Journal of Algorithms, vol. 37, 2000, pp. 538–569.
13. T. Ohtsuki, *Layout Design and Verification*, North-Holland, Amsterdam, 1986.
14. S. K. Pal and P. Mitra, *Case Generation Using Rough Sets with Fuzzy Representation*, IEEE Trans. on Knowledge and Data Engg., vol. 16(3), 2004, pp. 292–300.
15. S. K. Pal and P. Mitra, *Pattern Recognition Algorithms for Data Mining*, Chapman and Hall/CRC Press, Bocan Raton, FL, 2004.
16. N. Sherwani, *Algorithms for VLSI Physical Design Automation*, 3rd Edition, Kluwer Academic Publishers, Boston, 1999.
17. G. Taylor and L. Kleeman, *Grasping Unknown Objects with a Humanoid Robot*, Proc. Australasian Conf. on Robotics and Automation, 2002, pp. 191–196.

An Evolutionary SPDE Breeding-Based Hybrid Particle Swarm Optimizer: Application in Coordination of Robot Ants for Camera Coverage Area Optimization

Debraj De[1], Sonai Ray[1], Amit Konar[1], and Amita Chatterjee[2]

[1] Department of Electronics and Telecommunication Engineering, Jadavpur University,
Kolkata- 700032, India
debraj00@rediffmail.com, ssonai2003@yahoo.com,
amit_konar@vsnl.net
[2] Centre of Cognitive Science, Jadavpur University,
Kolkata- 700032, India
amita_ju@yahoo.com

Abstract. In this paper we propose a new Hybrid Particle Swarm Optimizer model based on particle swarm, with breeding concepts from novel evolutionary algorithms. The hybrid PSO combines traditional velocity and position update rules of RANDIW-PSO and ideas from Self Adaptive Pareto Differential Evolution Algorithm (SPDE). The hybrid model is tested and compared with some high quality PSO models like the RANDIW-PSO and TVIW-PSO. The results indicate two good prospects of our proposed hybrid PSO model: potential to achieve faster convergence as well as potential to find a better solution. The hybrid PSO model, with the abovementioned features, is then efficiently utilized to coordinate robot ants in order to help them to probe as much camera coverage area of some planetary surface or working field as possible with minimum common area coverage.

1 Introduction

Particle Swarm Optimization (PSO) is a population based self-adaptive search optimization technique, first introduced by Kennedy and Eberhart [1] in 1995. One of the latest promising quality models in PSO technique is the Particle Swarm Optimizer with Random Inertia Weight (RANDIW-PSO model). Evolutionary algorithms [5] are a kind of global optimization techniques that use selection and recombination as their primary operators to tackle optimization problems. *Differential evolution* (DE) is a branch of evolutionary algorithms developed by Rainer Storn and Kenneth Price for optimization problems over continuous domains. Of the latest Pareto Differential Evolution (PDE) algorithms, the Self-Adaptive Pareto Differential Evolution Algorithm (SPDE) [6] has the important property to self adapt the crossover and mutation rates.

The proposed hybrid PSO model incorporates crossover which is motivated by SPDE evolution. Here for some randomly selected dimensions particles are reselected and refined from SPDE crossover pool and goes under position updating. The paper is organized as follows: section 2 presents proposed hybrid PSO model, results and comparisons with some other PSO models are exhibited in section 3 and finally the hybrid PSO model is applied to solve coordination problem of robot ants which are engaged in covering some planetary surface by their camera, such that the common area coverage is minimum.

2 New Hybrid PSO Model

Here we propose a Hybrid Random Inertia Weight (RANDIW)-PSO model, in which breeding is performed by the Self Adaptive Pareto Differential Evolution (SPDE). The total algorithm is illustrated as follows:

A. Randomly generate the initial population.
B. Repeat
  until number of generation reaches its maximum limit:
  1. Randomly generate m number of dimensions that will be bred.
  2. For $i=1$ to m, do
     a. Construct SPDE breeding pools, each of which contain position values of i-th dimension (x_i) of three particles, chosen randomly.
     b. In each of the breeding pools, do
        i. Mark the minimum of three x_i values as the main parent α_1. Other two are supporting parent α_2 and α_3.
        ii. The crossover rate of each individual is chosen as $(1-x'_{ij})$, where x'_{ij} is the normalized position value of i-th dimension of j-th particle.
        iii. Calculate Crossover rate (x_c) of child:

$$x_c^{child} \leftarrow x_c^{\alpha 1} + r1 \cdot (x_c^{\alpha 2} - x_c^{\alpha 3}). \tag{1}$$

        Where r1 is a random number [0, 1].
        iv. Crossover: Select a random variable j [1, 3]
              For each variable k (value 1 or 2 or 3)
                With some random probability $[0, 1] > x_c^{child}$ or if $k = j$,
                do
                  Crossover between that α_k and the main parent α_1.
        Crossover is performed by arithmetic crossover on the position of the parents as follows:

$$child_1(x_i) = p_i.parent_1(x_i) + (1.0-p_i).parent_2(x_i). \tag{2}$$

$$child_2(x_i) = p_i.parent_2(x_i) + (1.0-p_i).parent_1(x_i). \tag{3}$$

Where p_i is uniformly distributed random value between 0 and 1. The velocity of the offspring is calculated as the sum of velocity vectors of the parent normalized to the original length of each parent velocity vector.

$$child_1(v) = [\{parent_1(v) + parent_2(v)\} / |parent_1(v) + parent_2(v)|] \cdot |parent_1(v)|. \tag{4}$$

$$child_2(v) = [\{parent_1(v) + parent_2(v)\} / |parent_1(v) + parent_2(v)|] \cdot |parent_2(v)|. \tag{5}$$

The arithmetic crossover of positions and velocity vectors used were empirically tested to be the most promising. The arithmetic crossover of positions in the search space is one of the most commonly used crossover methods with standard real valued GAs, placing the offspring within the hypercube spanned by the parent particles.

    iv. After the crossover, from the three parent and children, three minimum individuals are retained.

3. Apply PSO equation: The PSO equation follows the TVIW-PSO model:

$$v_i = w \cdot v_i + \varphi_{1i} \cdot (p_i - x_i) + \varphi_{2i} \cdot (p_g - x_i) . \tag{6}$$

$$x_i = x_i + v_i . \tag{7}$$

Where the inertia weight w is set to change randomly according to the following equation:

$$w = 0.5 + \{rand(.)/2\} . \tag{8}$$

The term rand(.) is a uniformly distributed random number within the range [0,1], thus with mean value 0.75. φ_{1i} and φ_{2i} are random values different for each particle and for each dimension. If the velocity is higher than a certain limit, called v_{max}, this limit will be used as the new velocity for this particle in this dimension, thus keeping the particles within search space.

3 Experimental Results

Our proposed SPDE breeding based hybrid RANDIW-PSO was compared with basic RANDIW-PSO and TVIW-PSO models on five standard test functions and it exhibited two important striking features of proposed hybrid PSO: faster convergence and resulting better solution, as illustrated clearly by the following tables and graphs.

Table 1. Initialization range, dynamic range and maximum for benchmarks

Test function	Range of search	Range of initialization	v_{max}
Sphere (f1)	$(-100,100)^n$	$(50,100)^n$	100
Rosenbrock (f2)	$(-100,100)^n$	$(15,30)^n$	100
Rastrigrin (f3)	$(-10,10)^n$	$(2.56, 5.12)^n$	10
Griewank (f4)	$(-600,600)^n$	$(300,600)^n$	600
Schaffer (f6)	$(-100,100)^2$	$(15,30)^2$	100

Table 2. Average value of the benchmarks for 50 trials

Function	Dimension	Generation	Average		
			PSO-RANDIW	PSO-TVIW	Proposed SPDE based hybrid PSO
f1	10	1000	0.01	0.01	0.01
	20	2000	0.01	0.01	0.01
	30	3000	0.01	0.01	0.01
f2	10	3000	2.212	26.840	2.002
	20	4000	28.332	53.653	26.708
	30	5000	38.227	63.352	36.586
f3	10	3000	1.001	1.989	1.989
	20	4000	19.984	3.979	8.944
	30	5000	44.772	15.919	10.823
f4	10	3000	0.0372	0.0765	0.0276
	20	4000	0.0074	0.0812	0.0070
	30	5000	0.0932	0.1048	0.01478
f6	2	100	0.00247	0.00246	0.00240

References

1. Kennedy, J., Eberhart, R.: Particle Swarm Optimization. Proc. IEEE Int. Conf. Neural Networks (1995) 1942-1948
2. Ratnaweera, A., Halgamuge, S.K., Watson, H.C.: Self-Organizing Hierarchical Particle Swarm Optimizer with Time-Varying Acceleration Coefficients. IEEE Transactions On Evolutionary Computation, Vol.8. (2004)
3. Kennedy, J.: The Particle Swarm: Social Adaptation of Knowledge. Proc. IEEE Int. Conf. Evolutionary Computation (1997) 303-308
4. Lovbjerg, M., Rasmussen, T.K., Krink, T.: Hybrid Particle Swarm Optimizer with Breeding and Subpopulation. Proc. 3rd Genetic Evolutionary Computation Conf. (GECCO-2001), San Fransisco, CA (2001) 469-476
5. Coello, C.A.: A Comprehensive Survey of Evolutionary-based Multiobjective Optimisation Techniques. Knowledge and Information Systems (1999) 269 – 308

An Improved Differential Evolution Scheme for Noisy Optimization Problems

Swagatam Das and Amit Konar

Dept. of Electronics and Telecommunication Engineering, Jadavpur University,
Kolkata-700032, India
swagatamdas19@yahoo.co.in

Abstract. Differential Evolution (DE) is a simple and surprisingly efficient algorithm for global optimization over continuous spaces. It has reportedly outperformed many versions of EA and other search heuristics when tested over both benchmark and real world problems. However the performance of DE deteriorates severely if the fitness function is noisy and continuously changing. In this paper we propose an improved DE scheme which can efficiently track the global optima of a noisy function. The scheme performs better than the classical DE, PSO, and an EA over a set of benchmark noisy problems.

1 Introduction

The problem of optimizing noisy or imprecise (not exactly known) functions occurs in diverse domains of engineering application, especially in the task of experimental optimizations. A number of methods for dealing with these noisy optimization problems have been proposed in the last few years by various experts in the fields of evolutionary programming (EP) [1], evolutionary strategies (ES) [2], genetic algorithms (GA) [3] and particle swarm optimization (PSO) [4]. Although DE is a simple and very fast technique for numerical optimization, it is reported in [5] that the performance of DE becomes poorer in comparison to EA when the function to be optimized is corrupted by noise and accuracy of the results is a vital factor.

In this study we propose an improved DE (DE/Rand1/Exp) algorithm where the scalar factor used to weigh the difference vector has been made completely random. We also introduce a novel threshold based selection strategy for the DE algorithm. Under this scheme an offspring vector replaces its parent in the next generation only if its fitness is greater than the parent's fitness by a certain threshold value. This provides prevention from accepting poor candidate solutions, which may deceptively appear fitter due to noise.

2 The Classical Differential Evolution – A Brief Introduction

DE [7], [8] searches for a global optimum point in an N-dimensional hyperspace. It begins with a randomly initialized population of N-dimensional real-valued parameter vectors. Each vector forms a candidate solution to the multi-dimensional optimization problem. Unlike the conventional GA, the reproduction scheme in DE is maintained as follows. For each individual vector G_k^D belonging to generation D, randomly sample three other individuals G_i^D, G_j^D and G_m^D from the same generation (for distinct *i, j, k and m*), calculate the difference of the components (chromosomes) of G_i^D and G_o^d, scale it by a scalar R ($\in [0,1]$) and create a trial vector by adding the result to the chromosomes of G_k^D.

$$\begin{rcases} G_{k,n}^{D+1} = G_{m,n}^D + R.(G_{i,n}^D - G_{j,n}^D) & \text{if rand}_n (0, 1) < CR \\ = G_{k,n}^D, & \text{otherwise.} \end{rcases} \quad (1)$$

for the n-th component of each parameter vector.

CR ($\in [0,1]$) is the crossover constant. The trial solution is evaluated and replaces its parent G_k^D. deterministically if its fitness is better.

3 The Newly Proposed Scheme

It is an observed fact that DE needs hardly any parameter tuning and converges surprisingly faster than PSO, GA and EA in most of the cases of static optimization problems. But we strongly feel that DE uses a less stochastic and greedier approach which makes the situation difficult for it whenever there is noise in the scenario.

In the original DE (1) the difference vector (G_i-G_j) is scaled by a constant factor 'R'. Usually the most popular choice for this control parameter in DE is in the range of (0.4, 1). However, we set this scale factor to change in a random fashion in the range (0.5, 1) by using the relation [11]

$$R = 0.5*(1+ \text{rand} (0, 1)) \quad (2)$$

where rand (0,1) is a uniformly distributed random number within the range [0, 1]. The mean value of the scale factor remains at 0.75. This allows for stochastic variation in the amplification of the difference vector and hence helps retain the population diversity as the search progresses.

Following the work done on EA in [6] we take up a threshold based selection procedure for DE. Here the offspring vector substitutes its parent vector in the new generation if its fitness is lesser than the fitness of the parent (in case of minimization problems) by a threshold margin τ. We keep the threshold margin proportional to the noise strength or variance (σ_n^2) i.e.

$$\tau = k.\sigma_n^2. \quad (3)$$

4 Experimental Setup and Simulation Strategy

We have used the noisy versions of the following benchmark functions enlisted in table 1. All of these are minimization problems. The noisy versions of the benchmark functions are defined as:

$$f_{noisy}(\vec{x}) = f(\vec{x}) + N(0, \sigma^2) \quad (4)$$

with N(0, σ^2) = Normal (or Gaussian) distribution with mean 0 and variance σ^2. To obtain N we take up the Box and Muller method [9] with various values of σ^2. In this work, we compare the performance of Particle Swarm Optimization (PSO), classical DE, the new scheme and Evolutionary Algorithm [10] over the noisy benchmarks listed above. Due to space limitations, it is not possible to give the brief description of the competitor algorithms.

Table 1. Benchmark functions for simulation

Name of the Function and Dimension	Mathematical Representation
Sphere function (50D)	$f_1(x) = \sum_{i=1}^{n} x_i^2$
Rosenbrock function (50D)	$f_2(x) = \sum_{i=1}^{n} [100 \ (x_{i+1} - x_i^2)^2 + (x_i - 1)^2]$
Griewank function (50D)	$f_4(x) = \frac{1}{4000} \sum_{i=1}^{n} x_i^2 - \prod_{i=1}^{n} \cos(\frac{x_i}{\sqrt{i}}) + 1$
Rastrigin function (50D)	$f_3(x) = \sum_{i=1}^{n} [x_i^2 - 10 \cos(2\pi x_i) + 10]$
Levy No. 5 (2D)	$f_5 = \sum_{i=1}^{5} i \cos[(i+1)x_1 + i] \times \sum_{j=1}^{5} j \cos[(j+1)x_2 + j] + (x_1 + 1.42513)^2 + (x_2 + 0.80032)^2$

5 Results of Simulation

Although we have experimented with noise variance values 0, 0.1, 0.2 ...1, due to space limitations we tabulate the final result in table 2 only for $\sigma_n^2 = 1.0$ i.e. when the noise strength is highest.

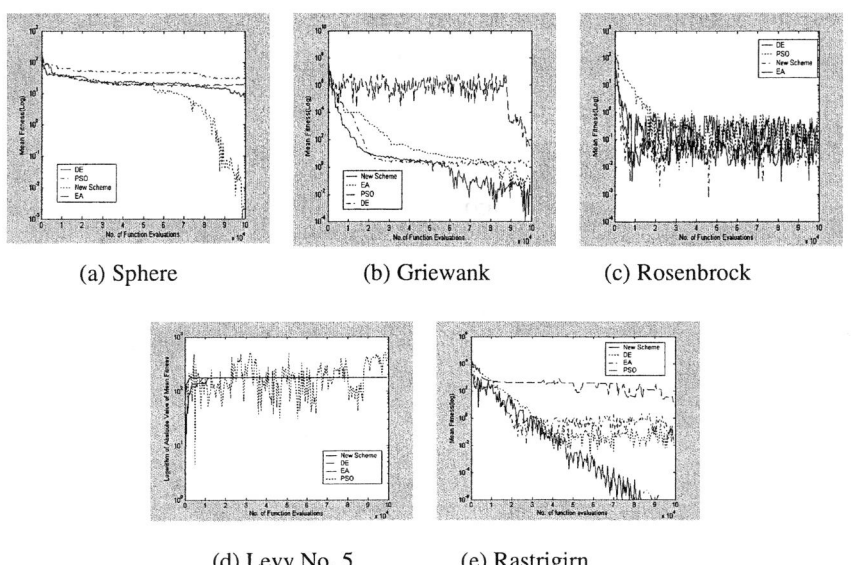

(a) Sphere   (b) Griewank   (c) Rosenbrock

(d) Levy No. 5   (e) Rastrigirn

Fig. 2. Progress to the optimum solution

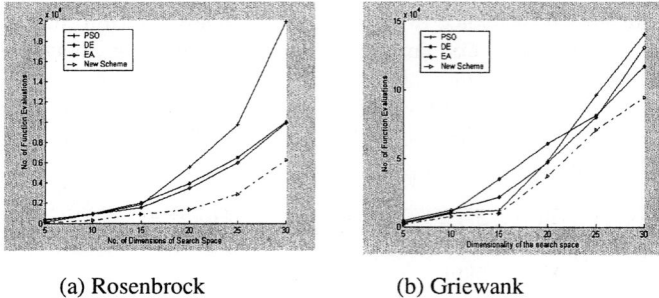

(a) Rosenbrock   (b) Griewank

Fig. 3. Variation of mean convergence time with increase in dimensionality of the search space. (Shaded graph accounts for the new algorithm).

Table 2. Mean and Standard Error (±SE) of the Final Results after 10^5 Function Evaluations

Function	DE	PSO	EA	New Scheme
f_1	0.2145±0.02408	0.3562±0.06021	0.05002±0.0056	**6.123E-6±0.0002**
f_2	42.2748±0.1741	4559.75±867.89	114.25±12.68	**1.27±7.363**
f_3	2.4169±0.04591	51.4508±3.0067	32.7144±1.656	**2.6148±0.0474**
f_4	3.7142±0.0766	13.6445±1.4435	1.0975±0.0026	**0.2113±0.00054**
f_5	0.1386±0.0309	0.7765±0.1137	0.0982±0.02573	**0.02215±0.00663**

6 Conclusion

In this paper we firstly point out that, DE due to employing a deterministic selection scheme and having no random mutation process becomes 'greedy' and fails to optimize noisy functions satisfactorily. As a remedy to this problem, we equip the basic algorithm with a randomly changing scale factor and a threshold based selection scheme. Substantial empirical evidence has been provided to justify the usefulness of the proposed approach. The new method has been compared against (a) the basic DE, (b) the PSO, and (c) EA using a five-function test suite.

References

1. Fogel, L.J, Owens, A.J, Walsh, M.J.: Artificial Intelligence through Simulated Evolution. John Wiley & Sons, New York, (1966).
2. Rechenberg, I.: Evolution Strategy: Optimization of technical systems by means of biological evolution. Fromman-Holzboog, Stuttgart, (1973).
3. Holland, J.H.: Adaptation in Natural and Artificial Systems. University of Michigan Press, Ann Arbor, MI, (1975)
4. Kennedy, J, Eberhart R.: Particle swarm optimization. Proc. IEEE Int. conf. Neural Networks. (1995) 1942-1948
5. Krink, T, Bodgan, F, Fogel, G.B., Thomson, R.: Noisy Optimization Problems – A Particular Challenge for Differential Evolution? Proc. Sixth Congress on Evolutionary Computation (CEC-2004). IEEE Press.

6. Markon, S, Arnold, V, D, Bäck, T, Beislstein, T, Beyer, G.-H.: Threshholding – a Selection Operator for Noisy ES. Proc. Congress on Evolutionary Computation (CEC-2001). 465-472
7. Storn, R., Price, K.: Differential evolution – A Simple and Efficient Heuristic for Global Optimization over Continuous Spaces, Journal of Global Optimization, 11(4) (1997) 341–359.
8. Price K. V.: An introduction to differential evolution. In New Ideas in Optimization. Corne, D, Dorigo, M, Glover, F, Eds. McGrow-Hill, London. (1999) 79-108.
9. Box, G. E. P, Muller, M. E.: A note on the generation of random deviates, Ann. Math. Statistics, vol. 29, (1958) 610-611.
10. Michalewicz, Z, Fogel, D. B.: How to Solve It: Modern Heuristics. Springer, Berlin, 2000.
11. Das, S., Konar, A., Chakraborty, U.K., Two improved differential evolution schemes for faster global search, to appear in the ACM-SIGEVO Proceedings of GECCO, Washington D.C., June 2005.

Facial Asymmetry in Frequency Domain: The "Phase" Connection

Sinjini Mitra[1], Marios Savvides[2], and B.V.K. Vijaya Kumar[2]

[1] Department of Statistics, Carnegie Mellon University,
Pittsburgh, PA 15213
smitra@stat.cmu.edu

[2] Electrical and Computer Engineering Department,
Carnegie Mellon University,
Pittsburgh, PA 15213
msavvid@cs.cmu.edu, kumar@ece.cmu.edu

Abstract. Facial asymmetry has now been established as a useful biometric for human identification in the presence of expression variations ([1]). The current paper investigates an alternative representation of asymmetry in the frequency domain framework, and its significance in identification tasks in terms of the phase component of the frequency spectrum of an image. The importance of the latter in face reconstruction is well-known in the engineering literature ([2]) and this establishes a firm ground for the success of asymmetry as a potentially useful biometric. We also point out some useful implications of this connection and dual representation. Moreover, the frequency domain features are shown to be more robust to intra-personal distortions than the corresponding spatial measures and yield error rates as low as 4% on a dataset with images showing extreme expression variations.

1 Introduction

Human faces have two kinds of asymmetry - intrinsic and extrinsic. The former is caused by growth, injury and age-related changes, while the latter is affected by viewing orientation and lighting direction. We are however interested in intrinsic asymmetry which is directly related to the individual facial structure while extrinsic asymmetry can be controlled to a large extent or can be pre-processed or normalized. Psychologists say that the more asymmetric a face, the less attractive it is and more recognizable ([3], [4]). This indicates the potential significance of asymmetry in automatic face recognition problems.

A commonly accepted notion in computer vision is that human faces are bilaterally symmetric ([5]) and [6] reported no differences whatsoever in recognition rates while using only the right and left halves of the face. However, a well-known fact is that manifesting expressions cause a considerable amount of facial asymmetry, they being more intense on the left side of the face ([7]). Indeed [8] found differences in recognition rates for the two halves of the face under a given facial expression.

Despite extensive studies on facial asymmetry, its use in human identification started in the computer vision community only in 2001 with the seminal work by Liu ([9]), who for the first time showed that certain facial asymmetry measures are efficient human identification tools under expression variations. This was followed by more in-depth studies ([1], [10]) which further investigated the role and locations of different types of asymmetry measures both for human as well as expression classifications. But people have not so far utilized the frequency domain for developing facial asymmetry measures for recognition. This is a natural extension given that there exists much correspondence between the two domains. We explore this in depth in this paper.

The paper is organized as follows. Section 2 describes the dataset used and Section 3 introduces the new asymmetry measures in the frequency domain and presents some classification results. Section 4 describes the connection with Fourier domain phase and finally a discussion appears in Section 5.

2 Data

The dataset used here is a part of the "Cohn-Kanade AU-coded Facial Expression Database" ([11]), consisting of images of 55 individuals expressing three different kinds of emotions - joy, anger and disgust. Each person was asked to express one emotion at a time by starting with a neutral expression and gradually evolving into its peak form. The data thus consists of video clips of people showing an emotion, each clip being broken down into several frames. The raw images are normalized using an affine transformation, the details being included in [1]. Each normalized image is of size 128 × 128. Some normalized images from our database are shown in Fig. 1. This is the only available database for studying facial asymmetry and we use this smaller subset as out initial testbed.

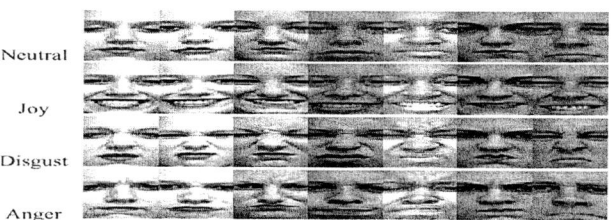

Fig. 1. Sample images from our database

3 The Frequency Domain

Many signal processing applications in computer engineering involve the frequency-domain representation of signals. The frequency spectrum consists of two components at each frequency: magnitude and phase. In 2D images particularly, the phase component captures more of the image intelligibility than magnitude and hence is very significant for performing image reconstruction ([2]). [12] showed that correlation filters built in the frequency domain can be used for efficient face-based recognition, and moreover, those based only on the phase component performed as well as the original filters ([13]). [14] demonstrated that performing PCA in the frequency domain by eliminating the magnitude spectrum not only outperformed spatial domain PCA, but also have attractive properties such as illumination and occlusion tolerance. These hence show that frequency domain features (particularly phase) possess the potential for improving classification results.

Symmetry properties of the Fourier transform are often very useful ([15]). Any sequence $x(n)$ can be expressed as a sum of an even part $x_e(n)$ and an odd part $x_o(n)$. Specifically, $x(n) = x_e(n) + x_o(n)$, where $x_e(n) = \frac{1}{2}(x(n) + x(-n))$ and $x_o(n) = \frac{1}{2}(x(n) - x(-n))$. Now, the even part actually corresponds to the *symmetry* part of the face and the odd part refers to the *asymmetry*. In other words, the more asymmetry a facial region possesses, the higher its value of the odd part and vice versa. Similarly, the more symmetric a particular face part is, the higher its value of the even part and vice versa. When a Fourier transform is performed on a real sequence $x(n)$, the even part $(x_e(n))$ transforms to the real part of the Fourier transform and the odd part $(x_o(n))$ transforms to its imaginary part (Fourier transform of any sequence is generally complex-valued). This implies that the asymmetry of the face (spatial domain) corresponds to the imaginary part of the Fourier transform and the symmetry part corresponds to the real part. This lays the ground for exploiting this correspondence between the two domains for developing more refined face identification tools based on asymmetry. Moreover, all these relations hold mainly for one-dimensional sequences alone, and hence we will define all our asymmetry features based on the Fourier transforms of row slices of the images.

3.1 The Asymmetry Biometrics

Following the notion presented in the earlier section, we define our asymmetry biometrics as:

- **I-face:** frequency-wise imaginary components of Fourier transforms of each row slice - 128 × 128 matrix of features
- **Ave I-face:** frequency-wise imaginary components of Fourier transforms of averages of two-row slices of the face - 64 × 128 matrix of features
- **E-face:** *energy* of the imaginary components of the Fourier transform of averages of two-row slices of the face - a feature vector of length 64

For all three sets of features, the higher their values the greater the amount of asymmetry, and vice versa. The averaging for E-faces is done in order to study if smoothing out noise in the image can reduce artificial asymmetry artifacts that gives misleading results. To the best of our knowledge, these frequency-based features as a means of representing facial asymmetry are fairly novel in any computer vision and pattern recognition problems.

3.2 Some Classification Results

Of the various classifiers tried (including SVM, LDA, FF), the best results are obtained with Individual PCA (IPCA) which we report here. The IPCA method ([13]) is different from the global PCA approach ([16]) where a subspace W is computed from all the images regardless of identity. In individual PCA, on the other hand, subspaces W_p are computed for each person p and each test image is projected onto each individual subspace using $y_p = W_p^T(x - m_p)$. The reader is referred to [13] for more details about the procedure.

Table 1. Error rates for human identification using frequency-domain measures

I-face	Ave I-face	E-face	Spatial D-face	D-face PCs
4.85%	3.64%	6.36%	17.58%	3.03%

The training is done on the neutral frames of the 55 individuals in the dataset and testing on the peak frames of the three emotions from all the people. Hence this represents an expression-invariant human identification problem, similar to the one reported in [1] which uses a simplistic measure of facial asymmetry in the spatial domain called D-face. The identification results in Table 1 show that our proposed frequency domain measures are significantly better than D-face (p-values <0.0001) and have no statistically significant differences with the D-face PCs at the 1% level (p-values nearly 1). This shows quite convincingly that the frequency-domain measures are at least as robust to expression changes as their spatial domain counterparts. Further, the I-faces proved to be significantly better than the E-faces, which may be due to the loss of discriminative information caused by the feature reduction in the E-faces.

4 Connection with Phase

In this section we investigate in depth the correspondence of facial asymmetry with phase, that was briefly mentioned in Section 3. The symmetric part of a real sequence transforms to the real part in a Fourier transform whereas the asymmetric part transforms to the imaginary part. Thus the Fourier transform of a real symmetric sequence is real; that of a real asymmetric sequence is purely imaginary. Now, since phase is defined as $\theta = \tan^{-1}\left(\frac{I}{R}\right)$, where R and I are respectively the real and the imaginary parts of the Fourier transform, $\theta = 0$ in case the imaginary component I is zero. In other words, a completely symmetric sequence gives rise to zero-phase frequency spectrum. In other words, absence of asymmetry implies zero phase, and vice versa. An important thing to note here is that all the above relations hold for 1D sequences $x(n)$ only (that is, when performing 1D Fourier transforms), as also pointed out in Section 3.

Interpreting these relations in terms of a face image, a completely symmetric face does not typically imply a zero-phase spectrum when applying a 2D Fourier transform. However, if we treat each row slice of the face as a 1D sequence and apply a 1D Fourier transform, the above relations will hold and each symmetric row will give rise to a 1D zero-phase spectrum. This is one primary reason we defined our asymmetry features the way we did. To make this study more rigorous, we constructed similar asymmetry features as before, using 1D row slices or averages of two-row slices but now based on "phase-only images" which have constant unit magnitude (obtained by dividing the Fourier transform by its magnitude). We call them I-face$_\theta$, Ave I-face$_\theta$ and E-Face$_\theta$.

Table 2. Error rates based on asymmetry features from phase-only images

I-face$_\theta$	Ave I-face$_\theta$	E-face$_\theta$
4.85%	5.45%	7.27%

Table 2 shows the results from these phase-only features using the same experimental setup as before. They help establish, although empirically, an interesting connection between facial asymmetry and phase for human identification. The I-face features based on the actual images and the phase-only images produce exactly same classification results. This indicates that phase contains all the asymmetry of the original face, at least to the extent that is necessary for identification purposes, and no crucial information is lost by removing the magnitude. This leads us to believe that asymmetry may provide an alternative means of representing phase information. The Ave I-face$_\theta$ and E-face$_\theta$ results are different from Ave I-face and E-face (not significantly though) and this may be an artifact of averaging invloved in computing these features.

5 Discussion

We have shown in this paper that facial asymmetry measures in the frequency domain offer a promising potential as an useful biometric in practice, especially, in the presence of expression variations in face images. An error rate of less than 5% is impressive and desirable given that the test images are very different from the training ones. This in turn is very important for recognition routines in practice, for example, surveillance photos captured at airports are expected to be quite diverse with respect to facial expressions.

Moreover, our features are very simple and easy to compute, and they are based on well-known techniques such as Fourier transforms and phase which have well-established themselves as efficient face recognition tools in computer vision. However, the particular representations of them in terms of facial asymmetry that we consider in this paper are novel. It helped show that facial asymmetry, which has so far been treated only in the spatial domain, also has an analogous frequency domain version - a fact that can be utilized in signal processing applications too. More importantly, we have established an interesting connection between facial asymmetry and the phase component. Given the utter significance of phase in face-based identification, this helps in strengthening the scientific basis for the success of facial asymmetry in telling human beings apart. This relationship is a novel one and have not been explored earlier. It adds a whole new dimension to the concept of facial asymmetry and lays the ground for much further research in different directions. Particularly, the fact that asymmetry has an analogous spatial domain representation, provides a potential means of studying phase behavior in the image domain, and can be useful from several viewpoints such as, modeling, inference, etc.

Future research directions include investigating the role of the frequency domain features for expression classification, their tolerance to illumination changes, increasing the efficiency of the features, not only from classification point of view but also from storage and computational standpoints and application to larger and more diverse databases.

References

1. Liu, Y., Schmidt, K., Cohn, J., Mitra, S.: Facial asymmetry quantification for expression-invariant human identification. CVIU **91** (2003) 138–159
2. Hayes, M.H.: The reconstruction of a multidimensional sequence from the phase or magnitude of its fourier transform. ASSP **30** (1982) 140–154
3. Thornhill, R., Gangstad, S. W.: Facial attractiveness. Transactions in Cognitive Sciences **3** (1999) 452–460
4. Troje, N. F., Buelthoff, H. H.: How is bilateral symmetry of human faces used for recognition of novel views? Vision Research **38** (1998) 79–89
5. Seitz, S.M., Dyer, C.R.: View morphing. SIGGRAPH (1996) 21–30
6. Gutta, S., Philomin, V., Trajkovic, M.: An investigation into the use of partial-faces for face recognition. In: International Conference on Automatic Face and Gesture Recognition, Washington D.C. (2002) 33–38
7. Borod, J.D., Koff, E., Yecker, S., Santschi, C., Schmidt, J.M.: Facial asymmetry during emotional expression: gender, valence and measurement technique. Psychophysiology **36** (1998) 1209–1215
8. Martinez, A.M.: Recognizing imprecisely localized, partially occluded and expression variant faces from a single sample per class. PAMI **24** (2002) 748–763
9. Liu, Y., Schmidt, K., Cohn, J., Weaver, R.L.: Human facial asymmetry for expression-invariant facial identification. In: Automatic Face and Gesture Recognition. (2002)
10. Mitra, S., Liu, Y.: Local facial asymmetry for expression classification. In Proceedings of CVPR (2004)
11. Kanade, T., Cohn, J.F., Tian, Y.L.: Comprehensive database for facial expression analysis. In: Automatic Face and Gesture Recognition. (2000) 46–53
12. Savvides, M., Vijaya Kumar, B.V.K., Khosla, P.: Face verification using correlation filters. In: 3rd IEEE Automatic Identification Advanced Technologies, Tarrytown, NY (2002) 56–61
13. Savvides, M., Kumar, B.V.K.: Eigenphases vs.eigenfaces. ICPR (2004)
14. Savvides, M., Kumar, B.V.K., Khosla, P.K.: Corefaces - robust shift invariant PCA based correlation filter for illumination tolerant face recognition. CVPR (2004)
15. Oppenheim, A.V., Schafer, R.W.: Discrete-time Signal Processing. Prentice Hall, Englewood Cliffs, NJ (1989)
16. Turk, M.A., Pentland, A.P.: Face recognition using eigenfaces. In CVPR (1991)

An Efficient Image Distortion Correction Method for an X-ray Digital Tomosynthesis System

J.Y. Kim

Dept. of Mechatronics Engineering,
Tongmyong University of Information Technology,
535 Yongdang-dong, Nam-gu, Busan 608-711, Korea
kjy97@tit.ac.kr

Abstract. Among X-ray cross-sectional imaging methods, digital tomosynthesis (DT) is very useful to PCB inspection because it can obtain a cross-sectional image of a local inspection area quickly. The image intensifier, which is usually used in DT systems, distorts X-ray images in shape and intensity. Therefore, image distortion correction is one of the most important issues in realizing a DT system. This paper presents an image distortion correction method to acquire an arbitrary cross-sectional image of an object by using a distance ratio function in an X-ray DT system. The method uses a simplified distortion model made by a distance ratio function in intensity correction, and by the 2D point mapping polynomials in shape correction.

1 Introduction

X-ray technology has been widely used in many industrial applications for inspecting inner defects which can hardly be found by normal vision systems. PCB solder joint inspection such as ball grid array (BGA) or flip chip array (FCA) is one of the applications that require such an X-ray inspection system[1,2]. An X-ray cross-sectional image can be obtained from two or more images projected from different directions by the methods such as tomography, laminography, or digital tomosynthesis.

Tomography has been mainly used in medical area, but recently it is being applied in industrial fields such as precision inspection of casting products[3]. Laminography was originated by Bocage[4]. Its principle comes from the geometric focusing effect by a synchronized motion between an X-ray source and a detector, which is shown in Fig. 1. Digital tomosynthesis is a digital version of laminography, where a set of images of different views are stored and synthesized through computational operations in a computer[5]. It is one of the most useful X-ray cross-sectional imaging methods for PCB inspection because it can obtain a cross-section of a local inspection area quickly. Thus it has been often applied to PCB solder joint inspection[5-8]. However, the shape and the intensity of the X-ray images obtained by DT are distorted because of the image intensifier used in DT systems. This distortion breaks the correspondences between those images and prevents us from acquiring accurate cross-sectional images. Therefore, image distortion correction is one of the most important issues in realizing a DT system.

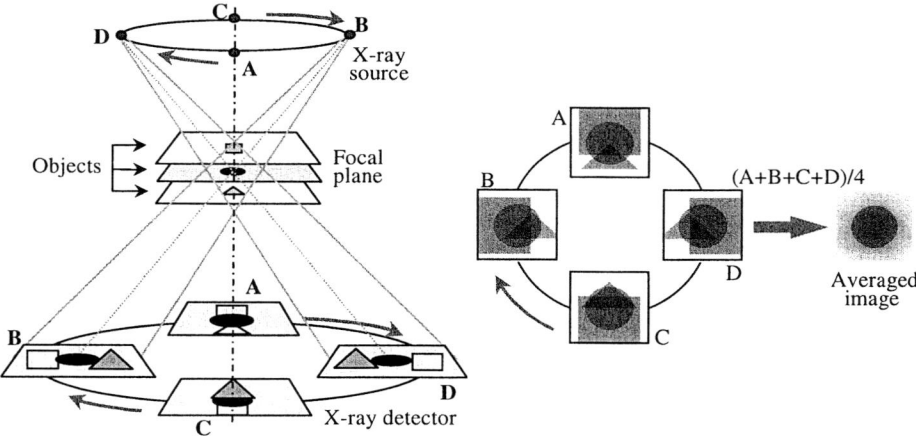

Fig. 1. The principle of Laminography and Digital Tomosynthesis

In this paper, an image distortion correction method for an X-ray DT system is presented. The method uses a simplified distortion model that is built by uniformly spaced grids and their distorted images. The intensity distortion model is based on the distance ratio function between two grids, and the shape distortion model is based on the two-dimensional point mapping polynomials. Also this paper performs a series of experiments to acquire PCB solder joint images by the presented correction method.

2 System Configuration and Image Distortion

Fig. 2(a) shows a configuration of the developed X-ray DT system, which is composed of a scanning X-ray tube, an image intensifier, a view selector and a zoom camera. An image intensifier with a large input screen is used as an X-ray detector so as to get all images projected at various directions. The area of interest of a PCB is projected on a circular trajectory on the image intensifier as the X-ray is steered on the trajectory, and eight or more images are sequentially acquired by the zoom camera through a view selector. A galvanometer or a rotating prism can be used as a view selector. The captured images are saved in the digital memory of a computer, and then synthesized to generate a cross-sectional image.

The curved image input surface of the intensifier, however, distorts both of the shape and the intensity of the X-ray images. Fig. 2(b) shows eight distorted images of an uniformly spaced grid pattern projected onto the image intensifier according to the steered X-ray source location. It is shown that the images are distorted more severely in the peripheral area than the central area. It is not possible to get an accurate cross-sectional image from these distorted images, since the correspondences between the images are not maintained anymore.

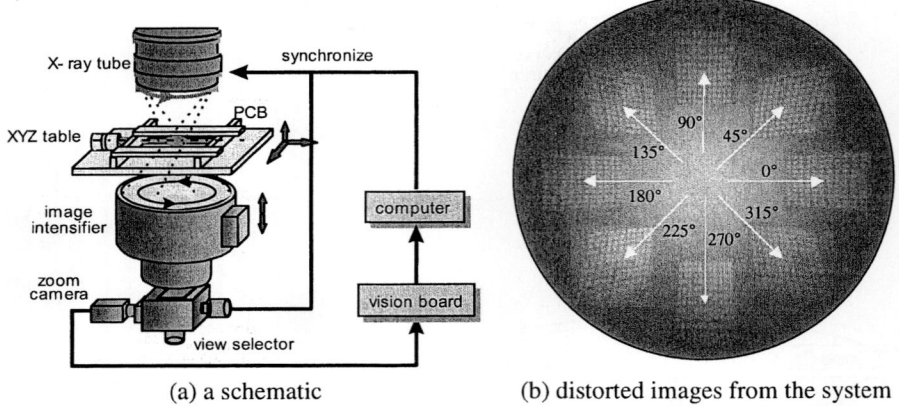

(a) a schematic (b) distorted images from the system

Fig. 2. The configuration of an X-ray Digital Tomosynthesis system

3   Intensity Distortion Correction by Using a Distance Ratio Function

The central area of the image intensifier is brighter than the peripheral area, since the incident angle of the X-ray to the curved input surface of the intensifier varies with the incident locations. In each projected image, therefore, intensity is the highest in the vicinity of the image intensifier center and gets lower toward the peripheral area. To compensate for the distorted intensity and make it uniform over the image, the distorted intensity should be scaled on the same level with an intensity value, for example, the maximum intensity level of the image. In order to do it, intensities are sampled over the image area and the distribution is modeled numerically.

The distorted intensity $\Phi_d(i, j)$ at a point (i, j) of an image can be corrected to the compensated intensity $\Phi_c(i, j)$ by dividing by the distance ratio function $f(L_d)$ for the point, as given in Eq. (1).

$$\Phi_c(i, j) = \Phi_d(i, j) / f(L_d). \tag{1}$$

$$f(L_d) = c_0 + c_1 L_d + c_2 L_d^2 + c_3 L_d^3. \tag{2}$$

$$L_d(i, j) = \sqrt{(i - i_H)^2 + (j - j_H)^2} \tag{3}$$

where $L_d(i, j)$ is defined as the distance from the highlight point $H = (i_H, j_H)$ to the point (i, j). The distance ratio function $f(L_d)$ has a value decreasing with L_d between 0 and 1, thus plays a role of correcting an intensity Φ_d to Φ_c. To build the ratio function $f(L_d)$, 10 intensity values are sampled from the 10 small areas on the path from the point H to the point L, as shown in the Fig. 3. The coefficients of the polynomial $f(L_d)$ can be determined by least square method.

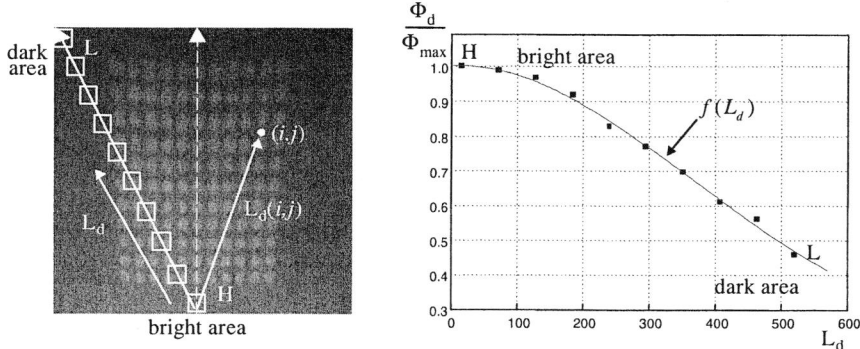

Fig. 3. Distorted intensity profile for a distance ratio function

4 Shape Distortion Correction by Using a Simplified Polynomial Model

The shape distortion can be corrected by finding a mapping relationship between the uniformly spacing grid image and its distorted image. Thus, a point (i, j) in the original undistorted image is mapped to a point (x, y) in the distorted image by the mapping relation, as shown in Fig. 4. As the sample data for distortion modeling, this paper used the data sets which consist of the uniformly spaced grid points of 11*11. There are two features in the shape distortion. One is that the distorted images are always symmetric with the projection center-line of the x-ray. Another one is that the peripheral area of the image intensifier is more elongated than the central area. Based on the two features, the mapping relationship can be modeled and represented by the following equations.

$$y_k(i,j) = \alpha_k(j)\{x(i,j) - x_c\}^2 + P_k(j) \cdot \quad (4)$$

$$x_k(i,j) = \beta_k(j) \cdot i + i_c \cdot \quad (5)$$

$$\begin{aligned} P_k(j) &= p_0^k + p_1^k \cdot j + p_2^k \cdot j^2 + p_3^k \cdot j^3 \\ \alpha_k(j) &= a_0^k + a_1^k \cdot j + a_2^k \cdot j^2 + a_3^k \cdot j^3 \\ \beta_k(j) &= b_0^k + b_1^k \cdot j + b_2^k \cdot j^2 + b_3^k \cdot j^3 \end{aligned} \quad (6)$$

A distorted line, which is a distortion of an original horizontal line, is modeled by using a 2nd order polynomial as shown in Eq. (4). On the other hand, the x coordinate values $x_k(i,j)$ of the distorted line are modeled as shown in Eq. (5). The parameters $P_k(j)$, $\alpha_k(j)$, $\beta_k(j)$ are functions of j, and they are modeled by using 3rd order polynomials as shown in Eq. (6). The coefficients $p_0^k \sim p_3^k$, $a_0^k \sim a_3^k$, $b_0^k \sim b_3^k$ are determined by using least square fitting.

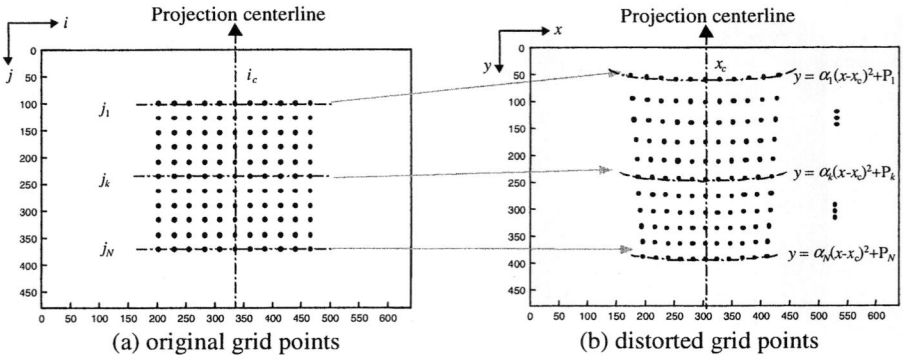

(a) original grid points   (b) distorted grid points

Fig. 4. Two-dimensional point mapping for shape distortion correction

5 Experiments for PCB Solder Joint Image Acquisition

A series of experiments to get the DT images of BGA was performed by using the X-ray DT system shown in Fig. 2(a). In the acquired images shown in Fig. 5, the dark regions represent the cross-sections of the corresponding focal planes. The cross-section at the middle of the lead ball has the maximum diameter. These DT images were acquired by integrating the 8 images taken from 8 different off-axis images. In each image of them, the intensity and shape distortion was corrected by using the correction method presented in above sections. These cross-sectional images provide a good cue or a unique solution to inspect the inner defects of the objects such as BGA or J-lead typed chips.

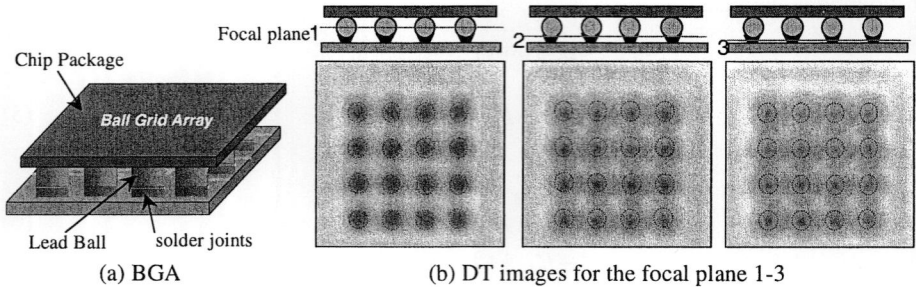

(a) BGA   (b) DT images for the focal plane 1-3

Fig. 5. X-ray DT images of BGA

6 Conclusions

In order to obtain an arbitrary cross-sectional image with high quality in an X-ray DT system, this paper presented a method to correct the distortion of image intensity and image shape. The method uses a simplified distortion model made by a distance ratio function in intensity correction, and by the 2D point mapping polynomials in shape correction. And a series of experiments to get DT images of BGA was performed by using the presented correction method. The experimental results show that the presented correction method is effective in acquiring an arbitrary cross-sectional image of an object.

References

1. Adams, J.: X-ray laminography analysis of ultra fine pitch solder connections on ultra-thin boards. SPIE Integrated Circuit Metrology, Inspection, and Process Control V, Vol. 1464. (1991) 484-497
2. Moore, T. D., Vanderstraeten, D., Forssell, P.M., Three-dimensional x-ray laminography as a tool for detection and characterization of BGA package defects. IEEE Tr. on Components and Packaging Technologies, Vol. 25. No. 2. (2002) 224-229
3. Bossi, R. H. and Georgeson, G. E.: Casting development savings with X-ray computed tomography. Casting (1993) 181-188
4. Bocage, E. M.: French Patent 536464 (1922)
5. Rooks, M. and Sack, T.: X-ray inspection of flip chip attach using digital tomosynthesis. Circuit World, Vol. 21. No. 3. (1995) 51-55
6. Bord, S., Clement, A., Lecomte, J. C., Marmeggi, J. C.: An X-ray tomography facility for IC industry at STMicroelectronics Grenoble. Microelectronic engineering, Vol. 62. (2002) 1069-1075
7. Sumimoto, T., Maruyamay, T., Azuma, Y., Goto, S., Mondo, M., Furukawa, N., Okada, S.: Detection of defects at BGA solder joints by using X-ray imaging. 2002 IEEE Int. Conf. on Industrial Technology, Vol. 1. (2002) 238-241
8. Roh, Y. J., Ko, K. W., Cho, H. S., Kim, J. Y., Byun, J. E.: The calibration of X-ray digital tomosynthesis system including the compensation of the image distortion. SPIE Symp. on Intelligent Systems and Advanced Manufacturing VII, Vol. 3528. (1998) 248-259

Eigen Transformation Based Edge Detector for Gray Images

P. Nagabhushan, D.S. Guru, and B.H. Shekar

Department of Studies in Computer Science, University of Mysore,
Manasagangothri, Mysore- 570006, Karnataka, India
pnagabhushan@hotmail.com, guruds@lycos.com,
bhshekar@yahoo.com

Abstract. In this paper, a simple and a robust algorithm to detect edges in a gray image is proposed. The statistical property of the small eigenvalue of the covariance matrix of a set of connected pixels over a small region of support is explored for the purpose of edge detection. The gray image is scanned from the top left corner to the bottom right corner with a moving mask of size k x k, for some integer k. At every stage, the small eigenvalue of the covariance matrix of the connected pixels that are having approximately same intensity as that of the center pixel of the mask is computed. This small eigenvalue is used to decide if a pixel is a potential edge pixel based on a pre-defined threshold value. The set of all identified potential edge pixels are then subjected to a pruning process where true edge pixels are selected. Experiments have been conducted on benchmark gray images to establish the performance of the proposed model. Comparative analysis with the Canny edge detector [1] and Sun et al. [15] is made to demonstrate the implementation simplicity and suitability of the proposed method in vision applications.

Keywords: Gray image; Small eigenvalue; Eigen image; Edge detection.

1 Introduction

Extraction of edges from an image for analyzing and understanding of the image is a fundamental task in computer vision applications. Edge detectors are used to locate significant variations of gray images and hence useful to provide meaningful description for objects under inspection. As edges play a dominant role in machine vision applications, the continued development of edge detectors is producing increasingly complex edge detection algorithms. Based on the behavioral study of the edges with respect to the differentiation operator, these models are broadly classified into five categories viz., Gradient edge detector [14, 11, 10], Zero-crossing [5], Laplacian of Gaussian [9], Gaussian edge detectors [1, 2, 12] and Colored edge detectors [3]. The most widely used among gradient edge detector based algorithms is Nevatia and Babu [10] technique which consists of determining the edge magnitude and direction by convolving the image with a number of masks followed by thinning and thresholding edge magnitudes. Haralick [5] proposed zero crossing approach which uses second directional derivative and includes Laplacian operator. Marr and Hildreth [9] proposed an edge detector which combines Gaussian filtering with the

Laplacian. The methods that convolve the image with the derivative of Gaussian are called Gaussian edge detectors. Among these Gaussian edge detectors, Canny edge detector [1] is being widely used in most of the applications. The algorithm is suitable especially in noise conditions. Deriche [2] extended Canny's initial filter to two dimensions, Shen and Castan [13] derived an exponential filter and implemented it using recursive filtering. Sarkar and Boyer [12] propose an optimal infinite-response edge detection filter using an ideal step edge and Canny's criteria.

On contrary to the models that are based on the differential operators using single scale information, there exists another class of edge detection techniques that fuse the multiscale edge information of an image to obtain a robust edge map [4, 8, 15]. As the wavelet transform is a better tool which can provide multiscale information of an image and has good time frequency characteristics, many techniques have been developed using the wavelet transform for the purpose of edge detection. The method proposed by Sun et al. [15] is one such recent technique in which statistical properties of multiscale information and multidirectional wavelet coefficients of an image have been explored.

Thus, although the field has come a long way since the algorithms of Roberts and Sobel, there is a belief that the increased sophistication is not producing a commensurate improvement in performance [6, 7]. In order to evaluate the performance of edge detectors, several factors need to be considered as addressed by Heath et al. [6, 7]. As noted in Heath et al. [6], at a minimum, these are: (1) the algorithm itself, (2) the type of images used to measure the performance of the algorithm, and (3) the edge detector parameters used in the evaluation. No doubt, Canny edge detector outperforms most of the edge detection algorithms that exists even today, however, a clever choice of threshold value is required. In the similar line, in this paper we propose a novel method of detecting edge pixels in gray images. Like Canny edge detector, our model is also a parametric and thus has been compared with Canny edge detector. The major intension behind detecting edges in any gray images useful for vision applications is to identify main objects without requiring fine textures. Sun et al. [15] have proposed an approach useful for detection of main objects and this model is also considered for comparative analysis. The obtained results are highly comparable and in addition our model is simple to implement and computationally efficient as it involves only small eigenvalue computation.

The rest of the paper is organized as follows. The proposed methodology is presented in section 2. Results of the experiments conducted on benchmark images chosen from many research papers are presented in section 3. Discussion on the comparative study made with Canny edge detector [1] and Sun et al. [15] is given along with conclusions in section 4.

2 Proposed Methodology

In this section, we present an algorithm for extracting edge pixels from gray images. The model first transforms a gray image into an image called eigen image from which potential edge pixels are extracted and then subsequently an edge pruning process is employed for selecting true edge pixels.

2.1 Transformation of Gray Image to Eigen Image

The suitability of the statistical property of the small eigenvalue of the set of connected pixels is explored for the purpose of edge detection. The proposed transformation is based on mask processing. A window W, of size $k \times k$ for some odd integer $k > 1$, is used for mask processing (here k is chosen to be odd since the pixel to be processed is to be the center pixel of the window). The proposed method places the window W at a pixel say p_i and computes the small eigenvalue of the covariance matrix of the set of all connected pixels covered by the window W and having approximately the same intensity as that of p_i. The set of all connected pixels covered by W and having approximately same intensity as that of p_i is defined to be the family of p_i. The computed small eigenvalue is said to be the value of all the pixels corresponding to each member in the family of p_i. When W is moved onto the next pixel say p_j, the family of p_j is worked out and the associated small eigenvalue is computed. The small eigenvalue computed at p_j is said to be the value of all the pixels corresponding to the members of the family of p_j. As the successive windows overlap each other, it is not uncommon that there are some pixels which are the members of the families of two or more pixels and hence these common pixels obviously bear more than one small eigenvalue. Therefore the number of eigenvalues associated with a pixel, say p in general, is equal to the number of families for which p is a member. It is well known fact that the small eigenvalue and large eigenvalue are same if all the pixels present within a window are considered for eigenvalue computation purpose. Moreover, the number of connected pixels nearer to an edge pixel within a window having approximately similar intensity is less. Hence, the smaller the number of families associated with a pixel, stronger is the evidence that the pixel is an edge pixel. It is proposed to associate each pixel with the average of all the small eigenvalues that are assigned to it. The image obtained in this way is termed as the eigen image.

More formally, let $g(N \times M)$ be the gray image. Let n $(= N \times M)$ be the total number of pixels in g. Let W be the window of size $k \times k$ for some odd integer $k > 1$ used for mask processing. Let $p_1, p_2, \ldots, p_n$ be the pixels in g and $F_1, F_2, \ldots, F_n$ be their respective families. That is, each F_i is the set of all pixels p_j such that p_j is having similar intensity as that of p_i, covered by W when placed at p_i, and connected to p_i, as shown in Fig. 1. Let $\alpha_1, \alpha_2, \ldots, \alpha_n$ be the small eigenvalues of the families $F_1, F_2 \ldots F_n$ respectively. The procedure for small eigenvalue computation is given in appendix-A. All the pixels that are the members of F_i are said to bear the value α_i. The small eigenvalue is assigned to members of a family since it represents small variations for any k-dimensional data (in our case, it is 2-dimensional data which are the coordinate positions of pixels). It can be observed from Table 1 that the small eigenvalue is approximately same as the large eigenvalue in the image region where there are no edge pixels and is considerably small when compared to large eigenvalue in the image region containing edge pixels. The eigen image is obtained by associating each pixel with the average of small eigenvalues assigned to it. Therefore, the proposed transformation function T:g(gray image) $\rightarrow g^1$ (eigen image) is defined as follows:

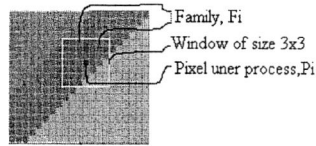

Fig. 1. Instance of an image during the process of eigen transformation

Table 1. Small eigenvalue and large eigenvalue in the region of edge pixel and non-edge pixel with window size 5 and intensity threshold value 10

Image (White pixel is the pixel under process)	Small eigenvalue	Large eigenvalue
	4.328312	10.056468
	9.663194	10.083333

$$g^1(x, y) = T(g(x, y)) = avg\{\alpha_j \mid g(x, y) \in F_j \ \forall j = 1, 2, ..., n\}$$
$$1 \leq x \leq N,$$
$$1 \leq y \leq M$$

The image $g^1(x, y)$ is called the eigen image. The potential edge pixels are those that are having smaller average eigenvalue and non-edge pixels are those that are having larger average eigenvalue. It is required to choose the threshold value, say eigen threshold, to identify potential edge pixels and non-edge pixels in an eigen image. The non-edge pixels in the eigen image are eliminated with the help of eigen threshold. Choosing such an eigen threshold is however application dependent. Like any other edge detection algorithm, the proposed model also requires post-processing to eliminate non-edge pixels among the potential edge pixels. Hence, we considered Canny like criterion to fix the threshold in order to eliminate non-edge pixels and to retain edge pixels among potential edge pixels.

2.2 Edge Pruning

The magnitude of the gradient image is computed only at potential edge pixels. It is well known fact that the magnitude is high in the case of edge pixels and almost zero in the case of non-edge pixels. Thus, edge magnitude information is used to extract the edge pixels thereby eliminating non-edge pixels among the potential edge pixels. A threshold value for this selection is fixed up empirically based on the histogram of the magnitude of the potential edge pixels. It is observed that the true edge pixels are those that are having low average eigen value and higher magnitude, and such true edge pixels are identified among the potential edge pixels. Therefore, in the output image, pixels that are above the gradient magnitude threshold and below the eigen threshold are set to high value (1) and the other pixels are set to low value (0). This binary image is the desired image consisting only edge pixels. Therefore, the combined transformation to obtain an edge image from a given gray image is as follows:

$$G(x,y) = \Gamma(g(x,y))$$
$$= \begin{cases} 1 & \text{if } avg\left\{\alpha_j \mid g(x,y) \in F_j \; \forall j = 1,2,\ldots,n\right\} < eigen \;\; threshold \\ & \text{and } magnitude \; (g(x,y)) > magnitude \;\; threshold \\ 0 & \text{otherwise} \end{cases}$$

3 Experimental Results

This section presents the results of the experiments conducted to study the performance of the proposed algorithm. The method has been implemented in the C language on a Pentium-III 200 MHz with 640x480 resolution. Experiments are conducted on benchmarks images that are chosen from various research papers [6, 15]. Two such benchmark images are shown in Fig. 2(a). Edge images obtained on application of the proposed methodology are given in Fig. 2(c) along with their average small eigenvalue images shown in Fig. 2(b) with window size 5 and intensity threshold 10.

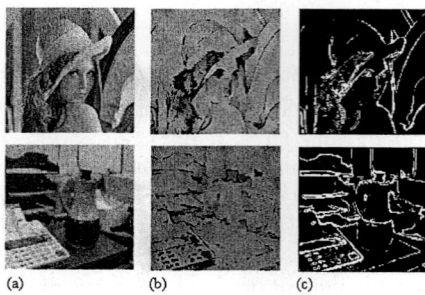

(a)   (b)   (c)

Fig. 2. Obtained edge images from the proposed methodology (a) Gray images; (b) Average small eigenvalue images; (c) Obtained edge images

4 Discussion and Conclusions

For the purpose of establishing the suitability and the usefulness of the proposed model for many computer vision applications, the output images of our model are compared with that of the Canny edge detector [1] and Sun, et al. [15] edge detector. The canny algorithm is a well-known edge detection algorithm. We used its implementation provided in the image processing toolbox of Matlab. Sun et al. [15] is an unsupervised learning algorithm to detect edges. In that work, the statistical properties of multiscale and multidirectional wavelet coefficients are explored for the purpose of edge extraction. We have chosen this method also as it is the most recent edge detection algorithm and able to extract the main objects rather than fine textures in the image unlike Canny's edge detector.

It is very clear from these output images (Fig. 3(b)) that the Canny model able to detect main objects and the fine textures which are slightly better at precision of edges. However, the results obtained using the proposed algorithm capture main objects (Fig. 3(d)) and remove most of the fine textures and the results are comparable with that of the results obtained using Sun, et al. [15] (Fig. 3(c)). The Canny algorithm extract edges by a step function corrupted by Gaussian noise while our model captures the edge information from the statistical property of small eigenvalue. Similar to Canny's algorithm, our model takes only single scale information unlike multiscale information captured by Sun, et al. [15] model. No doubt that the main objects are more likely to be highlighted even at single scale in the proposed model. Extending the proposed model to capture the main objects with multiscale information along with adaptive window-size, intensity threshold and eigen threshold values to fine tune the results is our future target.

In summary, a simple and useful parametric approach to detect edges in gray images is presented in this paper. The statistical property of the small eigenvalue of the connected set of pixels within a window is explored for the detection of edges. The method captures the main objects that are suitable for many computer vision applications.

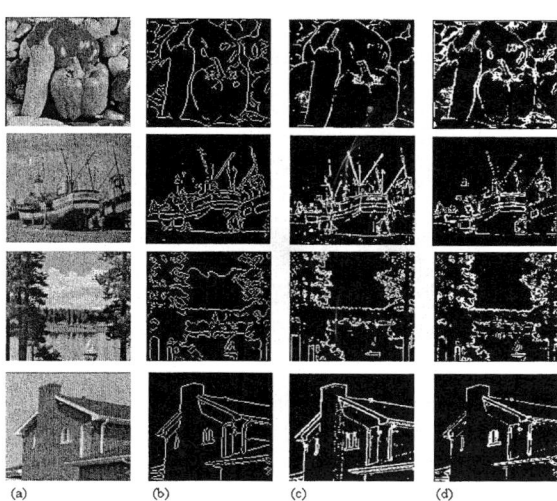

Fig. 3. Comparisons between the Canny[1], Sun, et al. [15] and our algorithm (a) Gray images; (b) Edge maps produced by Canny [1] algorithm; (c) Edge maps produced by Sun et al. [15] algorithm; (d) Edge maps produced by our algorithm.

References

1. Canny, J.F. A computational approach to edge detection, IEEE Transactions on Pattern Analysis and Machine Intelligence, vol. 8(6), pp. 679-698, 1986.
2. Deriche, R. Using Canny's criteria to derive a recursive implemented optimal edge detector, International Journal of Computer Vision, vol. 1(2), pp.167-187, 1987.
3. Garcia, P., Pla, F., and Garcia, I. Detecting edges in color images using dichromatic differences, Seventh International IEEE Conference on Image Processing and its Applications, vol. 1, pp. 363-367, 1999.
4. Gunsel, B., Panayirci, E., and Jain, A.K. Boundary detection using multiscale Markov random fields, Proc. of 12th International Conference on Computer Vision and Image Processing, Jerusalem, Israel, vol. 2, pp. 173-177, 1994.
5. Haralick R. M., Digital step edges from zero-crossings of second directional derivatives, IEEE Transactions on Pattern Analysis and Machine Intelligence, vol. 6(1), pp. 58-68, 1984.
6. Heath, M., Sarkar, S., Sanocki, T., and Bowyer, K. A robust visual method for assessing the relative performance of edge detection algorithms, IEEE Transactions on Pattern Analysis and Machine Intelligence, vol. 19(12), pp. 1338-1359, 1997.
7. Heath, M., Sarkar, S., Sanocki, T., and Bowyer, K. Comparison of edge detectors: A methodology and initial study, CVGIU, vol. 69(1), pp. 38-54, 1998.
8. Lu, R., Jain, R.C. Reasoning about edges in scale space, IEEE Transactions on Pattern Analysis and Machine Intelligence, vol. 14(7), pp. 710-732, 1992.
9. Marr, D., and Hildreth, E. C. Theory of edge detection, Proceedings of the Royal society of London, B207, pp. 187-217, 1980.
10. Nevatia, R., and Babu, K. R. Linear feature extraction and description, Computer Vision, Graphics and Image Processing, vol. 13, pp. 257-269, 1980.
11. Prewitt, J. M. S. Object enhancement and extraction, In Picture Processing and Psychopictorics, B.S. Lipkin and al., Eds. Academic Press, New York, 1970.
12. Sarkar, S., and Boyer, K. L. On optimal infinite impulse response edge detection filters, IEEE Transactions on Pattern Analysis and Machine Intelligence, vol.13(11), pp. 1154-1171, 1991.
13. Shen, J., and Castan, S. An optimal linear operator for step edge detection, CVGIP: Graphical Models and Image Processing, vol. 54(2), pp. 122-133, 1992.
14. Sobel, I. E. Camera models and machine perception, Technical report, Stanford University, pp. 277-284, 1970.
15. Sun, J., Gu, D., Chen, Y., and Zhang, S. A multiscale edge detection algorithm based on wavelet domain vector hidden Markov tree model, Pattern Recognition, vol. 37(7), pp. 1315-1324, 2004.

Appendix–A: Small Eigenvalue Computation Procedure

Given a set $S = \{p_i (x_i, y_i) \mid i=1,2,\ldots,n\}$ of n pixels, the small eigenvalue, α of the covariance matrix of S is computed by $\alpha = \frac{1}{2}\left[c_{11} + c_{22} - \sqrt{(c_{11} - c_{22})^2 + 4c_{12}^2}\right]$ where $\begin{bmatrix} c_{11} & c_{12} \\ c_{21} & c_{22} \end{bmatrix}$ is the covariance matrix of S and the coefficients c_{11}, c_{12}, c_{21} and c_{22} are given by $\frac{1}{n}\sum_{i=1..n} x_i^2 - c_x^2$, $\frac{1}{n}\sum_{i=1..n} x_i.y_i - c_x.c_y$, $\frac{1}{n}\sum_{i=1..n} x_i.y_i - c_x.c_y$ and $\frac{1}{n}\sum_{i=1..n} y_i^2 - c_y^2$ respectively. Here $c_x = \frac{1}{n}\sum_{i=1..n} x_i$ and $c_y = \frac{1}{n}\sum_{i=1..n} y_i$ are the respective mean values of the X and Y coordinates of the points in S.

Signal Processing for Digital Image Enhancement Considering APL in PDP

Soo-Wook Jang[1], Se-Jin Pyo[2], Eun-Su Kim[1],
Sung-Hak Lee[1], and Kyu-Ik Sohng[1]

[1] School of Electronic Engineering and Computer Science,
Kyungpook National University,
1370, Sankyug-Dong, Buk-Gu, Daegu, 702-701, Korea
{jjang, saeloum, shark2, kisohng}@ee.knu.ac.kr
[2] Digital Media R&D Center, Samsung Electronics Co., LTD.,
416, Maetan-3Dong, Yeongtong-Gu, Suwon, Gyeonggi-Do, 443-742, Korea
sejin.pyo@samsung.com

Abstract. In this paper, a method for improvement of image quality using the error diffusion which considers the APL process is proposed. In the proposed method, the APL process is performed before the error diffusion process. Simulation results showed that the proposed method has better performances for resolution in images and CCT uniformity according to each grayscale than the conventional method.

1 Introduction

Plasma display panel (PDP), which is researched actively in recent years, is new flat display technique that replaces flat CRT and TFT-LCD. It is attracting attention as new display device because it has merits that are absolute flat, the maximum of space efficiency, wide sight angle, high luminance and facility of a large display size. In spite of these merits, it has problems such as consumption of high power, high cost and degradation of image quality. The luminance of CRT is controlled by the amount of electro beam adjusted by current. On the other hand, the luminance of panel can't be controlled by amount of current in PDP due to uniformity of light discharged from a phosphor. So the number of sustain pulse is adjusted by desired luminance of panel for constant time. The integral effect or after image effect is used: human perceives the brightness of light by integrating the amount of light generated by sustain pulses for one field. The addressing time is needed to decide discharge of the PDP cell. And it is impossible to control the address electrode every gray-level 1 within one field time in this current PDP driving method. Therefore, the sub-field is used to display 256 gray-levels. One field is separated into several sub-fields and the on or off of each sub-field is controlled.

In current PDP, the major image processing consists of inverse gamma correction, error-diffusion and average picture level (APL). The quantization error, a decrease of number of the gray-scale, occurs during the inverse gamma correction. The digital halftoning method is used to solve this problem and it gives an effect which looks like more gray-levels is used as only few gray-levels. Now the most popular method of the digital halftoning is the error-diffusion. Although the error-diffusion is used to distribute this quantization error into the neighboring pixels, the worm-like pattern is inevitably produced [1],[2]. And the worm-like pattern is increased after APL which prevents the excessive temperature of panel and enhances the luminance efficiency of PDP.

However, there are some disadvantages and one of them is the image quality degradation, which is dependent on the digital signal processing. Although image quality of PDP is improving by many researches and experimentations, it still isn't as good as that of CRTs because of various factors. One of them is worm-like pattern generated by an error diffusion process. And the worm-like pattern is severely increased after an average picture level (APL) process. An increased worm-like pattern occur a drop of resolution in image and a change of correlated color temperature (CCT) according to each grayscale.

In this paper, we propose new method for digital image enhancement considering the APL in PDP. In the proposed method, the APL process is performed before the error diffusion process. Simulation results showed that the proposed method has better performances for resolution in images and CCT uniformity according to each grayscale than the conventional method.

2 Image Processing in the Current PDP

In current PDP, the major image processing consists of inverse gamma correction, error-diffusion and APL. Fig. 1 shows the block diagram of image processing in the current PDP. The inverse gamma correction is needed to display the gamma-corrected image, because PDP has nearly linear characteristic about output luminance for input gray-level. Digital input data of 8 bits is transformed into the data of bits more than 8 bits in inverse gamma correction processing. Generally, the relationship of input gray-level and output luminance in the image display device is shown in Eq. (1). In this Eq., i is the digital input gray-level, γ is display gamma value and k is constant for normalization.

$$Y(i) = k \cdot \left(\frac{i}{255}\right)^{\gamma} \qquad (1)$$

The error-diffusion of various digital halftoning methods is used to distribute the errors which occur during the preprocessor. It is mainly used to reduce the quantization error produced by the inverse gamma correction. The difference between the ideal output value of image and the actual output value of it is considered as error in this method. Generally, if the number of output data bits is increase, the quantization error produced by the inverse gamma correction is reduced. And the APL processing is mainly used to prevent the excessive temperature of panel and enhances the luminance efficiency of PDP. The APL maintains a uniform average level of the picture signal during active scanning time integrated over a frame period.

Even though the numerous digital halftoning techniques had been developed in the last twenty years, the one that has emerged as a standard because of its

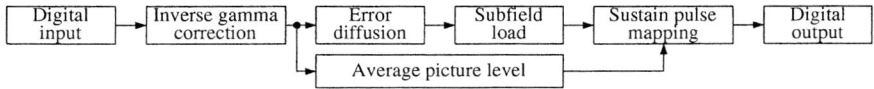

Fig. 1. Block diagram of signal processing in current PDP

simplicity and quality of output is the so-called error-diffusion algorithm [2]-[4]. This algorithm, first proposed by Floyd and Steinberg [5], is schematically shown in Fig. 2. The error-diffusion is used to solve the problem about the degradation of grayscale resolution in the dark area. The error-diffusion can be considered as a feedback system with two major operations - quantization and filtering, as illustrated in Fig. 2. The thresholding operation determines the values of output halftone. The filtering operation is usually implemented by diffusion the weighted binarization error to the anti-causal nearest neighbors. The weights are specified by the filter [6]. The difference between the pixel's ideal output digital value and the actual output digital value is considered as error in this method. To achieve the effect of continuous-tone illusion, this error is distributed to the four neighboring pixels that have not been processed yet, according to the matrix proposed by Floyd and Steinberg [5]. Despite widespread usage in many applications, worm-like patterns at some tone levels and limit-cycle behavior in mid-tones and quartertones are two major artifacts associated with Floyd and Steinberg error-diffusion. This worm-like pattern reduces especially the image quality of the PDP, because it is increased by the next processing like the APL. Also, it is easily detected by human's visual perception, because the most of current PDP is the standard definition panel and the size of one pixel is large relatively.

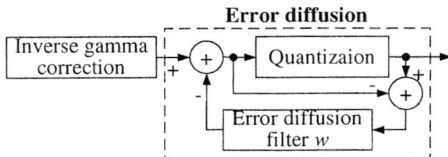

Fig. 2. Error diffusion algorithm

3 Proposed Method for Digital Image Enhancement Considering APL

Fig. 3 shows the flow chart of proposed method to improve the digital image quality considering the APL. The proposed method performs all image processing before the error-diffusion processing. 8 bits digital input data are stored with 12 bits after the inverse gamma correction and it is transformed into 16 bits data according to average level of the picture signal during active scanning time integrated over a frame period. The 11 bits data of 16 bits is the integer part and

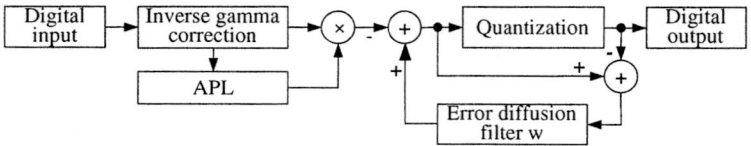

Fig. 3. Flow chart of proposed signal processing with error diffusion

the 5 bits data of it is fraction part for the error-diffusion. Finally, 10 bits data is used to load the subfield memory. The each processing of the proposed method to improve the digital image quality considering the APL is illustrated closely in the next paragraph.

CRT, which is widely used as image display device until now, has nonlinear characteristic about output luminance for input gray-level. On the other hand, PDP has nearly linear characteristic about output luminance for input gray-level. Therefore, inverse gamma correction is needed to display the gamma-corrected image. When the inverse gamma correction is applied, the difference between the target luminance and actual output luminance is produced because the number of grayscale which can be actually displayed in PDP is decreased specially in the dark area. In PDP, we define inverse gamma correction Eq. (2) to show luminance characteristic like the CRT's.

$$R(r) = R_{white} \cdot \left(\frac{r}{255}\right)^{\gamma}, G(g) = G_{white} \cdot \left(\frac{g}{255}\right)^{\gamma}, B(b) = B_{white} \cdot \left(\frac{b}{255}\right)^{\gamma} \quad (2)$$

The r, g, and b are the digital input values of each color channel and the R_{white}, G_{white}, and B_{white} are white level values of each color channel. The results of Eq. (2) show the digital output values for digital input values r, g, and b. Although it is computed to a fraction, it can be displayed with only integer values. Therefore, ideally computed fraction values have to be transformed into integer values. Table 1 shows the number of grayscale as output data bits in inverse gamma correction processing. It illustrates that the number of grayscale is 255 when the number of output data bit is infinity. In the proposed method to improve the digital image quality considering the APL, the 12 bits are used to minimize a decrease of the number of grayscale generated by inverse gamma correction processing and consider the design of hardware. The degradation of the grayscale resolution is produced in the low gray-levels despite an increase of the number of output data bit.

The great variety of image processing methods using digital halftoning has been suggested to improve this grayscale resolution in the low gray-levels. The

Table 1. The number of grayscale as output bits in inverse gamma corrention

The numver of output bit	8	9	10	11	12
The numver of output bit	183	215	233	243	248

digital half-toning is the process of transforming images with only a few discrete tone levels into the continuous-tone images.

4 Experiments and Results

A comparison of simulated images using the conventional and proposed signal processing method is shown in Fig. 4. The simulated images are one which video-gamma correction is processed, because it is displayed on standard CRT. The proposed PDP signal processing method has improved performance especially in aspect of increase of the number of grayscale and reduction of distributed error. The PSNR of the proposed method are 7.2 dB higher than that of the conventional method at gray scale image, and the PSNR of the proposed method are 6.9 dB higher than that of the conventional method at color image respectively.

(a) (b)

Fig. 4. A comparison of simulated images: (a) Conventional and (b) proposed signal processing method

The proposed signal processing method enables to display the luminance with one step of the sustain pulse and prevents the increase of the worm-like patterns generated by error-diffusion. Table 2 shows the number of grayscale for the number of sustain pulse in the several the APL, namely, the maximum number of sustain pulse. These illustrate that the luminance of panel is controlled by one step of the sustain pulse and the digital image quality is improved by preventing the increase of the worm-like patterns generated by error-diffusion.

Table 2. The number of grayscale for the number of sustain pulse in the several APL

Maximum numver of sustain pulse	The number of grayscale	
	Conventional	Proposed
200	207	222
255	230	230
510	230	242
1020	230	249

5 Conclusions

APL processing method is useful technique which prevents the excessive temperature of panel and enhances the luminance efficiency of PDP by maintaining a uniform average voltage of the picture signal during active scanning time integrated over a frame period. In the signal processing method of current PDP, although the error-diffusion is used to distribute this error into the neighboring pixels, the worm-like pattern is inevitably produced. And the worm-like pattern is increased after APL. So the proposed signal processing method enables to display the luminance in one step of the sustain pulse and prevents the increase of the worm-like patterns. In conclusion, the proposed signal processing method gives the excellent effectiveness for improve-ment of the digital image quality considering the APL processing for PDP.

References

[1] Li, P., Allebath, J. P.: Tone-dependent error diffusion, IEEE Transactions on Image Processing, Vol. 13, (2004) 201-215.
[2] Ulichney, R.: Digital Halftoning, MIT Press, Cambridge, Mass., (1987).
[3] Yoichi Sato, Kimio Amemiya, and Masataka Uchidoi: Recent Progresses of Device Per-formance and Picture Quality in Color Plasma Displays, IDW'00 Digest, (2000) 695-698.
[4] Peter R. Jones: Evolution of halftoning technology in the United States patent literature, Journal of Electronic Imaging, Vol. 3, No. 3, (1994) 257-275.
[5] Robert W. Floyd and Louis Steinberg: An Adaptive Algorithm for Spatial Grayscale, Proceedings of the Society for Information Display, Vol. 17, No. 2, (1976) 75-77.
[6] Ti-chiun Chang and Jan P. Allebach: Memory Efficient Error Diffusion, IEEE Transactions on image processing, Vol. 12, No. 11, (2003) 1352-1366.

A Hybrid Approach to Digital Image Watermarking Using Singular Value Decomposition and Spread Spectrum

Kunal Bhandari, Suman K. Mitra, and Ashish Jadhav

Dhirubhai Ambani Institute of Information and Communication Technology,
Gandhinagar, Gujarat, India, 382007
{kunal_bhandari, suman_mitra, ashish_jadhav}@da-iict.org

Abstract. This paper compares the most utilized spread spectrum technique with the newly evolved technique based on Singular Value Decomposition (SVD) for watermarking digital images. Both techniques are tested for a variety of attacks and the simulation results show that the watermarks generated by these techniques have complimentary robustness properties. A new hybrid technique, combining both paradigms, is proposed that is capable of surviving an extremely wide range of attacks. An image is first watermarked using spread spectrum and then a SVD based watermark is added to the watermarked image. The resulting double watermarked image is extremely robust to a wide range of distortions.

1 Introduction

Past few years have seen an explosive growth in digitization of multimedia (image, audio and video) content. The advancements in Internet technologies have largely increased the distribution of multimedia material. The possibility of infringement of digital media has also increased. The replication, manipulation and distribution of the digital multimedia content causes considerable financial loss to the media owners.

Digital watermarking [1] techniques offer a better solution as compared to encryption for the protection of such intellectual properties. Watermarking is a concept of embedding an unobtrusive mark into the data. This embedded information can later prove ownership, identify un-authorized copy, trace the marked data's dissemination through the network, or simply inform users about the rights-holder or the permitted user of the data. In sections 2, 3 and 4 we describe the basic spread spectrum approach, the SVD technique and the proposed hybrid scheme, respectively.

2 Watermarking Using Spread Spectrum [2]

Let N be the total number of pixels in an image, r_c be the chip-rate and $\{a_j\}:(a_j \in \{-1,1\})$ be the sequence of information bits to be embedded into the image. Then the spread sequence,

$$\{b_i\}: b_i = a_j; \text{ where } j.r_c \leq i < (j+1).r_c \quad . \tag{1}$$

The spread sequence {b_i} is then modulated by a pseudo-noise sequence {p_i}, where $p_i \in \{-1,1\}$. The modulated signal scaled with α is arranged into a matrix with size equal to the image. The watermark, w_i, is added to the image pixel values, v_i, to give the watermarked image, v_i^*.

$$w_i = \alpha.b_i.p_i \quad \text{and} \quad v_i^* = v_i + w_i . \quad (2)$$

The watermark could be extracted by means of a correlation receiver. The original image is first subtracted from the watermarked image to remove components of the image itself. The second step is demodulation, which is the multiplication of the subtracted watermarked image with the same pseudo-noise signal {p_i} that was used for embedding. This is followed by summation over a window of length equal to the chip rate, yielding the correlation sum S_j for the jth information bit. Therefore

$$S_j = \sum_{i=j.r_c}^{(j+1)r_c -1} p_i.w_i = \sum_{i=j.r_c}^{(j+1)r_c -1} p_i^2.b_i.\alpha = a_j.r_c.\alpha . \quad (3)$$

Now, sign (S_j)=sign ($a_j.r_c.\alpha$) = sign (a_j). This is because $r_c > 0$, $\alpha > 0$, $p_i^2 = 1$ and $a_j = \pm 1$. Thus the embedded bit can be retrieved without much loss. Therefore the embedded information bit is 1 if the correlation is positive and -1 if it is negative.

3 Watermarking Using Singular Value Decomposition [4] [5]

Singular value decomposition (SVD) is a linear algebra technique used to diagonalize matrices (image in this case) and it packs most of the signal energy into very few singular values (SVs). The SVs of an image remain un-changed even if the image is perturbed. This property is primarily used in image watermarking. Let the SVD of the host image X (M x N: M≥N) and the watermark W (P x Q: P≥Q) are as follows,

$$X = U S_x V^T \quad \text{and} \quad W = U_w S_w V_w^T . \quad (4)$$

Here S_x and S_w are diagonal matrices and represent the SVs of X and W, respectively and are represented by $S_x = [K_{x1}\ K_{x2}.....K_{xN}]$ and $S_w = [K_{w1}\ K_{w2}.....K_{wQ}]$. The watermark is embedded into the singular values of X according to the relationship

$$S_y = [K_{y1}\ K_{y2}\ ...\ K_{yN}] \quad \text{where,}\ K_{yi} = K_{xi} + \gamma.K_{wi} . \quad (5)$$

Here γ is a scaling factor that determines the embedding strength and accounts for the perceptual quality of the watermarked image Y ($Y = U S_y V^T$). The extraction process requires SVs of the host image and the watermark. The extraction process is as explained in (6). Here Y* is the possibly attacked watermarked image and W* is the recovered watermark.

$$Y^* = U^* S^*_y V^{*T},\ S^*_w = (S^*_y - S_x)/\gamma,\ \text{and}\ W^* = U_w S^*_w V_w^T . \quad (6)$$

4 Proposed Scheme

The SVD watermark interferes with the original image and original image is needed at the receiver to extract the watermark. It increases the robustness against attacks of low pass nature like blurring and lossy compression [3] [4] [5]. It also provides good performance against rotation attack [3]. It is susceptible to histogram based attacks and addition of noise. The spread spectrum based noise like watermark is statistically orthogonal to the host image and is spread throughout the image [2]. It uses correlation sum to extract the watermark and is highly sensitive to resynchronization attacks [6]. It performs quite well for addition of noise and gamma correction.

The range of attacks, these two techniques survive or succumb, are complimentary. Thus if we combine these two techniques then we can achieve robustness against a very wide range of intentional and unintentional attacks. We propose a hybrid SVD-SS method designed such that the two watermarks interfere very little with each other. The host image is marked with a spread spectrum based watermark and then the resulting image is re-watermarked using the SVD approach. The proposed scheme enjoys the benefits of both the methods and at least one of the watermarks survives under various attacks. The proposed embedding method is shown in Fig.1. The recovery procedure is just a reverse mechanism of embedding.

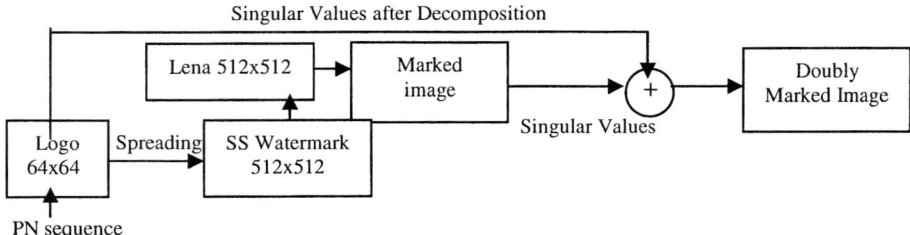

Fig. 1. Block diagram representing the embedding process of the proposed scheme

5 Experimental Results

The standard Lena 512 X 512 uncompressed image was used as the host and DA-IICT logo 64 X 64 as a binary watermark. The parameters r_c, α and γ for the embedding process are taken as 64, 5 and 50 respectively. The robustness of the algorithm is tested for 14 different attacks as illustrated in Fig.2. The JPEG compression, rotation, addition of Salt & pepper and Gaussian noise, intensity adjustment, gamma correction, histogram equalization, median filtering and dithering are applied from inbuilt functions of MATLAB. Attacks like Pixelate5 (Mosaic) and intentional pixel exchange are done in Photoshop. Print and scan (300dpi) is also considered as an attack.

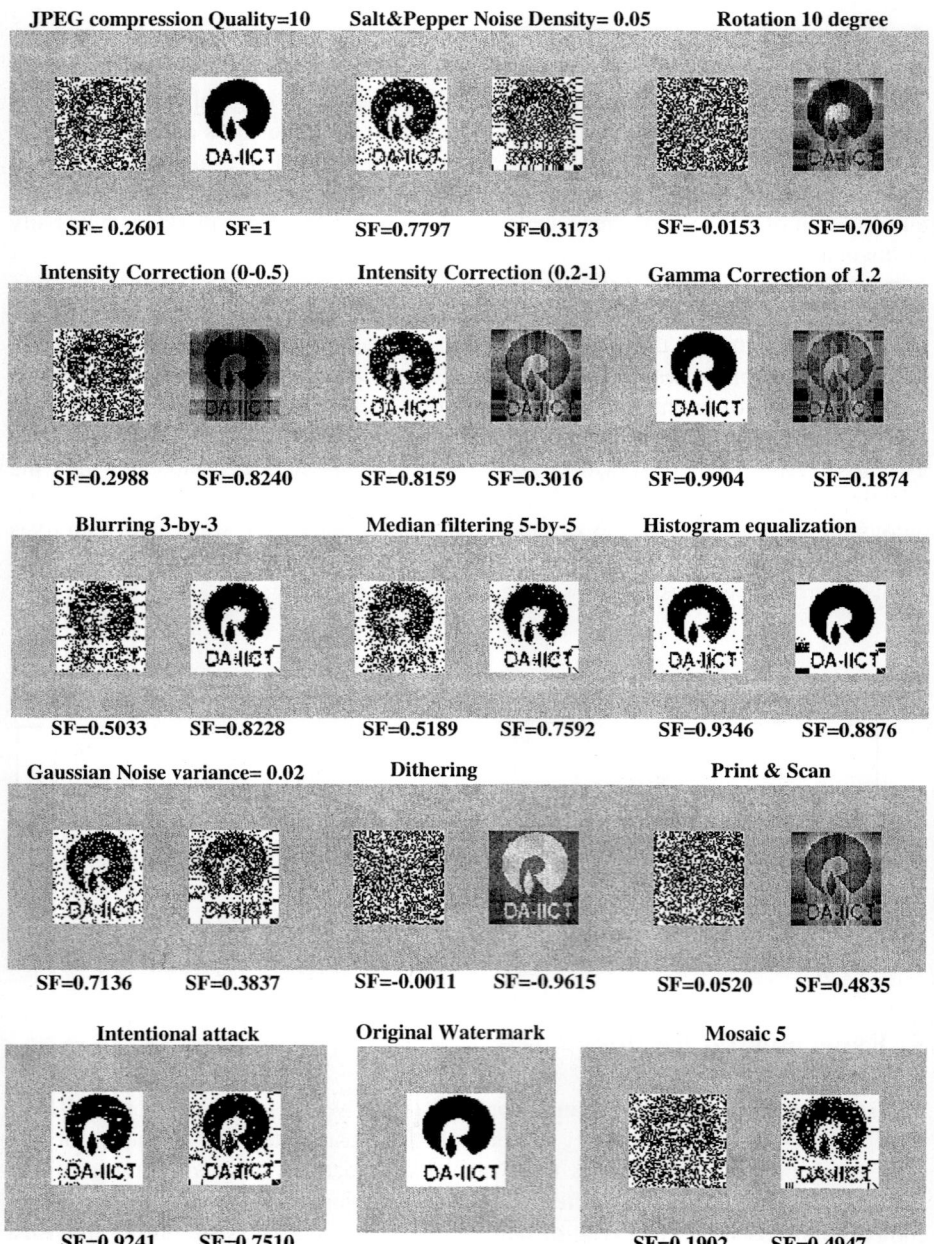

Fig. 2. Watermarks, with the similarity factors (SF), recovered after various attacks on the doubly marked image. The first logo shown, for each attack, is the one recovered by spread spectrum and the second by SVD extraction methods. The original logo is also shown.

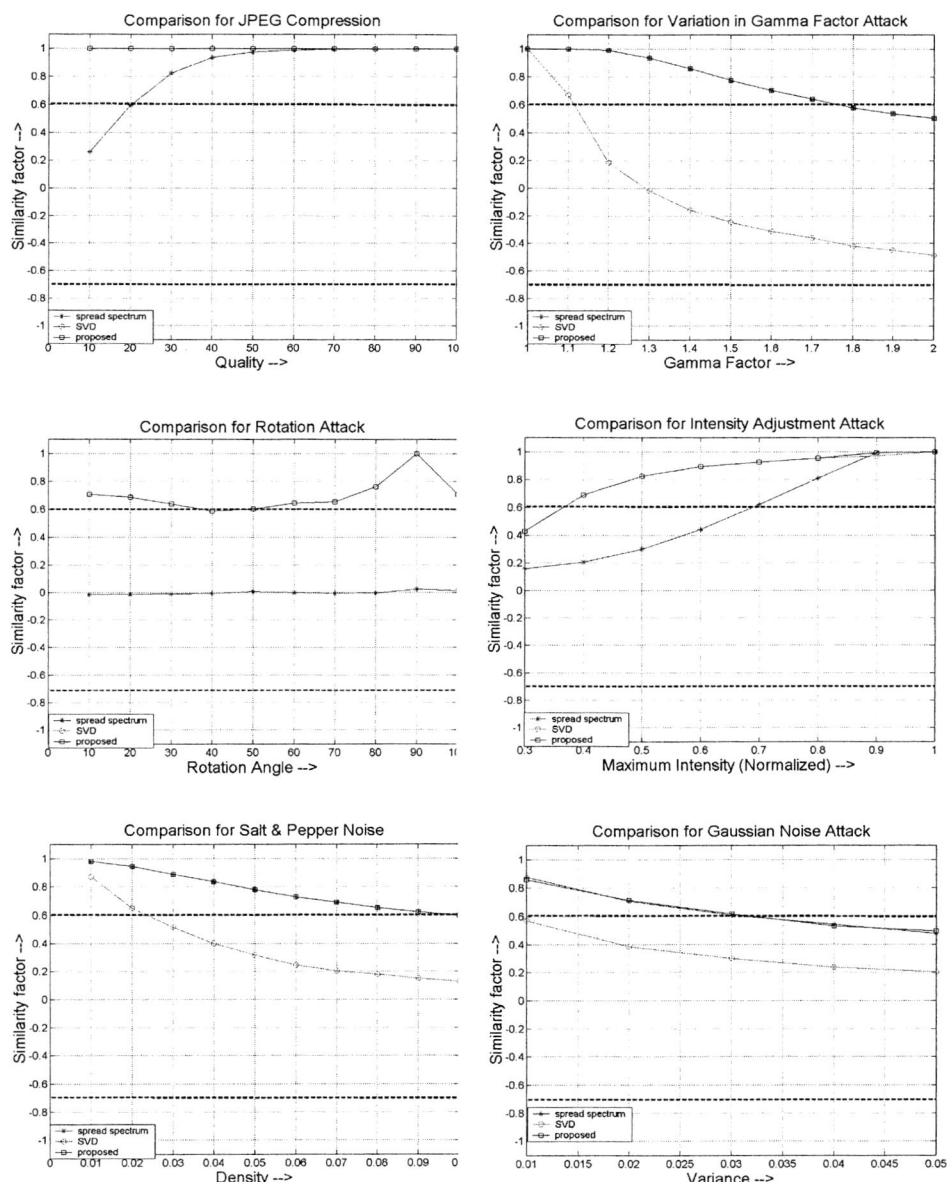

Fig. 3. Various plots showing comparison between SVD, Spread spectrum and the proposed hybrid scheme

The spread spectrum approach survives addition of noise, intensity adjustment k to 1 (k>0) and gamma correction while the SVD based approach outperforms spread spectrum in rotation, cropping, JPEG compression for quality below 30, intensity adjustment 0 to k (k<1) and filtering attacks. The extracted watermark W* is correlated with the original watermark W to quantitatively measure the similarity. It ranges between -1 to 1. More is the similarity factor better is the retrieval of the watermark. Fig.3 shows plots of similarity factors for various attacks. It is evident from Fig.3 that the performance of the proposed method is better than a non-hybrid scheme employing either of the techniques. It has been observed that under some attacks the visual quality of the extracted watermark is poor even if the similarity factor is high. By applying proper scaling, the visual quality of such watermarks can be enhanced. The simulation results validate our assertion that the proposed algorithm is resilient to a very broad category of intentional and unintentional attacks.

6 Conclusion

This paper presents a novel SVD-SS hybrid watermarking technique that embeds two watermarks, one by spread spectrum and the other by SVD approach. The two techniques of embedding watermarks separately are found to be complimentary to each other as far as robustness against various attacks is concerned. The proposed scheme being a union of both the schemes, survives the union of the attacks survived by each scheme independently. The scheme is designed such that there is negligible degradation of the image on addition of the second mark.

References

1. I. Cox, M. Miller and J. Bloom, "Digital Watermarking," Morgan Kauffman Publisher, 2001.
2. M. George, J. Y. Chouinard and N. Georganas, "Digital Watermarking of Images and Video using Direct Sequence Spread Spectrum Techniques," IEEE Canadian Conference on Electrical and Computer Engineering, vol. 1, 9-12 May 1999, pp. 116 – 121.
3. R. Liu and T. Tan, "A SVD-Based Watermarking Scheme for Protecting Rightful Ownership," *IEEE Transactions on Multimedia*, 4(1), March 2002, pp.121-128.
4. Chandra D.V.S, "Digital Image Watermarking using SVD". Circuits and Systems, MWSCAS-2002., vol. 3 , 4-7 Aug. 2002, pp.III-264 - III-267.
5. V.I. Gorodetski, L.J. popyack, V. Samoilov, and V.A. Skormin, "SVD-Based Approach to Transparent Embedding Data into Digital Images" proc. Int. Workshop on Mathematical Methods, Models and Architecture for Computer Network Security, LNCS, Vol. 2052, pp. 263-274, Springer Verlag, 2001.
6. F. Hartung, J. K. Su, and B. Girod, "Spread spectrum watermarking: Malicious attacks and counterattacks," in Security and Watermarking of Multimedia Contents, Proc. SPIE 3657, Jan. 1999, pp.147-158.

Image Enhancement by High-Order Gaussian Derivative Filters Simulating Non-classical Receptive Fields in the Human Visual System

Kuntal Ghosh, Sandip Sarkar, and Kamales Bhaumik

Microelectronics Division, Saha Institute of Nuclear Physics,
1/AF Bidhannagar, Kolkata-64, India
kuntal.ghosh@saha.ac.in

Abstract. The non-linearity exhibited by the non-classical receptive field in human visual system has been combined with the linear classical receptive field model. This enables us to construct higher order Gaussian Derivatives as a linear combination of lower order derivatives at different scales. Based on this, a new kernel which simulates non-classical receptive fields with extended disinhibitory surrounds, has been proposed. It is easy to implement and finds justification from an old psychophysical angle too. The proposed kernel has been shown to perform better than the well-known Laplacian kernel, which models the classical excitatory-inhibitory receptive fields.

1 Introduction

David Marr [1] introduced the Laplacian of Gaussian (LOG) kernel for the purpose of edge detection and demonstrated the equivalence of this operator to the classical centre-surround Difference of Gaussian (DOG) [2,3] based receptive field model in Human Visual System (HVS). The reason behind Gaussian smoothing prior to differentiation (Laplacian in this case), as is well known in Computer Vision, is to well-pose an ill-posed problem [4,5]. But even a simple Laplacian kernel, used for the purpose of image enhancement [6], may also be looked upon as a mimetic representation of the excitatory-inhibitory mechanism of visual receptive field. In this paper we are going to incorporate a physiologically reported disinhibitory mechanism[7,8] into the classical excitatory-inhibitory DOG model of visual receptive field, by including two additional Gaussians with larger variances representing an extended surround to the classical receptive field. It has been shown [9] with the help of a theorem by Ma and Li [10] that the DOG-LOG equivalence can be proved through a more rigorous approach as compared to that of Marr [1] and can also be generalized for any number of multi-scale Gaussians. As a continuation of this approach we have, in this paper, been able to express a sixth order derivative of Gaussian as a sum of second and a fourth order derivative in any scale ratio. This has enabled us to construct a generalization of the traditional Laplacian kernel that has been found to exhibit better performance for image enhancement.

2 The Proposed Model

It is well-known that DOG model of receptive field is the classical model for the centre-surround antagonistic effects observed in HVS. However physiological experiments [7] also lend support to the existence of an extended disinhibitory surround that is also capable of modulating the behaviour of the cell in question in a non-linear fashion. Though there is confusion regarding the polarity of this extended surround, recent experiments [8] suggest the existence of both positive as well as negative sub-units in this region. We are now going to show that such a scheme fits quite rigorously into Ma-Li's theorem [10] of construction of higher order Gaussian Derivatives which are a likely possibility in HVS according to the works of Young [11] and Koenderink [12].

Ma-Li's theorem states that any $2k$th order derivative filter which is generally a $2k$th order derivative of an analytical smooth function derivable up to $2k$th order, can be expressed as a weighted sum of $k+1$ components equal to an even function at different scales, the weights depending upon the corresponding scale ratios. In other words if g is the primitive Gaussian filter, then any $2k$th order derivative filter $h_{2k}(x)$ may be expressed as:

$$h_{2k}(x) = \sum_{j=0}^{k} \frac{\alpha_j}{\sigma_j} g\left(\frac{x}{\sigma_j}\right), \tag{1}$$

$$\text{where, } g\left(\frac{x}{\sigma}\right) = \frac{1}{\sqrt{2\pi}} e^{-\frac{x^2}{2\sigma^2}} \tag{2}$$

In order that $h_{2k}(x)$ may represent a derivative filter, the following conditions need to be satisfied:

$$\alpha_0 + \alpha_1 + \alpha_2 + \cdots + \alpha_k = 0$$
$$\alpha_0 \sigma_0^2 + \alpha_1 \sigma_1^2 + \alpha_2 \sigma_2^2 + \cdots + \alpha_k \sigma_k^2 = 0$$
$$\vdots$$
$$\alpha_0 \sigma_0^{2k} + \alpha_1 \sigma_1^{2k} + \alpha_2 \sigma_2^{2k} + \cdots + \alpha_k \sigma_k^{2k} = \frac{(2k)!}{m_{g,2k}}$$

and if the matrix M_σ where

$$M_\sigma = \begin{bmatrix} 1 & 1 & \cdots & 1 \\ \sigma_0^2 & \sigma_1^2 & \cdots & \sigma_k^2 \\ \vdots & & & \\ \sigma_0^{2k} & \sigma_1^{2k} & \cdots & \sigma_k^{2k} \end{bmatrix}$$

is non-singular, and $m_{g,2k}$ represents the $2k$th order moment of the function $g(x)$.

Using the above conditions it can be shown [9] that for a fourth order derivative filter we have:

$$\alpha_0 = c(\sigma_2^2 - \sigma_1^2) \tag{3}$$
$$\alpha_1 = -c(\sigma_2^2 - \sigma_0^2) \tag{4}$$
$$\alpha_2 = c(\sigma_1^2 - \sigma_0^2) \tag{5}$$

where c is a constant.

The above equations clearly show that a fourth order derivative filter, thus designed out of three Gaussian filters at different scales, is inherently non-linear. This is because the co-efficients of each of these Gaussian filters is a function of the scales of the other two, which is not the case in case of the DOG equivalence to LOG, where the two coefficients are simply equal to one another [10]. It is however difficult to ascertain whether this non-linearity is exactly akin to the non-linearities observed in the non-classical receptive field, since the nature of the non-linearity in the physiological system is yet to be properly identified. But there are some close similarities of the above model with the physiological system. Polarities of the three Gaussians, defined through equations (3) to (5) indicate the possibility of considering the three Gaussians as representatives of the centre, surround and disinhibitory extended surround portions of the non-classical receptive field respectively. Now in the limit of a large extended disinhibitory surround, evidences of which exist in physiology [8], it is possible to apply a limiting condition to the smallest of the three variances, which represents the excitatory centre, so that $\sigma_0 \to 0$, whereby :

$$h_4(x,\sigma) = mh_2(x,\sigma') + h_2(x,\sigma'') \tag{6}$$

where σ' and σ'' are two arbitrary scales and m is an amplitude scale factor.

So in two dimensions:

$$\nabla^4 G(r,\sigma) = m\nabla^2 G(r,\sigma') + \nabla^2 G(r,\sigma'') \tag{7}$$

Following the same procedure for a sixth order derivative, we find that two additional Gaussians represent contributions from the positive and negative subunits in the extended surround. It has also been shown [9] that the two new Gausssians in order to satisfy the derivative condition do indeed come in opposite polarity. Thus in two dimensions we arrive at:

$$\nabla^6 G(r,\sigma) = m\nabla^2 G(r,\sigma') + n\nabla^2 G(r,\sigma'') + \nabla^2 G(r,\sigma''') \tag{8}$$

for two amplitude scale factors m and n, and another arbitrary scale σ''' so that with the help of equation (7) we finally arrive at:

$$\nabla^6 G(r,\sigma) = m\nabla^2 G(r,\sigma') + \nabla^4 G(r,\sigma'''') \tag{9}$$

where the final two scales are designated as σ' and σ''''.

We thus arrive at a new, more general model for the Human Visual System that accounts for both linear, classical as well as non-linear, non-classical receptive fields in terms of even-order derivatives of Gaussian, up to the sixth order. Following the methodology described above, the eighth and the tenth order Gaussian Derivatives can also be similarly designed. Thus, through a multi-scale combination of various smoothing layers of neurons in retina and LGN, even order Gaussian Derivatives starting from the second order up to at least the tenth order can definitely be computed in visual cortex. The present model therefore justifies the experimental and theoretical findings of Young [11] and Koenderink [12] who also suggest the existence of Gaussian Derivatives up to the order ten in HVS.

3 Results and Discussion

The advantage of expressing a sixth order Gaussian derivative as a linear combination of a second order and a fourth order one at two different possible scales may be easily understood. Visual processing operates through a very flexible methodology that always changes according to the situation. By changing the value of m and operating at various combinations of scales, that may be dealt with a top-down approach, the visual system is capable of functioning bottom-up by taking advantage of both the classical as well as the non-classical receptive field. It has already been shown [13] that such a tuning of scale is capable of explaining many low-level brightness-contrast illusions as perceived by HVS. In figure 1, we are only giving two examples where such a combination clearly surpasses the standard LOG filter in terms of both enhancement and localization capability. In the first case the value of m is 0.5, which implies that the fourth order derivative is more dominant as compared to the second order one. In the second case, the value of m is 9, which implies that the fourth order derivative is less dominant as compared to the second order one.

As early as in 1868, the great physicist E. Mach provided a psychophysical model of visual computation [14] where he claimed that visual response is determined through a combination of absolute light intensity and its Laplacian. The present model for any order of derivative reduces to Mach's model if the scale of the higher derivative goes to zero in the limit i.e. in the present case if $\sigma'''' \to 0$. Using finite difference approximation theorem, it has been shown [15] that for $m = 9$, it is possible to construct a new kernel for the purpose of image enhancement that far exceeds the traditional Laplacian kernel in performance. If we take a look at the two kernels given below,

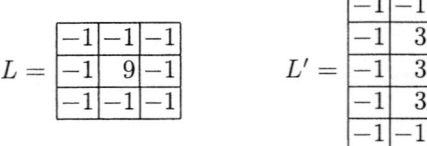

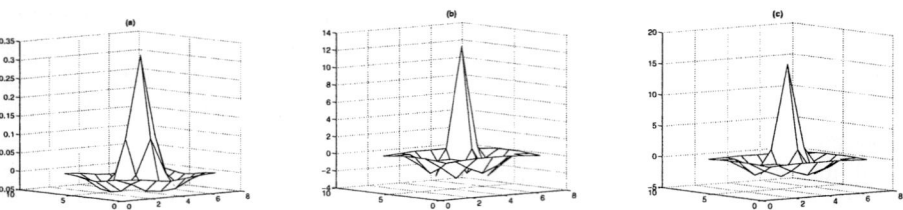

Fig. 1. (a) A Laplacian of Gaussian Mask (b) A combination of Laplacian and Bi-laplacian at $m = 0.5$ (c) A combination of Laplacian and Bi-laplacian at $m = 9$. Variances have been fixed at unity in all the cases for the sake of comparison.

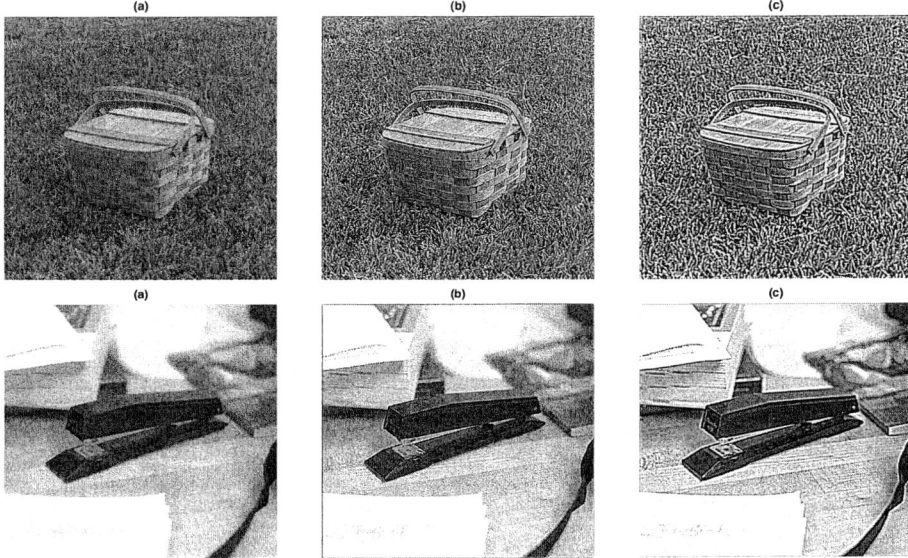

Fig. 2. (a) Two images of basket and stapler (b) the images enhanced with the Laplacian-based kernel (c) the images enhanced with the kernel derived from the proposed methodology

it is easy to see from the polarities of the weight factors that while the one constructed out of Laplacian (L) may clearly represent the classical excitatory-inhibitory model, the other one (L') represents the non-classical excitatory-inhibitory-disinhibitory model of receptive field. In figure 2, we show the results of convolving two images with L and L' kernels. The results clearly show that the new kernel L' outperforms the Laplacian based kernel L in terms of image enhancement. The parameters of m that have been chosen here are certainly not unique. It can be easily verified that one shall get similar results for other values as well.

Acknowledgement

We thank Mr. Ratan kumar Saha, Mr. Sankhasubhra Nag, Mr. Arunabha Adhikary and all members of Microelectronics Division, SINP for their help and cooperation.

References

1. Marr, D., Hildreth, E.: Theory of edge detection. Proceedings of Royal Society of London B **207** (1980) 187–217
2. Rodieck, R. W.: Quantitative analysis of cat retinal ganglion cell response to visual stimuli. Vision Research **5** (1965) 583–601

3. Enroth-Cugell, C., Robson, J. G.: The contrast sensitivity of the retinal ganglion cells of the cat. Journal of Physiology (London) **187** (1966) 517–552
4. Poggio, T., Torre, V.: Ill-posed problems and regularization analysis in early vision. MIT AI Memo **773** (1984)
5. Poggio, T. Voorhees, H., Yuille, A.: A Regularized solution to edge detection. MIT AI Memo **833** (1985)
6. Gonzalez, R. C., Woods, R. E.: Digital image processing. Second Ed. Third Indian Reprint, Pearson-Education (2003) 125-131
7. Ikeda, H., Wright, J.: Functional oganization of the periphery effect in retinal ganglion cells. Vision Research **12** (1972) 1857–1879
8. Passaglia, C. L., Enroth-Cugell C., Troy J. B.: Effects of remote stimulation on the mean firing rate of cat retinal ganglion cells. Journal of Neuroscience **21** (2001) 5794–5803
9. Ghosh, K., Sarkar, S., Bhaumik K.: A bio-inspired model for multi-scale representation of even order gaussian derivatives. Proceedings of International Conference on Intelligent Sensors, Sensor Networks and Information Processings (ISSNIP), IEEE EX **994** ISBN: 0-7803-8893-3 (2004) 497–502
10. Ma, S. D., Li, B.: Derivative computation by multiscale filters. Image and Vision Computing. **16** (1998) 43–53
11. Young, R. A.: The gaussian derivative theory of spatial vision: analysis of cortical cell receptive field line weighing profiles. GMR-**4920** (1985)
12. Koenderink, J. J., van Doorn, A. J.: Receptive field families. Biological Cybernetics **63** (1990) 291–297
13. Ghosh, K., Sarkar, S., Bhaumik, K.: Low-level brightness contrast illusions and non-classical receptive field of mammalian retina. Proceedings of Second International Conference on Intelligent Sensing and Information Processing (ICISIP), IEEE EX **979** ISBN: 0-7803-8840-2 (2005) 529–534
14. Mach, E.: On the physiological effect of spatially distributed light stimuli (1868). Mach Bands: Quantitative Studies On Neural Network In The Retina, F. Ratliff (Ed), Holden-Day, San Francisco (1965) 299–306
15. Ghosh, K., Sarkar S., Bhaumik, K.: A new mask for unsharp masking based on human visual system. Proceedings of National Conference on Image Processing (NCIP), IEEE Conf. Rec. **10435** (2005) 113–116

A Chosen Plaintext Steganalysis of Hide4PGP V 2.0

Debasis Mazumdar[1], Soma Mitra[1], Sonali Dhali[1], and Sankar K. Pal[2]

[1] CDAC,Kolkata, Plot E2/1, Block – GP, Sector V, Salt Lake City, Kolkata – 700091
[2] Machine Intelligence Unit, Indian Statistical Institute, Kolkata - 700108, India

Abstract. A chosen plaintext steganalysis algorithm is described to isolate the corrupted bits in an image tampered with Hide4PGP V 2.0. The method is developed from the notion of representation of two dimensional image data in terms of a linear bit stream consisting of a set of basic building blocks. Its performance for message extraction is demonstrated on different 24 bit BMP images.

1 Introduction

Hide4PGP V 2.0 is a steganography tool, which is readily available and used frequently to tamper both image and audio files. It encrypts the message before distribution; thereby making the tool robust. Some schemes are reported in this regard based on statistical measures [1] and pallet color [2]. First and higher order statistics are also used to discriminate between images with and without hidden messages using LSB embedding stego tools like Hide4PGP ([3],[4]). M.K.Johnson et. al. [5] has used frequency domain analysis for audio signals to detect the existence of hidden message embedded using Hide4PGP. However, these methods can only detect the presence or absence of hidden message within a cover. In the present article, we describe a steganalysis algorithm based on chosen plaintext attacking scheme, which can identify and isolate the corrupted bits. The isolation of corrupted bits helps us to get back the ciphertext. To reconstruct the plaintext message out of the ciphertext one may use further cryptanalysis. The algorithm uses a unique method of representing two dimensional image data as a linear bit string consisting of a set of basic building blocks. The effectiveness of the method is demonstrated on a set of 24 bit BMP images of varying sizes.

2 Characteristics of Message Distribution

After a series of experiments using monotonic (single color) cover image (having p no. of pixels) and known plaintext we found the following characteristics (patterns) of the distribution used in embedding a message in 3p number of LSB positions.

    i) The message, of length m_L, is embedded symmetrically within the LSBs of R, G and B components of p number of pixels. These LSBs, when arranged in a linear string, shows reflection symmetry with respect to centre position. Also in each part the arrangement is same when read from left to right or vice-versa. These are illustrated in (Fig. 2), where the black and white squares represent tampered and untampered bits respectively.

ii) Each part of the string, if further divided into two equal parts, the same symmetrical properties, as stated above, are observed. This continues up to a critical segment of the string beyond which its further splitting does not result in the said symmetrical property. Let this segment be defined as minimum unit M of length ℓ_M.

iii) Untampered ones separate tampered LSBs. No two tampered bits can occur together. Number of white squares (i.e. untampered bits) separating two black squares is variable. Let this number of such consecutive white squares be called the run length (ℓ).

iv) In any tampered image, there exist only two types of run lengths (even and odd), and they differ in length only by unity. The run length depends on both p and m_L.

Note that, all the aforesaid characteristics are valid only when $m_L < 3p/2$. If $m_L > 3p/2$, the same properties hold good with the black and white squares interchanged. When $m_L = 3p/2$, the LSB positions are alternatively occupied by the message bits and there exists only one type of run length of value unity. Beside these, the following special cases may be noted regarding message embedding.

Case I: $m_L = 3p$, Here all the LSBs are tampered; i.e., only one type of run length, having zero value, exists.

Case II: $3p < m_L \leq 6p$, All the 3p LSBs get tampered first and then the remaining ($m_L - 3p$) message bits are distributed in the next significant 3p bits following the aforesaid symmetrical characteristics ((i) – (iv)).

Case III: $m_L > 6p$, Hide4PGP V 2.0 fails to embed the message.

2.1 Linear Bit-String and Basic Building Blocks

A linear bit string consisting of tampered (black squares) and untampered bits (white squares), as shown in Fig. 2, can be viewed as an ensemble of basic building blocks, where each block consists of three elements nomenclatured as black ball (●), white ball (o), and the message bit (♦) of unit length. Black ball represents even run length ℓ. White ball represents odd run length $\ell + 1$ (or $\ell - 1$). Depending on the combinations of black ball, white ball and message bit, different building blocks such as, u_1, u_2, u_{2R}, u_3, u_4 and u_5 can be defined, as shown in Fig 1.

Basic building block	Structure	Lengths in Bits
u_1	♦ o ♦	$\ell + 3$ (or $\ell + 1$)
u_2	● ♦ o	$2\ell + 2$ (or 2ℓ)
u_{2R}	o ♦ ●	$2\ell + 2$ (or 2ℓ)
u_3	♦ ● ♦	$\ell + 2$
u_4	o ♦ o	$2\ell + 3$ (or $2\ell - 1$)
u_5	● ♦ ●	$2\ell + 1$

Fig. 1. Different basic building blocks and their lengths in bits

3 Method of Message Extraction

Let ξ be a tampered bit string containing n number of minimum units represented by the building blocks as shown in Fig. 2.

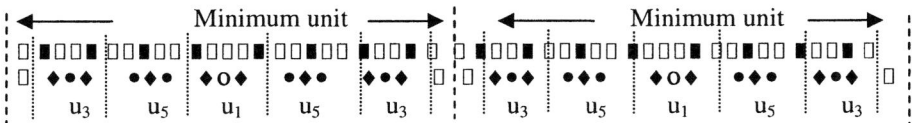

Fig. 2. Representation of minimum unit length of a bit string in terms of basic building blocks

Here all the diamonds (♦) in the n minimum units contain the hidden message. Therefore, determining their locations is necessary for extracting the message. In order to do that, the following steps may be taken:

Step 1: Compute the minimum unit length l_M in ξ.
Step 2: Compute all possible combinations of u_1, u_2, u_{2R}, u_3 and u_4 (or u_5) as determined by their number of occurrences within l_M.
Step 3: Determine that combination(s) of the building blocks within l_M, which shows the symmetry property.
Step 4: Isolate the diamond bits (♦) in all the n minimum units, arrange them linearly and extract the message contained in the string ξ through decryption using the descrambler [6].

In certain cases ξ may have more than one combination of building blocks having symmetry property. In that case, except one other would be (syntactically/ semantically) incorrect.

In the following sections we explain the methods of computing the length (l_M) of the minimum unit (Step 1), determining the number of basic building blocks in the minimum unit (Step 2), detecting the combinations of the building blocks which posses the symmetry (Step 3), and extracting the message bits from the entire string ξ (Step 4).

3.1 Computation of Length of Minimum Unit

Within the linear bit string ξ having 3p number of available LSBs, let, m_L message bits be distributed symmetrically. Let, in ξ, two consecutive message bits be separated by q number of untampered bits. The difference between the total number of available LSBs (3p) in ξ and the number of message bits m_L, therefore, gives the number of positions occupied by all the untampered bits. So, one can write:

$$3p - m_L = qm_L \tag{1}$$

For integral values of p and m_L, q may be either an integer or a real number. Since the number of untampered bits separating two message bits is always an integer, the adjustment (or justification) of the fractional part of q is made considering the occurrences of the even and odd run lengths of unit difference as follows:

If floor of q (i.e., $\lfloor q \rfloor$) is odd, then the even run length $\ell = \lfloor q \rfloor + 1$ and the odd run length $\ell - 1 = \lfloor q \rfloor$. When $\lfloor q \rfloor$ is even, the even run length $\ell = \lfloor q \rfloor$ and the odd run length $\ell + 1 = \lfloor q \rfloor + 1$. If q is an integer, then obviously there exists only one type of run length (either even or odd) separating two consecutive message bits. Let there be x number of black balls and y number of white balls in ξ. Since a message bit always follows each of black and white balls, total number of message bits is equal to the sum of the number of black and white balls. Thus,

$$x + y = m_L \qquad (2)$$

In terms of x and y, and the even and odd run lengths, Eq. (1) can be written as,

$$3p - m_L = \ell x + (\ell \pm 1)y \qquad (3)$$

'+' stands for even run length ℓ and odd run length $\ell+1$ while '-' stands for even run length ℓ and odd run length $\ell-1$.

Solving the above linear equations for x and y, one can compute the ratio (k) of the number of black balls to the number of white balls in the entire string ξ.

Since the data distribution in ξ follows the symmetrical properties (described in Section 2), the value of k computed over the entire string ξ would be the same even if computed within the minimum unit ℓ_M. Let, b_b and b_w be the number of black and white balls in the minimum unit length ℓ_M. Then,

$$b_b / b_w = k \qquad (4)$$

where b_b and b_w represent two smallest possible integers satisfying Eq. (4).

Therefore, the length of the minimum unit ℓ_M can be computed as:

$$\ell_M = b_w (\ell (1 + k)+ k) \qquad (5)$$

After obtaining ℓ_M, the next task is to determine all possible combinations of the basic building blocks u_is in it (Step 2), and then find the one, which shows symmetry property (Step 3). In Section 3.2 we explain the way of computing all such combinations of u_is with different n_i values in ℓ_M. The method of determining the symmetrical sequence out of them is then described in Section 3.3.

3.2 Computation of the Number of Basic Building Blocks in the Minimum Unit

Let n_i be the number of ith basic building block u_i of length ℓ_i (i = 1, 2, 2R, 3, 4 and 5) occurred in the minimum unit of length ℓ_M. While representing the minimum unit in terms of basic building blocks, as discussed in Section 2.1 and represented in Fig. 2, ℓ/2 number of white squares are seen to remain unaccounted both at the beginning and end points of the minimum unit. Hence the remaining ($\ell_M - \ell$) number of bits are represented by n_i number of u_i units. Therefore one can write,

$$\sum_i n_i \ell_i = \ell_M - \ell \qquad (6)$$

Three independent equations can be derived from Eq.(6) expressing the number of black balls, white balls and message bits in u_i in terms of the number of black balls (b_b), white balls(b_w) and message bits. In any minimum unit ℓ_M, five different n_is, namely, (n_1, n_2, n_{2R}, n_3, n_4) or (n_1, n_2, n_{2R}, n_3, n_5) can occur. Since it involves computation of five variables from three equations, the algorithm will give degenerate solutions. Further, units u_2 and u_{2R} are of equal length; hence, although the algorithm needs to compute only one n_i value for them, it is not possible to identify whether that value corresponds to u_2 or u_{2R}. Under the above circumstances, for a string ξ having Σn_i number of basic building blocks, the total number of degenerate solutions is

$$N = \sum_{k=1}^{\Sigma n_i/2} ((\Sigma n_i + 3 - 2k)^2). \qquad (7)$$

Out of them, usually the distribution (arrangements) of u_is corresponding to only one solution will posses the symmetry property, as stated in Section 2.

3.3 Determination of Minimum Unit with Building Blocks

In order to determine the solution(s) with symmetry property, one needs to check several conditions with the arrangements of u_is in ℓ_M. To articulate them, let us divide the set of basic building blocks i.e., $\{u_1, u_2, u_{2R}, u_3, u_4 \text{ (or } u_5)\}$ into two subsets, namely, $S_1 = \{u_1, u_3\}$ and $S_2 = \{u_2, u_{2R}, u_4 \text{ (or } u_5)\}$. With S_1, S_2 and the ratio k (Section 3.1), the conditions are stated below:

Condition 1: The even positions in the minimum unit ℓ_M are always occupied by the elements of S_2 while elements of S_1 always occupy the odd positions.
Condition 2: The number of consecutive white balls and black balls can be determined depending on the value of k, as follows:

i) If $k > 1$ and $k \in Z$ (Z is the set of positive integers) then each white ball will be followed by maximum k number of black balls. ii) If $k > 1$ and $k \in R$ (R is the set of rational numbers) then each white ball will be followed by either $\lceil k \rceil$ or $\lfloor k \rfloor$ number of black balls. iii) If $k < 1$ and $1/k \in Z$ then each black ball will be followed by maximum k number of white balls. iv) If $k < 1$ and $1/k \in R$ then each black ball will be followed by either $\lceil 1/k \rceil$ or $\lfloor 1/k \rfloor$ numbers of white balls.

3.4 Extraction of Message from ξ

After obtaining the solutions having symmetry property from the previous phase (Section 3.3), perform the following tasks:

i) Select one such solution. ii) Repeat it so as to construct the entire string ξ. iii) Isolate all the diamond ($\blacklozenge$) bits and put them consecutively to form a cipher string. iv) Decrypt the cipher string using the Descrambler function [6]. v) Check the decrypted message (text) syntactically/semantically, and accept it as the correct message. Otherwise select another solution with symmetry property and perform the above tasks (ii – iv).

4 Experimental Results

To demonstrate the effectiveness of our algorithm, two hundred 24-bit BMP images of different sizes, ranging from (8x8) to (512x512) pixels, are tampered using Hide4PGP V 2.0. The hidden text message is of different lengths covering 2 to 25% of the cover image. All these tampered images are then decrypted with the method described in Section 3. In all the cases the algorithm has been able to extract the hidden message.

5 Conclusions

We have described an attacking algorithm for extraction of hidden message out of stego images created using Hide4PGP V 2.0. The effectiveness of the methodology is demonstrated over a large number of 24 bit BMP images of different sizes. This algorithm is also applicable to WAV and VOC file formats tampered with Hide4PGP V 2.0.

Acknowledgements

The authors gratefully acknowledge the financial support through project no. 12(20)/04-IRSD of the DIT, MCIT, Govt. of India, New Delhi.

References

1. Dumitresu, S., Wu, X., Wang, Z.: Detection of LSB Steganography Via Sample Pair Analysis. Lecture Notes in Computer Science, Vol. 2578. Springer-Verlag, Noordwijkerhout, The Netherlands (2002) 355-372
2. Johnson, N.F., Jajodia, S.: Steganalysis of Images Created Using Current Steganography Software Lecture Notes in Computer Science, Vol. 1525. Springer-Verlag, Portland Oregon USA (1998) 273-289.
3. Lyu, S., Farid, H.: Detecting Hidden Messages Using Higher-Order Statistics and Support Vector Machines. Lecture Notes in Computer Science, Vol. 2578. Springer-Verlag, Noordwijkerhout, The Netherlands (2002) 340-354
4. Westfeld, A.: Detecting Low Embedding Rates. Lecture Notes in Computer Science, Vol. 2578. Springer-Verlag, Noordwijkerhout, The Netherlands (2002) 324-339
5. Johnson, M.K., Lyu, S., Farid, H.: Steganalysis in Recorded Speech. SPIE Symposium on Electronic Imaging San Jose CA (2005)
6. Hide4PGP Homepage: http://www.heinz-repp.onlinehome.de/Hide4PGP.htm

Isolation of Lung Cancer from Inflammation

Md. Jahangir Alam[1], Sid Ray[1], and Hiromitsu Hama[2]

[1] Clayton School of Information Technology, Monash University,
Victoria 3800, Australia
{md.alam, sid}@csse.monash.edu.au
[2] Faculty of Engineering, Osaka City University,
3-3-138 Sugimoto, Osaka, Japan
hama@info.eng.osaka-cu.ac.jp

Abstract. In this paper we propose an efficient new algorithm for making an intelligent system for isolating the lung cancer from the inflamed region using needle biopsies. The best way among the cancer treatments, surgery, is the way that can be used for the removal of a malignant tumor in an operation. It is most effective when a cancer is small and localized. Identification and removal of the cancer cells in their earliest formation are very much important. Almost all of the diagnostic laboratories in the world use experts to identify the suspected cells of the lung tumors under microscope. Due to the smaller number of experts, the proposed method, derived based on image contour analysis, has an important significance to replace the manual methods by an intelligent system.

1 Introduction

Cancer is a group of diseases characterized by the uncontrolled growth of abnormal cells in the body. Once cells become malignant, they multiply more rapidly than usual. Then they often form masses called tumors that invade nearby tissue and interfere with normal bodily functions. Cancer cells also have a tendency to spread to other parts of the body, where they may form a secondary tumor. The surgical approach, the best way among the existing cancer treatments, is most effective when cancer is small and localized.

Due to the rapid developments of image processing and pattern recognition techniques, computer-aided lung cancer diagnosis has drawn additional attraction. Many accomplishments have already been achieved [1],[2],[3]. In an effort to improve accuracy and the speed of lung cancer pulmonary radiology, an artificial neural network-based hybrid lung cancer detection method was designed [4]. The false-negative cases in mass screening of lung cancer were analyzed in [5], [6]. Koizumi [7] showed how cancer cell could be separated from the inflammation by analyzing the high and low components of Fourier Descriptors of cell contours. A system that extracted and analyzed features of the lung and pulmonary blood vessel regions for the detection of tumor candidate from helical CT images is described in [8].

In the work reported in this paper we use the compactness of the cell contour, in conjunction with the equilibrium number of curvature zero-crossing points, to analyze the contour of the suspected cancer cell. The method of compactness analysis is used based on the fact that the cancer cells (type-C1 and type-C2) have spike-wheel contours. Due to the wheel shape, this type of cell is more compact, unless the contour contains high frequencies. On the other hand, the inflmatory cells type-B1 and type-B2 have non-wheel contour without spikes on them. The rest of the paper is organized as follows. Section 2 presents the proposed cancer cell isolation system. Section 3 shows the experimental results and conclusion follows in Section 4.

2   Cancer Cell Isolation System

The typical cancer cell isolation system has four parts: image and contour extraction, estimation of equilibrium number of curvature zero-crossing points, compactness analysis varying scale-space parameter and cancer cell isolation decision. The following three sub-sections describe these components.

2.1   Image Capture and Contour Extraction

A digital camera is mounted with the light microscope for capturing the suspected cell images of the specimens of needle biopsies. Four cancer cell countours: type-B1, type-B2, type-C1, and type-C2 are shown in Fig. 1(a). It is to be noted here that cancer cells type-B1 and type-B2 are not dangerous; these cells form the inflammatory area in the lung region. In this paper, details of image capture, preprocessing and contour extraction are not included. All the cell contours are stored in the database. Each contour is normalized with 360 points implementing interpolation using FFT method [9]. Other interpolation methods are also checked in but FFT method provides the best outcome.

2.2   Equilibrium Number of Zero-Crossing Points

The equilibrium number of curvature zero-crossing points is found by varying the scale-space parameter. The scale-space parameter is chosen in such a way that its value is neither too small nor too large so that we can avoid the influence of noise effects and the loss of important features of the contour. When the contour attains the equilibrium number of zero-crossing points, it remains unchanged for a sufficient range of scale-space parameter values.

Of the many approaches to shape representation and analysis that have been proposed, the notion of curvature of planar curves has emerged to be one of the most powerful. There is psychophysical and physiological as well as computational and mathematical support in favor of using curvature as a representation for contours.

Let us suppose $\beta(s)$ is a parameterized contour defined by $\beta(s) = (x(s), y(s))$, $s \in [0, 1]$. An evolved version of the contour $\beta_\sigma(s)$ can be computed as follows:

$$\beta_\sigma(s) = (x(s,\sigma), y(s,\sigma)), s \in [0,1] \qquad (1)$$

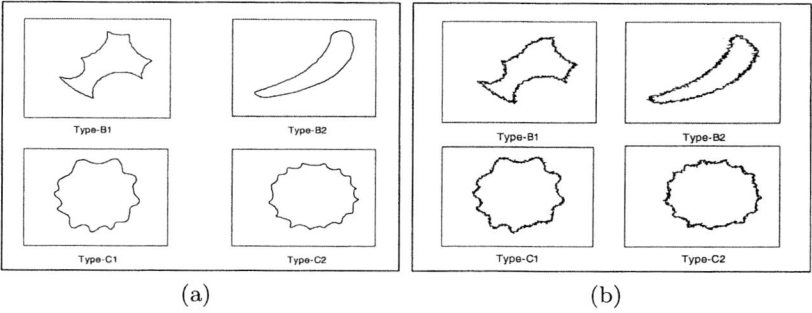

Fig. 1. Different types of cell contours: (a) database contours and (b) test contours

where $x(s, \sigma) = x(s) \otimes g(s, \sigma)$, $y(s, \sigma) = y(s) \otimes g(s, \sigma)$, $\otimes$ is the convolution operator and $g(s, \sigma)$ denotes a Gaussian kernel of width σ:

$$g(s, \sigma) = \frac{1}{\sigma \sqrt{2\pi}} e^{\frac{-s^2}{2\sigma^2}} \quad (2)$$

The curvature K on β_σ is given by [10]

$$K(s, \sigma) = \frac{x'(s, \sigma) y''(s, \sigma) - x''(s, \sigma) y'(s, \sigma)}{(x'^2(s, \sigma) + y'^2(s, \sigma))^{\frac{3}{2}}} \quad (3)$$

The curvature zero-crossing points can be found by setting $K(s, \sigma) = 0$. There is no way to know a priori what scale to search to smooth the contour. One strategy followed is to search for the position in scale-space where the number of dominant points is stable over the largest range of scales. We select a particular value of σ for which the contour of the object attains a certain number of curvature zero-crossing points, which remains unchanged for a long period of its changes. Fig. 2 shows an evolving contour of cancer type-B1 using different levels of scale-space parameter.

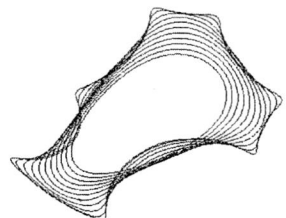

Fig. 2. Evolving contour using different levels of scale-space parameter

2.3 Compactness Analysis and Cancer Cell Isolation

The estimated values of the compactness for the input and database contours at an equilibrium number of zero-crossing points condition are used for the isolation of each cancer cell. As in [9], we measure the compactness of a contour by

$$\gamma = \frac{(perimeter)^2}{4\pi(area)} \qquad (4)$$

Fig. 3 shows the variation of the compactness of the database (see Fig. 1(a)) and test contours (see Fig. 1(b)) for various levels of the scale-space parameter.

The test contours are identified based on two conditions: equilibrium number of zero-crossing points (N_{eq}) and the compactness at the equilibrium (γ_{eq}). If the number of zero-crossing points (N) is high ($N > N_{eq}$) and the compactness (γ) is low ($\gamma < \gamma_{eq}$), the cell is malignant. This means that the person whose lung cells have been tested, is very likely to be suffering from lung cancer. The person should go for further investigation to identify the level and the location of the tumor in the lung region. If N is low ($N < N_{eq}$) and γ is high ($\gamma > \gamma_{eq}$), the cell is inflammatory (not dangerous). The conditions, when γ is low and N is also low or γ is high and N is also high, represent undecided cases.

To find out the values of N_{eq} and γ_{eq} we use the findings from our experimental observation. We know that the structure of a malignant cell is spike-wheel-shaped. From the investigation of the experimental findings, the values of N_{eq} and γ_{eq} have been chosen as 15 and 1.5, respectively. The number of zero-crossing points sustain at the equilibrium level for a certain range of scale-space parameter. The compactness of each contour has been calculated when the equilibrium number of zero-crossing points first appears corresponding to the value of σ. To find out the equilibrium number of zero-crossing points, we change the value of σ sufficiently small in each step.

3 Experimental Results

In examining the performance of the proposed method, experiments were conducted on different cancer cells. Twenty sets of test cancer cell contour are constructed using noise and removing a small portion of the contour to show the robustness in the case of contour deformation. Fig. 1(b) shows one set of constructed test contours corresponding to the database contours in Fig. 1(a). The algorithm has been programmed in Matlab and implemented on a Pentium III personal computer.

From Fig. 3 it is clear that even if the test contours contain noise, the ultimate variation of the compactness remains in the same level for a sufficient range of scale-space parameter. For the cells type-C1 and type-C2, the compactness value (N) becomes almost 1.0 (contour becomes round shaped) for scale-space parameter (σ) values in the range 18-20. At the same level of the scale, the compactness for both cells type-B1 and type-B2 is more than 1.5. Cells type-B1 and type-B2 take far higher range of σ values for the contour shape to be elliptical.

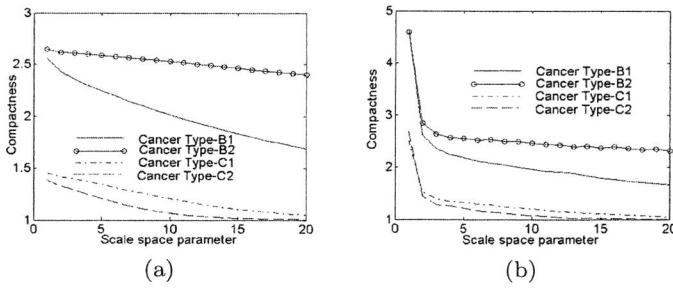

Fig. 3. Compactness variation for (a) database and (b) test contours

Fig. 4 shows the variation of the number of curvature zero-crossing points for various levels of the scale-space parameter for the database and the test contours. For the test contour of type-B1, the equilibrium number of zero-crossing points becomes 10, whereas for the same type in the database contour this number is 12. For the test contour of cancer cell type-B2, the equilibrium number of zero-crossing points is attained at the value of 2, which is the same for the database contour. For cancer cell types-C1, the number of zero-crossing points becomes 19, which is very close to the number of zero-crossing points for the database contour of the type-C1. For the case of cancer cell type-C2, the number of zero-crossing points is 30, which is almost the same number as in the database contour.

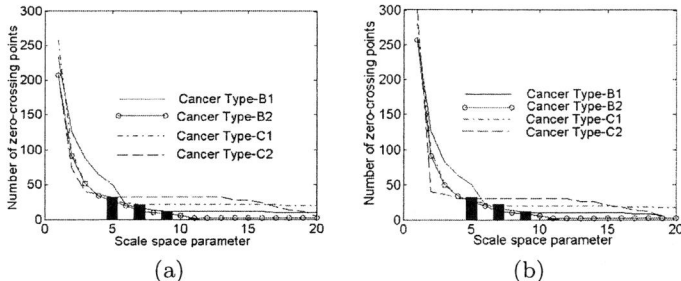

Fig. 4. Equilibrium zero-crossing points (bar) for (a) database and (b) test contours

4 Conclusion

In this research study we have dealt with the problem of cancer cell isolation from inflammation using needle biopsies. From the the compactness analysis at the equilibrium number of curvature zero-crossing points, each test contour is correctly identified. In most cases, the equilibrium number of zero-crossing points for cancer cell contours type-C1 and type-C2, is higher than 15 and the compactness value is less than 1.5. On the other hand, for the non-dangerous cells type-B1 and type-B2, the compactness value does not go bellow 1.5 in the equilibrium range of zero-crossing points. Furthermore, the number of zero-crossing points maintains its value under 15. The proposed method is very simple but effective in its use for the isolation of lung cancer from inflammation. A limitation of this study is that the test cases are made artificially. Our future goal is to implement the proposed system on a set of real data obtained from a sufficient number of suspected lung cancer sufferers.

References

1. K. Mori, Y. Saito, K. Tominaga, K. Yokoi, N. Miyazawa, A. Okuyama, and M. Sasagawa. Small nodular lesions in the lung periphery: New approach to diagnosis with CT. *Radiology*, 177:843–849, 1990.
2. Y. Kawata, N. Niki, and H. Ohmatsu. Curvature-based Internal Structure Analysis of Pulmonary Nodules Using Thoracic 3D CT Images. *Systems and Computers in Japan*, 32(11), 2001.
3. T. Masami, E. Masahiro, N. Koji, K. Masayuki, Y. Satory, K. Kiyomitsu, and H. Kazuyuki. Conceptual design of a synchrotron light source used for medical diagnoses at NIRS. In *SPIE*, volume 3770, pages 213–220, 1999.
4. Chiou YSP, Lure YMF, Ligomenides PA. Neural Network Image Analysis and Classification in Hybrid Lung Nodule Detection (HLND) System. In *IEEE-SP Workshop on Neural Networks for Signal Processing*, pages 517–526, 1993.
5. T. Tanaka, K. Yuta and Y. Kobayashi. A Study of False-Negative Case in Mass-Screening of Lung Cancer. *Jap. Thor. Med.*, 43:832–838, 1984.
6. J. Oda, S. Akita and K. Shimada. A Study of False-Negative Case in Comparative Reading of Mass-Screening of Lung Cancer. *Lung Cancer*, 29:271–278, 1989.
7. M. Koizumi. Medical Image Analysis for the Diagnosis of Chest X-ray. Doctor of Engineering Dissertation, Graduate School of Engineering, Osaka City University, Osaka, Japan, 2003. 37–47.
8. K. Kanazawa, M. Kubo and N. Niki. Computer Aided Diagnosis System for Lung Cancer Based on Helical CT Images. In *13th International Conference on Pattern Recognition*, volume 3, pages 381–385, 1996.
9. A.K. Jain. *Fundamentals of Digital Image Processing*. Prentice-Hall Inc., 1989.
10. Mokhtarian F and Machworth. A Scale-Based Description of Planner Curves and Two-Dimensional Shapes. *IEEE Trans. on Pattern Analysis and Matching Intelligence*, 8:34–43, 1996.

Learning to Segment Document Images

K.S. Sesh Kumar, Anoop Namboodiri, and C.V. Jawahar

Centre for Visual Information Technology,
International Institute of Information Technology, Hyderabad, India

Abstract. A hierarchical framework for document segmentation is proposed as an optimization problem. The model incorporates the dependencies between various levels of the hierarchy unlike traditional document segmentation algorithms. This framework is applied to learn the parameters of the document segmentation algorithm using optimization methods like gradient descent and Q-learning. The novelty of our approach lies in learning the segmentation parameters in the absence of groundtruth.

1 Introduction

Document image layout has a hierarchical (tree like) representation, with each level encapsulating some unique information that is not present in other levels. The representation contains the complete page in the root node, and the text blocks, images and background form the next layer of the hierarchy. The text blocks can have a further detailed representations like text lines, words and components, which form the remaining layers of the representation hierarchy. A number of segmentation algorithms [1] have been proposed to fill the hierarchy in a top-down or bottom-up fashion. However, traditional approaches assume independence between different levels of the hierarchy, which is incorrect in many cases. The problem of document segmentation is that of dividing a document image ($\mathcal{I}$) into a hierarchy of meaningful regions like paragraphs, text lines, words, image regions, etc. These regions are associated with a homogeneity property $\phi(\cdot)$ and the segmentation algorithms are parameterized by θ.

The nature of the parameters θ depend on the algorithm that is used to segment the image. Most of the current page segmentation algorithms decide the parameters θ, apriori, and use it irrespective of the page characteristics as shown in [2]. There are also algorithms that estimate the document properties (like average lengths of connected components) and assign values to θ using a predefined method [3]. Though these methods are reasonably good for homogeneous document image collections, they tend to fail in the case of wide variations in the image and its layout characteristics. The problem becomes even more challenging in the case of Indian language documents due to the presence of large variations in fonts, styles, etc. This warrants a method that can learn from examples and solve the document image segmentation for a wide variety of layouts. Such algorithms can be very effective for large and diverse document image collections such as digital libraries. In this paper, we propose a page segmentation algorithm based on a learning framework, where the parameter vector θ is learnt from a set of example documents, using homogeneity properties of regions, $\phi(\cdot)$. The feedback from different stages of the segmentation process is used to learn the parameters that maximize $\phi(\cdot)$.

Hierarchical framework: The hierarchical segmentation framework is characterized at each level i, by a parameter set $\theta_i, 1 \leq i \leq n$. The input to the segmentation algorithm is the document image, ($\mathcal{I}$), which is generated by a random process, parameterized by θ. Given an input document $\mathcal{I}$, the goal is to find the set values for parameters $\theta = (\theta_1, \theta_2, \ldots, \theta_n)$, that maximizes the joint probability of the parameters for a given ($\mathcal{I}$), using (1).

$$\hat{\theta} = arg \max_{\theta_1, \theta_2, \ldots, \theta_n} P(\theta_1, \theta_2, \ldots, \theta_n | \mathcal{I}) \tag{1}$$

$$= arg \max_{\theta_1, \theta_2, \ldots, \theta_n} P(\theta_1 | \mathcal{I}).P(\theta_2 | \mathcal{I}) \ldots P(\theta_n | \mathcal{I}) \tag{2}$$

$$= arg \max_{\theta_1, \theta_2, \ldots, \theta_n} P(\theta_1 | \mathcal{I}).P(\theta_2 | \mathcal{I}, \theta_1) \ldots P(\theta_n | \mathcal{I}, \theta_1, \ldots, \theta_{n-1}) \tag{3}$$

On assuming independence between different levels of the hierarchy, the parameters are conditionally independent of each other as they characterize the segmentation process at each level. Hence (1) can be rewritten as (2). However, this is not a valid assumption as errors at a level of the hierarchy is propagated downwards deteriorating the overall performance of the segmentation system. Hence the segmentation algorithm and its parameters at the lower levels depend on the parameters of the upper levels and the input image $\mathcal{I}$. To incorporate this dependency into the formulation, we need to rewrite (1) as (3).

To achieve optimal segmentation the joint probability of the parameters $P(\theta_1, \cdots \theta_n)$ needs to be modeled. However, the distribution is very complex in case of page segmentation algorithms. In addition a large set of algorithms that can be used at different levels of hierarchy. Hence a fitness measure of segmentation is defined that approximates the posterior probability at each stage. Our goal is to compute the parameter θ_i that maximizes the posterior $P(\theta_i / \mathcal{I}, \theta_1, \theta_2, \ldots, \theta_{i-1})$ or the fitness function at level i.

Conventionally, segmentation has been viewed as a deterministic partitioning scheme characterized by the parameter θ. The challenge has been in finding an optimal set of values for θ, to segment the input Image $\mathcal{I}$ into appropriate regions. In our formulation, the parameter vector θ is learned based on the feedback calculated in the form a homogeneity measure $\phi(\cdot)$ (a model based metric to represent the distance from ideal segmentation). The feedback is propagated upwards in the hierarchy to improve the performance of each level above, estimating the new values of the parameters to improve the overall performance of the system. Hence the values of θ are learned based on the feedback from present and lower levels of the system. In order to improve the performance of an algorithm over time using multiple examples or by processing an image multiple times, the algorithm is given appropriate feedback in the form of homogeneity measure of the segmented regions. Feedback mechanisms for learning the parameters could be employed at various levels.

2 Hypothesis Space for Page Segmentation

A document image layout is conventionally understood as a spatial distribution of text and graphics components. However, for a collection of document images, layout is characterized by a probability distribution of many independent random variables. For example, consider a conference proceedings formatted according to a specific layout style sheet. The set of values for word-spaces, line spaces etc. will follow a specific statistical distribution. For a new test page, segmentation implies the maximization of the likelihood of the observations (word-spaces etc.) by assuming the distribution. In our case, the objective is to maximize the likelihood of the set of observations by learning the parameters of the distribution, indirectly in θ-space.

We assume the existence and possibly the nature of a distribution of the region properties, but not the knowledge of the ground truth. For the problem of page segmentation, assumption of an available distribution (ground-truth) may not be very appropriate. Hence the problem is formulated as learning of the parameter vector θ, which minimizes an objective function $J(\mathcal{I}, \phi, \theta)$. The function $J(\cdot)$ could be thought of as an objective quality measure of the segmentation result. The parameter θ includes all the parameters in the hierarchy of document segmentation, $\theta_1, \cdots, \theta_n$. In this case, the objective function, $J(\cdot)$, can be expanded as a linear combination of n individual functions. Objective functions can be defined for different segmentation algorithms based on the homogeneous properties of the corresponding regions it segments.

Segmentation Quality Metric: A generic objective function should be able to encapsulate all the properties associated with the homogeneity function ϕ. In the experiments, a function is considered that includes additional properties of the layout, such as density of text pixels in the segmented foreground and background regions and a measure that accounts for partial projections in multi-column documents. In this work, the inter line variance (σ_1), the variance of the line height (σ_2), the variance of the distance between words (σ_3), the density of foreground pixels within a line (ILD) and between two lines (BLD), the density of foreground pixels within a word(IWD) and between words (BWD) are considered. We use the following objective functions $J(\mathcal{I}, \phi_l, \theta_l)$ and $J(\mathcal{I}, \phi_w, \theta_w)$, that needs to be maximized for best line and word segmentation respectively:

$$J(\mathcal{I}, \phi_l, \theta_l) = \frac{1}{1+\sigma_1} + \frac{1}{1+\sigma_2} - BLD + ILD \qquad (4)$$

$$J(\mathcal{I}, \phi_w, \theta_w) = \frac{1}{1+\sigma_3} - BWD + IWD \qquad (5)$$

The value of each of the factors in the combination in the above equations falls in the range $[0, 1]$, and hence $J(\mathcal{I}, \phi_l, \theta_l) \in [-1, 3]$ and $J(\mathcal{I}, \phi_w, \theta_w) \in [-1, 1]$.

3 Learning Segmentation Parameters

The process of learning tries to find the set of parameters, θ, that maximizes the objective function $J(\mathcal{I}, \phi, \theta)$: $\arg\min_\theta J(\mathcal{I}, \phi, \theta)$. Let $\tilde{\theta}_i$ be the current estimate of the parameter vector for a given document. We compute a revised estimate, $\tilde{\theta}_{i+1}$, using an update function, $D_\theta(.)$, which uses the quality metric $J(\cdot)$ in the neighborhood of $\tilde{\theta}_i$ to compute $\delta\theta_i$.

$$\tilde{\theta}_{i+1} = \tilde{\theta}_i + \delta\theta_i; \quad \delta\theta_i = D_\theta(J(\mathcal{I}, \phi, \tilde{\theta}_i)) \qquad (6)$$

In order to define the parameter vector θ, we need to look at the details of the segmentation algorithm that is employed. The algorithm used for segmentation operates in two stages. In the first stage, image regions are identified based on the size of connected components (size $\geq \theta_c$) and are removed. The remaining components are labeled as text. The second stage identifies the lines of text in the document based on recursive XY cuts as suggested in [1]. The projection profiles in the horizontal and vertical directions of each text block are considered alternately. A text block is divided at points in the projection, where the number of foreground pixels fall below a particular threshold, θ_n. In order to avoid noise pixels forming a text line, text line with a height less than a threshold, θ_l is removed. The lines segmented are further segmented into words using a parameter θ_w. We also restrict the number of projections to a maximum of 3, which is sufficient for most real-life documents. One could employ a variety of techniques to learn the optimal set of values for these parameters ($\theta_c, \theta_n, \theta_l$ and θ_w).

The parameter space corresponding to the above θ is large and a simple gradient-based search would often get stuck at local maxima, due to the complexity of the function being optimized. To overcome these difficulties, a reinforcement learning based approach called Q-learning is used. Peng et al. [4] suggested a reinforcement learning based parameter estimation algorithm for document image segmentation. However, our formulation is fundamentally different from that described in [4] in two ways: 1) It assumes no knowledge about the ground truth of segmentation or recognition, and 2) The state space is modeled to incorporate the knowledge of the results of the intermediate stages of processing unlike in [4] that uses a single state after each stage of processing.

3.1 Feedback Based Parameter Learning

The process of segmentation of a page, is carried out in multiple stages such as separation of text and image regions, and the segmentation of text into columns, blocks text lines and words. The sequential nature of the process lends well to learning in the Q-learning framework.

In Q-learning, we consider the process that is to be learned as a sequence of actions that takes the system from a starting state (input image $\mathcal{I}$) to a goal state (segmented image) [5]. An action a_t from a state s_t takes us to a new state s_{t+1} and could result in a reward, r_t. The final state is always associated with a reward depending on the overall performance of the system. The problem is to find a sequence of actions that

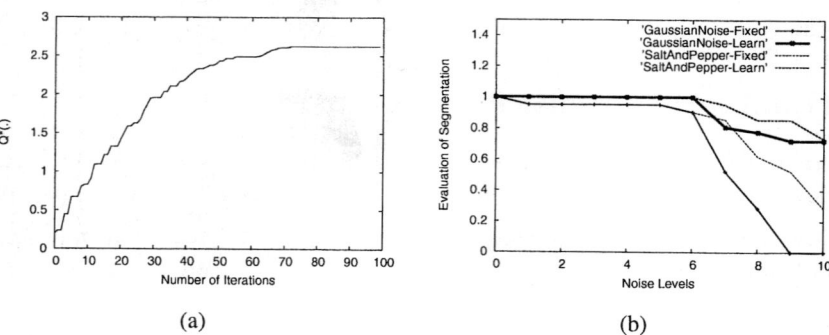

Fig. 1. (a): $Q(\cdot)$ over iterations, (b): segmentation accuracy of our approach and that of using fixed parameters in the presence of noise

maximizes the overall reward obtained in going from the start state to the goal state. The optimization is carried out with the help of the table $(Q(s_t, a_t))$ that maintains an estimate of the expected reward for the action a_t from the state, s_t. If there are n steps in the process, the Q table is updated using the following equation:

$$Q(s_t, a_t) = r_t + \gamma r_{t+1} + \ldots + \gamma^{n-1} r_{t+n-1} + \gamma^n \max_a (Q(s_{t+n}, a)) \qquad (7)$$

In the example of using XY cuts, the process contains two stages, and the above equation would reduce to $Q(s_t, a_t) = r_t + \gamma \max_a Q(s_{t+1}, a)$, where r_t is the immediate reward of the first step. Figure 1(a) shows the improvement of $Q^*(s_t, a_t) = \max_a Q(s_t, a_t)$ value over iterations for a particular document image. We note that the Q function converges in less than 100 iterations in our experiments.

4 Experimental Results

The segmentation algorithm was tested on a variety of documents, including new and old books in English and Indian languages, handwritten document images, as well as scans of historic palm leaf manuscripts collected by the Digital Library of India (DLI) project. Figure 2 shows examples of segmentation on a palm leaf, handwritten document, an indian language document with skew and a document with complex layout. Note that the algorithm is able to segment the document with multiple columns and images even when there is considerable variation between the font sizes, inter-line spacing among the different text blocks and unaligned text lines.

Performance in presence of Noise: Varying amounts of Gaussian noise and Salt-and-Pepper noise were added to the image and segmentation was carried out using the parameters learned from the resulting image. Figure 1(b) shows the segmentation performance of the learning-based approach as well as that using a fixed set of parameters, for varying amounts of noise in the data. We notice that the accuracy of the learning

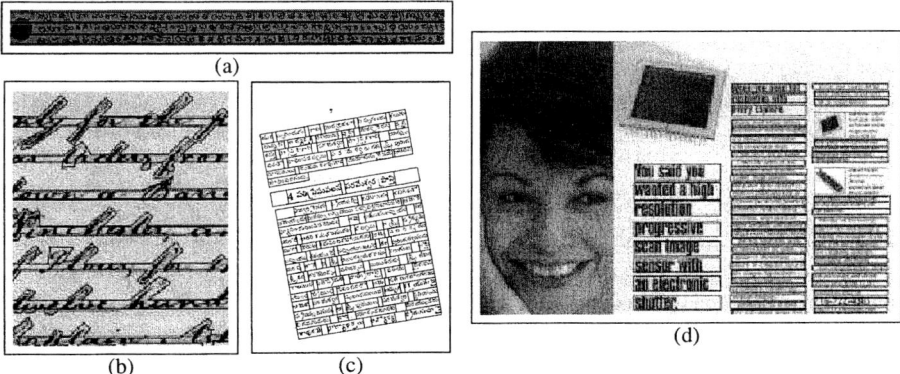

Fig. 2. Results of segmentation on (a) palm leaf, (b) handwritten document, (c) line and word segmentation of Indian language document with skew and (d) a multicolumn document

approach is consistently higher than that using a fixed set of parameters. At high levels of noise, the accuracy of the algorithm is still above 70%, while that using a fixed set of parameters falls to 20% or lower. The accuracy of segmentation, ρ, is computed as $\rho = (n(L) - n(C_L \cup S_L \cup M_L \cup F_L))/n(L)$, where $n(.)$ gives the cardinality of the set, L is the set of ground truth text lines in the document, C_L is the set of ground truth text lines that are missing, S_L is the set of ground truth text lines whose bounding boxes are split, M_L is the set of ground truth text lines that are horizontally merged, and F_L is the set of noise zones that are falsely detected [2]. We notice that the algorithm performs close to optimum even in presence of significant amounts of noise. Meanwhile, the performance of the same algorithm, when using a fixed set of parameters, degrades considerably in presence of noise.Our algorithm gave a performance evaluation of 97.80% on CEDAR dataset with five layouts and five documents of each layout and 91.20% on the Indian language DLI pages.

Integrating Skew Correction: Skew correction is integrated into the learning framework by introducing a skew correction stage to the sequence of processes in segmentation, after the removal of image regions. An additional parameter, θ_s, would be required to denote the skew angle of the document, which is to be rectified. The results of segmentation with skew can be viewed in 2(c). Defining an immediate reward for the skew correction stage, computed from the autocorrelation function of the projection histogram helps in speeding up the learning process.

The proposed algorithm is able to achieve robust segmentation results in the presence of various noises and a wide variety of layouts. The parameters are automatically adapted to segment the individual documents/text blocks, along with correction of document skew. The algorithm can easily be extended to include additional processing stages, such as thresholding, word and character segmentation, etc.

5 Conclusion

We have proposed a learning-based page segmentation algorithm using an evaluation metric which is used as feedback for segmentation. The proposed metric evaluates the quality of segmentation without the need of ground truth at various levels of segmentation. Experiments show that the algorithm can effectively adapt to a variety of document styles, and be robust in presence of noise and skew.

References

1. G.Nagy, S.Seth, M.Vishwanathan: A Prototype Document Image Analysis System for Technical Journals. Computer **25** (1992) 10–12
2. Mao, S., Kanungo, T.: Emperical performance evaluation methodology and its application to page segmentation algorithms. IEEE Transactions on PAMI **23** (2001) 242–256
3. Sylwester, D., Seth, S.: Adaptive segmentation of document images. In: Proceedings of the Sixth International Conference on Document Analysis and Recognition, Seattle, WA (2001) 827–831
4. J.Peng, B.Bhanu: Delayed reinforcement learning for adaptive image segmentation and feature extraction. IEEE Transactions on Systems, Man and Cybernetics **28** (1998) 482–488
5. Sutton, R.S., Barto, A.G.: Reinforcement Learning: An Introduction. The MIT Press (1998)

A Comparative Study of Different Texture Segmentation Techniques

Madasu Hanmandlu[1], Shilpa Agarwal[2], and Anirban Das[3]

[1] Dept. of Electrical Engineering, I.I.T Delhi, Hauz Khas,
New Delhi 110 016, India
`mhmandlu@ee.iitd.ernet.in`
[2] Dept. of Electrical Engineering, I.I.T Delhi, Hauz Khas,
New Delhi 110 016, India
`shilpadce@yahoo.com`
[3] Dept. of Computer Science, Jamia Millia Islamia University,
New Delhi 110 025, India
`anirban_das_jnu@rediffmail.com`

Abstract. Image segmentation techniques are very useful in the analysis of aerial images, biomedical images and seismic images as well as in the automation of industrial applications. The paper presents a few texture-specific features for the segmentation of texture images. We will present four approaches to texture segmentation, viz, descriptor based, heuristic function based, defuzzified feature based and Mask feature based. We have mainly used FCM for texture segmentation. Keywords- Texture segmentation, entropy, descriptors, texture energy measure, defuzzified feature

1 Introduction

The segmentation of textures requires the choice of proper texture-specific features with good discriminative power [1]. Generally speaking, texture feature extraction methods can be classified into three major categories, namely, statistical, structural and spectral. Various texture descriptors have been proposed in the literature. In addition to the aforementioned methods, Law's texture energy measures, Markov random field models, texture spectrum etc., are some other texture descriptors. A texture can be either regular pattern like man made texture, for e.g., "Mat" or "Fence" or it can be a random texture as in Natural images. We have implemented several methods for segmentation of Natural as well as mosaic images.

The paper is organized as follows: Section 2 gives an overview of the descriptor based approach for texture segmentation. In section 3, the feature based on heuristic function is explained. In Section 4, an overview of the mask-based feature for texture segmentation is discussed. Section 5 presents a comparison of results from different texture segmentation techniques.

2 Texture Image Segmentation Using Descriptors

The ambiguities in texture that arise due to fuzzy nature of image function give an opportunity to devise fuzzy texture features [2]. Since texture is region based, we consider arrangement of image functions (i.e., intensities) of pixels in a local region, say, a window, in order to characterize the texture. Spatial interaction model is used in the present work to evolve texture features. This approach brings into consideration the spatial arrangement of pixel intensities in a window. A pixel having similar intensity as that of its neighborhood will have a higher correlation.

The correlation of pixel $x(j)$ about its neighborhood $x(i)$ in a window of size pxp can be represented by a Gaussian membership function, which depends on the difference in their gray values. The membership function is defined as

$$\mu_j(i) = \exp\left[-\left\{\frac{x(j)-x(i)}{\tau}\right\}^2\right] \quad j=1,2,\ldots\ldots n \tag{1}$$

where τ is the fuzzifier selected as 10% of the size of window. We have calculated the membership value with the maximum gray level in a window as the reference. Accordingly, the membership function in (1) is modified to:

$$\mu_j(i) = \exp\left[-\left\{\frac{x(j)-x_{max}}{\tau}\right\}^2\right] \quad j=1,2,\ldots..8 \tag{2}$$

The membership value is $\mu_j(i)=1.0$ for $x(j)=x_{max}$. The membership values are less than or equal to 1 for the neighboring pixels in the window. Next, we obtain the cumulative response to the current pixel, x by taking weighted sum. So we have

$$y_i(x) = \sum_{j=1}^{n} \frac{\mu_j(i).x(j)}{\sum_{j=1}^{n}\mu_j(i)} \tag{3}$$

Where n is the number of pixels in a window. The output y(x) will be maximum when all the neighboring pixels are of the same value. Following this, the cumulative responses of all pixels are computed by forming 3x3 windows on original 512 x 512 image giving rise to an output image.

2.1 Texture Descriptors

If we use all the elements of Y ($Y=\{y_i(x)\}$), we would be bogged down by the computational problem. Instead, we derive texture descriptors that capture the essence of the texture subimage. If Y is of size MxM, it is then partitioned into sub-images, each of size wxw where $w \ll M$. We compute the n-descriptors for each sub-images, which results into a descriptor matrix, D of size RxR, where $R = M/w$. The element of D is a vector $[d_1, d_2,\ldots d_n]^T$, whose size n is equal to the number of descriptors. We want to capture the underlying structure of a texture through a few descriptors – Maximum occurrence, Difference moment of order k(for k=2)(also termed as 'inertia' feature), Entropy, Measures the similarity (also called 'Energy' feature).

3 Heuristic Function Based Feature

The following heuristic function is used to calculate the texture feature. This has been devised by experimentation.

$$E_T = \sum p(x)\left[t^2 f(x) + taf(x) + b\right] \tag{4}$$

The parameter "t" is obtained by optimizing the expression for E_T.

$$\therefore t = \frac{-a\sum f(x)}{\sum p(x)f(x)} \quad (5)$$

Here p(x) is the defuzzified response of the current pixel and f(x) is the fractal dimension for the current window. The expression for p(x) and f(x) are derived as under.

$$p(x) = \sum_{j=1}^{n} \frac{\mu_j(i).x(j)}{\sum_{j=1}^{n} \mu_j(i)} \quad \ldots(6) \quad \text{with} \quad \mu_j(i) = \exp\left[-\left\{\frac{x(j)-x_{max}}{\tau}\right\}^2\right] \quad j=1, 2\ldots 8 \quad (7)$$

Where x_{max} is the max gray level in current window with respect to which the gray levels of all neighboring pixels x (j) are compared and τ is the fuzzifier which is taken to be the initial size of the window.

Let us take (χ) as the initial window size for calculating the defuzzified response. Then fractal dimension is defined as

$$f_i(x) = \sum_{j=1}^{n} \ln_{s_j} \left\{\frac{y_i(s\chi)}{y_i(\chi)}\right\}. \quad (8)$$

4 Texture Feature Based on Masks for Image Enhancement

Laws' Texture Energy Measures (TEM) [3] determine textural properties by assessing average gray-level, edges, spots, ripples, and waves in texture. The measures are derived from three simple vectors: L3= (1,2,1) , E3 = (-1,0,1) , S3=(-1, 2 ,-1). After convolution of these vectors with themselves and each other, five vectors will result: L5 = 1,4,6,4,1), E5 = (-1,-2,0,2,1), S5 = (-1,0,2,0,-1), R5 = (1,-4,6,-4,1), W5=(-1,2,0,-2,-1) where L5 represents local averaging. S5 and E5 are spot and edge detectors; R5 can be used as "ripple" detector and W5 as "wave" detector.

The texture value of the pixel at coordinate (i,j) is defined as

$$f(i,j) = \sqrt{\left(\frac{f_{L5^T XE5}(i,j)}{f_{L5^T XE5_{Max}}}\right)^2 + \left(\frac{f_{L5^T XS5}(i,j)}{f_{L5^T XS5_{Max}}}\right)^2 + \left(\frac{f_{L5^T XR5}(i,j)}{f_{L5^T XR5_{Max}}}\right)^2 + \left(\frac{f_{L5^T XW5}(i,j)}{f_{L5^T XW5_{Max}}}\right)^2} \quad (9)$$

Where $f_{L5^T XE5}(i,j)$, $f_{L5^T XS5}(i,j)$, $f_{L5^T XR5}(i,j)$ and $f_{L5^T XW5}(i,j)$ are the convoluted results of the image with the four masks. These texture features can be directly used for segmentation.

5 Results of Comparison of Different Texture Features for Texture Segmentation

This section gives the simulation results for the Fuzzy Descriptors based texture segmentation. The descriptors used are Entropy, Energy, Inertia and Frequency. The segmentation is done using Fuzzy C-Means for both the Natural as well as mosaic images.

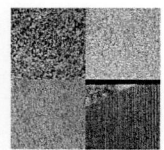 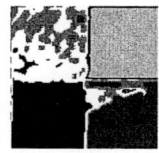 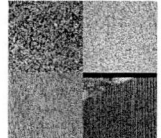 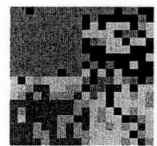

Original Mosaic-1   Segmented Mosaic-1   Original Mosaic-1   Segmented Mosaic-1

Fig. 1. Results for Mosaic Image-1 for segmentation using Descriptors

Fig. 2. Results for Mosaic Image-1 for segmentation using Heuristic Function

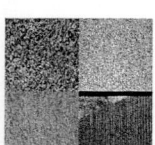   

Original Mosaic-1   Segmented Mosaic-1   Original Natural-1   Segmented Natural-1

Fig. 3. Results for Natural Image-1 for segmentation using Defuzzified Feature

Fig. 4. Results for Natural Image-1 for segmentation using Mask based Feature

6 Summary and Conclusions

In this paper, we have experimented on several features for texture segmentation keeping the clustering technique the same. The performance of descriptor-based approach is dependent on the surrounding texels. Heuristic based approach is found to be useful for random textures because of its property to capture randomness. The defuzzified feature based approach is amenable for regular patterns/textures. The mask- based approach is immensely appropriate for natural textures.

References

1. Chaudhuri, B.B., Sarkar, N.: Texture Segmentation Using Fractal Dimension. IEEE Transactions on Pattern Analysis and Machine Intelligence, Vol 17,No.1, 1995
2. Hanmandlu, M., Madasu, V. K., Vasikalra, S.: A Fuzzy Approach to Texture Segmentation. Proceeding of ITCC'04: Coding and Computing, 2004.
3. Laws, K.I.: Texture Energy Measures. DARPA Image Understanding Workshop. Los Angeles, CA, pages 47-51, DARPA, Los Altos, CA, 1979.

Run Length Based Steganography for Binary Images

Sos. S. Agaian and Ravindranath C. Cherukuri

ASPIIRE Lab, University of Texas at San Antonio,
6900 North Loop 1604 west, San Antonio, Texas-78249
`sagaian@utsa.edu, mailcravi@yahoo.co.in`

Abstract. Binary images (like cartoons, text documents, signatures captured by signing pads and/or 2-color imagery) are very commonly used in our daily life. Changing the pixel values in these images for hiding the data, may produce a noticeable change in the cover media. The primary problem is the capacity of the embedding technique and preserving the visible artifacts of the cover image even after embedding the secured data. In this paper, we present a run length based steganography algorithm for embedding the secured data into binary images. The proposed algorithm alters pixels of the embeddable blocks of cover image depending on there run length characteristics and chactersitics values of the block. In addition, the new algorithm is based on variable embedding rate for each block, which enhances the security of embedded data and the capacity of the embedding method. We test the performance of the algorithm over 50 various sizes of binary cover images embedding various sizes of secured data. Comparisons with existing algorithms will be presented.

Keyword: Run length, steganography, binary image.

1 Introduction

Steganography is the science that deals with the hiding of the secured information in a harmless signal. Binary images are two color (Black & White) images with pixel values (either 1 or 0). Therefore, embedding the secured data can easily distort the cover image. Hence, the amount of data that can be securely embedded into the binary cover image is very low. Several embedding algorithms have been developed for binary images using one of the frame work presented below:

- By altering the pixel value i.e. flipping of black pixel to white or vice versa.
- By changing the characteristics of the block in consideration i.e. thickness of strokes, curvature, spacing or relative positions.

For example, K.H. Hwang et.al [1] proposed an embedding algorithm that's embeds in the edge portion of the cover image. The prime factor is that modifications made to edge portions of the cover are more difficult to be recognized. Run length mechanism was introduced to make sure that pixel alterations are carried out in the edge portions only. Min.Wu and Bee Liu [2] proposed an embedding algorithm for binary images. The secured data is embedded into shuffled blocks by manipulating the flip able pixels. The shuffling of the blocks before embedding ensures the equalization of embedding capacity from region to region. H.K. Pan et.al [3] introduced the use of weighted matrix rather than secret key matrix and also altered the logical operation. The distortion in quality of the cover image remains. J. Chen et.al [5] proposed a technique that improves the effectiveness of the pan's technique [3]. The cover is decomposed into several 4x4 blocks. Each block is again portioned into four 3x3 overlapping blocks. The characteristic value of each sub-block defined by the number of ones in each block is determined for each block. For quality control no embedding is performed in when a sub-block characteristic value is 9 or 0.

In this paper, we investigate the following issues

1. How to select pixels for alteration so as to embed information with as little visual changes as possible to the cover.
2. How to enforce a relation ship between the blocks and Pn-sequence so as to embed information securely into the cover.
3. How to maximize the capacity of the proposed technique by employing a variable embedding rate for each block.

The rest of the paper is organized as follows. In Section 2, we introduce the proposed scheme for embedding the secured data into a binary cover image. Section 3 introduces the simulation results for the proposed algorithm for various images. And section 4 provides the conclusion.

2 Proposed Algorithm

The proposed algorithm embeds the secured information in secured regions and also increases capacity of the image by employing variably block embedding rate. The figure 1 shows the characteristics values of various blocks. The general steps in embedding the secured information into a binary cover media are:

Input: Binary cover and secured data

Step 1: Transform the data into binary format.
Step 2: Decompose cover into various blocks and determine their characteristic value and compute the runs in each block.
Step 3: Embedded binary secured data into cover depending runs and an embedding key.
Step 4: Measures are considered to ensure that the characteristic of blocks are unaltered.
Step 5: Recombine the blocks to retrieve the cover image with secured data.

Output: Cover image with secured data and key

The secured data embedded using the proposed scheme could maximize the capacity and limit the changes to those areas that are visibly hard to differentiate between the original and embedded cover images. Embedded information could be retrieved by exact inverse of the above steps.

3 Computer Simulation

Computer simulation was performed over 50 binary images of various sizes. Figure 1 original cover and the cover image after embedding 158 bits of the secured information in 82 blocks. The difference of 61 bits between the cartoon cover images before and after embedding the secured data of 158 bits is also presented.

Fig. 1. The original cartoon cover of size 160 by 171, the cover image after embedding 158 bits and the difference of 61 bits between the cartoon cover images before and after embedding the secured data of 158 bits

Fig. 2. The Map cover image before, after and difference in cover images

Table 1. Simulation results for embedded information and distorted bits along the embedding and security coefficients

Image	Bits embedded	Distorted bits	EC	SC
Cartoon	158	61	0.00164	6.177
Sarkis	603	258	0.00268	5.872
Rock	759	297	0.00290	6.261
Map	134	44	0.00818	5.253

Table 2. Simulation results for various algorithms that embedded information in similar number of blocks

CV =3	New Method	Hwang et.al [1]	J.Chen [6]
Sarkis	1721	1204	918
Rock	2617	1908	1092
Map	267	178	159
Cartoon	450	534	233

Figure 2 the original cover and the cover image after embedding 134 bits of the secured information in 57 blocks. The difference of 44 bits between the cartoon cover images before and after embedding the secured data of 134 bits is also presented.

Table 1 introduces the simulation results for various images of varying sizes. The amount of data that is securely embedded is shown by number of bits embedded. The distance between the binary cover before and after embedding the data is presented by number of distorted bits. The embedding and security coefficient should be optimal for high robustness. We could enhance the security level of the embedded information by minimizing the security coefficient. Table 2 shows the comparison between various other existing algorithms in terms of maximum embedded information. We also introduce a visual comparison for determining if there is any loss in the visible artifacts of the cover image

4 Conclusion

We have presented a new block based steganography algorithm that utilizes run length characteristics for embedding the secured data into binary images. We employ a variable embedding rate for each block depending on its characteristic value for maximizing the capacity of new technique. In addition, the new algorithm enhances the security level of secured data embedded into a binary cover image by limiting the altered pixels to edges only. We also present a visualization comparison between the new and existing algorithms.

Acknowledgement

This research was partially funded by Center for Infrastructure Assurance and Security (CIAS).

References

1. K. F. Hwang and C. C. Chang, "A Run Length Mechanism for Hiding Data into Binary Images", In proceedings of pacific rim workshop on digital steganography 2002, pp.71-74.
2. Min Wu; Bede Liu; "Data hiding in binary image for authentication and annotation" in proceedings of IEEE Transactions on multimedia, Vol: 6, Aug 2004 Pg: 528 – 538.
3. H.K. Pan, Y.Y. Chen and Y.C. Tseng, "A Secure Data Hiding Scheme for Two-Color Images", in proceedings of 5th IEEE Symposium on computers and communication, 2000 pp.750-755.
4. Yu-Chee Tseng; Hsiang-Kuang Pan, "Secure and invisible data hiding in 2-color images", in proceedings of 20 th IEEE Computer and Communications Societies, INFOCOM 2001 Volume: 2, Pg: 887 - 896 April 2001.
5. J. Chen; T. S. Chen & M. W Cheng, "A New Data Hiding Method in Binary Image", in proceedings of 5th IEEE international symposium on multimedia software engineering 2003

An Edge-Based Moving Object Detection for Video Surveillance

M. Julius Hossain and Oksam Chae[*]

Department of Computer Engineering, Kyung Hee University,
1 Seochun-ri, Kiheung-eup, Yongin-si,
Kyunggi-do, Korea, 449-701
`mdjulius@yahoo.com, oschae@khu.ac.kr`

Abstract. We present a novel approach for extracting moving objects, suitable for intrusion detection and video surveillance systems. Proposed method is characterized by robustness to illumination changes, acclimation to the changes in constituents of background and significantly reduced false alarm rate. We extract pieces of edge information from images and represent these segments with efficiently designed edge classes. Proposed algorithm for matching and updating of edges incorporates the robustness and resilience to intrusion detection system, which is illustrated by the results of our experiments.

1 Introduction

Automated video surveillance is an important research area in the commercial sector, as many organizations today want to shore up the safety and security of their employees, visitors as well as the premises and assets. The most significant demand from such systems is to isolate the events of potential interest from a large volume of redundant data. However, image data are often contaminated from various unimportant and nuisance noise which contribute unacceptably high false alarm rates. Due to the change of illumination, part of the background may be detected as moving object. The efficiency of surveillance technique lies in the successful detection of the regions with significant changes, ignoring the effect of noise and illumination [1].

We use edge information, which is more robust against illumination changes. Edges are extracted from input image as a unit of segment and a flexible method is proposed for the conformity between two edge segments. Representation of edge segment reduces the affect of noises as noises are found sparse and in a small group of points [2], which is simply ignored in edge extraction step. Reference edges are updated to adapt with the change in background scene as well as to the slow change of illumination. Proposed conformity method between corresponding edge segments of input image and reference image permits the fluctuation of camera focus or calibration error in a certain scale, which helps to reduce the false alarm rate.

---

[*] Corresponding Author.

2 Related Works

A lot of research effort is devoted detecting moving object with various processing steps and core algorithms. Early detection methods were based on difference image, obtained by subtracting the reference image from current input image where the resultant image is thresholded to obtain new objects. Many researchers surveyed and reported experiments on many different criteria to choose threshold value and achieve application specific requirements for false alarms and misses [3,4]. However, determination of an optimal threshold automatically is very difficult, where the applications are sensitive to noise and frequently affected with variations in illumination [1]. Some researchers detect the occurrence of significant change at a given pixel by choosing one of the competing hypotheses describing the intensity change on that pixel [5]. In some statistical approaches [6], the distribution of changes in brightness of reference image and input image are analyzed to discriminate the changes due to illumination variations from those due to new scene contents. It solves part of the problems contributed from illumination change but cannot obtain the complete structure of moving objects. Moving edge extraction method [7] utilizes only edge pixels to reduce the effect of noise and illumination. The performance of a change detection algorithm can be evaluated visually and quantitatively based on application needs. Quantitative evaluation is more challenging, primarily due to the difficulty of establishing a valid "ground truth" [8].

3 Description of the Proposed Method

We extract pieces of edge information from images by applying Canny edge extraction algorithm [9] and represent them as efficiently designed edge classes [10] where each segment can be accessed independently. Initially the extracted edge segments form the reference edge list. Input edges are extracted from current image, each segment is searched in the reference edge list and symmetric edges are eliminated. Moving objects are detected from the remaining edge segments, called moving edges. Finally, reference edge list and temporary edge list are updated by changing their weight values associated with them according to their availability in the same position in current fame. Accumulation of moving edges forms temporary reference edge list, which reflects the stability of respective edge. Figure 1 depicts the overall structure of the proposed method.

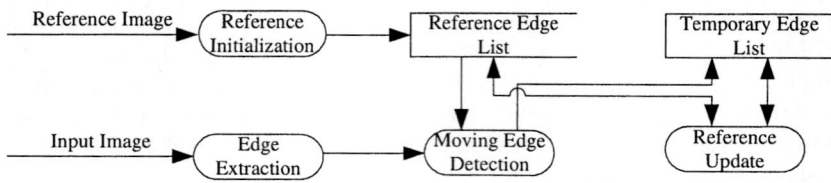

Fig. 1. Block diagram of the proposed method

4   Detection of Moving Object

Proposed method for detection of moving object is depicted in Figure 2. Edges, extracted from current image are not complete due to noise, breaks from non-uniform illumination and other effects that introduce spurious intensity discontinuities. To assemble edge pixels into meaningful edge segment, the characteristic of pixels of currently labeled edges in a small neighborhood is analyzed. All points that are similar according to a set of predefined criteria are linked to obtain edge segments. Each of the extracted input edge segments is searched in reference edge list. If there exist a similar edge segment in the reference list, corresponding edge is removed from current input edges. In this case, weight of the respective reference edge is increased, if the value is less than the predetermined threshold.

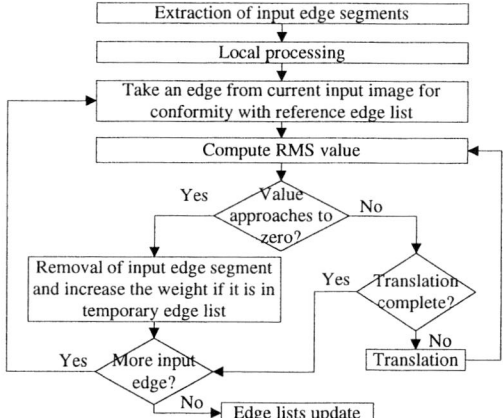

Fig. 2. Detection of moving object

For the conformity, between two edges, we assign a pixel with the value 1 if the pixel belongs to an edge otherwise assign it with 0. We take the root mean square (rms) value of two edges taken for the matching measure:

$$M = \sqrt{\frac{1}{n}\sum_{i=1}^{n} d_i^2}$$ (1)

where d_i is the difference of two corresponding pixel values and n is the number of points in the input edge. If the rms value approaches to zero, we consider them as instances of similar edge. Otherwise we translate the input edge and compute the rms value. In case of translation, we choose pixel following the non-decreasing order of city block distance. If these two edges do not match with in predetermined translation area, candidate edges are not considered similar. Translation of input edge in matching process tolerates minor change in camera focus and calibration error; and thus reduces the risk of false alarm.

To adapt the detection process with the change in environment, weight value of each edge segment of both edge lists is updated in every frame. If a moving edge is found in next frame at same position, the weight of that segment is incremented else it is decremented. If weight of any edge segment of the temporary edge list reaches specified threshold value, it is moved to the reference edge list from the temporary edge list. An edge segment is eliminated from the temporary edge list if the weight of the segment is zero. In similar fashion, if a reference edge is not found in current frame, the weight of the edge is decreased. The edge is removed from the reference list, if the weight is zero. Figure 5 reflects update in reference edge list and temporary edge list based on the associated weight value. Weight value of a temporary edge varies from 1 to 16 where the range is from 1 to 32 in case of a reference edge.

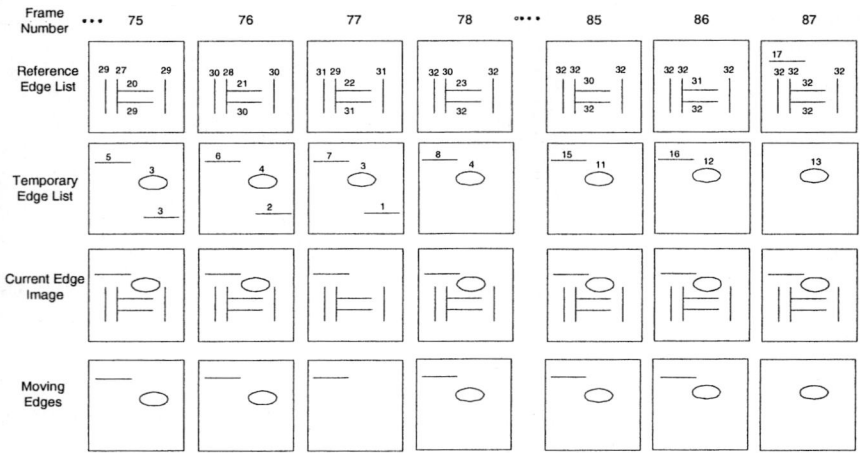

Fig. 3. Update of edge lists

5 Results

Proposed method is applied on a sequence of images of size 740 x 560 and intensity range 0-255. We used a system, which included processor of Pentium IV, RAM of 512MB. Visual C++ 6.0 and MTES [11], an image processing environment were used as environment tools. Above system processes 5 frames per second with the application of proposed algorithm and above mentioned environment tools.

Proposed method is adaptive to the change in illumination. Figure 4 shows an instant of reference images. A man is found in figure 5, where the illumination is relatively higher than that of reference image. The difference image is shown in figure 6. Figure 7 shows the edge image obtained by applying Cramer-von Mises approach [12], where they compare the cumulative distribution of the intensities in the two image windows. The result reflects that global thresholding method is not suitable for intrusion detection in dynamic environment. The removal of reference edges by the proposed method results the edge segments of the moving object and detects the intended man, shown in figure 8. Figure 9 to figure 14 reflect moving object detection by proposed method in dynamic background. Figure 9 shows edge image of current reference edge list at frame 84. Figure 10 is the current image at frame 120 and it

Fig. 4. Background image   **Fig. 5.** Current input image in different illumination   **Fig. 6.** Difference edge image

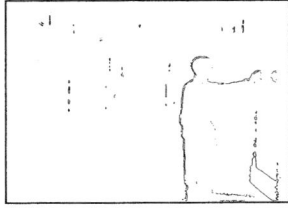 

Fig. 7. Detected moving object by Cramer-Von Mises method   **Fig. 8.** Detected moving object by proposed method

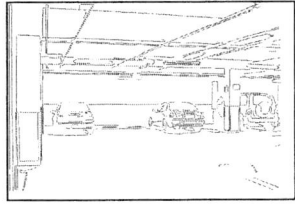  

Fig. 9. Edge image of reference edge list (frame 84)   **Fig. 10.** Input image at frame 120   **Fig. 11.** Edge image of updated reference edge list (frame 136)

Fig. 12. Input image at frame 147   **Fig. 13.** Edge image of frame 147   **Fig. 14.** Detected moving object with updated reference list

remains unchanged in next 16 frames. So the reference edge list is updated at frame 136 and shown in figure 11. In frame 147, a man is found in the scene, which is shown in figure 12, and corresponding edge image is available in figure 13. The man is detected by conformity and removal of updated reference edge list of figure 11. The resultant moving object is shown in figure 14.

6 Conclusions and Future Works

This paper presents edge extraction based moving object detection using fixed camera, suitable for intrusion detection as well as video surveillance. Proposed method for edge matching and reference update reduces the risk of false alarm due to noise and the change of illumination and contents of background. The proposed method has been tested on numerous real scenes and compared with some existing approaches to justify its effectiveness. However, still there are some scopes to improve the edge-matching algorithm. As a future work, our project pursues to detect moving object from panoramic view of background and to track the moving object.

References

1. Radke, R.J., Andra, S., Kofahi, O.A., Roysam, B.: Image Change Detection Algorithms: A Systematic Survey. IEEE Transactions On Image Processing, Vol. 14, No. 3 (2005) 294-307
2. Makarov, A., Vesin, J.M., Kunt, M.: Intrusion Detection using Extraction of Moving edges. International Conference on Computer Vision & Image Processing, Vol. 1 (1994) 804-807
3. Rosin, P.L.: Thresholding for Change Detection. Computer Vision and Image Understanding, Vol. 86 No. 2 (2002) 79-95
4. Smits, P., Annoni, A.: Toward specification-driven change detection. IEEE Transaction on Geoscience and Remote Sensing, Vol. 38, No. 3, (200) 1484–1488
5. Cavallaro, A., Ebrahimi, T.: Video Object Extraction based on Adaptive Background and Statistical Change Detection. SPIE conference on Visual Communications and Image Processing (2001) 465-475
6. Young, S., Forshaw, M., Hodgetts, M.: Image Comparison Methods for Perimeter Surveillance. International Conference on Image Processing and Its Applications Vol. 2 (1999) 799 - 802
7. Hossain, M.J., Lee, J.W., Chae, O.S.: An Adaptive Video Surveillance Approach for Dynamic Environment. IEEE International Symposium on Intelligent Signal Processing and Communication System (2004) 84-89
8. Rosin, P. Ioannidis, E.: Evaluation of global image thresholding for change detection. Pattern Recognition Letter. Vol. 24 No. 14 (2003) 2345–2356
9. Canny, J.: A Computational Approach to Edge Detection. IEEE Transactions on PAMI, 8-6, (1986) 679-698
10. Ahn, K.O., Hwang, H.J., Chae, O. S.: Design and Implementation of Edge Class for Image Analysis Algorithm Development based on Standard Edge. KISS Autumn Conference (2003) 589-591
11. Chae, O.S., Lee, J.H., Ha, Y.H.: Integrated Image Processing Environment for Teaching and Research. Proceedings of IWIEE (2002) 23-27
12. Sprent, P.: Applied Nonparametric Statistical Methods. Chapman and Hall, London (1993)

An Information Hiding Framework for Lightweight Mobile Devices with Digital Camera

Subhamoy Maitra[1], Tanmoy Kanti Das[2], and Jianying Zhou[2]

[1] Applied Statistics Unit, Indian Statistical Institute,
203, B T Road, Calcutta 700 108, India
subho@isical.ac.in
[2] Infocomm Security Department, Institute for Infocomm Research,
21 Heng Mui Keng Terrace, Singapore 119613
{tkdas, jyzhou}@i2r.a-star.edu.sg

Abstract. In this paper we present a paradigm for robust information hiding strategy designed with proper cryptographic and error correcting frameworks in mind that works for low end hardware devices like mobile phones with camera.

Keywords: Steganography, Digital Watermarking, Information Security, JPEG Compression, Mobile Devices.

1 Introduction

Information hiding has recently gained a lot of attention. The two main directions of information hiding are Steganography and Digital Watermarking. Though in terms of application these are completely different, the basic technical idea is same: to hide secret information in an innocent looking cover media, and the most frequently used cover media is image (in some cases audio also). In this paper we will consider image as the cover media.

In Steganography, secret message (binary string) is inserted in an image in a manner such that the visual quality of the image does not change at all. From the attacker side, the problem is given an image and the message embedding algorithm whether one can understand if there is any secret message contained in the cover media. Recovering the secret message is clearly a stronger attack, but this is elusive as the designer will not embed the plain message text in the cover, the encrypted version of the plain text will be used to communicate the secret. The state of the art encryption mechanisms are extremely robust and it is believed to be impossible to decrypt the encrypted message without knowing the secret key. Thus design of a robust steganographic scheme should satisfy that attacker will not be able to decide whether a media contains some secret information.

Digital watermarking is used for copyright protection. Given an image, the owner inserts a secret signature in it without making any visual change (we are only considering invisible watermarks). This is called the watermarked copy of the original image. If the watermarked copy is available from any resource, then the owner should be able to extract the secret signature to prove the copyright. Further, the owner may put buyer specific signatures in different watermarked copies of the same image. In that case the owner can prove the copyright as well as one can also pin down the buyer also, which is called fingerprinting. The attack model considers that the algorithms for watermark embedding and extraction are known and the attacker likes to destroy the watermark signal from the image. The robustness of the watermarking strategy is primarily evaluated on the following two criteria: (i) how well the malicious buyer is identified (who has intentionally attacked the watermarked image) and (ii) how infrequently an honest buyer is wrongly implicated. We like to refer [1,2,3,5] and references in these materials for more details on steganography and digital watermarking and their cryptanalysis.

In the last few years there is an enormous growth in mobile communication and mobile equipments. Mobile phones of different brands are available in the market which carry digital camera of considerably good quality. There are now standards proposed by Third-Generation Partnership Project (3GPP) and Internet Engineering Task Force (IETF) for voice calls enriched with live or pre-recorded video clips (see http://www.nokia.com). Given this growth there is a natural need to hide information in the images generated or stored in mobile devices, from both the angles of steganography and digital watermarking. Naturally JPEG CODEC is available in most of the processors, as example S1D13710/712 (see EPSON ED Journal, Vol 30, 2002). Thus we need a robust embedding scheme that uses JPEG image as the cover media. That is why we resort to the recent embedding scheme presented in [2].

Now we present the information hiding framework. In this case we will first take a message string M and encrypt it using a key K to get the cipher string C. Then C is encoded to generate an expanded string C_E. This is done for better error correction. Then the expanded string C_E is embedded to a cover image I using an image key K_I to generate a visually indistinguishable image I'. I' is then communicated through an open channel. At the receiver side I'' (a modified version of I' due to transmission error, signal processing, intentional attack etc.) is received and an extraction method is used (with the image key K_I) to get the encoded string C'_E (may not be same as C_E). Then we use the decoding strategy to get C' (may not be same as C) and then decryption is done using the key K to get the message M' (may not be same as M).

Towards the design, we consider that an adversary will know the complete algorithm with all the parameters except the keys K, K_I. For steganographic purposes we need: (i) nobody can identify whether a message is embedded in I', (ii) the recovered message M' should be as close as possible to M. For watermarking purposes a good correlation between M', M is sufficient for the owner to prove the copyright and identify the malacious buyer.

One may refer to [5] for a similar outline of a steganographic scheme in general. However, our attempt is more concrete in terms of design and implementation. We like to highlight the following issues that are addressed in this paper. We also like to mention that there are number of steganographic schemes that use LSB insertion, masking and filtering etc. However, since the schemes are basically based on image processing techniques only, they are not as robust as the scheme we propose here.

- There is an enormous development in mobile equipments where images can be captured and communicated. The hardware and software facilities are constrained in this environment. We like to explain a scheme which can be implemented in lightweight devices with sufficient amount of security for the purpose of information hiding.
- Note that even if a cryptosystem is designed very carefully, the security of the system is a conjecture. That is one needs to specify the scheme and then it is open to the community for cryptanalysis. Here we present a specific scheme with all the parameters so that the community may pay attention to the conjectured security of the system.
- We use the RC4 stream cipher (see [6] and references in this paper) for encryption/decryption, 1st order Reed-Muller code [4] for encoding/decoding and the modified DEW system [2] to embed/extract secret information in the cover image. Even if our scheme gets cryptanalysed over time, one can choose different options in terms of available schemes to build a more robust system depending on exact hardware facility. For our specific choice we also keep in mind that the complete scheme has to be implemented on low end hardwares, e.g., mobile phones etc.

2 Design and Implementation

In this section we outline the design and implementation strategy of our scheme. The framework is exactly described using RC4, Reed-Muller code and the modified DEW scheme.

2.1 RC4

The RC4 stream cipher has been designed by Ron Rivest for RSA Data Security in 1987, and was a propriety algorithm until 1994. It uses an S-Box $S = S_0, \ldots, S_{255}$ of length 256, with each location of 8 bits. It is initialized as $S_i = i$ for $0 \leq i \leq 255$. Another array $KEY = KEY_0, \ldots, KEY_{255}$ is used, where each location is of 8 bits. The minimum key size is 40 bits, i.e., in this case $KEY_0, \ldots, KEY_4$ will be filled by the key and then that is repeated number of times to fill up the entire array KEY. Initially an index j is set to 0 and for $(i = 0; i < 256; i++)\{ j = (j + S_i + KEY_i) \mod 256$; Swap S_i and S_j; $\}$

The following code is used to generate a random byte: $i = (i+1) \mod 256$;
$j = (j + S_i) \mod 256$;
Swap S_i and S_j; $t = (S_i + S_j) \mod 256$; $keyByte = S_t$;

The $keyByte$ is XORed with the message byte to generate the cipher byte at the sender end and again the $keyByte$ is XORed with the cipher byte to generate the message byte at the receiver end. The RC4 stream cipher has experienced a lot of cryptanalysis till date and it is well accepted to be used as a stream cipher for low end devices. An exact implementation of RC4 for low end sensor devices has been presented in [6] that takes only 8 machine instructions on ATMega 163L microcontroller to generate one byte of key stream after every 13 cycles. Thus it is clear that RC4 encryption methodology can be very well implemented in a mobile device since it works well for a very low end device as ATMega 163L.

2.2 Reed-Muller Code

The first order RM code [4] takes $(n+1)$-bit string and encodes it to 2^n-bit codeword. The minimum distance between any two codewords is at least 2^{n-1}, i.e., up to 2^{n-2} many errors can be corrected. The $(n+1)$-bit string $a_0, \ldots, a_n$ can be seen as an affine Boolean function $a_0 \oplus a_1 x_1 \oplus \ldots \oplus a_n x_n$ on n-variables. The codeword corresponding to this is the 2^n length truth table corresponding to the function. During decoding one calculates the Walsh spectra given the truth table of the Boolean function which is a collection of 2^n integer values and finds out the maximum absolute value in that collection which in turn gives the affine function $a_0 \oplus a_1 x_1 \oplus \ldots \oplus a_n x_n$.

For our purpose we take $n = 4$, i.e., we encode a 5-bit string to a 16-bit codeword. This requires 16 many logical operations and 16 more memory look-up's to encode a 5-bit string to a 16-bit codeword. During decoding we need 64 many ($n 2^n$) addition/subtraction operations and then finding the maximum out of 16 values. Given the low complexity of the encoding and decoding algorithm, it is clear that this strategy can be easily accommodated in a mobile device.

2.3 Modified DEW Scheme

Modified DEW scheme [2] embeds the message in a JPEG compressed image. It directly works with the DCT coefficients of the JPEG image. A JPEG image can be considered as a set of 8×8 DCT blocks, each block containing 64 DCT coefficients. This set is divided into different groups (known as lc-regions) and each group is further sub-divided into two sub-groups A and B. An lc-region contains t many blocks and each sub-group contains $\frac{t}{2}$ many blocks. Energy of a block is defined as the sum of q many low frequency DCT coefficient values. Energy of a group or a sub-group is the sum of the energies of the constituent blocks. Energies of sub-groups A, B are denoted as E_A, E_B. An energy difference is created among two sub-groups of a group to embed a message bit. The exact algorithm is as follows. Here the bit string to be embedded is denoted by $C_E = c_0, c_1, \ldots, c_{l-1}$ and the j-th DCT coefficient of the b-th block is represented by $\theta_{j,b}$.

Algorithm 1

1. *Randomly arrange the 8×8 DCT blocks of the JPEG image using some pseudo random generator and group them. Each group should be divided in two sub-groups such that sub-group A, i.e., E_A is almost equal to the energy of sub-group B, i.e., E_B. Store this group information which we call the image key K_I.*

2. FOR $k = 0$ to $l - 1$ DO
   (a) Select the k-th group consisting of z blocks.
   (b) Choose $\alpha_1 \in [0, 2\alpha]$ and set $\alpha_2 = 2\alpha - \alpha_1$.
   (c) IF $(c_k = 0)$ THEN
       i. $\theta_{j,b} = \theta_{j,b} * (1 + \alpha_1)$ for $b = 1, \ldots, \frac{t}{2} - 1$, and $j = 1, \ldots, q$.
       ii. $\theta_{j,b} = \theta_{j,b} * (1 - \alpha_2)$ for $b = \frac{t}{2}, \ldots, t - 1$, and $j = 1, \ldots, q$.
   (d) ELSE
       i. $\theta_{j,b} = \theta_{j,b} * (1 - \alpha_1)$ for $b = 1, \ldots, \frac{t}{2} - 1$, and $j = 1, \ldots, q$.
       ii. $\theta_{j,b} = \theta_{j,b} * (1 + \alpha_2)$ for $b = \frac{t}{2}, \ldots, t - 1$, and $j = 1, \ldots, q$.
3. Arrange back the DCT blocks to their original positions and write the image.

Message extraction algorithm is blind, i.e., the extraction process does not require the original host image. In Algorithm 1 all 8×8 blocks are shuffled according to a pseudo random generator. From these shuffled blocks, the groups are chosen. The image key K_I contains all the information about this region/subregion arrangement. Once the image key K_I is available, one can reorganize the blocks of the stego image in the manner that was used at the time of message embedding. Now one can calculate E_A, E_B for each lc-region and if $E_A > E_B$ then the recovered bit is 0 else it is 1.

The modified DEW scheme works on JPEG images and JPEG CODEC is available in most of the processors that are used for mobile phones with camera. The LCD controllers with built in image processing circuits contain good amount of memory and processing power, e.g., S1D13710/712 (see EPSON ED Journal, Vol 30, 2002) has embedded memory of 224/320 KBytes, and the CPU is of 16-bit with 32.768 kHz clock. Thus it looks feasible to implement modified DEW on a mobile device efficiently.

2.4 Experimental Results

The exact implementation of our complete scheme on low end devices is at its early stage. Sun Microsystems Java2 micro edition (J2ME) with Mobile Information Device Profile (MIDP) is one of the most used platforms for developing hardware and OS independent applications on mobile devices (see http://developers.sun.com/techtopics/mobility/midp/). The Symbian Application Development environment (see http://www.symbian.com) is also a popular platform. We are currently studying the feasibility of the implementation on such platforms.

The experimental result presented below is based on a standard C code implementation of the complete scheme on LINUX operating system in a PC. This has been done to study the the complete implementation and available from the first author on email request for public evaluation. In our experiment a message of length 10 characters (here the message is "attackOn8P") is embedded in the Lena image of size 512 × 512. The message is of $10 \cdot 8 = 80$ bits and encrypted using RC4 algorithm with a 40-bit key. The encrypted message is encoded using RM error-correcting code and generates $\frac{80}{5} \cdot 16 = 256$ bits. These 256 bits are embedded in the Lena image. Since the image is of size 512 × 512, we have total

$\frac{512 \times 512}{8 \times 8} = 4096$ many DCT blocks. The binary string to be embedded is 256 bits, so there are $\frac{4096}{256} = 16$ many DCT blocks in each lc-region, i.e., each sub-group contains 8 many DCT blocks. The experimental parameters for Algorithm 1 are as follows: $\alpha = .05$, $\alpha_1 = 0$, $\alpha_2 = 2\alpha = 0.1$, $q = 5$, $t = 16$, $l = 256$.

The image containing the secret information is of very high visual quality and the PSNR of the stego image is 41.6 dB with respect to the original image. The method can withstand image processing attacks, compression and filtering operations. As example, if the stego (or watermarked) image is re-compressed using a very low 10% JPEG quality, then also we can recover the message correctly. The comparison of our scheme with other schemes will be available in the full version of this paper.

3 Conclusion

Here we have presented a basic framework for information hiding on mobile devices with camera. For the basic assumption of steganography, the sender and receiver will share the secret private keys K, K_I at an earlier instance than when the exact transmission of the image takes place, i.e., there is no communication other than the image itself that contains the secret information. Thus, the cover image I and the corresponding image key K_I need to be fixed at an earlier instance while deciding the key K. This presents a restriction on online choice of the cover image. On the other hand, for the purpose of watermarking this is not at all a problem as the owner will store all the key information with him/her to prove the copyright and only the watermarked image will be communicated. Thus for watermarking application, choice of image could be online without any restriction.

References

1. R. J. Anderson and F. A. P. Petitcolas. On The Limits of Steganography. *IEEE Journal of Selected Areas in Communications. Special Issue on Copyright and Privacy Protection*, 16(4):474-481, May 1998.
2. T. K. Das, S. Maitra and J. Mitra. Cryptanalysis of Optimal Differential Energy Watermarking (DEW) and a Modified Robust Scheme. *IEEE Transactions on Signal Processing*, 53(2):768–775, February 2005.
3. S. Katzenbeisser, F. A. P. Petitcolas (edited). *Information Hiding Techniques for Steganography and Digital Watermarking*. Artech House, USA, 2000.
4. F. J. MacWillams and N. J. A. Sloane. *The Theory of Error Correcting Codes*. North Holland, 1977.
5. L. M. Marvel, C. G. Boncelet, Jr and C. T. Retter. Reliable Blind Information Hiding for Images. In *Information Hiding 1998*, LNCS 1525, Pages 48–61, 1998.
6. A. Seshadri, A. Perrig, L. v. Doorn, P. Khosla. SWATT: SoftWare-based ATTestation for Embedded Devices. *IEEE Symposium for Security and Privacy*, 2004.

Applications of the Discrete Hodge Helmholtz Decomposition to Image and Video Processing

Biswaroop Palit[1], Anup Basu[2], and Mrinal K. Mandal[1]

[1] Department of Electrical and Computer Engineering, University of Alberta,
Edmonton, AB, Canada T6G 2V4
{bpalit, mandal}@ece.ualberta.ca
[2] Department of Computing Science, University of Alberta,
Edmonton, AB, Canada, T6G 2E8
anup@cs.ualberta.ca

Abstract. The Discrete Hodge Helmholtz Decomposition (DHHD) is able to locate critical points in a vector field. We explore two novel applications of this technique to image processing problems, *viz.*, hurricane tracking and fingerprint analysis. The eye of the hurricane represents a rotational center, which is shown to be robustly detected using DHHD. This is followed by an automatic segmentation and tracking of the hurricane eye, which does not require manual initializations. DHHD is also used for identification of reference points in fingerprints. The new technique for reference point detection is relatively insensitive to noise in the orientation field. The DHHD based method is shown to detect reference points correctly for 96.25% of the images in the database used.

1 Introduction

In this paper we consider two applications where the DHHD can be used for efficient image analysis. We implement an algorithm to detect and locate the eye of a hurricane accurately. Most of the existing techniques, like [1], use feature matching for the analysis of satellite images. As mentioned in [2], feature matching is suitable for smaller sized images, but is not efficient for satellite images which span a large spatial area. In addition, several set of features have to be extracted at different positions for the satellite images, complicating feature matching further. Our technique does not involve feature matching. Our method is automatic and does not require human intervention for initialization. [3] developed a method to estimate accurately the nonrigid motion and the cloud structure in a hurricane. Our algorithm can locate the hurricane eye with only an approximate representation of the motion field, obtained using the simple Block Matching Algorithm (BMA).

Fingerprint matching is a widely used biometric technique for personal identification. Two fingerprint images need to be registered before matching them. Thus robust reference point detection is a crucial step in fingerprint matching and classification. As defined in [4], the point with the maximum curvature on a convex ridge is an apt choice for a reference point. Application of DHHD on the fingerprint orientation field can then be used to locate the reference point in the fingerprint. Our algorithm is robust to the noise in the orientation field.

The discrete Hodge-Helmholtz decomposition can be used to decompose a vector field into a sum of a curl free component, a divergence free component and a harmonic remainder. A field $\boldsymbol{\xi}$ is decomposed as:

$$\boldsymbol{\xi} = \boldsymbol{\xi}_{CF} + \boldsymbol{\xi}_{DF} + \boldsymbol{\xi}_{HR} \tag{1}$$

where $\boldsymbol{\xi}_{CF}$ is the curl free component, $\boldsymbol{\xi}_{DF}$ is the divergence free component and $\boldsymbol{\xi}_{HR}$ is the harmonic remainder. Associated with these different components, we have potential functions:

$$\boldsymbol{\xi}_{CF} = \nabla E; \; \boldsymbol{\xi}_{DF} = \nabla \times \boldsymbol{W} \tag{2}$$

Here E is a scalar potential and $\boldsymbol{W}$ a vector potential. The decomposed field, and its corresponding potential functions can be analyzed to predict singularities in the motion field. An implementation of the DHHD on regular triangular grids is developed in [5] and used for cardiac video analysis. We use a similar implementation for the DHHD.

Critical points like sources, sinks and rotational centers can be characterized on the basis of selected properties of the potential functions as follows:

- Point p is a source (velocity field diverges out of this point) if $E(p)$ is a minimum.
- Point p is a sink (field vectors converge to this point) if $E(p)$ is a maximum.
- A point p is an anticlockwise rotational center if $W(p)$ is a maximum.
- Point p is a clockwise rotational center if $W(p)$ is a minimum.

The subsequent discussion is organized as follows. Section 2 discusses the hurricane eye identification and tracking. Fingerprint analysis is described in Sect. 3. Some concluding remarks are outlined in Sect. 4.

2 Hurricane Tracking

Automatic analysis of satellite images is an extremely important application in meteorology. We propose to use DHHD for detecting the eye of a hurricane, and then track it using a level set algorithm. The first task is to be able to predict the approximate location of the eye of the hurricane. This is followed by segmentation of the eye structure using the level set method. The proposed hurricane eye detection technique has several steps:

- *Motion Detection:* Motion is estimated using the BMA. We also tried motion estimation using an optical flow algorithm and an affine motion model. However, block matching is the simplest of the aforementioned methods, and provides satisfactory results, so we just present the results obtained using this particular algorithm. The field extracted is shown in Fig. 1(a).
- *Motion Decomposition:* DHHD is applied on the extracted field. As we are trying to detect a rotational center in this particular application, only the divergence free component of the field is of importance to us. The divergence free potential obtained is shown in Fig. 1(b). Since the video sequence shows the hurricane rotating in an anticlockwise direction, we get a distinct maxima. We need to locate the extremum points on this potential surface.

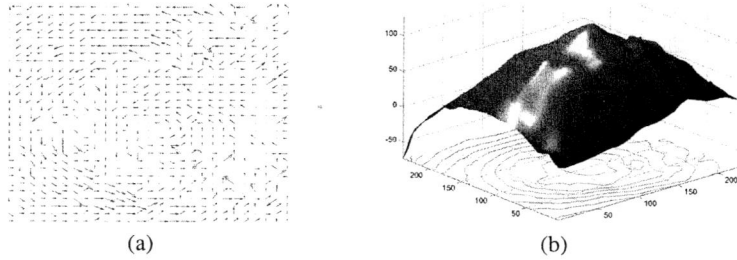

(a) (b)

Fig. 1. (a) Motion field in a anticlockwise rotating hurricane sequence extracted using the BMA. (b) The divergence free potential function with a distinct maximum and corresponding contours.

- *Locating the extremum point:* To detect points of extrema in the potential functions, we check the eight adjacent grid points of each grid node. If the point is a maxima or a minima in this neighbourhood it is chosen as an extrema point. This point is classified as a critical point of the vector field according to the conditions described in Section 1.
- *Segmentation of the eye:* We use the level set segmentation technique to segment out the eye from the hurricane image. The initial estimate for the location of the eye, obtained from the DHHD is used as the initial seed point. Details of the level set algorithm and its applications can be found in [6].

2.1 Implementation and Experiments

Image sequences of hurricane Luis (September 1995) and hurricane Isabel (September 2003), obtained from the NASA GOES satellites have been used for the experiments. Both sequences show the cloud mass rotating in an anticlockwise direction. The Hurricane Luis sequence has a smaller eye, compared to the Hurricane Isabel video sequence.

The motion field is estimated using the BMA with a block size of 8×8 and a search area of 16×16. This motion field is then fed into the DHHD subroutine and we extract the divergence free field and potential.

The initial estimate from DHHD turns out to be well within the eye of the hurricane. This extremum point indicated by the DHHD algorithm, and three other points in its neighborhood at a distance of 5 pixels each, are used as the initial points for the level set algorithm. The use of multiple initial seed points helps to speed up the level set algorithm. A narrow band fast marching implementation [6] of the level set method is used for reducing computational complexity. N_{iter} iterations of the fast marching step give satisfactory segmentation of the eye. N_{iter} depends on the size of the eye. For the video sequence Isabel, which has a bigger eye, $N_{iter} = 550$ gives good results; whereas for the Hurricane Luis sequence, 300 iterations of the fast marching method are sufficient.

The consecutive frames in the sequences do not have a significant burst of motion. Hence, the location of the eye can be assumed to be approximately the same in consecutive frames. The continuity is exploited in the initialization of points for the eye segmentation in the next frame. The center point of the segmented eye in frame N, and two neighbouring points at a distance of 5 pixels are chosen as the initial seed points of frame $N + 1$. Thus, we do not need to perform the DHHD step for every frame, which increases the computational speed.

Fig. 2. Sequence of images from the Hurricane Luis sequence, with eye segmented

The DHHD algorithm has been implemented in Matlab, while the level set tracking is a C program. For the 83 frames of the Isabel sequence, we call the BMA and DHHD once and the level set program 83 times. The total time taken by BMA and DHHD combined is about 39 seconds while the level set program requires 649 seconds for its 83 calls. All these experiments have been performed on a Pentium 4 3.2 GHz machine with 1 GB of RAM.

A series of segmented frames are shown in Fig. 2. As can be observed from these sequences, the performance of the tracking is accurate.

3 Fingerprint Analysis

Fingerprint recognition consists of reference point detection followed by feature extraction. Reference points are important for the registration of different fingerprint images [4]. We present a new algorithm for locating a reference point, which is defined as the point with maximum curvature in the ridge structure. The steps involved are described below.

- Preprocessing: The fingerprint image in consideration is preprocessed before analysis. An excellent source for fingerprint image enhancement is [7]. The fingerprint images are normalized. This process spreads the gray scale range of the given image over the entire spectrum of gray scales. Normalizing images makes it much easier to compare different images as all of them have the same range of gray scale. We use $\mu_0 = 100$ and $\sigma_0^2 = 100$ in the normalization algorithm from [7].
- Orientation field extraction: The orientation field is an estimate of the direction of the ridges and valleys in the fingerprint image. Since the valleys and ridges alternate periodically, the field direction can be estimated as the direction perpendicular to the intensity gradient. We follow the method described in [7] for extraction of the field.

  The extracted motion field has a discontinuity of π at certain locations. Such a discontinuity in the orientation field is observed in the circled part in Fig. 3(a). This will cause DHHD to fail as the direction of flow is reversed abruptly. To eliminate this discontinuity, the squared directional field is taken. The squared directional field is also used in [7] for eliminating the step of π in the orientation field, before detecting singular points. This is shown in Fig. 3(b).
- DHHD: DHHD is now applied onto the squared directional field. We are trying to identify the point with the maximum curvature and hence only the divergence free field and potential are considered. The potential function should have an extrema at the point of maximum curvature, hence identifying the point. A potential surface is shown in Fig. 3(c). To locate the extremum point, we use the same method as discussed in the case of the hurricane eye application. An extracted reference point is shown in Fig. 4(a).

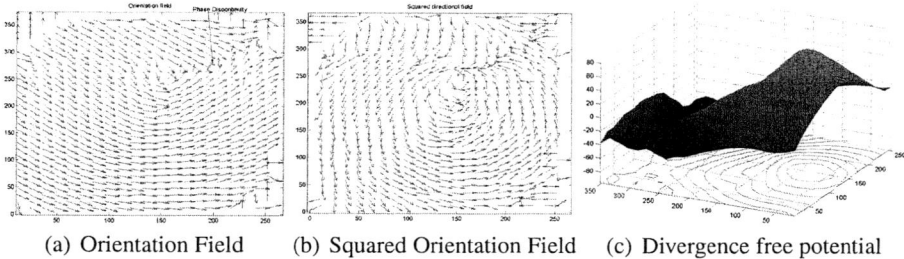

(a) Orientation Field (b) Squared Orientation Field (c) Divergence free potential

Fig. 3. (a) Fingerprint orientation field (b) Squared orientation field (c) Potential function obtained from squared orientation field

3.1 Experimental Results

The FVC2000 database is used to test our algorithm [7]. This has 4 datasets, each with 8 different images of the same finger. We use the images of 50 fingers from each data set to test our methods. Each image is 500 dpi. Reference points detected for different images of the same finger are shown in Fig. 4(a). Using the same criteria as in [4], the distance between the DHHD predicted reference point and the manually detected reference point is considered as a measure of the performance of our algorithm. If the detected point is within 10 pixels of the manually detected reference point, the localization is considered accurate. If it is 20 pixels away, we assume detection with tolerable error. If the distance between the detected reference point and the manually predicted reference point is greater than 20 pixels, the detection is erroneous. For a 500 dpi image, 20 pixels correspond to about 1 mm in physical distance.

(a) (b)

Fig. 4. (a) Reference point identified in two different images of the same finger (b) Images of the same finger with and without reference point, and the detected reference points

Table 1. Distance between reference point predicted by DHHD and point predicted manually

Distance (pixels)	Number of fingerprints	Percentage	Results from [4]
≤ 10	1355	84.69	81.07
> 10 and ≤ 20	185	11.56	13.72
> 20	60	3.75	5.21

There are some image sets where the reference point is not included in the fingerprint. Using the criteria described in [4], if the reference point is detected to be at the border as shown in Fig. 4(b), it is considered to be a correct detection. If it is elsewhere a faulty detection is reported. The results are shown in Table 1. We get a correct detection in 96.25% of the cases, which is better than the 94.79% correct detection reported in [4].

The algorithm has been implemented in Matlab. The entire algorithm (time includes preprocessing, field extraction and DHHD) takes 3.1 seconds on a 3.2 GHz Pentium 4 3.2 Ghz machine with 1GB of memory.

4 Conclusions

We applied the DHHD technique to two problems in image processing — hurricane tracking and fingerprint reference point identification. In the hurricane tracking application, motion between two consecutive frames was estimated using a block matching algorithm and then DHHD was used to identify the center of rotation (the hurricane eye). The estimate of the eye was then used to initialize a level set algorithm which tracked the eye over consecutive video frames. Thus, an automated system for hurricane eye tracking was developed. In the second application, DHHD is shown to be able to identify reference points in fingerprints. First the orientation field is extracted from the fingerprint image, after which DHHD is applied to the extracted field for critical point identification (the point with maximum curvature).

References

1. Mukherjee, D., Acton, S.: Cloud tracking by scale space classification. IEEE Transactions on Geoscience and Remote Sensing **40** (2002) 405–415
2. Bretschneider, T., Yikun, L.: On the problems of locally defined content vectors in image databases for large images. In: Proceedings of the International Conference on Information Communications and Signal Processing IEEE PCM. Volume 3. (2003) 1604–1608
3. Zhou, L., Kambhamettu, C., Goldgof, D., Palaniappan, K., Hasler, A.: Tracking nonrigid motion and structure from 2D satellite cloud images without correspondences. IEEE Transactions on Pattern Analysis and Machine Intelligence **23** (2001)
4. Jiang, X., Liu, M., Kot, A.: Reference point detection for fingerprint recognition. In: Proceedings of the 17th International Conference on Pattern Recognition, ICPR 2004. Volume 1. (2004) 540–543
5. Guo, Q., Mandal, M., Li, M.: Efficient hodge-helmholtz decomposition of motion fields. Pattern Recognition Letters **26** (2005) 493–501
6. Sethian, J.A.: Level Set Methods:Evolving Interfaces in Geometry,Fluid Mechanics, Computer Vision and Material Science. Cambridge University Press (1996)
7. Jain, A.K., Maltoni, D.: Handbook of Fingerprint Recognition. Springer-Verlag New York, Inc., Secaucus, NJ, USA (2003)

A Novel CAM for the Luminance Levels in the Same Chromaticity Viewing Conditions

Soo-Wook Jang, Eun-Su Kim, Sung-Hak Lee, and Kyu-Ik Sohng

School of Electronic Engineering and Computer Science,
Kyungpook National University,
1370, Sankyug-Dong, Buk-Gu, Daegu, 702-701, Korea
{jjang, saeloum, shark2, kisohng}@ee.knu.ac.kr

Abstract. In this paper, we propose the chromatic adaptation model (CAM) for the Variations of the Luminance Levels in the same Chromaticity Viewing Conditions. The proposed model is obtained by the transform the test colors of the high luminance into the corresponding colors of the low luminance. In the proposed model, the optimal coefficients are obtained from the corresponding colors data of the Breneman's experiments. In the experimental results, we confirmed that the chromaticity errors between the predicted colors by the proposed model and the corresponding colors of the Breneman's experiments are 0.004 in $u'v'$ chromaticity coordinates. The prediction performance of the proposed model is excellent because this error is the threshold value that two adjacent color patches can be distinguished.

1 Introduction

Color TV display systems have been designed and developed for the colorimetric and preferred color reproduction[1]. Preferred color reproduction is reproduction in which the colors depart from equality of appearance to those in the original in order to give a more pleasing result. This might be applicable in situations such as TV display in which consumers prefer to have pictures that reproduce colors closer to their memory colors for objects such as skin tones, foliage, sky, bodies of water, and so on. Colorimetric color reproduction in TV system is defined via metameric matches between the original and the reproduction such that they both have the same CIE xy chromaticity coordinates. In this case, the reproduced luminance levels are not equal with the original[2]. Real surround viewing conditions in watching TV and PC monitor are quite different from the photographing conditions in various luminance levels and chromaticities of illuminants. Human visual system (HVS) is adapted chromatically under the different viewing conditions in luminance levels and chromaticities of illuminants. Accordingly, the reproduced colors of the same chromaticity will appear as quite different color. Therefore, it is necessary that the displayed colors are reproduced to be appeared as the original colors in the photographing conditions.

Chromatic adaptation is one of the human visual characteristic that physically different colors look like equal according to the surround viewing conditions[2]-[7]. In this case, C2 under any other surround viewing conditions is called a corresponding color which C1 looks exactly the same color under a certain viewing condition.

There are various models that can be used to reproduce corresponding colors considering the chromatic adaptation according to the change of surround illuminants' chromaticity under the same luminance conditions[2]-[11]. However, there is almost unknown about the chromatic adaptation for the variations of the luminance levels under the same illuminants. And only the human visual characteristic about the variations of the luminance levels had been studied[6]-[7], [12]. Also, the CAMs for such phenomenon have not been proposed yet. In this paper, we propose the chromatic adaptation model for the variations of the luminance levels under the same illuminants.

2 The Proposed CAM

Under the sunlight conditions which have high luminance, the correlated color temperature (CCT) of clear sky is one of the popular research field at present and is about 5500 ~ 6000 K [13]. As shown in Fig. 1, the luminance level of white under the sunlight is about 10000 cd/m² and the luminance level of the living room is about 10 cd/m2 in average[14]. Thus, real surround viewing conditions in watching TV and PC monitor are quite different from the photographing conditions in various luminance levels of illuminants. HVS is adapted chromatically under the different viewing conditions in luminance levels of illuminants. Accordingly, the reproduced colors of the same chromaticity will appear as quite different color.

In this paper, the CAM is proposed according to the change of luminance level under the same illuminants. In Fig. 1, the proposed model is obtained by the transform the test colors of the high luminance into the corresponding colors of the low luminance. The proposed CAM is expressed in Eqs.(1) through (5). The first step is a transformation from the CIE tristimulus values XYZ to the fundamental tristimulus LMS. The Hunt-Pointer-Estevez transformation with illuminant D_{65} normalization is used[2],[11].

$$\begin{bmatrix} L_1 \\ M_1 \\ S_1 \end{bmatrix}_{Y_1} = \mathbf{M} \begin{bmatrix} X_1 \\ Y_1 \\ Z_1 \end{bmatrix}_{Y_1}, \quad \begin{bmatrix} L_2 \\ M_2 \\ S_2 \end{bmatrix}_{Y_2} = \mathbf{M} \begin{bmatrix} X_2 \\ Y_2 \\ Z_2 \end{bmatrix}_{Y_2} \tag{1}$$

$$\mathbf{M} = \begin{bmatrix} 0.4002 & 0.7076 & -0.0808 \\ -0.2263 & 1.1653 & 0.0457 \\ 0.0000 & 0.0000 & 0.9182 \end{bmatrix} \tag{2}$$

The next step is to apply the proposed model as shown in Eqs. (3) ~ (5).

$$\begin{bmatrix} L_2 \\ M_2 \\ S_2 \end{bmatrix} = \mathbf{M}_{\Delta Y} \begin{bmatrix} L_1 \\ M_1 \\ S_1 \end{bmatrix} = [M_{ij}]_{3 \times 3} \cdot \begin{bmatrix} L_1 \\ M_1 \\ S_1 \end{bmatrix} \tag{3}$$

$$M_{ij} = a_{ij} + b_{ij}\left(\frac{Y_2}{Y_1}\right) + c_{ij}\left(\frac{Y_2}{Y_1}\right), \quad (Y_2 \geq Y_1) \tag{4}$$

$$\begin{bmatrix} X_2 \\ Y_2 \\ Z_2 \end{bmatrix} = \mathbf{M}^{-1}\mathbf{M}_{\triangle Y}\mathbf{M} \begin{bmatrix} X_1 \\ Y_1 \\ Z_1 \end{bmatrix} \tag{5}$$

In these equations, Y_1 and Y_2 are maximum white luminance under a certain surround viewing conditions, and Y_2 is higher than Y_1. And $\mathbf{M}_{\triangle Y}$ represents 3×3 transfer matrix for chromatic adaptation according to the variations of the luminance levels under the same illuminants and also each element of transfer matrix is modeled by maximum luminance ratio, Y_2/Y_1, in Eq. 4.

In the proposed model, the optimal coefficients of each element in transfer matrix are obtained from the corresponding colors data of the Breneman's experiments[7]. And these optimal coefficients and element functions are shown in Table 1. Because transfer matrix of the proposed model is the square matrix, the proposed model can be transformed easily from high luminance conditions to low luminance conditions using the inverse matrix. And once the surround viewing condition is determined, the proposed model has the coefficient of linear transformation and can be easily applied to the color display devices.

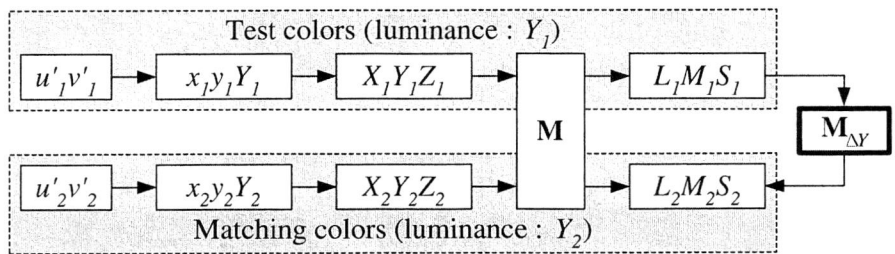

Fig. 1. Block diagram for the proposed model

Table 1. Element functions' coefficients of the transfer matrix $\mathbf{M}_{\triangle Y}$ of the proposed medel

M_{ij}	a_{ij}	b_{ij}	c_{ij}
M_{11}	0.2254	0.7691	0.0056
M_{12}	-0.1966	0.1993	-0.0026
M_{13}	-0.0186	0.0197	-0.0012
M_{21}	-0.1275	0.1306	-0.0031
M_{22}	0.1112	0.8873	0.0015
M_{23}	0.0104	-0.0112	0.0007
M_{31}	0.6355	-0.6743	0.0388
M_{32}	-0.8223	0.8645	-0.0422
M_{33}	0.2089	0.7989	-0.0077

3 Experiments and Results

The performance of the proposed model is evaluated in terms of color fidelity. The chromaticity errors, $\triangle u'v'$, and color reproduction errors, $\triangle E^*_{uv}$, are expressed in Eqs. (6) through (7). Table 2 shows the chromaticity errors and color reproduction errors between the predicted colors by the proposed model and the corresponding colors of the Breneman's experiments.

$$\triangle u'v' = \sqrt{(\triangle u')^2 + (\triangle v')^2} \tag{6}$$

$$\triangle E^*_{uv} = \sqrt{(\triangle L^*)^2 + (\triangle u^*)^2 + (\triangle v^*)^2} \tag{7}$$

In the experimental results, we confirmed that the chromaticity errors between the predicted colors by the proposed model and the corresponding colors of the Breneman's experiments are 0.004 in a $u'v'$ chromaticity coordinates. It is known that two adjacent color patches can usually be distinguished with a $\triangle u'v' \geq 0.004$, but for separated colors, a shift $\triangle u'v' \geq 0.04$ is often required to notice a color change in the $u'v'$ chromaticity coordinates system[1]. Therefore, the prediction performance of the proposed model is excellent because this errors are the threshold value that two adjacent color patches can be distinguished.

Table 2. The chromaticty errors and color reproduction errors of the proposed model

M_{ij}	Luminance of white					
	15 to 270 cd/m²		130 to 2120 cd/m²		850 to 11100 cd/m²	
Sample colors	$\triangle u'v'$	$\triangle E^*_{uv}$	$\triangle u'v'$	$\triangle E^*_{uv}$	$\triangle u'v'$	$\triangle E^*_{uv}$
Gray	0.002133	1.670525	0.001905	1.492598	0.005212	4.067244
Red	0.005458	2.804275	0.002450	1.221698	0.013313	6.889838
Skin	0.003970	3.067356	0.000886	0.694646	0.005590	4.372881
Orange	0.001528	1.193868	0.009350	7.312208	0.002032	1.548810
Brown	0.007249	3.777906	0.003234	1.673550	0.004054	2.088440
Yellow	0.003913	3.049058	0.006365	4.934431	0.005357	4.154822
Foliage	0.007803	4.074478	0.002105	1.080393	0.002801	1.446664
Green	0.006233	3.255593	0.003473	1.809795	0.004706	2.436179
Blue-green	0.001735	1.345712	0.003852	3.017073	0.000729	0.556415
Blue	0.004418	2.311566	0.006944	3.650813	0.012067	6.307394
Sky	0.001386	1.074741	0.001252	0.985754	0.004973	3.870815
Purple	0.004942	2.553928	0.003736	1.944588	0.002421	1.253062
Average	0.004231	2.514918	0.003736	2.484796	0.005271	3.249380

In subjective experiments, we use the predicted corresponding color images by the proposed model and the Breneman's corresponding color images according to the change of luminance level under the same D55 illuminants. These images are shown in Fig. 2. The predicted images by the proposed model were perceived the same as the corresponding color images of Breneman in all luminance conditions for the seven observers.

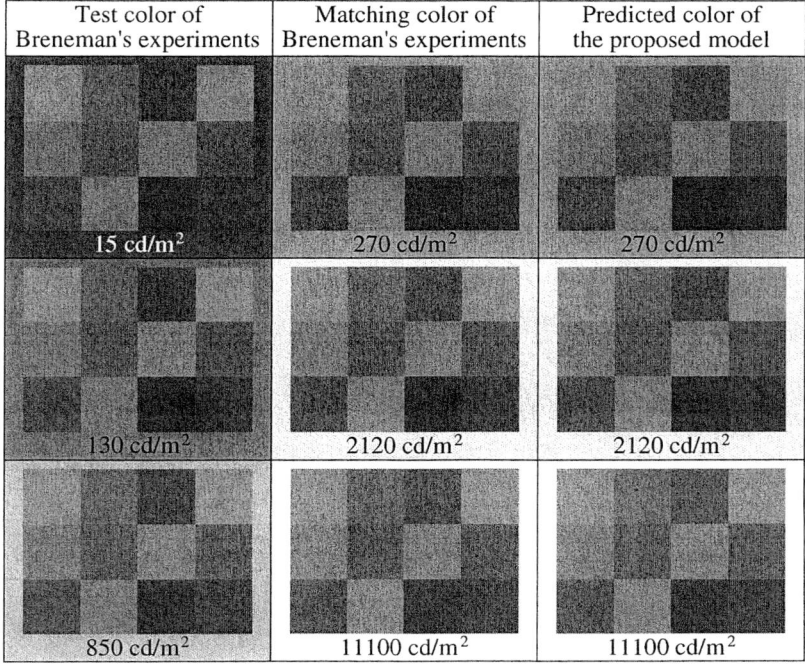

Fig. 2. Comparison between the predicted corresponding color images by the proposed model and the Breneman's corresponding color images according to the change of luminance level under the same D_{55} illuminants

4 Conclusions

In this paper, we propose the CAM for the different luminance levels under the same illuminant. The proposed model is obtained by the transform the test colors of the high luminance into the corresponding colors of the low luminance. In the proposed model, the optimal coefficients are obtained from the corresponding colors data of the Breneman's experiments. Because transfer matrix of the proposed model is the square matrix, the proposed model can be transformed easily from high luminance conditions to low luminance conditions using the inverse matrix. And once the surround viewing condition is determined, the proposed model has the coefficient of linear transformation and can be easily applied to the color display devices.

In the experimental results, we confirmed that the chromaticity errors between the predicted colors by the proposed model and the corresponding colors of the Breneman's experiments are 0.004 in $u'v'$ chromaticity coordinates. The prediction performance of the proposed model is excellent because these errors are the threshold value that two adjacent color patches can be distinguished. In subjective experiments, the predicted images by the proposed model were perceived the same as the corresponding color images of Breneman in all luminance conditions for the seven observers.

References

1. Hunt, R. W. G. : The Reproduction of Colour in Photography, Printing & Television, Fountain Press, England, (1987) 177-196.
2. Fairchild, M. D. : Color Appearance Models, Addison-Wesley, New York, (1998) 173-345.
3. Wyszecki, G. and Stiles, W. S.: Color Science: Concepts and Methods, Quantitative Data and Formulae, John Wiley & Sons, New York, (1982) 117-451.
4. MacAdam, D. L. : Color Measurement, Springer-Verlag Berlin Heidelberg, New York, (1981) 200-208.
5. Bartleson, C. J. : Comparison of chromatic-adaptation transforms, Color Res. Appl., Vol. 3, (1978) 129-136.
6. Bartleson, C. J. : Changes in color appearance with variations in chromatic adaptation, Color Res. Appl., Vol. 4, (1979) 119-138.
7. Breneman, E. J. : Corresponding chromaticities for different states of adaptation to complex visual fields, J. of Opt. Soc. Am., Vol. 4, (1987) 1115-1129.
8. Fairchild, M. D. : A model of incomplete chromatic adaptation, Proc. the 22nd Session of the CIE, Melbourne, (1991) 33-34.
9. Fairchild, M. D. : Formulation and testing of an incomplete-chromatic-adaptation model, Color Res. Appl., Vol. 16, (1991) 243-250.
10. CIE TC1-34 Final Report, The CIE 1997 Interim Colour Appearance Model (Simple Version), CIECAM97s, (1998).
11. Kim, E. S., Jang, S. W., Kwon, Y. D., Han, C. H. and Sohng, K. I.: Corresponding-color reproduction model according to surround viewing conditions, IEICE Trans. Fund., Vol. E87-A, No. 6, (2004) 1514-1519.
12. Hunt, R. W. G. : Light and dark adaptation and the perception of color, J. of Opt. Soc. Am., Vol. 42, (1952) 190-199.
13. Hernandez-Andres, J., Romero, J. and Nieves, J. L.: Color and spectral analysis of daylight in southern Europe, J. of Opt. Soc. Am., Vol. 18, (2001) 1325-1335.
14. Bartleson, C. J. : Predicting corresponding colors with changes in adaptation, Color Res. Appl., Vol. 4, (1979) 143-155.

Estimation of 2D Motion Trajectories from Video Object Planes and Its Application in Hand Gesture Recognition

M.K. Bhuyan, D. Ghosh, and P.K. Bora

Department of Electronics and Communication Engineering,
Indian Institute of Technology, Guwahati 781039, India
{manas_kb, ghosh, prabin}@iitg.ernet.in

Abstract. Hand gesture recognition from visual images finds applications in areas like human computer interaction, machine vision, virtual reality and so on. Vision-based hand gesture recognition involves visual analysis of hand shape, position and/or movement. In this paper, we present a model-based method for tracking hand motion in a complex scene, thereby estimating the hand motion trajectory. In our proposed technique, we first segment the frames into video object planes (VOPs) with the hand as the video object. This is followed by hand tracking using Hausdorff tracker. In the next step, the centroids of all VOPs are calculated using moments as well as motion information. Finally, the hand trajectory is estimated by joining the VOP centroids. In our experiment, the proposed trajectory estimation algorithm gives about 99% accuracy in finding the actual trajectory.

1 Introduction

The use of human hand as a natural interface for human-computer interaction (HCI) serves as the motivation for research in hand gesture recognition. While static hand gestures are modelled in terms of hand configuration, as defined by the flex angles of the fingers and palm orientation, dynamic hand gestures require hand trajectories and orientation in addition to these. So, appropriate interpretation of dynamic gestures on the basis of hand movement in addition to shape and position is necessary for recognition.

Another form of dynamic hand gesture that is in common use is in which the 2D gesture trajectory alone builds up a particular message. Examples of such gestures are shown in Fig. 1. Therefore, an essential step in dynamic hand gesture recognition is estimation of 2D gesture trajectory.

All approaches to hand/finger tracking require to locate hand regions in video sequences. Skin color offers an effective and efficient way to segment out hand regions. However, many of these techniques are plagued by some special difficulties such as large variation in skin tone, unknown lighting conditions and dynamic scenes. A solution to this is the 3D model-based approach, in which the hand configuration is estimated by taking advantage of 3D hand models [1].

However, they lack the simplicity and computational efficiency. Therefore, an alternative approach that is computationally simpler is the appearance-based model. Another important approach for hand tracking is the prediction algorithm combined with Kalman tracking and application of probabilistic reasoning for final inference [2]. But, this approach requires fine initial model and also requires additional computations to take care of rotation and changes in shape of the model. Moreover, it is very much sensitive to background noise. In this paper, we now propose a novel method for gesture trajectory estimation that is computationally much more simpler and also robust to background noise.

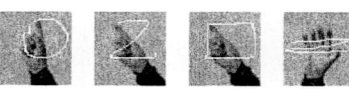

Fig. 1. Hand gestures for representing a circle, two, square and a wavy hand

In our proposed technique, we use the concept of object-based video abstraction for segmenting the frames into video object planes (VOPs), as used in MPEG-4, where hand is considered as a video object (VO) [3]. The VOPs are binarized to form binary alpha plane – the hand-pixels are assigned "**1**" and the background pixels are assigned "**0**". Thus, a binary model for the moving hand is derived and is used for tracking in subsequent frames. The Hausdorff tracker [4,5] is used for the purpose. The core of this algorithm is an object tracker that matches a two-dimensional (2D) binary model of the object against subsequent frames using the Hausdorff distance measure. The best match found indicates the translation the object has undergone, and the model is updated with every frame to accommodate for rotation and changes in shape. Next, we propose a centroid based method for estimating hand trajectory, where centroid of VOPs are calculated on the basis of moment as well as from respective motion vectors. The computed centroids are joined in the temporal sequence to get the final estimated trajectory.

2 Hausdorff Object Tracker for Hand Tracking

2.1 Hausdorff Distance

The Hausdorff distance measure can be used to measure the similarity between two shapes. It is defined as the maximum function between two sets of points:

$$H(O, I) = max\{h(O, I), h(I, O)\} \qquad (1)$$

where
$$h(O, I) = max_{o \in O} min_{i \in I} \| o - i \|$$
and
$$h(I, O) = max_{i \in I} min_{o \in O} \| i - o \|$$

$o_1, ..., o_m$ and $i_1, ..., i_n$ denote feature points in the sets O and I, respectively.

However, a computationally less expensive way to approximate the Hausdorff distance measure is the generalized Hausdorff distance in which the distances are sorted in ascending order and the kth value is chosen as

$$h_k(O, I) = k_{o \in O}^{th} min_{i \in I} \parallel o - i \parallel \qquad (2)$$

Similarly, $h_l(I, O)$ is defined as the lth value of the ordered distances. The maximum of these two gives the distance $H(O, I)$.

2.2 Hand Tracking and Model Update

The Hausdorff object tracker, which is based on the generalized Hausdorff distance, finds the position where the input hand model best matches the next edge image and returns the motion vector MV_i that represents the best translation from the $(i-1)^{th}$ frame to the ith frame.

As a tracked object moves in a video sequence, it might rotate or change its shape. To allow for this, the model must be updated in every frame. The model is updated by using the motion vector MV_i. First, the model image in frame $(i-1)$, say M_{i-1}, is dilated and shifted by MV_i. Then, the portion of edge image that overlaps this shifted model is selected as the new model image M_i in the ith frame.

2.3 Estimation of Motion Vector MV_i

In our hand tracking algorithm, we propose to use a simplified Hausdorff tracker with reduced computational load. Accordingly, we calculate generalized Hausdorff distance using distance transform algorithm [6]. Computation of distance transformation is accomplished using Chamfer $5-7-11$ mask. Further reduction in computation is achieved by searching the shifted hand model in subsequent VOPs only at some possible pixel locations around the model image. The algorithm for determination of motion vector MV_i for i^{th} VOP may accordingly be described as given below.

<u>*Algorithm 1 : Estimation of Motion vector*</u>

begin
  initialize translation vector t_x and t_y.
    Calculate distance transform of edge image.
      Calculate $h_k(O, I)$ for all translations (t_x, t_y).
      Calculate $h_l(I, O)$ for all translations (t_x, t_y).
      $H(O, I) = max\{h_k(O, I), h_l(I, O)\}$ for all translations (t_x, t_y).
      Find $min\{H_t(O, I)\}$ over all translations (t_x, t_y).
      Find translation vector $t^{'} = (t_x^{'}, t_y^{'})$ corresponding to $min\{H(O, I)\}$.
      $MV_i = (t_x^{'}, t_y^{'})$.
  return MV_i
end

3 Proposed Hand Trajectory Estimation Algorithm

3.1 Step 1: Determination of Centroid of Hand Image in a VOP

After determining the binary alpha plane corresponding to each VOP, moments are used to find the center of the hand. The 0th and the 1st moments are defined as:

$$M_{00} = \sum_x \sum_y I(x,y), \quad M_{10} = \sum_x \sum_y x I(x,y), \quad M_{01} = \sum_x \sum_y y I(x,y) \quad (3)$$

Subsequently, the centroid is calculated as

$$x_c = \frac{M_{10}}{M_{00}} \quad \text{and} \quad y_c = \frac{M_{01}}{M_{00}} \quad (4)$$

In the above equations, $I(x,y)$ is the pixel value at the position (x,y) of the image. Since the background pixels are assigned "0", the centroid of the hand in a frame is also the centroid of the total frame. Therefore, in moment calculation, we may either take the summation over all pixels in the frame or over only the hand pixels.

3.2 Step 2: Calculation of VOP Centroids

After determining the centroid of the first VOP in the gesture sequence, centroid of each subsequent VOP, say the ith VOP, is determined by shifting the centroid of the previous VOP by the motion vector MV_i corresponding to the current frame. However, since slight changes in the shape of the hand model in successive frames cause shifting of actual centroids than that computed from the motion vectors in the previous step, centroids are also computed using equations (3) and (4). Finally, the centroid c_i of the ith VOP is computed by taking the average of the two centroid values computed above.

3.3 Step 3: Trajectory Formation

In this step, the final trajectory is formed by joining all the calculated centroids in sequential manner. However, this trajectory may be noisy due to the following reasons.

- points too close.
- isolated points far away from correct trajectory due to change in hand shape.
- unclosed end points.
- hand trembling.
- unintentional movements.

Therefore, in order to take care of this, the final trajectory is smoothened out by considering the mean value of a specified point and its two neighboring points, *i.e.*,

$$(\hat{x}_t, \hat{y}_t) = ((x_{t-1} + x_t + x_{t+1})/3, (y_{t-1} + y_t + y_{t+1})/3) \quad (5)$$

So, dynamic hand gesture (DG) can be interpreted as a set of points in a spatio-temporal space as

$$DG = \{(\hat{x_1}, \hat{y_1}), (\hat{x_2}, \hat{y_2}), ..., (\hat{x_t}, \hat{y_t})\}. \qquad (6)$$

4 Key Frame Based Trajectory Estimation

The computational burden in estimating hand trajectory can be significantly reduced by selecting the key video frames in the gesture video sequence. The key VOPs are selected on the basis of Hausdorff distance measure, thereby transforming an entire video clip to a small number of representative frames that are sufficient to represent a particular gesture sequence [7,8]. These key frames form the set of gesture frames that best represents the content of the sequence in an abstracted manner. After getting the key frames, hand trajectories are obtained by following the same procedure as that of the previous one, but considering the key VOPs only.

5 Experimental Results

We have tested altogether eight different hand trajectories in view of special applications like robot control and gesture based window menu activation in the Human-Computer interactive (HCI) platform. They are gestures showing one, two, three, five, wavy hand, seven, square and circle as shown in Fig. 2. Figure 3 shows the extracted trajectories for four of these gestures, *viz.*, circle, square, one and two. First column shows the extracted trajectories, second column shows the smoothed trajectory and the third column shows the trajectories obtained from the key frames. Our proposed trajectory estimator gives about 99% of accuracy in finding the actual trajectory. The accuracy criteria is fixed in terms of shape similarity between the extracted gesture trajectory and the corresponding template/prototype trajectory.

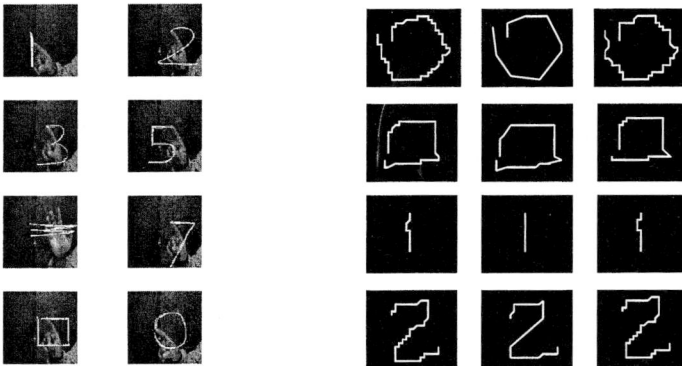

Fig. 2. Gestures showing 2D motion trajectory

Fig. 3. Estimated motion trajectories

6 Conclusions and Discussion

It is observed that the Hausdorff object tracker is capable of tracking hand motion in long gesture video sequences in an efficient manner. The VOP based method for segmentation requires no extra computation for rotation and scaling of the object, where the shape change is represented explicitly by a sequence of two dimensional models, one corresponding to each image frame. The major assumption is that the two dimensional shape of the hand changes slowly from one frame to the next. Moreover, trajectory estimated from the corresponding VOPs bears spatial information regarding hand positions in dynamic gestures, which is required in the gesture classification stage.

References

1. Pavlovic, V.I., Sharma, R., Huang, T.S.: Visual interpretation of hand gestures for human-computer interaction: A review, IEEE Trans. Pattern Analysis and Machine Intelligence, **19** (7) (1997) 677-695
2. Wu, Y., Huang, T.S.: Self-supervised learning for visual tracking and recognition of human hand, Proc. American Association for Artificial Intelligence (AAAI), (2000) 243-248
3. Bhuyan, M.K., Ghosh, D., Bora, P.K.: Automatic video object plane generation for recognition of hand gestures, Proc. International Conf. Systemics, Cybernetics and Informatics (ICSCI), (2005) 147-152
4. Huttenlocher, D.P., Noh, J.J., Rucklidge, W.J.: Tracking non-rigid objects in complex scene, 4th International Conf. Computer Vision, (1993) 93-101
5. Huttenlocher, D.P., Klanderman, G.A., Rucklidge, W.J.: Comparing images using the Hausdorff distance, IEEE Trans. Pattern Analysis and Machine Intelligence, **15** (9)(1993) 850-863
6. Borgefors, G.: Distance transformations in digital images, Computer Vision, Graphics and Image Processing, **34** (1986) 344-371
7. Bhuyan, M.K., Ghosh, D., Bora, P.K.: Finite state representation of hand gestures using key video object plane, Proc. IEEE Region 10 - Asia-Pacific Conf. (TENCON), (2004) 21-24
8. Bhuyan, M.K., Ghosh, D., Bora, P.K.: Key video object plane selection by MPEG-7 visual shape descriptor for summarization and recognition of hand gestures, Proc. 4th Indian Conf. Computer Vision, Graphics and Image Processing (ICVGIP), (2004) 638-643

3D Facial Pose Tracking in Uncalibrated Videos*

Gaurav Aggarwal, Ashok Veeraraghavan, and Rama Chellappa

University of Maryland, College Park MD 20742, USA
{gaurav, vashok, rama}@umiacs.umd.edu
http://www.cfar.umd.edu/~gaurav

Abstract. This paper presents a method to recover the 3D configuration of a face in each frame of a video. The 3D configuration consists of the 3 translational parameters and the 3 orientation parameters which correspond to the yaw, pitch and roll of the face, which is important for applications like face modeling, recognition, expression analysis, etc. The approach combines the structural advantages of geometric modeling with the statistical advantages of a particle-filter based inference. The face is modeled as the curved surface of a cylinder which is free to translate and rotate arbitrarily. The geometric modeling takes care of pose and self-occlusion while the statistical modeling handles moderate occlusion and illumination variations. Experimental results on multiple datasets are provided to show the efficacy of the approach. The insensitivity of our approach to calibration parameters (focal length) is also shown.

1 Introduction

Face tracking is a crucial task for several applications like face recognition, human computer interaction, etc. Most of these applications require actual 3D parameters of the location of the head. In this paper, we propose an approach based on a cylindrical model for the head for reliable tracking of position and orientation of the head under illumination changes, occlusion and extreme poses.

There has been significant work on facial tracking using 2D appearance based models[1][2][3][4]. Quite clearly, such 2D approaches do not explicitly provide the 3D configuration of the head. Recently, several methods have been developed for 3D face tracking. [5] uses a closed loop approach that utilizes a structure from motion algorithm to generate a 3D model of the face. In [6], techniques in continuous optimization are applied to a linear combination of 3D face models. [7] proposes a hybrid sampling solution using both RANSAC and particle filters to track the pose of a face. [8] shows examples of head tracking by posing it as a nonlinear state estimation problem. A cylindrical face model for face tracking has been used in [9]. In their formulation, they assume that the inter-frame warping function is locally linear and that the inter-frame pose change occurs only in one of the six degrees of freedom of the rigid cylindrical model. In our approach, we do not make any such assumptions. This improves both tracking accuracy and robustness. Moreover, unlike [9] we do not use information about

---
* Partially supported by the NSF-ITR Grant 03-25119.

the camera calibration parameters. Instead we analytically show the insensitivity of our approach to errors in focal length.

2 The Geometric Model

The choice of the model to represent the facial structure is very crucial for the problem of face tracking. There are several algorithms that do not assume an explicit structural model but track salient points, features or 2D patches [10] [11][4][2]. On the other extreme, there are algorithms like [5] that use a set of 3D laser-scanned heads. Though a planar model will probably be the simplest one to use, it does not have the capability to estimate the 3D configuration of the face. On the other hand, using a complicated face model makes the initialization and registration process difficult.

Similar to [9], we use a cylindrical model, though with an elliptical cross-section, to represent a face. Assuming that our cylindrical model reasonably approximates the 3D structure of a face, the problems related to pose and self-occlusion get automatically taken care of. Due to the absence of the calibration parameters, people usually assume orthographic projection. The use of orthographic projection is restrictive and introduces confusion between scale and pitch. These reasons motivate us to use perspective projection model. Since we do not know the camera focal length for un-calibrated videos, we show that our approach for pose recovery is robust to the errors in focal length assignment.

Let us assume that the true focal length of the camera imaging a cylinder centered at (X_0, Y_0, Z_0) with height H and radius R be f_0. Let us assume that we erroneously set the focal length to kf_0 (without loss of generality $k \geq 1$). The true projections of feature points on the cylinder are given by

$$x_f = \frac{f_0 X_f}{Z_0 + z_f} \qquad y_f = \frac{f_0 Y_f}{Z_0 + z_f} \qquad \text{where,} \qquad Z_f = Z_0 + z_f \qquad (1)$$

The projection of feature points of another cylinder with same dimensions but placed at (X_0, Y_0, kZ_0) and imaged by a camera of focal length kf_0 are

$$\hat{x}_f = \frac{kf_0 X_f}{kZ_0 + z_f} = x_f \left[1 + \frac{(k-1)z_f}{kZ_0 + z_f}\right] = x_f[1 + \delta_f] \qquad (2)$$

$$\hat{y}_f = \frac{kf_0 Y_f}{kZ_0 + z_f} = y_f \left[1 + \frac{(k-1)z_f}{kZ_0 + z_f}\right] = y_f[1 + \delta_f] \qquad (3)$$

If $\delta_f \ll 1$, the feature positions for the cylinder at (X_0, Y_0, Z_0) imaged by camera f_0 is equivalent to a cylinder at (X_0, Y_0, kZ_0) imaged by a camera with focal length kf_0. Therefore, when δ_f is small, our estimates of yaw, pitch and roll are reasonably accurate.

If the depth variations in the object (cylinder in our case) are smaller than the distance of the object from the camera center (i.e., $z_f \ll Z_0$) and the field of view is reasonably small, then

$$\delta_f = \frac{(k-1)z_f}{kZ_0 + z_f} \quad < \quad \frac{kz_f}{kZ_0 + z_f} \quad < \quad \frac{\frac{z_f}{Z_0}}{1 + \frac{z_f}{kZ_0}} \quad \ll \quad 1 \qquad (4)$$

The choice of features is extremely important for the task of 3D pose estimation of a moving face. The features should be easy to detect, robust to occlusions, changes in pose, expression and illumination. In this paper, we propose a hybrid approach which makes use of the advantages of a purely geometric approach and the power of statistical inference. We use an extremely simple and easily computable feature to stress-test the approach. We superimpose a rectangular grid all around the curved surface of our elliptical cylinder. The mean intensity for each of the visible grids forms the feature vector. Robust statistics makes the feature robust to moderate illumination changes, expressions and occlusions.

3 Tracking Framework

Once the structural model and feature vector have been fixed, the goal is to estimate the configuration (or pose) of the moving face in each frame of a given video. This can be viewed as a dynamic state estimation problem. Here the state consists of the six 3D configuration parameters. Particle filtering [12][13] is an inference technique for estimating the unknown dynamic state θ of a system from a collection of noisy observations $y_{1:t}$. The two components of this approach are the state transition model which models the state evolution, and the observation model which specifies the state-observation dependence:

$$\text{State transition model: } \theta_t = f(\theta_{t-1}, u_t), \quad (5)$$

$$\text{Observation model: } y_t = g(\theta_t, v_t), \quad (6)$$

where u_t is the system noise while v_t is the observation noise. In general, the functions f and g can also be time-dependent. The particle filter approximates the desired posterior pdf $p(\theta_t|y_{1:t})$ by a set of weighted particles $\{\theta_t^{(j)}, w_t^{(j)}\}_{j=1}^N$, where N denotes the number of particles. The state estimate $\hat{\theta}_t$ is recovered from the pdf as the maximum likelihood (ML) estimate. To keep the tracker as generic as possible, we use a random-walk model as the motion model:

$$\theta_t = \theta_{t-1} + u_t, \quad (7)$$

where u_t is normally distributed about zero. Based on the domain knowledge, one can come up with a motion model that will be capable of estimating the pdf better with lesser number of particles.

The observation model involves the feature vector described in the previous section. In our framework, we can rewrite the observation equation as:

$$z_t = \Gamma\{y_t; \theta_t\} = F_t + v_t, \quad (8)$$

where y_t is the current frame (the gray scale image), Γ is the mapping that computes the feature vector given an image y_t and a configuration θ_t, z_t is the computed feature vector and F_t is the feature model. The feature model is used to compute the likelihood of the particles (which correspond to different proposed configurations of the face). For each particle the likelihood is computed using the average sum of squared differences (SSD) between the feature model and the mean vector z_t corresponding to the particle.

On one extreme, the feature model can be a fixed template, while on the other hand one can use a dynamic template e.g, $F_t = \hat{z}_{t-1}$. Similar to [14], we refer to the fixed template $F_t = F_0$ as the lost model while the dynamic component $F_t = \hat{z}_{t-1}$ as the wander model. It is worthwhile to note that the wander component is capable of handling appearance changes due to illumination, expression, etc. as the face translates/rotates in the real world, while the lost component is resistant against drifts. In the current implementation, the likelihood of a particle is computed as the maximum of the likelihoods using the lost and the wander model. This gives us the capability both to handle appearance changes and to correct the estimation if the wander model drifts. The tracker performs well with as few as 200 particles. The performance does not show any appreciable improvement as we increased this number.

We use robust statistics in our likelihood model in order to make the feature robust to changes in illumination, expression and occlusions. We trust only the top half of the means and treat the rest as outliers as follows:

$$p(y_t|\theta_t^{(j)}) = e^{-\lambda dist} \quad \text{where,} \quad dist = \frac{\sum_{m,n} \eta(m,n) d(m,n)}{\sum_{m,n} \eta(m,n)} \tag{9}$$

where $\eta(m,n)$ is the visibility indicator variable, while $d(m,n)$ is computed as:

$$d(m,n) = \begin{cases} (F_t(m,n) - z_t^{(j)}(m,n))^2 & \text{if } d(m,n) < c \\ c & \text{otherwise} \end{cases}$$

$$\text{where,} \quad c = median(\{d(m,n)\}). \tag{10}$$

4 Experimental Results and Conclusion

Tracking under extreme poses: We conducted tracking experiments on 3 datasets (Honda/UCSD dataset [15], BU dataset [9] and Li dataset [16]). These datasets have numerous sequences in which there are significant illumination changes, expression variation and people are free to move their heads arbitrarily. Figure 1 shows few of the frames from three videos with grid points on the estimated cylinder overlaid on the image frame. The first and second columns show the ability of the tracker to maintain tracks in spite of considerable occlusion. The tracker does well even when confronted with extreme poses as shown in the third column. Moderate expressions do not affect the feature since it is the mean intensity within a small surface patch on the face. During certain severe expression changes robust statistics helps maintain the track. The tracker is able to maintain the track all along the sequences.

Ground Truth Comparison: The BU dataset [9] provides the ground truth for the pose of the face in each frame. We conducted tracking experiments on the BU dataset and compared the yaw, pitch and roll estimated by the tracker to the ground truth. Figure 2 shows the comparison for three sequences. We see that the tracker accurately estimates the pose of the face in most frames.

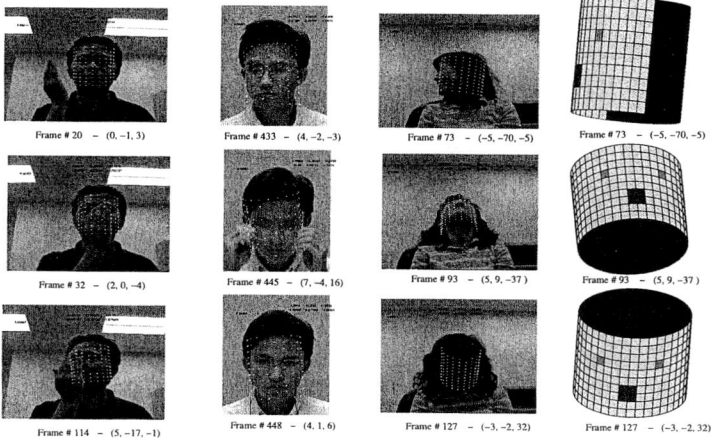

Fig. 1. Tracking results under severe occlusion, extreme poses and different illumination conditions. The cylindrical grid is overlaid on the image plane to display the results. The 3-tuple shows the estimated orientation (roll, yaw, pitch). The last column shows the cylindrical model in the pose estimated for the sequence in the third column.

Recognition with non-overlapping poses: Most recognition methods require the gallery and probe images to be in similar pose. Since the tracking method maintains explicit pose for each frame, we do not need this. We show this by performing recognition on non-overlapping poses. The closest poses in the gallery and the probe differ by at least 30 degrees. We used 10 subjects from the Honda/UCSD dataset [15] for this experiment. For each frame we build a texture mapped cylinder using the tracked pose. We used the minimum sum of squared distance between a gallery model and a probe model as the distance between two videos. This is a very challenging experiment since the poses exhibited by the gallery videos and those exhibited by the probe videos are very different. In spite of this, we obtained 100% recognition rate in this experiment.

Conclusions: We have proposed a method for tracking the facial pose in a video. The tracker is robust to moderate occlusions and illumination changes

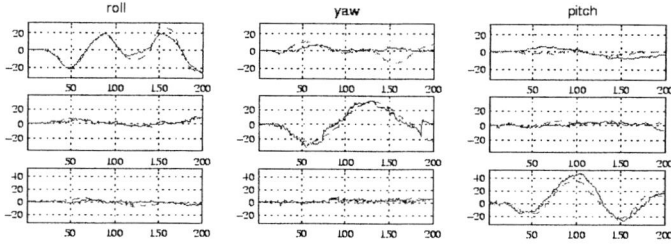

Fig. 2. Each row shows the 3 orientation parameters. The red/dashed curve depicts the ground truth while the blue/solid curve depicts the estimated values.

and maintains track even during extreme poses. We have also shown, how such 3D pose tracking can help in problems like face recognition from videos.

References

1. Lanitis, A., Taylor, C., Cootes, T.: Automatic interpretation and coding of face images using flexible models. IEEE Trans. on Pattern Analysis and Machine Intelligence **19** (1997) 743–756
2. Yuille, A.L., Cohen, D.S., Hallinan, P.W.: Feature extraction from faces using deformable templates. In: International Conference on Pattern Recognition. (1994)
3. Zhou, S., Chellappa, R., Moghaddam, B.: Visual tracking and recognition using appearance-adaptive models in particle filters. IEEE Trans. on Image Processing **11** (2004) 1434–1456
4. Hager, G.D., Belhumeur, P.N.: Efficient region tracking with parametric models of geometry and illumination. IEEE Trans. on Pattern Analysis and Machine Intelligence **20** (1998) 1025–1039
5. Jebara, T.S., Pentland, A.: Parameterized structure from motion for 3D adaptive feedback tracking of faces. In: IEEE Conference on Computer Vision and Pattern Recognition, San Juan, PR. (1997)
6. Pighin, F., Szeliski, R., Salesin, H.: Resynthesizing facial animation through 3D model-based tracking. In: Seventh International Conference on Computer Vision, Kerkyra, Greece. (1999) 143–150
7. Lu, L., Dai, X., Hager, G.: A particle filter without dynamics for robust 3D face tracking. In: IEEE Conference on Computer Vision and Pattern Recognition, Washington, D.C. (2004)
8. Moon, H., Chellappa, R., Rosenfeld, A.: 3d object tracking using shape-encoded particle propagation. In: International Conference on Computer Vision. (2001)
9. Cascia, M.L., Sclaroff, S., Athitsos, V.: Fast, reliable head tracking under varying illumination: An approach based on registration of texture-mapped 3D models. IEEE Trans. on Pattern Analysis and Machine Intelligence **22** (2000) 322–336
10. Birchfield, S.: An elliptical head tracker. In: Proceedings of the 31st Asilomar Conference on Signals, Systems, and Computers, Pacific Grove, California. (1997) 1710–1714
11. Fieguth, P., Terzopoulos, D.: Color-based tracking of heads and other mobile objects at video frame rates. In: IEEE Conference on Computer Vision and Pattern Recognition, San Juan, PR. (1997)
12. Doucet, A., Freitas, N.D., Gordon, N.: Sequential Monte Carlo methods in practice. Springer-Verlag, New York (2001)
13. Gordon, N.J., Salmond, D.J., Smith, A.F.M.: Novel approach to nonlinear/non-gaussian bayesian state estimation. In: IEE Proceedings on Radar and Signal Processing. Volume 140. (1993) 107–113
14. Jepson, A.D., Fleet, D.J., El-Maraghi, T.F.: Robust online appearance models for visual tracking. IEEE Trans. on Pattern Analysis and Machine Intelligence **25** (2003) 1296–1311
15. Lee, K.C., Ho, J., Yang, M.H., Kriegman, D.: Video-based face recognition using probabilistic appearance manifolds. In: IEEE Conference on Computer Vision and Pattern Recognition. (2003)
16. Li, B., Chellappa, R.: Face verification through tracking facial features. Journal of the Optical Society of America A **18** (2001) 2969–2981

Fusing Depth and Video Using Rao-Blackwellized Particle Filter

Amit Agrawal and Rama Chellappa

University of Maryland,
College Park, MD 20742 USA

Abstract. We address the problem of fusing sparse and noisy depth data obtained from a range finder with features obtained from intensity images to estimate ego-motion and refine 3D structure of a scene using a Rao-Blackwellized particle filter. For scenes with low depth variability, the algorithm shows an alternate way of performing Structure from Motion (SfM) starting with a flat depth map. Instead of using 3D depths, we formulate the problem using 2D image domain parallax and show that conditioned on non-linear motion parameters, the parallax magnitude with respect to the projection of the vanishing point forms a linear subsystem independent of camera motion and their distributions can be analytically integrated. Thus, the structure is obtained by estimating parallax with respect to the given depths using a Kalman filter and only the ego-motion is estimated using a particle filter. Hence, the required number of particles becomes independent of the number of feature points which is an improvement over previous algorithms. Experimental results on both synthetic and real data show the effectiveness of our approach.

1 Introduction

SfM refers to the estimation of 3D scene structure and sensor motion given monocular or stereo images. With increasing availability of range sensors in 3D modeling, the need for fusing the depth information from these sensors with information from intensity images naturally arises. However, the available depth data from range sensors is often noisy and coarse. We focus on using such coarse and noisy depth information along with sparse noisy features detected from intensity images to refine the depths and estimate the ego-motion under perspective projection. A moving camera can be viewed as a dynamical system where a state space model can be used to describe the motion and/or depths with the noisy 2D feature points denoting the observations. This approach was used in [1] where a Kalman filter was used to fuse information from a sequence of images. In [2], the problem was reformulated to reduce the size of the state space and an extended Kalman filter was used to handle the non-linearities. Recently, Sequential Monte Carlo (SMC) methods have emerged as a powerful tool for estimation, prediction and filtering of non-linear dynamical systems. Kitagawa [3] proposed a Monte Carlo filter for non-linear/non-gaussian dynamical systems. The bootstrap filter proposed by Gordon [4] is a similar variant of the SMC method. Several SMC methods have been proposed to handle various problems in computer vision such as shape and contour tracking [5], SfM [6], tracking [7], and self-calibration [8]. Most of the existing methods for SfM either *reduce* SfM such as [6]. These methods eliminate depths from the state space (e.g. utilizing the epipolar constraints) and estimate the camera motion. The structure can be estimated after motion estimation in a variety of ways such as using another Sequential Importance Sampling (SIS) procedure as in [6]. Or they attempt to estimate both structure and motion simultaneously. Here the state space consists of both structure and motion parameters and the size of state space increases linearly with the number of feature points.

With respect to the problem at hand, both approaches have limitations. The first approach eliminates depths in motion estimation. Thus, even if we have some prior depth information, such information can not be used to improve the motion estimates. The second approach has a considerable disadvantage that the size of state space increases linearly with the number of feature points as structure is also a part of the state space. Thus the number of particles in the particle filtering scheme needs to increase [9][10] which makes it computationally inefficient and unstable. To overcome the above limitations, we propose a formulation where both structure and motion are estimated *simultaneously* incorporating prior depth information. Thus structure is also a part of the state space. Thus our approach can deal with general 3D scenes and is *not* restricted. In addition, although structure is a part of state space, the number of particles required is independent of the number of feature points.

The approach proposed in this paper is based on the Rao-Blackwellisation [11] and marginalized particle filter schemes [9]. If one can find a linear subsystem in the state space model conditioned on the rest of the states, the distributions corresponding to linear states can analytically integrated. We show that by using a surface-parallax approach, the parallax magnitudes form a linear subsystem conditioned on the non-linear motion parameters. Thus, in our formulation, the non-linear part of the state space for which a particle filter is used consists of only the motion parameters and the distributions of the linear part (consisting of parallax magnitudes) is estimated using a Kalman filter. Prior information on depths can be transferred as prior information on parallax magnitudes and hence an efficient way of incorporating prior depth information can be obtained.

2 Algorithm

Let the Z axis of the camera point in the direction of the principal axis. At time instant 0, the camera coordinate system is aligned with the world coordinate system. We parameterize the motion at time t as $\mathbf{m}^t = (\omega_x, \omega_y, \omega_z, \alpha, \gamma, s)$ where $\Psi^t = (\omega_x, \omega_y, \omega_z)$ are the *total* rotational angles along the X, Y and Z axis upto current time t, (α, γ) denotes the elevation and azimuth angles and s denotes the scale. The translation direction is then $[\sin(\alpha)\cos(\gamma), \sin(\alpha)\sin(\gamma), \cos(\alpha)]^T$ and the *total* translation upto current time is $T(\alpha, \gamma, s) = \begin{bmatrix} T_x \\ T_y \\ T_z \end{bmatrix} = s \begin{bmatrix} \sin(\alpha)\cos(\gamma) \\ \sin(\alpha)\sin(\gamma) \\ \cos(\alpha) \end{bmatrix}$

Thus the overall camera motion in the world coordinate system is estimated. The rotation matrix R^t is then given by (1)

$$R^t = \begin{bmatrix} \eta_1^2 + (1-\eta_1^2)\tau & \eta_1\eta_2(1-\tau) + \eta_3\zeta & \eta_1\eta_3(1-\tau) - \eta_2\zeta \\ \eta_1\eta_2(1-\tau) - \eta_3\zeta & \eta_2^2 + (1-\eta_2^2)\tau & \eta_2\eta_3(1-\tau) + \eta_1\zeta \\ \eta_1\eta_3(1-\tau) + \eta_2\zeta & \eta_2\eta_3(1-\tau) - \eta_1\zeta & \eta_3^2 + (1-\eta_3^2)\tau \end{bmatrix} \quad (1)$$

where $\eta = (\eta_1, \eta_2, \eta_3)^T = \Psi^t/|\Psi^t|$ is the direction cosine vector, $\zeta = \sin|\Psi^t|$ and $\tau = \cos|\Psi^t|$. Let $P = [X, Y, Z]^T$ denote a 3D point on the rigid scene in the world coordinate system. The projection of P on to the image plane at time 0 is given by

$$\mathbf{p} = \begin{bmatrix} u \\ v \end{bmatrix} = \begin{bmatrix} X/Z \\ Y/Z \end{bmatrix} \quad (2)$$

where we assume that the focal length of the camera equals one (or the image pixels have been normalized w.r.t. focal length). Thus given the projection $\mathbf{p}$ at time 0, we can parameterize the 3D coordinates[1] as $X = uZ, Y = vZ$. At each time instant t, the 3D point P^t is given by the following motion model

$$P^t = R^t P + T^t \quad (3)$$

Let $R^t = \begin{bmatrix} r_{11} & r_{12} & r_{13} \\ r_{21} & r_{22} & r_{23} \\ r_{31} & r_{32} & r_{33} \end{bmatrix}$. Using (2) and (3), the projection of P^t, $\mathbf{p}^t = \begin{bmatrix} u^t \\ v^t \end{bmatrix}$ is

$$u^t = \frac{Za + T_x}{Zc + T_z}, v^t = \frac{Zb + T_y}{Zc + T_z} \quad (4)$$

where for simplicity $a = r_{11}u + r_{12}v + r_{13}$, $b = r_{21}u + r_{22}v + r_{23}$ and $c = r_{31}u + r_{32}v + r_{33}$. The prior depth information (also referred to as *reference depths*) gives us some estimate $\widehat{Z}$ of the 3D point P which essentially correspond to a different point Q along the 3D ray. Let $\mathbf{q}^t = h(\mathbf{m}^t, \widehat{Z})$ denotes the projection of Q^t at time t. Thus, from (4) $\mathbf{q}^t = \begin{bmatrix} u_q^t \\ v_q^t \end{bmatrix} = \begin{bmatrix} (\widehat{Z}a + T_x)/(\widehat{Z}c + T_z) \\ (\widehat{Z}b + T_y)/(\widehat{Z}c + T_z) \end{bmatrix}$. It is well known that $\mathbf{q}^t - \mathbf{p}^t$ lies along the epipolar direction $\mathbf{q}^t - \mathbf{e}^t$ where $\mathbf{e}^t$ denotes the epipole [12]. It is also the parallax due to $\widehat{Z}$. The parallax can be parameterized as a scalar (parallax magnitude β^t) times the vector along the epipolar direction, i.e. $(\mathbf{q}^t - \mathbf{p}^t) = \beta^t(\mathbf{q}^t - \mathbf{e}^t)$ The exact form of β^t (for $T_z \neq 0$) is then given by

$$\beta^t = \frac{\widehat{Z} - Z}{\widehat{Z}} \frac{T_z}{Zc + T_z} \quad (5)$$

Thus we have $\mathbf{p}^t = \mathbf{q}^t - (\mathbf{q}^t - \mathbf{p}^t) = \mathbf{q}^t - \beta^t(\mathbf{q}^t - \mathbf{e}^t)$

The above equation gives a *linear* relationship between the observed projection $\mathbf{p}^t$ and the parallax magnitude β^t. However parameterizing β with respect

---
[1] We assume the bias in feature points for the first image to be zero for simplicity.

to epipole will have a different equation when $T_z = 0$. To handle both cases, we propose an alternate formulation based on the projection of the vanishing point of the 3D ray corresponding to point P. Although the vanishing point is generally used in context of parallel set of lines, here by vanishing point (**vp**) we mean the intersection of the 3D ray corresponding to feature point **p** (in first frame) with the plane at infinity. Let **pvp**^{t} denote the projection of the vanishing point at time t. As $Z \to \infty$, using (4), we have $\mathbf{pvp}^t = \begin{bmatrix} a/c \\ b/c \end{bmatrix}$. Thus, if we write $\mathbf{p}^t = \mathbf{q}^t - \beta^t(\mathbf{q}^t - \mathbf{pvp}^t)$ one can solve for β^t as $\beta^t = -\frac{\widehat{Z}-Z}{Z}\frac{c}{c+T_z/Z}$. Thus when $T_z \ll Z$, i.e. motion in Z direction is small compared to the depths, we have

$$\beta^t \approx -(\widehat{Z} - Z)/Z \tag{6}$$

which is constant and **independent** of camera motion across all the frames.

2.1 State Space Model

Suppose we track N feature points $i = 1\ldots N$ across K time instants $t = 1\ldots K$. To capture the motion dynamics, we use a 1-step predictive model for motion. Let $\dot{\mathbf{m}}^t = (\dot\omega_x, \dot\omega_y, \dot\omega_z, \dot\alpha, \dot\gamma, \dot s)$. The state vector at time t is $\mathbf{x}^t = (\mathbf{x}^t_{nl}, \mathbf{x}^t_l) = (\mathbf{m}^t, \dot{\mathbf{m}}^t, \beta^t_1, \beta^t_2, \ldots, \beta^t_N)$ consisting of two parts: the *non-linear* states $\mathbf{x}^t_{nl} = (\mathbf{m}^t, \dot{\mathbf{m}}^t)$ and the *linear* states $\mathbf{x}^t_l = (\beta^t_1, \beta^t_2, \ldots, \beta^t_N)$ consisting of the parallax magnitudes for all the feature points. The state equations can then be written as

$$\begin{aligned}\mathbf{m}^{t+1} &= \mathbf{m}^t + \dot{\mathbf{m}}^t + \mathbf{n}^m & \dot{\mathbf{m}}^{t+1} &= \dot{\mathbf{m}}^t + \mathbf{n}^{\dot m} \\ \beta^{t+1}_i &= \beta^t_i + w_i \quad \text{for i=1}\ldots\text{N} & & \end{aligned} \tag{7}$$

where the state noise, $\mathbf{n}^m$ and $\mathbf{n}^{\dot m}$ is assumed to be Gaussian for the rotational velocities and uniform for the translational directional angles and scale. We also assume a IID gaussian state noise $w_i \sim \mathsf{N}(0, Q^l_i)$ with very low variance ($Q^l_i \approx 10^{-3}$) in β_i. The observation equation for $i = 1\ldots N$ can be written as

$$\mathbf{p}^t_i = \mathbf{q}^t_i - (\mathbf{q}^t_i - \mathbf{p}^t_i) + \mathbf{n}^p_i = h(\mathbf{m}^t, \widehat{Z}_i) - \beta^t_i C(\mathbf{m}^t, \widehat{Z}_i) + \mathbf{n}^p_i \tag{8}$$

where we assume the observation noise for each feature point to be distributed as $\mathbf{n}^p_i \sim \mathsf{N}(0, \sigma^2_p)$. For each feature point i, $\mathbf{q}^t_i$ is a non-linear function h of current motion $\mathbf{m}^t$ and reference depths $\widehat{Z}_i$. Similarly, $(\mathbf{q}^t_i - \mathbf{pvp}^t_i)$ is a non-linear function C of current motion and reference depths. Thus our state space model is of the form of diagonal model as in [9] and the marginalized particle filter described in [9] can be used to compute the posterior distributions of motion and parallax magnitudes. The filtering procedure then follows *Algorithm* 1 in [9] and we refer the reader to [9] for further details.

In general, the range sensor will provide some estimate of depth values along with their uncertainties (mean and covariances). For each feature point i, let the reference depth $\widehat{Z}_i$ be distributed as $\widehat{Z}_i \sim \mathsf{N}(Z_i + m_i, \sigma^2_i)$, where Z_i is the true depth value. Using (6), the prior distribution on the parallax magnitude β_i will be $\beta_i \sim \mathsf{N}(-m_i/Z_i, \sigma_i^2/Z_i^2)$. In practical scenarios, since Z_i is not known, we can use the given reference depth value. Thus we can assume $\beta_i \sim \mathsf{N}(-m_i/\widehat{Z}_i, \sigma_i^2/\widehat{Z}_i^2)$.

3 Experiments

Face Sequence. The face texture images and range data were downloaded from http://sampl.eng.ohio-state.edu/~sampl/data/3DDB/RID/minolta/faces-hands.1299. 20 frames of the face sequence were generated from a virtual camera with the ground truth focal length. Fig. 1(a) shows the tracked features overlayed on the first frame. The initial (reference) depths were chosen to be equal for all feature points as shown in Fig. 1(e). Figs. 1(b) and 1(c) show the estimates of translation direction and rotational velocities. Figs. 1(d) and 1(e) show the comparison of estimated β and depths with ground truth for all feature points for the last frame. The estimates are very close to the true values. Figs. 1(f), 1(g) and 1(h) shows novel views of texture mapped 3D model.

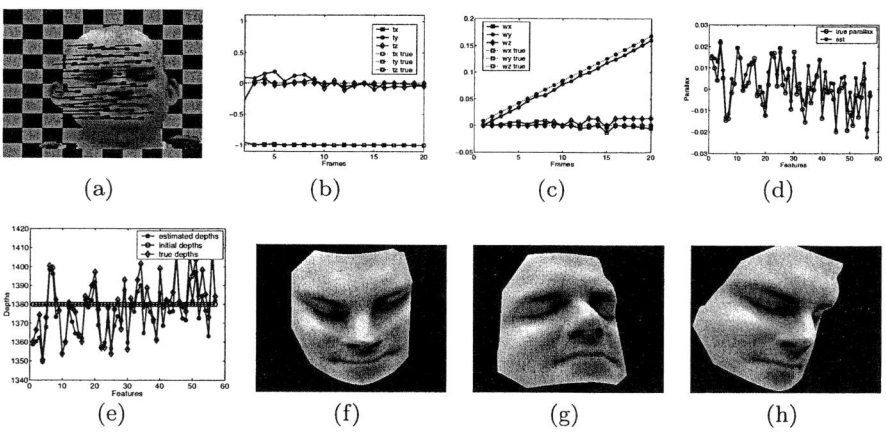

Fig. 1. Face Sequence: (Top Row) Tracked features; Translation direction estimates; Rotational velocities estimates; β estimates (Bottom Row) True, reference and estimated depths; Novel Views

Indoor Sequence. A video sequence of several toy objects was taken in a lab. The dominant camera motion was in the X direction. We choose the reference depths to be equal (500 units) for all feature points. The initial mean and variance for the parallax magnitudes were set to 0 and 1 pixel respectively. A total of 200 feature points were tracked for 30 frames with trajectories shown overlayed on first frame in Fig. 2(a). The estimates of translation direction and rotational velocities are shown in Fig. 2(b) and Fig. 2(c) respectively. The final depth map is obtained by interpolating the estimated depths. Fig. 2(d) to 2(g) shows novel views of texture mapped 3D model.

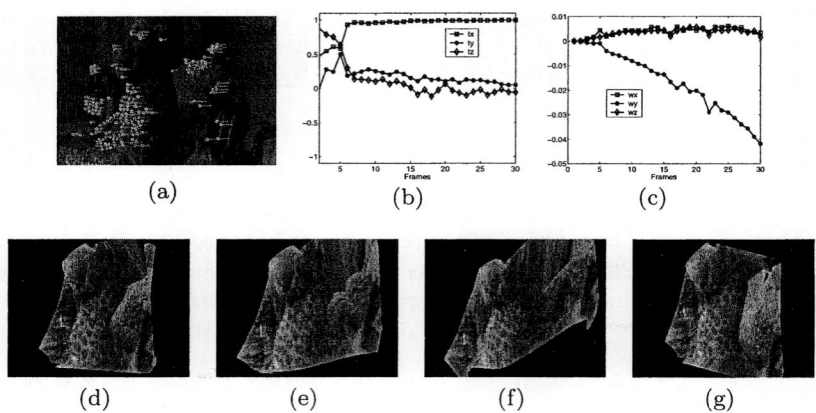

Fig. 2. Indoor Sequence: (Top Row) Tracked features; Translation direction estimates; Rotational velocities estimates (Bottom Row) Novel Views

References

1. Broida, T., Chellappa, R.: Estimating the kinematics and structure of a rigid object from a sequence of monocular images. IEEE Trans. Pattern Anal. Machine Intell. **13** (1991) 497–513
2. Azarbayejani, A., Pentland, A.: Recursive estimation of motion, structure, and focal length. IEEE Trans. Pattern Anal. Machine Intell. **17** (1995) 562–575
3. Kitagawa, G.: Monte carlo filter and smoother for non-gaussian nonlinear state space models. J. Computational and Graphical Statistics **5**(1) (1996) 1–25
4. Gordon, N., Salmond, D., Smith, A.: Novel approach to nonlinear/non-gaussian bayesian state estimation. In: IEE Proc. Radar, Sonar and Navig. (1993) 107–113
5. Isard, M., Blake, A.: Condensation – conditional density propagation for visual tracking. Int'l J. Computer Vision **29**(1) (1998) 5–28
6. Qian, G., Chellappa, R.: Structure from motion using sequential monte carlo methods. Int'l J. Computer Vision (2004) 5–31
7. Khan, Z., Balch, T., Dellaert, F.: A rao-blackwellized particle filter for eigentracking. In: Proc. Conf. Computer Vision and Pattern Recognition. (2004)
8. Qian, G., Chellappa, R.: Bayesian self-calibration of a moving camera. (to appear in *CVIU*)
9. Schon, T., Gustafsson, F.: Marginalized particle filters for mixed linear/nonlinear state-space models. (to appear in *IEEE Trans. Signal Processing*)
10. Khan, Z., Balch, T., Dellaert, F.: Efficient particle filter based tracking of multiple interacting targets using an mrf-based motion model. In: IEEE/RSJ Intl. Conf. on Intelligent Robots and Systems. (2003)
11. Casella, G., Robert, C.: Rao-blackwellisation of sampling schemes. Biometrika **83**(1) (1994) 81–94
12. Sawhney, H.: 3D geometry from planar parallax. In: Proc. Conf. Computer Vision and Pattern Recognition. (1994) 929–934

Specifying Spatio Temporal Relations for Multimedia Ontologies

Karthik Thatipamula[1], Santanu Chaudhury[1], and Hiranmay Ghosh[2]

[1] Department of Electrical Engineering, IIT Delhi
kashyap_karthik@yahoo.com, santanuc@ee.iitd.ac.in
[2] Research Group, Tata Infotech Limited, New Delhi
hiranmay.ghosh@tatainfotech.com

Abstract. This paper present a novel framework for formal specification of spatio-temporal relations between media objects using fuzzy membership. We have illustrated its use in multimedia ontologies and have described a reasoning framework for creating media based descriptions of concepts.

1 Introduction

An ontology to support multimedia applications needs to deal with media properties of concepts. Traditional ontology languages, e.g. OWL, does not support explicit assignment of media properties with concepts, and reasoning with the intrinsic uncertainties involved in media based concept recognition. We have proposed an extension of OWL to overcome these limitations [1]. The extended language M-OWL enables formulation of media based description of concepts and concept recognition through observation of media properties. Spatial and temporal relations between media objects are important for characterizing media events. We describe a new scheme for formal description of such spatio-temporal relations in this paper. We also describe a reasoning scheme to construct a media-based description of the concepts using these relations.

Papadias et al [2] have proposed a scheme for formal specification of spatial and temporal relations. This scheme is based on the relative positioning of the end points of the events in space and time axes. However, these definitions are crisp and cannot satisfactorily express the intrinsically uncertain nature of nearness relations. Moreover, it characterizes an event with the minimum bounding rectangle with the projections of its end-points on the space and time axes and cannot cope up with the relations associated with concave events. We have extended this scheme with fuzzy membership functions and additional relations based on RCC model [3] to overcome these limitations. We have also introduced a reasoning scheme that enables construction of media property based descriptions for concepts with these spatio-temporal relations.

The rest of the paper is organized as follows. Section 2 describes the motivation behind extension of OWL for multimedia Ontologies. Section 3 describes a new way of specifying semantics to spatio temporal relations and the extension to M-OWL to incorporate this information. Section 4 describes a Bayesian network based inference scheme to reason in context of spatio temporal relations. Section 5 concludes this paper.

2 Multimedia Ontology and Its Representation

A concept manifests itself as some media patterns in a multimedia document. The observation of the expected media patterns is the key to concept recognition. The traditional ontology languages, e.g. OWL, does not have a formal semantics for associating media patterns with the concepts. As a result, it is not possible to do reasoning with the media properties, e.g. a monument made of marble should "inherit" its color and texture properties. The crisp Description Logic based reasoning with OWL does not support the inherent uncertainties with semantic interpretation of media data.

Multimedia ontologies should enable construction of a model for the concepts in terms of media objects and their relations and enable reasoning with these properties and associated uncertainties. We have proposed M-OWL as an extension of OWL to incorporate these features [1]. M-OWL enables construction of an Observation Model (OM), which is a media-based description of a concept. It is organized as a Bayesian Network with the root node representing the concept and the leaf nodes representing a set of media patterns that are expected in a multimedia document where the concept materializes. The causal links connecting the concept with the media patterns in the Bayesian Network represents the uncertainties that are associated with semantic interpretation of media data. Observation of the expected media patterns in a multimedia document leads to concept recognition through belief propagation in the Bayesian Network [5].

Spatial and temporal relations between the media objects is another important aspect of multimedia. It should be possible for a multimedia ontology to Provide the capability for formal definitions for these relations and to reason with them. For example, a "goalScore" event in a football game can be described as ((ball *inside* goalPost) *followedBy* cheering). It should be possible to define the semantics of the relations *inside* and *followedBy* formally in a multimedia ontology, and use them to construct an observation model for the "goalScore" event with the media properties of the constituent concepts, namely "ball", "goalPost" and "cheering". Moreover, it should be possible to specify the degree of memberships for the spatio-temporal relations for different configurations of the connected concepts. We introduce a new method for formally specifying the spatio-temporal relations and reasoning with them in subsequent sections of this paper.

3 Encoding Spatio-temporal Relations

Padadias et al [2] proposes formal encoding of relation between two events in space-time encoded as a set of binary strings. If [a,b] be a closed and continuous 1D interval, we can identify five distinct regions of interest: $(-\infty, a)$, $[a, a]$, (a, b),

$[b, b]$, $(b, +\infty)$. The relationship between this primary interval and any other interval [z,y] can be specified by a binary string $< t, u, v, w, x >$ representing empty or non-empty intersections of [z,y] with the five regions of interest for [a,b]. Thus, the relation between two media events in a multimedia document can be represented by a 3-tuple $< C\_t, X\_p, Y\_p >$ denoting the binary intersection-strings in time, X and Y axes respectively.

This encoding scheme assumes that the events are are represented by convex regions in space-time and fails to unambiguously encode the relations when any of the events is concave. For example, the region B is contained in the region A in figure 1(b), while it is not in figure 1(a). Papadias'e encoding scheme cannot distinguish between the two scenarios. Motivated by RCC [3], we have introduced one more string C_s, which specifies the overlap or disconnectedness between the regions to solve this problem. C_s is represented by a string $< f\_0, f\_1, f\_2 >$ where

- f_0 - $A - (A \bigcap B)$
- f_1 - $B - (A \bigcap B)$
- f_2 - $(A \bigcap B) - (A \bigcap^* B)$ where $\bigcap^*$ denotes the regularized set operation.

Thus, the spatio-temporal relation is unambiguously defined as the 4-tuple $<C\_t, X\_p, Y\_p, C\_s >$.

Another weakness in Papadias'es scheme is in the definition of nearness relation in terms of a constant δ. The regions (a-δ,a) and (b,b+δ) are considered to be the neighborhood of [a,b]. This approach is unsatisfactory, since the definition of the constant δ is arbitrary and the nearness should not have a sharp cutoff and a-δ or b+δ. We solve this problem by introducing fuzzy membership functions in place of the binary intersection variables.

The membership function models the relation between intervals in a soft parametric fashion. For example consider the encoding of the fourth variable w for the temporal relation *followedBy* as shown in figure 2. The three different events [a, b], [a1, b1] and [a2, b2] are all after the event [x, y] but due to the membership function defined, the variable will have a very high value for [a1, b1] qualifying it for the relation *followedBy*, where as the event [a3, b3] will have a very low value and will not qualify.

Therefore in general, we can define temporal relations in 1D to be a 5-tuple $C_t = < t, u, v, w, x >$ each of which represents the membership function of the regions of intersection. The scheme of Papadias [2] is a special case of our scheme.

To encode the above primitives in M-OWL we propose a *STOp* class (Spatio Temporal Operator) which can have one or more of the components $< hasCs >, < hasXp >, < hasYp >, < hasCt >$. Each of them is a datatype property having the range as a string. The string gives the values of the parameters C_s, X_p, Y_p and C_t for any given spatio-temporal relation. Each component has a again five values $< t >, < u >, < v >, < w >$ and $< x >$, where each component specifies the membership function associated with each variable. The membership functions can be specified from a library of predefined functions and the parameters of the function can be specified in the definition. The function in figure 2 can be represented as

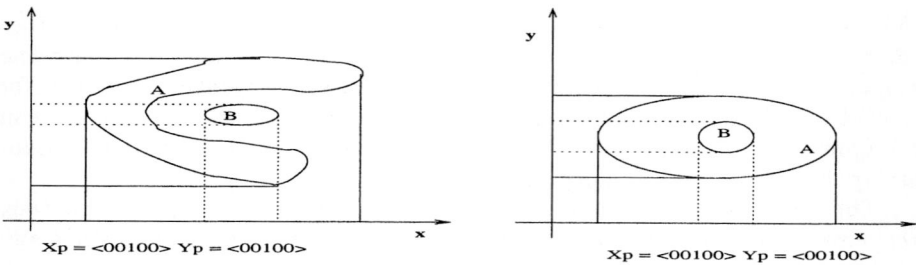

Fig. 1. Ambiguity due to concave regions

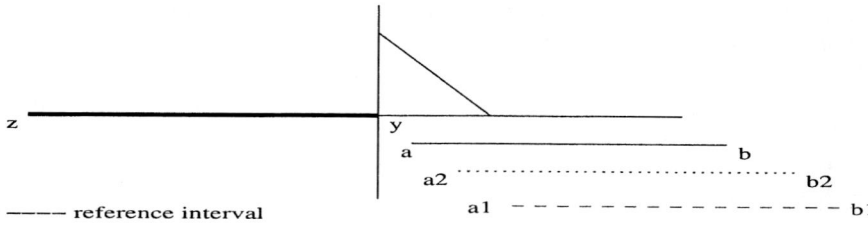

Fig. 2. Encoding a fuzzy temporal relation. The membership function is also shown.

a Piece-wise linear model as $<(-\infty\ 0),(0\ 0),(\ 0\ 1),(0.5\ 0.5),(1\ 0),(+\infty\ 0)>$. Not all of the components are required depending upon the relation as purely spatial or purely temporal or in general spatio-temporal. It is not necessary to specify all the membership functions for every relation.

4 Reasoning for Description Generation of Abstract Concepts

We define two more attributes for relations "propagate" and "hierarchy" as follows:

- **Hierarchy:** A relation between two concepts A and B has an attribute hierarchy true if an example of B is an example of A i.e B is a subconcept of A.
- **Propagate:** A relation between two concepts A and B has propagate true if the media features of A are inherited by B independent of the concept hierarchy.

With the above definitions, we propose a solution of the unique problem of Concept Description Generation. This involves the construction of media based description of concepts, via propagation and inheritance of media examples in an Observation Model. The steps for construction of OM from a M-OWL encoding and generating a description are

1. Every concept "C" is mapped to a node in the OM.
2. Every Property "P" with hierarchy true and with domain "D" and range "R"is mapped to a node in the translated network which has the set of individuals in the domain who have this property "P" .
3. Every property node has one more node as its child which has the individuals of the global range of the property.
4. Every spatio temporal relation is translated to a intermediate node between the composite concept and the sub concepts. It has a child node which denotes the operator defined for that property. The above rules construct an OM from any M-OWL encoding.
5. Now to generate a description of the composite concept we start with the media examples of the leaf nodes and transfer them *upwards* until we get a spatio-temporal node.
6. At a spatio temporal node the examples of individual concepts are composed according to the relation and then the composed example is transferred upwards.
7. The above step is repeated for each spatio temporal node until we reach the composite concept.

For the example concept of "goalScore" in section 2 the M-OWL encoding given in appendix 5. Following the rules mentioned above we get the OM shown in figure 3.The "STOp" nodes represent the operator of the spatio temporal relation. Note that the operator does not tell us any specific positioning of the examples of "goal" and "goalPost". As long as the positions are in accordance of the operator this will be an example of "goalScore" With this we can construct many such examples of the concept "goalScore". Similar scheme can be used for construction OM of an abstract concept in terms of media properties.

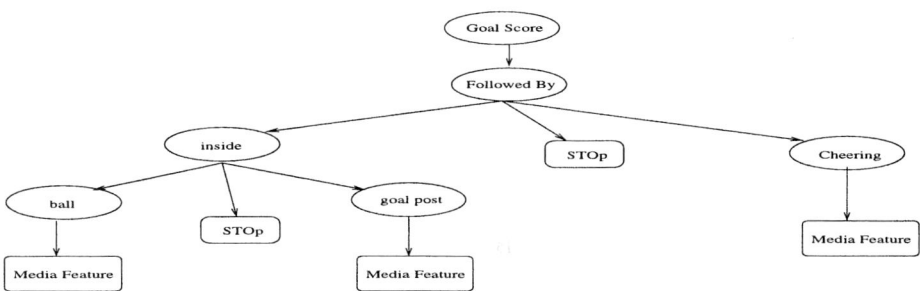

Fig. 3. Observation Model of spatio temporal relations

For the problem of concept recognition and retrieval we construct the propagate graph with all propagate relations and an OM is constructed as per the rules mentioned above.The conditional probabilities specified between concepts are included and the OM is now a belief network. A belief network based retrieval application with media features has been discussed in [4].

5 Conclusion

The above scheme of representing Spatio Temporal Relations and combining them with propagate and hierarchy gives a flexible way to deal with problems like concept description and concept recognition in in Multimedia Ontologies. We are working on other issues like – what is the interaction between an OWL ontology and a multimedia ontology and to what extent they can work together and to what extent Description Logic based inferencing of OWL can be applied to a multimedia ontology.

Acknowledgements. This work has been supported by the grant for DST project "E-Video: Video Information Processing with Enhanced Functionality."

References

1. H. Ghosh, S. Chaudhury, K. Kashyap, and B. Maiti, *Ontologies in Context of Information Systems*, ch. Ontology Specification and Integration for Multimedia Applications. Kluwer Press (Accepted for Publication).
2. Papadias, "Approximate spatio temporal retrieval," *ACM Transactions on Information Systems*, vol. 19, pp. 53–96, January 2001.
3. Cohn, "Qualitative spatial representation and reasoning with the region connected calculus," *GeoInformatica*, vol. 1, pp. 1–44, 1997.
4. S. Chaudhury and H. Ghosh, "Distributed and reactive query planning in RMAGIC:An agent based multimedia retrieval system," *IEEE Transactions on Knowledge and Data Engineering*, vol. 16, pp. 1082–1095, September 2004.

Appendix: M-OWL Encoding for Goalscore

```
<mowl:STOp rdf:ID="followedBy">
  <hasCt> <w>-INF 0 0 1 0.5 0.5 1 0 INF 0</w> </hasCt>
</mowl:STOp>
<mowl:STOP rdf:ID="inside">
  <hasXp><v>-INF 0 0 0 0.5 0.5 1 1 3 1 3.5 0.5 4 0 INF 0</v></hasXp>
  <hasYp><v>-INF 0 0 0 0.5 0.5 1 1 3 1 3.5 0.5 4 0 INF 0</v></hasYp>
</mowl:STOp>
<mowl:MediaFeature rdf:ID="ballShape">
  <Mpeg7: ..  ... a shape descriptor for ball shape </Mpeg7:..
</mowl:MediaFeature>
<mowl:MediaFeature rdf:ID="goalPostShape">
  <Mpeg7: ..  ... a shape descriptor for goal post shape </Mpeg7:..
</mowl:MediaFeature>
<mowl:MediaFeature rdf:ID="audioPatternForCheering">
  <Mpeg7: ..  ... an audio descriptor for cheering </Mpeg7:..
</mowl:MediaFeature>
<owl:Class rdf:ID="ball">
  <hasMediaFeature>ballShape</hasMediaFeature>
</owl:Class>
<owl:Class rdf:ID="goalPost">
  <hasMediaFeature>goalPostShape</hasMediaFeature>
</owl:Class>
<owl:Class rdf:ID="cheering">
  <hasMediaFeature>audioPatternForCheering</hasMediaFeature>
</owl:Class>
<owl:Class rdf:ID="goalScore">
  <mowl:followedBy rdf:parseType="Collection">
    <OWL:Class rdf:about="cheering"/>
    <mowl:inside rdf:parseType="Collection">
      <owl:Class rdf:about="goalPost"/>
      <owl:Class rdf:about="ball"/>
    </mowl:inside>
  </mowl:followedBy>
</owl:Class>
```

Motion Estimation of Elastic Articulated Objects from Image Points and Contours

Hailang Pan, Yuncai Liu, and Lei Shi

Institute of Image Processing and Pattern Recognition,
Shanghai Jiao Tong University, P.R. China 200030
{panhailang, whomliu, sl0030322014}@sjtu.edu.cn

Abstract. This paper presents two new methods of elastic articulated objects modeling and motion estimation based on a new revolving conic surface. The deformation of human body surfaces can be represented by adjusting only one or two deformation parameters for each limb. Then, the 3D deformation and motion parameters are estimated by corresponding 2D image points and contours from a sequences of stereo images.

1 Introduction

Elastic articulated objects are the combination of articulated objects and nonrigid objects. Human body is a typical elastic articulated objects. In the past researches, a number of method for human deformable body modeling have been proposed. Plankers[1] developed a framework for 3D shape and motion recovery of articulated deformable objects. Smooth implicit surfaces, known as metaballs, are attached to an articulated skeleton of the human body and are arranged in an anatomically-based approximation. Sminchisescu [2] built a human body model which consists of kinematic 'skeletons', covered by 'flesh' built from superquadric ellipsoids. A typical model has 9 deformable shape parameters for each body part. Apuzzo[3] presents simplified Model of a Limb. Only three ellipsoidal metaballs are attached to each limb skeleton. Each limb has twelve deformation parameters.

Our research focuses on two major points: 3D human body modeling and its parameters determination from images. The proposed human limb model is composed of two layers: a skeleton layer and a body surface layer. The body surface layer is expressed by revolving conic surfaces. We can deform the body surface layer during animation by adjusting only one or two deformation parameters for each human limb. 3D human arm parameters determination includes the skeleton motion parameters estimation and the deformable surfaces deformation parameters determination.

2 Establishment of Revolving Conic Surfaces and Human Skeleton

A 3D conic curve can be obtained by intersecting a conic surface with a plane that does not go through the vertex of the conic surface or by intersecting two conic surfaces. Consequently, a 3D conic curve S can be specified by the system of equations

$$\begin{cases} f_1(x_s, y_s, z_s) = 0 \\ f_2(x_s, y_s, z_s) = 0 \end{cases} \quad (1)$$

Where the equation $f_1(x_S,y_S,z_S)$ is a 3D conic surface and the equation $f_2(x_S,y_S,z_S)$ is a 3D plane or a 3D conic surface.

See Fig. 1, let $P_0=(x_0, y_0, z_0)$ be a point on the 3D straight line L which can represents the skeleton of a limb. Let e (m,n,p) be a non-zero vector parallel to the straight line L, then the straight line L has the canonical equation of the form

$$\frac{x-x_0}{m} = \frac{y-y_0}{n} = \frac{z-z_0}{p} = t \quad (2)$$

Let the curve S be a 3D conic curve. We can obtain a revolving conic surface by revolving the 3D conic curve S around the 3D straight line L. A revolving conic surface can represent the human body surface of a limb. It is defined as follows: Let $P(x,y,z)$ be a arbitrary point on the revolving conic surface. Let the plane U, passing through the point P and perpendicular to the straight line L. The point $P_S(x_S,y_S,z_S)$ is the intersection of the plane U and the conic curve S. The point $O(x_L,y_L,z_L)$ is the intersection of the plane U and the straight line L. Then the plane U, passing through the point P, P_S, O and perpendicular to the straight line L, has the equation of the form

$$m(x-x_S)+n(y-y_S)+p(z-z_S)=0 \quad (3)$$

The points P, P_S, O satisfy the relation $\overline{PO} = \overline{P_SO}$, namely

$$(x-x_L)^2+(y-y_L)^2+(z-y_L)^2 = (x_S-x_L)^2+(y_S-y_L)^2+(z_S-z_L)^2 \quad (4)$$

Since the point $P_S(x_S,y_S,z_S)$ lies on the conic curve S, its coordinates satisfy the equation (1). Hence, the system of equations (1),(3),(4) are the revolving conic surface.

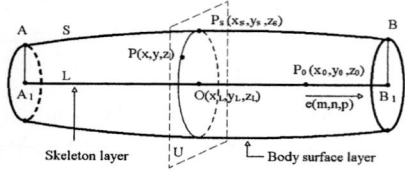
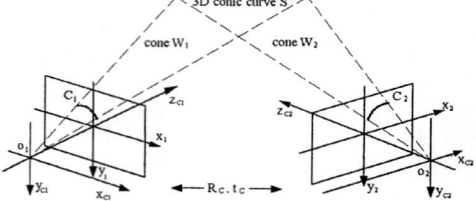

Fig. 1. 3D Revolving conic surface

Fig. 2. Stereo coordinate system of a 3D conic curve

The human skeleton system is treated as a series of jointed links(segments), which can be modeled as a articulated body. We describe the body as a stick model consisting of a set of fifteen joints (plus the head) connected by fourteen body segments [4].

3 Human Arm Modeling and Its Parameters Determination

3.1 Modeling from Image Points and Its Deformation Parameters Determination

A 3D conic curve S can be specified by the system of equations

$$\begin{cases} f_1(x_S, y_S, z_S) = (a_0+a_1x_S+a_2y_S+a_3z_S)(b_0+b_1x_S+b_2y_S+b_3z_S) - \rho(u_0+u_1x_S+u_2y_S+u_3z_S)^2 = 0 \\ f_2(x_S, y_S, z_S) = f_{ABC}(x_S, y_S, z_S) = a \cdot x_S + b \cdot y_S + c \cdot z_S + d = 0 \end{cases} \quad (5)$$

The first equation is a 3D conic surface. The second equation is a plane passing through the vertices A, B, C. Hence, the system of equations (3),(4),(5) are a revolving conic surface, which can represent deformable human body surface.

The input of our system of equations is (x,y,z), 3D coordinate of one arbitrary feature point on the revolving conic surface. The expected output is the parameter ρ that describes the model's deformation. Hence the deformation of one limb can also be determined with three feature points, two of them are points A, B and the third is a arbitrary point on the deformable surface. This is also a nonlinear system of equations, which can be solved by the Levenberg-Marquardt nonlinear least squares.

3.2 Modeling from Contours and Its Deformation Parameters Determination

The geometry of the stereo is shown in Fig. 2. Suppose there is a 3D conic curve S in space. Its two projections on two images are represented by two quadratic form C_1 and C_2 [5]:

$$C_i(x_i, y_i) = X_i^T Q_i X_i = 0 \quad i = 1,2 \tag{6}$$

where $X_i=[x_i,y_i,1]^T$. (x_i,y_i) are the 2D coordinates in two images.

Let $X_w=[x_w,y_w,z_w,1]^T$. (x_w,y_w,z_w) is a point in the world coordinate system. Then X_i and X_w are related to each other through the following equation:

$$z_{ci} X_i = M_i X_w \tag{7}$$

Substituting the equation (7) into the equation (6), we obtain the representations of the two cones W_1 and W_2 passing through the 2D conic curve C_1(or C_2) and the camera center o_1(or o_2):

$$\begin{cases} W_1(x_w, y_w, z_w) = X_w^T M_1^T Q_1 M_1 X_w = 0 \\ W_2(x_w, y_w, z_w) = X_w^T M_2^T Q_2 M_2 X_w = 0 \end{cases} \tag{8}$$

The 3D conic curve S in space is the intersection curve of two cones W_1 and W_2. Hence, the system of equations (3),(4),(8) are a revolving conic surface, which can represent deformable human body surface.

We fit one 2D conic curve to the contour of each limb in left or right images. We directly minimize the implicit form of a 2D conic curve to determine the best values of the deformation paramete ρ. We can get two deformation parameters $\rho_{i\text{-}left}$ and $\rho_{i\text{-}right}$ of each limb at a time.

3.3 Motion Parameters Estimation of Human Skeleton

We pick up the centers of the circles that pass through the vertices of the conic curve and are tangent to the boundary of each limb. We regard the points, lying on the sticks that linking these centers, as the skeleton points. The motion of one limb can be estimated with only three skeleton points correspondences[6].

4 Experiment Results

The controlled scenes are acquired by using a stereoscopic vision system. In the experiment of modeling from image points, six paper markers have been sticked on the body surfaces of the arm, three on the upper arm and three on the lower arm. On each limb, we detect three paper markers. The 3D coordinates of these feature points, acquired from the image planes, are used as the input data for determining the deformation parameters of two limbs. The estimated results are listed in Table 1 that describe the model's deformation. ρ_1 and ρ_2 are the estimated deformation parameters of the two limbs respectively. In the experiment of modeling from image contours, the human arm is nicely distinguishable against the simpler background using edge detection. The estimated results are listed in Table 2 that describe the model's deformation. Fig. 3 depicts the movement of human arm. We use OpenGL code to visualize the recovered 3D model.

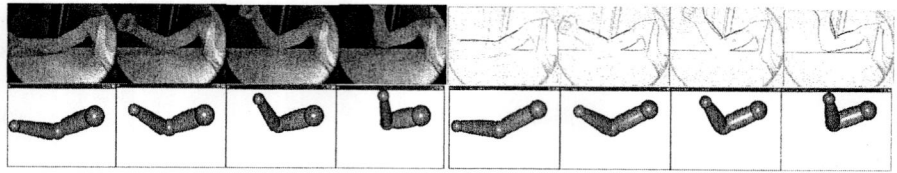

Fig. 3. Left first row: original images of left camera. Left second row: estimated 3D models from image points. Right first row: corresponding target contours and conic curve fitting results. Right second row: estimated 3D model from image contours.

Table 1. Estimated deformation parameters of modeling from image points

deformation parameter	Frame1	Frame2	Frame3	Frame4
ρ_1	0.5639	0.7995	1.5288	2.3358
ρ_2	0.0727	0.1775	0.0736	0.0052

Table 2. Estimated deformation parameters of modeling from image contours

Deformation parameter		Frame1	Frame2	Frame3	Frame4
ρ_{1left}	(upper arm)	81.2541	65.7300	30.2082	12.5882
ρ_{1right}	(upper arm)	-41.3898	-16.4795	-9.7585	-0.2843
ρ_{2left}	(lower arm)	-343.2955	-189.1445	-0.9332	-0.2642
ρ_{2right}	(lower arm)	25.0255	39.0449	18.7115	14.5475

5 Conclusion

We have presented two new methods of elastic articulated objects (human bodies) modeling based on a new revolving conic surface. Our experiments have demonstrated that our model can express the deformation of human body surfaces properly.

References

1. Ralf Plankers and Pascal Fua. Articulated Soft Objects for Multiview Shape and Motion Capture. IEEE Transaction on PAMI, 2003, 25 (9): 1182 ~ 1187.
2. ESTIMATION ALGORITHMS FOR AMBIGUOUS VISUAL MODELS (C.Sminchisescu), Doctoral Thesis, INRIA, July 2002.
3. D'Apuzzo N, Plänkers R, Gruen A, Fua F and Thalmann D, Modelling Human Bodies from Video Sequences, Proc. Electronic Imaging1999, San Jose, California, January.

4. Xiaoyun Zhang, Yuncai Liu and TS Huang. "Articulated Joint Estimation from Motion Using Two Monocular Images", Pattern Recognition Letters 25(10): 1097-1106, 2004.
5. Songde MA.Conics-Based Stereo, Motion Estimation, and Pose Determination. Intern. J. Computer Vision, Vol. 10, No.1, 1993.
6. Xiaoyun Zhang, Yuncai Liu and TS Huang. " Motion Estimation of Articulated Objects from Perspective Views", LNCS, Vol. 2492, pp.165-176 ,2002 .

Parsing News Video Using Integrated Audio-Video Features

S. Kalyan Krishna, Raghav Subbarao, Santanu Chaudhury[1], and Arun Kumar[2]

[1] Department of Electrical Engg., I.I.T,
New Delhi-110016, India
santanuc@ee.iitd.ac.in
[2] Centre for Applied Research in Electronics, I.I.T,
New Delhi-110016, India
arunkm@care.iitd.ac.in

Abstract. In this paper we have proposed a scheme for parsing News video sequences into their semantic components using integrated aural and visual features. We have explored use of the Token Passing Algorithm with HMM for simultaneous segmentation and characterization of the components. Experimentation with about 100 sequences have shown impressive results.

1 Introduction

Content of video sequences like News can be effectively analysed by considering both audio and video cues. For example, field reports in a News Video can not be recognised as an indivisible semantic component without the audio cue as, in general, it consists of multiple shots and scenes. In this paper, we propose a scheme that combines aural and visual cues for parsing a News video sequence into semantic components. This scheme will be useful for development of applications such as News Archival Systems, News-on-Demand Systems, etc.

Some work has been done in the past for interpretation of video sequences by integrating audio and video features. The approach proposed in [1] uses some audio properties along with color and motion information to detect scene and shot breaks. Adams et al. [2] have focused on semantic classification through the identification of meaningful intermediate-level semantic components using both audio and video features. In [3], a method is presented for analysis of News videos by sequentially identifying and segmenting semantic components by exploiting both aural and visual features. A scheme for classification of video scene breaks using both audio and visual features has been suggested in [4]. Dagtas and Abdel-Mottaleb [5] have presented a technique for detecting highlights in a multimedia content using multi-modal features. Another approach for using audio and video features has been suggested in [7].

The method we propose here is different from the previous approaches in many ways. In this approach we have considered a novel way of segmenting the sequence via recognition of its components through deferred decisions for exploiting contextual information. Use of token passing algorithm with HMM model for this purpose is a novel and useful contribution of this work. Further, it combines audio and video features in an integrated fashion instead of using independent decisions based on individual features. Another advantage of our scheme is its ability to handle large intra-class variations due to the use of a suitable set of stable features and their representation as mixture of Gaussians.

2 News Video Parsing Problem

We address the problem of parsing a News Video sequence into a given set of semantic components with no prior knowledge about the shots in the video sequence.The semantic classes that we have identified and are attempting to detect in a News Video sequence are:

1. Newsroom clips which consist of a News reader presenting News in a studio.
2. Field Report clips which consist of media personnel reporting from the field.
3. Field Interviews / Analysis clips which consist of reporters conducting an interview in the field, persons in the field being interviewed from the Newsroom, or speeches being made in the field.
4. Studio Room Interview / Analysis clips which consist of persons being interviewed by the News reader in the studio, panel discussions etc.
5. Headlines clips n which the News reader deals with multiple news item in brief.

On completion of the parsing process, the complete news sequence is segmented into these semantic components.

3 Feature Description and Extraction

3.1 Visual Features

Field Reports in News Videos have multiple and quick shot breaks whereas News Reader sequences are fairly static and have none or very few shot breaks. Features capturing information about shot breaks in the video sequence provide useful cues for parsing. We have used colour Histogram intersection between consecutive frames for capturing global change in colour distribution. For capturing local changes we have used L1 norm of the image difference between two consecutive frames

Relative motion in the scene is an important visual feature. In News reader and interview components, for example, the motion is less and is localized to small regions whereas in Field Reports, motion is significant and it is not localised. We have used bin-count of histogram of optic flow values as features. In our implementation we used the Lucas-Kanade algorithm for computing optic flow. We have also considered spatial distribution of motion by counting the number of of pixels with high optic flow value in each cell of a 7x7 grid overlaid on the frame.

Another visual cue that characterizes video sequences is the layout of the scene. The layout of News Reader scenes is stable and different from that of different Newsroom scenes or Interview scenes. In Field Reports and Headlines on the other hand the visual layout does not remain constant. We have used wavelet based layout features proposed in [6]. This scheme uses Daubechies Wavelets. We have used variance of wavelet coefficients at different levels as elements of feature vector. Use of layout based features for interpretation of News video has not been explored in the past.

3.2 Audio Features

The common audio scenarios found in news videos are silence, speech, music, environmental sounds and combinations of the latter three. For example, News reader and interview sequences in most News videos consist of pure speech. Field reports on the other hand contain a fair amount of noise due to environmental sounds. Headlines are often accompanied by music. Further, change in the speaker in videos provide a very powerful evidence for transition points and context of the content. Interview sequences, for example, consist of multiple speaker transitions as against News Reader clips which are monologues. Motivated by the above observations, we use statistics of Short Time Energy, Short Time Zero Crossing Rate and Short Time Fundamental Frequency to differentiate between different scenarios. In addition we capture speaker transitions by extracting Short Time Cepstral Coefficients.

3.3 Feature Vector Construction

Following the extraction of audio and visual features we use feature fusion to integrate the two to form one combined audio visual feature vector. The audio features (with the exception of short time fundamental frequency) are produced at the rate of 1 sample / sec. whereas video features are obtained at 25 samples / sec. In order to bring them both to the same temporal scale we repeat our audio features 25 times in every second and then combine them with the visual features. This gives us a feature vector that is generated at the rate of 25 samples / sec. Such a feature vector combines both the audio as well as the visual cues in the video sequence while taking into account their interdependence.

4 Parsing Scheme

The problem of parsing a News Video sequence into a given set of semantic components with no prior knowledge of the location of the breaks between them is very similar to a string parsing problem in continuous speech recognition. Taking into account the success of the Hidden Markov Model paradigm for this problem we decided to use an HMM based classifier for the semantic characterization of News videos.

4.1 HMM Model

A continuous HMM is determined by three groups of parameters: the state transition probability, the observation symbol probability $B = \{b_j(k)\}$; and the initial state distribution. In our case the observations are the feature vectors. We have modelled B as a mixture of Gaussian distribution with a diagonal covariance matrix. Therefore, we assume that the different elements of the feature vector are uncorrelated. We have used EM based approach for estimating Gaussians. The topology of a general HMM used for the semantic characterization is shown in figure 1. As can be seen the first and the last states are assumed to be *non-emitting* to facilitate embedded re-estimation of the HMMs. HMM's corresponding to each class of semantic components are first trained using Baum-Welch algorithm using example sequences. After training, we perform embedded re-estimation. For each training sequence, based purely on the sequence of labels (i.e. ignoring all boundary information) a composite HMM spanning the entire sequence is built. This HMM is retrained using sample sequences.

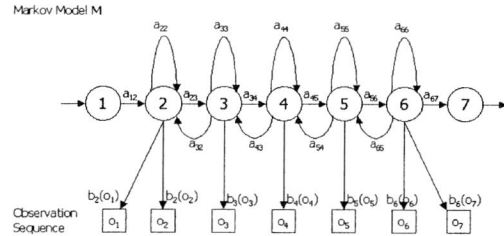

Fig. 1. HMM Generation Model

4.2 Description of the Parsing Algorithm

For a sequence with N frames every path which passes through N emitting states forms a potential transcription of the video sequence. Each of these paths has an associated log-probability which is obtained by adding the log probabilities of the transitions between the consecutive states and the log probability of each emitting state generating the corresponding observation vector. The decoding can now be viewed as the process of finding the path with the highest log probability. We use a variation of the standard Viterbi Algorithm known as the *Token Passing Algorithm* to achieve this.

5 Experimentation and Results

Experiments were conducted on a database consisting of a 100 news video clips (of duration one to three minutes) from 4 News channels broadcasting News in different languages (including BBC and CNN). We have experimentally determined the optimal HMM model for identification of each semantic component.

Using leave-one-out strategy we have obtained ROC curves for each semantic class by changing the number of nodes in the HMM model and obtained optimal configuration for HMMs. We have found that for optimal performance Newsroom HMM require 9 states, Field Report and Field Interview / Analysis HMMs require 10 states and the Headline HMM require 8 states.

Fig. 2. An example News Video sequence. The frames have been extracted from different semantic components to show the overall structure of the clip.

The figure 2 shows an example News Video sequence. Manual annotation for this News Video sequence (in terms of frame numbers) was as follows: 0 - 135: NEWSROOM; 136 - 1256: FIELD INTERVIEW; 1257 - 1690: NEWSROOM; 1691 - 3159: HEADLINE; and 3160 - 4010: NEWSROOM. The machine annotation produced by our system was: 0 - 132: NEWSROOM - 4501.437500; 133 - 1176 FIELD INTERVIEW - 35901.585938; 1177 - 1406 FIELD REPORT- 3241.435791; 1407 - 1690 NEWSROOM - 12143.261719; 1691 - 3251 HEADLINE - 49149.359375;and 3252 - 4010 NEWSROOM - 22067.953125. (The numbers on the side of each segment transcription represent the log probability of the transcription). As can be seen, that using our approach majority of the semantic components have been correctly detected.

We have validated our approach by carrying out leave-one-out test with the complete database. The results have been tabulated in the form of a Confusion Matrix (see table 1). We have found the approach to work well.

Table 1. Confusion Matrix (indicates frame based statistics); N.R: News reader, F.I: field interview, Int.: interview, Hdln: Headline

	N.R	Field	F.I	Int.	Hdln
N.R	87.90%	3.44%	3.14%	3.70%	1.83%
Field	5.83%	83.08%	7.40%	0.86%	2.83%
F.I	7.34%	8.00%	80.88%	2.62%	1.17%
Int.	0.69%	0.22%	2.46%	96.31%	0.32%
Hdline	4.74%	2.55%	4.32%	0%	88.38%

6 Conclusion

In this paper, we have presented a scheme for parsing News video using a combination of audio and video features. Since we have used mixture of Gaussians to handle variations in feature values and token passing algorithm for transcription enabling segmentation of the sequence by taking into account complete temporal context, we have obtained good classification results. Similar approach can be used for parsing other types of video sequences.

Achnowledgements

This work has been supported by the grant for DST project "E-Video: Video Information Processing with Enhanced Functionality."

References

1. Jincheng Huang, Zhu Liu and Yao Wang, "Integration of Audio and Visual Information for Content-based Video Segmentation," *Proc. of IEEE International Conference on Image Processing (ICIP'98)*, Invited Paper on "Content-based Video Search and Retrieval", Vol. 3, pp. 526 - 530, Chicago, IL, Oct. 4-7, 1998.
2. W.H. Adams, G. Iyengar, C.Y. Lin, M. R. Naphade, C. Neti,H. J. Nock, and J.R. Smith, "Semantic Indexing of Multimedia using Audio, Text and Visual Cues," EURASIP J. Appl. Signal Processing, pp. 170-185, 2003.
3. Qian Huang, Zhu Liu, Aaron Rosenberg, David Gibbon and Behzad Shahraray "Automated Generation of News Content Hierarchy By Integrating Audio, Video, and Text Information," *Proceedings of the International Conference on Acoustics, Speech, and Signal Processing*, 1999.
4. J. Huang, Z. Liu, and Y. Wang, "Joint Video Scene Segmentation and Classification based on Hidden Markov Model," *IEEE International Conference on Multimedia and Expo (ICME2000)*, August 2000, New York.
5. S. Dagtas, Mohamed Abdel-Mottaleb,"Multimodal detection of Highlights for Multimedia Content", Multimedia Systems, Vol. 9, pp. 586-593, 2004.
6. Wang J.Z., Wiederhold G., Firschein O., Wei Xin S., 'Content Based Image Indexing and Searching using Daubechies Wavelets', Digital Library (1997), Pg. 311-328.
7. Sofia Tsekeridou, Ioannis Pitas, "Content-based video parsing and indexing based on Audio-visual interaction", IEEE transactions on circuits and systems for video technology, vol. 11, no. 4, April 2001.

A Hybrid Data and Space Partitioning Technique for Similarity Queries on Bounded Clusters*

Piyush K. Bhunre[1], C. A. Murthy[2], Arijit Bishnu[3],
Bhargab B. Bhattacharya[2], and Malay K. Kundu[2]

[1] National University of Singapore,
3 Science Drive 2, Singapore 117543
[2] Indian Statistical Institute,
203, B. T. Road, Kolkata - 700108, India
[3] Indian Institute of Technology,
Kharagpur, Kharagpur - 721302, India

Abstract. In this paper, a new method for generating size-bounded clusters is proposed such that the cardinality of each cluster is less than or equal to a pre-specified value. First, set estimation techniques coupled with Rectangular Intersection Graphs are used to generate adaptive clusters. Then, the size-bounded clusters are obtained by using space partitioning techniques. The clusters can be indexed by a Kd-tree like structure for similarity queries. The proposed method is likely to find applications to Content Based Image Retrieval (CBIR).

1 Introduction

In a CBIR system, the images are indexed as points in the multidimensional feature space (mostly Euclidean space). Given a query image, the same features are extracted to perform a similarity query that basically is a search for the nearest neighbour(s) of the query point, or a range search around the query point in an Euclidean space [1]. Most of the nearest neighbor (NN) search techniques try to reduce the search time by using multidimensional indexing techniques. Multidimensional data structures can be classified as (i) *space partitioning* (e.g. Kd-tree and K-D-B tree) based techniques and (ii) *data partitioning* (e.g. R tree, R^+ tree, R^* tree, SS tree, and SR tree) based techniques [2]. The *space partitioning* techniques recursively partition the entire space into mutually disjoint sub-spaces. In *data partitioning* based index structures, the data points at a particular level are obtained by clustering them in the sibling nodes using different bounding regions like rectangular hyperbox, sphere, etc. For a survey on these, see [2]. Unlike the *data partitioning* index structure, range query on the multidimensional space using a *space partitioning* index structure like Kd-tree, requires only a single check at each node corresponding to the splitting dimension. Apparently these

---

* This work was supported in part by a grant from Intel Corp., USA (PO #CAC042717000).

methods offer logarithmic search time, but may be worse than linear search if $d > \log n$[3]. For all the above techniques, the problem increases manifold when the secondary memory, that is inherently non-random access, comes into play owing to huge image databases. On the other hand, clustering techniques have also been in use for image retrieval. Generally, clustering algorithms do not have any control over the number of points in a cluster. In addition, indexing clusters of arbitrary shape and size remains a problem. For such clusters spread over many disk pages, search time will be very high.

To address the above issues, we propose a method that generates clusters of bounded size (the size is an input to our method), which then can be indexed using a two-level multidimensional data structure for retrieval. We use set estimation techniques based on the data distribution to form a bounding box around each data point and then use rectangular intersection graphs to find clusters. Next, we use space partitioning techniques to further sub-divide the clusters so that the size of each cluster is less than the bounding size specified. This space partitioning technique is also used for indexing these bounded-size clusters.

2 Set Estimation and Clustering

In set estimation problem [4], the parameter to be estimated is a set. The cluster $\alpha (\subset \mathbb{R}^d)$, which is unknown is to be estimated. Below is the definition of the set of parameter $\mathcal{A}$ and a probability measure P_α on $\alpha \in \mathcal{A}$.

Definition 1. *[5,6]* $\mathcal{A} = \{\alpha : \alpha \subseteq \mathbb{R}^d, \alpha \text{ is path connected, compact, } cl(int(\alpha)) = \alpha \text{ and } \partial \alpha \text{ consists of finitely many analytic arcs } \}$ *Here cl represents "closure", int represents "interior" and $\partial \alpha$ represents the boundary of α and is defined as* $\alpha \cap cl(\alpha^c)$.

Definition 2. *[6] The properties of P_α are as follows: (i) $P_\alpha(\alpha^c) = 0$, (ii) $P_\alpha(\partial \alpha) = 0$; (iii) $P_\alpha(A \cap \alpha) > 0$, $\forall$ open set $A \subseteq \mathbb{R}^d$ with $A \cap \alpha \neq \phi$, and (iv) there exists a function $f : \mathbb{R}^d \to \mathbb{R}^+$ such that $P_\alpha(A) = \int_A f d\mu$, $\forall$ subset A in $\mathbb{R}^d$.*

Based on the above definition of the probability measure, we have the following definition for a consistent estimate of α.

Definition 3. *Let $X_1, X_2, \cdots, X_n$ be a random sample from P_α. Then α_n obtained from X_i's is said to be a consistent estimate of α if*

$$\lim_{n \to \infty} E_{P_\alpha}(\mu(\alpha_n \Delta \alpha)) = 0 \qquad (1)$$

where, μ is a Lebesgue measure in $\mathbb{R}^d$ and Δ denotes symmetric difference and E denotes expectation [4].

2.1 Estimation of α

In set estimation, depending on the sample points, we estimate the path connected set from which the sample points have come. We can estimate α by α_n

in the following way as proposed in [4,6]. Let d denote the dimension of the data. Let $\delta^n = (\delta_{n1}, \delta_{n2}, \cdots, \delta_{nd})^t \in \mathbb{R}^d$ with $\delta_{nj} > 0$, $\forall j$ such that the following conditions are met:

Condition 1. *(i)* $\delta_{nj} \to 0$*; and (ii)* $n \prod_{j=1}^{j=d} \delta_{nj} \to \infty$ *as* $n \to \infty$.

Define $A_i = \{X \in \mathbb{R}^d : |x_{ij} - x_j| \leq \delta_{nj}, \forall j = 1, 2, \cdots, d\}$, $\forall i = 1, 2, \cdots, n$. Then, form α_n as a union of connected subsets as $\alpha_n = \bigcup_{i=1}^{i=n} A_i$. It may be noted that α_n is taken as the union of closed axis-parallel hyper-rectangular neighborhoods around each sample point X_i. We now need to choose a suitable neighborhood so that Condition 1 and the consistency condition in Equation 1 are satisfied.

2.2 Choice of the Neighborhood δ_{nj}

We select the δ^n-neighborhood of the sample points as follows: the ranges $R_j = Max\{x_{ij}\}_{i=1}^{i=n} - Min\{x_{ij}\}_{i=1}^{i=n}$ (where x_{ij} is the jth component of X_i) for each of the components of the sample points are found out. Then, we choose each δ_{nj} as $\delta_{nj} = \frac{R_j}{n^{\frac{1}{2d}}}$, $\forall j = 1, 2, \ldots, d$.

Lemma 1. $\delta_{nj} = \frac{R_j}{n^{\frac{1}{2d}}}$, $\forall j = 1, 2, \ldots, d$*, satisfies Condition 1.*

Proof. $\lim_{n \to \infty} \delta_{nj} = \lim_{n \to \infty} \frac{R_j}{n^{\frac{1}{2d}}} = 0$. Also, $\lim_{n \to \infty} n \prod_{j=1}^{j=d} \delta_{nj} = \lim_{n \to \infty} \sqrt{n} \prod_{j=1}^{j=d} R_j = \infty$.

For a proof of the consistency property (see Equation 1 in Definition 3) of the above δ^n, see [6]. From the above discussions, we have the following observations.

Observation 1. *Any* $\alpha \in \mathcal{A}$ *is a path connected set by definition 1 and its estimate* $\alpha_n \to \alpha$ *as* $n \to \infty$ *[6] with respect to the consistency condition (1).*

Observation 2. *The set of all samples, which belongs to a connected subset is path connected and forms an estimate of the cluster of the sample point set. Thus, finding an estimate of the clusters of the sample points is same as finding the connected component of* α_n.

2.3 Generation of Clusters Using Rectangular Intersection Graph

The estimated set α_n is a union of some connected subsets with respect to the neighborhoods of the sample points.

Observation 3. *To find a path connected set, we observe that there is a path between two data points if their corresponding hyperrectangles intersect and a cluster is formed by a maximal set of data points such that there is a path between each pair of vertices.*

From the above observation, we can find the path connected set as a cluster by finding the strongly connected component in a Rectangular Intersection Graph (RIG). The RIG, $G = \{V, E\}$ is formed as follows. For each data point X_i, we assign a vertex $v_i \in V$ of the graph. Any two vertices v_i and v_j have an edge e_{ij} between them if the neighborhoods $N_{\delta^n}(X_i)$ and $N_{\delta^n}(X_j)$ intersect, i.e., $N_{\delta^n}(X_i) \cap N_{\delta^n}(X_j) \neq \phi$. Finding the connected component of an RIG having n vertices (i.e. n sample points) takes $O(n \log n)$ time and $O(n)$ space for $d = 2$ [7]. For $d > 2$, forming the RIG is equivalent to finding the k intersecting pairs in a set of n axis-parallel hyper-rectangles in d dimensions and can be done in $O(n\log^{d-1} n + k)$ time using only $O(n)$ space [8]. The RIG thus formed has $O(k)$ edges. We can find its connected component in $O(n+k)$ time [9]. Thus, the overall time needed for finding the cluster according to our method is dominated by the RIG formation and is $O(n\log^{d-1} n + k)$. Thus, from the above discussion, we have the following.

Theorem 1. *The clusters can be found as connected components in an RIG of the consistent estimate α_n of a path connected set α and can be computed in $O(n\log^{d-1} n + k)$ time.*

Remark 1. The clustering algorithm developed here is adaptive. A cluster of any shape (convex and non-convex) can be computed by the above method. The nearest neighbor of a point belongs to the same cluster.

3 Generation of Bounded Clusters and Their Indexing

We now have set estimated clusters, whose size and shape can be arbitrary. To partition the data and index it into small buckets, each of whose size does not exceed a threshold value (T), we use a two-level space partitioning tree.

We first find the set C of cluster centroids, $C = \{C_1, C_2, \ldots, C_m\}$, and the enclosing axis-parallel hyperboxes of each of the m clusters. These hyperboxes may be overlapping. We will now induce a recursive space partitioning, by splitting the centroids along a single dimension at each split, based on the spread of their enclosing hyperboxes. From the spread of the enclosing axis-parallel hyperboxes, we find the dimension j ($\leq d$), along which the data set has the largest elongation. Next, we find the median M_j of the jth component of the cluster centroids. Then, we split C into two subsets $C^{(1)}$ and $C^{(2)}$ such that $C^{(1)}$ contains all cluster centroids whose j^{th} component is less than M_j. Form $C^{(2)}$ as $C^{(2)} = C \setminus C^{(2)}$. To ensure that the splitting plane does not pass through any cluster centroid, we fix the splitting discriminant co-ordinate M_{nj} as the average of the maximum and minimum j^{th} coordinates of $C^{(1)}$ and $C^{(2)}$ respectively. This technique is applied recursively until each subspace has only one cluster centroid left. Thus, we generate a Kd-tree [7] using this method. At each split, we store the discriminant value M_{nj} at the tree node.

After the space partitioning for the cluster centroids ends, we have the first level Kd-tree, and corresponding to each cluster, we have the data points in that cluster. Now, we use the same recursive sub-division and stop when the cardinality of a set of points is just less than T, thus ensuring that the data is partitioned into buckets, each of which has size less than T. Note that, this has also a Kd-tree structure but unlike the level-1 tree, this level-2 tree may

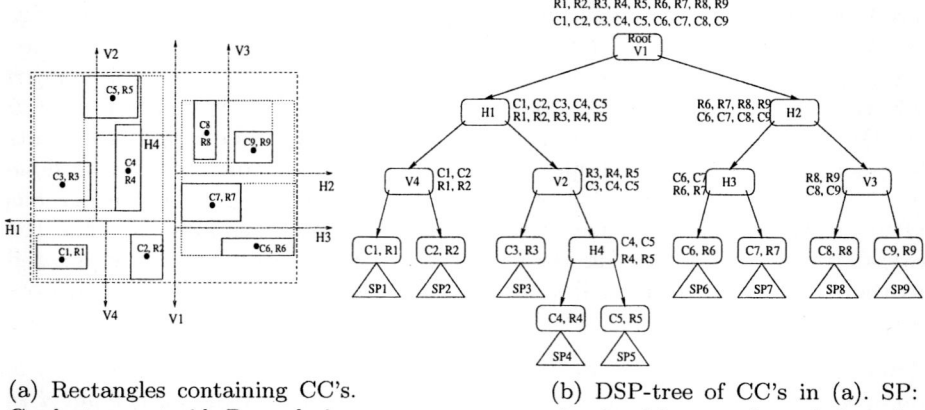

(a) Rectangles containing CC's. C: cluster centroid, R: enclosing boxes, V: vertical cut lines, H: horizontal cut lines

(b) DSP-tree of CC's in (a). SP: the level-2 tree formed by the points in that cluster.

Fig. 1. An example of space partitioning and indexing structure in 2D

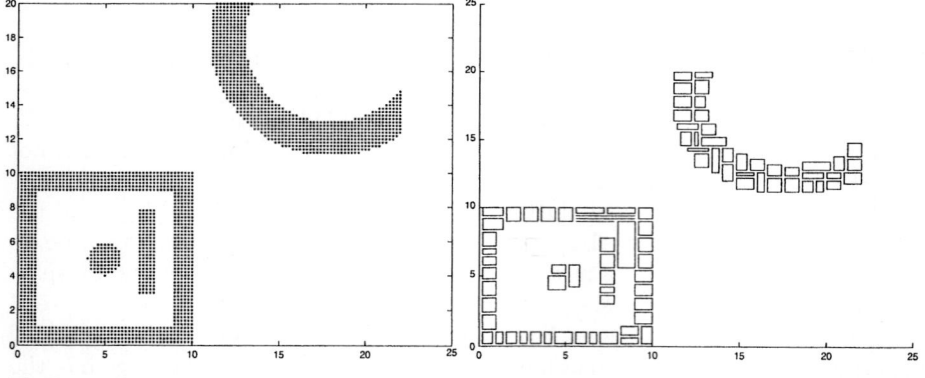

(a) Connected components of synthetically generated points in $I\!R^2$

(b) A program output showing splitting boxes generated by our method

Fig. 2. An example of adaptive clustering and space partitioning

not be balanced because of the arbitrary sized natural clusters generated using set estimation techniques. Henceforth, we term the two-level tree thus generated as a *DSP* tree (an acronym for Data and Space Partitioning). See Fig. 1 for an example. Fig. 2 shows an example of the adaptive cluster formation and its splitting into size-bounded clusters.

4 Similarity Query and Results

The image database used is the Columbia Object Image Library(COIL-20) [10] of 20 objects. There are 72 images per object, taken at pose intervals of 5 degrees, making a total of 1440 gray-scale images. We have taken feature vectors of dimension 7 whose first three components are the set of three invariant moments [12] and the other four components are the elements of the Euler vector [11], which is a 4-tuple, where each element is an integer representing the Euler number of the partial binary image formed by the gray code representation of the four most significant bit planes of the gray-tone image. As query, we have taken the front view of each of the 20 objects and an axis-parallel range query hyperbox around them. We have also performed the exhaustive search for testing the validity of the result of the experiment performed by our method. For each query, we have reported the first 10 (atmost) among the retrieved images. An output image is said to be accepted if it belongs to same COIL-object as the query image. The acceptance percentage is calculated as the ratio of the number of accepted output images by number of reported images. The results are given in Table-1. The purpose of the experiments reported here is not to achieve a high retrieval success for the COIL database, but to show that our scheme gives comparable retrieval success to exhaustive search with an appreciable savings in computation time.

Table 1. Search results

Input Images	DSP-tree Serach				Exhaustive Search			
	No. Of Ret. Im.	No. Of Acpt. Im.	% of Acpt.	Time (sec.) T_{DSP}	No. Of Ret. Im.	No. Of Acpt. Im	% Of Acpt.	Time (sec.) T_{EX}
obj1.raw	10	5	50	0.01	10	5	50	0.06
obj2.raw	10	6	60	0.00	10	6	60	0.06
obj3.raw	10	4	40	0.02	10	4	40	0.07
obj4.raw	10	10	100	0.00	10	10	100	0.05
obj5.raw	7	7	100	0.00	7	7	100	0.05
obj6.raw	10	1	10	0.02	10	1	10	0.05
obj7.raw	10	1	10	0.01	10	1	10	0.05
obj8.raw	10	6	60	0.00	10	6	60	0.05
obj9.raw	10	10	100	0.00	10	10	100	0.05
obj10.raw	10	4	40	0.01	10	4	40	0.06
obj11.raw	10	1	10	0.02	10	1	10	0.07
obj12.raw	10	2	20	0.01	10	2	20	0.07
obj13.raw	10	7	70	0.00	10	7	70	0.05
obj14.raw	10	4	40	0.01	10	4	40	0.05
obj15.raw	10	5	50	0.01	10	5	50	0.06
obj16.raw	10	5	50	0.02	10	5	50	0.06
obj17.raw	10	9	90	0.02	10	9	90	0.06
obj18.raw	10	8	80	0.01	10	8	80	0.05
obj19.raw	10	4	40	0.00	10	4	40	0.06
obj20.raw	10	2	20	0.00	10	2	20	0.06
Average	total = 197	total = 101	51.2690	0.0085	total = 197	total = 101	51.2690	0.0550

5 Discussions and Conclusion

In this paper, we first generated adaptive clusters using set estimation techniques and rectangular intersection graphs. Secondly, we devised a two-level space partitioned indexing scheme to generate indexed clusters of bounded size. We have evaluated our scheme against the exhaustive search method. In the future, we will elaborate the technique adopted to split and index a cluster whose enclosing box is completely contained in another. Further experiments are to be carried on image databases of larger size and with better representative features.

References

1. D. A. White, and R. Jain, "Similarity indexing with the SS-tree", *in Proc. of the* 12th *Int. Conf. on Data Engineering*, New Orleans, USA, pp. 516-523, Feb. 1996.
2. V. Gaede and O. Günther, "Multidimensional access methods", *ACM Computing Surveys*, pp. 170-231, vol. 30, No. 2, June 1998.
3. J. M. Klinberg, "Two algorithms for nearest neighbour search in higher dimensions", in Proc. 29th *ACM Symposium on Theory of Computing*, 1997.
4. U. Grenander, *Abstract Inference*, John Wiley & Sons, 1981.
5. H. L. Royden, *Real Analysis*, Prentice Hall of India, New Delhi, 2000.
6. C. A. Murthy, *On Consistent Estimate of Classes in $I\!R^2$ in the Context of Cluster Analysis*, Ph.D. Thesis, Indian Statistical Institute, Kolkata, India, 1988.
7. F. P. Preparata and M. I. Shamos, *Computational Geometry*, Springer Verlag, New York, 1985.
8. H. Edelsbrunner and M. H. Overmars, "Batched dynamic solutions to decomposable searching problems", *Journal of Algorithms*, vol. 6, pp. 515-542, 1985.
9. T. H. Cormen, C. E. Leiserson and R.L. Rivest, *Introduction to Algorithms*, Prentice Hall of India, 1998.
10. S. A. Nene, S. K. Nayar, and H. Murase, "Columbia Object Image Library: COIL-100", *Technical Report CUCS-006-96*, Department of Computer Science, Columbia University, February 1996.
11. A. Bishnu, B. B. Bhattacharya, M. K. Kundu, C. A. Murthy, and T. Acharya, "Euler vector for search and retrieval of gray-tone images", *IEEE Trans. SMC-B*, vol. 35, no. 4, pp. 801-812, 2005.
12. T. H. Reiss, "The revised fundamental theorem of moment invariants", *IEEE Trans. PAMI*, vol. 13, no. 8, pp. 830-834, 1991.

Image Retrieval by Content Using Segmentation Approach

Bhogeswar Borah and Dhruba K. Bhattacharyya

Tezpur University, Tezpur-784028, India
(bgb, dkb)@tezu.ernet.in

Abstract. This paper presents an efficient image retrieval technique based on content using segmentation approach and by considering global distribution of color. To cope with significant appearance changes, the method uses a global size and shape histogram to represent the image regions obtained after segmenting the image based on color similarity. The indexing technique can be found to be significant in comparison to its other counterparts, such as moment based method [12], due to its transformation invariance and effective retrieval performance over several application domains.

1 Introduction

Content-Based Image Retrieval (CBIR) is the retrieval of relevant images from an image database based on automatically derived features. Unlike keyword based databases content driven image databases are mostly queried by providing example images. It is the task of the search algorithm to find result images, which are most similar to the query image by computing the similarity, based upon extracted features. Primitive features such as color, texture, shape or a combination of these features are very useful for image description and retrieval. The need for efficient content-based image retrieval has increased tremendously in many application areas such as bio-medicine, crime prevention, the military, commerce, culture, education, entertainment, advertising, journalism, design, web-image classification and searching, etc .

As color plays an important role in image composition, many color indexing techniques have been developed including the original work by Swain and Ballard [1]. Although global color histograms and moments have been proven to be very useful for image indexing [2], they do not take color based spatial information into account resulting in many false hits as the image database size increases. The retrieval becomes more efficient when spatial arrangement of color is taken into account or when one or more low-level features, such as texture or shape, is added to the system. Several schemes [3,4,5,6,7] including spatial information have been proposed. An image can be partitioned into regions for the representation of spatial color distribution. A region-based retrieval system [8,9,10] applies image segmentation to decompose an image into regions, which correspond to objects if the decomposition is ideal. Color indexing can be obtained using global distribution or local distribution of color. Global color indexing enables whole image matching while regional indexing enables matching localized regions within images. However, if the image partition depends on the pixel positions, the approach may not tolerate significant appearance changes [11].

A compact and effective way of capturing the spectral content (i.e., chrominance) of an image is presented in [12]. This method is based on the *CIE xyY* color space. Each pixel in a given image yields a pair of *(x,y)* chromaticity values, thus forming a set of chromaticities for the entire image. This set of *(x,y)* pairs is called the *chromaticity set* of the specific image, while the corresponding *xy* Euclidean space is called the *chromaticity space*. Given an image, its chromaticities are characterized by two attributes, namely, their two-dimensional shape (*chromaticity set*) and their two-dimensional distribution (*histogram*). A set of moments are subsequently computed to capture the essence of these two attributes. These moments are called *chromaticity moments* and form a feature set for the corresponding image.

In this paper, we focus on region based retrieval of images considering global distribution of color. To cope with significant appearance changes, our method uses a global size and shape histogram to represent the image regions obtained after segmenting the image based on color similarity. The indexing technique is significant due to the following features: (1) the index has the property of translation, rotation and scaling invariance; it also has been found to be robust to significant appearance changes; (2) it is compact from the storage point of view; (3) it is comparatively effective in terms of retrieval performance and (4) it provides color indirect matching, i.e., similar objects with different colors can be matched;

Rest of the paper is organized as follows: In Section 2 the proposed image index is described. Section 3 presents experimental results. Finally, we conclude in Section 4.

2 Proposed Spatial Color Descriptor

The image is segmented into different color regions. The segment sizes are represented in an unnormalized size histogram. Similarly, for each segment a shape measure is computed and corresponding shape histogram is prepared. Both the histograms are concatenated into a single histogram. We define a similarity measure to compute the similarity of two images in the histogram space.

2.1 Image Segmentation

The objective of segmentation is to partition an image into non overlapped regions based on similarity of color. Let the color of a pixel be represented by the RGB vector $\mathbf{a}$. Let $\mathbf{z}$ denote a neighboring pixel of the pixel $\mathbf{a}$. We say that $\mathbf{z}$ is similar to $\mathbf{a}$ if the distance between them is less than a specified threshold D_0. The Euclidean distance between $\mathbf{z}$ and $\mathbf{a}$ is given by [13]:

$$D(\mathbf{z}, \mathbf{a}) = [(z_R - a_R)^2 + (z_G - a_G)^2 + (z_B - a_B)^2]^{1/2}$$

where, the subscripts R, G and B denote the RGB components of vectors **a** and **z**. If $D(\mathbf{z},\mathbf{a}) \leq D_0$ pixels **z** and **a** belong to the same color segment. Beginning with an arbitrary pixel at location (r,c) a region can be grown by examining the nearest neighbors $(8 - neighbours)$ of (r,c) one by one and accepting a neighboring pixel to belong to the same region as (r,c) if the distance between them is less than D_0. Once a new pixel is accepted as member of the current region the nearest neighbor of this new pixel is examined. This process goes on recursively until no more pixel is accepted. All the pixels of the current region are marked with a unique label. Then another unlabeled pixel is picked up and the same procedure is repeated. Scanning the image from left to right, top to bottom we go on labeling the regions until every pixel is assigned to some region or the other.

2.2 Color Segment Size and Shape Histograms

Let the total number of color segments in an image obtained by the segmentation process be t. The size of a segment, denoted by *segment_size* is the number of pixels present in the segment. The size histogram S is a list of $n+1$ integers:

$$S = \{s_0, s_1, s_2, \cdots, s_n | s_i \geq 0, \sum_{i=0}^{n} s_i = t\}$$

where, s_i is the number of segments such that $2^i \leq segment\_size < 2^{i+1}$.

The size histogram S is rotation invariant. With minor adjustment it becomes scale invariant. A nice property of the histogram is that for every horizontal or vertical scaling of the image by a factor of 2, the histogram is shifted by one location to the right. If the image is scaled up both horizontally and vertically by a factor of 2, the histogram is shifted to the right by 2 locations. In other words, if the overall image size is increased by $2^i (i = 1, 2, 3 \cdots)$ times then the histogram is shifted to the right i locations. Whether an image is scaled up one and if so, the number of bins the histogram should be shifted to the left to make it scale invariant can be obtained during segmentation.

A shape measure of a segment is a fraction in the closed interval $[0,1]$. It is defined as

$$Shape\_measure = \frac{segment\_size}{bounding\_rectangle\_size}$$

The *bounding_rectangle_size* is the area of the minimum rectangle whose sides are parallel to the axes and that completely encloses the segment. The shape histogram H is a list of $m+1$ integers :

$$H = \{h_0, h_1, h_2, \cdots, h_m | h_i \geq 0, \sum_{i=0}^{m} h_i = t\}$$

where, h_i is the number of segments such that $\frac{i}{m} \leq Shape\_measure < \frac{i+1}{m}$.

The shape histogram is invariant to scaling of the image. It is also invariant to rotation of the image by 90 degrees. In fact the size histogram and shape histogram can be concatenated into a single histogram, where the first n bins represent the size histogram and the last m bins represent the shape histogram.

2.3 Similarity Function for Image Comparison

Let, the combined histogram of size and shape be represented by Q for query image and D for any database image. Then the similarity measure between Q and D is a positive fraction ≤ 1. It is defined as

$$Similarity(Q, D) = \frac{1}{n+1} \sum_{i=0}^{h} \frac{|q_i - d_i|}{max(q_i, d_i) + w_i}$$

where, h represents the total number of bins in the combined histogram and w_i represents a non-zero positive weight assigned to bin i. Typical value for w_i is 1.

3 Experimental Results

We have implemented our approach in JAVA on an Intel workstation (1 Ghz CPU with 256 MB SDRAM). To test the technique we used an image collection of 4500 GIF, JPG and PNG images of size varying from 100x50 to 800x600 collected from various sources including $ETH-80$ database [14]. Images are segmented with distance threshold $D_0 = 4$. The combined histogram consists of 22 bins. First, the size histogram is computed and stored in bin numbers 0 to 10. Occurrence of segments of size bigger than $2^{10} = 1024$ pixels are very few. If such segments are found they are also counted in bin number 10. The shape histogram is stored starting from bin number 11 up to bin number 21. In this study, we use the efficiency of retrieval for the formal evaluation of retrieval effectiveness [3]. The efficiency of retrieval from a given output list of size T is defined as

$$E_T = \begin{cases} \frac{n}{N}, & \text{if } N \leq T; \\ \frac{n}{T}, & \text{otherwise.} \end{cases}$$

where n is the number of similar images retrieved and N is the total number of similar images in the database. We note that if $N \leq T$, then E_T becomes the traditional recall value of information retrieval, while if $N > T$, then E_T becomes the traditional precision value. Performance comparison of content-based image retrieval systems is a non-trivial task since it is very difficult to determine the relevant sets. Even if we do not exactly know the relevant sets, the observer's feel for relevant images in the retrieved set is what can be used as a measure of

Table 1. Comparison Results in terms of E_T

Size-of-list	Moment_based method [12]	Proposed method
5	0.58	0.70
10	0.43	0.52
15	0.40	0.45
20	0.35	0.43

precision. In each of the experiments performed, we have calculated the metric of precision for 50 randomly selected images and taken the average precision value. Precision is calculated for the first 5, 10, 15 and 20 nearest neighbor images of the result set. Also, for the same set of queries we have computed the precision values with the chromaticity moments based method proposed in [12]. The results are presented in Table 1.

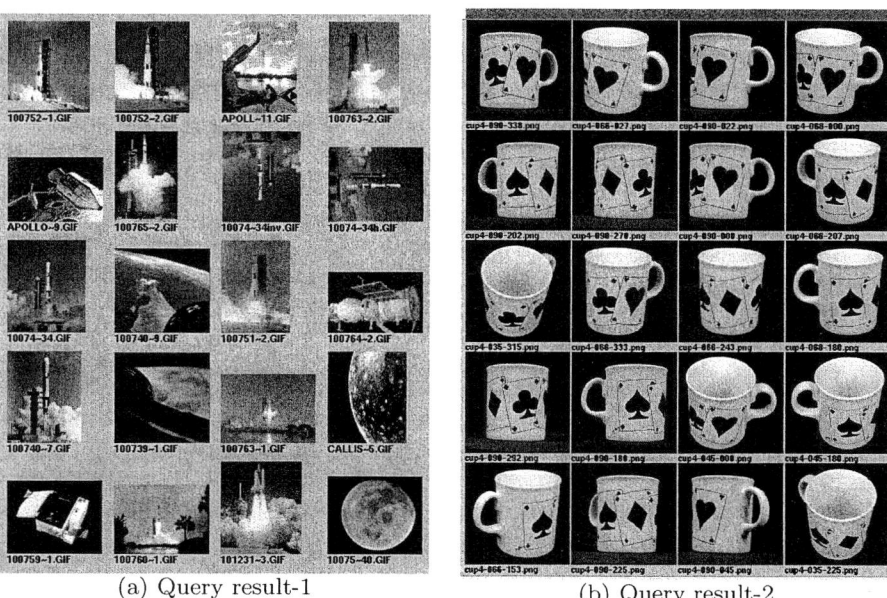

(a) Query result-1   (b) Query result-2

Fig. 1. Examples of Query results

Two query results are presented in Fig. 1. In all the results, the image at the top left corner is the query image. The retrieved list is ranked in order of decreasing similarity from left to right, top to bottom.

4 Conclusions

This paper has presented an efficient spatial color indexing technique designed using the segmentation approach. The technique has the property of translation, rotation and scaling invariance. The retrieval is tolerant to significant appearance changes and provides the facility of color indirect matching. The retrieval performance of the technique also has been established to be superior in comparison to its other counterparts, such as [12].

References

1. M.J. Swain and D.H. Ballard, "Color Indexing", International Journal of Computer Vision, Volume 7, Number 1, 1991, pp. 11-32.
2. M. Stricker and M. Orengo, "Similarity of Color Images", Proc. of SPIE Storage and Retrieval for Image and Video Databases, Volume 2420, February 1995, pp. 381-392.
3. Y. Tao, W.I. Grosky, "Spatial Color Indexing: A Novel Approach for Content-Based Image Retrieval", IEEE Intl. Conf. on Multimedia and Systems, Volume 1, June 1999, pp. 530-535.
4. W. Hsu, T.S. Chua and H.K. Pung, "An Integrated Color-Spatial Approach to Content-based Image Retrieval", Proc. of ACM Multimedia, San Francisco, California, November 1995, pp. 305-313.
5. H.Y. Lee, H.K. Lee and Y.H. Ha, "Spatial Color Descriptor for Image Retrieval and Video Segmentation", IEEE Transaction on Multimedia, Volume 5, Number 3, September, 2003.
6. G. Pass and R. Zabih, "Histogram Refinement for Content-Based Image Retrieval", IEEE Workshop on Applications of Computer Vision, 1996, pp. 96-102.
7. I.K. Park, I.D. Yun and S.W. Lee, "Color image retrieval using hybrid graph representation", Image and Vision Computing, Volume 17, Number 7, May 1999, pp. 465-474.
8. I.K. Sethi, I Coman, et al., "Color-WISE: A system for Image Similarity Retrieval Using Color", Proc. of SPIE Storage and Retrieval for Image and Video Databases, Volume 3312, February 1998, pp. 140-149.
9. S. Belongie, C. Carson, H. Greenspan, and J. Malik, "Color and texture-Based Image Segmentation Using EM and Its Application to Content-Based Image Retrieval", Proc. of the Intl. Conf. on Computer Vision (ICCV'98), 1998.
10. B.M. Mehtre, M.S. Kankanhalli, and W.F. Lee, "Content-Based Image Retrieval Using A Composite Color-Shape Approach", Information Processing and Management, Volume 34, Number 1, January 1998, pp. 109-120.
11. J. Huang, S.R. Kumar, M. Mitra, W.J. Zhu, and R. Zabih, "Image indexing Using Color Correlograms", Proc. of the 16th IEEE Conf. on Computer Vision and Pattern Recognition, June 1997, pp. 762-768.
12. G. Paschos, I. Radev, and N. Prabakar, "Image Content-Based Retrieval Using Chromaticity Moments", IEEE Ttransaction on Knowledge and Data Engineering", Volume 15. Number 5, Sept./Oct. 2003, pp. 1069-1072.
13. R.C. Gonzalez and R.E. Woods, "Digital Image Processing", 2nd ed., Pearson Education, 2003
14. http://www.vision.ethz.ch/projects/categorization/download.h tml

A Wavelet Based Image Retrieval

Kalyani Mali[1] and Rana Datta Gupta[2]

[1] Department of Computer Science, Kalyani University,
Kalyani 741 235, India
[2] Department of Computer Science & Engineering, Jadavpur University,
Calcutta, India
kalyani_mali@yahoo.com, rdg@ieee.org

Abstract. An wavelet based image retrieval scheme is described. Wavelet transforms are applied to compress the image space, thereby reducing noise. A combination of texture, shape, topology and fuzzy geometric features, that is invariant to orientation, scale and object deformation, are extracted from this compressed image. The use of wavelet based compression eliminates the need for any other preprocessing. The extracted features serve as the signature of the compressed images, in terms of their content. Their use in content based image retrieval is demonstrated.

Keywords: Image mining, wavelets, content based image retrieval, image compression.

1 Introduction

Wavelets [1] are found to be very useful in appropriately modeling the non-stationary property of image signals formed around the edges, as well as the correlation amongst the image pixels. The role of wavelets in different aspects of data mining is gaining significant importance, and it has become a very powerful signal processing tool in different application areas such as image processing, compression, image indexing and retrieval, digital libraries, image clustering and databases [2,3]. Most of the activities in mining image data have been in the search and retrieval of images based on the analysis of similarity of a query image or its feature(s) with the entries in the image database. In *Content Based Image Retrieval* (CBIR) systems, the images are searched and retrieved by extracting suitable features based on the visual content of the images [4,5]. CBIR has increasingly become a growing area of study towards the successful development of image mining techniques.

In this article we describe a wavelet based CBIR on real life digital images. Wavelet transforms are applied to compress the image space, thereby eliminating noise. The processing now needs to be done on subsampled images of smaller size. This also enables us to eliminate the need for any other preprocessing of the raw images. A combination of texture, shape, topology and fuzzy geometric features are extracted directly from this compressed image. The features are next used for CBIR in the compressed domain. The images retrieved, based on content, are always found to lie in the same partition as the query image.

2 Wavelet Transform

Wavelet transform is a signal processing technique that decomposes a signal or image into different frequency subbands at number of levels and multiple resolutions. In every level of decomposition, the high-frequency subband captures the discontinuities in the signals – for example, the edge information in an image. The low-frequency subband is a subsampled version of the original image, with similar statistical and spatial properties as the original signal. As a result, the low-frequency subband can be further decomposed into higher levels of resolution, and it helps in representing spatial objects in different coarser levels of accuracy in multiresolution subbands. The wavelet transform is typically represented as a pair of high-pass and low-pass filters, with many wavelet basis functions being available in literature [1].

Haar wavelet is one of the simplest wavelet. Daubechies wavelet family corresponds to a set of compactly supported orthonormal wavelets. These are denoted as db$N$, where N stands for the order of the wavelet. In this article we focus on Daubechies family of wavelets db-N ($N = 1, 2, 3, 4, 5, 6$) as well as db-9/7 [6]. The db-1 wavelet is the same as the Haar function.

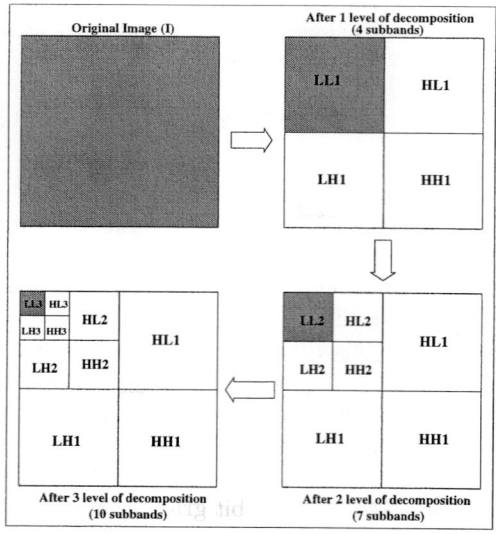

Fig. 1. Three level multiresolution wavelet decomposition of an image

In Fig. 1, we show an example of hierarchical wavelet decomposition of an image into ten subbands after three levels of decomposition [4]. After the first level of decomposition, the original image is decomposed into four subbands $LL1$, $HL1$, $LH1$, and $HH1$. Since the low-frequency subband $LL1$ has similar spatial and statistical characteristics as the original image, it can be further decomposed into four subbands $LL2$, $HL2$, $LH2$, and $HH2$.

3 Feature Extraction

In this section we mention the input features used. These include texture, fuzzy geometry, moment invariants and Euler vector. They are useful in characterizing images, and can be used as a signature of image content. Hence these features have promising application in CBIR.

3.1 Texture

Texture is one of the important features used in identifying objects or regions of interest in an image [7]. The contextual texture information is specified by the matrix of relative frequencies $P(i,j)$ with which two neighboring resolution cells, having gray levels i and j and separated by a distance δ, occur in the image. The angular second moment, inverse difference moment, Contrast, Entropy of the image are calculated four times, corresponding to each of the four directional cooccurrence matrices.

3.2 Shape

Shape can roughly be defined as the description of an object minus its position, orientation and size. Therefore, shape features should be invariant to *translation*, *rotation*, and *scale*, when the arrangement of the objects in the image are not known in advance.

Two of the seven *transformation invariant moments*, used here, are expressed as follows.
$$\left. \begin{array}{l} \phi_1 = (\eta_{2,0} + \eta_{0,2}) \\ \phi_2 = (\eta_{2,0} - \eta_{0,2})^2 + 4\eta_{1,1}^2. \end{array} \right\} \quad (1)$$

3.3 Topology

One topological property of a digital image is known as *Euler number*. Although typically computed in a binary image, it can be extended to characterize gray-tone images by defining the *Euler Vector* [8]. If an image has C connected components and H number of holes, the *Euler number* E of the image can be defined as $E = C - H$.

Intensity value of each pixel in an 8-bit gray-tone image can be represented by an 8-bit binary Euler vector b_i, $i = 0, 1, \cdots, 7$. The ith bit plane is formed with b_i's from all the pixels in the gray-tone image. We retain the first two most significant bit planes corresponding to (b_7, b_6), because they contain most of the information of the image.

3.4 Fuzzy Geometry

A fuzzy subset of a set S is a mapping μ from S into $[0,1]$ and denotes the degree of membership of an object. The *compactness* ($Comp$) [9] of a fuzzy set μ having area $a(\mu)$ and perimeter $p(\mu)$ is defined as

$$Comp(\mu) = \frac{a(\mu)}{p^2(\mu)}. \qquad (2)$$

Here the *area* is defined as $a(\mu) = \sum \mu$, the summation being considered over a region outside which $\mu = 0$. The *perimeter* of an image is expressed as $p(\mu) = \sum_{i,j} |\mu(i) - \mu(j)|$, where $\mu(i)$ and $\mu(j)$ are the membership values of two adjacent pixels.

4 Implementation and Results

A Content Based Image Retrieval were performed on 86 images, consisting of five different image categories such as 13 aeroplanes, 22 cars, 41 flowers of two types and 10 zebras. A sample image is presented to the system for content based retrieval of the closest match.

Wavelet transform is applied,followed by feature extraction. Performance is evaluated with each of these Daubechies functions in the LL1, LL2, LL3 subbands.The query image is identified as belonging to the majority class among the five nearest objects retrieved. Table 1 quantitatively evaluates the CBIR performance using Daubechies family wavelets on the basis of correct classification.

Table 1. CBIR Performance using different Daubechies wavelet functions

Wavelet		Aero	Car	Flow1	Flow2	Zebra	Average
	LL1	15.38	63.64	58.82	50.00	60.00	49.57
db1	LL2	30.77	54.55	52.94	70.83	90.00	59.82
	LL3	23.08	54.55	82.35	75.00	100.00	67.00
	LL1	46.15	50.00	52.95	75.00	60.00	56.82
db2	LL2	61.54	50.0	64.71	75.00	100.00	70.25
	LL3	53.85	45.45	64.71	87.50	100.00	70.30
	LL1	38.46	59.09	58.82	79.17	60.00	59.11
db3	LL2	23.08	63.64	70.59	75.00	100.00	66.46
	LL3	46.15	63.64	76.47	83.33	100.00	73.92
	LL1	46.15	45.45	70.59	75.00	80.00	63.44
db4	LL2	38.46	54.55	64.71	87.50	100.00	69.04
	LL3	38.46	68.18	47.06	83.33	70.00	61.41
	LL1	53.85	45.45	52.94	70.83	70.00	58.62
db5	LL2	53.85	68.18	70.59	87.50	100.00	76.02
	LL3	7.69	68.18	47.06	79.17	80.00	56.42
	LL1	61.54	59.09	52.94	70.83	70.00	62.88
db6	LL2	30.77	81.82	76.47	66.67	100.00	71.15
	LL3	15.38	54.55	58.82	83.33	100.00	62.42
	LL1	30.77	50.00	58.82	66.67	80.00	57.25
db9/7	LL2	30.77	40.91	70.59	75.00	100.00	63.45
	LL3	53.85	45.45	70.59	83.30	100.00	70.64
original		15.38	77.27	64.71	62.50	90.00	61.97

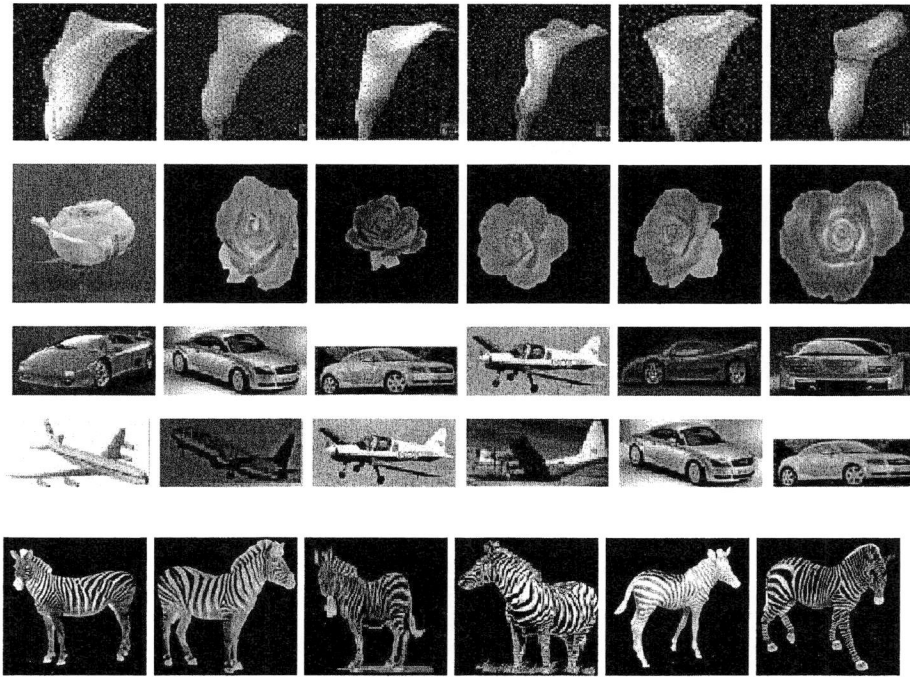

Fig. 2. CBIR for sample images in $LL2$ subband using db-5 function

The performance is compared with the results obtained from the original image. It is shown that performance is generally better in the higher subbands. Fig. 2 demonstrates sample CBIR results, from the $LL2$ subband of the wavelet decomposition, using db-5 function. The first column refers to the query image. The rest of the columns, along each row, depict the content-based retrieved images graded according to increasing distance from the corresponding query image. It is to be noted that most of the retrieved images are found to lie in the same subcategory as the query image.

On the whole, the results serve to highlight the utility of the extracted features, in the compressed domain, for CBIR.

5 Conclusions and Discussion

Wavelet transforms are employed to compress the image, and eliminate noise. This allows us to avoid the need for any other preprocessing of the raw image. The signature of the compressed images, in terms of their visual content, is extracted as features involving texture, shape, topology and fuzzy geometry. The features are invariant to orientation, scale and deformation of object, as well as the background intensity.

Use of these features for CBIR, in the compressed domain, is demonstrated. The retrieved images are always found to lie in the same partition as that of the corresponding query image. Since the processing is done on subsampled (compressed) images of smaller size, this strategy now opens up interesting propositions for large scale image mining.

References

1. Daubechies, I.: Ten Lectures on Wavelets. CBMS, Philadelphia: Society for Industrial and Applied Mathematics (1992)
2. Li, T., Li, Q., Zhu, S., Ogihara, M.: A survey on wavelet applications in data mining. ACM SIGKDD Explorations Newsletter **4** (2002)
3. de Wouwer, G.V., Scheunders, P., Dyck, D.V.: Statistical texture characterization from discrete wavelet representations. IEEE Transactions on Image Processing **8** (1999) 592–598
4. Mitra, S., Acharya, T.: Data Mining: Multimedia, Soft Computing, and Bioinformatics. New York: John Wiley (2003)
5. Castelli, V., Bergman, L.: Image Databases: Search and Retrieval of Digital Imagery. New York: Wiley-Interscience (2001)
6. Daubechies, I.: The wavelet transform, time-frequency localization and signal analysis. IEEE Trans. Infor. Theory **36** (1990) 961–1005
7. Haralick, R.M., Shanmugam, K., Dinstein, I.: Textural features for image classification. IEEE Transactions on Systems, Man, and Cybernetics **3** (1973) 610–621
8. Bishnu, A., Bhattacharya, B.B., Kundu, M.K., Murthy, C.A., Acharya, T.: Euler vector: A combinatorial signature of gray-tone images. Proc. of the IEEE Int. Conf. on Information Technology: Coding & Computing (2002)
9. Pal, S.K., Mitra, S.: Neuro-fuzzy Pattern Recognition: Methods in Soft Computing. New York: John Wiley (1999)

Use of Contourlets for Image Retrieval

Rajashekhar and Subhasis Chaudhuri

Department of Electrical Enginering,
IIT Bombay, Powai, India 400076
{raja, sc}@ee.iitb.ac.in

Abstract. We propose a simple technique for content-based image retrieval (CBIR) using contourlets that possess not only the multi-resolution time frequency localization properties of wavelets but are also good at capturing the directional information. Statistical features extracted from contourlet coefficients on each subband of the decomposed image, capturing the textural properties, are combined with the color feature while doing the CBIR. The retrieval performance on a large image database shows that the proposed technique provides a better accuracy compared to other multi-resolution based approaches.

1 Introduction

Content-based image retrieval is now an actively pursued research area, and a comprehensive literature survey can be found in [1, 2]. Although color is an effective feature, its use during retrieval may lead to some loss in discrimination power, if used alone. Texture is an important visual attribute whose properties are required for the identification of an object. Often one can efficiently encode the contents of many real world images, for example, cloud, bricks, building patterns, etc., in terms of textural characteristics. One such early work [3] is based on a statistical approach in which statistics derived from the cooccurence matrix are used to describe the texture. Another statistical scheme for wavelet-based texture retrieval scheme proposed in [4] is based on modeling the marginal distribution of the wavelet coefficients using a generalized Gaussian density (GGD) and computing the Kullback-Libler distance between the GGDs. Jhanwar *et al.* [5] have proposed a translation and illumination invariant retrieval scheme using motif cooccurence matrix. It uses an optimal Peano scan to locally encode the texture.

Normally the texture information is available at various scales. One natural method of texture analysis at various scales is to perform a multi-resolution analysis. Many researchers have explored the use of wavelets and Gabor filters for texture analysis at multi-resolution levels [6, 7, 8, 9]. Wavelets and Gabor filter approaches use separable bases during the image decomposition. However, the use of separable bases do not allow us to efficiently handle the presence of directional information hidden in the image. Indeed, this directional information is a very important cue in image content modeling since many natural images are not simply stacks of 1-D piecewise smooth scan-lines; discontinuity points (i.e. edges) are typically positioned along smooth curves along arbitrary directions owing to smooth boundaries of physical objects. Recently, Do et al. proposed in [10] the use of non separable bases in building contourlets for image decomposition which are very good in capturing the directional entities in the image. This inspired us to propose a simple technique of extracting the textural features using contourlets. We extract the statistical features such as mean and standard deviation on each subband of the decomposed Y component of the color image. We use these features to measure the similarity between two images. Subsequently we incorporate the color features. This method is simple and provides a favorably good retrieval accuracy compared to the existing texture retrieval methods. It may be noted that Do et al.[10] have also suggested the use of contourlet for image retrieval. However, their method requires the estimation of parameters for a hidden Markov model to parameterize the the contourlet tree structure. Thus it is computationally quite demanding and the performance depends on the fitness of the model. The proposed method is free from any model fitting.

2 Content Modeling Using Contourlet Statistics

The contourlet transform is an extension of the Cartesian wavelet transform in two dimensions using multiscale and directional filter banks. The contourlet expansion of an image consists of non separable bases oriented at various directions at multiple scales, with flexible aspect ratios. In addition to the multiscale time frequency localization properties of wavelets it offers a high degree of directionality (see more details in [10]). The Y component of the color image is decomposed into a lowpass subband and four, eight and sixteen bandpass directional subbands, respectively. Now we obtain 29 directional bandpass subbands at different scales for each image. Let $S_{m,n}$ be contourlet coefficients at the mth scale and n^{th} directional subband. For example, for a 3-layer decomposition, the subbands are $S_{0,0}$, $S_{1,1}, \cdots S_{1,4}$, $S_{2,1} \cdots \cdots S_{3,16}$. We then compute the mean $\mu_{m,n}$ and standard deviation (STD) $\sigma_{m,n}$ features of the computed contourlet coefficients on each subband of the decomposed image using the following equations.

$$\mu_{m,n} = \frac{\sum_{i,j} \mid S_{m,n}(i,j) \mid}{x_{m,n}}, \quad \sigma_{m,n} = [\frac{\sum_{i,j} \mid S_{m,n}(i,j) - \mu_{m,n} \mid^2}{x_{m,n}}]^{1/2}, \quad (1)$$

where $x_{m,n}$ is the number of components in the $(m,n)^{th}$ subband. A feature vector is now constructed using $\mu_{m,n}$ and $\sigma_{m,n}$. For 3 levels of decomposition, the resulting contourlet feature vector (CF) is given as $f = [\mu_{0,0}, \sigma_{0,0}, \mu_{1,1}, \sigma_{1,1} \cdots \mu_{1,4}, \sigma_{1,4}, \mu_{2,1}, \sigma_{2,1} \cdots \mu_{2,8}, \sigma_{2,8} \mu_{3,1}, \sigma_{3,1} \cdots, \mu_{3,16}, \sigma_{3,16}]$.

3 Textural Similarity

Measuring the similarity among images is of central importance for retrieving images by content. After having computed the textural features we match the textural features of the query and database images using the Canberra distance metric [7]. We weigh the standard deviations on each subband differently while computing this distance metric. Standard deviations of subband images give a measure of amount of details in that subband. Since a texture mainly consists of quasi-periodic spatial variations, we expect the higher frequency subbands (lower levels of decomposition) to contain more texture information, and we give a higher weight to these subbands. Also if the image is noisy, only the lower bands are affected and the overall distance does not change drastically due to lower weights. We do not weigh the mean of the subbands since it provides an average behavior over the subbands.

We normalize the individual feature vector components before finding the distance between the two images. If f_q and f_p are the feature vectors of the query image and the database image, the Canberra distance d_{cnt} [7] is given by

$$\text{Canb}(f_p, f_q) = d_{cnt} = \sum_{m,n} \frac{\mid \mu_{m,n}^p - \mu_{m,n}^q \mid + \omega_{m,n} \mid \sigma_{m,n}^p - \sigma_{m,n}^q \mid}{\mid \mu_{m,n}^p + \omega_{m,n} \sigma_{m,n}^p \mid + \mid \mu_{m,n}^q + \omega_{m,n} \sigma_{m,n}^q \mid}, \quad (2)$$

where $\omega_{m,n} = \frac{1}{2^{m-1}}$ and the superscript relates to a given image.

4 Inclusion of Color Feature

As discussed in section 2 we extract the contourlet features considering the Y component of the color image in YCbCr plane. We generalize the CBIR problem by incorporating the color information. The color histogram describes the global color distribution in an image [11]. We compute three separate histograms for R, G, and B planes of the color image. We use the Euclidean distance to compute the color similarity (d_c) between the query and database images. Then the over all similarity (d) is computed by combining both the similarities using appropriate weights.

$$d = d_{cnt} + \beta d_c, \quad (3)$$

where β the relative importance between the contourlet and color features. We select the weight β in an adhoc basis so that both the components in the distance measure d have nearly equal contributions.

5 Experimental Results

We tested the performance of the proposed method using various types of query images. The size of the database is about 5000, consisting of images of both natural and manmade objects. Each image in the database is decomposed upto 3 levels using the contourlet transform. In all the experimental results the image displayed first is the query image and ranking goes from left to right and top to bottom.

Fig. 1. Retrieved images using the contourlet features with the top left image as the query image. Here the contourlet features are computed up to the third level of decomposition.

Fig. 2. Retrieved images using the weighted contourlet features (WCF) with the top left image as the query image

First we demonstrate the performance using contourlet features having equal weights ie, $\omega_{m,n} = 1 \ \forall (m,n)$. Since contourlet features are good at capturing the geometrical structures such as smooth contours in natural images we retrieved a good number of relevant images. Since all the contourlet features are weighed uniformly, despite having top 5 relevant retrievals, we end up with a few false retrievals. The retrieved images using the zebra image as a query are shown in Figure 1. It may be noticed that although many retrieved images are relevant to the query a few images such as the images of the tiger and the horizontal texture do not correspond very well to the query image. We then consider the

Fig. 3. Retrieved images using the combination of WCF and color features

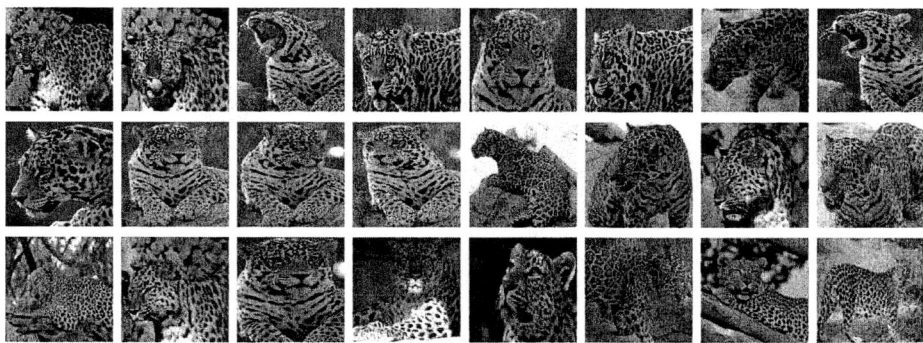

Fig. 4. Results of retrieval using both the WCF and color features for another query

use of the weighted contourlet features while doing CBIR. Figure 2 shows the corresponding retrieved images using the same zebra image as a query. In the top 15 retrieved images, shown here most of them correspond very well to the query image. Even then one may find a few irrelevant ones such as the tiger. This is due to the fact that the tiger has stripes similar to the zebra. We do note that a zebra and a tiger have different colors. We then combined the contourlet features with the color feature and repeated the CBIR experiment for the same image as the query. It may be noticed that in the retrieved list (see Figure 3), all the images correspond very well to the query image. This improves the retrieval accuracy further.

We then browsed the image database for similarity using a panther image as the query. The results in Figure 4 show the top 23 retrieved similar images. We compared the retrieval results of the proposed method with the results obtained using rotated wavelet filter (RWF), discrete wavelet filter (DWT) and RWF + DWT, and Gabor wavelets[6]. We find that the retrieval results of the proposed one is superior to the above CBIR methods.

The proposed method is also computationally very efficient. The table in Figure 5(b) provides a detailed comparison of average recall rates and retrieval time considering top 30 retrievals for combination of weighted contourlet feature (WCF) and color, contourlet feature (CF), DWT, RWF, combination of DWT and RWF, and Gabor wavelet method proposed by [6]. They have reported the Gabor wavelet-based texture image retrieval results using four scales and six orientations. For constructing the feature vector they have also used mean and standard deviation of the magnitude of the Gabor transform coefficients. The performance obtained with the standard DWT feature (81%) is better than that obtained with RWF (75.2%) features. The reason behind this is that RWF performs better for diagonally oriented texture images. The performance with combination of two feature sets (DWT + RWF) is better (85.50%) than that using any of them alone. The performance obtained with the combination of WCF and color feature sets (94%) is better than that using either WCF or CF as expected. In terms of retrieval time the existing Gabor wavelet based method

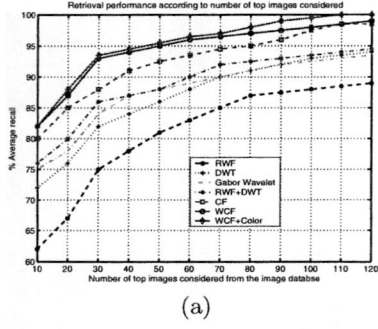

	Average recall rate (%)	Retrieval time/per 1000 search	Feature vector length
DWT	81.00	0.28sec	24
RWF	75.20	0.21sec	24
DWT + RWF	85.50	0.47sec	48
Gabor Wavelet	84.52	1.9sec	48
CF	90.50	0.19sec	58
WCF	92.50	0.18sec	58
WCF + Color	94.00	0.22sec	58 + 256

(a) (b)

Fig. 5. (a) Comparison of recall rates of the proposed method with the methods based on RWF, DWT, DWT+RWF and Gabor Wavelet, respectively, (b) Average recall rates and retrieval times for some of the related CBIR methods and the proposed method Here WCF stands for weighted contourlet feature.

is the most expensive. The proposed retrieval system has been implemented using a combination of MATLAB and C on a Pentium IV, 2.2GHz machine. The retrieval time for the proposed method is quite close to the other wavelet based methods. It may be noted that the retrieval times for the first four methods given in table shown in Figure 5(b) were on a P-III, 866MHz machine.

Figure 5(a) shows the recall rates for standard DWT, RWF, (DWT + RWF), Gabor wavelet, CF, and combination of WCF and Color based methods according to the number of top matches considered. From the figures it is clear that the retrieval performance of the combined WCF and Color feature set is superior to all the existing multi-resolution methods.

6 Conclusion

We have proposed the idea of using contourlet transform for CBIR. We have shown how the contourlet features are effective in capturing the directional information. The performance obtained with WCF is better than that of other multiresolution based CBIR schemes. We notice a further improvement in the retrieval accuracy with the inclusion of color feature. Computational requirement of the proposed method is very minimal. Thus the proposed method achieves both the important requirements such as high retrieval accuracy and less retrieval time for doing CBIR.

References

1. Bimbo, A.D.: Visual Information Retrieval. Morgan Kaufman Publishers, Inc., San Francisco, USA, (2001)
2. Rui, Y., Huang, T., Chang, S.F.: Image retrieval:current techniques promising directions and open issues. Journal of Visual Communication and Image Representation **10** (1999) 39–62

[3] Haralick, R.M., Shanmugam, K., Dinstein, I.: Texture features for image classification. IEEE Trans.on System, Man and Cybernetics **3** (1973) 610–621
[4] Do, M.N., Vitterli, M.: Wavelet-based texture retrieval using generalized gaussian density and kullback-liebler distance. IEEE Transactions on Image Processing **11** (2002) 146–158
[5] Jhanwar, N., Chaudhuri, S., Seetharaman, G., Zavidovique, B.: Content based image retrieval using motif coocurence matrix". Image and Vision Computing **22** (2004) 1211–1220
[6] Manjunath, B.S., Ma, W.Y.: Texture features for browsing and retrieval of image data. IEEE Trans.on Pattern Analysis and Machine Inelligence **8** (1996) 837–841
[7] Kokare, M., Chatterji, B.N., Biswas, P.K.: Rotated wavelet based texture features for content based image retrieval. In: Fifth International Conference on Advances in Pattern Recognition. (2003) 243–247
[8] Smith, J., Chang, S.F.: Visual seek: A fully automated conent based query system. In: Proc. ACM Multimedia ACM Press, Newyork (1996) 87–98
[9] Simoncelli, E.P., Adelson, E.H.: Non-seperable extensions of quadrature mirror filters to multiple dimensions. In: Proc.of IEEE: Special issue on Multidimensional Signal Processing. Volume 78. (1990) 652–664
[10] Do, M.N., Vitterli, M.: The contourlet transform:an efficient directional multiresolution image representation. IEEE Transactions on Image Processing (to appear) (2004)
[11] Swain, M.J., Ballard, D.H.: Color indexing. International Journal of Computer Vision **7** (1991) 11–32

Integration of Keyword and Feature Based Search for Image Retrieval Applications

A. Vadivel[1], Shamik Sural[2], and A.K. Majumdar[1]

[1] Department of Computer Science and Engineering, Indian Institute of Technology,
Kharagpur 721302, India
{vadi@cc, akmj@cse}.iitkgp.ernet.in
[2] School of Information Technology, Indian Institute of Technology,
Kharagpur 721302, India
shamik@sit.iitkgp.ernet.in

Abstract. The main obstacle in realizing semantic-based image retrieval is from the web that semantic description of an image is difficult to capture in low-level features. Text based keywords can be generated from web documents to capture semantic information narrowing down the search space. We use an effective dynamic approach to integrate keywords and color-texture features to take advantage of their complementing strengths. Experimental results show that the integrated approach has better retrieval performance than both the text based and the content-based techniques.

1 Introduction

Images are very frequently embedded in HTML documents to express the intended message effectively on the World Wide Web [16] (WWW). Conventional search engines use only keyword based search for retrieval and often takes many iterations to converge. Conventional search engines do not integrate low-level features to support image retrieval queries. On the other hand, a large number of content-based image retrieval systems have been developed in the academia and the industry [4,5,8,12] which use low-level features such as color, texture and shape. These approaches do not include keyword based textual information to complement the retrieval and narrow the search space. As result, precision of retrieval for general-purpose image retrieval applications tends to be very low. On the other hand text based retrievals like Google attend reasonably high precision. We feel that an effective image retrieval system should make use of both keywords and low-level features of an image and try to integrate keyword-based and content-based image retrieval techniques as a single system. Keywords-based capture high-level semantics but they cannot depict complicated image features very well. The key word extraction process also should be made dynamic to be really useful. On the other hand, content-based techniques can capture low-level image features and can accept images as queries. An image query process is hard to start, as the user has to specify a query image by selecting an existing image and the user normally does not have access to all the images, which can be used as queries. It is well established that while uploading images, one cannot possibly label or tag it with test. The reason is that, such labeling is subjective, often incomplete and heavily manpower intensive. On the other hand, it is not a difficult properties to include keywords along with sample images while preparing a query. Essentially, the user not only specifies a query image, but also mentions in text form, what is the semantic content of the image that he is interested in an information not captured just by the low-level features. In our system users can start their search process by providing keywords. A set of images are retrieved from the database and displayed to the user based on the keyword. From these initial results, user can further select image either as content-based queries or as content-based supplemented with keywords to narrow down the search space. The final retrieved images are based on combined scores of the keyword-based and the content-based searching. We have built a web-based application [13] which is available in the public domain for interested users to repeat our experiments and perform the searches.

In the next section, we explain our method for keyword-based indexing and retrieval of images. In section 3, we explain content-based image indexing and retrieval using COLTEX a color-texture retrieval technique. We describe the combined keyword and COLTEX based retrieval procedure in section 4. Experimental results are included in section 5 and we draw conclusions in the last section of the paper.

2 Keyword-Based Indexing and Retrieval of Images

Keyword-based image retrieval can be based on the traditional text information retrieval (IR) technique [7]. However, to improve retrieval performance, we should make use of the structure of HTML documents. This is because the words or the terms appearing at different locations of an HTML document have different levels of importance or relevance to related images [2]. Therefore, we need to assign term weights based on term positions. In our proposed approach, we extract texts around the images and calculate occurrence frequencies of the words in the text. The stop words are filtered out and others are stored in a database. Figure 1, shows the keyword based search interface and a typical output of the web-based application. In our database, a given image may be related to many keywords and a single keyword is related to many images. If a single keyword is provided as query string, the search space is wide and returned images may be from different categories. To minimize the search space, more than one keywords can be provided for performing the search.

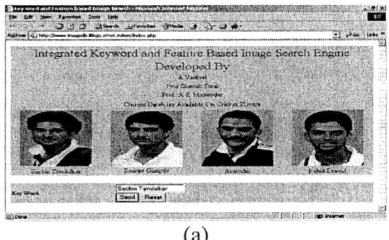
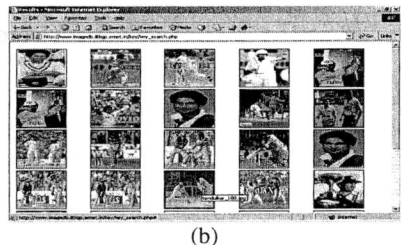

(a)   (b)

Fig. 1. Web – Based Image Retrieval System (a) Interface to perform keyword-based search (b) Results of a keyword-based search

3 Color-Texture Feature Based Indexing and Retrieval of Images

We use a combined color and texture feature called COLTEX for performing low-level image indexing and retrieval. While the method has been presented in [11], we give a brief overview here. COLTEX describes color and texture content of the images and is represented as a color texture matrix CTM where

$$CTM = \begin{pmatrix} CTM_{CC} & CTM_{CG} \\ CTM_{GC} & CTM_{GG} \end{pmatrix} \quad (1)$$

Each component of the COLTEX matrix $CTM_{ab}, a,b \in \{C,G\}$ is a sub matrix represents the combinations of color-color, color-texture, texture-color and texture-texture, respectively. This feature vector is based on human visual perception of the color and texture of an image pixel and its performance has been found to be encouraging [10]. Each sub matrix of COLTEX is given by

$$CTM_{CC} = ctm_{CC}(i,j) | i = 0 \ldots C_L, j = 0 \ldots C_L \quad (2)$$

$$CTM_{CG} = ctm_{CG}(i,j) | i = 0 \ldots C_L, j = 0 \ldots G_L \quad (3)$$

$$CTM_{GC} = ctm_{GC}(i,j) | i = 0 \ldots G_L, j = 0 \ldots C_L \quad (4)$$

$$CTM_{GG} = ctm_{GG}(i,j) | i = 0 \ldots G_L, j = 0 \ldots G_L \quad (5)$$

The values of C_L and G_L are as follows

$$C_L = \frac{2\pi}{Q_H} + 1 \quad (6)$$

$$G_L = \frac{255}{Q_I} + 1 \quad (7)$$

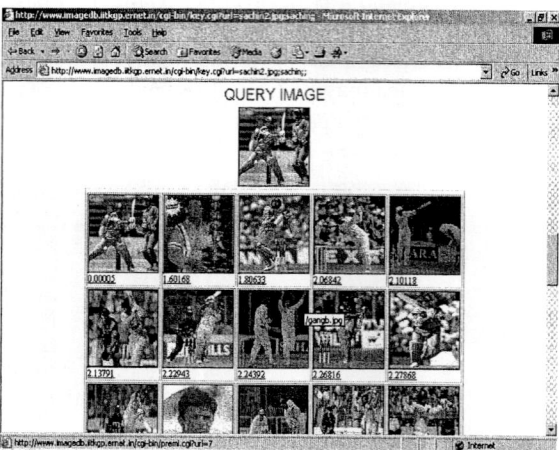

Fig. 2. Retrieval based on COLTEX

where Q_I and Q_H are the quantization values for color and texture respectively. 2π is the domain values for the hue and 255 is the maximum intensity level in the HSV color space [10].

For each image crawled from the web the COLTEX matrix is extracted and stored in a database. During image retrieval, COLTEX is extracted from the query image and compared with the all the features in the database. The Manhattan Distance is used to measure the similarity between COLTEX of the query image and each of the images in the database. Images with a distance smaller than a pre-defined threshold are retrieved from the database and presented to the user. Figure 2 shows the interface and retrieval results of feature-based extraction.

4 Image Retrieval by Combining Keywords and COLTEX

We combine keyword and COLTEX based search by the use of an input keyword and an image of interest from the set of images initially displayed. The keyword based retrieval is first applied based on the input keyword and COLTEX features of the retrieved images are extracted and compared with the database images to return the final set of retrieved images as shown in figure 3. The number of retrieved images depends on the search space. The result shows the final retrieved images and their distance values. If two images are close to each other in terms of their content the distance value is as close to zero. The distance value is more for images with different semantic content content.

Fig. 3. Image retrieval based on both keyword and COLTEX

5 Results

In this section, we show results of keyword-based, COLTEX-based and combined keyword and COLTEX based retrieval. Table 1 shows the average precision (P) in percentage for nearest neighbors 10, 20, 50 and 100.

Table 1. Precision of retrieval

Features	P(10) %	P(20) %	P(50) %	P (100) %
Keyword based	46.00	35.90	25.40	19.98
COLTEX	55.00	46.90	35.40	22.98
COLTEX and Keyword combined	**92.33**	**87.28**	**64.21**	**51.00**

We have used a large number of randomly selected images of different categories and content and calculated the average precision. Form the results, it is observed that the performance of the combined method is quite encouraging. We have earlier shown that COLTEX performance is better than other color-texture based methods. Hence, it is expected that the combined method have better performance compared to the existing approaches.

6 Conclusions

We have studied the important role of textual keywords in describing high-level semantics of an image. We have also described The COLTEX a feature represents color-texture content of images that can be used for image retrieval. We have combined both the high level and low level features effectively to achieve very high average precision of retrieval. An image retrieval system has been developed to demonstrate our work and interested readers are encouraged to use our system. Promising retrieval results are obtained from our web based system. We plan to increase the database size to about 10,000 images and compare our results with other keyword and low-level feature based retrieval systems [1,3,6,9,14,15].

Acknowledgement

The work done by Shamik Sural is supported by research grants from the Department of Science and Technology, India, under Grant No. SR/FTP/ETA-20/2003 and by a grant from IIT Kharagpur under ISIRD scheme No. IIT/SRIC/ISIRD/2002-2003. Work done by A. K. Majumdar is supported by a research grant from the Department of Science and Technology, India, under Grant No. SR/S3/EECE/024/2003-SERC-Engg.

References

1. Hyoung K. Lee and Suk I. Yoo: Nonlinear Combining of Heterogeneous Features in Content-Based Image Retrieval. International journal on Computer research, Volume 11, No. 3, (2002)
2. Lempel.R and A.Soffer: PicASHOW: Pictorial Authority Search by Hyperlinks on the Web. WWW10, May 1-5, Hong Kong, (2001).

3. Mezaris .V, et. al. : Combining Textual and Visual Information Processing for Interactive Video Retrieval: SCHEMA's participation in TRECVID 2004. *TRECVID 2004*. Text Retrieval Conference TRECVID Workshop, Gaithersburg, Maryland, 15-16 November (2004)
4. Niblack W. et al: The QBIC Project: Querying Images by Content using Color Texture and Shape. SPIE Int. Soc. Opt. Eng., In Storage and Retrieval for Image and Video Databases, Vol. 1908, (1993) 173-187
5. Ortega, M. et al: Supporting Ranked Boolean Similarity Queries in MARS. IEEE Trans. on Knowledge and Data Engineering, Vol. 10 (1998) 905-925
6. Pentland P.A., R. W. Picard, and S. Sclaroff : *Photobook:* Content-based Manipulation of Image Databases. Int. Journal of Computer Vision, Vol. 18, No. 3, (1996) 233--254, (1996)
7. Salton G.: Introduction to Modern Information Retrieval, McGraw-Hill Book Company. (1993).
8. Smith, J.R., Chang, S.-F.: VisualSeek: A Fully Automated Content based Image Query System. ACM Multimedia Conf., Boston, MA (1996)
9. Srihari.R.K: Combining text and image information in content-based retrieval. International Conference on Image Processing (Vol. 1)-Volume 1 October 23 - 26, (1995)
10. Vadivel.A , Shamik Sural and A.K.Majumdar: Human color perception in the HSV space and its application in histogram generation for image retrieval. International Conference on Color Imaging X: Processing, Hardcopy, and Applications, part of the IS&T/SPIE Symposium on Electronic Imaging, December (2005)
11. Vadivel.A, Shamik Sural and A.K.Majumdar: Color-Texture Feature Extraction using Soft Decision from the HSV Color Space", International Symposium on Intelligent Multimedia Processing, Hong Kong, 2004
12. Wang, J.Z., Li, J., Wiederhold, G.: SIMPLIcity: Semantics-sensitive Integrated Matching for Picture Libraries. IEEE Trans. on PAMI, Vol. 23 (2001).
13. Web Based On Line System: Http://www.imagedb.iitkgp.ernet.in/key/index.php.
14. Xiang Sean Zhou Huang, T.S.: Unifying keywords and visual contents in image retrieval. IEEE Multimedia Volume 9, Issue 2, 22-33, (April 2002)
15. Yixin Chen, James Z. Wang and Robert Krovetz : CLUE: Cluster-based Retrieval of Images by Unsupervised Learning. IEEE Transactions on Image Processing, vol. 14, 15 (2005) in press.
16. Zhuge. H. VEGA-KG: A Way to the Knowledge Web. In Proc. of 11th International World Wide Web Conference (WWW2002), May, Honolulu, Hawaii, USA, (2002).

Finding Locally and Periodically Frequent Sets and Periodic Association Rules

A. Kakoti Mahanta[1], F.A. Mazarbhuiya[1], and H.K. Baruah[2]

[1] Department of Computer Science, Gauhati University,
Assam, India
anjanagu@yahoo.co.in,
fokrul_2005@yahoo.com
[2] Department of Statistics, Gauhati University
hemanta_bh@yahoo.com

Abstract. The problem of finding association rules from a dataset is to find all possible associations that hold among the items, given a minimum support and confidence. This involves finding frequent sets first and then the association rules that hold within the items in the frequent sets. In temporal datasets as the time in which a transaction takes place is important we may find sets of items that are frequent in certain time intervals but not frequent throughout the dataset. These frequent sets may give rise to interesting rules but these can not be discovered if we calculate the supports of the item sets in the usual way. We call here these frequent sets locally frequent. Normally these locally frequent sets are periodic in nature. We propose modification to the Apriori algorithm to compute locally frequent sets and periodic frequent sets and periodic association rules.

1 Introduction

The problem of mining association rules has been defined initially by R. Agarwal et al [1] for application in large super markets. Large supermarkets have large collection of records of daily sales. Analyzing the buying patterns of the buyers will help in taking business decisions. Mining for association rules between items in temporal databases has been described as an important data-mining problem. The market basket transaction is an example of this type.

In this paper we consider datasets, which are temporal and the time in which a transaction has taken place is attached to the transactions. In large volumes of such data, some hidden information or relationship among the items may be there which do not necessarily exist or hold through out the period covered by the dataset. Such information may remain hidden because the support (as defined in [1]) of the association rules is less than the minimum support value provided by the user if the whole dataset is considered. It may be the case that these association rules hold for certain limited time periods and not through out the entire time period covered by the dataset. For finding such association rules we need to find itemsets that are frequent at certain time intervals but not frequent if the whole life span of the database is considered. We call such frequent sets locally frequent. From these locally frequent sets, associations among the items in these sets can be obtained. Since a periodic nature is there in any natural event this kind of association rules normally hold periodically. And if such locally frequent sets are periodic in nature then we call these sets periodic frequent sets and the associated association rules as periodic association rules.

In section 2 we give a brief discussion on the recent works in Temporal Data Mining. In section 3 we describe the terms and notations used in this paper. In section 4, we give the algorithm proposed in this paper for mining locally frequent sets and local association rules. In section 5 we describe a way of extracting periodic frequent sets and the related association rules. We conclude with conclusion and lines for future work in section 6.

2 Recent Works

Given a set I, of items and a large collection D of transactions involving the items, the problem is to find relationships among the items. A transaction t is said to support an item if that item is present in t. A transaction t is said to support an itemset if t supports each of the items present in the itemset. An association rule is an expression of the form $X \Rightarrow Y$ where X and Y are subsets of the item set I. The rule holds with confidence τ if $\tau\%$ of the transaction in D that supports X also supports Y. The rule has support σ if $\sigma\%$ of the transactions supports $X \cup Y$. A method for the discovery of association rules was given in [1]. This was then followed by subsequent refinements, generalizations, extensions and improvements.

The association rule discovery process is also extended to incorporate temporal aspects. In temporal association rules each rule has associated with it a time interval in which the rule holds. The problems associated are to find valid time periods during which association rules hold, the discovery of possible periodicities that association rules have and the discovery of association rules with temporal features. In [2], [3], [4] and [5], the problem of temporal data mining is addressed and techniques and algorithms have been developed for this. In [2] the problem of mining interesting associations with a high confidence level but with little support is addressed. This problem is caused due to the way in which supports of item sets are calculated. At the denominator we have the total number of transactions in the database. For this reason the support of itemsets that appear in the transactions for a short period, may not satisfy the minimum threshold criterion for becoming frequent. To handle this problem, in this paper for each itemset a lifetime is defined which is the time gap between the first occurrence and the last occurrence of the item in the transactions in the database. Supports of items are calculated only during its life span. Thus each rule has associated with it a time frame corresponding to the lifetime of the items participating in the rule. An algorithm, which is an extension of the A priori algorithm, is then given in order to extract the temporal association rules.

In [7], two algorithms are proposed for the discovery of temporal rules that display regular cyclic variations where the time interval is specified by user to divide the data into disjoint segments like months, weeks, days etc. Similar works were done in [6] and [8] incorporating multiple granularities of time intervals (e.g. first working day of every month) from which both cyclic and user defined calendar patterns can be achieved.

Our approach is different from the above approaches. We are considering the fact that some items are seasonal or appear frequently in the transactions for certain short time intervals only. They appear in the transactions for a short time and then disappear for a long time. After this they may again reappear for a certain period and this process may repeat. For these item sets if their life span is considered as defined in [2] in calculating their support values, they may not turn out to be frequent. These items may lead to interesting association rules with large confidence values. In this paper we calculate the support values of these sets locally in a particular season or in the time interval in which it is appearing frequently and if they are frequent in the time interval under consideration then we call these sets locally frequent sets. The large time gap in which they do not appear is not counted. This new method will be able to extract all frequent sets discovered by the algorithm described in [2] and some more sets that are frequent according to the way in which we are defining locally frequent sets. We also define periodic frequent sets and periodic association rules. As mentioned in the previous paragraph similarly works were also done in [7], [6] and [8]. But in all these methods the user should have prior information about the periods, which are required to be given as input. Also for different item sets the periods or cycles may differ. Our algorithm finds the periods for itemsets in a natural way without having any prior information about these.

3 Terms, Notations and Symbols Used

Let $T = <t_o, t_1,............>$ be a sequence of time stamps over which a linear ordering $<$ is defined where $t_i < t_j$ means t_i denotes a time which is earlier than t_j. Let I denote a finite set of items and the transaction database D is a collection of transactions where each transaction has a part which is a subset of the itemset I and the other part is a time-stamp indicating the time in which the transaction had taken place. We assume that D is ordered in the ascending order of the time stamps. For time intervals we always consider closed intervals of the form $[t_1, t_2]$ where t_1 and t_2 are time stamps. We say that a transaction is in the time interval $[t_1, t_2]$ if the time stamp of the transaction say t is such that $t_1 \leq t \leq t_2$. We define the local support of an itemset in a time interval $[t_1, t_2]$ as the ratio of the number of transactions in the time interval $[t_1, t_2]$ containing the itemset to the total number of transactions in $[t_1, t_2]$ for the whole database D. We use the notation $Sup_{[t_1,t_2]}(X)$ to denote the support of the itemset X in the time interval $[t_1, t_2]$. Given a threshold σ we say that an itemset X is frequent in $[t_1,t_2]$ if $Sup_{[t_1,t_2]}(X) \geq (\sigma/100)*$ tc where tc denotes the total number of transactions in D that are in the time interval $[t_1,t_2]$. We say that an association rule $X \Rightarrow Y$, where X and Y are itemsets holds in the time interval $[t_1, t_2]$ if and only if given threshold τ,

$$Sup_{[t_1,t_2]}(X \cup Y) / Sup_{[t_1,t_2]}(X) \geq \tau/100.0$$

and $X \cup Y$ is frequent in $[t_1, t_2]$. In this case we say that the confidence of the rule is τ.

For each locally frequent itemset we keep a list of time intervals in which the set is frequent where each interval is represented as [*start, end*] where *start* and *end* gives the starting and ending time of the time-interval. *end – start* gives the length of the time interval. Given two intervals [$start_1, end_1$] and [$start_2, end_2$] if the intervals are non-overlapping and $start_2 > end_1$ then $start_2 - end_1$ gives the distance between the time intervals.

4 Algorithm Proposed

4.1 Generating Locally Frequent Sets

While constructing locally frequent sets, with each locally frequent set a list of time-intervals is maintained in which the set is frequent. Two thresholds minthd1 and minthd2 are used and these are given as input. During execution, while making a pass through the database, if for a particular itemset the time gap between its current time-stamp and the time when it was last seen is less than the value of minthd1 then the current transaction is included in the current time-interval under consideration; otherwise a new time-interval is started with the current time-stamp as the starting point. The support count of the item set in the previous time interval is checked to see whether it is frequent in that interval or not and if it is then it is added to the list maintained for that set. Also for the locally frequent sets a minimum period length is given by the user as minthd2 and time intervals of length greater than or equal to this value are only kept. If minthd2 is not used than an item appearing once in the whole database will also become locally frequent.

Procedure to compute L_1, the set of all locally frequent item sets of size 1

For each item while going through the database we always keep a time-stamp called *lastseen* that corresponds to the time when the item was last seen. When an item is found in a transaction and the time-stamp is *tm* and the time gap between *lastseen* and *tm* is greater than the current minimum threshold given, then a new time interval is started by setting *start* of the new time interval as *tm* and *end* of the previous time interval as *lastseen*. The previous time interval is added to the list maintained for that item provided that the duration of the interval and the support of the itemset in that interval are both greater than the minimum thresholds specified for each. Otherwise *lastseen* is set to *tm*, the counters maintained for counting transactions are increased appropriately and the process is continued. Following is the algorithm to compute L_1, the list of locally frequent sets of size 1. Suppose the number of items in the dataset under consideration is n and we assume an ordering among the items.

Algorithm 4.1

$C_1 = \{(i_k, tp[k]) : k = 1, 2, \ldots, n\}$
  where i_k is the k-th item and tp[k] points to a list of time intervals initially empty.
for k = 1 to n do
   set lastseen[k], itemcount[k] and transcount[k] to zero
for each transaction t in the database with time stamp tm do
 {for k = 1 to n do
   { if $\{i_k\} \subseteq t$ then

```
        { if(lastseen[k] == 0)
           {lastseen[k] = firstseen[k] = tm;
            itemcount[k] = transcount[k] = 1;
           }
         else if (tm – lastseen[k] < minthd1)
            {lastseen[k]=tm; itemcount[k]++;
             transcount[k]++;
            }
         else
            {if (((\lastseen[k]–firstseen[k]\≥ minthd2)
              &&(itemcount[k]/transcount[k]*100 ≥ σ))
                 add(firstseen[k], lastseen[k]) to tp[k];
             itemcount[k] = transcount[k] = 1;
             lastseen[k] = firstseen[k] = tm;
            }
        }
       else transcount[k]++;
      } // end of k-loop //
    } // end of do loop //
    for k = 1 to n do
     {if (\lastseen[k]–firstseen[k]\≥ mintdh2 )and (itemcount[k] / transcount[k] * 100 ≥ σ)
         add (firstseen[k], lastseen[k] ) to tp[k];
      if(tp[k] != 0) add {i_k, tp[k]} to L_1
     }
```

Two support counts are kept, *itemcount* and *transcount*. If the count percentage of an item in a time interval is greater than the minimum threshold then only the set is considered as a locally frequent set.

After this Apriori candidate generation algorithm is used to find candidate frequent set of size 2. With each candidate frequent set of size two we associate a list of time intervals that are obtained in the pruning phase. In the generation phase this list is empty. If all subsets of a candidate set are found in the previous level then this set is constructed. The process is that when the first subset appearing in the previous level is found then that list is taken as the list of time intervals associated with the set. When subsequent subsets are found then the list is reconstructed by taking all possible pair wise intersection of subsets one from each list. Sets for which this list is empty are further pruned. Using this concept we describe below the modified A priori algorithm for the problem under consideration.

Algorithm 4.2

Modified A priori

Initialize
$k = 1$;
C_1 = all item sets of size 1
L_1 = {frequent item sets of size 1 where with each itemset {i_k} a list tp[k] is maintained which gives all time intervals in which the set is frequent}

L_1 is computed using algorithm 1.1 */
for(k = 2; $L_{k-1} \neq \phi$; k++) do
    { C_k = apriorigen(L_{k-1})
    /* same as the candidate generation method of the A priori algorithm setting tp[i] to
        zero for all i*/
    prune(C_k);
    drop all lists of time intervals maintained with the sets in C_k
    Compute L_k from C_k.
//L_k can be computed from C_k using the same procedure used for computing L_1 //
    k = k + 1
    }
Answer = $\bigcup_k L_k$

Prune(C_k)

{Let m be the number of sets in C_k and let the sets be $s_1, s_2,..., s_m$. Initialize the pointers tp[i] pointing to the list of time-intervals maintained with each set s_i to null
for i = 1 to m do
    {for each (k-1) subset d of s_i do
        {if d $\notin L_{k-1}$ then { $C_k = C_k - \{s_{i,} tp[i]\}$; break;}
        else
        {if (tp[i]==null) then set tp[i] to point to the list of intervals maintained for d
        else
            {take all possible pair-wise intersection of time intervals one from each
            list, one list maintained with tp[i] and the other maintained with d and
            take this as the list for tp[i]
            delete all time intervals whose size is less than the value of minthd2
            if tp[i] is empty then { $C_k = C_k - \{s_{i,} tp[i]\}$; break; }
            }
        }
    }
}

4.2 Generating Association Rules

If an itemset is frequent in a time-interval [t_1, t_2] then all its subsets are also frequent in the time-interval [t_1, t_2]. But to generate the association rules as defined in section 3, we need the supports of the subsets in [t_1, t_2] which may not be available after application of the algorithm as defined in 4.1. For this one more scan of the whole database will be needed. For each association rule we attach an interval in which the association rule holds.

5 Extracting Periodic Patterns

In the algorithm proposed in section 4 for each locally frequent set, a list of time intervals is maintained in which the set is frequent. In this list if we find that the distance between the intervals is almost equal (up to a small variation) then we call these frequent sets periodic frequent sets. Association rules that hold periodically are called periodic association rules.

Now if the time-stamps of the transactions are the calendar dates more interesting patterns may be seen. In a market-basket database we normally will see that the sales of cold drinks go up in summer. So in each year in summer cold drink will become frequent. But this periodicity is of a special type. If we consider only the month and day associated with the transactions, then the periods in which an item set is frequent will have large overlapping.

6 Conclusion and Lines for Future Work

An algorithm for finding frequent sets that are frequent in certain time periods called locally frequent sets in the paper is given. The technique used is similar to the A priori algorithm. From these locally frequent sets interesting rules may follow. Some of these locally frequent sets may be periodic in nature. We call these sets periodic frequent sets and the associated rules as periodic association rule and suggest methods of extracting these.

For further improvement, instead of maintaining the time intervals as lists, other suitable data structures such as a balanced binary search tree could be used. Further, we are in the process of implementation the algorithm and are planning to test the algorithm using some standard data generators and real life data sets available in http://www.ics.uci.edu/ and http://www.almaden.ibm.com/.

References

1. Agrawal,R.,Imielinski,T.and Swami, A.; Mining association rules between sets of items in large databases; Proceedings of ACM SIGMOD '93, Washington(1993).
2. Ale, Juan M and Rossi, G.H.; An approach to discovering temporal association rules; Proceedings of 2000 ACM symposium on Applied Computing (2000).
3. Chen, X. and Petrounias, I.; A framework for Temporal Data Mining; DEXA'98, Austria. Springer-Verlag, Lecture Notes in Computer Science 1460 (1998) 796-805
4. Chen, X. and Petrounias, I.; Language support for Temporal Data Mining; Proceedings of , PKDD '98, Springer Verlag, Berlin (1998) 282-290
5. Chen, X., Petrounias, I. and Healthfield, H.; Discovering temporal Association rules in temporal databases; Proceedings of IADT'98, 312-319
6. Li, Y., Ning, P., Wang, X. S. and Jajodia, S.; Discovering Calendar-based Temporal Association Rules, In Proc. of the 8th Int'l Symposium on Temporal Representation and Reasonong (2001)
7. Ozden, B., Ramaswamy, S. and Silberschatz, A.; Cyclic Association Rules, Proc. of the 14th Int'l Conference on Data Engineering, USA (1998) 412-421.
8. Zimbrao, G., Moreira de Souza, J., Teixeira de Almeida V. and Araujo da Silva, W.; An Algorithm to Discover Calendar-based Temporal Association Rules with Item's Lifespan Restriction, Proc. of the 8th ACM SIGKDD 2002.

An Efficient Hybrid Hierarchical Agglomerative Clustering (HHAC) Technique for Partitioning Large Data Sets

P.A. Vijaya, M. Narasimha Murty, and D.K. Subramanian

Department of Computer Science and Automation,
Indian Institute of Science,
Bangalore - 560012, India
{pav, mnm, dks}@csa.iisc.ernet.in

Abstract. In this paper, an efficient Hybrid Hierarchical Agglomerative Clustering (HHAC) technique is proposed for effective clustering and prototype selection for pattern classification. It uses the characteristics of both partitional (an incremental scheme) and Hierarchical Agglomerative Clustering (HAC) schemes. Initially, an incremental, partitional clustering algorithm - leader is used for finding the subgroups/subclusters. It reduces the time and space requirements incurred in the formation of the subclusters using the conventional hierarchical agglomerative schemes or other methods. Further, only the subcluster representatives are merged to get a required number of clusters using a hierarchical agglomerative scheme which now requires less space and time when compared to that of using it on the entire training set. Thus, this hybrid scheme would be suitable for clustering large data sets and we can get a hierarchical structure consisting of clusters and subclusters. The subcluster representatives of a cluster can also handle its arbitrary/non-spherical shape. The experimental results (Classification Accuracy (CA) using the prototypes obtained and the computation time) of the proposed algorithm are promising.

1 Introduction

Clustering is basically an unsupervised learning technique to divide the data into groups of similar objects by using a distance or similarity function. Clustering is mainly used for prototype selection/abstractions for pattern classification, data reorganization and indexing and for detecting outliers and noisy patterns. The earlier approaches do not adequately consider the fact that the data set can be too large and may not fit in the main memory of some computers. It is necessary to examine the principle of clustering to devise efficient algorithms to minimize the I/O operations and space requirements and to get appropriate prototypes/abstractions to increase the Classification Accuracy (CA). Clustering techniques are classified into hierarchical and partitional methods [3, 5]. Hierarchical clustering algorithms can be either divisive (top-down) or agglomerative (bottom-up). Single Link Algorithm (SLA) and Complete Link Algorithm

(CLA) are Hierarchical Agglomerative Clustering (HAC) schemes which require the distance/proximity matrix [3].

K-means, K-medoids and K-medians algorithms [3, 5] are partitional clustering approaches which are based on K centroids, medoids and median patterns of the initial partitions respectively and are iteratively improved. In data mining applications, both the number of patterns and features are typically large. SLA, CLA, K-means, K-medoids and K-medians based algorithms are not feasible for large data sets. Following are some of the clustering approaches that have been used on large data sets. CLARA, CLARANS and CURE [5] clustering schemes are designed to find clusters using random samples (subset of the original set). Divide and conquer scheme, a data partitioning technique, is used for disk resident data sets [3]. Incremental clustering methods such as leader based algorithm [3, 6] and BIRCH [5] are more efficient for clustering large data sets as they involve very few database scans (less I/O operations). Leader is a simple partitional clustering technique suitable for any type of data set such as numerical, categorical and sequence whereas BIRCH is an incremental hierarchical agglomerative clustering technique and is suitable only for numerical data sets. In [6], we had proposed an incremental top-down hierarchical approach for clustering large data sets using nearest leader based algorithm [7].

The problem we have considered here is: Given a large data set, design and implement an efficient hybrid technique to find a good set of prototypes from meaningful partitions/groupings so as to improve the CA and reduce the computation time and space requirements. In the literature, a fuzzy hybrid hierarchical clustering method has been used by Arnaud et al. [1] using fuzzy c-means and a hierarchical agglomerative scheme. A hybrid hierarchical clustering scheme has been designed for protein data set by Harlow et al. [2] using Markov clustering and a hierarchical agglomerative scheme. A hybrid clustering scheme has been developed by Mark et al. [4] for clustering genes using PAM (Partitioning Around Medoids) [5] and merging operations. Fuzzy c-means, PAM and Markov clustering methods are computationally expensive for large data sets when compared to leader based method. Also, a set of leaders may form a better set of prototypes than that of random samples chosen as prototypes. This is evident from Figure 4, drawn based on the experimental results for one of the data sets (Pendigits) used. Leader based algorithm is suitable for preprocessing or at the first level of a hybrid clustering scheme for large data sets.

In this paper, we propose a hybrid clustering method which combines the characteristics of an incremental, partitional clustering algorithm - leader and a hierarchical agglomerative clustering scheme. This clustering technique is suitable for numerical, categorical and sequence data sets with suitable similarity measures. In this paper, we report the results for numerical data sets and we use Euclidean distance for characterizing dissimilarity between two patterns. This paper is organized as follows. Section 2 contains the details of the proposed method. Experimental results and discussions are presented in section 3. Conclusions are provided in section 4.

2 Proposed Method

In the proposed Hybrid Hierarchical Agglomerative Clustering (HHAC) algorithm, there are two phases. In the first phase, leader based algorithm is used to generate subclusters (say S representatives, $S < n$, where n is the total number of training patterns) using a suitable threshold value. In the second phase, these S representatives are merged using a hierarchical agglomerative scheme such as SLA or CLA to obtain say K clusters and thus K cluster representatives. In SLA, the two clusters with the smallest minimum pairwise distance are merged at every level whereas in CLA, the two clusters with the smallest maximum pairwise distance are merged.

In leader algorithm, the first pattern is selected as the leader of a cluster and each of the remaining patterns is either assigned to one of the existing clusters or may become leader of a new cluster based on the user defined threshold value. There are two ways of assigning the next pattern to a cluster [7]. In one scheme, the next pattern is compared with the leaders created in the order one by one. It is assigned to the leader under consideration if the distance is less than or equal to the threshold value and the remaining leaders are not considered further. Let us refer to this method as **'Ordered Leader No Update (OLNU)'** as the cluster representative is not updated. In the other scheme, the next pattern is tested with all the existing leaders and is assigned to the nearest leader/cluster

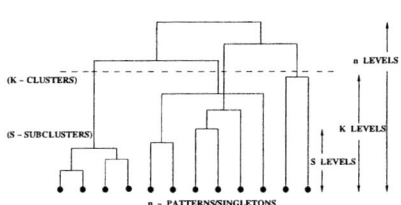

Fig. 1. Dendrogram of a HAC Algorithm

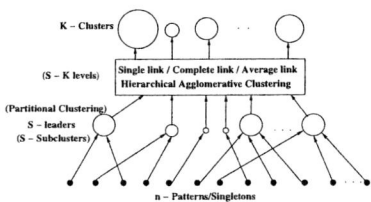

Fig. 2. Hybrid Hierarchical Agglomerative Clustering

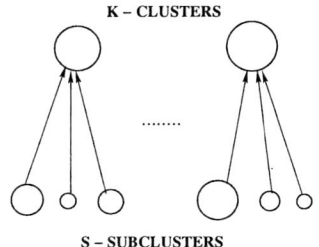

Fig. 3. Hierarchical Structure in HHAC Algorithm

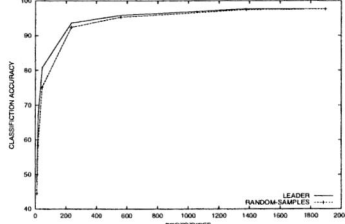

Fig. 4. Leader vs Random Samples

if the distance is less than or equal to the threshold value. Let us refer to this method as **'Nearest Leader No Update (NLNU)'**. OLNU/NLNU algorithm [7] requires only one database scan and its time complexity is $O(nSd)$, where d is the total number of attributes in a pattern. OLNU method takes less training time than NLNU method [7]. We use OLNU method in the preclustering process or at the first stage in a bottom-up hybrid hierarchical clustering technique such as HHAC for large data sets when the number of subclusters formed is large.

A small threshold value is chosen (for a dissimilarity index measure) to obtain a set of subclusters so that its size is larger than the number of clusters to be generated. In HAC schemes, the subclusters are formed in the beginning and these steps are replaced by the incremental partitional scheme - leader. This is used to save the operations performed in the first S levels in any HAC schemes as shown in Figure 1. These S representatives are merged using a HAC scheme to obtain say K clusters as shown in Figure 2. We use centroid as the cluster representative for numerical data at the second level.

Time and space complexity of the proposed method is less compared to the conventional HAC algorithms which use all the n training patterns as singleton clusters. As $S < n$, S representatives and $S \times S$ distance matrix may be accommodated in the main memory and hence reduces the disk I/O operations for large data sets. The space requirement of the HAC scheme in the second phase of HHAC is $O(S^2)$ instead of $O(n^2)$. Time complexity of the hierarchical agglomerative scheme is $O(S^2 d)$ instead of $O(n^2 d)$ for SLA and is $O((S^2 log S)d)$ instead of $O((n^2 log n)d)$ for CLA. Thus, HHAC algorithm generates a hierarchical structure as shown in Figure 3 and it consists of subgroups/subclusters within each cluster as required in many applications. Its time complexity is $O((nS + S^2)d)$ or $O((nS + S^2 log S)d)$ for leader with SLA or CLA respectively. There would be several subgroups/subclusters in each group/cluster of numerical data sets such as handwritten or printed character data sets. It is necessary to find these subgroups/subclusters also. Subcluster representatives of a cluster can take care of the arbitrary shape of that cluster. If a representative from each subgroup is chosen then naturally CA would be improved. Prototypes (representatives of the clusters and subclusters) are generated using the training data set. During classification/testing phase, for every test pattern, the nearest cluster representative is found first and then the nearest subcluster representative in that cluster is determined. Then the test pattern is classified based on the nearest of these two. For different values of threshold and K, experiments (both training and testing) are conducted and the results are evaluated. To evaluate the clustering quality (quality of the prototypes selected), labelled patterns are considered. During training phase they are treated as unlabelled patterns and the prototypes are selected. The quality of the prototypes is evaluated using the CA obtained on the test/validation data set. The experimental results of the proposed method are discussed in the following section.

3 Experimental Results

To evaluate the performance of HHAC algorithm, experiments were conducted on many data sets from machine learning repository of University of California, Irvine (http://www.ics.uci.edu/). Because of the space constraints, we are reporting few results for one of the data sets - Pendigits. There are 7494 patterns in the training set, 3498 patterns in the testing set and 10 classes with 16 numerical attribute values.

Table 1. Time and Classification Accuracy (CA)

Algorithm	Threshold	Subclusters (S)	Clusters (K)	Training time (s)	Testing time (s)	CA (%)
NNC	-	-	7494	-	135.57	97.74
SLA	-	-	861	61662.97	14.98	87.19
	-	-	2298	55018.08	40.73	96.65
CLA	-	-	861	68862.83	15.27	97.28
	-	-	2298	60241.55	40.76	97.88
LSLA(K)	20	4816	861	15380.90	15.89	86.62
	20	4816	2298	11977.26	41.58	96.45
	25	3361	861	4799.22	13.37	91.19
	25	3361	2298	2760.94	41.60	97.36
LCLA(K)	20	4816	861	16884.30	15.34	96.48
	20	4816	2298	12780.51	41.27	98.02
	25	3361	861	5021.54	13.08	95.91
	25	3361	2298	2839.51	40.16	97.51
LSLA(S+K)	20	4816	861	15380.90	18.35	88.67
	20	4816	2298	11977.26	46.10	96.51
	25	3361	861	4799.22	16.93	92.45
	25	3361	2298	2760.94	41.99	97.48
LCLA(S+K)	20	4816	861	16884.30	18.27	97.25
	20	4816	2298	12780.51	42.48	98.02
	25	3361	861	5021.54	14.33	97.02
	25	3361	2298	2839.51	40.55	97.62

LSLA - Leader and SLA, LCLA - Leader and CLA. K or S+K within brackets indicates the set of prototypes used during testing phase

The experiments were done on an Intel pentium-4 processor based machine having a clock frequency of 1700 Mhz and 512 MB RAM. In each case, different threshold and K values were used for HHAC algorithms. The performances of Nearest Neighbour Classifier (NNC) [3,6] and HAC schemes have also been reported in Table 1. Performance with CLA is the best among the four HAC schemes - SLA, CLA, Average Link algorithm and Weighted Average Link algorithm, for the data sets used. We have reported the results for SLA and CLA.

From the results obtained (as shown in Table 1), it is evident that HHAC algorithms performed well compared to HAC approaches in terms of computation time for almost the same CA or even more. Training time is the time taken for generating the prototypes. Testing time is the time taken for classifying all the test patterns. After the training phase, testing time is less when only cluster representatives are used but increases a little when subcluster representatives are also used. Even then, it is less when compared to NNC. The CA is greater than or as that of NNC when both cluster and subcluster representatives are used. Even if more number of prototypes are generated, classification time is less as only a part of the hierarchical structure is searched.

4 Conclusions

In this paper, experimental results of HHAC algorithm on numerical data sets show that it performs well by properly tuning the threshold and K values. HHAC algorithm is used to generate clusters and subclusters - a hierarchical structure. If both cluster and subcluster representatives are used then the CA is nearly same as that of NNC or even more. Subclusters can be obtained at low computation cost when compared to the conventional HAC schemes or other partitional methods, by using an incremental partitional approach such as leader. The performance of the hybrid technique with K-means or K-medoids at the second level is also found to be good. The proposed technique can also be used on protein sequence data sets, text and web document collection with appropriate distance measures.

References

1. Arnaud, D., Patrice, B., Gerard, V. L.: A Fuzzy Hybrid Hierarchical Clustering Method with a New Criterionable to Find the Optimal Partition. Fuzzy Sets and Systems. 128:3(2002) 323–338
2. Harlow, T. J., Gogarten, J. P., Ragan, M. A.: A Hybrid Clustering Approach to Recognition of Protein Families in 114 Microbial Genomes. BMC Bioinformatics. 5:45(2004) 1–14
3. Jain, A. K., Murty, M. N., Flynn, P. J.: Data Clustering: A Review. ACM Computing Surveys. 31:3(1999) 264–323
4. Mark, J. V., Katherine S. P.: A New Algorithm for Hybrid Hierarchical Clustering with Visualization and the Bootstrap. Journal of Statistical Planning and Inference. 117:2(2003) 275–303
5. Pujari, A. K.: Data Mining Techniques. Universities Press (India) Private Limited. (2000)
6. Vijaya, P. A., Murty, M. N., Subramanian, D. K.: Leaders-Subleaders: An Efficient Hierarchical Clustering Algorithm for Large Data Sets. Pattern Recognition Letters. 25(2004) 503–511
7. Vijaya, P. A., Murty, M. N., Subramanian, D. K.: Analysis of Leader based Clustering Algorithms for Pattern Classification, Accepted for publication in the Proceedings of the 2nd IICAI, Pune, India, Dec. 2005.

Density-Based View Materialization

A. Das and D.K. Bhattacharyya

Department of Information Technology,
Tezpur University, Napaam 784 028, India
dkb@tezu.ernet.in

Abstract. View materialization or pre-computation of aggregates(views) is a well known technique used in data warehouse design and Decision Support System(DSS) to reduce the query response time. Obviously, all the views cannot be materialized due to space-time constraint. So, one important decision in designing Data Warehouse and DSS is to select the views to be materialized, which will reduce the query response time to the minimum limit in a DSS. This paper presents a density-based view materialization algorithm with average runtime complexity O($n\log n$), where n is the number of views. We have used data cube lattice, view size, access frequency of the views and support(frequency) of the views in selecting the views to be materialized. Our algorithm works much faster and selects better views than other existing algorithms.

1 Introduction

OLAP operations deal with aggregate data(views). Hence, materialization or pre-computation of summarized data are often required to accelerate the DSS query processing and data warehouse design. In this context, there are three possibilities: materialize all the aggregates, no materialization and partial materialization. Among these, partial materialization is the most feasible solution.

View(cuboid) selection for materialization is a challenging task. Most of the algorithms to select views to be materialized have to work on some constraints. References [1,7] and [8] have discussed materialized view selection under disk-space constraint. *BPUS* [7] is a greedy algorithm, which selects the views with the highest benefits per unit space. Reference [1] has gone little further to present the *PBS*(Pick By Size) algorithm with the complexity O($n\log n$). However, PBS is meant for SR(Size Restricted)-Hypercube lattice. A^* algorithm [6] is interactive, flexible and robust enough to find the optimal solution under disk space constraint and the algorithm has been found to be useful when disk-space constraint is small. One important algorithm is *PVMA*(Progressive View Materialization Algorithm) [3]. This algorithm uses frequency of queries, updates on views, and view size to select views to be materialized using greedy algorithm. The algorithm has been found to be better than *PBS* and *PBUS*.

This paper presents a faster view materialization algorithm(*DVMA*) based on the notion of density, taken from the algorithm *DBSCAN* and support(frequency)

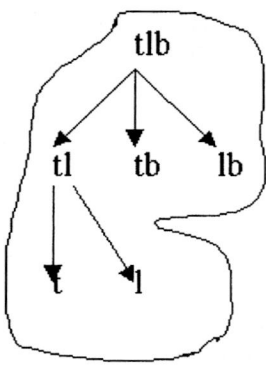

t, l, tb, lb : border points.
tlb, tl are core points.

tl is directly density-reachable from tlb.
t is density-reachable from tlb
t and lb are density connected by tlb

Fig. 1. Core points, border points and density-reachable points

of the sub-views. . Sub-view is nothing, but a subset of the view under consideration. The algorithm also has applied the concept of cost/benefit of *PVMA* to form the clusters of views.

The rest of the paper is organized as follows. Section 2 discusses density concept followed by section 3, which presents the Density-based View Materialization Algorithm. Section 4 gives the experimental results.

2 Density Concept

DBSCAN [4] uses the concept of density to find clusters of arbitrary shapes. We also have used the same density concept to form clusters of views and select the views to be materialized in a data warehouse system. A cluster in *DVMA* consists of views. The main concept of the *DVMA* algorithm is that *benefit* of the neighbourhood of any view in a cluster must be at least some pre-defined value. Here, benefit represents the quality of a cluster and has been defined in the following sections. Other important concepts are neighbourhood, minimum benefit, directly-density-reachable, density-reachable and cluster. Some concepts are defined below and other concepts can be found in [4]. For all the definitions, it is assumed that views are arranged in the form of a lattice as explained in [7].

- *Neighbourhood* : Neighbourhood of a view v with respect to $MaxD$, denoted by $N(v)$, is defined by $N(v) = v \cup \{w|w \in children(v)$ and $R(v) - R(w) \leq MaxD\}$.
- *Core View* : A view v is said to be core view if benefit$(N(v)) \geq MinBen$, where $MinBen$ is the minimum benefit.

There are basically three categories of views - *classified, unclassified* and *noise*. *Classified* views are already associated with a cluster; *unclassified* views are not yet associated with any cluster; *noise* views do not belong to any cluster . So it is understood that neighborhoods of classified and noise views are already calculated. Another category of views, called *leader* view, has been introduced. A leader view is an unclassified view, of which all the parents are either classified(not materialized) or declared noise.

3   Density-Based View Materialization Algorithm(*DVMA*)

The algorithm centers around forming the clusters of views. While creating clusters, the algorithm has to calculate benefits of neighborhoods. The benefit is based on the view size(number of rows), access frequency of view and supports of the sub-views. Supports of the frequent sub-views have been used to select the views because it has been observed that supports of the sub-views help select better views for materialization. Access frequencies of the views are easily available in any data warehouse system and support of the frequent sub-views can be generated by applying any association rule mining algorithm on the query database. View sizes also can be easily calculated [2,9].

The algorithm assumes that views are selected independently, there is no space constraint and OLAP uses relational database system. The algorithm also assumes that views are organized in the form of lattice as discussed in [7]. The algorithm first finds all the clusters of views and then selects the core views of the clusters for materialization. The algorithm always selects the top view(fact table) for materialization. So top view is not included in the formation of the clusters; clusters are formed from the rest of the views. In each iteration, the algorithm finds the smallest leader view v among the leader views with highest dimensions because we want to create clusters from the top of the lattice. Then it calculates the benefit of $N(v)$. If the benefit is less than the minimum benefit($MinBen$), it is marked as a noise. Otherwise, a cluster starts at v, and all the unclassified child views are put into a list of candidate views. Then one view from the candidate views is picked up and benefit is calculated. If it is a core view, all the unclassified child views are included in the list of candidate views. Otherwise, it is marked as classified. The process continues until the list becomes empty. Thus, one cluster is formed. Similarly, other clusters also are formed. When a cluster is formed , core view of the cluster is selected for materialization. The algorithm is given in *Fig* 2.

It is to be noted that Benefit of $N(v)$(*Formula* 1) is calculated in the same way as benefit of a view v was calculated in *PVMA* [3].

$$benefit(N(v)) = \left(R(NMPV(v)) - R(v) \sum_{p \in N(v) \cup v} f_p \right) + \sum_{p \in N(v) \cup F} s(v) \quad (1)$$

In the *Formula* 1, $NMPV(v)$ is the nearest materialized parent view of v, $R(v)$ is the size of v(number of rows), f_v is the access frequency of v, $child(v)$ is the set of children of v, F is the set of frequent sub-views and $s(v)$ is the support of v. F and $s(v)$ can be generated by transforming the query database into the

Algorithm : *DVMA*
Input : Lattice of the views, V= Set of views, Access frequency of the views access, F, $MaxD$, $MinBen$
Output: S = Views to be materialized.
Set all views of V as leader.
$S = \{v_1\}$ (S:set of views to be materialized, v_1: fact table}
$Temp$= "True"
$clid$ = Get a new cluster id.
Do while there is a leader view
       Find leader view v with smallest in size $(R(v))$ among leader views
           with maximum dimensions.
      $Temp$= CreateCluster(V, v,$clid$, $MaxD$, $MinBen$)
      If $Temp$ = "True" then
          clid = Get a new cluster id.
      Endif

End DO

CreateCluster(V, v,$clid$, $MaxD$, $MinBen$)
(Form the cluster with cluster id as $clid$)
If benefit$(N(v)) < MinBen$ Then
      v.noise= "True"
       Return "False"
Else
       v.classified="True"
      $S = S \cup v$
      seeds= $\{w|w \in N(v)$ and w.classified="False" $\}$
      For all $s \in seeds$ set s.classified= "True"
      While Empty($seeds$)="False" Do
          For each $s \in seeds$
             If benefit$(N(s)) \geq MinBen$ then
                $S = S \cup s$
                $Results = \{w|w \in N(s)\}$
                For each $r \in Results$
                    If r.classified = "False" then
                       $seeds = seeds \cup r$
                       r.classified="True"
                  Endif
                EndFor
            Endif
            $seeds = seeds - \{s\}$
          Endfor
      EndWhile
      Return "True"
Endif

Fig. 2. DVMA Algorithm

form of market-basket database and then applying any association rule mining algorithms on the database. Other symbols have been discussed in detail in [3]. Here, each view will require to compute the neighbourhood only once. So average run time complexity of the algorithm is $O(n \log n)$, where n is number of views. The time complexity is much less than that of *PVMA*. *MinBen* can be set to any arbitrary positive value according to requirement. However, optimum value can be calculated in the same way as cost of a view is calculated in *PVMA*. Similarly, optimum value for *MaxD* can be determined in the same way as *Eps* has been determined in [4].

4 Experimental Results

We compared the performance of *DVMA* with *PVMA* in terms of average query cost(average number of tuples to be processed) with two synthetic datasets (TD1 and TD2), because *PVMA* is one of the important algorithms to select the views for materialization. Each of TD1 and TD2 contained 8 dimensions without any hierarchy, one measure attribute and 2 lacs tuples. Each of 255 possible views was indexed from 1 to 255. Values of each dimension and measure attribute were chosen randomly. We used PIV machine 128 MB RAM for the experiments. We assumed that queries on any view were equally likely and we used the analytical formula presented in [2,9] to estimate the size of views. We created one view(query) database with about 1000 views to calculate access frequencies of the views and frequent sub-views. Frequent sub-views and their supports were calculated using *modified_Bit_AssocRule* [5] with minimum support as 5%. We took a constant value for *MinBen* and *MaxD*, because these parameters also do not change even if some views have been materialized. Fig 3 gives the average query cost in terms of average number of tuples (in '000) required to be processed against the number of materialized views for TD1 and TD2.

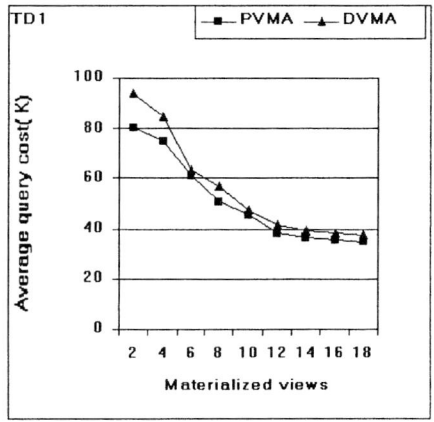
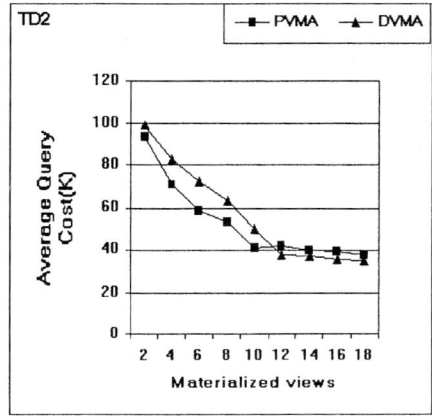

Fig. 3. Average Query Cost('K tuples)

4.1 Discussion

Experimental results showed that both the algorithms selected almost same views and average query costs were also almost same for both the algorithms. In case of TD1, *PVMA* selected slightly better views than that of *DVMA*, resulting in slightly better performance in terms of average query cost. In case of TD2, *PVMA* outperformed *DVMA* marginally in the beginning, when number of materialized views was small. However, as the number of materialized views increased, *DVMA* outperformed *PVMA* in terms of average query cost. This could be attributed to the selection of better views by *DVMA*. The main strength of *DVMA* is the execution time, which is much less than that of *PVMA*. However, due to space constraint, we could not present the execution time comparison.

References

1. A Shukla, P M Despande and J F Naughton. Materialized View Selection for Multidimensional Datasets. In *Proceedings of 24th VLDB Conference*, Newyork, 1998.
2. A Shukla, P M Despande, J F Naughton and K Ramasamy. Storage Estimation for Multidimensional Aggregates in the Presence of Hierarchies. In *Proceedings of 22nd International VLDB Conference*, 1996.
3. H Uchiyama, K Runapongsa and T J Theorey. A Progressive View Materialization Algorithm. In *Proceedings of 2nd International Data Warehousing and OLAP Workshop*, Kansas City, Nov, 1999.
4. M Ester, H P Krigel, J Sander and X Xu. A Density- based Algorithm for Discovering Clusters in Large Spatial Databases with Noise. In *Proceedings of 2nd International Conference on Knowledge Discovery and Data Mining*, Portland, 1996,pp 226-231.
5. A Das and D K Bhattacharyya. Faster Algorithms for Association Rule Mining. In *Proceedings of 12th International Conference on Advanced Computing and Communication*, Ahmedabad, India, Dec, 2004.
6. G Gang, Xu Jeffrey, C Chi-Hon, L Hongjun . An Efficient and Interactive A^* Algorithm with Pruning Power: Materialized View Selection Revisited. In *Proceedings of 8th International Conference On Database Systems for Advanced Application(DASFAA)*, 2003.
7. V Harinarayan, A Rajaraman and J D Ullman. Implementing Data Cubes Efficiently. In *Proceedings 1996 ACM-SIGMOD International Management of Data* Montreal ,Canada, 1996.
8. V Harinarayan, A Rajaraman and J D Ullman. Index Selection for OLAP. In *Proceedings for 13th International Conference on Data Engineering*, 208-219, 1997.
9. W Liang, H Wang and M E Orlowska. Materialized View Selection Under Time Constraint. *Data and Knowledge Engineering*, pp203-216, 2001.

On Simultaneous Selection of Prototypes and Features in Large Data

T. Ravindra Babu[1], M. Narasimha Murty[1], and V.K. Agrawal[2]

[1] Department of Computer Science and Automation,
Indian Institute of Science,
Bangalore, India
[2] ISRO Satellite Centre, Bangalore, India

Abstract. In dealing with high-dimensional, large data, for the sake of abstract generation one resorts to either dimensionality reduction or cluster the patterns and deal with cluster representatives or both. The current paper examines whether there exists an equivalence in terms of generalization error. Four different approaches are followed and results of exercises are provided in driving home the issues involved.

Keywords: Data Mining, prototype selection, frequent itemsets, clustering, feature selection.

1 Introduction

In a broad sense, any method that incorporates information from training samples in the design of a classifier employs learning [1]. Classification of Large Data is a challenging task, especially in the context of Data Mining. Occam's famous razor states that "Entities should not be multiplied beyond necessity". One may restate this as, "Given two models with the same generalization error, the simpler one should be preferred because simplicity is desirable in itself" [2].

With set of training patterns, each characterized by a large number of features the phenomena of "curse of dimensionality"[1] dominates. For a 'd' binary-featured pattern, the total number of possible distinct patterns is 2^d. This makes a classification algorithm unwieldy with large data, which is the focus of the current work. In view of this, one resorts to dimensionality reduction and less complex models, even though it amounts to discarding some information. At the same time, one would look to avoid overfitting and achieve smoother discrimination region. Alternatively, one can also find prototypes from the data by resorting to clustering. The approaches followed in the current work are novel and different from earlier work on the topic [8].

In the current work, we classify large Handwritten Digit data by four approaches combining dimensionality reduction and prototype selection. The compactness achieved by dimensionality reduction is indicated by means of number of combinations of distinct subsequences [5]. The concepts of Frequent items [3] and Leader cluster algorithms [4] are made use in the work. The k-NNC is the learner[1].

2 Training, Validation and Test Data

Large handwritten digit data of 10 classes is considered for the study. The data consists of 10003 labeled patterns, with 6670 training and 3333 test patterns. Each pattern consists of 192 binary features. The number of patterns per class is almost uniform. The above training data is further subdivided, for the current study, into training (6000) and validation (670) data. Figure 1 contains a sample set of handwritten data, which is under study.

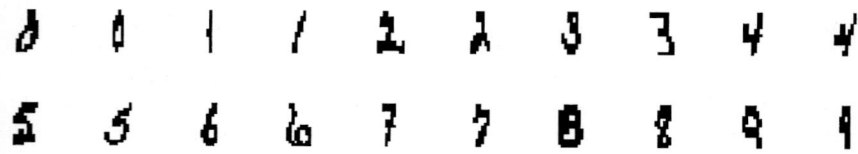

Fig. 1. A sample set of patterns of Handwritten data

3 Basic Terminology

Consider training data containing 'm' patterns, each having 'p' features. Let 'ϵ' and 'η' be minimum support [6,3] for considering any feature for the study and distance threshold respectively. Definitions of parameters which are used in the rest of paper are provided below.

Definition 1 *Sequence[7].* A sequence of integer numbers $\{s_1, s_2..s_p\}$ is a function from I to I' where I and I' are two sets of positive integers.

Definition 2 *Subsequence[7].* If $S=\{S_n\}$, n=1, 2..∞ is a sequence of integer numbers and $N=\{n_i\}$, i=1, 2..∞ is subsequence of the sequence of positive integers, then the composite function $S \circ N$ is called subsequence of S.

Definition 3 *Length of a subsequence.* Number of elements of a subsequence is the length of a subsequence.

Definition 4 *Block, Block Length.* A finite number of binary digits forms a block. Number of bits in a block is called the **block length**.

Definition 5 *Leader.* Leaders are cluster representatives obtained by using Leader Clustering algorithm[4]. The clustering algorithm is explained in Section 3.3.

Definition 6 *Support.* Support of a feature, in the current work, is actual number of patterns in which the feature is present[6, 3]. Minimum support is referred to as ϵ.

We use (a) pattern and transaction and (b) item and feature interchangeably in the current work. Following sections describe some of the important steps used.

3.1 Distinct Subsequences

The concepts of sequence, subsequence, length of subsequence are used in the context of demonstrating compactness of pattern. For example, consider a pattern containing binary features, as (0111 0110 1101 .. 0). Consider a block of length 4 and convert each subsequence to decimal code. Now the pattern will contain three blocks each of length of 4-bits, as (7, 6, 13...2). Let each set of three such codes form a subsequence, e.g., (7, 6, 13). In the training set all such distinct subsequences are counted. They form distinct subsequences. Original data of 6000 training patterns consists of 6000*192 features. When arranged as discussed in the current section and distinct subsequences are computed, they turn out to be 690. To elaborate further, consider two most frequent distinct subsequences, (0, 6, 0) and (0, 3, 0) in the entire data across all classes. Subsequence (0, 6, 0) repeats 8642 times and (0, 3, 0) repeats 6447 times. As the minimum support value, ϵ is increased, some of the feature values (binary) would be set to zero. This will lead to reduction in the number of distinct subsequences, as we would show later.

3.2 Computation of Frequent Features

This is intended to examine whether all features help discrimination. Number of occurrences of a feature in training data is computed. If the number is less than given ϵ, value of the features is set to be absent in all the patterns. The remaining features in the training data form 'frequent features'. Value of ϵ depends on the amount of training data, such as class-wise data of 600 patterns each or full data of 6000 patterns.

3.3 Computation of Leaders

The leader clustering algorithm [4] starts with first pattern as the first leader. With the given dissimilarity threshold, the algorithm scans the training data to place patterns within the same cluster. As a pattern that lies beyond the dissimilarity threshold is found, it is selected as next leader. The number of leaders depends on the value of dissimilarity threshold, η.

The leaders are considered as prototypes and they alone are used further, either for classification or for computing frequent items, depending on the adopted approach.

3.4 Classification of Validation Data

The prototypes containing frequent features are used for classifying validation data using k-NNC. Different approaches are followed to generate prototypes. They are described in the following section.

4 Considered Approaches

1. Consider Patterns containing Frequent Items alone
   (a) Identify frequent items for the given support considering (i) class-wise data and (ii) entire training data
   (b) Classify validation data with training data containing frequent features using kNNC
   (c) Compute number of distinct subsequences as an indicator of compactness of the pattern representation
2. Consider Cluster Representatives Alone
   (a) Generate leaders considering (i) class-wise data and (ii) full training data as two approaches
   (b) Classify validation data with leaders using kNNC
3. Computation of Frequent Items followed by Clustering
   (a) Identify frequent items using (i) class-wise data and (ii)the entire data and for the given ϵ
   (b) Generate leaders among the training data containing frequent items
   (c) Classify validation data with leaders containing frequent items using kNNC
4. Clustering followed by Frequent Item Generation
   (a) Generate leaders considering (a) class-wise data and (b) entire training data together
   (b) Identify frequent items in the leader patterns for the given η
   (c) Classify validation data with leaders using kNNC.

5 Discussion of Results

Extensive experimentation is carried out. Summary of results are provided in Table-1.

In Approach-1, we consider all patterns($\eta=0$) and frequent items are identified by considering support values (ϵ) from 0 to 200 for class-wise dataset handling. In case of full dataset ϵ is changed from 0 to 2000. Thus the number of effective items(or features) get reduced per pattern. This in turn results in reduction in distinct subsequences. For the case where best classification accuracy is obtained with validation data, the number of distinct subsequences in case of class-wise data is 507 out of 669 features and 450 out of 669 features. The Classification Accuracies(CA) with test data for class-wise data and full dataset are 92.32% and 92.05% respectively.

In Approach-2, only prototypes are considered($\epsilon=0$). The distance threshold values are changed from 0.0 to 5.0 in both the cases and prototypes are computed using leader clustering algorithm. For the best case with validation data, the C's with test data are 93.31% and 92.26% respectively. Observe that in this approach, the number of distinct features remain as in the original data.

In Approach-3, frequent items are computed first on the original data and then clustering is resorted to. Frequent items are computed with ϵ values ranging

Table 1. Results with each Approach

Sl No.	Approach	Description	ϵ	η	Prototypes	Distinct features	CA(kNNC) Valdn Data	CA(kNNC) Test Data
1	1	Class-wise data	160	0	6000	507	92.52%	92.32%
2	1	Full data	450	0	6000	361	92.09%	92.05%
3	2	Class-wise data	0	3.1	5064	669	93.14%	93.31%
4	2	Full data	0	3.1	5041	669	93.13%	92.26%
5	3	Class-wise data	40	3.1	5027	542	93.43%	93.52%
6	3	Full data	190	3.1	5059	433	93.58%	93.34%
7	4	Class-wise data	180	3.1	5064	433	93.58%	93.34%
8	4	Full data	300	3.1	5041	367	93.58%	93.52%

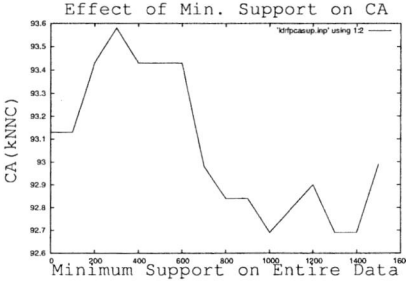
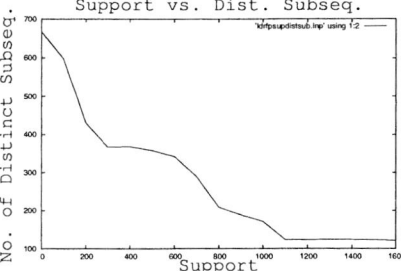

Fig. 2. (a)Support on C.A.(b) Support Vs. Dist. Subsequences in Approach-4 Full Data

from 0 to 200 in steps of 5.0. Subsequently, in each such case, prototypes are computed using leader clustering algorithm. The distance threshold values (η) are changed from 0 to 5.0 in steps of 1.0. The CAs obtained with test data, corresponding to best cases with validation datasets for class-wise data and full dataset are 93.52% and 93.34% respectively. Observe that number of distinct features of these two cases are 542 and 433.

In Approach-4, clustering is carried out first followed by frequent item computation. The CAs with test data corresponding to best cases with validation data are 93.34% and 93.52% for class-wise and full datasets respectivley. Further there is reduction in number of prototypes from original 6000 to 5064 and 5041 for each of these two cases. Significantly, the reduction in distinct subsequences is 433 and 367 respectively.

The number of distinct subsequences can be taken as an indicator of compactness. Another significant result is that there is no **significant reduction in Classification Accuracy(CA) even with good reduction in number of distinct subsequences**. This can be observed from Figure 2, corresponding to Approach-4 with full training data. Fig.2(a) displays CA for various values of support considering entire data and distance threshold of 3.1. Observe that CA with support of 300 reaches maximum. Fig.2(b) displays reduction in the number of distinct subsequences with increasing support considering full data.

6 Summary

With the objective of handling large data classification problem efficiently, a study is considered to examine the effectiveness of prototype selection and feature selection independently as well as in combination. In the process of the activity, the training data is considered both fully as well as class-wise. kNNC is considered for classifying given large, high-dimensional handwritten data. Extensive exercises are carried out and results are presented.

Important contributions of this work have been to show that combination of prototype and feature selection leads to better Classification Accuracy. Clustering data containing frequent features has provided good amount of compactness for classification. Such compactness did not result in significant reduction in classification accuracy. It is proposed to extend the current work to study the impact of maximum support of an item on compactness of representation as well as for classification.

References

1. Richard O. Duda, Peter E. Hart, David G. Stork.: Pattern Classification John Wiley & Sons, Inc, New York. (2002)
2. Pedro Domingos Occam's Two Razors: The Sharp and the Blunt.: American Association for Artificial Intelligence (1998)
3. Han, J., Pei, J., and Yin, Y. Mining frequent patterns without candidate generation Proc. 2000 ACM-SIGMOD Int. Conf. Management of Data(SIGMOD'00), Dallas, TX, May 2000 (2000) 1–12
4. H.Spath. : Cluster Analysis - Algorithms for Data Reduction and Classification of Objects Ellis Horwood Limited,West Sussex, UK (1980)
5. Ravindra Babu, T., Narasimha Murty, M., Agrawal, V.K. Hybrid Learning Scheme for Data Mining Applications Presented at Conference on Hybrid Intelligent Systems, HIS04, December 06-08, Kitakyushu, Japan (2004)
6. Agrawal, R., Imielinski, T., and Swami, A. : Mining association rules between sets of items in large databases Proc. 1993 ACM-SIGMOD Int. Conf. Management of Data(SIGMOD'93) 207–216, Washington,DC, May 1993 (1993)
7. Richard R. Goldberg : Methods of Real Analysis Oxford & IBH Publishing Co., New Delhi (1978) 24–25
8. Belur V. Dasarathy, J.S.Sanchez : Concurrent Feature and Prototype Selection in the Nearest Neighbour Decision Process Proc. of 4th World Multiconference on Systemics, Cybernetics and Informatics, Vol.VII, Orlando(USA), ISBN 980-07-6693-6 (2000) 628–633.

Knowledge Enhancement Through Ontology-Guided Text Mining

Muhammad Abulaish[1] and Lipika Dey[2,*]

[1] Department of Mathematics, Jamia Millia Islamia (A Central University),
New Delhi-25, India
mdabulaish@yahoo.com
[2] Department of Mathematics, Indian Institute of Technology,
New Delhi-16, India
lipika@maths.iitd.ernet.in

Abstract. In this paper we have proposed a system that performs both ontology-based text information extraction and ontology update using the extracted information. The system employs text-mining techniques to mine information from text documents guided by an underlying ontology. It also enhances the existing ontology with new concepts and their descriptors which may be precise and/ or imprecise, mined from the text. All extracted information related to concepts and concept descriptors are also stored in a structured knowledge base.

Keywords: Text mining, Information extraction, Ontology enhancement.

1 Introduction

Semantic analysis of texts with the help of structured domain knowledge can help in extracting information effectively from the documents. Ontologies store the key concepts and their inter-relationships thereby providing a shared common understanding of a domain [3]. Generally a concept in Ontology is defined in terms of its mandatory and optional properties along with the value restrictions on those properties. However, ontology-based text mining poses its own problems. Firstly, the concepts even if present in documents need not be present in conjunction with the same descriptors, rather may appear with new descriptors or even in association with qualifiers, which defines a fuzzy presence of the properties. Moreover, information extraction from web documents has to also account for imprecise concept descriptions presented by users while specifying a query [1]. A description is termed *imprecise* if it can have varying degrees of similarity with known descriptions. As of now, there is no general ontological framework for qualifying a property. Another bottleneck in designing ontology based information extraction systems arises from the fact that most of the existing domain ontologies are created and maintained manually by domain experts, which is a costly and time-consuming task. A critical issue in developing such systems therefore is the task of *identifying, defining* and *embedding* new concepts and concept descriptions into existing domain ontologies.

---
[*] Author for Correspondence.

This paper explores the possibility of focused information extraction from web documents in an ontology-guided way. The proposed text-mining system parses documents syntactically and then starts looking for known concepts present in the domain seed ontology. Thereafter it applies semantic analysis for inferring related concepts. The mined concepts are integrated into the existing ontological structure to enhance it. The rest of the paper is organized as follows. We present a brief overview of some related works on ontology learning and ontology-based text processing systems in section 2. Section 3 presents the system overview followed by some results that are given in section 4. Finally, we conclude the paper in section 5.

2 Related Work

The use of ontological models to access and integrate large knowledge repositories in a principled way has an enormous potential to enrich and make accessible unprecedented amounts of knowledge for reasoning [2]. Ontology representation languages like DAML+OIL and OWL are based on Description Logics (DLs) thus enabling the knowledge representation systems to provide reasoning support as well [4]. A number of systems exist to help in the process of construction of domain ontologies, of which the most famous one is the Protégé[1]. In [6] a java-based tool that helps domain experts by providing a graphical interface for domain ontology creation and testing is proposed. This is then used to extract data from web documents and to store them in structured form. [8] reported a text-mining tool to identify, define, and enter concept descriptions into ontology structures. In [5] an abstract Web mining model for gathering and extracting concepts by analyzing approximate concepts hidden in user profiles on the Semantic Web has been proposed. All the above works assume that concept descriptions are precise. Answering imprecise queries over structured databases have been addressed in [7].

3 Proposed Framework

Fig. 1 presents the architecture of the proposed system, which consists of five major modules – *Document Processor, Concept Miner, Fuzzy Description Generator, Ontology Editor* and *Ontology Parser*. The *Document Processor* applies shallow parsing techniques to identify relevant segments in a document and stores them into a tree structured form. Both *Concept Miner* and *Fuzzy Description Generator* work on these tree structures to enhance the ontology with new concepts extracted from documents and to instantiate the structured knowledge base. Ontology update is implemented through the *ontology editor*. The structured knowledge base is created to store the extracted information in a structured format. The design of the knowledge base is based on the ontology and is output by the *ontology parser*. The document processor outputs two similar tree structures differing in the information components contained in their nodes. For the *Concept Miner*, the nouns, adjectives and verbs identified in the document are stored in the tree generated as follows:

---

[1] http://protégé.stanford.edu

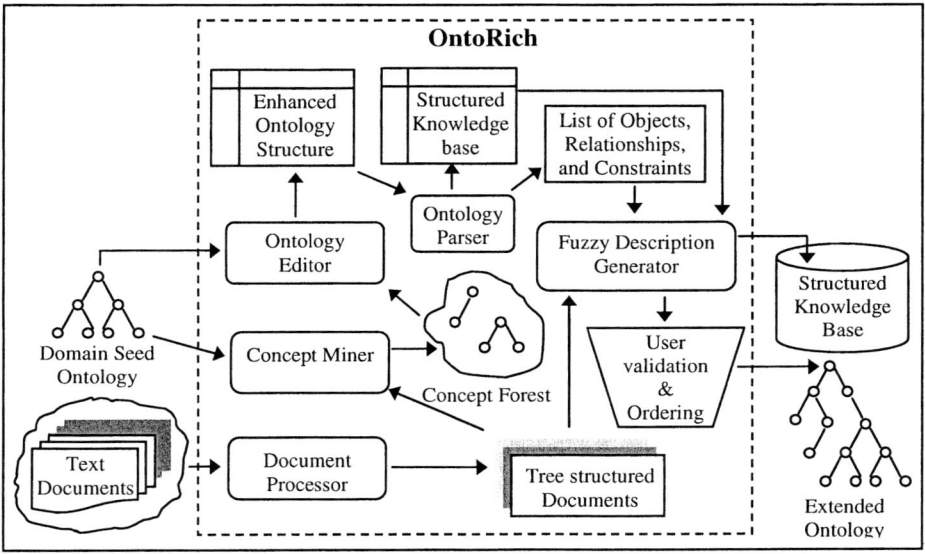

Fig. 1. Proposed system architecture for Ontology enhancement

Root (**R**):   A node that contains the *verb phrase* of a segment.
Lchild (**L**): A node that contains *noun phrase* left of the verb phrase considered at R.
Mchild (**M**): A node that contains *noun phrase* right of the verb phrase considered at R
Rchild: points to the root of the sub-tree constructed from the next segment.

The equivalent context-free grammar for this is given as follows:

Document (D) → S^*,   S → LRMS | ∈,   L → $(N+J)^*$,   R → V,   M → $(N+J)^*$

where, S denotes an English sentence, N, J and V are noun, adjective and verb tags respectively assigned by the POS tagger. Similarly, the tree for the *Fuzzy Description Generator* is created using nouns, adjectives, verbs and adverbs from the documents. The *Concept Miner* and the *Fuzzy Description Generator* mine the respective trees to locate ontology concepts and organize the extracted information into a structured knowledge base. They work in an interactive way to enrich the ontology structures with the newly mined concepts, relations, concept descriptions and qualifier sets for concept descriptions. Imprecise concept descriptions are stored using a fuzzy ontology structure, in which a concept descriptor is a combination of a qualifier and a value. Some new descriptors that were learnt for wine by the system are *exquisite flavor, indigenous red color* etc.

4 Experiments and Results

We have conducted experiments using a number of different domain ontologies like Wine, and the GENIA ontology for categorizing biological substances and locations

Table 1. Precision and recall of concept recognition in text documents

Domain	# Relevant Concepts Extracted	# Non-relevant Concepts Extracted	# Relevant Concepts Missed	Precision	Recall
Wine	209	16	50	92.89%	80.69%
Molecular Biology	137	41	10	76.97%	93.20%

(virus, mono-cell, body-part etc.) The GENIA ontology specifies only taxonomic relations among the basic classes and is enhanced by our proposed system to incorporate new biological relations like *"induce"*, *"activate"*, *"associate"*, *"bind"* *etc*. Since a biological relation may be associated with different pairs of biological concepts each relation is accompanied by a fuzzy membership value to represent its association strength. The membership value is directly proportional to the frequency of co-occurrences of a relation and associated biological concept-pairs. Table 1 summarizes the precision and recall values for identifying and storing relevant concepts and their descriptions from text documents for the two domains.

5 Conclusions and Future Work

In this paper we have presented an ontology-based text-mining system to enhance domain seed ontologies by extracting relevant concepts as well as precise and imprecise concept descriptors from text documents. The extracted instances of concepts are used to upgrade the ontology and answer user queries efficiently.

References

1. Abulaish, M., Dey, L.: Using Part-of-speech Patterns and Domain Ontology to Mine Imprecise Concepts from Text Documents. In Proceedings of the 6th International Conference on Information Integration and Web Based Applications and Services (iiWAS'04) Jakarta, Indonesia, (2004) 91-100
2. Crow, L., Shadbolt, N.: Extracting focused knowledge from the semantic web. Intl. Journal Human-Computer Studies 54 (2001) 155-184
3. Fensel, D., van Harmelen, F., Horrocks, I., McGuinness, D. L., Patel-Schneider, P. F.: OIL: An ontology Infrastructure for the Semantic Web. IEEE Intelligent Systems, 16 (2), (2001) 38-45
4. Horrocks I., Sattler, U.: Ontology Reasoning in the SHOQ(D) Description Logic. In Proceedings of the 7th IJCAI'01, (2001) 99-204
5. Li, Y., Zhong, N.: Web Mining Model and its Applications for Information Gathering. Knowledge-Based Systems 17 (2004) 207-217
6. Liddle, S. W., Hewett, K. A., Embley, D. W.: An Integrated Ontology Development Environment for Data Extraction. In Proceedings of ISTA'03, (2003) 21-33
7. Nambiar U., Kambhampati, S.: Answering Imprecise Database Queries: A Novel Approach. In Proceedings of the 5th ACM CIKM Workshop on Web Information and Data Management (WIDM'03), New Orleans, (2003)
8. Velardi, P., Fabriani, P., Missikoff, M.: Using Text Processing Techniques to Automatically Enrich a Domain Ontology. In Proceedings of ACM Conference on Formal Ontologies and Information Systems, FOIS, (2001) 270-284

A Novel Algorithm for Automatic Species Identification Using Principal Component Analysis

Shreyas Sen, Seetharam Narasimhan, and Amit Konar

Dept. of Electronics and Telecommunication Engineering, Jadavpur University,
Kolkata-700032, India
{shreyas.sen, mail.seetharam}@gmail.com,
babu25@hotmail.com

Abstract. This paper describes a novel scheme for automatic identification of a species from its genomic data. Random samples of a given length (10,000 elements) are taken from a genome sequence of a particular species. A set of 64 keywords is generated using all possible 3-tuple combinations of the 4 letters: A (for Adenine), T (for Thymine), C (for Cytosine) and G (for Guanine) representing the four types of nucleotide bases in a DNA strand. These $4^3 = 64$ keywords are searched in a sample of the genome sequence and their corresponding frequencies of occurrence are determined. Upon repeating this process for N randomly selected samples taken from the genome sequence, an N × 64 matrix of frequency count data is obtained. Then Principal Component Analysis is employed on this data to obtain a Feature Descriptor of reduced dimension (1 × 64). On determining the feature descriptors of different species and also by taking different samples from the same species, it is found that they are unique for a particular species while wide differences exist between those of different species. The variance of the descriptors for a given genome sequence being negligible, the proposed scheme finds extensive applications in automatic species identification.

1 Introduction

Genomic data mining and knowledge extraction is an interesting problem in bioinformatics. Identification of a species from its genomic database is a challenging task. The paper explores a new approach to extract genomic features of a species from its genome sequence.

Extensive works on local and global alignment of DNA sequences have already been undertaken by a number of researchers. The Smith-Waterman algorithm [1], [2] for local alignment and the Needleman-Wunsch algorithm [3] for global alignment of DNA-sequences, for instance, are two well-known algorithms for matching genome databases. These works have their own merits and limitations. The demerits include use of complicated matrix algebra and dynamic programming, and the results of sequence matching are not free from pre-calculated threshold value. It is to be noted that any of these methods stated above cannot be directly employed to identify the species from the structural signature of their genomes.

Rapid advancement in automated DNA sequencing technology [4] has generated the need for statistical summarization of large volumes of sequence data so that efficient and effective statistical analysis can be carried out leading to fruitful scientific results. The different known standard and popular sequence alignment algorithms and techniques for estimating the homologies [5] and mismatches among DNA sequences that are used for comparing sequences of relatively small sizes are not feasible to use when it comes to dealing with sequences having sizes varying between a few thousand base pairs to a few hundred thousand base pairs. Even for comparison of small sequences, the standard alignment and matching algorithms are known to be time consuming and laborious and the utility of more rapid and parsimonious procedures that may be somewhat rough in nature yet useful in producing quick and significant results is well appreciated. Effective analysis of large DNA sequences requires some form of statistical summarization by reducing the dimension of the data to facilitate numerical computations and at the same time to capture some of the fundamental structural information contained in the sequence data as efficiently as possible.

Traditional genetics and molecular biology have been directed towards understanding the role of a particular gene or protein in an important biological process [6]. A gene is sequenced to predict its function or to manipulate its activity or expression. This paper provides a statistical approach to handle the same problem by taking into account the genome database of a species for its identification.

The novelty of the work undertaken in the paper is summarised as follows. First, the paper takes into account frequency count of 64 three-lettered primitive DNA attributes in randomly selected samples of the genome sequences of different species like Escherichia coli (E. coli – a bacterium) [7], Drosophila melanogaster (fruit fly) [8], Saccharomyces cerevisiae (yeast) [9] and Mus musculus (mouse). Secondly, to reduce the data dimension of extracted features (here, frequency count), principal component analysis (PCA) [10] is employed on the N randomly selected samples of genome sequence. Thirdly, the variance of the extracted feature vectors being insignificantly small for any randomly selected input sequence, the accuracy of the results in identifying the species is very high.

The paper is divided into 5 sections. In section 2, we outline the proposed scheme for extracting the salient genomic features of a species from its genome sequence. Section 3 provides the detailed steps of using PCA in the proposed application. Diagrammatic representation of the results is presented in section 4. The conclusions are listed in section 5.

2 Selection of DNA-Descriptors

There are only 4 letters in a DNA-string; naturally the substrings could be one lettered, two lettered, three lettered or four lettered. To keep the search time optimum and moderately large search keys, we considered 3-lettered search keys only. Thus, we have $4^3 = 64$ search keys. Typical three-lettered search keys are AAA, AAC, AAG, AAT, ACA........ TTT. These 64 search keys are used to generate a (1 × 64) frequency count vector, whose each component denotes frequency of one of the 64 sub-strings or keys in a sample of the genomic data of a species.

To illustrate what we mean by frequency count, let us take the help of some examples. Consider a small portion of the sequence like ...AATCG.... It contributes a count of 1 each to the frequencies of occurrence of each of the 3 keywords AAT, ATC and TCG. Similarly for the substring ...TTTTT..., we get a count of 3 for the frequency of the keyword TTT. Proceeding similarly for a large sample sequence of 10,000 bases we get frequencies of all the 64 keywords in the form of a frequency count vector of dimension (1 × 64). The (1 × 64) vector is a DNA-descriptor of a given species. The DNA-descriptors are computed from different samples of a species and also for different species.

Experiments undertaken on DNA-string matching reveals that some typical substrings have a high population in the DNA-sequence of a given species. Naturally, this result can be used as a basic test criterion to determine a species from its DNA-sequence.

It is important to note that the frequency counts of 64 three-element keywords in a 10,000 element string of genome sequence are more or less invariant with respect to the random sampling of the genome sequence. Naturally, our main emphasis of study was to determine whether the small difference in the counts of a given keyword in N samples is statistically significant. PCA provides a solution to this problem. First, the dimension of (N × 64) is reduced by PCA to (1 × 64). Second, the (minor) disparity in the feature gets eliminated by PCA. Since PCA is a well-known tool for data reduction without loss of accuracy, we claim that our results on feature extraction from the genome database are also free from loss of accuracy.

3 Application of PCA

The methodology of employing PCA to the given problem is outlined below through the following steps:

INPUT: A set of N vectors (1 × 64) representing frequency count of 3-tuple keywords.

OUTPUT: A minimal feature descriptor vector sufficient to describe the problem without any significant loss in data.

1. Normalization: Let the ith (1 × 64) input vector be $a_i = [a_{i1} \; a_{i2} \; ..... \; a_{i64}]$

To get the vector normalized we use the following transformation:

$$a_{ik} \leftarrow a_{ik} / \sum_{j=1}^{64} a_{ij}$$

2. Mean adjusted data: To get the data adjusted around zero mean, we use the formula:

$$a_{ik} \leftarrow a_{ik} - \overline{a_i} \quad \forall k,i$$

where $\overline{a_i}$ = mean of the ith vector

The matrix (N × 64) so obtained is called the *Data Adjust*

$$= \frac{1}{64} \sum_{j=1}^{64} a_{ij} = \left[a_{ij} \right]_{N \times 64}$$

3. Evaluation of the covariance matrix: The covariance between any two vectors a_i and a_j is obtained by the following formula [10]:

$$cov(a_i, a_j) = c_{ij} = \frac{\sum_{k=1}^{64}(a_{ik} - \overline{a_i})(a_{jk} - \overline{a_j})}{(n-1)}$$

Covariance matrix is $C = [c_{ij}]_{N \times N}$ for the N different (1 × 64) vectors.

4. Eigenvalue Evaluation: Computing the roots of the equation $|C - \lambda I| = 0$, the eigenvalues of the covariance matrix C are obtained. There would be N eigenvalues of matrix C and corresponding to each eigenvalue there would be eigenvectors each of dimension N × 1.

5. Principal Component Evaluation: It is noticed that the eigenvalues have quite different values. In fact, it turns out that the eigenvector corresponding to the *highest* eigenvalue λ_{large} is the *Principal Component* (N × 1) *of* the data set.

$$\therefore Principal\ Component = [p_i]_{1 \times N}\ where\ \lambda_{large} \geq \lambda_i\ for\ 1 \leq i \leq N$$

6. Projection of the Data Adjust along the Principal Component: Now, to get the *Feature Descriptor*, the following formula is applied:

$$Feature\ Descriptor = Principal\ Component^T \times Data\ Adjust$$

where Principal Component^T (1 × N) is the transpose of the *Principal Component* vector.

Thus we get a *Feature Descriptor* vector of dimension 1 × 64 corresponding to N samples of the genome sequence database of the particular species.

7. Computing the Mean Feature Descriptor: We calculate M such *feature descriptors* from different random samples and calculate a mean of these vectors and also a variance vector (both 1 × 64).

4 Diagrammatic Representation of the Feature Descriptor

The *Feature Descriptor Diagrams* for different species are described here. We could represent the *Feature Descriptor* using bar diagram, pie-chart or any other standard representation. However, using the polar plot we get figures which are compact yet distinct representations of the *mean Feature Descriptor*.

As mentioned earlier the *mean Feature Descriptor* is a 1 × 64 vector. So to construct these diagrams 360^0 is divided into 64 equal parts, corresponding to 64 keywords. Plotting it in polar (r, ϴ) co-ordinates with r as the values of the *mean Feature Descriptor* vector and ϴ as these angles we get the *Feature Descriptor diagrams*. They were constructed for many species, some of which are shown below:

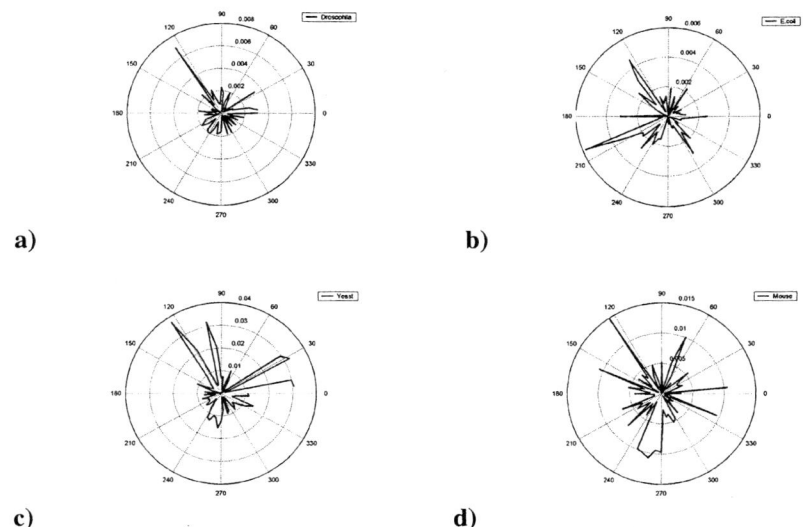

Fig. 1. Feature Descriptor Diagrams for a) Drosophila, b) E. coli, c) Yeast and d) Mouse

Plotting the *mean Feature Descriptor* in polar co-ordinates gives us a figure (*Feature Descriptor Diagram*) for each species which we can associate with it. This differs from species to species. We have plotted below the *Feature Descriptors* of similar species obtained from their mitochondrial genomes.

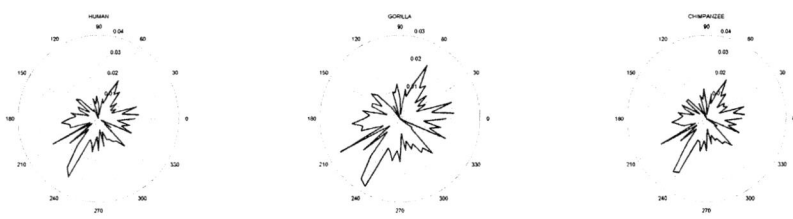

Fig. 2. Feature Descriptor Diagrams for Human, Gorilla and Chimpanzee

On observing these diagrams, we can correctly conclude that the species Human, Gorilla and Chimpanzee have many similarities in their genome characteristics which can be translated to a similarity in their biological characteristics. However it is also quite clear from these diagrams that these species have some distinctions in their genomic characteristics. So we can readily detect new species and identify known species by comparing their *Feature Descriptor diagrams*. Hence the *Feature Descriptor Diagrams* can be used as the unique representation of the genomic characteristics of the different species.

5 Conclusion

This is the first work of its kind to extract information from complete genome sequences and to distinguish between species by feature descriptor diagrams.

In this process we have used PCA to reduce the large dimensions of genome sequence data without loss of accuracy. If only the frequency count is plotted then we do get some difference from species to species but it is not enough to distinguish. This is where PCA comes in. When PCA is applied to original data we get enough differences between the *feature descriptor diagrams* of different species *which* enables us to distinguish a species from the other with the help of these diagrams.

By constructing *feature descriptor diagrams* for several species it has been observed that they are quite different from species to species indicating that we can certainly associate each figure with each species and claim that the figure represents the species. Moreover when *feature descriptor diagrams* for same species are calculated they came out to be almost identical with insignificant variance.

References

1. Smith, T. F., and Waterman, M. S., "Identification of common molecular subsequences," *J. Mol. Biol.* pp.147, 195-197, 1981.
2. Waterman, M. S., and Eggert, M., "A new algorithm for best subsequence alignments with applications to tRNA-rRNA," *J.Mol.Biol.*, pp. 197, 723-728, 1987.
3. Needleman, S. B., and Wunsch, C. "A general method applicable to the search for similarities in the amino sequence of two proteins." *J. Mol. Biol.* pp. 48,443-453, 1970.
4. Galperin, M. Y., and Koonin, E. V., Comparative Genome Analysis, In *Bioinformatics- A Practical Guide to the Analysis of Genes and Proteins*, Baxevins, A. D., and Oullette, B. F. F.(Eds.), Wiley-Interscience, New York, 2nd ed., p. 387, 2001.
5. States, D. J., and Boguski, M. s., Similarity and Homology, In *Sequence analysis primer* Gribskov, M., and Devereux, J. (Eds.), Stockton Press, New York, pp. 92-124, 1991.
6. Mount, D. W., *Bioinformatics: Sequence and Genome Analysis*, Cold Spring Harbor Laboratory Press, NY, 2001.
7. Blattner, F. R., Plunkett, G., Bloch, C. A., Perna, N. T., Burland, V., Riley, M., et al., "The complete genome sequence of Escherichia coli," Vol. K-12, *Science,* pp. 277, 1453-1462.
8. Adams, M. D., Celniker, S. E., Holt, R. A., Evans, C. A., Gocayne, J. D., Amanatides, P. G., Scherer, S. E., Li, P. W., et al, "The genome sequence of Drosophila melanogaster," *Science* pp. 287, 2185-2195, 2000.
9. Cherry, J. M., Ball, C., Weng, S., Juvik, G., Schimidt, R., Alder, C., Dunn, B., Dwight, S., Riles, L. et al., "Genetic and Physical maps of Saccharomyces cerevisiae," *Nature* (suppl. 6632) pp. 387, 67-73, 1997.
10. Smith, L. I., "A tutorial on Principal Components Analysis," 2002.

Analyzing the Effect of Prior Knowledge in Genetic Regulatory Network Inference

Gustavo Bastos and Katia S. Guimarães

Center of Informatics, Federal University of Pernambuco, Brazil
gbs@cin.ufpe.br, katia@cin.ufpe.br

Abstract. Inferring the metabolic pathways that control the cell cycles is a challenging and difficult task. Its importance in the process of understanding living organisms has motivated the development of several models to infer gene regulatory networks from DNA microarray data. In the last years, many works have been adding biological information to those models to improve the obtained results. In this work, we add prior biological knowledge into a Bayesian Network model with non parametric regression and analyze the effects of such information in the results.

1 Introduction

Gene regulation in eukaryotes is the result of interactions between proteins, genes, metabolites, enhancers, promoters, transcription factors and other biological elements. These interactions control when and with what intensity each gene is expressed in the genome and transcribed into RNA. In order to make it easier to discover the metabolical pathways which schematically describe such interactions, we can focus on just one kind of the elements cited above. For example, we can look only at genes, obtaining a network with gene-gene interactions, which is called a gene regulatory network. To infer the architecture of this type of network from gene expression microarray data is still a challenge in Bioinformatics.

Several mathematical models have been proposed to infer gene regulatory networks from microarray data: Boolean networks [1], differential equations [2], Bayesian networks [3,4], and others. These methods have achieved good results, but they still face hard problems, such as large computational demands and relatively poor quality in the results obtained, in the form of wrong edge directions and gene bypassing. Those problems may be due to the volume of data available to train the networks, usually far less than the proven number of samples needed, which for networks with binary nodes is $O(n^2 \log n^2 \log n^{k+1})$ [5], where n is the total number of genes and k is the maximum input degree of a node.

In order to try to overcome such problems, prior biological information is being added to some models. Hartemink et al. [6] have used Bayesian network with simulated annealing and Bayesian Scoring Metric (BSM) to choose the best network, and genomic location information to add prior knowledge to the model. Imoto et al. [7] designed a general framework for combining microarray data with biological information, and Tamada et al. [8] expanded this framework using motif detection to improve the model results. Kightley et al. [9] used an algorithm based on an epistemic approach and added prior knowledge to the input data.

In this work we perform a careful analysis of the effect that prior knowledge may have in the quality of the results obtained. We chose to use as reference a Bayesian network model and a combination of nonparametric regression with Bayesian Information Criterion (BIC), which was developed to infer the tricarboxylic (TCA) cycle of the *Saccharomices cerevisiae* cell cycle, with relatively good results [10]. Our analysis shows that, while adding prior knowledge actually yields better results to a certain extent, the degree of improvement is more attached to the quality of the information added than to its volume.

2 Network Inference Model

Under the Bayesian network model, nodes represent genes and edges represent relations between genes. Let $\mathbf{X} = (X_1, X_2, \ldots, X_n)^T$ be a random n-dimensional vector containing the genes to be analyzed, and assume that G is a directed graph. We use a joint density distribution where each gene follows a normal distribution with a β-spline non-parametric model with Gaussian noise. We define the density distribution as:

$$f(x_i|\theta_G) = \prod_{i=1}^{n} \prod_{j=1}^{s} f_i(x_{ij}|\mathbf{p}_{ij}; \theta_i),$$

where x_i is the vector of observations of the ith gene, s is the number of observations of a gene, x_{ij} is the jth observation of the ith gene, $\mathbf{p}_{ij}$ is the observation vector of parent genes, $\theta_G = (\theta_1, \ldots, \theta_n)^T$ is a parameter vector in graph G, and θ_i is a parameter vector in the model f_i, *i.e.*, the model of the ith gene.

In order to choose the network that best reproduces the relations between the genes, given the observations, we use BIC as follows:

$$\log p(G|\mathbf{X}) = -\log p(L_i) + \sum_{i=1}^{n} \sum_{j=1}^{s} \left\{ -\log f_i(x_{ij}|\mathbf{p}_{ji}, \theta_i) + \frac{d_i}{2} \log n \right\}, \quad (1)$$

where $p(G|\mathbf{X})$ is the probability of the graph, given the observations $\mathbf{X}$, and d_i is the dimension of θ_i. The chosen final graph is the one which minimizes (1), minimizing each node individually.

We used a 'voting' criterion to choose the edges of the final graph. The program was run a certain number of times and, after that, the edges which had a score above a threshold were selected. This score corresponded to the sum of the two possible relations between the two genes considered. The direction of the edge was chosen as the one which occurred the most. For example, suppose that we ran the program 10 times, and the results were such that in 3 of the executions, we obtained the edge (Gene_1, Gene_2); in 4 of the executions, we had (Gene_2, Gene_1); (Gene_3, Gene_4) was obtained only once, and (Gene_4, Gene_3) never appeared. According to our criterion, if the threshold is set to 5, (Gene_2, Gene_1) is the only chosen edge, as the relations between those two genes added up to 7, and (Gene_2, Gene_1) appeared more than (Gene_1, Gene_2).

3   Experiments and Results

We used the model described in the previous section to infer the aerobic respiration cycle (TCA cycle) of *Saccharomyces cerevisiae*. According to Hoffgen [5], it would be necessary to have more than 700 samples in order to guarantee estimation of the simplified network architecture. Such number of samples is too large and there are still no databases to provide them. Nevertheless, fairly good results can been obtained from the available microarray data, as shown in this work. In the experiments presented in this section, we used the *alpha* time series consisting of 18 time observations, which is one of the series of Spellman [11], using 600 iterations.

We build our analysis around a Bayesian network model that uses a combination of nonparametric regression with Bayesian Information Criterion (BIC), with no previous knowledge, which was developed to infer the tricarboxylic (TCA) cycle of the *Saccharomices cerevisiae* cell cycle [10]. We call that model Experiment 1, and its result is shown in Figure 1, where the reference network is shown on the left, while the network on the right was inferred by the model with threshold set to 50% of the total number of iterations.

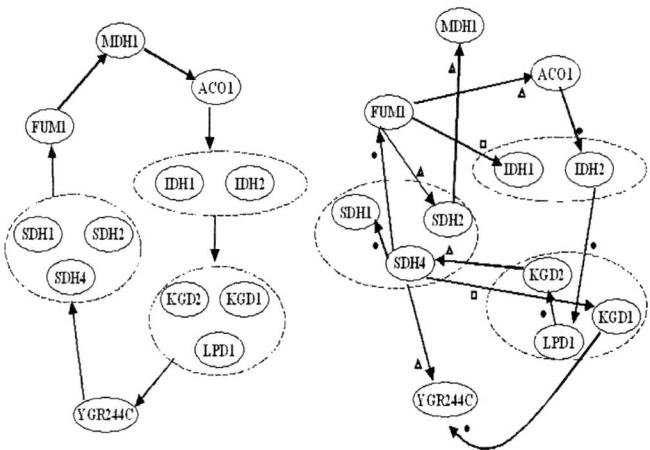

Fig. 1. Partial representation of respiration metabolic pathway of *S. cerevisiae*. On the left, the reference network; on the right, the network generated by the model without prior knowledge.

In all figures in this text, a circle represents a correct edge, while a triangle indicates inverted direction or gene bypassing, and a square represents an extra edge (not in the reference network).

In order to evaluate to which extent prior knowledge information could improve the results of the model, we ran several series of experiments fixing for each one the presence of a certain number of edges. The results in general clearly point to directions that can help one to choose which information to add when building a model.

An important general observation is that while the results almost always present some improvement, that is not highly significant, meaning that the number of samples is still a big factor. Another important result is that the number of edges informed is not as important as the correctness of those. That is, if one incorrect edge is informed, the model may have a performance that is actually worse than that of the model without prior knowledge.

To illustrate what may happen, we present the results of two experiments.

Experiment 2 consisted on adding biological information to the model of Experiment 1 through the preselection of five edges which had to appear in the final graph. We chose three edges corresponding to relations between co-regulated genes: (IDH2, IDH1), (LPD1, KGD1) and (SDH4, SDH2), and two edges corresponding to the beginning and end of the TCA cycle: (MDH1, ACO1) and (FUM1, MDH1).

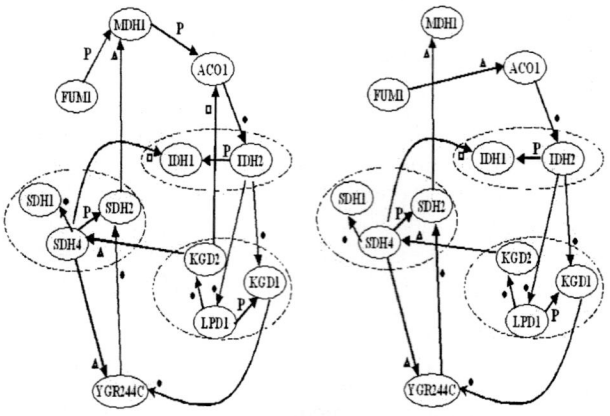

Fig. 2. Respiration metabolic pathway generated by our model. On the left, network inferred in Experiment 2. On the right, network inferred in Experiment 3.

The final network of Experiment 2 is shown in Figure 2, on the left. Circles, triangles and squares in this figure have the same meaning as in Figure 1, and a **P** indicates a preselected edge. The standard name of gene YFR244C, shown in Figure 2, is LSC2, but the systematic name was kept for having been used in Kim's work [12] and others [10]. We can notice that, by adding prior knowledge, we lost one of the correct edges [(SDH4, FUM1)] found in Experiment 1. However, we detected two other correct edges [(IDH2, KGD1) and (YGR244C, SDH2)] and eliminated two cases of bypassing or inverted edges [(FUM1, ACO1) and (FUM1, SDH2)]. The number of incorrect edges remained the same, although those edges differed: we had (FUM1, IDH1) and (SDH4, KGD1) in Experiment 1, and (SDH4, IDH1) and (KGD2, ACO1) in Experiment 2. This second model had 7 correct edges, 2 incorrect ones, and 3 occurrences of bypassing or inverted direction. One can say that some edges really improved the model's result, specially (LPD1, KGD1) and (SDH4, SDH2).

Experiment 3 consisted on choosing a subset of edges used in Experiment 2, namely: (LPD1, KGD1), (SDH4, SDH2) and (IDH2, IDH1). The result of Experiment 3 is shown in Figure 2, on the right, and is comparable to that of Experiment 2. An incorrect edge [(KGD2, ACO1)] was eliminated, while an occurrence of bypassing was introduced [(FUM1, ACO1)]. The number of correct edges of Experiment 3 was the same as in Experiment 2, in spite of the former's using less prior knowledge.

The experiments in general showed that relations of co-regulation are more effective information than causal relations. One difficulty common to all experiments was the fact that the part of the network next to the external "interference" signal was never correctly rebuilt. That can probably be explained by the large number of nodes (genes) in that region that were ignored in the reference model. That point will require more careful analysis.

More information on the experiments made can be found at [13].

4 Conclusion

Many mathematical models are being used to infer gene networks nowadays but all of them struggle to overcome two main problems, namely: determining the direction of edges and deciding whether a relation between genes is direct or not. These problems mainly arise due to the difficulty in obtaining reliable data in large quantities. The addition of prior knowledge to the models is a promising way of trying to overcome microarray data flaws.

In this work we presented the analysis of the behavior of a Bayesian Network model with non parametric regression and Bayesian Information Criterion in the presence of prior knowledge. Despite the small number of available samples to train the model, the results were encouraging. The experiments showed that relations of co-regulation is more effective information than causal relations. Furthermore, the correctness of the informed edges has a major impact on the results: informing incorrect edges produced worse results than those obtained with no prior knowledge at all.

As future work, the authors will add to the model more prior information about the beginning and end of the TCA cycle (upper part of the network shown in Figure 2), as this region presents the smallest number of correct guesses of the model. Experiments with other metabolic pathways are also being done.

References

1. Akutsu, T., Miyano, S., Kuhara, S.: Identification of genetic networks from a small number of gene expression patterns under the Boolean network model. In: Proc. of the Pacific Symp. on Biocomputing. Number 4 (1999) 17–28
2. Chen, T., He, H.L., Kuhara, S.: Modeling gene expression with differential equations. In: Proc. of the Pacific Symp. on Biocomputing. Number 4 (1999) 29–40
3. Friedman, N., Linial, M., Nachman, I., Pe'er, D.: Using Bayesian Networks to Analyze Expression Data. In: Proc. of the 4th Annual Intern. Confer. on Computational Molecular Biology, Tokyo, Japan, ACM, ACM Press (2000) 127–135
4. Imoto, S., Goto, T., Miyano, S.: Estimation of genetic networks and functional structures between genes by using Bayesian networks and nonparametric regression. In: Proc. of the Pacific Symp. on Biocomputing. Number 7 (2002) 175–186
5. Hoffgen, K.: Learning and robust learning of product distributions. In Pitt, L., ed.: Sixth Annual Workshop on Computational Learning Theory, New York, NY, ACM Press (1993) 77–83
6. Hartemink, A.J., Gifford, D.K., Jaakkola, T.S., Young, R.A.: Combining Location and Expression Data for Principled Discovery of Genetic Regulatory Network Models. In: Proc. of the Pacific Symp. on Biocomputing. Number 7 (2002) 437–449
7. Imoto, S., Higuchi, T., Goto, T., Tashiro, K., Kuhara, S., Miyano, S.: Combining Microarrays and Biological Knowledge for Estimating Gene Networks via Bayesian Networks. In: Proc. 2nd Computational Systems Bioinformatics. (2003) 104–113
8. Tamada, Y., Kim, S., Bannai, H., Imoto, S., Tashiro, K., Kuhara, S., Miyano, S.: Estimating gene networks from gene expression data by combining Bayesian network model with promoter element detection. BioInformatics **19**(Suppl. 2) (2003) ii227–ii236
9. Kightley, D., Chandra, N., Elliston, K.: Inferring Gene Regulatory Networks from Raw Data: A Molecular Epistemics Approach. In: Proc. of the Pacific Symp. on Biocomputing. Number 9 (2004) 510–520 Website: http://helixweb.stanford.edu/psb04/.
10. Bastos, G., Guimarães, K.S.: A Simpler Bayesian Network Model for Genetic Regulatory Network Inference. In: Proc. of the Intern. Joint Conference on Neural Networks 2005 (IJCNN'05), Montréal, Québec, Canada (2005) To be published.
11. Spellman, P., Sherlock, G., Zhang, M., Iyer, V., Anders, K., Eisen, M., Brown, P., Botstein, D., Futcher, B.: Comprehensive Identification of Cell Cycle-regulated Genes of Yeast *Saccharomyces cerevisiae* by Microarray Hybridization. Molecular Biology of the Cell **9** (1998) 3273–3297
12. Kim, S., Imoto, S., Miyano, S.: Dynamic Bayesian Network and Nonparametric Regression for Nonlinear Modeling of Gene Networks from Time Series Gene Expression Data. In Priami, C., ed.: Proc. of First Computational Methods in Systems Biology (CMSB). (Number 2602)
13. BioLab: Bioinformatics Laboratory at CIn/UFPE. Website: http://biolab.cin.ufpe.br/tools/ (2000)

New Genetic Operators for Solving TSP: Application to Microarray Gene Ordering

Shubhra Sankar Ray, Sanghamitra Bandyopadhyay, and Sankar K. Pal

Machine Intelligence Unit, Indian Statistical Institute,
Kolkata 700108, India.
{shubhra_r, sanghami, sankar}@isical.ac.in}

Abstract. This paper deals with some new operators of genetic algorithms for solving the traveling salesman problem (TSP). These include a new operator called, "nearest fragment operator" based on the concept of nearest neighbor heuristic, and a modified version of order crossover operator. Superiority of these operators has been established on different benchmark data sets for symmetric TSP. Finally, the application of TSP with these operators to gene ordering from microarray data has been demonstrated.

1 Introduction

The Traveling Salesman Problem (TSP) has been used as one of the most important test-beds for new combinatorial optimization methods [1]. Its importance stems from the fact there is a plethora of fields in which it finds applications e.g., scheduling, vehicle routing, VLSI layout, microarray gene ordering and DNA fragment assembly. Over decades, researchers have suggested a multitude of heuristic algorithms, including genetic algorithms (GAs) [1, 2, 3]for solving TSP. The classical formulation of TSP is stated as: Given a finite set of cities and the cost of traveling from city i to city j, if a traveling salesman was to visit each city exactly once and then return to the home city, which tour would incur the minimum cost?

Let $1, 2, \cdots, n$ be the labels of the n cities and $C = [c_{i,j}]$ be an $n \times n$ cost matrix where $c_{i,j}$ denotes the cost of traveling from city i to city j. The Traveling Salesman Problem (TSP) is the problem of finding the shortest closed route among n cities, having as input the complete distance matrix among all cities. The total cost A of a TSP tour is given by

$$A(n) = \sum_{i=1}^{n-1} C_{i,i+1} + C_{n,1} \qquad (1)$$

The objective is to find a permutation of the n cities, which has minimum cost.

The TSP, with some minor modifications, can be used to model the microarray gene ordering (MGO) problem. An optimal gene order provides a sequence of genes where the genes those are functionally related and similar are nearer in the ordering [4]. This functional relationship among genes is determined by gene expression levels from microarray by performing biological experiments [4]. Similarity between genes can be measured with Euclidean distance, Pearson correlation, absolute correlation, Spearman rank correlation, etc.

Two new genetic operators are proposed in this article for solving TSP. Consequently, the application of these operators are demonstrated for solving microarray gene ordering (MGO) problem efficiently.

2 Relevance of TSP in Microarray Gene Ordering

An optimal gene order, a minimum sum of distances between pairs of adjacent genes in a linear ordering $1, 2, \cdots, n$, can be formulated as [5]

$$F(n) = \sum_{i=1}^{n-1} C_{i,i+1}, \qquad (2)$$

where n is the number of genes and $C_{i,i+1}$ is the distance between two genes i and $i + 1$. In this study, the Euclidean distance is used to specify the distance $C_{i,i+1}$.

Let $X = x_1, x_2, \cdots, x_k$ and $Y = y_1, y_2, \cdots, y_k$ be the expression levels of the two genes in terms of log-transformed microarray gene expression data obtained over a series of k experiments. The Euclidean distance between X and Y is

$$C_{x,y} = \sqrt{\{x_1 - y_1\}^2 + \{x_2 - y_2\}^2 + \cdots + \{x_k - y_k\}^2}. \qquad (3)$$

One can thus construct a matrix of inter-gene distances, which serves as a knowledge-base for mining gene order using GA. Using this matrix one can calculate the total distance between adjacent genes and find that permutation of genes for which the total distance is minimized. This is analogous to the traveling salesman problem.

3 GA with New Operators for TSP

In this section, two new operators of GAs for solving TSP are described. These are nearest fragment (NF) and modified order crossover (MOC). The genetic algorithm designed using these operators is referred to as FRAG_GA. The structure of the proposed FRAG_GA is provided in Fig. 1. Here path representation [1], linear normalized selection and elitism operators are utilized [2]. For TSP, simple inversion mutation (SIM) [1] is employed.

3.1 Nearest Fragment (NF) Heuristic

The nearest-neighbor (NN) heuristic for creating initial population, have the advantage that they only contain a few severe mistakes, while there are long segments connecting nodes with short edges. Therefore such tours can serve as good starting tours. In NN the main disadvantage is that, several cities are

```
begin FRAG_GA
    Create initial population with Nearest-Neighbor Heuristic
    while generation_count < k do
        /* k = max. number of generations. */
        begin
            Apply NF heuristic
            Linear normalized selection
            MOC
            Mutation
            Elitism
            Increment generation_count
        end
        Output the best individual found
end FRAG_GA
```

Fig. 1. The Pseudo-code for FRAG_GA

not considered during the course of the algorithm and have to be inserted at high costs in the end. This leads to severe mistakes in path construction. To overcome the disadvantages of the NN heuristics, we propose a new heuristic operator, called the Nearest Fragment (NF) operator, which is used in every generation (iteration) of GA with a predefined probability for every chromosome in the population as a subsequent tour improvement method. In this process, each string (chromosome in GA) is randomly sliced in *frag* fragments. The value of *frag* is chosen in terms of the total number of cities (n) for a particular TSP instance. For tour construction the first fragment is chosen randomly. From the last city of that fragment, the nearest city that is either a start or an end point of a not yet visited tour fragment is determined from the cost matrix. The fragment containing the nearest city is connected to the selected fragment, with or without inversion depending on whether the nearest city is the last city of a fragment or not respectively. The process is repeated until all fragments have been reconnected.

3.2 Modified Order Crossover (MOC)

Order crossover [6] has been observed to be one of the best in terms of quality and speed, and yet is simple to implement for solving TSP using GA [1,2,3]. In order crossover the length of a substring is chosen randomly. Thus on an average, the length is equal to $n/2$. This can lead to a marked increase in the computational time, which can be reduced if the length of the substring for performing crossover can be fixed to a small value. However, no study has been reported in the literature for determining an appropriate value of the length of a substring for performing order crossover. Such an attempt is made in this article where it is found that a substring length $'y'$ for MOC provides good results for TSP if $y = \max\{2, \alpha\}$, where $n/9 \leq \alpha \leq n/7$ (n is the total number of cities). Unlike order crossover, where the substring length is randomly chosen, in MOC it is predefined at y. For example, for a 10 city problem the value of α

is predefined at 1.25, therefore $y = 2$. The rest of the process in MOC is same as order crossover.

4 Experimental Results

FRAG_GA is implemented in Matlab 5.2 on Pentium-4 (1.7 GHz). The experiment has two parts. In the first part we have compared FRAG_GA with SWAP_GATSP [3], and OX_SIM (standard GA with order crossover and simple inversion mutation) [1] for solving benchmark TSP instances like Grtschels24, kroA100, d198, ts225, pcb442 and rat783 [7]. In the second part for biological microarray gene ordering, Cell Cycle cdc15, Cell Cycle and Yeast Complexes datasets are chosen [8]. The three data sets consists of about 782, 803 and 979 genes respectively, which are cell cycle regulated in Saccharomyces cerevisiae, with different number of experiments (24, 59 and 79 respectively) [4]. Each dataset is classified into five groups termed G1, S, S/G2, G2/M, and M/G1 by Spellman et. al. [4]. Throughout the experiments the population size is taken to be 10 for smaller problems (<100 cities/genes), while for larger problems ($\geq$100 cities/genes) this is set equal to 20. Crossover probability is fixed at 0.85 and mutation probability is fixed at 0.015 across the generations.

For the nearest fragment (NF) operator, each string (chromosome in GA) is randomly sliced in *frag* fragments, where $frag \cong n/8$. Probability of NF operator was set to be 0.4 for n greater than 100 and 0.5, otherwise. The value of substring length for the modified order crossover operator (MOC) is kept in the range $n/7$ to $n/9$. All these values were obtained after extensive experiments, which are omitted here for the lack of space.

Table 1 summarizes the best results and average results obtained by running the FRAG_GA, SWAP_GATSP and OX_SIM on the aforesaid TSP instances.

Table 1. Cost values using FRAG_GA, SWAP_GATSP and OX_SIM for different TSP instances

Problem	Optimal	Best Results			Average Results		
		FRAG_GA	SWAP_GATSP	OX_SIM	FRAG_GA	SWAP_GATSP	OX_SIM
Grtschels 24	1272	1272 (130)	1272 (500)	1272 (8,000)	1272 (1000)	1272 (2000)	1322 (15000)
KroA 100	21282	21282 (800)	21504 (5000)	22,400 (25,000)	21,350 (2000)	21,900 (5000)	22670 (30000)
d198	15780	15834 (3000)	15992 (7000)	16,720 (25,000)	15964 (3500)	16,132 (10000)	18200 (40000)
Ts 225	126643	126730 (3000)	127012 (7000)	135800 (25,000)	126890 (3500)	128532 (10000)	138283 (40000)
Pcb 442	50778	51104 (8000)	52620 (15000)	53402 (40,000)	51930 (10000)	53,820 (20000)	59740 (65000)
Rat 783	8806	9007 (15000)	9732 (30000)	10810 (70,000)	9442 (20000)	10110 (40000)	11520 (100000)

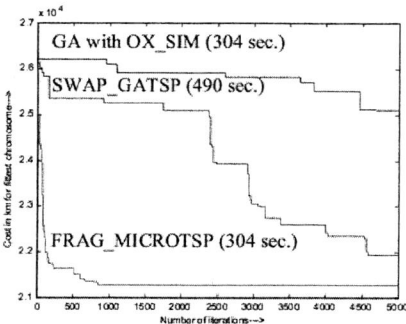

Fig. 2. Variation of cost of the best string with number of iteration for kroa100.tsp

For each problem the iteration in which the result is obtained is mentioned in columns 3-8 within parentheses. In SWAP_GATSP and OX_SIM the number of populations is taken to be 10 for 24 and 29 cities, 24 for 48 and 51 cities, 30 for 70 and 76 cities, and 40 for number of cities greater than or equal to 100 [3]. As can be seen from Table 1 FRAG_GA is superior in terms of quality of solution when compared with other existing GAs [1, 3].

Fig. 2 shows a comparison of FRAG_GA, SWAP_GATSP and OX_SIM when the fitness value of the fittest string is plotted with iteration. The three programs were run for 5000 iterations for kroa100.tsp with population 20. At any iteration, the FRAG_GA has the lowest tour cost. It took 304 seconds, 490 seconds and 304 seconds by FRAG_GA, SWAP_GATSP and OX_SIM respectively for executing 5000 iterations. Moreover, only FRAG_GA is seen to converge at around 800 iterations at the optimal cost value of 21,282 km. On the other hand, the cost is 21912 km for SWAP_GATSP and 25103 km for OX_SIM even after 5000 iterations.

The performance of FRAG_GA on microarray datasets is evaluated with a biological score (not used as fitness function of GA), defined by [5]

$S(n) = \sum_{i=1}^{n-1} C_{i,i+1}$ where $C_{i,i+1} = 1$, if gene i and $i+1$ are in the same group

$= 0$, if gene i and $i+1$ are not in the same group.

Using this, a solution of gene ordering has a higher score when more genes within the same group are aligned next to each other. Table 2 compares the performance of our FRAG_GA with other GA based methods in terms of S value. It is clear that FRAG_GA and NNGA [9] are comparable and they both

Table 2. Comparison of FRAG_GA with other algorithms in terms of best score

Algorithms	Cell cycle cdc15	Cell cycle	Yeast complexes
FRAG_GA	537	635	384
NNGA	539	634	384
FCGA	521	627	—

dominate FCGA [5]. Note that FRAG_GA is a conventional GA, while NNGA (hybrid GA) uses exhaustive local search methods [10], which provides the key contribution to optimality (not the GA itself). The main reason behind the good results obtained by FRAG_GA is that, biological solutions of microarray gene ordering lie in more than one sub optimal point (in terms of gene expression distance) rather than one optimal point.

5 Conclusion

A new "nearest fragment operator" (NF) and "modified version of order crossover operator" (MOC) of GAs are described along with their implementation for solving both symmetric TSP and microarray gene ordering problem. Appropriate number of fragments and appropriate substring length in terms of the number of cities are determined for NF and MOC respectively, and then applied on TSP and microarray data. It appears that NF operator is able to augment the search space quickly and thus obtains much better results compared to other heuristics. Moreover, MOC requires shorter computation time; thereby balancing the overhead corresponding to the NF operator.

Acknowledgement

This work is supported by the grant no. $22(0346)/02/EMR-II$ of the Council of Scientific and Industrial Research (CSIR), New Delhi.

References

1. Larranaga, P., Kuijpers, C., Murga, R., Inza, I., Dizdarevic, S.: Genetic algorithms for the traveling salesman problem: A review of representations and operators. Artificial Intell. Rev. **13** (1999) 129–170
2. Goldberg, D.E.: Genetic Algorithm in Search, Optimization and Machine Learning. Machine Learning, Addison-Wesley, New York (1989)
3. Ray, S.S., Bandyopadhyay, S., Pal, S.K.: New operators of genetic algorithms for traveling salesman problem. Volume 2., Cambridge, UK, ICPR-04 (2004) 497–500
4. Spellman, P.T., Sherlock, G., Zhang, M.Q., Iyer, V.R., Anders, K., Eisen, M.B., Brown, P.O., Botstein, D., Futcher, B.: Comprehensive identification of cell cycle-regulated genes of the yeast saccharomyces cerevisia by microarray hybridization. Molecular Biology Cell **9** (1998) 3273–3297
5. Tsai, H.K., Yang, J.M., Kao, C.Y.: Applying Genetic Algorithms To Finding The Optimal Gene Order In Displaying The Microarray Data. GECCO (2002) 610–617
6. Davis, L.: Applying adapting algorithms to epistatic domains. Proc. Int. Joint Conf. Artificial Intelligence (Quebec, canada, 1985)
7. TSPLIB: (http://www.iwr.uniheidelberg.de/groups/comopt/software/TSPLIB95/)
8. (http://www.psrg.lcs.mit.edu/clustering/ismb01/optimal.html)
9. Lee, S.K., Kim, Y.H., Moon, B.R.: Finding the Optimal Gene Order in Displaying Microarray Data. GECCO (2003) 2215–2226
10. Lin, S., Kernighan, B.W.: An effective heuristic for the traveling salesman problem. Operation Research **21** (1973) 498–516

Genetic Algorithm for Double Digest Problem

S. Sur-Kolay[1], S. Banerjee[2], S. Mukhopadhyaya[1,*], and C.A. Murthy[1]

[1] Indian Statistical Institute, Kolkata, India
[2] Honeywell Technology Solutions Lab Pvt. Ltd., Bangalore, India

Abstract. The strongly NP-complete Double Digest Problem (DDP) for physical mapping of DNA, is now used for efficient genotyping. An instance of DDP has multiple distinct solutions. Existing methods produce a single solution, and are slow for large instances. We employ a type of equivalence among the distinct solutions to obtain *almost* all of them. Our method comprises of first finding a solution from each equivalence class by an elitist genetic algorithm, and then generating entire classes. Notable efficiency was achieved due to significant reduction in search space.

1 Introduction

A DNA molecule can be represented as a string over the alphabet $\{A, C, G, T\}$ with its length in kilobasepairs, ranging from a few thousands for a yeast chromosome to billions for the entire human genome comprising of 23 pairs of chromosomes. A restriction enzyme can digest a DNA molecule and cut it at every occurrence of a short specific pattern. For example, the restriction enzyme PstI cuts each occurence of the string $CTGCAG$ in a DNA into two substrings $CTGCA$ and G. These locations are called *cut sites* of a DNA formed by the restriction enzyme. The sequence of cut sites constitute the *restriction map* of DNA [8], and the fragment between two consecutive cut sites is a *restriction fragment* for that enzyme. The lengths (but not the order!) of these fragments can be measured by gel-electrophoresis. In the Double Digest Problem (DDP), a restriction map is to be constructed from the fragment lengths obtained by applying *two* restriction enzymes separately as well as together.

Since the first successful restriction site mapping was achieved in 1970s [11], DDP has been studied intensely. It has been shown to be NP-complete [5] and then, strongly NP-complete [2]. Different heuristics such as integer linear programming, simulated annealing (SA), have been proposed [6,12,9]. Although SA was the best known method for solving DDP, its main drawbacks are that it produces only one solution and is fairly slow. A variation of DDP called *enhanced double digest (EDD)* problem [7], though NP-hard, can be solved in linear time only under certain constraints.

Finding all possible distinct solutions for a given instance, may be used for verifying the correctness of the sequence produced by fragment assembly. Though

---

* Partially supported by a grant from Dept. of Science and Technology, Govt. of India.

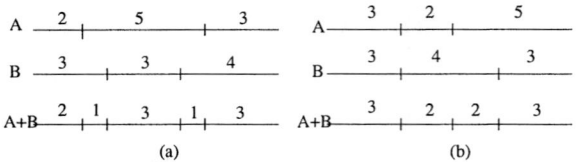

Fig. 1. Two distinct orderings of the fragment lengths for enzymes A and B

the number of solutions to DDP increases exponentially with the number of cut-sites, the entire set of solutions can be partitioned into a small number of equivalence classes [12,9].

In this paper, we design an *elitist* Genetic Algorithm to obtain all distinct *non-equivalent* solutions to DDP, from which the complete set of solutions is generated by applying simple transformations. The vanilla flavour genetic algorithm typically terminates with only one optimal solution even if there exist more than one. Hence, the proposed GA to produce all optimal solutions for DDP, which may be exponential in number of fragment lengths, is by itself novel.

2 Problem Formulation

The combinatorial description of Double Digest Problem (DDP) is as follows [12]: let $\mathcal{A} = \{a_i : 1 \leq i \leq m\}$, $\mathcal{B} = \{b_i : 1 \leq i \leq n\}$ and $\mathcal{A} + \mathcal{B} = \{d_i : 1 \leq i \leq l\}$ be the multisets of fragment lengths in non-decreasing order, obtained by application of restriction enzyme A, B, and $A + B$ (A and B together) respectively on a DNA string of length L. Thus, $\sum_{i=1}^{m} a_i = \sum_{i=1}^{n} b_i = \sum_{i=1}^{l} d_i = L$.

Let σ and μ be two permutations of the indices $(1, 2, \ldots, m)$ and $(1, 2, \ldots, n)$ respectively. In the restriction map M, the elements of $\mathcal{A}$ and $\mathcal{B}$ in their respective map orders σ and μ, are $A_\sigma = <A_1, \cdots, A_m>$ and $B_\mu = <B_1, \cdots, B_n>$ such that for $i < j$, A_i (B_i) appears to the left of A_j (B_j). While superposition of the sequences A_σ and B_μ yields the sequence of fragment lengths $C_{\sigma,\mu} = <C_1, \cdots, C_l>$, we term the multiset of fragment lengths in non-decreasing order $C(\sigma, \mu) = \{c_1, \cdots, c_p\}$ as the *configuration* (σ, μ). If a cut site in the superposition also occurs in both σ and μ, it is called *coincident cut site (ccs)*. DDP is to find possible configurations (σ, μ) such that $C(\sigma, \mu) = \mathcal{A} + \mathcal{B}$.

Example 1: Given $\mathcal{A} = \{2, 3, 5\}$, $\mathcal{B} = \{3, 3, 4\}$ and $\mathcal{A} + \mathcal{B} = \{1, 1, 2, 3, 3\}$, the first (σ, μ) in Fig. 1(a) yields $C(\sigma, \mu) = \{1, 1, 2, 3, 3\}$, whereas the second one in Fig. 1(b) gives $\{2, 2, 3, 3\}$. While the first matches $(\mathcal{A} + \mathcal{B})$, and hence corresponds to a correct restriction map, the second one is not a valid solution.

2.1 Classifying Solutions of DDP

The notion of equivalence has been defined over the large solution space of DDP in more than one ways [12]. Equivalence classes help in finding all solutions efficiently. Checking equivalence of two maps is non-trivial. Of the known types of equivalence, cassette equivalence is suitable for computation.

2.2 Cassette Equivalence

In a map M, any subsequence I_A (I_B) of A_σ (B_μ) is called a *block*. For $A_i \in A_\sigma$ ($B_i \in B_\mu$), each fragment in B_μ (A_σ), properly contained in A_i (B_i) is called a *non-border block* of A_i (B_i). For each pair i, j with $1 \leq i \leq j \leq l$, let I_C be the set of fragments from C_i to C_j. An extended definition of **cassette** for I_C is introduced for completeness' sake; earlier definition [9] assumed that coincident cut sites are absent. Two cases need to be considered:

Case 1: Neither of the boundaries of I_C is a coincident cut site (*ccs*).

A **cassette** defined by I_C is the pair of sets of intervals (I_A, I_B), where I_A and I_B are the sets of all blocks of A and B respectively that contain a block of I_C. In Fig. 2(b), the unique cassette defined by $I_C = \{C_4, C_5\}$ is shown.

Case 2: At least one of the boundaries of I_C is a *ccs* s_i, excepting either boundary of the DNA.

In this case, additional cassettes are also defined by I_C as follows. For a given I_C, we denote the predecessor of the left boundary of I_C and the successor of its right boundary by s_l and s_r respectively. If the *ccs* s_i is the left (right) boundary of I_C, then the interval (s_l, s_i) $((s_i, s_r))$ arising from either A_σ or B_μ may also be included in I_A or I_B respectively to form an additional cassette for this I_C. Further, if s_l (s_r) is also a *ccs*, then there are two additional cassettes depending on the inclusion of the interval (s_l, s_i) $((s_i, s_r))$ in either I_A or I_B.

Result 1: For a given I_C, the total number of possible cassettes may be 2, 3, 4, 6, and 9 depending on whether its adjacent cut sites are *ccs*'s.

Cassette Transformations: If two disjoint cassettes have their respective left and right overlaps equal [12], and each overlap comprises of only one double digest fragment C_i, then these two cassettes can be *exchanged* to form a new solution (Fig. 2(a)). If the two overlaps of a cassette have same absolute value but different signs, then the cassette can be *reflected* (Fig. 2(b)).

Definition: $[A_\sigma, B_\mu]$ and $[A'_\sigma, B'_\mu]$ are *cassette equivalent* if and only if there is a sequence of cassette transformations and permutations of the non-border block uncut fragments transforming $[A_\sigma, B_\mu]$ into $[A'_\sigma, B'_\mu]$.

Suppose X is a subsequence of A_σ or B_μ. Let $I(X) = \{C_i : C_i \subseteq X\}$, $I_s(X) = \{|C_i| : C_i \subseteq X\}$ and $I_s^*(X) = \{|C_i| : C_i$ is a border block of $X\}$ if $|I(X)| > 1$. The characteristic of a cassette equivalence class is defined as $I^*D = (\{(I_s^*(A_i), I_s(A_i)): A_i \in A\}, \{(I_s^*(B_j), I_s(B_j)): B_j \in B\})$.

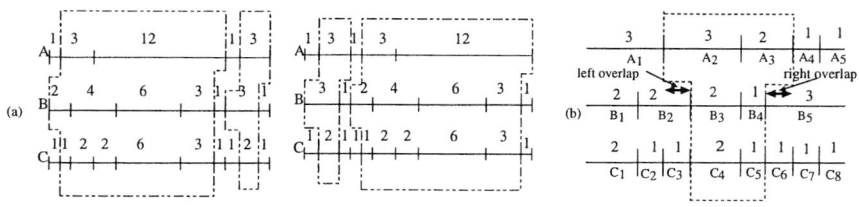

Fig. 2. Cassette transformations (a) exchange, (b) reflection

Result 2 [9]: $[A_\sigma, B_\mu]$ and $[A'_\sigma, B'_\mu]$ are cassette equivalent if and only if $I^*D[A_\sigma, B_\mu] = I^*D[A'_\sigma, B'_\mu]$.

This result provides an efficient method for checking cassette equivalence. But it does not hold for a *ccs* if the definition of a cassette is restricted to Case 1 only. This motivated us to introduce a complete definition of cassette above, thereby enabling us to employ Result 2 in general.

3 Proposed Algorithm for DDP

Our proposed algorithm consists of two parts: first, an elitist genetic algorithm [4] to generate all possible valid non-equivalent (w.r.t. cassette equivalence) solutions to a given instance of DDP, and second an algorithm to generate all valid solutions from the set of representative solutions obtained in the first part, by performing simple cassette transformations in an efficient manner.

3.1 GA for Finding Non-equivalent Solutions to DDP

In order to allow for multiple optimum solutions in GA, the structure of classical GA needs to be modified in our proposed algorithm, as outlined below followed by details of string representation, cost function and modified genetic operators.

begin ALGM_DDP
  Generate initial population at random.
  repeat
    (i) Natural selection; /* Select parents from the population. */
    (ii) Order preserving weighted crossover on selected parents;
    (iii) Partially deterministic compound mutation: mutate individuals;
    (iv) Equivalence checker elitism; /* Reserve solution (zero cost) individuals */
    (v) Form the next generation;
  until (termination condition)

String Representation and Cost Function: A string is a configuration in DDP represented as a 2-tuple (σ, μ). Its cost is defined as $\zeta = \sum_{i=1}^{max(p,l)} (d_i - c_i)^2$. If $p \neq l$, the shorter sequence is padded with zeroes. The optimum value of ζ is 0 which occurs if and only if the configuration is a valid solution.

Genetic Operators: Of the four genetic operations natural selection, crossover, mutation and elitism, which are applied stochastically, all operations save natural selection done by traditional roulette wheel, are modified to suit DDP.

Order Preserving Weighted Crossover: The single-point crossover on two configurations, where either the A_σs or the B_μs are chosen as parents, is demonstrated below.

Example 2: Suppose the randomly chosen crossover point is 3, p_1=(1,3,2,1,3,4,2,2) and $p_2 = $ (1,2,2,2,4,3,3,1). The child c_1 (c_2) is a permutation of p_1 (p_2) but inherits the order of the elements to the left of the crossover point from p_1 (p_2), and to the right from p_2 (p_1). Thus, $c_1 = $ (1,3,2,*2,2,4,3,1*) and $c_2 = $ (1,2,2,*3,1,3,4,2*).

Remark: The above crossover cannot generate any invalid permutation and can explore the search space efficiently.

Partially Deterministic Compound Mutation: Given a string to be mutated, either A_σ or B_μ is chosen randomly, say A_σ. All its elements are mutated by choosing a random number $r \in [0,1]$; if r is less than the mutation probability then for each i, $1 \leq i \leq m$, another random integer j, $1 \leq j \leq m$, is generated, and A_i and A_j are swapped. This guarantees that a string can be mutated to any other string in the search space in one step. This condition ensures uniform convergence of the elitist model of GA to optimal solution.

Equivalence Checker Elitism: This preserves best strings across generations in a special array, subject to checking cassette equivalence with all other existing non-equivalent solution strings in the array. For equivalence checking, *Result 2* of Sec. 2.2 is used. The next generation is formed from the union of the previous and present generations by including all the valid solutions, along with randomly chosen non-zero cost strings, keeping the population size invariant.

With this set of four genetic operations, the probability that all non equivalent strings are stored in the special array after sufficient number of iterations is almost 1.

3.2 Generating a Cassette Equivalence Class from a Representative

From a representative string s reserved in the special array above, GEN_CLASS(s) produces the set E-CLASS of all strings equivalent to s by calling PERMUT and CASS_EX_RF respectively for permutations of uncut fragments of non-border blocks and cassette transformations of s.

Procedure GEN_CLASS(string s)
 E-Class = {s};
 while (there is an unmarked string $s_1 \in$ E-Class) **do** E-Class = E-Class $\cup$ PERMUT(s_1)
 while (there is a marked string $s_2 \in$ E-Class) **do** E-Class = E-Class $\cup$ CASS_EX_RF(s_2)

Given a map M, not all the $O(l^2)$ possible cassettes where l is the number of cut sites in $(\mathcal{A}+\mathcal{B})$, are eligible for cassette transformations. We introduce a data structure called *cassette generation table (CGT)* to operate on only eligible cassettes. The ith row corresponds to cut site i and contains its distance from the left boundary of the DNA, name of enzyme(s) responsible for it, left and right overlaps if it is respectively the left and right boundary of a cassette. To reduce search, entries with equal left (right) overlaps form a singly linked list.

Complexity of the Proposed Approach: The time complexity for the GA is $O(Nkl^2\rho)$, where l, ρ, N and k are respectively cardinality of $\mathcal{A}+\mathcal{B}$, number of equivalence classes, size of the population and number of generations. The second phase requires $O(l^3 \cdot T)$ time for T distinct solutions. The space complexity of the GA is $O((N+\rho)l)$, and is output sensitive in second phase.

4 Experimental Results and Discussion

The ALGM_DDP was implemented in C, tested on DDP instances from laboratory data and artificial ones with fragment lengths rounded off (w.l.o.g.) to

Table 1. Results of proposed method

Problem Instance	# Equiv. Classes	# soln.	Problem Instance	# Equiv. Classes	# soln.
$\mathcal{A} = \{1,2,3,3,4,4,5,5\}$ $\mathcal{B} = \{1,2,3,3,3,7,8\}$ $\mathcal{A} + \mathcal{B} = \{1,1,1,1,1,1,2,2,2,2,3,4,4\}$	393	36660	$\mathcal{A} = \{1,2,2,3,3,4\}$ $\mathcal{B} = \{1,1,2,2,4,5\}$ $\mathcal{A} + \mathcal{B} = \{1,1,1,1,1,2,2,3\ 3\}$	18	3210
$\mathcal{A} = \{5509,5626,6527,6766,7233,16841\}$ $\mathcal{B} = \{3526,4878.5643,5804,7421,21230\}$ $\mathcal{A} + \mathcal{B} = \{1120,1868,2564,2752,3240,$ $3526,3758,3775,4669,5509,15721\}$	1	2	$\mathcal{A} = \{1,2,3,4,5,6,7,8,9\ \}$ $\mathcal{B} = \{15,15,15\}$ $\mathcal{A} + \mathcal{B} = \{1\ 1\ 1\ 1\ 2\ 2\ 2\ 3\ 6\ \}$	172	15840
$\mathcal{A} = \{7,\ 8,\ 18\}$ $\mathcal{B} = \{1,2,2,4,5,5,9\}$ $\mathcal{A} + \mathcal{B} = \{1,2,2,2,2,3,4,5,5,7\}$	52	686	$\mathcal{A} = \{7,\ 8,\ 18\}$ $\mathcal{B} = \{1,1,1,1,2,3,5,7,12\}$ $\mathcal{A} + \mathcal{B} = \{1,1,1,1,1,2,2,4,5,7,8\}$	65	930
$\mathcal{A} = \{1,1,1,1,2,3,5,7,12\}$ $\mathcal{B} = \{1,2,2,4,5,5,9\}$ $\mathcal{A} + \mathcal{B} = \{1,1,1,1,1,1,1,1,1,2,2,3,3,5,9\}$	376	92920	$\mathcal{A} = \{1,3,3,12\ \}$ $\mathcal{B} = \{1,2,3,3,4,6\}$ $\mathcal{A} + \mathcal{B} = \{1,1,1,1,2,2,2,3,6\ \}$	18	208

integral values keeping the sum of the lengthd invariant. The results appear in Table 1 for eight such problems, three being laboratory data for D10 using (BamHI, PstI), (BamHI, HindIII) and (PstI, HindIII) respectively.

The values of N and k were 50 and 10,000. For each instance, 5 initial populations and for each initial population, 10 trials were performed. Crossover probability was 0.85. Mutation probability was varied linearly in cycles of 200 iterations from $2/(m+n)$ to 0.45 and back to $2/(m+n)$, to enable efficient exploration of the search space and to prevent the GA from getting stuck in a local optima [1]. For all the instances, convergence occurred within the first 5,000 iterations. The number of distinct solutions was known *a priori* only for the last instance and it tallied with our results. For any instance, the proposed GA can theoretically produce *all the distinct solutions* after sufficiently large number of iterations [1].

Lastly, the efficacy of a search heuristic is judged by its reduction in search space. For Instances 1, 4 and 6 (in column-major order) of Table 1, the space reduction figures are 77%, 88% and 99% respectively.

In summary, our algorithm finds all valid solutions to a given instance of DDP efficently. For larger problem instances, the reduction in search space attained by the proposed method is remarkably high. It would be worth experimenting with the cost function as well as incorporate ideas of mulit-niche crowding [3]. Another future work is to tune the algorithm for either incompletely specified or inaccurate data.

References

1. Bhandari, D., Murthy, C. A., and Pal, S. K.: Genetic algorithm with elitist model and its convergence. *International Journal of Pattern Recognition and Artificial Intelligence*, 10, 1147 - 1151, 1999.
2. Cieliebak, M., Eidenbenz, S. and Woeginger, G. J.: Double digest revisited: Complexity and approximability in the presence of noisy data. *Technical Report No. 382*, ETH Zurich, Department of Computer Science, 2002.
3. Cedeno, W., Vemuri, V. Rao and Slezak, T.: Multi-niche crowding in genetic algorithms and its application to the assembly of DNA Restriction-fragments. *Evolutionary Computation*, 2(4), 321-345, 1994.

computational techniques are used in biological research areas such as *Sequence Alignment, Inductive Learning* and *Consensus Discovery*.

The well-known tool using the *Sequence Alignment*, such as BLAST [5], aligns uncharacterized sequences with the existing sequences in database and then assigns the uncharacterized sequences to the same class with one of the sequences in database that gets the best alignment score. This technique has to perform directly on all sequences in database, whose sizes are usually huge; therefore its processing time is much higher than other techniques. The *Inductive Learning* [9] and the *Consensus Discovery* [8] perform their tasks in a pre-process to derive rules that are used to perform the tasks during processing time. Although the use of the rules attains low processing time, the procedure for deriving rules still has too long computation time.

Our approach is to discover DNA signatures in the pre-process as the inductive learning and the consensus discovery. However, the proposed approach has much less pre-processing time. We apply an *n*-gram method and statistical scoring models for the signature discovery and evaluate the signatures over the influenza virus. Our system and methods are described in Section 2. Section 3 has a discussion on our experiments. Finally, we summarize the proposed approach in Section 4.

2 System and Methods

The signature recognition is a significant task in the Computational Biology research since the biological sequences are zero-knowledge based data. We do not know any "knowledge" of the biological data. Therefore, the recognition of the knowledge or informative signatures becomes more important. Our signature discovery framework of biological data is depicted in Fig. 1 as the four following steps.

Step I: *Pattern Generation* is to transform training data into *n*-gram patterns.

Step II: *Candidate Signature Selection* is to find the most significant *n*-gram patterns predicted as candidate signatures.

Step III: *Identifier Construction* is to create identifiers using the candidate signatures.

Step IV: *Performance Evaluation* is to estimate the goodness of the candidate signatures by comparing each identifier, generated by the different candidate signatures. If the accuracy of any identifiers is high, the candidate signatures used for constructing the identifiers are predicted as "Signatures" of the DNA sequences.

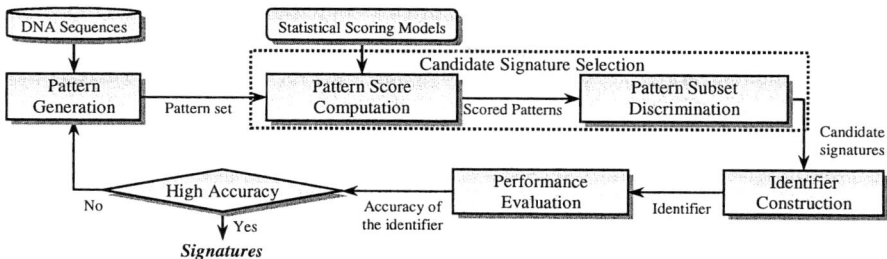

Fig. 1. Signature discovery framework

2.1 Pattern Generation

The Pattern Generation process is to find a data representation of DNA sequences. The data representation, called a pattern, is a substring of the DNA sequences. DNA sequences include four symbols {A, C, G, T}; therefore, the members of a pattern are also restricted to the four symbols. Let Y be a sequence $y_1y_2...y_M$ of length M over the four symbols of DNA. A substring $t_1t_2...t_n$ of length n is called an n-gram pattern [3]. The n-gram method generates the n-gram patterns representing the DNA sequences with different n-values. There are M-n+1 patterns in a sequence of length M for generating the n-gram patterns, but there are only 4^n possible patterns for any n-values. Notice that 1-gram patterns have 4 (4^1) possible patterns; while 24-gram patterns have 2.8×10^{14} (4^{24}) possible patterns. The numbers of possible patterns obviously vary from 4 to 2.8×10^{14} patterns. High n-values are not necessary since each pattern does not occur repeatedly and scoring models cannot discover signatures from these patterns. However, in our experiments, the patterns are solely generated from 1- to 24-grams since the higher n-values do not improve any performance.

2.2 Candidate Signature Selection

This process is to measure the significance of each n-gram pattern, called a score, using statistical models and then sort all n-gram patterns as their scores. Finally, the process selects the ten highest-score patterns as "Candidate Signatures". Let Pattern P represent a set of m members of n-gram patterns p_1, p_2 ... p_m generated by training data. The score of each pattern p_i, $score(p_i)$, is to measure the significance of each pattern using a statistical model. Let S be the candidate signatures, selected from the k highest-score patterns. The Pattern P and the candidate signatures S are defined by

$$P = \{p_1,...,p_{m-1}, p_m \mid score(p_{i-1}) \leq score(p_i) \wedge i = 2,3,...,m\}. \quad (1)$$

$$S = \{\forall_j s_j \mid s_j = p_{m-k+j} \wedge 1 \leq j \leq k\}. \quad (2)$$

For the statistical scoring models, we propose nine models to evaluate the goodness of biological data. Nine proposed models are *Term Frequency (TF)*, *Rocchio (TF-IDF)*, *DIA association factor (Z)*, *Cross Entropy (CE)*, *Mutual Information (MI)*, *Information Gain (IG)*, *NGL coefficient (NGL)*, *Chi-Square (X^2)* and *Weighted Odds Ratio (WOR)* [1,7]. We compare formulas of the models across four several criteria [6] that concentrate on pattern and class value as follows

Criteria I: *Common Patterns* computes pattern scores using the number of times pattern P occurs, $Freq(p)$, or the probability pattern P occurs, $P(p)$.

Criteria II: *Pattern Absence* computes pattern scores using the number of times or the probability that pattern P does not occur, $\overline{P}$.

Criteria III: *Class Value* computes pattern scores using the probability of the ith class value, $P(C_i)$, or the conditional probability given that pattern P occurs, $P(C_i|p)$.

Criteria IV: *Target Class Value* is a measure which emphasizes on difference between the target or positive class value, *pos*, and the non-target or negative class value, *neg*.

The criteria comparison of nine models is illustrated in Table 1. Where $Freq(p)$ is the number of times pattern P occurs; $DF(p)$ is the number of sequences pattern P

occurs at least once; $|D|$ is the total number of sequences; $P(p)$ is the probability pattern P occurs; $\overline{P}$ means that pattern P does not occur; $P(C_i)$ is the probability of the ith class value; $P(C_i | p)$ is the conditional probability of the ith class value given that pattern P occurs; $P(p|C_i)$ is the conditional probability of pattern occurrence given the ith class value; $P(pos | p)$ is the conditional probability of the 'positive' class value given that pattern P occurs; $P(neg | p)$ is the conditional probability of the 'negative' class value given that pattern P occurs; $P(p | pos)$ is the conditional probability of pattern occurrence given the positive class value; and $P(p | neg)$ is the conditional probability of pattern occurrence given the negative class value.

Table 1. Comparing nine statistical scoring models across four several criteria

Statistical Scoring Models	Common Patterns	Pattern Absence	Class Value	Target Class Value
$TF(p) = Freq(p)$.	Yes	-	-	-
$TF - IDF(p) = TF(p) \cdot \log (\frac{|D|}{DF(p)})$.	Yes	-	-	-
$Z(p) = P(C_i | p)$.	-	-	Yes	-
$CE(p) = P(p) \sum_i P(C_i | p) \log \frac{P(C_i|p)}{P(C_i)}$.	Yes	-	Yes	-
$MI(p) = \sum_i P(C_i) \log \frac{P(p|C_i)}{P(p)}$.	Yes	-	Yes	-
$IG(p) = P(p) \sum_i P(C_i | p) \log \frac{P(C_i|p)}{P(C_i)} + P(\overline{p}) \sum_i P(C_i | \overline{p}) \log \frac{P(C_i|\overline{p})}{P(C_i)}$.	Yes	Yes	Yes	-
$NGL(p) = \frac{\sqrt{|D|} \cdot [P(pos|p) \cdot P(neg|\overline{p}) - P(neg|p) \cdot P(pos|\overline{p})]}{\sqrt{P(p) \cdot P(\overline{p}) \cdot P(pos) \cdot P(neg)}}$.	Yes	Yes	Yes	Yes
$X^2(p) = \frac{|D| \cdot [P(pos|p) \cdot P(neg|\overline{p}) - P(neg|p) \cdot P(pos|\overline{p})]^2}{P(p) \cdot P(\overline{p}) \cdot P(pos) \cdot P(neg)}$.	Yes	Yes	Yes	Yes
$WOR(p) = P(p) \cdot \log \frac{P(p|pos) \cdot (1 - P(p, neg))}{(1 - P(p, pos)) \cdot P(p|neg)}$.	Yes	-	Yes	Yes

2.3 Identifier Construction

This process uses the candidate signatures to formulate a similarity scoring function. When there is a query sequence, the function is used to estimate the significance of candidate signatures of each class of DNA types (*SimScore*). If the *SimScore* of any class is maximal, the query is identified as a member of the class. On the other hand, if *SimScore* of every class is zero; the query is not assigned to any classes. Let X be a query sequence with cardinality m. Let $p_{x1}, p_{x2}...p_{xd}$ be a set of d ($m-n+1$) n-gram patterns generated by the query sequence. Let $s_{y1}, s_{y2}...s_{ye}$ be a set of e candidate signatures in a class Y. Then, $sim(p_x, s_y)$ is a similarity score of a pattern p_x and a candidate signature s_y, where $sim(p_x, s_y)$ is 1, if p_x is similar to s_y, and $sim(p_x, s_y)$ is 0, if not similar. The similarity score of a class Y, $SimScore(X, Y)$, is a summation of similarity scores of every pattern p_x and every candidate signature s_y as follows

$$SimScore(X, Y) = \sum_{1 \le i \le d, 1 \le j \le e} sim(p_{x_i}, s_{y_j}). \qquad (3)$$

3 Experiments

In our experiments, we compare the accuracies of identifiers by distinguishing the eight inner genes of Influenza in GenBank Database [2]. The accuracy is the ratio of the number of sequences correctly identified to the total number of test sequences. Each identifier is produced from the different sets of candidate signatures which each set is derived from one n-gram and one statistical model. Following the use of different criteria of models, we divide the experimental results into 3 ranges of n-grams, 1- to 6-grams, 6- to 11-grams and 11- to 24-grams, for more precise analysis.

The identifiers, constructed by 1- to 5-gram signatures in every scoring model, get poor results as shown in Fig. 2a; whereas the identifiers, constructed by 6- to 11-gram signatures in most models, achieve good results, except the models based on *Pattern Absence*, such as *IG*, *NGL* and X^2, as illustrated in Fig. 2b. In Fig. 2c, the use of signatures which are longer than 11-gram provides 10% less accuracy than the 6- to 11-gram, nevertheless the results are quite stable and good in several models, except the models based on *Target Class Value*, such as *NGL*, X^2 and *WOR*.

Following the results, the models based on frequencies of patterns solely, such as *TF* and *TF-IDF*, achieve good results; whereas the others depend on the length of n-gram signatures and the criteria used in the models. The models based on *Pattern Absence*, such as *IG*, *NGL* and X^2, between 6- to 11-grams produce poor results; whereas, longer than 11-gram, the model based on *Pattern Absence* but not based on *Target Class Value*, such as *IG*, gets good results. As discussed above, our discovery model selects the ten highest-score patterns to be signatures. The score comparison of each pattern, generated by the 6- to 11-grams, considers from frequencies of both presence and absence of pattern which may bring about unbalanced class and pattern score distribution. For longer than 11-gram, the score comparison mainly considers from frequencies of the pattern presence only, since the frequencies of pattern absence are very high in every pattern, because of the large number of possible patterns ($>4^{11}$ possible patterns) and the low probability of the same pattern occurrence. Hence, the performance of the models based on *Pattern Absence* in the long patterns is comparably equal with the models based on only *Common Patterns* owing to considering on the same only pattern presence.

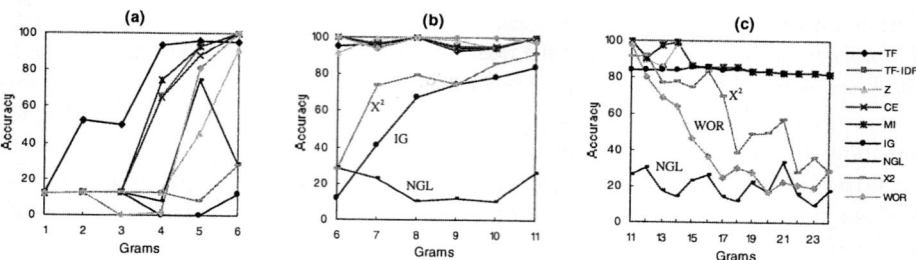

Fig. 2. Comparing the Accuracies of identifiers constructed using nine statistical scoring models and diverse n-grams: (a) 1- to 6-grams; (b) 6- to 11-grams; and (c) 11- to 24-grams

Next, we found that, longer than 11-gram, the accuracies of identifiers drop, when they use the models based on *Target Class Value*, such as *NGL*, X^2 and *WOR*, emphasizing on difference between the target and non-target classes. That the *Target Class Value* is not a good measure in the long n-gram patterns may be due to its unbalanced class and pattern score distribution. The use of long patterns generates the large number of possible patterns and the low probability of the same pattern occurrence; hence, the statistical analysis cannot handle with the too high pattern distribution which brings about the unbalanced score distribution.

However, from all results, several identifiers provide accuracy over 80% and up to 100% at 8- and 11-grams in several models. Hence, our proposed approach is highly possible to discover the actual "*DNA Signatures*" of the *Influenza virus*.

4 Conclusion

The signature discovery is an important task in the Computational Biology since the signature is more compact and more precise which helps reduce the high computation time. We propose a novel approach to discover "*Signatures*", which are sufficiently distinctive information for the sequence identification. We apply an n-gram method and statistical models in discovering the signatures. The signatures are derived from the best combination of the n-grams and the statistical models, which are evaluated by the identification system over the Influenza virus. The experimental results showed that the accuracies of several identifiers provide over 80% and maximal up to 100%, when the identifiers are constructed by the appropriate n-grams and statistical models. Hence, the candidate signatures used for the identifier construction are highly possible to be "Signatures" of the DNA sequences. Our approach succeeds in the signature discovery and also requires low computation time for the biological tasks.

References

1. Aalbersberg, I.: A document retrieval model based on term frequency ranks. Proc. of the 7th Annual International ACM SIGIR Conference on Research and Development in Information Retrieval (1994) 163-172
2. Benson, D.A., Karsch-Mizrachi, I., Lipman, D.J., Ostell, J., Rapp, B.A., Wheeler, D.L.: GenBank. Nucleic Acids Research 28(1) (2000) 15-18
3. Brown, P.F., de Souza, P.V., Della Pietra, V.J., Mercer, R.L.: Class-based n-gram models of natural language. Computational Linguistics 18(4) (1992) 467-479
4. Chuzhanova, N.A., Jones, A.J., Margetts, S.: Feature selection for genetic sequence classification. Bioinformatics Journal 14(2) (1998) 139-143
5. Krauthammer, M., Rzhetsky, A., Morozov, P., Friedman, C.: Using BLAST for identifying gene and protein names in journal articles. Gene 259(1-2) (2000) 245-252
6. Mladenic, D., Grobelnik, M.: Feature selection for unbalanced class distribution and naïve bayes. Proc. of the 16th International Conference on Machine Learning (1999) 258-267
7. Sebastiani, F.: Machine learning in automated text categorization. ACM Computing Surveys 34(1) (2002) 1-47
8. Wang, J.T.L., Rozen, S., Shapiro, B.A., Shasha, D., Wang, Z., Yin, M.: New techniques for DNA sequence classification. Journal of Computational Biology 6(2) (1999) 209-218
9. Xu, Y., Mural, R., Einstein, J., Shah, M., Uberbacher, E.: Grail: A multiagent neural network system for gene identification. Proc. of the IEEE 84(10) (1996) 1544-1552

Parallel Sequence Alignment: A Lookahead Approach

Prasanta K. Jana and Nikesh Kumar

Department of Computer Science and Engineering,
Indian School of Mines, Dhanbad-826004, India
prasantajana@yahoo.com, kumar_nikesh@yahoo.co.uk

Abstract. In this paper we present a parallel algorithm for local alignment of two biological sequences. Given two sequences of size m and n, our algorithm uses a novel technique namely, carry lookahead and requires $O(m/4 + n/2)$ time on a maximum of $O(m)$ processors.

1 Introduction

Sequence alignment is a very fundamental problem in modern molecular biology. Searching similarity or homologous sequences in the large biological databases through local alignment has now become a regular practice. Given two sequences S_1 and S_2, the problem of local alignment is to find two subsequences α and β of S_1 and S_2 respectively whose similarity (optimal global alignment value) is maximum over all pairs of subsequences from S_1 and S_2. The Smith-Waterman algorithm [5] is an optimal solution for the local alignment problem. A more restricted case of this problem known as the local suffix alignment is as follows. Let $V(i, j)$ be defined as the optimal alignment of prefixes $S_1[1...i]$ and $S_2[1...j]$. Given a pair of indices $i \leq m$ and $j \leq n$, the problem of local suffix alignment is to find a (possibly empty) suffix α of $S_1[1...i]$ and a (possibly empty) suffix β of $S_2[1...j]$ such that $V(\alpha, \beta)$ is the maximum over all pairs of suffixes of $S_1[1...i]$ and $S_2[1...j]$. Let $v(i, j)$ denote the value of the optimal local suffix alignment for the given index pair i, j. The dynamic programming solution for the local suffix alignment problem is based on the following recurrence relation [6]:

$$v(i, j) = max \begin{cases} 0 \\ v(i-1, j-1) + s(S_1(i), S_2(j)) \\ v(i-1, j) + s(S_1(i), \_) \\ v(i, j-1) + s(\_, S_2(j)) \end{cases} \text{ for } i > 0 \text{ and } j > 0 \quad (1.1)$$

with $v(i,0)=0$ and $v(0, j)=0\, \forall i, j$ where s denotes a scoring function and '–' denotes a space that implies an insertion or deletion. A solution to the local suffix alignment problem also solves the local alignment problem [6]. In the recent years many researchers have developed various parallel algorithms and parallel architectures for this problem which can be found in [1], [2], [3], [4],[7], [8], [9]. In this paper, we present a parallel algorithm for comparing two biological sequences through local alignment. In most of the dynamic programming based parallel algorithms, parallelism has been applied to calculate all the table elements concurrently on a *single diagonal only* and the computations proceed diagonal by diagonal. In contrast, our algorithm, however, computes all the table elements of *four diagonals* simultaneously using lookahead approach. This requires $O(m/4 + n/2)$ time using a maximum of $O(m)$ processors.

2 Proposed Parallel Algorithm

The basic idea of our algorithm is to first divide the entire dynamic programming table row wise into two equal parts, upper and lower using Hirschberg method [10]. Then we perform the computations to fill up the entries in the upper part and the lower part of the table concurrently in forward and backward direction followed by trace backs in both the parts and then combine the results of the trace backs. This is important to note that although the Hirschberg method is applicable to solve global alignment problem it can also be used for solving the local alignment problem for two sequences as explained in the section 12.1.5 of the text of Gusfield [6].

We now consider the lookahead approach for calculating the table elements for the upper part only. For symmetry, the elements of the lower part of the table can be calculated similarly. From (1.1) we have the following two equations

$$v(i-1, j) = max \begin{cases} 0 \\ v(i-2, j-1) + s(S_1(i-1), S_2(j)) \\ v(i-2, j) + s(S_1(i-1), \_) \\ v(i-1, j-1) + s(\_, S_2(j)) \end{cases} \quad (2.1)$$

$$\text{and} \quad v(i, j-1) = max \begin{cases} 0 \\ v(i-1, j-2) + s(S_1(i), S_2(j-1)) \\ v(i-1, j-1) + s(S_1(i), \_) \\ v(i, j-2) + s(\_, S_2(j-1)) \end{cases} \quad (2.2)$$

Substituting $v(i-1, j)$ and $v(i, j-1)$ from (2.1) and (2.2) in equation (1.1), we obtain

$$v(i, j) \leftarrow max \begin{cases} 0 \\ v(i-1, j-1) + s(S_1(i), S_2(j)) \\ v(i-1, j-1) + s(\_, S_2(j)) + s(S_1(i), \_) \\ v(i-2, j-1) + s(S_1(i-1), S_2(j)) + s(S_1(i), \_) \\ v(i-2, j) + s(S_1(i-1), \_) + s(S_1(i), \_), \\ v(i-1, j-2) + s(S_1(i), S_2(j-1)) + s(\_, S_2(j)) \\ v(i, j-2) + s(\_, S_2(j-1)) + s(\_, S_1(j)) \end{cases} \quad (2.3)$$

From the dependency graph (composite) as shown in Fig. 1, it is clear that computations of all three elements, i.e., $v(i, j)$, $v(i-1, j)$ and $v(i, j-1)$ are independent of each others. Therefore we can compute $v(i-1, j)$ and $v(i, j-1)$ using equation (1.1) from the values of the just two previous diagonals along with $v(i, j)$ using equation (2.3) from the values of the previous to previous two diagonal elements for all possible values of i and j. It means that all the elements of two consecutive diagonals (shown by solid lines in this figure) can be calculated concurrently. Since the table elements of the lower part will be calculated in the reverse direction, we replace '-' symbol by '+' for all the indices of $v(i, j)$ in equations (1.1) and (2.3).

We now formally present the parallel algorithm stepwise as follows. Since computing the table elements is the dominating one, in our parallel version, we only consider the generation of the entire table elements.

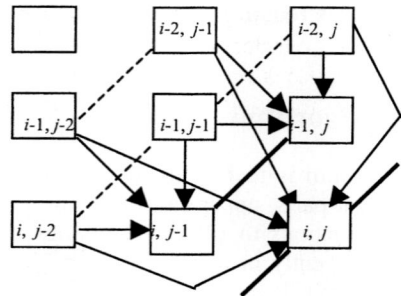

Fig. 1. Dependency graph of computing $v(i-1, j)$, $v(i, j-1)$ and $v(i, j)$

Algorithm Par_alignment:

1. **do** steps 2 and 3 **in parallel**
2. **for** $diag = 2$ to $m/2 + n$ **by step** 2
   for all i, j, $i = 1$ to $m/2$ **and** $j = 1$ to n **do** steps 2.1 and 2.2 **in parallel**
   2.1 **if** $(i + j = diag)$ **then**
   $$v(i,j) \leftarrow max \begin{cases} 0, \ v(i-1, j-1) + s(S_1(i), S_2(j)) \\ v(i-1, j) + s(S_1(i), \_) \\ v(i, j-1) + s(\_, S_2(j)) \end{cases}$$
   2.2 **if** $(i + j = diag + 1)$ **then**
   $$v(i,j) \leftarrow max \begin{cases} 0, \ v(i-1, j-1) + s(S_1(i), S_2(j) \\ v(i-1, j-1) + s(\_, S_2(j)) + s(S_1(i), \_) \\ v(i-2, j-1) + s(S_1(i-1), S_2(j)) + s(S_1(i), \_) \\ v(i-2, j) + s(S_1(i-1), \_) + s(S_1(i), \_), \\ v(i-1, j-2) + s(S_1(i), S_2(j-1)) + s(\_, S_2(j)) \\ v(i, j-2) + s(\_, S_2(j-1)) + s(\_, S_1(j)) \end{cases}$$

3. **for** $diag = 2$ to $m/2 + n$ **by step** 2
   forall i, j, $i = m$ **downto** $m/2 + 1$ **and** $j = n$ **downto** 1 **do** steps 3.1 and 3.2 **in parallel**
   3.1 **if** $(i + j - 2 + diag = m + n)$ **then**
   $$v(i,j) \leftarrow max \begin{cases} 0, \ v(i+1, j+1) + s(S_1(i), S_2(j)) \\ v(i+1, j) + s(S_1(i), \_) \\ v(i, j+1) + s(\_, S_2(j)) \end{cases}$$
   3.2 **if** $(i + j - 2 + diag = m + n - 1)$ **then**
   $$v(i,j) \leftarrow max \begin{cases} 0, \ v(i+1, j+1) + s(S_1(i), S_2(j)) \\ v(i+1, j+1) + s(\_, S_2(j)) + s(S_1(i), \_) \\ v(i+2, j+1) + s(S_1(i+1), S_2(j)) + s(S_1(i), \_) \\ v(i+2, j) + s(S_1(i+1), \_) + s(S_1(i), \_) \\ v(i+1, j+2) + s(S_1(i), S_2(j+1)) + s(\_, S_2(j)) \\ v(i, j+2) + s(\_, S_2(j+1)) + s(\_, S_1(j)) \end{cases}$$

4. **Stop**

Complexity: The steps 2 and 3 run in parallel each of which iterates $m/4 + n/2$ times and the other steps require constant time. So the above algorithm requires $O(m/4 + n/2)$ time. Since the maximum size of the diagonal of the upper or lower table is $m/2$, it requires maximum $2m$ processors to compute four diagonals in parallel.

3 Conclusion

A parallel algorithm has been presented for local alignment of two biological sequences based on lookahead approach. Given two sequences of size m and n respectively, our algorithm computes the dynamic programming table diagonal by diagonal requiring $O(m/4 + n/2)$ time and a maximum of $O(m)$ processors.

References

1. Huang, X.: A space efficient parallel sequence comparison algorithm for message-passing multiprocessors. International J. of Parallel Programming. 18 (1989) 223-239.
2. Lander, E., Mesirov, J., Taylor, W.: Protein sequence comparison on a data parallel computer. Proceedings of the 1988 International Conference on Parallel Processing (1988) 257-263.
3. Aluru, S., Futamura, N., Mehrotra, K.: Parallel biological sequence comparison using prefix computations. J. of Parallel and Distributed Computing. 63 (2003) 264 -272.
4. Edmiston, E., Core, N., Saltz, J., Smith, R.: Parallel processing of biological sequence comparison algorithms. International J. of Parallel Programming. 17 (1988) 259-275.
5. Smith, T. F., Waterman, M. S.: Identification of common molecular subsequences. J. of Molecular Biology. 147 (1981) 195-197.
6. Gusfield, D.: Algorithms on Strings Trees and Sequences. Cambridge University Press (1997).
7. Bokhari, S. H., Saurer, J. R.: Sequence alignment on the Cray MTA-2. Proceedings of Second IEEE International Workshop on High Performance Computational Biology, April 22, Nice, France (2003).
8. Schmidt, B., Schroder, H., Schimmler, M.: Massively Parallel Solutions for Molecular Sequence Analysis. Proceedings of 1st International workshop on High Performance Computational Biology (2002).
9. Martins, W. S., del Cuvillo, J., Cui, W., Gao, G., Whole genome alignment using a multithreaded parallel implementation. Proceedings of Symposium on Computer Architecture and High Performance Computing, Pirenopolis, Brazil, (2001) 1-8.
10. Hirschberg, D. S.: Algorithms for the longest common subsequence problem. *J. ACM* 24 (1977) 664-675.

Evolutionary Clustering Algorithm with Knowledge-Based Evaluation for Fuzzy Cluster Analysis of Gene Expression Profiles

Han-Saem Park and Sung-Bae Cho

Department of Computer Science, Yonsei University,
Biometrics Engineering Research Center,
134 Shinchon-dong, Sudaemoon-ku, Seoul 120-749, Korea
sammy@sclab.yonsei.ac.kr, sbcho@cs.yonsei.ac.kr

Abstract. Clustering method, which groups thousands of genes by their similarities of expression levels, has been used for identifying unknown functions of genes. Fuzzy clustering method that is one category of clustering assigns one sample to multiple groups according to their membership degrees. It is more appropriate than hard clustering algorithms for analyzing gene expression profiles since single gene might involve multiple genetic functions. However, general clustering methods have problems that they are sensitive to initialization and can be trapped into local optima. To solve the problems, we propose an evolutionary fuzzy clustering algorithm with knowledge-based evaluation. It uses a genetic algorithm for clustering and prior knowledge of data for evaluation. Yeast cell-cycle dataset has been used for experiments to show the usefulness of the proposed method.

1 Evolutionary Fuzzy Clustering with Knowledge-Based Evaluation

General clustering algorithms have common problems that they are very sensitive to initial values and they can be trapped by local optima since their processes are supposed to minimize objective function [1]. Besides, there is a problem of evaluating cluster results. Since gene expression profiles vary depending on their characteristics and environments that they were collected, it is not appropriate to evaluate them with the same criteria.

We propose an evolutionary fuzzy clustering and knowledge-based evaluation method to solve the problems. GA (genetic algorithm) that is an efficient method to solve optimization problem is applied for the evolutionary fuzzy clustering method. There have been many publications related to evolutionary computation for clustering. Maulik and Bandyopadhyay tried to minimize the distances between the data in the same clusters and cluster centers [1], and Hall used GA to minimize objective function value of the hard and fuzzy c-means algorithms. However, they fixed the number of clusters and used GA only for the minimization of objective function. We have encoded one cluster partition of variable number of clusters as one chromosome and formed various cluster partitions.

The proposed method is divided into two parts: an evolutionary clustering part, which searches optimal cluster partition using GA, and a knowledge-based evaluation part, which obtains the optimal α-cuts from several datasets for Bayesian validation (BV) method. Fuzzy c-means algorithm known as the most widely used fuzzy clustering method is used for clustering [2].

For knowledge-based evaluation, we have used BV and decision tree (DT) rule to decide the optimal α-cut value. Original BV [3] evaluates cluster partition with the same α-cuts for all datasets, but it cannot evaluate the cluster results correctly since each dataset has different distribution and they are extracted from different environments.

We have obtained α-cut value for each dataset using the DT rule. First, N gene expression profiles are clustered using the fuzzy c-means algorithm, and the results are evaluated by BV. Subsequently, the optimal α-cut for each dataset is decided, and they are used for the labels of DT training data. Rule production process trains DT, and produces rules. As Fig. 1 illustrates, the attributes of DT training data are produced using membership matrices that are the fuzzy clustering results of each dataset. Incrementing the membership degree value from 0.0 to 1.0 with the difference of 0.1, attributes are divided into 10 sections. Each section counts the frequency of samples and calculates the attribute by dividing the frequency by the total number of samples. These attributes calculated are $A_1 \sim A_{10}$.

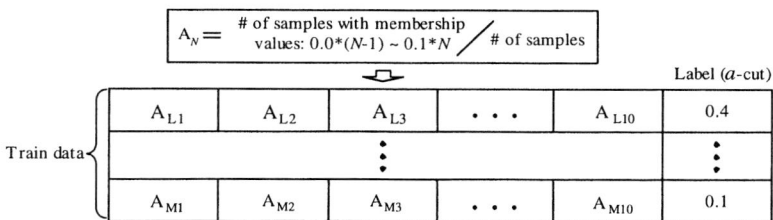

Fig. 1. Training data production process of decision tree

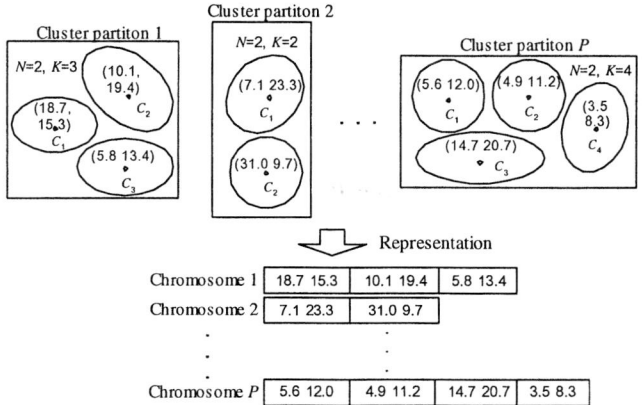

Fig. 2. Representation of variable length chromosome

The training process sets α-cut value when experimental dataset is inputted. Using these α-cut values, BV calculates the final Bayesian score (BS), which is the degree of fitness evaluation.

For evolutionary clustering, we have used floating point representation to represent a set of cluster centers of cluster partition. One cluster partition contains K clusters, and a chromosome is represented in a space of $N \times K$ in case that the dimension of each center is N. Fig. 2 illustrates several chromosomes that are in one cluster partition, and each chromosome can have different number of clusters and different values of cluster centers.

Population is initialized at random. The cluster numbers less than square value of the sample size have been used for clustering. The minimum number of clusters is set as 2. To evaluate fitness, all samples are clustered using fuzzy c-means algorithm, first. After cluster centers are updated, the chromosomes with updated centers are evaluated by BV. A roulette wheel strategy is used for selection. Crossover and mutation operations are performed considering variable length chromosomes.

2 Experiments and Analyses

We have performed experiments with yeast cell-cycle dataset, and it has expression levels of 6000 genes expressed during two cell cycles. 421 genes that show significant change of expression levels are used here, referring related work [4].

Maximum generation number of 1000 and population size of 200 have been used for experiments. Maximum numbers of clusters have been set by 20, and crossover rate of 0.8 and mutation rate of 0.01 have been used. The fuzziness parameter of the fuzzy c-means algorithm has been set as 1.2.

α-cut value of yeast cell-cycle dataset is decided as 0.4 by DT. Table 1 shows the training data extracted from yeast cell-cycle and SRBCT datasets. Comparing SRBCT, Values in A_2 and A_9 of yeast cell-cycle dataset are larger, and the value in A_{10} is smaller because the samples of yeast cell-cycle dataset have fuzzier cluster boundaries than SRBCT dataset. This shows that the characteristics of dataset should be considered since they are different.

Table 1. Training data of DT

Dataset	Attributes of training data									
	A_1	A_2	A_3	A_4	A_5	A_6	A_7	A_8	A_9	A_{10}
Yeast	1.000	0.231	0.114	0.086	0.071	0.064	0.059	0.069	0.162	0.546
SRBCT	1.000	0.016	0.000	0.016	0.000	0.016	0.000	0.000	0.048	0.937

We have compared the proposed method with the original FCM by means of BS and the objective function value (OF value) of the FCM. Table 2 shows 10 experimental results of yeast cell-cycle dataset. If BS is high and the objective function value is low, it means that clustering is performed well since the objective function value is based on the distances between cluster centers and samples. The proposed method shows better results than original FCM in both BS and OF value.

Table 2. Comparison experiments of original FCM and GA+FCM

Count	Original FCM		GA+FCM	
	BS	OF value	BS	OF value
1	0.03354	164.472	0.13256	166.883
2	0.00875	163.670	0.11246	161.542
3	0.03238	165.057	0.12661	162.911
4	0.03825	162.653	0.08058	162.073
5	0.02165	163.758	0.10667	162.798
6	0.04096	164.086	0.09778	162.312
7	0.02806	163.052	0.11873	162.042
8	0.04473	164.877	0.13659	162.773
9	0.02478	162.452	0.12898	162.905
10	0.04645	169.216	0.11246	161.542
Average	0.03195	164.329	0.11534	162.778

Finally, we have compared and analyzed the experimental result with the known genes of Cho's work [4]. We have focused on fuzzy genes that belong to several clusters at the same time with the membership degrees higher than 0.3. Fig. 3 illustrates the gene description and cluster number of fuzzy genes.

Gene	Gene description	Clusters
YPR019W	member of the Cdc46p/Mcm2p/Mcm3p family	10, 3
YHR113W	similarity to vacuolar aminopeptidase Ape1p	20, 21
YHR038W	killed in mutagen	20, 21
YNL078W	hypothetical protein	3, 19, 25
YBR160W	"g1,g2" CDC28 cyclin-dependent kinase	6, 12, 24
YDL227C	homothallic switching endonuclease	5, 12, 26
YER070W	ribonucleoside-diphosphate reductase, large subunit	12, 24, 26
YOL017W	similarity to YFR013w	12, 26
YDR464W	regulates spliceosome components	9, 11
YCR086W	hypothetical protein	9, 11
YKL052C	hypothetical protein	9, 11
YPR111W	kinase involved in late nuclear division	9, 13
YIL050W	cyclin like protein interacting with Pho85p	11, 13
YHR023W	myosin-1 isoform heavy chain	7, 18
YOR315W	hypothetical protein	7, 18

Fig. 3. Gene description and cluster number of fuzzy genes

Acknowledgements

This work was supported by the Korea Science and Engineering Foundation (KOSEF) through the Biometrics Engineering Research Center (BERC) at Yonsei University.

References

[1] U. Maulik and S. Bandyopadhyay, "Genetic algorithm-based clustering technique," *Pattern Recognition*, vol. 33, pp. 1455-1465, 2000.
[2] F. Hoppner, et al., *Fuzzy Cluster Analysis*, Wiley, 1999.
[3] S.-H. Yoo, et al., "Analyzing fuzzy partitions of Saccharomyces cerevisiae cell-cycle gene expression data by Bayesian validation method," *Proc. of the 2004 IEEE Symposium on CIBCB*, pp. 116-122, 2004.
[4] R. J. Cho, et al., "A genome-wide transcriptional analysis of the mitotic cell cycle," *Molecular Cell*, vol. 2, pp. 65-73, 1998.

Biological Text Mining for Extraction of Proteins and Their Interactions*

Kiho Hong[1], Junhyung Park[2], Jihoon Yang[2], and Sungyong Park[2]

[1] IT Agent Research Lab, LSIS R&D Center,
Hogae-dong, Dongsan-Gu, Anyang-Shi, Kyungki-Do 431-080, Korea
khhong1@lsis.biz

[2] Department of Computer Science and Interdisciplinary Program
of Integrated Biotechnology, Sogang University,
1 Shinsoo-Dong, Mapo-Ku, Seoul 121-742, Korea
jhpark@mllab.sogang.ac.kr, {yangjh, parksy}@sogang.ac.kr

Abstract. Text mining techniques have been proposed for extracting protein names and their interactions. First, we have made improvements on existing methods for handling single word protein names consisting of characters, special symbols, and numbers. Second, compound word protein names are extracted using conditional probabilities of the occurrences of neighboring words. Third, interactions are extracted based on Bayes theorem over discriminating verbs that represent the interactions of proteins. Experimental results demonstrate the feasibility of our approach with improved performance.

1 Introduction

In biologically significant applications such as developing a new drug and curing an inveterate disease, understanding the mutual effects of proteins (or genes which will be used interchangeably in the paper) are essential [1]. In order to achieve the goal, extracting gene names must be proceeded. Motivated by this background, we propose a new approach to extracting gene names and their relations.

2 Extraction of Protein Names

A protein is named either as a single word (i.e. singular protein name (SPN)) or multiple words (i.e. multiple protein name (MPN)). We describe extracting methods for each case.

2.1 SPN Extraction

A SPN is extracted by two steps:

1. Word Class Tagging: We used the Brill's tagger for tagging the text [2]. We added a word class GENE and prepared a list of words in the class.

---
* This work was supported by grant No. R01-2004-000-10689-0 from the Basic Research Program of the Korea Science & Engineering Foundation.

GenBank[1] database was adopted for making the list. To define lexicon rules and context rules during the tagger's learning stage, we used GENIA CORPUS [3,4].
2. SPN Extraction: Generally, protein names are usually irregular and ambiguous. Even though there exist some rules for protein naming (some can be found at Nature Genetics site [5]), it is hard to apply the rules to existing protein names. Also as the rules are not generalized, some of the special characters are used frequently. For this reason, processing them plays a great role for the whole efficiency. The HMM(Hidden Markov Model) with the Viterbi algorithm is applied for SPN extraction [6]. Also, in order to handle special characters, a substitution method was considered (e.g. & for digits and ? for roman letters).

2.2 MPN Extraction

Usually an SPN makes up an MPN with near (or neighboring) words. However, an MPN not including any SPN should be considered as well (e.g. tumor necrosis factor). Based on the technique used in TagGeN [5], we developed an enhanced probability model. First, if GENE tag is included, the range of an MPN is determined by expanding words in bidirection (i.e. right and left). If an MPN does not include any GENE word, we use SEED word (e.g. the words appearing in MPNs frequently). To determine the range of an MPN, it is needed to expand the search from a GENE word or a SEED word, considering the following probability:

$$P(W_{next}|W_{current}, M_{current} = 1) \qquad (1)$$

where W_i represents a word occurring at position i, and M_i is a binary value which represents whether the word at position i belongs to GENE word class or not.

3 Extraction of Protein Interactions

There could be a pattern like *'Protein(A)-Type(interaction)-Protein(B)'* [2]. We define the verbs for the interactions and extract events from these predefined patterns. Then we are able to know that entity A has a relation with B. We first extract the discriminating verbs and then extract associated protein interactions.

3.1 Discriminating Verb Extraction

A discriminating verb is extracted as follows:

1. Pre-processing: The set of types (i.e. interactions) we are interested in would be the discriminating verb set. To define the set, words tagged as verbs by Brill's tagger are extracted.

---
[1] http://www.ncbi.nlm.nih.gov/Genbank/index.html

2. P-Score: We use the Bayesian probability model for estimating the P-Score of each verb in the document. Then, we determine the set of discriminating verbs based on the P-Score. Therefore, the P-Score exhibits how well a verb describes the interaction between proteins. This was proposed for extracting a word set to classify documents by Marcotte [7]. We applied the method for extraction discriminating verbs and calculate the following probability:

$$P(n|N,f) \approx e^{-Nf}\frac{(Nf)^n}{n!} \qquad (2)$$

where n means how many times a verb is used as a protein interaction, N is the total number of words in a document, and f is the total occurrences of each verb. The Poisson distribution can be an alternative for $P(n|N,f)$ while N is big enough and f is fairy small.

3. Discriminating Verb Selection: Calculate P-Score for every word, and then choose a set of arbitrary number of words with the highest P-Scores.

3.2 Protein Interaction Extraction

The steps of extracting protein interactions are as follows:

1. Complex Sentence Processing: To handle the ambiguity in a sentence, we used Toshihide Ono's method [1] used for processing complex and negative sentences.
2. Interaction Extraction: If there is a pattern like *'Protein(A)-Type(Verb)-Protein(B)'* and a discriminating verb in a sentence, we calculate $Confidence$ of the sentence and then add the sentence into the $event$ (protein interaction) set. The $Confidence$ is calculated by sum of b (binary value which represents whether the pattern is included in the sentence or not) and a reciprocal of sd (sum of distances from proteins to a verb in the sentence). A sentence with no discriminating verb is added into candidate event set. We re-calculate $Confidence$ with $Frequency$ (how many times protein(A) and (B) are found in documents).

4 Experiments

We obtained the following extraction results of proteins and their interactions. Data used for the experiments are 600 papers from the GENIA Corpus. Our results are compared with those by ABGene and TagGeN [3,5] in Table 1.

- SPN: Since we used a substring matching method, our system produced high recall value at the cost of precision. Our system also showed outstanding extraction time than other methods.
- MPN: 'Exact' and 'partial' respectively mean perfect and subset match of MPN. Our approach outperformed TagGeN in MPN extraction.

Table 1. Performance of SPN and MPN Extraction

	SPN			MPN (exact/partial)	
	Precision(%)	Recall(%)	Time(sec)	Precision(%)	Recall(%)
Our system	85.00	96.27	6.23	86.65/91.35	84.25/91.56
ABGene	87.01	55.22	113.00	-	-
TagGeN	83.24	76.27	36324	87.81/91.15	80.23/86.51

– Protein Interaction Extraction: We used 80 discriminating verbs. Arbitrarily selected 100 sentences including 14 negative, 8 compound sentence structures, and 121 protein interactions were used. From the sentences, we extracted 139 protein interactions and obtained 76.58% precision, 92.70% recall and 83.87% F-measure value.

5 Conclusion

We developed an extraction system for proteins and their interactions. Our method with character substitution and abundant lexicon improved overall performance. We also defined discriminating verbs and extracted them using a probabilistic model. We extracted 80 discriminating verbs by Poisson distribution. Finally, we defined events, and extracted the interactions considering the confidence values of the events. We observed improved performance in all experiments.

References

1. Ono, T.: Automated extraction of information on protein-protein interactions from the biological literature. Bioinformatics **17** (2001) 155–161
2. Brill, E.: Some advances in transformation-based part of speech tagging. In: AAAI. (1994)
3. J. D. Kim, T. Ohta, Y.T., Tsujii, J.: Genia corpus - a semantically annotated for bio-textmining. Bioinformatics **19** (2002) 180–192
4. Rinaldi, F.: Mining relations in the genia corpus. In: Proceedings of the Second European Workshop and Text mining for Bioinformatics. (2004)
5. Tanabe, L., Wilbur, W.J.: Tagging gene and protein names in full text article. In: Proceedings of Association for Computational Linguistics. (2004) 9–13
6. Duda., R.O.: Pattern Classification. second edition edn. Wiley-interscience. Inc. (2000)
7. M.Marcotte, E.: Mining literature for protein-protein interactions. Bioinformatics **17** (2002) 359–363

DNA Gene Expression Classification with Ensemble Classifiers Optimized by Speciated Genetic Algorithm

Kyung-Joong Kim and Sung-Bae Cho

Department of Computer Science, Yonsei University,
134 Shinchon-dong, Sudaemoon-ku, Seoul 120-749, South Korea
{kjkim, sbcho}@cs.yonsei.ac.kr

Abstract. Accurate cancer classification is very important to cancer diagnosis and treatment. As molecular information is increasing for the cancer classification, a lot of techniques have been proposed and utilized to classify and predict the cancers from gene expression profiles. In this paper, we propose a method based on speciated evolution for the cancer classification. The optimal combination among several feature-classifier pairs from the various features and classifiers is evolutionarily searched using the deterministic crowding genetic algorithm. Experimental results demonstrate that the proposed method is more effective than the standard genetic algorithm and the fitness sharing genetic algorithm as well as the best single classifier to search the optimal ensembles for the cancer classification.

1 Introduction

The ensemble classifier, a combination of several feature-classifier pairs, has been regarded as promising due to the incompleteness of classification algorithms, the defects of data, and the difficulty of setting parameters. With the ensemble classifier, we can obtain more reliable solutions than with a single feature-classifier alone. However, because not all ensembles yield good classification performance, it is necessary to find the optimal\ ensembles in order to classify the samples accurately. In the neural network domain, it is well known that many ensembles instead of all neural networks were better. Therefore, forming an ensemble of all the feature-classifier pairs is not a good heuristic. A straightforward way of finding the optimal ensemble is to compare all the ensembles and simply select the best one. However, the possible number is too huge. In this paper, we used 42 feature-classifier pairs, indicating 2^{42} possible ensembles. It would be almost impossible to enumerate all the ensembles with even the most powerful computer.

Kuncheva et al. used the GA approach to design the classifier fusion system which was tested on a non-biological benchmark dataset [5]. In this paper, we propose the deterministic crowding genetic algorithm (DCGA) to search the optimal ensemble classifier. The reasons why we use DCGA rather than standard genetic algorithm (SGA) and fitness sharing genetic algorithm (FSGA) are summarized as follows:

(1) Geometry of the ensemble space is not known,
(2) Feature (gene) space is very huge,

(3) SGA tends to converge to only one local optimum of the function, and
(4) DCGA does not require prior knowledge.

The proposed method is unique to search the optimal ensemble evolutionarily from huge number of ensembles, whereas most of the other ensemble methods combine small number of classifiers according to specific rule.

2 Backgrounds

Studies for cancer classification based on gene expression data using ensemble approaches are summarized in Table 1. Most of the previous studies generate the base classifiers using different subsets of features to obtain diverse classifiers. Most of these studies have explored a small part of the ensemble space. However, the objective of this paper is to make a huge ensemble space and search optimal ensembles evolutionarily, which is the main contribution of this paper.

Table 1. Studies using ensemble approach for gene expression data classification

Researcher	Feature selection	Classifier	Ensemble method	Remark
Cho et al. [1]	Several methods	MLP KNN SVM SASOM	Majority voting Weighter voting Bayesian combination	Systematical comparison of features, classifiers and ensemble methods
Tan et al. [2]	Fayyad and Irani's discretization	C4.5	Bagging Boosting	Resampling
Tsymbal et al. [3]	N/A	Simple Bayesian classifier	Cross-validation majority Weighter voting Dynamic selection Etc.	Various ensemble method
Cho et al. [4]	Correlation Analysis	MLP	Majority voting	Ensemble classifier trained in mutually exclusive feature spaces

3 Proposed Method

GA (Genetic Algorithm) is stochastic search method that has been successfully applied in many search, optimization, and machine learning problems. However, standard GA has a defect which tends to converge to local minimum. DeJong's crowding is one of the niching methods which have been developed to reduce the effect of genetic drift resulting from the selection operator in the standard GA.

The structure of a chromosome is very important in the GA. In this paper, a chromosome corresponds to an ensemble. The chromosome is composed of 48 bits string, each of which indicates whether the corresponding FC (Feature-Classifier pair) is joined to the ensemble or not. In this paper, MLP (Multilayer-Perceptron), KNN (K-nearest neighbor), SVM (Support Vector Machine), and SASOM (Structure Adaptive

Self-Organizing Map) [1] are used as classification models. PC (Pearson Correlation), SC (Spearman Correlation Coefficients), ED (Euclidean Distance), CC (Cosine Coefficient), IG (Information Gain), MI (Mutual Information), SN (Signal-to Noise Ratio) and PCA (Principal Component Analysis) [1] are used as feature selection.

$$C_{fitness} = ENS_{accuracy} - k\,N_p$$

where k is a constant, N_p is the number of participant FCs to the ensemble and $ENS_{accuracy}$ is the accuracy of the corresponding ensemble on the validation data set.

$$ENS_{accuracy} = \frac{\#\,of\ exactly\ classified\ samples}{\#\,of\ total\ validation\ samples}$$

The crossover operation changes individual FCs partly between mated chromosomes, and the mutation operation either adds new FC to current chromosome or deletes a FC from it. The similarity between chromosomes is computed using hamming distance of genotypes. The algorithm of the procedure is described in Fig. 1. The majority voting scheme is used for combining the classifiers in an ensemble in this paper. This is a very popular combination scheme because of both its simplicity and its performance on real data.

```
 1: Initialize P individuals; {each individual represents an ensemble}
 2: Insert P individuals into Q; {Q holds individuals of the population}
 3: for (i = 0 ; i < MAX_GEN; i++)
 4:   Shuffle P individuals in Q;
 5:   while (Q is not empty) do
 6:     Delete (p1, p2) from Q;
 7:     q1, q2=Crossover p1, p2;
 8:     r1, r2=Mutate q1, q2;
 9:     if (distance (p1, r1)+distance (p2, r2) < distance (p1, r2)+distance (p2, r1)) then
10:       if (fitness (p1) < fitness (r1)) then Insert (r1) to Q2; else Insert (p1) to Q2; end if
11:       if (fitness (p2) < fitness (r2)) then Insert (r2) to Q2else Insert (p2) to Q2; end if
12:     else
13:       if (fitness (p1) < fitness (r2)) then Insert (r2) to Q2 else Insert (p1) to Q2; end if
14:       if (fitness (p2) < fitness (r1)) then Insert (r1) to Q2 else Insert (p2) to Q2; end if
15:     end if
16:   end while
17:   Q=Q2;
18: end for
```

Fig. 1. A pseudo code for crowding algorithm

If there are m classes and k classifiers, the ensemble result by majority voting is determined as follows:

$$c_{ensemble} = \arg\max_{1 \le i \le m} \left\{ \sum_{j=1}^{k} s_i(classifier_j) \right\}$$

where c_i is the class i, $i = 1, \ldots, m$, $s_i(classifier_j)$ is 1 if the output of the j-th classifier $classifier_j$ equals to the class i, 0 otherwise.

4 Experimental Results

B cell diffuse large cell lymphoma (B-DLCL) is a heterogeneous group of tumors, based on significant variations in morphology, clinical presentation, and response to treatment. Gene expression profiling has revealed two distinct tumor subtypes of B-DLCL: germinal center B cell-like DLCL and activated B cell-like DLCL. This lymphoma cancer dataset consists of 24 samples of GC B-like and 23 samples of activated B-like (http://genome-www.stanford.edu/lymphoma).

For the feature selection, we have selected top 25 genes or principal components (for PCA) considered as informative since a preliminary study suggested the optimal number of genes as 25~30 [1]. We have calculated PC, SC, ED and CC between each gene vector and 'ideal gene vector' in which the expression level is uniformly high in class 1 and uniformly low in class 2. IG, MI and SN are calculated using the feature values and the class label. Only PCA does not use the label information of samples.

For the classifiers, we have set the number of input-hidden-output nodes to 25-8-2. We also set 0.01~0.50 of learning rate, 0.3~0.9 of momentum, and 500 of maximum iterations. We let the back-propagation algorithm stop the training when it reaches to 98% of training accuracy. In the case of kNN, we have set the k from 3 to 9, and used Pearson correlation coefficients and cosine coefficients for the similarity measures. We have used Joachim's SVM^{light} with linear and radial basis function kernels (http://svmlight.joachims.org/). In SASOM, we have used initial 4×4 map which has rectangular shape. The details of parameters for each classification model can be found in [1].

For the DCGA, we have set the 0.9 of crossover rate, 0.05 of mutation rate, 500 of population size, and 2000 of maximum iterations and employed roulette wheel selection scheme. The value of k is set to 0.01. Fitness sharing which is for comparison, we set the sharing radius of 5. Table 2 shows the average accuracies of individual FCs for lymphoma dataset.

Leave-one-out cross-validation (LOOCV) is employed in our experiments both to overcome the number of samples and to just evaluate the proposed method. For LOOCV, dataset is divided into three parts: training samples, validation samples and one test sample. The FCs are trained by training samples. DCGA operates with validation samples to find the optimal ensemble. Finally, the best solution in the last generation is validated by test sample. These are repeated as many times as the number of data.

Table 2. The accuracy of individual FCs for lymphoma dataset

	MLP	SASOM	SVM(L)	SVM(R)	KNN(C)	KNN(P)	AVG
PC	77.6	67.7	66.4	55.6	78.4	78.0	70.6
SC	78.8	67.2	68.0	57.6	78.4	76.8	71.1
ED	75.2	62.8	66.4	64.0	76.0	77.6	70.3
CC	80.0	64.4	72.4	56.4	78.0	78.4	71.6
IG	85.2	75.2	77.6	66.8	81.6	83.2	78.3
MI	80.0	67.6	67.2	58.4	76.4	77.2	71.2
SN	81.2	70.8	68.0	58.4	78.8	79.2	72.7
PCA	87.2	84.0	88.4	58.4	86.0	86.4	81.7
AVG	80.7	70.0	71.8	59.5	79.2	79.7	73.5

Table 3. The comparison of performance (Average of ten runs)

Methods	LOOCV accuracy
Best single feature-classifier pair	95.3±3.05
Ensemble of all classifiers whose accuracy is larger than 80%	94.7±3.16
Simple GA	98.0±2.10
Crowding	98.8±1.93

DCGA found the optimal ensembles which exactly classify every validation sample. To demonstrate the superiority of our method, we have compared it with other methods and the result is in the Table. 3. The accuracy means the rate of exactly classified samples among test samples. Ensemble of good base classifiers (accuracy > 80%) is the combination of good individual FCs for classification. The performances of all GA strategies (SGA, DCGA and FSGA) are the best ensembles among 1 million ones which are generated by their operations. This shows that the combination of similar good ensemble classifiers degrades the performance and the proposed method performs well.

5 Conclusion and Future Work

This paper presents a DCGA-based method of searching the optimal ensemble for cancer classification using DNA microarray data. Though FSGA is also well known for one of good niching methods, we have employed DCGA because FSGA is known that it usually fails on hard problems and it requires prior knowledge for good result. Experiments have supported the use of DCGA for the optimal ensemble to classify cancers. The result of LOOCV also confirms the superiority of the proposed method.

Acknowledgement

This research was supported by Brain Science and Engineering Research Program sponsored by Korean Ministry of Commerce, Industry and Energy.

References

1. Cho, S.–B., and Won, H.–H.: Data mining for gene expression profiles from DNA microarray. Int. Journal of Software Engineering and Knowledge Engineering, 13 (2003) 593-608
2. Tan, A. C. and Gilbert, D.: Ensemble machine learning on gene expression data for cancer classification. Applied Bioinformatics, 2 (2003) s75-s83
3. Tsymbal, A. and Puuronen, S.: Ensemble feature selection with the simple Bayesian classification in medical diagnostics. Proc. of the 15th IEEE Symp. on Computer-Based Medical Systems (2002) 225-230
4. Cho, S.-B., and Ryu, J.-W.: Classifying gene expression data of cancer using classifier ensemble with mutually exclusive features. Proc. of the IEEE, 90 (11) (2002) 1744-1753
5. L. I. Kuncheva, and L. C. Jain, "Designing classifier fusion systems by genetic algorithms," IEEE Transactions on Evolutionary Computation, vol. 4, no. 4, pp. 327-336, 2000.

Multi-objective Optimization for Adaptive Web Site Generation

Prateek Jain[1] and Pabitra Mitra[2]

[1] IBM India Research Lab, New Delhi - 110016, India
prateekj@in.ibm.com
[2] Department of Computer Science and Engineering,
Indian Institute of Technology, Kanpur -208016, India
pmitra@iitk.ac.in

Abstract. Designing web sites is a complex problem. Adaptive sites are those which improve themselves by learning from user access patterns. In this paper we have considered a problem of *index page synthesis* for an adaptive website and framed it in a new type of *Multi-Objective Optimization* problem. We give a solution to *index page synthesis* which uses a popular clustering algorithm *DBSCAN* alongwith *NSGA-II*–an evolutionary algorithm–to find out best index pages for a website. Our experiments shows that very good candidate index pages can be generated automatically, and that our technique outperforms various existing methods such as PageGather, K-Means and Hierarchical Agglomerative Clustering.

1 Introduction

In todays society websites have become the primary source of information, but a major problem is to design a website so that it is lucid and presents its information in an efficient manner. The major problem here is that different users at different time have different goals and when a designer designs a website he has little or no idea of how this information is going to be used. Thus most of the times when complex web sites are surfed, an user has to traverse a number of pages before he obtains the relevant information. Thus comes the need for *adaptive websites*, websites that automatically improve their organization and presentation by learning from visitors' access patterns. Major problems posed here are, (a) Can adaptive websites do non-trivial adaptations and still lead to improvement?, (b) Can they be fully automated? To solve these problems an approach was suggested by Etzioni et al.[1], where he defined a problem called *index page synthesis* and have studied this problem empirically. An *index page* is a page consisting of links to a set of pages that cover a particular topic at a site, thereby leading to efficient navigation of site.

In this work, we have tried to solve *index page synthesis* problem by casting it in a new type of Multi-Objective Optimization Problem and compared our results to other standard algorithms. Our approach is to analyze Web Site's access logs to find groups of pages that are coherent i.e. occur together in user's visits. If a group of pages generally occur together in a user's visit it means that they are similar and if we link them from each other then user will reach to information required easily. Thus a technique is required to cluster similar pages and then there should be a mechanism to evaluate weblogs to determine if the clustering is good or not, and this information can be used to further improve clustering. Unsupervised learning algorithms such as *clustering algorithms* are of much importance here. Also, after clustering there should be a fine tuning mechanism which improves these clusters. In our solution, we use the DBSCAN algorithm [2] initially for finding close clusters and then use NSGA-II algorithm[3] for optimizing these set of clusters. Generally Multi-Objective Optimization algorithms are used to optimize functions which are independent of each other. But here our problem have set of functions which depend on each other too. A new method has been devised to handle this situation. Results obtained by empirical studies show that our system outperforms the existing methods.

2 Adaptive Wesites: Index-Page Synthesis

A number of different of approaches exists in field of adaptive websites. Two popular among them are *path prediction* and *index page synthesis* approach. In path prediction, the website guesses the user intent from user profile and tries to direct user to that page. This is used in the Web Watcher and AVANTI systems [4,5]. The index page synthesis approach, introduced by Etzioni et. al.[1], will be used by us.

We can define *Index-Page Synthesis* problem as: given a Web site and a visitor access log, create new index pages containing collections of links to related but currently unlinked pages. By visitor access log we mean log generated by web-server, which contains one entry for each page requested of the web-server. Each entry contains visitor's IP-Address, URL requested, time of request. *Related but currently unlinked pages* are pages that share a common topic but are not currently linked at the site. Two pages are considered to be linked if there exists a link from one page to the other or if there exist a page that links to both them. We are stressing on unlinked pages, because if two pages are linked then user can anyhow reach from one to other very easily. *Index Page Synthesis Problem* can be decomposed into following major subproblems: (i) What are the contents(i.e hyper-link) of the index page?, (ii) How are the hyper-links labelled?, (iii) What is the title of the page and does it correspond to a coherent concept?, and (iv) Where index page should be added to the site? To solve first problem we do clustering of pages, so that pages which are of related content gets clustered together and thus they form content of one index page. Hyper-links are labelled by name of target page to which they link. Third and fourth problems are handled by webmaster.

Etzioni et al.[1] suggested following criterion for evaluation of effectiveness of *index page synthesis*: (a) *Recall*: How much of the information sought by each user was actually found, (b) *Impact*: How many people use the new pages and how often, (c) *Benefit*: How much effort is saved by those who visit the page.

In our study we have compared competing solutions with respect to *impact* and *benefit*. For each cluster, we count the number of pages in the cluster viewed by each visitor to the site, and compute the total number of visitors who view at least one page, the number who view at least two pages, and so on. We then average over all the clusters generated by a particular algorithm. For each particular algorithm, we plot a line of the number of pages viewed(*benefit*) vs. the number of people who viewed that many pages(*impact*). If no users viewed more than m pages from any cluster for an algorithm, then the line for that algorithm will stop at m. We have represented *impact* on a log scale, as it often drops off exponentially with increasing benefit. Since index pages should not be too large or too small thus candidate index pages size have minimum and maximum size(5 and 100 respectively).

3 Proposed Approach for Index-Page Synthesis

In order to generate index-page, first we need to preprocess web logs and calculate co-occurrence frequency, followed by clustering and optimization of the results.

3.1 Pre-processing of Web Logs and Calculation of Co-occurrence Frequency

An web log is a sequence of page views, or requests made to the Web server. Each request includes time of request, URL requested, and the machine from which the request originated. Assuming each originating machine corresponds to a single visitor, single session for that visitor is defined as series of page views in one day's log. Thus we define a visit as ordered sequences of pages accessed by a single user in a single session. Now, co-occurrence frequency[1] of two pages p_1 and p_2 is defined as $min(P(p_1|p_2), P(p_2|p_1))$. $P(p_1|p_2)$ means probability of a visitor visiting p_1 if he/she has already visited p_2. We now form co-occurrence matrix,C, of size $n \times n$(n is total number of pages in website), where jth element of ith row, c_{ij}, represents co-occurrence frequency of Page p_i and Page p_j. Since we need to find out clusters of related but currently unlinked pages, thus to avoid finding cluster of pages already linked together, we set corresponding entries of linked pages as 0.

3.2 Clustering

We use DBScan clustering algorithm [2] for clustering similar pages. DBScan algorithm is a density based clustering algorithm, whose main principle is that if some $MinPts$ number of points are within ϵ distance of a given points then all the points belong to same cluster. Assuming pages which occur together are similar to each other, we can cluster them using DBScan algorithm, to obtain clusters of pages similar to each other. To do clustering, we have to first form feature space of each page. Each page is a point in n dimensional space, where ith co-ordinate corresponds to co-occurrence frequency of this page and p_i page.

Performance of DBScan algorithm depends largely on two parameters i.e. ϵ and $MinPts$. These parameters should be set such that quality of clusters, i.e. *Impact* and *benefit*, produced is very good. This necessitates use of an optimizer which sets ϵ and $MinPts$, such that *Impact* and *benefit* are maximized.

3.3 Multi-objective Optimization

Since, the functions to be optimized are greater than one, it is a case of multi-objective optimization, with two objectives, namely *Impact* and *benefit*. But here there is a trade-off. As benefit increases, impact decreases for a given ϵ and $MinPts$. So $f(\epsilon, MinPts)$ is a curve and not a point. Here x co-ordinate represents *benefit* and y co-ordinate represents *impact*. We have

$$Benefit(x_i) = i \text{ for } 0 \leq i \leq m, \qquad (1)$$

where m is maximum number of pages which at least one user visited. Hence, we need to apply optimizer so that *curve* is maximized. Now first we have to define what do we mean by maximization of a curve. Define,

$$Curve\ C_1(\epsilon, MinPts) = \{(x_1, y_1), (x_2, y_2), \ldots, (x_m, y_m)\}$$
$$Curve\ C_2(\epsilon', MinPts') = \{(x'_1, y'_1), (x'_2, y'_2), \ldots, (x'_{m'}, y'_{m'})\}$$

If $m' < m$, then extend Curve C_2 to x'_m with $y'_j = 0$ for $m' < j \leq m$. Now, we define a partial ordering on curves, $C_1 \geq C_2$ iff $\forall i \leq m \ \ y_i \geq y'_i$, else no relation is defined between C_1 and C_2.

We use a multiobjective algorithm named *Non-Dominated Sorting Genetic Algorithm (NSGA-II)* for optimization, which is an population based iterative algorithm. NSGA-II is based on principle of non-dominance of points i.e. let there are two variables x and y, and we have to maximize $f_1(x,y)$ and $f_2(x,y)$. Points (x_1, y_1) is dominated by (x_2, y_2) iff $f_1(x_1, y_1) \geq f_1(x_2, y_2)$ and also $f_2(x_1, y_1) \geq f_2(x_2, y_2)$. NSGA-II proceeds with a random generation of solutions (x, y) called population. Then a selection is applied to the generated solutions which takes out the best solutions out of current population. Best solutions are those which are least dominated. So from these best solutions, new solutions are formed using crossover operator and mutation operator and then this forms new population. Thus this process of selection and reproduction is continued till some terminating condition is satisfied.

For our problem, we have two variables namely ϵ and $MinPts$, which determines the clusters obtained. Quality of these clusters give curve of Impact vs Benefit. To apply NSGA-II in order to find out set of best ϵ and $MinPts$, we have to define domination of $(\epsilon, MinPts)$. $(\epsilon, MinPts)$ dominates $(\epsilon', MinPts')$ iff $C_1(\epsilon, MinPts) \geq C_2(\epsilon', MinPts')$ else $(\epsilon', MinPts')$ and $(\epsilon, MinPts)$ are non-dominated by each other, $C_1(\epsilon, MinPts)$ is produced by finding out cluster's(which is produced by applying DBScan with parameters ϵ and $MinPts$) impact vs benefit curve. Now we can directly apply NSGA-II to get optimized set of solutions.

Note that no curve can be said better than other in Pareto optimal set according to given objective functions. But after looking at all the pareto optimal curves, webmaster can decide to pick up one solution depending on targets of websites. For example a website which is targeted for a large number of visitors they will prefer curve which have high impact for benefit of 1 or 2 pages, though for higher benefits impact is not much. E.g. a website selling cheap electronic goods, not having alot of choices in products, will like that a large number of customers are attracted towards it though it maybe that they don't buy a lot of products. Where as websites for luxury cars will like to entice a few customers, but make sure that all of them get to know all the different varieties and are completely satisfied by their purchases.

4 Experimental Results and Comparison

We test our system on data collected from webpages of website *Music Machine*. Music Machine is a site devoted to information about many kinds of electronic musical instruments. Music Machines contains approximately 2500 distinct pages, including HTML pages, plain text, images, and audio samples. Music Machines receives approximately 10,000 hits per day from roughly 1200 distinct visitors. In our experiments, the training data is a collection of access logs for six months; the test data is a set of logs from a subsequent one-month period. NSGA-II is run for 50 Generation and 50 Population.

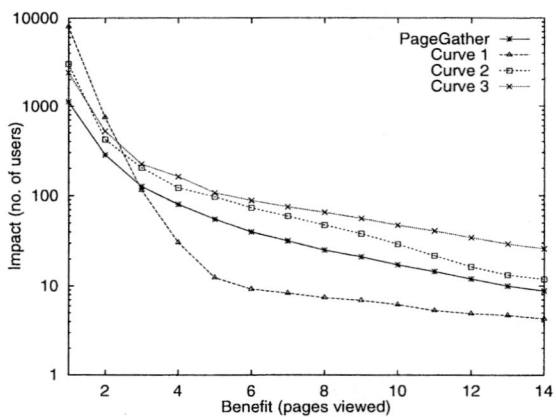

Fig. 1. Comparison of our algorithm and PageGather Algorithm

We compare our results with that of PageGather Algorithm which performed better than standard algorithms like K-Means, Hierarchial Agglomerative Clustering. Figure 1 shows Impact vs Benefit curve for both our system and for PageGather. We have compared our algorithm with PageGather Algorithm since it is known to perform better than the other algorithms [1].

Note that our algorithm gives a set of curves rather than just a single curve. These curves gives a wide range of choice to Webmaster to choose the one which suits his website the most. In the graph we have reported just few of those solutions else it would have become grossly confusing. Observe that out of set of pareto- optimal curves, two curves outperforms PageGather algorithm completely. Also none of our pareto-optimal curves were dominated by PageGather algorithm's solution.

5 Conclusion

The index page synthesis problem for adaptive web site design is formulated as a multiobjective optimization problem. A modified MOGA is used to optimize a page clustering clustering algorithm based on DBScan so as to give near optimal results on two parameters namely Impact and Benefit. Our better results goes onto indicate that Evolutionary Algorithms are quite suited to Webmining and Weblearning problems and can be used to obtain much improved performance than the present techniques.

References

1. Perkowitz, M., Etzioni, O.: Towards adaptive web sites: Conceptual framework and case study. Computer Networks **31** (1999) 1245–1258
2. Ester, M., Kriegel, H.P., Sander, J., Xu, X.: A density-based algorithm for discovering clusters in large spatial databases with noise. In: KDD. (1996) 226–231
3. Schoenauer, M., Deb, K., Rudolph, G., Yao, X., Lutton, E., Guervós, J.J.M., Schwefel, H.P., eds.: Parallel Problem Solving from Nature - PPSN VI, 6th International Conference, Paris, France, September 18-20, 2000, Proceedings. In Schoenauer, M., Deb, K., Rudolph, G., Yao, X., Lutton, E., Guervós, J.J.M., Schwefel, H.P., eds.: PPSN. Volume 1917 of Lecture Notes in Computer Science., Springer (2000)
4. Joachims, T., Freitag, D., Mitchell, T.M.: Web watcher: A tour guide for the world wide web. In: IJCAI (1). (1997) 770–777
5. Fink, J., Koenemann, J., Noller, S., Schwab, I.: Putting personalization into practice. Commun. ACM **45** (2002) 41–42

Speeding Up Web Access Using Weighted Association Rules

Abhinav Srivastava, Abhijit Bhosale, and Shamik Sural

School of Information Technology,
Indian Institute of Technology, Kharagpur
{abhinavs, abhijitb, shamik}@sit.iitkgp.ernet.in

Abstract. In this paper, we propose a data mining technique for finding frequently used web pages. These pages may be kept in a server's cache to speed up web access. Existing techniques of selecting pages to be cached do not capture a user's surfing patterns correctly. We use a Weighted Association Rule (WAR) mining technique that finds pages of the user's current interest and cache them to give faster net access. This approach captures both user's habit and interest as compared to other approaches where emphasis is only on habit.

Keywords: Data Mining, Web Server, Weighted Association Rule (WAR).

1 Introduction

Increasing popularity of the web has resulted in heavy traffic in the Internet. The effect of this growth is a significant increase in the user perceived delay. The reasons of delay are network congestion, low bandwidth, improper utilization of bandwidth and heavy load on web servers and propagation delay. The most obvious solution is to increase the bandwidth. But, it is not that easy because of required infrastructure and cost. The propagation delay cannot be reduced after certain stage, since it depends on the physical distance between source and destination. One way to speed up the web access is to prefetch those pages that show user's habit and interest and put them into the cache. When user requests for these pages, it will be served from the cache.

URLs requested by users are stored in the web logs. These URLs show information accessed by the users and give their surfing pattern. Data mining techniques can be used to mine these logs and extract association rules between the URLs requested by the users. The association rules will be of the form $X \rightarrow Y$ where X and Y are URLs. It means if a user accesses URL X then he would be accessing URL Y most likely.

Previous works in this field concentrate only on finding the user's habit. Srivastava et al [1] has attempted to provide a survey of web usage mining and its application in analyzing web usage data to better serve users. Nanopoulos et al [2] focus on the predictive prefetching and develop a new algorithm for the same. Woon et al [3] propose a novel and more holistic version of web usage mining named TRAnsactionized Logfile Mining (TRALOM) to effectively and correctly identify transactions as well as to mine useful knowledge from web access logs. Vaisman et al [4] study the data mining techniques (association rules, sequential patterns) and present a complete architecture of data mining proxy. However, most of these approaches only consider the user's habit and not the interest. User's interest keeps on changing while his habit typically remain constant. The existing approaches fail to capture this information.

In this paper, we show that both user's habit and interest can be captured by a Weighted Association Rule Mining (WAR) technique. We assign weights to all the URLs stored in a web log to distinguish recently accessed URLs from the old ones. The rest of the paper is organized as follows: In Section 2, we introduce the WAR technique and give salient features of our work. In Section 3, we present details of the experiment that we have carried out and give results. Finally, we conclude the paper with some discussions.

2 WAR Approach

User surfing patterns can be categorized into two types. (i) Regular accesses such as news, email etc. (ii) Occasional accesses based on the events such as Olympics. The former is known as habit and the later is known as interest. Users interest changes based on the events happening at any point of time.

Before we present our approach in detail, let us consider following situation: UserA logs on to Internet everyday for reading news and checking emails. He visits mail.yahoo.com and rediffmail.com in any order. However, because of the Olympics season, he starts visiting Olympics website to see the latest events and scores. In this case, Plain Association Rule (PAR) would give rules (UserA, mail.yahoo.com) → (UserA, rediffmail.com) ∧ (UserA, rediffmail.com) → (UserA, mail.yahoo.com). PAR will not detect association rules that contain the Olympics website because UserA has started visiting this website recently and to become the rule, it should be visited enough so that its support can go above the minimum support. On the other hand, using WAR scheme following rules will also be generated: (UserA, mail.yahoo.com) → (UserA, www.Olympics .com) ∧ (UserA, rediffmail.com) → (UserA, www.Olympics.com). These rules will provide real activity of UserA and captures both the habit (emails, news) and interest (Olympics) of the user. Hence, to come up with good frequent set of URLs accessed, it is important to consider user's interest also. Here are some salient features of the WAR technique:

For each URL stored in the web log, we assign a weight based on how recently it was accessed. The purpose of this weighting process is to categorize URLs into most recently accessed and less recently accessed. To achieve this, we divide the log file into different windows and assign each window a number known as windowIndex starting from the last window. The window with windowIndex 1 contains most recently accessed URLs, which are at the end of the log file. We assign all the URLs, which are in window 1, a highest weight $hWeight$, where $0 < hWeight < 1$. Let i, $weight_i$ and N be the windowIndex, weight of ith window and total number of windows (i.e. maximum value of i) respectively. $weight_i$ is calculated as follows:

$$weight_i = (hWeight)^i \tag{1}$$

It is evident from equation (1), that as we move from i to j where i and j are windowIndex and i < j, $weight_j < weight_i$. Since weight of a window represents weight of each URL in that window, weight assigned to a URL also decreases. So, the total weight of any URL u can be calculated as follows:

$$totalURLWeight = \sum_{i=1}^{N} weight_i \ (if \ u \ \epsilon \ i^{th} \ window) \tag{2}$$

Once the weight is calculated for all the URLs present in the web log, a minimum value of support is required. Unlike other approaches [2][3][4] where support is chosen only on the basis of count of URLs, we consider both weight and count of URLs for calculating support. So, for X % minimum support the weight would be:

$$(X * \sum_{i=1}^{N} weight_i)/100 \tag{3}$$

Finally, we modify the existing apriori algorithm [5] to support weighted URLs. In WAR, modified apriori algorithm works by counting the weight of each URL in all the windows in each phase using equation (2). Once we calculate the total weight of each URL, we eliminate those URLs which are below the minimum support. We iterate this process until no more frequent URLs set can be generated.

The URLs which a user accesses as a part of his habit, should be present in most of the windows including recent windows also. So, they must have high weights and will be part of frequent URLs set. The URLs which the user accesses as part of his interest should only present in the recent windows. Since recent windows have high weights, it is more likely that the total weight of a URL is above the minimum support and will be part of the frequent sets. Hence, the frequent URLs set generated by WAR contains mix of URLs capturing both habit and interest of the users. These frequent URLs can be used to speed up the web access by prefetching the URLs and present to the user whenever it is requested.

3 Experimental Results

A log file of a proxy server was used for the analysis of our work. The log was generated for a period of 8 working hours between 9 am and 5 pm. First, the log file is cleaned by removing the URLs of dynamic pages like jsp, asp etc. Then the log entries are separated as per requesting IP addresses. Here an IP address is considered as identifier for a user, assuming that only one user is using a particular computer, for accessing the web. The log entries of each IP address are processed separately. A window size is decided for a transaction. For experimental purpose, we have selected three different time windows of 1 min,

5 min and 10 min. Hence the log is partitioned in a group of URLs falling in a window, forming a transaction. Now, these transactions are used to find the frequent item sets of URLs.

We compare performance of our approach with Vaisman et al's approach that use PAR [4]. Here, due to size restriction we have included a few sample results of our experiments. We plot the Support vs. Number of Transactions graphs for different window sizes. Figures 1(a), 1(b) show graphical results for window size of 1 min, Figures 2(a), 2(b) show for 5 min and Figures 3(a), 3(b) show for 10 min window. The bold line is the minimum support value while others are for the sites accessed by the user. The Figures 1(a), 2(a) and 3(a) are results of PAR approach. In these Figures, access count of each URL is treated as the support. The Figures 1(b), 2(b) and 3(b) are results of WAR approach. In every graph a particular line represents how the support value changes with number of transactions. For example let us consider the regular continuous line, which represents the support values for site http://10.105.8.42. In Figure 2(a), at the time when total number of transactions generated from the log file is 50, the URL http://10.105.8.42 is accessed 8 times since beginning. While from Figure 2(b), we can observe that at the same time the calculated weight for the URL http://10.105.8.42 is little less that 1.

Consider Figure 2(a), if we notice the accessed site http://10.105.8.42 (regular continuous line), we can see that it is always above the minimum support and hence will be always become a part of the frequent item set. We can see that it is actually not accessed during the period of time from transactions 40 to 65. This means that user is not interested in this site, at least for some period. But still it is considered as a frequent item. Consider http://10.112.5.205 (dashed line with cross mark), which is accessed by the user for the first time in transaction number 60. After that, the user frequently accesses it since he gets interested in that side. But it still falls below the minimum support value and not considered as a frequent item.

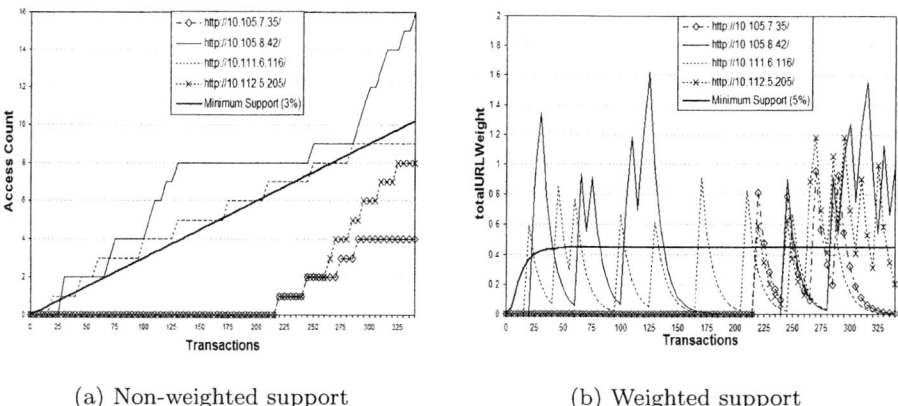

(a) Non-weighted support   (b) Weighted support

Fig. 1. Comparison of support vs. transactions for 1 minute window

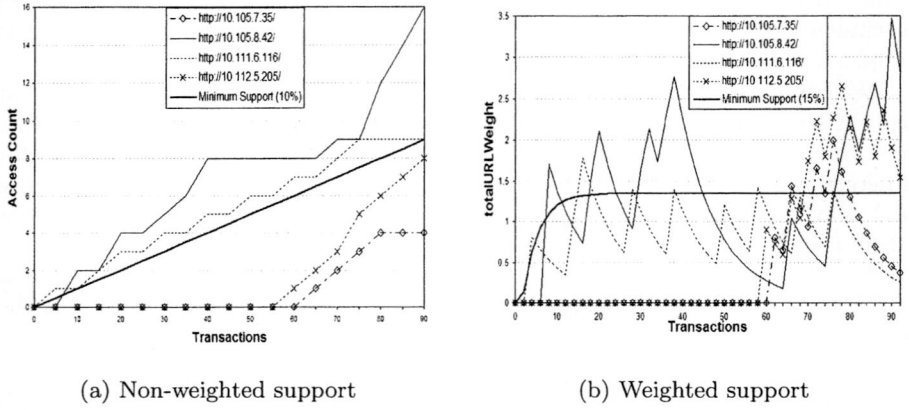

(a) Non-weighted support (b) Weighted support

Fig. 2. Comparison of support vs. transactions for 5 minutes window

Now, let us see how WAR helps in finding the user's interest that is not considered by PAR. In Figure 2(b), we can see that the weight for the site http://10.105.8.42 falls below minimum support at transaction number 46. Hence it will not be considered as frequent item during the period when the user in not interested in visiting that site. If we consider site http://10.112.5.205, we can observer that site is able to cross the minimum support at transaction number 66, just after 6 transactions of its first access. Hence a user's interest is better tracked in WAR.

The most critical part in the weighted support system is the selection of window size and minimum support, which need fine tuning as per the situation. In Figures 1(a), 1(b), where window size is 1 min, the support percentage needs

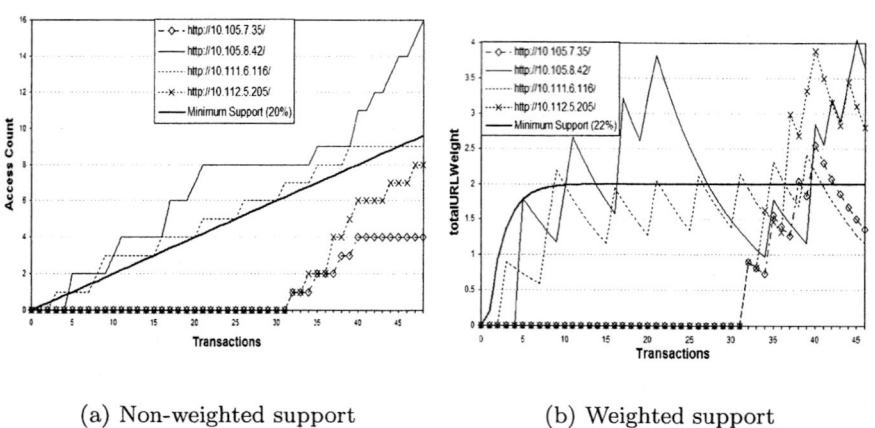

(a) Non-weighted support (b) Weighted support

Fig. 3. Comparison of support vs. transactions for 10 minutes window

to be lowered to get the similar results as we have obtained for 5 min window. On the other hand, as in case of Figures 3(a), 3(b) where the window size is 10 min, support percentage needs to be increased to obtain similar results. We can include a learning phase in our framework in which a sample log file will be used to find out the appropriate values of window size and minimum support percentage.

4 Conclusions and Discussions

In this paper, we have presented a new approach in which a weight is assigned to each URL for capturing its recency. We have used a weighted apriori algorithm to generate the frequent URL set . We also have suggested how this result can be used to speedup web access and reduce a user's perceived latency. This result can be improved by adding a learning phase in which window size and minimum support values can be tuned. Our work highlights the need for some mechanism to distinguish between frequently and recently accessed items by a user to predict his current interest and habits.

References

1. J. Srivastava, R. Cooley, M. Deshpande, P. N. Tan, *Web usage mining: Discovery and applications of usage patterns from web data*, SIGKDD Explorations, (2000) 12-23.
2. A. Nanopoulos, D. Katsaros, Y. Manolopoulos, *Effective prediction of web user access*, WEBKDD'01, (2001).
3. Y. Woon, W. Ng, E. Lim, *Online and incremental mining of separately-grouped Web access logs*, 3rd International Conference on Web Information Systems Engineering. (2002) 53-62.
4. A. A. Vaisman, G. Dandretta, M. Sapia, *Enhancing Web access using datamining techniques*, 14th International Workshop on Database and Expert Systems Application, (2003) 327-331.
5. A. Agrawal, H. Mannila, R. Srikant, H. Toivonen, A. Verkamo, *Fast Discovery of Association Rules*, 20th International Conference on Very Large Database, (1996) 307-328.

An Automatic Approach to Classify Web Documents Using a Domain Ontology

Mu-Hee Song, Soo-Yeon Lim, Seong-Bae Park, Dong-Jin Kang, and Sang-Jo Lee

Dept. of Computer Engineering, Information Technology Services,
Kyungpook National University, Daegu, The Korea
{mhsong, seongbae, djkang, sjlee}@knu.ac.kr
nadalsy@hotmail.com

Abstract. This paper suggests an automated method for document classification using an ontology, which expresses terminology information and vocabulary contained in Web documents by way of a hierarchical structure. Ontology-based document classification involves determining document features that represent the Web documents most accurately, and classifying them into the most appropriate categories after analyzing their contents by using at least two pre-defined categories per given document features. In this paper, Web documents are classified in real time not with experimental data or a learning process, but by similar calculations between the terminology information extracted from Web texts and ontology categories. This results in a more accurate document classification since the meanings and relationships unique to each document are determined.

Keywords: Document classification, Ontology, Web Page classification.

1 Introduction

In recent years ontologies have become a topic of interest in computer science. This paper suggests an automated method for document classification using ontology. In our research, Web documents are classified based on similarities determined by the ontology, which expresses the meaning structure of the Web documents' terminology information and vocabulary in a hierarchical manner. Identifying and comparing the meaning content and relationship of each document can perform document classification more accurately and efficiently. The ontology mentioned in this paper is comprised of concepts, concepts features, relations between concepts, and constraints for document classification, all in a hierarchical manner. Also, the ontology's hierarchical structure is applied to the document classification.

Our work is distinguished from others for the following reasons: (1) Rather than using a dictionary or knowledge index, ontology is used for document classification. (2) Our ontology is based on syntax information contained in the Web pages. (3) Mapping between the established ontology and terminology information extracted from Web pages is performed.

We wish our classification system could be used to classify current web pages into proper categories and to generate reports if the web pages belong to unwanted sites.

In the following section of this paper, we will discuss related approaches to our classifier. Section 3 describes the details of our framework how ontology, as suggested in this paper, is applied to document classification, and we show the experiments and evaluation of web page in Section 4. In conclusion we summarize our results and mention further research issues..

2 Related Works

This section describes research which has been carried out by people in the area of automatic document classification, and it examines the key difference between our work and other research.

The rule-based model [1] utilizes experts' help based on generally distinguished rules that appear in study texts or applies rules that are extracted by studying the documents. The Bayesian probability model [2] applies the probability theory to the document features extracted from the documents. The SVM (Support Vector Machine: SVM)[3] uses the machine learning method. Although these methods have some degree of accuracy, all of them require some rule learning level and they must have the training data as a reference.

There have been several approaches which focus on ontologies to classify Web pages [4,5,6]. Prabowo et. al. [4] defined ontology as "a single entity which holds conceptual instances of a domain, and differentiates itself from another," and used ontologies for web page classification with respect to the Dewey Decimal Classification(DDC) and Library of Congress Classification(LCC). The weakness of their approach is the fact that is not adaptive when users require more sophisticated classification, even if the approach follows the standard classifications. However, since our approach builds an adaptive ontology, we provide a flexible classification reflecting requests.

This paper suggests an ontology-based, automated document classification method, which does not require these learning processes and can be performed in real time.

3 Document Classification Using Ontology

3.1 Ontology Structure

In this paper, ontology is defined as one independent, collective representation of all standardized concepts for vocabulary and terms in one place. Here, we are not talking about collections of simple words, but we are referring to collection of vocabulary, which have relationships with both simple rules and meanings. Ontology expressions are based not only on the logical relations between term definitions and other meanings, but also on the bottom-out structure where the interpretation starts from primitive terms. We have decided to apply ontology to Web document classification, because it has the unique, hierarchical structure and characteristic of machine reasoning, starting from very primitive terms.

The advantages of an ontology-based classification approach over the existing ones, such as hierarchical[7], - and probabilistic – approach[8], are that (1) the nature of the relational structure of an ontology provides a mechanism to enable machine reasoning; (2) the conceptual instances within an ontology are not only a bag of keywords but have inherent semantics, and a close relationship with the class representatives of the classification schemes. Hence, they can be mapped to each other; (3) this is a kind of Web page and class representative. It also enables us to get insights into and observe the way the classifier assigns a class representative to Web pages by tracking the links between the conceptual instances involved and the associated class representative [4].

3.2 Building Domain Ontology for Document Classification

In this research, ontology for the 'economy' domain has been developed for experimental purposes of document classification. To configure and develop the ontology, it is first assumed that vocabulary which frequently appears in document collection is similarly related to other vocabulary. The second point is this frequently appearing vocabulary is used to build the basic network structure. Third, adding vocabulary that has a relationship with those selected words expands the ontology. Then, similarities between the terminology information extracted from Web page, and ontology terminology data are identified and compared in order to start the document classification process.

3.3 Document Classification Using Ontology

The process of Web document classification basically involves two procedures: Finding key vocabulary in the documents and mapping onto a node in the concept hierarchy (ontology) using the extracted words.

Table 1. The document-term frequency data matrix after the stemming and stopping processes

Doc_j	TF_1	TF_2	...	TF_m
Doc_1	2	4	...	5
Doc_2	2	3	...	2
Doc_3	2	3	...	2
...	...	...	...	...
Doc_n	1	3	...	7

As part of the key vocabulary extraction process from documents, the removal of stop words and the stemming of words, both as the pre-classification procedures as well as the application of information retrieval measurement, *tf×idf* (term frequency times inverted document frequency), take place. After the stemming and stopping process of the terms in each document, we will represent them as the document-term frequency matrix ($Doc_j \times TF_{jk}$) as shown in Table 1. Doc_j is referring to each web page document that exists in the news database where $j=1,....,n$. Term frequency TF_{jk} is the number of how many times the distinct word w_k occurs in document Doc_j where $k=1,...,m$. The calculation of the terms weight x_{jk} of each word w_k is done by using a method that has been used by Salton[9][10] which is given by

$$x_{jk} = TF_{jk} \times idf_k \qquad (1)$$

The similar calculation for classification is done using the following formula: The text is mapped onto a node with the highest similarity value, and one text is ultimately classified into one class.

$$Sim(Node, d) = \frac{\sum_{i=0}^{N} freq_{i,d} / \max_{i,d}}{N} \times \frac{V_d}{V} \qquad (2)$$

N is the feature frequency of a node. $freq_{i,d}$ represents the frequency of feature j that is matched in text d. $max_{i,d}$ is the frequency of the feature that is matched the most in Text d. V is the number of constraints, while V_d represents the number of constraints that are satisfied by Text d. The document classification takes place only when the use of the relations is "is-a", "has-a", "part-of", or "has-part". When another node is related, it is also included in the classification process to calculate the similarity. Using this approach, a more accurate classification can be performed.

The overall classification process for Web documents is as shown below (Figure 2).

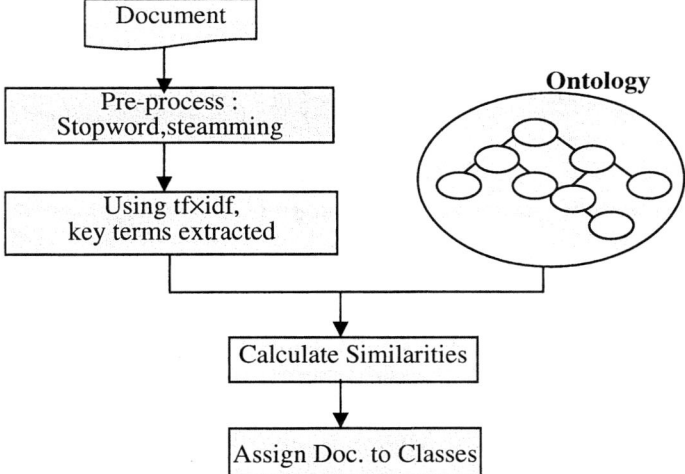

Fig. 2. Web Document Classification Process Using Ontology

4 Experimental Procedures

We have used a web pages dataset from Yahoo Economy news as shown in Table 2. The types of news in the database are Cooperatives, Employment, Finance, Marketing, Organizations and Trade. The total of documents are 5,235.

Automatic classification of web page is evaluated using the standard information retrieval measures that are precision, recall, and $F1$ [11]. The $F1$ measure is a kind of average of precision and recall.

Table 2. The number of document that are stored in the news database

Class no.	Class name	Number of Doc
1	Cooperatives	620
2	Employment	1,685
3	Finance	750
4	Marketing	680
5	Organizations	650
6	Trade	850
	Total	5,235

Table 3. The classification results

Class no.	Precision (%)	Recall (%)	F1 (%)
1	77.21	93.84	84.72
2	92.48	94.16	93.31
3	93.93	95.38	94.65
4	91.17	95.38	93.23
5	91.30	96.92	94.03
6	91.97	96.92	94.38
Average	89.68	95.43	92.39

(*These are the classes that exist in Economy category)

In Our the classification results, the precision, recall, and *F1* measures are 89.68%, 95.43%, 92.39%, respectively, as shown in Table 3.

A better document selection approach needs to be used for selecting the candidate documents from each class in order to increase the *F1* classification results.

5 Conclusion and Future Research

This paper introduced the use of ontology to conceptually express the meaning of relationships contained in Web documents and suggested an automated document classification method using the ontology. In particular, this paper focused on document classification based on the similarities of documents already categorized by ontology using terminology information extracted from the documents. Our work is distinguished from other studies in the following areas. (1) Rather than using a dictionary or knowledge index, ontology is used for document classification. (2) Our ontology is based on syntax information contained in the Web texts. (3) Mapping between the established ontology and the term information extracted from Web documents is performed. The document classification technique proposed by this paper does not involve any learning processes or experimental data and can be performed in real time.

Further research is required to develop more efficient and accurate ontological expressions and to document classification methods. We plan to conduct further studies on how to improve the efficiency of an information search using the document classification technique suggested in this paper and how to automatically determine the meaning of concepts and relations from Web documents.

References

1. Chidanand Apt, Fred Damerau, and Sholom M. Weis, "Towards Language Independent Automated Learning of Text Categorization models," *Proc. of the 17th annual international ACM-SIGIR, 1994.*
2. R.E.Shapire, Yoram Singhal, and Amit Singhal, "Boosting and Rocchio applied to text filtering,", *Proc. Of the 21th annual international ACM-SIGIR, 1998.*
3. Mart A. Hearst, "Support Vector Machines," *IEEE Information Systems, 13(4):18~28, 1998.*
4. Rudy Prabowo, Mike Jackson, Peter Burden, and Heinz-Dieter Knoell, 2002, "Ontology-Based Automatic Classification for the Web Pages:Design,Implementation and Evaluation,", *Proc. Of the 3rd International Conference on Web Information Systems Engineering, 2002.*
5. C.Jenkins, M.Jackson, P.Burden, and J.Wallis, "Automatic RDF metadata generation for resource discovery", *Proc. Of 8th International WWW Conference, Toronto, pp. 11-14, May 1999.*
6. Y.Ng, J.Tang, and M.Goodrich, "A binary categorization approach for classifying multiple-record Web documents using application ontologies and a probabilistic model", *Proc. Of 7th International Conference on Database Systems for Advances Applications, pp.58-65, April 2001.*
7. S.T.DUMAIS , and H.CHEN,"Hierarchical classification of Web content,", *Proc of the 23rd Annual International ACM SIGIR, July 24-28,2000, Arthens, Greece.*
8. N.GOEVERT, M.LALMAS, and N.FUHR, 1999, "A probabilistic description-oriented approach for categorisiong Web documents,", *Proc. Of the 8th ACM International Conference on Information and Knowledge Management, November 2-4, 1999,pp 475-482, Kansas City, U.S.*
9. Salton&McGill, Introduction to modern information retrieval, New York, Mcgraw-Hill, USA, 1983.
10. Andreas Hotho and Alexander Maedche and Steffen Staab, "Ontology-based Text Document Clustering", Http://www.aifb.uni-karlsruhe.de/WBS
11. D.D.Lewis, Evaluating and optimizing autonomous text classification systems, in: E.A.Fox, P.Ingwersen, R.Fidel(Ed.), *SIGIR'95: Proceedings of the 18th Annual International ACM SIGIR Conference on Research and Development in Information Retrieval*, New York, 1995, pp. 246-254.

Distribution Based Stemmer Refinement

B.L. Narayan and Sankar K. Pal

Machine Intelligence Unit, Indian Statistical Institute,
203, B. T. Road, Calcutta - 700108, India
{bln_r, sankar}@isical.ac.in

Abstract. Stemming is a common preprocessing task applied to text corpora. Errors in this process may be refined either manually or based on a corpus. We describe a novel corpus-based stemming technique which models the given words as being generated from a multinomial distribution over the topics available in the corpus. A sequential hypothesis testing like procedure helps us group together distributionally similar words. This stemmer refines any given stemmer and its strength can be controlled with the help of two thresholds. A refinement based on the 20 Newsgroups data set shows that the proposed method splits equivalence classes appropriately.

1 Introduction

Stemming is the process of clubbing together words that are similar in nature. This process improves recall and reduces the dictionary size of a corpus. Several standard techniques are available in the literature which perform stemming [1]. The strength of a stemmer is the amount of reduction in the size of the dictionary obtained by it [1]. Strong (or aggressive) stemmers may reduce the size of a given corpus drastically, but may result in a severe decrease in precision. Stemming is afflicted with two kinds of errors: under-stemming and over-stemming. These errors are either refined manually or automatically with the help of a corpus.

In this article, we describe the design of a corpus-based stemmer which makes use of the class information of the corpus. We model words as arising from a multinomial distribution [2] and club distributionally similar words together. The equivalence classes thus generated represent the proposed stemmer.

The article is organized as follows. The background on stemming and related work is provided in Section 2. Section 3 describes the errors accompanying stemming and methods for refinement. Then, we describe the proposed stemming technique and present the experimental results in Sections 4 and 5, respectively. Conclusions and future work are discussed in Section 6.

2 Stemming and Related Work

Documents are generally represented in terms of the words they contain, as in the vector space model [3]. Many of these words are similar to each other in the sense that they denote the same concept(s), *i.e.*, they are semantically similar.

Generally, morphologically similar words have similar semantic interpretations and may be considered as equivalent. The construction of such equivalence classes is known as stemming.

A number of stemming algorithms, or stemmers, have been developed, which attempt to reduce a word to its stem or root form. Thus, the document may now be represented by the stems rather than by the original words. As the variants of a term are now conflated to a single representative form, it also reduces the dictionary size, which is the number of distinct terms needed for representing a set of documents. A smaller dictionary size results in a saving of storage space and processing time.

Stemming is frequently used in the field of information retrieval [4], because it results in an increase in recall, as documents not containing the exact query terms are also retrieved. Moreover, the storage space for the corpus and retrieval times are reduced, without much loss of precision. Also, this give a system the option of query expansion to help a user refine his query.

Stemming also reduces the size of the feature set (when words are viewed as the features of documents). For the purpose of classification, this means that the models involved are far less complex than what would have been if the original set of words were used. This also means that it would lead to better generalization [5], in the sense that a small training error would imply a small test error too. It has been observed that the classification performance does not go down much due to the application of some of the standard stemmers. Also, this would lead to a reduction in the size of the corpus that needs to be stored.

Various stemmers are available in the literature. The most commonly used are the ones by Porter [6], Krovetz [7] and Paice/Husk [8]. Variants of these stemmers are available for non-English languages, too. The above stemmers apply a series of rules to a given word to obtain its stem.

3 Stemming Errors and Refinement

English, just like most other languages, is very diverse, and the morphological variants of all words cannot be obtained in the same manner. This leads to two kinds of stemming errors: under-stemming and over-stemming [9]. Understemming is the case where words that should have been grouped into the same class are not so. The more serious error is over-stemming, which results when too many unrelated words are merged together. This leads to a reduction in precision during retrieval and an increase in the error rate for classification. some examples of over-stemming by the Porter algorithm are:

- range and rang, even though unrelated, both stem to *rang*.
- petition, petit and petite are all stemmed to *petit* though petition is quite distinct from the rest.

These examples demonstrate how certain unrelated words may be grouped together on the basis of their morphological similarity. This problem is more pronounced in the case of stronger stemmers like Truncate(3) which clubs together all words whose first three letters are the same.

These errors may be manually corrected by specifying an exception list, or by means of modifying the rules of the stemmer. However, such refinements are labor intensive and may still not be appropriate. Moreover, the meanings and senses attached to a word vary a lot from corpus to corpus. An equivalence class considered appropriate for one corpus may not be so for a different one.

Xu and Croft devised a technique to automatically refine a stemmer. It was assumed that words with similar senses (which should be stemmed to the same stem) co-occur more often than dissimilar words. This co-occurrence information, obtained from a given corpus, is employed to split equivalence classes so that the resultant classes have larger co-occurrences between constituent words. The optimal algorithm that they provided for this purpose is computationally intensive and so, they opt for a suboptimal method based on connected component labeling to split large equivalence classes.

However, the basic assumption behind this co-occurrence based refinement, that similar words often co-occur may not hold in several instances. For example, documents describing an event of the past may use words related to the past tense only. Similarly, substitute words and word variants may not co-occur because an author of a document would generally stick to a single writing style throughout that document. The British and American variants of words form a prominent example of this kind. In all these cases, the co-occurrence based analysis splits several equivalence classes unnecessarily.

In the following, we consider a more general similarity measure between words for refining stemming algorithms.

4 Distribution Based Stemmer Refinement

We observe that though similar words might not occur in the same document, they are very likely to appear in similar documents of a corpus. So, instead of considering words to be unrelated when they do not co-occur in a single document, two words are considered dissimilar if they do not occur together in a class of documents. Thus, this methodology may be viewed as a generalization of co-occurrence based stemmer refinement. We utilize the information available in a classified text corpus to perform the splitting. The primary assumption behind the proposed methodology is that two words may be stemmed to the same stem if they are extremely similar in their distribution across various categories. This idea is similar to that described in [10].

Each word is assumed to have a multinomial distribution [2] over the set of categories of the given corpus. Words deemed to be arising from the same multinomial distribution are kept in the same equivalence class, whereas, those which are significantly different from each other are separated out. The distribution of each word is estimated from its frequencies in the various categories. Formally, the proposed methodology is as described below.

Let $\{w_1, w_2, \ldots, w_n\}$, be the set of words belonging to an equivalence class, i.e., they all stem to the same stem. Let K be the number of categories of the given text corpus. For each word w_i, we compute the occurrence vector

$n_{i1}, n_{i2}, \ldots, n_{iK}$, where n_{ij} is the number of occurrences of w_i under the jth category. We assume that each w_i arises from a multinomial distribution whose parameters are $p_{i1}, p_{i2}, \ldots, p_{iK}$, and $n_i = \sum_{j=1}^{K} n_{ij}$. Here, each p_{ij} denotes the probability of w_i appearing under the jth category and is estimated as the corresponding proportion of occurrences in the corpus, n_{ij}/n_i.

The aim is to partition this set of words into non-empty subsets such that each subset consists of words whose estimated distributions are not significantly different from each other. Moreover, this task needs to be done without a prior knowledge of the size of the partition.

We employ a procedure similar to sequential hypothesis testing [11] for attaining this goal. Two thresholds/cutoffs, say t_1 and t_2, ($t_1 <= t_2$), are chosen for this purpose, and for each given equivalence class, we try to split it as described hereunder. The words are sorted in descending order of their frequencies. Without loss of generality, we shall now denote this sorted list of words by $\{w_1, w_2, \ldots, w_n\}$. The most frequent word, w_1, is chosen and is considered to stem to itself. We denote this as $stem(w_1) = s_1$. Let S be the current set of stems. Right now, $S = \{s_1\}$. We shall also denote the equivalence class of stem s_j by S_j, defined as $S_j = \{w_k : stem(w_k) = s_j\}$.

Let, $(n_{i1}, n_{i2}, \ldots, n_{iK})$ and $(m_{j1}, m_{j2}, \ldots, m_{jK})$ be the topic vectors of w_i and S_j, respectively. Here, m_{jl}, $l \in \{1, 2, \ldots, K\}$, is defined as the number of occurrences of any of the words in S_j under topic l. It is assumed that the estimated distribution of S_j is the actual one. To test if $(n_{i1}, n_{i2}, \ldots, n_{iK})$ has arisen from the distribution of S_j, Pearson statistic is computed as: $\frac{m_j}{n_i} \sum_{l=1}^{K} \frac{n_{il}^2}{m_{jl}} - n_i$, where, n_i and m_j are the totals, as defined above. Since some of the n_{il}'s may be zero, we replace them by $n'_{il} = (1 - \alpha)n_{il} + \alpha \frac{n_i}{K} = n_{il} + \alpha \left(\frac{n_i}{K} - n_{il} \right)$. For small values of α, the frequencies, and hence, the test statistics, do not differ by much from those with α set to 0. We set $\alpha = 0.1$ in our experiments.

For a word w_i, and for each stem $s_j \in S$, we compute the Pearson statistic $d_{i,j}$. If each of these values is greater than the bigger cutoff, i.e., $d_{ij} > t_2 \; \forall j$, we shall call the current word as a new stem and add it to the set S. On the other hand, if any of the distances, say d_{ij}, is smaller than t_1, we shall add the current word to the equivalence class of s_j, so that $stem(w_i) = s_j$.

If $t_1 < t_2$, there may be some words which were neither merged with an existing class, nor put into a class of their own. Such words would be dealt with again in the next iteration. After each iteration, t_1 is increased and t_2 reduced. In the last iteration, t_1 is chosen to be equal to t_2.

When n_i is large, the Pearson statistic is known to approximately follow a χ^2 distribution with $K - 1$ degrees of freedom. Since we have sorted the words in descending order of their frequencies, the $\chi^2_{(K-1)}$ assumption is satisfied initially.

There are no strict guidelines for choosing t_1 and t_2. If $t_1 = t_2$, then we do not need multiple iterations in the given procedure. This would result in a reduction in computing time. However, it may miss out on some simple mergers of equivalence classes. This is so because, once a word is called a new stem, it cannot be merged with any of the existing stems at a later stage. Choosing $t_1 < t_2$ allows us to do just that. In this case, whenever one is sure of neither merging the current word with an existing stem nor assigning it to a new class of its own, this decision may be put off for later. In a following iteration, due to the change in the structure of the classes or the values of the chosen thresholds, the decision may become clearer. The strength of the stemmer would be proportional to the size of the thresholds t_1 and t_2, because the size of the dictionary reduces (due to more words being grouped together) with increasing thresholds.

5 Experimental Results

The 20 Newsgroups collection [12] is used to demonstrate the manner in which the proposed methodology splits stem classes as compared to that of the co-occurrence analysis based one. The 20 Newsgroups data set is a collection of 19,997 newsgroup documents, partitioned evenly across 20 different newsgroups. After stopword removal and lowercase conversion, the number of distinct words appearing in at least two documents of the corpus is 56436. These were stemmed by both Porter and Truncate(3) algorithms resulting in 40821 and 8158 stem classes, respectively.

Of the 40821 equivalence classes generated by the Porter stemmer, 32479 were singletons. So, only the remaining 8342 stem classes were considered for splitting. These were split into 16023 and 14962 classes by the distribution and co-occurrence based refinements, respectively. The 8158 equivalence classes generated by Truncate(3) have been split into 22643 and 30710 classes by the distribution and co-occurrence based refinements, respectively.

We examined the refinements of Truncate(3) stemmer and our observations are as follows:

- The co-occurrence based refinement resulted in several extremely large classes. For example, classes corresponding to account, accelerate, accident, accomplish, accuse, *etc.*, were all merged into one single class. Similarly, the classes corresponding to war, ware, ward, *etc.* were not separated out. This was referred to as the stringing effect in [13]. The proposed method split all of them into separate classes.
- Some classes were split unnecessarily by the co-occurrence based method. For example, angle, angles, angular, angstrom, *etc.* were all split into different classes. Our method, however, kept them all together.
- Classes containing certain words which are very similar to each other were split by the co-occurrence based method because they seldom occurred in together in the same document. For example, necessary, necessity, necessarily, *etc.* were all separated out into singleton equivalence classes, because documents containing necessity did not contain necessary and necessarily. Our method, which looks beyond just co-occurrences in a document, merged them all into a single class, with the stem being necessary.

Thus, the equivalence classes generated by the proposed refinement procedure are more appropriate than those by co-occurrence based analysis. Moreover, as seen above, our methodology may also result in fewer number of stems at the same time.

6 Conclusions

We have described the design of a stemming algorithm which uses the class information of a corpus to refine a given stemmer. The main advantage over other stemmers like co-occurrence based stemmers is its ability to drastically reduce the dictionary size. The refined stem equivalence classes are also more appropriate in comparison to those generated by alternative methods. These qualitative results need to be measured quantitatively in terms of precision and recall for retrieval tasks and accuracy for text classification tasks.

Acknowledgment

B. L. Narayan gratefully acknowledges the ISI-INSEAD (France) Fellowship to carry out his doctoral research. This work was also partially supported by CSIR Grant No. 22(0346)/02/EMR-II.

References

1. Frakes, W.B., Fox, C.J.: Strength and similarity of affix removal stemming algorithms. ACM SIGIR Forum **37** (2003) 26–30
2. Johnson, N.L., Kotz, S., Balakrishnan, N.: Discrete Multivariate Distributions. Wiley-Interscience (1997)
3. Salton, G., Wong, A., Yang, C.S.: A vector space model for automatic indexing. Communications of the ACM **18** (1975) 613–620
4. Kraaij, W., Pohlmann, R.: Viewing stemming as recall enhancement. In Frei, H.P., Harman, D., Schauble, P., Wilkinson, R., eds.: Proceedings of the 17th ACM SIGIR conference, Zurich (1996) 40–48
5. Vapnik, V.N.: The nature of statistical learning theory. Springer-Verlag, New York (1995)
6. Porter, M.F.: An algorithm for suffix stripping. Program **14** (1980) 130–137
7. Krovetz, R.: Viewing morphology as an inference process. In Korfhage, R., Rasmussen, E., Willett, P., eds.: Proceedings of the 16th ACM SIGIR conference, Pittsburgh (1993) 191–202
8. Paice, C.D.: A method for the evaluation of stemming algorithms based on error counting. Journal of the American Society for Information Science **47** (1996) 28–40
9. Yamout, F., Demachkieh, R., Hamdan, G., Sabra, R.: Further enhancement to Porter algorithm. In: Proceedings of the KI2004 Workshop on Machine Learning and Interaction for Text-based Information Retrieval, Germany (2004) 7–24
10. Pereira, F., Tishby, N., Lee, L.: Distributional clustering of English words. In: 31st Annual Meeting of the ACL. (1993) 183–190
11. Wald, A.: Sequential Analysis. Wiley and Sons, New York (1947)
12. http://kdd.ics.uci.edu/databases/20newsgroups/20newsgroups.html.
13. Xu, J., Croft, W.B.: Corpus-based stemming using coocurrence of word variants. ACM Transactions on Information Systems **16** (1998) 61–81

Text Similarity Measurement Using Concept Representation of Texts

Abhinay Pandya[1] and Pushpak Bhattacharyya[2]

[1] DA-IICT, Gandhinagar
abhinay_pandya@da-iict.org
[2] Dept. of CSE, IIT Bombay
pb@cse.iitb.ac.in

Abstract. Measuring *semantic nearness* of documents is important for accurate information retrieval, automated text categorization and classification. Inspired by the observation that text documents contain semantically coherent set of ideas/topics, this paper presents the design and experimental evaluation of a method to represent a text document as a set of concepts. Based on this, we propose a method to measure semantic nearness of texts. Our method makes use of WordNet which is a lexico-semantic network of words. We bypass word sense disambiguation. In order to show the effectiveness of our representation of texts, we compare experimental results of text classification and clustering with the results of classification and clustering with standard techniques.

1 Introduction

A key-step towards achieving the goal of retrieving *all and only the most relevant information*, is detecting semantic similarity, *i.e.*, judging how similar the contents of the two texts are. [1] has given an information theoretic definition of similarity. *Fundamentally, the similarity of two objects is measured by the number of features they have in common.* In contemporary IR, the words of a text are considered to be their features regardless of their meaning, and the similarity of texts is estimated based on the number of words they have in common (TF) and the relative importance of these in the corpus (IDF). Unfortunately, owing to the richness (and vagaries) of natural languages such as English, these methods fail to identify the actual semantic relatedness between texts if words from both texts are matched directly.

Many approaches have been proposed in the past to measure similarity between words based on their relationships such as *synonymy-antonymy, hypernymy-hyponymy, meronymy-holonymy*[1], *etc.* [9][6][4]. But these require finding the correct sense of each word in the text- *Word Sense Disambiguation (WSD)*- which in itself is a difficult problem to solve. Evidently, we need a method to represent a text in terms of its semantic features even when accurate sense information

---
[1] Hypernymy: is-a relationship, hyponymy: opposite of it, meronymy: has-a relationship, holonymy: part-of relationship.

of the words in the text is not available. Latent Semantic Indexing (LSI)[5] attempts to capture semantic information by observing co-occurrence of words. However, this will fail if semantically related words do not co-occur frequently.

Semantic similarity between two texts is perceived based on the commonness of the concepts contained in them. We propose a representation of a text as a set of concepts discussed in it. Similarity between two texts with this representation can then be estimated based on the *semantic relatedness*[2] of the concepts they describe.

Some works of relevance are mentioned now. [7] presents a method to represent text in the form of WordNet[2] hypernyms and shows improved performance for the classification task. [8] shows improvement in clustering task with synset representation of texts. These methods ignore all relationships between synsets other than hypernymy and relies on the WordNet structure without adapting it to the corpus (*i.e.*, non-information-theoretic).

In the next section we describe our methodology of text representation. Section 3 describes the experimental setup and the results. Section 4 concludes the paper.

2 Conceptual Representation of Texts

Finding a set of synsets as a representation of text is trivial if the correct sense (image of a word in the WordNet, synset) of each word in the given text is known. In the absence of WSD, we let each word in a given text map to all of its possible images in the WordNet and discard those synsets that are semantically very far from other synsets. Such synsets, which are far from the others, either do not represent the correct sense of words or are not representative of a given text.

Many approaches have been presented in the past to measure the semantic distance between synsets in the WordNet[9], [4], etc. [6]'s measure combines link-distance and information theoretic methods and also takes into account the type of relationship between synsets, depth of the synsets in the WordNet, and density of the region around the synsets. Based on these, a weight is attached to the edge between a child node c and its parent node p:

$$wt(c,p) = \left(\beta + (1-\beta)\frac{\bar{E}}{E(p)}\right)\left(\frac{d(p)+1}{d(p)}\right)^\alpha [IC(c) - IC(p)]T(c,p) \quad (1)$$

where $d(p)$ denotes the depth of the node p in the hierarchy, $E(p)$ the number of edges in the child links, $\bar{E}$ the average density in the whole hierarchy, and $T(c,p)$ the link relation/type factor such as *hypernymy/hyponymy*, *meronymy/holonymy*, etc. The parameters $\alpha(\alpha \geq 0)$ and $\beta(0 \leq \beta \leq 1)$ control the degree of how much the node depth and density factors contribute to the edge weighting calculation. Node density in different parts of the hierarchy

---
[2] Relatedness is more relevant than similarity: e.g., *doctor* and *hospital* are semantically related but not similar.

is different, and greater density around a node (e.g., *plant/flora* section of Word-Net) indicates more 'closeness'. Information content (IC) values for synsets can be calculated as follows:

$$IC(c) = -\log P(c) \qquad (2)$$

where $IC(c)$ is the information content value of synset c and $P(c)$ is the probability of encountering an instance of synset c. $P(c)$ can be calculated by finding the relative frequency of synset c in a sense-tagged corpus such as *SemCor*[3], in which each word is tagged with a WordNet synset identifier.

The overall distance between two nodes c_1 and c_2 would thus be the summation of edge weights (calculated as shown in equation (1)) along the shortest path linking two nodes:

$$dist(c_1, c_2) = \sum_{c \in \{path(c_1,c_2)\}} wt(c, parent(c)) \qquad (3)$$

The above measures rely only on the WordNet structure for semantic relatedness between concepts and do not take into account their pragmatic relationships. For example, the similarity between concepts *doctor#1* and *hospital#2* would be estimated lower than what actually is with all the above methods. We attempt to capture pragmatic associations between concepts by their gloss definitions in the WordNet. Very often the glosses of related concepts have a few words in common (see [10]). The word *medical* is in the intersection of glosses of *doctor#1* and *hospital#2*. Our measure of similarity between two concepts is as follows:

$$concept\_sim(c_1, c_2) = \frac{1}{dist(c_1, c_2)} \times \delta \times gloss\_intersect(c_1, c_2) \qquad (4)$$

where $\delta (0 \leq \delta \leq 1)$ controls the weightage of *gloss_intersection* in the similarity measurement.

2.1 Semantic Vicinity

With the enhanced notion of similarity between WordNet synsets as described above, we define *semantic vicinity* of a synset s as a set of all synsets that are within a specified link distance from s. Each node in the semantic vicinity of s is assigned a score (weight value) indicating its degree of relatedness with s. In order to select only the relevant concepts from the text, our method starts with building *semantic vicinities* for each input synset as described in the procedure (see algorithm 1). MAX controls the definition of similarity by specifying the maximum radius of influence of similarity measure. The more the value of MAX, the more is the dilution of similarity. Input to our algorithm is a list of unique nouns since nouns are the least polysemous compared to other parts of speech[3] and therefore believed to carry the *main burden of expression*. In addition to nouns, we consider *denominal* verbs, adjectives and adverbs that have only one sense[4]. For all practical IR applications, these POS are as informative as nouns.

---

[3] From http://www.cogsci.princeton.edu/~wn/man/wnstats.7WN.html
[4] This is achieved by following the "DERIVATION" pointer from the synset structures in WordNet.

We now present the algorithm as follows:

Data : list of unique nouns, *denomial* verbs, adjectives, and adverbs
Result : semantic vicinities corresponding to all senses of all input nouns
foreach *noun n_i in the noun-list* **do**
  foreach *sense s_j of noun n_i* **do**
    for *L = 0 to MAX* **do**
      for all synsets k_L, if $k_L \triangleleft s_j$ or $s_j \triangleleft k_L$, then $SNet(s_j) = SNet(s_j) \cup \{k_L\}$ where the symbol $\triangleleft$ between k_L and s_j denotes any of the following relationship types:

      - hypernymy: k_L is-a-kind-of s_j
      - hyponymy: s_j is-a-kind-of k_L
      - meronymy: s_j has-a k_L
      - holonymy: k_L has-a s_j
      - antonymy: k_L is-opposite-of s_j
      - gloss-overlap: k_L's gloss contains one or more words that are also a part of s_j's gloss.

      $score(k_L) = score(k_L) + concept\_sim(k_L, s_j)$ [see equation 4]
    end
  end
end

Algorithm 1. Procedure for building semantic vicinities

Representative synsets of a text among all synsets for a text can be found by discarding those synsets that are semantically distant from the rest. This is achieved by finding the intersection of semantic vicinities found in the algorithm above and selecting only those synsets that belong to majority of the semantic vicinities.

3 Experiments

3.1 Classification

250 documents in each of the categories *comp.graphics*, *rec.autos*, *rec.sport.hockey*, *rec.sport.baseball* from the *20Newsgroup* dataset (a collection of 20,000 USENET articles) were chosen for our classification experiments. Table 1 summarizes the results obtained when the following classification algorithms were run on our representation: *Naive Bayesian*, *k-NN* and *SVM*. For Naive Bayesian and k-NN, *Rainbow* utility provided as part of the *Bow* toolkit[5] was used and for SVM, SVM^{light}[6] was used.

The results are reported with the parameters that obtained the best performance. The first row shows the results obtained with the TFIDF vector representation of the documents. The second row displays the results when the

---
[5] http://www-2.cs.cmu.edu/~mccallum/bow/
[6] http://svmlight.joachims.org/

Table 1. Comparison of performance of classification experiments on 20 Newsgroup data

	Naive Bayesian	k-NN (k=35)	SVM (rbf, γ=1.1)
TFIDF, simi funct unchanged	0.98	0.98	0.66
CFICF, simi funct unchanged	0.88	0.80	0.77
bag-of-concepts, simi funct as Eq 5	—	0.87	0.76

documents are treated as bag-of-concepts. In this case, the similarity function in the classification algorithms is kept unchanged; only the representation of the documents is changed from TFIDF to CFICF (concept frequeny/inverse concept frequency). The third row of the table shows the results when the similarity function in each of the techniques was replaced with the following similarity function:

$$sim(D_1, D_2) = \frac{concept\_set\_sim(D_1, D_2)}{\sqrt{concept\_set\_sim(D_1, D_1) \times concept\_set\_sim(D_2, D_2)}} \times 100\% \quad (5)$$

where $concept\_set\_sim(A, B) = \sum_{c_1 \in A, c_2 \in B} concept\_sim(c_1, c_2)$ and $concept\_sim(c_1, c_2)$ can be calculated as shown in equation (4).

3.2 Clustering

The clustering experiments are performed with the same dataset as above. We used the Cluto[7] library for clustering. With Repeated Bisection and I2 criterion function, TFIDF-based clustering achieved **0.91** Fscore; whereas clustering based on conceptual representation of text (our method) achieved **0.79**.

Table 2. Results of clustering experiments with 20 Newsgroup dataset

	4 clusters	3 clusters
TFIDF (F-score)	0.97	0.57
our method (F-score)	0.79	0.61

4 Discussions, Conclusions and Future work

The reason for the higher score of TFIDF on both classification and clustering is the fact that replies to postings often include the original message in them, thereby duplicating words and increasing intra-class similarity based on TFIDF measure. The reasons for lower accuracy in cases where our approach is used are (i) shortness of articles in newsgroup articles, (ii) the fact that a small set of words are frequently used, and (iii) inaccurate IC values resulting from the smallness of the SemCor corpus. However, as evident from table 2, finding 3

---

[7] http://www-users.cs.umn.edu/~karypis/cluto/

clusters from the 4 categories of news items chosen will put *rec.sport.hockey* and *rec.sport.baseball* in the same cluster by our method. Lacking common set of frequent words, TFIDF-based measures cannot achieve this 'generalization'.

These observations are promising and confirm that *text similarity detection should be tackled from all three directions using lexical, syntactic and semantic knowledge.*

In future we would like to investigate if retrieval performance can be improved by *bridging* a query and a candidate document through WordNet with its conceptual representation.

References

1. Dekang Lin: *Information Theoretic definition of similarity.* Proc. 15th International Conf. on Machine Learning, 1998.
2. Christiane Fellbaum: *WordNet, An Electronic Lexical Database.* The MIT press, 1999.
3. Francis and Kucera: *Computational Analysis of present day American English.* Brown University press, 1967.
4. Philip Resnik: *Semantic Similarity in a Taxonomy: An Information-Based Measure and its Application to Problems of Ambiguity in Natural Language.* Journal of Artificial Intelligence Research (JAIR), 11: 95-130, 1999.
5. Michael W. Berry, Susan T. Dumais, Gavin W. O'Brien: *Using Linear Algebra for Intelligent Information Retrieval.* SIAM Review 37:4, 1995
6. Jiang and Conrath: *Semantic similarity based on Corpus statistics and lexical Taxonomy.* Proceedings of International Conference Research on Computational Linguistics, 1997.
7. Sam Scott and Stan Matwin: *Text classification using WordNet hypernyms.* Proc. of the COLING/ACL Workshop on Usage of WordNet in Natural Language Processing Systems, 1998.
8. Sam Scott and Stan Matwin: *WordNet improves text document clustering.* In Proc. of the Semantic Web Workshop at SIGIR-2003", 2003.
9. R. Rada and H. Milli and E. Bicknell and M. Blettner : *Development and Application of a Metric on Semantic Nets.* IEEE Transactions on Systems, Man and Cybernetics, vol. 1, no. 9: 17-30, 1989.
10. Michael Lesk: *Automatic sense disambiguation: How to tell a pine cone from an icecream cone.* In Proc. of the 1986 ACM SIGDOC conference, pages 24-26, New York.

Incorporating Distance Domination in Multiobjective Evolutionary Algorithm

Praveen K. Tripathi, Sanghamitra Bandyopadhyay, and Sankar K. Pal

Machine Intelligence Unit,
Indian Statistical Institute,
203 B. T. Road, Kolkata 700108
{praveen_r, sanghami, sankar}@isical.ac.in

Abstract. In this article we propose a novel distance domination parameter and describe a multiobjective evolutionary concept called distance domination based multiobjective evolutionary algorithm (DBMEA). The distance parameter drives the algorithm faster in approximating the Pareto optimal front. To ensure proper diversity in the solutions of the non-dominating set, a new method for incorporating diversity is explained. The DBMEA has been compared with the NSGA-II algorithm on different test functions using different performance measures.

1 Introduction

In this article, a new evolutionary multiobjective optimization (MOO) algorithm called "Distance-domination Based Multiobjective Evolutionary Algorithm (DBMEA)" is proposed. DBMEA uses the concept of distance domintaion parameter which refines the fitness function and helps in better convergence to the true Pareto-front. It incorporates non-dominated sorting and crowded-tournament selection as in NSGA-II [1]. The diversity parameter used here is also novel. DBMEA incorporates the concept of elitism, using archive concept as in SPEA-2 [2]. Comparative results of DBMEA and NSGA-II are provided for different standard test functions in terms of four performance measures.

2 Basic Principles

A general minimization problem of M objectives can be mathematically stated as:

- Minimize : $f(x) = [f_i(x), i = 1, \ldots, M]$, subject to :
  $g_j(x) \leq 0, \quad j = 1, 2, \ldots, J$, and
  $h_k(x) = 0, \quad k = 1, 2, \ldots, K$, where $f_i(x)$ is the ith objective function, $g_j(x)$ is the jth inequality constraint, and $h_k(x)$ is the kth equality constraint.

The MOO problem then reduces to finding x such that $f(x)$ is optimized. A solution is said to dominate another solution if it is not worse than that solution in all the objectives and is strictly better than that in at least one objective. The solutions over the entire solution space that are not dominated by any other solution are called *Pareto-optimal solutions*.

3 Distance-Domination Based Multiobjective Evolutionary Algorithm (DBMEA)

The basic structure of DBMEA is given in **Algorithm 1**. Different steps are described below in brief.

As is normally done, the parameters of the search space in DBMEA are encoded as string like structures called *chromosomes*. A *fitness* value is assigned to each chromosome that denotes the degree of goodness of the encoded solution. The fitness F_i of the ith chromosome is computed as:

$$F_i = f_{ri} + f_{di} \qquad (1)$$

where f_{ri} is the rank parameter as defined in [1] and f_{di} is the distance domination parameter proposed in this article.

- Rank Parameter (f_{ri}): The parameter f_{ri} is a measure of a solution's non-dominance. For computing f_{ri}, non-dominated sorting [1] is used to first determine the non-dominated fronts. f_{ri} is then set equal to the front number where i^{th} solution appears [1].
- Distance Domination Parameter (f_{di}): This new parameter is calculated as the normalized Euclidean distance of a dominated solution from its nearest non-dominated solution on the first front. The significance of this parameter is to give higher priority to those dominated solutions, that are closer to their dominating solution on the first front. As an example considering two functions minimization in Figure 1(a), the solutions 'g', 'h' and 'j' are dominated by solution 'c' on the first front. Normally, 'g', 'h' and 'j' would have the same status. However, it can be observed that 'h' is much closer to the first front. It is our intuition that 'h' should get higher priority over 'g' and 'j'. The parameter f_{di} (= 'd1' for, 'g', 'd2' for 'h' and 'd3' for 'j') takes care of this fact.

The *elitism* concept in DBMEA is similar to that in SPEA-2 [2]. An *archive* of fixed size (equal to the size of the population, N) is maintained, that gets updated at each iteration. After computation of the fitness archive is first filled by non-dominated solutions of the current archive and population, followed by the best (in terms of F_is) remaining solutions till the archive is full. In case of archive overflow at any stage, the density paramater d_i is used to truncate the archive. The parameter (d_i) (which is similar to crowded-distance [1], with some modification) is computed as the distance of each solution to its immediate next neighbour summed over each of the M objectives. For example in Figure 1(b), 'd1' and 'd2' correspond to the distances along $f1$ for solutions 'e' and 'f' respectively. Similarly 'd4' and 'd3' correspond to the distance along $f2$ for solutions 'c' and 'b' respectively.

After the fitness assignment, DBMEA uses *density-based binary tournament selection* on the archive to create the mating pool. This concept is inspired by the *crowded-tournament selection* [1], where crowded-distance has been used in order to overcome the tie in fitness values. Here if we get the solutions with the same F_i values, then we conside d_i and prefer the less crowded solution. The DBMEA uses *single-point crossover* and *bit-wise mutation* operation.

Algorithm 1. O_f= DBMEA(P_t,A_t,N,C) /*P_t: population at iteration t, A_t: archive at iteration t, N: size of the population and archive, C: maximum number of iterations. O_f: the final output */

1. $t = 0$, randomly initialize P_0 and compute the objectives, $A_0 = \Phi$.
2. non-dominated sorting on $P_t \cup A_t$.
3. $\forall i, \quad i \in \{P_t \cup A_t\}$, calculate f_{ri}, f_{di} and d_i.
   $F_i = f_{ri} + f_{di}$
4. $A_{t+1} \leftarrow$ non-dominated solutions from $P_t \cup A_t$
   – if $\{|A_{t+1}|\} > N$, truncate A_{t+1} to size N using d_i
   – if $\{|A_{t+1}|\} < N$, copy $\{N - |A_{t+1}|\}$ dominated solutions from $P_t \cup A_t$ to A_{t+1}.
5. If $t \geq C$ or other terminating condition is fulfilled, $O_f \leftarrow A_{t+1}$ and stop.
6. Genetic Operations:
   – Density-based binary tournament selection on A_{t+1} to get the mating pool.
   – Single-point crossover and bitwise mutation performed on mating pool to get P_{t+1}, compute objectives of P_{t+1}.
   $t \leftarrow t + 1$; goto (2).

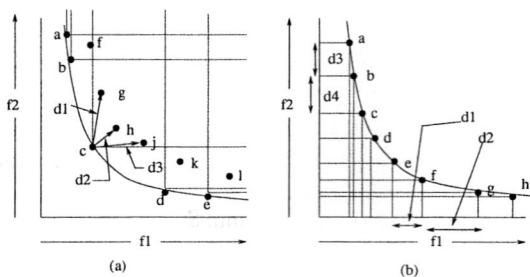

Fig. 1. (a): f_{di} parameter (b): diversity parameter

4 Simulation Study

DBMEA and NSGA-II have been compared on ten standard test problems. All the test problems studied in the present article involve minimization of the functions. Though the test problems have real domain, the binary encoded implementation of the algorithms (thus discretizing the domain, in practice) have been studied. The parameters used in these experiments are: *population size: 100, number of iterations: 250, crossover-probability: 0.9, mutation probability: inversely proportional to the chromosome length, chromosome-length: 10 bits per variable*. Ten runs of the algorithms were executed on each test problem, the mean and variance of the performance measures over these runs are reported.

Test Problems and Performance Measures

The set of test problems used in this article includes SCH1 and SCH2 [3], FON [4], KUR [5], POL [6], ZDT1, ZDT2, ZDT3, ZDT4 and ZDT6 [7]. The performance of DBMEA and NSGA-II is compared with respect to four performance measures: the convergence measure Υ [1], diversity measure Δ [1], purity value [8] and minimal-spacing [8]. The larger value of the purity measure and the smaller values of Υ, Δ and minimal spacing parameters signify the better performance. The details of the measures may be found in the respective references.

Results

Tables 1 and 2 represent the convergence measure and diversity measure, and the purity and minimal spacing measure respectively.

Table 1. Convergence and Diversity measure

Convergence Measure Υ								
Algorithm	SCH1	SCH2	FON	ZDT1	ZDT2	ZDT3	ZDT4	ZDT6
NSGA-II(Mean)	0.0144	0.0235	0.0032	0.0036	0.0027	0.0023	2.7681	0.0192
(Variance)	0.0000	0.0000	0.0000	0.0000	0.0000	0.0000	0.2939	0.0015
DBMEA(Mean)	0.0132	0.0167	0.0012	0.0050	0.0030	0.0033	1.2338	0.0048
(Variance)	0.0000	0.0000	0.0000	0.0000	0.0000	0.0000	1.2069	0.0000
Diversity Measure Δ								
Algorithm	SCH1	SCH2	FON	ZDT1	ZDT2	ZDT3	ZDT4	ZDT6
NSGA-II(Mean)	0.5763	1.4845	0.7713	0.9053	0.8322	0.7037	0.9474	0.9493
(Variance)	0.0068	0.0499	0.0004	0.0067	0.0059	0.0025	0.0011	0.0011
DBMEA (Mean)	0.3639	1.2623	0.7408	0.5758	0.3903	0.7304	0.8075	0.8188
(Variance)	0.0291	0.0795	0.0001	0.0573	0.0014	0.0072	0.0134	0.0023

Table 2. Purity and Minimal Spacing measure

	NSGA-II				DBMEA			
Test Function	Purity		Minimal Spacing		Purity		Minimal Spacing	
	Mean	Variance	Mean	Variance	Mean	Variance	Mean	Variance
SCH1	0.672	0.0639	0.0104	0.00	0.826	0.0528	0.0044	0.00
SCH2	0.808	0.0107	0.0524	0.00	0.818	0.0213	0.0497	0.00
KUR	0.811	0.0055	0.0897	0.00	0.943	0.0008	0.0877	0.00
POL	0.646	0.0465	0.0705	0.00	0.756	0.0403	0.0699	0.00
FON	0.680	0.0018	0.0084	0.00	0.944	0.0004	0.0005	0.00
ZDT1	0.989	0.0003	0.0113	0.00	0.397	0.0577	0.0069	0.00
ZDT2	0.998	0.0004	0.0142	0.00	0.187	0.0116	0.0114	0.00
ZDT3	0.957	0.0080	0.0358	0.00	0.410	0.0233	0.0369	0.00
ZDT4	0.200	0.1778	0.0164	0.00	0.800	0.1778	0.0064	0.00
ZDT6	1.000	0.0000	0.0146	0.00	1.000	0.0000	0.0087	0.00

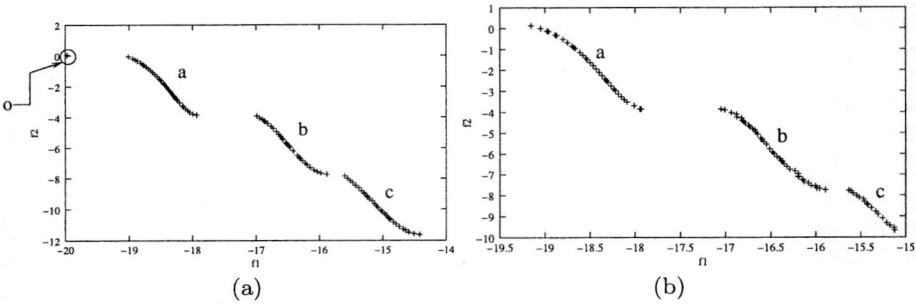

Fig. 2. Final Pareto-fronts of (a): DBMEA and (b): NSGA-II on KUR

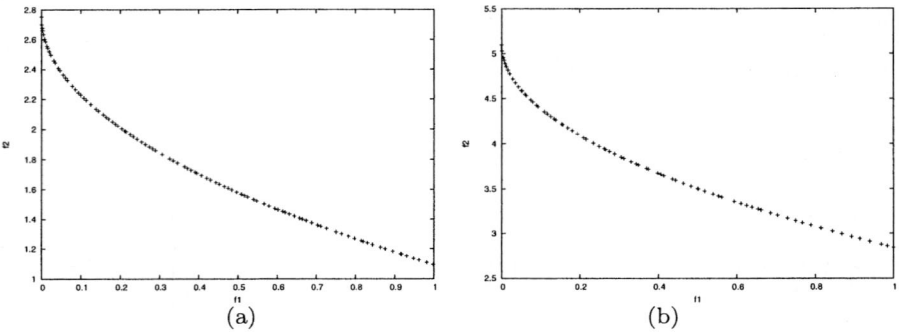

Fig. 3. Final Pareto-fronts of (a): DBMEA and (b): NSGA-II on ZDT4

As can be seen from Table 1, DBMEA has better convergence on test problems SCH1, SCH2, FON, ZDT4 and ZDT6, whereas NSGA-II has better convergence on functions ZDT1, ZDT2 and ZDT3. However it is interesting to note that except for ZDT3, DBMEA provides a better value of the diversity measure Δ for all other test problems. Again from Table 2, it is evident that DBMEA has better purity value for the test functions SCH1, SCH2, KUR, POL, FON, ZDT4 and ZDT6 compared to NSGA-II. The minimal spacing parameter shows that DBMEA has attained better spread of the solutions on the front for all test functions except ZDT3. Figures 2 and 3 show the final non-dominated fronts obtained by DBMEA and NSGA-II for two of the test functions (results for the others were almost similar). The better performance of DBMEA in terms of convergence and diversity is quite evident from Figure 3. In Figure 2, DBMEA is able to obtain the disjoint Pareto-optimal point 'o' at (-20,0) and the third disconnected component 'c' of the front, while NSGA-II fails to do that properly. From the results it can be concluded that DBMEA has comparable results with, often better than, NSGA-II in terms of the convergence to the Pareto-optimal front. In terms of the attainment of diversity on the Pareto-optimal front DBMEA is generally better than NSGA-II.

5 Discussion and Conclusions

In the present article, we have introduced a novel concept of measuring fitness function in MOEA by introducing a distance domination factor. A new way of computing density reflecting the diversity is explained that has resulted in much better spread of the solutions on the Pareto-optimal front. The MOEA based on this concept is not only good in approximating Pareto-optimal front, but also performs better in terms of diversity of the solutions on the front. Though the experiments done in this article have considered a good number of test problems with varying characterstics, a theoretical study dealing with the generalised performance of DBMEA is currently under investigation. It may be noted that the notion of distance domination is a general concept that can be used in other MOO algorithms also.

Acknowledgements. The present work has been partially supported by INSA funded project $No.BS/YSP/36/886$.

References

1. Deb, K., Pratap, A., Agarwal, S., Meyarivan, T.: A Fast and Elitist Multi-objective Genetic Algorithm: NSGA-II. Technical Report 200001, Kanpur Genetic Algorithms Laboratory (KanGAL), Indian Institute of Technology Kanpur, India (2000)
2. Zitzler, E., Laumanns, M., Thiele, L.: SPEA2: Improving the Strength Pareto Evolutionary Algorithm. Technical Report TIK-103, Computer Engineering and Network Laboratory (TIK), Swiss Fedral Institute of Technology (ETH), Gloriastrasse 35, CH-8092 Zurich, Swidzerland (2001)
3. Schaffer, J.D.: Some Experiments in Machine Learning using Vector Evaluated Genetic Algorithm. PhD thesis, Vanderbilt University, Nashville,TN (1984)
4. Fonseca, C.M., Fleming, P.J.: An Overview of Evolutionary Algorithms in Multi-objective Optimization. Evolutionary Computation Journal **3** (1995) 1–16
5. Kursawe, F.: A Variant of Evolutionary Strategies for Vector Optimization. In: In Parellel Problem Solving from Nature I (PPSN-I). (1990) 193–197
6. Poloni, C., Giurgevich, A., Onesti, L., Pediroda, V.: Hybridization of a Multiobjective Genetic Algorithm, a Neural Network and a Classical Optimizer for Complex Design Problem in Fluid Dynamics. Computer Methods in Applied Mechanics and Engineering (2000) 403–420
7. Zitzler, E., Deb, K., Thiele, L.: Comparison of Multiobjective Evolutionary Algorithms: Empirical Results. Evolutionary Computation Journal **8** (2000) 125–148
8. Bandyopadhyay, S., Pal, S.K., Aruna, B.: Multi-Objective GAs, Quantitative Indices, and Pattern Classification. IEEE Transaction on Systems, Man, and Cybernetics-Part B: Cybernetics **34** (2004) 2088–2099

I-EMO: An Interactive Evolutionary Multi-objective Optimization Tool

Kalyanmoy Deb and Shamik Chaudhuri

Kanpur Genetic Algorithms Laboratory (KanGAL),
Indian Institute of Technology, Kanpur,
Kanpur, PIN 208016, India
{deb, shamik}@iitk.ac.in,
http://www.iitk.ac.in/kangal

Abstract. With the advent of efficient techniques for multi-objective evolutionary optimization (EMO), real-world search and optimization problems are being increasingly solved for multiple conflicting objectives. During the past decade, most emphasis has been spent on finding the complete Pareto-optimal set, although EMO researchers were always aware of the importance of procedures which would help choose one particular solution from the Pareto-optimal set for implementation. This is also one of the main issues on which the classical and EMO philosophies are divided on. In this paper, we address this long-standing issue and suggest an interactive EMO procedure which, for the first time, will involve a decision-maker in the evolutionary optimization process and help choose a single solution at the end. This study is the culmination of many year's of research on EMO and would hopefully encourage both practitioners and researchers to pay more attention in viewing the multi-objective optimization as an aggregate task of optimization and decision-making.

1 Introduction

In the modern-day design and decision-making process, optimization plays a major role. Till now, most studies concentrated in finding the global optimum in a problem. However, with the advent of proper statistical tools designers and decision-makers are interested in introducing uncertainties and reliability-based concepts in the optimization process. These concepts are introduced simply because the real-world problem is full of such uncertainties and often the global optimum of an idealized deterministic optimization problem is not quite reliable.

In the context of multi-objective optimization and decision-making, there are additional problems of finding a set of optimal solutions and then making a scientific decision in choosing a particular solution. Often, such a decision making process is subjective and only when adequate information about the nature of the optimal solutions is provided to the *Decision Maker* (DM), a proper and reliable decision-making can be achieved. In this direction, the classical multi-objective literature provides a number of studies in which interactive methods were suggested. The sheer number of different methods also tells that none of these methods is widely accepted as a generic procedure. One common matter with all these methods is that they demand a lot of problem information from the DM without providing any idea of the nature of the resulting Pareto-optimal front. Thus, in most cases, the DM, while using these methods, rely on guesswork.

On the other hand, the research focus in evolutionary multi-objective optimization (EMO), was to find the nature and shape of the Pareto-optimal front by using a number of well-distributed solutions. In their history of about 10 years, the researchers did not seem to address the important issue of selecting one solution from the front. In this paper, for the first time, we suggest an interactive procedure (I-EMO), which takes the positive aspects of each field and attempts to suggest a procedure which can iteratively and interactively with a DM find the complete front and help focus to a single preferred solution. Based on the idea, we also provide some snapshots from a software which we are currently developing at Kanpur GA laboratory.

2 Related Works

There exists different interactive multi-objective optimization methods in the literature. But most of them are developed based on the classical optimization methods. Some of the most popular ones are Interactive Surrogate Worth Trade-off (ISWT) method [3], Reference Point method [11], the NIMBUS approach [9] etc. Each method is different from each other, but uses a single solution in each iteration. Based on particular multi-objective optimization procedure, a guess solution is modified to another solution iteratively and by gathering some information from a DM. Since a single solution is used in an iteration, the DM often has a local information (such as a local trade-off or search direction) and cannot make a decision using a more global picture of the true Pareto-optimal front. However, in the context of EMO, there does not exist many interactive studies. Tan et al. developed a GUI-based MOEA toolbox for multi-objective optimization [10]. The toolbox is designed with some classical decision-making aides, such as goal and priority settings. But a clear procedure of arriving at a single preferred solution is not present in the toolbox. Fonseca and Fleming [7] devised a GUI-based procedure which allowed a target value to be set for each objective and the effect of such a setting on the trade-off among different objectives was demonstrated. The procedure can be used to choose a preferred solution by visually comparing different solutions obtained using an EMO. However, the procedure did not provide any mean of relating the obtained solutions (closeness and location on the front) with the true Pareto-optimal front.

3 Interactive Evolutionary Multi-objective Optimization

In the proposed interactive EMO procedure, we attempt to put together some recent salient research results of EMO (described below) to constitute an interactive multi-criterion decision-making procedure:

1. An EMO is capable of finding the *entire* or a *partial* Pareto-optimal set, as desired [4,2].
2. An EMO is capable of finding the *knee* solutions from the Pareto-optimal set [1].
3. An EMO is capable of finding the *robust* solutions [5].
4. A local search starting from the EMO-obtained solutions has better convergence properties [6].
5. An EMO is capable of handling nonlinear constraints with extra additional parameter [4].

Further, in order to make a reliable decision, we ensure a verification procedure based on available multi-objective optimization techniques so that the decision-maker is satisfied and confident in deciding every step. The following classical principles can be used for this purpose and also for assisting in choosing a specific solution:

1. The extreme Pareto-optimal solutions can be verified by finding the individual optimum of each objective function (with constraints) [9].
2. Multiple applications of ϵ-constraint method can generate a set of Pareto-optimal solutions [9].
3. Interactive multi-objective methods, involving Tchebyshev methods or surrogate trade-off information [9] can be used to help choose a particular solution from the Pareto-optimal set.

In the following, we suggest an interactive-EMO procedure. The parameters to be supplied by the decision-maker (DM) are mentioned in parenthesis.

Step 1: Apply an EMO to obtain a non-dominated front close to the true Pareto-optimal front with following options:
    1.1 Compute the complete front (DM: no parameter)
    1.2 Compute a partial front (DM: limiting trade-off values)
    1.3 Compute *knee* solutions only (DM: limiting angle)
    1.4 Compute the *robust* Pareto-frontier using one of the following two strategies:
        1.4.1 Using mean objective values (DM: neighborhood size)
        1.4.2 Constrained approach (DM: neighborhood size and limiting robustness parameter)

Step 2: Improve the obtained non-dominated front using other optimization methods:
    2.1 Extreme solution improvement: Single-objective optimization of each objective
    2.2 Intermediate solution improvement: Local search from solutions chosen as follows:
        2.2.1 Automated selection of solutions from non-dominated front: Clustering (DM: number of solutions)
        2.2.2 User-defined solutions:
            2.2.2.1 Weighted-sum approach (DM: weight vectors)

      2.2.2.2 Utility function based approach (DM: utility functions)
      2.2.2.3 Tchebyshev function approach (DM: ideal points and L_p norm)
   2.3 Construct the modified front
Step 3: Final improvement (if any) with a classical approach
   3.1 ϵ-constraint method (one or multi-objective) (DM: ϵ-vector)
   3.2 Construct the final front
Step 4: User chooses a particular region of interest (single or multiply-connected) for focussed search using the above procedure
Step 5: Until satisfied, go to Step 1, else declare the chosen solution(s)

As clear from the above procedure, I-EMO proposes to first find the complete or a portion of the Pareto-optimal front in a problem. If desired, the DM can only consider the knee solutions or a robust frontier to start with. Thereafter, the obtained front can be improved by (i) finding individual optimum of each objective and (ii) performing a local search from a preferred set of intermediate solutions from the front. Finally, the classical ϵ-constraint method can be independently used to have a better confidence on the obtained front. Such a combination of a search based on optimization basics and a verification procedure will enable a DM to make his/her decisions more reliably and with confidence in an iterative manner till a single solution is identified. Another important matter is that the DM gets to analyze the true trade-off frontier before making any decision, a matter which makes this procedure different from other existing procedures.

3.1 In the Making of the I-EMO Software

At present to carry out such a rigorous interactive study, there exists no software. For an adequate user interaction we need a software with a powerful GUI and a good file-support facility. To this date, a major part of the above activities are coded and we give a flavor of the software using a few screen snap-shots.

In the first screen, the DM needs to define the main parameters of I-EMO, i.e. number of variables, objective functions and constraints to describe the problem. Each parameter is associated with an *Edit* button. Using this facility, further details of a parameter can be provided. An example is shown for the objective function button in Figure 1. In that window the DM can code his/her objective function(s) using the C-language syntax. There is a GA parameter window for providing population size, maximum generation number, crossover and mutation probabilities etc. Figure 2 shows the obtained non-dominated front for an example problem solved using NSGA-II. On this window, several menu buttons are available: *Point Menu, Utility Menu, ϵ-constraint Menu* and *Individual function Optimization Menu*. These menus can be used to choose a set of preferred solutions from which a local search can be performed. This is done to investigate if the solutions can be improved any further. The pop-up window for 'Utility' menu is shown in Figure 3. In the first option, the DM can give his priority of objective functions in the corresponding text-boxes and press the 'Find' button to get the best match on the non-dominated front. Similarly, there exists other

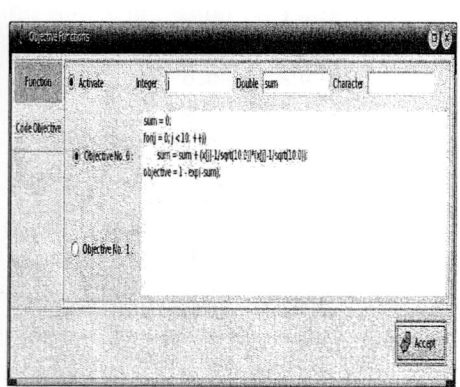
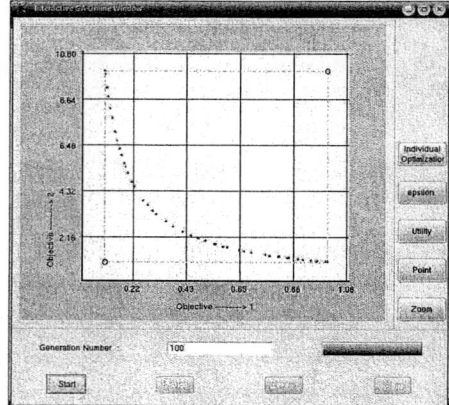

Fig. 1. Window for coding objective functions

Fig. 2. Plot window for two-objective problem

buttons for providing information via other methods. For example, for *Tcebycheff's* weight metric method, the DM can pick the *reference point* on the plot window and define the norm and weight-vector in the menu and ask for the best match. The software also allows the DM to find the individual optimum of each objective function. Then single objective GA is run with this modification and the data is shown in the same window.

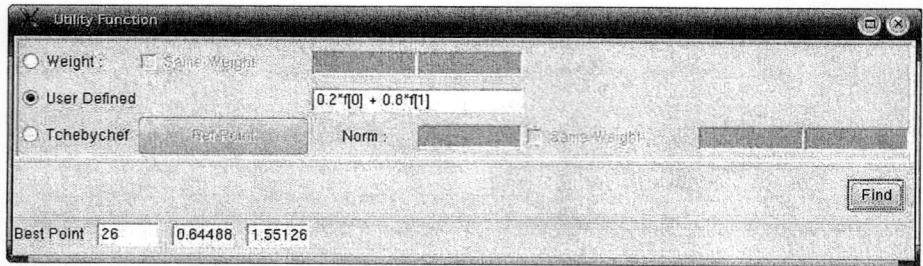

Fig. 3. Utility function window

Visualizing the Pareto-optimal front is an important part of an interactive EMO. However, due to the limitations in visualizing more than three objectives with current practices (albeit some recent suggestions [9,8]), our current implementation is restricted to three objectives only, although any number of objectives can be handled but visualization can be achieved by choosing any two or three objectives one at a time.

4 Conclusion

In this paper, we, for the first time, have proposed a truly interactive procedure for solving multi-objective optimization and decision-making problems. In order to arrive at the procedure, we have used most salient research results from classical and evolutionary multi-objective optimization literatures in a synergistic manner. The procedure not only finds the true Pareto-optimal front and then helps the DM to choose a particular solution, the procedure includes *checks and balances* at various steps so that the DM is more confident than ever in arriving at a particular solution. Till now, no such combined (classical and EMO) procedure is available for this task. With the ground-breaking research and application studies using EMO, it is now time for researchers to think and develop such interactive methods which will make the multi-objective optimization studies a real practical meaning and useful.

References

1. J. Branke, K. Deb, H. Dierolf, and M. Osswald. Finding Knees in multi-objective Optimization. Technical Report 2004010, Indian Institute of Technology, Kanpur: Kanpur Genetic Algorithms Laboratory (KanGAL), 2004.
2. J. Branke, T. Kaußler, and H. Schmeck. Guidance in Evolutionary Multi-objective Optimization. *Advances in Engineering Software*, 32:499–507, 2001.
3. V. Chankong and Y. Y. Haimes. *Multiobjective Decision Making Theory and Methodology*. New york: North-Holland, first edition edition, 1983.
4. K. Deb. *Multi-objective Optimization using Evolutionary Algorithms*. Chichester, UK: Wiley, second edition edition, 2001.
5. K. Deb and H. Gupta. Introducing Robustness in Multi-objective Optimization. Technical Report 2004016, Indian Institute of Technology, Kanpur: Kanpur Genetic Algorithms Laboratory (KanGAL), 2004.
6. K. Deb and S. Jain. Running performance metrics for evolutionary multi-objective optimization. In *Proceedings of the Fourth Asia-Pacific Conference on Simulated Evolution and Learning (SEAL-02)*, pages 13–20, 2002.
7. C. M. Fonseca and P. J. Fleming. Multiobjective optimization and multiple constraint handling with evolutionary algorithms–Part II: Application example. *IEEE Transactions on Systems, Man, and Cybernetics: Part A: Systems and Humans*, 28(1):38–47, 1998.
8. A. V. Lotov, V. A. Bushenkov, and H. K. Kamenev. *Interactive Decision Maps*. Kluwer, Boston, 2004.
9. K. Miettinen. *Nonlinear Multiobjective Optimization*. Kluwer's Academic Publisher, Boston, 1999.
10. K. C. Tan, T. H. Lee, D. Khoo, and E. F. Khor. A multiobjective evolutionay algorithm toolbox for computer-aided multiobjective optimization. *IEEE Transactions on Systems,Man, and Cybernetics - Part B: Cybernetics*, 31(4):537–556, 2001.
11. A.P. Wierzbicki. Reference point approaches. In T. Gal, T. Stewart, and T. Hanne, editors, *Multicriteria Decision Making: Advances in MCDM Models, Algorithms, Theory, and Applications*, pages 9.1–9.39. Kluwer Academic Publishers, Boston, 1999.

Simultaneous Multiobjective Multiple Route Selection Using Genetic Algorithm for Car Navigation

Basabi Chakraborty

Faculty of Software and Information Science,
Iwate Prefectural University,
152-52 Aza Sugo, Takizawamura, Iwate 020-0193, Japan
basabi@soft.iwate-pu.ac.jp

Abstract. A genetic algorithm (GA) based multiple route selection for car navigation device is proposed in this work. The proposed scheme offers the driver a choice from alternate near optimal solutions, each of which carries some specific characteristics based on the knowledge of the road map and the environment. The algorithm has been simulated on some real road map and it is found that it provides better solution compared to deterministic algorithms and other GA based algorithms in terms of driver's satisfaction.

1 Introduction

One of the essential component of a car navigation system is route planning. Given a set of origin-destination pair, there could be many possible routes for a driver. Search for optimal route from one point to another on a weighted graph is a well known problem and has several solutions. Though these algorithms can produce stable solutions in polynomial time, they exhibit high computational complexity specially in changing real time environment. In case of car navigation the shortest path may not be the best one from other considerations such as, simplicity, traffic congestion, environmental problem or simply user's satisfaction. So for an efficient practical car navigation device in dynamic environment, we need to specify multiple and different good (near optimal) choices accroding to multiple different criteria which make the search space too large to find out the solution in real time by deterministic algorithms.

A few research works on automated route selection for navigation are reported in literature [1] [2]. Genetic algorithms (GA) are now widely used to solve search problems with applications in practical routing and optimization problems [3]. GA includes a variety of quasi optimal solutions which can be obtained in a given time. Some works [4] [5] have also been reported for search of multiple routes for car navigation systems using GA. The problem in finding multiple semi optimal routes simultaneously is that the selected routes resemble each other i,e they partly overlap. Inagaki et.al [5] proposed an algorithm to minimize the effect of overlapping solutions. But the proposed algorithm requires a large solution space to attain high quality solution due to its inconsistent crossover mechanism. Inoue [6] proposed a method for finding out multiple different (non overlapping) routes by dividing the road map in multiple areas and putting different weights in each of them so that the selected routes are through different areas of the map. But as their is no direct method for comparing the overlapping of the selected paths this method is not guaranteed to select minimally overlapped multiple semi optimal paths. The author has previously proposed in [7] a GA based algorithm for finding out multiple nonoverlapping routes simultaneously while the selected routes did not possess any specific characteristics (i,e the objective of selection is not known) to be chosen by the driver. In this work a scheme for multiobjective multiple route selection on the basis of some specific characteristics of the route for car navigation using GA has been proposed. In the proposed method a set of nonoverlapping optimal routes are selected on the basis of different known criterion so that the driver can decide easily according to his choice. The proposed algorithm has been evaluated by simulation experiment with a piece of real road map and compared with Dijkustra and other GA based algorithms for multiple route selection.

2 Multiobjective Multiple Route Selection by GA

Genetic algorithm consists of three steps, problem coding, design of evaluation function and genetic operators (reproduction, crossover and mutation). The proposed GA is described below.

2.1 Problem Coding

The road map is first converted into a connected graph, considering each road crossing as a node (n) in the graph. The roads in map are represented by links (L) in the graph. The information of the road map is stored in a knowledge base in the form of the node numbers of the connecting node pair and a n-dimensional connecting link vector $(L = [l_1, l_2...l_n])$ whose components represent requisite knowledge regarding different choice of path such as the distance between the connecting node pair, the information of turnings (left or right), the information whether the link passes through mountain or by the side of the river etc. for every pair of connecting nodes. Any possible path from start node to goal node via other nodes is a possible solution and coded as a chromosome by using node numbers. However looping in the path is avoided.Population of chromosomes representing solution paths (routes) are generated by genetic coding. Chromosomes are equal length sequence of integers where each gene represents a node number.

2.2 Design of Fitness Function

In this work the fitness function has been designed with the objective of providing a set of alternate solution of routes with some knowledge about the individual routes such as the route passing through the side of a river, the route passing through mountain or the route has minimum number of turning or minimum number of signal. The knowledge based multiple choices of route will provide the driver better satisfaction and reasoning capability for selection of route.

The general fitness function F is defined here as follows:

$$F = \Sigma_1^n f_i(l_i) \qquad (1)$$

where $f_i(l_i)$ represents a function of the ith component of link vector. The idea is that the selection of optimum path according to ith choice of criterion will basically depend on the fitness function based on l_i, the requisite information regarding ith choice. Thus the design of f_i will depend on l_i. So depending on the choice of criteria, the value of the fitness function of same chromosome will be different. Here lower value of F corresponds to better solution.

2.3 Proposed Algorithm

The algorithm for finding out a set of solution containing 'm' alternate near optimal routes according to 'm' different criteria is as follows:

1. Initial population is formed by random selection of paths (chromosomes) from the entire solution space.
2. The individual chromosomes are evaluated multiply by the different component of the fitness function corresponding to different choices of criterion and 'm' group of chromosomes are formed by ranking corresponding to 'm' alternate selection. Any particular chromosome may belong to two groups. 'm' different groups are then subjected to genetic operation as follows:
   (a) For each group, the first few chromosomes (number to be selected according to the problem , we used 2 in our simulation) are retained as it is (elite selection) for the next generation.
   (b) For other chromosomes in the group crossover operation with probability P_c has been done with parents selected by Roulette selection with the group specific fitness function. The crossover position is selected at the place where the node numbers of the parents match.
   (c) Mutation with a very small probability P_m at a random position is done to generate new population in the group.
   (d) All the groups are then put together to form the next generation of population. The new population is then checked for duplicate chromosome and looping of path.
3. The new population is then ranked again by evaluating with the different fitness function and the procedure is repeated.(Go to step 2)
4. The stopping criterion is decided beforehand as a trade off between the availability of computation time and goodness of the produced solution.
5. The best route of each group 'm' after final iteration is selected to form 'm' alternate solutions.

3 Simulation Experiment

The simulation experiment has been done on a real road map. The road map is first converted into a graph with 130 nodes. The number of candidate paths from start(X) to destination node(Y) are found to be 100 (no looping is considered). The optimal path for different choices are considered in this experiment as 1) shortest route depending on total distance 2) optimal route with minimum number of turnings 3) optimal route through mountain and 4) optimal route passing by the side of a river. The link vector L with the road information has been calculated and stored as the knowledge base. The fitness function for different criteria (f_i)'s of Eq.(1) are designed as follows:

$$f_1(l_1) = \Sigma_1^n rlength(i) \tag{2}$$

where $rlength(i)$ represents the distance of the path between nth and $n-1$ node, the number of nodes in the path being n.

$$f_2(l_2) = \Sigma_1^n rlength(i) + \Sigma PR + \Sigma PL \tag{3}$$

ΣPR and ΣPL denotes the penalty for right and left turn respectively.

For choice 3 and 4, the following criterion function has been designed where $C < 1$ and $l(3) = 1$ represents that the node passes through the desired path of choice.

$$f_3(l_3) = \Sigma_1^n rlength(i) \times (2 - C) \text{ if } l(3) = 0 \tag{4a}$$
$$= \Sigma_1^n rlength(i) \times C \text{ if } l(3) = 1 \tag{4b}$$

C is problem dependent and set heuristically. We chose $C = 0.2$ for this problem. The algorithm has been run for several times.

Dijkstra's, Inagaki's method and author's earlier proposed method have also been used for simulation with same road map for comparison. The selected genetic parameters are represented in Table 1. In both the methods the parameters P_c and P_m have been changed to several values and the optimum values are noted in the table.

Table 1. Setting of parameters of GA

Method	Population size	No. of iteration	P_c	P_m	P_g
Inagaki	100	40	0.9	0.5	
Earlier	150	40	0.8	0.6	0.2
Proposed	150	40	0.8	0.2	

Table 2. Comparative Performance of different Algorithms

Algorithm	Time taken	Average. No. of overlapping nodes
Dijkstra	.014s	15
Inagaki	.182s	5
Earlier	.177s	2
Proposed	.167s	4

4 Simulation Results

Table 2. shows the comparative results of the different algorithms. Dijkstra algorithm takes much shorter time compared to other algorithms for finding out the

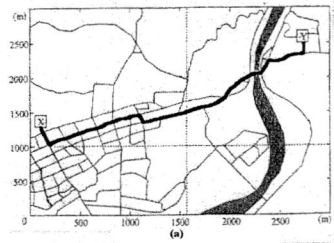
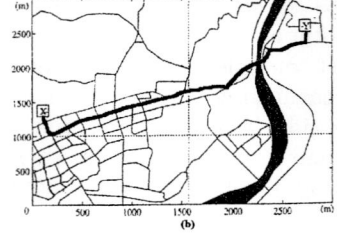

Fig. 1. Route by shortest distance   **Fig. 2.** Route by minimum turninng

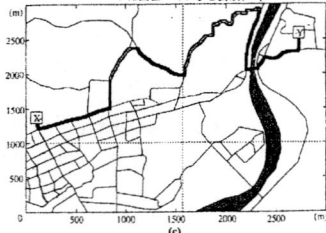
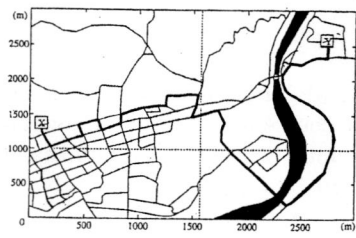

Fig. 3. Route through mountain   **Fig. 4.** Route by the side of river

shortest route and it also is able to find out better paths in terms of distance. But successive short routes are highly overlapped. Both Inagaki's method and the algorithms proposed by author's earlier and in this paper take longer time than Dijkstra's algorithm but alternate routes can be found out simultaneously. The proposed algorithms by author is found to be better than Inagaki's method in terms of nonoverlapping. In the newly proposed method only route 1 and route 2 has overlapping in between them but route 3 and route 4 are non overlapping with all others. The proposed algorithm in this work is also better than the earlier proposed algorithm in terms of the complexity and computation time of GA. One of the parameter P_g is not needed in the newly proposed algorithm. The alternate routes according to distance, number of turns, passing through mountain and passing by the side of river are found out and are shown. Though this simulation could not produce the best (optimal) routes the four alternate routes are quite independent and not much overlapping. As they satisfy some physical criterion based on the knowledge of the map the driver can use better reasoning capability while choosing from the alternatives.

5 Conclusion

In this work a Genetic Algorithm based solution technique for finding out m routes simultaneously with different characteristics for car navigation has been proposed. Simultaneous multiple route selection is difficult by popular optimization technique like Dijkstra algorithm. Currently available GA based algorithm can produce multiple routes simultaneously but selected routes resemble each other. Author has proposed a GA based technique in an earlier work for finding out multiple routes simultaneously with minimal overlapping by grouping m routes as one set of solution and designing fitness functions in such a way that it penalizes the function for overlapping. But though the algorithm produces better routes in terms of minimal overlapping, the alternate routes do not carry any meaning. It will be helpful to the driver to take decision and thereby get more satisfaction if we can provide the alternate routes with some special characteristics. In this work a GA based algorithm for finding multiple alternate routes have been proposed in which the fitness function is designed in such a way that the generated routes provide optimality according to some specific criteria and therefore satisfy the driver with some special knowledge about the generated routes. The simulation results with a real road map shows non optimality of some of the routes and the design of the fitness function depends on the map itself. Several experiments with different road maps are to be done to remove these two drawbacks. But from this limited experiment it is found that the alternate routes provide better satisfaction to the driver with a better computation time and complexity than other currently available methods.

References

1. Shapiro, J. et al., "Level Graphs and Approximate Shortest Paths Algorithms", Networks, Vol 22, pp. 691–717, 1992.
2. Liu, B.,"Intelligent Route Finding: Combining Knowledge, Cases and an Efficient Search Algorithm", in Proceedings of 12th European Conference on Artificial Intelligence, pp.380–384, 1996.
3. Ahn, C. W. and Ramakrishna, R. S. , "A Genetic Algorithm for Shortest Path Routing Problem and the Sizing of Populations", IEEE Trans. on Evolutionary Computations, Vol. 6, no. 6,pp. 566-579, December 2002.
4. Kanoh, H. and Nakamura, T.,*Knowledge based Genetic Algorithm for Dynamic Route Selection*, in Proceedings of International Conference on Knowledge based Intelligent engineering Systems and Allied Technologies, pp. 616–619, 2000.
5. Inagaki, J. et, al.,*A method of Determining Various Solutions for Routing Application with a Genetic Algorithm*,in Trans of IEICE, J82-D-I, No.8. pp.11 02-1111, August 2002.(in Japanese)
6. Inoue, Y., *Exploration Method of Various Routes with Genetic Algorithm*, Master's Thesis,Information System Engineering, Kochi Institute of Technology, 2001.(in Japanese)
7. Chakraborty, B.,'GA-based Multiple Route Selection for Car Navigation', Lecture Notes in Computer Science (Proceedings of AACC 2004), LNCS 3285 Springer, pp. 599–605, 2004.

Outliers in Rough k-Means Clustering

Georg Peters

Munich University of Applied Sciences,
Department of Computer Science, 80335 Munich, Germany
georg.peters@cs.fhm.edu

Abstract. Recently rough cluster algorithm were introduced and successfully applied to real life data. In this paper we analyze the rough k-means introduced by Lingras' et al. with respect to its compliance to the classical k-means, the numerical stability and its performance in the presence of outliers. We suggest a variation of the algorithm that shows improved results in these circumstances.

1 Introduction

In the past years soft computing methodologies like fuzzy sets [14], neural nets [3] or rough sets [9,10], have been proposed to handle challenges in data mining [8] like clustering. Recently rough cluster algorithms were introduced by Lingras et al. [5], do Prado et al. [2] and Voges et al. [11,12]. In rough clustering each cluster has a lower and an upper approximation. The data in a lower approximation exclusively belong to the cluster. Due to missing information the membership of data in an upper approximation is uncertain. Therefore they must be assigned to at least two upper approximations. The objective of this paper is to analyze Lingras et al. [5] cluster algorithm with respect to its compliance to the classical k-means, the numerical stability and outliers. In an example we show that a variation of the algorithm delivers more intuitive results in these circumstances. The structure of the paper is as follows. In Section 2 we introduce Lingras' et al. rough k-means cluster algorithm. In Section 3 we investigate the properties mentioned above and introduce an improved version of the algorithm. The paper concludes with a summary in Section 4.

2 Lingras' Rough k-Means Clustering Algorithm

Lingras et al. [5] assume the following set of properties for rough sets: (1) A data object can be a member of one lower approximation at most. (2) The lower approximation of a cluster is a subset of its upper approximation. (3) A data object that does not belong to any lower approximation is member of at least two upper approximations.

So their cluster algorithm belongs to the branch of rough set theory with a reduced interpretation of rough sets as lower and upper approximations of data constellation [13]. The algorithm proceeds as follows.

Let:

- Data set: X_n the nth data point and $\mathbf{X} = (X_1, ..., X_N)^T$, $n = 1, ..., N$.
- C_k the kth cluster, $\underline{C_k}$ its lower and $\overline{C_k}$ its upper approximation. $C_k^B = \overline{C_k} - \underline{C_k}$ the boundary area.
- Mean m_k of cluster C_k. $\mathbf{M} = (m_1, ..., m_K)^T$ with $k = 1, ..., K$.
- Distance between X_n and m_k: $d(X_n, m_k) = \|X_n - m_k\|$.

- **Step 0: Initialization.** Randomly assign each data object to one and only one lower approximation and its corresponding upper approximation.
- **Step 1: Calculation of the new means.**

$$m_k = \begin{cases} w_l \sum_{X_n \in \underline{C_k}} \frac{X_n}{|\underline{C_k}|} + w_b \sum_{X_n \in C_k^B} \frac{X_n}{|C_k^B|} & \text{for } C_k^B \neq \emptyset \\ w_l \sum_{X_n \in \underline{C_k}} \frac{X_n}{|\underline{C_k}|} & \text{otherwise} \end{cases} \quad (1)$$

with the weights w_l and w_b. $|\underline{C_k}|$ indicates the numbers of data objects in lower approximation, $|C_k^B| = |\overline{C_k} - \underline{C_k}|$ in the boundary area of cluster k.
- **Step 2: Assign the data objects to the approximations.**
  (i) For a given data object X_n determine its closest mean m_h:

$$d_{n,h}^{min} = d(X_n, m_h) = \min_{k=1,...,K} d(X_n, m_k). \quad (2)$$

Assign X_n to the upper approximation of the cluster h: $X_n \in \overline{C_h}$.
(ii) Determine the set T with ϵ a given threshold:

$$T = \{t : d(X_n, m_k) - d(X_n, m_h) \leq \epsilon \wedge h \neq k\}. \quad (3)$$

If $(T \neq \emptyset)$ Then $\{X_n \in \overline{C_t}, \forall t \in T\}$ Else $\{X_n \in \underline{C_h}\}$.
- **Step 3: Check convergence of the algorithm.**
  If (Algorithm converged) **Then**{Goto Step 1} **Else** {STOP}.

Lingras et al. applied their algorithm to the analysis of student web access logs at a university. Mitra [7] presented an evolutionary version and applied it to vowel, forest cover and colon cancer data.

3 Properties of the Rough k-Means

3.1 Compliance with the Classical k-Means

Lingras et al. propose [4,5,6] that their algorithm equals the classical k-means in the cases that the lower and upper approximations of the clusters are identical (the boundary areas are empty). However, Equation (1) becomes:

$$m_k = w_l \sum_{X_n \in \underline{C_k}} \frac{X_n}{|\underline{C_k}|} \quad (4)$$

Therefore we suggest to delete w_l in the second case of Equation (1) so that we obtain compliance with classical rough k-means:

$$m_k = \begin{cases} w_l \sum_{X_n \in \underline{C_k}} \frac{X_n}{|\underline{C_k}|} + w_b \sum_{X_n \in C_k^B} \frac{X_n}{|C_k^B|} & \text{for } C_k^B \neq \emptyset \\ \sum_{X_n \in \underline{C_k}} \frac{X_n}{|\underline{C_k}|} & \text{otherwise} \end{cases} \quad (5)$$

3.2 Numerical Stability

Lingas et al. algorithm is numerical instable in some circumstances. Consider the following data set:

$$\mathbf{X}^T = \begin{pmatrix} 0.2 & 0.1 & 0.0 & 0.4 & 0.4 & 0.5 & 0.6 & 0.8 & 1.0 & 0.7 \\ 0.0 & 0.2 & 0.2 & 0.5 & 0.6 & 0.5 & 0.5 & 0.8 & 0.8 & 1.0 \end{pmatrix}$$

For $K = 2$, $w_l = 0.7$, $w_u = 0.3$ and $\epsilon = 0.2$ a stable solution of the rough k-means is given by the following meaningful result (Figure 1):

Means

$$\mathbf{M}^T = \begin{pmatrix} 0.21250 & 0.72583 \\ 0.25083 & 0.76417 \end{pmatrix}$$

Approximations

$$\underline{\mathbf{C}}^T = \begin{pmatrix} 1 & 1 & 1 & 0 & 0 & 0 & 0 & 0 & 0 & 0 \\ 0 & 0 & 0 & 0 & 0 & 0 & 0 & 1 & 1 & 1 \end{pmatrix} \quad \text{and} \quad \overline{\mathbf{C}}^T = \begin{pmatrix} 1 & 1 & 1 & 1 & 1 & 1 & 1 & 0 & 0 & 0 \\ 0 & 0 & 0 & 1 & 1 & 1 & 1 & 1 & 1 & 1 \end{pmatrix}$$

However, the algorithm terminates abnormally if $|\underline{C_k}| = 0 \; \forall k$ which leads to a division by Zero in Equation (1). So there are not only data constellations that lead to empty boundary areas but it is also possible to obtain empty lower approximations. Therefore Equation (1) must be modified to:

$$m_k = \begin{cases} w_l \sum_{X_n \in \underline{C_k}} \frac{X_n}{|\underline{C_k}|} + w_b \sum_{X_n \in C_k^B} \frac{X_n}{|C_k^B|} & \text{for } C_k^B \neq \emptyset \wedge \underline{C_k} \neq \emptyset \\ \sum_{X_n \in \underline{C_k}} \frac{X_n}{|\underline{C_k}|} & \text{for } C_k^B = \emptyset \wedge \underline{C_k} \neq \emptyset \\ \sum_{X_n \in C_k^B} \frac{X_n}{|C_k^B|} & \text{for } C_k^B \neq \emptyset \wedge \underline{C_k} = \emptyset \end{cases} \quad (6)$$

Now, besides the solution above we obtain the following stable result where the lower approximations of both clusters are empty:

$$\mathbf{M}^T = \begin{pmatrix} 0.47 & 0.47 \\ 0.51 & 0.51 \end{pmatrix}$$

An expert now has to decide which solution is considered as optimal. In the present case it would properly be the first on.

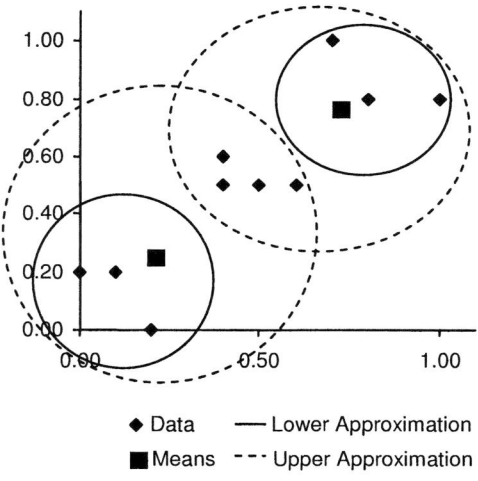

Fig. 1. Cluster results

3.3 Dealing with Outliers

To determine the set T Lingras et al. suggest to consider the *absolute* distance $d(X_n, m_k) - d(X_n, m_h)$. However consider the following data constellation incorporating an outlier A *inline* with Means 1 and 2 (Figure 2).

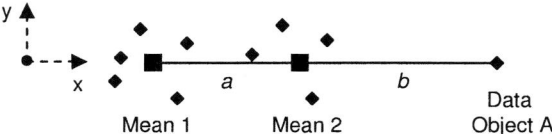

Fig. 2. Data with an outlier

Let $b = za$ ($z \in \mathbb{R}^+$) then A is an outlier for large z. For $a \leq \epsilon$ the data object A belongs to the upper approximations of both cluster:

$$\begin{aligned} d(X_n, m_k) \quad -d(X_n, m_h) &\leq \epsilon \\ \Rightarrow (a+b) \quad -b &\leq \epsilon \\ \Rightarrow a &\leq \epsilon. \end{aligned} \qquad (7)$$

It is member of the lower approximation of cluster 2 if $\epsilon < a$ respectively. Obviously this is independent of the selection of z. However, for large z the outlier should be assigned to the upper approximations of both clusters, indicating that the actual membership to *one* cluster is uncertain.

We suggest to use a *relative distance measure* instead of Lingras' et al. absolute to determine the set T:

$$T = \left\{ t : \frac{d(\boldsymbol{X_n}, \boldsymbol{m_k})}{d(\boldsymbol{X_n}, \boldsymbol{m_h})} \leq \zeta \wedge h \neq k \right\}. \tag{8}$$

The impact on the previous example is as follows. Let $b = za$ ($z \in \mathbb{R}^+$); then we get:

$$T = \{t : z \leq \zeta \wedge h \neq k\}. \tag{9}$$

Note that the set T depends on z now. In contrast to Lingras solution the data object A is assigned to the upper approximations of both sets for large z. This indicates its uncertain status.

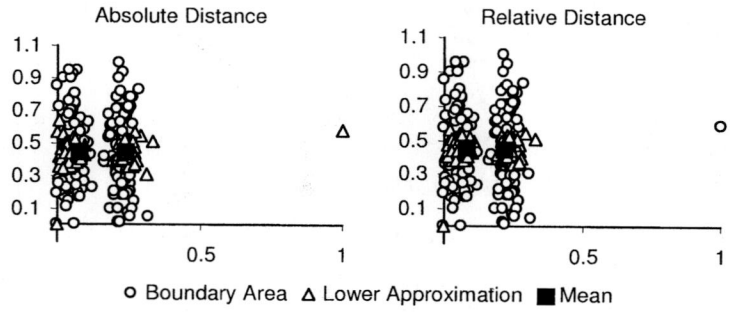

Fig. 3. Two clusters with absolute and relative thresholds

To test this an experiment was set up. We generated two normally distributed two-dimensional clusters each containing 100 data objects and added an data point representing an outlier (Figure 3). Let $w_l = 0.7$, $w_b = 0.3$ and Lingras' et al. threshold $\epsilon = 0.1$. The relative threshold was set to $\zeta = 1.86$ so that the boundary area has 130 data objects in both cases. While the outlier was assigned to the lower approximation in Lingras et al. case, it became a member of the boundary area when applying the relative threshold (Figure 3). Furthermore the Davies-Bouldin index [1], based on the data objects in the lower approximations, improved from $DB_{absolute} = 1.4137$ to $DB_{relative} = 0.9635$.

4 Conclusion

In the paper we investigated the performance of Lingras' et al. rough cluster algorithm with respect to its compliance to the classical k-means, the numerical stability and in the presents of outliers. We suggested an improved version of the algorithm that delivers more intuitive results in comparison to Lingras' et al. approach. In future research we will evaluate some other features of the algorithm, compare it to classical cluster algorithms and conduct experiments with real life data.

References

1. D.L. Davies and D.W. Bouldin. A cluster separation measure. *IEEE Transactions on Pattern Analysis and Machine Intelligence*, 1:224–227, 1979.
2. H.A. do Prado, P.M. Engel, and H.C. Filho. Rough clustering: An alternative to find meaningful clusters by using the reducts from a dataset. In *Rough Sets and Current Trends in Computing: Third International Conference, RSCTC 2002*, volume 2475 of *LNCS*, pages 234 – 238, Berlin, 2002. Springer.
3. S. Haykin. *Neural Networks: A Comprehensive Foundation*. Prentice Hall, Upper Saddle River, N.J., 2. edition, 1998.
4. P. Lingras and C. West. Interval set clustering of web users with rough k-means. Technical Report 2002-002, Department of Mathematics and Computer Science, St. Mary's University, Halifax, Canada, 2002.
5. P. Lingras and C. West. Interval set clustering of web users with rough k-means. *Journal of Intelligent Information Systems*, 23:5–16, 2004.
6. P. Lingras, R. Yan, and C. West. Comparison of conventional and rough k-means clustering. In *International Conference on Rough Sets, Fuzzy Sets, Data Mining and Granular Computing*, volume 2639 of *LNAI*, pages 130–137, Berlin, 2003. Springer.
7. S. Mitra. An evolutionary rough partitive clustering. *Pattern Recognition Letters*, 25:1439–1449, 2004.
8. S. Mitra and T. Acharya. *Data Mining: Multimedia, Soft Computing, and Bioinformatics*. John Wiley, New York, 2003.
9. Z. Pawlak. Rough sets. *International Journal of Information and Computer Sciences*, 11:145–172, 1982.
10. Z. Pawlak. *Rough Sets: Theoretical Aspects of Reasoning about Data*. Kluwer Academic Publishers, Boston, 1992.
11. K.E. Voges, N.K. Pope, and M.R. Brown. *Heuristics and Optimization for Knowledge Discovery*, chapter Cluster Analysis of Marketing Data Examining On-Line Shopping Orientation: A Comparision of k-Means and Rough Clustering Approaches, pages 207–224. Idea Group Publishing, Hershey PA, 2002.
12. K.E. Voges, N.K. Pope, and M.R. Brown. A rough cluster analysis of shopping orientation data. In *Proceedings Australian and New Zealand Marketing Academy Conference*, pages 1625–1631, Adelaide, 2003.
13. Y.Y. Yao, X. Li, T.Y. Lin, and Q. Liu. Representation and classification of rough set models. In *Proceedings Third International Workshop on Rough Sets and Soft Computing*, pages 630–637, San Jose, CA, 1994.
14. H.J. Zimmermann. *Fuzzy Set Theory and its Applications*. Kluwer Academic Publishers, Boston, 4. edition, 2001.

Divisible Rough Sets Based on Self-organizing Maps

Rocío Martínez-López and Miguel A. Sanz-Bobi

Computer Science Department, Escuela Técnica Superior de Ingeniería-ICAI,
Universidad Pontificia Comillas, 28015 Alberto Aguilera 25, Madrid, Spain
{rmartinez, masanz}@dsi.icai.upcomillas.es

Abstract. The rough sets theory has proved to be useful in knowledge discovery from databases, decision-making contexts and pattern recognition. However this technique has some difficulties with complex data due to its lack of flexibility and excessive dependency on the initial discretization of the continuous attributes. This paper presents the divisible rough sets as a new hybrid technique of automatic learning able to overcome the problems mentioned using a combination of variable precision rough sets with self-organizing maps and perceptrons. This new technique divides some of the equivalence classes generated by the rough sets method in order to obtain new certain rules under the data which originally were lost. The results obtained demonstrate that this new algorithm obtains a higher decision-making success rate in addition to a higher number of classified examples in the tested data sets.

1 Introduction

The rough sets theory [1], [2] is a powerful tool belonging to the inductive machine learning area which allows the recognition of hidden patterns in data. Additionally, it is capable of assigning uncertainty to the obtained knowledge and of identifying partial or total dependences in databases. The rough sets theory can also be applied to classification problems and to cases where elimination of redundant data is needed.

This paper proposes an improvement of the knowledge extraction technique based on rough sets. The aim is to overcome its inflexibility when dealing with inconsistent data. This is achieved by means of a new hybrid technique, "divisible rough sets", which combines variable precision rough sets [3] with other machine learning techniques such as neural networks, and, in particular with self-organizing maps (SOMs) [4]. Also, the modified Chi2 algorithm [5] is applied in the discretization process.

Previously, some hybrids have been developed involving rough sets and other statistical or machine learning methods improving both the performance and results [6], [7] and connections between rough sets and neural networks have been studied [8]. Specifically, in [9] another combination of SOMs and rough sets, where the first ones extract knowledge from the reducts obtained using rough set theory, is proposed.

The structure of this paper is as follows. First, the theoretical concepts of the divisible rough sets are described. Once the new technique has been detailed, its efficiency in knowledge extraction is tested in some real data sets and its results are then compared with those obtained with variable precision rough sets and self-organizing maps methods. Finally, some conclusions are presented.

2 Divisible Rough Sets Method Definition

Knowledge extraction based on rough sets suffers from some disadvantages, fundamentally, when it deals with very inconsistent data sets. Among them are the lack of flexibility and the excessive dependence on the chosen intervals in the discretization process. The suggested algorithm tries to overcome them improving the learning process, essentially using the information included in the equivalence classes belonging to the boundary region that do not produce any certain rule with the application of the classic rough sets method. In order to achieve this, these equivalence classes are split into several subsets after the clustering of the examples that compose them.

In addition, the divisible rough sets algorithm adds the notion of centre of an equivalence class, obtained from its examples. These centres are useful in the other possible equivalence class division, achieved from new examples examined once the rough sets regions are established, since it is considered that if a certain number of these examples are far from the centre of their class, it will be convenient to divide it.

These two possible equivalence class divisions create equivalence subclasses defined by the discrete values of the available attributes and by new attributes generated by means of mathematical equations where these attributes are numerically expressed. These new subsets will be able to create both certain and uncertain rules.

This analysis of the boundary region is similar to the one done with hierarchy-structured probabilistic tables [10], although here its reduction is carried out by means of new numerical attributes which come from the distances to the centres.

3 Divisible Rough Sets Algorithm

The divisible rough sets method consists of the following steps:

- Step 1: Creation of the decision table: data set examples are distributed in a table.
- Step 2: Initial knowledge extraction: the rough sets method is applied and the results are refined dividing the equivalence classes with clustering.
- Step 3: Knowledge update: via hyperplanes, the examples closer to other equivalence classes than to their own are separated.
- Step 4: Test: rules obtained in the previous steps are tested with new examples.

Now, these steps of the algorithm are briefly described.

3.1 Step 1: Creation of the Decision Table

The aim is to express the examples of the data set from which it is intended to extract knowledge so that they can be processed in the following step of the algorithm. First of all, the decision attribute, which classifies the examples, and the condition attributes, which are the factors a priori considered to be appropriate to make this classification, are selected. The final purpose will be to determine the value of the decision attribute from the information provided by the condition attributes, that is, to get the underlying knowledge rules which govern the relation between these attributes.

3.2 Step 2: Initial Knowledge Extraction

The objective of this step is the discovery of the rules hidden in the data set. In order to do this, the variable precision rough sets method and then clustering processes through self-organizing maps are applied to obtain more certain rules.

The initial knowledge extraction is divided into two phases:

- In the first one, the variable precision rough sets model is applied with a low error.
- In the second one, a clustering process is made in each one of the equivalence classes not included in the positive region in order to achieve new certain rules from equivalence classes that had only generated uncertain rules in the first phase.

At the end of both phases, each example has one more attribute: the distance to the centre of the equivalence class or group which it belongs to. Furthermore, the centres of each group or class will be useful in the following step: the knowledge updating.

The second phase, which constitutes the core of the new method, will be explained. At the end of the first one, the equivalence classes X_i of the partition A^*, which were induced by the equivalence relation of all condition attributes, were assigned to the positive or boundary region of the partition B^* induced by the decision attribute. Depending on the region, each of these equivalence classes will be treated as follows:

Case 1: Class X_i is included in the positive region. A single centre M average of the examples that constitute the equivalence class is calculated.

Case 2: Class X_i is included in the boundary region. One or several centres are calculated from its examples by means of a self-organizing map. Once the appropriate centres of the class X_i are calculated, they will be used to divide X_i in groups.

Let $P = \{p_1, p_2, ..., p_n\}$ be the obtained centres set, being each p_j a centre point defined by its values in the condition attributes. Each class X_i will be divided into as many groups as centres make the set P. Let $G = \{G_1, G_2, ..., G_n\}$ be the groups set composed from X_i, being each G_j a group which contains a subset of examples of the class X_i with an associated centre point p_j.

In order to assign all the examples belonging to X_i to the different groups of G, the Euclidean distance measure is applied. That is, an example $x \in X_i$ is included in the group G_j with the closer associated centre p_j to x. Therefore, the index j of the group which the example x should belong to, is calculated:

$$j(x) = \arg_j \min \|x-p_j\| \qquad (1)$$

Once the examples of the set X_i are distributed into the groups G_j, it is observed that G is a set of non-empty subsets of X_i, $G_1 \cup G_2 \cup ... \cup G_n = X_i$ and $G_i \cap G_j = \{\}$ for $i \neq j$. Therefore, G has the required characteristics to be considered a partition of the equivalence class X_i, and consequently G_j can be treated as a block of the partition G. The elements belonging to one of these blocks are characterized by the fact that they have the same discretized values in all the condition attributes and in the added attribute (being closer to the centre associated to the group than to the centres of the rest of the partition blocks). This last attribute makes some examples of an equivalence class to be equivalent and become members of the same group or "equivalence subclass".

Next, for each of the blocks of partition G it is checked to see if it can be included in the positive or boundary region of the partition B^*. The blocks of G belonging to the positive region, will produce certain rules, while the ones of the boundary region, will produce uncertain rules with a confidence factor given by:

$$\alpha_{Y_j}(G_j) = \frac{|G_j \cap Y_j|}{|G_j|} \qquad (2)$$

All these rules are more complex because the concept of nearness to the respective centre is added. As a result, a rule created from the group G_j of an equivalence class X_i is: *"if attribute c_1 is xx, attribute c_2 is yy, ..., and attribute c_n is zz, and also the closest centre of the equivalence class to the example is p_j, then attribute d is dd"*.

Centres estimation with self-organizing maps. A SOM is created to determine the centres of the groups of class X_i, which belongs to the boundary region.

The map of neurons is set up with its weight vectors randomly initialized and then each example of X_i is presented. Once the training process ends, the network is used as a classifier of the examples of X_i quantifying the number of examples that activate each neuron. Next, the neuron with the greatest amount of associated examples is selected, and then, also the neurons with at least half this amount. The reference vectors of the selected neurons will be part of the final centres set P used in this phase.

3.3 Step 3: Knowledge Update

The aim of this step is to obtain more certain rules besides those that were produced in the previous step. Thus, the equivalence class areas which are closer to groups of examples of neighbouring equivalence classes are studied with new update examples.

Let $Q = \{x_1, x_2, ..., x_n\}$ be the data set kept aside for knowledge update. For each $x_i \in Q$, with an unknown value for the decision attribute, this process is applied:

First, the equivalence class $X_i \in A^*$ which the example x_i belongs to is determined. Also, if this equivalence class has been divided in the previous phase, then the group G_j, where the example should be included, will be the one with its closest centre.

If the example does not belong to an equivalence class or group included in the positive region, then its Euclidean distances to the centres of the neighbouring classes or groups are calculated. If the nearest centre is closer than the one of its own equivalence class or group, the case is counted.

When a given rate of update examples are closer to another class or group than to their own one, then the original training examples of the class or group will be divided by means of the hyperplane equidistant to the centre of the own set and to the one which the update examples are closest to. This rate is estimated considering the training examples that compose the equivalence class or group.

This hyperplane is equivalent to that defined by a perceptron neuron. Henceforth, in the classes or groups divided like that, an example will be assigned to one of the two subsets depending on the output obtained when it is presented to the perceptron.

Next, it is verified if each of the generated subsets belongs to the positive or to the boundary region and the average centre of those subsets are calculated.

3.4 Step 4: Test

Let $T = \{x_1, x_2, \ldots, x_n\}$ be a set of examples not used in the previous steps. For each example $x_i \in T$ the following process will be carried out:

The first to be determined is the equivalence class $X_i \in A^*$ which the example x_i belongs to. Also, if X_i has been divided in the initial knowledge extraction phase, then the group where the example should be included in will be that with its closest centre. Likewise, if in phase 3 X_i or one of its groups have been divided by one or more hyperplanes, then the example must be presented to the perceptron.

If the set which the example belongs to is included in the positive region, the decision is directly assigned to the example. If it is in the boundary region, its decision will be the one with the highest confidence factor. If the test example does not belong to any equivalence class, the decision will be the one of the equivalence class or group belonging to the positive region with the nearest centre.

4 Experimental Results

In order to test the new proposed algorithm, its results have been compared with those obtained with VPRS and self-organizing maps. Five quite different real data sets from the UCI repository of machine learning databases [11] were used:

Table 1. Analysed Data Sets

Data sets	Characteristics			Success rate		
	Examples	Attributes	Classes	VPRS	SOM	Div. RS
Iris	150	4	3	92.00%	94.00%	94.00%
Liver Disorders	345	6	2	54.78%	61.74%	66.09%
Abalone	4177	4	9	55.46%	55.39%	54.53%
Glass	214	7	6	57.75%	63.38%	66.20%
Diabetes	768	7	2	59.77%	72.66%	70.31%

Each data set is randomly divided into the training set (two thirds), and the test set (one third). The divisible rough sets algorithm requires the additional division of the training set into initial training set (two thirds) used in step 2, and update set (the rest).

In order to carry out the discretizations, a variation of the Modified Chi2 algorithm [5] was applied. The variation proposed allows for the lowering of the initial consistency level so as to obtain equivalence classes with more examples. Other approaches to discretization, e.g. using hyperplanes or soft cuts, are expounded in [12].

The increase of the success rate with regard to VPRS is due to:

1. Test examples not belonging to any equivalence class created in the training process are assigned to the decision of the equivalence class or group belonging to the positive region with the nearest centre.
2. There are more certain rules, which are generated after the equivalence class divisions. As a result, more examples pertain to certain rules and this involves an increase of the confidence in the decision assignment, since the success rate in this case is greater than the one obtained when examples pertained to uncertain rules.

5 Conclusions

This paper proposes a new hybrid technique named "divisible rough sets", which combines a variable precision rough sets method with self-organizing. Additionally, in the data preprocessing phase a variation of the modified Chi2 algorithm was applied. The aim of this variation is the production of more relevant rules.

The objective of this new technique is to obtain certain rules from the uncertain rules provided by the rough sets method. Thus, it tries to increase the number of new examples presented to the knowledge database which can be assigned to a decision considered as certain. In addition, the class assignment to the examples that pertain to uncertain rules or to the examples that do not pertain to any rules (because there was no example similar to them in the training phase) has been allowed.

Finally, as a future extension of the present work the use of Radial Basis Function Networks (RBFN) is suggested instead of the perceptron applied in the knowledge update phase. These networks would allow a non linear division of the examples included in an equivalence class belonging to the boundary region, bringing a subsequent improvement of the success rate in complex data sets.

References

1. Pawlak, Z., "Rough Sets". International Journal of Computer and Information Sciences, vol. 11, no. 5, pp. 341-356. Oct. 1982.
2. Pawlak, Z., Grzymala-Busse, J., Slowinski, R. & Ziarko, W., "Rough Sets". Communications of the ACM, vol. 38, no. 11, pp. 89-95. Nov. 1995.
3. Ziarko, W., "Variable Precision Rough Set Model. Journal of Computer and System Sciences", vol. 46, no. 1, pp. 39-59. Feb. 2003.
4. Kohonen, T., "Self-organizing Formation of Topologically Correct Feature Maps". Biological Cybernetics, vol. 43, no. 1. pp. 59-69. 1982.
5. Shen, L., Tay, F.E.H., "A Discretization Method for Rough Sets Theory". Intelligent Data Analysis, vol. 5, pp. 431-438. 2001.
6. Browne, C., Düntsch, I., Gediga, G., "IRIS Revisited, A Comparison of Discriminant and Enhanced Rough Set Data Analysis". In: Polkowski, L., Slowron, A. (Eds.), "Rough Sets in Knowledge Discovery", Heidelberg: Physica Verlag, vol. 2, pp. 345-368. 1998.
7. Banarjee, M., Mitra, S., Pal, S.K., "Rough Fuzzy MLP: Knowledge Encoding and Classification". IEEE Transactions on Neural Networks, vol. 9, pp. 1203-1216. 1998.
8. Nguyen H. S., Szczuka, M.S., Slezak, D., "Neural Networks Design: Rough Set Approach to Continuous Data". Principles of Data Mining and Knowledge Discovery. First European Symposium, PKDD '97. Proceedings. Berlin, Germany: Springer-Verlag, pp. 359-366. 1997.
9. Pal, S. K., Dasgupta, B., Mitra, P., "Rough Self Organizing Map". Applied Intelligence, vol. 21, no. 3, pp 289-299. 2004.
10. Ziarko, W., "Acquisition of Hierarchy-Structured Probabilistic Decision Tables and Rules from Data". Expert Systems, vol. 20, no. 5, pp. 305-310. Nov. 2003.
11. Merz, C.J., Murphy, P.M., UCI repository of machine learning databases. http://www.ics.uci.edu/~mlearn/MLRepository.html. Irvine, CA: University of California, Department of Information and Computer Science. 1996.
12. Nguyen, H. S., Nguyen, S. H., "Discretization Methods in Data Mining". In: Polkowski, L., Slowron, A. (Eds.), "Rough Sets in Knowledge Discovery", Heidelberg: Physica Verlag, vol. 1, pp. 451-482. 1998.

Parallel Island Model for Attribute Reduction

Mohammad M. Rahman[1], Dominik Ślęzak[1,2], and Jakub Wróblewski[2]

[1] Department of Computer Science, University of Regina,
Regina, SK, S4S 0A2 Canada
{rahman5m, slezak}@cs.uregina.ca
[2] Polish-Japanese Institute of Information Technology,
Koszykowa 86, 02-008 Warsaw, Poland
{slezak, jakubw}@pjwstk.edu.pl

Abstract. We develop a framework for parallel computation of the optimal rough set decision reducts from data. We adapt the island model for evolutionary computing. The idea is to optimize reducts within separate populations (islands) and enable the best reducts-chromosomes to migrate among islands. Experiments show that the proposed method speeds up calculations and also provides often better quality of results, comparing to genetic algorithms applied so far to the attribute reduction.

1 Introduction

Feature Selection in KDD and Pattern Recognition is an essential task [6]. Rough set-based methods can measure multi-attribute relationships. Hence, they are used to identify (ir)relevant features. Selection of features that (approximately) preserve so called indiscernibility of objects leads to classifiers based on reducts – most informative, irreducible subsets of attributes [11].

There can be many reducts in a data set. Finding short reducts is a major task while developing a good rough set-based classifier. It enables to overcome weakness of other approaches that ignore the effects of the feature subsets on performance of the induction algorithms. The problem of finding minimal reducts is NP-hard [11]. Some heuristic approaches were developed. An order-based genetic algorithm (o-GA) for finding minimal reducts [14] is proposed as a hybrid process. Genetic algorithm (GA) greedily selects features and rough set methods measure a degree of their relevancy within a given subset.

o-GA for finding short reducts works on a single processor. Its weakness is that it takes more time to find out sufficiently good reducts in a large search space. We use distributed evolutionary computing [2] to exploit availability of computer networks and massive power of parallel computing. In distributed environment, the total population is divided into sub-populations evolving in parallel, which increases performance of calculations. But it declines the overall average quality of minimal reducts and sometimes it can not avoid local optima. It turns out that the proposed island model implementation in a distributed environment, which exploit migration technique to exchange genetic material between populations, increases quality along with performance.

The paper is organized as follows: Section 2 introduces basics of the rough set theory. Section 3 introduces order-based genetic algorithm for reduct generation. Section 4 gives an idea of the island model of distributed computing. Section 5 summarizes results comparing to the single processor-based rough-genetic approaches. Section 6 gives conclusions and discusses future work.

2 Rough Sets

Rough sets were introduced by Zdzisław Pawlak in 1982. It has become a popular theory in the field of data mining, derived from fundamental research on logical properties of information systems – pairs $A = (U, A)$, where U is a non-empty finite set called the universe and A is a non-empty finite set of attributes, i.e. $a : U \to V_a$ for $a \in A$, where V_a is called the value set of a.

With any $B \subseteq A$, there is associated the equivalence relation $IND(B) = \{(x, x') \in U^2 \mid \forall a \in B, a(x) = a(x')\}$, called the B-indiscernibility relation. If $(x, x') \in IND(B)$ then objects x and x' are indiscernible from each other by attributes from B. Equivalence classes of $IND(B)$ are denoted by $[x]_B$.

A decision system takes the form of $A = (U, A \cup \{d\})$ where d is the decision attribute. Elements of U are called objects. For every value $v_k \in V_d$ we define the k-th decision class $X_k = \{u \in U : d(u) = v_k\}$. For every $X_k \subseteq U$ and attribute subset $B \subseteq A$, we can approximate X_k by the B-lower approximation $\underline{B}X_k$ and B-upper approximation $\overline{B}X_k$ using knowledge of B. $\underline{B}X_k$ is the set of objects that are surely in X_k, defined as $\underline{B}X_k = \{x \mid [x]_B \subseteq X_k\}$. $\overline{B}X_k$ is the set of objects that are possibly in X_k, defined as $\overline{B}X_k = \{x \mid [x]_B \cap X_k \neq \emptyset\}$.

The positive region of d with respect to condition attributes B is denoted by $POS_B(d) = \bigcup \underline{B}X_k$. It is a set of objects of U that can be classified with certainty employing attributes of B. A subset $R \subseteq B$ is said to be a reduct of B if $POS_R(d) = POS_B(d)$ and there is no $R' \subsetneq R$ such that $POS_{R'}(d) = POS_R(d)$. In other words, a reduct is the irreducible set of attributes preserving the positive region. There can be many such reducts in a decision system.

3 Order-Based Genetic Algorithm

Genetic algorithm (GA) is an adaptive heuristic search method for solving optimization problems. It was introduced by John Holland in 1970s. As an alternative technique, it outperforms most of traditional methods. Finding the minimal reducts is a NP-hard problem [11]. Hence, GA is a good candidate as a methodology for finding minimal reducts.

In classical GA, individuals are encoded as binary strings of the attributes (e.g. $0100110100 \equiv \{a_2, a_5, a_6, a_8\}$). Each individual represents a set of attributes generated by mutation, crossover and selection procedures using some fitness criteria. Individuals with maximal fitness are highly probable to be reducts but there is no full guarantee. A hybrid approach using order-based encoding of the attributes is proposed in [14] where each individual will produce a reduct.

Algorithm 1. Reduct Calculation from a chromosome

Input: chromosome $\tau \equiv (a_1, a_2, a_3, ..., a_n)$
Output: reduct
1: $R = \{a_1, ..., a_n\}$
2: **for** $i = 0$ to n **do**
3:    **if** $POS_{R-\{a_{n-i}\}}(d) = POS_R(d)$ **then**
4:       $R = R - \{a_{n-i}\}$
5:    **end if**
6: **end for**
7: **return** R

Here, an individual is an ordered list of features $(a_1, a_2, a_3, ..., a_n)$. Order is a permutation of the features generated by GA operators. A deterministic algorithm is used to calculate the reduct (denoted by R) from an individual. Crossover, mutation and selection are applied to generate the next generation population. For selection method, length (denoted by L_R) of R is used as fitness. Deterministic procedure keeps removing each feature from the list's end as long as the remaining features maintain the same positive region.

4 Parallel GA and Island Model

Parallel GA was first attempted by Grefenstette in [5]. Parallelism refers to many processors, with distributed operational load. Each GA is a good candidate for parallelization. Processor may independently work with different parts of a search space and evolve new generations in parallel. This helps to find out the optimum solution for the complex problems by searching massive populations and increases quality of the solutions by overcoming premature convergence. Many complex problems like: set partitioning problem [8], RNA folding pathways [10], multiprocessor scheduling problem [2] are treated with Parallel GA.

The above traditional parallel GA is called a sequential GA. Another type is called the Island Model (IM) [12], where processors are globally controlled by message passing within master-slave architecture. Master processor sends "START" signal to the slave processors to start generations and continue sending "MIGRATION" message to partially exchange the best chromosomes between the processors. Time between two consecutive "MIGRATION" signals is called the migration step; percentage of the best chromosomes is called migration percentage. The worst chromosomes are replaced by the received ones. Migrations should occur after a time period long enough for allowing development of good characteristics in each sub-population.

5 Experimental Results

We calculate reducts within Cygwin-based (a Linux-like environment in Windows) parallel processing framework, using modified libGA [3]. We tested:

Algorithm 2. Island Model (master pc)

Input: number of processors N
Output: reducts
1: **for** $i = 0$ to N **do**
2:    SendMessage(i,START)
3: **end for**
4: **while** short enough reducts not found **do**
5:    **for** $i = 0$ to N **do**
6:      SendMessage(i,NEXTGENERATION)
7:    **end for**
8:    CollectReducts()
9:    **if** current generation such that migration time reached **then**
10:      **for** $i = 0$ to N **do**
11:        SendMessage(i,MIGRATION)
12:      **end for**
13:    **end if**
14: **end while**

1. Order-based serial GA (OGA) using a single processor
2. Parallel island model (PIM) over 10 computers

Each computer was Pentium 997 MHz, 384 Mb of RAM, using Windows 2000. We considered four UCI data sets. Partially matched crossover (PMX) with the rate of 70% and swap mutation, rate 1%, were used. We took a pool size 300 for OGA. We split it among 10 processors (30 chromosomes for each) for PIM.

PIM was done by two methods: with and without migration. In PIM with migration (further denoted by PIM-Mg), two new parameters are added: ms (migration step) is the number of generations between migrations; mr (migration rate) is the percentage of individuals migrating to the neighbor processors. In our experiment, we used $ms = 5$ and $mr = 25\%$.

For OGA, evolution was continued until the chance of getting new reducts was too low. Then we tried to find the same number of minimal reducts (only reducts of minimal length L and $L + 1$) by PIM methods. The process was repeated 20 times, given random initial pool. Average results are presented below.

Table 1. Average time taken in three different methods for four data sets, with different number of objects (m) and attributes (n). The top plus signs in the three results for PIM indicate that the minimal reducts could not be found within 500 generations.

m	n	No. of Min. Reducts	OGA	PIM	PIM-Mg
70	18	142	49.75	53.45^+	12.06
103	19	166	77.6	19.40	8.70
307	36	529	4980	1803^+	1289
592	19	1434	11219	2460^+	1778

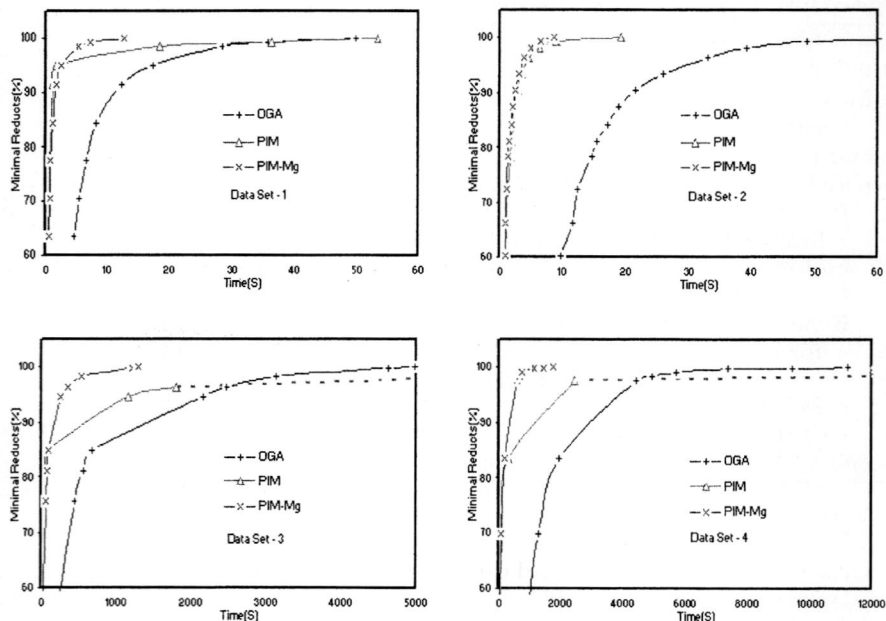

Fig. 1. The minimal reduct generation process for four different data sets, displayed in terms of "minimal reducts-time" graphs. The dotted lines in data sets 3 and 4 indicate that after some generations PIM without migration fell in local-optima. We considered the maximum time as the time needed for finding all the minimal reducts.

6 Conclusions

Results show that PIM takes less time in the initial stage because of not spending any time for migration and total population are distributed in 10 processors. But usually it got trapped in local optima because of its small population size. On the other hand, PIM-Mg outperforms all other methods in time and quality. Moreover, performance increased dramatically for larger data sets.

In conclusion, for feature selection/reduction problems with large search space, we can distribute the total population into islands (processors) to gain performance and apply migration to preserve quality.

In future, we will apply the island model strategy for finding high quality approximate and dynamic reducts. Especially the idea of dynamic reducts – subsets of features remaining reducts for different sub-samples of data [1] – fits the island model perfectly. Assigning different sub-samples to different islands, migrations may provide high stability of best found reducts. Also, we plan to check another possibilities of crossover operators, e.g. OX (order crossover).

Acknowledgments. The research reported in this article was supported in part by research grants from Natural Sciences and Engineering Research Council of

Canada awarded to the second author, as well as from Research Centre of PJIIT awarded to the third author.

References

1. Bazan, J., Skowron, A., Synak, P.: Dynamic reducts as a tool for extracting laws from decision tables. In: Proc the Symp. on Methodologies for Intelligent Systems, Charlotte, NC (1994) 16–19
2. Corcoran, A.L., Wainwright, R.L.: A parallel island modal genetic algorithm for the multiprocessor scheduling problem. In: Proc ACM/SIGAPP Symposium on Applied Computing (1994) 483–487
3. Corcoran, A.L., Wainwright, R.L.: LibGA: A user-friendly workbench for order-based genetic algorithm research. In: Proc ACM/SIGAPP Symposium on Applied Computing (1993) 111–118
4. Goldberg, D.E.: Genetic algorithms in search, optimisation and machine learning. Addison-Wesley, Reading MA (1989)
5. Grefenstette, J.J.: Parallel adaptive algorithms for function optimization. Technical Report CS-81-19, Computer Science Department, Vanderbilt University, Nashville, TN (1981)
6. Kittler, J.: Feature selection and extraction. In: Young and Fu (Eds.), Handbook of pattern recognition and image processing. Academic Press, New York (1986) 203–217
7. Knight, L., Wainwright, R.: HYPERGEN – A distributed genetic algorithm on a hypercube. In: Proc the Scalable High Performance Computing Conference. Williamsburg, Virginia (1992)
8. Levine, D.: A parallel genetic algorithm for the set partitioning problem. PhD thesis, Illinois Institute of Technology, Department of Computer Science (1994)
9. Pawlak, Z.: Rough sets – Theoretical aspects of reasoning about data. Kluwer Academic Publishers (1991)
10. Shapiro, B.A., Wu, J.C., Bengali, D., and Potts, M.J.: The massively parallel genetic algorithm for RNA folding: MIMD implementation and population variation. Bioinformatics 17 (2001) 137–148
11. Skowron, A., Rauszer, C.: The discernibility matrices and functions in information systems. In: Slowiński (Ed.): Intelligent Decision Support. Handbook of Applications and Advances of the Rough Sets Theory. Kluwer Academic Publishers, Dordrecht (1992) 331–362
12. Whitley, D.: A genetic algorithm tutorial. Technical report, Colorado State University (1993)
13. Wróblewski, J.: A parallel algorithm for knowledge discovery system, in: Proc PARELEC'98, Bialystok, Poland (1998) 228–230
14. Wróblewski, J.: Finding minimal reducts using genetic algorithms. In: Proc the Second Annual Joint Conference on Information Sciences. September 28 - October 1, Wrightsville Beach, NC (1995) 186–189
15. Wróblewski, J.: Theoretical foundations of order-based genetic algorithms. Fundamenta Informaticae 28(3-4) (1996) 423–430

On-Line Elimination of Non-relevant Parts of Complex Objects in Behavioral Pattern Identification

Jan G. Bazan[1] and Andrzej Skowron[2]

[1] Institute of Mathematics, University of Rzeszów,
Rejtana 16A, 35-959 Rzeszów, Poland
bazan@univ.rzeszow.pl
[2] Institute of Mathematics, Warsaw University,
Banacha 2, 02-097 Warsaw, Poland
skowron@mimuw.edu.pl

Abstract. We discuss some rough set tools for perception modelling that have been developed in our project for a system for modelling networks of classifiers for compound concepts. Such networks make it possible to recognize behavioral patterns of objects and their parts changing over time. We present a method that we call *a method for on-line elimination of non-relevant parts* (ENP). This method was developed for on-line elimination of complex object parts that are irrelevant for identifying a given behavioral pattern. Some results of experiments with data from the road simulator are included.

1 Introduction

Many real life problems can be modelled by systems of complex objects and their parts changing and interacting over time. The objects are usually linked by some dependencies, can cooperate between themselves and are able to perform flexible autonomous complex actions (operations). Such systems are identified as *complex dynamical systems* [2] or *autonomous multiagent systems* [9]. As an example of such a dynamical system one can consider *road traffic*. For experiments we have developed a road simulator, see [15] and [4] for more details.

The identification of behavioral patterns of complex dynamical systems can be very important for identification or prediction of global behavior of the investigated system, e.g., behavioral patterns can be used to identify some undesirable behaviors of complex objects (see [4] for more details).

Studying cognition, and in particular, perception based computing [1,7,8,6] [10,17] is becoming now one of the very active research directions for methods of complex concept approximation [3,4,11,12,14,18] and as a consequence for building intelligent systems.

We discuss an exemplary rough set [13] tool for perception modelling that was developed in our project for modelling networks of classifiers for compound concepts. Such networks make it possible to recognize behavioral patterns of complex objects and their parts changing over time. We use *behavioral graphs* (see Section 2) for representing *behavioral patterns* of complex objects. The behavioral pattern identification for a part of complex object is performed by testing properties of registered behavior of this part, often during a quite long period of time. However, in many applications, faster (often in real-time) testing if parts of complex objects are matching the given behavioral pattern is necessary. Hence, we have developed the ENP method for on-line elimination of non-relevant for a given behavioral pattern parts of complex object in a short observational period. In analysis of complex dynamical systems, we usually have to investigate very many parts of complex objects. Therefore, the fast verification of parts of complex objects can save time necessary for searching among parts matching the given behavioral pattern. In Section 3 we show that the testing of parts of complex objects can be speeded up by using some special decision rules. The presented ENP method makes it possible to achieve very fast elimination of many irrelevant parts of a given complex object in identification of a given behavioral pattern. To illustrate the method and to verify the effectiveness of classifiers based on behavioral patterns, we have performed several experiments with the data sets recorded in the road simulator [15]. We present results of our experiments in Section 4.

2 Behavioral Patterns

In many complex dynamic systems, one can distinguish some *elementary actions* (performed by complex objects), that can be expressed by a local change of object parameters, measured in a very short but a registerable period [4]. However, the perception of more complicated actions or behaviors requires analysis of elementary actions performed over a longer period. This longer period we often call as a *time window*. Therefore, if we want to predict more compound actions or discover a behavioral pattern we have to investigate all elementary actions, that have been performed by the investigated complex object in the current time window. Hence, one can, e.g., consider the frequency of elementary actions in a given time window and temporal dependencies between them. These properties can be expressed using *temporal patterns*. Any temporal pattern is a function defined by features parameters of an observed object over the time window [4]. We assume that any temporal pattern is defined by a human expert using domain knowledge accumulated for the given complex dynamic system.

The temporal patterns can be treated as new attributes (features) that can be used for approximation of more complex concepts. In this paper we call such concepts as *temporal concepts*. We assume that temporal concepts are specified by a human expert and are usually used in queries about the status of some objects in the given temporal window. The approximation of temporal concepts is defined by classifiers [4].

The temporal concepts defined over objects from some complex dynamical system and approximated by classifiers, are used as nodes of a graph, that we call as *a behavioral graph*. The branches in the behavioral graph represent temporal dependencies between nodes. The behavioral graph can be constructed for different kinds of objects appearing in the investigated complex dynamic system (e.g., for a single vehicle, for a group of vehicle, for a short vehicle like a small car, for long vehicle like a truck with a trailer) and it is usually defined for some kind of behavior of a complex object (e.g., driving on the strength road, driving through crossroads, overtaking, passing). For example, if one would like to investigate the overtaking maneuver, it is necessary to observe at least two vehicles: an overtaking vehicle and an overtaken vehicle.

In case of perception of a complex behavior (of parts or groups of objects), when we have to observe the behavior of dynamic systems over a long period of time, we can construct a behavioral graph for the investigated complex behavior. Next, using this graph, we can investigate a complex behavior of objects or a group of objects during some period. It is possible, by observing of transitions between nodes of behavioral graph and registering a sequence of nodes, that make some path of temporal patterns. If the path of temporal patterns (registered for an investigated object or group of objects) is matching a path in the behavioral graph, we conclude, that the behavior of this object or group is compatible with the behavioral graph. So, we can use the behavioral graph as a complex classifier for perception of the complex behavior of objects or groups of object. Therefore, the behavioral graph constructed for some complex behavior we call as *a behavioral pattern*.

3 Discovering Perception Rules for Fast Elimination of Behavioral Patterns

Let us assume, that we have a family of behavioral patterns $BP = \{b_1, ..., b_n\}$ defined for groups of objects (or parts of a given object). For any pattern b_i from the family BP one can construct a complex classifier based on a suitable behavioral graph (see Section 2) that makes it possible for us to answer the question: "Does the behavior of the investigated group (or the part of a complex object) match the pattern b_i?". The identification of behavioral patterns of any group is performed by investigation of a time window sequence registered for this group during some period (sometimes quite long). This registration of time windows is necessary if we want to avoid mistakes in identification of the investigated object group. However, in many applications, we are forced to make a faster (often in real-time) decision if some group of objects is matching the given behavioral pattern. In other words, we would like to check the investigated group of objects at once, that is, using the first or second temporal window of our observation only. This is very important from the computational complexity point of view, because if we investigate complex dynamic systems, we usually have to investigate very many groups of objects. Hence, the faster verification of groups can help us to optimize the process of searching among groups matching the given behavioral pattern.

The verification of complex objects consisting of some groups of objects can be speeded up by using some special decision rules. Such rules are making it possible to exclude very fast many parts (groups of objects) of a given complex object as irrelevant for identification of a given behavioral pattern. This is possible because these rules can be often applied at once, that is after only one temporal window of our observation.

Temporal patterns are constructed over temporal windows. At the beginning we define a family of temporal patterns $TP = \{t_1, ..., t_m\}$ that have influence on matching of investigated groups to behavioral patterns from family BP. These temporal patterns should be defined on the basis of information from temporal windows (for the verification of single object) or from information in behavioral graphs (for the verification of group of objects). Next, we construct classifiers for all defined temporal patterns (see [4] for more details).

For any temporal pattern t_i from the family TP we create a decision table DT_i that has only two attributes. Any object-row of the table DT_i is constructed on the basis of information registered during a period that is typical for the given temporal pattern t_i. The second attribute of the table DT_i (the decision attribute of this table) is computed using the classifier for t_i. The condition attribute registers the index of behavioral pattern from the family BP. This index can be obtained by using complex classifiers created for behavioral patterns from the family BP, because any complex classifier from the family BP can check for a single temporal window (and its time neighborhood) whether the investigated group of objects is matching the given behavioral pattern.

Next, we compute decision rules for DT_i using methods of attribute values grouping that have been developed in the RSES system [16]. Any computed decision rule expresses a dependency between a temporal pattern and the set of bahavioral patterns that are not matching this temporal pattern. Let us consider a very simple illustrative example. Assume we are interested in the recognition of overtaking that can be understand as a behavioral pattern, defined for the group of two vehicles. Using the methodology presented above, we can obtain the following decision rule: If the vehicle A is overtaking B then the vehicle B is driving on the right lane. After applying of the transposition low, we obtain the following rule: If the vehicle B is not driving on the right lane then the vehicle A is not overtaking B. The last rule allow us for fast verification whether the investigated group of objects (two vehicle: A and B) is matching the behavioral pattern of overtaking. Of course, in case of the considered complex dynamic system, there are many other rules that can help us in the fast verification of groups of objects related to the overtaking behavioral pattern. Besides, there

Table 1. Results of experiments for the overtaking pattern

Decision class	Method	Accuracy
YES	BP	0.923
(overtaking)	BP-E	0.883
NO	BP	0.993
(no overtaking)	BP-E	0.998
All classes	BP	0.989
(YES + NO)	BP-E	0.992

are many other behavioral patterns in this complex dynamic system and we have to calculate rules for them using the methodology presented above.

The ENP method is not a method for behavioral pattern recognition. However, this method allows us to eliminate some behavioral patterns that are not matched by a given group (or a part) of objects. After such elimination the complex classifiers based on a suitable behavioral graphs should be applied to the remaining parts of the complex object.

4 Experiments with Data

To verify the effectiveness of classifiers based on behavioral patterns, we have implemented our algorithms in the *Behavioral Patterns* programming library (BP-lib). This is an extension of the RSES-lib 2.2 programming library forming the computational kernel of the RSES system [16].

The experiments have been performed on the data sets obtained from the road simulator (see [15]). We have applied the "train and test" method for estimating accuracy. A training data set consists of 17553 objects generated by the road simulator during one thousand of simulation steps. Whereas, a testing data set consists of 17765 objects collected during another (completely different) session with the road simulator.

In our experiments, we compared the quality of two classifiers: BP and BP-E. The classifier BP is based on behavioral patterns (see Section 2) and the classifier BP-E is based on behavioral patterns too but with application of the ENP method (see Section 3). We compared BP and BP-E using accuracy of classification [3]. Table 1 shows the results of the considered classification algorithms for the concept related to the overtaking behavioral pattern.

One can see that in the case of perception of the overtaking maneuver (decision class YES) the accuracy of algorithm BP-E is 4% lower than the accuracy of the algorithm BP. However, the algorithm BP-E allows us to reduce the time of perception, because during perception we can usually identify the lack of overtaking much earlier than in the algorithm BP. This means that we do not need to collect and investigate the whole sequence of time windows (that is required in the BP method) but only an initial part of this sequence. In our experiments with the classifier BP-E it was only necessary to check on the average 47% of the whole window sequence for objects from the decision class NO (the lack of overtaking in the time window sequence).

5 Summary

We discussed some rough set tools for perception modelling. They make it possible to recognize behavioral patterns of objects and their parts changing over time. The presented approach is based on behavioral graphs and the ENP method. Note, that the ENP method is only one of the examples of perception methods that we have developed to speed up the identification of complex patterns (e.g., one can consider rules based on the hierarchical domain knowledge representation used for elimination of non-relevant parts of complex objects).

Acknowledgement. The authors gratefully acknowledge the suggestions made by Jim Peters concerning this paper. The research has been supported by the grant 3 T11C 002 26 from Ministry of Scientific Research and Information Technology of the Republic of Poland.

References

1. Anderson J.R. (1993). *Rules of the mind.* Lawrence Erlbaum, Hillsdale, NJ.
2. Bar-Yam Y. (1997). *Dynamics of Complex Systems.* Addison Wesley
3. Bazan J., Skowron A. (2005). Classifiers based on approximate reasoning schemes. In: Dunin-Keplicz B., Jankowski A., Skowron A., and Szczuka M. (Eds.), *Monitoring, Security, and Rescue Tasks in Multiagent Systems MSRAS*, Advances in Soft Computing, Springer, Heidelberg, 191–202.
4. Bazan J., Peters J.F., Skowron, A. (2005). Behavioral pattern identification through rough set modelling. Proceedings of the Tenth International Conference on Rough Sets, Fuzzy Sets, Data Mining, and Granular Computing (RSFDGrC 2005), August 31st - September 3rd, 2005, University of Regina, Canada (to appear).
5. Bazan J., Nguyen S. Hoa, Nguyen H. Son, Skowron A. (2004). Rough set methods in approximation of hierarchical concepts. *Proc. of RSCTC'2004*, LNAI **3066**, Springer, Heidelberg, 346–355
6. Kieras D., Meyer D.E. (1997). An overview of the EPIC architecture for cognition and performance with application to human-computer interaction. *Human-Computer Interaction* **12**: 391-438.
7. Langley P., Laird J.E. (2002). Cognitive architectures: Research issues and challenges. *Technical Report*, Institute for the Study of Learning and Expertise, Palo Alto, CA.
8. Laird J.E., Newell A., Rosenbloom P.S. (1987). Soar: An architecture for general intelligence. *Artificial Intelligence* **33**: 1-64.
9. Luck M., McBurney P., Preist Ch. (2003). *Agent Technology: Enabling Next Generation. A Roadmap for Agent Based Computing.* Agent Link.
10. Newell A. (1990). *Unified Theories of Cognition.* Cambridge, Harvard University Press, MA.
11. Nguyen S. Hoa, Bazan J., Skowron A., Nguyen H. Son (2004). Layered learning for concept synthesis. LNAI **3100**, *Transactions on Rough Sets* I: 187–208, Springer, Heidelberg,
12. Pal S.K., Polkowski L., Skowron A. (Eds.) (2004). *Rough-Neural Computing: Techniques for Computing with Words.* Cognitive Technologies, Springer, Heidelberg
13. Pawlak Z. (1991). *Rough Sets: Theoretical Aspects of Reasoning about Data.* Kluwer Academic Publishers, Dordrecht
14. Peters J.F. (2005). Rough ethology: Towards a biologically-inspired study of collective behavior in intelligent systems with approximation spaces. LNAI **3400**, *Transactions on Rough Sets* III: 153–174, Springer, Heidelberg
15. The Road simulator Homepage – logic.mimuw.edu.pl/~bazan/simulator
16. The RSES Homepage – logic.mimuw.edu.pl/~rses
17. Veloso M.M., Carbonell J.G. (1993). Derivational analogy in PRODIGY: Automating case acquisition, storage, and utilization. *Machine Learning* **10**: 249-278.
18. Zadeh L.A. (2001). A new direction in AI: Toward a computational theory of perceptions. *AI Magazine,* **22**(1): 73–84.

Rough Contraction Through Partial Meets

Mohua Banerjee and Pankaj Singh

Department of Mathematics and Statistics,
Indian Institute of Technology, Kanpur 208016, India
mohua,pankh@iitk.ac.in

Abstract. The paper addresses the problem of constructing rough belief change functions. Contraction and revision postulates using the notion of *rough consequence* and *rough consistency* have been proposed in [2]. The base logic is a reasoning framework $\mathcal{L}_\mathcal{R}$, that has a semantics of rough truth. We demonstrate here that functions satisfying the contraction postulates can be constructed through the method of *partial meets* [1]. As a result, a construction of rough revision functions is also obtained.

1 Introduction

Belief revision models the changes in beliefs of a person when some new information is provided or some earlier information has to be retracted. This kind of study helps in building intelligent agents, who have to manage information about the real world in order to achieve their goals. Beliefs may not represent complete or consistent information in all contexts, so one should be able to revise them when new correct or complete information is acquired. Thus a fundamental issue in belief revision is to decide upon the beliefs which should to be retracted in order to avoid contradiction.

The problem of belief change is well studied in the classical background, where any statement is either true or false – there are well-defined functions which model belief change. But clearly, there is need for appropriate methodology to deal with belief change in situations where information cannot be directly classified into a 'reject' or 'accept' category. Our idea is to be able to express through the base logic, vague/rough statements, and incorporate their properties in belief change. For instance, it is observed that a rough belief and its negation may not lead to a contradiction – motivating a relaxation in the definition of 'contradiction'. In this article, we further investigate an instance of *paraconsistent* belief change that is based on the logic $\mathcal{L}_\mathcal{R}$ of rough truth [2]. $\mathcal{L}_\mathcal{R}$ is, in fact, an alternative formulation of the well-known paraconsistent logic J due to Jaśkowski. It should be mentioned that one of the first studies in paraconsistent belief change is presented in [7], where a 4-valued base logic is used. Other work in the direction can be found in [6,9]. A comprehensive study on belief change in 3-valued and rough logics has been recently done in [8].

Postulates that rough belief change functions should satisfy, have been proposed in [2]. In this work, we show that rough contraction functions can be constructed through the method of *partial meets* [1]. Functions are defined using *maximal* subsets of belief sets that *do not* imply a belief A, and it is proved that they satisfy the rough contraction postulates with respect to A. The next section gives the requisite preliminaries. Section 3 presents the results on partial meet contraction in the rough context. Section 4 concludes the article.

2 Preliminaries

2.1 Partial Meet Contraction in Classical Belief Change

The base consequence relation $\vdash$ or operator Cn is assumed to be supraclassical (including classical consequence), and to satisfy cut, deduction theorem, monotonicity and compactness [4]. A set K of well-formed formulae (wffs) is a *belief set*, if $K = Cn(K)$. The three functions modelling belief change are *expansion*, *revision* and *contraction*. Incoming information may produce new beliefs (which may also lead to inconsistencies). Given a belief set K and a belief A, the expansion $K + A$ of K with respect to A is $Cn(K \cup \{A\})$. Sets of postulates [1,4] regulate revision and contraction functions to give belief sets $K * A$, $K - A$, revised and contracted with respect to a belief A respectively. The contraction and revision functions can be interrelated through the *Levi* and *Harper* identities.

One of the methods of constructing a contraction function is through *partial meets*. The central idea is that a reasonable $K - A$ must not contain A. One considers *maximal* subsets m of K not implying A. Formally, m is such that

(i) $m \subseteq K$,
(ii) $A \notin Cn(m)$, and
(iii) for any m' such that $m \subset m' \subseteq K$, $A \in Cn(m')$.

Let $K \perp A$ denote the collection of such sets m, and $M(K) = \bigcup_{A \in K} K \perp A$. Note that if $A \notin K$ then we take $K \perp A = \{K\}$, and if A is a theorem then $K \perp A = \emptyset$. A contraction $K - A$ is then the intersection of some 'preferred' elements of $K \perp A$. Let S denote the selection function for choosing these elements, i.e. $S(K \perp A) \subseteq K \perp A$. A contraction function can then be defined as:

$$K - A = \begin{cases} \bigcap S(K \perp A) \ if \ \nvdash A \\ K \ otherwise. \end{cases} \quad (1)$$

It turns out that the most appropriate S is the one picking the top elements in $K \perp A$, based on a reflexive and transitive preference relation $\geq$ over the maximal subsets in $K \perp A$, i.e.

$$S(K \perp A) = \{m \in K \perp A : m \geq m', \text{ for all } m' \in K \perp A\}. \quad (2)$$

2.2 $\mathcal{L}_\mathcal{R}$

The notion of rough truth was introduced in [5] to reflect 'inductive' truth, that, with gain of knowledge, leads to total, deductive truth.

The language of the system $\mathcal{L}_\mathcal{R}$ is that of a normal modal propositional logic. $\mathcal{L}_\mathcal{R}$ is, in fact, based on the modal system S_5. Let us notice that an S_5(Kripke) model $\mathcal{M} \equiv (X, R, \pi)$ is essentially an *approximation space* (X, R), where $X \neq \emptyset$, with the function π interpreting every wff of S_5 as a rough set in (X, R). If L, M denote the necessity and possibility connectives respectively, a modal wff $L\alpha(M\alpha)$, representing 'definitely' ('possibly') α, is interpreted by π as the lower (upper) approximation $\underline{\pi(\alpha)} \equiv \{x \in X : x' \in X, \text{ for all } x' \text{ such that } xRx'\}$ ($\overline{\pi(\alpha)} \equiv (\underline{\pi(\alpha)^c})^c$) of the set $\pi(\alpha)$.

A wff α is termed *roughly true* in $\mathcal{M}$, if $\overline{\pi(\alpha)} = X$. The notion of rough truth can be extended to *rough validity*. In the following, Γ is any set of wffs.

Definition 1. *An S_5-model $\mathcal{M} \equiv (X, R, \pi)$ is a* rough *model of Γ, if and only if every member γ of Γ is roughly true in $\mathcal{M}$, i.e. $\overline{\pi(\gamma)} = X$.*

Definition 2. *α is a rough semantic consequence of Γ (denoted $\Gamma \models \alpha$) if and only if every rough model of Γ is a rough model of α. If Γ is empty, α is said to be* roughly valid, *written $\models \alpha$.*

$\mathcal{L}_{\mathcal{R}}$ is defined through the *rough consequence* relation.

Definition 3. *α is a rough consequence of Γ (denoted $\Gamma \mid\sim \alpha$) if and only if there is a sequence $\alpha_1, ..., \alpha_n (\equiv \alpha)$ such that each $\alpha_i (i = 1, ..., n)$ is either (i) a theorem of S_5, or (ii) a member of Γ, or (iii) derived from some of $\alpha_1, ..., \alpha_{i-1}$ by R_1 or R_2 given below. If Γ is empty, α is said to be a rough theorem, written $\mid\sim \alpha$.*

$$R_1. \quad \frac{\alpha}{\beta} \quad \text{where } \vdash_{S_5} M\alpha \to M\beta \qquad R_2. \quad \frac{M\alpha \quad M\beta}{M\alpha \wedge M\beta}$$

$$DR1. \quad \frac{\alpha \quad \vdash_{S_5} \alpha \to \beta}{\beta} \qquad DR2. \quad \frac{(M\alpha)L\alpha \quad (M\alpha)L\alpha \to \beta}{\beta}$$

$$DR3. \quad \frac{M\alpha}{\alpha} \qquad DR4. \quad \frac{\alpha}{M\alpha}$$

$DR1 - 4$ are some derived rules of the system. The usual deduction theorem holds in $\mathcal{L}_{\mathcal{R}}$, though not its converse. $\mathcal{L}_{\mathcal{R}}$ is paraconsistent, i.e. there are α, β such that $\{\alpha, \neg\alpha\} \not\mid\sim \beta$. A set Γ is *roughly consistent*, if $M\Gamma = \{M\alpha : \alpha \in \Gamma\}$ is S_5-consistent: there is no $\alpha \in \mathcal{L}_{\mathcal{R}}$ such that $M\Gamma \vdash_{S_5} \alpha$ and $M\Gamma \vdash_{S_5} \neg\alpha$.

2.3 The Rough Belief Change Postulates

The changed belief set is denoted as $K *_r A$ ($K -_r A$) representing *rough revision (contraction)* of K with respect to A. The *expansion* $K +_r A$ of K by the wff A is the set $C_r(K \cup \{A\})$, where $C_r(K) = \{\alpha : K \mid\sim \alpha\}$. The *rough equality* connective $\approx$ [3] is used: $A \approx B \equiv (LA \leftrightarrow LB) \wedge (MA \leftrightarrow MB)$.

Postulates for Rough Revision

$K*1$ For any wff A and belief set K, $K *_r A$ is a belief set.
$K*2$ $A \in K *_r A$.
$K*3$ $K *_r A \subseteq K +_r A$.
$K*4$ If $\neg A \notin K$, then $K +_r A \subseteq K *_r A$.
$K*5$ If $K *_r A$ is not roughly consistent, then $\mathrel{|\!\sim} \neg A$.
$K*6$ If $\mathrel{|\!\sim} A \approx B$, then $K *_r A = K *_r B$.
$K*7$ $K *_r (MA \wedge MB) \subseteq K *_r A +_r B$.
$K*8$ If $\neg B \notin K *_r A$ then $K *_r A +_r B \subseteq K *_r (MA \wedge MB)$.

Postulates for Rough Contraction

K^-1 For any wff A and belief set K, $K -_r A$ is a belief set.
K^-2 $K -_r A \subseteq K$.
K^-3 If $A \notin K$, then $K -_r A = K$.
K^-4 If $A \in K -_r A$, then $\mathrel{|\!\sim} A$.
K^-5 $K \subseteq (K -_r A) +_r A$, if A is of the form LB or MB for some wff B.
K^-6 If $\mathrel{|\!\sim} A \approx B$, then $K -_r A = K -_r B$.
K^-7 $K -_r A \cap K -_r B \subseteq K -_r (MA \wedge MB)$.
K^-8 If $A \notin K -_r (MA \wedge MB)$ then $K -_r (MA \wedge MB) \subseteq K -_r A$.

Among other results, we can prove the following (partly done in [2]).

Theorem 1. *Let the Levi identity give $*_r$, i.e. $K *_r A \equiv (K -_r \neg A) +_r A$, where the contraction function $-_r$ satisfies $K^-1 - 8$. Then $*_r$ satisfies $K*1 - 8$.*

Observation 1. *Rough belief revision and contraction coincide with the corresponding classical notions if $\vdash_{S_5} A \leftrightarrow LA$ for every wff A, i.e. all beliefs are definable/describable (S_5 collapses into classical propositional logic).*

3 Partial Meet Contraction in Rough Belief Change

Similar to the classical case, we can construct partial meet contractions in the rough background. We refer to definitions (1), (2) of Section 2.1, modified to use C_r or $\mathrel{|\!\sim}$. The derived rules $DR1 - 4$ (cf. Section 2.2) are used in the proofs.

Lemma 1. *Let m be in $K \perp A$ for some A in K. Then (i) m is closed, and (ii) $C_r(m \cup \{\alpha\}) = K$ where $\alpha \in K \setminus m$.*

Proof. (i) Let $m \mathrel{|\!\sim} \alpha$ and assume $\alpha \notin m$. Now $m \mathrel{|\!\sim} \alpha$ implies $m \mathrel{|\!\sim} M\alpha$. So $M\alpha \in K$, as $m \subset K$ and K is closed. Hence $m \subset m \cup \{M\alpha\} \subseteq K$, which implies $m \cup \{M\alpha\} \mathrel{|\!\sim} A$ or $m \mathrel{|\!\sim} M\alpha \to A$. But then $m \mathrel{|\!\sim} A$, as $m \mathrel{|\!\sim} M\alpha$ and $M\alpha$ is modal – a contradiction. Hence $\alpha \in m$.
(ii) We already have $C_r(m \cup \{\alpha\}) \subseteq K$. $K \subseteq C_r(m \cup \{\alpha\})$: let $\beta \in K \setminus m$, and we show that $MA \to M\beta \in m$. Then any belief set containing MA and m (in particular $C_r(m \cup \{\alpha\})$) would have $M\beta$ and hence β. Suppose $MA \to M\beta \notin m$. Then $m \subset m \cup \{MA \to M\beta\} \subseteq K$ as $\vdash_{S_5} M\beta \to (MA \to M\beta)$ and $\beta(M\beta) \in K$. Thus $(MA \to M\beta) \to MA \in m$. But $\vdash_{S_5} ((MA \to M\beta) \to MA) \leftrightarrow MA$. So MA or $A \in m$, a contradiction. □

Importantly, Lemma 1(ii) says that all the beliefs in K outside m, behave identically with respect to m. Further, we have

Lemma 2. *Let $A \in K$ and $m \in K \bot A$. Then for all B in $K \setminus m$, $m \in K \bot B$.*

Using this result, we compare $K \bot (MA \wedge MB)$, $K \bot A$ and $K \bot B$. Note that $\{MA \wedge MB\} \hspace{0.2em}\mid\hspace{-0.5em}\sim\hspace{0.2em} A, B$, and $\{A, B\} \hspace{0.2em}\mid\hspace{-0.5em}\sim\hspace{0.2em} MA \wedge MB$. One can easily see that if $m \in K \bot (MA \wedge MB)$ then it is in $K \bot A$ or $K \bot B$ because $MA \wedge MB \notin m$ implies $A \notin m$ or $B \notin m$. What if m is in $K \bot A$? Conditions (i) and (ii) for membership in $K \bot MA \wedge MB$ are satisfied, and Lemma 2 implies (iii). Suppose $m \subset m' \subseteq K$. Then in addition to $A \in C_r(m')$, $C_r(m') = K$ also, implying that $B \in C_r(m')$ (as $B \in K$). Hence $MA \wedge MB$ is in $C_r(m')$.

Lemma 3. *Let A and B be in K. Then $K \bot (MA \wedge MB) = K \bot A \cup K \bot B$.*

As S is to select the 'best' elements of $K \bot A$, let us assume that it does so with the help of a reflexive and transitive *preference* relation $\geq$ over the maximal subsets in $K \bot A$. So S is defined through (2). The following then proves that such a selection works – definition (1) gives a rough contraction function.

Theorem 2. *Let $\geq$ be a reflexive and transitive relation on $M(K)$. Then the function defined through (1) with S as in (2) is a rough contraction function, i.e. it satisfies $K^- 1 - 8$.*

Proof. Let $A \hspace{0.2em}\mid\hspace{-0.5em}\sim\hspace{-0.5em}\mid\hspace{0.2em} B$ abbreviate $\{A\} \hspace{0.2em}\mid\hspace{-0.5em}\sim\hspace{0.2em} B$, $\{B\} \hspace{0.2em}\mid\hspace{-0.5em}\sim\hspace{0.2em} A$.

K^-1: Each maximal subset m in $S(K \bot A)$ is closed and intersection of closed sets is closed.

K^-2: Follows from the definition.

K^-3: If $A \notin K$ then $K \bot A = \{K\}$, and hence $K -_r A = K$.

K^-4: If $\not\hspace{0.2em}\mid\hspace{-0.5em}\sim\hspace{0.2em} A$ then $K \bot A$ is non-empty. Hence $A \notin K -_r A$.

K^-5: In fact, we obtain the classical recovery axiom (viz. $K \subseteq (K -_r A) +_r A$ for *any* A), and so, in particular, K^-5. Let $\alpha \in K$. Assume $\not\hspace{0.2em}\mid\hspace{-0.5em}\sim\hspace{0.2em} A$. We show that $(MA \to \alpha) \in K -_r A$. Using Lemma 1(ii), we get for all $m \in K \bot A$, $C_r(m \cup \{A\}) = K$, or $C_r(m \cup \{MA\}) = K$. Thus $MA \to \alpha \in m$, for all $\alpha \in K$, implying $MA \to \alpha \in K -_r A = \bigcap S(K \bot A)$. Hence $\alpha \in (K -_r A) + A$.

K^-6: Use, $\hspace{0.2em}\mid\hspace{-0.5em}\sim\hspace{0.2em} A \approx B$ implies $K \bot A = K \bot B$. In fact, $A \hspace{0.2em}\mid\hspace{-0.5em}\sim\hspace{-0.5em}\mid\hspace{0.2em} B$ gives the result.

K^-7: If $\hspace{0.2em}\mid\hspace{-0.5em}\sim\hspace{0.2em} A$ or $\hspace{0.2em}\mid\hspace{-0.5em}\sim\hspace{0.2em} B$ then obviously this holds: if $\hspace{0.2em}\mid\hspace{-0.5em}\sim\hspace{0.2em} A$ then $K -_r A = K$ and $K -_r B = K -_r (MA \wedge MB)$ (as $MA \wedge MB \hspace{0.2em}\mid\hspace{-0.5em}\sim\hspace{-0.5em}\mid\hspace{0.2em} B$). So let us assume $\not\hspace{0.2em}\mid\hspace{-0.5em}\sim\hspace{0.2em} A$ and $\not\hspace{0.2em}\mid\hspace{-0.5em}\sim\hspace{0.2em} B$. We have to show $(\bigcap S(K \bot A)) \cap (\bigcap S(K \bot B)) \subseteq \bigcap S(K \bot (MA \wedge MB))$. But $S(K \bot A \cup K \bot B) = S(K \bot A) \cap S(K \bot B) \subseteq S(K \bot A) \cup S(K \bot B)$. Hence $\bigcap (S(K \bot A \cup K \bot B)) \supseteq \bigcap (S(K \bot A) \cup S(K \bot B))$. Now $\bigcap (S(K \bot A) \cup S(K \bot B)) = (\bigcap S(K \bot A)) \cap (\bigcap S(K \bot B))$. By Lemma 3 we get $(\bigcap S(K \bot A)) \cap (\bigcap S(K \bot B)) = \bigcap (S(K \bot A) \cup S(K \bot B)) \subseteq \bigcap (S(K \bot A \cup K \bot B)) \bigcap S(K \bot MA \wedge MB)$.

K^-8: Let $A \notin K -_r (MA \wedge MB)$. Thus there exists an $m' \in K \bot (MA \wedge MB)$ such that $m' \geq m$, for all $m \in K \bot (MA \wedge MB)$ and $A \notin m'$. Note that $m' \in K \bot A$ as $A \notin m'$. Now we show $S(K \bot A) \subseteq S(K \bot (MA \wedge MB))$, whence $\bigcap S(K \bot (MA \wedge MB)) \subseteq \bigcap S(K \bot A)$. If $m'' \in S(K \bot A)$ then $m'' \geq m' \geq m$, for all $m \in K \bot MA \wedge MB$. By transitivity of $\geq$, $m'' \geq m$, for all $m \in K \bot (MA \wedge MB)$. Hence $m'' \in S(K \bot (MA \wedge MB))$, giving $S(K \bot A) \subseteq S(K \bot (MA \wedge MB))$. □

A rough revision function satisfying all the postulates K^*1-8 can thus be obtained through this method as well (using Theorems 2 and 1).

4 Conclusions

In rough belief change, the main consideration is to perform the change operations preserving rough consistency and rough truth. It is not surprising that the classical 'exact' notions are achieved as a special case, when a belief A can be identified with LA or MA. In this article, we show that the method of partial meets can be used to construct rough contraction and revision functions satisfying all the proposed rough postulates.

The next goal would be to study, in the rough context, the methods of Grove's spheres – focussing on *maximally consistent* sets of beliefs, and *epistemic entrenchment* – using an ordering on the beliefs. The latter, in particular, is expected to offer a more computationally tractable solution to the problem of constructing rough belief change functions.

References

1. Alchourrón, C.; Gärdenfors, P., Makinson, D.: On the logic of theory change: partial meet functions for contraction and revision. *J. Symb. Logic* **50** (1985) 510–530.
2. Banerjee, M.: Rough truth, consequence, consistency and belief revision. In: S. Tsumoto et al., editors, *LNAI 3066: Proc. 4th Int. Conf. On Rough Sets and Current Trends in Computing (RSCTC2004), Uppsala, Sweden, June 2004*, pages 95–102. Springer-Verlag, 2004.
3. Banerjee, M., Chakraborty, M.K.: Rough consequence and rough algebra. In: W.P. Ziarko, editor, *Rough Sets, Fuzzy Sets and Knowledge Discovery, Proc. Int. Workshop on Rough Sets and Knowledge Discovery (RSKD'93)*, pages 196–207. Springer-Verlag, 1994.
4. Gärdenfors, P., Rott, H.: Belief revision. In: D.M. Gabbay, C.J. Hogger and J.A. Robinson, editors, *Handbook of Logic in AI and Logic Programming, Vol.4: Epistemic and Temporal Reasoning*, pages 35–132. Clarendon, 1995.
5. Pawlak, Z.: Rough logic. *Bull. Polish Acad. Sc. (Tech. Sc.)* **35(5-6)** (1987) 253–258.
6. Priest, G.: Paraconsistent belief revision. *Theoria* **67** (2001) 214–228.
7. Restall, G., Slaney, J.: Realistic belief revision. In: *Proc. 1st World Congress in the Fundamentals of Artificial Intelligence, Paris, July 1995*, 367-378.
8. Singh, P.K.: *Belief Revision in Non-classical Logics*. Master's Thesis, Indian Institute of Technology, Kanpur, 2005.
9. Tanaka, K.: What does paraconsistency do ? The case of belief revision. In: *The Logical Yearbook 1997*, T. Childers, editor, Filosophia, Praha, 188–197.

Finding Interesting Rules Exploiting Rough Memberships

Lipika Dey[1], Amir Ahmad[2], and Sachin Kumar[1]

[1] Department of Mathematics, Indian Institute of Technology, Delhi,
Hauz Khas, New Delhi - 110 016, India
lipika@maths.iitd.ac.in

[2] Solid State Physics Laboratory, Timarpur, Delhi, India - 110 054
amir_ahmedsspl@ssplnet.org

Abstract. In this paper we propose a method to identify significant attributes which aid in good classification, as well as introduce certain degrees of roughness. Exception rules are formed with these attributes using the fact that exceptional elements have high rough memberships to more than one distinct class.

1 Introduction

Knowledge discovery refers to the generic task of discovering interesting, hidden, potentially useful patterns embedded in the data. Interestingness measure may be user or application dependent. In this work, we consider only rare or exceptional patterns as interesting. We propose a rough set-based method for mining rare and unexpected associations from a database in a guided fashion.

It is obvious that exceptions arise when the roughness of a set is high. An exceptional element has a high rough membership value to classes other than its defined class. Given a subset of attributes, it is easy to find the degree of roughness and this can be used to identify the exceptions. However, finding the ideal subset of attributes is a difficult task. We observe that though significant attributes which provide good classification are usually the ones which introduce low degrees of roughness, insignificant attributes do not provide correct classification knowledge. Thus our aim is to find rules based on significant attributes which also introduce roughness into a database. We propose methods to find two categories of exception rules. The first set identifies contradictions to usual classificatory knowledge. The second set of rules are compound in nature identifying combinations of appropriate features that lead to exception formation. This work is related to the classification scheme reported in [2]. The rest of the paper is organized as follows. In section 2 we provide a short overview of related work. Sections 3, 4 and 5 describe the proposed techniques for finding exceptions and interesting rules. We have explained the method through examples.

2 Rule Interestingness Measures – A Brief Survey

Interestingness measures proposed in literature are of two kinds - objective and subjective [5]. Among objective measures, Piatetsky-Shapiro's rule interestingness measure [8] quantifies the correlation between attributes in a simple classification rule. [11] proposed the J-measure which is the average information content of a probabilistic classification rule. Agrawal and Srikant's item set measures [1] identify frequently occurring associations in large databases. [3] proposes two objective rule-interestingness measures based on a one-attribute-at-a-time basis. In [10] interestingness is defined as the extent to which a soft belief is changed as a result of encountering new evidence i.e. discovered knowledge. In [14], a new interestingness measure, peculiarity, has been defined as the extent to which one data object differs from other similar data objects. [6] states how learned rules can be analyzed for interestingness using probabilistic measures. Objective measures do not take user perspective into account. [7] proposes a subjective approach for selecting interesting rules based on the notion of general impressions specified by users. [9] describes a genetic algorithm designed for discovering interesting fuzzy rules based on general impressions. The subjective approach assumes user is aware of common associations, while it may not be really so. [4] suggests use of objective interestingness measures to filter truly interesting rules and then use subjectiveness. Our approach is also intermediary.

3 Finding Significant Attributes

In [2] it has been shown that for a significant attribute with good classificatory power, there is a strong possibility that elements with complementary sets of values for this attribute, belong to complementary sets of classes. Alternatively, given that the class decisions for two sets of elements are different, the significant attribute values for these two sets of elements are usually different. These measures are computed as follows.

Let U be a collection of pre-classified elements belonging to m different classes, described by attributes $A_1, A_2, \cdots, A_g$. Let C represent any class from this set. Let J represent the set of attribute values that an attribute A_i can take. Let W denote a proper subset of J. We introduce $\alpha(A_i)$ to capture the cumulative effect of all possible values of A_i and their positive as well as negative associations to class decisions.

Definition 1. $\alpha(A_i)$ is called the discriminating power of A_i.

$$\alpha(A_i) = \Sigma_C(P_i^C(W') + P_i^{\sim C}(\sim W')),$$

where $W' \subset J$ such that $P_i^C(W') + P_i^{\sim C}(\sim W') > (P_i^C(W) + P_i^{\sim C}(\sim W)) \forall W \neq W'$
$P_i^C(W')$ = Probability that elements of U with class label C have their ith attribute value belonging to class W',
$P_i^{\sim C}(\sim W')$ = Probability that elements of classes other than C, do not have a value in W' as their ith attribute value.

W' is called the support set of C with respect to attribute A_i. Values in W' have maximal positive association to class C and maximal negative association to other classes. Both the probabilities can be computed from frequency counts. $\beta(A_i)$ is similarly computed as the cumulative effect of positive and negative class correlations to each value of attribute A_i. Details of these computations are available in [2].

Definition 2. *The significance of an attribute is denoted by $\sigma(A_i)$ and is the mean of $\alpha(A_i)$ and $\beta(A_i)$. A high value of $\sigma(A_i)$ denotes an attribute with more classificatory powers.*

Examples from heart database [15] are produced below to show how this measure can find contradictions. Elements of heart database are classified as non-heart patients and heart patients. A common user belief is *"Serum Cholesterol is High implies patient has heart disease."* However, using our method *serum cholesterol* is found to have $\alpha() = 0.132$ and $\beta() = 0.162$, which are low compared to the most significant attributes like *thal* or *number of major vessels colored by fluorosopy* (0-3). Hence, this is a contradiction. On verification with the database it is found that 38% of people with low cholesterol do have heart disease, and 46% of the people with high cholesterol actually are classified as non-heart patients. The support sets for non-heart and heart patients for *thal* are {3} and {6,7} respectively, and for the other attribute these are {0} and {1,2,3} respectively. These are used later to find interesting rules.

4 Finding Exceptions and Interesting Rules Using Support Sets and Rough Memberships

Significant attributes in a database can correctly classify elements of a class based on these attribute values only. However, exceptions to a class are elements which cannot be predicted correctly even by the significant attributes. Support set values have strong positive correlations to the class decision and negative correlation to the complement of the class. Elements of a class which do not have values for significant attributes in the support set can therefore be termed as exceptions. Exceptions can be found from a database using rough memberships of elements to various classes in conjunction with their support sets. Exception rules can thereafter be formed as specified by the following definitions.

Definition 3. *Let $S_A(C)$ define the support set of class C with respect to attribute A. $[S^C]_A$ is defined as the collection of all elements x whose values for attribute A lie in the support set of class C.*

Definition 4. *Given a subset of attributes A, rough membership of an element x to a class C is computed as $\mu_C^A(x) = \frac{|[S^C]_A \cap C|}{|[S^C]_A|}$.*

Definition 5. *Let A denote a set of significant attributes. An element x is said to be an exception to class C, if for a given set of significant attributes A, $\mu_{C'}^A(x) > \mu_C^A(x)$, for some class $C' \neq C$.
An exception rule is formed as $S_A(C) \implies C'$.*

We now present some sample exception rules extracted from the German credit card [15] and heart databases, using this approach. German credit card database has good and bad creditors. The most significant attribute identified is *Status of existing checking account* with values $A11 :< 0DM, A12 : 0 <= \cdots < 200DM, A13 : \ldots >= 200DM$ and $A14 :$ *no checking account*. $A13$ and $A14$ belong to the support set of good creditors. $A11$ and $A12$ lie in the support set of bad creditors. The second most significant attribute for the data set is *credit amount*, which being numeric, has been discretized to HIGH, LOW and VERY LOW. HIGH is in support set of bad creditor and the other two are in the support set of good creditor. With an expected minimum support of 2%, and confidence 10%, some interesting exception rules extracted from these two databases using this approach are shown in Table 1.

Table 1. Exception rules for German Credit card and Heart databases

Antecedent	Class	Support	Confidence
Status of existing checking account = A13 or A14 and Credit amount VERY LOW	bad creditor	4.8%	11%
Status of existing checking account = A11 or A12 and Credit amount = HIGH	good creditor	3.6%	41%
thal = 6 or 7 number of major blood vessels colored by fluoroscopy = 1, 2 or 3	not heart patient	2.2%	9%

5 Identifying Attribute Combinations That Cause Exceptions

While significant attributes help in classification, attributes which introduce roughness into a data set are the ones which cause exceptions. In this section we define *roughness coefficient* for each attribute. This along with the significance value enable us to formulate exception rules.

Definition 6. *Let* $s \in S_A(C)$. *Let* P *and* P' *denote the number of elements which have value* s *and belong to class* C *and* C' *respectively. Then,* $r_s(A) = \frac{|P'|}{|P|}$ *denotes the degree of roughness introduced by the value* s. *The* roughness coefficient *of the attribute* A *is computed as mean of* r_s *for all values* s *of* A *and is given by* $\rho(A) = 1/d * \Sigma_s(r_s(A))$, *where attribute* A *has* d *values.*

Following is a detailed scheme to find interesting rules from a pre-classified database, using roughness coefficient of significant attributes.

Step 1: Find the most significant attribute of database.
Step 2: Transform the given database by fusing the most significant attribute and the class decision to give new class decisions. Let A be the most significant

attribute of original data set, which has been fused with class column. If A had n distinct values and there were m distinct classes, then there will be mn new class decisions. Let $v \in S_A(C)$. Then vC and vC' are two new decision classes. Our aim is to find support set for vC' in the new database, since this identifies feature values that in combination with v changes the potential class of an element from C to C'. To do this we find the attributes with highest mean of significance and roughness coefficients with respect to the new fused decision.

Step 3: Find $\sigma(A_i)$ and the support sets for all remaining attributes A_i with respect to the new decision classes.

Step 4: Find roughness coefficients $\rho(A_i)$ for all attributes.

Step 5: Arrange attributes in decreasing order of mean value of $\sigma(A_i)$ and $\rho(A_i)$.

Step 6: Form compound exception rules with the new-found attributes and the most significant attributes of the original data set as follows:

$v \in S_A(C)$. Let s be a value of a top-ranking attribute A_i in fused data set, which belonged to the support set of class C' in original data set. If s belongs to support set of class vC' in fused data set, then an exception rule of the form $sv \implies C'$ is formed.

Step 7: Repeat steps 2-7 till no more rules satisfying user-given support can be extracted.

Table 2 cites some compound interesting exception rules identified for the German Credit card and heart databases using the above approach.

Table 2. Compound exception rules for German Credit card and Heart databases

Antecedent	Class	Support	Comment
Status of existing checking account = A13 or A14 and *Savings accountbond* < 100DM	bad creditor	3.6%	Low savings changes class from good to bad
Status of existing checking account = A11 or A12 and *Property* = real estate	good creditor	10.3%	Real estate changes class from bad to good
thal = 3 and *maximum heart rate* is LOW	heart patient	5.18%	Bad heart Rate causes heart disease
thal = 6 or 7 and *resting blood pressure* is LOW	not heart patient	7.4%	Low blood pressure changes class

6 Conclusion

Interestingness of a rule depends on the perspective of the user. In this paper, we have presented an approach which can help the user in finding contradictions to popular beliefs and also discover exceptions in data sets. The approach is based on rough memberships of elements to different classes and can yield surprising associations. The method has been shown to be useful in identifying interesting exceptions in financial and medical databases.

References

1. Agrawal, R., Srikant, R.,: Fast Algorithms for Mining Association Rules. In Proceedings of the 20th International Conference on Very Large databases, Santiago Chile (1994) 487-499.
2. Ahmad, A., and Dey, L.,: A Feature Selection Technique for Classificatory Analysis. Pattern Recognition Letters, Vol. 26, (2005) 43-56.
3. Freitas, A.A.,: On Objective Measures of Rule Surprisingness. In J.Zytkow and M.Quafou, editors, Proceedings of the Second European Conference on the Principles of Data Mining and Knowledge Discovery ,Nantes France (1998) 1-9.
4. Freitas, A.A.,: Data Mining and Knowledge Discovery with Evolutionary Algorithms. Springer-Verlag (2002), ISBN: 3-540-43331-7.
5. Hilderman, R., Hamilton, H.,: Knowledge Discovery and Interestingness Measures: A Survey. Technical Report CS 99-04, Department of Computer Science, University of Regina (1999).
6. Liu, B., and Hsu, W.,: Post-Analysis of Learned Rules. In Proceedings of the Thirteenth National Conference on Artificial Intelligence (1996) 828–834.
7. Liu, B., Hsu, W., Chen, S.,: Using General Impressions to Analyze Discovered Classification Rules, Proceedings of the Third International Conference on Knowledge Discovery and Data Mining (KDD-97, full paper), Newport Beach, California, USA (1997)pp. 31-36.
8. Piatetsky-Shapiro, G.,: Discovery Analysis and Presentation of Strong Rules. In Knowledge Discovery in Databases ,AAAI/MIT Press (1991) 229-248.
9. Romao, W., Freitas, A.A., Pacheco, P.C.S.Genetic. Algorithm for Discovering Interesting Fuzzy Prediction Rules: applications to science and technology data In WB Langdon and E Cantu-Paz et al, editors, Proceedings of Genetic and Evolutionary Computation Conference (GECCO-2002), San Francisco, CA, USA, (2002) 1188-1195.
10. Silberschatz, Avi., Tuzhilin, Alxender.,: What Makes Patterns Interesting in Knowledge Discovery Systems. IEEE Transactions on Knowledge and Data , Volume 8 (1996) 970-974.
11. Smyth, P., and Goodman, R.M.,: Rule Induction Using Information Theory. In Knowledge Discovery in Databases, AAAI/MIT Press (1991) 159-176.
12. Sahar, S.,: On Incorporating Subjective Interestingness Into the Mining Process. IEEE International Conference on Data Mining (2002).
13. Wang, K., Jiang, Y. and Lakshman, L.V.,S.,: Mining Unexpected Rules by Pushing User Dynamic. Conference on Knowledge Discovery in Data , Proceedings of the ninth ACM SIGKDD International Conference on Knowledge Discovery and Data Mining ,ACM Press New York USA (2003) 246-255.
14. Zhong, N., Yao, Y.Y., Oshuga S.,: Peculiarity-Oriented Multi-Database Mining. In J.Zytkow and J.Rauch (editors), Proceedings of the Third European Conference on the Principles of Data Mining and Knowledge Discovery, Czech republic (1999) 136-146.
15. www.liacc.up.pt/ML/statlog/dataset.html.

Probability Measures for Prediction in Multi-table Infomation Systems

R.S. Milton[1], V. Uma Maheswari[2], and Arul Siromoney[2]

[1] Department of Computer Science,
Madras Christian College, Chennai – 600 059, India
[2] Department of Computer Science and Engineering,
College of Engineering, Guindy,
Anna University, Chennai – 600 025, India
asiro@vsnl.com, umam@annauniv.edu

Abstract. Rough Set Theory is a mathematical tool to deal with vagueness and uncertainty. Rough Set Theory uses a single information table. Relational Learning is the learning from multiple relations or tables. This paper presents a new approach to the extension of Rough Set Theory to multiple relations or tables. The utility of this approach is shown in classification experiments in predictive toxicology.

1 Introduction

Rough set theory [Paw82, Paw91, KPPS99], introduced by Zdzislaw Pawlak in the early 1980s, is a mathematical tool to deal with vagueness and uncertainty. Rough set theory defines an indiscernibility relation that partitions the universe of examples into elementary sets. The indiscernibility relation is defined based on a single table. Relational Learning is based on multiple tables. A survey of research in Rough Sets and Relational Learning is presented in [MUS04]. *Statistical relational learning* (SRL) is a recent area of research, concerned with developing techniques to learn statistical models from relational data, and information is available at http://robotics.stanford.edu/srl/.

In this paper, a Multi–Table Information System (MTIS) is defined that extends the single information table of rough set theory to multiple information tables. The formalism used in this paper is based on tables and rows, rather than on universes and elements. Notions from the Variable Precision Rough Set model are introduced along with the notion of significant elementary sets (elementary sets in the β–positive or β–negative regions that also have a sufficiently large number of examples). This is used for prediction. An illustrative experiment in toxicology is then presented.

Another formalism for MTIS based on universes and elements is presented in [MUS05]. The universes correspond to the tables and the elements of the universes correspond to the rows of the tables. That formalism is applied in that paper to two special cases of MTIS. Whereas the formalism used in this paper is applicable to a general MTIS. The decision class of an unknown example is computed using the probability measures of the significant elementary sets in the individual tables. However, this formalism needs further study into the relationship between the probability measures of the overall system and those of the individual tables. A formal study based on probabilistic measures and distributed tables is found in [Ś05].

2 Multi-table Information System

2.1 Definitions

A table T is a set of *rows* $\{x_1, \ldots, x_m\}$ and is denoted as $T = (I, A, V, \rho)$, where I is a finite set of *row indices* (or row identifiers), with each row index $p, 1 \leq p \leq m$, corresponding to a particular row x_p of the table; A is a finite set of *attributes*; $V = \bigcup_{a \in A} V_a$ is the set of *attribute values* of all attributes, where V_a is the *domain* of attribute a; and $\rho : I \times A \to V$ is an *information function* such that for every row index $p \in I$, $\rho(p, a) \in V_a$ is the value of attribute a in the row x_p corresponding to the row index p. In other words, a row $x_p \in T = (I, A, V, \rho)$, $p \in I$, has the value $\rho(p, a) \in V_a$ for every $a \in A$. This definition is based on the definition of Rough Set Information System in [Paw82].

We define a *Multi-Table Information System (MTIS)* as a finite set of tables denoted as $T = \{T_0, T_1, \ldots, T_n\}$, where $T_0 = \{I_0, A_0, V_0, \rho_0\}$ is a decision table with two attributes in A_0, one of which is the *example identifier* which has a unique value for every row, and the other is a binary valued *decision attribute*. A similar definition is also found in [Wro00]. Here, each row of table T_0 corresponds to an example from the universe of examples as in the Rough Set Information System [Paw82].

An example MTIS follows. Let $T = \{T_0, T_1, T_2, T_3\}$. The values of I_i, A_i, V_i, ρ_i, $i = 0, 1, 2, 3$ can be easily seen from the figures of the tables given below.

Table T_0

drug	decision
d1	true
d10	true
d102	true
d110	false
d114	false

Table T_1

drug	atom	element	type	charge
d1	a1_1	h	1	p
d102	a102_1	h	2	p
d1	a1_2	o	1	n
d12	a12_1	o	2	n
d10	a10_1	c	1	p
d10	a10_2	c	2	p

Table T_3

drug	property	val
d12	salmonella	p
d205	chromaberr	n
d108	cytogen_sce	n
d1	cytogen_ca	p
d101	cytogen_ca	n

Table T_2

drug	atom1	atom2	bond-type
d12	d12_1	d12_2	7
d12	d12_1	d12_7	1
d1	d1_14	d1_22	2
d1	d1_17	d1_24	1
d101	d101_8	d101_9	2

2.2 Link Relation

Let $T_i, T_j \in T$ ($i \neq j$) be two tables in a MTIS T. T_i is said to be linked to T_j if there exists a set of common attributes $K_{ij} \subseteq (A_i \cap A_j) \neq \emptyset$, known as *link attributes*, between them. Let $x_{i,p}$ be the row in table T_i with row index $p \in I_i$, and $x_{j,q}$ be the row in table T_j with row index $q \in I_j$. We say that $x_{i,p}$ is *linked* to $x_{j,q}$ through the link attributes K_{ij} if $\rho_i(p,b) = \rho_j(q,b)$ for every $b \in K_{ij}$.

Formally, a binary relation $L(K_{ij})(K_{ij} \neq \emptyset)$, called *link relation*, is defined between two tables T_i and T_j as

$$L(K_{ij}) = \{(x_{i,p}, x_{j,q}) \in T_i \times T_j \mid \forall b \in K_{ij}. \rho_i(p,b) = \rho_j(q,b), \text{ where } p \in I_i, q \in I_j\}$$

A row $x_{i,p}$ in table T_i is linked to row $x_{j,q}$ in table T_j if $(x_{i,p}, x_{j,q}) \in L(K_{ij})$.

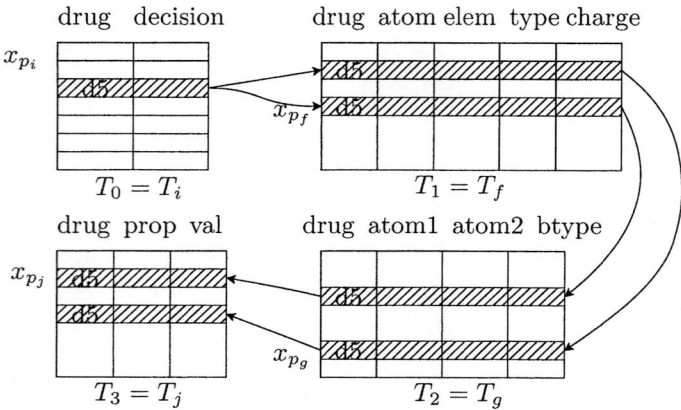

In general, a row x_{i,p_i} in table T_i is linked to another row x_{j,p_j} in table T_j iff there exist tables $T_f, T_g, \ldots, T_h \in T$, with rows such that $(x_{i,p_i}, x_{f,p_f}) \in L(K_{if})$, $(x_{f,p_f}, x_{g,p_g}) \in L(K_{fg})$, ..., $(x_{h,p_h}, x_{j,p_j}) \in L(K_{hj})$. We say that row x_{i,p_i} is *linked through* the rows $x_{f,p_f}, x_{g,p_g}, \ldots, x_{h,p_h}$ to row x_{j,p_j}, and the set of rows

$$C(p_i) = \{x_{f,p_f}, x_{g,p_g}, \ldots, x_{h,p_h}, x_{j,p_j}\}$$

is said to form of a *combination* of rows associated with x_{i,p_i}. We note that a row x_{i,p_i} in table T_i could have a number of such combinations of rows.

In this paper, we restrict K_{ij} to a singleton set, and consider only a single link attribute between any pair of tables. In the illustration, table T_0 is linked to tables T_1, T_2 and T_3 through the link attribute **drug**.

2.3 Elementary Sets

Let B_i be a subset of attributes in a table $T_i = (I_i, A_i, V_i, \rho_i)$, $B_i \subseteq A_i$, such that no attribute in B_i is either a link attribute or a primary key. A binary relation $R(B_i)$, called *indiscernibility relation*, is defined on a table T_i as

$$R(B_i) = \{(x_{i,p}, x_{i,q}) \in T_i \times T_i \mid \forall b \in B_i, \rho_i(p,b) = \rho_i(q,b), \text{ where } p,q \in I_i\}$$

We say that two rows $x_{i,p}$ and $x_{i,q}$ of table T_i are indiscernible and belong to the same elementary set iff $\rho_i(p,b) = \rho_i(q,b)$ for $p,q \in I_i$ and every $b \in B_i$.

The elementary set of table T_i, with respect to the indiscernibility relation $R(B_i)$, containing the row $x_{i,p}$ is

$$[x_{i,p}]_{R(B_i)} = \{x_{i,q} \in T_i \mid \forall b \in B_i, \rho(p,b) = \rho(q,b), \text{ where } p,q \in I_i\}$$

$[x_{i,p}]_{R(B_i)}$ is denoted as $[x_{i,p}]$ when B_i is known from the context. Even though each table is partitioned into elementary sets based on the attributes in B_i, yet it continues to have all the original entries.

2.4 Conditional Probabilities of Elementary Set

Each row in table $T_i \in T$, $i \neq 0$, is linked to one row in the decision table T_0. Hence, each row $x_{i,p}$ in an elementary set $[x_{i,p}]$ can be considered to be associated with a decision class. For a boolean decision class, let $[x_{i,p}]^+([x_{i,p}]^-)$ be the subset of the elementary set $[x_{i,p}]$ containing rows associated with the positive (negative) decision class.

The conditional probability that a row in the elementary set $[x_{i,p}]$ is positive is

$$P(+|[x_{i,p}]) = \frac{|[x_{i,p}]^+|}{|[x_{i,p}]|}$$

and $P(-|[x_{i,p}])$ is similarly defined.

2.5 Prediction

We now consider the prediction of the decision class of a test case. We assume that the test case has a row in the decision table T_0, but does not yet have a value for the decision attribute. The associated data for this test case is introduced as rows in the other tables.

A *combination* of rows $C(p) = \{x_{1,q}, \ldots, x_{n,t}\}$ linked to a test case $x_{0,p}$, has one row from each of the tables with rows linked to $x_{0,p}$. Every row in the combination is linked to the test case either directly or through other rows in the combination.

Each row $x_{i,p}$ in a combination falls in an elementary set of table T_i with the associated conditional probabilities $P(+|[x_{i,p}])$ and $P(-|[x_{i,p}])$. Hence, a row can be considered to have the conditional probabilities $P(+|[x_{i,p}])$ and $P(-|[x_{i,p}])$. We have also noted that a test case could have a number of combinations of rows.

Simple Approach: A simple approach that can be used for prediction follows. For every combination of rows corresponding to the test case with index p_0 of the decision table T_0, the product of positive conditional probabilities of rows is defined as

$$posprod = \prod_{x \in C_k(p_0)} P(+|[x])$$

Similarly, the product of negative conditional probabilities *negprod* is defined. If the sum of the *posprod*s of all the combinations is greater than the sum of *negprod*s of all the combinations, then the test case is predicted as positive; otherwise, it is predicted as negative. The posprod is the measure of the positive trend shown by the values of the attributes in each table. The summation of the posprod addresses the situation where a particular test case may be related to multiple rows in a table.

Significant Elementary Sets Approach: Many of the elementary sets are too small to be considered as representative of either positive or negative trend. We consider an elementary set to be a *significant elementary set*, if it has sufficiently large number of examples, and its $P(+|[x_{i,p}]) \geq \beta_u$ or $P(-|[x_{i,p}]) \leq \beta_l$, where $\beta_u \geq 0.5$ and $\beta_l \leq 0.5$. When $\beta_u = 1 - \beta_l$, we denote it as β, and note that $\beta_l = 1 - \beta$. An elementary set $[x_{i,p}]$ is said to be significant if and only if

$$|[x_{i,p}]| \geq \alpha \wedge ((P(+|[x_{i,p}]) \geq \beta_u \vee P(-|[x_{i,p}]) \leq \beta_l))$$

where α is a user-defined parameter.

If only k rows in the combination of rows fall in significant elementary sets, then we define the *Positive Conditional Probability* of the combination of rows as

$$\mathcal{P}_+ = \sqrt[k]{\prod P(+|[x_{i,p}])}$$

where $P(+|[x_{i,p}])$s are of significant elementary sets. Similarly, *Negative Conditional Probability* $\mathcal{P}_-$ is defined.

A combination of rows predicts the test case as positive if $\mathcal{P}_+ \geq \mathcal{P}_-$ and as negative otherwise. If the number of combinations predicting the test case as positive is greater than the number of combinations predicting it as negative, the final prediction of the test case is positive; otherwise, it is negative.

3 Application to Predictive Toxicology

The dataset used is the Predictive Toxicology Evaluation Challenge dataset found at http://web.comlab.ox.ac.uk/oucl/research/areas/machlearn/cancer.html. The database of compounds have been classified as carcinogens or otherwise. The challenge is to predict the carcinogenicity of previously untested chemicals. The dataset is in the form of the Multi–Table Information System described in Section 2.1.

An illustrative experiment is performed using this dataset, and the results of the ten-fold cross-validation and the summary of the results are presented in the the following tables. The results of one of the folds are not available due to an error in the experiment.

The average prediction accuracy using the simple approach is 60%, and that using the significant elementary sets approach is 59.6%. It is to be noted that there is no improvement in the prediction accuracy. However, the space requirement for the significant elementary sets approach is much less when compared to the simple approach. This is a difficult dataset and progol achieves only 64% even with the use of more background knowledge.

Simple approach				Significant elementary set approach			
Positive	Negative		Accuracy	Positive	Negative		Accuracy
+	−	+	−	+	−	+	−	
13	5	9	6	0.58	14	4	11	4	0.55
16	2	8	7	0.70	17	1	9	6	0.70
14	4	10	5	0.58	15	3	11	4	0.58
14	4	13	2	0.48	15	3	10	5	0.61
14	4	12	3	0.52	13	5	11	4	0.52
15	3	6	9	0.73	14	4	6	9	0.70
11	7	8	7	0.55	11	7	9	6	0.52
18	0	13	2	0.61	17	1	15	0	0.52
15	5	5	8	0.70	15	5	5	8	0.70

Simple approach			
	Actual +	Actual −	
Predicted +	130	84	214
Predicted −	34	49	83
	164	133	297

Significant elementary set approach			
	Actual +	Actual −	
Predicted +	131	87	218
Predicted −	33	46	79
	164	133	297

4 Conclusions

This paper presents an approach to learning from a Multi–Table Information System. The results of an illustrative example in toxicology are presented.

References

[KPPS99] J. Komorowski, Z. Pawlak, L. Polkowski, and A. Skowron. Rough sets: A tutorial. In S. K. Pal and A. Skowron, editors, *Rough Fuzzy Hybridization: A New Trend in Decision-Making*, pages 3–98. Springer-Verlag, 1999.

[MUS04] R. S. Milton, V. Uma Maheswari, and Arul Siromoney. Rough Sets and Relational Learning. *LNCS Transactions on Rough Sets*, Inaugural Volume, 2004.

[MUS05] R. S. Milton, V. Uma Maheswari, and Arul Siromoney. Studies on Rough Sets in multiple tables. In Dominik Ślęzak, Guoyin Wang, Marcin Szczuka, Ivo Duentsch, and Yiyu Yao, editors, *The Tenth International Conference on Rough Sets, Fuzzy Sets, Data Mining, and Granular Computing (RSFD-GrC 2005)*, pages 263–272. Springer-Verlag, 2005. LNAI 3641 (Accepted for publication).

[Paw82] Z. Pawlak. Rough sets. *International Journal of Computer and Information Sciences*, 11(5):341–356, 1982.

[Paw91] Z. Pawlak. *Rough Sets — Theoretical Aspects of Reasoning about Data*. Kluwer Academic Publishers, Dordrecht, The Netherlands, 1991.

[Ś05] D. Ślęzak. Rough Sets and Bayes Factor. *Transactions on Rough Sets*, III (LNCS 3400):202–229, 2005.

[Wro00] J. Wroblewski. Analyzing relational databases using rough set based methods. In *Proceedings of IPMU 2000*, volume 1, pages 256–262, 2000.

Object Extraction in Gray-Scale Images by Optimizing Roughness Measure of a Fuzzy Set

D.V. Janardhan Rao, Mohua Banerjee, and Pabitra Mitra

Indian Institute of Technology Kanpur,
Kanpur 208016, India
{dvjrao, pmitra, mohua}@iitk.ac.in

Abstract. Object extraction from gray-tone images involve handling of inherent uncertainties in an image. Traditionally fuzzy set theoretic techniques are used for this purpose. However, roughness and limited discernibility of objects is another important aspect of image uncertainty. In this article we propose an algorithm for selection of intensity threshold for object extraction by optimizing a roughness measure of the fuzzy set corresponding to the image object. The rough-fuzzy algorithm is tested on some benchmark images.

1 Introduction

The theory of Rough sets [1] has emerged as a major mathematical approach for managing uncertainty that arises from inexact, noisy, or incomplete information. The focus of rough set theory is on the ambiguity caused by limited discernibility of objects in the domain of discourse. The idea is to approximate any concept (a crisp subset of the domain) by a pair of exact sets, called the lower and upper approximations. On the other hand, fuzzy set theory hinges on the notion of a membership function on the domain of discourse, assigning to each object a grade of belongingness in order to represent an imprecise property. In practice, uncertainties of both the above type appear in nature, and it is apt to characterize both of them. Toward this goal several roughness measures of fuzzy sets (and vice versa) has been defined in literature [2,3]. The objective being to obtain more flexible representation of imprecise objects.

Object extraction refers to the task of segmenting the target image from its background. It is useful in a number of image processing and computer vision tasks. Images are inherently gray and of imprecise nature and can be modeled as a fuzzy set. The main challenge in object extraction from gray-tone images is that of handling uncertainties owing to grayness of the object boundaries. In literature several fuzzy set theoretic techniques has been proposed for this purpose. A review of these approaches is provided in [4]. Some of the poupular ones are based on the principle of minimizing fuzzy entropy [5]. It may be noted that probabilistic Shannon entropy can also be used for object extraction from gray-scale images [6].

Human vision system perceives objects only up to a limited (often variable and multiscale) spatial (and intensity) resolution or discernibility. It is expected that rough set representation of image objects in terms its lower and upper approximation would be beneficial in handling the image uncertainties in the border region of object and background. In this article we model an image as a rough-fuzzy set and use a 'roughness of a fuzzy set' measure to determine the gray-level threshold for segmenting an gray-tone object from its background.

The proposed approach for object extraction in gray-tone images comprises of the following steps. First we calculate the histogram of an image X and define a fuzzy object region over the image space with membership plane $A = \mu_X$ using a one-dimensional π-function with constant bandwidth. We control the thresholds α and β (which gives the lower and upper approximation of the fuzzy object region respectively) to minimize the roughness measure of the fuzzy object region. The threshold value is selected based on β for which roughness is minimum.

2 Rough Sets and Rough-Fuzzy Sets

We first define some basic concepts of rough set theory necessary for explanation of the object extraction algorithm. Let the domain U of discourse (also called universe) be a non-empty finite set, and R an equivalence relation on U. The pair $<U, R>$ is called an approximation space [1]. Let $X_1, \ldots, X_n$ denote the equivalence classes in U due to R, i.e., $\{X_1, \ldots, X_n\}$ forms a partition of U. If $A \subseteq U$, the lower approximation $\underline{A}$ and upper approximation $\overline{A}$ of A in the approximation space $<U, R>$ are respectively given as follows [1]:

$\underline{A} = \cup\{X_i / X_i \subseteq A\}$ and $\overline{A} = \cup\{X_i / X_i \cap A \neq \phi\}$, where $i \in \{1, \ldots, n\}$

$\underline{A}$ ($\overline{A}$) is interpreted as the collection of those objects of the domain U that definitely (possibly) belong to A. The pair $<\underline{A}, \overline{A}>$ may be called the rough approximation of the set A or simply rough set.

Roughness of a set A in the approximation space $<U, R>$ is reflected by the ratio of the number of objects in its lower approximation to that in its upper approximation - the greater the value of the ratio, the lower the roughness. More explicitly, a measure ρ_A of roughness of A in $<U, R>$ is defined thus [1]:

$$\rho_A = 1 - \frac{|\underline{A}|}{|\overline{A}|}, \qquad (1)$$

where $|X|$ denotes the cardinality of a set X.

We next come to the definitions of a rough fuzzy set and allied notions [3], roughness measure of a fuzzy set [2], that shall form the basis of this work. Let $A : U \to [0, 1]$ be a fuzzy set in U, $A(x)$, $x \in U$, giving the degree of membership of x in A.

Definition 2.1: The lower and upper approximations of the fuzzy set A in U, denoted $\underline{A}$ and $\overline{A}$, respectively, are defined as fuzzy sets in $U/R (= \{X_1, \ldots, X_n\})$, i.e., $\underline{A}, \overline{A} : U/R \to [0, 1]$, such that $\underline{A}(X_i) = Min_{x \in X_i} A(x)$ and $\overline{A}(X_i) = Max_{x \in X_i} A(x)$, where $i = 1, \ldots, n$ $<\underline{A}, \overline{A}>$ is called a rough fuzzy set.

Definition 2.2: Fuzzy sets $\underline{F}$ and $\overline{F}: U \to [0,1]$ are defined as follows:
$\underline{F}(x) = \underline{A}(X_i)$ and $\overline{F}(x) = \overline{A}(X_i)$ if $x \in X_i$, $i \in \{1, \ldots, n\}$,

$\underline{F}$ and $\overline{F}$ are fuzzy sets with constant membership on the equivalence classes of U. For any x in U, $\underline{F}(x)$ ($\overline{F}(x)$) can be viewed as the degree to which x definitely (possibly) belongs to the fuzzy set A.

3 Roughness Measure of a Fuzzy Set

In this section, we define the roughness measure of a fuzzy set [2] and state some properties and observations on this measure which are used in the present work. Let α, β be two parameters, where $0 < \beta \leq \alpha \leq 1$. Consider the α-cut $\underline{F}_\alpha$, β-cut $\overline{F}_\beta$ of the fuzzy sets $\underline{F}, \overline{F}$ respectively. $\underline{F}_\alpha = \{x/\underline{F}(x) \geq \alpha\}$ and $\overline{F}_\beta = \{x/\overline{F}(x) \geq \beta\}$.

It can then be said that $\underline{F}_\alpha$ ($\overline{F}_\beta$) is the collection of objects in U with $\alpha(\beta)$ as the minimum degree of definite (possible) membership in the fuzzy set A. In other-words, α, β act as thresholds of definiteness and possibility, respectively, in membership of the objects of U to A. $\underline{F}_\alpha, \overline{F}_\beta$ are called α-lower approximation and β-upper approximation of the fuzzy set A in $<U, R>$. $\underline{F}_\alpha = \cup\{X_i/X_i \in \underline{A}_\alpha\}$ and $\underline{F}_\beta = \cup\{X_i/X_i \in \overline{A}_\beta\}$, where $i = \{1, \ldots, n\}$ and $\underline{F}_\alpha, \overline{F}_\beta$ are the α- and β-cuts, respectively of the fuzzy sets $\underline{A}$ and $\overline{A}$ (cf. Definition 2.1). So, alternatively, $\underline{F}_\alpha$ ($\overline{F}_\beta$) can be looked upon as the union of those equivalence classes of U that have degree of membership in the lower (upper) approximation $\underline{A}$ ($\overline{A}$) of A at least α (β). Since $\alpha \geq \beta$, $\underline{F}_\alpha \subseteq \overline{F}_\beta$.

Definition 3.1: The roughness measure $\rho_A^{\alpha,\beta}$ of the fuzzy sets A in U with respect to parameters α, β where $0 < \beta \leq \alpha \leq 1$, and the approximation space $<U, R>$ is defined as:

$$\rho_A^{\alpha,\beta} = 1 - \frac{|\underline{F}_\alpha|}{|\overline{F}_\beta|} \qquad (2)$$

Lemma 3.1: (a) If β is kept fixed and α increased $|\underline{F}_\alpha|$ decreases and $\rho_A^{\alpha,\beta}$ increases.
(b) If α is kept fixed and β increased, $|\overline{F}_\beta|$ decreases and $\rho_A^{\alpha,\beta}$ decreases.
(c) If $A \subseteq B$ and $\overline{F}_\beta^A = \overline{F}_\beta^B$, then $\rho_B^{\alpha,\beta} \leq \rho_A^{\alpha,\beta}$.
(d) If $A \subseteq B$ and $\overline{F}_\alpha^A = \overline{F}_\alpha^B$, then $\rho_A^{\alpha,\beta} \leq \rho_B^{\alpha,\beta}$. These follow from the properties of rough and fuzzy sets.

4 Application to Object Extraction in Gray-Scale Images

The roughness measure ρ has many applications in pattern recognition and image analysis problems. Let X denote a gray-tone image or feature space, and $X_1, \ldots, X_n$ represent n regions. The fuzzy set A can be viewed to represent the ill-defined pattern classes or some imprecise image property such as brightness, darkness, edginess, smoothness etc. Relative to thresholds α, β roughness of such an imprecise property A can then be measured in terms of the ratio of number of feature points definitely satisfying A to the number of feature points possibly satisfying A. The concept of splitting $X_1, \ldots, X_n$ is analogous to increasing the resolution of a digital image, and can well be utilized for sub-pixel classification problems and for detecting the boundaries of regions precisely.

The algorithm for object extraction in gray-tone images using the roughness measure ρ is described below.

Algorithm
Step 1: Compute the histogram of the gray-tone image X and define a fuzzy object region over the image space with membership plane $A = \mu_X$. The one-dimensional π-function, with range [0,1], and constant bandwidth may be used as a membership function. It is represented as:

$$\pi(f_{ij}, c, \lambda) = \begin{cases} 2\left(1 - \frac{||f_{ij} - c||}{\lambda}\right)^2 & \text{for } \frac{\lambda}{2} \leq ||f_{ij} - c|| \leq \lambda \\ 1 - 2\left(\frac{||f_{ij} - c||}{\lambda}\right)^2 & \text{for } 0 \leq ||f_{ij} - c|| \leq \frac{\lambda}{2} \\ 0 & \text{otherwise} \end{cases}$$

where λ (> 0) is the radius of the π-function with c as central point.

We use the π-function as it is a general form which can present both S-function by the left part and the inverse of S-function by the right part. Therefore, the regions at the lowest and highest ends of features can also be represented by π functions.

Step 2: Partition the image X into $X_1, \ldots, X_n$, regions such that each X_i is a $w \times w$ pixel non-overlapping window of the image. Note that, any sub-image of X based on an arbitrary equivalence relation R may be used. The choice of w is determined by factors like amount of imprecision and computational complexity. We have done our experiments for different values of w.

Step 3: Vary the thresholds α and β which determine the lower and upper approximations according to Lemma 3.1. Determine α and β ($\alpha > \beta$) which minimises the roughness measure ρ (Equation 2) of the fuzzy object region A.

Step 4: Threshold the gray-tone image using β corresponding to minimum value of ρ. Note that, in conventional fuzzy segmentation, threshold is determined using only class membership information of pixels in the μ_X-plane. Here, in addition the lower and upper approximations of the μ_X-plane are taken into consideration.

Alternately, one can define a fuzzy object region over the image space with membership plane $A = \mu_X$ of constant bandwidth using a two-dimensional π-function. Vary the cross-over point of μ_X-plane and compute ρ for a fixed value of α and β. Find that μ_X-plane for which ρ is minimum. Such a μ_X-plane represents the fuzzy segmented version of the image (with lower and upper approximations as determined by α and β).

5 Experimental Results

The rough-fuzzy object extraction algorithm was tested on several images of different types. Figure 1, shows the extracted objects for the image of an airplane. The image contain objects with gray boundaries. Results are presented for thresholds obtained by optimizing probabilistic Shannon entropy [6] and the proposed rough-fuzzy uncertainty measure. The rough-fuzzy entropy measure was computed using granule sizes of 4×4 aqnd 8×8 respectively. It can be seen from the figures that the rough-fuzzy algorithm has extracted the objects with a high accuracy. It also outperforms the method based on probabilistic Shannon's entropy.

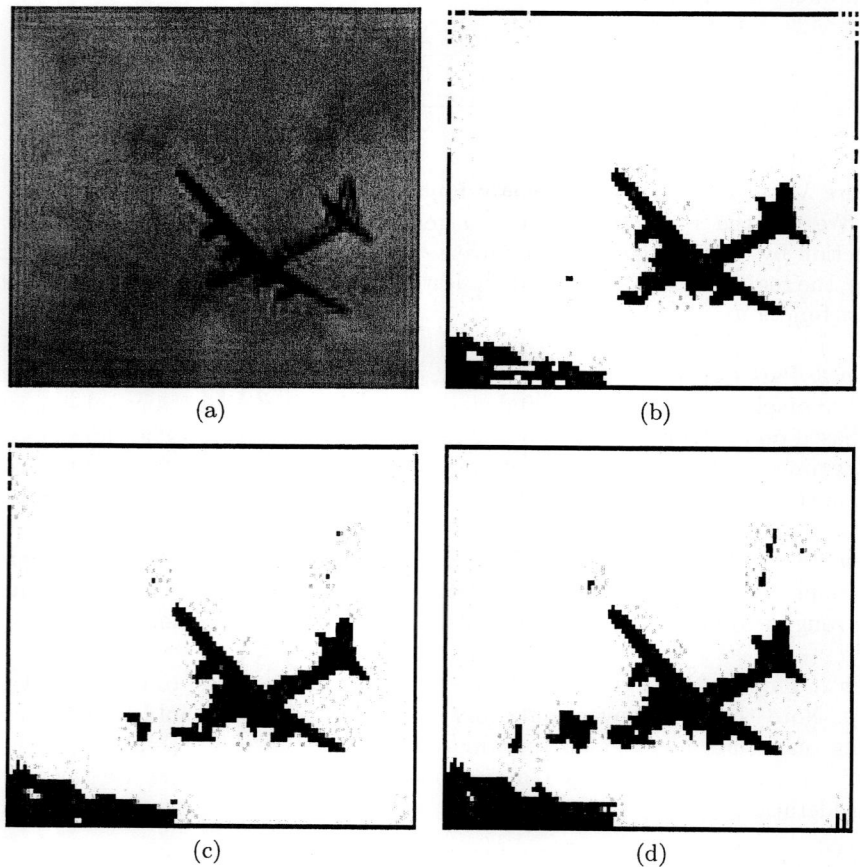

Fig. 1. Airplane image: (a) original image, and segmented images using (b) rough-fuzzy measure with 4×4 pixel granules, and (c) rough-fuzzy measure with 8×8 pixel granules, (d) Shannon entropy

6 Conclusions and Discussion

In this article we propose a method for object extraction in gray-scale images based on roughness measure of a fuzzy set.In conventional fuzzy segmentation, uncertainty is handled in terms of only class membership of pixels in the μ_X-plane. Here, in addition, the lower and upper approximations of the μ_X-plane are taken into consideration for managing uncertainty. Our future work would be to use this roughness measure for some other pattern recognition and image analysis problems like image enhancement and sub-pixel classification.

References

1. Pawlak, Z.: Rough sets : Theoretical Aspects of Reasoning about Data. Kluwer Academic (1991)
2. Banerjee, M., Pal, S.: Roughness of a fuzzy set. Information Sciences **17** (1996) 235–246
3. Dubois, D., Prade, H.: Rough fuzzy sets and fuzzy rough sets. Int.J.General Syst **17** (1990) 191–298
4. Pal, N., Pal, S.: A review on image segmentation techniques. Pattern Recognition **26** (1993) 1277–1294
5. Ruberto, C.D., Nappi, M., Vitulano, S.: Image segmentation by means of fuzzy entropy measure. In: ICIAP '97: Proc. 9th Intl Conf Image Analysis and Processing-Volume I, London, UK, Springer-Verlag (1997) 214–222
6. Kapoor, J., Sahoo, P., Wong, A.: A new method for gray-level picture thresholding using the entropy of the histogram. Comput. Vision Graphics Image Process **29** (1985) 273–285

Approximation Spaces in Machine Learning and Pattern Recognition

Andrzej Skowron[1], Jarosław Stepaniuk[2], and Roman Swiniarski[3,4]

[1] Institute of Mathematics, Warsaw University,
Banacha 2, 02-097 Warsaw, Poland
skowron@mimuw.edu.pl
[2] Department of Computer Science, Białystok University of Technology,
Wiejska 45a, 15-351 Białystok, Poland
jstepan@ii.pb.bialystok.pl
[3] Institute of Computer Science, Polish Academy of Sciences,
Ordona 21, 01-237 Warsaw, Poland
[4] Department of Computer Science, San Diego State University,
5500 Campanile Drive San Diego, CA 92182, USA
rswiniar@sciences.sdsu.edu

Abstract. Approximation spaces are fundamental for the rough set approach. We discuss their application in machine learning and pattern recognition.

Keywords: Rough sets, approximation spaces, concept approximation.

1 Introduction

Approximation spaces are fundamental structures for the rough set approach [3,9]. In this note we discuss a generalization of approximation spaces. We show how the rough set approach can be used for approximation of concepts assuming that partial information on approximation spaces is available only. We show that searching for relevant approximation spaces is one of the basic task in machine learning and pattern recognition.

2 Approximation Spaces

In this section we recall the definition of an approximation space from [6].

Definition 1. *A parameterized approximation space is a system* $AS_{\#,\$} = (U, I_\#, \nu_\$)$*, where*

- *U is a non-empty set of objects,*
- *$I_\# : U \to P(U)$ is an uncertainty function, where $P(U)$ denotes the power set of U,*
- *$\nu_\$: P(U) \times P(U) \to [0,1]$ is a rough inclusion function,*

and $\#, \$$ denote vectors of parameters (the indexes $\#, \$$ will be omitted if it does not lead to misunderstanding.

2.1 Uncertainty Function

The uncertainty function defines for every object x, a set of objects described similarly to x. The set $I(x)$ is called the neighborhood of x (see, e.g., [3,6]).

We assume that the values of uncertainty function are defined using a *sensory environment*, i.e., a pair $(L, \|\cdot\|_U)$, where L is a set of formulas, called the *sensory formulas*, and $\|\cdot\|_U : L \longrightarrow P(U)$ is the *sensor semantics*. We assume that for any sensory formula α and any object $x \in U$ the information if $x \in \|\alpha\|_U$ holds is available. The set $\{\alpha : x \in \|\alpha\|_U\}$ is called the *signature of x* in AS and is denoted by $Inf_{AS}(x)$. For any $x \in U$ the set $\mathcal{N}_{AS}(x)$ of *neighborhoods of x* in AS is defined by $\{\|\alpha\|_U : x \in \|\alpha\|_U\}$ and from this set the neighborhood $I(x)$ is constructed. For example, $I(x)$ is defined by selecting an element from the set $\{\|\alpha\|_U : x \in \|\alpha\|_U\}$ or by $I(x) = \bigcap \mathcal{N}_{AS}(x)$. Observe that any sensory environment $(L, \|\cdot\|_U)$ can be treated as a parameter of I from the vector $\#$ (see Def. 1).

Let us consider two examples. Any decision table $DT = (U, A, d)$ [3] defines an approximation space $AS_{DT} = (U, I_A, \nu_{SRI})$, where, as we will see, $I_A(x) = \{y \in U : a(y) = a(x) \text{ for all } a \in A\}$. Any sensory formula is a descriptor, i.e., a formula of the form $a = v$ where $a \in A$ and $v \in V_a$ with the standard semantics $\|a = v\|_U = \{x \in U : a(x) = v\}$. Then, for any $x \in U$ its signature $Inf_{AS_{DT}}(x)$ is equal to $\{a = a(x) : a \in A\}$ and the neighborhood $I_A(x)$ is equal to $\bigcap \mathcal{N}_{AS_{DT}}(x)$. Another example can be obtained assuming that for any $a \in A$ there is given a tolerance relation $\tau_a \subseteq V_a \times V_a$ (see, e.g., [6]). Let $\tau = \{\tau_a\}_{a \in A}$. Then, one can consider a tolerance decision table $DT_\tau = (U, A, d, \tau)$ with tolerance descriptors $a =_{\tau_a} v$ and their semantics $\|a =_{\tau_a} v\|_U = \{x \in U : v\tau_a a(x)\}$. Any such tolerance decision table $DT_\tau = (U, A, d, \tau)$ defines the approximation space $AS_{DT_\tau} = (U, I_A, \nu_{SRI})$ with the signature $Inf_{AS_{DT_\tau}}(x) = \{a =_{\tau_a} a(x) : a \in A\}$ and the neighborhood $I_A(x) = \bigcap \mathcal{N}_{AS_{DT_\tau}}(x)$ for any $x \in U$.

The fusion of $\mathcal{N}_{AS_{DT_\tau}}(x)$ for computing the neighborhood of x can have many different forms, the intersection is only an example. One can also consider some more general uncertainty functions, e.g., with values in $P^2(U)$ [9]. For example, to compute the value $I(x)$ first some subfamilies of $\mathcal{N}_{AS}(x)$ can be selected and next the family consisting of intersection of each such subfamily is taken as the value of $I(x)$.

Note, that any sensory environment $(L, \|\cdot\|_U)$ defines an information system with the universe U of objects. Any row of such an information system for an object x consists of information if $x \in \|\alpha\|_U$ holds, for any sensory formula α. Let us also observe that in our examples we have used a simple sensory language defined by descriptors of the form $a = v$. One can consider a more general approach by taking, instead of the simple structure $(V_a, =)$, some other relational structures R_a with the carrier V_a for $a \in A$ and a signature τ. Then any formula (with one free variable) from a sensory language with the signature τ that is interpreted in R_a defines a subset $V \subseteq V_a$ and induces on the universe of objects a neighborhood consisting of all objects having values of the attribute a in the set V. Note, that this is the basic step in hierarchical modelling [8].

2.2 Rough Inclusion Function

One can consider general constraints which the rough inclusion functions should satisfy. Searching for such constraints initiated investigations resulting in creation and development of rough mereology (see, e.g., [5,4] and the bibliography in [4]). In this subsection we present only some examples of rough inclusion functions.

The rough inclusion function $\nu_\$: P(U) \times P(U) \to [0,1]$ defines the degree of inclusion of X in Y, where $X, Y \subseteq U$.

In the simplest case it can be defined by (see, e.g., [6,3]):

$$\nu_{SRI}(X,Y) = \begin{cases} \frac{card(X \cap Y)}{card(X)} & \text{if } X \neq \emptyset \\ 1 & \text{if } X = \emptyset. \end{cases}$$

This measure is widely used by the data mining and rough set communities. It is worth mentioning that Jan Lukasiewicz [2] was the first one who used this idea to estimate the probability of implications. However, rough inclusion can have a much more general form than inclusion of sets to a degree (see, e.g., [5,4,9]).

Another example of rough inclusion function ν_t can be defined using the standard rough inclusion and a threshold $t \in (0, 0.5)$ using the following formula:

$$\nu_t(X,Y) = \begin{cases} 1 & \text{if } \nu_{SRI}(X,Y) \geq 1-t \\ \frac{\nu_{SRI}(X,Y)-t}{1-2t} & \text{if } t \leq \nu_{SRI}(X,Y) < 1-t \\ 0 & \text{if } \nu_{SRI}(X,Y) \leq t. \end{cases}$$

The rough inclusion function ν_t is used in the variable precision rough set approach [10].

Another example of rough inclusion is used for function approximation [9].

Usually, there are several parameters that are tuned in searching for relevant rough inclusion function. Such parameters are listed in the vector $\#$. An example of such parameter is the threshold mentioned for the rough inclusion function used in the variable precision rough set model. We would like to mention some other important parameters. Among them are pairs $(L^*, \|\cdot\|_U^*)$ where L^* is an extension of L and $\|\cdot\|_U^*$ is na extension of $\|\cdot\|_U$, where $(L, \|\cdot\|_U)$ is a sensory environment. For example, if L consists of sensory formulas $a = v$ for $a \in A$ and $v \in V_a$ than one can take as L^* the set of descriptor conjunctions. For rule based classifiers we search in such a set of formulas for relevant patterns for decision classes. We present more detail in the following section.

2.3 Lower and Upper Approximations

The lower and the upper approximations of subsets of U are defined as follows.

Definition 2. *For any approximation space $AS_{\#,\$} = (U, I_\#, \nu_\$)$ and any subset $X \subseteq U$, the lower and upper approximations are defined by*

$LOW(AS_{\#,\$}, X) = \{x \in U : \nu_\$(I_\#(x), X) = 1\},$
$UPP(AS_{\#,\$}, X) = \{x \in U : \nu_\$(I_\#(x), X) > 0\}$, *respectively.*

The lower approximation of a set X with respect to the approximation space $AS_{\#,\$}$ is the set of all objects, which can be classified with certainty as objects of X with respect to $AS_{\#,\$}$. The upper approximation of a set X with respect to the approximation space $AS_{\#,\$}$ is the set of all objects which can be possibly classified as objects of X with respect to $AS_{\#,\$}$.

Several known approaches to concept approximations can be covered using the discussed here approximation spaces, e.g., the approach given in [3], approximations based on the variable precision rough set model [10] or tolerance (similarity) rough set approximations (see, e.g., [6] and references in [6]).

In machine learning and pattern recognition many classification methods for concept approximation have been developed. They make it possible to decide for a given object if it belongs to the approximated concept or not. The classification methods yield the decisions using only partial information about approximated concepts. This fact is reflected in the rough set approach by assumption that concept approximations should be defined using partial information about approximation spaces only. To decide if a given object belongs to the (lower or upper) approximation of a given concept the rough inclusion function values are needed. In the next section we show how such values necessary for classification making are estimated on the basis of available partial information about approximation spaces.

3 Concept Approximation by Partial Information About Approximation Spaces

In machine learning and pattern recognition [1] we often search for approximation of a concept $C \subset U^*$ in approximation space $AS^* = (U^*, I^*, \nu^*)$ having only a partial information about AS^* and C, i.e., information restricted to a sample $U \subset U^*$. Let us denote the restriction of AS^* to U by $AS = (U, I, \nu)$, i.e., $I(x) = I^*(x) \cap U$, $\nu(X, Y) = \nu^*(X, Y)$ for $x \in U$, $X, Y \subseteq U$.

To decide if a given object x belongs to the lower approximation or the upper approximation of $C \subset U^*$ it is necessary to know the value $\nu^*(I^*(x), C)$. However, in case a partial information about the approximation space AS^* is available only, then an estimation of such a value rather than its exact value can be induced. In machine learning, pattern recognition or data mining different heuristics are used for estimation of the values of ν^*. Using different heuristic strategies values of another function ν' are computed and they are used for estimation of values of ν^*. Then, the function ν' is used for deciding if objects belong to C or not. Hence, we define an approximation of C in the approximation space $AS' = (U^*, I^*, \nu')$ rather than in AS^*. Usually, it is required that the approximations of $C \cap U$ in AS and AS' are close (or the same). If a new portion of objects extending the sample U to U_1 is received, then the closeness of approximations of C in the new approximation space $AS_1 = (U_1, I_1, \nu_1)$ (where I_1, ν_1 are obtained by restriction of I^*, ν^* to U_1) with approximations over AS' restricted to U_1 is verified. If the approximations are not close enough the definition of ν' is modified using new information about the extended sample. In this way we gradually improve the quality of approximation of C on larger parts of the universe U^*.

Now, we would like to explain in more detail a method for estimation of values $\nu^*(I^*(x), C)$. Let us consider an illustrative example. In the example we follow a method often used in rule based classifiers [9]. The method is based on the following steps. First, a set of patterns, that are used as left hand sides of decision rules, is induced. Each pattern describes a set of objects in U^* with a satisfactory degree of inclusion to one of decision classes (C or $U^* - C$ for the binary decision). Next, for any object the set of all such patterns that are matched to a satisfactory degree by the given object is extracted. Finally, it is applied a conflict resolution strategy (e.g., voting) for resolving conflicts between votes for different decisions by the matched patterns.

We now present an illustrative example to describe this process more formally in the framework of approximation spaces. First, we assume that among parameters of rough inclusion functions are pairs $(PAT, \|\cdot\|_{U^*})$, where PAT is a set of descriptor conjunctions over a set of condition attributes and $\|\cdot\|_{U^*} : PAT \longrightarrow P(U^*)$ is the semantics of patterns in U^*. Using such parameters we estimate the value $\nu^*(\|pat\|_{U^*}, C)$ by $\nu(\|pat\|_U, C \cap U)$ for any $pat \in PAT$ and we obtain, for a given threshold $deg \in [0, 1]$, the set S_1 of all patterns pat such that $\nu(\|pat\|_U, C \cap U) \geq deg$, i.e., consisting of patterns "for" the concept C. In an analogous way we obtain the set S_2 of all patterns pat satisfying $\nu^*(\|pat\|_{U^*}, U^* - C) \geq deg$. S_2 consists of patterns "for" the complement $U^* - C$ of the concept C. Next, we estimate $\nu^*(I^*(x), \|pat\|_{U^*})$ for $pat \in S_i$, for $i = 1, 2$. To do this we use our assumption on computing $I^*(x)$ for $x \in U^*$. We assume that the sensory formulas from L are descriptors $a = v$ over the condition attributes from a given set of condition attributes A with the semantics in U^* defined by $\|a = v\|_{U^*} = \{x \in U^* : a(x) = v\}$ for $a \in A$ and $v \in V_a$, where V_a is the value set of a. We also have $I^*(x) = \{y \in U^* : Inf_A(x) = Inf_A(y)\}$, where $Inf_A(x) = \{(a, a(x)) : a \in A\}$. Often, we estimate $\nu^*(I^*(x), \|pat\|_{U^*})$ using a matching strategy based on similarity of the syntactic description of x by $Inf_A(x)$ and the pattern pat. In this way we obtain for a given x the set S'_i of all patterns $pat \in S_i$ (for $i = 1, 2$) such that $\nu(I^*(x) \cap U, \|pat\|_U) \geq deg_1$ where $deg_1 \in [0, 1]$ is a given threshold. Finally, the estimation $\nu'(I^*(x), C)$ of the value $\nu^*(I^*(x), C)$ is obtained by application to the sets S'_1, S'_2 a conflict resolution strategy for resolving conflicts between patterns "for" and "against" the membership of x to C.

Usually, the function ν' is parameterized, e.g., by a threshold to which at least the patterns should be included into the decision classes. Also the discussed sets of patterns are among parameters of ν' tuned in the process of rule based classifier construction. Moreover, matching strategies used for estimation of matching degrees are usually parameterized and such parameters are also among tuned parameters of ν'. In machine learning, pattern recognition and data mining many different searching techniques have been developed for inducing concept approximations of the high quality. Among such components are relevant features, patterns, measures of closeness, model quality measures.

The approximation spaces defined above have been generalized in [9] to approximation spaces consisting of information granules.

4 Conclusions

In the paper we have discussed a role of approximation spaces in the rough set framework for machine learning and pattern recognition. We emphasized that approximation spaces are fundamental objects constructed for concept approximation. In our project we are developing evolutionary strategies searching for relevant approximation spaces for a given ontology [7] of concepts. We also investigate properties of evolutionary strategies for constructing sequences of approximation spaces in adaptive approximation of concepts.

Acknowledgements

The research has been supported by the grants 3 T11C 002 26 and 4 T11C 014 25 from Ministry of Scientific Research and Information Technology of the Republic of Poland.

References

1. Hastie, T., Tibshirani, R., Friedman, J.: *The Elements of Statistical Learning.* Springer-Verlag, Heidelberg, 2003.
2. Łukasiewicz, J.: Die logischen Grundlagen der Wahrscheinilchkeitsrechnung, Kraków 1913. In: Borkowski, L. (ed.), *Jan Lukasiewicz - Selected Works*. North Holland, Amstardam, Polish Scientific Publishers, Warsaw, 1970.
3. Pawlak, Z.: *Rough Sets. Theoretical Aspects of Reasoning about Data.* Kluwer Academic Publishers, Dordrecht, 1991.
4. Polkowski, L.: *Rough Sets: Mathematical Foundations.* Advances in Soft Computing, Physica-Verlag, Heidelberg, 2002.
5. Polkowski, L., Skowron, A.: Rough mereology: A new paradigm for approximate reasoning. *Journal of Approximate Reasoning* 15(4), 1996, 333–365.
6. Skowron, A., Stepaniuk, J.: Tolerance approximation spaces. *Fundamenta Informaticae* 27, 1996, 245–253.
7. Staab, S., Studer, R., (Eds.): *Handbook on Ontologies.* International Handbooks on Information Systems, Springer, Heidelberg, 2004.
8. Skowron, A., Synak, P., Complex patterns. *Fundamenta Informaticae* 60(1-4), 2004, 351–366.
9. Skowron, A., Swiniarski, R., Synak, P: Approximation spaces and information granulation. *Transactions on Rough Sets III: LNCS Journal Subline*, LNCS 3400, Springer, Heidelberg, 2005, 175–189.
10. Ziarko, W., Variable precision rough set model, *Journal of Computer and System Sciences* 46, 1993, 39–59.

A Rough Set-Based Magnetic Resonance Imaging Partial Volume Detection System

Sebastian Widz[1,2], Kenneth Revett[3], and Dominik Ślęzak[4,2]

[1] Deforma Sebastian Widz, Warsaw, Poland
[2] Polish-Japanese Institute of Information Technology, Warsaw, Poland
[3] University of Westminster, Harrow School of Computer Science, London, UK
[4] Department of Computer Science, University of Regina, Regina, Canada

Abstract. Segmentation of magnetic resonance imaging (MRI) data entails assigning tissue class labels to voxels. The primary source of segmentation error is the partial volume effect (PVE) which occurs most often with low resolution imaging – With large voxels, the probability of a voxel containing multiple tissue classes increases. Although the PVE problem has not been solved, the first stage entails correctly identifying PVE voxels. We employ rough sets to identify them automatically.

1 Introduction

Image segmentation is the process of assigning the class labels to data containing spatially varying information. In case of Magnetic Resonance Imaging (MRI) of the brain, segmentation relies on the magnitude values of voxels collected during the scanning procedure [6, 13]. The brain is imaged through the 2D slices sampled at a particular thickness. The goal is to classify every voxel within a slice to one of the tissue classes. It has been demonstrated that their relative distribution is diagnostic for specific diseases [3, 4].

Among many difficulties in segmenting MRI data, there is the partial volume effect (PVE) [2, 9]. In this paper, we focus on the automated detection of voxels subject to PVE. mthods developed for this problem so far do not provide satisfactory solution [1, 7]. We consider the theory of rough sets [8], particularly the approach based on approximate reducts [11, 12], as an alternative tool. Results are obtained for the data from Simulated Brain Database (SBD)[1]. They can be incorporated with our previous work on MRI segmentation [14, 15].

2 Data Preparation

The magnitudes of voxels are given in three modalities (T1, T2, PD). Under normal circumstances, the magnitudes of voxels form Gaussian distributions corresponding to the following tissue classes: bone and background (BCG), Cerebral Spinal Fluid (CSF), Grey Matter (GM), White Matter (WM), and others (fat, skin, muscle), as visible Figure 1. We focus on CSF, GM, and WM.

---
[1] SBD database is provided by the Brain Imaging Centre, Montreal Neurological Institute http://www.bic.mni.mcgill.ca/brainweb

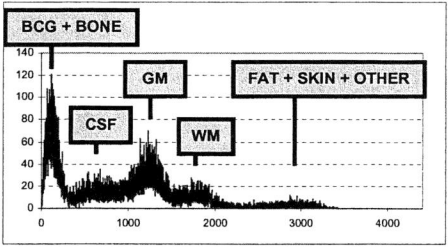

Fig. 1. The magnitude histogram obtained from a T1 slice. The x-axis corresponds to the magnitude of voxels. The peaks are likely to correspond to particular tissue classes.

To develop the PVE identification procedure, we first generate the training data. Following the standards of the theory of rough sets [5, 8], we form a decision table $\mathbb{A} = (U, A \cup \{d\})$, where each attribute $a \in A \cup \{d\}$ is a function $a : U \to V_a$ from the universe U of voxels into the value set V_a. The elements of U are voxels. The set A contains the following binary attributes extracted for each modality:

EDGE attributes are derived by a modified Discrete Laplacian method – a non-directional gradient operator determining whether neighborhood of a voxel is homogenous within a specified tolerance. We use a threshold for homogeneity tuned separately using the T1, T2, and PD training images. We consider this attribute type because voxels on tissue edges are more likely to suffer from PVE. We put the voxel's value as 1 in case inhomogeneity is detected and 0 otherwise.

MAGNITUDE attributes are derived using the magnitude histogram clustering [14]. Its idea is to produce clusters as intervals around the histogram's peaks and within the gaps. The distance between the magnitude levels is illustrated by Figure 2. The algorithm is controlled by parameters deciding about the number of peaks detected and size of intervals around them, which are tuned as in case of the edge attributes. Since the histogram's peaks are likely to correspond to particular tissues, we define this attribute's value as 1 for voxels with magnitudes within the peak intervals and 0 for those dropping into the gaps.

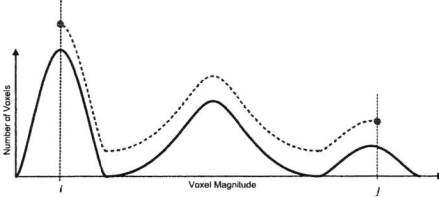

Fig. 2. Illustration of the histogram distance between magnitude positions i and j

NEIGHBOR attributes are derived from the edges and magnitudes. If the edge is not detected for a given voxel, the neighbor attribute's value is copied from the magnitude attribute. Otherwise, it is equal to the magnitude attribute's value (0 or 1) occurring more frequently within the direct voxel's neighborhood.

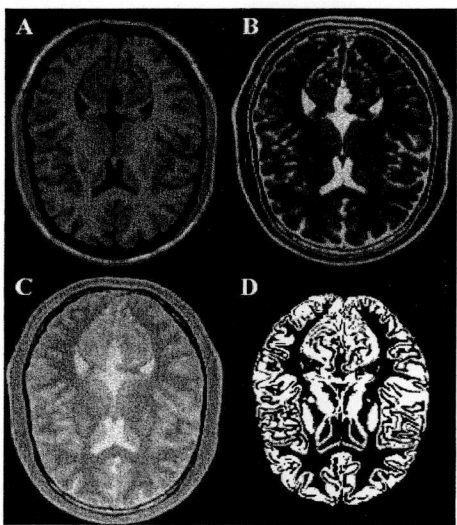

Fig. 3. Modalities T1 (A), T2 (B), and PD (C). D presents PVE (black) and NOE (white) decision classes obtained from the fuzzy SBD phantom for the same slice.

Attribute $d \notin A$ indicates whether voxels belong to PVE or NOE (NO-Effect) decision classes. For training and evaluation of the PVE identification accuracy, it is derived from so called fuzzy phantoms taken from SBD data, where each voxel is labeled with memberships to particular tissue types. We use the threshold to decide whether a given voxel belongs to the NOE class (if its membership to one of tissues exceeds enough the average tissue content level for the given slice) or to PVE class (if memberships are not diversified enough to decide). The threshold is tuned over the middle brain slice to get approximately 30%/70% distribution between the PVE and NOE classes, as illustrated by Figure 3.

3 Attribute Tuning and Reduction

While classifying new cases, one must strike a balance between accuracy and computational complexity. It can be achieved through the use of a decision reduct [5, 8]: an irreducible subset $B \subseteq A$ determining d in decision table $\mathbb{A} = (U, A \cup \{d\})$. Reducts are used to produce the decision rules from the training data. Sometimes it is better to remove more attributes to get shorter rules at the cost of their slight inconsistencies. Let us consider the following measure:

$$R(d/B) = \sum_{\text{rules } r \text{ induced by } B} \left(\frac{\text{number of objects recognizable by } r}{\text{number of objects in } U} * \max_i \frac{\text{probability of the } i\text{-th decision class induced by } r}{\text{prior probability of the } i\text{-th decision class}} \right)$$

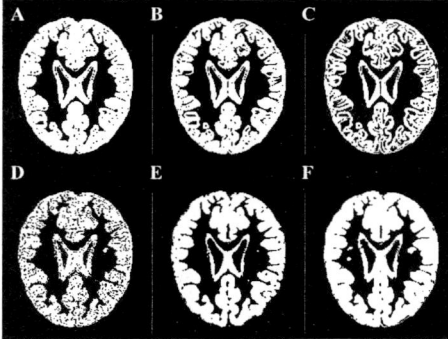

Fig. 4. Attributes derived for a single slice from the phantom data set. Image A corresponds to the edge attribute based on modality T1. B and C correspond to T2 and PD, respectively. The second row of images corresponds to the magnitude attributes.

Measure R expresses the average gain in determining decision classes under the evidence provided by the rules generated by $B \subseteq A$ [11, 12]. Given approximation threshold $\varepsilon \in [0, 1)$, let us say that $B \subseteq A$ is an (R, ε)-approximate decision reduct, if and only if it satisfies inequality $R(d/B) \geq (1 - \varepsilon) * R(d/A)$ and none of its proper subsets does it. We derive such approximate reducts from the MRI-related training data described in the previous section, using the order-based hybrid genetic algorithm adapted from [10, 16]. The results of applying the reduct-based rules to the testing images are presented in the next section.

R can be used also to evaluate single attributes. In particular, we apply it to tune the previously-mentioned parameters of the edge and magnitude attributes. The resulting attributes approximate very well the less frequent and actually more important PVE decision class – its area is almost perfectly contained in the borderline regions indicated by attributes $a \in A$ maximizing $R(d/\{a\})$. Examples of such obtained regions are illustrated by Figure 4. Consequently, the PVE identification procedure based on such attributes is expected to avoid misclassifying the PVE voxels as the ones which do not suffer from PVE.

4 Preliminary Results

The SBD phantoms have a complete set of MRI volumes, including partial voxel volumes of varying slice thickness (3-9 mm). For this study, we employed the 3mm thick volumes. We selected a range of slices from the center of the volume (27-36) for training/testing purposes. Reducts and rules were generated from the training set. The results are presented in Figure 5. For high $\varepsilon \in [0, 1)$, the reducts are empty, leading to a blind guess classification of all voxels to the larger class (no partial volume effect). In practice, however, we are more interested in sensitivity (accurate recognition of PVE), even if it leads to an increase of the false positive fraction. The accuracy curve suggests that for intermediate approximation thresholds the obtained non-empty reducts still provide a reasonable overall score and may better approximate PVE by decision rules.

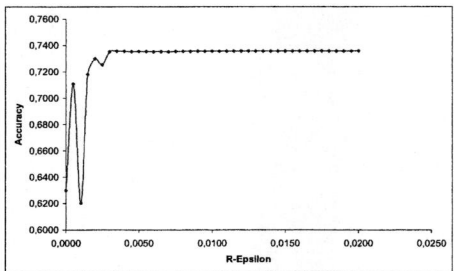

Fig. 5. Average accuracy of PVE identification with respect to the choice of $\varepsilon \in [0, 1)$

In Figure 6 it is visible that the shape of PVE classified area matches the actual one. Moreover, our method provides valuable results targeted at better PVE sensitivity and specificity. The amount of misclassified PVE voxels is considerably smaller than for NOE. Further research is needed to improve overall accuracy.

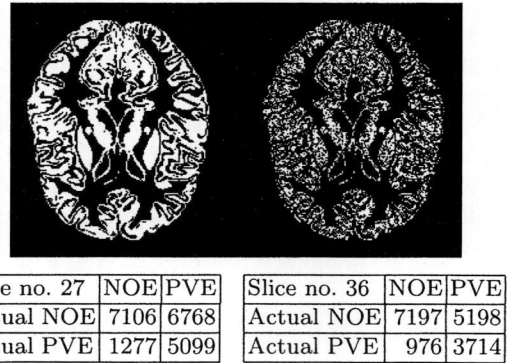

Slice no. 27	NOE	PVE
Actual NOE	7106	6768
Actual PVE	1277	5099

Slice no. 36	NOE	PVE
Actual NOE	7197	5198
Actual PVE	976	3714

Fig. 6. Example of PVE-identification for intermediate $\varepsilon \in [0, 1)$. Top left: The actual PVE area (black) taken from the phantom. Top right: the result of classification. Below: Confusion matrices for two other testing slices, obtained using non-empty reducts.

5 Conclusion

We presented a rough set-based system for partial volume voxel detection in multi-modal MR images. To extract relevant attributes, we utilized the edge detection and magnitude clustering methods on three imaging modalities. Decisions were obtained from fuzzy phantoms, taken from Simulated Brain Database. The obtained preliminary results show that the proposed method, based on simple binary attributes, is worth further development. Our approach forms the basis of a comprehensive automated segmentation algorithm. First, voxels not subject to PVE may be identified and segmented using previously developed methodology [14, 15]. The remaining voxels, presumed to suffer from PVE, may be processed accordingly. It provides the first instance of a rough set system that is capable of segmenting MR images regardless of occurrence of PVE.

Acknowledgments. The research reported in this article was supported in part by research grants from Natural Sciences and Engineering Research Council of Canada awarded to the third author.

References

1. Aston, J.A.D., Cunningham, V.J., Asselin, M.-C., Hammers, A., Evans, A.C., Gunn, R.N.: Positron emission tomography partial volume correction: estimation and algorithms. J Cereb Blood Flow Metab 22 (2002) 1019–1034
2. Atkins, M.S., Mackiewich, B.T.: Fully Automatic Segmentation of the Brain in MRI. IEEE Transcations on Medical Imaging 17(1) (1998)
3. Kamber, M., Shinghal, R., Collins, L.: Model-based 3D Segmentation of Multiple Sclerosis Lesions in Magnetic Resonance Brain Images. IEEE Trans Med Imaging 14(3) (1995) 442–453
4. Kaus, M., Warfield, S.K., Nabavi, A., Black, P.M., Jolesz, F.A., Kikinis, R.: Automated Segmentation of MRI of Brain Tumors. Radiology 218 (2001) 586–591
5. Komorowski, J., Pawlak, Z., Polkowski, L., Skowron, A.: Rough sets: A tutorial. In: S.K. Pal, A. Skowron (eds): Rough Fuzzy Hybridization – A New Trend in Decision Making. Springer Verlag (1999) 3–98
6. Kovacevic, N., Lobaugh, N.J., Bronskill, M.J., Levine, B., Feinstein, A., Black, S.E.: A Robust Extraction and Automatic Segmentation of Brain Images. NeuroImage 17 (2002) 1087–1100
7. Matsuda, H., Ohnishi, T., Asada, T., Li, Z., Kanetaka, H., Imabayashi, E., Tanaka, F., Nakano, S.: Correction for Partial-Volume Effects on Brain Perfusion SPECT in Healthy Men. J Nucl Med. 44 (2003) 1243–1252
8. Pawlak, Z.: Rough sets – Theoretical aspects of reasoning about data. Kluwer Academic Publishers (1991)
9. Pham, D.L., Prince, J.L.: Unsupervised partial volume estimation in single-channel imaging data. In: Proc MMBIA'00. Hilton Head Island, SC (2000)
10. Ślęzak, D., Wróblewski, J.: Order-based genetic algorithms for the search of approximate entropy reducts. In: Proc RSFDGrC'2003. Chongqing, China (2003)
11. Ślęzak, D., Ziarko, W.: Attribute Reduction in Bayesian Version of Variable Precision Rough Set Model. In: Proc. of RSKD'2003. Elsevier, ENTCS 82(4) (2003)
12. Ślęzak, D., Ziarko, W.: The Investigation of the Bayesian Rough Set Model. International Journal of Approximate Reasoning (2005)
13. Van Leemput, K., Maes, F., Vandermeulen, D., Colchester, A., Suetens, P.: Automated model-based tissue classification of MR images on the brain. IEEE Trans Med. Imag. 18 (1999) 897–908
14. Widz, S., Revett, K., Ślęzak, D.: A Hybrid Approach to MR Image Segmentation Using Unsupervised Clustering and Approximate Reducts. In: Proc RSFDGrC'2005. Regina, Canada (2005)
15. Widz, S., Ślęzak, D., Revett, K.: An Automated Multi-spectral MRI Segmentation Algorithm Using Approximate Reducts. In: Proc RSCTC'2004. Uppsala, Sweden (2004)
16. Wróblewski, J.: Theoretical Foundations of Order-Based Genetic Algorithms. Fundamenta Informaticae 28(3-4) (1996) 423–430

Eliciting Domain Knowledge in Handwritten Digit Recognition

Tuan Trung Nguyen

Polish-Japanese Institute of Computer Technology,
ul. Koszykowa 86, 02-008 Warsaw, Poland
nttrung@pjwstk.edu.pl

Abstract. Pattern recognition methods for complex structured objects such as handwritten characters often have to deal with vast search spaces. Developed techniques, despite significant advancement in the last decade, still face some performance barriers. We believe that additional knowledge about the structure of patterns, elicited from humans perceptions, will help improve the recognition's performance, especially when it comes to classify irregular, outlier cases. We propose a framework for the transfer of such knowledge from human experts and show how to incorporate it into the learning process of a recognition system using methods based on rough mereology. We also demonstrate how this knowledge acquisition can be conducted in an interactive manner, with a large dataset of handwritten digits as an example.

1 Introduction

Most existing pattern recognition systems use a descriptive language and a reasoning scheme, both assumed *a priori* for the learning process and only final quantitative parameters for the model's description are extracted from data. The development of rough set methods, however, have shown that the language, or the scheme itself can, and should, be determined by the data rather than assumed *a priori*. We show that this process can be further refined using background knowledge provided by a human expert.

The main challenge here is that an expert's explanations are usually expressed in his own descriptive language, often heavily based on natural language constructs (a *foreign language* L_f), while classifiers are based on a rather low-level language designed to facilitate the computation of physical traits of the images (a *domestic language* L_d). The knowledge passing process hence can be considered as the approximation of expert's concepts such as '*necks*' or '*circular*' by the classifier construction system. From a broader point of view, the expert's *ontology* on the domain is approximated within the ontology used by the computer system. Not only concepts, but the *reasoning schemes* of the expert about investigated samples are carried onto the recognition system as well.

We propose a method for transferring the expert's reasoning scheme into the recognition system, based on the rough mereology approach to concept's approximation [4], [8]. In particular, we show how complex spatial relations between parts of graphical objects can be approximated.

2 Knowledge Transfer

2.1 Foreign Language

An expert is supposed to provide explanations *why*, and perhaps more importantly, *how* he classifies a certain sample. This is denoted in the form of a rule:

$$[CL(u) = k] \equiv \Im(EFeature_1(u), ..., EFeature_n(u))$$

where $EFeature_i$ represents the expert's perception of some characteristics of the sample u, while synthesis operator $\Im$ represents his perception of some relations between these characteristics.

For example, the expert may express his perception of digit '5' as:

$[CL(u) =$'5'$] \equiv a,b,c,d$ are parts of u; 'Above_Right'(a,b); 'HStroke'(a); $b = Compose(c,d)$; 'VStroke'(c); 'WBelly'(d); 'Above'(c,d),

where *Compose* is an assembling operator that produces a bigger part from smaller components.

The above means if there is a west-open belly below a vertical stroke and the two have a horizontal stroke above-right in the sample's image, then the sample is a '5'. *'Above'*, *'WBelly'*, *'HStroke'* and the like are expert's concepts that may not be readily comprehensible for the classification system and need to be translated into its language.

2.2 Domestic Language

The classifier construction and sample classification algorithms view image samples as sets of black and white pixels. Basic features are constructed using Enhanced Loci coding, which reflects both local and global relations between regions of black and white pixels in the image. For example, each white pixel is assigned a code that denotes whether it has a black neighbor pixel to one of the four directions: North, East, South, West. For a more detailed description of this coding scheme, see [1]. A classifier may be expressed in this domestic language, for example, as:

$$[CL(u) =\text{'0'}] \equiv |\{\text{pixel } p\text{: code}(p)\text{=NESW}\}| > 35.$$

2.3 Approximation of Expert's Concepts

Expert's Features. Knowledge from the expert has to be somehow translated from the foreign language into domestic language. For instance, the presence of a concept *'a belly open to the east'* in a sample might be expressed as a following test: $|\{\text{pixel } p\text{: code}(p)\text{=NSW}\}| > 17\% \times |\{\text{all pixels}\}|$.

Since expert's features are expressed with natural language constructs, the notion of *'concept matching'* here must not be crisp, but should allow for a tolerant matching to a degree. A natural choice of tool for this problem is the rough inclusion measure, established as a basis of the theory of rough mereology

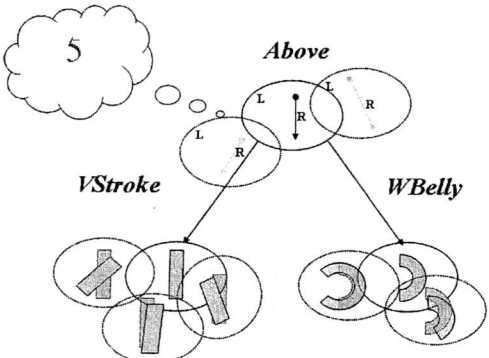

Fig. 1. Tolerant matching by expert

[4,8] to deal with the notion of inclusion to a degree. For instance, a stroke at 85 degree to the horizontal can still be regarded as a vertical stroke, though obviously not a 'pure' one (see Fig.1). Instead of just answering in a *'Yes/No'* fashion, the expert may express his degrees of belief using such terms as *'Strong'*, *'Fair'*, or *'Weak'*.

Relations Between Features. Relations between expert's features may include concepts such as *'Above'*, *'Below'* or simply *'Near'*. They express not only expert's perceptions about particular concepts, but also the interdependencies among them. Similarly to the stand-alone features, these relations can also be described by the expert with a degree of tolerance (See Fig. 1).

The approximation of these relations has been formalized within the framework of perception structures recently developed by Skowron [7]. A *perception structure S*, in a simpler form, is defined as:

$$S = (U, M, F, \models, p)$$

where U is a set of samples, F is a family of formulas expressed in domestic language that describe certain features of the samples and M is a family of relational structures in which these formulas can be evaluated, while $p: U \to M \times F$ is a *perception function* such that $\forall u \in U : p_1(u) \models p_2(u)$ (p_1 and p_2 are the first and second component projections of p) which means that $p_2(u)$ is satisfied (is true) in the relational structure $p_1(u)$. This may express that some relations among features within samples are observed.

Perception structures, following natural constructs in the expert's foreign language, can involve tolerant matching. Two relational structures might be considered approximately *the same* if they allow for similar formulas to yield similar results in majority of cases when these formulas are applicable.

Quality Constraints. The knowledge transfer process aims to find sets of patterns $Pat, Pat_1, ..., Pat_n$ and a relation $\Im_d$ in domestic language such that:

if $(\forall i : Match(Pat_i, EFeature_i) \geq p_i) \wedge (Pat = \Im_d(Pat_1, ..., Pat_n))$ **then**
$$Quality(Pat) > \alpha$$

Quality criteria are introduced so we can generalize the expert's reasoning to the largest possible number of investigated samples. The requirements on inclusion degrees ensure the *robustness* of the target reasoning scheme, as the target pattern Pat retains its quality regardless of deviations of input patterns. Another important aspect of this process is its *global stability*, which guarantees that if we have some input patterns Pat'_i equally "close" or "similar" to $EFeature_i$, then the target pattern $Pat' = \Im_d(Pat'_1, ..., Pat'_n)$ will meet the same quality requirements as Pat to a satisfactory degree. This leads to an approximation of $EFeature_i$ which is *independent* from particular patterns Pat_i, allowing for approximation schemes that focus on inclusion degrees p_i rather than on a specific input patterns Pat_i.

3 Implementation

3.1 Learning Expert's Features

In this step, we have to approximate expert's concept such as '*Circle*' or '*WBelly*'. The expert will explain what he means when he says, e.g. '*Circle*', by providing a decision table (U, d) with reference samples, where d is the expert decision to which degree he considers that '*Circle*' appears in samples $u \in U$. (See Tab. 1). The samples in U may be provided by the expert, or may be picked up by him among samples explicitly submitted by the system, e.g. those that had been misclassified in previous attempts.

Table 1. Perceived features

	Circle
u_1	Strong
u_2	Weak
...	...
u_n	Fair

Table 2. Translated features

	#NESW	Circle
u_1	252	Strong
u_2	4	Weak
...	...	...
u_n	90	Fair

We then attempt to find domestic feature(s) that approximates these degrees of belief. This can be conducted using, among other means, genetic algorithms (For example, [3] reported using this kind of tools and methods for a similar problem). In this example, such feature may be the number of pixels that have black neighbors in all four directions (See Tab. 2).

3.2 Learning Expert's Relations

Having approximated the expert's features $EFeature_i$, we can try to translate his relation $\Im$ into our $\Im_d$ by asking the expert to go through U and provide

Table 3. Perceived relations

	V Stroke	W Belly	Above
u_1	Strong	Strong	Strong
u_2	Fair	Weak	Weak
...	...	...	...
u_n	Fair	Fair	Weak

Table 4. Translated relations

	#V_S	#NES	$S_y < B_y$	Above
u_1	0.8	0.9	(Strong,1.0)	(Strong, 0.9)
u_2	0.9	1.0	(Weak, 0.1)	(Weak, 0.1)
...	...	...	...	...
u_n	0.9	0.6	(Fair, 0.3)	(Weak, 0.2)

us with the additional attributes of how strongly he considers the presence of $EFeature_i$ and to what degree he believes the relation $\Im$ holds (See Tab. 3).

We then replace the attributes corresponding to $EFeature_i$ with the rough inclusion measures of the domestic feature sets that approximate those concepts (computed in the previous step). In the next stage, we try to add other features, possibly induced from original domestic primitives, in order to approximate the decision d. Such a feature may be expressed by $S_y < B_y$, which tells whether the median center of the stroke is placed closer to the upper edge of the image than the median center of the belly. (See Tab. 4) Again, this task should be resolved by means of adaptive or evolutionary search strategies without too much computing burden, although it is more time-expensive.

The expert's perception "A '6' is something that has a 'vertical stroke' 'above' a 'belly open to the west'" is eventually approximated by a classifier in the form of a rule:

if $S(\#BL\_SL > 23)$ AND $B(\#NESW > 12\%)$ AND $S_y < B_y$ then CL='6',

where S and B are designations of pixel collections, #BL_SL and #NESW are numbers of pixels with particular Loci codes, and $S_y < B_y$ reasons about centers of gravity of the two collections.

3.3 Experiments

In order to illustrate the developed methods, we conducted a series of experiments on the NIST Handwritten Segmented Character Special Database 3. We compared the performances gained by a standard learning approach with and without the aid of the domain knowledge. The additional knowledge, passed by a human expert on popular classes as well as some atypical samples allowed to reduce the time needed by the learning phase from 205 minutes to 168 minutes, which means an improvement of about 22 percent without loss in classification quality. In case of screening classifiers, i.e. those that decide a sample *does not* belong to given classes, the improvement is around 60 percent. The representational samples found are also slightly simpler than those computed without using the background knowledge.

4 Conclusion

We presented a general yet powerful framework for the transfer of human domain knowledge to adaptive learning systems. Approximate reasoning schemes based on rough mereology can be effectively used to incorporate human ontology, expressed in natural language, into processes constructing computable features. We demonstrated that this communication and knowledge transfer process can be conducted in a convenient, interactive manner. We have shown how granular computing, equipped with rough mereology concepts can be effectively applied to highly practical fields such as OCR and handwritten digit recognition. Preliminary experiments conducted showed that presented methods can help improve the learning process and provide a better understanding of the dataset investigated.

Acknowledgment. This work has been partly supported by Grant 3 T11C 002 26 funded by the Ministry of Scientific Research and Information Technology of the Republic of Poland.

References

1. K. Komori, T. Kawatani, K. Ishii, and Y. Iida. A feature concentrated method for character recognition. In Bruce Gilchrist, editor, *Information Processing 77, Proceedings of the International Federation for Information Processing Congress 77*, pages 29–34, Toronto, Canada, August 8-12, 1977. North Holland.
2. T. T. Nguyen and A. Skowron. Rough set approach to domain knowledge approximation. In G. Wang, Q. Liu, Y. Yao, and A. Skowron, editors, *Proceedings of the 9th International Conference: Rough Sets, Fuzzy Sets, Data Mining, and Granular Computing, RSFDGRC'03. Lecture Notes in Computer Science Vol. 2639*, pages 221–228, Chongqing, China, Oct 19-22, 2003. Springer Verlag.
3. L.S. Oliveira, R. Sabourin, F. Bortolozzi, and C.Y. Suen. Feature selection using multi-objective genetic algorithms for handwritten digit recognition. In *International Conference on Pattern Recognition (ICPR02)*, pages I: 568–571, 2002.
4. L. Polkowski and A. Skowron. Rough mereology: A new paradigm for approximate reasoning. *Journal of Approximate Reasoning*, 15(4):333–365, 1996.
5. L. Polkowski and A. Skowron. Constructing rough mereological granules of classifying rules and classifying algorithms. In B. Bouchon-Meunier, J.Rios-Gutierrez, L. Magdalena, and R.R. Yager, editors, *Technologies for Constructing Intelligent Systems I*, pages 57–70, Heidelberg, 2002. Physica-Verlag.
6. R. J. Schalkoff. *Pattern Recognition: Statistical, Structural and Neural Approaches.* John Wiley & Sons, Inc., 1992.
7. A. Skowron. Rough sets in perception-based computing. In *First International Conference on Pattern Recognition and Machine Intelligence (PReMI'05)*. Springer-Verlag, 2005.
8. A. Skowron and L. Polkowski. Rough mereological foundations for design, analysis, synthesis, and control in distributed systems. *Information Sciences*, 104(1-2):129–156, 1998.

Collaborative Rough Clustering

Sushmita Mitra[1], Haider Banka[1], and Witold Pedrycz[2]

[1] Machine Intelligence Unit, Indian Statistical Institute,
Kolkata 700 108, India
{sushmita, hbanka_r}@isical.ac.in
[2] Dept. of Electrical & Computer Engg., University of Alberta,
Edmonton, Canada T6G 2G7
pedrycz@ece.ualberta.ca

Abstract. A novel collaborative clustering is proposed through the use of rough sets. The Davies-Bouldin clustering validity index is extended to the rough framework, to generate the optimal number of clusters during collaboration.

Keywords: Rough sets, collaborative clustering, cluster validity.

1 Introduction

A cluster is a collection of data objects which are similar to one another within the same cluster but dissimilar to the objects in other clusters. Clustering large data is a mining problem of considerable interest. A recent trend in intelligent system design for large-scale problems is to split the original task into simpler subtasks and use a module for each of the subtasks. It has been shown that by combining the output of several modules in an ensemble, one can improve the generalization ability over that of a single model [1].

Collaborative clustering deals with revealing a structure that is common or similar to a number of subsets [2]. For example, let us consider a large population of data about client information, distributed over multiple databases. An intelligent approach to mine such large volume of information would be to analyze each individual database of sub-population locally and subsequently combine (or collaborate on) the results at a globally abstract level. This also satisfies certain security (or privacy) concerns of clients in not allowing the sharing of individual data (or samples).

Recently various soft computing methodologies have been applied to handle the different challenges posed by data mining [1], involving large heterogeneous datasets and clustering [1]. Fuzzy sets and rough sets have been incorporated in the c-means framework to develop the fuzzy c-means (FCM) [3] and rough c-means (RCM) [4] algorithms. Typically, rough sets [5] are used to model the clusters in terms of upper and lower approximations. Collaborative clustering has been investigated by Pedrycz [2], using the FCM algorithm.

In this article we present a novel collaborative clustering through the use of rough sets. The Davies-Bouldin (DB) index is extended to the rough framework, and helps in determining the optimal number of clusters during collaboration. Section 2 provides the basic description of the c-means and RCM clustering algorithms, along with the modified DB index. Collaboration in the RCM framework is presented in Section 4. Experimental results are demonstrated in Section 5. Finally Section 6 concludes the article.

2 Rough Clustering

The c-means algorithm proceeds by partitioning N objects into c nonempty subsets. During each partition, the centroids or means of the clusters are computed. The main steps of the c-means algorithm [6] are as follows:

1. Assign initial means $\mathbf{m}_i$ (also called centroids).
2. Assign each data object $\mathbf{X}_k$ to the cluster U_i for the closest mean.
3. Compute new mean for each cluster using

$$\mathbf{m}_i = \frac{\sum_{\mathbf{X}_k \in U_i} \mathbf{X}_k}{|c_i|}, \qquad (1)$$

where $|c_i|$ is the number of objects in cluster U_i.
4. Iterate **until** criterion function converges, *i.e.*, there are no more new assignments.

The theory of *rough sets* [5] has recently emerged as another major mathematical tool for managing uncertainty that arises from granularity in the domain of discourse. The intention is to approximate a *rough* (imprecise) concept in the domain of discourse by a pair of *exact* concepts, called the lower and upper approximations. These exact concepts are determined by an *indiscernibility* relation on the domain, which, in turn, may be induced by a given set of *attributes* ascribed to the objects of the domain. The lower approximation is the set of objects definitely belonging to the vague concept, whereas the upper approximation is the set of objects possibly belonging to the same.

In the rough c-means (RCM) algorithm, the concept of c-means is extended by viewing each cluster as an interval or rough set [4]. A rough set Y is characterized by its lower and upper approximations $\underline{B}Y$ and $\overline{B}Y$ respectively. This permits overlaps between clusters. Here an object $\mathbf{X}_k$ can be part of at most *one* lower approximation. If $\mathbf{X}_k \in \underline{B}Y$ of cluster Y, then simultaneously $\mathbf{X}_k \in \overline{B}Y$. If $\mathbf{X}_k$ is not a part of any lower approximation, then it belongs to two or more upper approximations.

Adapting eqn. (1), the centroid $\mathbf{m}_i$ of cluster U_i is computed as

$$\mathbf{m}_i = \begin{cases} w_{low} \frac{\sum_{\mathbf{X}_k \in \underline{B}U_i} \mathbf{X}_k}{|\underline{B}U_i|} + w_{up} \frac{\sum_{\mathbf{X}_k \in (\overline{B}U_i - \underline{B}U_i)} \mathbf{X}_k}{|\overline{B}U_i - \underline{B}U_i|} & \text{if } \underline{B}U_i \neq \emptyset \wedge \overline{B}U_i - \underline{B}U_i \neq \emptyset \\ \frac{\sum_{\mathbf{X}_k \in \underline{B}U_i} \mathbf{X}_k}{|\underline{B}U_i|} & \text{if } \overline{B}U_i - \underline{B}U_i = \emptyset \\ \frac{\sum_{\mathbf{X}_k \in (\overline{B}U_i - \underline{B}U_i)} \mathbf{X}_k}{|\overline{B}U_i - \underline{B}U_i|} & \text{otherwise,} \end{cases} \qquad (2)$$

where the parameters w_{low} and w_{up} correspond to the relative importance of the lower and upper bounds respectively. Here $|\underline{B}U_i|$ indicates the number of patterns in the lower approximation of cluster U_i, while $|\overline{B}U_i - \underline{B}U_i|$ is the number of elements in the rough boundary lying between the two approximations.

The RCM algorithm is outlined as follows.

1. Assign initial means $\mathbf{m}_i$ for the c clusters.
2. Assign each data object (pattern point) $\mathbf{X}_k$ to the lower approximation $\underline{B}U_i$ or upper approximation $\overline{B}U_i$, $\overline{B}U_j$ of cluster pairs U_i, U_j by computing the difference in its distance $d_{ik} - d_{jk}$ from cluster centroid pairs $\mathbf{m}_i$ and $\mathbf{m}_j$.
3. Let d_{ik} be minimal.
   If $d_{jk} - d_{ik}$ is less than some *threshold*
      then $\mathbf{X}_k \in \overline{B}U_i$ and $\mathbf{X}_k \in \overline{B}U_j$ and $\mathbf{X}_k$ cannot be a member of any lower approximation,
      else $\mathbf{X}_k \in \underline{B}U_i$ such that distance d_{ik} is minimum over the c clusters.
4. Compute new mean for each cluster U_i using eqn. (2).
5. Iterate **until** convergence, *i.e.*, there are no more new assignments.

The expression in eqn. (2) boils down to eqn. (1) when the lower approximation is equal to the upper approximation, implying an empty boundary region. It is observed that the performance of the algorithm is dependent on the choice of w_{low}, w_{up} and *threshold*. We allowed $w_{up} = 1 - w_{low}$, $0.5 < w_{low} < 1$ and $0 < threshold < 0.5$.

3   Clustering Validity Index

The partitive clustering algorithms, described above, require prespecification of the number of clusters. The results are dependent on the choice of c. There exist validity indices to evaluate the goodness of clustering, corresponding to a given value of c. In this article we compute the optimal number of clusters c_0 in terms of the Davies-Bouldin cluster validity index [7].

The Davies-Bouldin index (DB) is a function of the ratio of the sum of within-cluster distance to between-cluster separation. Let $\{\mathbf{x}_1, \ldots, \mathbf{x}_{|c_k|}\}$ be a set of patterns lying in a cluster U_k. Then the *average distance* between objects within the cluster U_k is expressed as $S(U_k) = \frac{\sum_{i,i'} \|\mathbf{x}_i - \mathbf{x}_{i'}\|}{|c_k|(|c_k|-1)}$, where $\mathbf{x}_i, \mathbf{x}_{i'} \in U_k$ and $i \neq i'$. The *between-cluster separation* is defined as $d(U_k, U_l) = \frac{\sum_{i,j} \|\mathbf{x}_i - \mathbf{x}_j\|}{|c_k||c_l|}$, where $\mathbf{x}_i \in U_k$, $\mathbf{x}_j \in U_l$, such that $k \neq l$. The optimal clustering, for $c = c_0$, minimizes

$$DB = \frac{1}{c} \sum_{i=1}^{c} \max_{j \neq i} \left\{ \frac{S(U_i) + S(U_j)}{d(U_i, U_j)} \right\}, \qquad (3)$$

for $1 \leq i, j \leq c$. Thereby, the within-cluster distance $S(U_i)$ is minimized while the between-cluster separation $d(U_i, U_j)$ gets maximized.

The rough within-cluster distance is formulated as $S_r(U_i) =$

$$\begin{cases} w_{low} \frac{\sum_{\mathbf{x}_k \in \underline{B}U_i} ||\mathbf{X}_k - \mathbf{m}_i||^2}{|\underline{B}U_i|} \\ + w_{up} \frac{\sum_{\mathbf{x}_k \in (\overline{B}U_i - \underline{B}U_i)} ||\mathbf{X}_k - \mathbf{m}_i||^2}{|\overline{B}U_i - \underline{B}U_i|} & \text{if } \underline{B}U_i \neq \emptyset \wedge \overline{B}U_i - \underline{B}U_i \neq \emptyset \\ \frac{\sum_{\mathbf{x}_k \in \underline{B}U_i} ||\mathbf{X}_k - \mathbf{m}_i||^2}{|\underline{B}U_i|} & \text{if } \overline{B}U_i - \underline{B}U_i = \emptyset \\ \frac{\sum_{\mathbf{x}_k \in (\overline{B}U_i - \underline{B}U_i)} ||\mathbf{X}_k - \mathbf{m}_i||^2}{|\overline{B}U_i - \underline{B}U_i|} & \text{otherwise,} \end{cases} \quad (4)$$

using eqn. (2). Rough DB now becomes

$$DB_r = \frac{1}{c} \sum_{i=1}^{c} \max_{j \neq i} \left\{ \frac{S_r(U_i) + S_r(U_j)}{d(U_i, U_j)} \right\}. \quad (5)$$

4 Collaborative RCM Clustering

In this section a collaborative rough c-means clustering is proposed, by incorporating collaboration between different partitions or sub-populations. Let a dataset be divided into P sub-populations or modules. Each sub-population is independently clustered to reveal its structure. Collaboration is incorporated by exchanging information between the modules regarding the local partitions, in terms of the collection of prototypes computed within the individual modules. This sort of divide-and-conquer strategy enables efficient mining of large databases. The required communication links are hence at a higher level of abstraction, thereby representing information granules (rough clusters) in terms of their prototypes. There exist two phases in the algorithm.

- Generation of RCM clusters within the modules, without collaboration. Here we employ $0.5 < w_{low} < 1$, thereby providing more importance to samples lying within the lower approximation of clusters while computing their prototypes locally.
- Collaborative RCM between the clusters, computed locally for each module of the large dataset. Now we use $0 < w_{low} < 0.5$ (we chose $w_{low} = 1 - w_{low}$), with a lower value providing higher precedence to samples lying in the boundary region of overlapping clusters. Here a cluster U_i may be merged with an overlapping cluster U_j

$$\text{if} \quad |\underline{B}U_i| \leq |\overline{B}U_i - \underline{B}U_i| \quad (6)$$

is maximum for all $i = 1, \ldots, c$ and $d(\mathbf{m}_i, \mathbf{m}_j)$ is minimum for $j \neq i$.

Let there be c_1 and c_2 clusters, generated by RCM, in a pair of modules ($P = 2$) under consideration. During collaboration, we begin with $c_1 + c_2$ cluster prototypes and merge using eqn. (6).

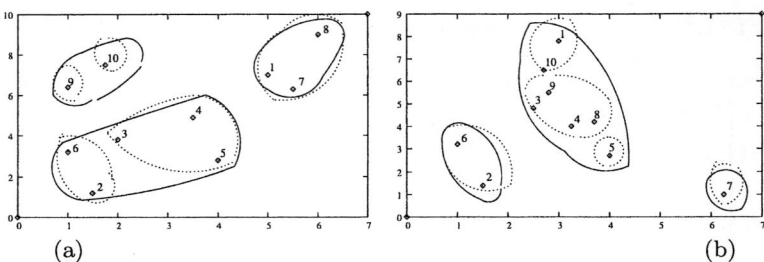

Fig. 1. Collaborative rough clustering on synthetic dataset for (a) Module A and (b) Module B, with RCM

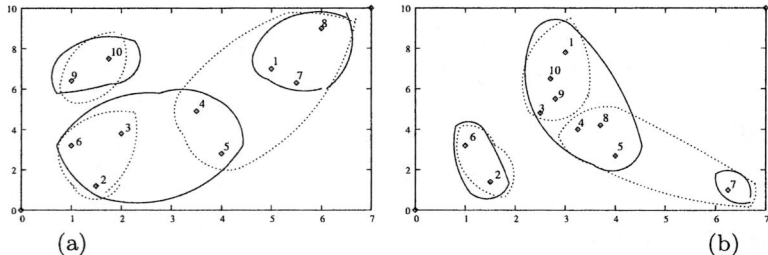

Fig. 2. Collaborative fuzzy clustering on synthetic dataset for (a) Module A and (b) Module B, with FCM

Table 1. Sample comparative performance of collaborative RCM on synthetic data

	Before collaboration			After collaboration		
Module	Prototypes	Samples in lower approximation	Rough DB	Prototypes	Samples in lower approximation	Rough DB
A	(3.35, 6.42) (6.0, 9.0) (2.13, 2.75)	1, 4, 7, 9, 10 8 2, 3, 5, 6	0.789	(1.75, 7.5) (5.5, 7.43) (3.17, 3.83) (1.0, 6.4) (1.25, 2.2)	10 1, 7, 8 3, 4, 5 9 2, 6	0.732
B	(6.25, 1.0) (3.14, 5.07) (1.25, 2.3)	7 1, 3, 4, 5, 8, 9, 10 2, 6	0.567	(2.85, 7.15) (4.0, 2.7) (6.25, 1.0) (3.06, 4.63) (1.25, 2.3)	1, 10 5 7 3, 4, 8, 9 2, 6	0.441

5 Results

Results are provided on a two-dimensional synthetic dataset [2], using RCM and FCM, as shown in Fig. 1 and Fig. 2 respectively. There are two modules (A and B) corresponding to ten samples each, partitioned into three clusters. Sample results using $threshold = 0.2$, $w_{low} = 0.9$ for RCM, and $w_{low} = 1 - 0.9 = 0.1$ for collaborative RCM, are provided in Table 1. It is observed that the Rough DB decreases for both modules after collaboration. Figs. 1(a) and (b) indicate the clustering before (solid line) and after (dotted line) collaboration, using modules A and B respectively with RCM.

6 Conclusion

Collaborative clustering is a promising approach towards modeling agent-based systems. While handling large data in this framework, each intelligent agent may concentrate on information discovery (or clustering) within a module. These agents can communicate with each other at the cluster interface, using appropriate protocol, their cluster profiles represented in terms of the centroids.

In this article, we have presented a novel collaborative clustering using the RCM algorithm. The Davies-Bouldin clustering validity index is modified, by incorporating rough concepts, to determine optimal clustering during collaboration.

Acknowledgement

This work is partly supported by CSIR (No. $22(0346)/02/EMR-II$),New Delhi.

References

1. Mitra, S., Acharya, T.: Data Mining: Multimedia, Soft Computing, and Bioinformatics. John Wiley, New York (2003)
2. Pedrycz, W.: Collaborative fuzzy clustering. Pattern Recognition Letters **23** (2002) 1675–1686
3. Bezdek, J.C.: Pattern Recognition with Fuzzy Objective Function Algorithms. Plenum Press, New York (1981)
4. Lingras, P., West, C.: Interval set clustering of Web users with rough k-means. Technical Report No. 2002-002, Dept. of Mathematics and Computer Science, St. Mary's University, Halifax, Canada (2002)
5. Pawlak, Z.: Rough Sets, Theoretical Aspects of Reasoning about Data. Kluwer Academic, Dordrecht (1991)
6. Tou, J.T., Gonzalez, R.C.: Pattern Recognition Principles. Addison-Wesley, London (1974)
7. Bezdek, J.C., Pal, N.R.: Some new indexes for cluster validity. IEEE Transactions on Systems, Man, and Cybernetics, Part-B **28** (1998) 301–315

Learning of General Cases

Silke Jänichen and Petra Perner

Institute of Computer Vision and applied Computer Sciences, IBaI,
Koernerstr. 10, 04107 Leipzig
ibaiperner@aol.com
www.ibai-institut.de

Abstract. Case-based object recognition requires a general case of the object that should be detected. Real world applications such as the recognition of biological objects in images cannot be solved by one general case. A case-base is necessary to handle the great natural variation in appearance of these objects. We present our conceptual clustering algorithm to learn a hierarchy of decreasingly generalized cases from a set of acquired structural cases. Due to its concept description, it explicitly supplies for each cluster a generalized case and a measure for the degree of its generalization. The resulting hierarchical case base is used for applications in the field of case-based object recognition.

Keywords: Case Mining, Case-Based Object Recognition, Cluster Analysis.

1 Introduction

In case-based object recognition, a group of similar objects is represented by a generalized case for efficient matching. If this representative case is not known *a-priori* it must be learnt from real examples. Special problems arise if the objects of interest have a great variation, so they cannot be generalized by one single case. A case base is necessary which describes the different appearances of the objects. But then it is not known in advance how many cases are necessary to detect all objects with a sufficiently high accuracy.

Clustering techniques can be used to mine for groups of similar cases in a set of acquired cases. For each group it is possible to determine a generalized case to represent this group. Because we do not know the number of cases in advance, we will use the hierarchical cluster-analysis method to learn a hierarchy of increasingly generalized cases. Applying a hierarchical instead of a flat case-base for case-based object recognition might speed up the recognition process especially in CBR applications with very large case bases.

When learning a representative case of a cluster, this case should average over all cases in this cluster by generalizing common properties of the instances. We offer two different approaches to calculate such a representative. While the first one is to learn an artificial case that is positioned in the centroid, the second one selects that case out of a cluster which has the minimum distance to all other cases in this cluster. It is also important to know the permissible dissimilarity from this generalized case because it has to be taken into account in the matching process. The more groups are established in a hierarchy level, the less generalized these representatives will be.

We will present in this paper our study on learning generalized cases. First we review related work on clustering in Section 2 and describe the material used for our study in Section 3. After having reviewed some agglomerative clustering methods in Section 4, we describe our novel algorithm for learning general cases in Section 5. The description of the calculation of cluster representatives is given in Section 6. We discuss experimental results in Section 7 and, finally, give conclusions in Section 8.

2 Related Work

Cluster analysis [1], [2] is used to mine for groups of similar observations in a set of unordered observations. There are plenty of different clustering algorithms [3], [4] and which one is best suited depends on the dataset and on the special properties and aims coupled with the cluster analysis. One main difference is the resulting organization of the instances. In our application, we prefer disjunctive clustering algorithms, because every case has to be assigned to exactly one cluster. If the number of clusters is known *a-priori*, partitioning clustering [5] can be used. If it is unknown or impossible to determine the number of clusters in advance, it might be better to create a sequence of partitions using hierarchical clustering methods.

A hierarchical clustering method [1], [4] divides the set of all input cases into a sequence of disjunctive partitions. They can be distinguished between agglomerative and divisive methods. The main drawback of conventional hierarchical clustering algorithms is that once a cluster has been formed, there is no way to redesign this cluster if necessary after other examples have been seen. Another main problem is that it is only possible to draw conclusions about the composition of the clusters. They do not explain why a cluster was established and they supply no real indication about the quality of single partitions. To determine the optimal number of clusters, different cluster validity indices [6] can be used. However, these indices have to be calculated in an off-line phase after the clustering has been done. Besides, conventional clustering methods supply no precise description about the clusters. One has to calculate this manually for each cluster in a post-processing step.

Alternatively, different conceptual clustering algorithms [7], [8] were developed. They establish clusters with a utility function, which can be built on a probabilistic concept [8], or a similarity-based concept [8]. On the basis of this function they explain why a set of cases confirm a cluster and automatically supply a comprehensive description of the established concepts. Their concept-forming strategy is more flexible than the one of the conventional clustering algorithms.

3 Material

In our application we are studying the shapes of six different airborne fungal spores. Table 1 shows one of the images for each analyzed fungal strain. The objects have a great variance in appearance, so that it is impossible to represent their shape by only one case. From the real images, we acquired a set of shapes for each species. These shapes were pair-wise aligned to obtain a measure of distance between them. A detailed description of our shape acquisition and alignment process was presented

Table 1. Images of six different fungal strains

Alternaria Alternata	Aspergillus Niger	Rhizopus Stolonifer
Scopul. Brevicaulis	Ulocladium Botrytis	Wallenia Sebi

in [9]. The alignment of every possible pair of shapes leads us to $N \times N$ distances between N acquired cases. These distances can be collected in a square symmetric distance matrix, which will be used as input for the hierarchical cluster analysis.

4 Agglomerative Clustering Methods

There are plenty of different agglomerative clustering methods. We have analyzed how they can be used for our problem of learning groups of similar cases and group representatives with its concept description. In agglomerative clustering methods, initially each case forms its own cluster. They become merged with increasing distances until all cases are combined in only one cluster. The distance where two clusters become one for the first time is called cophenetic proximity measure. Note that this proximity measure is not equal to the pair-wise dissimilarity measure. The clusters are merged together on specific converted distances, so every method establishes an own ultra-metric [2].

In summary, it can be said that the agglomerative hierarchical clustering methods give a good impression about the organization of the underlying dataset. However, these algorithms only produce a sequence of partitions, but give no further indication about why this cluster was established. Thus, all other information concerning a more detailed description of a cluster has to be calculated manually. The agglomerative clustering methods are simple but also rigid and inflexible. They offer merging as the only possibility to incorporate a case into a hierarchy. Once a case is merged, it is impossible to separate it or to change the cluster again. If it turns out later that a classification was wrong, this is irreversible. Beside that, these clustering methods cannot be used for incremental learning.

5 Our Conceptual Clustering Algorithm

Conceptual clustering is a type of flexible learning of the hierarchy by observations. The partitioning of the cases is controlled by a category utility function [1], which can be based on a probabilistic [7], or a similarity concept [8]. Our conceptual clustering algorithm presented here is based on similarities, because we do not consider logical but numerical concepts.

The algorithm results in a sequence of partitions (concept hierarchy) where the root node contains the complete set of input cases and each terminal node represents an individual case. Initially the concept hierarchy only consists of an empty root node. The algorithm implements a top-down method. Each new case is successively incorporated, so the algorithm dynamically fits the hierarchy to the data. A new case is tentatively placed into the actual concept hierarchy level by level beginning with the root node until a terminal node is reached. In each hierarchy level, one of these four different kinds of operations is performed:

- The new case is incorporated into an existing child node,
- A new empty child node is created where the new case is incorporated,
- Two existing nodes are merged to a node where the new case is incorporated, and
- An existing node is split into its child nodes.

Finally that operation is performed which gives the best score to the partition according to the evaluation criteria. A proper evaluation function prefers compact and well-separated clusters. These are clusters with small inner-cluster variances and high inter-class variances. Thus we calculate the score of a partition by

$$SCORE = \frac{1}{m} \sum_{i=1}^{m} p_i \left(SB_i - SW_i \right), \qquad (1)$$

where m is the number of clusters in this partition, p_i is the relative frequency of the i-th cluster, SB_i is the inter-cluster variance and SW_i is the inner-cluster variance of the i-th cluster. The normalization according to m is necessary to compare partitions of different size. The algorithm automatically determines how many clusters are necessary to obtain the best score.

We introduced a pruning criterion into the algorithm, which can be used optionally. It says that the clusters in one partition are removed if the sum of their inner-cluster-

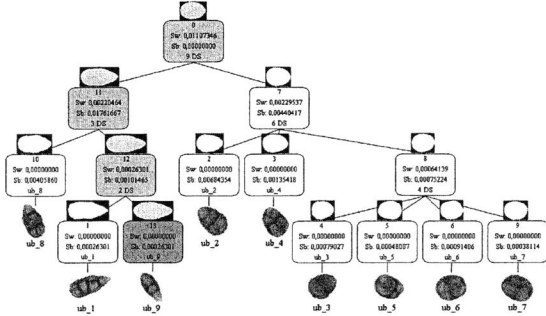

Fig. 1. Concept hierarchy after incrementally incorporating a new case. The *darker* nodes are those clusters which are modified because the new case was inserted. For these nodes the concept description and the representative cases had to be updated.

variances is *zero*. Fig. 1 shows the complete, not pruned concept hierarchy, where a new case was incorporated supplementarily. The darker nodes were those clusters, which had to be updated because the new case was incorporated into them.

6 Calculation of General Cases

The representative case of a cluster is a more general representation of all cases hosted in this cluster. Since this case should average over all cases in that cluster, a good case might be positioned in the centroid of the cluster. In our conceptual clustering algorithm the concept description is based on the inner-cluster-variance. The inner-cluster-variance of a cluster X is calculated by

$$SW_X = \frac{1}{n_X} \sum_{i=1}^{n_X} d(x_i, \overline{\mu}_X)^2 , \qquad (2)$$

where $\overline{\mu}_X$ is the centroid and n_X is the number of cases in the cluster X. Since the cluster centroid is represented by an artificial case, a second approach is to select the medoid as a natural representative case for a cluster. The medoid x_{medoid} of a cluster X is the shape case that has the minimum distance to all other cases in the cluster

$$\overline{\mu}_X = x_{medoid} = \arg \min_{x \in X} \sum_{i=1}^{n_X} d(x_i, x) . \qquad (3)$$

When matching objects with a hierarchical case-base of increasingly specialized cases, it is important to know the degree of generalization for each case. This measure will be used as a threshold for the similarity score while matching. Therefore, we calculate the maximum permissible distance D_X from this generalized case

$$D_X = \max_{x \in X} d(x, \overline{\mu}_X) . \qquad (4)$$

7 Experimental Results

Our conceptual clustering algorithm was directly applied to the set of shape cases instead of the matrix of pair-wise distances between those cases. The established groups appear useful and logical. If we compare this hierarchy to the outputs of the agglomerative clustering algorithms, it is very similar to the median method, which is based on the distances between un-weighted cluster centroids. The outputs are similar, but the main difference is how these results were obtained. In comparison to the agglomerative methods, our conceptual clustering algorithm is incremental and more flexible. If during the process it turns out that a classification was wrong, it is still possible to split or merge a formed cluster afterwards. If a new case is incorporated into the concept hierarchy, the algorithm dynamically fits the hierarchy to the new data. It has linear time complexity $O(N)$. By contrast the agglomerative clustering methods have to calculate the complete hierarchy again if a new case should be incorporated supplementary. Thus, conceptual clustering is better suited for huge databases and all applications where it is necessary to adapt the hierarchy by learning new cases over time. Our algorithm brings the right concept description for our purpose of learning case groups and generalized cases. The calculated general cases represent the clusters and are stored into the case base. The measures inner-cluster variance, inter-cluster variance, and maximum permissible distance to the cluster centroid help us to understand on what hierarchy level we should stop to generalize the cases, so that we can achieve good results during the matching process.

8 Conclusion

We have described how to learn a hierarchical case base of general cases from a set of acquired cases. It has shown that classical hierarchical clustering methods give a good impression about the organization of the cases, but fail if further information is necessary. We have also shown that our algorithm is more flexible since the establishing of the hierarchy is not only based on merging, but it is also possible to split, incorporate, and create clusters. In addition to that, it allows incremental incorporation of new cases, while the hierarchy is only adapted to fit the new data. Due to its concept description, our conceptual clustering algorithm supplies for each cluster a generalized case and a measure for the degree of its generalization. This output in form of a hierarchical case base with decreasingly generalized cases is the basis for efficient application in case-based object recognition.

Acknowledgement

The project is sponsored by the European Commission within the project "Multimedia Understanding through Semantics, Computation, and Learning" No. 507752.

References

1. P. Perner, Data Mining on Multimedia Data, Springer Verlag Berlin, 1998
2. H.J. Mucha, Clusteranalyse mit Mikrocomputern, Akademie Verlag, Berlin, 1992
3. A.K. Jain and R.C. Dubes, Algorithms for Clustering Data, Prentice Hall, 1988
4. E. Rasmussen, Clustering Algorithms, In W.B. Frakes and R. Baeza-Yates (Eds), Information Retrieval, pp. 419-442, Prentice Hall, 1992
5. J.B. MacQueen, Some Methods for classification and Analysis of Multivariate Observations, Proc. of 5th Berkeley Symposium on Mathematical Statistics and Probability, pp. 281-297, Berkeley, University of California Press, 1967
6. D.L. Davies and D.W. Bouldin, A cluster separation measure, IEEE Transactions on Pattern Analysis and Machine Intelligence, Vol. 1, No. 2, pp. 224-227, 1979
7. D. Fisher and P. Langley, Approaches to conceptual clustering, Proc. of the 9th International Joint Conference on Artificial Intelligence, pp. 691-697, Los Angeles, 1985
8. P. Perner, Different Learning Strategies in a Case-Based Reasoning System for Image Interpretation, In B. Smith and P. Cunningham (Eds.), Advances in Case-Based Reasoning, pp. 251-261, Springer Verlag, lnai 1488, 1998
9. P. Perner and S. Jänichen, Case Acquisition and Case Mining for Case-Based Object Recognition, In: Peter Funk and Pedro A. Gonzalez Calero (Eds.), Advances in Case-Based Reasoning, Proc. of the ECCBR 2004, pp. 616-629, Springer Verlag, 2004

Learning Similarity Measure of Nominal Features in CBR Classifiers

Yan Li[1], Simon Chi-Keung Shiu[1], Sankar Kumar Pal[2], and James Nga-Kwok Liu[1]

[1] Department of Computing, Hong Kong Polytechnic University,
Kowloon, HongKong
[2] Machine Intelligence Unit, Indian Statistical Institute,
Kolkata, 700 035, India
{csyli, csckshiu, csnkliu}@comp.polyu.edu.hk,
sankar@isical.ac.in

Abstract. Nominal feature is one type of symbolic features, whose feature values are completely unordered. The most often used existing similarity metrics for symbolic features is the Hamming metric, where similarity computation is coarse-grained and may affect the performance of case retrieval and then the classification accuracy. This paper presents a GA-based approach for learning similarity measure of nominal features for CBR classifiers. Based on the learned similarities, the classification accuracy can be improved, and the importance of each nominal feature can be analyzed to enhance the understanding of the used data sets.

1 Introduction

In the past decades, CBR systems [1, 2] have been successfully applied to various domains, among which those used in classification problems are called CBR classifiers. Since the basic assumption in CBR is that similar problems should have similar solutions, the similarity metric plays a critical role in case matching and retrieval. In this paper, we develop a GA-based method for learning the similarity measures of nominal features for CBR classifiers.

Nominal feature is one type of symbolic features whose values are completely unordered. Obviously, the unordered values provide less information than the ordered ones. This is reflected in comparing two cases in a case base. Based on the ordered feature values, we can not only identify whether a given pair of cases has the same feature values or not, but also find out the ordered relation between the two feature values. In contrast, based on the completely unordered feature values, there are only two relationships for a given pair of cases: same or different. From the point of view of information system, these unordered domain values of nominal features lead to coarse information granules, which may bring the difficulty of determining an accurate similarity measure in case matching and retrieval.

There are various forms of distance metrics and similarity measures for different types of features. The most common metrics are Euclidean Distance, Hamming distance, and Cosine coefficients. Among them the Hamming metric is the most often used for nominal features, where the similarity of two different nominal feature values is defined as zero and the similarity of two equal feature values is one. To deal with both numerical and symbolic features, many researchers proposed various heterogonous similarity measures [3-6]. However, in their definitions, the similarity measure of the nominal features is still the same to that in Hamming metric. In this research, we make a first attempt to show that, when two nominal feature values are different, the similarity should not always be set as zero. The domain of the similarity will be extended from {0, 1} to [0, 1] to obtain a fine-grained measure of nominal features.

A GA-based supervised learning approach is developed to obtain the similarity measure of nominal values for a given classification problem. Here we assume that there are only limited feature values in the domains of each nominal feature. Theoretically, if there are n elements in the domain of a feature, $n \cdot (n-1)/2$ similarity values need to be learned to determine the similarity measure of this feature. In practice, it is not necessary to determine so many similarity values. If two different nominal feature values certainly lead to different class labels, the similarity between these two nominal values is assumed as zero. The GA-based method is then used to learn the similarity values of other nominal feature values. The learned similarity values improve the classification accuracy and can be used to analyze the importance of each feature in the given CBR classifier.

2 Significance of Learning Nominal Feature Similarity: An Illustrative Example

Table 1 describes a case base with nominal features. The classification problem is to predict which continent a person comes from depending on his hair color and complexion. The features "Hair_Color" (H) and "Complexion" (C) are conditional features; and the last feature, "Place", is the class label. The domains of the two conditional features are represented by $D_H = \{Bl, Br, G, R\}$ and $D_C = \{Ye, Bl, W\}$, respectively.

Table 1. A case base with nominal features

ID	H	C	Place
1	R	Bl	Asia
2	R	Ye	Asia
3	Bl	W	Europe

Table 2. Testing cases

ID	H	C	Place
1	Bl	Ye	Asia
2	Br	Bl	Asia
3	G	Ye	Asia
4	G	W	Europe
5	Br	W	Europe
6	R	W	Europe

Traditionally, the similarity between every two different nominal feature values is zero. However, from the class labels of the cases in Table 1, Ye and Bl should be more similar than Ye and W does. This is based on the observation that either a person has the complexion of *Ye* or *Bl*, he comes from Asia; while if the person has *W* complexion, he surely comes from Europe. If we still assume that the similarity of *Ye* and *Bl* is zero, problems will arise when classifying new problems (unseen cases). Given a problem e, $e = \{H = R, C = Bl\}$, based on the similarity metric in [6], cases 2 and 6 are retrieved with $sim(e, 2) = sim(e, 6) = 0.5$. Therefore, e cannot be classified to "Asia" or "Europe".

To address the problem, we can adapt the similarity measure of *Ye*, *Bl*, and *W* for the feature *C* by making use of the hidden information in the class labels. For example, if we redefine that $sim(Ye, Bl) = 1 > 0$, then the retrieved cases will be 1, 2, 3, and 6. Based on the majority voting rule, the class label of the unseen case e is determined as "Asia".

This redefined similarity measure can be also used to analyze the goodness of each nominal feature. In this paper, the contribution of a feature to the given classification problem is evaluated by the inconsistent degree caused by using the feature for case retrieval. The smaller the degree, the more useful is the feature. The inconsistency arises when cases have the same feature values but belong to different classes. In this sense, the best two situations (when the inconsistency degree = 0) of a feature f are (i) all cases with different feature values are certainly classified to different classes; (ii) all cases with different feature values belong to the same classes. In the first situation, all the similarities of different feature values of f are equal to zero, and in the second situation, they are equal to one. Therefore, a feature is said to be more useful when its learned similarity values are closer to zero or one. We define a distance d between the similarity values of a feature f and the set $\{0, 1\}$ as

$$d(\{s_1, s_2, ..., s_L\}, \{0,1\}) = \sum_{i=1}^{L} \min\{s_i, 1-s_i\}, \quad (1)$$

where $\{s_1, s_2, ..., s_L\}$ is the learned set of similarity values of f. In the following sections, d is also denoted as $d(f, \{0, 1\})$.

3 Using GA to Learn Similarity Measure for Nominal Features

This section describes a supervised GA algorithm for learning the similarity values falling in [0, 1] instead of {0, 1}. Let there be a case base consisting of N cases e_1, e_2, ..., e_N, m nominal features $f_1, f_2, ..., f_m$. The domain of each feature has limited elements represented by $D_i = \{v_{i1}, v_{i2}, ..., v_{m,l_i}\}$, $i = 1, 2, ..., m$; v_{ij} is a nominal value, l_i is the number of different values of the i-th feature. As we have mentioned in Section 1, $L_i = l_i \cdot (l_i - 1)/2$ similarity values should be learned at most for the i-th feature.

Encoding rule
In the GA algorithm, each chromosome is encoded as a string consisting of m parts corresponding to the m features. A chromosome c takes the form shown in Fig. 1. For the i-th part, there are L_i genes represented by L_i decimals: $s_{ip} \in [0, 1]$, $(1 \leq p \leq L_i)$, representing the similarity measure for the i-th feature. The initial values of $s_{ij} (1 \leq p \leq L_i)$ is randomly generated for $i = 1, 2, ..., m$.

s_{11}	s_{12}	...	s_{1L_1}		s_{21}	...	s_{2L_2}		...		s_{m1}	s_{m2}	...	s_{mL_m}
0.25	0.10	...	0.83		0.62	...	0.35				0.74	0.40	...	0.56

Fig. 1. A chromosome c

Fitness Function
In this research, the fitness function of a chromosome c is the corresponding classification accuracy using the similarity values indicated in c. The classification accuracy is the ratio of the number of correctly classified cases, n_c, over the whole number of unseen cases, N_P. The fitness function is then defined as: $fitness(c) = n_c / N_P$.

The GA Algorithm
a) Initialize the population of the chromosomes. A population set is represented by $\{c_1, c_2, ..., c_P\}$, where P is the size of the population. Each chromosome is encoded as in Fig. 1. Each gene is a randomly initialized to be a decimal in [0, 1], representing the similarity value between two nominal values in the domain of each nominal feature.
b) Selection and crossover. Here the selection probability is set as 1 and the whole set of population is considered to be the mating pool. These settings let the modal to be closer to a random search. In each generation, two chromosomes are randomly selected to perform crossover. The cutting point for crossover is randomly generated and the genes in the two chromosomes that lie behind the cutting point are exchanged to produce an offspring.
c) Mutation. Let the mutation probability be p_{muta}. Randomly select one gene g (with value v_g) in the newly generated offspring string, and convert the value v_g to $(1-v_g)$.
d) End condition. Repeat (a)-(c) until the number of generations attains a predefined threshold.

4 Simulation Results and Analysis

Two examples are used in the simulations to show the effectiveness of learning similarity measure using the GA algorithm. The used data sets include the example case base in Table 1 and the Balloons database from the UCI repository [7].

4.1 Example 1

The cases in Table 1 are used as training data, and those in Table 2 are used as testing cases. There are totally 6 similarity values which need to be determined, five for the feature H and one for the feature C. Therefore, each chromosome has two parts, the first of which consists of 5 genes and the second part has only one gene. Here the size of population $P = 10$, the terminal number of generations is from 100 to 20000, and the mutation probability $P_m = 0.05$.

Table 3 shows the results of the learned similarity measure for the nominal features. For feature H, Bl and Br is the most similar feature values, and then comes

Table 3. Learned similarity measure of nominal features (testing accuracy = 1)

Number of Generations	sim(Bl, Br)	sim(Bl, G)	sim(Br, G)	sim(G, R)	sim(Br, R)	sim(Ye, Bl)
100	0.38	0.07	0.29	0.74	0.19	0.45
500	0.69	0.72	0.53	0.45	0.50	0.55
1,000	0.66	0.55	0.50	0.44	0.46	0.54
5,000	0.72	0.49	0.49	0.52	0.47	0.51
10,000	0.76	0.50	0.50	0.50	0.51	0.50
20,000	0.84	0.49	0.49	0.51	0.50	0.50
Avg.	0.68	0.47	0.47	0.53	0.44	0.51
$d(*, \{0, 1\})$		0.36			0.16	

the pair of G and R; and for feature C, $sim(Ye, Bl) = 0.51$ is much greater than $sim(Ye, W) = sim(Bl, W) = 0$. With these similarity values, all the testing cases in Table 2 can be correctly classified by the training cases.

Here $d(*, \{0, 1\})$ in Table 3 denotes the distance of the learned similarities to the set of $\{0, 1\}$ defined by Equation 1, where * means the feature H or C. Therefore, the feature C is more important for classifying unseen cases than the feature H does.

4.2 Example 2

The Balloons Database consists of 16 cases and 4 nominal features. There are two nominal values in the domain of each conditional feature. It is found that there are 4 similarity values which need to be learned.

Six cases are firstly selected as the training data and the remaining 10 cases are used as testing cases. The original classification accuracy based on the majority voting principle is 0.70. In the learning process of the GA algorithm, the mutation probability is also set as 0.05 as in Section 4.1.

Table 4. Learned similarity values on Balloons Database (Original accuracy = 0.70)

Number of Generations	sim(Yellow, Purple)	sim(Small, Large)	sim(Stretch, Dip)	sim(Adult, Child)	Accuracy
100	0.55	0.43	0.69	0.28	1.0
500	0.56	0.86	0.83	0.38	0.9
1,000	0.57	0.55	0.79	0.24	0.9
5,000	0.63	0.51	0.29	0.03	1.0
10,000	0.65	0.31	0.84	0.25	1.0
20,000	0.70	0.33	0.79	0.23	1.0
Avg.	0.61	0.50	0.71	0.24	0.97
$d(*, \{0, 1\})$	0.39	0.36	0.23	0.23	-

Note: * denotes the features, Color, Size, Act, and Age, respectively.

Table 4 shows the learned similarity values for the four nominal features. With these similarity values, the accuracy increases from the original 0.70 to 0.97. The distances of similarity values to $\{0, 1\}$ for "Act" and "Age" are the smallest compared with that of other features. Therefore, the features "Act" and "Age" are the most critical features to make the classification decisions. In fact, using only these two features, all the testing cases can be correctly classified based on the majority voting principle. In contrast, with the other two features "Color" and "Size", five out of ten cases are classified to the wrong classes.

5 Conclusions

In this paper, we make a first attempt to learn the similarity measures of nominal features using a GA-based approach. Two examples are used to illustrate the effectiveness of the developed learning method. The simulation results show that the testing accuracy increases and the importance of each feature is reflected in the learned similarity values. To summarize, the main contributions are as follows: (i) the similarity between the nominal features has been extended from {0, 1} to [0, 1], which can make the best out of the available information; (ii) this GA-based method is an alternative way to improve the classification accuracy; (iii) based on the learned similarity values, we can further analyze the importance of each nominal feature which can provide potential useful information to enhance the understanding of the data sets.

Acknowledgement

This work is supported by the CERG research grant #BQ-496.

References

1. J. Kolodner. *Case-Based Reasoning*. Morgan Kaufmann, San Francisco, 1993.
2. S. K. Pal and S. C. K. Shiu. *Foundations of Soft Case-Based Reasoning*. John Wiley, New York, 2004.
3. D. W. Aha, K. Dennis, and K. A. Marc. Instance-Based Learning Algorithms. *Machine Learning*, Vol. 6, pp. 37-66, 1991.
4. D. W. Aha. Tolerating noisy, irrelevant and novel attributes in instance-based learning algorithms. *International Journal of Man-Machine Studies*, Vol. 36, pp. 267-287, 1992.
5. D. R. Wilson and T. R. Martinez. Improved Heterogeneous Distance Functions. *Journal of Artificial Intelligence Research*, Vol. 6, pages 1-34, 1997.
6. K.C. Gowda and E. Diday. Symbolic clustering using a new similarity measure. *IEEE trans. Systems, man Cybernetics*, Vol. 22, pp.368-378, 1992.
7. S. Hettich, C. L. Blake, and C. J. Merz. UCI Repository of Machine Learning Databases: [http://www.ics.uci.edu/~mlearn/MLRepository.html]. Irvine, CA: University of California, Department of Information and Computer Science.

Decision Tree Induction with CBR

B. Radhika Selvamani and Deepak Khemani

A.I. & D.B. Lab, Dept. of Computer Science & Engineering,
I.I.T. Madras, India
bradhika@cs.iitm.ernet.in, khemani@iitm.ac.in

Abstract. This paper describes an application of CBR with decision tree induction in a manufacturing setting to analyze the cause for defects reoccurring in the domain. Abstraction of domain knowledge is made possible by integrating CBR with decision trees. The CID approach augments the recall and reuse done by CBR with statistical analysis that is focused towards the discovery of connections between specific defects and their possible causes. We show that this discovery also gives a pointer towards a corresponding corrective action.

1 Introduction

In most domains we can acquire the initial seed cases from the experts, documents or databases in the domain. However such a case base may fail to respond to a query due to: (1) Lack of adequate coverage (2) Presence of noisy cases (3) Occurrence of a novel case. The problem of case coverage may be solved over time when the experts update the case base periodically. Instance-based learning (IBL) is a carefully focused case-based learning approach that contributes evaluated algorithms for selecting good cases for classification, reducing storage requirements, tolerating noise and learning attribute relevances. Handling noisy instances has been widely explored in the IBL framework [1,2]. Occurrence of a novel case can be viewed as a gap in the case base. That is, a query case may find a similar case in the case base, but the retrieved case may be incomplete for solving the given problem. The case needs to be completed with the appropriate solution before it contributes to the case base. Traditional process of reminding as in CBR cannot address the problem at hand. The domain expert may complete an incomplete case after analysis. Other machine learning techniques like case adaptation, decision trees [7], data mining [4] etc., can be combined with CBR [3,10] to handle the problem. One such situation is that in which diagnosis of a frequently occurring fault has to be done. The fault may not have a corrective action identified, or the corrective action in current practice may not be working anymore. In the absence of a well-defined underlying theory, the first step in diagnosis would be the identification of possible parameters that could be causally linked to the fault. This task can be done by a statistical analysis of the past data, and it has been proposed as the construction of a Cause Induction in Discrimination Tree (CID Tree) [8]. We apply the technique to a real world problem from the manufacturing domain[1]. The paper is organized as follows. The earlier work relating induction with CBR has been

---

[1] This research work has been supported by a grant from Tube Products Investments, Carborundum Universal Ltd., Madras, India.

discussed. The domain where the algorithm has been applied and the experimental set up are explained. Finally the results obtained and the conclusions are given.

2 Domain

The domain is manufacturing steel strips. The raw material is in the form of a coil that passes through various process departments as follows. The pickling department first treats the coil with acid. The coils are then cut into strips of required length and width in the slitting department. The strips are reduced to the required thickness by drawing the steel sheets through a number of passes in a cold roll mill (CRM). Then the strips are subjected to annealing. Tests are done on the strips to check if they satisfy the required physical and mechanical properties. The parameters affecting the final product are the chemical properties of the raw coil used, the preprocessing parameters, the load and pressure parameters during drawing and the annealing parameters. The final steel sheets may have various defects like scratches, edge cracks, dent punch etc. When a defect is found, the strip is remade with modified parameters.

A CBR system was installed to capture the case history in the domain. All the cases manufactured are added to the case base. The case base evolves with each instance of manufacturing. Whenever a defect is seen, the case base is consulted for remedies. If no case is found, the defective case is added to the case base after appropriate analysis on the defect. The aim of the current work is to help the experts analyze the defects when the CBR system lacks the required information explicitly.

2.1 Case Structure

The cases are sought for a solution whenever there occurs a defect in the products. The problem space of the case is made up of the design attributes, the process parameters and the defect description. The solution space consists of possible remedies, which are suggested changes to the process parameters. The solution hence depends on the context provided by the problem space. A case is incomplete when it describes a defective with no corresponding solution. A case without a solution has no utility and hence considered a gap. The aim is to provide the experts with a set of suggestions to complete these cases and thus eliminate the gaps in the system

3 CBR with Cause Induction

CBR with cause induction algorithm CID Tree [8,9] was applied in the domain. The CIDTree method has two phases. The construction of the discrimination tree based on defect clusters constitutes the first phase and the induction process the second phase. During the first phase, the cases are labeled as good or bad based on the presence or absence of the defect to be analyzed. The labeled cases are then used in building up a discrimination tree (We used c4.5 induction algorithm for the experiments). Investigating the possible causes for the defect forms the second phase of the method. The aim of the analysis is to select a pair of nodes under the same parent, such that each has high importance with respect to the alternative classes (Good, Bad). One can observe that if there were a single identifiable cause for the defect in the case records then it would show up at the root of a three-node induction tree. The fact that in practice the induction trees are layered implies that this is not the case. In this situation, the CID algorithm inspects the tree to locate the most likely cause or causes for the given defect. The data is presumably noisy as well. The relevance score for each node P in causing the defect is calculated as follows. $Score_p = (D_p^2 * N_s^2)/(N_p^2 * D_s^2)$

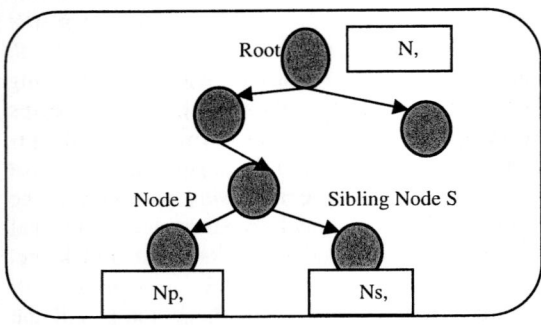

Fig. 1. Distribution of Cases at the Nodes

N_p, D_p are the number of good and bad cases under the node P.

N_s, D_s are the number of good and bad cases under the sibling node S.

N, D are the numer of good and bad cases present at the root.

Note that relevance score depends only upon the number of cases under the two nodes. It is high when the node P has relatively high number of defective cases compared to S. If P has more than one sibling, their numbers are clubbed into the parameters Ns and Ds.

3.1 Relevance of the Node

A node represents a pattern observed among the instances, which is the path of the node from the root (Fig.1). A decision tree holds all patterns that provide better classification accuracy within an optimum height. The number of defective/good instances classified under a node can be used to measure the support and confidence of the pattern causing a defective/good case. Let P be a node representing a pattern, the alternative pattern formed by changing the last decision is the sibling node S. We look at the statements (P => Defect), which is to be read as node P is the cause of the defect and (P=>Good) read as P reduces defects.

Support(P => Defect)   : Fraction of defects under node P over all cases = $D_p/(N+D)$.   (1)
Confidence(P=>Defect) : Fraction of defects among those under the node P=$D_p/(N_p+D_p)$ (2)
Support (P => Good)   : Fraction of good cases under node P over all cases = $N_p/(N+D)$.   (3)
Confidence(P=>Good): Fract. of good cases among those under the node P = $N_p/(N_p+D_p)$.   (4)

Maximize support and confidence (P => Defect):

$$D_p^2 / (N+D) * (N_p+D_p) \quad . \tag{1x2}$$

Minimize support and confidence (P => Good):

$$N_p^2 / (N+D) * (N_p+D_p) \quad . \tag{3x4}$$

Minimize support and confidence (S => Defect):

$$D_s^2 / (N+D) * (N_s+D_s) \quad . \tag{5}$$

Maximize support and confidence (S => Good):

$$N_s^2 / (N+D) * (N_s+D_s) \quad . \quad (6)$$

Relevance of Node P in causing the defect

$$D_p^2 N_s^2 / D_s^2 N_p^2 \quad . \quad (1 \times 2 \times 6 / 3 \times 4 \times 5)$$

Score(P=>Defect): $(D_p^2 N_s^2 + \text{residue}) / (D_s^2 N_p^2 + \text{residue})$

Score(P=>Good) : 1/Score

We have avoided division by zero by adding a residue to the formula.

Earlier work to convert decision trees to rules focused on extracting more comprehensive structures from the tree preserving the accuracy of classification [7]. We are extracting the patterns those are more relevant with respect to the defect used to label the instances. In our earlier work [8,9] we had tried out the algorithm with defects in a refractory blocks manufacturing setting [5,6]. The induction tree classifying the defects in the case base was instrumental in the diagnosis process. The correlations suggested by the trees were in agreement with the experts' intuitions in creating trials during failures. These are rules, which extracted the domain knowledge from the collected cases. The experiments, done on the steel strips manufacturing domain, are described in the following section.

4 Experiments

Data was obtained for 130 parameters from the domain. We have 1168 records from the domain and have done the analysis for three different types of defects namely scratch, edge cracks and dent punch. There were 231 records with scratches, 16 records with edge cracks and 51 with dent punch. The attributes Si (silicon) and others1 (other chemicals) are chemical characteristics of the raw material, the attributes A, B, C are the different vendors (names changed) of raw materials, CRMPasses is the number of times the sheet is passed through the CRM mills to reduce the thickness. The cases were labeled as D-defective case and N-Good case, based on the occurrence of the particular defect in the case to be analyzed.

4.1 CBR C4.5 and CID

The primary goal of the CBR implementation is to suggest process changes when there occurs a defect. When the CBR has cases, which do not provide any solution there is a gap in the system. The system retrieves cases based on the similarity of the problem, but lacks information to solve the problem. The case completion requires acquiring a solution for the problem. Note that all cases have defect description as part of the problem space, which is used to label the cases for induction There is enough information available for building the decision tree though cases are incomplete in the case base. The decision tree obtained using C4.5 is in Fig 2. Now to obtain a solution for a particular defect, we obtain the prominent patterns from the c4.5 using CID scoring. The results are shown in the Table1. This information when added to the cases, which have the particular defect, fills the gap in the system.

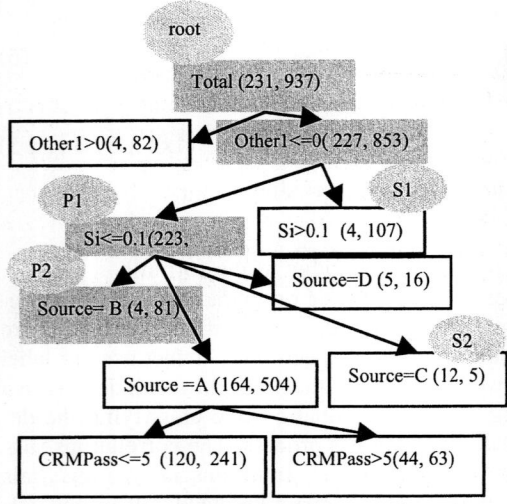

Table 1. The Scores Obtained by CID

Attribute	D	N	Scor	1/Sc
Others	231.3	936.7	0	0
Other1<=0	227.4	853.6	33.6	0
Other1 > 0	3.8	83.2	0	33.6
Si<= 0.1	223.4	746.3	62.0	0
Si > 0.1	4.1	107.3	0	62.0
Source =A	164.3	504.8	1.8	0.6
Source = B	3.8	81.2	0	49.1
Source = C	11.4	4.6	73.5	0
Source =D	4.8	15.8	1.1	1
CRMPass<=5	120.5	242.0	8.9	0.1
CRMPass>5	43.8	262.7	0.1	8.9

Fig. 2. Analysis of scratch in strips manufacturing

4.2 Results

The objective is to learn the causes for certain defects from the cases collected in the case base to complete the cases without solution. The incomplete cases may be filled up with their respective solutions based on the results obtained from the algorithm.
Scratches

- If the raw material for the sheet had silicon < 0.1 % then there were more scratches. The experts agreed upon this. (Shown as P1 and S1 in Fig. 2).
- The algorithm also identified that raw materials purchased from sourceB had less scratches and that from C had more (shown as P2 and S2 in Fig. 2).

Cracked Edges
- Similarly %carbon being less was found to be the cause for cracked edges.

Dent Punch
- Analysis on dent punch showed that pass2thickness being less (mechanical property) caused the defect. But dentpunch is known to occurr due to use of defective raw material (chemical property). The nonconforming results were attributed to the scratch data being misclassified as dentpunch.

In the above experiment the experts could suggest a change in source raw material for better results in cases with scratches. Better classification of the defects scratch and dentpunch may avoid erroneous cases.

5 Conclusions

Case Based Reasoning is built on the foundation of accumulating experience and reusing it to solve problems. Traditionally this reuse is direct, in the sense that the most similar case or a set of k most similar cases are retrieved and used directly. But combined with other machine learning techniques a case base can yield more information by looking at some level of abstraction. Machine learning has been used in case acquisition and in indexing [11]. In this paper we demonstrate that a decision tree learnt to separate defective cases from non-defective cases can be used to identify attributes whose value choices could be the causes of defects. The few experiments we have done with limited data corroborate the findings. As more data accrues, we hope that in future we will develop techniques that would help shop floor personnel choose effective corrective actions when faced with previously unsolved defect problems. Closing the feedback loop in CBR [12] is very important in managing the flow in a domain using CBR. Our future work is towards generating trial cases when the case base lacks enough domain expertise. After the remedy in the trial case is tested on the shop floor, the case can be stored permanently in the case base.

References

1. Aha, D.W., Kibler, D., Albert, M. K. Instance Based Learning Algorithms, Machine Learning, 6:37-66, 1991.
2. Cost S. Salzberg. A Weighted Nearest Neighbor Algorithm for Learning with Symbolic Features, Machine Learning, 10:57-78, 1993.
3. Janet Kolodner. *Case-Based Reasoning*, Morgan Kaufmann Publishers, 1993.
4. Jiawei Han and Micheline Kamber. *Data Mining: Concepts and Techniques*, Morgan Kaufmann Publishers, 2001.
5. Khemani, D., Radhika Selvamani, B., Ananda Rabi Dhar, Michael S.M. InfoFrax: CBR in Fused Cast Refractory Manufacture. *In proceedings on the European Conference on Case Based reasoning*, Lecture Notes in Computer Science 2416 Springer, 560 – 574, 2002.
6. Michael, S. M., and Khemani D. Knowledge Management in Manufacturing Technology. *In Proceedings of the International Conference on Enterprise Information System*, Ciudad Real, Spain, Vol. I, 506-512, 2002.
7. Quinlan, J.R., *C4.5: Programs for Machine Learning*, Morgan Kaufmann Publishers, 1993.
8. Radhika Selvamani, B., Deepak Khemani. Investigating Cause for Failures in Discrimination Tree from Multiple Views. In the proceedings of the *International Conference of Knowledge Based Computer Systems*, Mumbai December 11-14, 2002.
9. Radhika Selvamani, B., Deepak Khemani. Managing Experience for Process Improvement in Manufacturing. In the proceedings of the *International Conference of Case Based Reasoning ICCBR-2003*. Trondheim Norway, June 23-26, 2003.
10. Watson, I., Applying Case Based Reasoning: Techniques for Enterprise Systems, Morgan Kaufmann Publishers, 1997.
11. Patterson, D., Anand, S S., Dubitzky, W., Hughes, J G. : Towards Automated Case Knowledge Discovery in the M2 Case-Based Reasoning System. In Knowledge and Information Systems: An International Journal. Springer Verlag, Vol. 1 61-82, 1999.
12. Price, C.J., Pegler, I.S. Ratcliffe, M.B. and McManus, A. From troubleshooting to process design: closing the manufacturing loop. In proc. *2nd International Conference, ICCBR-97*, Providence, Rhode Island, USA, Lecture Notes in Computer Science 1266 Springer, 1997.

Rough Set Feature Selection Methods for Case-Based Categorization of Text Documents

Kalyan Moy Gupta[1,2], Philip G. Moore[1,2], David W. Aha[1], and Sankar K. Pal[3]

[1] ITT Industries,
2560 Huntington Ave, Alexandria, VA, USA
[2] Naval Research Laboratory,
4555 Overlook Ave., SW, Washington, DC, USA
[3] Indian Statistical Institute,
203 Barrackpore Trunk Road, Kolkata, India
{firstname.lastname}@nrl.navy.mil, sankar@isical.aci.in

Abstract. Textual case bases can contain thousands of features in the form of tokens or words, which can inhibit classification performance. Recent developments in rough set theory and its applications to feature selection offer promising approaches for selecting and reducing the number of features. We adapt two rough set feature selection methods for use on n-ary class text categorization problems. We also introduce a new method for selecting features that computes the union of features selected from randomly-partitioned training subsets. Our comparative evaluation of our method with a conventional method on the Reuters-21578 data set shows that it can dramatically decrease training time without compromising classification accuracy. Also, we found that randomized training set partitions dramatically reduce training time.

1 Introduction

Textual Case-Based Reasoning (TCBR) is a methodology that retrieves and reuses decisions from stored documents (i.e., *cases*) to solve new problems. Some TCBR methods can be used for supervised learning tasks. For example, they have been used to assign one or more topics to a document (Wiratunga, 2004). A problematic issue in TCBR, and text categorization in general, is the high dimensionality of the feature space. Most current approaches consider the unique terms and phrases that occur in the set of documents as features. These frequently number in the tens of thousands, which is prohibitively high for most learning algorithms. A variety of feature selection techniques can be used to address this issue. Conventional filter feature selection approaches for textual data have predominantly used statistical and entropy approaches such as document frequency, information gain, and mutual information (Yang & Pederson, 1997). Previously, rough set feature selection techniques have been applied to structured data with much success (Pal & Shiu, 2004), and may be a promising alternative for textual data. In this paper, we extend and evaluate two rough set feature selection methods on n-ary class text categorization problems. We also investigate and demonstrate the effectiveness of feature selection methods using randomly partitioned training sets to reduce training time.

We organize this paper as follows. In Section 2, we briefly review feature selection techniques that have been applied with TCBR methods. In Section 3, we adapt two rough set feature selection techniques to the n-ary class problem and present a feature selection methodology using randomized training set partitions. We present their evaluation in Section 4 and Section 5 concludes the paper.

2 Related Work

Feature selection is imperative for categorization with massive textual databases. A variety of filter metrics (e.g., document frequency, information gain, mutual information) can be effectively used to select features (Yang & Pederson, 1997). These techniques, while effective, have two shortcomings. First, they have high average computational complexity. For example, the information gain measure has a complexity of $O(NVM)$ where N is the number of documents, V is the vocabulary size, and M is the number of topics. Second, the user must specify a threshold (i.e., indicate when to stop selecting features).

Rough set methods have recently been used to select features from textual data (Chouchoulas & Chen, 2001; Li et al., 2005), and have the advantage of not requiring a threshold setting. However, because finding optimal feature subsets using rough set methods is computationally intractable (i.e., NP hard), heuristic approaches (e.g., QuickReduct) have been developed. Still, the computational complexity of heuristic techniques is still problematic for massive data. For example, its worst case computational complexity is $O(RVN^2)$ where R is the size of reduct. Li et al. (2005) address this issue by developing an approximate reduct computation method that has a complexity of $O(VN)$.

Chouchoulas and Chen (2001) explored the applicability of QuickReduct to a strict categorization problem (e.g., placing an email in exactly one folder). However, they did not explore its application to n-ary classification problems in large datasets. Li et al. (2005) applied their approximate reduct computation method to small sets of n-ary classification problems, but also did not examine performance issues pertaining to massive data sets. Alternative heuristics for rough sets include Johnson's algorithm and the Best Reduct Method (Popova, 2004). In this paper, we adapt QuickReduct and Johnson's algorithm to n-ary categorization problems and examine the impact of randomized partitions on their training time and classification performance.

3 N-Ary Classification with Rough Set Feature Selection

Assigning more than one class label to an object is an *n-ary* classification task. For example, assigning multiple keywords or topics to a document is an n-ary classification task. Rough set feature selection techniques can be applied to reduce the dimensionality of datasets used for n-ary classification.

Rough set approaches view a decision system as a table, where attributes are columns and objects are rows (Pawlak, 1991). For a set of conditional attributes **C**, decision attributes **D**, and universe of objects U, let $f(x,q)$ denote an attribute value, where

$x \in \mathbf{U}$ and $q \in \mathbf{A}$ (where $\mathbf{A}=\mathbf{C}\cup\mathbf{D}$). Then $f(x,q)$ defines an equivalence relation R_q over $\mathbf{U}$ that can be used to partition $\mathbf{U}$ into its disjoint subsets as follows:

$$R_q = \{x: x \in \mathbf{U} \land f(x,q)=f(x_0,q) \ \forall x_0 \in \mathbf{U}\} \qquad (1)$$

A key concept in rough set theory is *indiscernability*. Two objects x and y are indiscernible given a subset of attributes $\mathbf{P}$ iff $f(x,q)=f(y,q) \ \forall q \in \mathbf{P}$. Let IND($\mathbf{P}$) be an indiscernability relation that partitions $\mathbf{U}$. Then rough set theory approximates traditional sets using a pair of sets called *lower* ($\underline{P}\mathbf{D}$) and *upper* ($\overline{P\mathbf{D}}$) as follows:

$$\underline{P}\mathbf{D} = \cup\{X: X \in \mathbf{U}/\text{IND}(\mathbf{P}), X \subseteq \mathbf{D}\} \qquad (2)$$

$$\overline{P\mathbf{D}} = \cup\{X: X \in \mathbf{U}/\text{IND}(\mathbf{P}), X \cap \mathbf{D}\} \qquad (3)$$

The *positive region* of $\mathbf{P}$, denoted by $\text{POS}_\mathbf{P}(Q)$ where Q is the set of decision attributes, includes all the objects that are contained by the lower approximation. These objects can be classified using the information contained only in the attributes $\mathbf{P}$. Therefore, the information contained by a set of attributes can be measured by the *degree of dependency* as follows:

$$\gamma_\mathbf{P}(Q) = \|\text{POS}_\mathbf{P}(Q)\| / \|\mathbf{U}\| \qquad (4)$$

where, $\|\ \|$ denotes a set's cardinality.

Feature selection involves removing those attributes that have no significant information pertaining to the decision task. In a rough set method, the set of attributes $\mathbf{R}$, called the *reduct*, is a set of conditional attributes such that $\gamma_\mathbf{R}(\mathbf{D})=\gamma_\mathbf{C}(\mathbf{D})$ for decision attributes $\mathbf{D}$. Computing the minimal reduct is an NP hard problem. Hence, we discuss our adaptation of heuristic methods below.

3.1 QuickReduct

QuickReduct greedily selects attributes by computing the marginal increase in the degree of dependency for every attribute it chooses to add to the reduct (see (Chouchoulas & Shen, 2001) for details). At each iteration, it chooses the attribute with the maximum marginal increase in γ. It starts out with an empty reduct and terminates when there is no change in the degree of dependency of the reduct.

We adapt QuickReduct for n-ary classification using the following indiscernability relations for conditional and decision attributes. We compute the similarity $\sigma(\mathbf{D})$ of decision attribute values V of two objects x and y follows:

$$\sigma(\mathbf{D}) = \|(V_x \cap V_y)\| / \|(V_x \cup V_y)\| \qquad (5)$$

When $\sigma(\mathbf{D}) > \tau$, where τ is a user specified threshold ($0 \leq \tau < 1$), then the two objects are considered to be indiscernible. Two text documents x and y are indiscernible with respect to a given term t (i.e., a potential conditional attribute), if either both the documents contain t or both exclude it. That is, we ignore the frequency of term occurrences in a document for establishing indiscernability.

The computational complexity of QuickReduct is $O(RVN^2)$, where V is the vocabulary size of the text collection, N is the number of documents, R is the size of reduct, and we assume that $(R<<V)$. For massive data sets, where N and V are in the tens of

thousands, this method can be computationally infeasible. Below we present Johnson's (1974) heuristic, which has a lower computational complexity.

3.2 Johnson's Heuristic

Johnson's heuristic operates on the discernibility matrix that describes how two objects x and y differ from each other given the condition attributes (see Figure 1). Each cell $c_{x,y}$ in the matrix is defined as:

$$c_{x,y} = \{\{ a \in C: a(x) \neq a(y)\} \text{ for } \mathbf{D}(x) \neq \mathbf{D}(y), \text{ and } \phi \text{ otherwise }\} \quad (6)$$

```
JOHNSONSREDUCT(C, D, U)
Input   C-conditional attributes, D-decision attribute,
        U-universe of objects
Output  R, Attribute reduct R ⊆ C
1       R←φ, O←U, A←C
2       do
3           M← computeDiscernibilityMatrix(O, A, D)
4           a_h← selectHighestScoringAttribute(M)
5           R ←R ∪ a_h
6           O ← O − entriesContaining(M, a_h)
7           A ← A - a_h
8       until O = φ
9       return R
```

Fig. 1. Pseudocode for Johnson's heuristic

Given such a matrix M, for each attribute, it counts the number of entries in the matrix. The attribute a_h with the highest number of entries is selected for addition to the reduct **R**. Then all the objects that contain a_h are removed and the procedure is repeated until no objects remain. We adapt Johnson's heuristic for n-ary classification problems as follows. For each attribute, we compute a score equivalent to the highest number of entries by weighting the respective entries with a *dissimilarity factor* $(1- \sigma(\mathbf{D}))$, which represents the value differences in the decision attributes of objects x and y. If $\sigma(\mathbf{D})= 0$, then it reduces to the standard heuristic.

The *worst case* computational complexity of JOHNSONSREDUCT is $O(RN^2)$, which is independent of the vocabulary size V. Therefore, we expect it to be much faster than QuickReduct. However, like QuickReduct, the computational cost still increases as a square of the number of documents in the database. To combat this problem, we introduce the following feature selection method.

3.3 Feature Selection with Randomized Partitions

Feature selection with randomized partitions builds on the idea of divide and conquer. By reducing the number of documents that must be processed at one time, it can significantly reduce the training time. It proceeds as follows:

1. Randomly create m partitions of the training set.
2. From each partition, select features using a rough set approach such as QuickReduct or JOHNSONSREDUCT.
3. Define the final feature set as the union of features selected from each partition.

This approach should reduce the training time by a factor $1/m^2$. Next, we describe an evaluation of the rough set approach with randomized partitions.

4 Evaluation

We designed an experiment to measure the classification accuracy and training time of the rough set feature method. We also examined the effectiveness of randomized partitions for reducing the training time.

We selected the Reuters-21578 data set (Reuters, 2005) for our evaluation. It includes 11,330 news briefs (i.e., *cases*) with one or more topics (the number of topics ranges from 1 to 16, with an average of 1.26 per case). Each brief has an average of 137 words. In addition to the two rough set methods we described in Section 3, we implemented an information gain feature selection method for comparison (see (Yang & Pederson, 1997)). Part-of-speech tagging and morphotactic processing were used to create the features prior to their selection. Finally, we used the k-nearest-neighbor (kNN) classifier, where k was empirically set to 100.

We measured the three algorithms using *11-point average precision*, which is the average precision obtained at recall thresholds of 0%, 20%, ... 100%. The system assigns as many topics as needed until a given recall is achieved (Yang & Pederson, 1997). We also measured the *training time* in seconds (we ran our experiments on a Mac Power PC G4, 1.5 GHz). Each algorithm was run multiple times with a varying number m of training set partitions (1, 10, 20, and 40) and a varying percentage of cases used for training (30%, 50%, and 70%).

QuickReduct could only be run on a small number of documents due to its long training time (270 seconds for 100 cases, and 15,500 seconds for 200 cases). On this basis, we concluded that it is not suitable for large scale n-ary classification tasks.

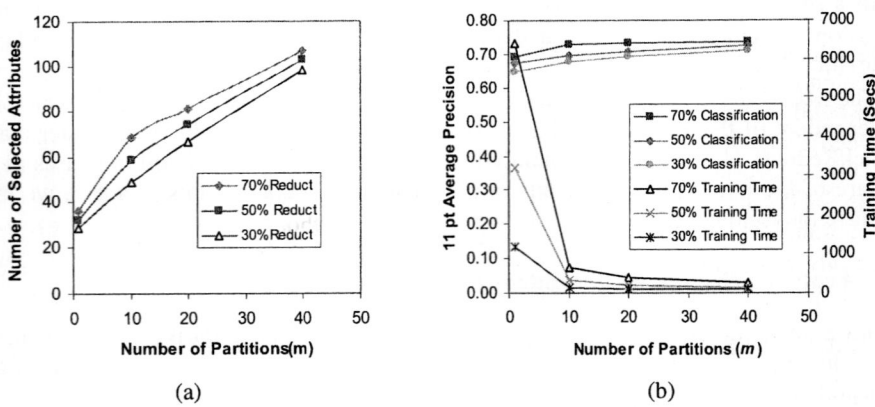

Fig. 2. (a) JOHNSONSREDUCT attribute selection performance. (b) JOHNSONSREDUCT classification and training time performance.

Figures 2(a) and 2(b) display the average (over 5 runs) performance of JOHNSONSREDUCT for feature selection, classification accuracy, and training time. It dramatically reduced the number of attributes (e.g., 11,500 to 32 for no partitions and to 107 for 40 partitions). Increasing the number of randomized partitions increased the number of selected attributes and increased the classification accuracy (69.3% for no

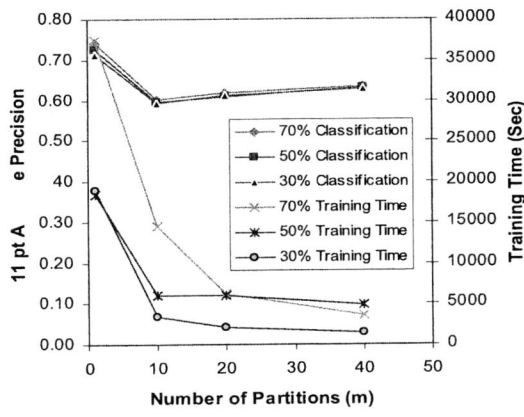

Fig. 3. Information Gain performance

partitions to 73.7% for 40 partitions). Increasing the number of partitions also drastically reduced the computation time (6400 seconds for no partitions to 260 seconds for 40). Furthermore, decreasing the percentage of training cases from 70% to 30% of the dataset only marginally reduced the classification accuracy. Thus, JOHNSONSREDUCT is effective for feature selection, and using randomized partitions is effective for reducing training time. For comparison, Figure 3 shows the classification and training time performance of information gain (IG) at the same number of attributes as JOHNSONSREDUCT. Classification accuracy is significantly lower with randomized partitions (e.g., 61% for 10 partitions). This is consistent with our expectations that IG relies on more data for reliable statistics. Further, IG training time (e.g., 37,000 seconds for no partitions) is substantially higher than JOHNSONSREDUCT (6000 seconds). This was expected due to IG's dependency on the vocabulary size.

5 Conclusion

We adapted two rough set feature selection techniques for n-ary text categorization problems. We also introduced a method of training with randomized partitions to drastically reduce their training time. Based on our preliminary evaluations, we concluded that the JOHNSONSREDUCT technique is a robust and feasible technique for feature selection for n-ary text categorization problems, while QuickReduct is unsuitable for the same. Although randomized partitions are effective for rough set feature selection, it is not effective for some conventional methods (e.g., information gain). In our future work, we will extend our evaluations to additional data sets.

Acknowledgement

We thank the Naval Research Laboratory for supporting this research.

References

Chouchoulas, A., & Shen, Q. (2001). Rough-set aided keyword reduction for text categorization. *Applied Artificial Intelligence*, **15**, 843-873.

Johnson, D.S. (1974). Approximation algorithms for combinatorial problems, *Journal of Computer and System Sciences*, **9**, 256-278.

Li, Y., Shiu, S.C.K., & Pal, S.K. (2005). Combining feature reduction and case selection in building CBR classifiers. To appear in S.K. Pal, David W. Aha, & K.M Gupta (Eds.) *Case-based reasoning in knowledge discovery and data mining*. New York, NY: Wiley.

Pal, S.K., & Shiu, S.C.K. (2004). *Foundations of soft case-based reasoning*. Hoboken, NJ: Wiley.

Pawlak, Z. (1991). *Rough sets: Theoretical aspects of reasoning about data*. Dordrecht, Poland: Kluwer.

Popova, V.N. (2004). *Knowledge discovery and monotonicity*. Doctoral dissertation, Rotterdam School of Economics, Erasmus University, The Netherlands.

Reuters (2005). [http://www.daviddlewis.com/resources/testcollections/reuters21578]

Wiratunga, N., Koychev, I., & Massie, S. (2004). Feature selection and generalization for retrieval of textual cases. *Proceedings of the Seventh European Conference on Case-Based Reasoning* (pp. 806-820). Madrid, Spain: Springer.

Yang, Y., & Pederson, J. (1997). A comparative study of feature selection in text categorization. *Proceedings of the Fourteenth International Conference on Machine Learning* (pp. 412-420). Nashville, TN: Morgan Kaufmann.

An Efficient Parzen-Window Based Network Intrusion Detector Using a Pattern Synthesis Technique

P. Viswanath[1], M. Narasimha Murty[2], and Satish Kambala[3]

[1] Dept. of CSE, IIT-Guwahati, Guwahati-781039, India
viswanath@iitg.ernet.in
[2] Dept. of CSA, IISc, Bangalore-560012, India
mnm@csa.iisc.ernet.in
[3] Dept. of CSE, NIT, Tiruchirapalli-620015, India
satish_kambala@yahoo.co.in

Abstract. The problem of detecting anomalous network connections caused by intrusion activities is called Network intrusion detection. Conventional classification methods use data from both normal and intrusion classes to build the classifiers. However, intrusion data are usually scarce and difficult to collect. Novelty detection approach overcomes this problem which depends only on normal data. For this purpose, nonparametric density estimation approaches based on Parzen-window estimators are proposed earlier. Two fundamental problems faced are, (i) due to curse of dimensionality, for high dimensional data with a limited training set, the estimation can be biased and (ii) high computational requirements. We propose, (i) a novel pattern synthesis technique to synthesize artificial new training patterns to increase the training set size and thus to reduce the curse of dimensionality effect, and (ii) a compact data representation scheme to store the entire synthetic set to reduce the computational costs. The effectiveness of our methods are experimentally demonstrated.

1 Introduction

Intrusion detection is the process of monitoring events occurring in a computer system or network and analyzing them for signs of intrusions, defined as attempts to bypass the security mechanisms of a computer or network. From a high-level view, the goal is to find out whether or not a system is operating normally. Network-based intrusion detection systems monitor network behavior by examining the content as well as the format of network data packets, which typically are not specific to the exact operating systems used by individual computers as long as these computers can communicate with each other using the same network protocol. For these types of systems, one may take a data mining approach by "mining" through the data to detect possible attacks.

Typical *classification* problems can be formulated as follows. A discriminative classifier is built using training examples from all c (≥ 2) classes, so that it can classify the given pattern into one of c classes. Many network intrusion methods are based on this approach [1,2]. This means, they have to use normal as well as intrusion data for training the classifier. But the main drawback in the case of intrusion detection is that there may not exist any valid underlying model from which the intrusion data is generated. So, one needs to differentiate between normal and abnormal (novel) data by using only normal data. This is called novelty detection.

Recently, Yeung and Chow [3] have proposed a novelty detection method using Parzen-Window based density estimation approach. For a given test pattern, its class conditional density for the normal class is obtained by using Gaussian kernel based Parzen-Window method. If this density exceeds a threshold density then the pattern is classified as normal, otherwise as novel. But two main drawbacks are, (i) due to curse of dimensionality, the estimated density can be biased with a limited training set, and (ii) the computational requirements are very high.

In this paper we propose (i) a pattern synthesis technique called *partition based pattern synthesis* to increase the training set size which in turn can reduce the curse of dimensionality effect, and (ii) a compact representation called *partitioned pattern count tree (PPC-tree)* to store the synthetic set which can reduce the computational requirements. Experimentally it is shown that our approach can outperform some of the related methods.

The rest of this paper is organized as follows: Section 2 gives a brief description of the density estimation approaches to novelty detection. Section 3 describes pattern synthesis. A Compact representation for the training set will be presented in Section 4. In Section 5 we will describe our method. Experimental results will be presented in Section 6. Finally, some concluding remarks will be made in Section 7.

2   Parzen-Window Based Density Estimation

Parzen introduced a nonparametric method for estimating density functions [4]. Let $p(x)$ be the density function to be approximated. Given a set $D = \{x_1, x_2, ..., x_n\}$ of n i.i.d. samples drawn according to $p(x)$, the Parzen-window estimate of $p(x)$ based on the n examples in D is

$$\hat{p}(x) = \frac{1}{n} \sum_{i=1}^{n} \delta_n(x - x_i)$$

where $\delta_n(.)$ is a kernel function with localized support and its exact form depends on n.

We choose to use Gaussian kernel functions for two reasons. First, the Gaussian function is smooth and hence the estimated density function $\hat{p}(x)$ also varies smoothly. Second, if we assume a special form of the Gaussian family in which the function is radially symmetrical, the function can be completely specified by a variance parameter only. Thus $\hat{p}(x)$ can be expressed as a mixture of radially symmetrical Gaussian kernels with common variance σ^2:

$$\hat{p}(x) = \frac{1}{n(2\pi)^{d/2}\sigma^d} \sum_{i=1}^{n} \exp\left\{-\frac{\|x - x_i\|^2}{2\sigma^2}\right\} \quad (1)$$

where d is the dimensionality of the feature space.

3 Partition Based Pattern Synthesis

We present in this section an instance based pattern synthesis method called partition based pattern synthesis where the given training set and some of the properties of the data are used to generate new artificial patterns.

Let $F = \{f_1, \ldots, f_d\}$ be the set of features, $\mathcal{X}$ be a set of patterns. For a pattern X, let X_B be the projection of X onto features in B where $B \subseteq F$. Let $\pi_B(\mathcal{X}) = \{X_B \mid X \in \mathcal{X}\}$.

Let us define a product ($\times$) similar to cartesian product over the sets of projected patterns as follows. Let $Z = (X_{B_1}^1, X_{B_2}^2, \ldots, X_{B_p}^p)$ be a pattern such that $Z_{B_1} = X_{B_1}^1, Z_{B_2} = X_{B_2}^2, \ldots, Z_{B_p} = X_{B_p}^p$ where $\{B_1, B_2, \ldots, B_p\}$ is a partition of F and $X^1, \ldots, X^p$ are p patterns (not necessarily distinct). Then

$$\pi_{B_1}(\mathcal{X}) \times \pi_{B_2}(\mathcal{X}) \times \ldots \times \pi_{B_p}(\mathcal{X}) = \{(X_{B_1}^1, X_{B_2}^2, \ldots, X_{B_p}^p) \mid X^1, \ldots, X^p \in \mathcal{X}\}.$$

The synthetic set of patterns for a class with label l is,

$$SS_{Q_l}(\mathcal{X}^l) = \pi_{B_{l1}}(\mathcal{X}^l) \times \pi_{B_{l2}}(\mathcal{X}^l) \times \ldots \times \pi_{B_{lp}}(\mathcal{X}^l)$$

where $\mathcal{X}^l$ is the set of given pattens which belongs to the class with label l and $Q_l = \{B_{l1}, B_{l2}, \ldots, B_{lp}\}$ is a partition of F.

Example: This illustrates the concept of partition based pattern synthesis. Let $F = (f_1, f_2, f_3, f_4)$, $\mathcal{X}^l = \{(a,b,c,d), (p,q,r,s), (w,x,y,z)\}$ be the given training set for class with label l, and $\pi_l = \{B_{l1}, B_{l2}\}$ such that $B_{l1} = (f_1, f_2)$ and $B_{l2} = (f_3, f_4)$. Then, the synthetic set for the class is $SS_{Q_l}(\mathcal{X}^l) = \pi_{B_{l1}}(\mathcal{X}^l) \times \pi_{B_{l2}}(\mathcal{X}^l)$ $= \{(X_{B_{l1}}^a, X_{B_{l2}}^b) \mid X^a, X^b \in \mathcal{X}^i\} = \{(a,b,c,d), (a,b,r,s), (a,b,y,z), (p,q,c,d), (p,q,r,s), (p,q,y,z), (w,x,c,d), (w,x,r,s), (w,x,y,z)\}$.

It is easy to see that the original set of patterns $\mathcal{X}^l$ and the synthetic set $SS_{Q_l}(\mathcal{X}^l)$ are from the same probability distribution if the subsets of F viz., $B_{l1}, \ldots, B_{lp}$ are statistically independent for the given class. But unfortunately, such a partitioning of F may not exist and even if they exist, finding it would be a computationally demanding problem. So, an approximate partitioning method is used based on correlation coefficient between pairs of features. The set of features is partitioned such that on average features in different blocks are least correlated with each other.

4 A Compact Representation

Partition based pattern synthesis can generate synthetic set of size $O(n^p)$, where n is the original set size and p is the number of blocks in the partition. Hence explicitly storing the synthetic set is very space consuming. In this section we present a compact representation of the original set which is suitable for the synthesis. For large data sets, this representation requires less storage space than that for the original set. This is called *partitioned pattern count tree (PPC-tree)*.

PPC-tree is a generalization of a data structure called *pattern count tree (PC-tree)* [5]. PC-tree, as well as PPC-tree are suitable when each feature can take discrete values (can be categorical values also). For continuous valued features, an appropriate discretization needs to be done first. PPC-tree structure is described with an example below.

Example: Let $\{(a,b,c,x,y,z), (a,b,d,x,y,z), (a,e,c,x,y,u), (f,b,c,x,y,v)\}$ be the original training set for a class with label i. Let the partition chosen is $Q_i = \{B_{i1}, B_{i2}\}$ such that $B_{i1} = \{f_1, f_2, f_3\}$ and $B_{i2} = \{f_4, f_5, f_6\}$, respectively. Then the PPC-tree is shown in Fig. 1. Each node of the tree (except root) is of the format *(feature : count)*.

The PPC-tree is a set of tree structures (called PC-trees) $\{\mathcal{T}_{i1}, \mathcal{T}_{i2}\}$, where $\mathcal{T}_{i1}$ represents the set of projected patterns $\mathcal{X}^i_{B_{i1}} = \{(a,b,c), (a,b,d), (a,e,c), (f,b,c)\}$. Similarly $\mathcal{T}_{i2}$ represents the set of projected patterns $\mathcal{X}^i_{B_2}$.

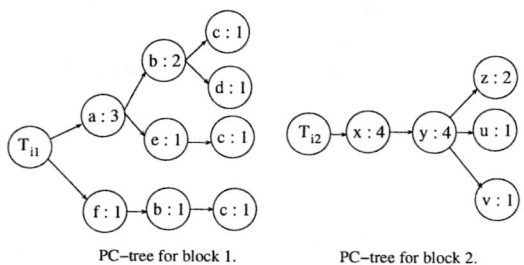

Fig. 1. PPC-tree $\mathcal{T}_i = \{\mathcal{T}_{i1}, \mathcal{T}_{i2}\}$

A path from root to leaf of $\mathcal{T}_{i1}$ represents a projected pattern onto features in B_{i1} and that of $\mathcal{T}_{i2}$ represents a projected pattern onto B_{i2}. Merging the two projected patterns gives a synthetic pattern according to the partition.

The space and time (to build) requirements for the representation is $O(n)$ where n is the number of original patterns.

5 Novelty Detection Using Synthetic Patterns

For the normal class, partition the set of features into p blocks (p is chosen based on a three-fold cross-validation) using the approximate partitioning method. Let the partition be $\{B_1, \ldots, B_p\}$. Let the PPC-tree representation for the synthetic set be $\mathcal{T} = \{\mathcal{T}_1, \ldots, \mathcal{T}_p\}$. Let T be the given test pattern. For each tree structure $\mathcal{T}_i \in \mathcal{T}$, we maintain two lists $dist_i$ and $dist\_count_i$ each of length equal to the number of paths (same as the number of leaf nodes i.e., l_i) in the tree structure

$\mathcal{T}_i$. The jth entry in the list $dist_i$ is $dist_{ij}$ and this gives squared Euclidean distance between T_{B_i} and a projected pattern corresponding to a path in the tree, whereas the corresponding entry in the $dist\_count_i$ list is $dist\_count_{ij}$ which gives the number of times the projected pattern (given by the count field of the leaf node of the corresponding path) is repeated. Find the set of pairs $\mathcal{S} = \{(\text{dist}_{1j_1} + \ldots + \text{dist}_{pj_p}, \text{dist\_count}_{1j_1} \times \ldots \times \text{dist\_count}_{pj_p}) \mid 1 \leq j_i \leq l_i,\ 1 \leq i \leq p\}$, where first member of each pair gives squared Euclidean distance between T and a synthetic pattern and second member gives number of times the synthetic pattern is repeated. These distances are used to estimate the density at the given test pattern T by using the Equation 1 whose modified version is given below.

1. Let $\mathcal{S} = \{(d_1, c_1), (d_2, c_2), \ldots, (d_m, c_m)\}$ where $m = |\mathcal{S}| = (l_1 \times l_2 \times \ldots \times l_p)$.
2. Density at T is found by using

$$\hat{p}(x) = \frac{1}{n^p (2\pi)^{d/2} \sigma^d} \sum_{i=1}^{m} c_i \exp\left\{-\frac{d_i}{2\sigma^2}\right\} \qquad (2)$$

{Hence, a total of $m = l_1 \times l_2 \times \ldots \times l_p$ computations are required. But according to the experimental studies, the values of each of l_i is much smaller than n. So m is much smaller than n^p, the total number of synthetic patterns.} If the calculated density, $p_m(x)$ exceeds a threshold value (chosen based on a three-fold cross-validation) then the test pattern T is classified as normal, otherwise as novel (abnormal).

6 Experiments

In our experiments, we use KDD Cup 1999 dataset (for details refer [3]) which was obtained from a real-world military network environment with simulated intrusions.

The dataset has four intrusion categories: *probing*, *denial-of-service* (DoS), *user-to-root* (U2R), and *remote-to-local* (R2L). We use the performance measures *true acceptance rate* (TAR) and *true detection rate* (TDR) as given in [3]. TAR measures the percentage of normal connections in the test set that are classified as normal, whereas TDR measures the percentage of intrusive connections in the test set that are detected as intrusions.

We use the training dataset consisting of 97276 patterns, all from normal class to estimate the density model. The test dataset consists of 311029 patterns. Each test pattern is classified as either normal or abnormal based on a threshold value which is fixed based on a three-fold cross-validation using training dataset.

We have compared our results with those of Yeung and Chow [3], KDD Cup winner and KDD Cup Runner. Table 1 gives the TAR and TDR values for all the methods. The results of Yeung and Chow are taken from [3]. Since the KDD Cup is concerned with multi-class classification but we are interested only in normal/intrusion discrimination, we have converted the results of KDD Cup winner and Runner into our format (as done by Yeung and Chow [3]). The best results in each category are highlighted.

Table 1. Comparison of our model with others (showing (%))

Method	TAR	TDR				Cost
	Normal	Probing	DoS	U2R	R2L	
Ours	96.20	**99.76**	97.59	**96.49**	**37.12**	**0.1796**
Yeung and Chow	97.38	99.17	96.71	93.57	31.17	0.2024
KDD Winner	**99.45**	87.73	**97.69**	26.32	10.27	0.2260
KDD Runner	99.42	89.01	97.57	22.37	7.38	0.2339

The proposed method is also compared with others based on a scoring scheme. KDD Cup scoring scheme uses a cost matrix which is modified (as done by Yeung and Chow [3]) to suit the given approach.

Although our method is not always better because its TAR is lower, it is fair to say that our method can achieve performance comparable to the best methods, with the favorable characteristics that it requires no intrusion data at all and effectively uses very large number of synthesized training patterns.

7 Concluding Remarks

The paper presented a novelty detection approach to detect abnormal patterns. This is useful when the normal class is well defined and abnormal class does not have an explicit definition apart from saying that it is not normal. Parzen-Window based novelty detection is presented. To reduce the curse of dimensionality effect we used partition based synthetic patterns. To reduce the computational requirements we used PPC-tree representations. The results are compared with other related approaches and found to be encouraging.

References

1. Lippmann, R., Cunningham, R.: Improving intrusion detection performance using keyword selection and neural networks. Computer Networks **34** (2000) 579–603
2. Lee, W., Xiang, D.: Information-theoretic measures for anomaly detection. In: Proceedings of the IEEE Symposium on Security and Privacy. (2001) 130–143
3. Yeung, D.Y., Chow, C.: Parzen-window network intrusion detectors. In: Proceedings of the 16th International Conference on Pattern Recognition. Volume 4. (2002) 385–388
4. Parzen, E.: On estimation of a probability density function and mode. Annals of Mathematical Statistics **33** (1962) 1065–1076
5. Ananthanarayana, V., Murty, M., Subramanian, D.: An incremental data mining algorithm for compact realization of prototypes. Pattern Recognition **34** (2001) 2249–2251

Author Index

Abulaish, Muhammad   601
Agaian, Sos.S.   481
Agarwal, Shilpa   477
Aggarwal, Gaurav   11, 515
Aggarwal, J.K.   39
Agrawal, Amit   521
Agrawal, V.K.   595
Aha, David W.   30, 792
Ahmad, Amir   732
Aibar, P.   310
Ajishna, G.   108
Alam, Md. Jahangir   465
Amaral, Alexandre Marques   294
Anami, B.S.   388
Angadi, S.A.   388

Bandyopadhyay, Sanghamitra   617, 684
Banerjee, Mohua   726, 744
Banerjee, S.   623
Banka, Haider   768
Baruah, H.K.   576
Bastos, Gustavo   611
Basu, Anup   497
Basu, Dipak Kumar   236, 364
Basu, Subhadip   236
Bazan, Jan G.   720
Bhandari, Kunal   447
Bhattacharya, Arya K.   318
Bhattacharya, Bhargab B.   407, 544
Bhattacharya, Binay   60
Bhattacharyya, Dhruba K.   551, 589
Bhattacharyya, Pushpak   678
Bhaumik, Kamales   453
Bhosale, Abhijit   660
Bhowmick, Partha   407
Bhunre, Piyush K.   544
Bhuyan, M.K.   509
Bishnu, Arijit   544
Biswas, Arindam   407
Blat, F.   310
Bora, P.K.   509
Borah, Bhogeswar   551
Bose, Smarajit   170
Bouguila, Nizar   200

Bovolo, Francesca   260
Braga, Ana Paula M.   332
Braud, Agnès   300
Bruzzone, Lorenzo   40, 206, 260
Buller, Andrzej   70

Cao, Wenming   254
Carnevalli, Ricardo   332
Carvalho, Milene Barbosa   294
Castro, M.J.   310
Chae, Oksam   485
Chakraborty, Basabi   696
Chakraborty, Rupsa   344
Chandra, Suresh   360
Chandran, Sharat   242
Chaoji, Joe Urban Vineet   91
Chatterjee, Amita   413
Chaudhuri, Shamik   690
Chaudhuri, Subhasis   206, 563
Chaudhury, Santanu   527, 538
Chellappa, Rama   11, 515, 521
Cherukuri, Ravindranath C.   481
Chithra, K.   318
Cho, Sung-Bae   222, 640, 649
Cook, Diane J.   80

da Costa, Pyramo Pires Jr.   248, 287
Damle, Santhosh S.   382
Das, A.   589
Das, Anirban   477
Das, Jadav   318
Das, Nibaran   236
Das, Sajal K.   80
Das, Swagatam   369, 417
Das, T.   325
Das, Tanmoy Kanti   491
Datta Gupta, Rana   557
De, Debraj   413
De, Nilanjana   91
Deb, Kalyanmoy   690
de la Fuente, Pablo   218
Demir, Güleser K.   182
Desai, U.B.   108, 306
Dey, Debangshu   369

Author Index

Dey, Lipika   601, 732
Dhali, Sonali   459
Di Gesù, Vito   50
Díaz, W.   310
Dinesh, M.S.   338
Dinesh, R.   382
Dooley, Laurence S.   401

Ekel, Petr   294, 332
España, S.   310

Fabiano Alves, Mário   248
Fernandes, Délio E.B.   248
Ferri, F.J.   310

Gao, Feng   91
Ghosh, Anil Kumar   170
Ghosh, D.   509
Ghosh, Hiranmay   527
Ghosh, Kuntal   453
Gökmen, Muhittin   118
Golbeck, Jennifer   160
Gomide, Fernando   287
Gontijo, Marcelo   332
Gowda, K.C.   338
Grau, Bernardo Cuenca   160
Grau, S.   310
Grevera, George J.   137
Griol, D.   310
Guha, Prithwijit   212
Guimarães, Katia S.   611
Gupta, Kalyan Moy   792
Guru, D.S.   382, 434

Halaschek-Wiener, Christian   160
Hama, Hiromitsu   465
Hanmandlu, Madasu   477
Hasan, Mohammad Al   91
Hell, Michel   287
Hendler, James   160
Hiremath, P.S.   266
Hommet, Jean   300
Hong, Kiho   645
Hossain, M. Julius   485

Jadhav, Ashish   447
Jaime-Rivas, R.   310
Jain, Anil K.   1
Jain, Prateek   654
Jana, Prasanta K.   636

Janardhan Rao, D.V.   744
Jang, Soo-Wook   441, 503
Jänichen, Silke   774
Jatla, S.V.   318
Jawahar, C.V.   276, 471
Jayadeva   360
Jayaraman, V.K.   242
Joshi, Aniruddha   242
Junges, Marcio   332

Kahraman, Fatih   118
Kalyan Krishna, S.   538
Kalyanpur, Aditya   160
Kambala, Satish   799
Kang, Dong-Jin   666
Kar, I.N.   325
Karmakar, Gour C.   401
Keinduangjun, Jitimon   630
Khairnar, D.G.   306
Khemani, Deepak   786
Khemchandani, Reshma   360
Kim, Eun-Su   441, 503
Kim, J.Y.   428
Kim, Kyung-Joong   649
Konar, Amit   413, 417, 605
Kong, Adams Wai-Kin   147
Koo, Ja-Min   222
Korczak, Jerzy   300
Kulkarni, B.D.   242
Kumar, Arun   538
Kumar, B.V.K. Vijaya   422
Kumar, M.N.S.S.K. Pavan   276
Kumar, Nikesh   636
Kumar, Sachin   732
Kundu, Mahantapas   236, 364
Kundu, Malay K.   544

Lachiche, Nicolas   300
Law, Martin H.C.   1
Lee, Sang-Jo   666
Lee, Sung-Hak   441, 503
Leu, Ming C.   280
Li, Yan   780
Lim, Soo-Yeon   666
Liu, James Nga-Kwok   780
Liu, Jiming   157
Liu, Yuncai   533
Lovell, Brian C.   128
Lu, Fei   254
Lu, Guangming   147

Mahanta, A. Kakoti 576
Maitra, Anutosh 272
Maitra, Subhamoy 491
Majumdar, A.K. 570
Mali, Kalyani 557
Mallikarjun Reddy, G. 350
Mandal, Mrinal K. 497
Marconcini, Mattia 40
Martínez-González, Mercedes 218
Martínez-López, Rocío 708
Martins, Carlos Augusto Paiva
  da Silva 294
Mazarbhuiya, F.A. 576
Mazumdar, Debasis 459
Mehra, Ankit K 206
Merchant, S.N. 108, 306
Milton, R.S. 738
Miranda, Jaime 188
Mitra, Pabitra 212, 654, 744
Mitra, Sinjini 422
Mitra, Soma 459
Mitra, Suman K. 272, 447
Mitra, Sushmita 768
Mohan, B.Krishna 350
Montoya, Ricardo 188
Moore, Philip G. 792
Mukerjee, Amitabha 212
Mukherjee, Kaustav 60
Mukhopadhyaya, S. 623
Murthy, C.A. 544, 623
Mylaraswamy, Dinkar 176

Nagabhushan, P. 193, 338, 388, 434
Namboodiri, Anoop 471
Narasimha Murty, M. 583, 595, 799
Narasimhan, Seetharam 605
Narayan, B.L. 672
Nasipuri, Mita 236, 364
Neta, Bernadete Maria de
  Mendonça 332
Nguyen, Tuan Trung 762
Niu, Ben 315

Oz, Cemil 280

Palhares, Reinaldo M. 332
Palit, Biswaroop 497
Pal, Sankar Kumar 315, 459, 617,
  672, 684, 780, 792
Pan, Hailang 533

Pandya, Abhinay 678
Parimi, Nagender 91
Park, Han-Saem 640
Park, Junhyung 645
Park, Seong-Bae 666
Park, Sungyong 645
Parsia, Bijan 160
Pedrycz, Witold 768
Perner, Petra 774
Peters, Georg 702
Phadke, Sanjay 242
Phanish, H.S. 108
Phoophakdee, Benjamin 91
Piamsa-nga, Punpiti 630
Ponce, Claudio 356
Ponce, Ernesto 356
Poovorawan, Yong 630
Prabhakar, C.J. 266
Proctor, Jason M. 376
Purohit, Manoj 108
Pyo, Se-Jin 441

Radhika Selvamani, B. 786
Rahman, Mohammad M. 714
Rajashekhar 563
Rajshekhar 242
Ramos, Luiz Eduardo da Silva 294
Rangarajan, Lalitha 193
Ravindra Babu, T. 595
Ray, Shubhra Sankar 617
Ray, Sid 465
Ray, Sonai 413
Revett, Kenneth 756
Ruiz-Pinales, J. 310

Salem, Saeed 91
Sanz-Bobi, Miguel A. 708
Sarkar, Ram 236
Sarkar, Sandip 453
Savvides, Marios 422
Schain, Andrew 160
Secco, Luiz 287
Sen, Shreyas 605
Sesh Kumar, K.S. 471
Shekar, B.H. 434
Shetty, Pradeep Kumar 229
Shi, Lei 533
Shiu, Simon Chi Keung 315, 780
Sil, Jaya 344
Sing, J.K. 364

Singh, Pankaj 726
Sirin, Evren 160
Siromoney, Arul 738
Skowron, Andrzej 21, 720, 750
Ślęzak, Dominik 714, 756
Sohel, Ferdous Ahmed 401
Sohng, Kyu-Ik 441, 503
Song, Mu-Hee 666
Srinivas, P.S. 318
Srivastava, Abhinav 660
Stepaniuk, Jarosław 750
Subbarao, Raghav 538
Subramanian, D.K. 583
Sural, Shamik 570, 660
Sur-Kolay, S. 623
Swiniarski, Roman 750

Tallur, Basavanneppa 395
Thatipamula, Karthik 527
Toussaint, Godfried 60
Tripathi, Praveen K. 684
Trivedi, Jigish 272
Tyagi, Mayank 206

Udupa, Jayaram K. 137
Uma Maheswari, V. 738

Vadivel, A. 570
Vaghela, Pradeep 212
Veeraraghavan, Ashok 11, 515
Venkatesh, K.S. 212
Vicente, Dámaso-Javier 218
Vijaya, P.A. 583
Viswanath, P. 799

Weber, Richard 188
Weber, Rosina 376
Widz, Sebastian 756
Wong, Michael 147
Wróblewski, Jakub 714

Yang, Jihoon 645

Zaki, Mohammed J. 91
Zaveri, Mukesh 108
Zavidovique, Bertrand 50
Zhang, David 147
Zhang, Michael Q. 31
Zhong, Ning 98
Zhou, Jianying 491
Ziou, Djemel 200

Lecture Notes in Computer Science

For information about Vols. 1–3737

please contact your bookseller or Springer

Vol. 3837: K. Cho, P. Jacquet (Eds.), Technologies for Advanced Heterogeneous Networks. IX, 307 pages. 2005.

Vol. 3835: G. Sutcliffe, A. Voronkov (Eds.), Logic for Programming, Artificial Intelligence, and Reasoning. XIV, 744 pages. 2005. (Subseries LNAI).

Vol. 3833: K.-J. Li, C. Vangenot (Eds.), Web and Wireless Geographical Information Systems. XI, 309 pages. 2005.

Vol. 3829: P. Pettersson, W. Yi (Eds.), Formal Modeling and Analysis of Timed Systems. IX, 305 pages. 2005.

Vol. 3828: X. Deng, Y. Ye (Eds.), Internet and Network Economics. XVII, 1106 pages. 2005.

Vol. 3826: B. Benatallah, F. Casati, P. Traverso (Eds.), Service-Oriented Computing - ICSOC 2005. XVIII, 597 pages. 2005.

Vol. 3824: L.T. Yang, M. Amamiya, Z. Liu, M. Guo, F.J. Rammig (Eds.), Embedded and Ubiquitous Computing. XXIII, 1204 pages. 2005.

Vol. 3823: T. Enokido, L. Yan, B. Xiao, D. Kim, Y. Dai, L.T. Yang (Eds.), Embedded and Ubiquitous Computing. XXXII, 1317 pages. 2005.

Vol. 3822: D. Feng, D. Lin, M. Yung (Eds.), Information Security and Cryptology. XII, 420 pages. 2005.

Vol. 3821: R. Ramanujam, S. Sen (Eds.), FSTTCS 2005: Foundations of Software Technology and Theoretical Computer Science. XIV, 566 pages. 2005.

Vol. 3820: L.T. Yang, X. Zhou, W. Zhao, Z. Wu, Y. Zhu, M. Lin (Eds.), Embedded Software and Systems. XXVIII, 779 pages. 2005.

Vol. 3818: S. Grumbach, L. Sui, V. Vianu (Eds.), Advances in Computer Science – ASIAN 2005. XIII, 294 pages. 2005.

Vol. 3815: E.A. Fox, E.J. Neuhold, P. Premsmit, V. Wuwongse (Eds.), Digital Libraries: Implementing Strategies and Sharing Experiences. XVII, 529 pages. 2005.

Vol. 3814: M. Maybury, O. Stock, W. Wahlster (Eds.), Intelligent Technologies for Interactive Entertainment. XV, 342 pages. 2005. (Subseries LNAI).

Vol. 3810: Y.G. Desmedt, H. Wang, Y. Mu, Y. Li (Eds.), Cryptology and Network Security. XI, 349 pages. 2005.

Vol. 3809: S. Zhang, R. Jarvis (Eds.), AI 2005: Advances in Artificial Intelligence. XXVII, 1344 pages. 2005. (Subseries LNAI).

Vol. 3808: C. Bento, A. Cardoso, G. Dias (Eds.), Progress in Artificial Intelligence. XVIII, 704 pages. 2005. (Subseries LNAI).

Vol. 3807: M. Dean, Y. Guo, W. Jun, R. Kaschek, S. Krishnaswamy, Z. Pan, Q.Z. Sheng (Eds.), Web Information Systems Engineering – WISE 2005 Workshops. XV, 275 pages. 2005.

Vol. 3806: A.H. H. Ngu, M. Kitsuregawa, E.J. Neuhold, J.-Y. Chung, Q.Z. Sheng (Eds.), Web Information Systems Engineering – WISE 2005. XXI, 771 pages. 2005.

Vol. 3805: G. Subsol (Ed.), Virtual Storytelling. XII, 289 pages. 2005.

Vol. 3804: G. Bebis, R. Boyle, D. Koracin, B. Parvin (Eds.), Advances in Visual Computing. XX, 755 pages. 2005.

Vol. 3803: S. Jajodia, C. Mazumdar (Eds.), Information Systems Security. XI, 342 pages. 2005.

Vol. 3802: Y. Hao, J. Liu, Y. Wang, Y.-m. Cheung, H. Yin, L. Jiao, J. Ma, Y.-C. Jiao (Eds.), Computational Intelligence and Security, Part II. XLII, 1166 pages. 2005. (Subseries LNAI).

Vol. 3801: Y. Hao, J. Liu, Y. Wang, Y.-m. Cheung, H. Yin, L. Jiao, J. Ma, Y.-C. Jiao (Eds.), Computational Intelligence and Security, Part I. XLI, 1122 pages. 2005. (Subseries LNAI).

Vol. 3799: M. A. Rodríguez, I.F. Cruz, S. Levashkin, M.J. Egenhofer (Eds.), GeoSpatial Semantics. X, 259 pages. 2005.

Vol. 3798: A. Dearle, S. Eisenbach (Eds.), Component Deployment. X, 197 pages. 2005.

Vol. 3797: S. Maitra, C. E. V. Madhavan, R. Venkatesan (Eds.), Progress in Cryptology - INDOCRYPT 2005. XIV, 417 pages. 2005.

Vol. 3796: N.P. Smart (Ed.), Cryptography and Coding. XI, 461 pages. 2005.

Vol. 3795: H. Zhuge, G.C. Fox (Eds.), Grid and Cooperative Computing - GCC 2005. XXI, 1203 pages. 2005.

Vol. 3794: X. Jia, J. Wu, Y. He (Eds.), Mobile Ad-hoc and Sensor Networks. XX, 1136 pages. 2005.

Vol. 3793: T. Conte, N. Navarro, W.-m.W. Hwu, M. Valero, T. Ungerer (Eds.), High Performance Embedded Architectures and Compilers. XIII, 317 pages. 2005.

Vol. 3792: I. Richardson, P. Abrahamsson, R. Messnarz (Eds.), Software Process Improvement. VIII, 215 pages. 2005.

Vol. 3791: A. Adi, S. Stoutenburg, S. Tabet (Eds.), Rules and Rule Markup Languages for the Semantic Web. X, 225 pages. 2005.

Vol. 3790: G. Alonso (Ed.), Middleware 2005. XIII, 443 pages. 2005.

Vol. 3789: A. Gelbukh, Á. de Albornoz, H. Terashima-Marín (Eds.), MICAI 2005: Advances in Artificial Intelligence. XXVI, 1198 pages. 2005. (Subseries LNAI).

Vol. 3788: B. Roy (Ed.), Advances in Cryptology - ASIACRYPT 2005. XIV, 703 pages. 2005.

Vol. 3785: K.-K. Lau, R. Banach (Eds.), Formal Methods and Software Engineering. XIV, 496 pages. 2005.

Vol. 3784: J. Tao, T. Tan, R.W. Picard (Eds.), Affective Computing and Intelligent Interaction. XIX, 1008 pages. 2005.

Vol. 3783: S. Qing, W. Mao, J. Lopez, G. Wang (Eds.), Information and Communications Security. XIV, 492 pages. 2005.

Vol. 3781: S.Z. Li, Z. Sun, T. Tan, S. Pankanti, G. Chollet, D. Zhang (Eds.), Advances in Biometric Person Authentication. XI, 250 pages. 2005.

Vol. 3780: K. Yi (Ed.), Programming Languages and Systems. XI, 435 pages. 2005.

Vol. 3779: H. Jin, D. Reed, W. Jiang (Eds.), Network and Parallel Computing. XV, 513 pages. 2005.

Vol. 3778: C. Atkinson, C. Bunse, H.-G. Gross, C. Peper (Eds.), Component-Based Software Development for Embedded Systems. VIII, 345 pages. 2005.

Vol. 3777: O.B. Lupanov, O.M. Kasim-Zade, A.V. Chaskin, K. Steinhöfel (Eds.), Stochastic Algorithms: Foundations and Applications. VIII, 239 pages. 2005.

Vol. 3776: S.K. Pal, S. Bandyopadhyay, S. Biswas (Eds.), Pattern Recognition and Machine Intelligence. XXIV, 808 pages. 2005.

Vol. 3775: J. Schönwälder, J. Serrat (Eds.), Ambient Networks. XIII, 281 pages. 2005.

Vol. 3774: G. Bierman, C. Koch (Eds.), Database Programming Languages. X, 295 pages. 2005.

Vol. 3773: A. Sanfeliu, M.L. Cortés (Eds.), Progress in Pattern Recognition, Image Analysis and Applications. XX, 1094 pages. 2005.

Vol. 3772: M. Consens, G. Navarro (Eds.), String Processing and Information Retrieval. XIV, 406 pages. 2005.

Vol. 3771: J.M.T. Romijn, G.P. Smith, J. van de Pol (Eds.), Integrated Formal Methods. XI, 407 pages. 2005.

Vol. 3770: J. Akoka, S.W. Liddle, I.-Y. Song, M. Bertolotto, I. Comyn-Wattiau, W.-J. van den Heuvel, M. Kolp, J. Trujillo, C. Kop, H.C. Mayr (Eds.), Perspectives in Conceptual Modeling. XXII, 476 pages. 2005.

Vol. 3769: D.A. Bader, M. Parashar, V. Sridhar, V.K. Prasanna (Eds.), High Performance Computing – HiPC 2005. XXVIII, 550 pages. 2005.

Vol. 3768: Y.-S. Ho, H.J. Kim (Eds.), Advances in Multimedia Information Processing - PCM 2005, Part II. XXVIII, 1088 pages. 2005.

Vol. 3767: Y.-S. Ho, H.J. Kim (Eds.), Advances in Multimedia Information Processing - PCM 2005, Part I. XXVIII, 1022 pages. 2005.

Vol. 3766: N. Sebe, M.S. Lew, T.S. Huang (Eds.), Computer Vision in Human-Computer Interaction. X, 231 pages. 2005.

Vol. 3765: Y. Liu, T. Jiang, C. Zhang (Eds.), Computer Vision for Biomedical Image Applications. X, 563 pages. 2005.

Vol. 3764: S. Tixeuil, T. Herman (Eds.), Self-Stabilizing Systems. VIII, 229 pages. 2005.

Vol. 3762: R. Meersman, Z. Tari, P. Herrero (Eds.), On the Move to Meaningful Internet Systems 2005: OTM 2005 Workshops. XXXI, 1228 pages. 2005.

Vol. 3761: R. Meersman, Z. Tari (Eds.), On the Move to Meaningful Internet Systems 2005: CoopIS, DOA, and ODBASE, Part II. XXVII, 653 pages. 2005.

Vol. 3760: R. Meersman, Z. Tari (Eds.), On the Move to Meaningful Internet Systems 2005: CoopIS, DOA, and ODBASE, Part I. XXVII, 921 pages. 2005.

Vol. 3759: G. Chen, Y. Pan, M. Guo, J. Lu (Eds.), Parallel and Distributed Processing and Applications - ISPA 2005 Workshops. XIII, 669 pages. 2005.

Vol. 3758: Y. Pan, D.-x. Chen, M. Guo, J. Cao, J.J. Dongarra (Eds.), Parallel and Distributed Processing and Applications. XXIII, 1162 pages. 2005.

Vol. 3757: A. Rangarajan, B. Vemuri, A.L. Yuille (Eds.), Energy Minimization Methods in Computer Vision and Pattern Recognition. XII, 666 pages. 2005.

Vol. 3756: J. Cao, W. Nejdl, M. Xu (Eds.), Advanced Parallel Processing Technologies. XIV, 526 pages. 2005.

Vol. 3754: J. Dalmau Royo, G. Hasegawa (Eds.), Management of Multimedia Networks and Services. XII, 384 pages. 2005.

Vol. 3753: O.F. Olsen, L.M.J. Florack, A. Kuijper (Eds.), Deep Structure, Singularities, and Computer Vision. X, 259 pages. 2005.

Vol. 3752: N. Paragios, O. Faugeras, T. Chan, C. Schnörr (Eds.), Variational, Geometric, and Level Set Methods in Computer Vision. XI, 369 pages. 2005.

Vol. 3751: T. Magedanz, E.R. M. Madeira, P. Dini (Eds.), Operations and Management in IP-Based Networks. X, 213 pages. 2005.

Vol. 3750: J.S. Duncan, G. Gerig (Eds.), Medical Image Computing and Computer-Assisted Intervention – MICCAI 2005, Part II. XL, 1018 pages. 2005.

Vol. 3749: J.S. Duncan, G. Gerig (Eds.), Medical Image Computing and Computer-Assisted Intervention – MICCAI 2005, Part I. XXXIX, 942 pages. 2005.

Vol. 3748: A. Hartman, D. Kreische (Eds.), Model Driven Architecture – Foundations and Applications. IX, 349 pages. 2005.

Vol. 3747: C.A. Maziero, J.G. Silva, A.M.S. Andrade, F.M.d. Assis Silva (Eds.), Dependable Computing. XV, 267 pages. 2005.

Vol. 3746: P. Bozanis, E.N. Houstis (Eds.), Advances in Informatics. XIX, 879 pages. 2005.

Vol. 3745: J.L. Oliveira, V. Maojo, F. Martín-Sánchez, A.S. Pereira (Eds.), Biological and Medical Data Analysis. XII, 422 pages. 2005. (Subseries LNBI).

Vol. 3744: T. Magedanz, A. Karmouch, S. Pierre, I. Venieris (Eds.), Mobility Aware Technologies and Applications. XIV, 418 pages. 2005.

Vol. 3742: J. Akiyama, M. Kano, X. Tan (Eds.), Discrete and Computational Geometry. VIII, 213 pages. 2005.

Vol. 3740: T. Srikanthan, J. Xue, C.-H. Chang (Eds.), Advances in Computer Systems Architecture. XVII, 833 pages. 2005.

Vol. 3739: W. Fan, Z. Wu, J. Yang (Eds.), Advances in Web-Age Information Management. XXIV, 930 pages. 2005.

Vol. 3738: V.R. Syrotiuk, E. Chávez (Eds.), Ad-Hoc, Mobile, and Wireless Networks. XI, 360 pages. 2005.